A SURVEY OF MUSICAL INSTRUMENTS

A SURVEY

HARPER & ROW, PUBLISHERS

OF MUSICAL

INSTRUMENTS

Sibyl Marcuse

NEW YORK, EVANSTON, SAN FRANCISCO, LONDON

FIRST EDITION

Designed by Lydia Link

Library of Congress Cataloging in Publication Data.

Marcuse, Sibyl.
  A survey of musical instruments.
  Bibliography: p.
  1. Musical instruments. 2. Musical instruments—
History. I. Title.
ML460.M365S94   781.9′1′09   72–9135
ISBN 0–06–012776–7

75 76 77 78 79 10 9 8 7 6 5 4 3 2 1

Contents

v

Part Two
MEMBRANOPHONES

Part Three

CHORDOPHONES

viii | *Contents*

Part Four
AEROPHONES

Illustrations

Pitch letters printed without further identification, such as B♭, C, do not connote any definite pitch. Definite pitches are indicated as in the following diagram.

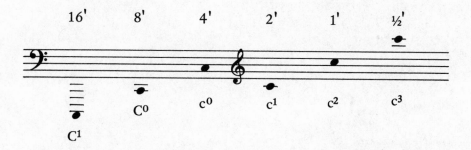

Directions concerning left and right. The left and right sides of necked chordophones (violins, lutes, guitars, etc.) are those to left and right of the viewer, when the instrument is placed strings up, neck pointing away from him.

Part One

IDIOPHONES

CONCUSSION IDIOPHONES

Concussion idiophones, more commonly called clappers, are of world-wide distribution and of unknown if very great age. Several forms are distinguished: concussion sticks, plaques, troughs, and vessels, of which the last category is perhaps the best known to the West, embracing as it does castanets and cymbals. Clappers originated as a substitute for hand clapping, the ageless rhythm marking of dancers—which they may also complement—and also as noisemakers to dispel evil spirits or to imitate thunder. The Thonga people of South Africa have clappers made of rectangular slats of wood furnished with a leather band so that they can be worn as mitts; male dancers clash them to enhance the sound of hand clapping. And to this day Celebes Islanders exorcise evil spirits by striking metal rods together, while the North American Mono imitate thunder in magical ceremonies by sounding their stick clappers. Such examples could be multiplied.

Clappers are struck or clashed together either by holding one in each hand, or by holding a pair in one hand or by hinging several together. They are made of a variety of materials and may be composed of independent pieces, or two or more may be hinged together. The holding of two concussion sticks in one hand is depicted on predynastic Egyptian vases of about 3000 B.C., held in the hands of female dancers, and shortly thereafter, around 2800 B.C., the use of a single clapper in each hand is documented on a seal from Ur. Clappers from prehistoric times have been preserved and are also depicted on monuments from Sumer; the earliest museum specimen dates from about 3200 B.C. A seal of Ur of around 2700 B.C. shows attendants striking curved sticks together in rhythmic accompaniment of a dancer. Clappers from Bronze Age Babylon have

3

been found, generally in pairs, made of flat, curved pieces of wood or metal, some mounted on wooden handles. Egyptian necropolises of the predynastic Badarian culture have yielded three different forms, all elongated: straight, with a rectangular curve, and boomerang shaped; all three coexisted. Some of those in boomerang form follow the natural curve of the hippopotamus ivory from which they were made (they are not, however, identical with early Egyptian boomerangs, with which they were coeval). Others, dating from the First Dynasty, represent a pair of hands, either straight or curved, or else hands and forearms; later models, made of wood or of ivory, imitate a lotus flower. Surviving hand-shaped clappers of the New Kingdom, made of hippopotamus or elephant ivory, have become extremely fragile with age. A priestly implement in its early history, the Egyptian clapper degenerated later into a dancer's rhythm instrument.

Vessel clappers made of ivory, with both plain and ornamented ends, are encountered in Egypt about 2000 B.C.; on some instruments the vessel is formed by the natural hollow inherent in the material—such as hippopotamus tooth—but in others the natural cavity has been enlarged, presumably to increase the volume of sound. A single hole was pierced in each shank for tying a pair together; later specimens exist made not only of ivory but also of bone and wood, straight or curved, and in greatly varying dimensions. Pairs of clappers are shown, held two in a hand rather like "bones" in the late Eighteenth Dynasty (fourteenth century B.C.), always by females (two and a half millennia later they appear, held in precisely the same manner, in the thirteenth-century Spanish *Cantigas de Santa María*). The use of concussion sticks seems never to have died out in Egypt, where they are still played, and where the Copts even have ritual clappers of a type probably in use already by the third or fourth century A.D.; these are of bone, with two shorter sections hinged to a larger central one; a flick of the wrist sends the former striking against the latter.

If Egypt had its hand-shaped clappers, those of ancient Greece were by contrast boot shaped: the wooden Greek *krotala* were made in several shapes but chiefly that of boots joined together at one end. As they were used in pairs, they are generally referred to in the plural (*krotalon* is the singular form). *Krotala* were mentioned by Homer and by Sappho, and continued in use until Roman times. Rome then took them over, modified their shape, made them of wood, metal, horn, even of clay or shells, and put them in the hands of dancers. Shorter two-piece clappers are frequently depicted in the hands of both male and female players in Greece; they may have been hinged at one end. Fifth-century B.C. Greek pottery—such as, for example, the Douris Cup—shows a female player, her arms extended to right and left, a two-piece clapper in each hand. Dancing satyrs are also portrayed holding this type of clapper.

The Greek *kroupalon* or *kroupezion,* first depicted in the third century B.C., was a different form, made of hinged wooden plaques attached like a sandal to the right foot of a Greek chorus leader in order to mark the rhythm, actually more like a conductor's baton than a musical instrument. This also was adopted by the Romans, who called it *scabellum.* Clappers played with the feet are not otherwise known in Europe, but they occur in Hawaii, where a hollow rectangle of wood is placed over a short transverse stick under the performer's naked foot, worked rather like a *kroupezion,* and sounded simultaneously with hand-held concussion sticks.

We are not informed as to the precise nature of the *tabulae,* mentioned by Amalarius of Metz as being in the hands of church cantors during liturgical services of the early ninth century A.D.—he writes that they were of bone—and again by Sicard of Cremona (d. ca. 1215); quite possibly they were similar to the "bones," which were two-piece, one-hand clappers, so called because they were originally made of ox rib, and known to have been introduced into medieval Europe by the *joculatores,* who brought them from Rome. In the present century they are played only as toys, but they also appeared in eighteenth-century Turkey, played by female dancers, who held a pair in each hand. From 1590 on the English word "bones" took on a second sense, that of clappers made of bone or ivory, but, although these were later made of flat, hardwood sticks, the old name persisted. A pair was held in each hand and clicked by a flick of the wrist. Shakespeare knew the word in this sense, for in A *Midsummer Night's Dream* (act IV, scene 1) Bottom says: "I have a reasonable good ear in music. Let's have the tongs and the bones." But in medieval times among the chief users of clappers were lepers, who were obliged to sound them as a warning of their impeding approach and also when begging for alms. In Spanish they were known as *tablillas de San Lázaro, lazarus* being a medieval Latin synonym of "leper"; the French called them *tablettes.* Spanish *tablillas* were made of three pieces of wood joined at one end by a cord, the central piece furnished with a handle. Guillaume de Lorris (ca. 1240) puts *tablettes* into the hands of jongleurs.

A clapper composed of three identical pieces of flat, spoon-shaped wood, hinged together at the handle ends and clicked so that the outer two struck against the inner one, was also known to western Europe: Virdung (1511) calls it *Britsche*. Modernized and spelled *Pritsche*, this has survived as a carnival instrument: longitudinal saw cuts are made in an oblong piece of wood to form a switch. In his *Wilhelm Meisters Lehrjahre*, published in 1795–1796, Goethe describes Pagliaccio mingling with the crowd and jesting by kissing a girl here, applying the switch to a boy there (. . . *bald ein Mädchen küsste, bald einen Knaben pritschte* . . .). An equivalent of the older, three-piece *Britsche*, made in rectangular form and provided with a handle, was used by beggars in Italy in the eighteenth century, according to Buonanni (1722), and is still in use in Sicily; and the three-piece *olezkilla* of the Basques serves during Easter Week in lieu of church bells—the name means "wooden bell." Although clappers have almost died out in the West, one form that has been retained is that of the slapstick that gave its name to "slapstick" comedy—a clapper of modern rhythm bands consisting of two wooden slabs hinged together. But whereas in the West clappers remain crudely or simply made, those of Asia often become artifacts of great beauty.

Clappers of the high-culture areas of Asia are, or were, also associated with the cult. In China, formerly, clappers made of twelve narrow bamboo slips were tied together so as to fan out at their free ends; they were held by temple singers, who struck them against the palm of one hand, causing the sections to click against one another. A highly refined version of the three-piece clapper is to be found in Vietnam; made of lacquered wood, the longer, central portion is carved to resemble a dragon, and pellet bells attached to the outside sections add their jingling to the crisp sound of the clapper. Here again, far from being a folk instrument, this is reserved for religious ceremonies. A scraped clapper is played in the same area: while it is clicked with one hand, it is simultaneously scraped with a notched stick held in the other hand.

Clappers made of circular wooden plaques with a short handle are seen in the hands of Persian girl dancers in miniatures of the sixteenth and seventeenth centuries. Similar objects are still in use on the Indian subcontinent, one held in each hand; in some areas this is an instrument of fakirs and mendicants, while in others it is provided with a cluster of pellet bells and serves as a rhythm instrument. Square metal clappers held pairwise like castanets are met with in northern India. Metal is also used for the *kechrek* of Java, with its two or more iron slabs loosely tied together; instead of being held in the hand, as might be expected, it is played with the performer's toes. In the theater such clappers imitate the noise of battles, but itinerant tinkers also sound them to announce their presence. On the same island the ancient tantric *kepyak*, a quadruple clapper, is made from buffalo bones.

The Japanese *hyōshige* not only offers an illustration of twofold use—in *kabuki* theaters as rhythm instruments and by fire watchers as signal instruments—but also that of a transition from concussion to percussion instrument: solid blocks of hardwood are either struck together or struck against a wooden board. And the *yotsu dake*, meaning "four bamboos" in Japanese, are put to three different uses: made of split bamboo, a pair is held in each hand and serves as a rhythm instrument in the theater, as a signal to draw attention to their presence by beggars, and, on the Ryukyu Islands, to accompany traditional dances—doubtless its original function.

Turning to Africa, a very large form of clapper is played in Morocco; shaped like a dumbbell split lengthwise, and with the heads hollowed out, a pair measuring perhaps 30 centimeters (12 inches) is held in each hand of a singer, who may accompany himself by their clicks. A similar form, composed of flat iron disks joined by a bar of the same material, with the connecting bar serving as a handle, is found in the Sudan, and a three-piece bone clapper, with a rigid central piece to which two thin bones are hinged by leather thongs, is found in Dahomey. But the most interesting of African clappers are probably the South African *spagane*, which consist of rectangular wooden slats with a leather band attached to the narrow end, thus permitting them to be worn as mitts; they are played only by male dancers, for the purpose of augmenting the sound of hand clapping.

In the Americas, certain North American tribes formerly made use of concussion sticks as game calls, others associated them with funeral rites, and both men and women participated in war dances at which clappers were struck together. Antlers and bones served as materials for stick clappers to the ancient Mexicans.

Clappers are not common in the Pacific area, but in New Guinea they are to be found made of fruit shells; on the south coast a more fanciful material, namely lobster pincers, meet the requisite for natural concussion. Australian aborigines clash wooden boomerangs together, and this usage, coupled with the finding of very early boomerang-shaped concussion sticks in Egypt, caused organologists to believe until recently that clappers were an outgrowth of boomerangs.

Finally, mention must be made of concussion stones, clashed ritually by some North American Indians to make thunder, and formerly also played in Hawaii by dancers of the pebble dance, *ili-ili;* these dancers held pebbles in each hand and clashed them during the dance. Their use is also attested in Europe, and Buonanni (1722) illustrates both "bones" and concussion stones over a caption reading "Children's instruments."

To these may be opposed the extremely delicate Aeolian concussion plaques of the Far Eastern high cultures, consisting of a piece of flat, open metalwork representing a flower sprig or other object, often of exquisite workmanship, to which small pendants in the form of leaves, for example, are attached by silk threads. When stirred by the wind, a tinkling or clashing takes place, depending upon the force of the breeze.

VESSEL CLAPPERS

CASTANETS

Despite the fact that vessel clappers were known at an early date in ancient Egypt, it was not until the Twenty-fourth Dynasty (eighth century B.C.) that the true castanet appeared there, together with small cymbals and crotals (forked cymbals), imported instruments all. Beautiful little castanets from early Coptic times (second century) are shaped like Egyptian ointment flasks, with rounded or rectangular bodies and short, narrow necks topped by a wider rim, apparently made from a piece of wood cut in half and hollowed out in the center to form a hemispheric cavity, with a broad edge left all around; the two halves were then connected by a cord. In modified form they have retained their use among Copts until the present time; they are played in church during Mass.

The origin of these instruments has not been determined with any degree of certainty. In view of their subsequent development in Spain and South Italy, Sachs's suggestion of a Phoenician ancestry is now accepted, for Spain, like southern Italy, was once a Phoenician colony and already a center of dancing in antiquity (in Roman times the dancers of Cadiz are known to have played metal castanets). The bivalve scallop shell form of the modern European instrument is said to indicate a shell prototype, and this would certainly point to provenance from a coastal region.

The Spanish wooden castanet, the *castañeta* (from the Latin *castanea,* "chestnut"), as we know it today, is thought to derive from one of the areas where it is still played: Spain, the Balearic Islands, or southern Italy. Castanets characteristically consist of two almost circular disks, hollowed in the center of their striking side, connected pairwise by a cord like half shells, a pair held in each hand, with the cord passing over the thumb of one hand and the middle finger of the other. However, not all European castanets are shell shaped, as both Spain and the Baleares also know them in rectangular form, and Buonanni (1722) illustrated rectangular ones from Italy. Their name is derived not from the chestnut form, but rather from the wood of which they were traditionally made, though today boxwood, grenadilla, walnut, or other hardwoods are preferred. A pair of good castanets is extraordinarily resonant. Spanish dancers consider the larger of the two pairs as male, to be worn on the left hand, and the slightly smaller pair as female.

Castanets were played in Spain throughout the Middle Ages; they were illustrated from the eleventh century on and later became virtually a national instrument. In sixteenth-century Spain the saraband was usually danced to the accompaniment of a guitar or of castanets, and when the saraband crossed the frontier and proceeded north in the second half of the century, castanets went with it. By 1588 both dance and instrument were known in France, for in that year Richelieu, castanets on his fingers and bells on his shoes, danced the saraband at a court ballet. Early eighteenth-century writers of several countries refer to the castanets of Spaniards and Bohemians in connection with their dancers, and Stendhal, in an entry of his *Journal* for 1811 comments on the great use made in Naples of *tambours* (here, frame drums), castanets, "and other instruments said to be of Greek origin."

Today as in the past castanets are chiefly dancers' instruments, either clicked rhythmically or sounded in sustained rolls, with great emotional impact on their audience. Many nineteenth- and twentieth-century orchestral works dealing with Spanish themes score for them, and recently they have been adopted by rhythm bands, with one or two single castanets, or even a pair, made of Bakelite or of wood, attached to a long handle for ease in clicking, for the true castanet is difficult to master.

CYMBALS

Cymbals are another, specialized, form of vessel clapper; their two metal plates with concave centers are usually of indefinite pitch owing to the production of inharmonic partial tones. Generally they are made of copper or brass, in India additionally of "white" metal (i.e., bell metal), and the best finger cymbals are said to be those of silver. One of a pair is held in each hand and the two are clashed together. Originally a ritual instrument, the cymbal passed into martial use and was also admitted to the theater. Both the materials from which it is made and the intricacies of its manufacture preclude its use in primitive societies.

Its origin is Asiatic and probably Mesopotamian, from which area it radiated north, west, and east. A unique form of ancient Assyria was funnel shaped, with a long neck serving as a handle; two of these were held horizontally and clashed with a vertical motion. On a Phoenician bronze figure from Cyprus, small cymbals with big, bosslike handles are held vertically and clashed horizontally, in contrast to Assyrian usage. Cymbals made of shell appear in Egypt under the Eighteenth Dynasty (1580–1350 B.C.), but the true cymbal of metal is not encountered there until the Twenty-fourth Dynasty (eighth century B.C.), and then as an imported instrument. In Israel, where they were known from about 1100 B.C. on, cymbals were the only permanent idiophones of the Temple orchestra, and David's chief musician, Asaph, "made a sound with cymbals" (1 Chron. 16:5). An eleventh-century B.C. Babylonian plaque depicts a seated performer clashing, horizontally, a pair of flat cymbals at the same time that a large drum is being struck; both instruments accompany, or perhaps encourage, two boxers. Assyrian reliefs of the seventh century B.C. show, in addition to the above-mentioned conical form, flat cymbals held vertically and clashed horizontally.

Two forms of cymbals were distinguished in ancient and modern Asia, as well as in medieval Europe: (1) broad-rimmed, with a small central boss, held in horizontal position and clashed vertically; and (2) narrow-rimmed, with a large central boss, sometimes nearly hemispheric in shape, held vertically and clashed horizontally (rimless versions are also known). As metal disks are almost devoid of vibrations in the center, the tone of a cymbal is not impaired by grasping it on the boss or by drilling a hole through the vertex for suspension by a leather strap or other means. Both the broad- and the narrow-rimmed versions appear on the Hindu-Javanese temple sculptures of Borobudur, Java, of about A.D. 800, both exist in Tibet, and both were probably known to ancient Israel, as two different kinds of cymbal are mentioned in the Bible; Sachs (1940) has discussed this question in detail. As stated, they were ritual instruments in ancient Israel, as they remain today in Japan, Tibet, and Vietnam. In the present century, according to Gradenwitz (1949), women in Jewish communities of Oriental-Sephardic districts and of Yemen still accompany their songs with frame drums or cymbals beaten with their hands. The combination of cymbal and drum is an ancient one in Asia; Fa-Hsien, the Chinese Buddhist priest who set out for India in A.D. 399, relates how "those in charge of the shrine" in what is nowadays eastern Afghanistan beat on a big drum, blew a shell trumpet, and clashed copper cymbals.

Egyptian cymbals had large bosses and flat rims and were not unlike modern Western instruments, though smaller, judging by preserved specimens: two pairs housed in the British Museum have a diameter of some 13½ centimeters (over 5 inches). From the Near East and Egypt cymbals traveled to Greece with the cult of Kybele. Greek cymbals, called *kymbala* (plural of *kymbalon*) were about as large as a plate; frequently two were attached pairwise by a strap or a chain and were usually clashed horizontally. From the cult of Kybele they passed to that of Demeter and of Dionysus, and eventually were also played in the theater.

Etruria and Rome took them, in turn, from Greece. The Romans retained their Greek name (but wrote it *cymbalum*, pl. *cymbala*). Ever a practical people, they not only clashed them in honor of Bacchus and Cybele, but also in animal husbandry to prevent the flight of bees. (A similar usage obtained in Italy until Buonanni's time: he shows a beekeeper striking a large caldron to recall a swarm.) Bronze cymbals from Pompeii were held together by a metal wire passed through the vertex, while others were provided with a metal ring at the vertex for holding them; usually they were of small size with large boss and reduced rim, sometimes with rim even curved upward. Rimless, cup-shaped cymbals formed like resting bells, with a diameter of perhaps from 7 to 10 centimeters (3 to 4 inches) appear in Pompeiian mosaics.

Western writers of classical and early medieval times report the use of cymbals by Parthians, Persians, and Arabs as instruments of war, and describe the crashing din they made. In his enumeration of the martial instruments of different peoples, Clement of Alexandria (d. A.D. 215) links cymbals specifically with the Arabs: *In bellis suis tuba utunturi. Hetrusci, fistula, Arcades, Siculi pictidibus, Cretenses lyra, Lacedemones tibia, cornu Thraces, tympano Aegyptii, et Arabo cymbalo.*

Before the end of the first millennium we hear nothing of the regular cymbal, but other versions were inherited from antiquity: the crotal and the finger cymbal. The crotal, also called forked cymbal, was actually a forked clapper shaped like a pair of short tongs, with a miniature cymbal attached to the inner surface of each free end, facing each other pairwise.

A curious form, it turned up under the Twenty-fourth Dynasty in Egypt (eighth century B.C.), probably imported together with other instruments —castanets, goblet drums, and small cymbals—that also made their first appearance in Egypt at that time. Forked cymbals continued in use in Coptic Egypt and also appear on Persian silver vessels of the seventh to ninth centuries, a pair held in each hand of female dancers. They then made their way to Greece and Rome—where they were portrayed unmistakably in the fourth century A.D.—and then, presumably by intermediary of the *joculatores,* to western Europe by early medieval times (outside Europe, forked cymbals are played in modern Turkey and, strangely, also in Burma).

The Hebrew word *selslīm* was translated by the Septuagint as *cymbala,* and was so defined by such early writers as Augustine, Isidore, and Cassiodorus. In archaizing illustrations of the Carolingian period *cymbala* are rendered as forked cymbals, with the tong portion usually longer than it had been in antiquity, and, as always, a pair held in each hand. It is difficult to determine whether they were indeed played so late, or whether they merely represented nostalgic reminiscences of a better order. However, the eighth-century *Psalterium aureum* of Saint Gall depicts two crotal players flanking a central figure holding an elongated postclassical chordophone, and the ivory relief cover of a late eighth-century psalter presented by Charlemagne to Pope Hadrian I depicts several contemporary instruments: a short-necked lute and a harp or a rote, in company of which are also two pairs of crotals, a pair in each hand of a performer whose left foot is about to descend upon what can only be described as a foot crotal, a *scabellum* with small cymbals attached to the inner surfaces. Quite possibly this represents the instrument known to contemporary Byzantium as *kymbala podōn* ("foot cymbals"); the term occurs, together with *kymbala cheirōn* ("hand cymbals"), in an anonymous Greek treatise of ca. A.D. 800 devoted to alchemy, one section of which contains an enumeration of musical instruments. Another late illustration is one from the ninth-century Utrecht Psalter, in which two extremely large disks are held by far too delicate a pair of tongs.

At the end of the ninth century the word *cymbala* changed its meaning and came to denote a set of small bells, and from then on the crotal is neither seen nor heard of in Europe.

Finger cymbals are miniature cymbals, also of Asiatic origin, played chiefly by dancers who attach a pair to thumb and fore- or middle finger of each hand. Though they are usually made with both boss and rim they also occur in thimble form, and these are worn exactly like thimbles.

Known since antiquity, they became cult instruments among the Copts, with whom they still fulfill this function. Buonanni (1722) described them as "Coptic instruments," and shows a priest wearing one on thumb and middle finger of his left hand and one on thumb and forefinger of his right hand. But far from being restricted to the Copts, finger cymbals—usually made of brass, exceptionally of silver as this gives a brighter tone—are still played over an area extending from North Africa to China. The Chinese *p'eng chung* are of the deep, thimble type, and are worn on thumb and middle finger. Earlier in our century they were also worn by Greek dancers, but are currently scorned as being of Turkish derivation; however, they can still be heard in dance halls outside the mother country, where dancers prefer the two of a pair to be of slightly different pitches—about a semitone apart. This preference may be compared to the use of the small Javanese cymbal *engkuk*, inseparable from its twin, *kemong*; the two, with their gonglike rims, are identical except for their pitch.

The small, cup-shaped early medieval cymbals called *acetabula*, a Latin word for "vinegar containers," were described by Isidore of Seville (seventh century) and by Cassiodorus (sixth century) as being made of brass and silver. They must have been identical with the *oxybapha* (Greek for "vinegar cups") listed with other idiophones in the Byzantine alchemy treatise of around A.D. 800 already cited. As to their form, one can only surmise that they were deep and practically rimless. The notion of striking one cymbal alone instead of clashing two together was already known, for both Isidore and Suidas (tenth century) relate that a single cymbal could be played with a stick. From the tenth century on, regular cymbals are depicted, at first in illustrations of Eastern derivation: a Byzantine miniature of that century (MS grec. 752 of the Vatican Library) shows a pair being clashed horizontally, while, in a Beatus commentary of the same century in Madrid, the two forming a pair are connected by a long cord; here they are about to be clashed horizontally, but one of the player's hands is held higher than the other, suggesting familiarity with the modern sideswiping motion. A pair are held vertically by their handles in an eleventh-century fresco at Kiev Cathedral, to be clashed horizontally; this was to become the prevailing mode of playing in the West. Cymbals of thirteenth-century Spain, as portrayed in the *Cantigas de Santa María*, had virtually modern form and were larger than those of antiquity; in France and Britain they are depicted in the same century. They are allied to a pipe-and-tabor player in several thirteenth- and fourteenth-century miniatures of dance scenes.

The fourteenth-century *Echecs amoureux* includes *cymballes* among the loud instruments that accompanied dancers; at this period they are generally depicted as flat, held by leather strap handles, one above the other, and clashed vertically; the same position was current in fifteenth-century Italy, while, in the rare instances in which they can be observed in the sixteenth century, they are held in the modern edge-up position and clashed horizontally. Apparently forgotten thereafter, they reappear—but only to create local color—in the 1680 opera *Esther* of Nicholas Adam Strungk, then are once more forgotten until the introduction of "Turkish" music, that is, Janissary music, in the second half of the eighteenth century, through which they reentered the opera orchestra. Grétry used cymbals in the "Turkish" music of his *L'Amitié à l'épreuve* (1770), but so strange were they that Mme Favart, the harpist, was obliged to explain them to her fellow musicians as being little basins of bronze or silver having a diameter of 8 to 10 *pouces* (inches), a concavity of about 2 *pouces* depth, a flat rim of as much, with handle soldered to its convex side; she furthermore explained that they were clashed together. In 1779, in his *Iphigénie en Tauride*, Gluck introduced cymbals to lend local color to his chorus of Scythians, and soon thereafter they gained a permanent position in the orchestra. They were new to Burney in 1770—he called them "crotala." In the last quarter of the century military bands adopted the "clashpans," as they were familiarly known, also as a result of the impression created by "Turkish" music.

As folk instruments, cymbals have been played for centuries in Provence, probably as the continuation of a far older tradition. Made of bronze or steel and called *cymbalettes,* or *palets,* they formed an ensemble with a pair of miniature kettledrums; combined with a fife, these constituted a trio that, by long-established tradition, participated up to the outbreak of the French Revolution in the processions of Notre Dame de la Garde, Marseilles, and that survives at present in the little town of Salon.

The cymbals that had been brought to Europe by the Janissary bands were imported from Turkey, and ever since then Western orchestras and bands have depended almost exclusively on Turkey and China for their supply, although a few have been made in Italy. In recent years their manufacture has been undertaken—with greater or lesser degrees of success—in several other Western countries.

Apart from the ancient Near East, Asiatic cymbals appear in Central Asia in the early Christian era, and deep, almost campaniform varieties are seen on East Turkistan art objects of the third to seventh centuries.

Finger cymbals appear there from the sixth to the ninth centuries, while a plate-shaped version, first seen during this period, continues in existence thereafter. Cymbals are mentioned in the annals of the T'ang dynasty of China (A.D. 618–907); but they have no ritual tradition in China, unlike the adjacent countries, and in modern times have been given a prominent part in the theater. They are made in different sizes, and some attain a diameter of 60 centimeters (2 feet). Chinese orchestral cymbals have definite pitch; they are made of thin metal and grasped by the boss. The *po*, popular in both theater and opera, have peaked bosses and either flat or slightly turned rims. In neighboring Vietnam, cymbals are ritual instruments, except for some very large models that are at home in the theater. Thailand and Cambodia have small, bowl-shaped ones of brass, thick and heavy, with small rims, a pair of which are held in one hand to beat the measure in orchestras; that of the Mon is similar, hemispheric and rimless, and Jones (1964) reported a form exactly like it, albeit made of hemispheric fruit shells, in use in Africa by the Kissi. In Java, the *kechicher*, made in three sizes, is restricted to a few *gamelans* (Indonesian orchestras), except in eastern Java, where it is commonly encountered; one of a pair is affixed to a carved frame while the other is clashed against it. In some areas of the Malay archipelago an ancient function still prevails, namely that of dispelling evil spirits by terrifying them with the loud clashing of cymbals.

Not until the fifth century A.D. are cymbals represented in the plastic arts of India, at first bowl shaped, with or without handles, with flat models occurring from the sixth century on. By the sixteenth century large cymbals with small bosses appear in paintings, held in the same position as those of Western orchestras. Ancient Indian cymbals were not bossed, but in modern times have been made in many forms and sizes, varying from those resembling teacups to large models that look like gongs. The smallest, known as *mandirā*, often made in cup shape, are not only struck together by their rims, but also by their exterior surfaces so as to produce two different sounds. Their function is to accompany singers or to perform in instrumental ensembles. Some larger varieties actually sound more like gongs than cymbals; in north India they participate in religious ceremonies as well as in civilian festivities. Occurrence of the crotal, or forked cymbal, in neighboring Burma has already been mentioned.

In Turkey the old Anatolian cymbal was established as a martial instrument by the seventeenth century, and the tradition of its military use spread from there to the Balkan peoples and to the Kurds. In their homeland, cymbals were never accepted in art music. Called *zil* in Turkish, a word cognate with the Arabic *salāsil*, Hebrew *selslīm*, Pahlevi *sil*, Tibetan *sil-sil*, they are thicker, heavier, and flatter than those of China and are judged tonally superior by Western players. They have indefinite pitch. Today they are held by a leather strap passed through the vertex; their exact composition is a carefully guarded trade secret, but the alloy employed is known to consist of roughly 80 percent copper and 20 percent tin. As folk instruments, the crotals are still played.

Modern Western orchestras demand heavy cymbals with a diameter of at least 35 centimeters (14 inches), although rhythm bands frequently make use of lighter ones. Turkish cymbals are struck with a sideswiping, brushing motion, as clashing them together full force might cause them to crack, and, furthermore, a direct clash deadens the vibrations. By contrast, the Chinese cymbal—played singly—is struck with a beater (and thereby joins the group of percussion instruments). Though cymbals are clashed together in orchestral writing, in military bands one plate is often affixed to a bass drum while its performer strikes both the drum and clashes the cymbal against its fixed twin. In addition to traditional playing techniques, many modifications have been developed by rhythm band players: a single cymbal can be "crashed" by suspending it from a cord and then hitting it with a drumstick; or "choked" by immobilizing the lower of a pair on a metal rod so that it lies horizontally, leaving its upper twin mobile, with a pedal to lower it and cause the two to clash, or "choke." The opposite of "chokes" are "sock" cymbals: here the lower of a pair is moved upward against its fixed partner; finally, a variety called sizzle or rivet cymbals are drilled with holes for the attaching of jingles or rivets.

PERCUSSION IDIOPHONES

STAMPED IDIOPHONES

Just as the origin of concussion idiophones may be sought in hand clapping and body slapping, another body motion, that of stamping the feet, is the very distant ancestor of percussion idiophones (also called struck idiophones). This ancient rhythmic movement continues in existence, not only in relatively archaic cultures, but also among such sophisticated musicians as, for instance, Scottish bagpipers.

But the simple practice of ground stamping may be extended and its result enhanced by various means; sometimes a beam is placed upon the ground to produce greater resonance when stamped or drummed upon. Such beams have been reported from Africa, Asia, Surinam, the Pacific, and from the Negro population of Brazil. Another version is the stamped pit: greater sonority can be obtained by digging a pit or trench and covering it with a board. Thus the Modoc Indians of Tule, California, lay a board over a pit some 90 centimeters (3 feet) deep and about 60 centimeters (2 feet) long and wide; this is then stamped rhythmically by a barefooted man during certain ritual dances.

Finally, the motion of the foot is transferred to stamping sticks or poles, played either singly or in pairs. And if hollow bamboo shafts are selected in preference to sticks or poles they are termed stamping tubes. When one of a pair of sticks or tubes is of a different length from the other, the two will resonate at different pitches.

PERCUSSION BEAMS

Wooden boards are transformed into percussion instruments, but not necessarily stamped, in many parts of the world. In Madagascar a bamboo plank several meters long is either laid on the ground or suspended horizontally about 1 meter (40 inches) above it, and struck by several persons simultaneously, each holding two sticks. The occasions on which it is sounded include funeral wakes and dances. In one form or another, percussion beams are found in parts of all continents, frequently as signal instruments: in Zaire the *bomo,* a horizontally suspended beam, is struck with wooden sticks; the *o le polotu* of Samoan and Tongan chieftains accompanies solo singing; in Buddhist monasteries of Japan percussion beams are struck with a small mallet; in eighteenth-century Saint Petersburg, watchmen announced the hours by striking a free-hanging iron beam; and in North Germany the ancient *Hillebille,* originally a signal instrument of the Erzgebirge, has survived as a carnival instrument, struck with two mallets.

Use of a percussion beam in the Christian church is said by Amalarius of Metz (ninth century) to go back to the days when early Christians assembled in secret in crypts, but this is unlikely, if for no other reason than that the noise would have betrayed their presence. Nevertheless, it entered monastery and church at an early date, best known by its Greek name of *sēmantērion,* meaning "signal." Before the introduction of bells in the

Greek Orthodox church in the eleventh century, the faithful were summoned to worship by the *sēmantērion*, and during Easter Week, when church bells may not be rung, it still serves as their substitute, struck with a hammer. In the Eastern church and in monasteries, the *sēmantērion* is held in the left hand and struck alternately on each side with a wooden mallet. A smaller board is called *cheirosēmantron*, or "hand signal," to distinguish it from a larger model, found suspended in the tower by iron chains and called *megasēmantron* ("great signal"). Occasionally metal beams are substituted for those of wood; long and narrow, such a beam is known as *hagiosideron*, or "holy iron." During the period of Turkish domination of Greece, church bells were forbidden, and both *sēmantērion* and *hagiosideron* took their place. The *sēmantērion* has also substituted for bells in the Roman Catholic church during Easter Week, and is still sounded in Mediterranean countries; it is called *lignum sacrum* in church Latin. Richelet recorded its use in seventeenth-century France.

Outside Europe, *sēmantēria* are found in the Coptic churches of Egypt, and in Ethiopia a *hagiosideron* or a lithophone (see page 29) may be strung to a tree near a church, or suspended at its entrance.

Sets of tuned, hanging wooden beams are found among the Magindanao of the Philippines, who play melodies upon them.

A different form is met with in eastern Siberia, where among the Orochi of the Amur region and the Nivikhi of the same area and of Sakhalin, a percussion log is suspended from a rough framework of poles during the bear festivals, to be struck by women only.

PERCUSSION DISKS

Struck bronze disks, suspended from a circular wooden frame, have long been in use in East Asia, and the practice of sounding single disks in Indian temples still obtains. The ancient Roman *discus*, a metal plate with large central hole for suspension that served as a signal giver derives from such Eastern forebears.

The sound of beaten bronze or iron objects was believed in antiquity to cause specters to flee. Thus in Rome, after the annual visit to their former homes that ghosts of the dead were believed to pay, these were shown to the door with the request to depart, the request being emphasized by the clanging of a bronze plate. Like the bell, another bronze object, such disks had great apotropaic powers. (Kouretes danced over the infant Zeus in the Idaean Cave of Crete, beating their bronze-covered shields with their bare swords to protect him from Kronos. And when

Idaean Zeus became identified on Crete with Dionysus, the latter was depicted as an infant, surrounded by armed Kouretes clashing swords on circular bronze shields.)

A more sophisticated version of the percussion disk has existed ever since ancient times, namely the twirled disk (cf. rattle drums, page 151). As it exists today, a metal disk is affixed to a long handle; around the disk's periphery are attached a number of pellet bells that strike the disk when it is twirled. During the excavation of a tomb at Colci, Etruria, two thin bronze disks were found, hung with small rings around the rim and affixed to metal handles, and at Pompeii a metal disk hung with pellet bells, also on a handle, was brought to light. It is more than likely that these were already ritual instruments at the time, for the percussion disk has come down to the present century in connection with rites of the Eastern Christian churches. Bianchini (1729) illustrated an instrument purportedly in use by Armenians in their religious services; it was a disk on a stick, with pellet bells strung around the rim. In Egypt today the same instrument is called *marawe* or *maruwe*. Usually the disk is of silver and the pellet bells of copper. When twirled by its long handle, the pellet bells strike against the disk. Curiously enough, this instrument has a double: it is also made as a membranophone, specifically as a rattle drum.

Other Oriental churches employing the *marawe* are the Syrian-Christian, the Lebanon Maronites, the Greek Orthodox church in Egypt, and the Christian Copts of Egypt, already mentioned. It is twirled during Mass and also at important feast-day services. In an Egyptian variant, little rattles are threaded to iron rings, which are in turn attached to the disk.

The secular *gong beri* of Java has a curious history: it started life as a drum, and as such was used for both signal and martial requirements; later it was transformed into a bossless and rimless "gong"—actually a percussion disk—but was denied admittance to the *gamelan* because of its martial antecedents.

So far only single disks have been discussed, but percussion disks are also made as chimes in eastern Asia: in Japan a chime of bronze plaques of irregular shape and graduated sizes, sometimes gilded, is struck with a wooden mallet in those Buddhist temples where it is encountered.

PERCUSSION STICKS

Percussion sticks occur either singly or as a set; or several sticks may be united so as to form one instrument, such as, for instance, a xylophone.

Their function today is not only that of accentuating rhythm, but in some areas it continues a tradition of magic associations: on Celebes and Banks Island they serve to ward off evil spirits. In parts of Uganda their use is ritual—sets of sticks are struck at circumcision ceremonies—while elsewhere in Uganda Lango boys make purely secular use of them as practice drums: they break a length of cane into three sections, leaving them attached to one another, and bend the outer sections so as to form a U; the ends are then inserted into the ground, and the center, now forming a bridge, is drummed upon.

As rhythm instruments they occur in many forms: for example, large percussion logs of wood or of bamboo are beaten with a stick to accompany dances or singing, sometimes as part of magical rites. Although they are usually played by men, women strike them in certain areas, notably in southern Celebes: a long bamboo pole is struck with two shorter switches on that island. A Cuban form, derived from the Nigerian Yoruba, consists of a bunch of nine twigs; another Cuban instrument, the *jicarita*, is shaped like a short, deep spoon of wood; it is played in pairs by striking two rhythmically and alternately against the ground or against a table. The Chinese *pang tse*, a half-round redwood stick, is cupped in the hollow of the left hand and tapped with a second stick of identical length; in small theater orchestras and in opera it not only provides rhythmic accents but also determines the tempo. The same instrument is known in Haiti and Cuba as a *clave*; there it is made of lignum vitae and played in the same manner as in China. Western rhythm bands have appropriated it, naming it *claves*. Percussion sticks exist in Southeast Asia, Negro Africa, Madagascar, North America, the Pacific, and among Afro-Americans of South America. In Europe the only older single percussion stick to have continued in existence until now is the metallic triangle.

THE TRIANGLE

This little instrument in its modern form is but a round metal rod bent to form an equilateral triangle, left open where the ends meet in order to permit the whole length to vibrate, and suspended by a fine thread so as not to interrupt the vibrations produced by striking it with a beater of the same metal. Due chiefly to the many inharmonic overtones, a triangle's indefinite pitch can be heard above a full orchestra.

When it first appeared in the fourteenth century it was named *trépie* or *trepit* in French; Machaut mentions a *trespié*, and in 1396 a player of the *tripet* was recompensed at the court of the princes of Savoy. Early forms were usually trapezoid or stirrup shaped, and the rod was closed at its juncture; yet in the Book of Hours of Jeanne d'Evreux of 1325 a triangular instrument is twice depicted. In fifteenth-century Italy, probably the country of its origin, it was called *staffa* ("stirrup"), and in 1404 Eberhard Cersne referred to it as *Stegeryff*, the German word for "stirrup." During the greater part of its history the triangle is generally seen with a number of loose rings threaded on it; prior to 1660 three are standard (Filippino Lippi [ca. 1490] shows but two in his *Ascension of the Virgin*) and thereafter as many as five appear, strung as they had been on the sistrum, as though that instrument had projected itself across the centuries (and indeed, Jan Komenský, writing as Comenius in 1664, translates "triangle" into Latin as *sistrum*). These rings do not disappear completely before the early nineteenth century. Judging by Flemish art works, the North seems to have favored the trapeze form with rings more than did Italy, for a perfectly plain triangular instrument, devoid of rings and held just as it is today, appears on an inlay from Orvieto Cathedral, now in the local museum of the Duomo, dating from the first half of the fourteenth century. The late fourteenth-century Bible of King Wenceslav of Bohemia also contains the representation of a ringless triangle, and in 1417 a stirrup-shaped version, equally devoid of rings, is illustrated in the Olomouc (Olmütz, Moravia) Bible.

Despite its acceptance in religious art, the triangle was a dance instrument; Jean de Gerson (d. ca. 1429), the chancellor of Paris University, mentions a *tripos* of steel that was played at dances, and in 1475 *staffetti* ("little stirrups") and other instruments resounded at the wedd'ng of Camilla of Aragon and Costanzo Sforza. The change from stirrup to triangular form is possibly reflected in the change of terminology, even though, as has been shown, the triangular form had existed earlier. Sachs (1940) pointed out that its designation as a triangle does not occur prior to 1589. Perhaps the first description of the manner in which it was played is that of Jacques Cellier (1585); his *cimballe* is a closed triangle provided with six rings: "the *cimballe* hangs from the left hand thumb and is struck on its inside by a steel stick in the right hand." He specifies that the beater is of the same material as the instrument proper and as its rings.

During his visit to Dresden in 1629, Philip Hainhofer noted *ain dreyandel mit Schellen* ("a triangle with pellet bells") in the ducal *Pfeiffen-*

kammer. Yet its continued presence in the hands of angels and even of muses in the fifteenth and sixteenth centuries could not prevent its being found increasingly in the hands of persons of lower quality, and Mersenne (who calls it a *cimbale*) remarks (1636) that it was a beggar's instrument. A Stuttgart regulation of 1721 governing cornett players lists triangles together with bagpipes and hurdy-gurdies "and similar nonmusical instruments," all forbidden to cornettists, be they master or apprentice, and to Grassineau (1740) "the modern Cymbal is a paultry instrument, chiefly in use among vagrants & gypsies . . .," yet in 1732 it shared the distinguished company of a horn and a bandora in the frontispiece to Walther's dictionary; the author called it *cymbalum*, but gave no indication of its status.

The triangle's acceptance in the orchestra predates its appearance in the "Turkish" music by several decades. Sachs (1940) reported its employment in the opera at Hamburg as early as 1710; in the second half of the century it was added to the various components of "Turkish" music, and in Germany it seems to have passed into the realm of folk music, for in Goethe's *Wilhelm Meisters Lehrjahre* of 1795–1796 some miners accompany their songs with zithers and a triangle. It entered military bands in the nineteenth century. Vaclav F. Červeny, the brass instrument maker, attempted to develop the simple triangle; to this end he built a *Glockentriangel* ("bell triangle") in 1877, in form of an inverted V, made of a four-sided metal bar; when struck with a wooden mallet this emitted a bell-like tone, but when struck in the usual manner it sounded like an ordinary triangle. This experiment did not find favor, however, and the round rod remains in use.

XYLOPHONES

Fundamentally, xylophones are nothing more than a set of percussion sticks, usually tuned; they are played in both very primitive and in highly developed forms and societies, and are among the few instruments that can be followed through all stages of their evolution by actual observation. Developed forms consist of a series of tuned keys laid parallel to one another, each supported at the two points forming vibrational nodes; on primitive instruments, the keys are not necessarily tuned. All are played with sticks or with knobbed beaters. Xylophone keys, as well as those of the related metallophones, are subject to the laws governing free bars. When struck, they form a transverse node near each end, at about two-ninths of the total length, where no vibrations occur. Consequently, these are the points at which a key can be pierced or placed upon straw, cushions, and so on, without impairment of tone. And as their vibrations are inversely proportionate to the square of their length, the keys can be kept relatively short for the pitch required: a slat twice as long as another but of the same thickness will sound two octaves lower; conversely, if two keys are of the same length but one is twice as thick as the other, they will sound one octave apart. Width is not critical. Tuning is effected by reducing the length to raise the pitch, or by reducing the thickness to lower it (cf. music boxes, page 104). Both in Southeast Asia and in Africa wood is pared away from the central portion on the underside to lower the pitch. In fine tuning, keys may be sharpened if necessary by paring the undersides of the ends. The higher the pitch, the shorter and thicker a key becomes, until the treble keys of some instruments are virtually round rods. As to the resonators, they are graduated in size to roughly conform to the pitch of the individual keys to which they are attached, and are then fine tuned, both in Indonesia and in Africa, by building up a collar of beeswax on the mouth of the resonator until the latter is in tune with its key.

Primitive Xylophones

In its simplest form, the pit or ground xylophone is merely a pit or trench acting as resonator for a few wooden bars placed over it; the bars are isolated from the ground by setting them on bundles of grass or on wooden members at their nodal points. This form is still played in East and West Africa (Uganda, Kenya, Guinea, Nigeria, Dahomey), as well as by children on the Middle Chari and parts of the Central Congo basin. The eight-key pit *ndara* is kept only by the sultan of Alur, Uganda; its keys are supported by bundles of grass and are pegged to the ground over a pit.

Log xylophones have no resonator of any kind but are composed of two banana stems or other logs placed on the ground, with a few keys laid across them. This form is found in East and West Africa, Indonesia, New Britain, and Papua. A leg xylophone is formed by placing a few keys across the outstretched legs of a person sitting on the ground— usually a woman—and is an extension of the log xylophone. It occurs in Africa (Guinea, Dahomey, and Zambia), on Madagascar, and in Indonesia. Sometimes this type is struck by a second person, at other times by the sitter. In Nias a combination leg-log xylophone is played by women who sit with their legs extended over a trench dug in the ground, with three or four keys laid over their thighs. The Orang Belende and Orang Mentera of Malaya have a four-key leg xylophone with keys placed across the outstretched legs of two performers who sit facing one another; a similar instrument is played in like manner by the Land Dayak of Borneo. The more archaic peoples of Sumatra play xylophones with bamboo keys, and bamboo also occurs as material in Thailand and Cambodia.

In more developed forms the keys are graduated in size and are always tuned; they are placed upon logs that assume both the form and function of a frame, and finally the frame becomes a trough. Individual gourd resonators are suspended from the keys of African xylophones to augment the sound, and often a membrane is affixed over a hole cut in each resonator—a mirliton device for the modification of timbre. A small, portable version of Nigeria has oxhorn resonators.

Xylophones in Asia

The xylophone's highest development took place in Southeast Asia, its territory of origin, where it is found both on the mainland and in the archipelago, and where trough xylophones were depicted in the four-teenth century (in Java) showing two keys being struck simultaneously, just as they are in certain regions of Africa today. But trough xylophones are not the only form met with in Southeast Asia—all known forms occur there in one area or another—nor is their Asian distribution restricted to that region, as the *mokkin* of Japan, for example, is a trough xylophone having from thirteen to sixteen keys, a rhythm rather than a melody instrument, that is played chiefly in *kabuki* music. On all such instruments the trough itself is an open-top box on which the keys are laid, and which acts as resonator for all keys on a nonselective basis. Older Indonesian examples were carved from a single block of wood but today they are built up of boards. Although they are typical of Indonesia, the solid-box type occurs also in the Niger delta region of West Africa.

The royal xylophone of Burma, the *pattala*, is a large instrument with up to twenty-three keys of different lengths, suspended over an elaborately carved trough; keys are fine tuned by affixing wax pellets to the underside, a system used elsewhere in Indonesia and also in Africa. Trough forms exist also in Thailand and Cambodia, and in the archipelago. They are prominent in the *gamelans* of Java, where the largest used in the *gamelan pelog* (orchestra tuned to the *pelog* scale), has from sixteen to twenty-one keys of teak or other hardwood, sometimes even bamboo, laid on small isolating cushions and held in position by pins; their compass extends usually from three to four octaves, lacking keys for the notes called *pelog* and *bem* (or *barang*); exchange keys for the different tunings are kept inside the trough. The player holds mushroom-shaped beaters between forefingers and thumbs.

Xylophones of Indonesian (and some mainland) percussion orchestras have various compasses and pitches, systematically determined. In addition to large, multioctave instruments there exist several smaller ones, each of which represents tonally a cutout of the large models. Together these single-octave models duplicate the entire range of the multioctave sizes. Tuning is either to the scale known as *pelog* or to that named *slendro*, the former pentatonic, the latter heptatonic.

Two beaters are commonly used in Indonesia, but in Bali the *gambang* players use four, two in each hand, each pair held so as to form a V. As early as the seventh or eighth century B.C., such forked beaters can be seen in sculpture. Today a beater is held typically—and elegantly—between the second and third fingers, thumbs up, a position similar to that in which curved dulcimer beaters were held in fifteenth- and sixteenth-century Europe.

Xylophones in Africa and the Americas

In a brilliant study, A. M. Jones (1964) has demonstrated beyond reasonable doubt what several earlier investigators suspected, namely the provenance of African xylophones from Southeast Asia. Not only are the instruments themselves similar, but unmistakable parallelisms exist in playing techniques, in tunings, and even in the music performed. Kirby (1934) was already convinced that African xylophones with resonators were of Malayan origin. The playing of two or more together is another feature common to both areas. Exactly when or how the migration took place from Asia has not yet been elucidated, but it certainly occurred before the arrival of the Portuguese: Jones points out that ibn-Battuta, the Arabic traveler, reached the Niger River around 1352, and in his description of the kingdom of Mali referred to a musical instrument struck with sticks that was undoubtedly a xylophone provided with resonators. Later, in the sixteenth century, the Portuguese João dos Santos found a xylophone he called *ambira* in use among the Karanga of Ethiopia, furnished with resonators and spider's-egg membranes; its beaters had knobs made of balls of sinew. Dos Santos commented on the fact that certain instruments had their treble keys at the right, others at the left, from which it may be gathered that then as now some African xylophones were built for both right-handed and left-handed players. The *mbira* or *mbila*, as it is now called, is still played, not only by the Karanga but also in the Congo area and in South Africa.

Developed African xylophones consist of a variable number of graduated, tuned keys, usually of hardwood, suspended by thongs or cords at their nodal points over a rectangular wooden frame; each key is provided with a tuned resonator of calabash or other hard fruit, into which a hole is generally cut for the insertion of a spider's-egg or other thin membrane—a mirliton device that was described by eighteenth-century travelers. Some are solo instruments, others are intended for ensemble playing only. The Chopi of Portuguese East Africa have a *gamelan*-type orchestra consisting of xylophones, drums, and rattle. Their xylophones are made exclusively for ensemble playing, and are built in five sizes, roughly corresponding to soprano, alto, tenor, bass, and double bass, the four highest of which all overlap, and together have a compass of just over four octaves. In pitch, compass, and scale, these are substantially the same as those of Thailand, and are played with rubber-headed beaters similar to those of Indonesia. Chopi orchestras may have anywhere from five to thirty xylophone players. Further north, the Baganda have a large xylophone with from sixteen to eighteen keys, slightly convex, and played simultaneously by five performers, each wielding two strikers. Ensemble playing was already noted by seventeenth-century travelers, who reported seeing near the mouth of the Congo River three, four, and even five xylophones being played together.

African xylophones are tuned to the same system as those of Indonesia; furthermore, Jones ascertained that both African and Indonesian instruments have in common intercalary tones at or close to the same positions, as well as gaps of a fourth and a bisect fourth. Players generally hold one beater in each hand but sometimes a pair is held in each, just as in Indonesia (cf. similarities between African and Asian metallophones, page 33).

Distribution of the xylophone in Africa is not continent wide, but is restricted to an area roughly south of 15° north latitude on the west coast, and of 5° north latitude on the east coast, down to Angola and Mozambique. Historically they have been associated with royalty in Africa, and, according to Olga Boone (1936), all those of Zaire are prerogatives of the chiefs; in Uganda some are still royal instruments, but there the status is changing rapidly. As implements of protective magic they are still found in Angola; the museum of Dundu preserves a number of musical instruments of reduced form, notably xylophones with from two to five keys, magical objects all, to be suspended above doorways to protect the inhabitants from being murdered or carried off.

The marimba, a xylophone supplied with gourd resonators, known to have existed in the Congo region ever since the seventeenth century, is still played there and in neighboring areas of Angola, and may derive its name from the Bantu root *imba* ("song"). Under this name it was introduced to Central and South America. Cubans make it both in its traditional form and also as a metallophone. In Mexico the keys are laid on a large rectangular frame with legs, big enough for its complement of four performers, who play it simultaneously, each provided with two beaters; elongated cedarwood resonators furnished with mirliton devices are suspended from the keys. Most investigators believe that xylophones reached America in the early days of the slave trade, but Izikowitz (1935) was of the opinion that it had arrived in pre-Columbian times, as it is found not only among the Negro but also among the Indian population. However, Amerinds who have xylophones are either coastal peoples or they have had contacts with coastal areas or populations; some thirty years ago the Colorado Indians of western Ecuador informed the author that they had received theirs from Guatemala.

Xylophones in Europe

The xylophone reached Europe from Indonesia, and curiously enough it was first heard of as an organ stop in 1506, when it was termed a new register. It is then mentioned in 1511 by both Schlick and Virdung; they called it *hültzig glechter* ("wooden sticks"). But between the introduction of an instrument and its imitation as an organ stop there must be a time lapse during which the instrument becomes sufficiently well known to warrant its imitation; the xylophone's arrival in Europe can therefore be placed at not later than the final decade of the fifteenth century. After 1517 it does not seem to have been built as an organ register any more. A woodcut of Hans Holbein the Younger from his *Dance of Death* series, originating between 1523 and 1525, is the earliest known representation of the new instrument: Death carries it suspended horizontally like a tray by a strap from his neck, with the biggest key closest to his body—or, rather, skeleton. Agricola's followed shortly thereafter (1528), with twenty-five cylindrical keys, and Praetorius was first to show flat ones. The keys were insulated by a bed of straw, giving rise to such names as "straw fiddle," *Strohfiedel, madera y paja.* From the late sixteenth century on it was also called *régale de bois* in French, a name later Englished to "rigols."

Xylophones composed of graduated bars strung on a cord and suspended vertically like a ladder, the smallest at the top, became known a little later. Called *ginebras* in Spanish, where they are recorded from 1628 on, this form was also illustrated by Mersenne in 1636, with twelve graduated keys; he took it for a Turkish instrument and called it *échelette* ("small ladder"). German writers of the seventeenth century referred to it as *Xylorganum*; Caspar Schott stated that he had heard them in Rome and Würzburg.

A third form had appeared by Mersenne's time, the keyed xylophone. In his day it was in use by "the Flemings" as a practice instrument for carillonneurs; in the following century Majer (1732) went so far as to call it "the xylophone of the Flemings." Its use by carillonneurs is also attested by other writers.

The old, horizontal form remained a folk instrument, best known in the northern countries: Austria, Germany, Poland, and Russia. During the 1830s it was further popularized by the efforts of Michael Joseph Gusikow, a Pole who concertized extensively with it from 1832 on, covering an area from Odessa to Paris. A new artist named Eben appeared in Berlin in 1839, and critics reported that the public loved "this musicless instrument." Little original music for the xylophone was written down, but during his last years Ignaz Schweigl (d. 1803) wrote a number of concertante pieces for it, marking the end of an era. Saint-Saëns reintroduced it into the orchestra with his *Danse macabre* of 1874, and from then on it has been admitted to symphony orchestra and variety entertainment alike, ultimately to become an important component of rhythm bands.

German, Austrian, and East European makers did not arrange their xylophone bars in keyboard form, as did their competitors elsewhere; instead they utilized a four-row system analogous to the Alpine dulcimer (*Hackbrett*) stringing, placing the diatonic tones in the two center rows. Up to the early 1920s such instruments were built with their wooden keys resting on straw, and they are still called *Strohfiedel* in rural Germany.

Today's developed instruments were made possible by the 1927 invention by Hermann E. Winterhoff of the arcuate notch, an arc cut on the underside of each key to improve the tone quality and to give greater definition of pitch. Modern Western instruments are built with varying compasses, that of the larger models reaching from c′ to c⁴, with keys arranged in two rows like those of a piano keyboard. Each key is furnished with a tubular metal resonator suspended vertically beneath it. Large xylophones with resonators and a four-octave compass are known as marimbas; they have been made commercially in the United States since 1910.

CRYSTALLOPHONES

Percussion sticks can also be made of glass, in which case they are known as crystallophones. Played with two sticks like a xylophone, small diatonic instruments were made in Europe as children's toys in the nineteenth century and possibly earlier. Larger models were played as true musical instruments, and those that were chromatic had their bars arranged in two rows in piano keyboard formation. In the late eighteenth and early nineteenth centuries, crystallophones were furnished with regular piano keyboards and were struck with hammers. Apparently the first successful such combination was the *pianoforte à cordes de verre* ("pianoforte with glass strings") by Beyer of Paris, said to have been named "glasschord" by Benjamin Franklin. But there may be confusion here, as Franklin's glass harmonica was known not only by its original name, armonica, but also as "glassychord" and variants thereof. One surviving instrument is inscribed *Glasscord* [sic] *de Beyer approuvé par l'Académie Royale des Sciences de Paris le 18 mars 1785*; it has a three-octave compass from g° to g³. The tuned glass bars were laid horizontally on strips of thick cloth and struck from above by small wooden hammers. Modifications, elaborations, and imitations of this were made well into the nineteenth century, with the bars arranged in either one or several rows. But interest flagged after a while, and the crystallophones joined other ephemera of the day.

LITHOPHONES

Various types of stone are capable of vibrating when struck with a heavy beater, provided they are of suitable thinness, and of emitting a bright, clear tone that may continue to reverberate for several minutes. The acoustical potentialities of such stones have been exploited in ancient and modern times in areas as far apart as Venezuela and Vietnam, Ethiopia and Europe. Single stones having musical properties are referred to as sonorous stones, musical stones, or phonoliths; when forming sets they are called stone chimes, while the word "lithophone" denotes more loosely any sounding instrument of stone. The origin of their use as musical instruments has not been determined, but their dispersal points to South China as a possible point from which diffusion may have taken place, if indeed the sonority naturally inherent in certain stones was not a polygenetic discovery.

Lithophones occur as plaques and as bars; as plaques they are suspended vertically, while the oblong bars, rather like oversized xylophone keys, are suspended or placed horizontally. Larger chimes are tuned to the intervals of a musical scale. Just as the xylophone can be followed and observed through the different stages of its development from archaic to sophisticated, so can the lithophone.

The bar type of chime remained unknown to the West until 1949, when one of undeterminable age came to light in rural Annam; in 1958 three bars, the surviving portion of a once larger set, were encountered in actual use in the same region, placed across the seated player's thighs in the same position that leg-xylophone keys would occupy. Several other chimes of a similar nature have been found since, the largest of which consists of ten bars varying in length from 65 centimeters (26 inches) to 1 meter (40 inches), said to yield a pentatonic scale of uneven intervals. So far it has not been possible to date any of the Vietnamese bar lithophones.

Plaque lithophones have long been cult instruments in Vietnam, with those in temple service attaining up to 1 meter (40 inches) in diameter and a thickness of 10 centimeters (4 inches), assuming the form of an irregular disk; from this usage it is thought likely that bar lithophones once had a ritual character. Musical stones in plaque form are also met with on Samoa and have been reported from Venezuela and Ecuador; in the latter country a green stone was formerly cut to a length of about 30 centimeters (12 inches) and suspended vertically.

On the island of Chios and in Ethiopia, resonant stones substitute for bells in some Christian churches, suspended either from a tree or from a frame set up outside the church door; in Ethiopia they are struck with a pebble, almost in the manner of a gong. Although they occur as single phonoliths, they are also formed into sets of two, three, and even four stones, rough and crudely fashioned.

But the country in which the lithophone reached the height of its development is China. There the generic name for instruments made of stone is *ch'ing*. Musical stones and the art of tuning them have been known to the Chinese since antiquity. Single stones often assume symbolic forms, such as that of a lucky cloud, a fish, or even two fishes side by side, a bat with outspread wings, a bell, and so on. These are suspended from a frame so as to hang freely and, providing that shape and fashioning have not impaired the vibrations, will continue to emit a clear sound for several minutes when struck with a mallet. The single *te ch'ing* is more often cut into a shape resembling a square or an L, the larger portion of which is struck, and, in addition to the more common stones, it is also made of marble or even agate or jade. Sometimes a *te ch'ing* receives an application of lacquer and is then painted, or the surface may be engraved.

Sixteen L-shaped *te ch'ing* form a *pien ch'ing*, or stone chime, probably the best known of all lithophones. A ritual and imperial instrument at a very early date, the chime has since been restricted to Confucian temples. Its stones are all of identical length and width but of different thicknesses; they are suspended in two rows of eight stones each, one above the other, by the "knee," or juncture of the two branches, in a large rectangular frame, the upper row of which contains the male *lü* ("semitones"), the lower the female *lü*. The L shape is a very ancient one; a sonorous stone from the Anyang period of the Shang dynasty (ca. 1401–ca. 1123 B.C.) was found in a tomb at Anyang, made of gray limestone, decorated with a stylized tiger, and pierced with a hole for suspension. As chimes, such stones are depicted, together with other instruments, on bas-reliefs of Wu tombs in Shantung Province. A ninth-century poem of the T'ang poet Tu Mu compares the sound of a lithophone to that of a beautiful bird, and in the thirteenth century Kublai Khan is said to have augmented the orchestra of his day by addition of the lithophone.

The same ancient Chinese form is found in Korea, where it is also a Confucian instrument, and where the oldest chime dates from the fourteenth century.

Sonorous stones were also known to Europe in antiquity, for Pliny mentions the black *chalcophonos*, a stone ringing like brass, but its musical possibilities were apparently not exploited at that time. Only after the xylophone had been popularized in the nineteenth-century West were attempts made to imitate it in stone. A *Lithokymbalon* of alabaster was produced in 1837 by Franz Weber of Vienna, to be followed in 1841 by the "rock harmonicon" of an English stonemason named Richardson— it was the age of the harmonicon—a series of tuned basalt bars, originally composed of ten or twelve stones, later enlarged to a five-and-one-half-octave compass and played with wooden beaters; several other efforts were followed in 1883 by the *clavier de silex* of Baudres, which had twenty-six flint and two schist bars, all in natural formation, but shortly thereafter interest in musical stones died out in Europe.

METALLOPHONES

Asian Metallophones

The oldest known metallophones occur in Asia, where they have remained in use until the present time. Like the lithophones, they are found in two forms, in bars or in plaques, and either in a vertical arrangement suspended from an upright frame or in a horizontal version, resting on a rectangular frame that is often elaborately carved. Of these the second, horizontal, variety is by far the most common. To the first belongs the Chinese *fang hiang*, a metal imitation of the older lithophone, with its sixteen bars suspended in two rows. Known since the seventh century, when it was introduced by the orchestra of a Turkic people, this form proceeded to Korea in the twelfth century; it may still be encountered there, albeit infrequently, now made of iron plates. The single metal plaque, called *hsiang pan* in China and made of thick brass, assumes the same form as its stone counterpart, both being struck with a long stick; it exists also in Japan, where it is found in Buddhist temples.

Indonesia and Indochina have metallophones constructed like xylophones, and are indeed metal counterparts of the latter. They reach their highest development in the archipelago, chiefly among the Javanese and Balinese. But even the less advanced Dayak of Borneo have a metallophone with seven bars set on a common resonator. On the mainland iron (in Cambodia) or steel (in Thailand) is the material from which the bars are made, but on the islands bronze is usual. Important components of the *gamelan*, metallophones of Java and Bali are grouped as *sarons* and *genders*. The former are trough metallophones, with the trough functioning as a nonselective resonator for all the bars, just as it does for xylophone keys. The bars are secured by metal pins passing through holes at the nodal points and insulated by resting on some soft material. Frequently the trough is carved to resemble a dragon. A version with bamboo bars—actually a trough xylophone, but it bears the name *saron*—exists in rural areas, and Kunst (1949) suggested it might represent

the survival of a premetallic form. As a metallophone, the *saron* goes
back in this area to at least A.D. 800, when it is seen on the Borobudur
reliefs in Java. Largest in compass is the *gambang gangsa,* a multioctave
instrument now dying out, which forms part of the *gamelan;* all other
sarons are smaller, with a one-octave compass. Those tuned to *slendro*
scales have six, seven, or eight bars, those tuned in *pelog* have seven. Each
of these represents a tonal cutout of the larger *gambang gangsa,* and,
taken together, they cover its entire range. According to Kunst, the
gambang gangsa is representative of an older period when the four smaller
sarons had not come into existence, and together they have been likened
to a *gambang gangsa* "fallen apart."

The second type of Indonesian metallophone is the *gender,* with bronze
bars strung on cords passed through holes at their nodal points, and suspended over a carved wooden frame; usually each bar lies above a tubular
resonator hanging in the frame. In most cases these are of bamboo,
closed at the lower end by a node and tuned in unison to the key to which
each lends acoustic support. Newer instruments, however, may have metal
or glass resonators, half stopped so that the whole instrument can be
built lower, in order to enable the player to sit on the ground. *Gender-*
type metallophones, though not always provided with resonators, are
known to have existed in the archipelago as early as 1157, and early
genders with ten bars in *slendro* tuning have been excavated; nowadays
they have eleven or thirteen bars, and the smaller, one-octave versions
have but six or seven bars. All are played with mushroom-shaped beaters
held loosely between fore- and middle fingers.

In construction, tone sequence, and pitches, African xylophones closely
resemble these Indonesian metallophones; in structure the *genders,* with
their individual resonators and cord-strung bars are closest to the African
instruments; as regards pitch, compass, and tonal sequence, the *genders*
and all *sarons* except the *saron panerus* have their African counterparts
in wood. The metallophone itself is not entirely absent from the African
xylophone "belt," for Nigeria has one with fourteen bars of iron and
with calabash resonators. The inference seems inescapable that migration
from Indonesia to Africa took place at a period that cannot yet be pin-
pointed.

Another Javanese form of metallophone is the *gong kemodong,* consisting of two large bronze or iron bars with bosses (in West Java it is a
single bar) suspended on cords over a hollow frame like a miniature
gender; two earthenware pots are frequently set in the frame below the

bars to act as resonators. Its chief use is to substitute for the large *gong ageng*, a true gong, and hence an expensive object.

European Metallophones

By the second half of the seventeenth century metallophones had reached the Netherlands from Indonesia, and in 1695 an Amsterdam *klokenist* had for sale *"eenige staeff spellen"* ("several bar chimes") of his own make, with a three- or four-octave compass, available at either cornett or organ pitch. *Staafspel*, as it is now spelled, could of course mean either xylophone or metallophone, but a bell founder may be presumed to prefer making metal instruments. A few years later, in 1703, Brossard referred to a "carillon" of pieces of metal; Quirijn van Blankenburg described a *staafspel* of bronze in the early eighteenth century, and from that time on metallophones served as practice instruments for carillonneurs in the Low Countries—one dated 1720 with steel bars was preserved in the Berlin Hochschule collection—some furnished with a piano-type keyboard and hammers, others with a carillon manual and a pedalboard. But apart from their usefulness to carillonneurs, metallophones in Europe always led a peripheral existence: Grassineau (1740) writes of "a kind of instrument which we likewise call a cymbal," having bars made of a compound of bell metal and silver, all pierced at both ends for support by pins set in wooden members and grouped in two rows to correspond to piano keyboard disposition; its near-forty bars were struck with knobbed sticks and its sound was pronounced agreeable, "being something exceeding soft, the low notes resembling the Flute."

Among the instruments inventoried at the death of the Parisian harpsichord maker Galland in 1760 was a *carillon à lames* ("bar carillon") of two octaves. Steel, rather than bronze, was the metal that came to be employed both in the Low Countries and in the areas to which metallophones spread from there. Provided with a keyboard, one served in Handel's *Saul*; as "carillon" and struck with a beater, another appears as the *stromento d'acciaio* of Mozart's *The Magic Flute*. But the form in which it gained a Western identity from the eighteenth century on was as the glockenspiel.

The glockenspiel. The glockenspiel originated as a miniature carillon, a series of small tuned bells, as its name indicates (it is the German for "bell chime"). When, in order to render it portable, its bells were transformed into metal bars, the old name was retained. Exactly the same process can be followed in India, where the *septaghantika* (Sanscrit for "seven bells") originally was composed of seven bells, struck with a single hammer, but now it either has fourteen bells with individual hammers or it is made as a metallophone. Transformation of bells into bars was effected in the glockenspiel's case in order to obtain not only greater portability, but also greater ease of manipulation and surer tuning. The bars are arranged in two rows like the keys of a piano and are played with two knobbed beaters. Since the latter part of the eighteenth century it has been an orchestral instrument, at first used for special effects only, but now it is an integral part of symphony and opera orchestras, and lately also of dance bands. The bars are flat rectangles of steel of graduated lengths, with a usual compass of two and one-half octaves from G to C, notated as g° to c³ regardless of absolute pitch. Resonators were added in 1935 by William F. Ludwig of Chicago. Some models are additionally furnished with a small keyboard and metal hammers that strike the bars from beneath; these are known as keyboard glockenspiels and were already in use in the eighteenth century, but, at that time, with a spring rather than with a hammer action.

As a portable instrument designed for the use of marching bands, the glockenspiel had about an octave's worth of flat metal bars hung in a lyre-shaped metal frame, which form caused it to be known as bell lyre, or even as plain lyre. Set upon a wooden handle and tapped with a metal beater, this was carried in front of the player with the lyre on a level with his head. As a nonportable military instrument it was given a larger compass, made fully chromatic, with bars laid out on a framework in a box. Except for its being struck with round, metal-headed beaters, the "bells," "carillon," "lyre," or glockenspiel does not differ from Grassineau's "cymbal." An attempt was made to give it a more appropriate name during the period of the "harmonicon" craze, when it was dubbed metal harmonica. But the addition of pellet bells and horsetails to portable glockenspiels—a form of instrumental cross-fertilization from the pseudo-Janissary jingling johnny—by some military bands from the 1860s on did not help matters of nomenclature: ultimately the English had "lyra-glockenspiels," the French remained true to the traditional *carillon*, the Germans abandoned *Glockenspiel* in favor of the more logical *Stahlspiel* for the orchestral instrument, accepting *Lyra* for the portable model.

The celesta. A radical departure from existing keyboard metallophones was made in 1847 by Papelard of Paris, who patented in that year his claviola, with two steel bars for each tone, tuned an octave apart. They were placed horizontally, fixed at one end, left free to vibrate at the other, and varied from 1.5 centimeters to 4.7 centimeters in length. A year later its maker replaced his claviola with a new instrument he called *clavi-lame* ("keyed bar"), also with metal bar action. Both of these instruments are now long forgotten, but they remain important as forerunners of another metallophone that has found a permanent place in the Western orchestra, the celesta, or *célesta*, as its inventors called it.

The celesta, in the form of a small upright piano, was invented by Auguste and Alphonse Mustel of Paris (sons of the better known Victor Mustel) and patented in 1886. Its graduated steel bars are suspended over boxlike wooden resonators and struck by piano hammers: weights are soldered to both ends of the bars so that the length may be kept to a minimum without raising their pitch. The intermediary action is a simplified piano action, and a set of dampers is worked by a pedal. From its original compass of four octaves it has grown to one of five octaves, and a second pedal for *piano* has been added. The celesta's timbre has been described as possessing "exquisite purity," and, although it is thin, celestas have been scored for in both symphonic and opera orchestras.

The application of resonators to European metallophones proved so successful that it was exploited further in the present century, even without the adjunct of a keyboard: the vibraharp is an American development of the 1920s (known in Europe as vibraphone), with tuned, graduated metal bars arranged in two rows like piano keys, below which tubular metal resonators are suspended; these not only sustain the tone but impart a characteristic vibrato by means of a motor-driven propeller affixed to the top of each resonator. Similarly, the marimba gongs of rhythm bands are actually a metal marimba (xylophone) fitted with resonators and, like the vibraharp, struck with padded beaters.

The tuning-fork piano. A now largely forgotten type of European metallophone was the so-called tuning-fork piano. After the invention of the tuning fork, which probably took place in the 1750s, experimentation with sets of graduated tuning forks combined with a keyboard resulted in a short-lived idiophone called tuning-fork piano for want of a better name. Its forks were set on a single large resonator and struck by hammers. Charles Claggett of London seems to have been the first to experiment in this direction when, in 1788, he proposed "a new instrument composed of a proper number of these tuning forks or of single prongs or rods of metal fixed on a standing board or box . . ." and sounded from a keyboard. Between Claggett and the first practical tuning-fork piano lay the entire gamut of friction-bar pianos (page 108).

After the latter had been abandoned, Victor Mustel of Paris created the earliest tuning-fork piano in 1865, calling it typophone; it had forty-nine tuning forks set in resonator boxes that were struck by hammers from a keyboard. Three years later he improved upon the typophone, and then apparently abandoned tuning forks altogether in favor of metal bars, which he then used in the construction of his successful celesta. Following Mustel, a series of tuning-fork pianos were brought out in the second half of the nineteenth century, among them the *Adiaphon* of Fischer and Fritz of Leipzig, patented in 1882, with horizontal tuning forks struck from below and pressed against a soundboard; Thomas Machell and Sons of Glasgow produced the dulcitone, and A. Appunn of Hanau the *Euphonium*, all of which were soon forgotten.

PERCUSSION TUBES

STAMPING TUBES

Among the age-old magicoritual instruments still played in many parts of the world (Africa, Central and South America, Asia, and the Pacific), the stamping tube has by now been desacralized to the extent of serving primarily to define the rhythm of dances. Made of a natural tube such as bamboo, with one end usually left closed by a node, or else made of wood, they are beaten rhythmically against the ground. Sometimes the simple tube is left intact, but often it is modified in some way, as, for example, the ancient Chinese bamboo *ch'ung tu*, which was split several times for part of its length in order to add percussive sound when stamped; its Korean derivative reached 2 meters (6½ feet) in size. Among several peoples the tube is not only stamped, but is often struck additionally with a stick: Indians of São Gabriel, Brazil, strike theirs with a palm-leaf beater; the Washambala of East Africa augment its sonority by means of longitudinal slits, and also strike the tube with a stick while it is stamped at dances. Similarly the Dayak of Borneo insert dried fruit seeds that rattle when the bamboo tube is stamped during dances. Often stamping tubes are played in pairs of different sizes, and in Malaya the larger are called father and those of intermediary sizes mother; the smallest, formerly called children, are no longer in use; these tubes are either stamped against the ground or against a wooden log. The *pu ili* of Hawaii consists of two tubes, a longer and shorter one, both of bamboo; the bark is detached from the longer of the two, giving it the appearance of a switch; it is then either stamped, shaken as a rattle, struck with the smaller tube, or even struck against the player's body, a most versatile sound producer. Dancers among the Wapare of Tanzania hold stamping tubes pairwise, one in each hand, and the *ohe ke eke* of Hawaii are held in like manner. In Haiti several *gambo* are played together; originally they came from Angola, where they are called *dikanmbo*. On Fiji also, stamping tubes are played together. The Afro-Cuban *págugu* is named from the Yoruba *okpa* ("stick") and *egungun* ("spirits of the dead"): it is a symbolic substitution used at funeral rites, and as such must necessarily be of the same length as was the deceased person.

Other types of bamboo or wooden percussion tubes in different stages of evolution occur in horizontal form, such as the *ubar* of western Arnhemland, Australia, a short, hollow tree trunk generally painted red, the color of life, as instrument both sacred and secret. As it is hollow it is considered to be female and to represent the belly; it is beaten with a pandanus-leaf rib. Hollowed tree trunks are struck with two sticks in eastern Cuba, where they are made of mahogany or other hardwoods, left open at both ends, and laid horizontally on a stand. Older specimens reached considerable proportions but modern ones are smaller; a recent variety, however, is longer and narrower, with patches of metal from gasoline cans affixed to the upper surface; the metal patches are then struck. On Haiti, a small, hollow wooden cylinder, often a headless drum, is suspended by a rope or strap from the player's neck. Another form encountered there is a bamboo section with the node removed, placed in the cleft of two Y-shaped sticks inserted in the ground; the tube is then struck during dances. The Javanese have a bamboo segment cut so as to leave a node above the center; both ends are left open, and one surface is planed down lengthwise. Because of the position of the node, the tones yielded when both sections are struck sound a fifth apart. Several such tubes may be suspended in a frame in *jemblung* ensembles.

SLIT DRUMS

The slit drum, often erroneously called drum or gong, is in fact a percussion tube, and a very ancient one, its existence from the beginning of the Paleolithic Age having been proven. In its earliest form it was merely a branch or tree trunk with a slit or some holes, placed over a pit and stamped with the feet. The Witoto and Bora Indians of Colombia still use it in such a manner: they cut a flat gutter from a slender tree trunk;

the trunk is then set on two logs over a pit, which acts as resonator. Both ends are sculptured, one to resemble a woman's breast, the other in form of a lizard's head; men dance upon it and stamp it with their feet. In the next stage of its development it was still a tree trunk, but hollowed out through a narrow longitudinal slit, first struck on the inside, later on the outside—a fertility symbol. Primitive versions are often extremely large, varying from 2 to 7 meters (6½ to 23 feet), and serve to relay messages or information. Those of the New Hebrides are left upright *in situ*, carved with the faces of ancestors.

The Maori of New Zealand have no membrane drums, but know the slit drums; sometimes they suspend these in the open from a simple frame on a raised platform and use them as signal instruments; they are struck with a wooden mallet and are occasionally shaped to resemble a canoe. In some instances the Maori form a slit drum by cutting a long tongue from a living tree that is naturally hollow. The Muria of Bastar, India, also have a canoe-shaped slit drum, the bottom of which they pierce with a small hole, allegedly to improve the tone. The slit is long and deep, but the remainder of the log is not hollowed; prior to marriage ceremonies it is worshiped by the bridal pair. In New Guinea giant slit drums are usually placed in special, roofed-over drum houses to protect them from the weather.

From an initial length of some 10 meters (33 feet) or even more, the slit drum becomes increasingly smaller in later stages, until finally it is a diminutive, portable signal instrument, such as that carried by Malayan watchmen. Early types are stamped with large sticks, while later ones are drummed against the edges of the slit, which is purposely left of different thicknesses so as to yield several pitches. Apart from its use as a stamped log and a signal instrument, later also as a musical instrument, the slit drum is credited with magical powers in certain areas; in South America and the Pacific it participates in lunar rites, and, as mentioned above, it is worshiped by the tribal Muria of India.

With the exception of Europe, slit drums are found on all continents and the Pacific. Many specimens, particularly the smaller ones, are beautifully carved; from Assam to Melanesia and Polynesia, these ornaments are often anthropomorphic or zoomorphic.

Slit Drums in Asia

Of great antiquity and of a high degree of development are the slit drums of East Asia and Java. In China the *mu yü* is still a ritual instrument played by Taoist and Buddhist priests alike to mark time when

reciting prayers, or when collecting alms; carved out of a block of cam-
phorwood, it was formerly made in the form of a fish with a loose ball in
its open mouth, but recently it has assumed the form of a human head; its
exterior is lacquered. The *mu yü* can be placed on a cushion or it may be
suspended, but in either case it is sounded with a stick. The same instrument is known in Japan as *mo kugyu*. There it is also a Buddhist ritual
object, formerly made in the form of a fish with its tail in its mouth, but
nowadays it resembles a bird. The Korean equivalent is of far larger
dimensions, made up to 2 meters (6½ feet) long, and the related *cai mo*
of Vietnam takes the shape of a fish, fruit, even that of a pellet bell. The
Vietnamese instrument serves both in temple and in orchestra, and to
announce the hours of the night.

North Celebes has an imaginative Aeolian slit drum put to purely
utilitarian purpose, namely that of keeping animals away from fields
under cultivation. The object itself is a bamboo internode with single
longitudinal slit; a pole is driven into the ground and from its upper end
are suspended (1) the slit drum, (2) a piece of palm or palm-leaf matting,
(3) a striker. The matting is so disposed as to catch the breeze, and when
this takes place the striker keeps hitting the slit drum. On Java, where
several forms are known, slit drums can be traced back to the Hindu-
Javanese period; indeed, the ancient *tong tong*, made of bronze, was
known there by the fourth century (the name is now given to a wooden
equivalent found in western New Guinea). Others, of bamboo or wood,
vary from those small enough to be held in the hand to specimens with
a slit 180 centimeters (6 feet) long. Small, portable models are generally
suspended vertically, whereas the larger ones rest horizontally. Some serve
as signal instruments, others underline the rhythm of dances.

Slit Drums in Africa

African slit drums are distributed in the western "Bend" and in the
Congo River basin, areas in which the xylophone is also present. Apart
from the usual elongated form, Africans also make theirs in scaphoid,
cuneiform, or even crescent shape, or else zoomorphic with a dorsal slit,
sometimes with dumbbell slits. Africans also use their slit drums for the
transmission of messages in much the same way as the "talking" drums
(see page 156). That of the Batatela of Kasai Province, Zaire, called
lukumbi, is capable of emitting six different pitches. Regardless of its
size, the relative tuning is always T 2T 1½T 1½T, where T stands for
tone (e.g., A B D♯ F♯ A B). *Lukumbis* are also played as musical instruments.

A variant form, possibly related to the drummed tube zither, is encountered in the Guineas, Sierra Leone, and Liberia: a cylindrical slit drum with from two to five longitudinal slits forming from one to four narrow slats, rough tuned by varying the length of the slit, and then fine tuned by inserting a small wedge into the slit near the end; occasionally a slat is even detached at one end. The Nalu of Portuguese Guinea formerly had a large instrument of this nature with two slats; it was played by hitting the slats with a length of rope, but this method is now extinct. The Kissi of Guinea have a similar instrument with up to four slats sounded by three male players; one strikes the slats with two sticks while the others strike the ends of the tube, also with two sticks each. Outside Africa such instruments occur only on Java, where they are made of bamboo, have two slits forming a single slat, and are played with a single beater. As their African distribution is limited to the area where xylophones are also played, the probability of their introduction from Indonesia cannot be overlooked.

Slit Drums in the Americas

Other areas where these instruments are demonstrably of considerable age are Central and South America. The *teponaztli*—the word means "wooden drum" in Nahuatl—is probably the best known of all Amerind instruments. In pre-Columbian times some small specimens were made of stone, beautifully carved and occasionally zoomorphic in decoration, but wood remained the chief material there as elsewhere. The Ixtepeji Zapotec warriors reportedly went to battle carrying an idol and singing to the accompaniment of a *teponaztli*, and of two musicians represented on a stone statue of the Olmec culture (ca. 800 B.C.), one is playing the slit drum. Now little known in South America, its use is virtually restricted to Central America, where it is played as a musical—not a signal—instrument. Oblong, and made from a block of very hard wood, its characteristic feature in that region is the form of its slits, an H obtained by making three incisions, thereby creating two tongues facing each other. The interior is chiseled out so as to leave different thicknesses of wood, resulting in as many pitches when the tongues are struck with rubber-knobbed beaters; the sound is as clearly defined as that of a kettledrum, and carries for several miles. Some are small enough to be carried around the player's neck suspended by a strap, others are over 1½ meters (5 feet) long; smaller models may also be placed on tripod stands to avoid deadening the sound by contact with the ground. When struck the tongues vibrate, while the hollow body acts as a resonator.

Teponaztli were not the only slit drums to have H slits, for the mid-sixteenth-century chronicler Gonzalo Fernandez de Oviedo y Valdes wrote that the Indians of Hispaniola frequently accompanied their songs with a slit drum that was often as large as a man, and danced to it; the two tongues formed by an H slit were beaten with a stick, and a rectangular hole was cut into the wall opposite the slit. Its name is given, in a later source, as *maguay* or *maguey*, and the Bora of the Upper Amazon have to this day a slit drum named *manguare*, which they play both as a signal and as a musical instrument. The custom of cutting holes in the bottom persists, for a Guatemalan instrument still in use has several such apertures, in addition to the two or even three slits on its upper surface. Sometimes slit drums are made in pairs on this continent, rather than singly; among the Bora the *huare* is made in pairs of male and female, each emitting two tones and sounded only as signal instruments. Due to its great carrying power, some Ecuadorian tribes employ the slit drum for the transmission of messages.

Slit Drums in the Pacific

The large size of primitive slit drums in this area has already been referred to above. A related form, somewhat reminiscent of the leg xylophone, occurs on the Fiji Islands, elongated with a short slit; it is struck with two sticks while lying athwart the ankles of a female player seated on the ground, or else held against the well-oiled chest of a seated man, with the drummer kneeling in front of him. Here, however, it is the side opposite to the slit that is beaten.

TUBULAR CHIMES AND BELLS

Southeast Asia is the home of another variety of percussion idiophone, the tubular chime, despite the fact that we tend to think of it as a European invention. Resonant, tuned bamboo segments forming a chime are still to be found in rural Annam and in Java, areas in which a number of primitive instruments have survived, including bamboo chimes. The West Javanese *chalung* is composed of twelve, fourteen, or sixteen tuned bamboo segments, graduated according to length, closed at one end by a node, and cut back at the other so as to form a long tongue capable of vibrating; the tongue itself is tuned to the pitch of the tube. All the tubes are then strung in ladder formation with the smallest on top, and suspended from the wall of a house or from a tree and played with padded beaters. In East Java, where it is called *angklung,* the twelve to fourteen tubes are attached to a wooden frame, and the frame is then set up in a slanting position against a wall; this is a development of the shaken (rattle) *angklung,* now obsolete in East Java but still played in the western part of the island.

The principle of resonant tubes did not remain confined to Southeast Asia, but in due course became known in Europe, possibly by independent discovery. However, as bamboo does not grow there, the material employed was metal. True bells have always been both expensive and cumbersome, but not until the first half of the nineteenth century did various bell substitutes begin making their appearance. Before the mid-century steel bars were serving as clock chimes; yet steel did not prove to be a satisfactory material, and after much experimentation John Harrington of Coventry, in about 1885, succeeded in producing a bronze tubular bell. This was not a true bell but a hollow cylinder, struck on the outside with a hammer, and one end pierced with two holes for suspension.

By 1890 whole sets of tubular bells could be played from an organ manual. Today they are made of brass in graduated lengths, all tubes of a chime having the same diameter; furthermore, they are provided with dampers, a signal advantage over real bells. As an independent instrument, a whole set can be suspended in a frame and struck with wooden mallets. In the organ, tubular bells are controlled directly from the manual. Many churches that cannot afford a true carillon prefer to install a chime of tubular bells, the tone of which is picked up, amplified, and fed into a system of loudspeakers in the tower. Such carillons are usually arranged so as to serve both as organ chimes and for tower music; as a result of the application of electronics to the field of musical instruments, they have been available since the 1930s.

When the metal tube replaced the bell in orchestra and church, it also replaced the steel bar of the military: the tubaphone is a descendant of the glockenspiel, its tubes arranged in the same pattern as that of its parent instrument.

PERCUSSION VESSELS

Percussion vessels in one form or another are sounded in most parts of the world; they range from the ultrasimple to the highly evolved, and are played in archaic and high-culture societies alike; in parts of Asia, Africa,

and among Afro-Americans they retain their ancient connections with
ritual life.

PERCUSSION GOURDS AND POTS

Among the least developed of percussion vessels are the stamped
gourds, still to be found in Africa and the Pacific; such are the large and
hollow calabashes of West African *griots* and Moors, with an orifice cut
in the top, held in both hands by the player, who stamps it on the ground,
and the double calabash of Hawaii, which has been restricted around its
middle during growth. Hawaiians also join two calabashes together to
form a figure eight, then either stamp it against the ground or drum
upon it with bare hands. Large calabashes struck with a stick were taken
to the Americas from West Africa; in northern Haiti today they sometimes substitute for drums, played with thimble-covered fingers; and,
during the *canari*-breaking (jar-breaking) voodoo rite, a group of priests'
assistants drum on the calabash with sticks—an adaptation of Dahomey
funerary rites in which special rhythms were beaten on calabashes.

Another simple variety arises from a substitution for hand clapping,
namely hand cupping. Cupped hands can beat the surface of a body of
water, and by extension so can a half gourd or half calabash. In New
Guinea such gourds are found in hourglass form, open at both ends and
provided with a handle at the top; when plunged in and out of water they
emit the sound *uh-ah-uh-ah*; New Guinea also has a technically more
advanced form made of an oblong board, hollowed, and with a handle at
each end.

Half gourds or calabashes may also be floated, open side down, in a
pan of water and struck rhythmically with small sticks. In this form they
are often called water drum, a misnomer apt to cause confusion with the
true drum that is partly filled with water, and for which the term "water
gourd" seems preferable. A water "bowl" is known to the Saharan
Tuaregs, who have no calabashes; they place an inverted bowl in a large,
water-filled pan or bowl and drum on it with a stick. Gourds are played in
this manner in West Africa—in Guinea they consist of tuned pairs; their
chief use in Dahomey is during funeral rites, and a Cuban variety is
played during funeral rites of the African population.

The Mexican half gourd or inverted bowl is floated in water and
struck with a stick; it was probably introduced by Africans. Indians of the
Southwest United States place large half gourds on the ground and beat
them, also with sticks. They likewise drum upon shallow, circular baskets,

generally made of woven grasses and roots, inverted on the ground. Several drummers together slap one with their open hands. These are held to be of pre-Columbian origin.

More widely diffused is the percussion pot; this consists of a clay pot or a gourd, its mouth left open, which is either drummed upon with bare hands or beaters, or else the mouth is alternately opened and closed by the player's hand or by a flat beater, thereby causing the air inside to vibrate. Sometimes a lateral aperture is perforated in the pot, or it may be provided with a pouring spout. Formerly, percussion pots were known in Europe; Buonanni (1722), an excellent source for European folk instruments of the eighteenth century, illustrates a *brocca di terra*, or earthenware jar, so played. Nowadays they are found in Asia, Africa, and among Afro-Americans. This simple device is exploited in a surprisingly large number of ways: in Korea it is struck with a bamboo switch; in India its open mouth is pressed against the player's stomach while he strikes it alternately with both wrists. Among the Ibo of Nigeria only women may play it; they strike it with a palm leaf. Its use in Guinea is restricted to members of a secret society, who hold their right hand at the open mouth while the left hand opens and closes a lateral aperture, thereby modifying the pitch; the Vili of the Lower Congo employ a baobab fruit, open at both ends, which they either strike against their thigh or hit with the flat of their palm. The Bambara of the western Sudan sound theirs by vigorously closing its aperture with the hand; as many as fifty initiates play it at rites of the god Ko Man; the Fan of Dahomey make use of a flat, spoonlike beater formed to fit the open mouth. From Dahomey, where its playing formed an integral part of funeral ceremonies, it was taken to America, and among the Dahomey Negros of Cuba and Brazil it is sounded in like manner at funeral rites. The same instrument, as played by Afro-Bahians, is struck with a double fire-fan during death rites. Haitians beat a large clay vessel with sticks, or they may sing into it, thus transforming it into a voice distorter, or even cover its opening with a goat- or sheepskin membrane and then beat it as a drum, thereby accomplishing its transition to the realm of membranophones.

The venerable Chinese *chu* is a percussion vessel of a different order. Its name occurs in a poem dating from around 1100 B.C. and it was still being sounded in the mid-twentieth century. Its characteristic form is that of a square box with walls sloping outward so that the top is larger than the bottom—the form of an ancient grain measure. The sides are struck on the inside by a wooden mallet, which remains in the interior; as the *chu* is closed, the mallet is reached through a round aperture cut in one of the walls. It is found only in Confucian temples, where, according to ancient tradition, its place is in the northeast corner. The similar—and derived—*chuk* of Korea is sounded by a phallic-shaped pestle passed through an aperture in the lid.

GONGS

Gongs in Asia

Gongs are usually circular (in Borneo a polygonal form is encountered), always have turned rims (which feature differentiates them from percussion disks), and are always made of metal. The surface is either flat or has a central boss, or it may be shaped like a soup plate turned bottom side up. Most often it is made of thin bronze, the traditional metal. Other metals or alloys occur, however, as for example a bell-metal alloy in India, beaten iron in Africa, silver in Tibet. They are made in a great variety of sizes and have either definite or indefinite pitch, depending upon whether they are bossed or not. Those with bosses have definite pitch and are known in East Asia as female gongs; those devoid of boss have indefinite pitch and are known there as male gongs. In general, single gongs are suspended vertically so as to hang freely—although the *chempung* of Sumatra rests on a bed of banana leaves. All are sounded by being struck in the center, either with a beater or, as in Java, with the player's fist. The fundamental difference between gong and bell—another percussion vessel—is that the gong's vibrations issue from its center while its rim is virtually dead, whereas the bell, on the contrary, is most resonant on the soundbow and dead at the vertex.

The gong's early history has not yet been fully elucidated—the word itself is Javanese. Although first recorded in sixth-century China, Chinese tradition ascribes it to "barbarians" (i.e., foreigners) farther west, probably indicating a Turkic people; at present, Asia is considered to be its homeland.

The oldest form of gong appears to have been flat, and Sachs surmised that it might have been a descendant of the frame drum. From China it spread to Southeast Asia, reaching Java by the eighth century, when it was represented on the Borobudur reliefs (ca. A.D. 800); then it proceeded west through Asia to Africa and Europe. Gongs of China are both bossed and flat; those of the archipelago are bossed, those of India flat; no flat gongs occur in Africa.

Probably its oldest use was as a protective device against evil spirits. In Chinese processions it both terrified and dispersed them, just as it terrified the malevolent dragon attempting to devour the moon during eclipses, when it was beaten as loudly as possible. Among certain peoples a stormy wind is considered to be an evil being, and both the Sea Dayak and the Kayan of Borneo beat gongs loudly during a storm to apprise this spirit of their whereabouts, lest he blow down their houses. The old, boss-less *lo* of China, made in many sizes and struck with a copper beater, is a Buddhist ritual instrument; other small gongs have been desacralized and are employed as signal instruments. Until the beginning of the present century, when an important personage was conveyed by sedan chair, it was customary for servants to precede him, beating a single gong; the rank of the personage would be indicated by the number of strikes sounded from time to time. A gong was struck at the gate of a mandarin's residence to announce a visitor, and, at the other end of the social scale, gongs were sounded by beggars in Shantung Province. Other uses were in the army to sound a retreat, or to stress rhythm when accompanying a song. In Japan small gongs are played both in *kabuki* and at folk festivals, but the larger, gilded *waniguchi*, still a ritual gong, is hung at shrine entrances and struck by the worshipers.

So far only the directly struck gong has been considered, but a number of indirectly struck varieties are at home in East Asia, and in analogy to the rattle drum they may be termed rattle gongs. An example is the Chinese *ling tse*, with one or two beads attached to a strap in such a manner as to hit the gong when the latter is twirled. In Shanghai, formerly, two gongs were superposed in metal frames attached to a handle; cords terminating in knots were tied to the frame, and when twirled the knots would strike the gongs, making a deafening noise. Sets of such superposed gongs were far from rare in both China and Japan.

Gong chimes. Indonesian and East Asian gongs are played both singly and in tuned sets known as gong chimes. Some of these are upright, but most are horizontal. The Chinese *yün lo* consists of ten small bronze gongs rather like soup plates, suspended vertically in three rows of three each, plus a single one on top, in an upright frame; sometimes the individual gongs vary little in diameter but considerably in thickness, on others the components have identical diameters. Such chimes are not orchestral, but Confucian and Buddhist cult instruments, and were formerly also played at court; at present they are carried in funeral processions. A Vietnamese chime is derived from the *yün lo* and resembles it. Neighboring Thailand has both vertical chimes of three, five, or seven gongs, and larger horizontal chimes composed of sixteen or eighteen *bonang* gongs, the latter inspired by the better-known horizontal chimes of Indonesia, called *bonang* in Java, and outstanding components of the Southeast Asian orchestra. *Bonang* gongs are sharply bossed and deep-rimmed, which form has given rise to the misleading terms of *bonang* kettle or even gong kettle. The age of the *bonang* is not known, but the word *brekuk*, which occurs in A.D. 902, is believed to have referred to it. A little later, about 1000, the Javanese chime was known as *kangsi*.

When forming part of a *gamelan*, both single *bonang* gongs and chimes are laid horizontally, boss up, on a low, horizontal frame, often elaborately carved; each gong rests upon taut, crossed cords attached to the frame. The fact that its rim is in contact with the cords does not impair its resonance, since, as already noted, the rim is virtually dead. Frames are in general circular or semicircular, with the player sitting on the floor in the center, surrounded by his gongs, the lowest in pitch to his left. He strikes them with short sticks, usually knobbed, right on the center of the boss, often in octaves. Formerly the *bonang* gongs were cast in molds, but today the metal is heated and forged; older instruments have four small holes in the rim, as do those of modern Indochina—for a different method of mounting—and sharply peaked bosses. Fine tuning is accomplished by filing the boss to raise its pitch or by filing the rim to lower it, or even by pouring lead into the hollow of the boss. The timbre of these gongs is very noticeably modified by polishing the surface. The higher-pitched gongs of *gamelans* have deeper rims and are considered to be male, the lower pitched and smaller gongs are considered female; this seeming contradiction in sound-to-size ratio is explained by the fact that the smaller gongs emit a lower tone because they are made of considerably thicker metal than are the larger models.

Today's *bonangs* usually consist of two rows of seven gongs, but in *slendro* tuning twice five or six suffice; those with twice six gongs have a compass of two closed octaves, whereas in *pelog* tuning the compass is always two uncompleted octaves. Elsewhere in the archipelago other arrangements are common; on Banda, for instance, the nine gongs of the local *bonang* are grouped in three rows of three, and on Amboina twelve gongs are placed in four groups of three each. In the southern Philippine

Islands, *bonang*-type chimes of Indonesian derivation combine with drums to form a percussion ensemble.

A gong of unusual form called the *reyong* first appeared on twelfth-century reliefs in Java. The instrument resembles a dumbbell, consisting as it does of two *bonang* gongs connected by a cylinder; it is now extinct on Java but exists on Bali and Lombok, played in pairs (and consequently emitting four tones). The horizontal chimes of Thailand present another peculiarity in that, instead of resting on a frame, forming the usual semicircle or circle, the gongs are placed on a perpendicularly arched frame, with the low central portion supported by a small stand; both ends of the frame curve upward to form a vertical semicircle. Certain xylophones of Zaire assume exactly the same form and are believed to be derived from this type of gong chime.

Gongs of Africa are met with in the western part of the "xylophone belt," where they are made of iron and serve both as signal and as cult instruments.

Kettlegongs. A particularly rare and beautiful kind of gong, the kettlegong, has given classifiers much difficulty due to its peculiar shape, for its rims are so deep that they form an incurved wall. The surface is always flat, and on older instruments is typically ornamented with concentric circles or other engraved designs and with several small cast figures of frogs (the Thais call their kettlegong *ka si* ["frog drum"], from the four pairs of small frogs posed on the surface); on such older instruments the walls are also decorated. Invariably made of metal and usually of bronze, kettlegongs are suspended so that the flat striking surface hangs vertically; they are struck on the center of this head. The edges of the head generally form a sharp angle to the walls, but in northern Indochina, among the Abor, they are rounded.

This ancient form of instrument is found from Mongolia, via South China and Indochina, to Indonesia as far as the Kai Islands (near the New Guinea coast). Products of the Bronze Age culture, they have been ritually connected with rainmaking ceremonies; indeed, the *ch'eng* of China, a kettlegong varying from 50 to over 100 centimeters (20 to 40 inches) in diameter, is also called rain drum for its former cult associations. Among the Garo, the Karen, and other related peoples, kettlegongs are associated with the cult of the dead. Furthermore, the Karen of Burma and western Thailand make offerings of food to the deceased by placing it on the flat surface of a kettlegong, utilizing it in the manner of an altar. They distinguish between "hot" kettlegongs, reserved for death cults, and "cold" ones, which serve all other purposes.

In the archipelago older specimens are believed by the local population to have had a supernatural origin and to have fallen from heaven. Several kettlegongs found among the Muong of North Vietnam were still in use at funeral rites in the early twentieth century. Archaeologists are unable to ascertain whether the specimens found in Indonesia were actually made there, or whether they were imported from the mainland, particularly as many were not cast by the cire perdue method. The same doubt is attached to the so-called moon of Bali, the largest known kettlegong— 186 centimeters (73½ inches) high, 160 centimeters (63 inches) in diameter—made of bronze and elaborately decorated, found near Pedjeng on Bali, despite the fact that fragments of a stone mold designed for a similar but smaller kettlegong were found close by.

Smaller specimens of more recent date have been looked upon as bride price on Alor Island, and on Sangland Island in the Lesser Sundas three specimens found standing on ancient graves were still employed at rain-making ceremonies at the time of their discovery; the entire surface of the heads was decorated with festive scenes of village life, showing definite Chinese influence. Difficulties encountered in attempting to date these instruments has led to widely diverging estimates of their age, but perhaps the third or fourth century A.D. is not too far from the mark. Ancient kettlegongs from the Dong-Son culture area of North Vietnam range in size from miniature grave goods 4 centimeters high to large instruments of over 1 meter (40 inches) in height, and with a diameter of 120 centimeters (51 inches), all provided with four handles; the larger models were made in molds, with their seams still visible. They may be dated from between the fifth and the third or second century B.C., as the Dong-Son culture came to an end with the Han conquest in 111 B.C. Older specimens have also been found in Yunnan, Laos, and on Salajar Island near Celebes. Their manufacture did not cease simultaneously in all regions, however; it continued in southern China until the eighteenth century, and in the Shan State of Burma even up to the beginning of the present century.

The Gong in Europe

The Idaean Cave on Crete has yielded an eighth-century B.C. bronze tympanum with the scene of a deity astride a bull, flanked by two winged men generally described as each clashing a pair of cymbals; these objects are circular, bossless, and are held by means of handles attached to the periphery, similar to those appearing at a later date on eastern Mediterranean frame drums. Rather than cymbals, they may well represent gongs, for the action depicted does not suggest clashing. In this connection it may be mentioned that the large Chinese gong *ta lo* has a *torii*-shaped handle set in the rim, a similarity that may not be entirely coincidental.

The identity of form shared by frame drum and gong may authorize the assumption that the bronze or copper drums with which Parthian troops are said (e.g., by Plutarch in his life of Crassus) to have frightened their enemies were in fact gongs. Although we cannot be sure that gongs were known to Greece, their existence in Rome has been proven, and a rimmed gong of Roman provenance has been found as far away as Westbury, Wiltshire.

The gong then disappears until late medieval times. In the Book of Hours of Catherine of Cleves (ca. 1440), in the margin of a scene depicting the mocking of Christ, a soup-plate type of gong is held by one of the tormentors, a shape associated in the East with gong chimes rather than with single gongs. Several other late medieval miniatures show what appear to be badly delineated gongs. But, although the word "gong" was known in Europe in the sixteenth century, its use there is not further recorded until the end of the eighteenth century. Praetorius knew of the gong chime but not of the single gong. He depicts both a vertical and a horizontal chime of four soup-plate gongs each, and calls them American cymbals. Both are again depicted by Buonanni (1722), who correctly ascribes their origin to Indonesia; the single gong he calls drum (*tamburro*). Meanwhile Johann Christoph Lorber had given a description of the gong in 1696; he still called it cymbal (*Becken*), described it as an "Indian" (i.e., Asian) instrument, and interestingly stated that it was made of bell metal. From him we learn the origin of the word *gom-gom*, the Indonesian colonists' name of the *bonang*: it was the phonetic rendering of "gong-gong" (plural of "gong"); today the word "gong-gong" is given to iron bells of Africa. In addition to purely musical functions, native oarsmen sounded it rhythmically to help a crew pull together, Lorber related. His comments were quoted by Walther (1732).

The gong's use in Western orchestras has been restricted to obtaining special effects, and dates from 1791, when Gossec included a gong in his *Musique funèbre à la mémoire de Mirabeau*, followed by Cherubini in his Requiem, and Steibelt in his *Roméo et Juliette* (1793). Since then it has been accepted as an orchestral instrument of indefinite pitch. To quote Carl Engel, gongs were introduced into modern orchestral scores "for the purpose of producing terrific effects." For generations, in both its bossed and flat forms, it also fulfilled the domestic role of summoning the family to meals. But its true musical value has never been exploited by the West.

THE ĒCHEION

Perhaps the mysterious *ēcheion* of ancient Greece should be given a place among the percussion vessels. From the fairly numerous and somewhat contradictory references, primarily in Greek but later also in Roman literature, it seems justifiable to assume that the word identified a percussion vessel of sorts, probably a bossless gong that, when inverted, could act as a sound amplifier or resonator. Certainly it was made of bronze, but the *ēcheion* seems to have been more than a simple bronze plaque beaten solely for apotropaic purposes. Apollodorus, as quoted by the scholiast of Theocritus, mentioned that "they sound the *chalkos* [bronze] at eclipses of the moon," and proceeded to state that "at Athens, the hierophant of her who had the title of Kore sounded what was called an *ēcheion*"; presumably a percussion instrument.

As to its form, we may attempt to reconstruct it from a passage in Vitruvius (first century B.C.). Bronze vessels, he wrote, are placed in theaters in order to amplify actors' voices. He recommends that a whole series—tuned to fundamental, fourth, fifth, octave, and superoctave—be placed upside down in special niches built in the semicircular aisle between the rising banks of seats, with the smallest *ēcheia* at the extreme sides and the lowest-pitched ones in the center. The voice will be amplified, he states, and, when directed at it, will also cause a given *ēcheion* to reverberate if its pitch corresponds to that of the voice. Individual *ēcheia* were kept in position by wedges set in the side facing the stage; they were needed only when a theater was built of nonresonant materials such as stone or masonry (it will be recalled that Greek theaters were not roofed over), and not in wooden buildings. Some architects, he continues, have taken large clay jars for use as *ēcheia* when building theaters in small towns: they are cheaper. This sounds as though *ēcheia* might have been deep-rimmed gongs paced upright on their rim; their sound-reflecting and amplifying qualities are further brought out by equations with the soundboard of a lyra.

(Parenthetically, clay pots were frequently installed in churches to amplify the preacher's voice in medieval times, or even to augment the sound of the organ; one still remains in the Chapel of the Chartreuse in Villeneuve-lès-Avignon, and Dufourcq [1934–1935] found an invoice entry in the church records of Saint Germain, Argenteuil, made in 1463, for a pipe of lime for the making of "windows" [i.e., niches] in the nave, as well as for clay pots [*pots de terre*] set in said "windows" to improve the sound of the organ.)

Echeia have puzzled musicologists from the sixteenth century on, when Ercole Bottrigari made them a subject of his investigations in his unpublished *La mascara* of 1598, to Jaap Kunst in the twentieth century, who was inclined to identify them as gongs, and to transfer the gong's putative Asiatic origins to the eastern Mediterranean area. In this, as archaeological evidence accumulates, he may possibly be proved correct. Perhaps a connecting link may be seen in the bronze tympanon of the Idaean Cave already described.

THE STEEL DRUM

The steel drum is a twentieth-century variety of percussion vessel, analogous to the gong, that originated in Trinidad during the Second World War. Of simple construction, it consists of an ordinary fifty-gallon oil drum stood upright, with one head divided into sections of different sizes by means of punched grooves. Each section is tuned to its own pitch, so that one head may produce as many as twenty-five or even thirty pitches when struck with a rubber-tipped drumstick. Originally the containers were left whole, but now the drum is usually severed at a desired distance from the end, depending upon the range required. Steel drums, also called pans, are played in sets, with the highest-pitched instrument, the ping pong, reserved for the melody. Ping pongs have a chromatic scale of about two octaves, ascending approximately from c'. Other pans forming a band are tuned to lower pitches. While a ping pong retains only from 13 to 15 centimeters (5 to 6 inches) of body, a bass pan may be 60 centimeters (2 feet) deep. During parades it is suspended by a strap from the player's neck. From Trinidad, where some two hundred steel drum bands have been reported, they have spilled over and have become a vehicle for popular music in the United States.

BELLS

Although both bells and gongs belong to the group of percussion vessels, they differ fundamentally, as stated, from one another in that the bell is resonant at the soundbow—close to its rim—when it is struck, and almost dead at the vertex, whereas the opposite is true of the gong, which must be struck at the center in order to obtain maximum vibration, while its rim is dead. Bells can be broadly classified as those having an inside clapper and those which, lacking clappers, are struck on the outside by an unconnected hammer or rod. The Chinese differentiate categorically between these two types, applying the name *ling* to clapper bells, *chung* to clapperless ones.

Bells as Instruments of Magic and Ritual

In one form or another bells are known to virtually all peoples, and, although their origin has not yet been fully determined, we know that, like so many other musical instruments, their earliest uses were magical and ritual, not musical, and in many parts of the world they remain so to this day.

The Near East. Their apotropaic nature is well illustrated by the Near Eastern usage of Biblical times: in Exodus 28 instructions are given for the making of an ephod for Aaron: "And beneath upon the hem of it thou shalt make pomegranates . . . and bells of gold between them round about; a golden bell and a pomegranate . . . And it shall be upon Aaron to minister: and his sound shall be heard when he goeth in unto the holy place before the Lord, and when he cometh out, that he die not. . . ." And in Exodus 39 we are informed that "they made bells of pure gold . . . round about the hem of the robe to minister in; as the Lord commanded Moses." Whether these were true bells or pellet bells (see page 81) is unknown—their Hebrew name was *pa'anim* (s. *pa'amon*), but in either case their function would have been identical, that of protecting the priest against evil spirits by their magic power. To this day, Jewish ceremonial objects are frequently ornamented with small campaniform bells, as for example the Torah crowns and headpieces, sometimes the Torah breastplate, even Sabbath lamps and spice containers. This custom was probably taken from the Egyptians, for it is known that priests of the temple of Hathor in Dendera wore little bells (or pellet bells) on their garments or sandals as apotropaic amulets.

Europe. The practice of thus ornamenting the vestments of priests was continued in the Christian church; the cope of Conrad, abbot of Canterbury, was edged with 140 little silver bells, and that of Lanfranc, eleventh-century archbishop of Canterbury, with 51 bells, and stoles with similar ornamentation are mentioned by the bishop of Soissons in his will, dated 915. Nonetheless, Saint John Chrysostom (d. 407) had felt it necessary to protest against the custom of attaching bells to the clothing and bracelets of children in order to protect them against demons.

Not only persons, but also animals benefited by the wearing of bells to ward off evil, and they were attached to horses' heads at a very early date; Assyrian bas-reliefs represent horses with clapper bells around necks or affixed to collars, and in Zechariah 14:20 "the bells of the horses" are also mentioned. Bells preserved horses from the evil eye in European antiquity. "Little bells" hung around dogs' necks and birds' feet were documented in 1372 by Robert Bossuat in his translation into French of Bartholomaeus Anglicus's *De proprietatibus rerum;* they were the indirect descendants of those little clapper bells of the Assyrian reliefs. On festive occasions large silver bells formed part of the caparisons of princely horses in fifteenth-century France, such as were seen on the occasion of Louis XI's entry into Paris in 1461. Even today, in Siberia and parts of Russia, small bells on the yokes of horse-drawn vehicles divert both wolves and devils, and Neapolitans suspend tiny bells from silver amulets *contra la jettatura* ("against the evil eye").

With the adoption of bells the Christian church also adopted the belief, so common in antiquity, that ghosts and demons could be put to flight by the sound of metal. To this was added the protective power inherent in bells, now consecrated by their association with the sacred cult. Thus an exorcising celebrant often sounded a handbell or wore small bells on some portion of his garment; furthermore, devils were scared away by the sound of bells, and bells were credited with the power of being able to ring of their own accord. The Roman Catholic church still recognizes the power of church bells to divert both evil spirits and those of the dead. In the Lötschental of Switzerland, pieces of a bell traditionally given to Saint Theodul, first bishop of Sion, by the pope, were incorporated into other bells during casting, thereby lending them the ability to dispel evil spirits; their ringing is still said to offer protection, particularly against frost or rime. Writing prior to 1286, Guillaume Durand, bishop of Mende, tells us in his *Rationale divinorum officiorum* that bells are rung during processions in order that devils may flee, as they are known to be afraid of bells, and that bells are rung at the onset of a storm for the same reason. In Rome, up to the beginning of the present century, it was the custom to ring innumerable clay bells on Saint John's Day (June 24), in order to chase away the witches that teemed in the air on the Eve of

Saint John's; these bells, which were made in a variety of sizes, were furnished with clay clappers. The age-old belief in demons has not altogether died out in Europe: in the Engadine Valley boys proceed through the villages ringing cowbells early on the morning of *Chalanda marz* (March 1), and a bell in a nearby village is inscribed *daemones pello* ("I flee the demons").

Exorcising with bells was a practice not confined to Europe, for the sixth-century Byzantine writer, Menander Protektor, describes an exorcism he had witnessed among Turkic tribes of Central Asia that included noise-making by ringing a bell and beating a drum. The institution of the passing bell must fall within the same province; its tolling in England was already recorded by Bede (d. 735) when the objective was that of keeping evil spirits away from moribund persons; in many parts of Central Europe handbells were rung when a person was at the point of death (although passing bells are no longer sounded in England, the death knoll is still rung there). Indeed, the defunct were protected by bells until interment; Bede mentions their sounding at funerals, and the Bayeux tapestry shows two boys, each carrying a pair of handbells, accompanying the coffin of Edward the Confessor.

Asia. Belief in the magical power of bells in relation to the dead is not confined to Europe, and in the gentle spirit of Japanese Buddhism the bell acts as a guide to the deceased. Lafcadio Hearn wrote of the bell tower of the Buddhist Tennōji temple in Osaka "where there is a bell called Indo-no-kane, or Guiding-Bell, because its sound guides the ghosts of children through the dark"; its bell rope was made of bibs of dead children. "Every moment some bereaved father or mother would come to the door, pull the bell-rope, throw some copper coins on the matting, and make a prayer. Each time the bell sounds, some little ghost is believed to hear—perhaps even to find its way back for one more look at loved toys and faces." And in India also, the bell sound was said to be heard by moribund persons—but the sound was an abstraction, not that of a physically audible bell.

The use of bells in connection with fertility and rain ceremonies is attested on three continents, Europe, Asia, and Africa; being made of bronze, they shared their magical qualities with other bronze implements, including percussion plaques (page 18). Metal objects, and particularly those of bronze, are sounded in certain parts of the world, notably Southeast Asia, to dispel thunderstorms. Such a practice was rare in Europe, yet Jules Renard could record in his journal entry of June 18, 1900: *À Germenay, ils sonnent encore les cloches pour éloigner l'orage* ("At Germenay they still sound bells to drive off storms").

Bells: Their Composition and Shape

Bells have historically been made in a large variety of shapes and of many materials. The oldest known forms are those quadrangular in cross section, and the beehive shape so typical of China. Many beehive-shaped bells have also been excavated in Mesopotamia, and analysis has shown them to consist of copper with about 14 percent of tin; bells of this shape are still played in East Asia. Quadrangular bells have been found in areas extending from Ireland to the Shan State, Burma. In India, the earliest bells represented in the plastic arts look like upside-down flower-pots. European bells are usually "campaniform," a convenient term to denote an outward curve at the soundbow; furthermore, hemispheric, rectangular, troncoconical, tulip-shaped, cylindrical, and flattened forms also exist, the last chiefly in Asia.

Today the most common material in use is bell metal (see below) but many ancient specimens excavated in Europe were found to have been made of two hammered iron sheets riveted together, and of quadrangular form. Pottery appears to have preceded metal, and may have been the oldest material, which would place the origin of bells in the Neolithic rather than in the Bronze Age. Ancient pottery bells have not only been excavated on Crete, but they also numbered among the musical instruments of Guatemala of about A.D. 700–1000. Apart from clay, wood, and metals ranging from gold and silver to sheet iron, glass and porcelain have been occasionally transformed into bells. Glass handbells were a specialty of nineteenth-century Bristol glass makers, and in the same century porcelain bells, including sets of small carillons, were produced at Meissen. Also, cheap clocks formerly manufactured in the Black Forest contained from eight to sixteen small glass bells that played folk tunes and were once popular export wares. Wood has served chiefly for Asian cowbells and for camel bells in North Africa. Wooden bells of India are frequently flattened, whereas those of China are quadrangular. Africans, and to a lesser degree also Asians, make some smaller bells of fruit shells or even palm seeds.

The composition of bell metal has not undergone any substantial modification since Theophilus wrote (ca. 1100), recommending an alloy of one-fifth to one-sixth tin, the remainder to consist of copper. Precisely the same formula was said by Walter Odington (ca. 1300) to have been in use in his day. Present-day bells are made from about 78 percent copper and 20 percent tin, with very small amounts of other materials added.

Bells in Antiquity

The origin of bells, both with regard to time and place, is unknown. Though the vast majority are made of metal, and are indeed typical products of the Bronze Age, they may have been preceded by bells of clay.

This theory now appears to be confirmed for the eastern Mediterranean at least (although the genesis of the soldered bells of Africa may prove to be quite different). So far the oldest bells found are those excavated at Knossos, Crete; they are of clay and include one double bell; specialists have dated them between 2000 and 1850 B.C. As might be expected, they were cult objects. Chronologically China follows next; the older of the two types of Chinese bells (page 54) is probably the clappered variety called *ling*, which has been found, together with other ritual bronzes, in sites dating from before the founding of Anyang in the fourteenth century B.C. In India, bronze bells, presumed to have been horse or cattle bells, made around 1000–800 B.C., were found in a northwest-frontier cemetery near Afghanistan. Numerous others have been excavated from southern India Iron Age graves (ca. 1050 B.C.), one complete with its bronze band for attaching to an animal's neck. Indian sculpture represents clapper bells with suspension loops, shaped like inverted flowerpots, from the second century A.D. on. Ancient bronze bells have also come to light in Cambodia and Laos, in the Dong-Son culture style (fifth to second century B.C.), and a tulip-shaped bell of the same culture decorates a bronze belt buckle from North Vietnam.

Turning west, bronze bells from Assyria of about 700 B.C. on have been preserved. A. H. Layard, who found eighty such during his excavation of Nimrud (the ancient Kalakh) in the last century, wrote that they were beehive shaped, the largest measuring 3¼ inches with a diameter of 2½ inches, the smallest 1¾ inches both in height and in diameter. Some had iron clappers, and most had a hole in the vertex, presumably for suspension of a clapper, and a loop handle. As to ancient Egypt, despite the lack of pictorial or literary records, actual bronze bells have been removed from tombs of the Twenty-second Dynasty (945–745 B.C.) and later; some are hemispheric resting bells (see page 77), others are quadrangular.

Small golden and silver bells from Hellenistic times are also found, but bells in Egypt are clearly of late introduction and minor importance.

Bells in Europe

In classical and in Hellenistic times, anklets adorned with small bells are frequently seen on figures of jesters, dancers, and courtesans portrayed on art objects. Greek bells were of bronze, and their principal uses seem to have been utilitarian, that of a (night) watchman's, guard's, or sentinel's signal, both in peace and in war. In his *Seven Against Thebes*, Aeschylus describes Tydeus' shield as having bronze bells attached to its underside in order to terrify the enemy by their clamor; and in *Rhesus*, Euripides has clapper bells attached to the shields' handles for the same purpose. Bronze objects, it will be recalled, were believed to displease hostile spirits and to keep them away (the British Museum houses a small bronze bell, inscribed, that formerly protected the temple of the Kabeiroi at Thebes). Little bells of terra-cotta and also of bronze have been found in Greek tombs. Bronze bells do not emit the clear, ringing tone we associate today with those made of bell metal; those of antiquity clanged rather than rang.

Roman bells, usually of bronze and always small, have reached us in a great variety of forms—tulip shaped, quadrangular, cylindrical, hemispheric—and from many parts of the empire. Some bells of iron have also been found, and iron was the material commonly used for Roman bell clappers; oxidation is held responsible for many bells having reached us minus their clappers. Exceptionally, bells were also made of gold, silver, and glass. The Roman *tintinnabulum* served both as a signal bell when affixed to a door to summon an attendant, or in the hands of watchmen to give the alarm in case of fire, and as a herd animal bell. *Tintinnabula* are recorded in Nonsberg, Tirol, in 397, as animal bells. The word is still occasionally used to designate a small bell in English and some Romance languages. Another early word for bell is the Latin *signum*; in ancient Rome, this denoted a sign or signal, such as might be sounded by a *tuba*, and when this function was transferred, or partly transferred, to the signal bell, the word's meaning changed also; from the sixth century on, *signum* indicated a bell. Numerous derivations and corruptions of the word occur in Romance languages: the Old French *sein*, denoting a church bell, survived into the nineteenth century (Stendhal writes of the *sein, sing, saint*, sounded at Grenoble during his childhood) and in

Rhaeto-Romanic *zenn* is still the name of the church bell. The Latin *cloca* or *clocca,* documented since the seventh century, gave rise to the terms *cloche* (French), *Glocke* (German), *klok* (Dutch), and others, all meaning "bell," and our "clock"—an indication of one major use of the bell in its early Christian history, that of timepiece, of announcer of the hours: an audible clock.

Early bells were signal instruments in a very real sense of the word; thus the *carroccio,* a bell cart of Italy, consisted of a big clapper bell mounted on a wheeled cartlike framework and surmounted by a standard. The bell was sounded by means of a bell rope while the cart was in motion, and constituted an effective military signal instrument; as such it outlived the Middle Ages and was in use as late as the seventeenth century. But traditions die slowly in the Old World, and in one town of Italy the *carroccio* is not forgotten, for at the Palio festival of Siena it forms the rearguard of the procession. Drawn by four white oxen, it proudly bears the banner of the commune, the *palio,* and the bell, now diminutive but with bell rope intact, perched high in the air on the banner pole: the *carroccio* has become the "triumphal car."

In France the term *beffroi,* derived as is our "belfry" from the Middle High German *bercvrit,* a watchtower, originally designated a tower where the watch was kept with an alarm bell; in the fifteenth century it came to denote the alarm bell itself, and *sonner le beffroi* ("to sound the belfry") was synonymous with ringing the alarm bell. *Beffroi* soon degenerated by the laws of folk etymology to *effroy,* meaning dread or fear, whence *sonner l'effroy,* a really impressive alarm.

Among the more curious rites of the Christian church is that of baptizing bells, already mentioned in a capitulary of Charlemagne in 789 (*cloccae non sunt baptizandae* . . .), and virtually unchanged since the ninth century. Bells were often known by their names, and many of those of important proportions bore inscriptions. Several that were cast in the fifteenth century carry the motto "*Vivos voco—mortuos plango—fulgura frango*" ("I call the living, I weep for the dead, I break the lightning"). By early medieval times bells had assumed a major role in church and monastery, and in eighth-century Ireland they seem to have been an attribute of higher ecclesiastics; several carvings of this period represent a bell beside a crozier or together with a crozier and a book, and a number of bells of the period have reached us, unfortunately all unornamented, as ornamentation came later. In the monasteries they acted as timekeepers to the monks who assembled for prayer at the canonical hours: matins, lauds, prime, tierce, sext, nones, vespers, and compline; moreover, they called the faithful to worship and participated in the Mass itself. The very casting of bells in medieval times was one of the monastic arts, brought to the Continent from Ireland, where it had fled at the collapse of the Roman Empire. Bells announced joy and suffering; they pealed continuously when a new pope was elected and on other solemn occasions, such as at the conclusion of peace between Burgundy and Armagnac in the early fifteenth century, when bells of all the churches and monasteries in Paris rang continuously from morning until well into the night, and, in our own century, at the liberation of Paris in 1944: "the immense hosanna of bells filled the night of deliverance" (Malraux, 1971). The divers functions of the church bell in the Middle Ages is perhaps best summarized by Jean de Gerson's text, doubtless that of a bell inscription:

> *Laudo deum verum, plebem voco*
> *Congrego clerum, defunctos ploro*
> *Pestem fugo, festa decoro.*

> I praise the true god, call the people,
> Convoke the clergy, mourn the dead,
> Chase disease, adorn festivities.

In order to be heard at a distance, larger bells were installed in elevated bell towers, and each time the hour was sounded, a bell ringer was obliged to climb the tower and strike them by hand. His labors did not cease until the invention of the bell wheel in the fourteenth century. Prior to the introduction of visual clocks, that is, of the clock dial, automatic figures were made to strike bells on the outside with a hammer at regular intervals; these are known to have existed as early as the thirteenth century. In England they were known as Jacks, in France as *jaquemarts*, a word derived from the medieval Latin *jaccomarchiadus* ("man in armor"), and these tower figures are always represented as such. When clock dials came into use the old oral clocks were not abandoned: time was both seen and heard.

In some countries, notably Italy and Spain, church bells are hung in a separate campanile, or bell tower, which does not form part of the church building. And, in secular life, handbells large and small were common during the Middle Ages; with one in each of the player's hands they formed part of small mixed ensembles at pastoral dances and other forms of rural merrymaking.

Over the centuries, bigger and ever bigger bells were cast, until a halt was made with the giant *tsar kolokol* ("emperor bell"), produced in Moscow in 1734; this stood 21 feet high and weighed 12,000 *pud* or 433,200 pounds avoirdupois, self-defeating in stature as it proved too big and too heavy for incorporation in a tower. Broken in a fire a few years later, it remained unhung, and in 1836 it was cautiously raised onto a platform in the Kremlin.

Bells have been introduced to the orchestra, but some composers have preferred merely to imitate their sound. Gevaert pointed to problems of notation, such as that in Meyerbeer's *Les Huguenots* (1836), where the *tocsin* of Saint Barthélemy is to sound f° and c′, which would necessitate the presence of bells weighing some 20,000 and 6,000 pounds, respectively. (Tubular bells did not come into use until later.) In his "Russian Easter" Overture of 1888, Rimski-Korsakov preferred to imitate the sound by a combination of triangle, cymbals, and gong, combined with pizzicato and sustained chords of strings and winds.

Unlike the majority of European bells, the cowbell is not cast. It is a clapper bell, bent and soldered (in Asia it is often made of wood). All metal cowbells assume one of two forms: either the height is greater than the diameter or, conversely, the diameter exceeds the height. The name itself is a misnomer, for such bells are also suspended from the necks of other herd animals left free to stray, and then a proud herd owner will sometimes hang a cast, campaniform bell on his prize stock. Soldered cowbells are still employed in the Alps, Pyrenees, and the Aveyron, France. Clapperless cowbells form part of the percussion section of modern rhythm bands, where they are struck with a drumstick.

Bells in Islam

Although Islam has always known the bell, Moslem countries have never used it in ritual, nor even to exhort the faithful to worship; instead, the latter role was given to the human voice (when Constantinople fell in the fifteenth century all its bells were silenced). Possibly influenced by the Prophet's at least partial proscription of musical instruments, bells in Islam were sublimated to become bell *sounds*. Thus Hafiz, the great mystical poet of the fourteenth century, could write that

> No one knows where my beloved stays
> The only thing one knows is that the sound of
> bells approaches.

And the seventeenth century treatise *Dabistan*, compiled by Mobed Shah, goes as far as to assert that the revelation of mystic bell sounds was known to the Prophet himself. Consequently the bell's chief practical use in Arab countries has been restricted to that of herd animals; its principal name, *juljul*, lives on in disguise in many Mediterranean derivatives, from the Spanish *cencerro* and Basque *zinzerri* to the Sicilian *cianciana*.

Bells in Asia

Mention has already been made of the metal bells found in both northern and southern India dating from about 1000 B.C., believed to have been cattle bells, and to the appearance of bells on sculptured monuments from the second century A.D. on. From early literary sources and later usages the intimate connection in India between bell sound and mystic experience becomes evident; already the Pali canon likens the voice of a heavenly *deva* and *yaksha* to that of a golden bell, and the Buddhist monk Fo t'u teng, after visiting Kashmir and other parts of India, arrived in China in the year 310 and prophesied from the sound of bells. In modern times the meditation of *shabd-yoga*, the yoga of sound, as practiced by the Radhaswami sect near Kapurthala, has been described (i.a., by Mircea Eliade) as a meditation during the course of which it is possible to attain a degree of concentration so intense that the bell sound is heard. But mystic revelation is granted only to the few, and for the multitude temple ceremonies must suffice; in these, handbells have long been in use. Bells are also sounded in the religious rites of those countries that came under Indian influence. The Hindu-Javanese stupa of Borobudur contains a charming scene in high relief of the Buddha expounding the Law to his mother, who is seated beneath a stylized tree from whose branches a number of tulip-shaped bells are suspended. Best known of the Indian bells is perhaps the *ghanta*, a small campaniform handbell, a temple bell of the Brahmin, whose use has been compared to that of the Roman Catholic Sanctus bell; in Tibet and Ladakh it serves in Buddhist temples under the name of *dril-bu*. The *dril-bu* is also one of the two chief attributes of sorcerers and sorceresses of Sikkim and Bhutan, the south Tibetan hinterlands, the other being the rattle drum *rnga-ch'un*; during ecstatic dances bell and drum are sounded simultaneously, the former grasped by the left hand, the latter by the right hand of the practitioner. Java has a very similar bell; its handle is either ornamented with the figure of a bull, in which case it is dedicated to Shiva, or with that of a wheel, in which case it serves either Vishnu or the Buddha.

Even though the clappered Chinese *ling* may be older than the clapperless *chung* (see page 58), temple bells of China, as those of Japan, are always clapperless. Moreover, they generally take the form of bell chimes.

A single, clapperless *po chung*, suspended in an ornamental frame and struck on the outside by a slender wooden stick, was traditionally placed to the east of the Moon Terrace of Confucian temples; it served to indicate the pitch for voices chanting the verses of Confucian hymns, and was also an imperial instrument and as such found in the imperial palaces. But, regardless of its emplacement, the *po chung*'s pitch always corresponded to one of the *lü* (see page 67). Japanese bells of the larger varieties, such as the Buddhist *o gane*, are struck horizontally by a suspended wooden beam resembling a battering ram; in many Japanese and Burmese temples worshipers strike large bells placed at the entrance as they enter and again as they leave the temple.

Wooden bells, round, square, or flat, are typical of rural Asia. Among the more primitive examples is the *keretok* of Thailand, a herd animal bell, which is made from the seed of the *tah*, or sugar palm, its lower end cut off for insertion of a palmwood clapper. Another characteristic bell is the square buffalo bell of Shan State herders, with its three wooden clappers suspended on a wire. Rectangular wooden bells with several clappers occur on some Indonesian islands, also in Burma, and—rather unexpectedly—in Estonia.

Bells in Africa

A wide variety of bells are sounded in Negro Africa, metal and wooden, single and double, clapperless or having one or several clappers, signal or rhythm instruments. Among the Bobati of Zaire bells are associated with chieftainship; their possession is a sign of independence. During battle they may serve as signal instruments, but always remain close to the chieftain's person. Their apotropaic quality was recognized on this continent also: both the Bobati and the Zande rang a bell whenever the chief drank or smoked, in order to prevent evil influences from entering his body, and a bell preceded him whenever he went abroad. Such bells were of two pieces of metal soldered together and provided with a clapper. In East Africa the Teso exorcise storm spirits for weeks after they have suffered from lightning or storm-caused conflagration by wearing bells around their ankles; and the Bakrewi of Lake Victoria fasten a bell to the entrance of their houses, which visitors are careful to ring so as to ward off evil spirits.

Several peoples of the Lower Congo basin have a wooden bell, the generic name of which is *dibu*, patterned on the shape of the Borassus fruit; smaller specimens are attached to dogs during the hunt, but larger and more ornate models are restricted to the cult. Many African bells have more than one clapper; the Bemba, for instance, have a variety with five clappers that they consider to be male, and a smaller one with three clappers, considered female. Other wooden bells of Central Africa are flat, usually ornamented with carvings and furnished with several clappers. Double bells are quite common; they are usually made of soldered metal, infrequently of wood, and consist of two single bells connected by a common handle. If this is sharply bent, the bells lie side by side; if it is straight, they are shaped like a dumbbell. Those of any given pair differ either in length or in diameter and always in pitch. When made of metal they are clapperless, but those of wood may have one or even several clappers. The *apolo* of the Nzakara and the *aporo* of the Zande are double bells made of sheet iron soldered down the side, but in view of the fact that *aporo* is the name of a wood, these bells must originally have been made of wood. Wooden double bells are found elsewhere in the Congo basin, often with multiple clappers, usually troncoconical, and occur both in the straight and the bent-handle varieties. Clapperless, conoid metal bells were reported by a late sixteenth-century traveler to Africa, and the areas in which they are found today, either in single- or double-bell form, are precisely those in which the xylophone is also present. All such clapperless bells are struck on the side, usually with short metal rods.

Nonmetallic bells of Africa are often connected with ritual: the Bemba of Zaire make a *kitsika* from a fruit shell of the *kitsika* tree and furnish it with a wooden clapper; women wear it during rites for the protection of a newborn child. In the east the Washambala have a wooden hourglass bell hollowed out at both ends and provided with three iron clappers, an instrument of magicians who sound it in their efforts to drive off demons.

Yet another type exists, a metal bell of sheet iron bent into shape but not closed, a slit being left open all the way down the side; as the top is of course also open, the handle projects from the side opposite the slit. This open-sided bell occurs in West Africa and among the African population of Cuba, who brought it from their homeland; in both areas it is held horizontally and struck on the outside close to the slit. A similar form but with longer handle and near-cylindrical body exists on Java and Bali and constitutes, according to Kunst, the principal variety of the *kemanak*.

The kemanak. This peculiar instrument, technically a clapperless bell, is now obsolescent. It consists of a pair of bronze or iron objects that Kunst aptly described as having the form of a banana opened lengthwise on its convex side, with the pulp removed; two such instruments are attached together by means of a cord. In Cheribon and East Java they are struck crosswise, the back of one striking the slit side of the other, and vice versa, but elsewhere they are played by two persons, each holding a single *kemanak*, and striking it with a short, padded beater. The pitch, both absolute and relative, varies from set to set. *Kemanaks* are recorded from the twelfth century on in East Java; as rhythm instruments they accompany the hieratic dances of *bedayas*, court dancers of noble birth.

Outside Indonesia this same instrument is found among several West African peoples (in Ghana, Guinea, Mali, Benin, Cameroun, Gabon) and in Zambia. More important is probably the fact that it has also been found at Zimbabwe, South Africa. In Africa the two *kemanaks* forming a pair are of slightly different sizes, and there also they serve to accompany liturgical dances. The playing technique is that of Indonesia. *Kemanaks* of both types—with and without handle—have been excavated in the Kendiri region together with an object dated from 1263 A.D., and in a prehistoric rock painting of the Southwest African Brandberg Mountain, Kunst identified as *kemanaks* a pair of banana-shaped implements held by one of the figures. Attempts at dating these paintings have so far not been successful. Such similarities of type, playing techniques, and employment can scarcely be coincidental, and here once more one must conclude that an early wave of immigration or trade carried the *kemanak* to Africa.

Bells in the Americas

When West Africans were forcefully settled in the New World they took their religious rites and their musical instruments with them. Some of the latter continued to be played without further development, others, such as the banjo, underwent transformation. Bells were modified relatively little. The *gankogui*, a double bell of the Ewe, for instance, is made of beaten iron in Ghana, of sheet metal soldered up the side in Afro-Cuba, and in Haiti it has become a ritual voodoo instrument. Hand-bells play a part, albeit a minor one, in voodoo rites of both Afro-Cubans and Afro-Brazilians; in Cuba, such a bell, named *agogo*, is made in several shapes, often conical tapering to a handle, or made as a multiple bell, with several strung on a vertical or even a horizontal handle; some have clappers, others not. The same bell in Bahia, Pernambuco, and Rio is tulip shaped, clapperless, or occurs as a double bell.

Bells have played a negligible part in American Indian musical cultures. Ancient Peru is known to have had small, clapperless bells of metal, some of which were founded, others bent into a conical shape; all were ritual instruments. Multiclapper, rectangular bells of wood were also known, similar to those found in Southeast Asia and in Estonia.

Bell Chimes

Bells assembled into tuned sets have been played for three millennia, first in China and in areas under her cultural influence, later in Europe. So far, the oldest chime recovered in China dates from the ninth century B.C., and during the 1957 excavations at Hsin-yang, Honan Province, a series of thirteen bells came to light, datable from an inscription to the year 525 B.C. The bells composing these early chimes were ritual bronze objects; they have a series of raised knobs on their surface, arranged in three double rows. Whether they are purely ornamental, or ritually significant, or whether they also contributed to accurate tuning, has not yet been established. It appears likely that in China, at least, bells were played as chimes before they were sounded singly, as early sources refer to the bell in the plural. The first chimes consisted of bells quadrangular in cross section; this shape gave way to the beehive form, and chimes of this shape are still played. Like the lithophone *pien ch'ing*, to which it corresponds closely in all but materials and shape, the modern *pien chung* comprises sixteen (clapperless) bells of uniform size but graduated thicknesses, suspended in two rows of eight each in an ornate, upright frame, one row containing the female *lü* (semitones), the other, the male *lü*; in past ages the precise number of bells has varied with the dynasty. As a ritual Confucian instrument, appropriate bells of the *ko chung*, a chime pitched one octave higher than the *pien chung*, and composed of from fourteen to twenty-four bells, were struck with a small beater to indicate pitch. The same ancient Chinese form is also found in Korea.

Though small, hemispheric bells may have been strung together in chains in Rome, the bell chime is not found outside East Asia until early medieval times, when it developed independently in Europe. The old meaning of the Latin word *cymbala* (see page 11) was changed in the tenth century to denote a bell chime, and, when the word *cymbala* occurs in illustrated texts, it is depicted from the eleventh century on as a bell chime, whence the obsolete English form *chimbe*, and the German *Zimbel*. The uncertain transition terminology is evident in the Schoenborn (Pommersfeld) Codex 2777, a Bible of about 1070, which illustrates the words *non cymbala desunt* with a seven-bell chime, its seated player holding a hammer in one hand while the other hand taps with forefinger somewhat ambiguously on an instrument that looks more like a frame drum than a cymbal.

Early European chimes were most often represented as a number of clapperless, hemispheric bells: inverted resting bells (see page 78); those consisting of campaniform bells are rarer. Infrequently, a set of clapper bells is portrayed with a seated musician pulling on cords attached to the clappers. The number of bells in a set varied from three to fifteen, arranged in a series forming a tuned scale and suspended either in a frame or from a horizontal rod, and sounded by being struck on the outside with one or, more often, two hammers. A single chime of seven, eight, or nine bells forming a diatonic octave (if nine, with synemmenon) is frequently illustrated in manuscripts of the eleventh to the fifteenth centuries; in the plastic arts, chimes first appear in the twelfth century. In the eleventh and twelfth centuries bells are sometimes marked with their letter names; the Glasgow Psalter (Hunterian Museum) for instance, shows a double chime of campaniform bells marked *ut re mi fa sol la fa mi sol fa mi re ut*, all apparently of the same size.

The casting of church bells during the greater part of the Middle Ages was restricted to monasteries. In making a series of bells tuned to a scale, any given weight would serve for the first bell; a model was made of wax, the amount of metal then determined, and the sizes, that is, the weights, of the remaining bells then computed by monochord ratios—which formula could not and did not work, as is evident from the numerous variant formulas for the proportions of bells given by medieval authors. Theophilus, a monk who lived probably around 1100, devoted a section of his *Diversarum artium schedula* to the art of casting bells for a chime. The pertinent passage may be summarized as follows:

Start by making the highest pitched bell and proceed to the lowest; take two parts of wax of equal weight, one for the *a* (highest) bell and the other for the G bell. Divide the *a* mass into eight equal parts and add one-eighth for G. Similarly, divide G into eight equal parts and give F as much as the total amount of G plus one-eighth of G, and this will give two contiguous tones. Here there must be a semitone; divide the amount of *a* into three parts, and the total amount of *a* plus one-third will give E. Then give to D as much as the total of *a* plus one-half of *a*; give C the same amount as G and half as much again; this will give two tones below the semitone. Then allot to B as much as the total of F plus one-third, and this will result in another semitone. For the octave A, double the amount of wax of the first *a*. For the synemmenon (i.e., B♭), weigh the total amount given to F and add one-half more to obtain B♭.

Today we know that the pitch of a bell is inverse to the cubic root of its weight. If a bell sounding C weighs, shall we say, 800 pounds, a bell sounding one octave higher will weigh 100 pounds—and, furthermore, allowance must be made for equal temperament if this is desired. But bell founders of the Middle Ages, with their faith in monochord ratios, had to proceed by trial and error. Yet Europeans were not alone in tuning bell chimes by means of monochord ratios, for during the Chou dynasty of China (1050–256 B.C.) a multistringed "monochord" with center string laid over a calibrated scale served for determining the pitches of bell chimes.

A turning point in the evolution of chimes was reached in the thirteenth century when the bells were first mechanized, that is, struck mechanically and connected to clockwork. New, to all intents and purposes, these instruments continued to bear their old name, and in addition they became known as *horologium* in Latin and *orloge* in French, a term that already appears in the *Roman de la rose* of around 1280:

> *Et refait sonner ses orloges*
> *Par ses sales et par ses loges*

> Where the *orloges* resound in the halls

and, in the fourteenth century, Eustache Deschamps (*Art de dictier*) speaks of *cloches mises en diverses orloges, lesquelles par le touchement des marteaux sonnent des sons accordables selon les six notes* ("bells placed in different *orloges*, which by the striking of hammers emit harmonic sounds of the six tones" [the hexachord]). Jean de Gerson in his *Tractatus primus de canticis* written a little later defines the *cymbala* as small bells for melody arranged in a *horologium: Sunt et campanulae pro melodia velut in horologiis aliquidibus ordinatae.*

The oldest mechanical chime of which any detailed information is available is that of the astronomical clock at Strasbourg Cathedral, erected in 1354. It was weight-driven, and contained a mechanical chime. A description of it was made two centuries later, by Dasypodius in 1578, prior to his installation of a new clock. The original clockwork had rotated a wheel upon which stood statues of the Three Kings and the Virgin, toward whom the kings bowed whenever the clock sounded; connected to the clockwork was a chime that could play several tunes, upon completion of which a cock would crow. Astronomical clocks were in great vogue in the fifteenth and sixteenth centuries, and, when their bells were ultimately transferred to a separate bell tower, a distinction can perhaps be drawn between chime and carillon.

The Zimbelstern. One of the earlier ecclesiastical uses of small bells within the church proper was the *rota tintinnabulis,* the belled wheel, also called *rota campanarum, nolarum circulis,* later known as the wheel, *roue à clochettes* (French), *cascabeles* (Spanish), *Zimbelrad* and *Glockenrad* (German), and recorded from the tenth century on. Here a number of tiny clapper bells, about the size of a human thumb, were attached to the periphery of a large wheel made to revolve either by rope and handcrank or—at a later date—by clockwork. In the tenth century the wheel is known to have been set in motion on feast days. Often it would be attached to the front of the organ; subsequently it was transformed into a large star, and in this form it evolved during the Renaissance into the earliest known auxiliary organ stop, known in German as *Zimbelstern.* These tiny bells were made of silver or of bell metal in various sizes and, according to older authors, emitted a confused but delightful high-pitched tinkling. For reasons of symmetry a second star, devoid of bells, was usually added to the organ front. Prior to the application of pneumatics to the organ, the star was revolved by a wind wheel—a device similar to the waterwheel of a mill—connected to a roller. Later the bells were disconnected from the star—which continued nevertheless to revolve—and their continued tinkling was ensured by wind supplied as theretofore. The star of Fulda Cathedral, an exceptionally large one completed in 1415, no less than 24 feet in diameter, had some 350 bells attached to its 14 rays, and was suspended from the church ceiling. But it caused a disaster in 1781 when its rope broke and it came crashing down into the assembled congregation. Athanasius Kircher, a product of the Jesuit school of Fulda, illustrated this star in his *Musurgia universalis* of 1650; he had suggested (according to his *Machinamentum* V) working it without human labor by affixing windmill arms to the cathedral roof. However, the star was never mechanized, and in the present century it still retained about 150 of its bells and was rotated by a person walking a treadmill inside it.

By the late Baroque the tinkling *Zimbelstern* no longer pleased, and was transformed into a series of three or four bells tuned to a chord, as a rule g' b' d^2 g^2, provided with metal hammers and springs to ensure their release, and attached in a horizontal row to a roller, one end of which was connected to a wheel. Such bells were either of bell metal or of brass. Adlung (1758) states that the preferred tunings in his day were C or G chords, as most chorales were sung in those tonalities. *Campanella, campanulae, campanetta, carillon, Glockenspiel* are some of the names by which these chimes were known. Bach's cantata, *Schlage doch, gewünschte Stunde,* calls for a *campanella.* In an extended version it formed an auxiliary organ stop consisting of an octave's worth of bells tuned to a scale and worked from the manual, usually repeating. An extant Gottfried Silbermann organ in Ponitz, built in 1738, had a chromatic, two-octave bell chime added in 1782, with all bells suspended from an iron bar and struck by felt-wrapped hammers. Today the older form, that of a small wheel set with minute bells, is being revived.

Bell wheels were also known in Britain, but were less used there. In the sixteenth century "viij lytel belles in a chyme hanginge on a wheel" were reported, and again "viij lytle bells upon a wheel." In Spain the *cascabeles,* made of a set of harness bells attached to a paddle wheel, maintained itself up to the nineteenth century. Completely detached from the organ, "lytel belles" were transformed into yet another ecclesiastical instrument, the Elevation bell wheel (as distinct from the single Elevation bell): some churches of Spain and Italy had a bell wheel attached high upon the church wall, preferably the north wall, rotated by rope and crank handle, and set in motion only during the Mass at the moment of the Elevation of the Host.

Despite its long history within the church, the bell wheel followed an example set by so many far older instruments—the rattle comes immediately to mind—it degenerated from its association with the sacred to that of the profane: the Dutch *hoepelspel,* known in the eighteenth century, was a child's noisy toy consisting of a large wheel strung with small bells, its axle serving as a handle.

Carillons. The distinction between chime and carillon is merely one of size and compass; at present, if a set of bells exceeds a compass of one and one-half or two octaves, it is considered to be a carillon. Historically, criteria were size and location of the set, with the term "carillon" reserved for bells in a tower. However, the word has indicated different things at different times: in French-speaking areas today, *carillon* denotes a tune, not the instrument that plays it, whereas formerly it designated a set of tuned bells, regardless of number, hung dead (i.e., stationary) and sounded by clockwork. In English-speaking areas it denotes a set of tuned bells hung dead in a tower and played either from a keyboard or mechanically. The word itself, which is French, derives from *careignon, carenon, quarregnon,* the last already in use in the thirteenth century, whereas the word "carillon" is not recorded before 1343. All these terms are cognate with the medieval Latin *quadrilionem* ("quatenary"), and point to a chime originally composed of four bells.

With the gradual progress in casting methods, bells grew larger, leaving the small chime bells behind by the thirteenth century. The resting bell form (see page 77) was entirely abandoned, and at the same time chimes were mechanized by connecting their bells to the town clocks, with a cogwheel causing exterior hammers to strike against the bells in a given sequence and at a given time. Weights had to be wound by hand daily: one for the clock, another for the hours, a third for the chiming cylinder. The Low Countries and northern France were destined to bring the art of carillon founding and playing to its greatest perfection, and in these countries a more elaborate system prevailed; there the bells were suspended from a framework in a tower and their outside hammers were automatically released by iron pegs set in a large wooden barrel (later a metal cylinder) revolved by weight and pulley, thereby making it possible to play a whole tune automatically. The principle upon which the barrels were pinned was later transferred to other mechanical instruments (e.g., barrel organs, music boxes); the function of the pegs was to trip levers connected to the hammers by means of wires, thus raising the hammerheads and releasing them, whereupon the bell was struck. In order to ensure good repetition, bells were provided with as many as six hammers, depending upon their size. All mechanically played carillons, then as now, are hung dead.

Tower bells, as already mentioned, sounded the hours by clockwork. In order to alert the population to the coming announcement of time, this was preceded by ringing a few smaller bells mechanically by means of the rotating barrel. In the Low Countries such introductory playing was called *voorslag* ("prestrike"), and when the *voorslag* developed into a melody, this was called *voorspel* ("preplay"). *Voorslags* were sounded in Mons in 1328, and in other towns later in the century; the *voorspel* appeared in Audenarde in 1501, elsewhere soon thereafter.

An innovation of signal importance took place around 1500 when a keyboard was added to the carillons of Antwerp and the surrounding countryside—one is mentioned in Audenarde in 1510—thus making it possible to play the bells manually as well as mechanically, provided of course that the bells were first disconnected from the barrel and the hammers; instead, they were connected directly to the manual by wires and levers, in an arrangement similar to that of an organ tracker action. Later the bells were furnished with clappers, as these were easier to connect than were the hammers. This type of action still prevails, although electropneumatic actions have been installed in the twentieth century.

Finally, as the compass was extended downward, it became impossible to play larger bells with their heavy hammers by hand, and so a pedal-board was added. That of Mechelen (Malines) of 1583 may have been the earliest. Pedalboards, usually of a compass of one and one-half octaves, were connected to the manual by pulldowns. By the end of the sixteenth century the people of the Low Countries were fortunate in possessing public outdoor clocks with dials and a chime mechanism for announcing the time every quarter hour, the *voorspel*, which could be changed periodically to avoid monotony, and furnished additionally with manual and pedalboard from which nonrepeating music could be performed.

Although carillons spread to other European countries in the sixteenth and seventeenth centuries, and to North America even later, most carillon towers are still to be found in the Low Countries and northern France. While the majority of old French carillons were destroyed during the French Revolution and their bells melted down, some were replaced in the course of the nineteenth century. In 1557 the Milanese physician Geronimo Cardani described the carillons he had heard on his travels to Brussels, Louvain, and Antwerp, played for all the citizens to hear, as he relates. Unfortunately, he does not say whether they were played automatically or manually. The combination of both playing methods was mentioned in the early seventeenth century by another Italian writer, Angelo Rocca (*De campanis commentarius*, 1612), in connection with Liége; Saint Paul's Church there had a carillon of twenty-four bells, played manually, but upon which an antiphon was performed mechanically every hour before the clock struck—a good example of the old *voorspel*.

Many treatises of the seventeenth century advocate water as a motive force for carillons; Robert Fludd (*De natura simia*, 1618), Salomon de Caus (*Les raisons des forces mouvantes*, 1615), Athanasius Kircher (*Musurgia universalis*, 1650), Caspar Schott (*Technica curiosa*, 1664), all favored water power, yet in practice the old clock-driven mechanism continued to be used. At the same time, small carillons for indoor performance enjoyed a certain vogue. Philip Hainhofer's description of the

Dresden *Kunstkammer* in 1629 includes *ain clavir instrument mit 42 gloegglen, sehr lieblich* ("a keyboard instrument with forty-two small bells, very pleasant").

By far the most famous of the carillon bell founders were the seventeenth-century Van der Gheyn and Hemony families. The brothers Pierre and François Hemony came to Amsterdam from Lorraine in 1655, and the ensuing decade was perhaps the most fruitful one in the history of carillon founding. From their arrival in Amsterdam until the French Revolution, some two hundred carillons were manufactured in the Low Countries, of which an estimated three-quarters were installed there and the remainder exported. Carillons with from thirty-seven to forty-seven bells were not uncommon, and the largest produced in the seventeenth century—by Pierre Hemony—had fifty-two bells. Of this maker it is said that he required his bells to contain the overtones of three octaves, two fifths, and one major and one minor third. Needless to say, the expense of so large an instrument precluded its acquisition by any but municipalities, religious institutions, or princes. Yet virtually every town in the Low Countries had its carillon, installed either in the church tower or in a separate neighboring carillon tower, and occasionally even in the town hall tower. Then as now a carillonneur's duties consisted not only of playing at stipulated times and on stipulated occasions, but of being responsible for the maintenance and repegging of his instrument. In order to change a tune it was necessary to reset all the pegs on the cylinder, a major undertaking, and in past times tunes were not changed more than eight, or at most ten, times a year, as a consequence of which the population had ample time to familiarize itself with the repertoire.

Carillon cylinders revolve at an invariable speed; the circumference is pierced, somewhat in the manner of a sieve, with rows of orifices into which metal pegs are inserted and firmly screwed down from the inside. If the pegging is not accurate or if the speed varies, the music will not be correctly rendered. Accurate insertion of the pegs ensures proper pitch and precise timing, for their position with respect to the cylinder's length controls the pitch (the left end corresponds to the bass bells) and their location along the periphery controls the timing. Because the pegs are mobile, they can be removed and the whole cylinder repegged with a different tune; one regrettable consequence of this system is that no tunes pegged in former centuries have come down to us. Once the cylinder had made a complete revolution, all its music had been played, and in order to accommodate larger pieces, huge cylinders were made with diameters of up to 2 meters (over 6 feet).

Up in the tower the smaller bells are suspended above the larger ones; the manual from which a carillon is played is laid out in two rows of "keys," disposed in the same order as piano keys, but they consist of wooden cylinders of some 2 centimeters diameter and have to be spread far enough apart to permit each to be struck without touching its neighbor. As these "keys'" are connected to hammer or clapper by wires and levers, a certain amount of force is needed in order to depress them, and traditionally they have been played with the outside of the hand (little-finger end) formed into a fist. John Evelyn went up the bell tower of Saint Nicholas, Amsterdam, in 1641, and found the carillonneur wearing wooden guards to protect his hands while playing. One advantage of manual playing is that the greater the force deployed by the player, the greater the force with which the bell is struck and hence the louder its tone, in contrast to mechanically played instruments, where no dynamic shadings are possible.

To the already considerable difficulties inherent in tuning bells were added those caused by the necessity of preparing a whole set intended for polyphonic playing; a far greater degree of precision is required for these than for clock bells or chimes destined for change ringing (see page 76). Tuning takes place at the time of casting, and only limited fine tuning can be accomplished later by filing or turning. A real crisis in the carillon's history occurred when mean-tone tuning no longer sufficed for the playing of music containing more chromatic notes than had been customary. Both a qualitative and a quantitative decrease in carillon making resulted, and the crisis was not entirely overcome until carillons were finally divorced completely from clocks and tuned in equal temperament, an event that originated outside the Low Countries. Price (1933) states that in the nineteenth century no bell founder pretended he could tune bells satisfactorily for carillons, except perhaps in the belief that he could sell one to an ignorant customer.

At no time has the number of bells comprising a carillon been standardized, so that, although there exists a large body of traditional melodies and of compositions written specially for it, most carillonneurs must often make their own arrangements to accommodate the range of their particular instrument. A larger carillon may have from thirty-seven to fifty-two bells.

Despite improvements made to the hammer-release mechanism in the nineteenth century, the touch on a modern instrument varies considerably from bass to treble, with about 3 pounds weight required for the center of the manual, and about 9 pounds for a 150-pound clapper in the bass. Electropneumatic actions were introduced in the twentieth century, yet the old system of working hammers on the outside of the bell is still preferred and prevails. Carillon bells have occasionally been made of materials other than bell metal; several were made of glass in the eighteenth century, and there exist at least two German porcelain carillons. Today the far cheaper tubular bells, amplified electronically, are being used increasingly as substitutes for the bell carillon (see page 43).

Change ringing. Whereas the European continent had listened for centuries to chorales and other melodies preludizing the announcement of the time, England had listened to "chimes," short sequences played on a small number of bells at every quarter hour, the length of the chime increasing as the hour progressed, and known as quarter chimes. They were monophonic and always played mechanically. Chimes were not altogether known on the Continent, as Mattheson relates that a certain kapellmeister found inspiration even in the bells of Saint Peter's in Hamburg, which sounded a tetrachord by means of clockwork.

In Britain the bells of a church tower do not play melodies but are rung in "changes." A change is defined as the ringing of bells in a series of mathematical permutations, in canon form. The larger the number of bells in a set, the greater the number of possible combinations in which they can be rung. Thus three bells contain six possible changes: 123, 213, 231, 321, 312, 132. All changes, or "rows" as they are called, rung through once constitute a "peal." A peal of four bells contains 24 changes, that of five bells 120 changes, that of six bells 720 changes, that of eight bells 40,320 changes, and so on. The number of bells involved practically in change ringing varies between four and twelve, but eight is the most common number. Such bells are hung dead with their crowns secured to a headstick of metal, which in turn is attached to a large wheel; the rim of the wheel is grooved to hold a rope, and this in turn "raises" the bell when pulled, causing it to swing forcibly until its mouth is high enough for the clapper to strike it. The bells are tuned to a diatonic scale, with the biggest, called tenor, always sounding the keynote. Change ringing is so popular in England that one might define it as an enthusiastically followed participant's sport; it is not even restricted to church bells, for aficionados frequently gather to ring changes with large handbells, holding one in each hand—and sometimes they may even hold two in each hand.

Aeolian Bells

When clapper bells are suspended in the open and sounded by the wind, they are called Aeolian bells. Known to both Europe and Asia in antiquity, they exist today only in East Asia and East Africa. In ancient Greece bells were allegedly hung from chains in the sanctuary of Zeus at Dodona and set in motion by the breeze; others were suspended over the tomb of the Etruscan king Porsenna, according to Pliny, so that the wind might sound them and thereby banish evil spirits from the premises. Flavius Josephus recounts that Solomon caused bells to be hung from the Temple roof, allegedly to keep birds away, actually an apotropaic charm. The medieval chronicles of Ceylon describe balustrades of royal buildings hung with a network of small silver bells, and relate that the sleeping apartment of the king's palace contained "a network of tiny golden bells suspended here and there [that] gave forth a sound." They bore the onomatopoeic name of *kinkinijāla*. Further east, Marco Polo commented in the thirteenth century on the Aeolian bells of Burma that tinkled in the wind. Small bells are still suspended from the projecting eaves of Buddhist pagoda roofs in Burma, with a thin plate of metal, shaped like a leaf, attached to the clapper. Similarly, Aeolian bells of Japan and Korea have clappers in the form of a cross, from which a thin brass fish or fishtail is suspended; such bells are hung from pagoda, temple, and palace eaves, as well as from those of some private residences. In China, the famous Porcelain Tower of Nanking, destroyed in the past century, was built of white brick and had numerous porcelain bells appended to its nine stories.

During a visit to Montmartre Cemetery in 1855, the Goncourt brothers came across the grave of a child whose father had suspended Aeolian bells from a series of rods, to lull the little boy by their music—probably a unique occurrence of wind-activated bells in modern Europe.

Resting Bells

Another type of bell is the Oriental hemispheric resting bell; this is a heavy bowl of bronze, devoid of handle or clapper, generally small enough to be held in the palm of the hand, its open side up, or else laid on a cushion, and always struck on the rim. Resting bells are encountered from China to Rome, and from antiquity to modern times, invariably as ritual instruments. In China they have been made in the usual small sizes, but also in far larger dimensions, for Moule reported one in a Hangchow monastery of some 75 centimeters (2½ feet) diameter. Chinese, Japanese, and Indochinese resting bells are instruments of Buddhism, and a single one is to be found nestled on a cushion in temples.

Another variety of hemispheric bell differs from the resting bell in that it is provided with a handle or with a metal suspension loop for attaching to a chain, cord, or the like, and, instead of lying rim up, characteristic position of the resting bell, it is suspended rim down. The ancient Romans had such bells and passed them on to Christian Europe, where they were combined into bell chimes (see page 67) at an early date. Today in the Near East the hemispheric bell is provided with a handle and is known as *nāqūs*, a word closely related to *nuqaisāt* (actually a diminutive of *nāqūs*), the name of finger cymbals among the Berbers; as a liturgical instrument of Syrian and Lebanese Christians, and of the Egyptian Copts, it is primarily used in processions, when it is held rim down and struck with a metal rod. The Armenians, great lovers of percussion during their religious services, sound the *nāqūs* during Mass; the Christians of Egypt make it too large to be held in the hand and therefore it is mounted on a support, but it is not part of the instrumentarium of the Orthodox church. Among the Shluh of southern Morocco it is a true resting bell, isolated from the ground on a *babouche*, a slipper, and struck with two short beaters.

Musical cups. Resting bells were combined into sets or chimes both in Asia and in Europe; some were of metal, others of porcelain. The true resting bell (rim up) united with others of its kind were known as musical cups, and are presumably the ancestors of our musical glasses (see page 111). Cup or bowl shaped, they were either beaten with little rods, just as their single precursors had been or, as in India, rubbed around the rims with wetted fingers (friction vessels); sometimes they were tuned by being partly filled with water.

A set of bowls, struck with rods, is portrayed in a Greek manuscript of the fourth century, according to Sachs; in the form of little cups they appear in seventh-century Turkistan, and by the end of the eighth century they are represented on the Borobudur reliefs of Java, but here the cups are sounded by being touched together; they accompany a dance. Later they are identified as *cheluring,* and their transformation can be followed until they have become a set of bronze cups nailed down side by side on a wooden frame and struck with small metal rods. The number of component cups varies; if there are but few, they serve to indicate rhythm, but if there are as many as seven, and this is frequently the case, they become a melody chime.

Although our evidence for such chimes in India is of later date, they must have existed there prior to appearing at Borobudur. Modern India has a set of cups called *rastrarang* that can be played either with sticks or as a friction instrument, by rubbing wetted fingers along the rim (the cups do not contain water). By contrast, the *jaltarang,* also of India, makes use of water for fine tuning; each bowl, when empty, has a different pitch, modified when necessary by the addition of water. A *jaltarang* usually consists of eighteen small bowls, but the compass can vary from two to three octaves; its bowls form a semicircle in front of the player, with the lowest in pitch on his left, and are played with two very slender bamboo sticks with padded tips. Actually the water fulfills three distinct functions: it modifies the pitch, sustains the tone, and permits the playing of *gamakas* (ornaments) by carefully bringing the beaters into contact with the surface of the water. Unfortunately these instruments are becoming increasingly rare.

Turkish writers of the fifteenth century describe sets of porcelain bowls tuned by adding small amounts of water, and ascribe their origin to India; they were still played in the seventeenth century. In Japan a set known as *orugōri* is still found in Buddhist temples and in *kabuki* music; here the bowls are inserted into a wooden board and played with rods. Central Asia is another area where musical cups were recently in use for entertainment, perhaps descendants of those of medieval Turkistan. A traveler named Eugene Schuyler wrote that in 1877, of a trio of musicians playing in Kuldja, northern Sinkiang, "the third filled in the harmony by beating with a little stick on three porcelain bowls of different sizes, which he held in his hand."

The tuned cups or bowls of the East reached Europe—where they were transformed into tuned glasses—no later than the fifteenth century, for they are seen in a woodcut of Gafori (1492). Gafori is demonstrating the intervals of the musical scale by different means, including a set of six drinking glasses marked with the ratio numbers 4:6:8:12:16; all the glasses are of the same size but contain varying amounts of water, ranging from very little (4) to full (16) via half full (8); two of the glasses are being tapped with small rods. Whether or not they were also used for simple music making at that time is not known, and little more is heard of them thereafter except as curiosities. A *glas werck* inventorized at Ambras in 1596 apparently contained a set of percussion bowls; it was described in the early nineteenth century as a decorative box containing glass bowls (*Glassglocken*) having a chromatic compass of over three octaves, F° to a². The remnants of what apparently constituted this very instrument have survived, and, although unfortunately the action is now missing, the housing itself is complete, with a small keyboard, from which it may be concluded that the glass *Glocken* were struck. Thereafter, in Europe, they were to be rubbed (see page 111).

SHAKEN IDIOPHONES (RATTLES)

Whatever their form, rattles are sounded by shaking and therefore are also known as shaken idiophones. Distinction is made between vessel rattles, usually containing hard objects that strike against the container; suspension rattles, comprising stick and strung rattles; and frame rattles, a group that includes pendant and sliding rattles (the cog rattle, despite its name, is a scraped idiophone).

Among the oldest instruments of mankind, rattles were originally apotropaic amulets, dancers' rhythm markers, and children's toys, later to become cult instruments. Magical and profane functions coexisted as late as Roman times, when *crepundia* (from *crepere*, "to rattle") were both charms against evil and a child's toy. In the Americas they were—and still are—also shaman's instruments shaken during healing ceremonies.

Prehistoric pottery vessel rattles in a great variety of forms, some zoomorphic, have been found in Europe and in Mesopotamia. Clay vessel rattles were found in children's graves of the east European Usa Tovo culture (which is contemporaneous with the late Tripolye culture, probably second half of the fourth millennium B.C.). Metal forms from northern and western Europe have been dated from the Late Bronze Age on. Egypt and India have also yielded prehistoric rattles, and some of clay dating from around 1000 B.C. have come to light in Palestine. Egypt developed the sistrum at a very early date; some Roman authors, e.g., Martial and Apuleius, called it a *crepitaculum*, a name they also applied to the child's rattle. Next to the sistrum, the most highly developed form of rattle is the pellet bell—another cult instrument—whose history reaches from antiquity to the present day.

In modern times rattles retain as their chief functions those of past millennia: the stressing of dance rhythm and the amusement of small children.

VESSEL RATTLES

PELLET BELLS

Although customarily referred to loosely as a bell in English (French and German have specific names for it), the pellet bell is in reality a small vessel rattle, and, in its Western form, a metal sphere enclosing one or more pellets. Due to the lack of precise nomenclature it is often impossible to distinguish between the true bell and the small vessel rattle in older literary sources, particularly Biblical ones, and modern English-language writers have often felt obliged to denote the rattle variety by the term "jingle." One early author who devised a compound pellet bell and called it a bell was "Muristus," a Greek writer known only by this name through Arabic sources from the eighth century on; his instrument was a hollow sphere divided internally into ten sections of different sizes, each containing pieces of metal; the globe was suspended by a ring and gave off harmonious sounds when shaken.

Found in most parts of the world, pellet bells are usually globular or ovoid in form; the enclosed materials may be pebbles, dried seeds, or similar materials. Like true bells, they have been credited with possessing magical powers in some areas of the world, and appear as cult instruments in others. In medieval Europe they were worn as apotropaic amulets, made of metal, and from the twelfth century on became objects of personal adornment, often made of precious metals, either spherical or piriform, worn as necklaces, attached to clothing, or dangling from a lady's belt. The Middle High German *Tristan und Isolde*, written in the early thirteenth century, relates that the sound of a *schelle* (pellet bell) suspended by a chain from the neck of the little dog Petitcriu, had the magic power of dispelling the listener's sorrow. Pellet bells were also attached to the numerous garters of morris dancers—they wore several pairs on each leg—and their hobbyhorse boasted horse bells.

Horse and mule bells of Europe were generally large spherical pellet bells with a slit at the bottom and a loop on top for attachment to the harness. A horse bell of silver was awarded the winning horse of English horse races in the sixteenth century, as, for example, those of Haddington, where annual races were established in 1552 and the winner received a silver bell. Jesters wore pellet bells on their caps, and the official court jester of Charles II, Tom Killigrew, received "a fee out of the wardrobe" for cap and bells, as Pepys noted in a diary entry of 1667. Miniature sizes, attached to the legs of hawks, are known in falconry as hawking bells; those from the city of Milan were renowned for their workmanship and sound, for such bells had to be "well sounding and shrill, yet not both of one sound, but one at least a note under the other." Italy had a long tradition of bell and pellet bell making, going back to Roman times, and Roman pellet bells are in existence with a suspension loop, sometimes ornamented with the most delicate workmanship. The sound of pellet bells was added to that of the frame drum in certain areas, including Galicia and Turkey, by adding several to the frame of the drum, a custom probably reaching back to antiquity. Today the *cabrette* (bagpipe) players of Auvergne thread pellet bells around their ankles to enhance the foot stamping with which they accentuate their rhythms, and the regional *bourrée montagnarde* is danced by men only, some of whom wear pellet bell anklets. Such usage represents the end of a dying and formerly more widespread European tradition. When Emperor Charles V was welcomed by a group of twenty singing and tambourine-playing girls in Spain in 1517, they were dressed *à la morisque* and wore pellet bells on arms, legs, and around their waists; a *putto* of Bronzino's *Allegory with Venus and Cupid*, painted in the same century, wears a band studded with pellet bells on his left ankle. In our unimaginative age their use is restricted to the sleigh.

But Europe is by no means the only area in which pellet bells were credited with magical powers; their apotropaic use in the ancient Near East is discussed above (see page 54), and it is from there that they are believed to have reached Europe some five centuries before the Christian era. Faith in their magical powers has been noted in peoples as far apart as the Eskimo, whose shamans formerly tied pellet bells to their garments, and magicians among the West African Fan, who today attach them to their hands and feet.

As cult instruments pellet bells appear in widely separated areas: in Japan they are ovoid, made of copper or brass, and form part of the Shinto ceremonial; very often a whole cluster is attached by metal rings to a handle. On the African continent, Christian priests of Ethiopia attach a cluster to a leather band and shake it at the moment of the Elevation; the East African Washambala place iron pellets inside globules of the same material and string them on strips of leather; they are then worn by men as dancing rattles, or during death rituals. The greatest variety of materials occurs whenever pellet bells serve simply as dancing rattles, as they do in many parts of Asia and Africa, strung together and worn as anklets or bracelets, or else twined about a dancer's calves or waist. Long strings of cocoons containing pebbles are sewn in pairs to a fiber cord by the Pedi of South Africa; a completed cord, which is worn as a leg rattle by women only, may measure 1½ meters (5 feet) in length. Africans often make their pellet bells of small gourds, fruit shells, or even hollowed wood, and Zande dancers make theirs of sheet iron.

Both male and female dancers of India wear pellet bell anklets to accentuate the stamping of their feet; in Japan, movements in certain *kabuki* dances are stressed with a rattle of pellet bells. Their clear but indeterminate pitch makes them acceptable to the highly evolved Vietnamese orchestra and as adjunct to the musical bow of the Congolese Bariri alike.

In pre-Columbian Mexico and Peru pellet bells were made of metal and contained pebbles; whole clusters have been recovered in Mexico, and it is known that Mayan dancers wore them. Ohio prehistoric mound builders made use of small turtle shells, a religious emblem of both prehistoric and contemporary Amerinds alike, and imitations in copper of such shells are found in the Hopewell culture. A belt on which eighteen miniature copper turtles, each 5 centimeters (2 inches) long, sewn side by side, was recovered from the Mound City Group, Ross County, Ohio, each filled with shell beads or quartz pebbles. (For other instruments of turtle carapace, see scraped idiophones, page 91.)

GOURD RATTLES

Next to the pellet bell, the most widely distributed form of vessel rattle is probably the gourd rattle, made of a dried calabash or of a gourd having a neck, usually piriform, with the neck serving as natural handle. In regions where gourds do not grow, their form is imitated in clay, wood, basketwork, metal, and even leather. Clay versions particularly are numerous. Gourd rattles are met with predominantly in Africa and America; on the Indian subcontinent they retain the form of a calabash but are made of metal, wood, clay, or basketry, into which pebbles or dried seeds are inserted.

Both gourd rattles and their pottery imitations have been in use in Mexico from Aztec times on, those of gourd containing seeds, their modern clay counterparts slit at one end for the insertion of a clay ball. Rattles, cult instruments in prehistoric America, were also used by medicine men during their incantations; a dried calabash rattle is still sounded by shamans of the Amazon, Pueblo, and Bison regions when treating the sick. In tropical South America the maraca gourd rattle is considered sacred and it even receives offerings of food from the Tupinamba. Shamans of the Barama Carib put pebbles representing spirits in their rattle so as to be able to invoke them at will. Today in Peru calabash rattles are encountered only in the northeast among the Bora and Muinanne; calabashes do not grow in other areas, and this fact has led at least one specialist (Izikowitz [1935]) to surmise that Peruvian rattle drums (see page 151) may have originated due to a lack of calabashes.

Prehistoric Ohio mound builders made vessel rattles of turkey skulls (and smaller ones of turtle carapaces, as described); several have been excavated from human burials and found to contain pebbles. Wildduck-skull rattles have been retrieved from other sites in Ohio. Many Plains and Northwest Coast Indians formerly made rawhide imitations of gourd rattles by sewing wet leather into a spherical bag, filling the bag with sand, and leaving it to dry, after which the sand was removed and the bag attached to a stick by the opening. Hollow wooden rattles are also made by Northwest Coast Indians.

Gourds with natural handles are commonly transformed into rattles in Negro Africa. Among the Bakongo, Bemba, and neighboring peoples of Central Africa these are filled with seeds of *Canna indica* and serve in religious cults and magical rites in addition to their profane role as rhythm makers. West Africans developed a variety with external percussion; the Sehgura of the Mende in Sierra Leone partly cover the exterior of their gourd rattles by a network of dried fruit seeds threaded on a cord; the gourd is then held by its handle in the player's left hand, while with his right hand he holds taut the ends of the cords, plaited into a rope, and agitates them. The Ewe of Ghana cover theirs with a mesh of beads and small pieces of bamboo threaded on a string. Such gourds do not contain rattling objects in their interior.

Afro-Americans play both types—gourds with internal and with external percussion—as well as a distinct variety made of two metal cones soldered together at the widest part, perforated, filled with seeds or pebbles, and furnished with a handle. All three types are found in Afro-American communities of the Caribbean and South America, where they play an important role in African cults. Furthermore, Afro-Americans may have adopted indigenous gourd rattles, for the maraca is said originally to have been a pellet-filled gourd rattle of pre-Columbian Araucanian derivation. Also, the Araucanian word *quiqui* forms the root of *quiquia*, name of a South American gourd rattle and of the Haitian *quiaquia* rattle. The name "maraca" has been given to Afro-American rattles of gourd, to those of the soldered cone type, and also to some in shape of a dumbbell or cross. Western rhythm bands have incorporated the net-covered gourd rattle, but the gourd is now synthetic and the beads are strung on gut.

Calabash rattles are ritual implements of the Haitian voodoo priests: the *baksor*, covered with a network of beads, assists in summoning either African gods or the dead; another, the *asson*, after being dried and emptied of its pulp and seeds, is covered with a network of beads and snake vertebrae, and generally furnished with a small bell that the priest sounds during the ceremony; but before it can serve in any cult, the *asson* must be baptized. During mystic voodoo marriages the celebrant invokes African gods to the shaking of the *asson:* he "makes *sesheshet*" see page 88).

BASKETRY RATTLES

Vessel rattles of basketry were known in ancient Egypt and are found today in Africa, America, and the Pacific. From Gabon to South Africa, little basketwork boxes woven from palm leaves or other materials are filled with pebbles, threaded on cords, and tied to dancers' legs during circumcision rites. Sometimes rattling is combined with drumming, as in East Africa, where the Ganda hold a cane basketwork box filled with seeds in their upturned palms to provide a shaking motion, while their thumbs beat a rhythm on the box. Gourds are imitated in wickerwork both in Africa and by Afro-Brazilians, but on the South American continent basketry rattles are restricted to the coastal rim.

HOLLOW RING RATTLES

Hollow rings are another popular form of vessel rattle, widely distributed. In Asia hollow copper rings with enclosed pellets are worn as anklets by dancers of India and Japan. A pair of similar rings serve in South India as temple rattles, one held in each hand and gently shaken to provide rhythm. Further east, itinerant physicians of China rapidly twirl a hollow, pebble-filled metal ring mounted on a stick handle to announce their presence; hollow staffs serve the same purpose. A curious, multitube rattle of Borneo rice planters has seven bamboo or hardwood tubes of different lengths containing wooden fragments studded with antler points; seven men sound it, each wielding a single tube—a rare occurrence of a rattle chime.

Ceremonial rattles of the Aztec and Maya called *chicahuaztli* were simply hollow, seed-filled staffs several feet long that, when shaken, were said to make the sound of falling rain; beautifully decorated descendants of these are still played by the North American Cora and Huichol Indians. A bamboo internode can be put to the same use, as is the case in coastal Ecuador, where both ends of the section remain closed and rattling objects are introduced through a longitudinal slit. Later the bamboo is imitated in metal, as, for example, in Brazil, where a closed cylinder of tinplate is substituted.

In East Africa multiple hollow cane or rush segments are tied together raftwise and secured by three transverse sticks by the Washambala, who fill the tube with peas and shake them during dances.

SUSPENSION RATTLES

STICK RATTLES

Rattling objects strung together on a rigid bar or a ring are known as stick rattles, and are differentiated from strung rattles, described below, in that the latter consist of rattling objects strung on a pliant cord. A Viking grave at Oseberg, Norway, dating from the ninth century, was found to contain a rattle consisting of a short metal handle onto one end of which was hooked a large metal ring; five smaller rings were threaded to this, and to each of these a still smaller one was suspended, causing a whole series of clashes when the rattle was shaken. Because of the great distance both in time and in space it is particularly interesting to discover a very similar stick rattle in present-day Tibet and in Buddhist Mongolia, with a ring onto which smaller rings are strung; and a related instrument of Kashmiri fakirs is made of a hooked metal bar along which a number of metal rings are threaded. In Japan this rattle becomes an attribute of the god Jizo and is restricted to ritual use. Called *shaku gyo*, it can be described in the same terms as the Oseberg rattle but for the fact that the short metal handle of Oseberg is here a wooden staff.

Several rural districts of Europe, among them the Val d'Anniers of Switzerland and some horse-herding regions of northern Germany, still have, or until very recently had, a ring-strung stick rattle, the long handle of which is a wand.

The Sistrum

But by far the best known of stick rattles are the sistra of antiquity. The word "sistrum," Roman name of the Greek *seistron* (from *seiein*, "to shake") is allied in most people's minds with Egypt, yet, although it probably originated and certainly reached the height of its development there, its use was by no means restricted to that area; indeed, it was known over a considerable portion of the ancient world.

Primitive varieties made of a forked stick are still encountered in many parts of the world: shark fishermen of Malaya and Melanesia make common use of a type of giant sistrum composed of a split bamboo or rattan section, its prongs held apart by a stick on which coconut shells are strung in facing pairs; the shells clash together when the implement is shaken. It is credited with having the power of magically attracting sharks. In Mali, West Africa, forked sticks are strung with pairs of calabash fragments threaded on a tine, and such rattles play an important role in fertility and initiation rites. And, in the Americas, the Yaqui of Mexico and the United States, and the Kadiuveo of Brazil, have sistrumlike rattles, those of the latter consisting of a forked stick with jingles strung on wires.

The earliest form of developed sistrum is U shaped, open at the top, with a short handle at the juncture of the prongs, and two horizontal bars inserted loosely enough to rattle when the object is shaken. The bars might be threaded with disks or with rectangular jingles. This form of sistrum is usually referred to as the spur type. Such an instrument was known to the Sumerian civilization of the mid-third millennium B.C. On the inlay work of a lyre excavated at the royal tombs of Ur of Bronze Age Babylon, now in the University of Philadelphia Museum, a spur-type sistrum is shown in the hands of a fox, its horizontal bar or bars strung with large disks. Fragments of an actual instrument were found at the same site, its bars strung with white shells.

Somewhat later, by about 2100–2000 B.C., a rectangular version appeared at Horoztepe in Anatolia, also with two horizontal bars on which rectangular jingling disks were threaded, and ornamented with little animal figures—either bulls or stags—around the frame. Bronze Age spur-type sistra from about the same period have also been found there; sometimes the frames were ornamented with bull horns: these were Hatti (Hittite) instruments. This people, it will be recalled, took over the cuneiform script of the Assyrians and adapted it to their own language; apparently they took over the Mesopotamian sistrum as well. Sistra of similar form have been discovered near Tiflis, Georgia. Only a single example of the spur type has come to light so far in Egypt, a specimen dating from about 2000 B.C. found at Asyût, with jingles on its bars.

The Egyptian sistrum is characterized, however, by being closed at the top. Of the two known closed forms, the *sesheshet* was shaped like a *naos* (temple) and the *iba* had the form of a horseshoe closed on top; both had handles. The *naos* sistrum first represented the front view of a house, later that of a temple, and had two, subsequently three or four horizontal bars—in Greco-Roman times even five—with or without jingles. This particular form, the *naos*, is restricted to Egypt and has not been encountered elsewhere so far. It was usually made of metal, bronze or brass, although pottery specimens have also been excavated, their frames pierced for the insertion of three horizontal bars. Some of these pottery sistra show signs of wear, hence they cannot have been mere grave goods. On several the crossbars are wrought in the form of snakes.

Ibas were made of metal generally, but wooden and pottery versions are known. Metal disks were added to the bars of sistra of the Old and Middle Kingdoms, a practice discontinued in the New Kingdom. Primitive sistra were already known in prehistoric Egypt; the horseshoe form (*iba*) first occurs in the Fifth Dynasty (2500–2350 B.C.), the *naos* first in the Sixth Dynasty (2350–2200 B.C.). As bronze implements, sistra also possessed apotropaic powers; Egyptians shook them, according to Plutarch (*Isis and Osiris*), in order to frighten away Typhon by their horrifying noise.

The Egyptian sistrum remained a cult instrument throughout its history and was sacred to Hathor. Wall paintings in tombs occasionally depict the deceased standing in the Barge of the Dead while gliding through a papyrus thicket, seizing the stalks in passing, and shaking them in order to attract the goddess by their noise; and in early times young maidens would pick the rushlike papyri of Nile thickets and shake them so that they rattled, an age-old cult gesture called "to make *sesheshet*."

Later, when Hathor was metamorphosed into Isis, the sistrum became sacred to Isis and continued to be played only by women. Then, toward the end of Egypt's independence, it passed into the hands of male priests of the Isis cult (in the Brember-Rhind Papyrus, Osiris is invoked as the "fair sistrum player," and his priestesses carried frame drums). When the cult of Isis spread to Greece and Rome, so did her sistra, still in the hands of priests. A wall painting from Herculaneum, now in the Naples Museum, depicts a scene of worship in which the celebrant is flanked to his left by a Negro priest shaking a sistrum, to his right by a priestess holding another; the background of palm and ibises indicates that the action was laid in Egypt.

That the Romans themselves did not accept the sistrum may be gathered from their calling it *crepitaculum* ("rattle"), as in Apuleius' *Golden Ass* (second century B.C.), where the goddess *nam dextra quidem ferebat aereum crepitaculum, cuius per angustam laminam in modum baltei recurvatam traiecta mediae paucae virgulae, cripante brachio trigeminus iactus reddebant argutam sonorem.* (". . . in her right hand carried a bronze *crepitaculum*, the narrow blade of which, curved in the form of a baldric, was transversed by several small rods.") When this passage was translated by William Adlington in 1566, the sistrum, long forgotten, became a "timbrel of brass."

Actual instruments of the closed type have been found not only in Italy but as far away as France, where two were removed from the tomb of a priest of Isis at Nîmes, and a Bronze Age rattle from Blödesheim, Rhine-Hesse, is clearly derived from the sistrum; its U shape, closed at the top by a yoke, is attached to a handle, but in lieu of the horizontal wires it has rings with metal jingles attached to either side of the bottom of the frame.

From Egypt the sistrum traveled to the Aegean and to Palestine, areas in which its use remains problematic. A single appearance on Minoan Crete is also known, that of a horseshoe type represented in the hands of a man on the so-called Harvesters Vase in the Heraklion Museum. As to the Levant, the *mena'anim* was a rattle of the ancient Hebrews (*nu'a* means "shock") and is believed to have been a sistrum; but the identification of many instruments of ancient Israel is difficult, and there is still a question mark regarding this one.

The present-day Ethiopian horseshoe type, *tsanatsel*, is doubtless a direct descendant of the ancient Egyptian sistrum. Today it is some 15 to 18 centimeters (6 to 7 inches) high, with a metal frame and wooden handle; strangely enough its sole use is in the Christian Monophysite church where it is held in the same manner and position as that depicted millennia ago, namely, in the left hand with arm bent at shoulder height. Shaken gently, it follows a prescribed rhythmic pattern, which it shares with a double-headed drum. The frame is ordinarily of copper or iron, but some have been made of silver and even of gold, and all have wires threaded with jingling rings.

In Europe and the Near East, the sistrum did not outlive antiquity. This did not prevent the continued use of its name, though, transferred to other instruments as need arose; thus sistrum, *cistrum*, or *cistro* turn up in the enumerations of stringed instruments from late medieval to baroque times, when reference is usually to a "cittern"—a good example of etymological back formation.

STRUNG RATTLES

A primitive form of rattle still found on all continents, the strung rattle consists typically of a number of objects threaded together on a cord loosely enough to permit their clashing together when shaken. Such are the rattle anklets worn by dancers in many societies, originally protective amulets designed to ward off evil spirits, while today their function is that of underscoring the rhythmic stepping or stamping of legs, or the motions of body or arms.

American Indians of pre-Columbian times wore rattles both on clothing and as necklaces made of dried cocoons, bear teeth, and similar objects, pierced and strung together. In ancient Mexico a string of sea-snail shells was worn as anklet or as breast ornament. The same materials are used today in New Guinea, where they are strung on bark fiber to form dancers' bracelets. Rattling bands of dried fruits threaded on a string of liana are worn below the right knee of Witoto dancers in Colombia. Deer-hoof rattles were formerly much in demand among the Plains Indians of North America and those of the North American Southwest; the hooves were either strung along a stick or they were attached to one end in a bunch (a form also called bunch rattle), but nowadays hoof and dewclaw have given way to metal jingles. When the strung material consists of a dead enemy's teeth, as among the Brazilian Munducurú, the rattle becomes a source of magic strength to the wearer.

African dancers often wear bands of rattling objects around the calf, the waist, the ankles or wrists, or else wind them about the leg. In function if not in form, these are identical with the threaded pellet bells worn in identical fashion.

FRAME RATTLES

One form of frame rattle, the pendant rattle, consists of a carrier from which rattling objects depend; when set in motion objects strike the carrier. In many areas where turtles are found they have become religious emblems to the peoples whose habitat they share. This has been true since prehistoric times (cf. pellet bells in the Americas, page 81). Some East African dancers wear frame rattles made of a complete tortoise carapace from which a number of short iron chains dangle; the carapace is affixed to the dancer's arm by a thong and his movements cause the chains to strike against the shell. Medicine men of the North American Pueblo Indians tied a similar rattle, also a tortoise carapace, but with hoof and metal jingles for attachments, to their left knee.

Another variety of frame rattle, the tuned sliding rattle, is played only in Indonesia. Actually it is a rattle chime, known as *angklung* in western Java and as *grantang* in Bali. Formerly played over a wider territory, it is now restricted to these two areas. Two or three bamboo tubes are cut back for over half their length so as to form a tongue; the lower end is closed by a node and terminates in two "feet." Tuned in octaves, these tubes are suspended upright in a bamboo frame in which they slide back and forth when the frame is shaken, their "feet" fitting through a slit in the framework to prevent their falling out. A number of *angklungs*— from nine to fifteen—of different sizes form a set with a pentatonic tone sequence. Each player shakes his instrument when his turn comes to play, much as certain aerophones are played in South America. An *angklung* from Java in the Brussels Conservatoire Museum has fifteen frames of two tubes each, with a range from $b\flat^\circ$ to $b\flat^2$, extended by the octave tubes to $b\flat^3$. A similar instrument of Java is composed of tubes no longer shaken but struck; it has become a percussion idiophone (see page 38).

SCRAPED IDIOPHONES

Scraped idiophones are solid objects such as sticks, bones, et cetera (stick scrapers), or hollow objects such as gourds, shells, et cetera (vessel scrapers), notched on the surface and scraped with a stick. The quality of sound emitted hardly qualifies them as musical instruments; rather, they serve to underscore rhythmic patterns, often in a ritual context. Scrapers were known to Paleolithic and Neolithic Europe and in modern times they are found on all continents and the Pacific.

From the Paleolithic on, scraped, notched bones have been in use in Europe, but whether they were merely held in one hand and scraped, or were rested on or against some form of resonator to increase the volume of sound, is unknown. In our era they can be documented from the Middle Ages on: a wooden scraper with two opposite rows of notches dating from the twelfth century was excavated in Poland. Two centuries later scraped pots are recorded in western Europe; one, scraped with a two-pronged, curved stick, is depicted on a French miniature from the first quarter of the fourteenth century illustrating the *Roman de Fauvel*, and the beautiful *Glorification of the Virgin* by Gerard of Saint John, painted about 1490, includes among numerous instruments a pot rather like the *Hafen*, a scraped pot of sixteenth-century Germany, first mentioned (and also illustrated) by Virdung (1511). By now such objects have all but disappeared from Europe. At the carnival of Binche, Belgium, is played a violin-shaped scraper, made of a wooden board with a rectangular opening into which three wooden tongues are introduced; these are scraped with a notched stick. A simpler form played in the Campagna, southern Italy, consists of two sticks scraped with a saw-shaped wooden "bow." Catalonia has retained two scrapers, one of gourd;

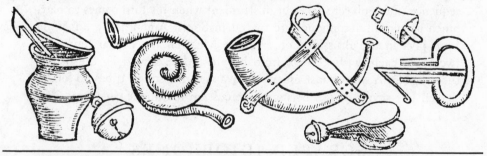

Trumpeln/Schelle/Jeger horn/Acher horn/Kůschellen. Brütsche/vff dem hafen

Scraped pot and other Renaissance folk instruments: pellet bell, horns, clappers, bell, Jew's harp. As may be seen from the German enumeration, the woodcut is reversed. From Sebastian Virdung, *Musica getutscht*, 1511.

the other, called *peixet* ("fish"), is a sheet-metal imitation of a fish with raised scales that are scraped with a metal rod.

To China belongs the distinction of possessing a scraper that has remained in continuous use for three millennia, ever since the Chou dynasty (1050–256 B.C.), the *yü*, or tiger. This is a vessel scraper carved of wood to resemble a crouching tiger, with a series of notches running the length of its back. These are scraped with a bamboo stick split half-way down its length to form twelve or more switches; as a Confucian ritual instrument it is sounded three times to mark the end of religious services. The same instrument is found in Korea, also restricted to Confucian ritual, and in Japan. Both countries received their "tiger" from China. The Javanese have a scraper shaped like a shrimp, covered with a notched bronze plaque that is scraped with a bronze rod.

Elsewhere in Asia scrapers are sometimes combined with another instrument, as in Vietnam, for instance, where a pair of hardwood clappers provided with jingling cash (small coins) is held in one hand, and, while they click and jingle, they are simultaneously scraped with a notched stick. A musical bow of Mirzapur, India, is notched along its surface; one end is rested on a basket set on the ground, the other on the ground itself; when scraped, the basket reverberates. Notched poles of bamboo or metal are frequent in other areas of the Indian subcontinent.

Africans also make use of various forms of both solid and hollow scrapers. One of the latter is, perhaps coincidentally, akin to the Asiatic "tiger": the *nkumbi* of Angola is carved to resemble an antelope with a notched stick laid along its back. Nearby in the Lower Congo the Bwende have a scraper formed like a slit drum, with one extremity carved to represent a head and a notched stick placed over the slit. Another scraper of Angola, the *quilando*, a large calabash with notched surface, was described in 1692 by Girolamo Merolla; today it is played together with a second scraper made of a hollowed piece of wood covered by a notched board.

Of the scrapers played by Afro-Americans, the *güira* has now been adopted by Western rhythm bands. Afro-Cubans call it *guayó*, Haitians *gragé*, and on the mainland it goes by the name of *güiro* or *güira*; all are made from an oval gourd of that name that has a natural handle by which it is held, the gourd's surface being notched. Afro-Cubans also make various forms of scraper-rattles; one is a notched turtle carapace impaled on a stick and filled with pebbles; another, played also in Haiti, is a pole having a short crossbar, to which four globular gourds are attached so as to form a cross; the lower portion of the cross is notched. Both types are shaken and at the same time scraped.

A curious variety is the *quijada* (Spanish for "jawbone"), which is simply the lower jaw of a horse, mule, or donkey with all its teeth left in. Played on the mainland and in the Caribbean, its use among the Negroes of coastal Peru goes back to the late eighteenth century. The English traveler, William Walton, described one in 1810 when he observed it in Santo Domingo as "the teeth fixed in the jaw-bone of a horse, scraped with rapid motion." The *quijada* is also a rattle, for the teeth chatter when the jawbone is shaken, and it doubles as a percussion instrument, since it can be hit with the player's fist. Under the name of "jawbone" the same implement is scraped by Negroes of Louisiana and the Carolinas.

The use of scrapers in Central America is very ancient; frescoes of the Bonampak temple of Chiapas State, Mexico, believed to date from the eighth or ninth century A.D., show scrapers and gourd rattles played in a procession. The scraper portrayed is the *ayotl*, a turtle carapace, here carried in a vertical position with its player holding a forked antler in each hand. Today the *ayotl* resounds from Mexico and Guatemala, usually suspended from the performer's neck. Ancient Mexicans also had the *omichicahuaztli* of animal bone or antler, in pre-Columbian times also of a human femur. Scrapers were ritual instruments, sounded by slaves at the funerals of rulers—before the slaves themselves were sacrificed—and at commemorations of dead warriors or of sacrificed prisoners.

In North America scrapers of deer and elk bone of the prehistoric Ohio Indians have been excavated, their notches cut at one-half to one-quarter inch intervals. A common scraper, formerly much in use among Plains and southwestern tribes is the *morache*, the Spanish name having become established by usage. This was generally a notched stick or bone scraped with a smaller stick or bone. Typically it was placed on a resonator, such as a half or a whole gourd; the Ute formerly set an upturned basket on the ground, now make use of a piece of zinc; the Papago also had upturned basket resonators, while Plains Indians made use of a piece of parfleche or folded rawhide. Other objects, such as a tub, gourd, or box, also serve as resonators, depending upon the area. Some tribes sound the scraper as accompaniment to drums during dances, or as a time beater; among the Pima it is a rhythm instrument to accompany ceremonial songs, and also plays an important part in their rainmaking ceremonies.

The implement with which the scraping is done is usually a wooden stick, but numerous other materials have been or are still in use.

Although rarely encountered in the Pacific, scrapers there participate in death and funerary rites on Torres and Banks islands in the New Hebrides.

COG RATTLES

Scraped wheels, or ratchets, are commonly referred to as cog rattles, but they are actually cogwheels with a prolongation of the axle serving as a handle, and with a wooden tongue affixed to the frame. When whirled, the tongue strikes the cogs one after the other, causing a loud, clappering noise. Here the notched and the scraping sticks are mechanized and combined into a single unit that can be both held and sounded by one hand. Such mechanized scrapers are found in Europe, Asia, and North and Central America.

Their use in Europe extends back to the late medieval period, and their functions were varied. Principally they served in monasteries of the Orthodox church and in Roman Catholic churches of Romance countries to replace bells during Easter Week; in some areas they still do so. Formerly, children were free during that week to run around sounding them as mere noisemakers also; additionally they were signal instruments in the hands of night watchmen, occasionally of beggars and of lepers, and since the sixteenth century if not earlier small models have been made as toys. At a funeral procession in Paris in 1478, four town criers carrying cog rattles preceded the bier.

Spain and Portugal had a distinct and very large cog rattle called the *matraca*—the word has been in use since 1570—up to 2 meters (6½ feet) in diameter, installed in or outside the church tower, and rotated during Easter Week to summon the worshipers. From the Iberian peninsula the *matraca* was taken to Mexico, where it serves the same purpose, and to the Philippine Islands, where it was set up to frighten off locusts from fields under cultivation. A *matraca* is suspended in one of the arches of the Giralda Tower in Seville, a minaret abandoned by the Moors, and there is another above the nine great bells of Toledo Cathedral, worked by a "curious mechanism," and sounded continuously for forty-eight hours before the *Gloria in excelsis* on Saturday preceding Easter. These church *matracas* were so arranged that the axle could be rotated by means of a large hand crank. The French called them *moulinet* ("little mill") in the sixteenth century, from the resemblance to a windmill of the enlarged cogs that were struck by hammers as they revolved.

In India, as in North America, cog rattles are now reduced to the role of a child's toy. However, formerly among the Ingaliks AmerInds its sound was said to attract evil spirits and for that reason it was used only during daylight.

SPLIT IDIOPHONES

One of the most peculiar of all idiophones is without doubt the "tuning fork" idiophone of Southeast Asia. After originating in Yunnan, South China, it is believed to have reached the Malayan peninsula via the Philippine Islands; on the peninsula it is now known as *genggong sakai* ("Jew's harp of the Sakai people"). It is nothing more than a piece of bamboo in the shape of a tuning fork or an old-fashioned clothespin. The cane is hollowed, then split between nodes so as to form two prongs and a handle; the prongs are forced apart by insertion of a small stick at the joint. The handle—also hollow—serves as a resonator and is pierced with two holes for changing the pitch; if both tone holes are closed, the pitch is lowered by a major second. When slapped against the player's wrist or thigh, or struck with the knuckles of the free hand, a fixed-pitch buzzing emanates.

On Celebes these instruments attain a length of from 40 to 70 centimeters (19 to 27 inches). Two are played together on Nias, where one of a pair is smaller than the other and is pitched a third higher, so that a tone sequence of TTT can be obtained from the two instruments, the tritone on which most southern Nias songs are based. The same idiophones are played on other islands of the archipelago and along the Torres Straits, where they are sounded by rainmakers to imitate thunder. The Maori of New Zealand have a similar instrument made from the thick part of a flax leaf, and on the Chinese mainland tuning fork idiophones are now made of metal and have become the signal whereby itinerant barbers announce their presence.

A split idiophone known as chapstick is made by North American Indians, usually of wood but sometimes of reed or cane. About 60 centimeters (2 feet) long and split part of the way, it does not assume tuning fork shape, as the prongs are not forced apart. But the playing method is identical, for the Indians hold theirs in one hand and strike it against the palm of the other hand, and some Amerinds even play them in pairs. More developed models are hollowed out. Seder (1952) reports that wide use is made of these idiophones by California Indians, especially at girls' puberty rites.

A percussion switch made of wood or cane split at one end into numerous segments is also found in North America, chiefly in California, and again in connection with girls' puberty ceremonies. It can be struck or shaken, indiscriminately. Percussive switches of similar nature are also known in Tibet and Assam, and among the Dayak of Borneo and the Grebo of West Africa.

Buonanni (1722) illustrated its use in eighteenth-century Europe by depicting a monk waking his brethren by beating on their cell doors with just such a switch.

PLUCKED IDIOPHONES

Plucked idiophones, also known as linguaphones, have as their distinguishing feature an elastic lingua, or series of linguae, fixed at one end and left free to vibrate at the other. The free end is flexed and promptly released; this flexing can be either manual or, as in more developed forms, mechanical.

One of the simplest forms of linguaphone is the Melanesian *cricri*, a fruit shell, nut, or other substance that serves as resonator, with a tongue carved from its surface. This is then plucked by the player's thumb. A more sophisticated application of the same principle is found in the Jew's harp, with its single lamella. Linguaphones with multiple tongues constitute such seemingly disparate instruments as the African *sansa* and the European music box. Yet the latter may conceivably have been inspired by the former.

THE JEW'S HARP

The Jew's harp is neither a harp nor a Jewish instrument, nor even, as some would have it, connected with jaws. Prior to being called Jew's harp (from 1595 on) it was known as Jew's trump in English, in northern England and Scotland as plain "trump." Its present French name is *guimbarde,* but before the eighteenth century it was known as *gronde* or *trompe,* and earlier still as *rebube* (whence "ributhe" in a fifteenth-century Scottish poem entitled "Houlgate"); Spanish equivalents, *trompa de Paris, trompa gallega, trompa inglesa,* all point to a foreign origin. In Germany its earliest recorded name (sixteenth century) was *Trumpel,* changed in the seventeeenth century to *Maultrumpe* and *Brummeisen* ("drone iron"). These numerous occurrences of *trompe* and variants thereof indicate an etymological affiliation with "trumpet," an instrument with which, curiously enough, it has something very fundamental in common, namely its scale. (Italians call the instrument by the charming name of *scacciapensieri,* "chase away thoughts").

Jew's harps assume two principal forms, the older that of a clothespin, to the closed end of which a flexible lamella is attached, its other end remaining free to be plucked. This type is made of bamboo, wood, or metal. In the younger form, a slender frame of metal assumes the outline of an onion, its two ends just far enough apart to give free passage to the tongue. Jew's harps can have either idioglot or heteroglot tongues; idioglot tongues are encountered in Indonesia and Melanesia, heteroglot tongues in Europe; both forms occur on the Indian subcontinent and in China. In the more widely employed playing technique, the broader end of the frame is steadied with one hand and the narrow end is held loosely between the teeth, leaving the lingua free to swing. The player plucks it with his finger so that it vibrates in his mouth, using the oral cavity as a resonator. The tones produced are those of the harmonic scale of the trumpet, but infinitely soft. Actually the first, second, and third harmonics do not speak at all, but the fourth to the tenth harmonics speak clearly. By altering the position of lips, tongue, and cheeks—and consequently of the air mass—the player is able to isolate and reinforce one or another of the harmonics. Modification of the lamella's fundamental pitch is made possible by an application of wax or similar substance to its free end. Metal instruments sound louder than those of wood or bamboo.

Other than by importation, Jew's harps are unknown to Africans and American Indians. They may have originated in southern China or Southwest Asia; the oldest types are still to be found in these regions, played by several of the peoples bordering on South China, as well as by the more archaic populations of Java. Laurence Picken, noted for his studies of musical instruments in this area, writes that among the Naga, Mosua, and Minjia, the Jew's harp is only a step removed from the free reed of the mouth organ, another ancient instrument common to the area, and, furthermore, that evidence exists showing that the Chinese have always considered the free reed as an instrument in its own right, independently of its occurrence in the mouth organ.

The free reeds of some of the less developed mouth organs (see page 731) and the form of the Jew's harps under discussion are both slender rectangles, both have an idioglot tongue, and both are set in vibration by the player's breath. Thus the monophonic mouth-organ reed, detached from its instrument, is in many ways analogous to the "solo" Jew's harp, the latter rendered "polyphonic" by its complex playing technique. That of the Mosua group of Luo in southwestern Yunnan is shaped like an elongated clothespin made of bamboo, with small idioglot tongue set in motion by jerking a silk cord attached to one end, while the other is held steady. Although it is held horizontally in front of the player's parted lips, it does not touch them. The area in which this form occurs reaches as far as New Guinea, where the inhabitants of Nassau Range know of no other musical instrument. Three separate, tuned Jew's harps, formed into a triple instrument, are also played in southwestern Yunnan and areas bordering on southern China, no longer jerked by a cord but vibrated by plucking a slender projection of the free end. Picken relates that by means of such triple instruments, where pitch differences are sufficiently pronounced, young people exchange messages with one another, as in speech (cf. "talking" drums, page 156).

Somewhat younger types on Taiwan and Cape Engaño (Philippines) have the same form but heteroglot reeds of metal; these are plucked directly by the player's finger. The evolution is continued with instruments having the outline of an onion, of metal, and with a metal lamella. In northern China these are cut out of a single piece of flat iron with idioglot tongue; this is broad at the vertex, tapering toward the free end, typical of the tongues of onion-shaped versions. Elsewhere this form—almost always made of iron—is composed of two pieces soldered together at the vertex, with metal lamella affixed at that point; it projects beyond the frame at both ends, the free end upturned for ease in plucking.

In this form the Jew's harp found its way to ancient Rome, whence it passed to Egypt; there it is seen from 30 B.C. on, according to Hans Hickmann, a specialist in Egyptian instruments both ancient and modern. Rome also transmitted it to postclassical Europe. In its final form, assumed in Europe, only the plucked end of the tongue projects beyond the frame. Virdung (1511) depicts the new shape, but the older continued to be made for centuries thereafter.

The earliest evidence of the Jew's harp's presence in postclassical Europe so far known is from a mid-fourteenth-century sculpture at Essex Cathedral. An actual instrument of the same century was found while the remains of Tannenberg Castle in Hesse, destroyed in 1399, were being excavated. When Virdung illustrated the *Trumpel*, it was part of *musica irregularis*; Emperor Maximilian's court jester played one, and both jester and instrument were included in one of Burgkmair's engravings of *The Triumphs of Maximilian*. Apparently Jew's harps were part of the regular stock-in-trade of certain merchants and instrument dealers during the sixteenth and seventeenth centuries, for in the town of Brunswick two dozen Jew's harps formed part of a shopkeeper's estate in 1553, while in 1647 a merchant's inventory included nine dozen Jew's harps. Seven years later another shopkeeper, obviously an instrument dealer judging by his large and assorted store of goods, had no fewer than thirty dozen Jew's harps and an extra six bundles of brass Jew's harps on hand.

The tiny instrument had amazing staying power: Adlung (1758) recalled having heard eight Jew's harps played simultaneously in—of all places—Erfurt Cathedral; in the late eighteenth and early nineteenth century it was temporarily transformed into a virtuoso instrument by performers such as Koch (who started playing around 1785), Carl Eulenstein of Württemberg, and Johann Heinrich Scheibler of Krefeld—and in his *Wilhelm Meister*, published in 1795–1796, Goethe's pedant plays a concert "pianissimo" on the *Maultrommel*. Eulenstein traveled to London in 1827 and concertized there on sixteen Jew's harps. Some time thereafter his teeth had become so damaged by the iron instrument that he could not play without great pain, and so he started to cultivate the guitar; finally a dentist was able to grant him relief by concocting a cover for his teeth, whereupon he resumed the playing of his favorite instrument. After further concertizing he established himself at Bath from 1834 to 1845 as "teacher of the guitar, concertina, and the German language"—the day of the Jew's harp was over.

Due to the fact that only an incomplete scale is obtainable on any Jew's harp, it becomes necessary to add a second instrument pitched a fourth lower if a diatonic scale is desired, so that performers employed simultaneously two or more Jew's harps of different fundamental pitches. Such a combination was the *Aura* of Johann Heinrich Scheibler, designed in 1816; he combined ten of differing pitches into two groups of five each on frames provided with handles—he called them holders—one group held in each hand; later he apparently combined up to twenty in circular fashion, with their lamellae radiating all around. They were fine tuned by having sealing wax placed on the tip of the tongue. Perhaps it was one of these that Eulenstein had played.

After its brief glory on the concert platform, little more is heard of the Jew's harp in Europe, for its successor, the mouth organ, supplanted it in the third decade of the nineteenth century. However, it may have influenced the development of free-reed keyboard instruments, since two makers of these professed having transferred the principle of a Jew's harp lamella to the free reed. But the small linguaphone continued to be played up to the end of the century in more isolated regions such as the Austrian Alps. Today it is a shepherd's instrument in parts of Spain and a toy elsewhere.

Ever since 1679 there existed a guild of Jew's harp makers in Mölln, Upper Austria; by 1818 the membership of this organization had grown to thirty-three masters and fourteen apprentices, who together accounted for an annual output of some 2½ million pieces, all made by hand. A good century after manufacture of the competitive mouth organ had started, in 1935 to be exact, ten masters and their families were still producing annually an estimated 1½ million pieces for export. A similar enterprise existed on Lake Garda, near Riva (Austrian at the time); its output was exported overseas via Genoa and Livorno. Other European countries also engaged in manufacture, but on a smaller scale. Such export items have turned up as far away as the Republic of Cameroun.

Although most of its music was not written down, a nineteenth-century *Partita* in C by Johann Heinrich Hörner exists in manuscript (Landesmuseum, Innsbruck), for two unison Jew's harps and other instruments; the "crembalum" parts double muted violins, chiefly at the lower octave. Currently Jew's harp playing enjoys a certain vogue in the United States, where both instrument, imported from England, and tutor are available. Outside Europe its soft and sweet tone has often caused it to be connected with courtship, particularly so in Asia. A small drum or other rhythm instrument frequently accompanies it in Cutch, western India, where it is called *murchang* ("mouth harp"), or just *chang* ("harp").

THE SANSA

African sansas consist of a varying number of split cane or metal tongues fitted to a wooden board or resonator so as to permit one end of each lamella to vibrate freely. Pitch is determined by the length of the individual lamellae and can be adjusted quickly and easily; fine tuning is possible, where necessary, by affixing small balls of beeswax or rubber to the underside of the free ends. While played the instrument is grasped by both hands, the free ends of the tongues are flexed and released by the player's thumbs, or by his thumbs and forefingers. In some areas of Central Africa the sansa is attached to a gourd resonator, which is pressed against the performer's body, but more often resonators take the form of a box having soundholes. Split-cane sansas are believed to be older than those of metal. Usually the tongues are graduated so as to form a definite scale sequence; less commonly they may be arranged in a particular melodic pattern. Sometimes the tongues are even arranged on several levels, like miniature keyboards (this type may have given rise to the term "Kaffir piano"); they occur on two or even three levels in Zaire and in Angola. On multitier sansas the longest tongues form the lowest level for ease of access, while the shorter ones have upcurving, spatulate ends. Sometimes jingles are added, or else a buzzing effect is obtained by placing loose sleeves around the individual lamellae. The Bapende of Zaire hollow out the cane lamellae and fill them with rattling seeds.

Sansas are played over a very wide area, and special effects such as those just described vary according to the aesthetic preferences of the different peoples who play them. To the Lunga (Marunga) of Zaire, as well as to Westerners in general, sansa is the name by which this linguaphone is known. Among Bantu speakers it is more commonly called *mbira*, but a number of local names exist; in some regions along the Congo River it is referred to as *marimba* or *marimbula*, and apparently this name has not changed for centuries, as Buonanni (1722) depicted a sansa called *marimba dei Cafri*.

Age and genesis of the sansa are unknown. The West became aware of its existence by João dos Santos's description of the nine-tongued *ambira* (variant of *mbira*) in 1586, and through other early writers. Studies of the sansa's area of distribution, tuning, and nomenclature that have been undertaken, notably by A. M. Jones (1964), have led to some interesting findings: their area of distribution falls within that of the African xylophone; in many instances the words for the sansa or its keys are the same as those of the xylophone or its keys; sansas show heptatonic and equipentatonic tunings, as do the xylophones, and the tuning of a given instrument corresponds to that of a xylophone or of part of a xylophone.

Consequently Jones considers the sansa to be a small, portable version of the xylophone, and thus linked again with Indonesia.

Africans took the sansa with them to the New World, where it is still played by their descendants (in Central and South America only). Its Cuban name is *marimbula*, its Brazilian name, *marimbao*, clear indications of the locus of their origin. A greatly enlarged form, of soap-box size, is played in Haiti, with the player sitting astride it and manipulating the tongues with both thumbs between his knees.

THE MUSIC BOX

In the latter part of the eighteenth century musical clocks (see page 645) underwent a sort of "miniaturization," from which they emerged as music boxes. Essentially, the pipework disappeared, to be replaced by a comb mechanism (the term itself was sometimes applied to pipework automata of small sizes in the 1760s). At the height of its development the music box comprised a comb of tuned metal teeth—their free ends pointed—a pinned cylinder, and a watch spring, all housed in a wooden box. Small boxes furnished with a hand crank instead of a spring were also made, but in other respects they were identical.

The early history of these minute automata is far from clear. For one thing, it is not known whether the idea of slender, tunable metal tongues may not have been inspired by the African sansa, as Algernon Rose suggested already in 1904, nor is the precise date of the first music boxes known, nor yet the identity of the earliest maker (Louis Favre of Geneva has been proposed), but it seems likely that their originator was a Swiss, for the history of the music box has always been associated with Switzerland, and particularly with Geneva. The first models were actually not music "boxes" at all, but simply movements placed first in pocket watches and subsequently in snuff boxes, before they came to be housed in the rectangular wooden receptacles they were to remain in for over a century.

About 1770 small models with combs having from fifteen to twenty-five teeth were made in Switzerland and called *carillons à musique*. Their combs were made up either of separate teeth, or of several combs composed of four or five teeth each, with their free ends radiating out like a fan. Pinned cylinders—often said to have been the invention of David Lecoultre of Geneva around 1780—are now known to have existed by the decade of the 1770s. However, another arrangement was also in use until about 1810: instead of a cylinder, steel pins were set on both surfaces of a small steel or brass disk, some 3 centimeters in diameter. This concept of the "notated" disk was to return later in the century. From about 1820 on it became possible to cut entire combs from a single sheet of steel, and concurrently the cylinders started assuming greater proportions; they grew to 50 centimeters (20 inches) in length, as more and more tunes were pinned cheek by jowl. Some of the larger models were provided with a second, interchangeable cylinder.

From the mid-century on attempts were made to vary the rather monotonous sound by adding a variety of "improvements," among which were featured drums, bells, castanets, mandolin or zither effects, even a row of air-actuated free reeds worked by bellows and known as flutina, or by modifying the comb itself to gain special effects; an imitation harp or zither tone, for instance, could be produced by placing a sheet of paper on the comb. The great century of the music box was roughly from 1810 to 1910, and it was from the mid-nineteenth century on that these accessories were introduced.

But the really important improvements were those of a technical nature: greater accuracy in pinning, in the tuning of the teeth, of adjusting the cylinder so that a given tune could be played without first having to play through any preceding ones, standardization of cylinder sizes so that they would fit different boxes, perfection of a system of interchangeable cylinders (the last was accomplished in 1862).

The sound-producing elements of a music box are of course the tuned metal teeth of the comb. A separate tooth is necessary for each tone to be played, and tuning was accomplished by varying the lengths of each tooth: the deeper the desired pitch, the deeper a tooth was cut. According to the laws of acoustics governing bars—and the tooth of a comb is acoustically speaking a bar—the pitch is raised by two octaves if its length is halved (cf. xylophones, page 23). For keyboard instruments sounded by pipes or strings there exist certain means of reducing the length of bass pipes and strings without modifying their pitch, and the same is true of bars: from the 1820s on tiny lead weights were placed on the underside of the bass teeth, permitting a reduction in their length; and because the width of a tongue is not acoustically critical, teeth could be made extremely narrow. The pinning of a cylinder demanded meticulous workmanship in order to assure correct and uniform tempo and accurate rendition of the tune; in France, this art was known as *tonotechnie*. Although pinned cylinders and pegged barrels of tower instruments have much in common, one fundamental difference is that the pegs of a carillon barrel are movable, while the pins of a music-box comb are permanent.

When fashioning a cylinder, first the positions of the pins were marked off, then the corresponding holes were drilled, after which the pins were inserted and tested for uniformity of length, and the cylinder tested for uniform speed of rotation. The position of a given pin in the cylinder determined which tooth was to be sounded; if ten pins are set in a straight line around the circumference of a cylinder, then a given tooth will sound ten times during one revolution (provided they are not set too closely together). On some instruments several teeth were tuned in unison because a tooth can only be sounded by its pin when in a position of rest, so that if rapidly repeated notes are to be played, a duplication will be necessary. If ten pins are set side by side in a straight horizontal row, ten teeth of different pitches will sound simultaneously. Given these basic factors, makers used their ingenuity to enhance the musical possibilities of their products. Some of the more expensive boxes, for instance, contained groups of teeth tuned in unison as a means of increasing the dynamics, resulting in the creation of instruments with over a hundred teeth to a comb.

The type of music pinned on these cylinders varied with the prevailing public taste: opera arias, folk songs, popular tunes, waltzes (after the mid-century), and other forms of light music formed their repertoire. Meanwhile the Swiss industry was providing a wide range of models, from small and cheap instruments to very elaborate and expensive ones. Several types were differentiated, such as the *tabatière* ("snuffbox"), in which two tunes were pinned side by side on a cylinder; the large *cartel* with its music pinned spirally around the cylinder; the *forte piano* with two combs of different sizes, one for soft, the other for loud tones. Manufacture spread to other countries, competition increased, and makers were obliged to keep abreast of the shifts in musical taste and to bring out the latest airs, waltzes, and so on, that had become "hits." In its heyday the music box was the only modestly priced automatic instrument available.

A totally new concept was introduced in 1885 by Paul Lochmann of Gohlis and mass produced a year later: instead of a pinned cylinder, a perforated cardboard disk sounded the comb, and the entire mechanism was housed in an upright cabinet. This was called the *Symphonium*. Soon after 1886, the Polyphon company of Leipzig brought out its competing *Polyphon* with punched metal disk; both enjoyed considerable popularity, and the *Libellion* of Thost and Richter of Rudolstadt was similar, also operating by means of a metal disk. But the changing of disks by hand remained an inconvenience until the Regina Company, in the United States, patented an automatic changing device and also brought out its Regina, containing up to twenty punched metal disks with a diameter of 18 centimeters (7 inches), each with a playing duration of two minutes, and two combs with a combined compass of seven octaves. Both the Polyphon and the Regina companies continued making music boxes up to 1912. Cylinder instuments are still being made in Switzerland, although more as curiosities than as music-making machines.

Classification of music boxes as plucked linguaphones is of course due to their plucked teeth. But final developments remove them from this category, for in the late nineteenth century P. and P. E. Ehrlich of Gohlis introduced a free-reed music box with perforated disk and hand-cranked bellows called the *Ariston,* and the British Organette and Music Manufacturing Company, of Blackburn, competed with a model having two rows of free reeds, working on suction wind provided by hand-cranked bellows, and strips of perforated paper fed by the crank. Thus the music box was finally transformed into a free-reed aerophone. Combinations of reeds and comb were also built; two Swiss firms, Lecoultre and Heller, went as far as adding a small keyboard outside the case so as to permit manual accompaniment by the reeds, otherwise worked mechanically. But neither comb nor free reed could withstand the impact of the phonograph, and ultimately the musical automaton was replaced by the reproduction machine.

FRICTION IDIOPHONES

Idiophones sounded by means of friction vary from simple sticks rubbed with the fingers (direct friction) to friction vessels such as the glass harmonica of Benjamin Franklin, in which the friction is indirect.

FRICTION STICKS

Relatively simple implements, friction sticks seem to be confined to Europe. In Catalonia a folk instrument named *ossets* is made by stringing on a rope a series of bird bones, graduated in size and threaded at both ends like the steps of a ladder; the completed instrument is then suspended from the player's neck, held taut at the lower loop by one hand and the bones rubbed with a ring held in the other hand. This type of idiophone is frequently confused with the scraped idiophones.

At the other end of Europe the relatively modern nail violin, a friction idiophone consisting of a set of fixed nails, was invented by Johann Wilde, a violinist in the court orchestra at Saint Petersburg in the eighteenth century. The story is told of his returning home one day after a concert in or about 1740, and hanging his violin bow up on a convenient nail, accidentally producing a musical sound as the bow was drawn over the iron nail. This supposedly led to his invention of the nail violin, a circular, flat-topped wooden resonator, around the circumference of which a number of nails or iron pins were driven more or less deeply into the wood; the shorter the protruding section of the nail, the higher its pitch. The nail also diminished in thickness toward the treble, and to facilitate bowing, those pins producing diatonic tones were set straight, but the accidentals were slightly curved at the top. As nails fixed at one end are governed by the same acoustical laws as metal bars (if one is as long but twice as thick as another, the thicker will sound two octaves higher than the thinner), a fairly wide range was practicable without resort to unwieldy long nails. Originally nail violins had twelve, eighteen, or twenty-four nails; some had a semicircular resonator, from which they were known as semi-luna. As time went on, the number of nails was increased until thirty-seven became standard, and their shape was changed to that of a staple. Nail violins were held in the left hand by a handhole under the resonator, and bowed with a violin bow, usually one furnished with coarse black hair and heavily rosined. The sound was said to resemble the flageolet tones of a violin.

Manufacture of these instruments was restricted almost exclusively to Germany and Sweden, and toward the end of the century they were improved and transformed: around 1780 Senal of Bohemia increased the resonance by adding fifteen sympathetic strings, placed across the top of the resonator. He called his new model *violino harmonico* and made it known to the public by his concertizing. In 1791 a teacher named Träger created the nail piano by dividing the nails into four horizontal tiers set in an oblong block of wood connected to a keyboard and sounded by a continuous belt of rosin-coated linen rotated by a treadle. Other improvements followed, but, despite such latter-day efforts, the nail violin's popularity waned by the mid-nineteenth century when it slowly gave way to the harmonium.

FRICTION-BAR "PIANOS" AND THEIR PRECURSORS

The acoustical experiments of Ernst Friedrich Chladni made in the latter part of the eighteenth century, and particularly those connected with direct and indirect transmission of vibrations by means of friction, led to the creation of a series of friction-bar instruments, most of which were provided with a keyboard. In contrast to the tuning-fork "pianos," in which a series of tuning forks were struck with hammers (percussion idiophones), the bars of the friction "pianos" were set in vibration by the friction of a revolving cylinder or cone.

The earliest of Chladni's own instruments was the euphone (*Euphon* in German), invented in 1790. Its action consisted of a series of tuned, upright glass cylinders about the size of a pen, rubbed lengthwise by the player's wet fingers; the cylinders were connected to metal rods, to which they imparted their vibrations. Franklin's glass harmonica and the older musical glasses may possibly have suggested the materials for the experimental euphone. Charles Claggett, a violinist and inventor of several musical instruments, had patented a tuning-fork "piano" (see page 36) in 1788, and followed this by a friction-bar instrument he called the aiuton, in which a number of forks were actuated from a keyboard and pressed against a rotating horizontal metal cone. Chladni meanwhile had continued his experimentation, and in 1799 produced a successor to the euphone, naming it clavicylinder, the definitive version of which was not developed until 1814, when it emerged in the shape of a square piano; C-shaped metal bars of graduated lengths were attached horizontally to the rear of the keys; on depressing one of these, the corresponding bar was pushed against a wet glass cylinder kept in rotation by a treadle. Early clavicylinders had a compass of c° to f^3, later enlarged to from G' to a^3. Imitations and adaptations attested, if not its success, at least the great interest it evoked.

Starting with the first decade of the nineteenth century, the impetus provided by Chladni's work caused makers to follow two distinct directions: one group continued to produce true friction idiophones; another, apparently influenced by the bowed keyboard instruments (see pages

307 ff), no longer used friction bars autonomously but rather as inter-mediaries to set strings in vibration, and although these are chordophones by virtue of the addition of their sound-producing strings, they will be mentioned here as outgrowths of friction-bar idiophones. The first of these was the *Cölison* brought out by Maslowski of Poznan in 1804 in the form of an upright piano minus the keyboard; instead of keys, a number of wooden bars were stroked by the player's fingers, therby trans-ferring their vibrations to the appropriate strings. A year later, Johann Christian Dietz the Elder, best known for his claviharp, brought out his *Melodion* and his *Chalybssonans*—we are back in the classic era—at about the same time; both instruments had metal friction bars sounded by a revolving cone. Uthe of Sangerhausen reverted to finger-stroked bars in his *Xylosistron* of 1807 or 1808, later added a keyboard, and called the new model *Xylharmonikon*. In or by 1809, Johann Friedrich Kaufmann and his father, Johann Gottfried, invented the *Harmonichord* in the form of an upright grand piano; like Maslowski, they made use of indirectly vibrated strings; these were held in the forked ends of a series of wooden bars, which, when the corresponding keys were depressed, moved against a leather-covered wooden cone, the ensuing friction causing the strings to vibrate. An ingenious system of dampers was provided. Kaufmann concertized successfully on this instrument in Germany, and also in Amsterdam, Paris, and Stockholm. Carl Maria von Weber composed an Adagio and Rondo for it, first performed in 1811. But Kaufmann was apparently not interested in building any further models, for even Liszt's repeated requests for a harmonichord remained unfilled. What may be the only specimen to have been completed is now housed in the Leipzig University instrument collection.

Euphone and clavicylinder imitations continued making their appear-ance: that of Weidner of Frauenfeld, devoid of keyboard, was one of three new models introduced in 1810; of the others, the second had rectangular metal bars, while the third, by Johann David Buschmann, was identical except for its cloth-covered cylinder to his later and better known *Terpodion*, which he introduced in 1816; this had wooden friction bars and a resin-coated wooden cylinder. In 1812, Louis Klatte of Erfurt paid homage to Chladni by naming his totally unoriginal version *Euphonia*, and in the same year Dietz, apparently not satisfied with his earlier *Melodion*, brought out the technically more original *Trochleon*, its metal bars bowed by a continuous, felt-covered band. Other attempts made during the decade included an instrument with a series of lead forks brought into contact with brass disks attached to the rotating cylinder, and brass springs replaced bars in a British patent of 1821. Wheatstone and Green patented in 1837 a piano with "continuous sounds produced from strings, wires, or springs," probably a friction instrument.

None of these instruments was successful, and shortly thereafter the novelty of experimentation had worn off and the free reeds took over—except for a late-comer, that is: Gustave Baudet of Paris spent many years perfecting the action of his *piano quatuor*, patented in England as piano-violin and introduced in 1865. A complicated and ingenious instrument, it was an extension of Kaufmann's harmonichord, although Baudet may not have been aware of this. In appearance an upright piano with a seven-octave range, his instrument had one string per key—thicker than contemporary piano strings—a rosined metal cylinder covered with papier-mâché reaching the entire length of the keyboard; each string had a gut or fiber tie wound around it at or close to a nodal point; when a key was depressed, a spiral spring and abstract were raised, pressing a tie against the rotating cylinder, and the strings were sounded by the transmission of vibrations from the tie. The *piano quatuor* won a medal at the 1873 Vienna Exhibition.

Belatedly, Chladni's euphone seems to have been a source of inspiration for the *orgue de cristal* brought out in France in 1956, with glass rods rubbed with wetted fingers transferring their vibrations to metal bars.

FRICTION VESSELS

Simple friction vessels either emit sounds of indefinite pitch or else they can be tuned. To the former category belong the rubbed tortoise carapaces of Central and South America, taboo to the uninitiated (and not to be confused with those carapaces turned into rattles or scrapers in these regions). To the latter category belong the curious rubbed wooden vessels of New Ireland, known chiefly as *nunut* or *livika*, consisting of a rounded block of wood, hollowed, with three tongues of differing lengths and thicknesses cut into its upper portion; these sound at as many pitches. The seated player grasps the vessel between outstretched legs and, after oiling his hands with palm juice, proceeds to rub the tongues. The resultant tune, always the same, resembles the song of the hornbill (whose native name is *vika*). Taboo to women and children, who may not see or even hear it, the *livika* is played at death memorial rites (not at funerals).

MUSICAL GLASSES

Apparently the offspring of tuned metal or porcelain cups of the East, and played in India both as percussion and as friction vessels (see also bells, page 78), European musical glasses can be followed from the seventeenth century on. Kircher (1673) shows a set of large wine glasses standing on a table and being played with the fingertips, four years later an echo from England described "gay wine music" performed by rubbing the rims of wine glasses with wet fingers, and in the same year Harsdörfer's *Mathematische und philosophische Erquickungen* mentions an identical manner of playing. Both in England and Germany these glasses were known by their French name, *verrillon*; Walther (1732) refers to them as such in his dictionary.

An Irishman named Richard Pockridge concertized on the musical glasses in Dublin in 1743 and in England a year later, paving the way for Gluck, who on April 23, 1746, played in the Haymarket Theatre of London "a concerto on twenty-six drinking glasses tuned with spring water," and while visiting Copenhagen in 1750 he was heard in a concert of vocal and instrumental music, during the course of which he introduced the "hitherto unknown instrument consisting solely of glasses." Pockridge and his contemporary, Delaval, made use of glasses tuned by the addition of more or less water and rubbed by wet fingers. The compass of the verrillon at that time, as given by Eisel (1738), was two and one-half octaves, from $g°$ to c^3, composed of eighteen tuned beer glasses, fine tuned by the addition of water (he adds that they were played in churches).

By 1761 musical glasses had not only become a "fashionable topic" of conversation, along with "pictures, taste, Shakespeare" and the like, according to Goldsmith's *Vicar of Wakefield*, but, more important, they had also attracted the attention of Benjamin Franklin, who had watched performances of both Pockridge and Delaval, noted the glasses' limitations, and proceeded to transform them into both a more efficient and, above all, a polyphonic instrument. This he accomplished by taking a series of tuned, graduated glasses in the shape of resting bells, drilling a small hole in the vertex of each, and stringing them on a wire spindle, one nestled inside the other so as to form a horizontal row; the spindle was rotated by means of a treadle, and the row of glasses was placed in a shallow trough with the largest glass to the left. All that was then needed was to touch the revolving rims lightly with wet fingers; their compactness enabled the performer to sound several simultaneously and with both hands. Fully chromatic compasses were now practicable, and the rim—or the entire glass—could be marked with differentiating colors, a system later simplified by bronzing the rims of the accidentals. Dynamics were varied chiefly by rotating the spindle more or less rapidly, but also by regulating the pressure of the player's fingertips. Of this instrument, created in 1761, Franklin wrote to Padre Beccaria of Torino in a letter dated July 13, 1762: "In honor of your musical language I have borrowed from it the name of this instrument, calling it Armonica." Today we call it the glass harmonica. According to the London *Universal Directory* for 1763, it was first made by Charles James, listed as the "original maker of the Armonica, a Musical Instrument, composed of Glasses (without water) capable of Thorough Bass, and never out of tune."

The armonica's popularity was immediate. From the start it became both a household and a virtuoso instrument, and makers brought out models with varying numbers of glasses. Marianne Davies was the first to concertize on the new instrument: starting in 1762, she played for four years in London, Paris, Vienna, Florence, and several German cities; Hasse composed armonica pieces for her. She was followed by Philipp Frick, an organist who gave concerts extensively in Germany in 1769. Thus popularized, makers set about "improving" the glasses, and from 1769 on efforts were made to combine the harmonica with a keyboard, but they were not successful until 1784, when the keyed glass harmonica, furnished with a button-type keyboard arranged in piano sequence, was marketed. Here the glasses were arranged in two rows and sounded by a series of levers connected to the keys by abstracts; the ends of the levers were covered with cloth and moistened.

The composer and pianist Dussek concertized throughout Germany on both the piano and the keyed harmonica in 1784 and 1785, and afterwards in Milan. The French builder, Deudon, brought out in 1787 an ingenious transposing harmonica with a movable, identifying band placed above the cone of nestled glasses. Perhaps the best known, and certainly the best remembered of the harmonica's virtuosi was the blind Marianne Kirchgessner (1770–1808), whose teacher, Joseph Aloys Schmittbauer, extended the instrument's compass to $e°-f^2$. Mozart wrote his Adagio and

Rondo in C (K. 617) for her; she performed the work, which was scored for harmonica, flute, oboe, viola, and cello, on August 19, 1791. His Adagio for Harmonica (K. 356), first played in Vienna in 1791, was probably also written for her.

Further improvements included those of Francis Hopkinson of Philadelphia, who, in 1787, substituted metal bowls for those of glass, and the organized harmonica constructed in 1795 under the auspices of Wilhelm Christian Müller, kapellmeister of Bremen and author of a harmonica tutor. His instrument combined four stops of flue organ pipes played from a separate manual with a keyed harmonica. A year later, in 1796, Grassa, a Bohemian virtuoso in Paris, built his *instrument de parnasse*, a harmonica with added pedalboard for the left foot, the right foot being engaged, as usual, in working the treadle. Yet another "improvement" was the organ-harmonica patented in 1800 and named *Cölestine* by its inventor, Zinck; and, perhaps inevitably, a set of musical glasses was added to the piano, with the glasses sounded by hammers. A patent for such an instrument was granted to John Day. Zinck's invention was expanded by Henry Whitaker to a piano-organ-cum-harmonica, for which he received a patent in 1859.

Once the utmost limits to which the glass harmonica could be improved had been reached, the inevitable reaction set in: the old, unimproved model was taken up again in the nineteenth century and its compass enlarged to three or even four octaves. Preserved in the Brussels Conservatoire Museum is a *vis-à-vis* model for two performers facing each other, probably from this time. The court orchestra at Darmstadt had a harmonica, and in 1818 engaged C. F. Pohl (senior) to play it; his son was to publish a history of the *Glasharmonika* (musical glasses) in 1862. Among the last composers to write for it was Berlioz, who scored a part for it in his Fantasia on *The Tempest* of 1830. A decade later it was a thing of the past or an accessory stop of certain keyboard instruments.

Before playing the Franklin harmonica, a performer thoroughly washed his hands. Then, after the rims of the glasses were moistened with a wet sponge, the glasses were set in rotation by the treadle, the rotation being toward the player. The tone quality of both musical glasses and harmonica was allegedly so enervating that Marianne Davies had to abandon playing after four years, and it is said to have affected the nerves of many young ladies who were merely auditors.

At the time of their nineteenth-century revival, the old-fashioned musical glasses reappeared as a set of stemmed glasses of graduated sizes, rough tuned, each glass inscribed with its pitch name. Fine tuning was accomplished by adding a little water to the glasses; all were inserted upright into a wooden holder housed in a cabinet, and were played by rubbing the rims with wet fingers. A large variety of substantially identical models were patented and known by a succession of trade names, from the grand harmonicon of 1828 to the *Glasharfe* of the present century.

Part Two

MEMBRANOPHONES

CLASSIFICATION AND ACOUSTICS

Any instrument sounded by means of a taut membrane is classified as a membranophone, and this very large group is divided into four categories:

1. Tubular drums which have either one or two membranes (heads) and assume many forms, chief among which are those of a cylinder, cone, barrel, hourglass, goblet, or frame. Numerous intermediary forms are also encountered. Shallow drums and rattle drums are included in this category.

2. Drums with basin- or bowl-shaped shells (bodies), called kettle-drums.

3. Friction drums, sounded by friction rather than by percussion.

4. Mirlitons.

Furthermore, there exist primitive "predrum" membranophones known as ground drums and pot drums.

This classification is unsatisfactory insofar as it does not take variant forms into account, particularly with regard to the first group, but it is useful as an overall framework.

Membranes of instruments comprising the first three groups are either glued, nailed, lapped, or laced to the body. If they are glued or nailed, the pitch can be somewhat modified by exposure to heat, whereas lapped or laced heads are readily tunable by tightening the cords or screws; sometimes wooden wedges are inserted between shell and lacings to further increase tension, and the application of tuning paste to a portion of the head will also influence pitch (but the origins of tuning paste were probably ritual rather than musical). Membranes are commonly set in vibration by percussion, but friction is another mode of tone production, and the membrane of a mirliton is caused to vibrate by the action of sound waves.

117

By far the largest category of membranophones is that of tubular drums, and, of these, those with single heads are earlier than the double-headed varieties. In one form or another drums are played the world over, with the exception of a few archaic peoples (Australians have no membrane drums). Their age is unknown, and we can follow them back no further than about 3000 B.C. Both in ancient and in modern times they have been ritual and even sacred objects; some were believed to be endowed with magical powers, others were status symbols or emblems of royalty. Their functions have always been manifold, divided between musical and nonmusical activities.

Acoustically, all membranophones are conditioned primarily by the membrane; the shell merely acts as a resonator, and is of secondary importance to tone production. According to the laws governing membranes, the greater the diameter the deeper the sound, while the greater the tension the higher the pitch will be. The only drums tuned to a definite pitch in Western musical culture are kettledrums, but this does not hold true in other areas.

All drums sound loudest and clearest when raised off the ground; hence, the lower ends of many tubular drums are prolonged to form "feet," such drums then being known as footed drums. Some may terminate in a series of tooth- or sawlike projections, others are given an openwork base, and in certain areas of Asia and Africa the "foot" takes the form of a pair of human legs. Great cylinder drums that may be up to 3 meters (10 feet) high, reminiscent of their ancestral tree trunk, can only be played by slanting them to an angle sufficient to bring the head within the performer's reach; such drums are usually cleared from the ground by a foot (drums of unusual height are played in parts of Asia, Africa, and the Pacific). An ancient playing stance still encountered in East, West, and South Africa, along the Amazon River, and formerly also in Mexico, has the drum slanted to an obtuse angle and held between the standing player's legs like a hobbyhorse. Contemporary North American Indians have many short drums that are cleared from the ground by being suspended by handles from upright forked sticks.

THE DRUM AS INSTRUMENT OF MAGIC AND THUNDER

Long before the drum became a musical instrument its noisemaking qualities endowed it with the power of making thunder and of chasing evil spirits, and were also exploited to frighten the enemy. In the ancient Near East the hide of a sacred animal—the bull—was used as drumhead, thereby transferring sanctity to the finished instrument (see goblet drum, page 147). Not only was the bull sacred throughout the ancient East, from Sumer to Egypt and over to Minoan Crete, but in pre-Aryan India the *Bos primigenius* figured on seals is sometimes seen standing in front of an altar, whereas the indigenous *Bos indicus* is never so depicted.

As creators of thunder, drums were connected with the Near Eastern cult of Kybele (who is identical with Rhea and Kotys), which passed to mainland Greece, an area where thunder had already been summoned by beating on shields made of tightly stretched oxhide, objects hardly to be differentiated from large frame drums. In *Bacchae* Euripides refers to skin-stretched orbs (and in our times South African Zulu warriors drum on their hide shields). However, it is in China and Japan that thunder drums achieved their highest development. The Chinese Duke of Thunder, Lei Kung, has been worshiped since the beginning of our era; he is traditionally surrounded by numerous drums, which he beats in order to obtain the noise of thunder, and it is the sound of his drums—not the lightning—that is said to cause death. Half bird, half man, the thunder god Zin Shin is surrounded by a revolving wheel to which a number of alternating barrel drums and kettledrums are affixed; the god holds a knobbed drumstick in one hand, a thunderbolt in the other. The revolving wheel may be genetically related to the Buddhist prayer wheel, a connection in greater evidence in Japan, where drums make thunder mechanically and in the absence of any god, simply by being attached to the outer circumference of a wheel that, when revolved, causes them to rattle. Clearly such drums must have been partly filled with pebbles or similar materials that struck against the membrane when the drum was rotated (cf. rattle drums, page 151). Sets of thunder drums also appear in East Turkestan from the ninth century on, as attributes of the thunder god and of demons. It may be assumed that thunder drums were always untuned, yet the fact that they are present in sets suggests the possibility of a relationship to the Southeast Asian drum chimes.

A major role of the drum in many parts of the world was, and still is, as cult instrument. Such usage was known in the Orphic rites of Greece, and in Asia, Africa, and America cult drums have been associated with sacrifices, including those of human beings. Among the sacrifices prescribed by the Atharva Veda of India is the application of blood, or a red imitation thereof, to the head of a drum, and this is said to account for the practice of applying tuning paste to the heads of certain drums on the subcontinent (tuning paste is also employed in Africa). Bon priests of Tibet play hourglass-shaped drums made from two human skullcaps fastened together, probably leftovers from the ritual cannibalism that lasted there up to the beginning of the nineteenth century.

Along the same lines, the Chinese *Tso Chuan* mentions for the years 627, 588, and 537 B.C. the consecration of drums by smearing them with the blood of a sacrificed person, usually a war captive. Inca priests were found by mid-sixteenth-century missionaries to be beating drums covered with blood; they had developed a gruesome habit of flaying dead enemies and stuffing their skins to make drums, using the dead person's arm as a drumstick. Among the Ashanti of Ghana the sacrificial drum is covered with a membrane of human skin and ornamented with human skulls. Afro-American cults, both in South America and in the Caribbean, center around blood-smeared drums to which sacrifices are offered (see drum sets, page 154). Drumming is the prerogative of men in all Afro-American communities and is taboo to women; in the hinterland of Guiana women dare not even simulate drum rhythms for fear that their breasts may lengthen until they reach the ground.

"PREDRUM" MEMBRANOPHONES

GROUND DRUMS

One of the most primitive forms of membranophone is the ground drum, a simple animal skin stretched taut over a pit, with the pit functioning as resonator. The skin of a sacrificial animal would serve in this manner and be struck with the animal's tail. Pots could be placed in the pit to enhance the resonance. Such ground drums are beaten chiefly by women in Australia and in Africa, but in North America generally by men. Among the Jicarilla Apache of North America, during healing ceremonies for a sick person ground drums of buffalo skins are beaten with the patient's moccasins.

When pits are no longer dug, the ground serves as reflector of the sound issuing from the stretched membrane; girls among the Dogon of Mali stretch their skirts over their thighs and drum upon them. Further south, among the Xhosa, a dried ox skin or bullock hide is stretched between poles driven into the ground and beaten; another variety has been reported as having loops of hide fastened at intervals around a skin held taut by the left hands of several players, while the right hands strike the surface with a stick. Similarly, at a former time in North America, on occasions when drums were not available, a circle of drummers would hold a rawhide with one hand, stretching it taut, and slap it with the other hand, thus improvising a dance drum. The primitive "drum" of the Xhosa mentioned above is an evolutionary step behind a dance drum the Chippewa formerly made: they drove split poles into the ground in a circular fashion, so close together that the poles touched, thereby forming a fixed circular frame some 60 centimeters (2 feet) high and wide, over which they stretched a hide that they laced to notches cut in the pole. Evolution from ground drum to tubular drum was completed when they made their dance drum by bending a thin cedar board about 30 centimeters (1 foot) wide into a hoop to which they added a membrane.

POT DRUMS

Ground drums were by their very nature impermanent and nonportable, and when the need arose for drums that could be made available repeatedly, a skin was tied over a gourd, coconut, clay pot (household or other), or similar object. Such implements, known as pot drums, are still found in Asia, Africa, and the New World. In many areas the skin acts as a sympathetic resonator and is not struck; elsewhere a dull thud is emitted by hitting the skin with the flat of the hand.

On the Indian subcontinent, pots are made specially for transformation into pot drums, with large, spherical bodies and narrow apertures to be covered with parchment. Wrists, fingers, and even fingernails are used in playing, but it is the body of the pot and not the membrane that is drummed upon to produce a rhythmic accompaniment for stringed instruments. The Swazi of South Africa employ a primitive type of pot drum to exorcise spirits: a goatskin head, stretched but not tied over the pot's mouth, is held taut by an assistant while one or two persons play upon it simultaneously with sticks. Among the Hottentot a wooden jar or a pot is covered with a goatskin membrane and struck, by women only, with the flat of the hand. Goatskin also forms the membrane of a gourd or clay drum in the Moroccan Rif; there the performer presses the rim with his thumb in order to obtain a hollow sound, while drumming with his fingers.

TUBULAR DRUMS

THE TUBULAR DRUM IN HISTORY

Regardless of the form they assume, the earliest drums were all struck by hand. Neolithic pottery drums of unusual shape have been found in central and eastern Europe: the upper portion is cylindrical, the lower, truncoconical, with closed, flat bottom—the same form as that of some modern East African wooden drums that Sachs (1940) counts among kettledrums. Most of these Neolithic artifacts are plain, but one specimen from Egeln near Magdeburg, Germany, is provided with handles and with holes for lacing a head. Other prehistoric pottery drums of Stone Age Europe have been found as grave goods in central and southeastern Europe, chiefly in form intermediate between goblet and hourglass, and open at both ends; they have projections around the bowl portion over which the membrane could be stretched. Some fragmentary goblet drums dating from about 2000 B.C. assume the shape of a diminutive Babylonian *lilissu* (see goblet drums, page 147), and are not unlike the modern *darabuka* of India. Until recently the identification of these objects as drums was not clearly established, but it is generally accepted at present.

Specialists are inclined to agree that, whereas the portable, single-headed drum was originally modeled of clay and later imitated in wood, the larger double-headed cylinder and conoid drums were first made of wood, their prototype being a branch or the section of a tree trunk. Prehistoric drumsticks, most frequently consisting of perishable wood, are even rarer finds, but bone drumsticks have been found at a site dated about 500 B.C. on Odeny Island in Barents Sea, and the theory has been advanced (by Horst Kirchner) that the so-called *bâtons de commandement*, otherwise unidentified objects found at some prehistoric sites, may in reality be drumsticks.

ANTIQUITY

Bronze Age Babylon had drums of a great variety of forms—cylindrical, hourglass, goblet, and bowl shaped—all of which were made of clay and could be stood upright or be suspended by a strap from the player's neck when carried in processions, leaving the player free to strike them with both hands. Assyrians also had a conical drum that was carried at the player's side and played with bare hands. Temple instruments were considerably larger: the frame drum attained some 150 centimeters (5 feet) in diameter and had to be stood upright on edge. A seal of the third millennium B.C. shows Ishtar before an altar having exactly the same shape as an upended hourglass drum; possibly it still was a drum (the metal kettle-gongs of Southeast Asia have fulfilled the function of altar for over two millennia). The ancestor of the kettledrum appears in Babylonia as a temple instrument also.

Large double-headed cylindrical or barrel-shaped drums appear in Egypt in the early Middle Kingdom, believed to have been imported from Negro Africa and adapted for local use. In New Kingdom times, drums are seen played by both Egyptians and Negroes, sometimes suspended horizontally from a strap around the player's shoulders and struck with both hands. An instrument excavated at Thebes was some 60 centimeters (2 feet) long and 45 centimeters (1½ feet) in diameter. None of these Egyptian drums appears to have been played widely, but frame drums of different shapes were known (they are discussed on pages 130 ff) and seem to have been more common.

Although European antiquity probably knew of no drum other than the Semitic frame drum—the *tympanon* of the Greeks and *tympanum* of the Romans—other forms were introduced from Asia in the early Christian era. A small barrel drum with V lacings and a central ligature is portrayed on a sculptured frieze found at the fortified site of Airtam, some three hundred kilometers southeast of Samarkand, dating from the Kushan period, probably of the first century B.C. The drum is held almost horizontally in front of the player, who is apparently sounding both heads with his bare hands (one hand is broken off). That the drum did not die out in this area may be deduced from the description of an entertainment at the court of the (Central Asian) Ghazawids (962–1186) at which the *rebab*, harp, and drum were played, as well as from pictorial materials from this area showing ensembles with cylinder drums. A two-headed waisted drum, held horizontally in front of the player, appears on the bas-reliefs of Taq i-Bustan (590–628 A.D.), also played with bare hands, and a Sassanid silver vessel of approximately the same period depicts another, its two heads clearly of different sizes—indicating different pitches—and with what appears to be a central ligature, an early form of hourglass drum that continued to be played in the Near East throughout the Middle Ages.

The double-headed drum was also known to the Romans and was spread abroad by them, and has been found as far north as the Isle of Wight, where a Roman pavement portrays a dancing girl with two-headed drum suspended at her side while she accompanies a man playing panpipes. Both Greece and Rome made considerable use of the frame drum, but in Byzantium this was gradually displaced by the cylinder drum of Asiatic origin; tenth-century and later manuscript illustrators interpret the Greek names with pictures of new instruments, and the *tympanon* becomes a cylinder drum in the tenth and eleventh centuries.

POSTCLASSICAL EUROPE

That the two-headed drum was still known, or had been reintroduced, in the West in the sixth century is clear from Cassiodorus (d. 575): *Tympanum est quasi duobus modiis solis capitibus convenientibus supra eos tensi corii sonora resultatio; quod musici disciplinabili mensura percutientes, geminata resonatione modulantur.* The Latin is difficult, but clearly refers to "geminated sounds," and taken in conjunction with two passages of Isidore of Seville (d. 636), his text leaves little room for doubt. The passages from Isidore read: *Tympanum est pellis vel corium ligno ex una parte extensum. Est enim pars media symphoniae in similitudinem cribri* (. . . "It is a half symphony, similar to a sieve"), a fair description of the frame drum, while the double-headed drum now receives a name of its own, symphony: *Symphonia vulgo appellatur lignum cavum ex utraque parte pelle extensa, quam virgulis hinc inde & inde musici feriunt, sitque in ea ex concordia gravis & acuti suavissimus cantus,* or, that it is the common name of a hollowed wood having its ends covered by skins and struck with sticks to produce high and low sounds; and we learn here for the first time of its being struck with drumsticks, a characteristic adopted from Asia. The two heads of the symphony were presumably of different sizes, as they sounded at different pitches. Because of the very early date for a drum sounding two different pitches, this passage has been taken to be a later addition, yet it is in no way incompatible with our knowledge of double-headed drums. Certainly such an instrument (not too unlike the Stone Age grave goods referred to above) is depicted in the ninth-century Utrecht Psalter, held horizontally in front of its player.

By the tenth century the hourglass drum had been introduced to

Europe from the East and is represented, held vertically by its waist while its lower head is played with the bare hand, in a tenth-century Beatus commentary codex in Madrid and in later Spanish manuscripts; in the thirteenth-century *Cantigas de Santa María* the same drum is depicted resting horizontally on the player's shoulder, its struck head facing forward, being held by one hand while the other hand taps it. These instruments still closely resemble their Oriental counterparts as we can observe them in modern times. From the ninth century on a double-headed cylinder drum is played in Byzantium with a single crozier stick; in the eleventh century the Old French word *tabur* is first recorded, giving us the English "tabor" in the twelfth century (the corresponding Middle High German was *Trumme*, whence the English "drum"). This denoted a small cylinder drum, very shallow at first, provided with a snare placed traditionally on the outside of the upper membrane; it was struck with a single stick in the center of the head, right on the snare. Played together with the three-holed pipe, this formed the one-man pipe and tabor ensemble (for details of which, see pipe and tabor, page 559).

By the twelfth century the barrel drum is illustrated in England; it was held horizontally, both heads played with bare hands. In English and continental miniatures of the thirteenth century, a crozier-shaped stick is often seen being applied to cylinder and kettledrums. Meanwhile the Old French word *tabur* had become *tabour*, finally changed to *tambour*, a generic term for drums from the fourteenth century on; even in Trichet's day (ca. 1640) it could denote a frame drum as well as a side drum or a kettledrum. Tabors of the fourteenth and fifteenth centuries were usually small both in diameter and in depth, but in the sixteenth century they grew deeper—notably in France—until the depth was about twice the diameter. These proportions were the reverse of those of earlier instruments. Arbeau's tabor (in 1589) has those of a diminutive long drum.

Cylinder drums played as independent instruments and beaten with two sticks continued to coexist with the tabor. In the fifteenth century they were occasionally portrayed with tiny bells strung along the snare. They remain small in the West until they are "contaminated," as anthropologists would have it, by, or merged into—documentation does not yet afford precision—the Byzantine type, large, hooped, and braced, physically more important. Depth is notably greater than diameter by the early fourteenth century; they have a snare on the struck membrane, hooped and laced heads, and are the ancestors of our side drum and our long drum.*

Quite apart from the pipe and tabor ensembles, cylinder drums also became associated with fifes in the late Middle Ages, and to this association of drum and fife corps of foot troops may be juxtaposed the trumpet and kettledrum combination of the cavalry, despite the differences of their functions: the long fifes provided melody (which the cavalry never needed), the drums rhythm for the soldiers to march to. Swiss drummers and fifers had already participated in the battle of Sempach (1386), and by the latter part of the fifteenth century Swiss mercenaries were much sought after; their "Swiss pipes" (*Schweizerpfeiffen*) and drums rapidly became famous throughout Western Europe; as far away as Scotland their drum became known as the *swech* or *swisch*.

The English called the instrument drom or drum, and the contemporary expression "dromslade" or "drumslade" is an Englishing of the Dutch *trommelslag* ("drumbeat"), at first designating the drummer, later the drum itself. In German, these mercenaries were referred to as *Landsknechte,* from which the term Landsknecht's drum is derived, becoming *tambour de lansquenet* in French. This was a large cylindrical drum of wood or metal, complete with hoops and braces, struck on the upper head only with two sticks, and to which a snare on the lower membrane added great brilliance of tone. Pieter Brueghel the Elder's painting of a fifer, drummer, and standard bearer (*The Three Soldiers*) of 1518, gives an idea of the important dimensions the drum had attained by then; its snare is shown placed across the outside of the lower membrane, as it remains today. When Arbeau wrote (1589) of the *tambour* having reached a height of 2½ feet and the same diameter, it is this instrument he was describing. (A curious auxiliary use of the Renaissance infantry drum was that of drumhead triangulation, with two drums serving in the measurement of angles of elevation for computing distances or heights.)

Praetorius (1619) gives two views of a "soldier's drum" of about 2 Brunswick feet in height and diameter; a Moorish timbrel, the ubiquitous tabor with its pipe, a pair of kettledrums, and the soldier's drum exhaust his repertoire of membranophones. Side drums of the military fife and

* The type of military drum called snare drum in the United States is known as side drum in Britain, as it is suspended from the player's side; in order to avoid confusion with other drums provided with snares, the (U.S.) snare drum will here be referred to as side drum.

Lansquenet drum and Swiss fife. *The Three Soldiers* by Pieter Brueghel the Elder, 1518. Copyright The Frick Collection, New York.

drum corps underwent modifications, both with respect to dimensions and to head-tensioning methods—braces or rods—in different countries and over a period of time; no uniform model existed other than locally. Diameter and length remained equal until the instrument was considered too unwieldy, causing it to be shortened considerably by the nineteenth century, with the result that the modern and the traditional versions have little in common except the name and the snare.

So similar in every respect to the older and longer side drum is the tenor drum—except for the absence of snares—that it probably represents a petrifact of a seventeenth-century type. Its French, German, and Italian names (*caisse roulante, Rollier-* or *Wirbeltrommel, cassa rullante*) are indications of its function, that of playing rolls. During the nineteenth century it was gradually eased out of most military bands in favor of the side drum, a far lighter instrument as its shell was being made of metal by this time, while that of the tenor was still wooden, but several countries, among them England and Spain, have retained it both as an orchestral and as a military band instrument.

The designation of bass drum has been applied to two separate instruments by modern writers, some preferring thereby to indicate a short and wide drum, others a long cylindrical one. The confusion is due to the fact that the latter form was modified in the nineteenth century until it came to resemble the former; for the sake of clarity the short form will be referred to hereafter as shallow drum, the long drum as bass drum (shallow drums are also discussed separately; see page 141).

Among the instruments in the hands of angel musicians portrayed in the Angers Tapestry of the Apocalypse, completed in 1380, is a wide but short drum—a shallow drum—with a snare on its struck surface, its two heads secured by the Oriental method of nailing, suspended from a narrow, ill-attached neckband, and beaten with a stick on each of its heads; although positioned so as to render the depth visible, the presence of a second drumstick implies that its shell must have rested against the player's chest, with the heads facing sideways; a curious round aperture in the shell is too large for a vent. Drums of this type had been unknown in Europe up to then: both shallow form and nailed head point to a Near Eastern origin. Perhaps this is what the Turkish *tabl baladi* or larger *tabl turki* looked like at the time.

Some seventy years later the same shallow drum is figured in Agostino di Duccio's *Musical Angels* at Rimini (1447–1454), but by then suitably Occidentalized: instead of two drumsticks, a single knobbed stick is now in use, striking the snare head; the neckband has disappeared and, instead, a looped strap handle rises from an aperture in the shell, an aperture that occurs in exactly the same position as that of the Angers Tapestry. Was the designer of the tapestry working from a model with lost strap handle, for which he substituted an imaginary if more familiar neckband? When the same instrument appears in the hands of a Turkish drummer in a painting by Vittore Carpaccio of about 1500, no snare is shown and the drum has become, if anything, even shallower than before: an oversized frame drum, held with heads facing sideways. This is the drum known to the West until the nineteenth century as the Turkish drum; Villoteau still described it as such in 1823, just about the time it began to be called bass drum.

With its diameter expanded and its frame lengthened, the bass drum, as it was thereafter known, retained its proportion of a diameter at least twice as great as its depth. It is set, or carried, with shell resting against the drummer's chest, heads facing sideways, and played close to the rim with a single, padded stick. (An exception to this mode of playing is made by Scottish regimental bagpipe and drum bands; here the Turkish manner is still preserved, with the single stick supplemented by a switch.) The original shell of wood has been replaced by metal and, in recent times, laminated wood. Today it is made in different sizes, depending upon whether it is to serve in the orchestra or the military band, and the tension of its heads is adjusted by thumbscrews, but its form remains that of a shallow drum. Gluck was an early writer for the then new instrument in his *Les pèlerins de la Mecque* of 1764, and Mozart scored for it in his *Die Entführung aus dem Serail* (1782).

Another variety known as bass drum, already referred to, was the long drum, a cylinder having a length up to twice that of its diameter. A military drum, it remained in favor until it was displaced by the *dawūl* of Turkish mounted Janissary bands: this was another great drum, but of different proportions, diameter and length being about equal; it was carried to the left side of the saddle, often in a broad cloth sling, or else tilted across the rider's left knee, leaving him free to strike its upper head with a heavy drumstick curved at the tip, reaching the lower at the same time with a very slender stick; sometimes the latter was exchanged for a shorter switch. In such bands, seven, eight, or nine *dawūls* followed as many shawms, to be followed in turn by camel- or horse-mounted kettle-drums, their drummers gesticulating extravagantly, then by a row of cymbals and one of slender, folded trumpets. Whole Janissary bands reached Europe in the early eighteenth century, were imitated, and by the nineteenth century "Turkish" music was an established factor in European military band life (the Turkish horsetail standard became transformed into a jingling johnny by the addition of numerous small bells) as well as in the home: drums, triangles, and bells were built into pianos for which special "Turkish" music had been composed. Unlike some other components of Janissary bands, the "Turkish drum" was more than a temporary showpiece in Europe: great battle-scarred specimens of the eighteenth and early nineteenth centuries in our museums vouch for their continued use in Europe in their original form. After the Janissaries were disbanded in Turkey in 1826, the drum continued its existence there paired with a *zurnā* (shawm), its length slightly reduced so that both heads could be more conveniently reached; today it is suspended in a near-horizontal position from a band passing around the player's neck.

Under the name of *daoúli*, the *dawūl* also lives on in Greece, played in the Turkish manner, a switch in the left hand, a drumstick in the right. The same instrument is called *tupan* in Yugoslavia, and is a great, bulky affair, with diameter larger than the length and heads tuned a fifth apart, held in front of the player in a tilted position, and sounded with a combination of switch and stick; there also, it usually accompanies a shawm. It has been said that the unwieldy proportions of the *dawūl* caused it to be cut down in the West so as to form the modern bass drum; however, to transform it thus would have required, not only cutting down considerably on the length, but also increasing the diameter.

Modern orchestral bass drums have a minimum diameter of 80 centimeters (32 inches), though rhythm band requirements are less. The original wooden shell is now made of brass, and tension of the heads is by thumbscrews.

FRAME DRUMS

Portable drums with a narrow frame and one or two heads stretched over a hoop, if round, or a square frame, if four-cornered, include the smaller, tambourine type of frame drum; the larger shaman's drum, with or without handle; and the deeper variety, for which Sachs coined the name of shallow drum, to be described separately. Most frame drums are single headed and therefore can be held by the rim; in one form or another they are distributed over most parts of the world, although they do not occur in the Pacific.

FRAME DRUMS IN ANTIQUITY

Frame drums first appear in ancient Mesopotamian art from the third millennium B.C. Giant drums, to all appearance double-headed, their skins attached by large nails, are shown from about 2200 B.C. on. A drum on the Gudea Relief in Paris, dating from this period, rests upright on its rim, standing as high as a man: another is depicted on the Stele of Ur-Nammu of about 2100 B.C., now in Philadelphia. The tension on such huge instruments would have been great, so much so that the frame was thought by Sachs to have been similar to a type still current in Japan, that of a narrow barrel drum.

Smaller instruments, reaching from knee to shoulder, also with nail-fastened membranes and struck by two players, date from the same period. On a small vase of the twenty-second century B.C. in the Louvre, both players (women?) are depicted striking each head alternately. The earlier giants had been struck by men, but from about 2000 B.C. on, smaller frame drums—believed to have been called *balag-di* in Sumerian and *timbuttu* in Akkadian—appear in Sumer in the hands of women. Of great significance is the information supplied by a Sumerian text to the effect that the granddaughter of a king was appointed player of the *balag-di* in the Temple of the Moon at Ur around 2400 B.C., for the frame drum is known to have been a woman's instrument in the Near East for millennia, long after its connection with the moon goddess was forgotten.

Relatively large instruments were still played by men in late Hittite civilization: a shield-sized drum is seen on a relief from Carchemish of about 900 B.C., being held by a central figure and flanked to left and right by a male musician, each with one hand on the visible front membrane, the other presumably striking the invisible second head. The nails have disappeared, and were it not for the striking lateral figures, one might imagine a warrior with his shield.

From Asia the frame drum, together with other instruments, traveled to Egypt in the wake of the slave girl trade in the Eighteenth Dynasty (1570–1350 B.C.). A rectangular form occurs under Queen Hatshepsut (1520–1481 B.C.) and a large rectangle with incurved sides is represented at Thebes under Thutmose III (1501–1447 B.C.). Circular instruments are smaller, and, although the iconography is not clear on this point, they appear to have been double headed, judging by the manner in which they are held. But no matter what the form, they are always played by females, socially ranging from priestesses of Osiris (mentioned in the Brember-Rhind Papyrus) to dancing girls.

The frame drum of Israel was called *tof* (pl. *tupim*); circular, probably provided with two heads, it was almost exclusively in the hands of women. The word *tof* was translated as "timbrel," of which the Bible says: "Miriam the prophetisse . . . toke a tymbrell in hir hand, and all the women followed out after hir with timbrels in a daunse" (Clover-dale's Exodus 15:20). The *tof* was an instrument of the people, and it accompanied their songs; Gradenwitz (1949) relates that even today, in Oriental-Sephardic Jewish communities and those of Yemen, women still accompany their songs on a frame drum or on cymbals beaten with their hands. Elsewhere in the Eastern Mediterranean the round frame drum appears on Cyprus in the eighth century B.C., shown in com-pany with auloi and a kithara on a bronze disk depicting a cult scene.

European frame drums are descended from those of the Eastern Mediterranean culture, and in Greece, where it was known as *tympanon*, the frame drum was still a woman's instrument. Generally it was provided with two membranes, was held in one hand, upright on its rim as thereto-fore, and struck with the fingers of the other hand. Probably introduced from the East in connection with the cult of Kybele, which reached Greece in the sixth century B.C., it is not mentioned prior to Pindar (fifth century B.C.) nor portrayed before his century; it is shown last on an Attic vase painting of the third century B.C.

On Greek vases of both the fifth and the fourth centuries, frame drums are often played by maenads; a vase by the Dinos painter of about 420 B.C. shows two holding their instruments by a cord loop passed over the open hand below the knuckles, while six pairs of ribbons (or leather thongs?) dangle on the membrane. A mid-fourth-century vase depicts several looped handles spaced around the rim of the frame that look like short cords or knots, which would presumably strike against the head if twirled; if so, this would be evidence of the rattle drum (see page 151) in European antiquity, but one argument against such an identification is that rattle drums with external percussion are twirled by a rigid handle. From the fourth century on, jingles were added to some Greek frame drums (ancient Israeli instruments were devoid of jingles); sometimes the struck head was painted or strap handles were provided for easier grasping.

From Greece the frame drum passed to Rome, where it was called *tympanum*. From its inception it was connected with the cult of Cybele. Roman instruments portrayed are frequently quite large, sometimes held horizontally, and with ribbons dangling gaily from the frame. Strabo (d. ca. 25 A.D.) and Clement of Alexandria after him state that Parthians and Egyptians employed the *tympanum* as a war drum; in view of the frame drum's historical association with ritual and its almost exclusive appearance in the hands of women, their information seems improbable until it is realized that the Arabic *duff*—its name corresponds to *tof*—was a martial instrument in the seventh century A.D. (played, of course, by men). Also, *tympanum* could have been the name of a different drum. And by the time Strabo wrote the frame drum's use may no longer have been restricted to women even in Rome, for in the later days of the empire it became an instrument of the *joculatores,* who are sometimes depicted throwing it up in the air and catching it again.

FRAME DRUMS IN POSTCLASSICAL EUROPE

Postclassical Europe may have received the frame drum at different times and by different routes. The *joculatores* are believed responsible for spreading it beyond the confines of the Italian peninsula, and the pre-Islamic East may also have made a contribution: a group of musicians depicted in the Sassanid bas-reliefs of Taq i-Bustan (590–628) includes a player of the square frame drum. Arabs may have introduced it to Spain, and the crusaders certainly brought it back from the Levant, and finally it was reintroduced in the eighteenth century with the advent of "Turkish" music. From the onset its sievelike appearance was noted; Isidore of Seville (d. 636) writes that the *tympanum est pellis vel corium ligno ex una parte extensum. Est enim pars media symphoniae in similitudinem cribri . . .,* ("half a *symphonia* [two-headed drum] resembling a sieve . . ."), and even later they were sometimes described as sieve drums, for *girbal,* the Arabic word for sieve, is also the name of a now obsolete circular frame drum of Islam. Isidore further stated that the *tympanum* was played with a stick, and in this he is supported by the testimony of our earliest depictions of frame drums: the *Hortus deliciarum* (twelfth century) of Abbess Herrad of Landsberg shows two women playing frame drums with curved sticks of the type that Sachs has termed "crozier stick"; here the drums are suspended from the players' necks. In the thirteenth-century *Roman de la rose,* female dancers and players throw the *timbre* up in the air and catch it again; other medieval French texts refer to it as being in the hands of female dancers. A French miniature of the first quarter of the fourteenth century illustrates a *charivari* in the *Roman de Fauvel,* with several frame drums being played with a stick. Square models are struck either with a stick or by hand in the thirteenth and fourteenth centuries (e.g., MS 24 of Munich University). Jingles and pellet bells are frequently added from the fourteenth century on, and occasionally a snare is also visible. If a drum were furnished with jingles it would of course have to have been shaken by hand, but until these were added there could have been little difference between tapping the membrane with the fingers or striking it with a stick. Sometimes the two methods are shown together, as in the *Christ in Glory* of Fra Angelico (ca. 1430); here the beaten drum is the slightly larger of the two and has snares. An early frame drum seen from the back in a fresco by Ambrogio Lorenzetti (d. ca. 1348) at the Palazzo Pubblico, Siena, has a single head and jingles but no snare; it is the sole instrument accompanying a dance in progress. Single-headed instruments were more convenient for dancers to hold.

The Tambourine

The Old French word *timbre*, first used in the twelfth century and now obsolete in the sense of frame drum, gave rise to the English "timbrel," and is cognate with the Old Provençal *temple*; both derive from *tympanum*, as does probably the Middle High German *Rotumbes*. The modern "tambourine" is a diminutive of the French *tambour*, a generic term for drums ever since the fourteenth century, but the modern French for tambourine is *tambour de Basque*, from the older *tabourin de Basque*, which points to a reintroduction through Spain. An early Italian word for the same instrument was *cembalo*; during the first half of the thirteenth century the city of Siena employed *suonatori di cembali e di tamburi*; in the second half of the same century it boasted *trombone* (trumpets), *ceramelle* (shawms), and *nacchere* (kettledrums), with the last replacing the *cembali*. When Boccaccio wrote in the fourteenth century that the *cembalo* served to accompany the voice, he was not alluding to the harpsichord (*clavicembalo*), which did not exist at that time, but to the frame drum. *Cembalo* is still in use in Italy in this sense, and particularly in the combined form of *cembalo loreto*.

In the fifteenth century not only jingles but also pellet bells were appended to the frames of some tambourines, while in Italy a frame "drum" consisting of hoop and jingles but no head was shaken; it is one of the instruments lying at the feet of Raphael's *Saint Cecilia* (ca. 1513), where a true tambourine with two rows of jingles is also seen. Around 1600 the term *cimbaletto con sonaglie alla spagnuola* occurs, indicating a Spanish-style tambourine with pellet bells. Cotgrave might have described it—as he did the *tabourin de Basque*—as having "small bells and other jingling knacks of lattin"; Praetorius called it *Morenpäuklein* a little later; and Mersenne, the *tambour de Biscaye*. The conjunction of *tabourin de Basque, tambour de Biscaye,* the Spanish-style *cimbaletto,* and the Moorish *Päuklein* can scarcely be coincidental: Moorish instruments had risen to new heights in the hands of Spanish dancers. The Spaniards themselves called their instrument *pandair* (twelfth century) or *pandero* (fifteenth century), or *panderete* (fourteenth century), the last a diminutive of *pandero.* Lazarillo de Tormes, titular hero of the mid-sixteenth-century picaresque novel, earned his living for a while by working for a *maestro de pintar panderos* (a master *pandero* painter). And although work was not Lazarillo's forte, he may well have been kept busy, for the popularity of *panderos* was such that, while traveling in Spain in 1517, the Emperor Charles V was greeted at San Vicente de la Baquera by a group of twenty young girls, all singing and playing *tambourins à ung fond bien estoffé de sonnettes* ("single-membrane tambourines well furnished with pellet bells").

From Spain the *pandero* migrated to Hispaniola, where a sixteenth-century chronicler likened the songs and dances of Santo Domingo to those of the peasants in certain parts of Spain, where both men and women engaged in *pandero* playing during the summer months.

The tambourine of Europe remained first and foremost a dancer's instrument, and to a lesser degree one of street musicians and performers of popular music. In certain areas it has even managed to retain its age-old traditions: the Sicilian *tamuredda,* for instance, is played by women only. Presumably as part of the vogue for rustic instruments exemplified by the French court, eighteenth-century French society brought the tambourine to the status of a salon instrument; it could be heard at fashionable soirées combined with harp or keyboard instrument up to the Revolution. Rarely written for, von Weber nonetheless included a tambourine for local color in his *Preciosa* (1820), as did Berlioz in his *Le Carnaval romain* (1844).

Today the instrument has a single head nailed to a wooden hoop of 25 to 30 centimeters (10 to 12 inches) diameter and a depth of some 8 centimeters (3 inches); it lacks snares, but metal jingles are inserted pairwise in holes cut from the frame for this purpose, and fixed loosely enough to permit them to rattle freely when the drum is shaken. Three manners of playing are current: (1) it is simply shaken to set the jingles ringing; (2) the performer holds it in the left hand and strikes the membrane with fingers or closed knuckles of the right hand; or (3) the membrane is rubbed with a wet thumb or forefinger to produce a buzzing sound. Modern Spanish *panderetes* are either round or square and are furnished with both jingles and pellet bells. These same forms are encountered along the North African coast and also in South America, where they were introduced from Europe.

Because of its similarity to North American frame drums, that of the northern Scandinavian Lapps is discussed below with American frame drums.

FRAME DRUMS IN ASIA AND AFRICA

In pre-Islamic Arabia the round frame drum was known as *da'ira,* meaning "circle," and in Islamic times the term came to denote round frame drums throughout Islam, including Moslem Spain. Both jingle and pellet bell were added later to the frame but have since disappeared in many countries, among them Arabia and Turkey, and the former Islamic territories of Albania and Serbia. Numerous variants of the word enable us to follow it along North Africa, through the Balkans, the Caucasus, Afghanistan, and over to northern India. In this last area it is also met with in octagonal form, with wooden or metal frame and either a glued or a nailed membrane.

The custom of affixing membranes by nail is an ancient one, and is characteristic of the Orient. Japanese drums are still nailed, authorizing the belief that this method represents the continuation of a now defunct tradition of Chinese drum making. Sumerian drumheads, as has been pointed out, were attached by nails; their instruments and those of China (from whom Japan received most of its instruments, including drums) may possibly have sprung from a common source. Today, Near and Far Eastern traditions of membrane securing meet on the Indian subcontinent.

Frame drums of the above-mentioned areas are usually held in the left hand, with the player's right-hand fingers alternating between center and edge of the membrane. In North Africa, the *tār* is played by both men and women; Algerians sound it together with the *rebab.* Egyptian and Sudanese *tārs* are sometimes inlaid with mother-of-pearl, tortoiseshell, or ivory; in Egypt they have an important part in art music and are provided with two rows of five pairs of jingles. Those of Upper Egypt are occasionally furnished with snares; their principal use is at funerals by the traditional wailing female mourners. The word *tār* traveled as far south as Swahili territory, where it designates a tambourine with handle.

The Arabic *duff,* cognate with the Hebrew *tof,* is not only a generic designation for all frame drums but denotes in particular the square and octagonal forms with two heads and snares. Variants of the word describe the same instrument in Islamic-influenced regions and also in Brazil, where it was imported by the Portuguese. Indian frame drums are usually very large, their single head fastened by tension thongs of leather laced across the open back, but the octagonal *dampha* of Bengal, played by mendicant monks, has a nailed head, as it does in Nepal.

Another North African form is the *bendair*, a term clearly related to *pandair*, but, as the Spanish word form is known to have occurred earlier than the Arabic, it has been argued that the North African instrument was imported from Spain; yet in view of the fact that the Arabic term is first recorded on Spanish soil, it may well be that the Spaniards merely named an Arabic instrument. Today this is a very large tambourine with two snares, known in Algeria and Morocco, exclusively a rural instrument among the Berbers, with a goatskin head stretched over a 20-centimeter (8-inch) deep frame having a diameter of perhaps 50 centimeters (20 inches). Liberia and Nigeria have a form with clay frame and pegged single head, played with a curved beater.

Frame drums are also known in Africa outside the Islamic sphere of influence: the Thonga of South Africa, for instance, have circular single-headed shallow instruments played by their medicine men while exorcising (cf. the use of frame drums by shamans of Asia and America, pages 138 ff).

The southern Indian frame drum is known as *tambattam*, a word clearly cognate with the *Akkadian timbuttu*. In some areas its head is nailed, in others laced. Large and of circular form, it is made in sizes up to 120 centimeters (4 feet) in diameter and is struck with a short stick while held horizontally in front of the player. Another large drum is that of the Tibetan lamas, with a diameter of 90 to 120 centimeters (3 to 4 feet), set on an upright pole and struck with a sickle-shaped beater; a smaller version, only 40 to 60 centimeters (16 to 24 inches) in diameter, with an antelope head laced across the open back, is struck by southern Tibetan sorcerers of Bonnag from below, with the membrane facing the ground. A further form occurs in southern India, restricted to temple use: here the diminutive metal frame is fastened by a handle to a ring encircling the player's forehead and struck with a stick.

China has a great variety, some with single nailed head, played with a withy, others with single head and metal hoop, played with thin bamboo sticks during funeral processions; others again with two nailed heads tapped with the fingers; and finally a small octagonal model with glued snakeskin membrane and provided with brass jingles, possibly an importation from the West.

Ethnologists have noted the resemblances between the Lapps of northern Scandinavia and the American Indian tribes, especially those of the Northeast, resemblances that include such details of culture as similarities of the shamanic song and, of more interest to organologists, the shamanic drum. Furthermore, identity of structure and of function of these peoples' frame drums with those of some northern Siberian peoples is striking. Symbolism and magical functions of the shamanic drum are complex and multiple: among the peoples noted, shamanic drums are made of wood from the Cosmic Tree itself; they are then ceremoniously "animated" (by sprinkling with alcoholic spirits), after which the shaman by his drumming is enabled to fly away on his drum, that is, to mystically transcend both time and space. Usually it is oval, with a membrane of reindeer, elk, or horsehide. Ostyak and Samoyed shamans of eastern Siberia do not paint their membrane, nor do the Ugrian peoples, but the Tungus, Yakut, Yenisei Ostyak, and Tatar tribes do: the designs are symbolic, with the center of the head left unadorned; among the Lapps, both sides of the membrane are covered with images. Some Siberian drums have a vertical handhold of wood and iron at the open back, and the horizontal bracings hold a number of metal jingles, bells, or other rattling objects, all of which have symbolic meaning; drums of Tungus shamans are gripped by the cords that stretch the membrane across the open back.

An early eye-witness account of the drum and its stick is furnished by the English traveler Richard Johnson, who wrote in 1556 of the Samoyeds encountered on the banks of the Pechoza:

And first the Priest doeth beginne to playe upon a thing like a great sieve, with a skinne on the one ende like a drumme: and the stick that he playeth with is about a spanne long, and one end is round like a ball, covered with the skin of an Harte. Then he singeth as wee use heere in Englande to hallow, whope, or showte at houndes . . .

Eliade (1964) has pointed out that the shamanic drum is distinguished from all other "magical" instruments by virtue of the fact that its *musical* magic determined its shamanic function, not the antidemonic magic of noise. He further states that several data indicate that the North Asian shamanic drum was originally disseminated from South Asia, and that the lamaist drum indubitably influenced the shape not only of the

Siberian but also of the Chukchi and Eskimo drums. As a result of recent studies on the origin of shamanic drums in Central and North Asia, several disparate conclusions have been advanced: (1) their prototype is the Tibetan "double drum," that is, the hourglass-shaped rattle drum composed of two human skullcaps; (2) the Tibetan frame drum on a handle was the first to reach North Asia (including the Chukchi and the Eskimo); (3) their prototype was the drum in shape of a winnowing basket that is found today among magicians of several archaic peoples of India. As to nonshamanic frame drums of these same northern areas, they have identical form but their heads are never painted; double-headed circular versions are sounded by the Altai and Buryat of Siberia.

FRAME DRUMS IN THE AMERICAS

Equally rich in its variety of frame drums is the American continent. Comparatively little is known of their use in prehistoric times, but evidence points to a preference having been given to the larger membranophone. However, double-headed shallow drums (page 128) have been played in Peru since pre-Columbian days, and frame drums are known in Bolivia today.

Amerind frame drums have several notable features in common with those of the Far East: their heads are often painted, they are commonly played with a stick, and the form intermediate between frame and tubular drum—the shallow drum—now exists in these two areas exclusively.

North American frame drums are single or double headed, and generally played with a single, straight stick. Drums with a single head prevail among the Plains and Northwest Coast Indians, those with two heads among woodland dwellers. Most single-headed frame drums are tensed by radial lacings, or an extra piece of skin is tied in the center of the back to form a handhold. Formerly the Sioux pegged the membrane all around its circumference and stretched thongs across the back for the same purpose. Heads of the two-headed drums are neatly sewn together all around the hoop so as to meet and to hide the hoop, and are provided with a thong handle.

Square frame drums have been made on the Northwest Coast and are becoming increasingly popular for purely utilitarian reasons: they can easily be assembled from packing cases. Several Plains peoples make them occasionally because of the difficulty in procuring wood suitable for hoops.

The Dakota Indians peg the heads of their square frame drums. Rectangular versions are found in Mexico, Bolivia, and in California, and octagonal ones among the Cherokee. Both single- and double-headed drums of the North American Indians were war drums; they accompanied warriors on fighting expeditions and provided the rhythm necessary to war dances.

Outside southern Europe, the custom of painting the membranes of frame drums is common to North American Indians, Lapps, and some Siberian peoples; the Japanese paint those of their shallow drums and of some tubular drums. Originally symbolic, the meaning of the designs is now forgotten by Amerinds and has become purely ornamental. Formerly the heads were painted with natural dyes, but commercial products are now in use. Many of the older, two-headed drums bear a design on the inside as well as on the outside of the membrane; in Alaska and rarely on the Northwest Coast, decorations appear on the inside only.

By adding to an ordinary frame drum certain rattling devices, it is transformed into a medicine (i.e., magic) drum, with power over spirits. Two such types may be distinguished: struck frame drums furnished with rattling, snarelike appurtenances, and smaller shaken rattle drums. Devices added to the conventional drum can vary from a number of small sticks around 5 centimeters (2 inches) in length, threaded at the center and tied across the diameter so that they lie against the inside of the head, or wooden needles about twice as long, strung through their eyes, or quills, even beads, all affixed in the same manner. On double-headed drums these objects may be strung on the exterior of a head, but this is rare. In the northwestern Canadian woods a regular cord or buckskin snare is occasionally added. Whatever the material, the effect is similar to the conventional snare.

But the shaken frame drum containing pebbles is considered to be the true medicine drum and is used by the medicine men of many woodland tribes in curing the ill. Typically it is smaller than the war drum, varying generally from 5 to 20 centimeters (2 to 8 inches) in diameter; it is held by the medicine man and shaken over the patient. Rarely is it played as a struck drum, and, as a great volume of sound is not required, its diminutive size is an advantage.

A different type is played by the Eskimo over an area comprising Greenland, arctic North America and northern Siberia, namely one with a fixed handle. This always has a single head and very thin membrane of seal or walrus bladder or intestine, tied through slits in the narrow frame by a sinew. The drum is either round, oval, or even fan shaped. Unlike all other frame drums, that of the Eskimo is struck on the hoop—not on the membrane—by a slender stick, so that the membrane acts merely as an amplifier. The drum is flat and of considerable proportions, attaining in Canada a diameter of 1 meter (40 inches). Its sound enhances the player's voice, so to speak, for a singer will direct his voice against the membrane, utilizing it as a mirliton for color and amplification; hence this version stands halfway between a true drum and a mirliton. Use of the same instrument, particularly in Greenland, in connection with contests of insults and legal disputes, is now dying out. The hooked beaters with which the Eskimo and Lapp strike them are found elsewhere chiefly among North American Indians. This type of drum is sometimes referred to as a shaman's drum, but, according to Eliade (1964), the Eskimo shaman is conspicuous for his lack both of ritual costume and drum.

SHALLOW DRUMS

Shallow drum (*Flachtrommel* in German) is a modern designation (of Sachs) for a frame drum with higher than ordinary frame, the diameter of which always remains greater than its height, although the proportions vary in different parts of the world, with those of the American Indians being characteristically taller. They are believed to be of Turkish or Arabian origin and occur typically in the Near East, but the American shallow drum, known to predate Columbus, probably had an independent genesis.

A second-century B.C. relief at Bharahat, central India, depicts a large drum, held with the player's left arm bent around the shell and the right hand striking its head with a stick; from the playing position, Sachs was inclined to identify this as an early appearance of the Near Eastern shallow drum.

European shallow drums may be an offshoot of the ancient Semitic frame drum; the latter was light enough to be held in one hand, but shallow drums are large enough to require bracing against the player's body or else setting on the rim, even suspending from a handle, forked stick, et cetera. Among the objects found in a Scythian tumulus at Chertomlyk in the lower Dnieper region of southern Russia, dating from the fourth century B.C., is a *gorytus* (bow and arrow case) of precious metal; its low-relief ornamentation includes a seated figure holding a drum approximately the size of Carpaccio's shallow drum of 1505, but deeper. One head (or the open bottom?) is held against the player's torso; the upper head faces forward and is tapped with the fingers of both hands. No fastening is visible. The *gorytus* belongs to the classical period of Greco-Scythian art and is believed to have been executed by Greek craftsmen to a Scythian pattern; it is now housed in the Hermitage Museum in Leningrad. After this brief appearance, the shallow drum is not seen again until it surfaces in Turkey and passes from there to Europe by the fourteenth century, as has already been noted, and where it was long known as the Turkish drum.

In America, shallow drums were small enough to be held in one hand in the days of the Inca empire. Today those of North America are either medicine or dance drums, with heavy hide head struck by a hard beater in order to produce a loud and staccato sound. One type of drum is suspended a few inches off the floor by four upright notched poles right in the center of the dance house, playing head horizontal, and beaten by approximately ten drummers seated in a circle around the drum, all striking the head simultaneously. At present, drummers regrettably prefer to buy a ready-made washtub rather than construct their own instrument (although the Dakota still play a shallow drum with bent frame and sewn heads, struck with a single stick). Shallow tub-shaped drums are sounded by Indians of the North Central woods, also by the Iowa, Dakota Sioux, Shoshoni, and other tribes further west. Identical with the foregoing instrument is the so-called dream-dance drum, except for the latter's elaborate decoration and for a bell suspended in its interior; this form is said to have powerful medicine (i.e., magical) properties.

Present-day drumming practice in North America calls for straight sticks, with wrapped, not knobbed, ends, held parallel to the drum and struck sideways against the head of both the smaller hand frame and larger tub-shaped drums. Most interesting are the beaters of the Chippewa, with a curled prolongation resulting in a small circular striking end —like a crozier stick with the end filled in—and the rattle drumstick sometimes used in conjunction with medicine drums. Here the circular end is enlarged to about one-half of the length of the handle, and covered on both sides with rawhide sewn together after a handful of pebbles has been introduced, thus transforming it into a miniature rattle drum on a handle (however, this is probably *not* the genesis of rattle drums). For conversion of shallow drum to rattle drum with internal percussion, see rattle drum (page 153).

CYLINDER DRUMS

So far cylinder drums have not been traced back further than about 2000 B.C., when they were first seen in Egypt. An actual specimen believed to date from the Twelfth Dynasty (2000–1788 B.C.) is housed in the Cairo Museum; it measures 65 by 29 centimeters (25½ by 11½ inches), and its heads are laced by a network of thongs. With the advent of the New Kingdom the cylinder drum disappeared, to reappear nearly a thousand years later in India.

Outside Europe, cylinder drums always remained on a comparatively primitive level, even in the high-culture areas of the East. A short cylinder drum, its two heads laced, is first depicted in the plastic arts of India in the last pre-Christian centuries, when it was played with sticks and suspended in a horizontal position by a strap from its player's neck. The Southeast Asian archipelago is not rich in drums, as gongs are the preferred rhythm instruments there, yet a cylinder drum is among the instruments depicted on the Borobudur reliefs on Java, of about A.D. 800. Primitive, 3-meter- (10-foot-) high cylinder drums, reminiscent of their ancestral tree trunk, are slanted to a playable angle on Nias, their lower end carved to form a foot (footed drum). In China, small cylinder drums were formerly popular, to judge from a scene on an ink-on-paper drawing of Li Kung-lin (d. 1106) of dancing peasants, one of whom carries such a drum suspended from his neck; he is playing it with both bare hands while another peasant plays a cross flute. (For cylinder drums played in pairs, see drum sets, page 154.)

As in Indonesia, footed cylinder drums also attain a height of 3 meters (10 feet) in Loango, West Africa; too large to permit being played upright, they have to be tilted to bring the head within the player's reach. Many other African drums are created by the simple expedient of hollowing out a section of a tree trunk, a procedure that results either in a cylinder form or one that tapers slightly toward the base, that is, conical. A now obsolete form from West Africa can be seen on a sixteenth-century bronze plaque from Benin, now in the Lagos, Nigeria, museum, where a "dancing king" with ceremonial sword is flanked by two musicians, one holding a short cylinder drum with hooped heads projecting far beyond the rim of the shell, in the manner of some Far Eastern drums, and the other holding a side-blown trumpet.

Evidence for the existence of both pottery and wooden drums in ancient America is available from excavations and also from iconographic materials. Apparently they were beaten without sticks. Slender pottery drums, open top and bottom, were among the instruments played in the Guatemala highlands in the late classical period (A.D. 700–1000); Sachs has shown that not only these but also other central American drums were played with bare hands. Remnants of a small cylinder drum from ancient Peru present evidence of a most unusual form: the "shell" is merely a skeletal framework comprising two horizontal wooden rings forming the upper and lower rims, connected by a group of three vertical laths 17 centimeters (7 inches) high, a form not known to exist elsewhere. Most Amerind drumheads of modern times are sewn (a few are nailed), and we can assume that this early Peruvian structure was provided with two skins large enough to be sewn together so as to form closed sides. Pre-Columbian *huehuetls* of Mexico were beautifully carved, as may be ascertained from extant specimens; today they are made as footed drums and with European-inspired lacings.

Cylinder drums of the Indians of the southwestern United States have long been made of a log of hollowed wood—traditionally cottonwood; historically they were war and dance drums, today they are sold in tourist shops. With a height twice that of the diameter, the two heads are laced together. In order to obtain maximum volume of sound the drum is raised off the floor and suspended by its handles from a forked stick inserted in the ground. A similar drum, but taller and with open bottom, is played by the Assiniboin of the northern Plains.

HOURGLASS DRUMS

Small, portable drums fashioned in the shape of an hourglass, with two cuplike sections joined so as to form a waist, are generally made of wood or of clay. In some areas, notably in Africa and the Pacific, they may have a monoxylous handle carved at the waist; others, laced from head to head in various cord patterns, are gripped by a band around the waist (tension ligature), thereby increasing the tension of the heads and raising the pitch.

Known since the late Neolithic period in Europe, in historical times the hourglass drum first appeared in India, when the second century B.C. Bharahat reliefs portrayed such a drum suspended from its player's shoulders in a horizontal position, both its heads beaten with sticks. Modern drums of this form on the subcontinent are made of clay, wood, or brass, and have tension ligatures. In the north, a large wooden model is played with sticks, while in the south the small *udukkai*, a temple instrument, is held in the left hand and tapped with bare fingers. Closely re-sembling it is the rattle drum in hourglass form, the *dāmaru* (see rattle drums, page 151).

Prior to their introduction from Eastern Turkistan in the fourth cen-tury A.D., hourglass drums were unknown in China. There, and in the areas under her cultural influence, both heads are played. Via Korea, China exported her hourglass drums to Japan, where the many varieties in existence are known collectively as *tsuzumi*. Among them the o *tsuzumi* may be compared to the *ko tsuzumi*—both of which are played in *no ku* music—and the *san no tsuzumi* played in *gagaku*. Of the three, the first is grasped by its cords with the player's left hand, and one head is played with the right hand; the second drum, placed on the performer's shoulder, has its forward-facing head played with the right hand; the third drum is struck on its right head with a stick. The characteristically hooped heads, extending far beyond the body, are shared with East Asian barrel drums. A very squat and rather gruesome variety found in Tibet has already been mentioned: the ritual instrument of Bon priests that consists of human skullcaps joined together. (Asian hourglass drums transformed into rattle drums are discussed on page 152.)

On the African continent hourglass drums spread clear across the north-ern coastal area with the Islamic conquests, and penetrated into West and Central Africa. Among the Berber, women are the chief players. Formerly laced, the larger of the drum's two heads is now glued; this is held so it faces down, to be tapped by the player's bare hand. In Zaire, the Balunda carve their hourglass drums and nail the playing head; furthermore, they pierce a hole in the body and cover this with a vesicle—a mirliton device, such as they also apply commonly to their xylophones. Hourglass drums of the western "Bend" are also played as "talking" drums (see page 156).

In the Pacific, such drums are single headed, with membrane consist-ing of varan, heated and glued, and a monoxylous carrying handle is carved; on New Guinea they are said to symbolize the transition from earth to heaven. The elongated *kunda* drums of the western New Guinea Wapenamunda have heads of reptile skin, lack handles, and may be played at war dances.

CONICAL DRUMS

Conical drums made of clay were known in ancient Mesopotamia, as already noted, but, with the notable exception of India, this form is now found chiefly in an undeveloped condition, probably due in part to the fact that a tree trunk cut into segments provides readily available if not always easily worked raw material (some are burned out), offering two apertures of differing dimensions, transformable if so desired into heads of different pitches. A set of three conoid drums is figured on the Hindu-Javanese reliefs of Borobudur, Java, of about A.D. 800, played with bare hands on the smaller of the heads; and in the present-day Balinese *gamelan gong* orchestra, two conical drums mark changes of tempo. On the mainland, the Garo of Assam, an archaic people, play a conical drum with heads tensed by V lacings. (For double conical drums joined at the widest part, see barrel drums, page 148.)

In Africa, the Ethiopian *kabaro* is distinguished by its position in the Christian Monophysite church, where it is played on secular occasions. When made from a tree trunk section it is conical, but otherwise it assumes the shape of an egg with a slice removed from top and bottom; both forms are double headed. If only the upper head is to be played, the drum is stood upright; if both, then it is suspended in front of its player at a slant, supported by a neck band. *Kabaros* can attain a height of 90 centimeters (3 feet) and considerable width, and are always beaten with bare hands. Form and playing technique have been likened by Wellesz (1954) to that of the ancient Egyptian tubular drums. Conical drums hollowed out of a block of wood with the bottom left open, and provided with two monoxylous handles are played in South Africa by women—an exception to the tradition requiring drums to be played by men only; that of the Pedi has a membrane secured by pegs, while another shared by the Pedi, Venda, Chwana, and Sotho peoples of South Africa has a laced head; women tap it with their fingers or palms while standing, with the drum held between the thighs, hobbyhorse fashion, a stance convenient for reaching the head of a drum large enough to require tilting, and at the same time leaving both hands free to play. Another South African people, the Berg Dama, reserve the use of their *arub*, formed like a wooden bucket, for occasions when the medicine man is called in to treat an ill person; its membrane is played with the thumbs of both hands. A vast number of drums from Central and West Africa are truncoconical, made from hollowed tree trunks, and in West Africa these are often played in sets (see page 154). From the coastal regions they were taken to the New World, where they still participate in Afro-American cult life. Names such as Ibo drum, Dahomey drum, and so on, clearly indicate their provenance.

African drums of Haiti are sacred objects and may even represent the divinity itself. As such they receive libations: sacrifices and offerings of blood are part of the voodoo ritual. Most sacred of these instruments is— or was—the *assoto*, which stands over 2 meters (6½ feet) high (most *assotos* reportedly disappeared during antisuperstition campaigns waged some years ago). Truncoconical in form and with pegged head, it must be made of wood of the *Ochroma pyramidalis* (said to contain "a lot of blood") cut at full moon; after baptism, it receives the sacrifice of a red-coated bull or a white or black he-goat, from whose blood a cross is then painted on the shell.

As for the Pacific area, Polynesians have a generic name for their membranophones: *pahu*. These are usually made from the wood of the breadfruit tree or from a hollowed coconut palm, resulting in a natural conical shape; the single head is then laced with sharkskin. Always large, on some islands they reach a height of 2½ meters (8 feet). Many assume the form of footed drums with elaborately carved pedestals; those of Hawaii were imported to the islands from more southerly islands some six centuries ago.

GOBLET DRUMS

A Babylonian plaque from about 1100 B.C., now in the British Museum, depicts a large, ovoid drum on a very short stem, reaching from the ground to the player's waist—perhaps some 90 centimeters (3 feet) or so high—and struck by a man with his bare hands: this is the prototype of the goblet drum. Our next glimpse of one is some eight centuries later.

Thureau-Dangin (1921) published in his *Rituels accadiens* the text— in Akkadian cuneiform and a French translation—of a *kalu* (temple priest) rite involving the ritual immolation of a bull for the sake of its hide, needed to form the membrane of the temple drum *lilissu* (*lilis*, in Sumerian). The admittedly late text is taken from an inscription at Erech (Uruk, the modern Warka) of about 300 B.C., but undoubtedly represents an earlier and well-established usage. Both bull and drum are figured, and the latter has the shape of a goblet; more specifically, it is that of a hemispheric bowl set on a short stem terminating in a low, flat base. The bull is apparently a *primigenius*. Now, the function of the *kalu* was to appease the gods by his singing, and the principal instrument with which he accompanied his song was the *lilissu*, a metal drum with bull-hide membrane. Bulls were sacred in the ancient world, from Mesopotamia west to France at least (beneath Notre Dame Cathedral in Paris lies a sanctuary of the horned god, Cernunnos), and east to pre-Aryan India (where, as already mentioned, the *Bos primigenius* is sometimes represented with an altar, whereas the indigenous *Bos indicus* never is); hence the use of a bull skin for the head of a temple, that is, sacred, drum. Only a bull resembling the celestial bull might be ritually slaughtered for this purpose; he must be black and free of blemishes.

Both the immolation ritual involving incantations of magical efficiency and the preparation of the hide itself are dealt with in detail: the membrane was stretched over varnished *sikkatu*, pegs of box, cedar, or other woods inserted in the bowl. Fifteen days after application of the drumhead, sacrifices were made to the now divine *lilissu*, and seven small figurines called "hands," representing the children of Enmesharra, the supreme *kalu* (but seven was a sacred, ergo a symbolic, number in Mesopotamia), were placed in the interior of the shell (in another version it is stated that twelve bronze figurines of divinities were placed inside it). Their rattling must have added considerably to the noise of the beaten drum. Of its size we are not informed. Here, then, is a metal basin set on a stand, a sacred instrument by virtue of its bull-skin membrane and its dedication to temple service. Sumerian texts indicate that the *lilissu* also participated in processions.

Large drums of antiquity such as this (and the Mesopotamian frame drum) were subsequently reduced in size, "miniaturized" to the extent that when they reappeared they were portable and the proportion of shell to stem had been modified—a form that lends itself admirably to being gripped firmly between the player's upper arm and thorax, with head facing forward. Such a drum can also be stood upright, or even held upside down with head facing the ground, in which case it is tapped from below.

This small version became known to the Arabs and was disseminated by them. Extinct in western Europe, it is today a drum of the Islamic world par excellence. The modern *darabuka* of North Africa and the Near East, known by a number of variant names from Morocco to Iran and north as far as Bulgaria, is made of metal or of pottery. Further east, a primitive form in Malaya has a snakeskin head laced with split cane to a wooden body, and still farther it is found in Indonesia, made of wood; on Celebes one form remains a temple instrument, set on the ground when played.

BARREL DRUMS

Barrel-shaped drums are widest at the center, with rounded outline narrowing toward the ends, but a variant that is wider at the center and has rectilinear narrowing is usually included in this classification. The latter form existed in ancient Egypt and is found in India and East Asia today. A characteristic of both types is their horizontal position when played, both heads being struck.

The barrel drum was first seen in Egypt, during the Middle and New Kingdoms, and two small wooden drums with braced heads, dating from the New Kingdom (1580–1090 B.C.), about 30 centimeters (1 foot) long, have been excavated.

But the continent on which the barrel drums have continued to thrive in abundance since antiquity is Asia. A wide variety is played on the Indian subcontinent, many connected with ancient traditions: Brahma himself is said to have invented the *mridanga*. In historical times the portable barrel drum is first shown in the first century B.C., being played with bare hands. Brahma's *mridanga* was and still is the classical barrel drum of the subcontinent; *mrd* means "clay," pointing to the material from which it may have been made originally, but throughout its known history wood has been the material employed for its fabrication. Its heads are lapped over hoops and laced from end to end, tensed by wedges placed under the lacings and tuned by application of tuning paste.

Tuning paste is a mixture of several ingredients that vary with the locality, but in general the right head receives a permanent application of black paste composed nowadays of manganese dust, boiled rice, and tamarind juice, or of iron filings and boiled rice. A different paste is applied —always temporarily—to the left head shortly before the drum is to be played, in order to tune it to the octave below the right head; this paste is scraped off after each performance. A number of other drums, both in India and in other Asiatic countries, are likewise tuned by paste applied to the center of the head, or to the side of the head, and in Africa the (low-caste) smiths of Egidi, Zazawa, in the Sahara, tune their drum with a paste concocted of goat's brains and the soot of cooking pots; in fact, the use of tuning paste extends as far south as Nigeria, and, as stated above, its origin is probably to be sought in ritual.

To return to the *mridanga*: this drum is played with both wrists and fingertips, and, indeed, most Indian drums are played by hand and in this manner. In northern India the same instrument is called *pakhawaj*; in early seventeenth-century Mogul dance scenes it is shown held by a strap at the player's waist. A form considered to be a descendant of the *mridanga* is widely disseminated as a clay drum in the shape of two truncated cones joined at the wide part, with heads smaller than those of the *mridanga* and tuned a fourth or a fifth apart by tension cords. The *tabla*, its name derived from the Arabic *tabl,* has a shell of wood, metal, or clay, is closed at the bottom, and has the same shape as the *pakhawaj;* its single head is tuned with tension wedges and permanent tuning paste, on account of which it is often compared to or even identified with the right head of the *mridanga.* The *tabla* constitutes the right-hand drum of a pair, the other half of which is a small metal kettledrum called *bāmyā;* together these two have the tuning of a *mridanga. Bāmyās* are played exclusively as partners of the *tabla.* Other barrel drums are the ancient *mādalā,* of clay with laced heads, nowadays also of wood, and the *dhol,* sacred to the Chamar of Uttar Pradesh, among whom it is played chiefly by women, only its left head being struck and then always with a drumstick; the Muria of Bastar play the same instrument in the same fashion. The related *dhōlaka,* encountered all over the subcontinent, is hollowed out of a block of wood; both its heads are played.

To the east, the predominant form of drum throughout Indochina is that of a barrel, introduced from China. A hand-beaten barrel drum is depicted on the Hindu-Javanese reliefs of Borobudur of about A.D. 800. In Vietnam, Laos, and Cambodia today a double-headed barrel drum is tapped with the fingers, its heads usually tuned by tension ligatures and tuning paste. Regional variations are of course numerous: in Thailand the large *klong* has nailed heads, only one of which is played, and this is tuned by means of tuning paste. It emits soft tones when struck with padded sticks and loud ones when bare bamboo is employed. The *klong* is always propped up so that the lower membrane (not played) may vibrate freely; the similar *tapone* is laid horizontally in a framework. In Vietnam, shells are usually lacquered and the larger instruments are struck with a stick; the heads of lacquered instruments are attached by nails. Both lacquer and the nailing of heads indicate a Chinese influence.

In China of yore, barrel-shaped containers served as rice or other grain measures, and in time these came to be transformed into drums. Such is the genesis of the *po fu,* at present—or until recently—a Confucian temple instrument held horizontally on its player's knees, its two heads tapped with the fingers of both hands. The heads of all Chinese barrel drums are secured with nails, and it is probable that this system of attaching them originated here or in the territory between China and Mesopotamia. Large barrel drums, such as the 2-meter (6½-foot) long *tsin ku* were suspended in an upright frame; if, as was sometimes the case, the heads were also lacquered, they were struck with two drumsticks; others were war drums.

China's musical instruments, including its drums, traveled east to Korea and thence to Japan. Both the barrel drum and the hourglass drum have counterparts there, although the proportions are not always those of their ancestors. A form particular to Japan is the short, bulging barrel drum with projecting heads mounted on hoops laced to each other, with the hoops projecting beyond the shell. Such is the *kakko*, its two heads always played with slender drumsticks while the shell rests horizontally on a sculptured stand. A now obsolete form, known as *kaiko*, was formerly played with the fingers of the player's right hand during processions.

Counterpart of the great Chinese *tsin ku* is the somewhat smaller *da daiko*, the slightly barrel-shaped shell of which is some 1½ meters (5 feet) long. Typical of this and of some other *daikos* are heads with hoops that project so far that they virtually hide the shell from view with their lacings. Too large to be portable, the *da daiko* is suspended from a frame or set on a stand and struck with two heavy, lacquered beaters, always in left-right sequence, its use restricted to *gagaku* and, occasionally, *bugaku* music. Smaller *daikos* are set on low stands in front of the player, tilted, and played with two sticks. When *tsuzumi* (hourglass drums) and smaller *daikos* are employed in *samisen* music, they are played by women. Some other *daikos*, such as the *tsuri daiko* ("hanging" *daiko*) have nailed heads, and both their body and heads are painted; a patch of deerskin applied to the center of the head guards the decoration from damage by the knobbed stick with which it is beaten.

For barrel drums as components of tuned drum chimes in Burma and Thailand, see drum chimes (page 158).

RATTLE DRUMS

Rattle drums are shaken membranophones, and, as their name indicates, they combine elements of both the rattle and the drum, and percussion is either by impact of the knotted ends of attached cords or leather thongs, or by partly filling the drum with pebbles. The former type is referred to as rattle drum with external percussion, the latter as rattle drum with internal percussion. In the former, the striking action of the human hand or drumstick has been abolished, and a simple twirling suffices to sound the membrane. Today such drums are found chiefly in Asia— from India to Japan and in the Syria-Lebanon area—in Arabia and modern Egypt, and also among Amerinds of the Americas. Some frame drums depicted on Greek vases of the fourth and third centuries B.C. look suspiciously as though short cords terminating in knots were appended to the frame.

The ancient practice of placing or suspending votive objects in the interior of drums has been suggested as a possible origin for these curious instruments, whose history can be traced to the Shang dynasty of China, a theory that would account for the ritual character of rattle drums with internal percussion. Another hypothesis may be formulated from the fact that in ancient Japan both drums and rattles are known to have been professional tools of shamanesses; possibly the two were once combined into a single instrument for ritual use, but not necessarily in Japan.

The rattle drum of modern China assumes the form of a small drum with two snakeskin heads impaled on a handle; two wax balls are suspended from the drum by cords so they will strike against the heads when the drum is twirled; its principal use is by itinerant vendors or as a child's toy. In ancient times, however, it consisted of two or more drums impaled on a stick, one above the other, or else suspended in a frame, and was dedicated to service in Confucian temples. This older form has survived in Korea and Japan, where two drums are still superposed. The Chinese populations of Java and Bali have a miniature barrel drum with snakeskin heads that are struck by wax balls on the ends of cords affixed to the drum; it is known as *klontong*. An ancient *klontong* of bronze, 14 centimeters (6 inches) long, has been excavated.

In India and Tibet hourglass drums are transformed into rattle drums by the addition of a cord wound around the waist, terminating in knotted ends that strike the heads. As an attribute to Shiva, the Indian rattle drum *dāmaru* is sacred; nonetheless, it is now played by beggars all over the subcontinent and is also found in the hands of snake charmers; a miniature form is played by Gypsies and jugglers. But in Sikkim and Bhutan the "small drum" (*rnga ch'un*) is still an attribute of male and female sorcerers, together with a handbell.

Among the Yemeni rattle drums were still known in the eighteenth century but are now extinct; in this area also there were hourglass drums of very small dimensions.

A third form is in use in the Eastern churches of modern Egypt (including the Greek Orthodox church), as well as by Syrian Christians and Lebanese Maronites: a frame drum on a handle. The frame is about 4 centimeters (1½ inches) deep, its diameter 14 centimeters (5½ inches); the two membranes are of skin or of thick paper, and the two maize seeds that are attached to strings secured to the frame strike the membranes when the drum is twirled. The prototype of this instrument is the metal percussion disk (see page 18), to which pellet bells or other materials are attached and which can be traced back to antiquity. Yet another form is the Chinese combination of rattle drum and gong: a small rattle drum on a handle is surmounted by a gong suspended in a circular frame; two wooden balls are attached to the frame and strike the gong when the instrument is twirled, with the drum sounding at the same time. This combination, called *lo ku,* is to be found in the hands of itinerant vendors.

So far the rattle drums discussed have been of the type with external percussion. That with internal percussion is found chiefly in the Americas, where pebbles are inserted into the body of the drum before it is completed, usually by sewing the heads together. As the drum rattles when shaken, the need for belaboring it with drumsticks is obviated. This type is known from South America via Central America, where the Puralla of Guatemala make it, to North America. The Chippewa and the Cree have a unique two-headed frame drum filled with pebbles; when making the drum, instead of cutting off the excess board after the frame is completed, an extra length is left to form a handle. Izikowitz (1931) believed that this might represent a transformation of the calabash rattle, due to the absence of calabashes in the areas where this variety occurs. Shallow drums converted into rattle drums, having bent frames and heads sewn together, pebble-filled and shaken, are found among the Ojibwa. Those of Amerind medicine men are discussed on page 142.

WATER DRUMS

Some Indian tribes of both North and South America possess a ceremonial drum known to anthropologists as a water drum, from the fact that it is partly filled with water. Such instruments are made either of wood or of pottery and have a common characteristic: virtually every description of these water drums is accompanied by the remark that it sounds dull when heard at close quarters but that it has far greater carrying power than other drums, due to the water inside (one investigator adds, alas, that the carrying power of water is a well-established fact). Perhaps a description will help evaluate such reports.

These drums fall into two categories, those of pottery and those of wood. The former are potbellied, bowl shaped, or footed, and were formerly common among eastern and southern tribes of the United States. The potbellied type is still played by the Pueblo Indians, who make it of undecorated pots varying in size from 15 centimeters (6 inches) to over 76 centimeters (30 inches); the Chippewa consider it a potent medicine (magic) drum, and it was the sacred drum of their medicine society.

Wooden drums, on the other hand, are made from a hollowed log with a thick, wooden bottom inserted slightly above the lower rim, and a bung-hole pierced in the side. Both pottery and wooden varieties are filled about one-quarter full of water, after which a wet and well-soaked head of heavy tanned buckskin is put on; this is tied on with a thong if the drum is of pottery, but is held down by a hoop on those of wood. This head is applied temporarily before each use, then removed and placed inside the drum. Pottery water drums are played with a special beater about 30 centimeters (1 foot) long, a stick thinned toward one end, its thin portion then bent into a circle and lashed so as to form a circular knob; wooden drums are played with a curved stick ending in a small knob occasionally covered with buckskin.

Most pottery drums of South American Indians were or are "water" drums, according to Izikowitz (1931). The Brazilian Chiriguano and the Mataco and Toba Indians of the Chaco play a wooden mortar drum as water drum, while the Lengua, also of the Chaco, have clay pots with deerhide heads; the Lengua fill theirs with variable amounts of water in order to obtain different pitches.

The alleged unusual carrying power of these drums, as well as their dullness of sound when heard close by, has been reported by so many investigators independently that it cannot be questioned, but that the water in the interior is responsible for these effects must be disallowed. Heads of water drums are of tanned buckskin, *wetted*—other drums of the same tribes, not containing water, have heads of rawhide. When beaten, water drums would therefore emit a tone composed of considerably more fundamental than would a dry membrane—and the fundamental of a tone is louder and has greater carrying power than have its overtones.

DRUM SETS

Apart from chimes, with their individual drums tuned to the intervals of a musical scale (see page 158), and from the "talking" drum ensembles (see page 156), small batteries of two or more drums have been played for many a century, most of them by as many drummers as there are drums.

Cylinder drums were played in pairs in ancient India, either by one or by two persons, and in present-day Korea two cylinder drums with nailed heads are suspended, one above the other, from an upright frame; the pairing of kettledrums is discussed on page 160. Among the membranophones shown on the Borobudur reliefs of Java (ca. A.D. 800) is a battery of three conical drums, two of which are set upright while the third lies horizontally on the ground, all three apparently beaten with bare hands on the smaller of the heads.

Small sets are important at present in West Africa, as well as in Afro-American cults. Apart from the *dundun* ensemble that doubles as a set of "talking" drums among the Yoruba (see page 157), the four-drum *asiwui* battery of the Ewe of Ghana may be mentioned. This comprises the Ewe's master drum, called *atsimevu*, standing 1½ meters (5 feet) high, and three smaller drums. All are single headed, slightly barrel shaped, and with open bottoms; their duiker-skin heads are secured by wooden hoops somewhat larger than the shell, and each drum is struck with two drumsticks. Before playing the drums are turned upside down and a small amount of water is poured in; when the head is deemed sufficiently soaked, the drums are rolled over so as to swell the wood. The *atsimevu*'s shell is brightly painted and encircled by iron hoops to strengthen it.

Afro-Bahians have sets of three drums of graded sizes; according to a local tradition, drums with cord bracings should be played with bare hands, but those with pegged membranes with beaters. Only the skins of sacrificial animals may be used for the heads, and the shell is built up of staves to resemble a half barrel. But the "power" of these drums resides not only in the instrument but also in the drumstick, and is conferred by means of prolonged rituals and ceremonies during which the drums are "fed"; baptism is the initial rite, a feature of such African cults as have been retained in New World Catholic countries. Unbaptized drums are termed "pagan" and should not be played. "Feeding" consists of sacrificial offerings of chicken blood, palm oil, honey, holy water (baptism is by holy water obtained from a Catholic church), with the blood being made to flow freely over the drum; drum sounds may then become so potent that the gods themselves must respond.

In Haiti the different Afro-American cults have their sets of two or three drums; the *loa petro* cult employs two truncoconical drums with cord bracings, played with the flat of the hand (cf. the Afro-Bahian tradition mentioned above); the *congo* cult set comprises three cylindrical double-headed drums, their heads lapped over hoops; that of intermediate size leads the ensemble, resting horizontally on a support and played with sticks. Most interesting is the manner of playing the three "Dahomey" drums of the *loa rada* cult: all three are sections of hollowed tree trunk, truncoconical, with single ox skin or goatskin head pegged and corded, their shells usually painted. The largest of the set, over 1 meter (40 inches) tall, is played with one bare hand and a wooden, hammer-shaped beater, either on the membrane or on the shell, by a standing or sitting player, with the drum tilted toward him; the second drum is held between a seated player's knees and beaten either with both palms, or with the left hand and a forked or crozier-shaped stick; finally, the third drum, always in a vertical position, is struck with two sticks. This ensemble is completed by the ritual bell *ogùn*.

"TALKING" DRUMS

The problem of transmitting information with greater speed than can be conveyed by messenger has preoccupied populations both in the technological era and prior thereto. Classical examples that come to mind are the employment of carrier pigeons among literate peoples and of smoke signals by the nonliterate Amerinds. On Gomera, one of the Canary Islands, the art of conveying speech by whistling has been developed, the Gomerans having learned it, according to tradition, from the aboriginal Guanches, who are now extinct. By using their lips, tongues, and oral cavities much as they would in normal speech, and by introducing two fingers into their mouth, Gomerans are able to produce sounds that closely imitate Spanish speech, notably its tones and rhythms. By such means they can carry on a dialogue over greater distances than ordinary conversation would permit. Mountain goatherds in particular are said to be expert at this form of communication. This method of speech whistling was reported already by Jean de Béthencourt, conqueror of the Canary Islands in 1402.

A somewhat comparable means of communication exists in the portion of West Africa known as the "Bend"; there, messages are conveyed by "talking" drums over distances reportedly as great as twenty miles, where they may be relayed by another drummer. As in Gomera, there can be no question of a code: the languages of the messages to be transmitted are characterized by pronounced high- and low-pitched tones, a quality skillfully exploited by the drummer. Two drums are essential for the sending of messages, a lower-pitched (male) and a higher-pitched (female) variety. Accent, number, and pitch of the syllables are drummed. To a person unfamiliar with the language in which the messages are conveyed, such drumming is merely a jumble of confused noise, as tonal patterns and rhythms must be recognized before any meaning can be discerned. The Ashanti place a small piece of iron called *akasa* on the head of their male drum; this creates an additional jingling and gives rise to discordant sounds, possibly suggesting consonants.

The Ashanti have several "talking" drums, principal among which is the *atumpani* (pl., *ntumpani*); only chieftains may possess them. The trees from which they are to be made must be felled ritually; the trunk is then hollowed, its final shape being that of a barrel on a cylindrical base. Membranes are always made of elephant ears, tied on "like jam pot covers," to quote Rattray (1923); they are laced to wooden pegs driven into the body and then tuned. Two natural branches with shoots forming an acute angle serve as drumsticks. This type of "talking" drum is tilted on wooden supports and positioned with the male drum to the standing player's left. Another Ashanti "talking" drum, the *fontomfrom*, serves only for the sounding of drum proverbs. Each drum of a pair has its own drummer, who engages in a sort of duet with his colleague.

Among the Yoruba, mixed sets of tubular drums and of kettledrums are employed both as "talking" drums and in their more customary role of musical instruments. The more common combination, called *dundun*, comprises four hourglass drums and a kettledrum; the leather lacings of the former are gripped firmly by the player to raise the pitch, while playing them with a hooked stick, the blunted end of which—not the curve—strikes the head; they are held under the left arm, suspended by a band from the player's shoulder, with head facing forward. The most important *dundun* drum is the *lya-ilu* ("mother of drums"), which has the range of an octave; not only does it produce the tones, but it also renders the glides of the Yoruba language by manipulation of its lacings. The small kettledrum of the ensemble is also suspended from the player's neck by a strap and struck with a leather beater held in each hand.

Another set of "talking" drums is composed of three *bata*, double-headed conical drums of different sizes, plus two small kettledrums, all having applications of tuning paste on their playing surfaces. The *bata* hangs horizontally from its player's neck so that both heads can be played;

by virtue of the conicity these have different pitches. Sometimes they are played with bare hands, at other times with beaters. Having fixed pitches, these drums are, of course, not capable of reproducing glides.

DRUM CHIMES

Sets of drums tuned to a musical scale are found on two continents, Asia and Africa. On both they occur in areas where xylophones are also played, and investigators are beginning to consider a possible similarity of patterns between drum chimes and the chimes of xylophone keys. Moreover, the fact that drum chimes occur only in Southeast Asia and in Africa tends to confirm the probability (discussed in connection with xylophones) that the African chime is an importation from Southeast Asia and, more specifically, Burma.

Burma and neighboring Thailand have very similar chimes, composed of from sixteen to twenty-four drums; made of wood, they are barrel-shaped, the heads are tensed by lacings, and, in addition, tuning paste is applied to the played head. All the drums of a chime are suspended in a low, circular wooden frame or pen, often elaborately carved, with an opening to admit the single performer. The smallest drum is to the right of this entrance, the largest to the left. The player uses both his fingers and his palms, occasionally also a stick. Such chimes form part of the theater orchestra, and are even played in processions when the cumbersome frame containing the drums is carried by two men, with the player walking along in the center.

The Toba Bataks of southern Nias have drum chimes tuned according to a scale found in Java (some of the Nias drums are made locally, others are imported from Java); these are played with beaters. Of Nias it may be noted that, although the north lost its indigenous culture as a result of rigorous Christianizing, a highly interesting native musical culture survives in the south.

Drum chimes of Africa have royal status: the *entenga*, largest of the chimes known in Uganda, was traditionally played only at the court of the *kabaka*, and only he might own one. The fifteen drums of an *entenga* require six musicians to play them; twelve of the drums, permanently combined pairwise, are attached to a horizontal beam, the smallest on the left, with heads tilted toward four crouching players, who strike them with long and very thin curved sticks; the reach of these players overlaps. The three remaining drums are large enough to be played standing, and are also struck with beaters. A smaller chime of the Bugwere of Uganda is now gradually replacing their *entala* xylophone, and the Lango, also of Uganda, possess a seven-drum chime, six components of which are sounded by a single performer, the last by a second. East African drum chimes must not be confused with the batteries of "talking" drums found on the west coast "Bend"; the two differ fundamentally in that the drums of a true chime are tuned to a series of musical intervals, and a whole range of pitches is controlled by one performer—the chief performer, not necessarily the only one—whereas the elements of a "talking" drum battery are not so tuned, and generally each drummer manipulates but a single drum.

With the craze of nineteenth-century Europe for playing every conceivable kind of music from a keyboard, even the drum, ill adapted for this purpose though it might be, was not spared, and the tambourine was transformed into a mechanical drum chime. In 1841 Paul-Joseph Sormani of Paris patented his *piano basque*, actually a set of tambourines, each of which was provided with two drumsticks worked from a keyboard. As each drumstick was linked to a separate key, the manual required two keys for every pitch. No compass was specified in the patent, where it is merely mentioned that thirteen tambourines were necessary for a chromatic octave. Six years later Nunns and Fisher of New York patented a piano with a set of chromatically tuned kettledrums, but such experiments are now fortunately forgotten.

KETTLEDRUMS

Drums with bodies in form of hemispheric or ovate bowls or basins are termed kettledrums, and very shallow specimens are also known as bowl drums; they have definite pitch, the quality and evenness of which depend upon the membrane.

Kettledrums are found on all continents and in the Pacific. Those of Europe, Asia, and Africa originated in western Asia, while the bowl drums of the Americas and the Pacific may be presumed to be autochthonous to one or the other of these regions (the direction of influence between South America and the Pacific has not yet been established). Those of the Old World cannot lay claim to great antiquity, according to Sachs, who saw the earliest record of their existence in a Persian relief at Taq i-Bustan of about A.D. 600, on which a bowl drum is represented, struck with one or perhaps two sticks; it may have corresponded to the contemporaneous *tās*. The larger type does not appear until the twelfth century—again, according to Sachs—when it is shown on Mesopotamian miniatures; it is first seen as flat bottomed like a pot drum, rather than rounded. From such evidence Sachs concluded that kettledrums were originally a primitive form of clay drum, an assumption that seems to be borne out by the fact that even today Oriental kettledrums are more frequently made of clay than of metal, and that Amerind bowl drums are also of clay.

Eastern kettledrums are differentiated from those designed for European military and art music in that heads of the former are secured by braces, while those of the latter are provided with tension screws.

Both types, the large and the small, were propagated by Islam, westward to the Near East, Europe, and Africa, eastward to the Indian subcontinent, and down to Malaya. From India to Africa and Europe, certain common features are shared: (1) kettledrums are emblems of royalty; (2) they are associated with (royal) trumpets; and (3) small kettledrums are always, larger ones often, played in pairs.

Throughout the Orient, a player has two kettledrums tuned a fourth or a fifth apart; in Africa they are even kept in pairs when they form part of a larger set, in which case they are tied together pairwise (see drum chimes, page 158). Furthermore, African royal drums are distinguished by always being beaten with sticks, although kettledrums played in popular performances may be played with bare hands. A parallel distinction is made on the Indian subcontinent, where drums are generally beaten with the hands, but the large metal kettledrum mounted on elephant or camel back in processions or in battle is struck with sticks. The same remark is valid for the Ethiopian highland *nagarit*.

The reasons why kettledrums were emblems of royalty, why they were associated with (royal) trumpets, and why they have traditionally been played in pairs have not yet been fully elucidated; and, mutatis mutandis, the same questions concern the trumpets. A cult origin doubtless furnishes at least partial answers, and may be postulated for the gemination of kettledrums and trumpets that Islamic culture transmitted to the West, documented for close to a millennium. However, it is likely that the tradition is considerably older, and that Moslem invaders may have encountered it in similar combinations during the course of their Asian conquests (in India perhaps?), for certain archaic or static societies still employ drum and lip-vibrated aerophone duos in shamanic and tantric

ceremonies. Among the Lolo of the South China border area, the shaman still recites prayers to the sounds of drum and horn for the guidance
of a dead man on his journey to the other world, and a dance forming
part of a Tibetan tantric rite is accompanied by a drum made of human
skulls and a trumpet of a human femur. Quite possibly, a derivation from
hide and horns of the sacred bull will ultimately be traced.

The assertion frequently made to the effect that kettledrums are always
played in pairs is, however, inaccurate, for the large type, from India to
Russia, has historically remained a single instrument, and only the small
version is invariably paired.

KETTLEDRUMS IN ASIA

The Persian, Kurdish, and Arabic name for kettledrums is *naqqāra*.
Specifically, this denotes a pair of copper-shelled instruments, ancestors
of the large kettledrum that gained acceptance in Europe at court and
with the cavalry. (In Iran today they are made of pottery.) But the cognate *naqqāra* designates a different type, the smaller, paired kettledrum
of wood or metal that has been in use since the Middle Ages in Turkey,
Egypt, and Syria, carried on horseback or camelback, one to either side
of the rider, and beaten with a stick, with the higher pitched of the two
placed to the rider's left. In Turkey, where it is retained both in military
and civilian use, the *naqqāra* may also be played singly, in which case it
is held in the left hand or suspended from the neck.

This is the instrument that spread to Europe during the Crusades, and
also to India by way of the Islamic trade route. Some idea of its importance and diffusion may be gathered from a few of its etymological derivatives: the French *anacaire* and *nacaire*, which gave rise to the English
"naker," the Spanish *nacara*, and Italian *nacchera* together with its augmentative, *naccherone*; the obsolete *nakri* of Russia and Yugoslavia; the
na'ra of Turkish Gypsies; the *nuqairat* of North African Berbers and of
Syria; the potbellied *naqāra*, now a Punjabi toy; the *naguar* of southern
India; and the *nagarit* of Ethiopia. *Nagarits* in particular have been symbols
of power for many a century; those belonging to princes have traditionally
had shells of silver, those of high officials of copper, while those permitted
lesser personages had shells of wood. Up to the time of the Ethiopian war
with Italy, Emperor Haile Selassie maintained a band of four hundred
nagarits. Despite its martial origin, the *nagarit* has now found its way into
the Ethiopian church and has also been taken over—as a symbol of power

—by the neighboring Galla and Somali peoples. Modern Ethiopian *nagarits* are of metal, extremely shallow, with a ratio of diameter to depth of three to one at least; they are always played with sticks, never with bare hands.

Large kettle and smaller bowl drums are played all over the Indian subcontinent, made of silver, copper, brass, wood, or clay, their heads laced, some played with bare hands, others with sticks, the lower pitched of a pair placed to the performer's left. A very large Arabic kettledrum called *naubat* gave its name to the *nabat* of Russia, and also to the largest of Indian kettledrums (variants are *nobut*, *nahabat*); these may attain a diameter of 1½ meters (5 feet); a pair is mounted on elephantback, each drum having its own player who strikes it with a silver stick, while the *sutri nahabat* are mounted on camelback, both drums played by the same drummer. A seventeenth-century *naubat khana* (royal band), actually a drum and trumpet ensemble, is portrayed in a painting of the period: to the left of a row of drummers, a standing player raises his bare fists high over his head to bring them down on a single large kettledrum; two musicians next to him, seated in Oriental fashion, belabor their pairs of kettledrums alternately with one bare hand and a stick; to the right of a central player are three more kettledrummers holding two sticks each. All drumsticks are straight, and the kettledrums forming a pair are in each case tilted toward one another; the trumpeters are seen standing behind the drummers. Contemporary with this painting is a description of the luxuriant participation of large brass kettledrums at a Moslem festival in Turkey, when eighty kettledrums were carried in procession on forty white camels.

From a martial and ceremonial instrument, the kettledrum finally succeeded in entering the realm of art music and in participating in true musical ensembles in the East. In the Caucasus, for instance, among *sazanda* ensembles, the leader—a singer—accompanies himself on a frame drum, joined by a spike fiddle, long-necked lute, shawm, and kettledrums; and in Turkey classical vocal monody is accompanied by a kettledrum struck either in the center of its head or close to the rim, depending upon whether clear or muffled sounds are desired.

KETTLEDRUMS IN AFRICA

Phonetically, at least, Islamic kettledrums can be followed as far south as Nigeria; the Hausa of Socotra play a *tambari*, both name and instrument being derived from the Arabic *tabl*. Kettledrums of Negro Africa are royal, ritual, or ceremonial; instead of metal or clay resonators they utilize wood or even basketry, and thus, unlike their Asian counterparts, the heads are sometimes nailed and the resonator can be sculptured or provided with monoxylous handles. Frequently a solid block of wood is hollowed out to form the shell. The traditional gemination of kettledrum and trumpet extends to south of Zaire: the two are combined at funerals and at public festivities in the San Salvador region of Angola.

African drums in general are notorious for their multiplicity of forms, some conditioned by the materials from which they are made, as a more or less conical tree trunk, for example, leads to an overlap of forms that cannot be pigeonholed into the convenient Western classifications of drums. This applies also to kettledrums; they are found as oversized, flat-bottomed bowls, made of basketry or wood, or as cylindroconical wooden vessels with flat bases, a form also known to Neolithic Europe, and in many shapes approaching the ovoid and the hemisphere; in East Africa (apart from Ethiopia) a blending of form and function suggests native forms in the service of originally foreign functions, probably due to the indirect influence of Islam. Furthermore, lacing patterns are extremely varied.

KETTLEDRUMS IN EUROPE

When kettledrums were introduced to Europe from the Islamic world, their well-established traditions were inherited: the smaller sizes continued to be played in pairs, and they were coupled with trumpets.

Their route of travel was twofold, the earlier, concerning which too little is known, led through the Eastern empire to eastern Europe. Already in the eleventh century kettledrums were known in Russia, and in 1216 the royal standards, trumpets, and kettledrums of troops are listed there as though they formed a unit: the military tradition had also been inherited. Three centuries later, in 1557, shipmaster Anthony Jenkins reported that the Russians "use little drummes at their sadle bowes, by the sound whereof their horses use to runne more swiftly." In addition to such smaller paired instruments, the Russians also made use of single "drummes of a huge bignesse" set on a board laid on four horses and played by eight drummers, according to the sixteenth-century traveler Dr. Giles Fletcher (quoted by Bessaraboff, 1941). A single large drum called *tulumbaz*, carried on horseback, was primarily a hawking drum;

it was struck with a single *voshaga*, a small wooden ball affixed to a leather strap that in turn was attached to a handle—a barely modified Oriental beater. The word *tulumbaz* is Turkish, composed of *tulum* ("bag") and *baz* ("hawk"); as *talambasi* it denotes very small kettledrums of Yugoslavia, now obsolete, a pair of which were carried on horseback to either side of the saddle, their diameter no more than 20 centimeters (8 inches). Both are closely related to the Near Eastern metal *tabli bāz*, hawking kettledrums known in Turkey from the seventeenth century on and still played there and in Egypt; a pair of the very small models is beaten with a strap. As *daulbas* the term describes the small Bosnian and Serbian copper kettledrum, still in use, its thick leather membrane beaten with two leather straps attached to the shell. Rather curiously, the word turns up at the other end of Europe, in Gerona, Spain, as *trampes* (*r* is interchangeable with *l*), a pair of kettledrums mounted on horseback; the singular form of the noun does not exist. So much for the etymological excursus.

To return to Russia: the large *nabat* referred to above was a signal instrument, serving instead of an alarm bell; Bessaraboff (1941) relates that, within his time, fire alarms in Russia were sounded by a bell called *nabatniy kolokol* ("kettledrum bell") and that the bell ringer was instructed to "beat the *nabat*."

Kettledrums remained unknown in western Europe until the crusaders encountered the small variety in the East, probably in the late twelfth century, as some time prior to 1216, when he was last known to be alive, the crusader Robert de Clari related in his memoirs that, at the crusaders' departure from Venice in 1202, one hundred pairs of *buisines* were sounded together with *timbres et tabours* and other unspecified instruments; furthermore, the Doge's galley was preceded by four silver *buisines* and *timbres, qui grant joie demenoient* ("that expressed great joy"). Here the word *timbre* (from the Latin *tympanum*, "drum") is obviously used in the sense of kettledrum, and may perhaps be compared with the passage from Jean de Meung's *Roman de la rose* of around 1280:

> Par toneire et par esparz
> Qui tabourent, timbrent et trompent

where thunder and lightning are compared to drumming, kettledrumming (?), and trumpeting.

The term *anacaire* had probably given birth to *nacaire* by the time Joinville wrote his *Histoire de Saint Louis*, completed in 1309 (all surviving manuscripts of this work are of a considerably later date); in it he described the great noise of *nacaires, tabours,* and *cor sarrazinois* made by the enemy at Damietta in 1249. This was the small form of geminated kettledrum. (The larger basins were not recorded in western Europe until the fifteenth century.) It is tempting to see a kettledrum in the *tabor* of the *Chanson de Roland* (ca. 1100) rather than a cylinder drum; the term is used twice, each time as an instrument in the hands of the pagan enemy.

The township of Siena employed trumpet, shawm, and *nacchere* (kettledrums) players in the second half of the thirteenth century, and in England "Janino *le nakerer*" figured among Edward I's minstrels, while the court minstrels of Louis of Navarre (1305–1316) included two trumpets and "Michelet *des naquaires.*" The combination of drums, kettledrums, and trumpets is clearly recorded in 1314 by Guillaume Guiart who writes of *tabours, trompes, et anacaires.*

At this period the instruments were small hand drums, usually seen suspended by a strap from the player's waist or shoulder, one straight stick in each hand, although occasionally, as in the early fourteenth-century Luttrell Psalter, curved ("crozier") sticks are depicted. Despite their essentially military character they are also seen in the hands of female angels—for angels were still sexed *in illo tempore*—sometimes furnished with a snare. Jean de Gerson (1362–1429) appears to have been the first to corroborate the fact that the twin drums—he calls them *tympanula*—were at different pitches, one with a dull, the other with a very bright sound. But although small nakers were coupled with trumpets, they are seen in paintings of the period together with other instruments, even in groups that might be devoid of trumpets. Not until the second half of the fourteenth century do kettledrums appear that are too large to be attached to the player; instead, they are placed on a stand. During this and the following century the small type remained in use but disappeared completely toward the end of the fifteenth century, except in those areas already mentioned and in Provence, where little *tymbalons* with diameters about equal to their depth, 20 centimeters (8 inches) or so, are still suspended in medieval fashion from their players' waists.

The earliest recorded appearance of the great horse-borne kettledrums in western Europe dates from 1457, when Ladislas of Hungary sent an impressive embassy to France, his envoys accompanied by "drums like great kettles carried on horseback," the great metal drums of the Ottoman Turks. Thirty-five years later, the emperor Maximilian gave the good people of Metz an opportunity to marvel at his enormous copper drums. By the turn of the sixteenth century this large model shows up in Germany as *Heerpauke* ("army drum"). Virdung (1511) depicts an amazingly modern form, complete with hoops and screws; these two items distinguish the European from the Eastern kettledrum, but screws did not become common until the end of the sixteenth century. At a joust at Valladolid in 1517, held in the presence of Emperor Charles V, massed groups of twelve and twenty *ataballes* were mounted on muleback *menant grant bruyt* ("making a great noise"), but their size is not indicated. Their arrival in England was late; Henry VIII ordered from Vienna kettledrums "after the Hungarian manner" in 1542, and they were still new enough to be called "drummes made of kettylles" in 1554, and did not take their present name until about 1600.

Kettledrums formed part of the band welcoming the French bride of Philip II of Spain at the Spanish border in 1559 with music for *cornets, haultbois, trompettes, tabartz, qui sont tabourins à cheval à la moresque, comme les avoit le duc de Saxe au camp dernier de France* ("cornetts, shawms, trumpets, *tabartz*, which are Moorish-type horseborne drums like those of the Duke of Saxony at the last French camp"). The frequent early references to the clamor of kettledrums are doubtless based on the manner of playing at the time, which can perhaps be resuscitated by modern comparison: Powne (1968) recounts that the kettledrums at Emperor Haile Selassie's silver jubilee in 1955 were not beaten rhythmically in unison, but rather they created a large volume of sound, alternating with that of the trumpets. Thoinot Arbeau (1589) still writes of the *tambour des Perses* and gives it a diameter of some 2½ feet. (This would be about the size of the deep-bodied drums drawn by Leonardo da Vinci as studies for automatic kettledrums.) One only, not a pair, was carried on horseback by "certain Germans," he states.

Following the Hungarian fashion—taken in turn from the Arabs—of carrying a kettledrum slung on either side of the saddle, European noblemen kept mounted kettledrummers to support their trumpeters. Trumpeters and kettledrummers enjoyed a privileged position among the musicians of Europe; both belonged to the same guild, and their sphere of action was restricted to court and to the military (for further details, see trumpets, page 794). In these circles pomp was an indispensable prerequisite; not only were horses and drums elaborately decorated, but the drummers adopted and improved upon the already exaggerated motions of Turkish military kettledrummers, whose arms were flung high above their heads when playing. Originally the large instruments were played with the same knobbed sticks that the Turks were using, but in the late seventeenth century the knob was transformed into a small disk called a rosette; the entire drumstick measured less than 25 centimeters (10 inches). This type remained in use throughout the eighteenth century.

By the last quarter of the seventeenth century kettledrums came to be considered as possible orchestral instruments, and less martial playing techniques are first heard of: Speer (1687) comments that echo effects could be obtained by playing softly close to the rim and then striking hard near the center. For orchestral use the timpani, as they then came to be called, were placed on tripod metal stands (known, in German, as Spanish riders). Up to Speer's time the secrecy enjoined upon guild members had prevented music for trumpets and kettledrums from being written down— it had been memorized and freely improvised upon where necessary— but from then on the orchestral parts were notated. The smaller of the two drums was tuned to C°, the larger to G' (i.e., to tonic and lower dominant of the trumpet); the C drum was placed to the left of the G drum.

Lully was the first to admit *hautbois*, trumpets, drums, and kettledrums to the opera and even into church music, according to Titon du Tillet (1727); thus the French would have been the first to take advantage of the added sonorities these instruments could provide. For the year 1713, Laborde (1780) records a *timbalier* (kettledrummer) among the personnel of the Paris opera—but no trumpeter. In 1687, five years after Lully's death, Purcell scored for kettledrums in *The Fairy Queen*. Extended use of the kettledrum became more general in the eighteenth century; Majer (1732) writes of their participation in the field, in church, and in opera, as well as at "solemnities." For funerals they could be muffled by draping the heads in a cloth, or the drumsticks could be covered with chamois. Several authors recommend treating a new drumhead with a brandy and garlic mixture—a prescription frequently advocated at the time for rendering wooden organ pipes wormproof.

On the European continent, trumpets were considered to be at choir pitch, and consequently kettledrums were also; Altenburg states in 1795 that the larger drum was said to be in G, despite the fact that it was often tuned to A, and the smaller C drum was then tuned a tone higher to D. The need for timpani at different pitches, or for means of retuning them, became increasingly greater as writing for the instruments became freer, leading in the eighteenth century to different forms of machine drum.

Today both the hand-tuned and the machine drum are played; both have hemispheric shells of copper or of brass, with calfskin head adjustable as to tension; on both types the head is stretched over a hoop, that of the hand drum made of wood with a metal counter-hoop fitted over it.

Hand-drum heads are tightened by working a number of handles disposed around the circumference, each of which turns a large screw. Machine drums were invented to render the turning of so many screws unnecessary, and are provided with a mechanical device for tuning them all simultaneously. Three systems are in current use: (1) pedal drums, (2) drums tuned by a single handle, and (3) drums that rotate on a stand. A device that acted on all screws simultaneously was invented in 1812 by Gerhard Cramer of Munich, and in 1821 J. C. N. Stumpff of Amsterdam discovered a means for tuning the drum itself, without recourse to screws. Pedal drums are furnished with a single pedal that turns a central tuning screw; the farther the pedal is depressed, the higher the pitch is raised. The pedal drum was a mid-nineteenth-century invention, and led to further experimentation; in an attempt to satisfy the pitch requirements of the modern orchestra, a French inventor patented, before 1855, a series of eight pedal drums tuned to a diatonic scale (cf. drum chimes, page 159). The fertile brain of Adolphe Sax produced in 1857 the *timbales-chromatiques*, a series of shell-less "kettledrums," each consisting of two concentric metal hoops, reminiscent of an embroidery frame, with a supporting cross member and a membrane. Tuned to the diatonic scale, they were superposed so as to save space, and could furthermore be tilted as desired. According to Pontécoulant, Sax based his timpani experiments on the physicist Félix Savart's observations of vibrating membranes; in 1855 he also brought out a *trompette-timbale*.

Today the problem of pitch has been solved by employing two or sometimes three timpani able to span an octave between them; if two are used, one is pitched in F and can be tuned to any pitch between $F°$ and $c°$, and the other, in B♭, can be tuned from $B♭°$ to $f°$. The old cavalry drum disposition with the smaller drum to the left has been reversed—it now stands to the right.

Drumsticks for timpani were in former centuries of flexible material terminating in a hard ball or head, like those of their Oriental precursors. Flexible straps were replaced by increasingly stiffer materials, and the head was made of wood. Casings of chamois leather were fitted over the heads when a muffled tone was desired, as at funerals, and as long as the chief use of kettledrums was in military music, such relatively crude contrivances sufficed. But an outcry from Berlioz condemning the unmusical character of timpani sticks brought about reform, and sticks were henceforth made of whalebone, wood, or metal, those of whalebone being declared best. The head of the stick was transformed into a wooden disk covered with hide, felt, or sponge, depending upon the degree of firmness required. Today's timpanist makes use of several pairs of drumsticks of variable weight, with heads of different degrees of hardness, varying from felt or lamb's wool to wood or even ivory; sometimes a composer will specify the type of stick he wishes to be used.

FRICTION DRUMS

The membrane of a drum can be sounded not only by percussion but also by friction, and this can be accomplished in a variety of manners. Sometimes the skin is rubbed with a piece of hide, as in Africa, or by the more general means of a stick or a cord passed through the membrane. Such drums are found in Europe, parts of Asia, Africa, the Americas, and the Pacific (Hawaii), and great ingenuity is displayed by some of their users. In many countries they are or were a folk instrument; in parts of Europe and in India they have degenerated into a child's toy. Elsewhere they assume the function of a ritual instrument, and in Europe are thought to have been originally pagan cult instruments.

In its simplest form the friction drum is merely a wooden bucket or clay pot with the top left open and the bottom closed by a membrane. A small hole is pierced in the center of the membrane and a wooden stick is inserted; the stick is then either alternately pulled up and pushed down again, or it is rubbed with the player's wet fingers, in each case causing the skin to vibrate. Sometimes the stick is replaced by a friction cord or by other material. Acoustically these instruments are subject to the same laws as other membranophones, but, in addition, friction drums are influenced by the speed with which the stick or cord is made to vibrate and to pass its vibrations on to the membrane; the pressure of the player's fingers modifies this speed of vibration so greatly that sounds produced by a given friction drum may vary by as much as a fourth.

The late twelfth-century sculptures of the Archbishop's Palace at Santiago de Compostela clearly show a friction drum with rod, yet Mersenne was the first author to mention it in Europe, and he took it for a non-European instrument. His contemporary, Jan Molenaer's, painting of children making music (1629) testifies to its popularity in his day—it forms an ensemble with a violin and a helmet used as a percussion pot; Frans Hals's and Abraham Bloemaert's *rommelpot* players—the latter is holding a carnival instrument—both date from the same period. More recently, the *rommelpot* of Flanders was played at Christmas, New Year's, and Epiphany; three singers, one holding a *rommelpot*, wandered through the countryside singing and playing at farmhouses for a few pennies—a custom that was discontinued after the First World War. Up to about 1875 a *rommelpot* traditionally accompanied Christmas carols. Made of wood or clay, it sometimes contained water and it had a membrane made of an animal bladder, the "stick" often a straw rubbed between wetted fingers; but in neighboring Frisia the *rummelpot* was merely a child's toy.

Carol singers of Bohemia still play a friction drum, holding it between their knees and stroking its horsehair cord with wet fingers, and the Polish *buk* is also played only at Christmas. Formerly, the Provençal *pignato* was played on Ash Wednesday; and in Naples the friction drum is, or until quite recently was, played at carnival time, as it was formerly also in Austria, where it was formed by covering a clay pot with a pig's bladder; in Slovenia one served as bass accompaniment to the mouth organ up to the First World War. The Romanian *buchaĭŭ*, meaning "bull," is made of a watering can and is said to roar like a bull (as is also the *brau* of Aveyron, France); in Moldavia and Walachia, the "bull" was combined with a flute to greet the New Year. The "jackdaw" of Lincolnshire was obviously milder, and Andalusia had its "cricket" (*chicarra*). Mahillon relates that hawkers used to sell a toy they called *cri de la belle-mère* ("mother-in-law's scream"), made of a tin can, which was nothing but a friction drum. These descriptions could be continued, but should suffice to show the wide distribution of friction drums in Europe as folk instruments.

But, if the European friction drum is often likened to a bull, that of Africa is said to resemble a leopard. Such is the *dingwinti* (from *kwinta*, Kongo for "to roar like a leopard") of the Bwende and Sundi of the Lower Congo, formerly a ritual instrument exclusively, now increasingly a secular one, and the "village leopard" of the Bapende of the same region, with its friction stick of palm-leaf rib rubbed with a handful of grass or leaves, and played only during secret society initiations or at the death of members. The pattern of ritual use is manifest again among the Mamvu and the Mambutu of Zaire, among whom it is exclusively a man's instrument; women are not permitted to see it under penalty of stillbirth. By contrast, among the Pedi of South Africa only old women play it, but then only during the initiation of young girls.

A friction drum of Venezuela is made of a small barrel over which a piece of leather is stretched, then perforated in the center to admit a friction stick.

A modification of the friction drum is the whirled friction drum, an implement whirled through the air by means of a cord (not to be confused with the buzzer, page 551). The friction drum usually consists of a cardboard box, at least in Europe; its cord is rosined, and the pitch rises with the increase in speed of the whirling; the sound is said to be loud but not very musical. The hummer, known in Coventry up to the nineteenth century, was made of paper and a thread; it migrated to the New World, where it was sold in Philadelphia in the early nineteenth century under the name of locust, sometimes with a tin cylinder body. Its German equivalent, the *Waldteufel* ("forest devil"), was held by a stick to which the friction cord—a horsehair string—was attached; in France the same instrument is known as *diable des bois*, also "forest devil." Similar contrivances are found as far east as Russia. They are also played in southern India and in Hawaii, where a large hollow nut or calabash is furnished with a friction cord.

MIRLITONS

"Mirliton" is the collective French name for a group of musical auxiliaries, rather than true musical instruments, membranophones that modify the sound of the human voice or of a musical instrument. The sympathetic vibrations of the membrane act as amplifiers and color the tone with a buzzing nasal timbre. The membrane may be free, as it is in the familiar comb-and-paper combination played by generations of children (Buonanni depicted it in 1722), when it is called a free mirliton, or it may be stretched across the aperture of a tube or vessel, in which case it is termed tube or vessel mirliton. Membranes are most frequently of parchment or paper, and were formerly also made of onion skin, that is, the skin of an onion—not the paper of that name; in Africa spider-egg tissue is a material of choice. If it is the human voice that is to be modified, this is either directed against the membrane, thereby setting it in vibration (see also frame drums, page 141), or the membrane is held against the player's throat; to modify the timbre of an instrument, the vibrating air column of a sounding tube is directed against the membrane.

Tube mirlitons have been known in Europe since the sixteenth century, and possibly earlier; Gérold (1932) has suggested that Machaut's *flûte brehaigne* is to be interpreted literally, that is, as sterile flute, rather than as a derivation of Behaigne, Bohemia, which would place the mirliton in Europe considerably earlier. In form the mirlitons resembled flutes, shawms, or other instruments, and were generally furnished with a parchment membrane. Sir Francis Bacon was probably referring to a mirliton when he wrote in his *Sylva sylvarum:* "If you sing into the hole of a drum, it maketh the singing more sweet. And I conceive it would, if it were a song in parts sung into several drums. . . ." Mersenne describes and illustrates the onion-skin flute, or eunuch flute, as it was also called then (cf. *flûte brehaigne*), with its slightly flared open bell, upper end closed by a membrane, and a removable cap set over the top to protect the delicate tissue; pierced in the wall of the tube was a mouthhole into which the performer directed his voice. Mersenne refers to the membrane top as a "little drum," and his statement that four- and five-part music was performed with these instruments tends to confirm the notion that Bacon's part singing into "several drums" may indeed have referred to the mirliton. Sometimes the structure of a woodwind instrument was imitated to the point of adding simulated or real "fingerholes," which of course had no effect on the pitch, as the latter was entirely dependent on the player's voice.

Possibly inspired by Asiatic flutes furnished with an added mirliton membrane, Malcolm McGregor of London patented in 1810 his *flauto di voce*, a mirliton in form of an alto flute with a large hole in the second body joint covered by a thin mirliton, and by the middle of the century mirlitons were played as toys in most of Europe. A French toy maker named Bigot brought out from 1883 on a bigotphone, or bigophone, as it is also spelled, a zinc reproduction of several orchestral instruments, with mouthhole covered by tissue paper. As late as 1910, gatherings of enthusiastic "bigotphonists" were held in Paris, later to be spoofed in a delightful passage of André Malraux's *Lunes en papier*. In the 1920s, the *varinette* was another popular mirliton, and wooden or cardboard toys with membrane-covered apertures were sold under a multiplicity of names, some Anglo-American terms being bazoo, hewgag, kazoo, tommy talker, zarah. As a toy it is still encountered, and as a folk instrument it continues in existence among the mountain populations of Switzerland

and Austria. The *Flatsche* of Carinthia, for example, is made of very thin bark held taut in front of a humming or singing performer's mouth, and such natural material may well have led to the more developed mirlitons.

Outside Europe this device is primarily a means of obtaining a characteristic timbre on musical instruments played in normal fashion; thus in East and Southeast Asia many woodwinds have a lateral hole covered by a membrane in addition to the regular blowhole or reed, and in Burma even horns are so provided. The Chinese *ti*, a cross flute of lacquered bamboo that originated as an endblown flute, has a membrane-covered aperture in its wall between blowhole and fingerholes, and its Japanese counterpart, the *sei teki*, has a similar arrangement. A double flute of Java, made of a bamboo section with interior node, has both ends covered by a thin membrane and an oval mouthhole pierced close to each end.

African mirlitons are frequently very imaginative: the Fan of Gabon, for instance, make theirs from a section of cane closed at one end by a spider-egg membrane, and insert it into one nostril in the manner of a nose flute; they also make other mirlitons out of small wooden boxes, while the Lango and Madi of Uganda make theirs of elongated gourds. But mirlitons in Africa are noted chiefly for their connection with xylophones, as their xylophone resonators commonly have an aperture pierced in the bottom or the side that is then covered by a delicate spider-egg membrane.

An entirely different application of the mirliton principle is encountered in India, where the *nyastaranga*, or throat trumpet, is a tube mirliton in the form of a short brass trumpet, with a membrane located just below the cup mouthpiece; when such trumpets are applied, always pairwise, against the vocal chords of a humming performer they impart their vibrations to the air column inside the tube; the resultant tone is said to sound very like that of a reed instrument.

During the 1950s a technique probably derived from the *nyastaranga* was evolved in the United States for the recording of anthropomorphic effects, whereby certain objects, such as train whistles, organs, and so on, were made to "talk"; an amorphous and sustained musical chord was generated, usually by an electronic organ, while a girl held a device like a microphone to her larynx and then mouthed the words to be "spoken," but without uttering any sound; the generated tone and the vibrations picked up by the device were then mixed. Although popular for a time for the recording of "commercials," it proved too monotonous to be anything but short lived.

Part Three

CHORDOPHONES

ZITHERS

A zither in the wider, organological sense of the word is any simple (i.e., not composite) chordophone, consisting as such of a string bearer. Any other appurtenance, such as a resonator, must be an accessory, so that if removed it will not destroy the sound-producing apparatus. In a more restricted sense, the term "zither" is applied to an Alpine folk instrument. Zithers in the broader sense comprise a whole gamut of instruments, ranging from the primitive ground zither and the musical bow to the highly complex piano (which is a developed box zither).

GROUND ZITHERS

Stretch a cord horizontally between two short, upright posts, beat it with a stick or two, and you have an elementary—and probably the oldest—form of ground zither. Generally the string passes over a previously dug pit that has been covered with bark, and the bark weighted down with a stone; a second and shorter string is then attached to the original one and pegged to the bark. The role of the pit is now clear: it has become a resonator. The horizontal (long) string is struck with small sticks.

Evidence of such instruments has been found in Neolithic excavations on several continents; they are still played in Indonesia, Indochina, East Africa, and on Madagascar and Fernando Poo. Malayans make use of a cord 2 meters (6½ feet) long; they cover their pit with a palm leaf, and both strings and palm leaf are struck. On Java an earthenware jar is placed in the pit to augment the volume of sound, and in rural areas of North Vietnam it is a man's instrument exclusively; one of its uses is that of accompanying courtship songs.

In Uganda the zither string is divided into sections, not by a cord, but by being passed over a central supporting pole, and is beaten by two or more players.

Multiple ground zithers have been reported from areas as far apart as Java and Fernando Poo in the Gulf of Guinea, comprising several strings of different lengths, each with its own pit. When the string of a single or of a multiple ground zither is divided into unequal lengths by cord or pole, each section emits a different pitch when struck.

MUSICAL BOWS

Another primitive chordophone, the musical bow, is shaped exactly like a shooting bow. Opinion is still divided as to its origin: Sachs pointed to what appears to have been its earliest form, that of a bow 3 meters (10 feet) long, useless for shooting, while other investigators, including Kirby, have derived it from the shooting bow. Fusion of function has obviously occurred at different times; Kirby (1934), for instance, observed the daily use by Bushmen in South Africa of their shooting bows as musical bows, and the Damara, also of South Africa, convert their shooting bow into a musical one by the simple expedient of adding a tuning loop. The root of the word meaning "war" in Sudanic languages, *ta*, is also the root of the word for musical bow in both the Sudanic and the Bantu language families. A wall painting in the Trois Frères Caves, Arriège, dated about 15,000 B.C., depicts an object said to represent either a musical bow or a flute, but this is too tenuous an identification to be useful.

Musical bows are found in almost every part of the world except Europe: in Asia, Central and South Africa, in America from California to Patagonia, and in the Pacific—but both shooting and musical bows are unknown in Australia, a fact that weights the evidence in favor of the latter being derived from the former. In all bows, a flexible wooden stick is held under tension by a string stretched between its two ends; either the bows are plain, without a resonator of any kind, such as those still played in Assam, or they have detached resonator, such as a half gourd, pot, and so on; or else a truncated resonator of gourd, tin can, or other material may be affixed, with the open end pressed against the player's body. Finally, in a version known as the mouth bow, the player's mouth acts as a resonator. All these varieties can be held either horizontally or vertically; their string is set in vibration by tapping it with a small stick or by plucking it, or else by stroking it with a plectrum; it may even be bowed with a short bow. Longer bows are less highly curved than are shorter ones, some of the latter being bent until they are almost semicircular. Sometimes the bow is notched and the notches are scraped with a stick while the string is being tapped. At first musical bows were plucked with the fingers or tapped with a stick; later they were rubbed, and in the last stage of their development they were bowed with a second bow.

This simple instrument is amazingly versatile. Its string can be divided into two sections by means of a tuning loop, whereby two fundamentals are obtained; the player can create a third by stopping the string with the back of his finger while striking it with a stick held in the other hand. Bows with two or more strings are also encountered. Finally, several bows may be stuck upright in the ground and played together. Pitch is varied by stopping the string either with a stick or with the player's thumb and index finger; even flageolet tones can be produced by touching it very lightly. The harmonics of mouth bows can be reinforced by changing the size of the oral cavity, with the fundamental serving as a drone. Comparison with the Jew's harp (see page 97) immediately comes to mind, and indeed the two instruments have much in common. As a further refinement, breathing upon a horizontally held bow is said to impart a tremolo and to augment the volume of sound.

An ingenious bow and scraper of Mirzapur, India, is no more than a notched bamboo bow with one end placed on a basket set on the ground bottom up, the other end resting on the ground proper; when the bow is scraped it causes the basket to reverberate. Further north, among the Lebed Tatars and certain Altaic peoples the bow is an instrument of magical music in the hands of shamans, replacing the shamanist drum. Shamans of the Yurak Samoyed go as far as naming their drum "bow" or "singing bow"; like the drum, it is deemed capable of driving away evil spirits, an unusual attribute for a chordophone.

Multistringed instruments are preferred in the Pacific: New Britain, New Ireland, and eastern New Guinea had two-stringed bows, which in New Guinea might be played by women only; in New Britain the two-stringed bow became obsolete in the 1880s, when it was replaced by the Jew's harp. The Hawaiian *ukeke* had three strings originally made of sennit. After the white man's arrival the strings were made of horsehair, and later of gut; they were tuned to fundamental, third, and fifth, and plucked with the bare fingers or with a plectrum.

Musical bows are said to have reached the Americas from Africa. This

statement, however, needs qualification, as it applies only to those instruments found in parts of Central America and in the eastern coastal
regions of South America. It is doubtless true of the marimba played in
northern Colombia, which happily combines a musical bow and a scraper.
Further south, the Tehuelche Indians of Patagonia "bow" the string of
their instrument with a condor bone. And the Araucanians go further:
their *kunkulkawe*, a ritual instrument played to induce trances or mystic
exaltation, consists of two interlocking bows, the string of one bowing
that of the other. Bows of the Caingua have no resonators, but the player
hums while striking the string with a small stick. In Costa Rica and
Nicaragua a small jar sometimes serves as a resonator, in which instances
its mouth is opened more or less by the player's left hand while his right
hand taps the string with a stick.

Musical bows of the North American West are related to those of the
Pacific and of Asia and do not suggest African derivation. They can be
classified, according to Helen Roberts (1936), as (1) long single-stringed
bows held between teeth and lips, and plucked; (2) short two-stringed
bows with the player's mouth acting as a resonator; (3) single-stringed
bows with a tuning peg at one end; and (4) ceremonial instruments of
West Central Mexico with a pot or inverted gourd resonator.

But it is in Africa that the musical bow received its greatest development and that the most imaginative playing techniques evolved. The
Acoli of Uganda, for example, bend their bow into a U shape and then
lace the string through it so as to form a Z; the bottom of the U is rested
on a gourd resonator placed open side down on the player's lap; the top
section of the string is stopped by the performer's chin while all three
sections of the Z lacing are plucked. Only women may play it. A similar
technique is employed by the South African Berg Dama, who set their
bow on a block of wood that serves as the resonator, and hold the
other end of the bow in position with their chin in order to have both
hands free for playing. Here the pitch is varied by changing the string's
tension with the left hand; often a second person taps the string with
a rod. Several South African peoples add a rattling quality to the
sound by impaling on their bow a number of dried, globular fruit shells
filled with seeds or pebbles; elsewhere, metal jingles are attached to one
end of the bow. Half-gourd resonators are often pressed against the
player's chest or stomach, and the Xhosa of South Africa can modify the
bow's dynamics by displacing the gourd to a greater or lesser degree. The
Konjo of Uganda place the gourd resonator over the mouth or across

mouth and cheeks. Double bows are found in Zambia; here the Plateau Tonga combine two bows, one end steadied against the player's chest; with his left hand he plucks a drone, while the string of the right bow is stopped by his chin and plucked by his forefinger.

Two further developments must be mentioned: in South Africa the musical bow is also played as a friction instrument, one type making use of a rough stick or stalk to vibrate the string, the other of a small bow. Mouth-held bows without resonator or tuning loop are played—chiefly by young women—with stick 'or stalk in Xhosa-speaking areas of the eastern Cape, formerly also by the Zulu and Swazi. The bow is held vertically between the lips, with the player's left hand supporting its lower end, leaving only the thumb free to stop the string; but harmonics are obtained by varying the size of the oral cavity and of the tongue position. Melodies thus produced are audible up to 3 meters (10 feet) away. The second type of friction bow is held in the hand, has an empty oil can resonator on which it rests upright, and is played by Xhosa-speaking boys of the same area. Friction is produced by cowtail hair, one end secured in the notch of a bow stick, the other end sometimes left unattached; in such cases it is gripped with the fingers. The bow is moved with a circular motion, counterclockwise, with variable tension.

Finally, the musical bow impinges on the features of a blown idiophone. Described as early as 1686, the *gora* originated with the Cape and Korana Hottentots and has since been adopted by the Bushmen, Chwana, Sotho, Xhosa, and Zulu. Here the string is passed through a flattened ostrich quill tied to the bow and taken between the player's lips—but not touched by them. Quill and string are set in vibration by inhaling and exhaling sharply. By modifying the shape of the oral cavity and the force of the breath, the fifth to ninth harmonics can be obtained, while the quill, when breathed upon heavily, can be made to vibrate twice as fast as the string and thereby to provide the second harmonic or, with still heavier breath, even the third harmonic.

AEOLIAN BOWS

Musical bows can also be sounded by the wind, in which case they are known as Aeolian bows. These can be suspended from a tree, as in Indonesia; swung by the player's hand, as in Java, Malaya, and West Africa; or attached to a kite, as in China, Korea, Japan, Thailand, and parts of Indonesia.

Structurally the Aeolian bow is identical to that sounded by hand; bamboo is a favored material. The Javanese affix a bamboo bow with rattan or horsehair string to treetops or to a kite. Of the several types made by the Chinese, one formerly in use in Shanghai was actually a composite instrument of seven strings attached to as many lengths of bamboo laid parallel to one another and fixed to a frame. Attached to a paper kite, it made a loud humming sound when flown. (Not content with musical bows, the Chinese also produced musical arrows: regular arrows were provided with perforated tubular tips that sang while flying through the air.)

THE PLURIARC

The term "pluriarc" was coined by the late organologist George Montaudon to describe a West and Southwest African chordophone to which the misleading name of bowlute has also been applied. As the name suggests, the pluriarc is generally considered to be a form of multiple musical bow. The South African Bushmen stick a number of shooting bows—seven or more—upright in the sand, and a single performer then plays them to accompany a dance. Pluriarcs are believed to represent a step in the evolution of such multiple but separate bows to a conglomeration of bows in fixed state, and a comparison may be made with the traditional origins of the Japanese *wagon* (see page 195).

The pluriarc has a common resonator for all of its bows, usually a wooden box of irregular rectangular form, from the back of which rise a varying number of flexible sticks, each held under tension by a taut string attached by one end to the resonator front and by the other to the top of the stick. These bowlike projections number from two to eight and are of approximately equal length. Their strings are tuned to differences of tension, which in turn cause differing curvatures of the bows. In some areas the resonator is not even built up to form a box, but is a wooden cylinder or hollowed wooden rectangle. Pluriarcs are held horizontally, with the resonator pressed against the player's stomach, and are more often played with the bare fingers of both hands, but in parts of the Lower Congo area a plectrum is attached to the right index finger. This mode of playing recalls that of the harp lute (see page 404).

Together with other instruments, West Africans took the pluriarc with them to the New World: the Afro-Cuban *kissanga*, still in use, was known to Praetorius, who depicted it as an "Indian" instrument and commented that it had the sound of a harp. Perhaps the very uncertainty of its genesis has caused it to be given so many names in modern times—bow-lute, Congo guitar, West African guitar—and to be confused at times with the harp zither (see page 404).

STICK ZITHERS

Zithers consisting of no more than a rigid stick and one or more strings can be played without further amplification of sound, but generally a resonator in one form or another is appended: a gourd, coconut, inflated vesicle, and so on. The stick itself can be round, as in India and Indochina, or a flat bar, as in Indonesia and Africa. On the Indian subcontinent stick zithers vary from primitive, as played by some aboriginal tribes, to the most elaborate *vīnās*; neither those of Southeast Asia nor those of Africa attain a similar development. Those of Europe are poor relatives, surviving in the form of the ancient folk instrument known as bladder and string.

Simple bar zithers of Indonesia and Africa have but one idiochord string; in Central and East Africa, as on Madagascar, up to four occur, and three raised frets are sculptured from the material of the bar. However, on polychord models one of the strings is "off board," that is, it passes along but not over the frets, and is a drone. This African type is known by its Swahili name of *seze*. Stick zithers were brought to Madagascar in the fifteenth century by the Hova, a people of Malaya. Here they are both plucked and tapped, while on continental Africa they are usually tapped only. Both in Indonesia and in Africa the resonator is pressed against the player's stomach or chest. Some African models of Ruanda and of the Congo basin assume considerable proportions, from 75 centimeters to 1 meter (30 to 40 inches); of the two strings one lies over the frets and the other is raised on a movable bridge; the player's right hand plucks the melody string and the drone is plucked by his thumb.

On the American continent stick zithers have no resonators. In New Mexico a concave agate stalk has a single horsehair string held by a large wooden peg. The same instrument, with minor variations, is played from Mexico to Argentina.

Both in Indonesia and in Indochina, single-resonator instruments are pressed taut against the player's body by the resonator, but a Thai instrument has two calabash resonators and as many strings; the upper calabash rests against the player's shoulder, with stick dangling downward; his left hand stops the strings, his right hand plucks them: this is the playing position seen on ancient Indian monuments, first at Mavalipuram Temple (seventh century) and on the Borobudur stupa of Java (ca. A.D. 800). Such instruments, but with single string and resonator, can be matched with the name of *kinnara* in Hindu and Old Javanese literature, and were described by the early Arabic writers al-Jahiz (d. 868) and al-Masudi (d. 956).

Known nowadays as *kinnari* in southern India, the stick zither is made of bamboo there, has two or three metal strings, raised frets, three gourd resonators, and is played only by members of lower castes. Among the Dhenka (Madras area) a far more primitive form has coconut resonators and cowrie-shell frets, and on the west coast of the subcontinent a long lacquered stick to which a single string of hide is attached rests on an upturned clay pot set on the ground; several persons alternately strike the string with short sticks. Clusters of small bells suspended from the stick add their tinkling to the dull sound of the string. Punjabi equivalents have the related name of *king*. Many of these undeveloped forms consist of a bamboo stave, to the underside of which a gourd is attached at each end, and a variable number of strings pass from tailpiece to tuning pegs over several raised frets. The latter are usually secured by wax; in other words, they are left mobile for the performer to reposition according to need. Gourd resonators have a large hole cut in their underside. During performance the zithers are either laid horizontally on the ground, resting on their gourds, or they are held almost vertically against the body in the position described above.

THE VĪNĀ

But the glory of all stick zithers is the Indian *vīnā*, or *bīn*, as it is called in the north. Already mentioned in the *Yahur Veda* (the word then probably designated the harp), the term is clearly related to *bint*, the harp of ancient Egypt. After the harp disappeared from India some thousand years ago, the word was apparently transferred to the stick zither. It is also possible that theretofore *vīnā/bīn* was a generic term for chordophones; at any rate, the word is older than the form of instrument it designates today.

Vīnās are consecrated to Sarasvati, goddess of wisdom, and differ according to the regions in which they are encountered. Generally speaking, those of southern India are longer than those of the north, and the most highly developed southern models resemble lutes more closely than they do stick zithers. Characteristic of all is the long string carrier, the presence of melody and drone strings and of at least one gourd resonator. A simpler northern Indian *bīn* may consist of a bamboo stave with nineteen or even more chromatic raised frets affixed with wax, three off-board drones and four melody strings—all of metal—and two gourd resonators. Best known of the *vīnās* is the *mahati vīnā*, or great *vīnā*, representing the acme of stick zither development. Two large gourds are suspended from the ends of its round stick; its four or five melody strings are of metal, and the one or two drones are shorter, higher pitched, and secured to tuning pegs inserted into both sides of the string bearer. From twenty to twenty-four high frets are affixed with wax. Melody strings are usually plucked with ring plectra (occasionally with the fingernails), the drones being reached by the player's two little fingers. Rare today, the *mahata vīnā*, known as *naradiya vīnā* in the south, is a solo instrument with a very complicated playing technique.

South Indian development, as exemplified by the three-century-old *sarasvati vīnā*, caused the lower gourd to be replaced by a wooden bowl hollowed out of jackwood or blackwood, the string bearer to become a hollow neck terminating in a sculptured head and bearing twenty-four high, adjustable frets; the upper gourd remains but is now detachable; the four melody strings pass over a metal-topped wooden bridge and three off-board drones run over an auxiliary bridge to lateral pegs. When played it rests horizontally on bowl and gourd, the performer plucking its strings with bare fingers. Still younger is a similar but unfretted form known principally as *gotuvādyam*, the strings of which are stopped by means of a wooden or crystal cylinder held in the left hand and glided over the melody strings in a manner reminiscent of the Hawaiian guitar or the Appalachian dulcimer. Furthermore, the drones are now replaced by seven sympathetic strings placed beneath the melody strings. Finally, the *vīnā* possesses a regular body, which may be octagonal or gourd shaped, with neck and pegbox; it has become a long-necked lute, and its only claim to relationship with a stick zither is a leftover, redundant second gourd, now diminutive, made of wood and detachable; drones have been abandoned. With the exception of such late derivations, the melody is played on the four strings that pass over the entire length of the string bearer; accompaniments are played on the three shorter drones, reached by the player's little fingers, that lie off board to either side and sound at a higher pitch. A note may be ornamented by first plucking a string and then pulling it sideways.

Today the term *vīnā* is used rather loosely on the subcontinent to designate plucked chordophones, and in this sense it includes the popular sitar, a long-necked lute. Understandably, one may add, for the true stick zither had become refined to the point that its complex playing technique took it from the hands of the many to the hands of the few, then adopted elements of the lute and discarded those of the zither's overdevelopment.

THE BLADDER AND STRING

The only form of stick zither known in Europe, once apparently spread over the entire continent, is the bowed bladder and string, formerly called drone in Britain. Its stick is held under tension by a thick gut string attached to its ends; an inflated pig or ox bladder acts as combination bridge and resonator, being wedged between stick and string at the lower end, and the string is bowed by a short, curved stick, tensioned by copiously rosined horsehair.

The age of this peculiar instrument cannot be determined precisely, but the oldest reference to it occurs—as *bumba*—in Nordic sagas. An Icelandic version of the bladder and string bearing this name was described in the seventeenth-century Icelandic lexicon of Ion Olafsson as having two strings, two bladders, pellet bells, and jingles, and producing a "dull sound." Generally, however, its sound was said to resemble the roll of a drum. Two details may be indicative of considerably earlier origins: in some areas the string is scraped with a notched stick, not bowed, and elsewhere it was played with the bladder end pointing up, projecting above the player's head—like the trumpet marine in medieval times. An illustration in Pougin's *Dictionnaire du théâtre* of 1885 shows an Italian bladder and string player of 1759 holding his instrument with its rigid stick and oblong bladder high in the air and bowed at waist level. In Poland it is still played as the *luk muzycyny* (musical bow); the fact that it has no fewer than five names there points to its considerable age in that region.

Philip Hainhofer in his travel diary for 1629 comments that a three-stringed *Bumbass* he saw was a new instrument, but this seems most unlikely. Jan Steen's painting, *The Serenade*, of the mid-seventeenth century,

portrays a flutist, lutenist, and bladder and string player (the latter holding his bow palm up in a-gamba playing style). Hogarth's well-known
parody of *The Beggar's Opera* includes a man-high bladder and string; in
England the instrument continued to be played by wandering minstrels
well into the nineteenth century. The German and Bohemian *Bumbass*
was "bowed" with a notched stick, and by the nineteenth century it had
become a kind of one-man band, with cymbals and pellet bells suspended
from the stick, a beggar's instrument. Early in our century it was transformed: the bladder gave way to a circular frame covered by a membrane
—perhaps influenced by the banjo of minstrel shows—and the stick was
stamped against the ground, its string "bowed" with a notched stick. In
this form it was adopted as a carnival instrument in southern Germany,
and has since been manufactured at Markneukirchen. A modern model,
the "devil's fiddle," is also known in the United States, with string passing
over a circular frame provided with a parchment head and snares, the
stick itself surmounted by a pair of brass cymbals.

In two areas a *bumba*-like instrument has had its bladder replaced by a
gourd: Olivone, in Italian-speaking Switzerland, and East Africa. The
Olivone version, bearing the onomatopoeic name of *turututela*, was introduced by Italians. The related East African instrument has a half
gourd inserted between a metal string and a bamboo stick, and is bowed,
certainly under the stimulus of Western inspiration.

RAFT ZITHERS

Any number of slender canes or raffia segments can be combined side
by side in raft fashion to form a single entity. An idiochord string is detached from each, and two common bridges, one inserted under the
strings at each end, join the tubes together. When the number of tubes
is augmented to the point where the bridges no longer provide sufficient
stability, the ends are tied together by in-and-out weaving; as many as
sixteen tubes are combined in this manner. Very rarely, a calabash resonator is added. These simple raft zithers are met with in East Africa and
in the Congo region.

Larger instruments need greater solidity; this is obtained by detaching
an idiochord string from the underside of the tubes and inserting sticks
at right angles between strings and tubes; these lower strings are not
sounded but serve structural purposes only. Such zithers are found in
East Africa, in West Africa down to Angola, and in the Chittagong dis-

trict of Bengal. Indian instruments have a greater number of tubes— from twenty to forty have been reported—whereas in Africa the number does not exceed twenty-two. As the tubes often have very small diameters, some are left with their upper surface intact to provide space for ease in plucking the others. On some of the larger Indian instruments the strings are divided into two speaking sections by an additional bridge, placed diagonally, recalling the disposition of Islamic psalteries. Although they did not originate in imitation of the *santir* (see page 221), Indian raft zithers were certainly contaminated with it: fourteen courses of four strings each is standard *santir* stringing, and fourteen courses of three strings each is that of some of the larger northern Indian raft zithers.

Heterochord specimens are comparatively rare and consist of relatively few canes, the usual number being eight; one length of cord is woven back and forth to form all of the strings. This type is apparently confined to the African continent.

TROUGH ZITHERS

A purely African form of zither—found in continental Tanzania, Uganda, Burundi, Ruanda, and Zaire—is the trough zither, in which a length of cord is laced up and down the opening of a flat wooden trough. Often small, cruciform soundholes are pierced, and sometimes a calabash resonator is added to smaller specimens. The zither itself is a hollowed-out board with or without a monoxylous handle. The latter may be elaborately sculptured. Seven or nine strings are usual in some areas, eight are preferred in others; they are of vegetable fiber or of cow tendon. The Bashi and Fuliri of the Congo set their trough zither horizontally on their knees and brush, rather than pluck, the strings. The Hutu (Rundi) of Ruanda, on the other hand, hold theirs horizontally under one arm and pluck the strings with both hands. Among the Bahaya of Tanzania only men may play it; with them it is an honored instrument, played in the chief's residence by professional musicians.

FRAME ZITHERS

A form of zither consisting of strings attached across an open framework is found in West Africa, played by the Kru of Liberia—hence often called the Kru harp—as well as in Sierra Leone and in Guinea. This curious instrument has, as played by the Kru, seven fiber strings stretched over a triangular wooden frame composed of three sticks arranged in form of an inverted delta, with the horizontal stroke on top; the ends of the down-facing sticks are wedged into a calabash resonator from which the strings are cleared by means of a bridge. During performance the resonator is held against the player's chest or stomach, with the frame projecting in front of him.

The yokes (arms and crossbar) of modern East African bowl lyres form a blunted triangle, an inverted delta; the arms penetrate the proportionally small resonator and help to maintain the belly's rigidity. Frame zithers likewise consist of a triangular yoke and smaller resonator. Tunings and strings of East African lyres are variable and may not be of value for purposes of comparison, and the number of strings of the Kru variety of frame zither may only be coincidentally the same as that of the classical lyre. Yet the possibility—indeed, the probability—cannot be overlooked that the West African frame zither is another petrifact of the Grecian legacy.

TUBE ZITHERS

The tube zither is a relatively primitive form of zither characterized by the convex surface of its string bearer. This can be either a tube, such as a bamboo internode (whole-tube zither), or the tube may be halved lengthwise (half-tube zither); in either case, strings are stretched over the convex surface so that the tube or half tube forms both resonator and string bearer. In its basic form the strings are idiochord, cut from the periphery but left attached at both ends and given the necessary tension by being raised on two minuscule nuts. To prevent them from tearing at the ends, a ligature or metal ring is sometimes applied beyond the nuts. The latter are mobile, and tuning is accomplished by displacing them in order to change the string's length. In more developed forms strings are heterochord; finally the bamboo gives way to more permanent wood.

Such instruments are plucked, struck, drummed upon, even bowed, and in Malaya and Guyana they are also made as Aeolian zithers: those of the Malayan peninsula are of bamboo, idiochord, and are suspended from a treetop to catch the breeze, while those of Guyana consist of a long palm-leaf rib, also with idiochord strings, and are stuck perpendicularly in the ground to await the wind.

Tube zithers are found chiefly in Asia (India, Indonesia, Indochina, Moluccas, Philippines, Burma, Malaya, Hainan, Eastern Turkistan, and among the Ainu of Japan), but also in Africa (Madagascar, West Africa, and a bowed half-tube zither in South Africa), southeastern Europe, where a bowed type is encountered (Romania, Slovenia, Serbia, Macedonia), and the Americas (post-Columbian). Sachs has pointed out that back formations met with in the Balkans and Eastern Turkistan indicate a greater area of distribution in the past.

What is probably the most ancient manner of bowing—exciting the strings of one instrument by those of another identical instrument—is still practiced in two entirely separate parts of the world: southeastern Europe and eastern Bengal. In Europe tube zithers are mere toys nowadays, but their playing method alone is witness to their age. Made from a piece of cane (*Arundo donax*), with two idiochord strings stretched over the same nut at each end of the tube, they always occur in pairs, the second instrument being used as a bow. This is true of the areas mentioned above, with the exception of Slovenia, where a plucked idiochord toy is made from a cornstalk. According to Sachs, the Lushei of eastern Bengal also bow their tube zither with another one-string idiochord bamboo segment.

In Asia both idiochord and heterochord tube zithers seem to be more frequently struck than plucked. Often small, primitive instruments have a hole pierced in the tube to augment the sonority, sometimes a tongue may be cut in its wall, to be struck alternately with the tube itself; or a bamboo or wooden plaque is strung on two strings to form a striking surface immediately above the hole; in such cases the string bearer, the string(s), the tongue if present, and the plaque, all can be struck alternately. Other models have a long slit rather than a soundhole.

Some Asiatic instruments are plucked and struck together, the striking being done by a beater or by the player's thumb. Frequently there is only one string. An idiochord tube zither of Java, called *gambeng* in fourteenth-century records and still known by that name in Bali, is of bamboo, sometimes has a spoon-shaped drumming bridge inserted under its single string (cf. the trumpet marine of Europe, page 202). On Buru island and Halmahera in the Moluccas the zither has five strings plucked by the player's left hand while his right hand drums on the resonator; and, on Mindanao in the Philippines, up to six idiochord strings are cut along opposite sides of the circumference. In Shan State, Burma, a rectangular hole is pierced in the underside of the tube and covered by a wooden plaque, which is drummed upon with the player's left thumb while he simultaneously plucks the single string. A half-tube bamboo zither with from six to nine idiochord strings is struck on Flores and neighboring islands with two small sticks. The archaic Ainu of Japan have exceptionally few musical instruments, but among these is a half-tube zither with five strings that they pluck with bare fingers.

Sometimes two instruments—be they idiochord or heterochord—are joined together so as to form a single unit, each tube having but a single string; two common nuts in the form of sticks inserted under the string of each instrument effectively hold them together. Such double tube-zithers have become children's toys among the Sarts of Eastern Turkistan.

Heterochord tube zithers also can be plucked or drummed, or even bowed; here the strings are attached to pegs inserted in the upper node. As no account need be taken of incisions in the tube's periphery, hetero-chord instruments can be given a far greater number of strings. Those of the Vietnamese Moi have ten strings, and the sonority of their tube is en-hanced by the addition of two gourd resonators. A more common reso-nator is, however, the palm leaf: the Malayan *keranting* has up to twenty strings and an enveloping palm-leaf resonator attached so as to reflect the sound. A sister instrument on Timor occurs in both idiochord and hetero-chord form; in the latter, up to eighteen copper strings are strung pair-wise all around the tube; this is then surrounded by a palm-leaf resonator. The strings are tuned by shifting small, movable bridges. This palm-leaf reflector type was taken by the Hova of Malaya to Madagascar in the fifteenth century; there it was called *valiha*, the name by which it is generally known today, regardless of whether a given specimen is Malagasy or Asian. Apart from Malaya and Madagascar, *valihas* are found in the Moluccas and western New Guinea. Instead of resting horizontally, as do the simpler forms, these are held vertically and plucked with bare fingers.

Tube zithers reach their highest development on the Indochinese peninsula, and spill over as far as Assam. Bamboo is forsaken in favor of wood—a material suitable for carving—and the resultant freedom has produced the enchanting whole-tube zither sculptured to resemble a croco-dile. Usually the tube is lacquered and set on a lacquered stand; its three strings, which are of silk or metal and are secured to pegs in the croco-dile's tail, pass over a number of movable or fixed frets. A long soundslit is cut in the underside, and it is by means of this slit that the wood is hollowed out. The player depresses the strings against the frets and plucks them with a plectrum. Burmese orchestras include a *mi gyaun*, as this instrument is called, for the accompaniment of dramatic performances. Strings of the corresponding Cambodian *takhe* are tuned A° e° a°.

A number of South African peoples, including the Venda, Xhosa, Zulu, Swazi, Chwana, and Sotho, play a half-tube zither called *tsijolo* by the Venda. Made of bamboo, a section is cut away for most of the length, the intact tubular portion left expressly for insertion of a tuning peg; the string's tension is modified by the introduction of the player's hand between tube and string, and pressure on the latter by the third and fourth fingers. The convex side of the far end rests against the player's face, his oral cavity serving as a resonator, while the string is bowed with a short cowhair bow. More recently a tin can has been added to the tube, replacing the need for the player's mouth. Only men and boys may perform on this instrument.

Apart from Madagascar, whole-tube zithers are played only on the western coastal regions of the African continent. They do not resemble the *valiha* but are made of a raffia-palm stalk with from one to four idiochord strings, and sometimes attain the respectable length of over 2 meters (6½ feet).

Tube zithers in the Americas do not antedate the colonial period (that of modern Mexico is significantly called the *harpa*) and are not encountered frequently. Both whole- and half-tube forms occur and, as already mentioned, an Aeolian tube is known in Guyana.

BOARD ZITHERS

Zithers in which a rectangular board serves as string bearer occur in simple form in Africa—in Zaire and neighboring areas of Tanzania—often set upon a calabash resonator. The stringing method, characteristic of African instruments, is shared with the trough zithers: a single long cord is laced back and forth to form as many strings as desired.

African board zithers present so many features of the East Asian long zithers (see page 193) that we are entitled to consider them as a heritage from the East. Norlind (1939) pointed out that on all older specimens the cord is threaded through apertures in the ends of the board and tied on the underside (as on long zithers), whereas on later ones they are simply notched. Furthermore, the board itself is sometimes convex, reminiscent of the vaulted zither. Finally, the presence of individual bridges, some provided with a hole for the passage of a string, is a sure indication of a former connection with East Asia. The preferred size of

African instruments is about 40 centimeters (15 to 16 inches), with the number of strings varying considerably, from five to fourteen or more.

Similar zithers are found on Borneo. The older type of Javanese *chelempung* exemplifies an intermediary stage of development: this was a squat trapezoid with vaulted surface, flat bottom, and twenty-six metal strings that passed over a common bridge and were played with two metal plectra. Tuning pegs were inserted in the long sides of the board at its wider end. The same system of lateral tuning pegs is met with on Javanese flat-board zithers with upturned ends, but these have the individual bridges of the vaulted zithers.

Several ancient Greek authors wrote of a *simikion* with thirty-five strings and of an *epigoneion* with forty strings, neither of which has yet been identified conclusively. So large a number of strings points to a zither rather than to a harp, and Sachs (1940), deriving *epigoneion* from *epi* ("upon") and *gony* ("knee"), believed that the board zither laid across the knees of a seated performer might fit the etymology, and also that the Persian word *sim* ("string") might explain that of *simikion*, in preference to Julian Pollux's unlikely interpretation that the latter was invented by a man named Simos. However, there exists no pictorial evidence of a zither in Greece or Rome.

LONG ZITHERS

The term "long zither," or "vaulted zither," is applied to an East Asian form intermediate between a half-tube zither and a board zither. As the names indicate, such zithers have a slightly arched surface and are typically narrow, forming an elongated rectangle or trapeze that can attain 2 meters (6½ feet) in length. The bottom is flat. The vaulted upper and flat lower surfaces are said in China to be symbolic of heaven and earth. Most of them are plucked, but one type is bowed. Characteristically they lack tuning pins or pegs; when in playing position (set horizontally in front of the performer with the left long side facing him) the silk strings are seen to be fastened to a string holder at his right, whence they pass over a nut on his left, to be attached on the underside of the instrument, usually in two groups.

The area over which these instruments are played reaches from western Mongolia south to Vietnam and east to Japan. Their country of origin is believed to be China, where they are documented from about 1100 B.C., first in an ode mentioning the *ch'in* and the *shē*.

East Asian long zithers fall into two categories: they either have a series of individual bridges or else they are furnished with the equivalent of frets. Those having bridges are by far the most numerous. Structurally they differ from the fretted models by their long middle section and short end sections, the latter set on a downward incline, whereas the fretted models consist of a single section. According to Chinese tradition, unfretted zithers were originally made of bamboo, which makes it likely that they were derived from a half-tube prototype (Sachs has likened the transnodes of the latter to the end sections of the long zither with bridges). Such an origin would account for the vaulted surface and explain the individual, movable bridges derived from the need to raise each string separately from an idiochord tube.

INDIVIDUALLY BRIDGED LONG ZITHERS

Foremost among the group having individual bridges is the *shē* of China, a Confucian temple and court ceremonial instrument. Its convex surface is almost semicircular in circumference, and richly ornamented with lacquerwork. At the time of the emperor Shih Huang Ti (third century B.C.), or so it is said, its strings were reduced from fifty to the present twenty-five, under each of which is a small, two-footed bridge. Like all bridges, these divide the string into a "speaking" and a "dead" section, but the dead section of the *shē's* strings is brought into play to furnish vibrati and intermediate pitches not otherwise available from the speaking length. In order to facilitate playing by making the strings more readily recognizable, bridges are grouped together in fives of the same color. The *shē* has a total compass of five octaves, is tuned pentatonically, and played in parallel octaves. In Korea the same instrument is known as *sul*; its Vietnamese equivalent, the *cai tung shac*, now obsolete, traditionally also had fifty strings reduced to twenty-five. Like the *shē*, the Japanese *hitsu no koto* is said to originally have had fifty strings, subsequently reduced to twenty-five or fewer. Now obsolete, it is replaced by its descendant, the *sō no koto*, known simply as the *koto*, whose thirteen strings pass over as many bridges. An instrument of court music (*gagaku*) for over a thousand years, it was reserved exclusively for classical Chinese music, but has been popularized in modern times and is now a household instrument, and especially one of women. Thimble-like plectra are worn on the player's right thumb, fore-, and middle fingers, while the left hand damps the strings and changes their pitch by pressing down on the dead section; by such means the pitch can be raised up to a whole tone.

With only thirteen or fourteen strings, and sometimes fewer, but otherwise similar to the *shē*, the smaller *cheng* of China is still played on festive occasions. Closely allied to it is the Mongolian long zither *yatag*, now rare, with its left end forming an obtuse angle. Usually this instrument has twelve silk strings, tuned to a pentatonic scale and played only as open strings, either plucked with a plectrum or with bare fingers. The same instrument is in use among the Volga Kalmuck and the Kirghiz, the latter having a flat model with seven wire strings.

The classical unfretted long zither of Japan is the *wagon*, or *yamato koto*, said to be indigenous and to have developed from six hunters' bows laid side by side, strings uppermost. Such bows once played an important role in persuading the Japanese sun goddess to issue from a cave in which she had hidden. Nowadays the *wagon* is a slender trapezoid, flatter than most long zithers, but its right end still has five notches cut into it for the attachment of six silk strings to the six projecting "bows" thus created; these serve in lieu of a common string holder. The basic relative tuning of its strings is d²a′d′b′g′e′; all are plucked simultaneously with a sweeping plectrum stroke at the same time that the player's left little finger plays the melody and the left hand damps the strings. Nowadays it is heard but rarely.

One of the most interesting zithers by virtue of its history is the bowed zither of northern China now known as *la ch'in*. It differs from those just discussed only by having its ten pairs of silk strings attached not to the underside but to iron pegs driven into the short end. Furthermore, it is held in a semiupright position, with two small holes at the base serving as fingerholds. Its slightly curved horsehair bow is nearly as long as the instrument itself, which averages 65 centimeters (26 inches). Picken (1965) informs us that Chinese musicologists have equated the *la ch'in* with the *ya cheng* of the T'ang dynasty (A.D. 618–907) at which time it was played with a friction stick (the bow had not yet come into existence); a contemporary reference states that it "was made to creak with a slip of bamboo moistened at its tip." In the twelfth century *Yüeh shu* by Ch'en Yang, the *ya cheng* is classified as a folk instrument. Although defunct elsewhere, it lives on under its original name in Wu-an County, Hopei, bowed with a *kao liang* (sorghum) stem dusted with resin.

FRETTED LONG ZITHERS

Most prominent among the second category of long zithers—those that are fretted—is the Chinese *ch'in*. Here frets take the form of small ivory or mother-of-pearl disks inlaid in the wood underneath the single melody string to indicate the stopping points. China's greatest classical instrument, it appears on a late Han dynasty (A.D. 25–220) relief in Szechwan and is considered to be its oldest chordophone. A beautifully ornamented seven-stringed *ch'in*, probably of the fifth century, is preserved with other historical instruments in the Shōsoin at Nara, Japan, measuring 114.5 centimeters (about 45 inches) in length. The *ch'in's* seven strings—there were only five originally—are stretched across the narrow trapezoid and attached to two stubs on the left and right underside at the narrower end. At the wider end they pass over a nut, then through holes in the board, to be secured by individual plugs.

Tradition and myth combine to explain the dimensions and components of the *ch'in*: its length is 3.66 (Chinese) feet, corresponding to the 366 days of the year, and the original five strings are said to have symbolized the five elements; the upper and under surfaces represent heaven and earth; the inlaid fingering disks, thirteen in number, represent the twelve regular months and one leap month. Unlike other fretted chordophones, the disks are not disposed so as to produce increasingly smaller spacings; their widest spacing occurs at the center of the string length and proceeds symmetrically to ever closer spacings on left and right. Sachs (1940) calculated the divisions of the string length at which the disks are placed as ½, ⅓ and ⅔, ¼ and ¾, ⅕ and ⅘, ⅙ and ⅚, ⅛ and ⅞, resulting in a scale of $c°d°e♭°e°f°g°a°c'e'g'$-$c^2e^2g^2c^3$; this becomes meaningful only once the technique of playing in harmonics is recalled.

Six of the seven strings are played as open strings to provide accompaniment for the stopped melody string. All are of equal length but their thicknesses are of Pythagorean proportions, being composed—at least theoretically—of 48, 54, 64, 72, 81, 96, and 108 strands of silk, producing ratios of 9:8 (204 cents) and 27:32 (294 cents). The scale is pentatonic without semitones; an ancient tuning is given as $c°d°e°g°a°$-$c'd'$, changed to $g°a°c'd'e'g'a'$, and an official tuning was $d°e°g°a°b°d'e'$. When playing, the performer plucks the strings with his right hand while his left hand stops the melody string, gliding from one stopping point to another chiefly in harmonics (obtained by not pressing the string against the board). Plectra are dispensed with, as more subtle control can be exercised by the bare fingers. To the Chinese intellectual the *ch'in* was at least as important a symbol of culture as it was a musical instrument; historically its music has been his domain.

From China the *ch'in* traveled to Korea, where it was adopted as the *komunko* and where it currently has six strings; thence to Japan where it is known as *shi chi gen kin* ("seven-stringed *kin*"). It retains the Chinese form, fingering disks, and method of string attachment. With the left hand stopping the melody string, the performer's right thumb arpeggios over the remaining strings; here again no plectrum is used. The *gin dai*, or great *kin*, is similar in all respects except for its having thirteen strings. Another Japanese long zither, the *go kin*, retains the Chinese features but reduces the stringing to five strings and secures these to tuning pegs. Other Japanese fingering-disk zithers survive that may well represent now obsolete Chinese forms. Among these are the single-stringed *ichi gen kin* ("one-stringed *kin*"), played with a plectrum and usually made of wood; tradition derives it from a bamboo half-tube, and some specimens made from this material are known. The *ni gen kin* ("two-stringed *kin*") has two unison strings and lacks the usual bottom. Very similar is the *yakumo koto*, which was formerly made of a bamboo half-tube with a closed wooden bottom, now always of paulownia or cedarwood.

The *ch'in*'s Vietnamese equivalent, the *cai cam*, is now obsolete. It had a lacquered board and, we are informed, originally five strings, later augmented to seven, and it shared the Chinese traditional length of 3.66 feet. Earlier in our century the *cai cam* was exhibited at rituals of the imperial temple, where it symbolized harmony.

BOX ZITHERS

Zithers with built-up string bearers of slats, forming boxlike resonators, are relatively young. Their home may prove to be western Asia, but the sparse information we have concerning early Eastern (Phoenician) zithers does not as yet permit us to establish their initial history.

Subsequently diffused by Islam, box zithers reached their greatest development in Europe, where they evolved into keyboard chordophones.

THE MONOCHORD

Greek authors are unanimous in attributing the invention of the *kanōn*, that is, the monochord, to Pythagoras in the sixth century B.C. This device was utilized in antiquity for measuring, testing, and mathematically demonstrating musical intervals (possibly even earlier than the sixth century). Through the writings of Boethius (ca. A.D. 500) it became known to medieval theorists, with the result that treatises on monochord ratios began to appear in the tenth century. During the Middle Ages and into the sixteenth century, monochords were invaluable adjuncts to the teaching of solmization: in his mid-fifteenth-century treatise, Chilston mentions "the monochord that is called the instrument of plain-song."

In its earliest known form the monochord was an elongated rectangular box with a single string stretched across its calibrated upper surface; shortly after 1000 it was enlarged and improved by the addition of a movable bridge of the same height as the semicircular nuts placed at each end (known as *hemispherium, hemipherium,* or *stefanos*). After the bridge had been shifted to the desired position, the string was pressed firmly against its top by the player, who then plucked the string either by bare finger of the other hand or by a plectrum (in practice it is difficult to obtain a clear tone in this manner). Tension was obtained by a weight added to the string during the Middle Ages, thereafter by a tuning peg.

From a piece of musical equipment the monochord seems to have become a musical instrument, a transformation at first partly functional—not structural—that took place by the late eleventh century. Both pictorial and literary sources point to the existence of a single-string apparatus (devoid of keys) used as a plucked chordophone, sometimes in a setting of *joculatores* and tumblers; Wace's *Roman de Brut* of about 1155 enumerates *symphonies, psalterions, monachordes,* and Guiraut de Calenson in the thirteenth century writes of a *manicorda una corda* at a time when it also appears as a tuning device:

> L'un mandura e l'autre acorda
> Lo salteri ab manicorda

> One played the *mandura*
> And the other tuned the psaltery by the monochord

as it is stated in the *Roman de flamenca* of about 1250. Machaut (ca. 1300–1377) still assures us of the one-stringer's presence:

> . . . *monocorde*
> *ou il n'y a qu'une seule corde*

Medieval theorists recommended the addition of extra strings to permit the comparison of intervals; Simon Tunstede in the fourteenth century recommends two, others write of a larger number either as desirable or as existing. In other words, they describe a polychord (but Labeo Notker [d. 1022], who has been said to describe such an instrument, was actually referring to a single-string monochord with sixteen divisions, or tones). Interesting in this connection are the remarks of al-Farabi (d. 950), who, after describing the Greek perfect system, suggests constructing an instrument for the verification of musical theory: a rectangular box with a top large enough to permit the alignment of fifteen pegs or more, for as many strings at the same tension and pitch, and fourteen small ivory or hardwood bridges with perfectly rounded tops and flat bottoms, very slightly higher than the hemispheric nuts.

Polychord "monochords" mentioned by medieval theorists fall into two categories: either they are monochords with an additional string or two (Johannes de Muris in the fourteenth century appears to have suggested four; but Fogliano's *Musica theoretica* of 1529 shows a monochord—*unica chorda*—with string doubled back on itself to permit the sounding of intervals), or they are early clavichords with all strings the same length, still called by the older name.

A different problem arises with regard to its potential confusion with the trumpet marine (see page 209). Praetorius assures us—wrongly, I believe—that the latter was descended from the monochord. When the *Echecs amoureux* of about 1375 mention this as a musical instrument, or Eberhard Cersne (1404) lists it among the instruments of his day—he mentions the clavichord also—may these references not in reality be to the trumpet marine, which at that time appears to have had no name of its own? It is true that Paulus Paulirinus (ca. 1460) describes as a musical instrument the monochord with single gut string stretched over a hollow body and plucked *cum penna aut ligno* ("with quill or stick"), and we know that by then the trumpet marine was bowed, not plucked; but in the next century Glareanus calls it a monochord, which, of course, is technically correct.

The role in which the monochord lived longest was that of organ tuner's accessory. Prior to the adoption of equal temperament, organ tuning presented complications unknown in our day, and organ literature, particularly that of the baroque era, contains many descriptions of the problems inherent in correct calibration of monochords. On arrival at a church the tuner, accompanied by his monochord-carrying apprentice, would first proceed to tune the monochord to a trumpet brought along for this purpose—it being an instrument of "fixed and unalterable" pitch—then to tune the organ to the monochord. Its string was by now of metal, that is, louder than gut. Whatever its deficiencies may have been, the eighteenth century held it to be vastly superior to the human ear in matters of tuning, and monochords continued to be built commercially for tuning purposes as late as the 1820s in France. And in 1860 Oscar Paul described monochords as indispensable for the determination of pitch. Ethnomusicologists still use a (bowed) monochord for measuring musical intervals.

Various improved versions were "invented" from the seventeenth century on, including a four-string and four-jack model; a keyed monochord with keyboard and bowed strings; and, to make the circle complete, a London artist named Higgs built in 1843 a monochord with movable bridge for the teaching of singing.

The relationship between the medieval monochord and the dichordium remains unknown.

THE STRING DRUM

During the Middle Ages there appeared in Europe an oblong box across the top of which were stretched two strings that were struck with a heavy stick. In the fourteenth century we can match illustration with text: the Angers Tapestry of the Apocalypse, designed about 1375, shows a cumbersome instrument of this nature being carried by an angel, who is in the process of striking its strings with a club. At about the same time Jean Lefebvre describes the *choron* as a *grant boise* ("great log"), with a string that is beaten, and Aimeri de Peyrac, also in the fourteenth century, writes of the chorus with its doubled string:

> *Quidam choros consonantes*
> *Duplicem chordam perstringentes*

A little later, Jean de Gerson (d. ca. 1429) gives details of an instrument commonly called a *chorus*, an oblong piece of hollowed wood with two or three strings, much thicker than those of a harp, struck with a stick (*Sic chorus vocatur a nonnullis vulgaribus instrumentum quoddam, instar trabis oblongum & vacuum, chordas habens grossiores multo plus quam cithara, duas aut tres, quae baculis erutis percussae varie variant rudem sonem*). Now *chorus* was a handy name for any instrument with a plurality of strings or pipes, especially for one not yet well enough established to have a specific name of its own. Had not Saint Augustine (d. 430) "enumerated" it in his list of musical instruments recognized by the church? *Vos estis tuba, psalterium, cithara, tympanum, chorus, chordae, et organum, et cymbala jubilationis bene sonantia* (Enarr. in ps. 150). Accordingly the name was also bestowed upon several other instruments capable of emitting two tones simultaneously.

Several Netherlandic documents of the fourteenth and fifteenth centuries contain references to a mysterious *bonge* or *bonghe*, a chordophone with struck strings that, according to a fourteenth-century ditty, accompanied songs. The term is cognate with the Middle High German *bunge*, denoting a drum, and the *bonge* was in all likelihood the same instrument as that described by Gerson.

Our instrument appears, played by a fabulous half man, half beast, carved on a choir stall, completed in 1432, of Basel Minster. By the mid-fifteenth century a refined form appears in Italy, played in conjunction with a one-hand flute, and from then on, wherever it is found, the two instruments are sounded simultaneously by one performer. This new form is known chiefly by its French name, *tambourin à cordes* ("string drum"); as it was popular in Béarn and Gascony it is also known as the *tambourin de Béarn* or *de Gascogne*. Zarlino informs us (1588) that the Italian equivalent was called by its Venetian name, *altobasso* ("highlow"). All told, this is one of those unfortunate instruments of immense innate vitality that never had specific names of their own. The Basque people and the Spaniards also played it, and still do—in the Basque country it has from six to nine strings—but the string drum and *galoubet* combination does not seem to have spread beyond the area of the Mediterranean.

From the time it was painted by Filippo Lippi (d. 1469) it has undergone little change. The oldest instruments are rectilinear, later ones have incurved or bulging long sides, and the number of strings increases. These are of gut, stretched as theretofore over one long surface; all are struck simultaneously with a stick and are tuned to tonic and dominant of the pipe they accompany. The performer suspends the string drum from his left forearm by means of a strap, and holds his flute in the left hand, the stick in his right.

In the second half of the eighteenth century attempts at "improving" the string drum resulted mainly in the placing of a set of sympathetic strings immediately below the struck ones, and a Paris advertisement of 1764 concerning a *tambourin à cordes à 2 faces pouvant être monté sur deux tons* ("with two surfaces, for stringing in two tonalities") gives added evidence of the interest taken by French eighteenth-century society in rustic instruments, for, despite its appearance in the hands of angels or in the distinguished company of *lyras* and gambas (as in Abraham Bosse's illustration of about 1650 of the Hypolydian mode, for Denis Gaultier's *La rhétorique des dieux*), it was, and remained, an instrument of the people.

The string drum was not the only instrument to become closely associated with a pipe, for the pipe and tabor combination was even better known. Gaudenzio Ferrari's dome at Saronno, painted around 1535, depicts both types of ensemble. Apparently they were interchangeable at times, for Pierre de Lancre, writing in the early seventeenth century (*Tableau de l'inconstance des mauvais anges*, Paris, 1613), as quoted in Murray (1921), describes the dancing of witches in France to the music of tabor and flute, and sometimes with that long instrument that is placed on the shoulder and reaches to the waist and is struck with a little stick (*Elles dancent au son du petit tabourin & de la fluste, & parfois avec ce long instrument qu'ils posent sur le col, puis s'allongeant iusqu'aupres de la ceinture, ils* [sic] *le battent avec un petit baston* . . .). It was on the shoulder that the angel of the Angers Tapestry had carried its string drum.

THE TRUMPET MARINE

A folk instrument of unusual features and a long history, the trumpet marine—neither a trumpet nor yet marine—first appeared in the twelfth century; it seems not to have survived the Renaissance in southern Europe, but somehow managed to continue its existence in some isolated communities of the north until the nineteenth century, for it is reported as having been played in the mountain districts of Silesia in 1845 under the name of *Trompeta Maria*.

In shape the trumpet marine had an elongated prismatic body varying in length from perhaps 1 meter (40 inches) in its early days to over 2 meters (6½ feet) by the seventeenth century, tapering toward the upper end, and originally triangular in cross section. The three thin boards of which it was made—one of them formed the soundboard—were later increased to as many as eleven in the eighteenth century, terminating in a very short neck with a frontal peg to hold its single gut string. During the fifteenth century the resonator was made of three or four tapering boards and the bottom end was left open.

The earliest instruments portrayed, those of French twelfth- to fourteenth-century art works, are all plucked with bare fingers; the bow is not shown until the fifteenth century. A second string, half as long as the first, was added in the fifteenth century, to be supplemented later by a third or even a fourth, each half the length of the preceding one. By 1400 or so trumpets marine were being made in two sizes, the shorter of which—obsolete already in the sixteenth century—was played in a most unusual manner: the upper (tuning peg) end was held against the player's chest with the lower end projecting forward and overhead in the air, and the string was stopped by the player's left thumb. This mode of playing is shown e.g. on a miniature in a Netherlandic Bible of 1425, where two trumpets marine participate in an instrumental ensemble, and in a woodcut of Sebastian Brant's *Ship of Fools* (1494), and is described by Glareanus in 1547. The better-known Memling angel of about 1480 is, however, stopping the string as though she were playing a fiddle.

The larger models of the fifteenth and later centuries are shown held with pegbox or neck resting against the performer's shoulder, with the lower end placed on the ground in front of him. Other characteristic features of the trumpet marine are its peculiar bridge and the fashion in which it is bowed. As hinted at by Paulus Paulirinus (ca. 1460), described by Glareanus, and depicted by Mersenne (1636–1637), the bridge had feet of unequal size and shape: the broader right foot bore the weight of the string and was set firmly on the belly, whereas the slender left foot barely came in contact with the belly and rattled when the string was vibrated. Sometimes a small ivory or metal plaque was affixed to the belly under the left foot in order to augment the rattling, or a nail might be driven into its underside. Instead of pressing the string down hard against the body, in the absence of a fingerboard, the player touched it lightly with his thumb and consequently produced only flageolet tones; the bow was kept close to the pegbox, always held between the latter and stopping thumb (not in the expected position between stopping thumb and bridge). Later, during the seventeenth century, when the trumpet marine changed its shape and developed a long, rounded neck, the different stopping points of the string were often marked by inscribing their pitch names on the neck; these corresponded to the series of harmonic tones. Traditionally the string was tuned to C (Glareanus comments that only the Ionian and Hypo-ionian modes sounded well on it).

Certain Near Eastern chordophones lack a fingerboard and are played by stopping the strings with the fingertips without pressing them against the neck. Nineteenth-century investigators took it for granted that this technique would of necessity produce flageolet tones only, and thereby gave rise to the theory of an Oriental origin for the trumpet marine, a theory that has since been abandoned. Actually the Oriental and Slavonic technique consists in stopping a string at any point of its length and with sufficient pressure to obtain the fundamental pitch.

Wantzlöben (1911) seems to have been the first author to draw attention to the occurrence of the *monacorde* in medieval French poetry among the instruments employed by jongleurs, and to have ascertained that manuscripts of the period depict only two instruments with a single string, in addition to the true monochord, namely the pear-shaped *lira* (of Gerbert's well-known drawing) and the trumpet marine. Certainly the possibility, indeed the probability, exists that prior to the sixteenth century the trumpet marine's identity was often hidden under the appellation of monochord, and some otherwise puzzling descriptions of the monochord as a musical instrument become more comprehensible if one considers that they might have pertained to trumpets marine.

Passages that would benefit by such an interpretation are, for instance, Wace's reference (twelfth century) to King Arthur's court: *mult ot a la cort juglors/chanteors/estrumenteors/ . . . symphonies, psalterions/monacordes, cymbes, chorons . . .* ("many jugglers, singers, instrumentalists were at the court . . . symphonies, psalteries, monochords, *cymbes, chorons . . .*"); or a sermon entitled *Grant mal fit Adam*, where the *gigue, monacorde/harpe, siphome* together make a *concorde*. Also, Guiraut de Calenson, a troubadour of the early thirteenth century, expects strolling players to master no fewer than nine instruments, among which was the aforementioned *manicorda/una corda*. Guillaume de Machaut (ca. 1300–1377) enumerates *buisine, eles, monocorde/ou il n'y a qu'une seule corde* ("buisine, psaltery, monochord where there is but one string"); the *Echecs amoureux*, written between 1370 and 1380, has *qui sonnent moult doucement/chyffonies et monocordes/et maint aultre instrument de corde* ("who sounded very softly symphonies and monochords and many other stringed instruments"), and in the fifteenth century we may note Holland's *Buke of the Howlat* (ca. 1450), with "the crowde and the monocordy, the gythornis gaye/the rote and the recordour." And when Simone Prodenzani writes (by 1420) of sending for a monochord of such *alta voce* that it made a lute sound muted:

> *Do puoi fecer venire un menacordo*
> *Che avia si alta voce, che un liuto*
> *Appresso a quello gli parebbe sordo*

he is more likely referring to a trumpet marine than to a monochord. Eberhard Cersne's well-known enumeration of the instruments of his day in *Der Minne Regel* of 1404, exhaustive as it is, does not mention a *Trumscheit*, as the trumpet marine was known in German a century later, but he does list among the chordophones . . . *harffe edir flegil/ noch schachtbrett, monochordium* ("harp or wing-shaped psaltery, also chekker, monochord"). These and other examples indicate participation of a single-stringed chordophone in ensembles or as melody instrument, uses with which the classical monochord can hardly be reconciled. Therefore we may perhaps also consider the term as a name of the trumpet marine, which in its early history was known to be in the hands of strolling players, Memling's angel notwithstanding.

When Paulirinus described it as a hollow wooden instrument "like a triagonal monochord" he called it a *tubalcana*, from which we may gather that it lacked a name of its own both in Latin and in the vernacular at that time; its bow *facit precise sonum tube* ("produced the sound of a trumpet"): his is the first association in literature of trumpet marine and trumpet, and a clue to the peculiar name he bestowed upon it. Virdung (1511) called it a *Trumscheit* and dismissed it as an "unnecessary" instrument. *Trumscheit* derives from *scheit* ("log") and *trumba*, an Old High German term for both trumpet and drum. Five years later, Nicholaus Faber equates monochord with *Drumelscheit*.

Glareanus's testimony is most important: trumpets marine were played, he relates, by the Germans, French, and Netherlanders and, to a lesser extent, also by the Italians; yet he has no name for them and is obliged to graecize the word *Trumscheit* to *tympanischiza*; the two-stringed version he refers to as a diachord. We do not know whether the trembling foot formed part of the fittings from the inception, or whether it was added later on, but certainly it existed by Glareanus's time, as he describes it minutely, and from him we learn that the older, short instrument constructed from three boards was still in use, played by ambulant musicians in the old overhead position. On a contemporary Nativity scene painted by Il Bramantino (d. 1536) a slender, tapering model is still shown in this manner, while in an engraving by Giambattista Bracelli of 1599 the new long version is held at the player's shoulder and rests on the ground.

Not only did the slight thumb pressure on the string result in the exclusive production of flageolet tones, but, as the string is stopped only at nodal points, all were harmonics. Glareanus notes that solely thirds, fourths, fifths, and octaves could be obtained, that semitones or tones were more difficult, and that the rattling foot made them indistinct. Investigations into the acoustics of the trumpet marine were carried out in France and in England in the latter part of the seventeenth century and in 1691 *The Philosophical Transactions* printed a report by Francis Ribert that stated in part:

The sound is so like [that of a trumpet] as not to be easily distinguishable by the nicest Ear, and as it performs the very same Notes, so it has the very same defects as the Trumpet, for if the String be stopt in any part, but such as produces a Trumpet Note, it yields a harsh and uncouth (not a Musical) sound. . . . Now in the Trumpet-Marine you do not stop close as in other Instruments, but touch the string gently with your thumb. . . . The Trumpet-Marine will yield no Musical sound but when the stop makes the upper part of the string an *aliquot* of the remainder, and consequently of the whole.

Canon Galpin summed up the situation somewhat more concisely when he wrote (1904): "Played by stopping in the usual way, the marine trumpet produces tones far less melodious than the bray of an ass."

Praetorius, who quotes Glareanus extensively on the subject of the trumpet marine, owned one himself, still made of three tapering boards, but already over seven feet in length, and with four strings tuned c°c°g°c′, only one of which was stopped, as the three shorter ones were drones. The comments of Mersenne are of particular interest, because in France the trumpet marine gained a status it lacked elsewhere. He calls it *trompette marine*, an expression possibly derived by confusion with the megaphone (Buonanni [1722] depicts a giant megaphone and entitles it *tromba marina*), as he credits sailors with its invention. (Hence Lully wrote a *divertissement* for sailors—*pour les matelots*—to Cavalli's *Xerxes* [1660] for a trumpet marine with string accompaniment.) Mersenne also wrote of the difficulty in playing it and commented that few indeed could play it well; that often several hours were needed to properly adjust the bridge in order to obtain desired results, but that once correctly placed the string spoke with great ease. (Modern experiments have shown that a very thick string produces best results and that the bow needs to be heavily rosined.) Not only was it dignified by an appearance in opera, but from 1679 to 1767 the *Bande de la Grande Écurie du Roi* included five ostensible trumpet marine players, alternately listed as players of the *basse de cromorne*; however, both terms seem to have pertained to the office rather than to the instrument, and to have in fact referred to performers on the *hautbois*.

In England the trumpet marine seems to have been unknown until the mid-seventeenth century, when Pepys heard it and reported in his diary for October 24, 1667:

. . . we in to see a Frenchman, one Monsieur Prim, play on the Trump-marine, which he do beyond belief, and, the truth is, it do so far outdo a trumpet as nothing more . . . and at first was a mystery to me that I should hear a whole concert of chords together at the end of a pause, but he showed me that it was only when the last notes were 5ths or 3rds, one to another, and then their sounds like an Echo did last so as they seemed to last altogether. The instrument is open at one end, I discovered; but he would not let me look into it . . .

Seven years later "a rare concert of four Trumpets marine, never before heard in England" was given at the Fleece Tavern "every day of the week except Sundays. Every concert shall continue one hour, and so begin again'" starting at 2:00 P.M. The "Monsieur Prim" heard by Pepys was Jean-Baptiste Prim, a French virtuoso performer who also wrote a *Traité de la trompette marine* and who claimed to have been the first to have added sympathetic strings to the interior; these were of metal, tuned in unison or an octave above the bowed gut string. Their number was variable; a seventeenth-century Italian specimen in the Boston Museum of Fine Arts has the unusually large number of fifty such strings, their tuning pegs concealed by a sliding door; and James Talbot at the end of the century examined an instrument with twenty-one strings of brass wire "within the belly."

By the time Pepys first heard it, the trumpet marine already had a rounded neck, and the bowed string was tuned by a ratchet-wheel machine head. This system had already been known to Praetorius, who saw it applied to a double bass. It was to be refined or reinvented by Carl Ludwig Bachmann in the last quarter of the nineteenth century. Museum instruments from the latter part of the seventeenth century and later are not uncommon; they often have a pronounced flare at the bottom, occasionally resulting in a near-campaniform outline; some have a violin-type pegbox. At times a metal hook was affixed to the back of the resonator to hold a band passed around the player's neck to prevent the instrument from slipping.

From *Trumscheit*, the German name was changed to *Marien-Trompete*, no doubt under the influence of *trompette marine*, and also to the very logical *Trompetengeige* and to *Nonnengeige*, the latter Englished as "nun's fiddle." This last term, and latest of the three, is said to have arisen from its use in convents by nuns, who were either forbidden or unable to play real trumpets. While such assertions have been deprecated in recent years, they may well hold true for Germany at least, in contrast to Italy, where Bottrigari praised the performance of nuns on cornetti and trumpets at the close of the sixteenth century, and where we know that trumpet playing was taught to girls in the mid-eighteenth century at the Naples Conservatorio della Pietà dei Turchini. Our first information for the hitherto disputed German usage is from Samuel Petri (1767); he does not use the term *Nonnengeige* but instead refers to the *Trompete marine . . . welche die Töne der Trompete nachahmt, und jetzt nur noch in Jungfernklöstern gebraucht wird, wo man keine Trompeterinnen hat* ("trumpet marine . . . which imitates the sounds of the trumpet and now is used only in women's convents, where there are no woman trumpeters").

Petri's statement is corroborated a century later: three trumpets marine were said by Rühlmann (1882) to have been in use in his day by nuns of the Marienthal Convent near Ostritz in Saxony, as replacements for the trumpet, and at the same time trumpets marine were also being played in the Mariastern Convent in nearby Kamenz (the instrument collection of the Karl Marx University, Leipzig, contains four trumpets marine of eighteenth-century workmanship from the Marienthal Convent). But if convents utilized them, so did monasteries: Kremsmünster Monastery in Austria purchased two trumpets marine in 1655; music flourished at Kremsmünster, and the monastery owned a considerable number of instruments. In the first half of the seventeenth century, Father Lechler, the house composer, wrote music for violins, viols, *viola bastarda*, viola da gamba, for *tromba marina*, and for various other instruments. Perhaps the two trumpets marine were bought for performances of his compositions.

Early eighteenth-century German opinions on the instrument were mixed: Mattheson (1713) characterizes it as "contemptuous," and Majer (1732) mentions it only in his appendix of foreign words, and yet the 1773 inventory of instruments belonging to the court *Kapelle* at Coethen, of which Bach had had charge half a century earlier, lists a trumpet marine, possibly a leftover from Bach's time. Still in the eighteenth century, "trumpet marines" were being made, sold, and played in England, and are included in Longman & Broderip's sales list of 1782, placed strategically between "trumpets" and "kettledrums" (Daniel Speer in 1687 had also mentioned them in connection with kettledrums).

The dearth of literature for this instrument is out of proportion to its documented use and to the number of surviving instruments.

THE PSALTERY

Alien finger-plucked chordophones of Greece were known in the classical age as *psaltēria*, from *psalmos* ("finger"), because their strings were plucked with bare fingers, in contradistinction to other instruments played with a plectrum, it is believed; the verb *psallein* in its restricted sense means to sound with the fingers, hence an instrument so played was a *psaltērion* (a word that passed unchanged into French). Although in Greece this denoted principally the harp, the term is now used for plucked zithers in general, and specifically for the plucked box zithers known to Europe from medieval times on. These may have a Phoenician origin.

The Biblical *asor*, meaning "ten," mentioned three times only (in the Psalms), is thought to have indicated a ten-string Phoenician psaltery with rectangular frame, plucked with bare fingers. The earliest positive identification of a psaltery, however, is that depicted on a Phoenician ivory box of the eighth century from Nimrud palace (ancient Kalakh), Assyria; it is rectangular, apparently with ten parallel strings running from one long side to the other, and played by a woman. The Book of Daniel, written probably not before the second century B.C., speaks of the *psanterin*; its name alone vouches for a foreign origin.

When Christian writers from the third century on mention the *psaltērion* they are probably referring to the ancient Hebrew harp, and it is possible that the word continued to designate a harp in the earlier Middle Ages, as well as the triangular rote or cruit. During the latter part of the Middle Ages, "psaltery" came to denote both the finger-plucked psaltery and the struck dulcimer.

Medieval European psalteries could be either plucked with bare fingers or with a plectrum, and by the late Middle Ages had assumed a variety of forms: triangular, trapezoidal, semitrapezoidal, wing shaped, or harp shaped. The latter—the early and important rote, or cruit, as it was variously known—is discussed separately (see page 215). From the ninth century on we hear of a psaltery in form of a square shield with ten strings, the *psalterium decacordum*, presumably a rectangular instrument held upright with strings running from top to bottom. The term continued in use long after psalteries had acquired additional strings: King David is shown busily tuning a twenty-one-string rote inscribed *psalterium dicitur decacordum* in the *Hortus deliciarum* of Abbess Herrad of Landsberg (1167–1195). Late medieval French literature still mentions the *décacorde*, and the thirteenth-century troubadour Guiraud de Calenson wrote of playing an *estampie* on the strings of a psaltery:

> *del salteri*
> *faras X cordas estampir*

Julian Pollux in his *Onomasticon* (IV, 61) of the second century describes the *plinthion* as a musical instrument, double strung, and one ell long. Still unidentified, the *plinthion* crops up again in a Byzantine treatise on alchemy of the eighth or early ninth century by Pseudo-Zosimo, a section of which is given over to an enumeration of musical instruments; here it is given thirty-two strings. As the word denotes a square, hollow figure or base, the *plinthion* may have been a large box zither. A very big, wide, and rectangular psaltery, held upright, with short sides at top and bottom and strings running from one to the other, and with tuning pegs on top, occurs in a Byzantine manuscript of the tenth century (MS graec. 752, Vatican Library) as part of a symbolic representation of the eight church modes. Similar instruments appear in German manuscripts of the eleventh century, depicted as being plucked by the fingers, and in the thirteenth-century Spanish *Cantigas de Santa María*, where it has a rounded top and is held obliquely by a seated player.

Meanwhile the *qānūn*, a Near Eastern trapezoid psaltery held vertically, had evolved by the tenth century and was introduced into Moorish Spain in the eleventh century, when it is also first mentioned. Its extra-European aspects and playing technique are discussed on page

220. By the twelfth century, the *qānūn* had passed from Spain to non-Moorish Europe in two forms, large and small, known as *caño* and *medio caño* in Spanish, *canon* and *micanon* in French, *canone* and *mezzo canone* in Italian, *canon* and *medius canon*, or *ala* ("wing") in Latin, *Kanon* and *Metzkanon* in German. An alternative Latin designation was *canale*, with its *medium canale*, the latter then corrupted to *medicinale*. The early fifteenth-century *Der Minne Regel* of Eberhard Cersne enumerates—and thereby distinguishes between—both *medicinale* and *psalterium*. *Ala integra* and *media ala* are terms employed by Paulirinus about 1460 for psalteries he describes as triangular and semi-triangular, plectrum played, with wire strings running vertically (*sursum levatas*); some other psalteries are shaped like the harpsichord, he writes. European "canons" were held in the same upright position as the *qānūn*.

Excepting the rote, medieval psalteries as portrayed in works of art fall into the following categories:

1. Large, wide rectangles with tuning pegs on top, held upright.

2. Large, square, slightly rectangular models resting on their long side across a seated player's knees, its back to his torso, strings running from left to right.

3. Small instruments, square or slightly trapezoid, strings running horizontally, played with two plectra, depicted from the twelfth century on. Some appear to be bichord.

4. Small trapezoid form with incurved sides laid on the player's lap, long side and longest string next to the player's body, played with two plectra, strings running from left to right, depicted from the twelfth century on.

5. The same instrument as (4) but cut in half—presumably the *micanon*; it has one incurved side.

6. Semitrapezoid—a trapezium cut in two—held with its back to the torso, long side on top, short side facing down, left side oblique and containing the tuning pins. Trichord stringing, played with a plectrum or with bare fingers. Depicted in the fifteenth century.

7. Semitrapezoid; the same as (6) except that the oblique side is now stepped. Trichord stringing, tuning pins to the left, plectrum played. Depicted from the fourteenth century on.

Psaltery-type chordophones in the form of an equilateral triangle with the point on top occur in copies of the ninth-century Epistle to

Trichord semitrapezoidal psaltery played with a plectrum. Fifteenth century. Detail of *The Coronation of the Virgin* by Paolo and Giovanni Veneziano, 1458. Copyright The Frick Collection, New York.

Dardanus by Pseudo-Jerome, in the eleventh-century Ivrea Psalter, the twelfth-century South German MS Pal. lat. 39 of the Vatican Library, MS 5371 of the Bibliothèque nationale of the eleventh century, superscribed *David basileus psallans;* their vertical stringing from short to long and back to short does not make sense, and the instruments can be taken as illustrations or interpretations of the psaltery "in form of the letter delta." Psalteries were evidently considered important in the Middle Ages; they are mentioned frequently in literature and in court records. Thus the *Clef d'amour* of about 1280 mentions indiscriminately the sounding of a psaltery, a drum, or other chordophone:

> *a sonner le psalterion*
> *ou timbre ou quinterne ou cithole*

About 1310 Louis of Navarre had a psaltery player in his employ; a document from the reign of Louis X (1314-1316) lists the following minstrels:

> *Jehannot trompeur*
> *Ernault trompeur*
> *Michelet des naquaires*
> *Le Roy Robert*
> *Le Borne du psalterion* . . .

John of Normandy (king in 1350) had a *micanon* player, and a minstrel of the psaltery received payment at the court of Philip the Bold in the mid-fourteenth century.

Two variant types branched off in the fourteenth century: the central European instrument given in modern times the name of *ala bohemica* ("Bohemian wing") and the eastern European *gusli*. The former usually assumed the form of an elongated rectangle ending in a flat, circular head, actually an outsize peg disk (showing contamination from the lute family) and had a variable number of strings. Numerous forms are depicted in the fourteenth and fifteenth centuries, not necessarily wing shaped, but all have retained the vertical playing position of the *qānūn*.

The word *gusli* is translated in medieval texts chiefly as "kithara," *lyra*, and *organon*, the last a generic designation for stringed instruments. More recently the term has been restricted to denote a triangular psaltery with incurved sides, a medieval petrifact, now a folk instrument of several peoples of the Soviet Union. In fourteenth-century Russian manuscripts it is seen as a triangle, with point on top, held vertically against the body, its strings horizontal and the shortest uppermost (in western Europe on the same instrument the longest string was uppermost); by the sixteenth century the point disappeared, the sides are incurved—its shape has become more campaniform in outline than trapezoidal, and it rests upright on the seated player's lap. Modern instruments have the same form, are laid flat on the seated player's lap, and are usually strung with gut, seldom with metal. The strings may vary from twelve to thirty-six in number, depending upon the size of the *gusli*. All are of the same diameter, but vary in length and are plucked with the bare fingers of both hands. In shape many *guslis* still resemble those seen in the hands of medieval angels; others are rectangular. Nowadays they are played chiefly by the Cheremis of the Volga area, the Votyak, and the Chuvash. During the 1880s Vassil Vassilyevitch Andreyev proceeded to modernize the *gusli* and even attempted to combine it with a keyboard.

Another type, called "old *gusli*," has the form of a Finnish *kantele* (see page 221), and from seven to thirteen strings that fan out toward the diagonal end. This contains the tuning pins and is placed to the player's left during performance. The seated player holds it horizontally on his lap, plucking the strings with bare fingers of the right hand, his left hand damping the unwanted ones in a technique reminiscent of lyre playing.

By the sixteenth century, medieval psalteries in western Europe were being relegated to the background, if not already obsolete as art music instruments. And precisely at this time a totally new form became popular—totally new to the West, that is. Best known as the *arpanetta*, it is described separately on page 219. Virdung (1511) writes of the psaltery "that is still in use, I have never seen other than the triangular." The trapezoid with incurved sides (number 4, above) was called *istromento di porco* in Italy according to Praetorius, who translates the term into German as *Sawkopf* or *Schweinekopf* ("sow's head" or "pig's head"). Although it was no longer in use in his day—doomed by the stringed keyboard instruments—he portrays it with the old Oriental feature of wooden tuning pegs. Mersenne, writing soon thereafter, noted that psalteries could be played indiscriminately as dulcimers, that is, struck or plucked. In eighteenth-century Italy the *salterio* attempted a comeback.

As to the mode of playing, Jacques Cellier's *Recueil de plusieurs singularités* of 1585 describes two methods: the first, with plectrum in each hand, he characterizes as imperfect, as one can only sound two courses simultaneously; the second, by plucking the strings with bare fingers, in which manner three or four courses could be plucked together. A tutor of 1770 gives instructions for playing a trapezoid-shaped psaltery strung with steel in the treble, brass in the bass, and having a series of individual, mobile bridges; the author recommends plucking with thumb and first two fingers, the thumb to be reserved for the playing of arpeggios. As might be expected with a metal-strung instrument, plectra were to be employed. Eighteenth-century psalteries were placed horizontally on the lap or on a table. Ring plectra called *dediles* were fixed on thumb and fingers in Spain, two or three on each hand, and instruments had up to five or six strings per course. As late as the last quarter of the nineteenth century psalteries were popular in Murcia and Alicante as accompaniments to songs and dances.

The Rote

An instrument known in medieval times on the European continent as *rota, rote, rotta, rotte, hrota, chrotta, hruozza* and further variants, and in England as *rote, crot(t),* or *cruit,* has been identified by Steger (1961) from a capital, dating from 1085–1115, in the Moissac Cloister on which a figure holding a triangular psaltery is inscribed *Eman cum rotta.* The rote has about thirty strings; its form is that of an inverted Δ, horizontal side uppermost, and tuning pins are set in the horizontal side. Such instruments appear frequently in contemporary art works, both sculptural and pictorial, and clearly imply the presence of a soundboard, thus distinguishing them from the harp. The rote was mentioned from the sixth to the sixteenth century and depicted from the ninth to the fifteenth. For many years it was believed to have been a form of medieval harp—understandably so, as the triangular rote coexisted with the triangular harp—and in the early Middle Ages it was referred to as *cythara*—a term that apparently included all chordophones having open strings exclusively. It is recorded in the oft-quoted passage from Venantius Fortunatus, poet and churchman, who lived in the sixth century:

> *Romanusque lyra, plaudat tibi barbarus harpa*
> *Graecus achilliaca, chrotta britanna canat*

where the barbarian praises with harp, the Roman with lyre, the Greek sings songs of Achilles, and where *britanna* probably stands for Bretons rather than Britons (the author was a North Italian who lived in Poitiers), although at that time the two would have probably been almost identical. However, it is quite possible that the *chrotta* mentioned here refers to the crwth, a late form of lyre. Another somewhat doubtful identification is that of Isidore of Seville in the seventh century (or a later copyist?), who wrote of a *cithara barbarica in modum deltae litterae,* probably a rote.

By the eighth century we are on firmer ground: the English bishop

Cuthbert wrote to Boniface, bishop of Mainz (d. 730): *delectat me quoque cytharistam habere, qui possit cytharizare in cithara, quam nos appellamus rottam, quia citharum habet,* requesting a *citharista* capable of playing the "cithara that we call *rotta*." Our first representation appears in the Utrecht Psalter of the ninth century, in company with a spade-shaped lute, to illustrate the passage of Psalm 108, *exsurge psalterium et cythara,* showing six strings but eight tuning pegs, with the shortest string nearest to the player. The triangular psaltery had great appeal to the Church Fathers because of its symbolism, and early theorists were not slow to describe it, following Isidore, as an instrument *in figura deltae litterae.* In the eleventh-century German poem *Ruotlieb,* King David is credited with inventing the "triangular psaltery called *rotta*," and it is frequently depicted in his hands thereafter. The vocabulary of Papias, written about 1040 (again: or a later copyist's addition?) amplifies and explains that the psaltery is like a *cythara barbarica,* delta shaped, but different in that "the psaltery's hollow wood whence the sound issues is above, with strings running downward and tuned on top, while the cithara has its hollow wood below." Several passages ascribed to Notker Labeo (formerly to his namesake, Notker Balbulus) or to a copyist, and probably dating from the twelfth century, give valuable information: in his commentary on Psalm 80 the author writes: *daz psalterium, saltirsanch, heizet nu in diutscum rotta* ("the psaltery, *saltirsanch,* is now called *rotta* in German"), and elsewhere that the old, ten-stringed psaltery had subsequently been transformed by the *symphoniaci* and *ludicratores* who changed the shape to a more convenient one, added strings, and called it by the barbarous name of *rotta.* Several early sources describe it as a plucked instrument, as for example, *als Her David sein Rotten spien/ wan er darauf harpfen wolt* ("when Lord David espied his rote, then he wished to harp on it"). Neither size nor stringing was standardized at any period of its existence.

French literature of the twelfth and thirteenth centuries contains numerous references to the rote, sometimes coupled with the harp, a combination that also occurs in the English *Cursor mundi* of about 1300. A rote appears among the sculptures of the twelfth-century Archbishop's Palace at Santiago de Compostela, those of the mid-twelfth century Abbey of Saint George de Boscherville in Normandy, and at the twelfth-century Baptisterio of Parma. The strings are always vertical, or nearly so. The *Hortus deliciarum* of Abbess Herrad of

Landsberg, also of the twelfth century, shows a realistic instrument in the hands of a seated King David who holds a long plectrum in one hand, a tuning key in the other; the tuning pins remain on the upper, horizontal side; another picture of the same work portrays a harpy holding a similar instrument with eleven tuning pins and strings, grasping the board with her left hand.

In the thirteenth century we hear and see further details: strolling players from Wales were, according to Gottfried von Strassburg's *Tristan und Isolde*, written about 1210, famous as performers on the rote; one player carried his on his back, a small instrument adorned with gold and precious stones:

> *Ueber sinen ruecke fuort er*
> *eine rotten, diu was kleine*
> *mit gold und mit gesteine*
> *geschoenert und gezieret*
> *zu wunsch geaccordieret*

In the same poem a small dog was transported inside a rote, our first literary evidence that the rote was a box zither, not a mere board with a few strings strung across the top. Guiraut de Calenson, also of the early thirteenth century, tells a jongleur to string his rote with seventeen strings (*e faitz la rota a deszest cordas garnir*). Two rotes are shown in the thirteenth-century *Cantigas de Santa María*, still with tuning pins along the top and with a large rose set into the soundboard: our first pictorial evidence of the rote's identity as a box zither, since the object of soundholes was to permit sound to escape from an otherwise closed resonator. Soundholes are also visible in later illustrations, as, for example, a French fourteenth-century Bible (Codex 27, Burger Bibliothek, Bern) with three soundholes. Transition instruments of France and Germany with aberrant forms also depict them, and a total of four soundholes are visible on the beautiful instrument of the *Coronation of the Virgin* by Paolo and Giovanni Veneziano, dated 1458, in the Frick Collection, New York. That such instruments were ever strung on both sides of the resonator is improbable, as one hand was needed to hold it while the other plucked the strings. Rotes were gut strung according to *Le bon berger* of 1379:

les menus cordes de boyaux, bien lavez, sechez, tors, rez, essuez, et filez, sont pour la melodie des instruments de musique, de vielle, de harpes, de rothes, de

Rote. Detail from *The Coronation of the Virgin* by Paolo and Giovanni Veneziano, 1458. Copyright The Frick Collection, New York.

luthz, de guiternes, de rebecs, de choros, de almaduries, de symphonies, de cytholes et de aultres instruments que l'on fait sonner par dois et par cordes.

Fine gut strings, well washed, dried, wrung, wiped, and spun, are for the melody of musical instruments, of vielles, harps, rotes, lutes, gitterns, rebecs, chorus, mandoras, symphonies, citoles, and other instruments sounded by fingers and strings.

—and here again harp and rote appear cheek by jowl. (This passage, incidentally, is an early reference to the method of spinning gut.) Rotes were instruments of the *joculatores*, for the *routte* was represented at their gathering at Wismar in 1343.

English use of the word "rote" continued from the thirteenth century right up to the sixteenth, although one might expect it to have become obsolete by then. Spenser, in his *Faerie Queen*, pays at least lip service to the instrument:

> There did he find her in delitious boure
> The faire Paeana playing on a rote

Chaucer still knew it, and passages such as "wel coude he singe and playen on a rote" caused Dr. Burney to erroneously identify rote with hurdy-gurdy, for he writes: "I have not the least doubt but that the instrument called a *rote*, so frequently mentioned by our Chaucer, as well as by the old French poets, was the same as the modern *vielle*, and had its first name from *rota*, the wheel with which its tones were produced."

But by the late fourteenth century the rote had outlived its usefulness; French and Bohemian miniatures show transient forms: early harp shapes with a partial soundboard in France, a vertical *gusli* in Bohemia. Harps were coming to the forefront at this time, and the rote, requiring as it did one hand to steady it, was no longer competitive with the harp, whose strings could be plucked with both hands.

The Arpanetta

Never sufficiently known in Britain to receive an English name, the *arpanetta* (Italian), or *Spitzharfe* (German), also called *Harfenett*, is a shallow box zither rather than the "little harp" that these appellations imply. It was generally said to be harp shaped and credited with being a descendant of the medieval rote, but its form is actually that of a semitrapezoid with incurved sides. It was always held upright or placed upright upon a table or other piece of furniture. The *arpanetta* bears two sets of strings, one on each side of the box resonator. Elongated and narrow, when it was positioned close to the player he had the steel-strung treble section to his right, the brass-strung bass section to his left, with tuning pins set in the bottom.

The *arpanetta* betrays its Oriental origin by its form—that of a *qānūn* (which in its earlier days was played upended)—by its multiple (bichord or trichord) metal stringing, and by the carved roses in its wooden soundboard. An eastern instrument with two sets of strings separated by a wooden soundboard and known by the name of *jank misrī* (Egyptian harp), was in existence by the fourteenth century and might well be the *arpanetta*'s ancestor.

In Italian paintings of the sixteenth and seventeenth centuries such as Tintoretto's *Musical Ladies* and Il Padovanino's *Nozze di Canaan*, the *arpanetta* appears to be about 60 centimeters (2 feet) high, but museum specimens average around 90 centimeters (3 feet). What were presumably the inherited three rows of tuning pins for trichord stringing are Occidentalized to two straight rows for the diatonic strings, the third, uppermost, being reserved for chromatic strings and arranged in groups of two and three, conforming to the disposition of black keys on a piano. Compasses varied from two-and-a-half to over four octaves. Italy seems to have known the *arpanetta* earlier than did the northern countries, but it enjoyed its greatest vogue in eighteenth-century Germany. Indeed, Walther (1732) could write that three kinds of harp were in existence: "1. the common one, known everywhere, strung with wire and called *harpanetta*. 2 . . ." But in France it was so little known that, at the end of the seventeenth century, Abbé du Mont could "invent" the *consonnante*, which was nothing but a large *arpanetta* placed on a pedestal. A mechanized version with spring-driven barrel was brought out in the eighteenth century and called *Harfenett d'amour*; in addition to its plucked strings it had a number of sympathetic ones. A *succès d'estime* at best, it signaled the demise of an instrument that had long outlived its musical usefulness. The chromatic harp took over.

The Qānūn

The *qānūn* of Arabian culture, a rectangular psaltery with the uppermost part cut off diagonally, derives its name from the Greek *kanōn* ("law"). It had appeared in the Near East by the tenth century, at which time it is depicted as having ten strings. The name by which it was known in the *Arabian Nights*, *qānūn miṣrī*, or Egyptian *qānūn*, may indicate the locus of its origin.

From the twelfth to the fifteenth centuries it was held upright, with the bottom of the soundbox resting against the player's chest, and kept in position by one hand, while the other was engaged in plucking the strings. A fourteenth-century Persian treatise describes it as trapezoidal, with 64 strings in courses of three each; in the early fifteenth century it is said to have had 105 strings of copper, also in courses of three. During the same century it reached Turkey. Ultimately it succeeded in radiating to all areas under Moslem influence, from Spain and North Africa to India and Indonesia. Today it survives in Arabic-speaking countries and on the Indian subcontinent—where such names as *qanum* and *kanuna* betray its descent—and in Central Asia.

Modern instruments of the Near East are gut strung and held horizontally, resting across the player's lap with the tuning pegs to his left, longest string closest to the body. The stringing varies from seventeen to twenty-five trichord courses, with a compass usually of three octaves within a range of c' to g³. In typical Eastern fashion the soundboard consists half of wood and half of skin. Thimble plectra are worn on both forefingers. In Egypt the *qānūn* is an art music instrument, not employed in folk or popular music, generally with twenty-six trichord courses tuned to the particular *makām* (mode) about to be played. The strings are plucked in octaves with both hands, but an additional function of the left hand is that of stopping the strings about to be plucked by the right hand, a procedure necessary when modulating; intervals of up to a whole tone may be stopped in this manner. Sometimes a series of movable bridges is provided, enabling strings to be sounded a quarter tone or so higher.

Turkish musicians still play both *santir* (see dulcimer, page 222) and *qānūn*; in the Maghrib the *qānūn* shows signs of becoming obsolete; in Iran it has already died out, but it still flourishes in Egypt, Syria, and Iraq. On the Indian subcontinent it has retained the features of the older instrument: its strings are still of metal, plectrum plucked, and it is held in the original vertical position; called *satatantri vīnā* (hundred-stringed *vīnā*), it now has from twenty-two to thirty-six metal strings, but probably had more originally. West of India, wooden tuning pegs and three roses covering the soundholes are typical of the *qānūn*. Among its descendants are a number of folk instruments of northern Europe, some obsolete, others still played, chief of which is perhaps the *kantele*.

The kantele. National instrument of Finland, and invented in legendary times, according to tradition, the *kantele* is still played in our day. Its name is cognate with those of the same instrument in neighboring areas: the Estonian *kannel*, the Lettonan *kohkles*, the Lithuanian *kanklys* or *kenkles*, the Livonian *kanala*, an indication that it was received from these more southerly peoples. All these variants are believed to derive ultimately from the Greek word *kanōn*. Not only does this seem likely from a philological viewpoint, but we may further surmise that their striking similarity of form to the *qānūn* is no coincidence. Their age is unknown but is believed to reach back to medieval times, despite the fact that no specimen prior to the early seventeenth century is in existence from any area.

The *kantele* approximates the *qānūn* in shape, with its resonator cut off diagonally at the upper, peg-carrying end, but it is more elongated by virtue of having few and comparatively long strings; these fan out toward the top so that the long sides diverge slightly. In common with the *qānūn* it is held horizontally across the lap with oblique side to the player's left. Fundamentally different, however, is the small number of strings, originally five, tuned $g'a'b\flat'c^2d^2$, and now sometimes seven. *Kanteles* were made from a single block of wood, hollowed out to form sides and belly, with the back left open; an even older type was hollowed from above with the soundboard then added. The first type is found from Finland to Lithuania; the second is larger than the first, assumes several forms, and is found chiefly in Estonia. Given the same number of strings, Lithuanian specimens are generally wider than Estonian or Finnish ones. A nineteenth- and twentieth-century revival form arose, played chiefly in Finland: nearly 1 meter (40 inches) in length, it has up to thirty-four strings, nowadays of steel, plucked with bare fingers.

The trumpa. Similar to the *kantele* is the *trumpa* or *tromba* found in the old Swedish colonies of Estonia and in Karelia; it differs by being rectangular, with tuning pegs set in an oblique line, corresponding to that of the diagonal cutoff of the *kantele*. Its eleven or twelve strings are tuned $F°c°d°e°f°g°a°b°c'd'e'$ and are played with or without a plectrum.

Dulcimers

Trapezoidal psalteries are not always plucked. When they are struck—usually with curved, blade-shaped beaters or padded sticks—they are known as dulcimers. The origin of struck zithers is clearly an Eastern one, but their history is not easy to follow before their arrival and dispersal in Europe.

Persia is probably their homeland, and they may have evolved at the same time as the *qānūn* (tenth century). Their Persian name, *santir*, derived from the Greek *psaltērion*, may serve as a possible clue in dating. More important is the fact that struck strings are usually of metal, whereas plucked ones are preponderantly of gut, silk, or other soft substances. If the *santir* was originally strung with metal it could scarcely have evolved much earlier. From Persia it proceeded to the surrounding areas of the Caucasus, Armenia, and Western Turkistan, where the Georgians and Kurds still play it, and to East Anatolia and Arab lands from Iraq to North Africa.

The modern Eastern instrument retains the form of a shallow, symmetrical, trapezoidal box, always metal strung, always placed horizontally when played. Generally there are fourteen or more courses of four strings, each course having its own movable bridge, with all sharing a common nut. The bridges are arranged in two rows of long and short strings for easier reach by the curved blades (it is the curve, not the tip, that strikes the strings). Typically the tuning pegs are inserted into the side of the case, not in its upper surface (belly), as might be expected.

Sea-lanes rather than overland routes seem to be responsible for the dulcimer's appearance in East Asia, introduced from either Turkey or Europe. According to a local tradition, the *yang kum* ("foreign zither") reached Korea around 1725 from India (where it is, however, unknown). Despite its name it has now become a very popular instrument in Korea, struck with a single bamboo stick while held by the player's free hand. The *yang ch'in* ("foreign zither") of China was introduced either from Turkey or from Europe around 1800, and varies considerably as to details of form, size, and stringing. Generally the very shallow, trapezoidal box, furnished with a lid, is smaller than its European counterpart. It is struck with two bamboo sticks. The same instrument is played in Japan as the *san gen da kin*.

Our first glimpse of a struck zither in Europe is in the first half of the twelfth century, in a Byzantine ivory bookplate from the Egerton Codex in the British Museum, where King David strikes a trapezoidal psaltery with two long and seemingly straight sticks. Later in the century, in 1184, we find it depicted at the other end of the Mediterranean on the sculptured portico of the cathedral at Santiago de Compostela. The presence so far apart geographically of these earliest European occurrences suggests two separate paths of entry, both occasioned by the Arabs, who took the *santir* west across Africa with them. It was played in the Maghrib in the early fifteenth century, according to ibn-Khaldun, but fell into disuse among the Arabs there later. From Spain it traveled north to France, from Byzantium to the Balkans: in modern Greece it is still called *santoúri* and *sintīr* in Egypt and Syria. By the fifteenth century we know its name in the Romance countries and England: *dulce melos* in Latin, *dulcema* in Spanish, *dolcemela* in Italian, *doucemelle* or *doulcemer* in French and English. Later the French and English were to call it *tympanon*, by which name it is known in France today (this is the old word for drum, transferred to chordophones by the tenth century). Germans called it *Hackbrett* ("chopping board") from 1477 on, possibly an indication of its preferred use as a folk instrument in German-speaking areas; as a folk instrument it appears in Switzerland in the fifteenth century, and Luscinius (1536) characterizes it as an *instrumentum ignoble*. Two distinct forms are shown in art works of the second half of the fifteenth century and the earlier sixteenth century, one trapezoidal, the other a narrow triangle; both are played with curved beaters. Sometimes these are held loosely between the second and third fingers, thumbs up, in exactly the same manner as some Indonesian xylophones are sounded. Typically the dulcimer is seen in the hands of angel musicians at this time.

Writers of the fifteenth century make no distinction between the struck and the plucked instruments. Henry Arnaut (ca. 1440) knew of two instruments by the name of *dulce melos,* one a rectangular keyboard instrument discussed below (page 244), and a simpler, nonkeyboard version played with beaters. Both had a narrow, rectangular form and strings divided by two bridges (in addition to nuts). This type can be seen played by an angel holding two light beaters, thumbs up, in the Book of Hours of Catherine of Cleves, dating from the same period. Some twenty years later, about 1460, Paulus Paulirinus said it could be played with *ligniculo aut penna* ("a small stick or a quill"). In sixteenth-century Italy the dulcimer was still an instrument of some refinement: Alessandro Citolini (1561) listed among the chordophones of his day having metal strings *dolcemele, con le verghette sue,* and Sabba da Castiglione was the owner of several *dolcemele.*

Luscinius, quoted above, seems to have expressed the German attitude toward the *Hackbrett* for his century and the next; a document dated 1586 records a blind dulcimer player among the free musicians of Breslau, probably a sign of disrepute, and Praetorius enumerates it with hurdy-gurdy, keyed fiddle, xylophone, and other components of *musica irregularis*. But elsewhere in the seventeenth century the dulcimer continued to flourish. Mersenne, it is true, depicts an instrument with only thirteen bichord courses and a two-octave compass (from g°), the dimensions of which might vary "one foot each way." Museum specimens from his time are generally larger, with about double the number of courses, and having four or five strings to a course. A bridge divides the strings into a ratio of $2:3$ in such a manner that, when struck on their left portion, they sound a fifth higher than when struck on the right. However, in practice two bridges are required, for in order to create space for the beaters, the courses are led alternately over and under the bridge. At this time, tuning pins and hitchpins were set in an additional narrow board, projecting beyond the sides of the instrument and tilted to a slightly different plane. Pepys records in his diary for May 23, 1662: "I first saw a dulcimer played on with sticks knocking of the strings . . ." probably a rare appearance of the instrument in England, where dulcimers followed the *Hackbrett*'s example. Grassineau in the next century found them "not much used except among puppet shows."

At the end of the seventeenth century the dulcimer was enlarged and modernized by Pantaleon Hebenstreit, whose instrument deserves discussing in some detail if only because of its alleged role in the creation of the pianoforte.

The pantaleon and its influence. Around the year 1690, Hebenstreit, a dancing master of Leipzig, heard a dulcimer while evading his creditors in a village near Merseburg, so the story goes, and conceived the notion of improving it. He proceeded to add the accidentals missing up to then and extended the compass at treble and bass. The resultant instrument was about twice the size of the unimproved version, some four feet long, with two soundboards "opposite one another," that is, juxtaposed, one steel strung, the other with metal-covered gut strings. By 1697 Hebenstreit was making a name for himself as a virtuoso on his new instrument, and in 1705 he had the honor of playing before the king of France. Louis XIV called the instrument pantaleon, and it has been known as such ever since, albeit more often corrupted to "pantalon."

Various modifications were added by others in the course of the eighteenth century, and accounts vary as to size and stringing. The usual compass was five octaves, from G' to g^3, but Kuhnau owned one with a compass of E^2 to e^3, diatonic up to G', chromatic thereafter. Hebenstreit himself played with two different beaters, a padded one for the soft tones, the other presumably of bare wood. The possibility of making rapid changes from *piano* to *forte* left a marked impression upon his audience, but this advantage was partly offset by the lack of damping, and here, as with the Hungarian *cimbalom*, the player's hand or sleeve had to help out. Hebenstreit had his pantaleons built by Gottfried Silbermann up until 1727, at which time they quarreled and engaged in a legal battle. Hebenstreit had several pupils, and after his death in 1750 they continued concertizing (until 1787), but by the time Burney saw a pantaleon in Dresden, in 1772, it lay unused, nearly all of its strings broken. Diderot was fascinated by the *pantaleone* he heard in Paris in 1765, which he described as being four feet wide by eight feet long, with seventy-four *tons*, evidently capable of all shadings from *pianissimo* to the most thunderous *forte*, played by a musician able to "make his audience pass from fury to joy, and from joy to fury" (letter to Sophie Volland).

The role that Hebenstreit and his invention played in the emergence of the piano has undoubtedly been exaggerated by many writers. Schroeter claimed to have been first to invent it: he had "had the opportunity of hearing the world-renowned virtuoso, Herr Pantalon [*sic*] Hebenstreit" perform on the instrument of his—that is, Hebenstreit's—invention, which was strung with gut strings and played with *Klöppel* (beaters) like a dulcimer; this, Schroeter admitted, gave him the idea of inventing a keyboard instrument on which he could play both *piano* and *forte*. (For further details, see pianoforte, page 325). "Pantaleon" was a household word in Germany when piano building started there, and early pianos were often called *Hämmerwerk* or *Hämmerpantaleon*, sometimes abbreviated to plain *Pantaleon*; and "pantalon" stops appeared on clavichords and pianos alike in the mid-eighteenth century. The name "pantalon" lingered on into the nineteenth century, although the instrument itself had died out by then.

Such was the impact of the pantaleon that from about 1750 on the dulcimer was remodeled and taken up by virtuosi. Its case was enlarged, the projecting tilted boards for tuning pins and hitchpins abolished, and the former inserted into the case proper; the large number of thin strings per course was likewise abolished and replaced by thicker bichord or at most trichord courses under greater tension; the left bridge was either divided or split up to form individual bridges. As these divided the sounding length of the string their position was critical; hence they were always set loosely upon the soundboard, never glued on. The string's tension kept them in place. Finally, in order to obtain maximum string length for the basses, the lowest strings were given the entire length of the soundboard.

English dulcimers of the eighteenth century had a compass of three diatonic octaves, whereas in Germany one result of the pantaleon's influence had been to render the dulcimer's compass chromatic. This transformed "chopping board" became known as *Cimbal* in German; in America it went by the unlovely name of whamdiddle. Ironically, dulcimers underwent the fate of so many other eighteenth-century instruments: from 1783 on patents were granted for the addition of a keyboard.

More often this spelled the death blow, but the dulcimer managed to survive. Throughout the eighteenth and well into the nineteenth century it remained an instrument of polite society, but, from the delicate, highly ornate objects they so often were in the eighteenth century, they grew into cumbersome and coarse pieces of four-legged furniture. By the mid-nineteenth century they were completely vanquished by the piano.

Folk dulcimers. Defunct as art instruments in Europe, dulcimers live on there as folk instruments, albeit in a smaller area than that which they once covered. Formerly folk instruments from Bohemia to Yugoslavia, their territory is now restricted to Switzerland and countries east thereof; they survive as *Cimbal* in Appenzell, Switzerland, and in the Austrian Alps—usually trichord, with a compass of C° to c³—as *zimbel* in Russia, in Hungary as *cimbalom*, in Romania as *țambal* (pron. *tsambal*) — all words derived from the Greek *kymbalon*—and as *santoúri* in Greece.

For Hungarian Gypsies the *cimbalom* forms the basic orchestral unit. Up to the second half of the nineteenth century it was a true folk instrument, but at that time it was modernized by Schunda of Budapest, who transformed it into a shallow, trapezoidal box resting on four legs, with a compass of E° to e³, and a pedal to raise a series of dampers. Wherever these improvements have remained unknown or neglected, the old version may still be heard. From Hungary the *cimbalom* passed to Romania in the first half of the nineteenth century, before it underwent modernization.

AEOLIAN HARPS

Despite its name, the wind god's harp is but a zither, traditionally a box resonator strung with gut strings of identical length and pitch but of different thicknesses, and at low tension. The resonator of most models is a rectangle of a few feet's length, its surface provided with soundholes. It is placed in an open window or suspended elsewhere so as to catch the breeze, when its dozen or so strings are set in vibration by the action of the wind and sound in soft chords.

The principle of the Aeolian harp was already known by Biblical times; the strings of King David's *kinnōr*, a lyre, sounded in the north wind at night. In another age such manifestations were regarded with the greatest suspicion: Saint Dunstan (d. 988) was suspected of sorcery for having experimented with a "harp" that played of its own accord when hung in the breeze. We hear no more of such attempts until the mid-sixteenth century, when Giovanni Battista Porta mentions strings sounded by the wind (in 1558). Not until a century later was the idea taken up again, when Athanasius Kircher (1650) designed elaborate wind catchers and managed to arouse, at least temporarily, a measure of both theoretical and practical interest in the phenomenon. A further century passed before the poet James Thompson discussed the Aeolian harp (1746), after which the "ghostly sound of chords" was retained by the popular imagination and assumed a definite place in eighteenth-century *Affekten*. Probably still influenced by Kircher's writing, the Abbate G. C. Gattoni of Como concocted his *armonica meteorologica* in 1785—it was also dubbed *arpa gigantesca*—with fifteen metal strings tuned diatonically. This he caused to be strung up between his house and a nearby tower; the strings were to be vibrated by the wind to serve as a weather-forecasting device, and due to vagaries of the weather it seems to have been more successful as a "barometer" than as a musical instrument.

Far more sophisticated was the *anémocorde* invented by Johann Jacob Schnell of Paris, court instrument maker to the Comtesse d'Artois, who created in 1789 what was in effect an Aeolian harp controlled from a keyboard. When a key was depressed, the corresponding (trichord) strings were set in vibration by wind conducted through tubes leading from bellows. Although dynamic variation was made possible by registers, the tone remained soft, and only slow pieces could be executed upon it. In appearance it was like a claviorganum, some seven feet long and standing four and one-half feet high; its three upper octaves were strung with silk strings. Queen Marie Antoinette heard of the *anémocorde* and sent word to its maker requesting him to reserve it for her until more favorable conditions prevailed. But Schnell managed to escape to Germany at the outbreak of the Revolution and was later able to exhibit his invention. In 1803 it was purchased by the British physicist Robertson, who took it to London.

The *anémocorde* seems to have aroused sufficient interest to warrant imitation, for the *piano éolien*, a similar instrument, was devised in 1837 by Isouard, who then sold his patent to the pianist and piano builder, Henri Herz of Paris.

Aeolian harps in the simple form that we still occasionally encounter were even produced by such builders of repute as Johann Christian Dietz, who set his boxes on feet to enable them to be placed in the most advantageous possible position, and Friedrich Theodor Kaufmann of Dresden, of the famous family of musical automata builders, also produced a version, probably around 1850. The craze for such instruments that had started in the mid-eighteenth century continued until the mid-nineteenth. In 1841, for instance, Aeolian harps were being manufactured for garden owners on the continent of Europe. Such outdoor versions had already been mentioned in 1784 by Matthew Young (*Enquiry into the Principal Phenomena of Sounds and Musical Strings*) who credited William Jones with their invention. A whole book was devoted to Aeolian harps in 1808 (*Nature's Music*, by Robert Blomfield), another in 1856 (by Georges Kastner). Today they are met with as curiosities only.

FRETTED ZITHERS

Although its derivation cannot be proved, the fretted folk zither of northern Europe is believed to be descended from the medieval monochord. First mentioned by Praetorius (1619), it is undoubtedly older. In Germany it was called *Scheitholt* ("wooden log") except in the maritime area, where it was known as *Hummel* ("drone"); in the neighboring Low Countries it was either a *noordsche balk* ("northern log") or a *hommel*; in northern maritime France it was usually a *bûche* ("log") or else an *épinette des Vosges*, probably so called because the Val d'Ajol in the Vosges Mountains became a center of their manufacture in the eighteenth century; in French-speaking Belgium its name was *bûche de Flandres* ("Flemish log"), indicating an alien provenance. The sparse references in Denmark are to a *humle*, again "drone." Iceland, Sweden, and Norway have another common terminology: *langspil, langspel, langleik,* respectively, whereas to the Finns it was a sort of *kantele*. All these instruments resemble one another closely: they are rectangular like a narrow log, usually tapering at the upper end, with a series of wooden or metal frets, sometimes with a fretted fingerboard taking up almost the total length of the left flank, a single melody string, and most have in addition one or more drone strings. In some areas the strings are plucked, in others bowed, but regardless of the method of sound production these zithers are always placed horizontally on a table when played. From Europe—more precisely, probably from Germany and Holland—the fretted zither was introduced to the United States, where it survives in a relatively small area as the Appalachian dulcimer.

Of the Central European group, the French *bûche* lasted longest, up to the mid-nineteenth century. Its two melody strings were plucked by the right thumb, while the left hand held a small rod with which the strings were depressed onto the frets (as is the case with all these fretted zithers, the frets do not extend under the drone strings). Later the manner of playing was changed and a plectrum came into use. Both melody strings were tuned to g', the three drones to g'g'c'. Unison playing was not adhered to exclusively: the melody strings could also be stopped so as to sound the interval of a third, or some other interval; in such cases they were depressed by index and middle finger, whereas, when unisons were desired, both were stopped by the rod. The *bûche* remained a regional instrument in France, restricted to the northwest maritime areas and to the Vosges Mountains.

When Claas Douwes (1699) described the Flemish *noordsche balk* it had three or four strings and diatonic frets. Colloquially it was simply called "drone," *hommel,* and when it was bowed the left hand stopped the melody strings. Older instruments were hollowed out of a block of wood, the back being left open (cf. the northern psalteries). A *balk* dating from about the time when Douwes wrote has three melody and five drone strings and measures 151 centimeters (59½ inches). By the nineteenth century it was extinct.

The German *Scheitholt* was described by Praetorius as a *Lumpen Instrument* ("instrument of the riffraff"—today we would probably qualify it as a popular instrument) with usually three and sometimes four strings. The melody string was made to sound a fifth higher than the other strings by the simple expedient of running it through a hook placed two-thirds of the length of the fingerboard, and apparently obtaining the necessary downbearing by means of a fret. All the strings were "strummed" with the right thumb as a smooth stick glided from position to position on the fingerboard (cf. Hawaiian guitar, page 457; *gotuvādyam* stick zither, page 183). *Scheitholts* were built up of slats, either as a closed box or, less frequently, with open back. By the middle of the eighteenth century they were known to the literati by name only, and even that was not entirely clear: Adlung (1758) calls it *Scheitholt* or Spanish *Hummel,* and refers his readers to Praetorius. Actually it lived on as *Hummel* or *humle* in remoter areas such as the North Sea islands, the Ditmarsh regions of Schleswig-Holstein, and southern Denmark.

Tradition ascribes its introduction to these North Sea areas to seamen of the Low Countries. *Humles* of Denmark have a larger number of strings than those further south; four melody and six drone strings are still common, the latter tuned pairwise to tonic and dominant, and all are played with a plectrum. Several variant forms are encountered, some rectangular, some tapering, others with a bulging of the lower right side.

Of the northern group, the Norwegian *langleik* may well be oldest; it can be traced back to the mid-sixteenth century and has remained in use ever since. With a greater number of strings than other instruments of the group, it is occasionally made with a pegbox at each end. The strings, all of steel, vary in number from four to fourteen, with one or more melody strings. Stopping is effected by a back-and-forth gliding motion of three fingers, with the right hand holding a long plectrum. Tunings are varied: that of an eight-stringed instrument has G melody strings with drones $c°c'g'e^2e^2g^2$, that of a seven-stringed instrument $a°a°/a°a°e'e'e^2$ or $c\sharp^2$. The high strings are brought up to pitch by means of a small nut wedged between soundboard and string at an appropriate position, analogous to the hook of Praetorius (a specimen in the Brussels Conservatoire Museum has a hook for shortening the string close to the fourth fret, at precisely the same position as that of Praetorius's illustration). In rural areas the *langleik* serves to accompany dances. The same instrument was played in seventeenth-century Denmark, called *langeleg* by the peasants who played it. Some of the older *langleiks* were hollowed out of a block of wood and left bottomless, a feature shared with the *kantele*.

The *langspil* of Iceland was first mentioned in eighteenth-century literature when it was described as a bowed chordophone with six strings; this relatively large number may indicate that it was originally plucked there, and indeed it appears to have also been plucked on occasion. Subsequently the number of strings was reduced to two or three, a single melody and one or two drone strings, the latter tuned to tonic and dominant of the melody string. Generally it was made in slender, rectangular *bûche* form, fretted along one side, but some models bulged out at the right lower end. When revived in the mid-nineteenth century, the *langspil* was invariably bowed, as it is today; but nowadays it is rarely encountered. A modern variety with a single metal string exists.

Sweden adopted both the bowed form called *langspel*—it corresponds to the Icelandic variety—and in addition had a plucked model with a larger number of strings. Finland formerly had a bowed variety also, the *kantele-harpe,* now obsolete. Like those of other areas, its back was generally left open and a rectangle bulged out at the lower right. Of its two brass strings, that for the melody passed over fourteen fixed frets of wood, and the shorter drone was attached to a peg inserted partway down the right side.

A rectangular "log" type was formerly played in Pennsylvania but is now obsolete there; it had been imported, probably from Germany. Either as a rectangle or of more fanciful undulating form with symmetrical bulges on both sides of a central fingerboard, it survives as the Appalachian dulcimer, mountain zither, or simply dulcimer, a folk instrument of the southern Appalachian mountains and foothills and of the Upper Ohio Valley. Its general use has been ascertained only from the turn of the nineteenth to the twentieth century, but its presence there doubtless goes back further. Playing technique is that of its European ancestors: either it is placed horizontally on a table or across the lap; plucking is with bare fingers or a plectrum. Traditionally the latter is a turkey or goose quill called a pick. A similar quill, called a noter, is held in the left hand for stopping—or "noting"—the melody string with gliding motions. Some players, however, "note" the string with their fingers. The zither often has cordiform soundholes and the usual fixed frets—only here they are wire staples driven into the fingerboard —and from three to five metal strings. The more common number is three, tuned $C°f°c°$ or $C°g°c°$ or $c°g°g°$ (relative pitches all). The fretting of most instruments is diatonic starting with the third fret and comprises a compass of over two octaves; the tone sequence, starting with the open string, is generally TTSTTSTTT . . . Formerly, metal strings were handmade on an anvil or, if unavailable, gut substitutes were used; now, however, banjo or guitar strings are preferred. Despite the fact that its route of introduction to the southeastern United States is not known, the form of the instrument combined with known patterns of population movements point to Germany via Pennsylvania as the probable path taken.

The Alpine Zither

Obsolete though most of the north European instruments have become, they nevertheless left descendants in the mountainous regions further south in form of the Alpine zither, also called mountain zither. Characteristically these are wider in relationship to their length and have a greater number of strings than did their ancestors. They survive not only in the Bavarian and Austrian Alps but are also found in Slovenia. Transition from the *bûche-Scheitholt* rectangle to the broader build appears at a relatively early date: a Paris-made instrument of 1787 is only some three times as long as it is wide, and in addition to its two pairs of melody strings it has seven pairs of drones spread out over the resonator. The zither's apogee as a folk instrument was reached in the latter part of the eighteenth century and the early nineteenth century, before its transformation into a popular instrument took place. Until the late eighteenth century the fretted mountain zither was not found outside the Alpine regions, but at that point the Alps were "discovered" by travelers, and with them the zither. This resulted in a flurry of building and commercialization. The rectangular form was preserved until the 1830s, at which time two schools of zither building developed: that of Mittenwald in Bavaria, another in the Salzburg area, the former with bulging projections on both lower flanks, the latter with a bulge on the right flank only. Sometimes the Salzburg type terminated in a helmet-like pegbox, in which case it was known as a helmet zither (*Helmzither*); such instruments date from the 1840s and 1850s.

Zithers were built in various sizes in order to encourage ensemble playing; fostered by the concert tours of virtuosi such as Johann Petzmayer in the 1830s, and by publication of Nikolaus Weigl's tutor of 1838, with its standard stringing and tuning, the zither came close to entering the domain of art instruments. At the mid-century it had assumed its modern form, basically that of a flat rectangular box, with the long side nearest the player carrying a chromatically fretted fingerboard. Today its stringing varies considerably, but four melody strings tuned $c°g°d'a'$ are common, and the drones—now referred to as accompaniment strings—may number from thirty-eight to forty-two. Melody strings are of metal, sounded with a ring plectrum worn on the player's right thumb, and are stopped by his left hand; the drones are of gut and are strummed with the right-hand fingers. By the 1870s it had "come into fashion, especially in the south of Germany."

Bowed zithers in shape of cordiform violins or viole da gamba were also introduced, but did not outlive the century. Simple zithers are rarely heard now, because in the late nineteenth century their place was partly taken by an "improvement," the chord zither. This was, however, a popular rather than a true folk instrument. Here, a series of chord bars lie across all the strings; when the bars are depressed the unwanted strings are damped, thereby permitting persons of little or no musical ability to play in chords.

THE BELL HARP

In the early eighteenth century a wire-strung box zither was invented by John Simcock of Bath, allegedly named bell harp in honor of his commanding officer, a Captain Bell. The trapezoidal box was suspended from a cord and created much effect by the manner in which it was played: it was kept swinging. The strings of brass or steel varied from fourteen to twenty-three courses of three or four strings each, sixteen being a common number. They were tuned to the D major scale and divided into two sections, those in the bass plucked by the left thumb, those in the treble by the right thumb, both armed "with a little wire pin," a finger plectrum. According to Tans'ur (1772) the plectra could also be of quill, whalebone, or horn. Although the outline is described by him as campaniform, actual specimens are either trapezoidal or rectangular.

A sales list of Longman & Broderip of London, dated 1782, offers among many instruments "Aeolian and Bath harps," the latter presumably our bell harp invented in Bath, and its juxtaposition with the Aeolian harp may point to its author's probable source of inspiration.

KEYBOARD CHORDOPHONES

THE KEYBOARD

Before summarizing the history of individual keyboard instruments, a brief survey of the keyboard itself may serve as a connecting link to their disparate developments.

Unlike present-day piano keys, pivoted on a fulcrum, the earliest keys were of a push-pull variety. Keys forming part of a Roman organ dating from the third century had the shape of an L square, the short foot of which was pushed by the player and returned by means of a spring; the top of the long foot was connected to a flat slider, pierced so as to open or close access to the pipe feet, depending upon its position.

For western Europe all details concerning keyboards are lacking until roughly the end of the millennium, after which realistic representations of organs start appearing. Their keyboards were of the slider-key variety, with each broad key terminating in a handle, also of a push-pull kind (the return springs were absent at first). Not more than two such keys, one in each hand, could be pulled simultaneously. They were flat, no longer L shaped, and no doubt represent simplification of the older type. The compass of the earliest Western organs was of two octaves, increased in the thirteenth and fourteenth centuries to three octaves. Because all the keys looked exactly alike, their alphabet names were marked on each key, as they also were on some early organistrums. This is already visible on the organ illustrated in the Bible of Saint Stephen Harding, completed between 1098 and 1109, where the letters CDEFGab♮ can be seen, that is, with both B♭ and B♮. (It will be recalled that B♭ was an integral part of the hexachord system, hence not considered as an accidental. Cf. the *Buxheimer Orgelbuch* of about 1460: *Voces ut re mi fa so la. Et duae conjunctae h durum b molle. Et distribuntur per litteras c d e f g a h b. quatuor semitonia cis dis fis gis.*) On the preserved keyboards of four late fourteenth-century Swedish organs both B♭ and B♮ still appear as "white" keys.

Organ keyboards did not become fully chromatic until about 1400, but it must be stressed that neither compass nor disposition were standardized at any time. The organ of Sainte Marie de la Mer in 1425 had thirty-five keys; a drawing of Henry Arnaut's manuscript of about 1440 shows a compass of $B°$ to a^2 with thirty-five keys, but many organs of the period had fewer. Arnaut also gives the length of the front (i.e., visible) portion of the keys of organ, harpsichord, clavichord, and *dulce melos* as twice their width. From about 1490 to the mid-sixteenth century the lowest manual key was usually F on an organ; during the sixteenth century a four-octave compass became common, increased to four and one-half octaves in the course of the seventeenth century. However, organ manuals were increased earlier in Spain and Italy than they were in the north, probably because organs there lacked independent pedals.

North of the Alps the compass of stringed keyboard instruments expanded in advance of that of the organ, as the chordophones had no built-in 16′ or 2′ stops to draw upon. Italian harpsichords maintained from the sixteenth to the eighteenth century a four-octave compass with relatively few exceptions, while that of contemporary Italian spinets was four and one-half octaves: $C°$ to c^3 and $C°$ to f^3, respectively, both with bass short octave.

The short octave, called *mi re ut* in Italian, was an arrangement designed to save space and pipes (ergo, money) in the lowest octave of organs, both in the manual and in the pedal, by omitting those keys and corresponding pipes that were deemed unnecessary or could be dispensed with. Such a practice seems to have existed by the fourteenth century, arising no doubt from the downward extension of the compass, and was adopted by keyboard chordophones in the late fifteenth century (Ramis de Pareja knew of it). Both the organ and keyboard chordophones retained at least vestiges of the system until the late eighteenth century. The system expanded with the instrument, for when the bass compass was extended from C or B down to F, the accidentals of this extension were omitted (B♭ was still not considered to be an accidental),

so that the lowest octave consisted of FGA BC $\overset{\text{B♭ C♯ E♭}}{\text{D}}$ E. But then it was discovered that, by adding a single key to the bass and inserting two more accidentals, the compass could effectively be lengthened to C, for

a half-octave extension: CF G A BC $\overset{\text{D E B♭ C♯ E♭}}{\text{D}}$ E. This pattern is also known as the C short octave. By the early seventeenth century the lacking low F♯ and G♯ keys were needed, and in order to obtain these without actually enlarging the keyboard—an expensive affair—two split sharps were introduced, the front portions of which communicated with the pipes sounding D and E, as theretofore, the rear portions with new pipes sounding F♯ and G♯, respectively.

This type of bass octave is rarely encountered on keyboard chordophones before 1700. Although the C short octave was by far the most common, other arrangements existed, notably the G short octave, resulting from the extension down to G, and occasionally also completed by split sharps:

$$\overset{\text{A B F♯}}{\text{GC D EF G} \ldots}$$

Here only the G key has been added, and the former C♯ pipes were replaced by A pipes for a downward extension of a fourth, but lacking the low B♭. Although found on the European continent only occasionally, this was a common short octave pattern in England after the Restoration (Father Smith, for one, made use of it). Subsequently, the G short octave was enlarged to G long octave (instruments with a full bass octave are said to be long octave), and this continued in use until the nineteenth century, to judge from Sutton's A *Short Account of Organs*

(1847). Other patterns of short octave have been met with on organs, but only in isolated instances.

Memories of the B♭ as an integral part of the hexachord system lingered on in Italy into the seventeenth century; describing the organs of his day, Banchieri (1609) gives them a compass of twenty-eight white keys plus four *b molle naturale & 4 accidentali,* eight all told, as well as the *diesis posti nelle corde* CFG—the theorist in him is coming out—and the three added keys for the short octave, for a total of fifty keys. Other organs, he continues, have a compass of fifty-four, forty-two, or thirty-eight keys.

But to return to the compasses of stringed instruments: Flemish keyboard chordophones terminated in the bass on C° at the time of the *ravalement* (a bass extension of the eighteenth century), when the compass was gradually taken down to F'. In England, organ builders stayed with the Γ ut of yore and consequently the practice of also terminating other keyboard instruments on G was adhered to up to the time of Kirkman in the eighteenth century. Harpsichords first attained a five-octave compass around 1700; the first pianos had a four-octave span, rapidly increased to five octaves. Organs did not achieve five-octave manuals until far later. By the end of the eighteenth century some pianos had already expanded their keyboard to six octaves, F' to f⁴, increasing further to six and one-half octaves during the course of the nineteenth century (C' to f⁴); Broadwood reached this compass by 1811. That of modern pianos extends for seven octaves and a minor third, from A² to c⁵.

Split keys occurring outside the bass octave had a function different from that mentioned above; their division into front and rear sections, each connected to different pipes, was primarily in the interest of intonation, and was resorted to in the organ from the mid-fifteenth century on, with the keyboard chordophones following suit for the same reason. Splitting the G♯ and E♭ keys throughout the compass became the usual way of eliminating the "wolf" tone of nonequal temperaments. Thus if the pitch of the E♭ keys was not satisfactory in relation to certain intervals in a given tonality, those keys could be divided to give the player the option of E♭ or D♯. Similarly, the G♯ was sometimes split in order to obtain an additional A♭; thus the organ contract for Saint Martin's, Lucca, which instrument was completed in 1484, called for split D♯ and G♯ keys. Throughout the sixteenth and seventeenth centuries, numerous organs had one or more of their keys split throughout the compass, and pedal keys were treated in the same manner. Schlick (1511) wrote that twelve years earlier an organ had been built with "double semitones" in both manual and pedal. It was customary to allot the front portions of split keys to the sharps, the rear portions to the flats. Split keys were unknown to the ultraconservative organ builders in England until after the Restoration, when Father Smith (né Bernhard Schmidt, a Dutch builder who had settled in England) introduced them in his Temple Church organ built by 1685; this was said to contain "extraordinary Stopps, quarter Notes, and other Rarityes," the quarter notes in question being split C♯ and G♯ keys on the great and choir organ. When split keys are situated in the lowest octave of any keyboard instrument, it should be noted, they are the result of attempts to extend the compass, and are independent of any question of intonation.

EXPERIMENTAL KEYBOARDS

After the adoption of equal temperament in the nineteenth century, unrestricted transposition was possible, thus distracting attention from the relative importance of the diatonic keys and hence also of their position; as a consequence, a number of reforms and would-be improvements to the existing keyboard were suggested, none of which has, however, been accepted so far. Curiously, and perhaps illogically, these have their roots in pre-equal temperament times, and are known collectively as chromatic keyboards. According to Mattheson (1722), the mathematician Conrad Henfling invented one as early as 1708; Gerber (1812–1814) relates that in 1791 a chromatic keyboard was presented to the Berlin Academy by Johann Rohleder, with diatonic and accidental keys alternating uninterruptedly, with C D E F♯ G♯ B♭ as natural keys, C♯ D♯ F G A B as accidental ones, the latter spaced regularly between the former. This type was built in the nineteenth century, notably by several German piano makers, and, once the new system had been mastered, fingering was considerably simplified. Another chromatic keyboard, that of Arthur Wallbridge, pseudonym of the Englishman A. B. Lunn, built in 1843, had equally spaced keys and was called sequential keyboard. In 1882 Paul von Jankó invented what was subsequently known as the Jankó keyboard, originally built by R. W. Kurka of Vienna; in addition to the objectives of his precursors, namely those of giving equal emphasis to all tonalities and to simplify fingering, von Jankó also wished to reduce the octave span. His octave therefore had a span of 13 centimeters (ca. 5 inches) as opposed to the 16½ centimeter (6½ inch) standard. The keys, shaped like square buttons, were arranged in six tiers, alternating and repeating whole-tone sequences, one starting on C, the next on C♯.

Experimental keyboards have also been produced in crescent or curved form, to permit the maintenance of the same hand position throughout the range; with two manuals, the upper of which was reversed in pitch, with the lowest-sounding string in the treble (the *piano à queue à double clavier renversé* exhibited in the 1878 Paris Exposition by Edouard Mangeot); with two manuals and an octave coupler; with two manuals tuned a quarter tone or semitone apart, such as that designed by Pierre Hans, an engineer of Liége, in 1920 and built by Pleyel, with upper manual tuned a semitone higher than the lower in order to facilitate fingering in difficult passages; and others. None of these gained general acceptance.

TRANSPOSING KEYBOARDS

Difficulty and, in certain cases, even the impossibility of transposition experienced by keyboard instrument players of past ages are said to have been responsible for the invention of a number of devices to transpose pitch. But this is true only in part, for transposing keyboards were built right through the nineteenth century, and for other purposes also. They were created in response to various requirements, the most common of these being:

1. At a time when the absolute pitch of organs differed by as much as half an octave, to permit organists to play solo works, such as intonations, at the same pitch level on different instruments, but without change of fingering.

2. Prior to the adoption of equal temperament, to furnish accidentals not otherwise available (e.g., D♯ in lieu of E♭), although this defect was sometimes remedied by split keys.

3. To enable players to accommodate singers or instrumentalists— particularly the higher-pitched wind instruments of the nineteenth century—by playing at different pitch.

4. To enable unskilled performers to play pieces having several sharps or flats in the signature in "easy" keys.

The first of these requirements was met by creating practice instruments for organists in the form of two-manual harpsichords, one manual at the pitch of the higher organ, the second at that of the lower organ, with the F key of one manual plucking the C key of the other. Several Flemish harpsichords dating from the first half of the seventeenth century with such keyboards are still in existence, and this type was also depicted by the Velvet Brueghel in his *Allegory of Hearing* (ca. 1620) in the Prado, and by the anonymous painter of *Music* (attributed to van Kessel) in the museum of Saint Germain-en-Laye. But such instruments existed only in Flanders. Italian makers solved the problem in a different manner: they seem to have pitched their spinets (normally with a four-and-one-half-octave compass) half an octave lower than their harpsichords (normally with a four-octave compass).

The second requirement was met by including in certain organs (such as that of the Foundling Hospital, London) a special transposition register whereby those accidental keys normally tuned C♯ D♯ G♯ A♯ could be changed to provide D♭ E♭ A♭ B♭.

The third requirement was furnished commonly by a shifting keyboard. This device was already known to Schlick in 1511; he states that he had in daily use an organ that could transpose one tone, with the C key sounding D pipes. Shifting keyboards have been in intermittent use ever since, and were applied to harpsichords from the seventeenth century on; Praetorius describes one with nineteen microtones to the octave and a keyboard that could be shifted seven times, or "three full tones." In a letter addressed to Constantijn Huygens, dated July 31, 1648, the Sieur de la Barre, organist and harpsichordist to the king of France, takes credit for its invention. He writes of a two-manual harpsichord with shifting keyboards for playing in "all tones and semitones" of his own invention, a *clavecin . . . à deux claviers et triples cordes, avec l'invention de faire mouvoir les claviers pour jouer en touttes sortes de tons et demy tons: cette derniere invention est de moy, il n'y a que les miens en france* [sic] *ou cela se trouve.* Huygens in turn wrote to Mersenne on August 14 of the same year to inquire whether he, Mersenne, knew anything about the *certain clavier d'espinette mouvante* ("the shifting harpsichord keyboard").

Shifting keyboards could be of two kinds: the first could move, for example, the C key so that it communicated with a C♯ pipe or string (in which case there would be corresponding extra pipes or strings at the treble end), or the shift would cause the keys to communicate with extra sets of pipes or strings for intermediary pitches, such as that of the harpsichord described by Bontempi (1695), with fifteen strings to the (closed) octave, the extra two for additional tones between D♯ and E, G♯ and A, the traditional "wolf" tones. Clearly this was an alternative to split sharps. Shifting keyboards on pianos were popular for accompanying wind instruments, as the pitch could thus be raised by a semitone or a tone; but once metal struts were incorporated into pianos between pinblock and belly rail it was found that they obstructed the shift, and as a result the shift was discontinued shortly before Lehmann (1827) wrote his tuner's manual; yet an upright piano dated 1841 in the Leipzig University collection still has a shifting keyboard permitting transposition up to three semitones.

Finally, a false keyboard solved the problem of the fourth requirement. This relatively modern idea found application on pianos after 1801, the year in which Edward Ryley patented a piano with a false keyboard placed over the real one; it could be shifted to any semitone of the octave, enabling a performer to play any piece in C major if so desired. Later, in 1872, the Paris firm of Pleyel, Wolff & Cie patented a false keyboard with a six-octave compass moved by means of a rack.

Organs of former centuries also made use of a transposition stop that brought different pipes into play without recourse to a shifting keyboard; many eighteenth- and nineteenth-century *Kammerton* ("chamber pitch") stops fall into this category. The ranks in question sounded generally a tone lower than the rest of the organ and were needed when playing with other chamber pitch instruments. A variation on this theme was the 1844 patenting in England by Sébastien Mercier of Paris of a piano with split keys, the rear portions of which caused a second set of hammers to strike the neighboring course of strings. Mercier's patent was worked by Robert Addison, and such a piano was shown in the 1851 Exposition—but a patent for a similar action had already been granted in 1843 to Le Bihan of Carhaix (Finistère). However, shifting keyboards remained by far the more common and were even applied to clavichord and square piano (where the motion is of necessity one of pushing the keyboard *in*, not sideways, because of the transverse direction of the strings).

Samuel Petri (1782) epitomizes the problems encountered by organists of the past when he relates that most organs then in use had been built in the (higher) *Chorton* ("choir pitch"), partly to save on expensive tin, partly to be at the same pitch as trombones and trumpets (however, it should be noted that trombones and trumpets were built at choir pitch in those days because the organ was at choir pitch, not vice versa). But later, Petri continues, other instruments [at *Kammerton*] were introduced into the church and the organist's part was then notated a tone lower. As long as church modes only remained in use there were few problems, but once music was written in all tonalities transposition became complicated indeed, partly due to the unequal tuning of the various tonalities, and partly because of the short octave in manual and pedal "so that the whole bass has but a single F♯ C♯ and D♯ and the pedal merely a single C♯," thus constantly obliging the organist to transpose the prescribed key. Hence some builders helped the organist, he says, by arranging a shifting keyboard in such a manner that the keys acted on the neighboring abstracts. Now that equal temperament is taken for granted, it is often difficult to realize the extent to which preceding tunings affected musical life.

THE CHEKKER

A keyboard instrument that has hitherto defied identification made its appearance around 1350: the chekker. Guillaume de Machaut in his exhaustive list of musical instruments of *Li temps pastour* (1340) does not mention it. But two decades later, in July 1360, to be precise, Edward III gave an *eschequier* to John II of France, then his prisoner. A further decade later, Machaut mentions the *eschaquier d'Engleterre* and some other instruments in his *Prise d'Alexandrie*, written shortly after 1369, from which it may be gathered that the chekker had probably been introduced to France from England or by English players (but was not necessarily invented there).

Chekkers enjoyed quite a vogue during the latter part of the fourteenth and all through the fifteenth century, during which time they were often cited together with the *manicordion* and, by Jean Molinet in his *Naufrage de la Pucelle*, with the *dolce melos* (*doucemelle*), thus precluding identity with either of these. What little evidence exists has suggested a small, upright harpsichord of high register, no larger than a portative organ, such as the late fifteenth-century sculpture in Kefermarkt, Austria, which shows an upright harpsichord played in portative organ position. Short keyboard chordophones could be made by the second half of the fourteenth century because the production of wire, formerly restricted to the almost exclusive service of the church and the crusaders, was developing into an independent industry.

Although the drawplate had been invented in the tenth century, wire continued to be forged for centuries thereafter; in Nuremberg the term *Drahtschmieder* ("wire smith") remained current until the mid-fourteenth century when, significantly, first at Augsburg in 1351, then at Nuremberg in 1360, the newer name of *Drahtzieher* or *Drahtmueller* ("wire drawer" or "wire miller") occurs. From 1414 on, drawers of wire for musical instruments were established at Nuremberg (*Leyrendrotzieher*), presumably drawers of wire for lute, citole, or harp. The length of any instrument—particularly any keyboard instrument—sounded by means of metal strings would at that time have been dependent on the maximum length to which a given thickness of wire could be drawn.

As to its name, *echiquier*, Latinized to *scacarum*, both meaning "chessboard," it is tempting to postulate black and white or black and yellow keys for the chekker, similar to the colors of chessboard squares, and to compare them with those of the portative organ, which at that time were rather like typewriter keys, as it seems fairly certain that the feature to which the chekker owes its name was somehow connected with an innovation of keyboard pattern. A chekker player was rewarded by the Duke of Burgundy in 1376; Deschamps praises the young Pierre of Navarre's playing of it in 1379; *un instrument nommé echaquier* was purchased in 1385 for the chapel of Philip of Burgundy, yet all details are lacking until 1387, when Juan I of Aragon sent for an instrument *appelat exaquier*, which was in the hands of his valet, and gives directions for careful packing and for its transportation by pack animal—an indication of its size or weight. Several of his communications of 1388 are known, from one of which it transpires that a certain Devisa possessed an instrument *semblant d'orguens que sona ab cordes* ("resembling an organ but sounded by strings"); the word "chekker" does not occur, however. He orders its purchase, and subsequent letters addressed by him to the Duke and Duchess of Burgundy request a "good Flemish minstrel named Johan dels orguens" ("John of the organs") and later contain a second request for the same minstrel, who is described as *apte de tocar exaquier* [and] *los petits orguens* ("able to play the chekker and the small organs"). In the same year he writes yet another letter to ensure Johan's bringing with him the book in which are notated pieces of music he knows how to play on the chekker and the organ. Finally, in 1394, the king expressed the wish to acquire some instruments but specifically excluded *orguens de coll* (portative organs), *harpa, exaquier, rota, organs de peu* (positive organs), as he already owned a sufficient number of these.

In England, Bishop Braybrooke of London gave three shillings and four pence in 1390 to a player of the chekker, and references occur to *le chekker* there in the last decade of the century. Eberhard Cersne's well-known enumeration of the musical instruments of his day (1404) contains a *Schachtbrett* ("chessboard"), and Isabeau of Bavaria, Queen of France, owned a chekker, according to Alain Chartier's *Livre des quatre dames* (1416). Jean de Gerson (d. ca. 1429), humanist and chancellor of Paris University, lists it among chordophones whose strings are shortened when played, as opposed to the harp and the psaltery. This differentiation between stopped and open strings may be a real clue, for the strings of a harpsichord are open, whereas those of the early clavichord were stopped. Could the chekker have been an upright form of clavichord? We shall probably never know. Yet it is curious that Henry Arnaut did not mention any upright keyboard chordophone in his treatise of about 1440.

Interest in the chekker died down as the century progressed, and finally, in 1511, Antoine, Duke of Lorraine, purchased in Valence from the organ builder Loys Rodilli an instrument *faisant archiquier, orgues, espinettes, et fluttes,* where chekker and spinet represent the strings, organ and flutes—an early term for gedackt pipes—the pipework of a claviorganum (nearly a century and a half later, Kircher depicted in his *Musurgia universalis* a combination instrument contained in a coffer, comprising symphony, spinet, and organ, to be played together or separately, manually or mechanically. *Plus ça change . . .*). Later references are either historical or else they form part of conventional catalogs of instruments, such as the amusing macaronic enumeration by Antoine d'Arena (first edition ca. 1519) of instruments to which one dances.

A harpsichord played by a monkey depicted in a fifteenth-century French *Conquest of the Golden Fleece* (Bibl. nat. MS Fr 331) has unfortunately been reproduced in a modern publication on musical instruments as a line drawing, shown in vertical position to better fit the page, and minus its monkey, thereby causing a recent investigator to identify this "upright" harpsichord as a chekker.

THE DULCE MELOS

The chekker was not the only ephemeral keyboard instrument of the late Middle Ages, for Henry Arnaut's treatise of about 1440 describes two types of instrument called *dulce melos,* one of which was an early

form of dulcimer, the other a short-lived keyboard instrument. He qualifies the former as rustic, and nowhere does he hint that the keyboard
version might be its development, yet this was most likely the case, as
the Near Eastern dulcimer was already known in Europe by then and
Arnaut's bridge dispositions make great sense on a dulcimer but were not
suited to a key action. Not surprisingly, the keyed version is not heard of
further, unless the *dulcemel para tañer* that belonged to Isabella the
Catholic in 1503 was, as seems indicated by the wording, of the keyboard
type.

Both of Arnaut's models are rectangular, with his keyboard of thirty-
five keys, B° to a², set at one of the long sides, slightly right of center;
the action was formed by one of the four different jacks he depicts (see
harpsichord, page 261), but the feature that distinguishes the *dulce melos*
from the clavichord and other rectangular keyboard instruments is its
string division. Twelve pairs of strings, one for each semitone of the
octave, were divided by a bass nut and three bridges, their emplacements
calculated to produce the ratio of 1:2:4, by partitioning the strings into
three sections of one octave each; the lowest key of the bass octave struck
the lowest section of the string nearest the player, and the lowest key
of the second octave struck the same string, but in the section bounded
by two bridges, while the lowest key of the top octave struck the same
string between the second and the treble bridge. All strings were of
identical length, as on the contemporary clavichord.

In the first of two models for which he gives drawings, Arnaut shows
that bridges and nut ran parallel to the narrow sides of the case; but
as this necessitated the same string length throughout an entire octave,
resulting in an unsatisfactory scale, the bridge and nut positions were
set obliquely at different angles, acute in the bass, increasingly obtuse in
the treble. Yet even with this improvement the *dulce melos* could not
survive, and in the sixteenth century its name lived on only in connection with the struck "village" variety, the dulcimer.

THE CLAVICHORD

After experimentation with "monochords" of two, three, or even four
strings had occupied theorists and probably musicians also in the fourteenth century, it seems that the monochord was transformed into an
instrument of some eight strings tuned in unison, with multiple mobile

nuts, one for each pitch: these were nothing less than a new form of key, very long as compared with those of the organ, each carrying implanted a perpendicular blade; it was this blade that represented a segment of the nut. This transformation occurred toward the end of the fourteenth century, as far as is known. Like so many other newly developed instruments, the clavichord had initially no name of its own, and so continued to be referred to as monochord (a "pare of monochordis" figure as late as 1497 in the accounts of the Lord High Treasurer of Scotland); when early in the fifteenth century the importance of the new keys became evident, the name of clavichord (from *clavis*, "key") was bestowed upon it, but the old term lived on for at least another century. Eberhard Cersne was the first to use the new word in his *Der Minne Regel* of 1404. (Identification of a nineteen-stringed "monochord" in a fourteenth-century text formerly attributed to Johannes de Muris rests on a misinterpretation, for the author was describing the theoretical division of a string into nineteen parts.)

Whether or not the clavichord preceded the harpsichord is unknown

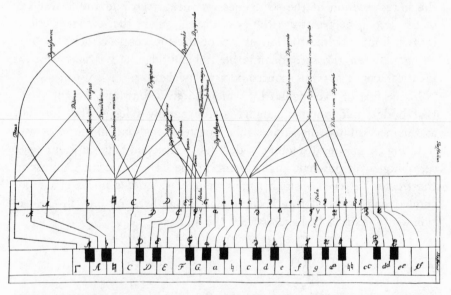

Copy of a schematic drawing of a clavichord by Johannes Keck, ch. 1442, showing computation of intervals determining the rack layout. "Steffanus," at extreme right, denotes the bridge. From Martin Gerbert, *De cantu et musica sacra*, 1774.

—Cersne mentions both instruments—but the simpler construction and action of the former militates in favor of its priority. Structurally the clavichord is a narrow, shallow, rectangular box, with keyboard in one long side, pinblock and soundboard to the right. The keys reach to the back of the case, where each is engaged in a groove—a mere sawcut—and free to ride up and down. Actually it is a slender prolongation of whalebone, wood, or metal, inserted in the rear of each key that rides in the grooves, and the most critical feature in clavichord making was for centuries the precisely calculated positioning of these grooves, known collectively as rack (*diapason* in French, *Rechen* in German). Upon them depended the accuracy of intervals as long as clavichords remained fretted, because they corresponded exactly to the striking point of the blade (tangent) set upright on each key; to a great extent they represent built-in tunings in an era of unequal temperaments, carefully worked out by monochord divisions. On the first clavichords, the tangents simply replaced the monochord's movable bridge.

The action is simplicity itself: when a key is depressed, its metal tangent rises to strike the string from below and remains in contact with the string until the key is released. Thus the string is divided into two sections of unequal length, both of which would continue to vibrate if the unwanted portion were not silenced by listing or by a damper board. As the tangent is placed in line with its apposite groove, it executes so to speak the preset interval provided by the groove. Clavichord tangents therefore have a triple function: they constitute the action, form a series of individual nuts (there is no single, long nut on a clavichord), and determine the intervals of a particular built-in musical scale.

On early clavichords all strings were of the same diameter, length, and tension, with the varieties of pitch being obtained solely by stopping them at different points. Such instruments coexisted for a while with the clavichord as we know it today, with its strings of different diameters, lengths, and pitches. Ramis de Pareja (1482) described both types and called both "monochord," and even in 1511 Virdung depicted the older model.

The treatise of Giorgio Anselmi of Parma of 1434 refers to a "monochord" with eight strings at unison pitch and up to twenty-nine keys; he stipulates that the keys for the semitones must be shorter and raised slightly above the others. In the Weimar *Wunderbuch* of about 1440 a rectangular instrument with projecting keyboard is inscribed *clavicordium;* its strings are of equal length and a large rose is set in its soundboard. Also dating from about 1440 is the Arnaut treatise, the earliest known work devoted to the making of musical instruments, with carefully drawn illustrations. Paintings, intarsia, and illustrations of the clavichord do not start in Italy until the 1530s, with a fresco by Leonardo da Besozzo in Naples (ca. 1533) showing a two-octave instrument of the early type, fully chromatic, with perhaps half a dozen strings. The small number of strings need not surprise us; with six strings, two octaves' worth of keys would indicate that in the treble there would be three or four keys to a string, fewer in the bass.

All early clavichords were fretted, regardless of whether their strings were of equal or of differing lengths. When applied to the clavichord, "fretting" means that two or more keys struck the same string, or pair of strings, producing differing pitches by striking at different points (the German equivalent, *gebunden*, and the French *lié*, both mean "tied"). No standardization of fretting ever existed, but after the early model with strings of uniform length was abandoned and the clavichord's compass notably increased, the middle section had two or three keys per string, the treble two, three, or four, while the bass octave was left unfretted. Of the keys thus fretted together, only one could be sounded at a time, namely that which was highest in pitch. Tangents were so spaced as to sound a semitone apart, but as this arrangement was not feasible with straight keys of equal size, some keys had to be made in curved or angled form, and the rear portion of the treble keys had to be made increasingly narrower to permit the tangents to lie ever closer together.

Despite the lack of standardization, one system of fretting is encountered frequently enough to form a pattern, to wit, that of fretting keys together pairwise and leaving the D and A keys unfretted. This system has led to several varying interpretations. Actually, once it is decided to fret no more than two keys together, it becomes logical to fret one diatonic key to its accidental, and, as there are only five accidental keys for each seven diatonic ones, two of the diatonic keys must of necessity remain unfretted. D and A were obvious choices because of their important position in modal music and in the instruments of the period: D was the lowest tone of many a stringed and a wind instrument, as it was of the Dorian mode. But the prime consideration must have been musical writing; manuscripts of the fourteenth century already included signs for C♯ F♯ G♯ E♭ (B♭, it will be recalled, was an integral part of the hexachord system). The only keys that were not sharped or flatted were D and A, and these were consequently left unfretted, resulting in the fol-

lowing pattern: C/C♯ D E♭/E F/F♯ G/G♯ A B♭/B, which is found
on Italian clavichords of the sixteenth century and later also on German
and Swedish ones. Praetorius's report of a clavichord with unfretted Ds
and As having been sent to Meissen in Saxony some thirty years before
he wrote, that is, around 1590, suggests that it may have been a novelty
in Germany then, and indeed Virdung (1511) considered the E♭ as a
D♯ and the B♭ as an A♯, resulting in the fretting: C/C♯ D/D♯ E F/F♯
G/G♯ A/A♯ B, five sharps and no flats, and this is the identical pattern
adopted by Iberian makers, as evidenced by a number of older clavichords made on the peninsula.

But to return to Henry Arnaut and the mid-fifteenth century: the
clavichord that Arnaut delineated had nine pairs of strings and thirty-
seven keys, with a compass of three octaves, from B° to b², about the
same as that of the contemporary organ. From the 1440s date the first
records of the clavichord's presence in England; in the year 1447 William Horwood was appointed instructor of choristers at Lincoln Cathedral, and those whom "he shall find apt to learn the clavycordes"
were to be taught organ playing, a very early reference to the clavichord's
historical role as a teaching and practice instrument for organists. In
the same year John Prudde designed the Beauchamp window of Saint
Mary's church, Warwick, showing a clavichord with six strings of identical length in a long and very narrow box with projecting keyboard, very
similar to a northern Netherlands wood sculpture of about 1450 in the
Rijksmuseum, Amsterdam, also with six strings. By the 1460s the clavichord had not only spread as far south as Portugal (where it continued
to be called *monacord*) and east to Poland, but it could also when necessary be furnished with a pedalboard. Paulus Paulirinus (ca. 1460) defined the clavichord as an oblong instrument in form of a box with
geminated metal strings *quo cum suo calcatorio datur magnum pream-
bulum in studium organorum et aliorum* ("which with its *calcatorium*
serves in the initial study of organ playing"); he also wrote of the
organ's *claves calcantes* for the low tones, so there can be no doubt but
that by *calcatorium* pedals are meant. Jacques Handschin published
the drawing of a late-fifteenth-century pedal clavichord (in *Zeitschrift
für Musikwissenschaft* XVII, 1935) taken from a manuscript of Hugo
von Reutlingen's *Flores musices* of 1467, but the drawing itself is somewhat later. (A fresco in Tierps Church, Upland, Sweden, of 1469, also
includes a small clavichord.)

Early pedalboards on stringed keyboard instruments were simple affairs, mere pull-downs whereby the keys of an organ pedalboard (short and straight in those times) were connected to the front portions of manual keys by wires or even cordage.

An idea of the clavichord's popularity on the Iberian peninsula may be gained from the fact that during the reign of Alfonso V (1448–1481) three organ builders and no fewer than twelve clavichord makers were established in Lisbon; a number of instruments from former centuries are preserved in Portugal today. In Spain, Barcelona, Seville, and Zaragoza became centers of clavichord production in the sixteenth century, and Santiago Kastner, writing on Iberian music and instruments, has termed the clavichord the peninsula's traditional keyboard instrument. Both in Spain and in Portugal the word *monocordio* was reserved for the clavichord (and the harpsichord was known as *clavicordio*); sixteenth-century Italy often understood by *clavicordio* a pentagonal spinet. Furthermore, *clavicordio* later became a generic term for stringed keyboard instruments in Spain, a usage to which the twelve sonatas for "clavichord" by Domenico Scarlatti published in London in 1752 bear witness. Before the end of the fifteenth century organists could own several of these small and relatively cheap instruments. Thus Godefroid van Neve, an Antwerp organist, bequeathed "his best clavichord" to a friend in 1496.

With the advent of the sixteenth century written documents flow more freely, and the first preserved instruments corroborate the written sources. Virdung (1511) mentions pedals and gives us information no longer obtainable from any extant instrument, namely the first data concerning stringing, when he points out that brass strings were used for the basses and steel for the trebles; he is also the first author to mention the addition of a third string to each course. This, as is known from later sources, was at 4' pitch, and optionally added to the bass section. Use of brass and steel wire is confirmed by Johannes Cochlaeus in 1512. Virdung's instrument had a compass from $F°$ to g^2 without the low $F\sharp$, and thirty-eight keys, but many new clavichords, he wrote, have four octaves' worth of keys or even more; these were, however, duplications of the "voices" (i.e., pitches) of the other keys, usually added for the purpose of hanging pedals from them; in other words, a duplication of some keys so that those to which pulldowns were attached could—by duplication—be played *manualiter* or *pedaliter*.

A manuscript tablature of 1513 containing keyboard music—chiefly that of Johann Cotter—gives the clavichord's compass already as $F°$ to c³, without the low F♯, a very wide range for the period. The Art Museum of Worcester, Massachusetts, houses a painting attributed by Max Friedländer to van Hemessen (ca. 1500–1566); theretofore it was said to be a portrait of Eleanor of Portugal playing the clavichord, painted by the Master of the Half Lengths; the clavichord has a typical organ keyboard with its three white keys (F°G°A°) terminating the bass compass; its range, F° to g², places it around 1510–1520 rather than in van Hemessen's *floruit*; the very young player might conceivably be the archduchess, for Antoine Mors is known to have built a clavichord for her in 1514, when she was still Eleanor of Austria.

The earliest preserved clavichord, dated 1543, is by Domenico of Pesaro; made of cypress, it has a four-octave compass and bass short octave (see keyboards, page 236), from C° to c³, with twenty-two pairs of strings and three independent, straight bridges, a typical feature of early Italian clavichords (as of the Burgundian *dulce melos*), and a double soundboard. Undoubtedly influenced by Italy, Flemish clavichords (and some virginals) of the second half of the sixteenth century changed shape, abandoning the narrow rectangle in favor of a flattened pentagon. During this period, the clavichord was also much in favor in England, although it was discarded there earlier than elsewhere, probably replaced by the rectangular virginal, to become almost nonexistent by the eighteenth century; in English cathedral and monastery schools children still received their fundamental organ instruction on the clavichord. "Pairs" of clavichords also figure in household accounts. Many may have been imported from the Low Countries; duty of a pair of "clarycordes" (i.e., one instrument) in 1545 was two shillings, that of a pound of clavichord wire, four pence. Another country where the clavichord was discarded early is France, yet we have sixteenth-century documents relating to various Parisian makers as well as to organists offering instruction on both the "manicordion" and the spinet.

Spain in the mid-sixteenth century had an outstanding theorist with a yen to build keyboard instruments, Juan Bermudo, whose *Declaración de instrumentos musicales* of 1555 is a veritable mine of information concerning the instruments and musical practices of his day. The keyboard of his "ordinary" clavichord had forty-two keys with a compass of C° to a², and short octave; his Ds and As are unfretted, the number of strings is not given. On some clavichords the G♯ key strikes the F strings, he states, which implies four keys to a pair of strings at some point of the range. A passage on the derivation of the clavichord from the monochord, in which he gives the word *cuerda* the two senses of the Greek word *chordē*, namely "string" and "pitch," and in which he mentions the forty-two *cuerdas* of contemporary instuments, has led some recent writers to conclude he is advocating an unfretted clavichord, an assumption not warranted by the context. Bermudo had also seen foreign instruments, for by his time the Low Countries were already exporters of keyboard chordophones, and not only to Spain, as may be seen from the inventory taken at the death of Ratsherr Otto Spigel of Nuremberg in 1560, who left 1 *niderlandisch clavicordium* and from the fact that the Fuggers, a banking family of Augsburg, obtained their clavichords (and cornetts) from Antwerp in the third quarter of the century.

By the dawn of the seventeenth century the clavichord's compass had been extended generally to four octaves, from C° to c³, slightly in excess of that of the contemporary organ manual, as Calvisius noted in 1600. Every increase in compass necessitated not only a longer case, but also a wider one to accommodate the additional strings, yet until unfretted clavichords were built in the eighteenth century the rectangles remained of modest size. A drawing by Jacques Cellier of about 1585 is noteworthy for its detailed rendering of the listing—strips of damping cloth woven between the courses of strings behind their striking points —and for the two separate, straight bridges, one for the bass, the other for the treble strings. Listing is a feature maintained until the nineteenth century, but replaced on modern instruments by a felt-lined damper board; this lends a little more resistance to the touch and greatly facilitates the replacement of strings.

Cellier's details are of particular interest when contrasted with the three clavichord models shown by Praetorius (1619); all three have modern damper boards instead of listing, his "regular" clavichord (reversed in the illustration) has an S-curved bridge, while his Italian model —an elongated polygon—has four separate, straight bridges (a putative fifth duplicating the treble bridge is a draughtsman's error), each for a different section of the compass. Such divisions are perfectly logical; nonetheless, the question arises as to whether the *dulce melos* may not have influenced clavichord making in Mediterranean countries. Praetorius's third clavichord is a very small model at 4' pitch; in analogy to the Bible regal, small clavichords at 4' pitch were also built as Bible clavichords; one dating from the eighteenth century measures but 37 centimeters (14½ inches) in length, 28 centimeters (11 inches) in width, and is 7 centimeters (less than 3 inches) deep, with fifteen pairs of strings providing a range of from g° to c³, two and one-half octaves. Sometimes a third set of strings, tuned to 4′ pitch, was added to the regular 8′ clavichords in the bass section, a procedure still advocated in the early nineteenth century; frequently the lowest strings lacked definition, and the addition of octave strings helped to bring out the fundamentals.

The clavichord shown by Mersenne is already unfretted except for the top octave, but an unfortunate disparity between text and illustration, and contradictions between statements in the text itself render his testimony on this point unreliable. Italianate, his drawing also shows five bridges. Later in the century Furetière (1685) misunderstood the purpose of listing cloth, and took it to be that of suffocating the sound, an opinion iterated continuously for the next century (one of the clavichord's names in France was *sourdine*, "mute"). For the remainder of the seventeenth century small fretted models continued to be made, while better instruments were larger, with the bass and middle sections unfretted, that is, with each key sounding its own strings. Claas Douwes (1699), to whose writings much valuable information concerning keyboard instruments of the late seventeenth century is due, recommends that small clavichords have four keys to a treble course, three to a bass course, so that with eight courses a compass of two octaves and a tone may be obtained. This could scarcely be anything but a teaching instrument.

One reason for the continued popularity of the smaller instruments, quite apart from their cheapness, was that they were easier to tune. This is expressed with the greatest clarity by Andreas Werckmeister in his *Generalbass* of 1698. One can tune fretted clavichords with little trouble, he writes, provided the tangent emplacement has been correctly calculated to provide a good temperament, for after tuning C, then G D A E and B, and their octaves, all the chromatic keys will automatically be in tune. The large and partially unfretted models were referred to as unfretted by contemporary writers, so that it is difficult to say exactly when the first completely unfretted version was produced. Thus Adlung (1758) defines as "unfretted" a clavichord in which each diatonic key had its own strings, and as "fully unfretted" one in which each chromatic key had its own strings, certainly a liberalization of Werckmeister's definition of 1698.

The designing of completely unfretted clavichords was certainly accomplished by the early eighteenth century, but ascription of its "invention" to Daniel Tobias Faber is a misreading of Johann Walther

(1732), who refers to a Coburg newspaper of April 1725, wherein it was stated that Faber had "invented a clavichord, completely unfretted, which could be varied by different 'machines' to sound like (1) a lute (2) a damped (3) an undamped bell chime," the invention referring here to the variations of tone and means of obtaining them, not to the emancipation of the keys. The maker Barthold Fritz kept annual lists of the purchasers of his clavichords; these show that up to 1744 most of his instruments were fretted; in his 1757 list some are still fretted but most are unfretted. Standardization was nonexistent and space saving, fretted instruments continued in use. (The *cimbal d'amour* of Gottfried Silbermann, which chronologically belongs here, is discussed separately on page 258.)

Daniel Faber's variations of tone of 1725 were harbingers of the latest keyboard craze, and one that was to become a major arm in the harpsichord's bitter struggle for survival later in the century, that of changing the tone quality to make it resemble that of some other instrument—the development of imitation stops. Such was, for example, the pandoret, a mid-century clavichord intended to imitate the sound of the bandora, with an extra and higher set of strings having its own mechanism, and the fad may be said to have culminated with Franz Jacob Spaeth's clavichord of 1751 with no fewer than fifty changes of tone, including *forte, piano, pianissimo,* echo, harp, lute, pantaleon, and cross flute.

Extension of the bass compass on the larger instruments brought about the introduction of wound strings by 1733, and although at mid-century most clavichords in use had but a four-octave range, newer ones already terminated on F in the bass. At the same time it became necessary to furnish separate stands for the increasingly bulkier and heavier instruments as the compass progressed to a span of five octaves; indeed, some were even enlarged to six octaves—Schubart in 1784 wrote enthusiastically: "Today they have five to six octaves, are fretted and unfretted, with or without a lute stop." Clavichords with octave (4') and even with superoctave (2') strings were being built, with the lowest twenty or so courses wound, the remainder of brass. From the mid-century on they were also built for "tone, that is, for loudness," and Adlung wrote that some could penetrate the sound of several violins. (Hipkins in 1946 mentioned the existence of cross-stringing as "already existing in some old clavichords" but regrettably gives no further details.)

Manufacture of the clavichord had ended by now in all but the German-speaking countries, Scandinavia (patterned on the German model), and the Iberian peninsula, and when the publisher Robert Bremner listed clavichords among the musical instruments obtainable from him in 1765, they would have been imported ones. *Un manucordion allemand* (a kind of small harpsichord) combined with five ranks of organ pipes—in other words, an organized clavichord (for which, see page 255)—was offered for sale in Paris in 1763. Shortly thereafter, the instrument was forgotten; the Lausanne edition of the *Encyclopédie* (1779) laments the fact that the clavichord was not known in France, and at the same time a German paper lamented its absence in England, causing Carl Engel, when he came across the article in question a century later, to instigate a strenuous search that resulted in his turning up but two or three instruments. Iberian clavichords did not participate in the development of those of central Europe; of thirteen extant Spanish and Portuguese instruments listed by Santiago Kastner, six are unichord and only four are unfretted; the keyboards of all are recessed.

The musical *Affektenlehre* of Germany, with its emotive stresses, gave great impetus there to clavichord playing and making in the second half of the eighteenth century. Carl Lemme was cited in the *Musikalisher Almanach* of 1782 for his unfretted clavichords with straight keys, in contrast to the crooked keys still in general use, and also for his use of "pressed" (*gepresste*) soundboards invented by his father in 1771—two-ply laminated wood—and finally, for his oval and round clavichords. C. P. E. Bach's advocacy and requirements also influenced makers; in a letter of November 10, 1773, Bach admits to preferring Friderici's clavichords to those of his competitors because of the touch (*Tractament*) and because the basses lacked octave strings "that I cannot stand."

A characteristic of the playing technique of that period was the *Bebung*, whereby a note could be graced or its sound sustained by "cradling the key with the finger as it were," as Bach put it, rapidly alternating the pressure of the finger on the key without releasing the latter. However, such increases in pressure could also affect the pitch, if not carefully controlled, and a century and a half earlier Praetorius had even suggested taking advantage of this feature to correct the tuning of (unequally tempered) thirds by means of pressure on the key. Tunings were still far from standardized in the eighteenth century, but their progressive evenness caused C. P. E. Bach, to quote him for the last time, to draw attention to the need for a new fingering system for those tonalities that formerly could not be played because the clavichord was "not as well tempered as it is nowadays."

Having arrived at the height of its development, it now became necessary for the clavichord to meet competition from the increasingly perfected piano, and so makers took to stringing their output more heavily in quest of greater volume. Possibly they were successful in this, for a Swedish builder in 1780 added a swell to his models—a more futile improvement would be difficult to imagine. In 1785 the *Schlesische Provinzblätter* accused makers of building *Claviere* in name only (*Clavier* was a German term for the clavichord from 1741 on; *Instrument* was another). Nonetheless, German makers withstood the competition and continued building uninterruptedly until the nineteenth century, and consequently music continued to be published—at least ostensibly—for the clavichord: Johann Nikolaus Forkel brought out in 1792 his "24 variations for clavichord or fortepiano on the English folk song [*sic*]: God Save the King," obtainable from the author at Göttingen or from Vandenhöck and Rupprecht (the fortepiano would have been a square piano). In rural areas clavichords continued to be played until the late 1820s, and the perhaps somewhat anachronistic tuning manual of Johann Traugott Lehmann of 1827 finds clavichords getting scarcer as they were pushed out by the piano; he is probably the latest writer to note brass stringing throughout, bichord, with wound strings in the bass. It comes as a distinct shock to find Gustav Schilling in 1835 so far forgetting the very nature of the clavichord to mention quilling it.

PEDAL, TWO-MANUAL, AND ORGANIZED CLAVICHORDS

Various compound types remain to be discussed: those with pedalboard, with two manuals, and with organ pipes. These all arose in response to the organist's need for a cheap practice and teaching instrument that would take up a minimum of space. Pedalboards with pulldowns had already been added by the 1460s, as noted, and clavichords with organ pedalboards were built intermittently up to the end of the eighteenth century; their keys did not radiate as on modern organs, but were straight and shorter.

Two forms of pedal clavichord existed: those with pulldowns (abstracts) connecting manual key to pedal key, and more elaborate versions with pedal keys acting on a separate set of strings (not connected to any keys), in reality a separate clavichord. It is difficult to determine just when the latter type came into use. On his death in Brunswick in 1571, Probst Johann Konen left *1 Clavichordium mit einem Pedal und Kasten darüber da man aufsitzt* ("a clavichord with a pedal and box above which one sits"), but this is not conclusive. The earliest unambiguous information is contained in the statement of Douwes (1699) to the effect that pedals must have a roller board (he is speaking of the clavichord). Kremsmünster Monastery in Austria had *2 clavicordi, darzue ein Pedall* ("2 clavichords, for which a pedal") in 1584, and in 1591 the local organ builder made a new clavichord with pedalboard for the abbot. (Earlier, in 1568, the organist's room there had contained, among other instruments, two clavichords, two virginals, and a regal.) Johann Christoph Bach received *3 Clavier nebst Pedal* from his father during the latter's lifetime; Adlung, who was also a builder, states that he made clavichord pedalboards with two bridges, one for a set of bichord strings at 8′ pitch, the other for a bichord, wound 16′.

Two-manual clavichords were created by the simple expedient of setting one instrument on top of the other (cf. virginals, page 299); they did not necessarily couple. A "double" clavichord figured in a 1633 inventory of instruments having belonged to a Brunswick musician, probably a two-manual affair. A unique two-manual clavichord with independent pedal instrument has survived, that of Johann David Gerstenberg, made in 1760; it has bichord manuals, and the pedal has no fewer than four strings per key. Pedal clavichords were built as late as 1800; one of that date by Johann Paul Krämer was destroyed during the Second World War. The organist, Heinrich Nicolaus Gerber, who had been a pupil of Bach's, invented an upright pedal clavichord in order to save space, and constructed one in 1742, with the help of a carpenter, in near pyramidal shape, with two manuals and pedal; it was nine feet high, with a depth of one foot and a maximum width of seven feet without the projecting keys.

The musical function of organized clavichords is not so clear; one tends to assume that strings and pipes were played alternately rather than together, but whether for instruction or for artistic purposes is unknown; possibly such instruments merely represented an "either-or" choice in space-saving form. Organized instruments of various types, that is, those combined with one or more ranks of pipes, were popular from the fifteenth century on; flue pipes were combined with harpsichord, spinet, hurdy-gurdy, and even clavichord. A Dresden inventory of 1593 lists two organized clavichords that had their pipework underneath. References to such instruments also occur in eighteenth-century documents (cf. the above-mentioned German "manucordion" offered for sale in Paris in 1763), and one such combination of 1772 is extant; it was built in Stockholm by Pehr Lundborg, triple-strung in the bass, with organ pipes enclosed in a separate housing under the string section. The Bayrisches Nationalmuseum of Munich formerly owned a combination clavichord and mechanical organ, the latter weight-driven, with two ranks of flue pipes, and the Carolino-Augusteum Museum of Linz owns an organ-clavichord made in 1699 by Valentin Zeiss. A *sordino . . . con graviorgano* was formerly in the Medici collection in Florence during Cristofori's curatorship.

Clavichord building had scarcely died out before its revival started in 1857 with the construction by Hoffmann of Stuttgart of an instrument made for an English purchaser. He was followed in the last decade of the century by Arnold Dolmetsch in London. In our century a number of makers have been active on both sides of the Atlantic, producing a variety of models from small and delicate to large and cross strung, with or without metal frame.

THE CIMBAL D'AMOUR

In or by 1721 the organ builder Gottfried Silbermann had designed a double-sized clavichord, named *cymbal d'amour* (from *cimbal*, dulcimer) by a group of his admirers, his object in creating it being to produce an instrument with clavichord dynamics but the volume of a harpsichord. This invention of his falls in the period between the piano's creation in Italy and its becoming known in Germany. The piano met precisely those conditions Silbermann required of his *cimbal d'amour*, namely dynamic flexibility coupled with volume, and Silbermann's instrument must be considered as one more of its immediate precursors.

The *cimbal d'amour* was first described in the *Breslauer Sammlungen* of July 1721, and illustrated in the February 1723 issue of the same periodical; Mattheson drew attention to it in his *Critica musica* of 1722. Silbermann was anxious to avoid imitation by other builders, and to this end he was careful not to permit publication of action details or indications of scale. In June 1723 he obtained a fifteen-year privilege for sole manufacture and sale of his instrument. Despite these precautions he became involved in a lawsuit—one of the results of which was the revocation in 1735 of his fifteen-year privilege—lasting from 1728 to 1733 with Johann Ernst Haehnel, who had not only copied the *cimbal d'amour* but had added insult to injury by providing "variations of tone" as well.

From the testimony of the expert witnesses, extant drawings, and the comments of J. F. Agricola (1768), a reasonably good idea of Silbermann's model can be gained: it was a large clavichord of irregular polygonal shape, 3 to 3½ ells (6 to 7 feet) long, partly strung with simple, partly with wound, metal strings. All of these were struck at precisely half of their speaking length, so that the two sections sounded at unison pitch, but also required two soundboards, one on either side of the keyboard. The crux of the action was its diagonal rack, designed to serve both as terminal guide to the keys, as on a clavichord, and, by padding its top with cloth, also as a damping system (the ends of the strings were not interwoven with listing). When a key was depressed, its pair of strings was raised by the tangent and on release of the key the strings fell back onto the cloth-covered rack and were silenced. According to a contemporary commentator, the new instrument sounded louder and had greater sustaining power than a clavichord, and *Bebungen* could be executed with greater ease.

Haehnel called his imitation the *Cimbal royal*; he had started manufacture in 1726, and improved upon his first model by adding a "*Cölestin* or pantalon" stop (heavy brass pins set close to the tangents against which the strings could jar), and another stop one can only describe as self-defeating: a cloth-covered batten was laid upon the strings on one or the other side of the rack, thereby damping half their vibrating length and reducing the volume to that of an ordinary clavichord. On another occasion he added a lute stop with extra-wide tangents, half their tops covered with leather; the keyboard could be shifted so that only the leather-covered portion of the tangents struck the strings.

Shortly thereafter, two Hamburg builders, Bartholomäus Oppelmann and H. A. Hass, started building *cimbals d'amour* also. An instrument maker named Kellner took one with him from Hamburg to Stockholm in 1728, where they were then manufactured by the builder Philip Specken. Nils Brelin of Sweden is said to have incorporated the principle of the *cimbal d'amour* in an "improved clavichord" of his dating from the 1730s.

Sibermann's instrument had little more than a *succès d'estime*; its early demise was no doubt due to its inherent problems: the great length of its bass strings and a striking point so far removed from either end must have caused floppiness and jangling and have been a deterrent to enlarging the compass (the 1723 drawing shows one of four octaves). Organologically its importance lies in the fact that it is a link in the chain leading to the piano: Silbermann was the first to utilize Cristofori's invention outside Italy.

THE HARPSICHORD

Just as the various components of the organ had been invented prior to the emergence of the hydraulus, so the various parts that make up a harpsichord were available before that instrument was invented or, rather, put together: the psaltery, complete with soundholes in its resonator, organ and probably clavichord keyboards, drawn wire—all that was needed was an action (the mechanism forming the connection between key and string). At least one such action, and possibly several, evolved by the end of the fourteenth century, for in 1404 Eberhard Cersne enumerated among the instruments of his day a *clavicymbolum*, or keyed *cymbalum* (subsequently spelled *clavicembalum*), the earliest name of the harpsichord. As iron wire could only be drawn to short lengths at that time, the earliest keyboard chordophones must of necessity have been restricted in length and thus comparatively high pitched, and in fact the earliest representations show them proportionately small in relation to their width (e.g., Henry Arnaut's treatise of ca. 1440, "The Monkey at the Harpsichord" from MS fr 331, Bibliothèque national; the Beauchamp window of Saint Mary's, Warwick, designed 1447; and the Weimar *Wunderbuch* of the same period); their form will be found to coincide exactly with that of a type of contemporary psaltery—minus the keyboard, of course. Even the roses of the soundboard are taken over. A late-fifteenth-century square-tailed harpsichord with no fewer than five such roses is depicted at Haverö Church, Sweden. Meanwhile *clavicimbel* and *clavicembalo* were glossed in a vocabulary of 1429 as *instrumentum musicum*, and in Zwickau payment was made in 1438 to a *spilman der da slug uff dem klavizimbel* ("minstrel who played the *klavizimbel*"), showing that the name was accepted in the vernacular by a very early date.

The new harpsichord must have been immediately successful, for it quickly spread all over Europe. Henry Arnaut, whose manuscript contains so much useful information concerning the organ of his time, was also interested in the construction of stringed keyboard instruments. He gives a drawing to scale of the *clavicimbalum*, and both illustrates and describes no fewer than four possible actions. His Latin is difficult and the illustrations of his actions far from clear, but it seems that in three of them the sound-eliciting parts—they cannot yet be called jacks—were not set freely on the rear of each key as they are today, but were attached in a groove running the breadth of the instrument and furnished with metal plectra. In the fourth action, weighted "jacks" furnished with clavichord tangents seem to have been propelled against the strings in the manner of eighteenth-century tangent pianos, to fall back under their own impetus. His keyboard shows a compass of B° to a², fully chromatic; his soundboard is graced with five rose-covered soundholes of differing sizes; and the bottom of the case is closed, as it was to remain until the present century.

Harpsichords could be built with one set of strings or two, and, if with two, Arnaut's bridgepins were notched in such a fashion that one string was higher than the other, but, since both retained the same vertical plane, a given plectrum would pluck each string in quick succession. That quill plectra were also known in his day transpires from a passage relating to the "monochordium." With the freedom offered by so many types of action it is not surprising that precision in terminology was slow to develop. The early harpsichord is another illustration of the fact that technology sometimes reverses itself as far as musical instruments are concerned, and proceeds from the complicated to the simple, for later harpsichords have vastly simpler actions than any of Arnaut's; however, modern instruments are rigid in comparison to his, for he writes of a given action that with it one could make a *clavicembalum* or a *clavichordium* or a *dulce melos*, and, in another passage, *posset fieri quod clavichordium sonaret clavicimbalum* ("it can be made that the clavichord sounds like a harpsichord").

The harpsichord's close association with the organ, which was to remain effective until the eighteenth century, starts at this time; a *clavicymbale* was sold in 1447 by a Paris organist (who may have used it as a practice instrument), and about two decades after Arnaut wrote, Paulus Paulirinus described a combination upright harpsichord and portative organ. From then on the keyboard chordophones remained to a large extent adjuncts of the organ, a relationship that did not cease until the advent of the piano. Their role as practice instruments for organists was of primary importance; their compass was correlated to the former's needs and their terminology taken over from organ building; until well into the eighteenth century they were constructed principally by organ builders (the articles of indenture of an apprentice builder of Amsterdam in 1625 stipulated his learning both organ and harpsichord building and playing from one and the same master); a second manual was added to some Flemish harpsichords in order to accommodate organists who had to deal with organs at different pitches; the "pair of organs" becomes a "pair of virginals," and so on; furthermore, the majority of great harpsichord players and composers were primarily organists and writers of organ music. As a secular instrument, the harpsichord was long restricted to lighter entertainment, and writers such as Diruta in the sixteenth century make it perfectly clear that performance of serious music on quilled instruments was considered bad form—partly because of their lack of sustaining power. Dance music was permissible, and in fact the sixteenth-century *balli* for harpsichord, spinet, or *arpicordo* are representative of the early literature for these instruments, their players being known as *sonatori di balli* ("dance music players").

Builders' names in southern countries are known from the fifteenth century on, for instance, Sesto Tantini in Italy requested payment for a *clavicimbalo* of his make in 1461. From the Iberian peninsula the constable of Portugal requests in writing in 1460 that a *claricimbal* be sent to him, and by the end of that century harpsichords were so common in Spain that an inventory of Isabella the Catholic's instruments in the Alcazar records two "old" *clavicímbanos*. Pedalboards, already adapted to the clavichord, were occasionally hung from harpsichord manuals from the late fifteenth century on; our oldest notice concerning such a combination is that of a *clavicimbalo cum pedali* mentioned in Cracow in 1497 (according to Adolph Chybinski in *Sammelbände der internationalen Musikgesellschaft*, 1911).

England initially adopted the term clavicymbal—it occurs in literature from 1502 on—sometimes corrupted to claricymbal, in which form it took its place with other stringed instruments in Stephen Hawes's *The Passetyme of Pleasure* of 1509:

> . . . taboures, trumpettes, with pypes melodyous
> Sackbuttes, organs, and the recorder swetely
> Harpes, lutes, and crouddes ryght delycyous

Cȳphans, doussemers, wᵗ clarycymbales gloryous
Rebeckes, clarycordes . . .

"Clavicymbal" was subsequently dropped in favor of "virginal," a term that referred indifferently to the long and the square forms, as may be seen from the seventeenth-century phrase: "harpsicon or virginal." The word "harpsichord," derived from the Italian *arpicordo* (see page 283), did not come into use prior to the early seventeenth century (1607, as far as is known). The terminology was just as slack in France, where both before the word *clavecin* was introduced (1611 on) and after, *épinette* indicated with impartiality both harpsichord and spinet (de La Barre was styled *épinette* and organist to the king).

A harpsichord with two "registers" was built for Pope Leo X in 1514, and, referring to organ terminology once more, this meant that it was furnished with two rows of jacks, plucking presumably as many sets of strings. Fortunately we have a contemporary woodcut depicting just such an instrument, indeed possibly the very same instrument; it occurs on the title page of the first book of *Frottole intabulate da sonare organi*, published in Rome in 1517 (the earliest printed Italian organ tablature), and bears the arms of Leo X on the turned-back front portion of the lid; two rows of tuning pins are visible, one immediately behind the other, indicative of two sets of strings; a dropleaf is also shown. The disposition of 2×8′ (two registers at 8′ pitch) is that of the earliest preserved harpsichord, by Jerome of Bologna, of 1521 (a harpsichord nameboard dated 1516 is preserved in Italy, fitted to an instrument for which it does not appear to have been made).

A 4′ stop is known on Italian harpsichords from the 1530s (e.g., on that by Alessandro Trasuntino, 1538, now in the Brussels Conservatoire Museum) and was sporadically built thereafter (by Francesco Patavini in 1561, by Francesco Antegnati of the famous organ-building family in 1564). On all of these, one of the 8′ stops is omitted in favor of the 4′ stop, resulting in a disposition of 1×8′+1×4′. It must be stressed that the occurrence of a 4′ register was quite unusual in Italy, at least prior to the eighteenth century, as the vast majority of extant instruments adhere to the basic 2×8′ registers, always with a single manual. Discounting the relatively few exceptions, their range was of four octaves from C° to c³, with short octave (Italian spinets, on the other hand, usually had a compass of four and one-half octaves, C° to f³, also with short octave). In general the compasses of keyboard chordophones expanded faster than did those of the organ (see keyboards, page 234). Jerome of Bologna's harpsichord already had a range of C° to d³, forty-seven keys, with short octave; and, following the organ, most keyboard chordophones of the sixteenth and seventeenth centuries had bass short octaves (for details, see keyboards, page 236) regardless of their country of origin.

Flemish instruments had, according to van Blankenburg (1739), a compass of F to A, or three octaves and a third, in the sixteenth century, subsequently taken down to C, and expanded around 1640 by the addition of one key in the bass and several in the treble to four octaves and a tone, B to C; this date seems a little late, for Jan Couchet, an Antwerp builder and nephew of Johannes Ruckers, wrote to Constantijn Huygens concerning a harpsichord he had just finished for him (in 1648; the letter is undated, but the date can be supplied from the Duarte-Huygens correspondence) à propos of its manual, which terminated on F: "this is the first that I have so built." It would have brought the compass to four and one-half octaves, F to C, a range the harpsichord was to retain up to the time of the *grand ravalement*, or extension to five full octaves, F to F, starting around 1700. In England, the lowest key of a harpsichord was commonly G up to Kirkman's time (eighteenth century), following British organ-building custom.

Harpsichords with three registers were built from the 1570s on, at least. *Ain clavicimbole mit drei registern* ("a harpsichord with three registers") was inventorized in Graz in 1577, unfortunately without further details, but probably an Italian instrument with $2 \times 8' + 1 \times 4'$ stops, for Austria procured her keyboard chordophones mainly from Italy at that time. But three-register harpsichords were by no means confined to the south; the earliest preserved English harpsichord—if indeed it can be called English (it was made by an Antwerp builder who emigrated to London), or harpsichord (it is a claviorganum)— that of Lodewijk Theeuwes dated 1579, has $2 \times 8' + 1 \times 4'$ stops; provision for the three rows of jacks was made by cutting mortises into the soundboard, which uninterruptedly also forms the wrestplank cover; registration was by means of a movable lower jack guide.

The record of a purchase of a *doppeltes venezianisches Clavicimbel* ("Venetian double harpsichord") in 1580 in Trento for the Innsbruck court is a puzzler, for two-manual harpsichords were not only a northern creation but had probably not even been built at that time. Possibly a claviorganum was meant. A *Symphonei* at the Brandenburg court two years later had four stops, perhaps a claviorganum also. The earliest record of an indubitable two-manual harpsichord is of one by Hans Ruckers the Elder of Antwerp, dated 1588, now lost; the first extant double manual dates from 1590. This, or rather, these, for there are two of that year, were made by the same Hans Ruckers the Elder, head of a family of harpsichord and virginal makers and indeed of the Antwerp school of keyboard chordophone building.

A cursory rundown of Antwerp makers, as listed in Stellfeld (1942), shows that that city housed six harpsichord makers in the first half of the sixteenth century, eighteen in the second half, and nineteen in the seventeenth century, based on archival entries alone (and excluding clavichord makers). It is probably no accident that Antwerp became a center of keyboard instrument making in the sixteenth century in preference to Amsterdam or some city of the northern Netherlands, for the Reformation did not take kindly to musical instruments in the church, and many an organ was silenced or its role curtailed, and when organists were unemployed so were the harpsichord makers. According to tradition, Hans Ruckers was responsible for many improvements to the harpsichord, and, although some ascriptions have been questioned or proved wrong, it is now generally conceded that he most probably created the two-manual harpsichord, and certainly created the transposing harpsichord aimed at providing organists with a practice instrument. Some practical implications of the coexistence of organs half an octave apart in pitch are outlined below (see also keyboards, page 239). Hans the Elder became master of his guild in 1579, and his earliest known extant instrument, a double virginal, dates from 1581. He not only made virginals and harpsichords but was also a repairer and tuner of organs in Antwerp. Of his surviving harpsichords the majority have two manuals, and it can be assumed not only that he inaugurated this method of construction but also that of transposing manuals. To anticipate a little: several transposing harpsichords by various members of the Ruckers family have come down to us, more or less modified yet recognizable for what they were, and one with its manuals intact, showing that each keyboard disposed of one 8′ and one 4′ stop, but at different pitches, for the C key of one manual plucked the string of an F key on the other and the two could of course not be coupled. Such instruments were still being made in the mid-seventeenth century, but only, as far as is known, in Flanders. Gradually the rows of jacks were put to less specialized use; an extra set of strings at 8′ pitch was added and one row of the 8′ jacks was made to pluck it, and the keyboards were rebuilt so that the C key of one was aligned with the C key of the other. From that point on it shared in the development of the fullblown classical expression instruments of the eighteenth century, disposing of 3×8′+4′, an (upper) piano and (lower) forte manual that could be coupled, and three sets of strings.

If Italian organ builders remained ultraconservative once they had found a satisfactory model, so did Italian harpsichord makers—often one and the same. They continued to produce simple, one-manual instruments, still very slight, in the seventeenth century, and with a separate case from which they were withdrawn for performance (known as *cassa levatora* in eighteenth-century Italy), somewhat more substantial in the eighteenth century, when they were built directly into an outer housing that might be decorated according to the taste of the period but were essentially still of cypress, whereas in Flanders the softwoods were preferred. Italian models had short but variable scales averaging 25 centimeters (10 inches) on c², as opposed to those of Italian spinets, averaging 33 centimeters (13 inches); the minor variations were in part due to dis-

Transposing manuals of a harpsichord by Johannes Ruckers, seventeenth century, showing the C keys aligned above the F keys. Courtesy of Mrs. Lotta Bizallion.

crepancies of local pitches, but the consistent and large divergence between harpsichord and spinet scales indicates that they were in all likelihood constructed with an eye to the high and low organs of the time. The Flemish scale was larger, around 35 centimeters (14 inches), also for c^2.

Organ influence is very much in evidence in Germany and France in the early seventeenth century, for both Praetorius and Mersenne after him write of harpsichords with up to four choirs of strings, and Mersenne speaks of three manuals; yet, despite their reference to such complex instruments, both authors depict simple, one-manual harpsichords of Italian style, with but one 8′ and a 4′ stop. Obviously then these were the typical models of their day. Praetorius adds to his delineation the comment: "Harpsichord, so a fourth lower than choir pitch" (by contrast, his spinet and virginal bear the annotation *so recht Chorton,* "at normal choir pitch"). In this connection it is of interest to note the inscription appearing on an Italian harpsichord exhibited in Paris in 1889: *Fait à Milan pour sonner à la quinte, refait pour sonner au ton par J. J. Nesle, 1780* ("made in Milan to sound at the fifth, rebuilt to sound at pitch by J. J. Nesle, 1780"); also, a small harpsichord built in 1627 by Praetorius's contemporary, Andreas Ruckers, has a scale roughly two-thirds of the standard Ruckers harpsichord scale, indicating that originally it sounded a fifth higher.

Mersenne, in various sections of his Book III, has several surprises, for he writes that "nowadays" harpsichords with seven or eight *jeux* (registration possibilities) and two or three keyboards were being made, and that the *jeux* could be varied (i.e., registration effected) by means of several *petits registres, chevilles & ressorts* ("little registers, pins and springs"); but that some players preferred the single manual, which was shifted in or out for changes of registration, to the springs in question, as these were ordinarily not accurate.

In another passage concerned with two-manual instruments he comments that small wedges (*calles*) were glued to the rear end of the keys in order to change registration (*afin de changer les jeux*) and that the key frame could be drawn out. This is a fair description—and the earliest—of a coupling system (short, cuneiform members affixed to the rear of the lower manual keys engaged those of the upper manual when this was pushed in; Mersenne's upper-manual keys were two French inches shorter than those of the lower manual). Furthermore, he writes of a four-jack, four-string *eudisharmoste* (harpsichord) that could be built with either one, two, or three manuals. He borrows his terminology from the organ and lists the *eudisharmoste*'s stops as being at 12', the octave, twelfth (a quint), and fifteenth (this implies F as the lowest key), regardless of the number of keyboards. The information of Praetorius is similar if less detailed; he had seen a harpsichord with 2 × 8', a quint, and a 4' choir. "One can also add a new stop of a tierce," continues Mersenne, or its repetition at the tenth or seventeenth, but this is presumably a mere theoretical suggestion. Among other new items of his century he reported that some builders caused two strings to speak by the single plectrum of one jack; this would be possible only if one string were situated above the other, as on Arnaut's instrument, otherwise a double-tongued jack would be necessary, and did in fact exist in the eighteenth century.

Seventeenth-century references to three-manual harpsichords are rare indeed, but such instruments seem to have been built sporadically if exceptionally then and in the eighteenth century, probably as special orders for organists. An advertisement in the *Amsterdam Courant* in 1694 offered *verschiedene clavecimbels met 2 en 3 claviere die continueel met 2 a 3 snaren konnen spreken naer men de registers trekt* ("several harpsichords with two and three manuals, which can sound continuously with two or three strings according to the registers drawn"), the property of an Amsterdam carillonneur.

Italian harpsichord actions differed from others in that they had, instead of the mobile jack slides and fixed lower guide usual elsewhere, a deep one-piece, mortised jack box; and the disengaging of strings, indispensable when tuning and desirable when playing, was brought about by pushing the keyboard in to engage the rear row of jacks, pulling it out to engage the front row, while a neutral center position caused both to pluck.

Keyboard chordophones must be unique in the extent to which their features were reinvented, sometimes over considerable time spans: Arnaut's fifteenth-century free "jack" action anticipated the eighteenth-century tangent piano; Mersenne's jack capable of plucking two strings appears on some Sodi harpsichords in the second half of the eighteenth century; Mersenne's contemporary, Giovanni Battista Doni (1640) suggested gradually raising the lid of a harpsichord "as necessary" in order to vary the dynamics, thus foreshadowing the swells of Shudi and Kirkman, also in the eighteenth century.

Apart from the spectacular instruments seen by Praetorius and Mer-

senne, a more conservative two-manual expression harpsichord came into
being, probably during the third decade of the seventeenth century,
with three rows of jacks and an undetermined number of choirs of
strings, probably three. Experiments with forms of double manuals had
already started by the last decade of the sixteenth century, when Hans
Ruckers produced a combination harpsichord-virginal, a long rectangle
with a harpsichord set in one of the narrow sides and a virginal built
in the far end of the right long side, intended for simultaneous playing
by two persons. The earliest of three such instruments to have come
down to us is dated 1594; its harpsichord has a single manual; the second,
by Hans's son Johannes, is dated 1619 and has a two-manual harpsichord section; another, undated, of the same maker, has a single manual.
Now lost is a "four-square" harpsichord with three rows of keys at one
end, a spinet on the side, made by Johannes Ruckers and listed in
1720 by Pepusch among the Duke of Chandos's instruments; and among
the musical instruments at the Dresden court, noted by Philip Hainhofer in 1629, was an *Instrument* "on which three can play simultaneously, on three keyboards, each on a separate side," probably identical
with the "large instrument with two small ones that the Leipzig organist sold" inventorized at Dresden in 1593, and perhaps conceived in
the manner of those just noted, with harpsichord at the narrow end,
spinets on the sides. This type of keyboard instrument seems to have
been little known outside the Low Countries, and was probably discontinued by the mid-century; a reference is contained in an Amsterdam
notary's act of 1654: . . . *seeckere clavicimbal daer twee personen gelijk
op spilen konnen . . . de clavicimbal self langwerpich vierkant van
ongemeene groote* (". . . certain harpsichord on which 2 persons can
play together . . . the harpsichord itself an oblong square of unusual
size"). Perhaps this form may be associated with the requirements of
organists, for in the next century it was revived by an organist, Johannes
Coenen of Roermond, who has left a rectangular harpsichord with two
manuals and a virginal built into the long side, made in 1735. Adlung
(1768) proposed a simplified model, with a player at each end of the
two narrow sides of a rectangular harpsichord, which, by virtue of its
form, becomes an *Instrument*, ergo, a virginal. But his suggestion had
already been anticipated by Philippe Denis of Paris, who in 1712 had
built a harpsichord with two keyboards at each end, one for solo, the
other for accompaniment—a *vis-à-vis*.

Another discovery of the seventeenth century was the registration pedal, but it proved to be premature and perhaps technically unsatis-factory as well, and did not catch on. Mace (1676) described a "Pedal, an instrument of a late Invention, contriv'd [as I have been informed] by one Mr. John Hayward of London . . ." consisting of a harpsichord with "a kind of Cubbord, or Box" containing "4 little pummels of wood," two for each foot, providing forte, piano, and "other Various Stops." Of this invention Mace further states that: "It is not very commonly used, or known; because Few make Them Well . . ." and also because of their great expense. English seventeenth-century refer-ences to a pedal in connection with the harpsichord must be taken to refer to such registration pedals and not to a pedalboard, since organ pedalboards were unknown in England prior to the eighteenth century. First mentioned in 1664 and then sporadically for three decades (Wil-liam Turner's comment in 1697 to the effect that "the harpsichord is of late mightily improved by the invention of the Pedal" is obviously out of date), they then disappear until 1741, when Nils Brelin of Sweden applied registration pedals to a clavicytherium of his invention.

THE HARPSICHORD AFTER 1700

Unlike Italian makers, who were satisfied to continue producing the same models they had standardized by 1520 and probably earlier, trans-alpine builders continued experimenting with both forms and additional means of expression. A folding harpsichord (*clavecin brisé*) was in-vented by Jean Marius of Paris, for which he received a twenty-year privilege in 1700. Marius was singularly attracted by anything foldable or collapsible, and he submitted for the Académie's approval a series of folding tents and folding umbrellas, the latter remarkably like modern beach umbrellas. His folding harpsichord was designed as a travel in-strument and was made in three hinged sections, the treble and center of which could be folded over the bass section to form a compact box. Marius claimed that it held its tuning better than did ordinary harpsi-chords, but its real merit lay in its portability (comments made later in the century were to the effect that folding harpsichords needed constant repairs). Frederick the Great owned one, and it was sufficiently popular to be imitated by other makers, both in France and in Italy (Farinelli left two folding harpsichords), and Galland's workshop in Paris con-tained in 1755, among other instruments, three folding harpsichords at 8′ pitch and another three at 4′ pitch. Today Marius is remembered chiefly as the independent inventor of several piano actions in 1716, but in addition to the foregoing he also assisted Sauveur in his acoustical experiments, for which he received acknowledgment in the *Mémoires de l'Académie des sciences*, 1713.

Larger harpsichords with three or four registers were becoming common; Mattheson (1713) writes of *grosse mit 3 à 4 Zuegen oder Register versehenen Clavicymbali*, one of which might have been the recently devised lute stop (*Nasalzug*, in German) of Quirijn van Blankenburg, who in 1708 cut a gap through the wrestplank of a two-manual harpsichord almost parallel to the nut, for the insertion of a fourth row of jacks. Their position so close to the nut set them off tonally from the remaining jacks by a strong nasal timbre. English builders became very partial to this stop and it was also used, albeit sparingly, on the Continent. It is first seen on a London-made instrument, dated 1721, of Hermann Tabel, a Netherlander who had learned his trade from the Couchets (but the date of this harpsichord is not altogether satisfactory). Van Blankenburg (1739) also summarized the steps in Flemish harpsichord development that led to its invention: until perhaps 1630 or 1640 the Ruckers' two-manual harpsichords were all transposing (with the lower manual a fourth lower than organ pitch), he writes—but he is in error on this point; then around the mid-century the compass was extended, and subsequently a third string was added, with one jack for each string, leaving the fourth row of jacks inactive, and it was this row that he put to work by transferring it to a position where it plucked the strings very close to the nut. The remaining row of jacks was doglegged to straddle the shorter keys of the upper manual and the longer lower-manual ones, and thus was available either for a one-string *piano* upper keyboard, or for a three-string *forte* lower keyboard. This juxtaposition of *piano* and *forte* manuals was not restricted to the Low Countries but became general wherever two manuals were built, including Germany, where this disposition was forgotten by the twentieth-century revival; Quantz (1752) refers to the advantage of having an upper manual for *pianissimo* on a two-keyboard harpsichord (*Auf einem Clavicymbal mit zweyen Clavieren, hat man über dieses noch den Vortheil, zum Pianissimo sich des obersten Claviers bedienen zu können*). Van Blankenburg's lute stop was not fitted to all two-manual instruments, either old or new, and on those unaffected by his discovery the fourth row of jacks shared an 8′ string with another row from which it was still sufficiently separated to serve as a color stop.

This was the period during which leadership in building was in the process of passing from the Ruckers-Couchet school at Antwerp to the Blanchet-Taskin dynasty of Paris. Stylistically and structurally the latter continued the tradition of the former, and the Flemish influence is evident as early as 1722, when the workshop of Nicholas Blanchet (founder of the dynasty, d. 1731) contained such items as "one harpsichord, 3 spinets and another small harpsichord, all from Flanders," as well as an "old" Flemish harpsichord; five years later its contents included two large Flemish harpsichords with *ravalement*, three small harpsichords, ten spinets, and one large harpsichord, all by members of the Ruckers family, as well as four plates for printing Flanders paper, the printed papers with which Flemish makers had decorated the cases and lids of their instruments. Of greater import perhaps is the presence in Jean-Marie Galland's workshop in 1760 of a harpsichord made in the Ruckers' style (the Ruckers had been dead for a century by then).

But innovations were not lacking: Thévenard designed a "new" harpsichord in 1727 in which half the strings could be abolished without impairment of tone, due to a novel form of jack containing a combination tongue-plectrum made in a special mold and designed to fall back under its own weight; from his drawings it seems as though the reduction of $2 \times 8'$ to $1 \times 8'$ was forced by the need of procuring extra space for his hook-shaped plectra, and that their author was making a virtue out of necessity. Preoccupation with plectra was not new—indeed, a whole treatise had been devoted to ideas for a new spiral plectrum in 1679 (by J. B. de La Rousselière)—as both adjustment and wear presented continuing problems; but despite much experimentation with new shapes and new materials the traditional raven or crow quill remained standard until the instrument's demise, even after the introduction of buff leather by Pascal Taskin, and the probable but unverifiable use of hard leather earlier in Italy, not to mention the silver, brass, or steel quills "invented" by William Burton in 1730.

Italian eighteenth-century instruments continued to be built right into an outer housing, but makers may have produced a proportionately larger number with 4' registers than theretofore, and also changed their basses from short octave to long octave. These practices seem to be borne out by details of the fourteen harpsichords possessed by Cardinal Ottoboni (d. 1740); eight of these had two registers and six had three registers, and, furthermore, a total of eight were *ottava stesa*, as the

Italians term the long octave. One maker who departed from the narrow path of established tradition was Vincenzo Sodi of Florence, who in the late eighteenth century put double-tongued jacks, capable of plucking two strings simultaneously, in his harpsichords, and also reverted to an ancient practice of cutting circular soundholes in the belly rail.

With Burkat Shudi (1702–1773) and Jacob Kirkman (1710–1792), both of Swiss extraction, the English school of harpsichord making came into existence. Prior to the Restoration many if not most keyboard chordophones seem to have been imported, and after the Restoration local manufacture was concentrated on virginals and spinets rather than on the larger instruments. Reformation, Puritanism, and civil disorders had disrupted church music to the point of rendering the profession of church organist unnecessary (as it had that of the organ builder), and the ranks of organ as of harpsichord builders were to be replenished by large infusions of foreign blood. Once settled, Shudi and Kirkman established what were to remain the norms of harpsichord making in England, to the detriment of such "classics" as the Ruckers. In a letter addressed to Dr. Burney, dated January 13, 1774, the Rev. Thomas Twining thanked him for advice concerning the purchase of a piano, and goes on:

I have hitherto made shift with a little Andreas Ruckers but the want of compass is miserable. The tone is very fine in the *middle*, & has a certain *crispness* (I cannot help my own ideas!) that is not in any other harpsichord that I know of. But the sweetness, the quality of the *firm bases* [*sic*] of Kirkman's are far beyond. I have likewise a 2 unis. Kirkman which was Mrs. T's, & has hitherto stood at Colchester. This I shall carry to Fordham, & sell my Ruckers if I can get anything for it. But I fear there are no Ruckers fanciers left. Do you know anybody that I could *impose* upon? It was the very harpsichord that Handel used for some years at Covent Garden: I think my father bought it of Kirkman—Shudi—I don't know which.

A marginal note informs us that in 1818 the Ruckers was still in the family.

A remark by Burney anent the Ruckers owned by Balbastre in Paris: "the touch very light, owing to the quilling, which in France is always weak" leads to the inference that the touch of English instruments was heavy, a heaviness perhaps passed on to the piano, for Shudi's daughter married John Broadwood, and under his direction the firm later became that of the piano house of Broadwood, whose pianos continued as robust as his father-in-law's harpsichords had been, and of notably heavier touch than those of the Viennese competitors.

As soon as the pianoforte assumed sufficient importance to be a potential threat to the harpsichord, makers felt obliged to strive for new effects, that is, choices of timbre, and dynamic nuances. Dynamic nuancing was the more difficult to obtain in view of the harpsichord's inherent rigidity, yet two means were employed with transitory success: Shudi, turning to the organ for inspiration, patented in 1769 a Venetian swell, a set of louvers placed over the soundboard in analogy to the organ swell box, a boxlike chamber furnished with shutters or louvers and containing pipes; it had been known in England for over half a century. A similar system, worked by a knee lever, was invented independently at about the same time, possibly earlier, by Ferdinand Weber of Dublin. Shudi's chief competitor, Kirkman, was thus forced to fall back on the one-piece swell that Roger Plenius had already incorporated into his lyrichord in 1741, a swell obtained very simply by making the lid of two hinged sections, the smaller of which could be raised and lowered independently. A second way of varying dynamics was to provide a "machine" or other mechanism for rapidly reversing the on-off position (i.e., plucking or silent positions) of one or of several rows of jacks simultaneously and without requiring the performer to remove his hands from the keyboard. Originally, the ends of jack slides had pierced, and projected beyond, the cheekpiece; later on drawstops were provided, and as these necessitated withdrawing the hand from the keyboard they were in turn replaced by knee levers or by registration pedals.

Registration pedals were reinvented, rather than merely revived, in 1741, when Nils Brelin incorporated eight into his clavicytherium; Shudi employed pedals by 1765, the year in which he built a two-manual harpsichord for the King of Prussia, and had it played for the first time by the nine-year-old Mozart. The *Salzburg Zeitung* of August 6 (as quoted in Kinsky, 1912) printed a London report of July 4 relating that Shudi had combined all the registers in a pedal, by the treading of which one register after another could be drawn off, increasing or decreasing the volume as desired. Also in 1765, von Blaha of Prague is credited with having invented the Janissary stop, operated by a pedal.

A knee lever (*genouillère*) mechanism was invented in 1762 by Joseph-

Antoine Berger of Grenoble, and Virbès of Paris applied two *genouil-lères* to a 1766 harpsichord of his make in an attempt to obtain *forte* and *piano* effects. Pascal Taskin was said (by Abbé Troufflaut) to have first adapted knee levers to his instruments in 1768. Like modern harpsi-chord pedals, their position could be fixed indefinitely by hitching. Taskin applied as many as six to a two-manual model, controlling the individual rows of jacks, the coupler, and machine stop. Paralleling these efforts was a progressively increasing production of bowed key-board instruments (see page 307 ff) whose makers apparently came to believe that their complicated mechanisms would be competitive with, and ultimately outdo, harpsichord and piano in the realm of dynamic nuances.

A different approach, again inspired by the organ, was taken by Ger-man makers, who occasionally added stops at 2' or at 16' pitch; the former were technically exacting to produce and their musical contri-bution limited, hence their documentation is rare. But the 16' stop offered scope for a new dynamic dimension, one that has been more fully exploited in the twentieth-century revival than it ever was in the eighteenth century. The easiest and cheapest way of adding a 16' was simply to replace one set of 8' strings with wound strings sounding an octave lower, and this procedure was followed more often; alternately, an additional choir of longer strings, with their separate bridge, nut, and sometimes even soundboard section, was added to an instrument built proportionately longer. Of the two types, only the second is recogniz-able today, as the first leaves, of course, no permanent trace.

H. A. Hass of Hamburg is the earliest known maker to have furnished some of his harpsichords with a 16' stop of the second type, from 1734 on. A large harpsichord by J. A. Hass with both 2' and 16' stops bears the date 1710, too early by far, for that maker was still building in 1768, and furthermore this particular instrument passed through the Berceau Royal's workshop in the 1920s, an establishment from which musical instruments are known to have occasionally departed in slightly dif-ferent form from that in which they entered. But harpsichords with 16' stops were rare until later in the century, and their construction may have been restricted geographically for a time, as a 1756 tuning manual by the well-known Brunswick maker, Barthold Fritz, makes no mention of any 16' stop, and a year later Mathias Koch, a Strasbourg builder, announced his completion of a three-manual harpsichord with four unison and one octave strings, again without a 16'. However, Johann

Andreas Stein built a combination harpsichord-piano (see page 332) in 1769 with a 16′ stop on the harpsichord, and Adlung (d. 1762) reported having seen a Breitenbach harpsichord with two manuals and three sets of strings: 4′, 8′, and wound 16′ (with 4′ and 16′ on the lower manual). From the details he gives it is clear that he considered it important enough to warrant description, and also that the 8′ and 16′ shared the same bridge; on a previous page he had written, apropos of 8′ strings: *wo man sie spinnt, können sie 16′ werden* ("if they are wound they can become 16′"). His *Anleitung*, written in 1754 and published in 1758, states that most harpsichords had two or three choirs, the latter with 2×8′+4′, that occasionally one of the 8′ choirs was replaced by a wound 16′, and that harpsichords with one or with four rows of jacks were rare; if four rows were present the disposition was either 2×8′+2×4′, or 2×8′+1×4′ with a wound or plain 16′, and this could be placed on a "third bridge," that is, one of its own—a true 16′.

He had also seen the cut-through lute stop, which, he says, was called spinet stop in Germany. And, good organist that he was, he suggested the addition of a quint stop to the bass section: "Here it does not cost as much as on the organ." He greatly admired a harpsichord with independent pedal, the latter strung with 2×8′ and a wound 16′, the top of which contained a "door" that could be opened to increase the volume. Such pedal cases were large boxes upon which the harpsichord was placed. Among the various auxiliary stops he described were the harp stop (*Harfenzug*), with bent pins set in a mobile batten adjacent to the nut, which could be moved until the pins touched the strings. "Praetorius (p. 67) calls an instrument with this stop arpichordum," he reminds us, and the fortepiano stop that was worked by a pedal but regrettably not further described: the piano was indeed infringing upon the harpsichord's rightful domain.

The pedal with independent harpsichord action was known as *clavecin de pédales* in eighteenth-century France and *Clavicymbelpedal* in eighteenth-century Germany, where it was described by Adlung as having a two-octave compass; its jacks and strings were spaced further apart than those of the manuals, so that the two octaves took up as much room as did four octaves' worth of manual action. Such pedal instruments extended the total compass to six octaves. Often it is difficult to tell whether reference was to a pedalboard with pulldowns or to that with its own action and strings; a one-manual harpsichord with *clavecin de pédales* was among the instruments in Jean Denis's workshop at his death in 1686; its appraisal at a sum close to that of the two-manual harpsichords is an indication that this was an independent instrument. In the case of Nicolas Gigault, organist, who in 1701 possessed a two-manual harpsichord with pedal, the same certainty obtains, for the pitch of the 16′ pedal is given. Georg Gebel (1685–1749), organist at Breslau and an almost exact contemporary of J. S. Bach, devised a harpsichord pedal housed in one case with the harpsichord, for an overall compass of six octaves, but whether it had trackers to relay pull-down motion sideways, or an independent pedal action with or without trackers, is impossible to tell, and details are also lacking concerning the pedal that Le Gay of Paris added to his combination harpsichord and bowed keyboard instrument in 1760.

Three-manual harpsichords were built, albeit exceptionally, in the eighteenth century; one is documented as having belonged to the organist Claude Jacquet in 1702. H. A. Hass of Hamburg left a three-manual dated 1740, most elaborate both as to disposition (it boasts five choirs of strings and six rows of jacks for 16′, 8′, 4′, and 2′) and as to decoration—certainly not a practice instrument conceived for underpaid organists. Koch of Strasbourg built a less impressive three-manual that he described in a letter published in Marpurg (1757); its lower manual was intended for preludizing and accompanying, the second manual for solo playing, the upper "contained" an echo, and it had four unisons and an octave (4×8′+4′) all told. Milchmeyer devised another, about 1780, with no fewer than 250 variations of tone, or so he claimed. The *clavecin royal* of Wagner of Dresden was, despite its name, a square piano imitating the harpsichord, not a three-manual harpsichord, an error of identity for which Fétis seems responsible (see piano, page 331). Johann Nikolaus Bach, the "Jena" Bach (d. 1753), made at least one three-manual gut-strung harpsichord (see page 268); Hullmandel in the *Encyclopédie* also mentions the existence of three-manual harpsichords. In the year 1901 two Italian instruments with three manuals purportedly came to light, and certainly came on the market, but no Italian three-manual instrument is now considered genuine.

The quarter century immediately preceding the outbreak of the French Revolution saw the apogee of harpsichord making in England and France, but the former great centers of building—Italy and the Low Countries—made no more contributions; in Italy at that time, if we can believe Burney, harpsichords were rarities, while spinets were common in private houses. In Germany makers were preoccupied chiefly with clavichord and piano building; a Cassel keyboard-instrument maker named Wilhelm (or Wilhelmi) was charging, in 1783, 140 *Reichsthaler* for a two-manual harpsichord, 100–110 for fortepianos, 40–47 for five-octave clavichords, 18–30 for four-and-one-half-octave clavichords—the race with the piano was a close one indeed. The Antwerp school died out with the last Couchets, and by 1740 the harpsichord makers' section of Saint Luke's Guild numbered only three members.

Yet the Ruckers instruments lived on; cherished at first for their tone quality, they were often decorated by painters of repute according to the prevailing fashion, and when their musical usefulness was impaired by age they were rebuilt and their compass was extended. They also continued to be imitated, *a s'y méprendre* ("so that one could be taken in by it") in fact, according to the 1779 Lausanne edition of the *Encyclopédie*; the writer goes on to say that Blanchet excelled in enlarging Ruckers harpsichords, which involved cutting into cheekpiece and spine, widening and even lengthening the case, adding old wood to complete the enlarged soundboard, and replacing the wrestplank, so that by and large only the main portion of the soundboard and some two and one-half feet of the bentside were original. Yet such was the reputation of the Ruckers that these operations not only paid but also enhanced the rebuilder's name (of twenty-three harpsichords inventorized in the king's library at Versailles in 1780, eleven were by members of the Ruckers family). This operation was called *ravalement* and started in the late seventeenth century. If the enlargement resulted in a compass of five octaves, F to F, it was known as *grand ravalement*; if less, either as plain *ravalement* or sometimes as *petit ravalement*.

Pascal Taskin, a Walloon who trained in the Blanchet workshop and ultimately took it over, was not only a builder of harpsichords and pianos, but he also made a reputation for himself as rebuilder of Ruckers harpsichords, and complained in a letter of having so many orders for *ravalements* that he lacked time to build his own instruments. Instead of cutting through the wrestplank for insertion of a lute stop, he made a novel use of the fourth row of jacks on Ruckers harpsichords by furnishing them with plectra of *peau de buffle* (buff leather), thereby adding a new dynamic level—that of *pianissimo*—as well as a new tone color. His *peau de buffle*, which became the rage of musical Paris, was first applied by him in 1768, according to Abbé Troufflaut. Other makers adopted it, including Sébastien Érard, of whom the *Almanach musical* of 1783 mentions a harpsichord with three quilled and one buff leather registers and several pedals, and remarks that Érard was the first to make all four jacks speak by means of the *grand clavier* (lower manual) alone. This is valuable information, for extant French harpsichords generally have only three registers in contrast to the Flemish instruments rebuilt in France. Taskin also applied buff leather plectra to his own, three-jack instruments. This leather is soft, porous, and spongy, and inability to distinguish between these qualities and those of ordinary hard sole leather has caused much misunderstanding in the past. The *Encyclopédie* of 1790 wrote of the *guinée ou buffle* that it

is an ox or cow leather, oiled by the chamois [leather] process to give it the strength and suppleness necessary for equipping the cavalry. . . . Although one works true buffalo skin very rarely because it is too hard and also too difficult to obtain, one always gives this name to the large ox or cow skins from which are made the large [military] belts and shoulders belts. For us it is a branch of trade in the Levant and in Africa, which lends it the name of *guinée* [Guinea] . . .

There no longer seems to be any doubt that Taskin was the first to apply buff leather plectra to his harpsichords, but ordinary hard leather may have been used earlier, particularly in Italy, and was certainly employed by 1760 when Le Gay submitted a combination harpsichord–bowed keyboard instrument to the Paris Académie, its jacks *garnis, au lieu de plume, d'un petit morceau de cuir dur* ("garnished, instead of quill, with a small piece of hard leather"). But despite such improvements and the numerous variations of tone designed to imitate the sounds of harp, lute, mandolin, bassoon, flageolet, oboe, and other instruments, the harpsichord was doomed. The year 1768, so auspiciously linked with Taskin's *peau de buffle*, was also the ill-omened year in which Johann Christian Bach played the world's first public piano recital in London. Nonetheless, there were still nineteen harpsichord makers active in Paris alone, as against sixteen piano makers, according to the *Calendrier musical universel* for that year, but by the time the French Revolution had abated, the harpsichord had become a museum object.

A museum object, that is, in most, but not all, of the Western world, for, like the Bronze Age, the harpsichord age lingered longer in Ireland than elsewhere in Europe, and builders in Dublin were still active in the first decade of the new century, with one maker, John Southwell, still producing harpsichords in 1822. By contrast, a contributor to the *Allgemeine musikalische Zeitung* of 1804 wondered "several years ago" if it would not be feasible to provide some of the originally so expensive harpsichords that had since been relegated to the attic with a piano action, and a builder to whom he suggested this did then transform an old harpsichord into a usable fortepiano. When Moscheles gave his musical soirées in London in 1837 he experienced great difficulty in finding a harpsichord, but finally procured a Shudi of 1771, upon which he performed some Scarlatti, the latter "received with considerable interest by the audience, on account of the introduction of the old harpsichord."

Modern revival of harpsichord playing was stimulated in the final decades of the past century, by, among others, keyboard player and collector Eugène de Bricqueville, in France; Érard restarted and Pleyel started building in 1888, to be followed in England by Arnold Dolmetsch in 1896, and by numerous others in the Old and New Worlds since. Two different conceptions of the modern instrument have been manifest almost from the beginning of their revival, one aimed at producing an instrument that will withstand the rigors of climate and transportation, combined with a tone powerful enough to fill a modern concert hall; the other, to reproduce as closely as possible the models of a specific school of the past, with due allowance for certain technological innovations.

THE CLAVICYTHERIUM

The clavicytherium or "keyed harp" (from *clavis* + *cythara*) was a harpsichord in upright form made from the fifteenth to the eighteenth century, with an action more complicated than that of an ordinary harpsichord since the jacks did not fall back of their own volition but had to be pulled back. The instrument existed before its present name, which is first mentioned by Virdung (1511) and occurs infrequently thereafter until the seventeenth century. Mersenne speaks of it as an instrument "in use in Italy," but then he was describing the true keyed harp (see page 398), whereas his contemporary in Rome, Athanasius Kircher, reported it as being played in Germany. Obviously it was scarce in their time. Kircher was also the first of several authors to point out that it had the great advantage of occupying very little space, a consideration that may account for its relative popularity in the eighteenth century, prior to its replacement by the upright piano—or its conversion into one (Eitner relates that Gerber in 1742 applied hammers to a clavicytherium and called it *Cabinetflügel*).

Writing about 1440, Paulus Paulirinus described an instrument he calls *-nnportile* (the initial letter is lacking), a small upright harpsichord combined with a positive organ; this earliest reference is at the same time the most complicated version known. A late-fifteenth-century sculpture in the Kefermarkt parish church, Upper Austria, shows a very small upright harpsichord with a large central rose being played in portative organ fashion, a psaltery to which a keyboard has somehow been added. Bass and treble are reversed; ten pairs of strings seem to be visible, and the maximum length of the whole instrument may have been some 60 centimeters (2 feet). Shortly thereafter, Virdung (1511) presents a woodcut—also reversed—of a clavicytherium having a compass of over three octaves, F to G, lacking the low F♯, its shape and general disposition inspired by the portative organ. The anonymous painting of about 1540, *Der castalische Brunnen*, in private ownership in Zurich, includes a clavicytherium among numerous other instruments, a rather uncertain affair set well in the background.

The Florentine organ and harpsichord maker, Vincenzo Bolcioni, proposed making for Cardinal Ferdinand Gonzaga in 1608 a clavicytherium strung both front and back; it was to have had 8′ strings on one side, 4′ strings on the other, both to have been playable from a single keyboard; the price was to have been sixty scudi (how it was to have been tuned he does not state). But the Cardinal ordered instead a bowed keyboard instrument and an organ. The pertinent correspondence repeatedly requests wood sufficient for the making of two soundboards and also records the presence in Mantua of a clavicytherium strung front and back; actually, no fewer than four clavicytheria were then in Mantua, all dating from the previous century.

In the north, construction remained more conservative. Praetorius (1619) was familiar with clavicytheria and depicted one with the rounded tail so typical of German instruments having a bentside. But it is not until the eighteenth-century revival that structural details are forthcoming: as the action was not housed perpendicular to the depth, the body was shallower than that of a harpsichord; the jacks were pushed out by means of squares, pulled back by wire springs that pressed against each jack; these wires could sometimes be dispensed with if the lower portion of the key was heavy enough to pull its jack back; however, the space-saving advantages offered were partly offset by the fact that these instruments were more difficult to play than were harpsichords. The actions of preserved eighteenth-century instruments differ somewhat in that springs no longer have to be relied upon to return the jacks, but instead the lower member of the square is weighted (it rests on an abstract set upon the rear of each key). Two 8′ registers formed the common disposition; rarely was a 4′ added.

In 1741, Nils Brelin of Sweden designed and built an "upright double harpsichord" with eight variations of tone—the latter indispensable by then, it seems—a drawing of which shows that the variations were controlled by as many registration pedals of the straight type in use on contemporary organs—the earliest recorded instance of the reinvention of registration pedals on a keyboard chordophone. His clavicytherium was "double" because its strings were double length for at least the treble half of the compass, as he stated, passing over two bridges, with both sections sounding at the same pitch, a very ingenious arrangement. And indeed his drawing shows an exceptionally tall instrument, over 6 ells high (probably the equivalent of 12 local feet) with what appear to be one set of strings at 4′ and another at 8′ pitch, the latter prolonged upward to pass over two bridges; these extra lengths vibrated sympathetically, for no plucking mechanism is provided for them. Brelin, who had learned instrument building abroad, may have been inspired by Silbermann's *cimbal d'amour*; he is said to have incorporated its principle in an "improved clavichord" of the 1730s. Later, the calculation of "dead" end string-lengths to enhance the sound of the struck strings became known as aliquot stringing.

Instruments were then being made from Italy to Dublin to Sweden, and even one of the models for a *clavecin à maillets* submitted to the Paris Académie des Sciences by Jean Marius in 1716 was a clavicytherium (see pianoforte, page 322). Builders such as Cristofori did not disdain to make upright harpsichords, for the Medici collection in Florence included an item entitled *un cimbalo da sonarsi ritto* ("a harpsichord to be played upright") made by him; three clavicytheria by Delin of Tournai, dating from the mid-eighteenth century, have survived; a Dublin organ builder offered for sale double and single upright harpsichords in the 1760s, and Laborde explained in 1780 that such instruments were built to accommodate persons dwelling in small apartments. Even gut-strung harpsichords (see page 283) were made in upright form. In the nineteenth century the name clavicytherium was transferred to the giraffe piano, logically enough, and even to the claviharp. Many museum instruments appear to be converted horizontal harpsichords and the dearth of authentic older specimens may be due to Gerber's example having been followed a little too freely.

GUT-STRUNG HARPSICHORDS AND SPINETS

Plucked keyboard instruments strung with gut were known by the early sixteenth century and continued to be made sporadically until the second half of the eighteenth century. At the time of their appearance they were given the name of *arpicordo* in Italian, *Harfentive* in German. The German expression, created apparently in analogy to *Positive*, is the earliest of the two to be documented, although the instrument itself seems to have originated in Italy. Long after the *Harfentive* was forgotten in the north it lived on by its Italian name—*arpicordo*—as a harpsichord or spinet stop. It also lent its name to the English "harpsichord."

In his discussion of lutes and their stringing, Virdung remarks that the strings of lutes, of the great and small *Geigen*, harps, *Harfentiven*, and trumpets marine were of sheep's gut. On an earlier page containing three woodcuts, two of which represent keyboard instruments—a rectangular one entitled *Clavicimbalum* and an upright one entitled *Claviciterium*—his accompanying text reads: "This is the same instrument as the virginal/only it has different strings of the intestines of sheep and nails that make it harp [;] has also quills like the virginal, is newly invented and I have only seen one of it," after which he proceeds directly to the discussion of fretted chordophones. His drawing of a virginal on the previous page is of the same instrument as the *Clavicimbalum*, differing only in very minor details. This passage has proved a stumbling block to organologists in the past. But clearly the *Clavicimbalum* was not new in Virdung's day, nor was it "like the virginal," nor was it gut strung. Obviously then the woodcut was mistitled by some error, and one may conclude that virginal and *Harfentive* differed not in form but in stringing and by the additional harping nails; the name itself is also obviously derived from its likeness to the bray harp (see page 390) with its nails.

The earliest Italian mention of the *arpicordo* that I have come across so far concerns a *maistro d'arpicordi* (an *arpicordo* maker, not teacher) whose *floruit* was 1515, the son of the Venetian *maistro da manachordi* Johane Antonio. From Lanfranco (1533) we learn that the lowest key

on organs and *arpichordi* [sic] was *ffaut gravissima,* and that Francesco
Antegnati of Brescia, one of the great organ builders of his century,
was also making *monochordi, arpichordi, clavacymbali* (several of
which are extant). A few years later, in 1540, Pietro Aretino wrote to
Alessandro degli Organi to suggest that he, Alessandro, make an *arpicordo*
for Titian, who in return would paint his portrait, but the answer to
this promising inquiry has not come down to us. From these last two
references, as well as from numerous later ones, it becomes clear that
the meaning of the term *arpicordo* must have become altered to designate both spinets and harpsichords, regardless of whether they were gut
or wire strung, and finally to denote no more than a mere accessory expression stop on these instruments, all this in the course of the sixteenth
century. A milestone date is 1561, year of the publication of Alessandro
Citolini's *La tipocosmia,* for this work includes a passage enumerating
metal-strung musical instruments, among which are specified the *mono-
cordo, arpicordo, clavicembalo, clavicordio,* and dulcimer.

Italian references to the *arpicordo* in the sixteenth and seventeenth
centuries were fairly numerous, northern ones less so. However, Elias
Ammerbach's *Orgel und Instrument-tabulatur* of 1571 contains a statement to the effect that whoever can play the organ can also play the
positive, regal, virginal, clavichord, *clavicimbalo, harficordo,* and "other
similar instruments," and the Dresden court inventory of 1593 included *ein Harf Cortium,* as well as "as instrument in form of a book,
strung with lute strings, which is broken, and none of the keys work,"
probably a 4′ *spinettino,* and at any rate evidence of the presence of
gut-strung keyboard instruments at the end of the sixteenth century.

What name, if any, was given to these in the seventeenth century is
unknown; the Innsbruck *Instrumentenkammer* had in that century a
"simple *spinetl thiorbata*" by Undeus of Venice, a gut-strung spinet, and
during his sojourn in Venice from 1656 to 1669 Eugen Casparini, the
noted organ builder, saw many instruments "strung in the manner of
theorboes or lutes" belonging to "gentlemen of the nobility." These
terms foreshadow the *Theorbenflügel* of the north. Casparini himself
made several, according to his son, Adam Orazio; those that his father
saw and made he referred to as plain *Instrumenta* (Orazio spoke German), not *Flügel,* a term in current use by the time he wrote (1718),
which fact suggests that they may have been rectangular in form. As
Hubbard has pointed out (1965), the fact that gut strings are thicker
than metal ones complicates the question of layout, and, together with

problems of tuning, this factor would have induced makers to keep their gut-strung models as simple as possible.

A few early Italian harpsichords with short scale were built for a single 8′ stop and could theoretically have been intended for gut stringing; perhaps they represent *arpicordi*. Praetorius does not mention a gut-strung harpsichord, but Mersenne refers to gut for the stringing of spinets and notes that such strings do not stay in tune as well as those of metal, as proven by experiments, an implication that gut was not used in practice in his day. The mathematician Claude Dechales suggested (1674) that harpsichords could be strung with gut, and apparently they were sporadically, for a harpsichord with "Cat's Gut string" was seen in England at about that time, and one made by a Mr. Longfellow that stood in the Duke of Chandos's house at Cambridge in 1720, the year in which it was made, is still in existence.

More information is forthcoming in eighteenth-century Germany, where these instruments seem to have enjoyed a certain vogue. Johann Christoph Fleischer of Hamburg built his first model in 1718 and wrote of it (in the *Breslauer Sammlungen* for that year): "the small 8′ lute-clavessin has a circular case," straight at the keyboard end, the whole instrument shaped like an amphitheater; its case was four feet long, had two choirs of gut strings at 8′ pitch, and in the bass additionally one octave at 4′ pitch, from C° to c°. He also made *Theorbenflügel*, distinguished from the others by their downward extension to the 16′ register; these had three sets of strings, two of gut and one of metal. Agricola (1768) relates having seen and heard in Leipzig around 1740 a lute-harpsichord suggested by J. S. Bach, and executed by the organ builder Zacharias Hildebrand; it had a shorter scale than ordinary harpsichords, he writes, with two choirs of gut strings—presumably at 8′ pitch —and a 4′ stop of brass strings, like those of Fleischer. (Hildebrand regularly tuned the harpsichord of the Leipzig Thomasschule between 1734 and 1744, when Bach was in Leipzig.) Among the instruments in J. S. Bach's possession at the time of his death was a lute-harpsichord, perhaps that of Hildebrand. Adlung's contemporary, Christian Ernst Friderici, a Silbermann pupil, well known for his organs and pianos, also made lute-harpsichords to which he added the increasingly indispensable "variations of tone."

Another maker was the "Jena" Bach, Johann Nikolaus Bach (1669–1753), a second cousin of Johann Sebastian, organist, composer, and maker of keyboard instruments, of whose gut-strung harpsichords Adlung writes in detail. Some were in harpsichord shape and differed from the metal-strung models chiefly by their shorter and less pointed form, their stringing, and their bridges, as each string had its individual bridge on the soundboard in order to approximate the vibrating string lengths (both open and stopped) of a real lute; in order to imitate the lute's dynamics, Bach made his instruments with two or three keyboards, one for *forte*, the second for *piano*, the third for *più piano*; all acted on a single choir of strings, but each manual had its separate row of jacks, and the difference in plucking points accounted for the dynamic gradations—which must have been minor, especially as the quills are stated to have been all of equal strength; the compass was from C° to c³. Adlung also saw several of Bach's gut-strung oval instruments (Cristofori had made at least one oval spinet) and relates that he painted and varnished the soundboards of his *Lautenwerke*, as they were called.

Johann Georg Gleichmann of Ilmenau seems to have had a predilection for gut-strung keyboard instruments, for about 1722 he brought out a gut-strung bowed keyboard instrument (see page 314) and was also a maker of gut-strung harpsichords, as a sideline to his bread-and-butter duties as organist. The Parisian harpsichord builder Le Gay managed to combine a bowed keyboard instrument with a gut-strung harpsichord in 1760 (see page 315). Writing in the 1776 supplement to the *Encyclopédie* and in the Geneva edition of the same work in the following year, V.A.L. states that in his day one could find old gut harpsichords in Paris and in the larger towns of the Low Countries, a statement that causes a raising of eyebrows on first reading, but that is found to have a basis in fact if one bears in mind the popularity of bowed keyboard instruments in the eighteenth century, many of which were gut strung, most of which were very short lived, and to all intents and purposes represented just another variety of harpsichord to the nonprofessional eye.

Gut-strung harpsichords were also made in upright form; Harding (1944) quotes a 1792 writer to the *Bataavisch genootschap der kunsten en wetenschappen* named Gratiaan, who noted that such instruments were built for ease in transportation, and that some were provided with three soundboards and had a very dull tone.

ENHARMONIC HARPSICHORDS

Musical theorists of the sixteenth century, intent on re-creating the music of the Greeks, attempted to reconstruct the three Greek genera—

diatonic, chromatic, and enharmonic—both in theory and in practice. They failed, but to their efforts we owe the birth of opera. Problems of tuning had to be reconciled, and demonstration instruments were needed to illustrate the finer points of dividing an octave into a specified number of microtones; to this end, harpsichords and organs with special features were built. Although both remained rarities, enharmonic harpsichords were cheaper to construct than enharmonic organs, as such instruments have since been called, and consequently more is heard of the former. Theories, discussions, and countertheories spilled over into the seventeenth century, and there even exist compositions from this period for the enharmonic harpsichord. The designation "enharmonic" was applied to such instruments in modern times—the sixteenth century called them *arcicembali*—and has now come to denote a harpsichord with more than twelve keys and strings to an octave, including later specimens designed for acoustical experimentation. Not considered enharmonic are those keyboards furnished with split sharps for the avoidance of "wolf" tones.

The first such instrument recorded was built in 1548 in Venice for the composer and theorist Gioseffo Zarlino by Domenico of Pesaro, *fabbricatore eccelente di simili instrumenti* ("excellent maker of such instruments"), as Zarlino terms him, in which not only "the major semitones are divided into two parts but also all the minor ones." Burney saw it in Florence in 1779, copied Zarlino's instructions for tuning it, and announced his intention of publishing them in his *History of Music* but did not do so. Yet at least one enharmonic harpsichord may have been built before Zarlino's, for Salinas (1577) knew of an *arcicembalo* in Italy, built "about forty years ago," in which each tone was divided into five parts. This represents thirty-one microtones to the octave, a favored division of the theorists; and shortly thereafter a two-manual instrument with sharps split throughout the compass was made—about 1550—by Cesare de Pollastris.

Arcicembalo was the name given by Nicola Vicentino to the enharmonic harpsichord in his treatise of 1555, in which he describes in detail an instrument then in his possession and which he had caused to be constructed. His tuning system called for thirty-one divisions of the octave; he furnished a large number of examples of all possible octave species, but he ultimately became lost in a labyrinth of theoretical tonalities far removed from his avowed purpose of demonstrating how the three genera could be practically incorporated in a keyboard instrument.

Bottrigari (1594) calls the *arcicembalo* "by Don Nicolo Vincentino [sic] *quasi unicum*," relates that it had twenty-six diatonic keys, over one hundred and thirty strings, and two keyboards with "doubled and split" accidentals—split sharps, plus additional accidental keys, he explains—and used but seldom due to difficulty of tuning and maintenance. However, Vicentino was a composer and theorist, not a builder, although he may have been responsible for some of the specifications.

At the time Bottrigari wrote, the *arcicembalo* in question was in the instrument collection of Alfonso, Duke of Modena, where it was duly inventorized in 1598 by the harpsichord builder, Ippolito Cricca, as *un clavacimbalo cromatico con due testadure* [sic], probably the same as that listed in an annotation as *cembalo unisono con li tasti spezzati, di Ferrara* [i.e. made in Ferrara], *da Camera: pretioso*. (Other keyboard instruments in the list rate a mere *buono* or at most *buonissimo*.) On Alfonso's death the instrument passed to Antonio Goretti, according to Artusi; and when Goretti died, his instruments were sold (ca. 1660) and went to Innsbruck. The 1665 inventory of the Innsbruck instruments mentions *ein doppeltes Instrument* made of cypress with two keyboards by Cesare de Pollastris of Ferrara, with split sharps throughout the compass, but like the earlier instrument seen by Burney, this one also has since disappeared.

Through their writings, Vicentino and Zarlino stimulated considerable interest both in the revival of the Greek genera and in the construction of further experimental instruments. Another *arcicembalo* was built for Camillo Gonzaga, Count of Novellara, in 1606 by Vito Trasuntino of Venice, who called it *clavemusicum omnitonum*, the only early baroque instrument of its kind to have come down to us, now housed in the Museo Civico of Bologna. Its single manual consists of natural keys like those of any harpsichord, but its accidentals are as wide as the naturals and are divided into alternating black and white sections, with added shorter and narrower keys inserted between the E and F, B and C keys, for a total of thirty-one microtones to the octave, and a four-octave compass, C° to c³ (illustrations appear in MGG *sub* Trasuntino, in Dupont 1955, in Russell 1959).

Fabio Colonna designed and described a *sambuca lincea* with four microtones to the tone, bichord stringing, and keys arranged in eight tiers, in 1618, the year before Praetorius devoted a substantial amount of space to the *clavecymbalum universale* he had seen; this belonged to

Carl Luython, court organist to Emperor Rudolf II at Prague, and had been built some thirty years earlier in Vienna, with nineteen microtones to the octave; it contained split sharps and extra accidentals inserted between the E and F, B and C keys, and had bichord 8′ stringing; furthermore its keyboard could be shifted seven times. Luython sold it in 1613. Praetorius also heard from an Italian musician in Kassel about an enharmonic "spinet" in Italy; this might have been one of Giovanni Battista Boni, who worked in the first quarter of the seventeenth century and who was praised by Mersenne for his enharmonic harpsichords having split sharps throughout the compass. Further north, Jan Ban, the Dutch theorist, owned an enharmonic harpsichord.

Literature for such instruments, although sparse, was not completely lacking. The *Secondo libro de ricercate* of Giovanni Maria Trabaci, published at Naples in 1615, included several pieces for enharmonic harpsichord, and Jean Titelouze, in a letter to Mersenne of March 2, 1622, referred to a *certaine espinette faite exprez* ("a certain harpsichord made expressly") for enharmonic compositions. Mersenne himself furnished diagrams of keyboards arranged for enharmonic tunings. About 1630 Giovanni Pietro Polizzino made an enharmonic harpsichord with two sets of strings, one for the Phrygian, the other for the Dorian and hypodorian modes, to the design of Pietro della Valle. Perhaps it was of such an instrument that André Maugars wrote from Rome in 1639: . . . *l'espinette . . . J'ai veu quelques curieux qui en ont fait faire à deux claviers; l'un propre pour sonner le mode Dorien, l'autre le Phrygien, divisant le ton en quatre chordes* (". . . spinets of several amateurs who had them made with two manuals, one for the Dorian mode, the other for the Phrygian, dividing the tone among four strings"). At the mid-century Francesco Nigetti of Florence, organist and harpsichord maker, created his *proteus*, with each tone divided into five microtones, and provided with five tiers of keys. This appears to have been sold to Innsbruck, as the same inventory that recorded the Pollastris instrument included "another instrument with many keyboards of white ivory on which are the Florentine arms and in the center the author's, Francesco Nigetti's, name . . ." Indeed, it may be gathered from Kircher that such instruments were fairly frequent in seventeenth-century Italy, where such outstanding personalities as Giovanni Battista Doni and Galeazzo Sabbatini not only advocated but also designed their enharmonic keyboards.

From Kircher it also transpires that Nicolò Ramerino of Florence devised a transposing keyboard in 1640; his tuning system called for nine commas to the tone, and by means of registers the pitch could be changed by the desired number of commas. Perhaps his system was similar to that of Dr. Robert Smith, the eighteenth-century Cambridge physicist whose "changeable harpsichord," an enharmonic instrument, was built by Kirkman about 1757, and who proposed facilitating performance by drawing upon additional "seven couples of secondary notes" controlled by stops, as required, for any given piece of music. Still later, Jacques Goermans of Paris made a *clavecin parfait accord* with twenty-one divisions of the octave as late as 1781 or 1782, by means of split keys (this implies all accidentals split, as well as all the Cs, Ds, Gs, and As). The multiplicity of strings required for even an octave's worth of microtones made tuning excessively complicated, a reason given for abandoning the earlier enharmonic instruments. Bottrigari relates (1594) that only Luzzasco Luzzaschi, organist and composer at the Ferrara court, was able to tune the 130 strings of the local *arcicembalo*, and next to the woodcut of an enharmonic harpsichord in Zarlino's *Istitutioni harmoniche I* is a quotation from Alciati: *Difficile est, nisi docto homini tot tendere chordes*, attesting to the difficulty experienced by all but the very skilled.

After the battle of the Greek genera had subsided, enharmonic harpsichords remained in use for theoretical demonstrations of temperaments, for prior to the adoption of equal temperament the tuning of keyboard instruments presented very real problems. All sixteenth- and seventeenth-century enharmonic instruments called for the normal seven diatonic keys to the octave, plus a variable number of accidentals —*semitonia* and *subsemitonia*, as they were called then. Structurally this was realized either by furnishing the instrument with a single manual and the usual complement of "white" keys, plus as many tiers of shorter "black" keys as necessary, or by dividing the keys on two manuals, each with its own (single) set of strings, in which case the accidentals were "doubled and split"; all strings corresponding to one manual would then be tuned a diesis higher than those of the other. Even after the introduction of equal temperament, the problem of microtones and the possibilities of exploiting them remained alive, and in the twentieth century quarter-tone pianos were built. The nineteenth century preferred the sustained tone of harmoniums for its experimental instruments.

THE SPINET

Spinets have the same action as harpsichords, but differ from the latter in shape and usually also in their lesser size, as well as by the direction of their strings, as these proceed diagonally from left to right of the player. With very few exceptions spinets have a single manual and single set of strings; their shape has varied with time and place. Those of rectangular form, known as virginals, are discussed separately (see page 297).

The manuscript of Henry Arnaut of about 1440, devoted primarily to keyboard instruments, does not mention the spinet as such. But a small and rather crude drawing of a rectangle (no keyboard or strings are shown) six and a half times as long as it is wide, is accompanied by the text: *monocordium sonans ita alte sicut clavicembalum,* and a subsidiary drawing of what might be a jack has the annotation: "this piece is inserted into the key and in its *fissura* is a quill (*pluma*)." Now the word *altus,* like the French *haut,* means both high and loud, so that the "monocordium" either sounded as high as a *clavicimbalum* (harpsichord) or as loud as one. The latter interpretation not only makes better sense but is all the more likely as Arnaut lived in the epoch of "high and low," that is, loud and soft, instruments. A monochord with quills is out of the question, as is a quilled clavichord, so we are left to surmise that the "monochordium" of Arnaut's day was an embryo spinet, an embryo that had then no name of its own.

Certainly its name existed by the last decade of the fifteenth century, for the household accounts of the Countess of Angoulême for 1496 record a payment made for an *espinete* as well as for a coffer in which to place it. This may conceivably have been a harpsichord, however, for the French term *épinette* became a generic word for all plucked keyboard instruments; what it specified in the fifteenth century we cannot tell. With a *spineta sive gravicordi* mentioned in an Avignon contract of 1503 we are on surer ground, for *gravichord* is a corruption of clavichord, and hence it is very unlikely that the "spineta" had harpsichord shape. Concerning the etymology of "spinet" we have the unsupported evidence of Banchieri (1609), who asserts that "the spinet received its name from the inventor of that form who was one Giovanni Spinetti, Venetian, one of whose instruments existed in the hands of Francesco

Stivorio, organist . . . inscribed Ioannes Spinetus Venetus fecit 1503."
But this derivation is most unlikely. *Spinetta* is a diminutive of the
Italian word *spina*, thorn, and the spinet is also said to have been named
for its thornlike plectra, a genealogy traceable to Scaliger (1484–1558)
who implied that quill plectra came into use in his lifetime (but they
were known to Arnaut) and stated that the instrument called *clavicym-*
balum and *harpichordum*—he wrote in Latin—when he was a boy "is
now" called spinet from its plectra, thus indicating that the word originated well after the turn of the century, which is erroneous.

If the French used the term indiscriminately to denote spinet, virginal,
and harpsichord, the English used the word virginal in the same multiple
sense, and in seventeenth- and eighteenth-century Germany *Instrument*
covered both spinet and virginal, as did occasionally the word *Symphonie*
(Adlung reserves *Instrument* exclusively for the spinet). Praetorius in
Syntagma III defines *Viereckicht Instrument, Instrumentum indiscrete*
sic dictum as *Spinetto, Virginal*, but in another passage he classes harpsichord and spinet as *instrumenta pennata*, "otherwise generally called
Instrument." In sixteenth-century Italy, the spinet also went disguised
under the name of *clavichordio* (Latinized to *clavichordium*); thus
Annibale Rossi and his son Ferrante, a number of whose polygonal spinets are extant, are recorded in 1595 as improvers and modernizers of
clavicordi. It is not sure that the *espinetta* with its case owned by Margaret of Austria in 1531 really was a spinet rather than a harpsichord,
and Antonio Gardano was taking no chances with the vocabulary when
he subtitled his 1551 *Intavolatura nova* specifically *per arpichordi, clavi-*
cembali, spinette e manochordi.

The classical spinet of sixteenth- and seventeenth-century Italy was
six-sided, with keyboard in the long side, projecting from the casework
like a balcony. Case and soundboard were of thin cypress, lacking lid
and stand, housed in a separate outer case from which they were withdrawn for performance. The compass was early standardized at four
and one-half octaves, from $C°$ to f^3, with short octave (rarely, four
octaves occur also, $C°$ to c^3). Around 1700 the structural case was
thickened, a lid was provided, and the outer case came to be dispensed
with.

Apart from the standard instruments at 8′ pitch, smaller models at 4′
pitch, termed *spinettino* or *ottavina* (the latter an abbreviation of
spinetta ottavina) and an intermediary size at 6′ pitch, were apparently
popular. These smaller sizes were generally made of the same materials

as the larger models, but in northern Italy some makers availed themselves of Brazilwood (e.g., Francesco of Padova, who was also an organ
builder) or pine (e.g., Adam Abel), and were built either in trapezoid
or in polygonal form. Those of trapezoid form had recessed keyboards
and were built directly into the outer housing.

In many such 4' *spinettini* the tuning pins were placed immediately
behind the nameboard, as they are in the harpsichord, in contrast to
the 8' models with tuning pins to the player's right along the treble
wall. This disposition of the 4' tuning pins was retained in a large model
with a greatly lengthened spine, developed by Italian makers at the end
of the seventeenth century, in which the keyboard was set at an oblique
angle. It had full harpsichord scale and sometimes reached the overall
length of the harpsichord, and was provided with more than the usual
single set of strings (always running from left to right, however). This
type was called *arcispinetta*; one example is known that measures 244.5
centimeters (8 feet), another, attributed to Cristofori, is a fraction
longer—246.0 centimeters; both have a set of 4' strings in addition to
the normal 8' choir. Registration is effected here, as on some Italian
harpsichords, by pulling the keyboard out a fraction, and by pushing it
in by the same amount. A similar instrument by Celestini, but of
smaller proportions, is even inscribed *arcispineta*.

But a far more successful form was obtained by replacing the cheekpiece by a bentside, thereby giving the spinet the wing shape familiarly
known as a "leg of mutton." The earliest extant example of this type
is one by its inventor, Girolamo Zenti, made in 1631. Zenti was credited
by Bontempi (1695) with having invented instruments *fatti in figura di
Triangolo non giustamente equicrure: ma vario, per haver tre lati in-
eguali, con due tastadure, collocate non gia nella base ma in uno de' lati
minori di quella* ("made in the shape of a not quite isosceles triangle
having unequal sides, with two keyboards set in one of the lesser sides").
They occupy little space, he adds. This model became known in France
as *épinette à l'italienne* and in Italy as *spinetta traversa*. But it was in
England that the "leg of mutton" was to achieve its greatest popularity.
In the last decade of the seventeenth century an elliptic form of spinet
was made by Cristofori for Ferdinand de' Medici, with two strings to
a key, and a similar instrument, also bichord, but octagonal due to its
corners having been squared, was made in the eighteenth century by
another Italian builder, Gozzini, possibly inspired by Cristofori.

Significantly, perhaps, Virdung does not depict nor even mention

Bird's-eye view of a "leg of mutton" spinet by John Hitchcock, ca. 1770.
Courtesy of Yale University.

the polygonal Italian spinet, although the year his book appeared the Duke of Lorraine purchased his complex chekker-cum-spinet-cum-organ. Despite the preponderance of virginals in the Low Countries, Italianate polygonal spinets do appear, if rarely, in sixteenth-century paintings from the north, for instance in Frans Floris's portrait of the Berchem family of 1561, now in the Lier Museum; and an instrument of 1591 by Hans Ruckers, founder of the Antwerp school of harpsichord builders, is now housed at Bruges.

Italian-type spinets prevailed in France throughout this and the following century, to judge from the sparse source material. Of the *spinettini* Mersenne wrote that those having two and one-half feet in length sounded one octave above the *ton de chapelle* (choir pitch), those of three and one-half feet a fourth above choir pitch, while the standard size was five feet in length. In fact the literature is so full of comments to the effect that the spinet was pitched a fifth higher than the harpsichord that Carl Engel could declare (in 1874) "the tone of the spinet was generally a fifth higher than that of the harpsichord." Certainly the word "spinet" identified the smaller, higher-pitched versions far and wide; Bermudo (1555) applied the term *espineta* in that sense. He is echoed by Praetorius, to whom spinets are small and are tuned a fifth or an octave higher than regular pitch and are set on, or in, a larger instrument. In Italy, he adds, large models are also called spinets.

At first glance one is at a loss to imagine what musical purpose a keyboard instrument at intermediary 6′ pitch could serve. As a household instrument for solo playing absolute pitch is not important, but, until their emancipation in the eighteenth century, spinets and other stringed keyboard instruments were also important as organists' practice auxiliaries, and their pitch—and to a lesser degree, their compass as well—followed organ-building conventions. It is known that organs existed at pitches about half an octave apart and the spinets of intermediary pitch will have corresponded to the "6′" or intermediary organs. Occasionally, spinets were also included in processional music: Philip Hainhofer saw at the Dresden court in 1629 an "*Instrument* with two leather straps to be carried round the neck, the keyboard (which is open) to be played while marching."

What the clavichord was to the German household and the virginal to that of the Low Countries, the "leg of mutton" became to English domestic life. The English school of spinet making followed chronologically upon that of virginal building (last quarter of the seventeenth century). Most surviving "legs of mutton" date from the second half of the eighteenth century, however. Intrinsically alike, they vary only in very minor details. Most British instruments have a compass of G' to g³, following British organ compasses, whereas on the Continent F' to f³ was standard. The Low Countries remained producers of virginals rather than of spinets, but the wing shape was occasionally made there during the eighteenth century, as it was in both France and Germany. This form was ultimately driven out by the square piano in the last quarter of the eighteenth century.

Reference has already been made to the early gut-strung chordophone called *arpicordo*, from which the English word "harpsichord" is derived. A series of metal hooks arranged under the gut strings caused a jarring or snarling sound when the strings were plucked, similar to that of the contemporary bray harp, and in analogy to which the *arpicordo* must have been named. Actually we do not know of what material the hooks were made until Praetorius mentioned brass, but that they were of metal from the onset seems probable, for Virdung described them as "nails." In the course of the sixteenth century the gut strings were replaced by metal ones, but the name continued to designate spinets retaining the metal hooks under their strings. Praetorius defines the *arpicordo* as: *Da in einer Symphoney oder Virginal durch sonderliche Züge von Messingshäcklein unter den Saitten ein Harffenirender Resonanz entsteht* . . . ("When in a symphony or virginal a harping sound is produced by special stops of brass hooks under the strings . . ."). After Praetorius, little more is heard of it. The young Walther in his *Praecepta* of 1708 iterates Praetorius except that the "symphony or virginal" has now become a harpsichord and the stop causes a shrieking (*kreischender*) harp tone (had he ever heard one?) but in his later dictionary he renders *arpicordo* as "spinet." Adlung in 1758 described the harp stop of a harpsichord as a mobile batten with bent wire pins or wooden brays acting on one register. Several Flemish virginals and at least one harpsichord bear witness to such stops having existed on instruments built up to the last quarter of the seventeenth century.

Neglected in Germany as a consequence of the clavichord's popularity, the spinet flourished longer in England; but there, as on the Continent, it was finally pushed aside by the square piano. Ungrateful instruments from the builders' point of view, it is probably no coincidence that over ninety harpsichords but only three spinets built by the Kirkmans prior to 1800 have come down to us.

Rarely, wing-shaped spinets were made with two manuals, both the larger 8′ models and, quite exceptionally, also the 4′ spinettini, but this development seems to have been restricted to Germany and was probably addressed to organists or to teachers.

THE VIRGINAL

The term "virginal" has been reserved for the rectangular form of spinet whose history starts, for practical purposes, about 1460 with the statement of Paulus Paulirinus that it had the form of a clavichord, the sound of a harpsichord, and was strung with thirty-two metal strings. Paulirinus taught at Cracow, had visited Italy, and may have heard the word on his travels. Its etymology has puzzled scholars for generations, and *virga,* Latin for "rod," or a compliment paid to the Virgin Queen, have in turn been adduced. The reasons for identifying virginal as a vernacular translation of *cembalo,* an instrument traditionally played by women for some two millennia, were set forth in an earlier book (Marcuse, 1964), pointing up a confusion of etymons, tympanum and cymbalum, due to which *cembalo* came to denote the tambourine in Italian (instrument of Miriam the prophetess, sister of Aaron), a translation of which further included such items as *Instrument vors Frauenzimmer,* abbreviated occasionally to simple *Frauenzimmer* in seventeenth-century Germany, while in France the *demoiselle,* otherwise unidentified, was included in a list of musical instruments played at the time of its compilation by the Académie des Sciences in 1702.

The virginal was mentioned in a proverb formerly inscribed on the wall of Manor House, Leckingfield, Yorkshire, dating from the reign of Henry VII (1485–1509). On the Continent, the court organist at Buda *ludebat in virginali infra prandia ante dominum principem* ("played the virginal at meals before the prince") on January 1, 1501, according to the household accounts of Sigismund of Poland, then on a visit to his brother Ladislas II of Hungary, and the Buda court purchased a new virginal the following year. Thus by 1500 the virginal is found to have been in use from Britain to Hungary.

Virdung corroborates Paulirinus's description of its clavichord shape, but believed it to be descended from the psaltery rather than from the clavichord, particularly as each string of the virginal was longer than that of its neighbor (whereas clavichord strings were all of one length at that time) so that they formed a triangle inside the case—a passage later paraphrased by Praetorius. The keyboard was placed either to left or to right of center on the long side, markedly so on Flemish models. As the keyboard emplacement determined the points at which the strings were plucked (plucking points), its position was critical in influencing timbre. When placed to the right (treble) side, the strings were plucked nearer their center than when the keyboard was placed to the left, producing a more nasal tone. Douwes (1699) called those virginals with keyboard to the left spinets, and those with keyboard to the right *muselaer*; van Blankenburg in the following century confirms the identification of the former type and writes of the latter that their basses "grunt like young pigs."

On Italian instruments the keyboard usually projected out from the case; like the contemporary Italian spinets, they were made of thin cypress, devoid of lid or stand; the shallow box was inserted into a separate housing from which it could be withdrawn when required. Flemish models, emanating chiefly from Antwerp, had recessed keyboards except for some 4′ models; they were made of thicker softwood and furnished with lid and dropleaf. When the latter was closed the instrument formed a neat oblong box requiring no further protective housing. In addition to the standard 8′ variety, makers also put out small ones at 4′ pitch and, according to Praetorius, others at intermediary 6′ pitch, a fifth above the standard version.

All surviving examples of English virginals known so far were made during the four decades between 1640 and 1680; they combine some Italian with chiefly Flemish features, are exceptionally deep, and are recognizable by what is tantamount to a national characteristic, a vaulted lid that lends them the appearance of *cassoni* when closed (and from which the feature was probably borrowed in the first place). Prior to the production of this vaulted type, English-made virginals had been housed in an outer case from which they, as their Italian counterparts, could be withdrawn, according to contemporary sources, but whether these were rectangular virginals or other forms of spinet or even harpsichords is uncertain, as during both sixteenth and seventeenth centuries the word "virginal" designated in England all plucked keyboard instruments indiscriminately. Thus in 1611 Cotgrave could translate *espinette* as "a pair of virginals"—a term derived, incidentally, from organ terminology—and in 1673 Henry Purcell was appointed "keeper of regals, virginals, flutes . . ."

Blunt's *Glossographia* of 1656, as quoted by Rimbault (1860), de-

fined the clavecymbel (harpsichord) as "a pair of virginals, or clavichords"; Henry VIII purchased five "virginals" from William Lewes for
seven pounds in 1530 and another five in the following year, but
whether they were virginals in today's sense of the word is a matter for
conjecture. Import duty on a "payre" of clavichords (i.e., a single instrument) in the mid-sixteenth century was two shillings, that of a
pair of virginals three shillings and four pence, less than double, hence
probably a true virginal or spinet. German nomenclature was not
much clearer: although a *Firginal* [*sic*] was bought for the Innsbruck
court in 1549, and a regal as well as two *Symphonei* and a *Virginal* were
purchased from an organ builder in Königsberg in 1542, virginals usually
hid under the name of *Instrument*, exceptionally also of *Frauenzimmer*
(Schütz and Praetorius avail themselves of this last term). In France,
épinette designated plucked chordophones at large in the same way
"virginal" did in England.

A special and extremely popular form was the double virginal of
Flemish invention, called "mother and child" locally because it combined a larger instrument at 8′ pitch cheek by jowl with a smaller one at
4′ pitch. This *ottavina* was mobile, set in a recess between the soundboard and the bottom of the case, usually to the left of the 8′ keyboard.
Their manufacture was restricted to the Low Countries, chiefly to Antwerp, and possibly imitated in Germany, for an *Instrument* with a small
one inside it (*darinnen ein kleines steckt*) at Dresden in 1593 was said
to have been made by master Hans of Augsburg. For performance the
smaller *ottavina* was withdrawn and could be placed on top of the 8′
virginal, the jack rail of which had previously been removed; a diagonal
slot cut from the bottom of the *ottavina* permitted the jacks of the
larger instrument to raise the keys of the smaller one—a simple form of
coupler—thereby transforming the two into a single combination of 8′ and
4′. This simple and convenient form of coupling may not have been
general, and the more usual manner of playing may have consisted of
superposing the two independently, as set forth in the 1771 advertisement of an Andreas Ruckers virginal for sale in Paris "with another
smaller one" that could be set on the larger *pour former deux claviers*
("to form two manuals"). The age of the double virginal is hard to
determine; it may antedate the Ruckers, for the merchandise inventory
of *Stadtpfeifer* and instrument dealer Krause of Leipzig in 1574 included 1 *Neu Instrument, m. 2 Claviren* ("one new instrument with

two keyboards"), and this is a little too early a date for a two-manual harpsichord.

Early French references to the *espinette double* are not uncommon; two occur in 1521, for example, and designate bichord instruments, doubtless harpsichords, if Furetière is correct in his interpretation of the term, not double virginals. Likewise, the English expression, "double virginals" or "pair of double virginals" pertain not to a mother and child but rather to the keyboard compass, as any notes below gamma ut were called "double" notes and written FF (pronounced "double F"), EE, and so on. Hence any instrument with a compass exceeding gamma ut in the bass was "double," be it virginal, curtal, or organ. Kremsmünster Monastery's inventory of its instruments in 1584 included one good virginal and four old ones, in addition to a *doppeltes Virginal; all of these were still there in 1600, as was another small virginal and a triple virginal (*dridopelts*); in 1617 two *doppelt Instrumente* were enumerated there, one of which was described as *dreifach*—the triple virginal of 1600; the change in terminology at the turn of the century from *Virginal* to *Instrument* is interesting. Another triple instrument is mentioned in Austria: an Innsbruck inventory of 1665 contains mention of a *spineta darinnen zway claine Spinetlin liegen und man alle drei aufeinander setzen und auf einmal schlagen kann*, or a triple instrument in which all three components could be superposed and played simultaneously; the simultaneous playing postulates some sort of coupling arrangement.

Two further varieties of virginal that were popular in their day were the organized virginal—one to which a rank or two of organ pipes were joined, in use by the mid-sixteenth century, when Rabelais referred to it —and the automatic, cylinder-driven virginal; such a "virginal that goethe with a whele without playing upon" was among the instruments of Henry VIII. The making of automatic keyboard instruments seems to have been a German and Netherlandish specialty; from Samuel Bidermann of Breslau three such virginals are extant, two of which can be played automatically only, the third, dated 1651, either manually or automatically. Of its forty-five strings, twenty-six are needed for the six tunes played by means of a pinned cylinder and spring mechanism. Its manual compass of four octaves, $C°$ to c^3, with bass short octave, is the standard virginal compass of the period. Philip Hainhofer, already quoted, saw in Dresden in 1629 "a long table . . . containing a pinned, self-playing instrument," probably the same as that inventorized in

1593—at which date it was already in a state of disrepair, lacking its strings—as an *Instrument* that could be played either manually or, when the keyboard was pushed in, automatically.

Judging by paintings and documents, virginals must have been extremely popular household instruments in the latter part of the sixteenth and all of the seventeenth century, at least in the Low Countries, England, and German-speaking areas. Evidence on this point is lacking for France and Italy, but the larger number of Italian polygonal spinets still in existence argue for preference accorded to this form south of the Alps. In England they were forced to give way to the "leg of mutton" spinet, in German-speaking countries to the clavichord; nowhere did they live long enough to enter into competition with the piano. Adlung (1768) had never seen any with a compass exceeding four octaves, and reported that in his day "these instruments are almost despised."

THE CLAVIORGANUM

Historically this term has designated the combination of harpsichord and organ, but more recently it has also been applied to any combination of keyboard chordophone and pipe or reed organ. Such combinations may result from a desire to alternate two different tone qualities or to prolong the sound of the stringed instrument, and conceivably, if less probably, to augment the attack of organ speech.

The earliest form of claviorganum known is also the most complicated one: an upright, metal-strung harpsichord combined with a positive organ was described about 1460 by Paulus Paulirinus of Prague (he is known to have visited Italy); both components were played by the same manual. The next reference comes from Spain, where two *clabiórganos* were in the possession of Don Sancho de Paredes at the Spanish court in 1480, and where Don Juan, Prince of Asturias (1478–1497) had in his chambers a *claviórgano e organos e clavecímbanos e clavicordio*, in addition to other musical instruments, and was able to play them all. Twelve years later, in 1492, Emperor Maximilian was entertained by the playing of a lute, viol, and claviorganum, the strings and pipes of which could be played separately or together.

In 1511 the Duke of Lorraine purchased an organized chekker, and in the same year Alessandro of Modena constructed for his patron, the Duke of Modena, an *organo cum el clavazimbano*. Some early claviorgana were clearly two separate instruments without coupling device, as certain texts refer to the organ component alone as a "claviorganum"; e.g., a Spanish inventory from the time of Philip II includes *un clavicordio* ("a harpsichord") *y llaviórgano todo junto en una pieza* (". . . all joined in one piece"), or *un clavicordio y llaviórgano grande, todo junto con muchas differencias de música y se tañe con manos y pies* ("a large harpsichord and claviorganum, combined together, with many variations of tone, and played with hands and feet"), which Don Juan of Asturias presented to Philip II.

Claviorgana seem to have spread rapidly and to have been well accepted throughout the sixteenth and seventeenth centuries; several are listed among the instruments of Henry VIII in 1547; their pipework usually consisted of one or two ranks of flue pipes, generally of wood, with bellows operated by the performer (hence the "hands and feet" of the above quotation).

The earliest preserved claviorganum, dated 1579, is that of the Anglo-Fleming, Lodowijk Theeuwes, an Antwerp émigré, now in the Victoria and Albert Museum, London—a harpsichord set over organ pipes and bellows. Unluckily little but the shell and soundboard remain. A combination spinet-regal of the same period, made by Anton Meidling in 1587, is in far better condition; it is extremely shallow, with a regal forming the left portion and a juxtaposed 4′ spinet hinged to the right, and when closed the surface represents a chessboard. A *sordino . . . con graviorgano*, a clavichord-organ combination, by Domenico of Pesaro, was in the Medici collection in Cristofori's day; such combinations were rare, however. The *épinette organisée* of French writers from Rabelais on did not refer to a spinet but to the far more common organ-harpsichord. A claviorganum by Alessandro Bortolotti dated 1585, now in Brussels, is sufficiently well preserved to demonstrate the means that the player of such an instrument had at his command: the harpsichord section has 1 × 8′ and 1 × 4′, the organ section three ranks of pipes at 8′, 4′, and a quint; each rank could be drawn on separately, as could the harpsichord registers (according to Mahillon [1909], but Hubbard [1965] writes that the harpsichord registers have no drawstops; in that case, they presumably shifted in and out), so that any combination of pipe and string was possible.

A metal-strung instrument combined with "hidden pipes" formed part of the estate of Archduke Carl of Austria in 1590, and no fewer than five combination instruments were inventorized at the Dresden court in

1593, two of which were clavichord-organs. A clavichord-organ made by Valentin Zeiss in 1639, with pedalboard connected to the manual by pulldowns, is the earliest of its kind to be preserved. Italy in particular prized these combinations of pipes and strings, for Banchieri (1594) wrote: "there are many chamber organs united with a harpsichord that together produce a delighting and pleasing sound, and above all, when they have more than a single register of pipes and strings."

In the last years of the sixteenth century an *instromento pian e forte* is mentioned several times by Ippolito Cricca, a maker of organs and keyboard chordophones; he wrote in 1598 to Alfonso II, Duke of Modena, regarding an *instromento pian e forte con l'organo di sotto*. Past writers have interpreted this and other passages as early references to a pianoforte, a most improbable conjecture, but they are more likely to have indicated the claviorganum, particularly as Cricca was a builder of both organs and stringed keyboard instruments; the phrasing is comparable to the earlier Spanish texts quoted above. It may be added that at that time the Duke had four claviorgana in his collection, all in need of repairs.

At the princely courts of Germany such instruments were no less rare: Dresden had four claviorgana in 1593 as well as two organ-clavichords made by the local organ builder, Georg Kretschmar. Landgrave William IV of Hesse made a hobby of them: he designed them himself and caused several to be built; one, containing both regal and flue pipes as well as strings was so successful that he promptly ordered another, larger model, with a tremulant, by 1575. Even a new organ for the court chapel, contracted for in 1592, shortly before his death, had provision for *ein geduppeldt Saittenwergk*, a two-choired chordophone, in addition to its eleven manual stops, and the pedal called for three ranks of pipework and another two-choir *Saittenwergk*, no less. The term *doppelt Instrument* occurs at this time in connection with one of these instruments and is employed at the end of the century at Kremsmünster, Austria, in connection with a combination of regal, pipework, and strings, and in Innsbruck a *doppelt Instrument in tono di Roma* is recorded in 1665; apparently this term, occurring sporadically in German-language inventories and other documents of the time, disguises the claviorganum and not a two-manual harpsichord.

The bulk of seventeenth-century information is derived from Italian sources, as claviorgana seem to have been considered from then on more of a curiosity than anything else farther north; mechanical models were exhibited at fairs in Holland in the 1620s, and when Samuel Pepys saw a claviorganum in 1667 he was not particularly impressed; in his opinion the organ was "but a bauble, with a virginal joining to it." At the opening of the century the organ builder, Domenico da Feltre, traveled through Italy with a combination *arpicordo*-organ; this could have been a useful practice instrument for organists and perhaps Domenico was looking for business during his travels. A noncoupling variety that probably went under the name of claviorganum is portrayed on the lid of a spinet in Nuremberg, painted in 1619; it shows an Italian polygonal spinet set upon a flat, table-model chamber organ, and the performer is playing the organ with the left hand, the spinet with the right. Table-shaped positives were easily combined with spinets and continued to be made in the eighteenth century, but usually with a single manual from which both or either component could be played; here again, the pipework was usually of wood and the whole instrument could be very reasonably priced.

Although the smaller instruments, the clavichord and spinet combinations that took up little space, were practice instruments of organists, this was apparently not true of the larger models in Italy at least, for G. B. Doni writes of *graviorgani* placed on the stage where, due to the amount of light (synonymous with heat at the time) to which they were exposed, the metal strings dropped in pitch so badly that they were out of tune with the pipework, and that such situations could be obviated by tuning the strings a quarter tone higher than the pipes in the first place. This is not the speculation of a theorist but the observation of a practical musician based on experience, and we are left wondering exactly what function a claviorganum fulfilled on stage in seventeenth-century Italy. It would have been an ideal continuo instrument, with its incisive harpsichord attack to support a singer, and sustained organ tone blending with the bowed strings; but information on this point is unhappily lacking. Probably the aim was to achieve greater sustaining power of the strings, as was the case with the later piano-organs.

Claviorgana continued to be built right through the eighteenth century, but the center of their production moved north, away from Italy, and in many instances they were built on more elaborate lines than in the past. Among several claviorgana housed in the Medici collection during Cristofori's curatorship was one consisting of an organ with several registers of pipes, both of wood and of tin, a rank of regal pipes, on top of which was set a one-register harpsichord and two *spinettini* (for the unusual combination of $1 \times 8' + 2 \times 4'$). In England, Crang built two-manual claviorgana, one of which, dated 1745, had $2 \times 8' + 4'$ on the harpsichord and six stops on the organ, two of which were divided. An instrument of similar disposition but with five stops on the organ was built a few years later by Kirkman in conjunction with the well-known organ builder Snetzler; its lower manual could be coupled to the organ. On the Continent, claviorgana were built from Prague to Grenoble, and in Dom Bédos de Celles's day, claviorgana with three manuals were being produced. He described one with the two upper manuals serving the harpsichord, the lowest reserved for the organ section; when this was drawn out so that it projected, the organ sounded, and when pushed back, the organ was silenced; furthermore, when it projected, both instruments were coupled on the second manual, with the upper manual for harpsichord solo. Reservoir and bellows were housed not, as was usual, under the harpsichord with the pipework, but instead under the organist's seat. Its disposition was that of a harpsichord with 8' and 4', combined with a four-rank organ.

The principle of the claviorganum was exploited in the first half of the seventeenth century by a mechanically gifted musician named Michele Todini, who spent eighteen years perfecting an instrumental monster while earning his living as violone player in Rome: an organ, a large harpsichord, two smaller ones, and a spinet, were all controlled by a secret mechanism from the lower manual of the large harpsichord. Any of the stringed instruments could be coupled to the controlling instrument, or else one could be coupled to another; the organ was not coupled to the strings but was played from a separate upper manual of the large harpsichord. When the smaller components were played from the controlling instrument, their keys were seen to move up and down as though moved by invisible hands, to the amazement of the audience. The idea of separated instruments controlled from one console was adopted in the following century at the giant Handel commemoration of 1784 in Westminster Abbey, when the conductor's harpsichord was connected to the organ erected specially for the performance, the two being separated by a distance of 5.7 meters (19 feet); each could be played individually. Nothing more is heard of claviorgana thereafter, but today the preserved thirty-odd harpsichord-organs attest to the once popular combination.

After the introduction of the piano, makers combined the newer instrument with an organ, and when the reed organ had successfully replaced the chamber organ, the original plucked strings and organ pipes of claviorgana were metamorphosed into struck strings and reeds. An interesting transition instrument was the bichord tangent piano (see page 353) combined with an organ, a specimen of which is preserved in the Bachhaus at Eisenach; a pedalboard added to the keyboard by pulldowns identifies it as a practice instrument for organists.

THE PIANO-ORGAN

Piano-organs were very popular during the last quarter of the eighteenth century, so much so, in fact, that German piano makers gave their customers the choice of piano or piano-organ, and in 1790 John Crang and Hancock (a partnership) patented a piano with organ attachment. Outstanding builders such as Johann Andreas Stein, Pascal Taskin, and L'Épine, organ builder to the king of France, did not disdain to build them. An instrument of Stein's in form of a grand piano, dated 1772, is housed in the Göteborg Museum, its upper manual for the piano, its lower for the organ. In the same year L'Épine designed one in form of a *secrétaire* (desk, i.e., of square form), again with two manuals. Also in 1772, Balbastre played a "new forte piano" "augmented by a rank of flue pipes" for an audience of the Concerts Spirituels in Paris; Taskin at his death left a piano-organ, possibly made at Balbastre's suggestion.

Dom Bédos de Celles depicts one of L'Épine's instruments, a square piano with two manuals—the upper for the piano, the lower, retractable, for the organ—and three organ registers. But interest was waning in France; Grétry advertised his organized piano for sale in 1776; its organ section was made by Cliquot, one of France's great builders, yet there were no takers for two years. Zumpe and Buntebart, to whom more than any other makers the popularity of the square piano is due, occasionally combined such instruments with organs; Longman & Broderip brought out the same combination, adding a pedalboard. Piano-organs were also built in Prague by Vincent von Blaha, inventor of the Janissary stop, about 1765; a "royal crescendo" by Hofrat Bauer of Berlin built in 1786 was composed of a four-and-one-half-octave piano combined with flue pipes. Sébastien Érard left two organized fortepianos of 1790 and 1791, respectively. A combination contrived with the organist in mind was the organochordon devised by Abbé Vogler and built to his specifications by Rackwitz of Stockholm in 1798, consisting of a square piano with three and one-half stops of organ pipes. Even upright pianos were combined with pipes before the craze died down, and not even the older harpsichord-organs were spared: one built by Hermann Brock of Hanover in 1712 was converted into a piano-organ.

Shortly after Friderici of Gera had produced a grand piano combined with organ pipes, around 1800, free reeds started to supplant the pipework, and in fact their introduction into piano-organs had constituted the first practical application of the free reed, then new to Europe, for Kirsnik, a Saint Petersburg organ builder, experimentally included a few free reeds in his piano-organs of 1780, but the first organ register composed exclusively of free reeds was not built before 1792 (see free reeds, page 737). An early builder to combine a piano with a reed organ was Jozé Dlugosz of Warsaw in 1824; each instrument could be played separately. Debain, inventor of the harmonium, created a piano-harmonium that he patented under the name of symphonium in 1845. By the mid-nineteenth century piano-harmoniums were enjoying a considerable vogue. Jacob Alexandre of Paris combined free reeds with a piano in order to obtain greater sustaining power and called his new instrument *piano à prolongement*; a variant model, presented at the Paris Exposition of 1855, he called *piano-mélodium*. Liszt commissioned a piano-harmonium, with piano section built by Érard, harmonium and pedalboard supplied by Alexandre, which instrument is now in Vienna. The aim of prolonging the piano's sustaining power was also admitted to by Jaulin of Paris when introducing his piano-organ in 1846. During the 1870s and 1880s piano-organs were produced by the organ builder Duvivier of Nevers, including a "magnificent salon organ" with four manuals and pedalboard, exhibited at Vienne in 1873, a three-manual organ combined with a piano.

Before their final disappearance in the twentieth century, a number of decadent combinations made their appearance, such as that of piano-organ–harp–glass harmonica, entitled Cherubine [sic] minor, or the two-manual giraffe piano with three stops of organ pipes and automaton in form of a flute-playing boy, called apollonion; as late as 1910 a combination of piano, pipework, and free reeds called *orphéal* was built. The United States contributed a combined mechanical (player) upright piano and reed organ, patented in 1896.

BOWED KEYBOARD INSTRUMENTS

Ever since the fifteenth century, musicians have expressed the desire for a keyboard instrument combining sustained tone with dynamic nuances. Marpurg (1754) summed up the situation well when he wrote, after discussing the *Flügel:* "All other ordinary instruments share with the human voice [the properties] of sustaining a tone and letting it increase in volume as well as diminish." The organ, although sustaining, is dynamically inflexible, and consequently makers concentrated their experiments on chordophones. Existing bowed chordophones offered both sustained tone and dynamic variations, and therefore a means was sought of combining the principle of bowed chordophone with that of the keyboard. The earlier of these attempts proved the more fruitful, but by the late eighteenth century a spate of such ephemeral combinations as keyed violin, keyed cello, bowed "piano," and so on, had been produced and the original issues lost sight of. It has been customary in the recent past to refer to the resulting instruments collectively as sostinente pianos in English, but, as many of them antedate the invention of the piano and none has a piano action, the term "bowed keyboard instrument," if awkward, seems preferable. Because the unattained ideal sound continued to preoccupy thinkers and builders continuously for nearly five centuries, a chronological if incomplete conspectus of their efforts follows.

The elements of continuous string sound and rudimentary keyboard are present in the organistrum, on which a modicum of dynamic variation was obtainable by manipulation of the wheel. The first to undertake further development of this principle was Leonardo da Vinci.

1488–1489. Leonardo's MS "B" of 1488–1489 contains several studies for an automatic musical instrument, the *viola organista.* Although never built, it represents the earliest known attempt to combine sustained string sound with a keyboard by means of mechanical bowing. In his notebooks, Leonardo wrote of his intention to obtain "with the help of the mill unending sounds from all sorts of instruments that will sound as long as the mill shall continue to move" (Codex Atlantico 271). One drawing shows his strings bowed by a revolving wheel, a somewhat later one by an endless bow of horsehair. After Leonardo, little is heard of such instruments for nearly a century; Vincenzo Galilei, however, wrote (1581) that such instruments were built before Haiden's day by "several makers." Unfortunately he mentions no names.

1575. Hans Haiden of Nuremberg was the first to translate the principle of Leonardo's *viola organista* into an actual instrument, and thereby created the most successful of all bowed keyboard instruments, the *Geigenwerk* (called arched viol in seventeenth-century England, *archiviole* in seventeenth-century France). His first playable *Geigenwerk* was completed in or by 1575; he then proceeded to improve its action, was successful in this in 1599, and received a privilege from Emperor Rudolf II in 1601 for his *instrumentum reformatum.* Haiden had concentrated his efforts on producing an instrument having all "modulations" of the human voice, and as this was unobtainable with conventional actions he combined strings, violin bow, and keyboard. Because of the repercussions his invention was to have, it may be of interest to summarize the disposition he made of his *Geigenwerke.*

His first was sold to August, Elector of Saxony; in 1576 Duke Albert V of Bavaria visited the Dresden court and saw it there; he received it as a gift and had it sent to Munich in the same year. There, Vincenzo Galilei saw it and described it in 1581 as being strung in the manner of a lute and bowed in the manner of a *viola*, with a special strand of the same hair as that of viol bows. This could be set in motion very easily by the foot, and it bowed continuously by means of a wheel over which it passed, "as many strings as the fingers demand. . . . I tuned this instrument two years ago when I was at that court, in the manner of a lute . . . and when well played it sounded like a consort of viols. . . ."

Thanks to Galilei's account we can reconstruct the improvements Haiden made to his later instruments: the bowing mechanism was changed from one continuous band to "five or six" steel wheels covered with parchment and coated with rosin ("like a fiddle bow," wrote Praetorius, who devoted several pages to the *Geigenwerk*, based on Haiden's own writings of 1610). In order to prevent breakage of strings and to better maintain the tuning, the original gut strings were replaced with brass or steel that gave a "purer and sharper" timbre. Apparently Haiden returned to gut stringing again later on, for Cristofori's inventory mentions *corde di budelle* (see page 312). The privilege granted in 1601 was renewed in 1612 for a ten-year period by Emperor Mathias, and this second privilege mentions the *Geigenwerk*'s crucial novelty: . . . *und dess Clavis also beschaffen, dass dieselbe allein durch eine freye Hand, ohne ab-oder zu-ziehen an Register (wie sonsten gebräuchlich) moderirt und je eines jedem Affekte nach, laut oder still gemacht werden kann* . . . (". . . its keys so fashioned that by the hand alone, without setting any register—as otherwise usual—[the tone] can be modified and made loud or soft, according to every mood"). A tremulant, either slow or rapid, was also obtainable, just as on the organ (this would have had the effect of a *Bebung*).

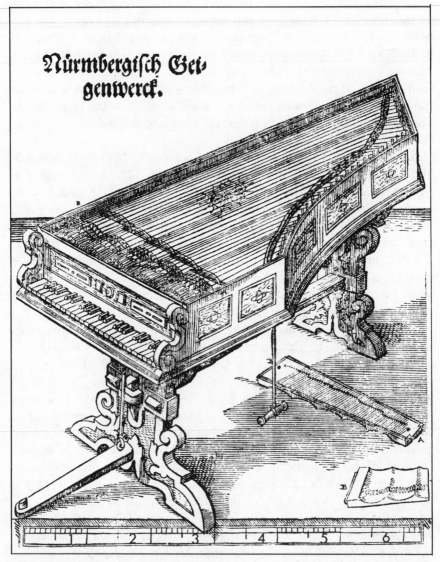

Hans Haiden's *Geigenwerk*. From Michael Praetorius, *Theatrum instrumentorum*, 1620.

Apparently satisfied with the performance of his improved model, Haiden set about the publication of no fewer than three promotional booklets, all entitled *Musicale instrumentum reformatum,* two of which appeared in German, one in Latin. The date of the first is not known, but must lie between 1600 and 1605, the second was published in 1605, the third in 1610. In the last Haiden specifically states that whereas on ordinary keyboard instruments the tone cannot be sustained, on the *Geigenwerk* it can be both sustained and "moderated," that is, dynamically modified. Fortunately for us, Haiden's son David kept an account of his father's instruments and of their disposal. He lists twenty-three *Geigenwerke,* of which four were given away, the remainder sold.

To resume our enumeration after this excursus: Numbers three and seven went to Emperor Rudolf II at Prague (who also bought another of Haiden's inventions, an outsized double bass with special tuning device); number fifteen went to Rudolf's successor, the Emperor Mathias (1558–1618) at Innsbruck; number five to Archduke Ferdinand of Prague (later Emperor Ferdinand II). Number one, as stated, was sold to August, Elector of Saxony; number twelve went to Hans Leo Hassler, the composer, who sold it to August's grandson, Christian II of Saxony. This instrument remained in Dresden and was still playable in the eighteenth century, for Christoph Gottlieb Schroeter recounted in his claim to the invention of the pianoforte that in 1715 he was shown a Nuremberg *Geigenwerk* that had met with his approval, except that he did not like having to work a treadle. Number four belonged to Duke Heinrich Julius of Brunswick, who had lived in Prague and knew the Hassler brothers; Praetorius became his kapellmeister in 1604, and this was presumably the instrument he described and depicted. Number eleven was sold to the Duke of Lignitz, numbers eighteen and nineteen to Churfürst Ernst zu Coelln (Duke Ernst of Bavaria); number eight was purchased by Christoph Fugger of Augsburg, and the remainder were sold to less exalted personages. The four that were given away went to (1) the church of Saint Sebald, Nuremberg, and was later removed to the Town Hall, where it was used in 1643 for a large concert and again in 1649 in a celebration of the ending of the Thirty Years' War, where, supported by a theorbo, it supplied the continuo to an ensemble of eight viols; (2) Caspar Hassler; (3) Haiden's son Christoph; (4) Haiden's son David. David sold his in due course to "Don Medicce of Florence," who had it sent to Florence. "Don Medicce" was none other than Archduke Ferdinand II (d. 1670). This instrument was later inherited by his grandson, Prince Ferdinand de' Medici (d. 1713), owner of a notable collection of musical instruments. On his death, an inventory of these was taken by their curator, no less a celebrity in his own right, Bartolommeo Cristofori, inventor of the pianoforte. The *Geigenwerk* appears as number 29 on his list, "with a device of five wheels in order to rotate the gut strings in the manner of a hurdy-gurdy, painted red, with gold . . . decorations." An assertion to the effect that Philip III of Spain (1598–1621) ordered a *Geigenwerk* and that this was found in the Escorial in 1872 seems to rest on confusion with the rediscovery of a similar instrument built by Truchador (see below).

1579. The immediate success of the *Geigenwerk* stimulated interest in copying it; a former apprentice of Haiden's named Rot, while working for the court organ builder of Landgrave Moritz of Hesse, constructed an imitation, thereby clearly infringing the terms of the originator's privilege.

ca. 1590. Prior to 1593, when it appeared in an inventory, Georg Kretschmar, instrument builder of Dresden, constructed a *Geigen-Instrument*, presumably another copy of Haiden's *Geigenwerk*.

1608. In June, the composer Marco da Gagliano, then in Florence, wrote to his patron, Cardinal Ferdinand Gonzaga, that the organ and harpsichord builder, Vincenzo Bolcione of Florence, wished to make for him *uno instrumento che suoni concerti di viole*; its price would be "at least 100 of our [i.e., Roman] scudi" (this compares with a price of sixty *scudi* Bolcione was then asking for an elaborate clavicytherium [see page 281]). Later, a firm order was placed, and Bolcione promised delivery in three months and not earlier, stating that he would be working on it full time during that period. The Medici *Geigenwerk* had not then arrived in Florence, so Bolcione could not have known it; but he may well have read Galilei's description or a copy of Haiden's booklet.

1625. The Spaniard Raymundo Truchador made an imitation of the *Geigenwerk*, sole instrument of its kind to have survived until now, housed in the Brussels Conservatoire Museum. Of harpsichord form, its strings are sounded by means of four vertical revolving wheels, hand cranked by a handle projecting from the tail of the case; this hand crank was supplied during restoration early in the present century, because the instrument is so low that a pedal was not feasible. Also the original soundboard, painted in the Flemish manner, has been replaced, and its present velvet covering, although old, is not original, for the case itself was painted. Unsubstantiated is the assertion that it was formerly housed in Toledo Cathedral, although it certainly was exhibited in Madrid in 1893 and has been in Brussels since 1903.

1636. Mersenne devoted a passage to the *jeu de violes*, pointing out the difficulty of getting a bow to touch the strings with controlled pressure. Although he does not mention Haiden by name, he states that Germans were mechanically more ingenious than other nations, having contrived the combination of viols with harpsichords, without bows but with four or five wheels "turned by the feet." "One presses the strings as little as one wishes against the wheel, which makes the sound last as long as the finger remains on the key," the sounds being *piano* or *forte* according to the player's touch.

1650. Athanasius Kircher claimed for himself invention of an instrument he called his *Machinamentum No. 6*: a strand of rosined horsehair passed over the vertex of a single wheel, while pressure on the keys caused the strings to be pressed against the horsehair. Kircher suggested automating it by the addition of a pinned barrel to actuate the keys and a weight for moving the wheel. Due to the large size of the wheel his whole contrivance is clumsy, and it is doubtful whether it ever progressed to the drawing-board stage.

1664.
To the musique meeting at the Post Office . . . and the new instrument was brought called the Arched Viall, where being tuned with lute-strings, and played on with kees like an organ, a piece of parchment is always kept moving; and the strings, which by the kees are pressed down upon it, are grated in imitation of a bow, by the parchment; and so it is intended to resemble several vyalls played on with one bow, but so basely and harshly, that it will never do. But after three hours' stay it could not be fixed in tune . . .

So wrote Samuel Pepys in his diary on October 5, 1664 (Evelyn heard the same instrument).

ca. 1673. Michele Todini of Rome constructed an *archicymbalum symphoniarca*, a combination of which Dr. Burney wrote, upon viewing its remains a century later: "under the frame is a violin, tenor and bass, which by a movement of the foot used to be played upon by the harpsichord keys." Todini, a professional violone player, is best remembered for his giant claviorganum (see page 301).

1674. Claude-François Milliet Dechales described an *archiviola* in his *Cursus seu mundus mathematicus*, vol. 3. His was only a theoretical instrument and does not seem to have ever been built: a large harpsichord was to be strung with gut and furnished with one large and three small wheels turned by a hand crank. When depressed, the keys, set above the strings, conducted the latter to the wheels. Dechales may well have inspired the next practical invention:

1708. Cuisinié of Paris invented a *clavecin-vielle*, a novel form of keyboard hurdy-gurdy; one hand played the keys of a regular keyboard, the other turned a crank handle. But instead of being touched sideways, as on the hurdy-gurdy, its six strings were sounded from below.

ca. 1722. Johann Georg Gleichmann, organist of Ilmenau and builder also of gut-strung harpsichords, built a *Claviergamba*, an imitation of Haiden's instrument, with body as long as a bass viol, gut strung, and five rosined wheels. The strings were wound at the points of friction. Its rapid changes from *forte* to *piano* were greatly praised.

ca. 1730. Wahlfried Ficker of Zeiss also made *Claviergambas*; in the 1750s he built pianos.

1741. Roger Plenius had invented his lyrichord in London by 1741. A wire- and gut-strung instrument with wheels, imitating both violin and organ sound, it could be played "loud and soft," produced "the close shake" (*Bebung*), and had a lid swell operated by a pedal. Metal struts separated wrestplank from soundboard, thus anticipating their introduction in the piano. The fifteen wheels that moved at different speeds were rotated by clockwork, and the bass strings were wound with silver. Later, his instrument was owned by the piano builder Frederick Neubauer, on whose death in 1772 it was sold at Christie's in London.

1741 (or earlier). Levoir of Paris built an *archiviole*, which could be played automatically by the addition of a weight-driven, pinned cylinder. The body actually consisted of a viola and a cello.

1745. Renaud of Orléans built his *épinette à archet* ("bowed spinet").

1749. Levoir built an enlarged *archiviole* in harpsichord form, with two violins, viola, cello, and drum.

ca. 1750. Daniel Bertin, Georg Matthias Risch, and Johann Michael Pachebel of Nuremberg (the last named a brother of the composer) are all said to have constructed bowed keyboard instruments at this time.

1750. Renaud, who by this time had moved to Paris, built an *épinette à orchestre*.

1753. Johann Hohlfeld of Berlin invented a *Bogelflügel*, characterized by a bow consisting of a continuous band of horsehair in lieu of the wheels generally employed, thus reverting to the earlier type of bowed keyboard instrument. A series of small hooks pressed gut strings against the bow. Shortly before he died in 1771, the King (Frederick II) bought his instrument and placed it in the Neues Palais of Potsdam. Both C. P. E. Bach (1753) and Marpurg (1765) had praised it. Bach also set a song entitled *Bey dem Grabe des verstorbenen Mechanicus Hohlfeld* ("At the grave of the deceased mechanic Hohlfeld"), which appeared in 1771 in the *Hamburger Unterhaltungen*. Marpurg noted that *piano, forte,* and *Bebung* were obtainable, and also that changes of *piano* and *forte* were possible only on a clavichord, "and better still, on a Hohlfeld *Bogenflügel.*"

1760. The Parisian harpsichord maker, Le Gay, built a bowed keyboard instrument worked by a horsehair bow that he transformed into a combination bowed keyboard instrument and gut-strung harpsichord by adding a pedalboard (with pulldowns from the manual) and a second manual with its own set of gut strings, played in conventional fashion by jacks furnished with hard-leather plectra rather than the usual quill, said to have sounded like a theorbo or guitar, whereas the first manual produced a timbre compared to a consort of viols. The combination, called *clavicordium*, was also noted for its production of *piano* and *forte*, and was submitted to the Académie in 1760. It had a total of 122 strings, probably two choirs of 61 each (five octaves).

ca. 1765. Nils Söderström of Nora, Sweden, built a *Clavier-gamba*, allegedly still another imitation of Haiden's work.

1769. De Laine of Paris built a combination bowed keyboard instrument and harpsichord; the mechanism of the former could be applied to any harpsichord.

1772. Adam Walker patented his *celestina* in London on August 29. As described in William Mason's correspondence with Mary Granville, it was a short harpsichord, only two feet long, played with the right hand while the left hand controlled a kind of violin bow. The patent specified one, two, or three wire or catgut strings, a bow of silk, wire, flax, leather, etc., placed over or under the strings and controlled by weights or springs. The *celestina*, the invention of which has been attributed to Mason in the past, was also adaptable as a separate stop attached to harpsichords.

(1773). Among the instruments inventorized as belonging to the Cöthen court in 1773 was a *Gambenwerk* said to date from Bach's time. (Bach had left Cöthen in 1723.)

1778. H. Schmidt, an organ builder of Rostock, improved Hohlfeld's instrument, giving it the form of an upright piano, but it was capable of playing only slow music.

1779. Johann Carl Greiner of Wetzlar started building bowed keyboard instruments in the form of square pianos. He called them *Bogenclaviere*, and the name has been used ever since in German to denote any bowed keyboard instrument. Unlike previous makes, his could allegedly play fast music. Later, at the suggestion of Abbé Vogler, he combined them with pianos and named the new models *Bogenhammerclaviere*. One of these, played at a concert in Hamburg, measured five feet, two inches by one foot, eight inches (local feet). C. P. E. Bach wrote a *Sonate fürs Bogen-Clavier*, probably composed in Hamburg in 1783, with Greiner's instrument in mind. The *Bogenhammerclavier* was also rectangular in form and had two manuals, the upper with a downstriking piano action and wire strings, the lower for bowed gut strings. A coupler, worked by a knee lever, permitted each manual to be played separately or both together.

ca. 1782. H. Schmidt built a *Harmonica* with continuous bow worked by a treadle and a compass of F′ to f³. Its sound was said to resemble that of a cello.

1783. Gottlieb Friedrich Riedeln of Bonn, harpsichord and piano maker, was also making bowed keyboard instruments by this year.

1789. Sachs (1913) wrote that Gerli of Milan built one in 1789.

1790. Garbrecht, a mechanic, and C. Wasiansky, the friend and biographer of Kant, together brought out a new bowed keyboard instrument in Königsberg, much praised in the early nineteenth century.

In 1790 Chladni's acoustical experiments and his use of friction bars, as applied to his *Euphon* (euphone) and later instruments, brought about a plethora of new keyboard instruments. (See friction bar "pianos," page 108.)

1795. Under Chladni's influence, von Mayer of Görlitz made an instrument in grand piano form with a single gut string for each key sounded by a horsehair bow set in motion by a treadle, and incorporating a flageolet register controlled by a knee lever.

1799. Thomas Anton Kunz of Prague improved on von Mayer's instrument, partly by lightening its touch.

1800. Carl Leopold Röllig of Vienna, musician, composer, and inventor of musical instruments, created the *Xenorphica*, a clumsy "musical violin bow instrument with keyboard" outwardly resembling the (later) claviharp, with a bow for each string and key; the series of bows was suspended in a common frame and set in motion by a treadle. When a key was depressed, the corresponding bow moved to the appropriate string and sounded it, the string remaining immobile. This instrument was improved by Matthias Müller, a Vienna piano builder who also played it in concerts.

ca. 1801. Huebner and Pouleau, the latter a French mechanic in Moscow, built an *orchestrine* also known as *clavecin harmonique*, with continuous bow, hand cranked.

1801. John Conrad Becker took out a patent for setting "piano" strings in motion by means of a wheel or wheels.

1802. The engineer John Isaac Hawkins invented the claviola, which he introduced to the public at a concert in Philadelphia on June 21, 1802. In shape a small upright piano, its strings were sounded by a continuous bow against which the strings were pressed. Hawkins complained in 1814 that, due to expiration of his patent, his idea had been appropriated by others. The claviola must have been popular for a long time, for the Metropolitan Museum of New York possesses a "late nineteenth-century" claviola of unknown make, with a violin-type bow, and a compass of just over two octaves. The keys were played with the left hand while the right hand moved the bow back and forth.

1803. Tobias Schmidt of Paris patented the *piano-harmonicon*, with a single choir of strings, which were raised to meet a band of flexible material. His patent covered both square and grand piano form.

1806. Johann Christian Dietz, Sr., exhibited his *organo-diapazo* in Paris.

1817. Piano builder Isaac Henry Robert Mott patented his *sostinente piano forte*. The tone of this instrument was sustained by means of a roller acting upon silk threads and rotated by a treadle. Mott claimed for it both sustaining power and the ability to increase or diminish the volume of sound at will. He may have been inspired by the friction bar "pianos."

1820. Taconi of Milan built a bowed keyboard instrument.

1820. In the *violicembalo* that Abbate Gregorio Trentino of Venice produced the strings were pressed against a continuous bow.

1823. Thomas Todd of Swansea, Wales, patented an instrument with endless rosined band and two rollers worked by a treadle.

1827. Johann Christian Dietz, Jr., of Paris invented the polyplectron said to have had a continuous bow for each string.

1828. The plectro-euphone, invented by Gama of Nantes, of unknown construction, is believed to have been a bowed keyboard instrument.

1830. H. Lichtenthal of Brussels patented his *piano-viole* and showed it at the Exposition Nationale there.

1830. Archotti of Rome produced a bowed keyboard instrument.

1833. Heinz of Toelz did likewise. This was said (by Closson) to have been a two-manual piano, with one conventional and one bowed keyboard.

1838. Lichtenthal brought out an improvement of his *piano-viole*, called *piano à sons soutenus*.

1861. Robert Thomas Worton patented his *vis-pianoforte*.

(1865). (For Baudet's *piano-violon*, see friction idiophones, page 110.)

1871. Stead brought out an improved version of Mott's *sostinente piano*, with clockwork replacing the treadle.

1909. Karl Beddies of Gotha built a model of his *Streichharmonium*, consisting of four octaves' worth of gut strings strung over as many fiddle-shaped resonators, and a silk-covered leather strap functioning as bow.

19... A Polish builder named Piatkiewicz built a bowed keyboard instrument concerning which no details are known.

THE PIANOFORTE

THE PIANO TO 1800

The rigid dynamics inherent in the harpsichord had long been the subject of complaints, and from the sixteenth century on attempts were made sporadically to overcome this defect. Means of swelling and diminishing the tone were sought by modifications of the action, chiefly by sounding the strings with a continuous bow or its analogue. Such instruments must be considered as immediate forerunners of the piano, and have been discussed collectively on page 307 ff.

Italy

The pianoforte, characterized by a striking mechanism, that of a hammer, was invented by 1709 by Bartolommeo Cristofori of Padua, but then in Florence. Cristofori was by profession a harpsichord maker, and he called his new instrument simply *gravicembalo col pian e forte*, ("harpsichord with loud and soft"); today it still has not been given a name, being merely referred to as piano or pianoforte, abbreviations of Cristofori's appellation (in the eighteenth century the word was reversed to fortepiano).

Our first knowledge of the new instrument's existence is due to Francesco Scipione, Marchese di Maffei, who published details of his 1709 visit to Cristofori's workshop in the *Giornale dei litterati d'Italia*, vol. 5, 1711. Maffei had seen four of the newly invented instruments, three in harpsichord form and one of an unspecified but different shape, *e alquanto più facile struttura* ("of somewhat easier structure"). To his description Maffei added a drawing of the action for the harpsichord-shaped version with which we can compare the actions of two extant grand pianos by Cristofori, one dated 1720, in the Metropolitan Museum of New York, the other dated 1726, in the instrument collection of the Karl Marx University, Leipzig (formerly the Heyer collection). The drawing shows small, square hammers topped with leather, pivoted by their butts inside a hammer rail, tuning pins inserted in the underside of the wrestplank, harpsichord jacks transformed into underdampers, with a *linguetta mobile*, or small jack, forming a single escapement.

The earlier of the two pianos is not in its original condition, having been restored both in Italy and in America, but fortunately drawings of its action were made in Italy in the last century and published in Leto Puliti's *Cenni storici* of 1874; comparison with that of Maffei shows that the actions were not identical. Furthermore, the discrepancies between the actions of the two extant pianos are even greater, an indication that Cristofori continued experimenting. Both pianos are bichord, have leather-covered hammers pivoted to a hammer rail, and overhead dampers. The New York piano has a compass of four and one-half octaves, $C°$ to f^3, and has discarded an intermediate lever apparent in Maffei's drawing; it already has a backcheck, hopper, and dampers resting on the rear of the keys. The later piano had a compass of only four octaves, $C°$ to c^3 (long octave); its tuning pins pass through the shallow pinblock and the strings are secured to them under the pinblock. A spring-regulated escapement is attached to each key, and the old intermediary lever is restored; the hitherto customary soundhole in the soundboard is abolished and, instead, Cristofori cut holes in the belly rail. A surprising innovation is an *una corda* shift worked by iron levers under the keyboard and controlled by two handstops; the keyboard shifts toward the bass. Maffei reported that the new *gravicembalo* was designed as a solo instrument, but, though not adapted for church music or large orchestras, was also useful as a chamber instrument, perfect for accompanying the voice and supporting another instrument, and that a larger volume of tone depended upon the force exerted to depress the keys. Apparently the tone of these first models was small—smaller than that of the standard Italian harpsichord.

In searching for a means of overcoming the harpsichord's dynamic inflexibility, Cristofori may have been influenced by the only really successful bowed keyboard instrument produced by then, the *Geigenwerk* (see page 308) of Hans Haiden, an example of which was in the Medici collection of which he became curator in 1716, but which must have been known to him earlier, as he had moved to Florence in 1693.

The *gravicembalo col pian e forte* was considered, as its name implies, merely as another kind of harpsichord, and there appears to have been no desire—either by its author or by his immediate successors—to create a new instrument with a different timbre. Early pianos, in Italy and elsewhere, encountered the criticism that they were tonally weaker than the harpsichord (this comment was made as late as 1802 by Koch in his lexicon) and that the sound was less distinct.

A pupil of Cristofori's, Giovanni Ferrini of Florence, continued building pianos in Italy, along with his harpsichords and dulcimers. Farinelli owned a piano of his dated 1730, originally made for Elizabeth Farnese, wife of Philip V of Spain. Sonatas for the new *cimbalo di piano e forte detto volgarmente di martinetti* by Lodovico Giustini—the earliest piano-forte music—were published in 1732, but Cristofori did not live to witness this recognition of his invention, having died the year before.

Although the first upright piano action had been designed by Marius in 1716, it was left to Domenico del Mela of Gagliano to create the vertical piano, a modernization of the older clavicytherium; an instrument of his dated 1739 is extant, housed in the Florence Conservatory. Its action is an adaptation of that of Cristofori, as might be expected, with the hammers striking from behind the strings. Italian pianos, some possibly from Ferrini's workshop, were exported to France and to Spain at an early date; one was advertised for sale in Paris in 1759, and among the musical instruments inventorized at the death of Queen Maria Barbara of Spain in 1758 were a Florentine piano of cypress, a harpsichord *que antes fue de piano echo en Florencia* ("which formerly was a piano made in Florence"), another Florentine instrument *que fue de piano y aora es de pluma* ("which was a piano and is now quilled"), and one more Florentine piano. After these early bursts of activity, Italian pianoforte making lapsed into a state of subservience to the harpsichord and never recovered its leadership.

France

That Cristofori was the first to apply a hammer mechanism to the harpsichord is no longer in doubt or dispute, but his priority was hotly contested in the eighteenth and even in the nineteenth centuries by other claimants and their defenders. Time and technology were ripe for the creation of a dynamically flexible keyboard instrument, and many experiments were made toward solving the inherent problems. Chief among these were the efforts of Marius in France and Schroeter in Germany, the runners-up. One of the numerous makers of bowed keyboard instruments was Cuisinié of Paris, who in 1708 had made, and submitted to the Paris Académie des Sciences, an instrument with *maillets* set on the end of the keys, tangents positioned like clavichord tangents, with the width of the blade parallel to the length of the key. His action was designed for a rectangular, clavichord-shaped instrument.

This was probably known to Jean Marius, the ingenious Paris inventor and harpsichord maker who had already produced a folding travel harpsichord, and who in 1716 submitted four different models of *clavecins à maillets* to the Académie. His first was on Cuisinié's principle, with *maillets* affixed upright to the rear of the keys, but this time the width of the maillets was parallel to the width of the keys, intended for a harpsichord-shaped instrument, and could be made in graduated thicknesses, larger in the bass than in the treble. It seems likely that both Cuisinié and Marius attempted to design actions that could swell and prolong sound in the manner of a clavichord, a logical point of departure. Marius's second model included three different types of action, all with *maillets* consisting of strips of wood about the length of the key, one end terminating in a striking head, a square block of wood; two of these actions call for down-striking *maillets*, the third for up-striking ones, and, although they are a far cry from our modern felt hammers, they are still unmistakably piano action components. His down-striking actions may possibly have been inspired by Hebenstreit's dulcimer (cf. the pantaleon, page 225). Marius's third model was a clavicytherium—the first upright piano action; his fourth combined a bichord piano and a harpsichord and was called by him *clavecin à maillets et à sautereaux.*

These pioneer experiments must have been regarded by his contemporaries more as curiosities than as viable instruments, for there was no follow-up of his efforts, and no further record of a French-built piano appears until 1759, when Weltmann submitted another piano-harpsichord combination, complete with two *genouillères* (knee levers) to the

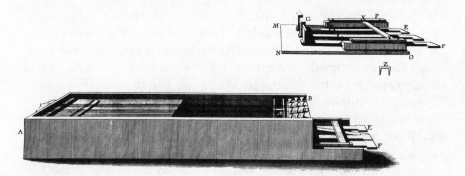

Marius's first action model, with *maillets* attached to the rear of the keys and trichord stringing, 1716. From *Machines et inventions approuvées par l'Académie Royale des Sciences*. Vol. 3, 1735.

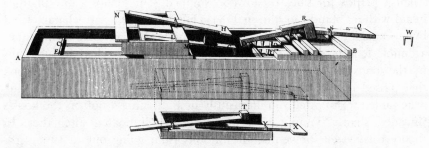

Marius's second model, combining various actions. The *maillet* O-R illustrates a down-striking action, 1716. From *Machines et inventions approuvées par l'Académie Royale des Sciences*. Vol. 3, 1735.

Académie des Sciences. The combination of these two distinct action types by early French makers points to a compromise transition instrument, with the piano action governing, so to speak, the harpsichord's set volume (see also harpsichord-piano, page 349). The knee levers in question were added to both harpsichords and pianos in the eighteenth century to effect registration and were succeeded by registration pedals.

Virbès, a mechanically inclined organist and builder of various keyboard instruments—the King of France possessed a harpsichord of his make—let his eight-year-old son perform in May 1769 on an instrument of his make, a *nouvel instrument à marteaux, espèce de clavecin*; a year later the boy played on a piano "in form of those from England," that is, a square piano, built to Virbès's specifications in Germany, and, also in 1770, he could proudly announce that his son had had the honor of playing the piano for the Dauphine.

Square pianos, already so popular abroad, were made from 1770 on in Paris by Johann Kilian Mercken (an example inscribed *Johannes Kilianus Mercken Parisiis 1770* is preserved in Paris), and an Italian maker named Barberini established in Grenoble was producing harpsichords and pianos there in the same year. L'Épine in 1772 submitted yet another combination harpsichord-piano to the Académie for approval, but piano making in France did not really flourish until after 1777, when Sébastien Érard started turning out square pianos on the English model, and a number of other makers were setting themselves up in Paris, to be joined by German competitors in the 1780s.

France's greatest harpsichord maker, Pascal Taskin, also devoted himself to the construction of grand pianos in the 1780s (he also imported

English pianos for sale; Broadwood shipped four pianos, "one plain, 3 inlaid without stand" to him in 1784). His instruments are characterized by an ingenious system of bichord stringing well in advance of his time: a double length of string looped at each end was attached to hitchpins by the loops while it was placed at exactly half its length over a hook that passed horizontally through the pinblock; both halves of the string were pulled up to pitch simultaneously by tightening a nut on the hook's threaded shank. Tuning pins were thereby eliminated altogether. In theory this system prevented the unisons from going out of tune separately; he hinged the hammers to the belly rail and then attached his overhead dampers to the hammers. Of the latter device Taskin wrote in a letter of 1786, terming it "a newly made action" (*une mécanique nouvellement faite*): . . . *je réduis à la dernier* [sic] *simplicité possible un forté piano qui a la forme d'un clavecin, dont j'ai fait porter a chaqu'un de ses étouffement* [sic] *reciproquement chaqu'uns leurs marteaux . . . qui . . . annule à chaque touche de cet instrument neuf frottement* [sic] . . . ("I reduce to the last possible simplicity a harpsichord-shaped piano, where I make each damper carry its own hammer, thereby avoiding nine friction points for each key of the instrument").

But despite such innovations, builders everywhere continued their individually looped method of stringing in the old harpsichord fashion, and it was not until 1827 that James Stewart, a partner of Jonas Chickering in Boston, Massachusetts, discarded looped unisons in favor of double-length strings passed over a hitchpin, the system now in universal use. Quite possibly a Marseilles builder named Jean-Louis Boisselot knew of Taskin's innovations, for in 1838 he built a *piano clédi-harmonique*, in which he suppressed the tuning pins, substituting an endless screw and hitching his double-length strings over special hitchpins.

But although French output remained negligible until the 1770s, both square and grand pianos had been imported there from the 1750s on, first from Italy, then from Germany, finally from England. New nomenclature was slow to become established, and in France the piano was still known as *clavecin à marteaux* into the nineteenth century.

Among the advertisements for secondhand keyboard instruments for sale in Paris in 1759 were an Italian piano and a newly invented harpsichord with *piano* and *forte* of unspecified nationality, capable of imitating a number of other instruments and of transposing by a semitone. The advertiser claimed that, unlike other harpsichords, it had no plectra. Other pianos were offered in the 1760s and thereafter.

The first public performance on a *clavecin forté-piano* in France was by Mlle Lechantre at a Paris concert on September 8, 1768, a year after its first public performance in England, and on an instrument imported from that country. In the 1770s, the decade in which French piano building started to prosper, makers had every reason to be discouraged by the now well-known opinions of their renowned countrymen: it was in December 1774 that Voltaire wrote to Mme du Deffand: *Le piano forté n'est qu'un instrument de chaudronnier, en comparaison du clavecin,* and Balbastre's prophecy: *Jamais ce nouveau venu ne détrônera le majestueux clavecin* was equally cheerless ("The piano is a mere coppersmith's instrument, in comparison to the harpsichord," and "Never will this newcomer dethrone the majestic harpsichord"). Nor did the Lausanne edition of the *Encyclopédie* (1779) offer much solace, when "FDC" (François de Castillon?) drew attention to foreign imports and also found the piano's touch detrimental to technique:

For some time *clavecins à marteaux* called *forté pianos* made in Strasbourg by the famous [Johann Heinrich] Silbermann have been brought to Paris, with walnut case and hammers of leather-covered cardboard that strike two unison strings or a single string, *mais ils sont plus pénibles à jouer* [but they are more troublesome to play] because of the weight of the hammers which tires the fingers and in time even makes the hand heavy.

Germany

In Germany the Dresden organist, Christoph Gottlieb Schroeter, designed, or claimed to have designed, two hammer actions in 1717, one downstriking, the other upstriking, both allegedly inspired by the pantaleon, an outsized dulcimer (see page 225) to which he sought to adapt a keyboard. He also claimed to have submitted models of both actions to the Dresden court in 1721. However, his claims were not made public until after Cristofori's invention had become known in Germany through a translation of Maffei's article made by the poet Koenig in Mattheson's *Critica musica* of 1725. Schroeter published his claim in Mizler's *Neueröffnete musikalische Bibliothek* of 1747 (diagrams appeared in Marpurg's *Kritische Briefe über die Tonkunst,* vol. 3, 1763). He also caused a piano of his design to be built under his supervision in 1739: it had a tangent action. Although Schroeter claimed, loudly and repeatedly, to have anticipated Cristofori's invention, it is far more likely that in reality Marius's drawings—they were published in 1735—had furnished the material for his upstriking and downstriking actions. Schroeter was a composer, a performing and theoretical musician, not an instrument maker, and it is difficult to see where else he could have found the necessary data on precisely these two types of action.

Once the translation of Maffei's article had appeared in Germany, German organ and harpsichord builders experimented with the new action. By 1730 or very shortly thereafter the renowned organ builder, Gottfried Silbermann of Freiberg, later of Dresden, started producing pianos. Zedler's *Lexicon* of 1733 reported that "a short while ago" he had invented another new instrument which he had presented to the Crown Prince of Poland (the Dresden-born future August III, King of Poland and Elector of Saxony). Silbermann submitted one of his earlier pianos to J. S. Bach, either in 1733 or in 1736, but Bach was of the opinion that the treble was too thin and that the instrument was too hard (*schwer*) to play, thereby possibly indicating a heavy action. In this connection it is interesting to note Agricola's comment (1768) on the *etwas schwächern Laut in der Höhe* ("the somewhat weaker tone of the treble") of pianos as represented by those of Silbermann. Silbermann experimented further, and by 1746 if not earlier, had built others with improved action; Bach saw one of these and pronounced it satisfactory. Frederick II of Prussia ordered a grand piano and was so pleased with it that he is said by Forkel to have ordered and received a total of fifteen, distributed among the Potsdam palaces. Three of these were extant until recently. At first Silbermann used Cristofori's action, modifying it later; he did away with the pivoting of hammer butts in the hammer rail and instead attached the hammers individually by strips of leather to a slighter rail. Following Cristofori, he and his immediate successors maintained bichord stringing throughout the compass, but, unlike him, Silbermann retained the harpsichord soundhole.

Contemporaries of Silbermann (and quite possibly the master himself) also produced small square pianos, about the size and shape of the contemporary clavichord. These had an early form of *Prellmechanik* ("*Prell* action"), named for the *Prelleiste*, or "rebound rail." In this action the hammers point toward the player and are attached either directly or indirectly to the keys; the hammer shank is tripped by an overhanging *Prelleiste*, a transformation of the upper portion of the clavichord or harpsichord rack. In its more developed form, found in both square and grand pianos, the hammers were pivoted in a so-called *Kapsel* —a forked sheath of metal or wood set on the key—instead of being attached to the key proper. The earliest example of a square piano known so far is that by Johann Socher, made in southern Swabia in 1742; its compass is four and one-half octaves from C° to f³, its action a *Stoss-mechanik* with underdampers, the damper butts made heavy enough to ensure the return of the dampers (later in the century Broadwood was to patent an underdamper using basically the same principle). In the *Stossmechanik* the hammers point away from the player; they are hinged to a hammer rail, which in turn is attached to the key frame at treble and bass ends. The hammers were set in motion by a jack or other device fixed to the key; in other words, it was a simplified form of the Cristofori action. Subsequently this was developed into the *Stosszungenmechanik*, in which the hammers are set in motion by a form of escapement fixed to the key (the *Stosszunge*), usually a check. The *Stosszungenmechanik* was later known as *englische Mechanik*, which, despite its name, is not identical with the English action.

An early maker of upright pianos was the organ builder, Christian Ernst Friderici of Gera, who from 1745 on brought out "pyramid" pianos—tall, truncated pyramids with oblique stringing, an innovation for any form of grand piano, but one that proved to be premature, and its potentialities were not realized until a later date.

Although early German square pianos usually retained both shape and overall construction of the clavichord, some were built in form of very small polygonal spinets. Many had no dampers, possibly—indeed, probably—due to the influence of the pantaleon (see page 225). Downstriking actions were common, in fact Adlung (1758) wrote that all the *Häm-merwerke* "here" (i.e., of Erfurt) were of that type. Square pianos of this period, and particularly those with downstriking actions, were known in Germany as pantaleons, possibly because of Schroeter's claim to have produced a pantaleon with keyboard.

This misleading term was in use up to the end of the century. Samuel Petri, for instance, wrote (1767) that formerly the "pantalon" had had either no damping system at all or a very deficient one, so that they all sounded like dulcimers (*Hackbretter*) and could not be used for good music, but that "now" they were vastly improved, not only by adequate damping but also by virtue of numerous variations of tone that could be brought into play by means of pedals; and in 1798–1799 the *Allge-meine musikalische Zeitung* could write of an instrument builder: "He made small pianofortes or so-called pantalons and also pianofortes in

Stein's manner." Marpurg (1763) brings out the difference between the two nicely and at the same time gives an interesting picture of the state of piano building in Germany in his day:

More than 20 towns and villages are known to me in which since 1721 [the date of Schroeter's alleged submission of his actions to the Dresden court] instead of the otherwise more common harpsichords, keyboard instruments with hammers or jacks [*Springern*] have been built which, when the striking of strings takes place from above are called *Pantalons* by their makers and purchasers. But when such an instrument with hammers is arranged so that the strings are struck from below then they call it pianoforte. Finally, if one asks each of these builders who really invented it, nearly every one of them passes himself off as the inventor.

These keyed pantaleons were said to lack the silvery tone of the harpsichord, but were loud enough for chamber music and—best of all—did not require any troublesome quilling. This last advantage was felt to be partly offset, however, by the difficulties experienced in tuning, due to the lack of registers for drawing off a course of strings.

The pantaleon's influence on German piano making is evident not only in nomenclature and downstriking actions, but also in the use by some builders of five and even six strings to a course in the treble of their instruments in an effort to compensate for its inherent weakness. This manner of stringing was first suggested by Schroeter. Adlung (1758) stated that Wahlfried Ficker of Zeiss made pianos with five strings in the upper octaves, four in the middle of the range, and three in the bass. A piano, "suitable for large concerts," which was offered for sale second-hand in Paris in 1759, had six strings in the two treble octaves and four in the remainder, and a compass reaching into the 16′ register (probably to F′, which in analogy to organ terminology would make it an instrument of 16′ pitch). This was probably a German piano, as were most of those in France at that time; it was also furnished with a pedal. At an unspecified date prior to 1768 a piano was used "successfully" in a (single) performance at the Berlin opera.

Shortly after Silbermann's death in 1753, the Seven Years' War broke out, causing the dispersion of Saxony's piano builders. England was to reap the benefits of this emigration. The first pianos in England had been imported, and manufacture there was started by such German makers as Johann Christoph Zumpe, a former Silbermann pupil who arrived in London about 1760 and established himself in that city a year later as a maker of square pianos, of which he was to build prodigious quantities. Zumpe had been accompanied to England by several other German builders, and together the group became known as the "twelve apostles." (Frederick Neubauer, possibly one of them, is known to have made pianos in London by 1763.)

The earliest extant English piano is a Zumpe square of 1766 (however, Fétis stated that he learned to play on a Zumpe dated 1762); this has a compass of just under five octaves, from G' to f³, and all accidentals from E♭° to b♭² are split. Zumpe was so successful that he could not keep up with the demand for his squares; his action is known as the single action, with jacks fixed to the keys, and hammers hinged to a rail, pointing away from the player. (Érard and other makers were also to use this action, an adaptation as it was of Cristofori's.) Zumpe's comblike damper system was of whalebone and his dampers could be raised by a hand stop.

The first public performance upon a piano in England took place at Covent Garden on May 16, 1767, at a benefit for Miss Brickler, who sang an aria from *Judith* by Arne, accompanied by Charles Dibdin on the piano. But the world's first public piano recital was not given until a year later, when Johann Christian Bach performed in London on one of Zumpe's square pianos "for the benefit of Mr. Fisher," the very year in which Taskin created the ne plus ultra of harpsichord refinement, his *clavecin à peau de buffle*. According to Dr. Burney, "after Bach's arrival [in 1762] all the harpsichord makers in this country tried their mechanical powers on pianofortes, but the first attempts were always on the large size," that is, the grand piano (harpsichord-shaped pianos were called "large pianos" in England until the term "grand" came into use). Of these attempts little is known, but certainly the popular English square was built in sufficient quantities to permit comparatively large-scale exports to France by the end of the 1760s.

From 1759 on, Johann Andreas Stein (1728–1792) of Augsburg, one of the great eighteenth-century makers of stringed keyboard instruments, started devoting less of his time to the organ—he was also an organist and organ builder—and more to the making and improving of pianos. He had been a pupil of Johann Andreas Silbermann, a nephew of Gottfried's, in 1748–1749. Stein transformed the *Prellmechanik* into the German action (*deutsche Mechanic*) by furnishing it with an escapement (which he did not evolve until 1773); he converted the fixed *Prelleiste* into an escapement by cutting it up into a series of hinged members, one for every hammer, each maintained in position by a spring; the old *Kapsel* was retained, and the hammers pointed toward the player. The German action, as it was henceforth known, could be applied to both square and grand forms; one effect of the new action was to lighten the touch, as the hammers were either pivoted to the *Kapsel* affixed to each key, or to the key itself. After Stein's children—Nanette Streicher née Stein and her brother Andreas Matthäus—had moved to Vienna where they continued building, the German action became known as the Vienna action. Stein contributed the shifting pedal in 1783, introducing it on his *Saitenharmonika*, a bichord piano with an additional string to each course (probably the earliest practical application of trichord stringing); the shift caused only this third string to be struck, and was consequently called *Spinett* or *Spinettchen* by its maker: we would call it an *una corda*.

Stein generally brought the art of piano building to so high a degree of perfection that a contributor to the *Allgemeine musikalische Zeitung* could state in 1804 that sixty years earlier a person was lucky enough if he possessed a grand piano; that Silbermann, Friderici, and others had made instruments with excellent tone, but that piano technique had progressed to such an extent during the past thirty years that those older pianos were now held to be unusable because of their actions, and had been completely replaced by Stein's instruments.

Not only building technique but also playing technique had changed indeed, for the early pianos had been played just like harpsichords; Maffei, it is true, had realized at once the implications of having *piano* and *forte* at his fingertips without changes of registration—he had undoubtedly received demonstrations from Cristofori—and Quantz (1752) with his instinctive feeling for instruments praises the piano's ability for dynamic modulation, in which he considered it superior to both the single- and two-manual harpsichords, but other German musicians of the mid-century were still relying for soft playing on mechanical "stops" rather than on touch. Square pianos of this time, provided as they were with little or no escapement, could be played from *mezzo piano* to *mezzo forte*, to use more modern expressions, but really soft playing was virtually unobtainable because of blocking hammers, a condition that favored the "piano" stop, a strip of cloth interposed between strings and hammers by means of a hand stop or pedal.

The extent to which the piano's true nature was misunderstood can be gathered from Adlung's comment that the most beautiful thing (*das schönste*) about a piano was the alternating of *forte* and *piano* by means of a pedal, without necessitating any interruption in playing, as pieces of cloth or leather could be pushed under the hammers. Anything more self-defeating than a fortepiano with a *fortepiano* stop is hard to conceive of. Strings on early pianos were as thin as those of the harpsichord, and only gradually were they increased in thickness when greater volume came to be desired. Wound bass strings came into use in the last quarter of the century.

To the challenge presented by the increasingly fashionable piano, harpsichord makers had responded by augmenting the number of accessory contrivances, many of which were taken over—experimentally or more permanently—by the piano. From the mid-century on the rage for imitating other instruments became apparent, and lute, harp, bassoon, and other stops were added; indeed, the harpsichord itself was imitated: a square piano of Johann Gottlob Wagner and his brother, Christian Salomon, both of Dresden, built in 1774 with a modified Cristofori action, was named *clavecin royal* by its makers; the uncovered hammers sounded like a harpsichord, and additionally it offered six variations of tone with lute, *forte, piano*, and swell worked by knee levers. The Wagners would doubtless have been complimented could they have foreseen that their instrument would be described as a harpsichord—and a three-manual one, to boot—in the nineteenth century.

The decade that contributed most to the spreading and adoption of the piano was perhaps that of the 1770s; France and England had made enormous strides in starting industries of their own, due in large measure to the presence of German and Alsatian makers and mechanics. In the United States the first mention of a piano occurs in 1774; there, pianos were at first imported from England and nothing is heard anent American makers until the close of the 1780s, when English and German piano builders immigrated. The first piano built in the New World is believed to have been by John Behrent of Philadelphia, and from the end of the century on American builders were making their own contributions to the piano's development.

At some time between 1772 and 1776 Americus Backers, a Dutchman working in England, invented the English action, a modification of the Cristofori-Silbermann action, but without the intermediary lever, and with hammers pivoted to a rail so as to point away from the player; the earliest drawing of this action is shown in Robert Stoddard's patent of

1777 for coupling a piano with a harpsichord; this patent is also note-worthy in that it contains for the first time the prefix "grand" in connection with a piano. John Broadwood, son-in-law and successor to Shudi, the harpsichord maker, was first to employ the new action, and other English makers followed. (As already mentioned, the English action is not identical with the *englische Mechanik*.)

Broadwood made his first piano in London in 1773, the year in which Johann Andreas Stein invented the escapement action. But up to 1780 Broadwood made only squares, and these were based on the Zumpe model. He then created his own design—in 1780—and patented it in 1783. Up to then, square pianos had closely resembled clavichords, both in form and construction methods, but once Backers had found the means of changing the action emplacement, Broadwood conceived the idea of moving the wrestplank away from the right side to the rear and thereby transformed the construction of the square. Other makers adopted his disposition after they became aware of the vastly augmented tone volume obtainable from the new model once the length of the strings' dead ends had been considerably reduced and the tension increased.

Broadwood's patent of 1783 also covered damper and *piano* pedals for a grand piano; these were transformations of the old English harpsichord machine stop and swell pedals, respectively. Another item of the patent was a soundpost that communicated with a second soundboard added one inch below the regular soundboard, with the object of further increasing the volume of tone; and finally, an underdamper system for squares.

"The earliest date for a Broadwood grand piano is 1781," wrote A. J. Hipkins, who was to become associated with the firm in the next century. It incorporated the English action from the beginning. Hipkins (1885) stated that Broadwood was the first maker to attempt to equalize the scale both in tension and in striking place, and that about 1788 he divided the bridge, shortening the great harpsichord-length bass strings by placing them on a separate bridge, thereby permitting the establishment of a striking point theoretically the same throughout the range. He aimed at that of 1/9th, with some latitude in the treble. Broadwood's pedals and divided bridge were universally adopted, and his soundpost was applied sporadically by other builders. Hipkins never encountered the striking point of 1/7th, repeatedly attributed to old keyboard instruments, although Carl Kützing (1844) seems to have met with it. Both

Kützing and Henry Fowler Broadwood preferred the striking point of 1/8th, and the latter incorporated it in his pianos in the nineteenth century; in the treble, though, the striking point is brought very close to the nut in order to obtain brilliance of tone.

The improvements brought about by Stein's invention of an escapement action in 1773 and that of the English action shortly thereafter caused composers to turn their attention to the piano, and the first compositions for piano rather than for harpsichord appear in this decade; it was also the era of the first great pianists—Mozart and Clementi. Mozart played a German, Clementi an English, action piano, and to judge from reports of their 1781 musical contest in Vienna, the influence of action on performer was greater than that of performer on action. Publication in 1777 of Burney's duets for two persons performing on one piano—the first duets of their kind—are said to have lent impetus to the building of *vis-à-vis* pianos with the players facing each other; but at least one harpsichord had been constructed in this fashion earlier in the century, and Stein's *vis-à-vis*, first built in 1777, were piano-harpsichord combinations.

Another giant in the piano-building world of the late eighteenth century was Sébastien Érard, who had devoted himself to harpsichord making in his youth but turned his attention to the making and, above all, the improving of pianos. His first piano, a square, was made in 1777, not to be followed by a grand until 1796, for the French Revolution, combined with his devotion to the construction of harps, interrupted his piano-making activities. His grands were built with English action until 1808, according to Fétis; in 1783 he (and Wagner in Germany) had abandoned knee levers in favor of pedals. But his great contribution was the repetition action for grand pianos, patented in its first form in 1809 (*mécanisme à étrier*, "stirrup action"), which patent included a disposition for upward bearing at the nut, and in its second and final form of double escapement action in 1821, when a patent was granted to his nephew, Pierre Érard, in London. This action has formed the basis of all double escapement actions made since, including the Schwander action (in which a double escapement enables the hammer to strike the strings any number of times without falling back all the way, that is, without completely releasing the key).

Among other late-eighteenth-century developments must be mentioned: the small harp-shaped pianos, such as those put out from the 1770s on by Johann Matthäus Schmahl and other makers, and imitations of the "leg of mutton" spinet, so popular in eighteenth-century England, transformed into pianos of the same shape by John Crang and Hancock (a partnership), the earliest of which dates from 1779. A very small portable piano of this form but of reduced proportions, called the orphica, was built by Carl Röllig of Vienna from 1795 on (it continued to be made until about 1830), with one string to the hammer, a compass varying from two to four octaves, and keys about half the standard width. Intended for open-air performances, it could be set on the player's lap or suspended by a band from his neck. The escapement lever or jack, known as hopper in England—an abbreviation of "grasshopper"—was due to John Geib, who patented it in 1786 in London, for inclusion in square piano actions; upon expiration of his patent it came into general use.

Early squares had had a five-octave compass generally, but from 1794 on, when William Southwell of London patented an extra compartment for a small key frame to be inserted under the treble soundboard, the compass was extended upward from f^3 to c^4. The extra keys were known as "extension" or "new extension"; a gap for passage of the hammers was cut from the soundboard, and the extra key frame partitioned off from the main body of the keys. Broadwood, as mentioned, had placed wrest-plank and tuning pins to the rear of his squares, but in 1792 George Garcka made another change, moving them to a position immediately behind the nameboard, a great convenience when tuning. Elongated uprights of harpsichord dimension were still being made, set on stands, their name changed meanwhile from "pyramid" to "giraffe." Hofrat Bauer of Berlin "invented" such a piano in 1780 and called it the crescendo. It stood eight and one-half feet high, had a five-octave compass, and a shifting keyboard to accommodate performances "with wind instruments that are one or two tones higher than chamber pitch" (for other transposing pianos, see keyboards, page 239). The strings of such instruments were of grand piano length. Uprights of the period were also built in cupboard form—huge rectangles—and have more recently been called grand upright pianos.

Much attention was also paid in the closing decades of the century to the materials from which the hammers were made, and attempts at rendering the heads more resilient led to experimentation with felt, wool, and cloth for the heads, which were then capped with leather. By the end of the century the compass had been extended to five and one-half octaves, from F' to c^4; a number of stops and gadgets had been fitted, not only in emulation of the now declining harpsichord, but apparently in an effort to create a one-man orchestra; piano reductions of orchestral scores, either for two or for four hands, fostered the demand for a number of imitative stops, calling for additional pedals and covered by patents from 1797 on. Some of these effects were incorporated in response to the introduction of "Turkish" (Janissary) music into military bands, causing composers both major and minor to write Turkish marches for the piano: triangle (one or more bells of the resting-bell type attached below the soundboard and struck with a metal beater), drum (a padded hammer that struck the underside of the soundboard), cymbals (several strips of brass "clashed" against the bass strings), bassoon (a batten to which a role of parchment was glued, to be lowered onto the strings—a very popular item), and similar devices could be added ad lib. French and German makers reversed the traditional color of the keys, preferring black naturals and white accidentals. Finally, the greater tension occasioned by the larger compass necessitated extra bracing of the wooden frame, and from 1794 on patents for various types of metal braces were applied for, resulting in a 1799 patent for the earliest longitudinal metal bracing with united components, to replace the wooden braces *under* the soundboard.

THE PIANO SINCE 1800

From 1800 on the pace of discoveries and improvements accelerated rapidly. During the entire period of transition from harpsichord to piano, combination harpsichord-pianos were built, some details of which are given separately (see page 349). Another transition type was the piano imitating the harpsichord, such as the *clavecin royal*. Square pianos with two sets of hammers were also constructed to this end, one set with padded, the other with bare, wood; they could be alternated as desired. Some of these pianos were provided in addition with stops for *forte* and *piano*; other square pianos had a single set of unpadded hammers. The *cembalo* stop was but one more form of imitation, consisting of a series of tongues of cloth or other material edged with brass that could be maneuvered between hammers and strings so as to cause the hammers to strike the hard edging against the strings.

Double Pianos

Influenced no doubt by the large amount of music for four hands made available to the public, pianos were built for two performers facing each other, a continuation of the double instruments of similar nature produced in the eighteenth century from Jean Denis on. In 1812 Érard patented a *piano secrétaire* (in the form of a desk), with two soundboards and trichord stringing; the upper set of strings could be sounded an octave higher than the lower one by octave coupling, or both could be sounded in unison; optionally, an additional keyboard could be incorporated. Octave couplers, copied from the harpsichord, became popular after the *piano secrétaire* was marketed and copied by other makers.

Not only grand pianos but also uprights were built for two performers: in 1800 Matthias Müller of Vienna constructed an upright with facing keyboards, sufficiently low for the players to see each other; he called it *Ditanaklasis*. The real innovation of this model, however, was that its structure reached down to the ground, whereas contemporary uprights were still being placed on stands, and as such it was the forerunner of our modern uprights. Müller also made regular, one-manual pianos on this pattern.

A double grand piano for two performers facing each other was patented in New York by Pirson in 1850; it had a single string-plate, "the short string of one being in line with the long string pianoforte of the other," as the patent specified. And at the very end of the century a maker in Lyons brought out a double grand piano of rectangular form with keyboard at each end and single soundboard, but independent stringing for each player.

Upright Pianos

Upright pianos evolved erratically for the first century of their existence, for despite the tendency to build them less and less high, with increasing compromises of scale as a result, the old models continued to be made side by side with lower and far more modern ones. According to the form they assume, uprights are known as pyramid, giraffe, cabinet, cottage piano, and so on. Today's low, vertical pianos are often called spinet pianos or consoles, both of which terms are misnomers. Pyramid pianos—traditionally so named by their inventor, Friderici—had the form of a truncated pyramid; owing in part to their decorative effect they remained popular as late as about 1825, when they were replaced by the smaller uprights. Pyramids overlapped and were succeeded by the giraffes; these were characterized by a straight, perpendicular bass side and a treble side usually curved to form a scroll at the tail. They were made from about 1798 to 1850, mostly with the type of action known as hanging action, in which the hammer is at rest in an upright position below the level of the keys (this idea was adopted for the very low-slung twentieth-century vertical pianos). Wachtel and Bleyel of Vienna laid claim to the invention of the giraffe.

Matthias Müller was not the only maker to abolish the stand and to rest his uprights directly on the ground, for in the same year—1800—and quite independently, John Isaac Hawkins, then of Philadelphia, did likewise. The overall height of uprights was thereby greatly reduced. In 1800, too, Hawkins patented his "portable grand pianoforte" a vertical grand with strings reaching to the ground, its soundboard set in a metal frame and braced with metal bars, a metal wrestplank, a five-octave compass, and cloth-covered hammers; its overall height was a mere 138 centimeters (54 inches). Hawkins's stringing was still vertical, but two years later, in 1802, Thomas Loud of London and New York produced a diagonally strung upright (Friderici had already strung his pyramid diagonally, it will be recalled). In 1807 William Southwell of London brought out the cabinet piano, a large and cumbersome rectangle up to 2 meters (6½ feet) high, with tuning pins at the top, and large cloth-covered front panel; he improved it in 1821. Despite its size it remained in demand until the mid-century.

Efforts at designing a really low upright were finally successful in 1811, when Robert Wornum of London developed his first upright piano with diagonal stringing that measured only 1 meter (3 feet 4 inches) in height; here also, the strings reached to the ground. In 1813 Wornum produced his "harmonic piano," better known by its subsequent name of cottage piano, a term extended to include the low uprights of other makers. This was vertically strung and only 117 centimeters (3 feet 10 inches) tall. By 1826 Wornum had developed an action for his uprights, patented that year, which, together with the final form of his tape check action patented in 1842 (and promptly copied abroad) remains the basic upright action of today. Success of the cottage piano was not confined to Britain but spread quickly to France, where Pleyel adopted it and named it *pianino*. Other French makers were quick to copy it, and so well received was the cottage piano that square pianos were neglected in its favor; German and Austrian makers became aware of the cottage piano through Pleyel's copies and began giving preference to the smaller upright over the square from about 1838 on.

During the first quarter of the nineteenth century German and Austrian makers had confined their vertical piano models to tall giraffes, but from about 1830 on they reduced these in size, stood them on four legs, strung them diagonally, and furnished them with a standing German action; this was an adaptation of Streicher's Vienna action, with hammers in upright position pivoted to a *Kapsel* set in the key. Some idea of the style of late giant uprights may be gathered from that of a giraffe by Caspar Schlimbach, about 1820, in Leipzig, which stands 2.74 meters (9 feet) high, has six pedals for *forte, piano, pianissimo, Verschiebung* ("shift"; in Beethoven's day this was not necessarily an *una corda* as it could work on one or on two strings), bassoon, and Janissary music, the latter setting in motion drum and bells, and also cymbals and a jingling johnny carried by two sculptured, 60-centimeter- (2-foot-) high Negroes, one to either side of the case. Another form of upright dating from this period is the lyra piano, with its outline of a *lyra* and symmetrically arched sides, attributed to J. C. Schleip of Berlin about 1824, and also made in France and in England for a quarter of a century thereafter; it had a standing English action.

If Wornum's cottage piano had been well received, Roller et Blanchet's *piano droit* of 1827 created a sensation; a small and low-strung upright, it measured only 1 meter (40 inches) in height, and 130 centimeters (51 inches) in width; it was strung diagonally and had an aperture in the bottom of the case for the performer's feet. Its success was such that it forced out the square piano. In the following year Jean-Henri Pape of Paris, another piano-building "great," brought out his competitive upright with the same height but with overstrung bass section. This not only permitted lengthening the bass strings—with concomitant improvement in tone—but also made possible a more even distribution of tension. Cross-stringing promptly spread to America, and has become universal on both uprights and grands ever since.

In the opinion of Harding (1933) it was the patenting of an action for small uprights by Martin Seufert of Vienna in 1836 that probably marked the introduction to Austria and Germany of this type of piano, for when the *pianino* first became known there in 1838 it was presented as a new instrument—and was manufactured locally from about 1840 on. The year 1846 saw the invention by Antoine-Jean-Denis Bord of Paris of a double escapement action for grands, which, notwithstanding, forms part of the modern upright piano action.

Although European makers had started emphasizing upright pianos at the expense of square models from the 1830s on, American builders had preferred to develop the square. Not until the Paris Exposition of

1867 did they change this policy. Large square pianos as produced in America in the second and third quarters of the nineteenth century seem to have been considered, both by purveyors and purchasers, as an alternate form of grand piano with some of the status symbolism of the latter, while uprights remained substitutes, so to speak, for the "real" piano. But the American squares attained such huge proportions that once space became a consideration, the upright found itself very acceptable.

Uprights of all forms have at all times suffered from the fact that their strings are enclosed from all sides, and the soundboard is always set against a wall, so that the tone cannot issue freely and remains muffled. Lid props are of little help in overcoming this deficiency. When Friedrich Hölling of Zeiss brought out his *Konsonanzpianino* in 1877, an upright with sympathetic strings on the reverse side of the soundboard, he may have hoped to thereby enhance the volume.

Square Pianos

In addition to the traditional rectangular form, small pianos in the shape of spinets were produced in Germany and known as *Querflügel*. Although they differ in appearance they belong structurally to the square rather than to the grand piano. Some were no more than 1 meter (40 inches) long and had but a single string to a key, with or without a damper system. In the first part of the nineteenth century they continue, and are often an enlargement of, the late-eighteenth-century models. The rectangular form continued to be made in considerable quantities and benefited from many improvements applied to the grand piano. From 1822 on, metal hitchpin plates had been developed for square pianos, and in 1825 Alpheus Babcock of Boston patented a complete cast-iron frame for squares.

In Germany square pianos took the place vacated by the clavichord—Thon (1843) even wrote that Spaeth converted many *Claviere* into fortepianos—but after about 1838 the development of upright pianos brought about their discontinuation, until manufacture stopped entirely around 1860. Certainly square pianos were being replaced all over Europe by uprights by the middle of the nineteenth century. American builders held out longer than did their European competitors, and Steinway caused a furore at the New York World's Fair of 1855 when he presented a square piano with full iron frame and an overstrung scale. Contrary to expectation it had no metallic tone, even in the susceptible treble section, and was capable of greater volume than were rival models. The production of square pianos continued in America until 1880, culminating in a cross-strung, metal-plated monster of seven octaves that took up as much space as a grand.

Soundboards often had their upper surface varnished, and in 1826 a patent was even granted for their varnishing on both sides. Why a patent should have been required, or granted, for a procedure already in use a good century earlier is not clear; Donat about 1700 had varnished the soundboards of his clavichords, and a long article on the advantages of varnishing soundboards with copal had appeared in Mizler (1742). A patent for a wooden or metal soundboard for square pianos was granted in 1828. The evolution of metal frames for squares is tied to those for grand pianos.

Grand Pianos

Piano compasses by the end of the eighteenth century had attained five and one-half and exceptionally six octaves, and rapidly increased to six and one-half in the nineteenth century (Broadwood reached this range in 1811). They were to expand further to the present compass of seven octaves and a major third, from A^2 to c^5. Actions were preponderantly those called English action and German action; however, the German action as modified by the Streichers after their removal to Vienna in 1794 became known as the Vienna action (see page 330), and because it resulted in a closer resemblance to the English action than to the German action it was also called *englische Mechanik*. Here the hammer points toward the player and is hinged to a rail placed behind the keys; escapement is provided by a jack set on the key.

Ever since the days when Marius had experimented with a downstriking action, makers had been faced with the problem inherent in all upstriking actions, namely that of the hammer's impact dislodging the strings from their position at the nut and at the bridge pins, with resultant ill effect on tone quality. This led to renewed experimentation in the late eighteenth and early nineteenth centuries and to the production of models with downstriking actions on which the hammers were returned by counterweights or springs. One maker, Johann Jacob Goll of Vienna, patented a construction in which the strings were placed on the underside of the soundboard so that each blow from the hammer drove the strings further home. Other patents of a similar nature were granted later. But once the agraffe had been invented by Érard (in 1838), this particular problem was solved.

Pianos were still very lightly strung at the beginning of the nineteenth century, and their tone was of short duration, as may be gathered from Rochlitz's advice—given in 1802—to play Bach's C major Prelude (and several others) of Book I of the *Well-tempered Clavier* with raised dampers. Trichord stringing had been introduced, but even this augmentation of tension was deleterious, and at least one bichord model— that of Tobias Schmidt, 1802—was built in the new century. Thinness of tone apparently did not become objectionable until the early nineteenth century, when many attempts were made to remedy it: Broadwood applied steel tension bars to the treble of his grands in 1808, but they were not satisfactory; the experiment was repeated in 1818 with as little success.

Several pianos having four strings to a course were patented, and one was even designed, by Pape, for six strings. With more than three strings, two hammer heads were necessary, however, and so double hammers with two heads were created. But the existing frames could not take the additional strain. Streicher of Vienna found a happier solution: they omitted the traditional closed bottom, and according to Blüthner and Gretschel (1886) this had a notable effect on tone production. Probably the 4' stop patented by Joseph Kirkman, a descendant of Jacob Kirkman, in 1816 was another attempt to increase volume and brilliance of tone; it had its own bridge and was clearly an adaptation of the harpsichord register.

By 1806 a contributor to the *Allgemeine musikalische Zeitung* could state that the harpsichord had been replaced twenty years earlier by the piano, and that "now" beauty of tone had been combined with strength, sustaining power had been realized to a certain extent, and touch had become lighter than that of a harpsichord. But this was only a beginning. In the same year that Broadwood had patented his treble tension bars and Érard his first repetition action, Wachtel and Bleyel, piano makers of Vienna, commenced the commercial production of artificially seasoned woods for soundboards; they steamed the wood for forty-eight hours, bringing up the resin to the surface in brown splotches, and then dried it in drying boxes. This is considerably earlier than the artificial seasoning in special chambers reported by Oscar Paul (1868) as having taken place from about 1856 on. Soundboards in those days were made thicker in the treble than in the bass, in conformity with harpsichord-making tradition; a piano patent of 1828 contains a mention of thinner bass sections.

Two distinct schools of piano building developed, known as the English and the Vienna schools, and they greatly influenced contemporary styles of playing. Hummel's celebrated *Piano School* of 1828 attributes the differences of technique to the differences of English and German actions. German pianos had a shallow key dip and light action, favoring rapidity in execution, in contrast to the deeper dip, heavier action, and greater volume of tone of the English grands; but their slower repetition and heavier touch permitted of less dynamic shading (hammers of English pianos had to travel farther to reach the strings). Hummel himself played a Vienna action piano. Writing in the same year as Hummel, the physicist Ernst Chladni reported in the *Allgemeine musikalische Zeitung* on having played several English pianos as well as a Streicher; the English pianos had greater volume of tone, he noted, but the Viennese instrument had a lighter action. Clementi's and Mozart's playing styles were later contrasted by Ernst Pauer (whose mother was a Streicher); he ascribed their disparity to the performers' instruments, for Clementi played an English, Mozart and his followers a Vienna, piano; the former had a fuller and more sonorous tone, the deeper key fall was favorable to the sure execution of thirds, sixths, and octaves, and to clarity and precision in playing chords successively; Pauer then contrasts these advantages with those of Vienna pianos, with their thin but pleasing tone of short duration and extremely light touch, responsive to the most delicate pressure. Another advantage of the Viennese piano was its price—it cost about half as much as the more solidly constructed English grand, as Hummel stated.

Ever since the changeover from bichord to trichord stringing in the late eighteenth century, it had become increasingly evident that the framework would have to be considerably strengthened if the piano were to evolve any further, but because of the strong prejudice against metal, said to be injurious to the tone, only wooden members could be utilized at first. These added considerably to the overall weight but did little to improve the structure. (The battle between metal and nonmetal frames, after having been settled for a good century, broke out anew in the twentieth century in connection with the revival of harpsichord making, and was carried on chiefly in the pages of the *Zeitschrift für Instrumen-*

tenbau.) Then, after the compass had been extended in the treble, some form of metal support was found indispensable.

The growing need for greater volume of tone felt from the 1820s on, involving as it did heavier stringing and yet greater compass extensions, coupled with the gradual rise in pitch in the nineteenth century, were further aggravating factors. Braces were first to be used; they took the form either of metal bars or of compensating tubes, the latter designed so as to contract and expand with the strings according to changes in temperature, and were only partially successful. From tubes they were developed into compensating frames; two workmen of William Stoddard patented such a frame in 1820—Stoddard purchased it from them —consisting of a series of tubes placed parallel to the strings, bound together by wooden crossbars. Érard patented a similar arrangement two years later "to enable the tuning to hold better by modifying the effect of hot and cold on metal strings." Both patents covered grand pianos. (Tubular bars for square pianos seem to have first been used in 1825 by Francis Melville.) Compensation tubes continued to be built in the United States until about 1840—but they were not the answer.

Although Broadwood's tension bars of 1808 had been a failure, it became clear that the solution to structural problems posed by increased tension lay rather in solid bars or plates, and experiments with these were now multiplied: by 1821 Broadwood had built up to five metal braces into grand pianos; the first metal hitchpin plate was incorporated into a square piano in the following year; a metal wrestplank was patented by J. Muller of Paris in 1823. Finally, in 1825, the first complete metal frame with hitchpin block (in one casting) was patented by Alpheus Babcock of Boston; it was for square pianos. Numerous patents were taken out in the United States from then on for metal plates and frames, fewer in Europe, where the need may have been less because of a more benign climate. Nonetheless, Broadwood patented in 1827 a combination of solid bars and fixed metal string-plate.

The piano's development henceforth was notably aided by technical improvements resulting from the Industrial Revolution: major factors affecting it were the invention of telegraphy, for example, as this led to vast advances in the manufacture of wire, thereby permitting both heavier stringing and an increase in scale; and the newfangled hot-air furnaces installed in basements of private homes in the United States caused perfectly good pianos to curl up promptly, making it imperative to stabilize them by taking advantage of the new metallurgical techniques by which the casting of plates became possible—at first partial, later whole plates. Overstrung grands were produced by Bridgehead and Jardine of New York in 1833, and patents gather momentum thereafter: Érard invented the important agraffe in 1838, and Jonas Chickering of Boston patented a cast-iron frame for square pianos in 1840. By then the delicate Vienna piano was doomed, and Breitkopf and Härtel of Leipzig were reported in 1839 to be building grand pianos *nach Broadwood*, like those of the London firm; Mme Pleyel chose one for her Leipzig concerts that year (Fischhof could still write in Vienna in 1853 that English and French pianos had a larger tone than did those of German make). In August 1842 the Danish piano builder C. C. Hornung applied for a patent for a one-piece cast-iron frame, which was granted in 1843, the year in which Jonas Chickering also was granted a patent for a frame for flat-scale grand pianos in one solid casting. Henceforth the Chickering concert piano was famous. In the same year Antoine-Jean-Denis Bord of Paris introduced his *capotasto* bar, a metal pressure bar that acts as a nut in the treble section, exerting downward pressure on the strings.

The old dichotomy of English versus Austro-German pianos gave way to a new alignment of the United States, Denmark, and France, with their preference for one-piece cast-iron frames, versus England, Austria, and Germany, where builders continued to prefer a composite frame for a while. Harding (1933) relates that cast-iron frames were generally considered as Americanisms, although Broadwood did make a grand piano with a complete metal frame in 1851. The year 1846 was another landmark, but of a nonstructural nature: Broadwood adopted intentional equal temperament, the first firm to do so.

Two writers of the 1840s in conjunction give us a good portrait of the piano of that era: Christian Thon (1843), and Carl Kützing (1844), the latter a piano and organ builder of Bern. Thon reminds us that the actions of English pianos were set directly on the bottom of the case, whereas German actions rest three finger-breadths above the bottom, on supports (to remove such an action the support battens were first withdrawn; this not only lowered the action but also cleared the hammer heads from the pinblock. As stated above, hammers of this system had less distance to travel than did those of English pianos). English actions are to be preferred, he goes on to relate, rather surprisingly, as they are lighter [sic], more precise and more elastic than German actions; English actions demanded greater accuracy in construction, a fact that may account for the German action not having gained acceptance everywhere. The latter, he adds, was made chiefly in Vienna.

What this amounts to is that after Beethoven—who played a Broadwood in his later years—the *englische Mechanik* emulated the increasingly influential English models without concomitant structural changes, resulting in an imbalance found in many Austro-German grands of the time. Downstriking actions were not yet forgotten; Thon praises their sound as better than that of upstriking models, for the latter had a tendency always to raise the string from the nut, so that some makers screwed a strip of brass to the wrestplank at the nut in order to hold the strings down (prototype of the *capotasto*). He also recalled that formerly both grands and squares with strings passing below the pin-block were built in Vienna. Pianos of his day had either a six-octave or a six-and-one-half-octave compass, but the tone of both extremities he qualified as bad.

Kützing a year later related that Vienna had lost ground as a school of piano building, and he would not discuss the Vienna action, he wrote, because it was outdated. With the iron strings formerly in use, and a scale far shorter than when he wrote, it had been necessary to place the striking point closer to the bearing (nut), but such proportions were rendered useless with the invention of metal string-plates and longer scale; furthermore, cast-iron string-plates permitted thicker stringing in the treble. While striking points varied from 1/8th to 1/9th, in his youth he had had to voice hammers with striking points varying from 1/12th to 1/7th; he himself advocated that of 1/8th as productive of the best tone. He quotes Scheibler in saying that pitch varied from A 425 to A 445, so that, when calculating the scale of a piano, the higher pitch should be assumed. Bridge pins were often too weak, resulting in impure tone, worst of all in the trichord square pianos that in practice could not be brought into a pure tuning.

Kützing had been to America and was very favorably impressed by American piano building. German pianos exported to America, he wrote, cracked up even before they arrived at their destination; they had cheap shellac finishes, whereas the American pianos were made of the most beautiful woods and were lacquered with copal, which lacquering made the wood less susceptible to atmospheric changes and thus assisted in maintaining the tuning. New York makers were first to adopt the string-plate, for when he was there in 1840 his examination of pianos with metal string-plates showed them to be at least twenty years old. The climate in the United States was, in his opinion—and he appears to have been the first to hold it—probably responsible for tuning problems, as the best London and Paris instruments did not hold their tunings there. To which we can only add: amen.

By the time Thon and Kützing wrote and the metal plate had been developed, other components had undergone considerable modifications since the beginning of the century: stringing had made great progress, due principally to wire drawing and to application of the metal string-plate; the introduction of wound strings (at an unknown date) also helped, but did not become general until a relatively late date, for Kützing commented that, if uncovered bass strings were slack, their tone would be improved by light "overspinning." And stringing was really modernized after James Stewart, partner of Jonas Chickering, abolished the loop in favor of double string lengths passed around a pin (in 1827), as Taskin had done in the preceding century. Stewart's idea was not generally applied for some years, as may be deduced from Kützing's statement that the ordinary method of stringing was by means of loops, which he condemned in favor of the double strings.

Attention was also being paid to the "dead" ends of strings beyond the bridge, and Frederick William Collard of London patented, in 1821, a "bridge of reverberation" designed to permit them to vibrate sympathetically with the sounding portions. On modern pianos, the lengths between bridge and hitchpins are proportioned so as to produce overtones of the struck strings; for a while, Blüthner of Leipzig added half-length sympathetic strings to the three treble octaves of their "aliquot" pianos. Montal in his tuning tutor of 1835 still knew brass-strung basses, both plain and wound—the latter very brittle and easily broken. Nuremberg wire drawing had long been famous, but the new technology of the Industrial Revolution had brought changes and challenges, with English cast-steel strings coming to the fore in 1834; these permitted a lengthening of the scale, particularly that of the treble, and at the same time heavier stringing, as they could withstand greater tension than those made in Berlin and Nuremberg. Cast-steel piano wire was first brought out by Webster and Horsfall of Birmingham in 1834 and was recognized immediately as being so superior to the old iron wire then in use as to render this obsolete. But then in 1840 a Vienna manufacturer made an even better piano wire, and competition was intensified until Moritz

Pohlmann of Nuremberg started about 1855 producing a variety of wire that was universally adopted.

The culmination of the bravura style of playing at the mid-century imposed severe strains on the piano; Fischhof wrote in 1853 of concert artists breaking strings and "dislocating" both hammers and keys by playing with too much force—and making a terrific din while doing so. Very à propos is the report of Heinrich Welcker von Gontershausen (1870) of a visit to hear Liszt play at his Paris flat in the rue de Provence: the ceiling had been removed and in its place a gallery built for an audience; four grand pianos stood next to one another, and Liszt slid from one to the other, playing at most eighteen bars on each, while a piano tuner stood by to remove the broken strings and to replace them. At the end of the performance Liszt fainted and was carried off by "satellites," who had anticipated this outcome. (An interesting comment in this connection is that of Eitner, made in 1896, to the effect that the heavy touch of organs and keyboard chordophones in Germany originated with the repairs these instruments underwent in the 1840s and 1850s, at the time of the Liszt enthusiasm, for Liszt had demanded a heavy touch; Eitner knew of three Silbermann pianos, all of which had a light touch.) On a more technical level, Welcker von Gontershausen recommended for striking points one-tenth the length of wound strings, one-eighth that of simple bass strings up to $a°$, gradually increasing thereafter to one-ninth, one-tenth, one-eleventh, reaching one-twelfth at a^4.

Hammers in the eighteenth century had been made, at least experimentally, of a number of materials. A writer on the history of inventions, Johann Beckmann (1786), states that they could be made of wood, sometimes of leather, paper pulp, papier-mâché, "or other materials," but leather had rapidly become the accepted and conventional material. When Jean-Henri Pape patented rabbit's-hair felt for hammers in 1826 after lengthy experimentation, the prejudice against it was hard to overcome, and as late as 1835 Schilling criticized Broadwood for using it (Broadwood had substituted wool for hair). A year after Pape's patent was granted, Edward Dodd of London received one for a hammer with outer covering of leather capable of being tightened or loosened, depending upon the timbre required. Clearly leather was no longer satisfactory, yet felt did not come into general use until 1855, and in fact deer leather was still being worked for the outer layer of hammer heads in Germany in 1856. To quote Welcker von Gontershausen once more, the thick "Verdian" tone quality that was preferred in France and Germany at the time he wrote could best be obtained by felt hammers; leather, he stated, without losing the necessary softness, gave a clearer tone with more brilliance and fire; it emitted the so-called Vienna tone. But the Vienna tone lost out, and in the present century felt may be losing out also, as a synthetic material is making its competitive presence known.

Some innovations in the preparation of soundboards have already been mentioned. In addition, two-ply soundboards had been inserted into clavichords by the Lemmes as early as 1772, but this did not prevent Carl Schmidt of Pressburg (Bratislava) from "inventing" one in 1826 that would, as he claimed, neither split nor sink. His idea was entirely viable, and later in the century, in 1891, two-ply soundboards ("duplex soundboards") were patented by Mathushek. This firm also experimented with different thicknesses of soundboard and found three-eighths of an inch to be most responsive for the treble, tapering to one-quarter inch in the bass. Metal soundboards, made of iron and copper, were subjects of experimentation by Johann Jacob Goll of Vienna in 1823 and also of Jean-Henri Pape in Paris, but proved unsatisfactory. In the present century laminated soundboards have been reintroduced and are currently common in both grand and upright pianos.

After Jonas Chickering patented his full iron frame in 1843, American piano building split temporarily into two "schools," that of Boston, where the majority of builders adopted the full metal frame, and that of New York, where makers objected to the metallic tone quality inherent in metal-frame pianos, particularly in the trebles, and consequently continued to favor braces and flat scales for a while. It is against this background that the tremendous impact of the square piano that Steinway exhibited at the 1855 World's Fair must be considered; it had an overstrung scale and a full iron frame capable of taking the increased tension of the new scale, and further had greater volume of tone than the squares exhibited by competitors, and—*mirabile dictu*—no metallic tone. The battle for the iron frame was won.

Until then Chickering had led the industry in importance, with Nunns and Clark running second, at least in production, both domestically and by its exports (of square pianos), but now these firms were to be overtaken by Steinway, at first by the revolutionary square piano alone; then,

in 1859, Steinway finally patented their own full iron frame for grands
—sixteen years after Chickering had done so—and this proved to be a
solid frame with overstrung scale and fanning-out strings, no less. The
modern grand was born.

After the London Exposition of 1862 prejudice against the iron frame
broke down sufficiently to permit its adoption in Germany and Austria,
where resistance had been the strongest, but strangely enough English
and French makers preferred to retain the flat scale and bracing system
for some time thereafter.

Modern pianos are standardized as to compass (although Bösendorfer
makes a grand with eight octaves) and today employ virtually identical
actions. But each maker has his own standard of length for his grands
and of height for his uprights. Stringing is universally trichord in the
treble, bichord in the center, unichord in the bass, the changeover points
being known as breaks. The metal frame covers both soundboard and
pinblock and carries the hitchpins; it takes a stress of some thirty-odd
tons imposed by today's heavy stringing. The soundboard, or belly, is
crowned, that is, it is forced into a convex shape and heavily barred while
in that shape and prior to its insertion in the piano; once the instrument
is strung, downward pressure of the strings causes it to flatten. It carries
a stout, S-shaped bridge and a separate bass bridge, the latter undercut
on the distal side and placed diagonally. European pianos are generally
furnished with two pedals, the *piano* or *una corda* pedal, and the sustaining or damper pedal. American pianos have additionally a *sostinente*
pedal placed between these two, originally called *pédale de prolongement*
when it was first shown in 1844 by its putative inventor, Dominique-
François-Xavier Boisselot of Marseilles. Although tuning in intentional
equal temperament was introduced experimentally by Broadwood in
1811, it was not in general use by that firm until 1844–1846 under A. J.
Hipkins, and it is probably safe to say that until the end of the century
it was universally more intentional than equal.

HARPSICHORD-PIANOS

Combinations of harpsichord and piano were built from the latter's
early days right into the nineteenth century. As transition instruments,
they bridge the entire period of competition between the two and appear only a few years after the first piano had been built.

One of the instruments submitted to the Académie des Sciences in 1716 by Jean Marius was a *clavecin à maillets et à sautereaux* ("harpsichord with hammers and jacks"), with the on and off positions of a set of hammers regulated by the height of the balance rail, while the jacks, placed behind them, were engaged and disengaged as usual by a movement of the jack slide. Marius's hammers were small blocks—rectangular in his drawing—fixed to the rear of each key, and cloth-covered dampers were also affixed to the keys. Nothing further is heard of such combinations until 1755, when the Reverend William Mason purchased one in Hamburg, with two choirs of strings on the harpsichord that could be silenced when the piano was played.

From then on, hybrids containing a hammer and jack, or hammer and tangent, action were frequently made in Germany. Indeed, the written evidence points to their having been common arrangements up to the time when Stein perfected the grand piano. Of the "fortepiano" Petri (1767) states: *Die grossen sind in der Gestalt der Flügel und haben Hämmer und Flügeltangenten zugleich, manche aber nur Hämmer allein, welche daher mehr Pantalons genent werden* ("The large ones are wing [i.e., harpsichord] shaped and have both hammers and jacks, but some only hammers alone, which are therefore more often called pantalons"). Another instrument was submitted to the Académie by Weltmann in 1759, but its piano action consisted of tangents rather than of normal jacks. 1769 saw the invention of Johann Andreas Stein's *Polytoni-Clavichordium*, not a clavichord despite its name, and probably inspired by an instrument of Marius's he saw while in Paris in 1758; it consisted of a two-manual harpsichord separated from a lower piano by a central soundboard; the harpsichord had three sets of strings at 8' pitch and one at 16', with the upper keyboard plucking only one 8'; all four choirs were available on the lower manual and dampers for the piano section were worked by a knee lever. Stein emphasized that his was not the type of instrument in which hammers and jacks acted on the same strings, as the strike of the hammers demanded a quite different string scale from that of a plucking jack action, a principle he later adopted in his *vis-à-vis*.

In reality the hammer impact, if at all forceful, would cause jarring and would tend to raise the strings from the harpsichord-type bridge and nut. Joseph Merlin, a London builder from the Low Countries, patented in 1774 a set of hammers "of the nature of those used in the kind of harpsichords called Piano Forte" for connecting to a harpsichord. Sometime during the 1770s—the precise date remains unknown—Sébastien Érard of Paris built his *clavecin mécanique,* a combination in which each instrument could be played separately or both together.

Stein then brought out in 1777 his *vis-à-vis* for two players seated opposite each other. Here again, the idea was not entirely new, for a harpsichord of Philippe Denis of Paris with four manuals, two at each end, intended for two players, had already been exhibited in Paris in 1712, and a somewhat crude sketch of a similar instrument had appeared in Adlung (1768). Two of Stein's *vis-à-vis* have come down to us, of which one, now in Verona, is from 1777; it is a long rectangle, with three manuals at one end, the two upper of which are for a harpsichord with four choirs, the lower for a piano, and with one manual for the piano only at the opposite end. Another Augsburg maker, Joseph Senft, thought to have been a pupil of Stein's, brought out his own *vis-à-vis* a little later. Also in 1777, Robert Stoddard patented a harpsichord-piano, the drawing for which shows for the first time details of the English grand action. A like combination was built by Hoffmann of Gotha in 1779, furnished with a coupler—a return to the principle of the old claviorganum, as it were.

Merlin left an elaborate instrument dated 1780, now in Munich, with single manual for both harpsichord and piano, the latter with downstriking hammers; the jacks plucked $1 \times 16'$, $1 \times 8'$, and $1 \times 4'$, and the hammers struck $1 \times 16'$ and $2 \times 8'$ (there are four sets of strings all told). In addition to this, an automatic notation device is attached to the instrument. A year later, Pehr Lindholm of Stockholm introduced his *Crescendo* with no fewer than fifty-five variations of tone. By 1783 the harpsichord and piano maker, Gottlieb Friedrich Riedeln of Bonn, was also producing combination instruments, according to the *Magazin der Musik* of that year. In the next decade, in 1792, the London organ builder, James Davies, combined an upper manual for piano with a lower manual for harpsichord, and during the same year John Geib invented a two-manual clavichord-piano or spinet-piano, the drawings for which show a combination clavichord-piano. Elias Schlegel of Altenburg likewise "invented" a harpsichord-piano combination called *Fortepiano-clavier* in 1794. As late as 1861 the lyro-pianoforte of Thomas Worton in England combined jack and hammer actions by affixing a jack directly to each hammer so that either could be played independently.

Undoubtedly many other makers also produced instruments of this type to accommodate performers wishing to have both the old and the new instrument at their disposal during the period of transition, and the above catalog may serve as an indication of the measure of their popularity. Such combinations were probably less expensive than two separate instruments would have been, and certainly took up only half the space.

TANGENT PIANOS

The English word "tangent," when applied to a keyboard chordophone, denotes the striking mechanism of a clavichord—a slender blade of metal affixed upright to a key. In German the word *Tangente* was formerly used in a far wider sense and covered both fixed and loose vertical members of metal or of wood, set at the rear of a key, and thus the term included clavichord tangents, harpsichord jacks, and the action components of several experimental or short-lived instruments including the *Tangentenflügel*, or tangent piano. This was an eighteenth-century creation of Franz Jacob Spaeth of Regensburg, with the shape of a grand piano or harpsichord, as its name indicates, and a characteristic action: a free "tangent" similar to a harpsichord jack, leathered top and bottom, rested on a lever at the end of each key; it was held in place by a harpsichord-style slide. When a key was depressed the corresponding lever propelled the tangent upward against the (bichord) strings. The keyboard could be shifted for an *una corda* stop by means of a knee lever, with a second knee lever raising the dampers to form a *forte* stop.

Although invention of the *Tangentenflügel* is attributed to Spaeth, the action as such was not new in his day. Schroeter's pianoforte, built in 1739, had had a similar action, with tangents about the thickness of harpsichord jacks, capped with leather, and to which dampers were attached; and then Weltmann in Paris had submitted to the Académie in 1759 a combination harpsichord and tangent-action piano; and to go back even further, Cuisinié in 1708 had made a clavichord-shaped instrument with tangent action (see pianoforte, page 321).

In the development of keyboard instruments, the tangent piano appears as an intermediary, or perhaps it is more accurate to say a compromise, between harpsichord and piano actions, for the structure was that of a harpsichord, stringing and scale those of a piano (a late *Tan-*

gentenflügel in the Neupert collection has virtually the same scale as that of a Johann Heinrich Silbermann grand piano of 1776 in Berlin); the old jacks are now replaced by far simpler tangents, but the old jack-slide is retained; the strings are struck from below by the top of the tangent, but, unlike those of a clavichord, they are released immediately, so that the string remains free to vibrate. Both in its day and in modern times its tone quality has been greatly praised, and dynamic variation could be obtained by changes of pressure on the keys, which in turn controlled the force with which the tangents were impelled against the strings.

Spaeth took his son-in-law, Christoph Friedrich Schmahl, into partnership, and from 1774 on the firm name appears as Spaeth and Schmahl; all extant instruments date from these partnership days. They enjoyed a short-lived popularity in the late eighteenth and early nineteenth centuries—the Leipzig University collection even contains an Italian harpsichord rebuilt into a tangent piano. Other makers imitated Spaeth and Schmahl's instruments at the end of the century, and a more complicated tangent action was patented in 1787 by Humphrey Walton; his model, of grand piano form, contained a piano action in which hammers were employed to propel the tangents against the strings. A claviorganum comprising tangent piano and organ is preserved in the Bachhaus of Eisenach.

SUSTAINING PIANOS

A criticism frequently leveled against the piano, both in the eighteenth and in the nineteenth centuries, was its lack of sustaining power, and many attempts were made to obviate this shortcoming. One of the earliest means resorted to for prolonging the tone was transferral of the clavichord's *Bebung*, which Friderici of Gera succeeded in accomplishing in 1770, if not a little earlier. In one form or another, this idea was taken up by one maker after the other: the *Bebung* was imitated by hammers repeating so rapidly that they created a tremolo. An action with rapidly repeating hammers was patented in England in 1800 by Isaac Hawkins (on behalf of his son John Isaac Hawkins, then in the United States). Throughout the nineteenth century and into the twentieth, makers sporadically took up this same idea, with the sustaining device consisting as a rule of a second set of small hammers placed over the regular hammers, suspended from a bar, and kept in motion by a fly wheel controlled by a pedal. Henri Herz of Paris marketed a similar contrivance, but with hammers controlled by clockwork.

Jean-Henri Pape, also of Paris, went a step further by abolishing the piano and retaining the *sostinente*, so to speak, in a series of patents taken out from 1824 on: he did away with strings altogether and substituted coiled metal springs, while hammers were made to repeat by means of a pinned cylinder.

Other systems included those of Jacob Alexandre of Paris, who combined his free reeds with a piano in order to prolong the latter's sound, calling his creation *piano à prolongement* (this was actually a claviorganum, and it is likely that many other nineteenth-century claviorgana were constructed for the same purpose). Jean-Louis Boisselot of Marseilles tried to obtain the same effect by building a piano in 1843 with five strings to a key, three at unison pitch and two tuned an octave higher that could be struck or not, at the discretion of the player. Early in the present century German makers experimented with an extra set of strings, shorter and pitched an octave higher than the main body of strings, placed above the latter but untouched by the hammer; their sympathetic resonance, undamped, was to add both to the brilliance of tone and to augment the sustaining power.

PEDALBOARD PIANOS

Pianos with independent pedalboards were made from the eighteenth century on, at first to permit pianists to play transcriptions of organ music or arrangements of symphonies, overtures, and so on. Action and strings were housed in boxes that followed the outline of the grand piano under which they were placed and from which the pedalboard projected. Such pedals were in effect separate and independent instrumental entities. The earliest of these had a two-octave compass and were pitched at 16' tone. Mozart had such a pedal built in 1785, when Leopold Mozart wrote to Nannerl of the large and extremely heavy pedal set under the piano from which it projected by about two feet. A concert was given in Leipzig in 1806 on such a "pedal." Usually, however, their function was that of practice instrument for organists, and in 1817 a *piano organistico* was devised by the Abbate Gregorio Trentino of Venice, its two-octave pedalboard furnished with two choirs of strings at 8' and one at 4' pitch.

A different type of pedalboard piano, no longer with independent pedal instrument, was that of a piano with pedalboard and abstracts for activating an extra set of hammers in the piano itself; these struck the piano's regular bass strings. Johann Andreas Stein left such an instrument from the year 1778.

A third type, for which patents were taken out from 1825 on, had a simple pedalboard connected by pulldowns to the piano keys, an idea taken from the organ, and occasionally upright pianos were also combined in this manner, without independent strings or hammers. Louis Schoene constructed pedalboard pianos in Leipzig in 1843 for both Robert Schumann and Felix Mendelssohn; that for Mendelssohn was to be used in conjunction with a grand piano, that of Schumann in connection with an upright; it called for a special action to be placed in back of the upright, with a separate soundboard to carry twenty-nine courses of strings for as many pedal keys. Both Érard and Pleyel built pedalboard pianos in Paris in the mid-nineteenth century. None of these types must be confused with the piano-organ combinations (for which, see claviorganum, page 301).

ENHARMONIC PIANOS

Tunings, their mathematics, and their amelioration had preoccupied musicians, instrument makers, and theorists alike ever since the early Renaissance, and the devising and demonstrating of new tuning principles gathered momentum from the latter part of the eighteenth century on, when a number of keyboard instruments were produced specifically for such purposes. Enharmonic harpsichords (see page 287) were succeeded by enharmonic pianos, until these in turn gave way to the enharmonic harmonium.

The earliest in a series of enharmonic pianos was the telio-chordon of Charles Claggett, patented in 1788, with thirty-nine microtones to the octave, thereby permitting the "temperature of all thirds and fifths" to be improved and eliminating the "wolf" tone. His thirty-nine microtones were for a closed octave, as his arrangement called for the control of three microtones by each key, through two additional mobile bridges; when these were brought into play the strings were retuned by means of a pedal, as on a harp. Two decades later, in 1808, William Hawkes added seven diatonic and five accidental tones per octave to obtain an enharmonic scale (it was a forerunner of the quarter-tone piano) with extra bichord strings controlled by a pedal; as this is said to have shifted the keyboard forward and backward, his must have been a square piano. A patent taken out in the following year called for twelve additional courses of strings and no fewer than six pedals. Finally, Roller et Blanchet of Paris constructed an enharmonic piano by 1866 for Bottée de Toulmon, an experimental instrument with two keyboards and a two-octave compass.

PLAYER PIANOS

The barrel organ's great success prompted piano makers in the early nineteenth century to imitate it, replacing organ pipes with piano strings; thus barrel pianos were actually the earliest form of mechanically played pianos. The pinned cylinder of the barrel organ was retained, set in motion by a hand crank. Dampers were lacking, and the weak treble section was reinforced by adding a fourth string to each course. Made at first in upright form, such pianos were mounted on little wheeled carts and played on the streets of English and Continental towns by street "musicians." They were made in Spain and Italy into the twentieth century and are often misnamed hand organ.

A totally new approach was that calling for attachments or devices for mechanically depressing the keys of certain keyboard instruments, starting in the mid-nineteenth century with those imagined for organs and harmoniums; these were subsequently adapted to the piano (cf. the "dumb organist," *sub* barrel organ). Essentially the problem was one of transferring the pneumatic organ action to a piano. The first piano players were separate cabinets set in front of the keyboard, hand-cranked, that depressed the keys by fingerlike levers. Later the mechanism was incorporated into the instrument proper, with the pneumatic action controlled by perforated paper rolls. Such was, for instance, the *pianista*.

An automatic player attachment was brought out by Alexandre-François Debain of Paris in 1846, intended for use in small churches and consequently called *antiphonel*. He pinned the music on an oblong board (the *planchette*) set with metal pegs; once the device was set in motion by a hand crank, the pegs engaged jacks that depressed the keys. Debain then adapted the *antiphonel* for application to cottage pianos and showed it in London in 1851; the device fitted on top of a piano, its music still pinned on a *planchette*. A year later, Martin de Corteuil patented a perforated paper strip to replace the *planchette*. A popular attachment was the *pianista*, patented by Fourneaux of Paris in 1863, which was in the form of a cabinet from which a set of horizontal levers extended; these depressed the appropriate keys, driven by a hand crank turned by the player's left hand, while his right hand controlled the dynamics.

Pneumatic self-playing pianos were built from 1880 on, but the older attachments continued to be manufactured; thus the *mélotrope*, a hand-cranked version, was patented by J. Carpentier in 1884, and even the renowned pianola was first made separately from the piano. The first automatic piano was brought out in 1880 by Needham & Sons of New York, built by R. W. Pain and Henry Kuster, either with or without an electric motor permanently installed in the interior of the piano, as well as a pneumatic mechanism operating upon the rear ends of the keys or, alternately, a treadle-worked exhaust bellows. A combination automatic piano and reed organ was patented in 1896.

The following year, the engineer Edwin S. Votley applied for a patent for his pianola, which was granted in 1900. Made at first as a separate entity, "pianola" was actually the trade name of a device manufactured by the Aeolian Piano Company of New York, but its popularity was such that it later came to denote any automatically played piano with a pneumatic system. It enjoyed a great vogue for decades, but, when the company tried to revive it after the Second World War, the effort met with no success, and production was discontinued in 1951. Several other manufacturers, both in the United States and in Europe, brought out pneumatic pianos. The Welte company in Germany started production of player pianos in 1904; their Welte-Mignon was well accepted on both continents.

Prior to 1898 all player actions were constructed to play only sixty-five keys of the piano's total of eighty-eight, but after that date they were extended to incorporate the entire compass. The 1928 American supplement to Grove's *Dictionary of Music and Musicians* lists no fewer than thirty-nine player mechanisms in production in the United States alone at that time, and adds that numerous additional types were known merely by the name of the firms employing them. But development of the phonograph effectively killed this widespread and highly lucrative production.

LYRES

In the wider, organological sense of the word, lyres are chordophones whose strings are attached to a yoke on the same plane as the resonator, the yoke consisting of two arms and a crossbar (in contradistinction to the harp, whose strings lie on a plane different from that of the resonator); they lack a neck. In the narrower sense, the term is applied to the Greek *lyra*.

Lyres are either bowl or box lyres, the former having a natural or artificially hollowed bowl as resonator and a membrane belly, whereas the resonator of box lyres is a built-up wooden box having a wooden soundboard. The two types are exemplified by the *lyra* and the *kithara* of ancient Greece. Box lyres of ancient Mesopotamia and Egypt, as well as those of modern Africa, tend to an asymmetrical design with arms of unequal length set at different angles in relation to the resonator.

LYRES IN ANTIQUITY

MESOPOTAMIA

Of the two forms, the box lyre is the elder. It first appears in Sumer about 3000 B.C., its earliest representation so far known being that on a seal from Farra of that time. Early Sumerian lyres are invariably shown held in a vertical position, whether they are being played or merely carried; they were large, cumbersome instruments, asymmetrical, the yoke having two straight, divergent arms, one longer than the other. Resonators were adorned (or consecrated?) with the figure of a bull or bull's head placed at the juncture of resonator and right arm, facing outward. From eight to twelve strings were fastened in a bunch on the lower left of the resonator, fanning out to the crossbar, to be plucked with the bare fingers of both hands. The effect of this diagonal pull on the strings of early instruments produced the distortion seen on unrestored museum instruments, and may have been responsible for subsequent structural modifications. Perhaps this early diagonal stringing of the lyre denotes a common origin with, or even a derivation from, the harp; the very early Megiddo harplike chordophone is suggestive of such a genesis.

However, on a relief from Telloh of the twenty-third century B.C., the strings apparently are vertical, no longer slanted.

We are fortunate in that excavations at the royal cemetery of Ur produced a total of eight actual lyres or fragments of lyres. From these we know that Sumerian lyres were large indeed—three of those excavated measure over 1 meter (40 inches) in height, the biggest 120 centimeters (ca. 47 inches). In one of the royal burials three lyres were found that had actually been played: the players' fingers were still touching their strings. The resonators were adorned with figures of bull, heifer, and stag. Such instruments correspond to those described in contemporary texts as employed in temple services; in dedication texts it is usually the bull that is brought into relationship with the lyre, and thus the sound of the lyre is likened to the roar of the bull. Bulls—sacred from India to Iberia in prehistoric times—not only lent their voice to the lyre but to other instruments as well (cf. the making of Sumerian temple drums, page 147).

In some instances the resonator itself becomes a bull, the projecting head its logical termination; this is clearly hinted on a plaque from Ur now in the Philadelphia University Museum. Two of the Ur lyres had eleven strings, another an estimated eight, yet another ten or eleven. Tuning rods for a silver lyre were found there *in situ*. On these lyres tuning was effected by winding each string around a small rod or stick tangential to the crossbar, and then winding it around the crossbar; the position of the stick against the crossbar (i.e., tension) could be regulated by displacing it slightly (later, as in Greece, the rods were to be replaced by tuning rings of leather).

Such giant instruments proved unwieldy in the long run, and were succeeded in Babylonian times by a smaller model, easier to hold. A relief of about 1700 B.C. in the Berlin Museum shows such a lyre played in horizontal position, with crossbar held away from the body and with gracefully curving (no longer straight) arms. Small rectangular and relatively primitive lyres, with perhaps five strings and lacking the bull's head, are illustrated in connection with both civil and domestic events. From Assyria come two cylinder seals of about 1900–1800 B.C., showing lyres, one with straight arms of unequal length and diagonal crossbar, the longer arm nearest the player, and with a rectangular resonator. Not only is the Sumerian type of asymmetrical lyre with its oblique yoke that holds strings of slightly uneven lengths representative of Assyria, but also of Phoenicia and of Asia Minor generally.

SYRIA, PALESTINE, AND PHOENICIA

From Mesopotamia the lyre proceeded west through Syria and Palestine into Egypt. A Carchemish seal of about 2000 B.C. shows an asymmetrical lyre with four strings, attesting to its presence in Syria at an early date, and a century later, about 1900, a lyre depicted on the walls of an Egyptian tomb at Beni Hasan is in the hands of one of the alien peoples represented, in this case presumably a Syrian or Hebrew. Here we see for the first time a lyre plucked with a plectrum; it is entirely symmetrical, with slightly curved arms of equal length, and is held horizontally, with the bottom of the resonator against the player's body, crossbar facing ahead; his left hand appears to be damping the strings, an easy undertaking, as they are all bunched close together on one plane. From Megiddo in Palestine we have an ivory of the thirteenth century B.C. showing an asymmetrical nine-stringed lyre played by a woman; she is holding her instrument horizontally, the longer of the curved arms uppermost, with crossbar horizontal. A painted pottery jar from the next century, also from Megiddo, shows a lyre with but four strings and the crossbar slanting steeply from longer to shorter arm. A heart-shaped lyre with extremely small body is held upright by a woman player on an early Phoenician terra-cotta; the same shape is met with on Crete.

Our main sources of knowledge of the music and musical practices of the ancient Hebrews are the Bible and the Talmudic commentaries. Among the instruments of the Hebrews' nomadic period was the *kinnōr* (a word cognate with the Egyptian *knr*) in use for the accompaniment of singers and now identified as a box lyre. Later we hear that the Temple orchestra included nine or more lyres. Actually the word seems to have been used both as a generic term for all chordophones and to designate the lyre in particular; the Septuagint translates it as *kinyra, psaltērion,* and the Vulgate (ca. 400) renders it as *cithara.* It was the "harp" of King David. Some Hebrew coins struck during the second century B.C. portray lyres with three, four, five, and seven strings —more often four—with arms clearly made of animal horn (or its imitation in wood). Resonators of the Hebrew instruments were of wood, the strings of sheep gut; when accompanying dances the lyres were played with a plectrum, otherwise with bare fingers (dances would demand a more staccato attack and greater volume than other types of performance—cf. the roles of harpsichord versus organ in sixteenth-century Europe). Flavius Josephus (b. A.D. 37) wrote that the *kinnōr* had ten strings and was played with a plectrum. Its pitch was higher than that of the contemporary harp, for we know its strings were thinner. In late reproductions the *kinnōr* comes to resemble the classical *kithara*.

The western Hittite site of Karatepe has yielded reliefs tentatively dated from the late eighth or early seventh century B.C. On one of these a banquet scene with musicians is depicted. Two of the four players hold lyres—but basically different instruments. The first is the Mesopotamian square-resonator type with diagonal crossbar, the second a Mediterranean form with rounded resonator, horizontal crossbar, and strings bunched close together. The former appears to have seven strings, those of the latter are unidentifiable.

EGYPT

Lyres came to Egypt from the north, making an isolated appearance in the above-mentioned tomb painting of Beni Hasan under Amenemhet II (1938–1903 B.C.) of the Twelfth Dynasty. During the early dynastic period Egypt knew relatively few musical instruments, and not until the reign of Thutmose III (1501–1447 B.C.) in the Eighteenth Dynasty, after the Hyksos invasions and subsequent foreign wars in Palestine, Phoenicia, and Syria (and reaching as far as the Euphrates), was musical tradition broken and lyre, lute, and frame drum followed south in the wake of the girl slave trade. From then on, until it disappears in Alexandrian times, the Egyptian lyre is played standing or walking, but always by women. It is an asymmetrical instrument, held horizontally with longer arm on top, the strings virtually of the same length. Also, from the beginning of the Eighteenth Dynasty we find animal heads adorning the ends of the crossbar or the arms—clearly another importation from the north. During the reign of Ikhnaton (1375–1358 B.C.) huge lyres appear, symmetrical forms during that of Ramses II (1292–1225 B.C.). As a rule, the large lyres that prevailed until about 1000 B.C. were held horizontally with crossbar away from the player; when a smaller model came into use thereafter, with parallel arms, it was held upright. During the New Kingdom the number of strings varied considerably: seven, eight, nine, ten, thirteen, and fifteen have been ascertained.

With a single exception, Egyptian lyres never had rounded resonators, the exception being one shown on a stele from Kom Firim in the Nile

Delta, dating from the Twenty-second Dynasty (945–745 B.C.); its arms
and the nine strings diverge. From the numerous and detailed portrayals
of musical performances, and from present-day playing techniques of
lyres in Nubia—direct descendants of those of ancient Egypt—we find
that the lyre was plucked with a long plectrum held in the right hand,
all the strings being struck with a sweeping movement while the left
hand silenced those that were unwanted (this identical method can be
observed on a Greco-Roman statuette). But, during the many centuries
in which lyres were played in Egypt, they never received a name of their
own and were designated as *knr*. Indeed, late Egyptian lyres were even
Greek imports.

THE AEGEAN

Lyres of the Minoan culture never had the rectangular resonators of
Near Eastern and Egyptian instruments but adopted a rounded form.
Minoans also made use of ibex horns for the arms. Lyrelike instruments
had already appeared on Crete about 1850–1700 B.C.; a few are almost
cordiform. In the era of the new palaces, after the earthquake of about
1700, a lyre player is depicted on a seal from Knossos; here the resonator
is seen to continue so as to form the arms. On a painted sarcophagus
from the Hagia Triada (1500–1400 B.C.), now in the Heraklion Museum,
a seven-stringed "horseshoe" lyre is portrayed, carried in upright position; a bronze lyre player, also from Crete, dated between 900 and 700
B.C., holds at a slant a four-stringed instrument. On Cyprus a tenth-
century B.C. lyre seen on an amphora has but three strings and cordiform
resonator; a four-stringed instrument is shown in the ninth century, and
from the eighth century we have a bronze disk depicting a cult scene
with lyre, auloi, and round frame drum; the lyre is asymmetrical, has
six strings, and is held horizontally. Western Anatolia and the Sporades
in the eighth century knew lyres with resonators ovate at the bottom
and but three strings; however, by the next century their number is
increased to seven and the resonator is of horseshoe form. Only two
examples of seven-stringed lyres prior to 700 B.C. are known from this
area, but in Minoan Crete and mainland Mycenaean sites eight are
more common. Terpander of Lesbos (seventh century B.C.) was credited
with having added a seventh string to the extant six of his day, but in fact
he seems to have introduced and popularized the seven-stringed *kithara*
in replacement of a tetrachord instrument.

GREECE

Box lyres, later to be called *kitharas*, appear on the Greek mainland in the second millennium B.C., toward the end of the Mycenaean era. Segments of several ivory lyres dating between 1400 and 1100 have been excavated, grave goods one and all, not built to be played. A horseshoe-shaped lyre is shown on the so-called singer's fresco of the Pylos palace, its resonator and arms apparently made of a single piece. After the collapse of Mycenaean culture there is a gap until the late geometric period, followed by sparse renderings on pottery of rather crudely drawn *kitharas* presumed to be of the ninth or eighth centuries; their resonators are semicircular. Figures of lyres resume again in the mid-eighth century with several shapes portrayed, all with rounded bottoms; sometimes the resonator is so diminished as to have no greater width than the arms, and assumes the form of a horseshoe. These have four strings and are believed to represent the *phorminx* of Homer.

The eventful seventh century saw the appearance of the plectrum-played seven-stringed *kithara*, thought to have entered the mainland from the Cyclades (as noted above, Terpander of Lesbos is credited by tradition with its introduction about 670), as well as the square-bottomed *kithara*, and the true *lyra*.

The *lyra* appears on an early seventh-century Orientalizing hydria, with small, round body, five strings, and straight diverging arms obviously of wood; it is held tilted. During the classical period it had a resonator of tortoiseshell or its imitation in wood (Pausanias writes that the tortoises used for lyre backs came from Mount Parthenion in Argolis), a skin belly, and two curved arms made of animal horn (probably from the sixth century on), later of wood. Herodotus (*Histories* IV) points to the oryx—a long-haired antelope—as the source (the word "oryx" literally means "to pick at," from the animal's pointed horns). A low bridge raised the strings off the belly of both *lyra* and *kithara*. Of simpler construction, the *lyra* became the instrument of amateurs as opposed to the professionally played *kithara*, and was not taken over by the Romans, although they adopted the box lyre. According to Greek tradition, the *lyra* came from Thrace and was considered an autochthonous, indeed, a national instrument; but a Near Eastern origin is generally postulated today. In the sixth century eight strings are met with on both *kithara* and *lyra*, and thereafter the number increases greatly, with from eight to twelve present in the fifth century.

The classical *kithara* achieved its final form in the sixth century; it had a square, flat box resonator of wood, and two symmetrical, thick, hollow arms connected by a crossbar. The strings, of equal length but of different tensions and probably varying slightly in thickness, were of gut and were always sounded by a plectrum. A heavy, cumbersome instrument, it was held upright when played—in contrast to the tilted *lyra*—while its weight was partly supported by resting against the player's body and partly by a band passing from his left wrist or over his shoulder and attached to the far end of the *kithara*, thus leaving the hand free to damp the strings. The *kollops* mentioned by several writers of antiquity was a small piece of thick bull- or sheepskin, a tuning ring wound around the crossbar, and around which in turn a string was tightly wound. Each *kollops* could then be turned sufficiently to adjust the tuning of its string. A bronze mirror attributed to the fifth century illustrates Orpheus surrounded by a gathering of animals; he is tuning, his right hand in the act of turning one of the tuning rings, while his spread left hand tests the pitch. Crossbar terminals, usually in form of a knob, are seen on later *kitharas*; they are not tuning arrangements as has been claimed, but purely ornamental devices, possibly indicative of Ionian influence. Because the strings were under varying tensions it would have been impossible to tune all simultaneously by a simple turn of the crossbar; that they could have been "rough tuned," that is, brought up to approximate pitch by turning or raising the crossbar is, however, theoretically feasible, but there exists no evidence that this was ever done. In modern Ethiopia wooden pegs replace the *kollopes* of box lyres but serve the same purpose. During preclassical times the *kithara* was an instrument of bards, who accompanied their epic songs on it, but by the classical age it had become that of professional players, the *kitharōedoi*.

Lyras follow the development of the *kithara* with respect to the number of strings. The two instruments are found side by side on Greek vases, played indiscriminately by men or women. The *lyra* is rarely held upright, generally at a tilt, occasionally at a horizontal stance. After the primitive tortoiseshell carapace had been abandoned, resonators continued to resemble this material outwardly at least: a bronze resonator worked to imitate tortoiseshell was excavated at Kerch (Crimea), the ancient Panticapaeum, and vestiges of a Greek *lyra* in the British Museum show that a presumably wooden resonator was faced with tortoiseshell. The decision to abandon the carapace must have been an especially hard one to make, because according to myth Hermes himself had invented the *lyra*: early in life he came across the shell of a tortoise to which he added a cowhide belly and cowgut strings; although some say his lyre had seven strings, others claim it originally had but three, yet others, four, and that Apollo added the remainder.

Lyra and *kithara* shared the same playing technique, with extended left-hand fingers on the back of the strings and a long plectrum held in the right hand, a combination suggestive of the ancient Egyptian and modern Nubian mode of fanning over all the strings with a plectrum while those not needed were silenced by the left hand.

Another variety of bowl lyre found in ancient Greece was the *barbiton* or *barbitos*, of which we know little more than that it sounded an octave lower than the *pēktis* (a hitherto unidentified instrument) and was played with a plectrum. We may gather that it had long strings. From the late sixth century to the mid-fifth century B.C. an elegant, elongated form of *lyra* appears on vases, with very slender incurved arms, and several modern writers associate this form with the *barbitos*. Roman poets used the term rather loosely to denote any kind of chordophone; the Renaissance applied it to the archlute—we read of *doulx barbitons* in this sense in sixteenth-century France.

Pictorially we can follow the *kithara*—but not the *lyra*—through Hellenistic and Roman times chronologically, and from Rome almost to the confines of her empire geographically. The *lyra* migrated to Etruria, however. Those of Etruscan tomb paintings of the fifth century have six or seven strings, heavy bridge clearly shown, and small body with long arms.

ROME

At the turn of the sixth to the fifth century the round-bottomed *kithara* appears, complete with plectrum, on the Roman peninsula. The *lyra* was at least known to the Romans, who appear to have played it little if at all, and is found chiefly on Greco-Roman funerary monuments. Nonetheless, the Romans called both instruments *testudo*, a translation of the Greek *chelys*, meaning "tortoise."

In Roman times the *kithara*—now *cithara*—became heavier, rectangular in form, overornamented, although a simple rectangular model is occasionally depicted in the hands of women players. Neither harp nor lyre could play an important role in the musical life of as martial a people as the Romans, and if the Greeks constituted preponderantly a "string audience," as we should say today, the Romans remained primarily a "wind audience." Pompeiian wall paintings include several *citharoedi*, some with plain, others with fanciful, instruments. Although most of the later models must have looked as tasteless in reality, to judge by contemporary comments, as their portrayals appear to us today, most of them seem organologically realistic. But in a Pompeiian wall painting Orpheus is seen playing an impossible *cithara*, its scythelike arms tilted to an angle that require the strings to cross before reaching the bridge.

Orpheus playing his lyre to assembled beasts is a subject encountered rather frequently in Roman art, from statue to hand mirror to coin, and the association of player surrounded by animals was transferred in the early days of Christianity to symbolize the figure of the Good Shepherd; as such, he appears in the Christian catacombs. His audience, which at the beginning contains a pair of lions, becomes reduced little by little to a flock of sheep, and Orpheus or the Good Shepherd then is metamorphosed into King David with his "harp." In the Christian era the *cithara* continued to be depicted both in Rome and throughout the empire: on a third-century sarcophagus from Rome an instrument of classical form has strings held firmly by tuning rods rather than by the usual *kollopes*—perhaps a back formation, probably a link to the future, for when the rod is inserted in the wood instead of abutting it, the mobile tuning peg is born.

EUROPE

Lyres were known outside Greece and the Italian peninsula in the Hallstatt age. On an incised urn from a grave at Marz near Sopron (Ödenburg), Hungary, of about 650 B.C. can be seen a primitive four-stringed upright *kithara*, and another two, less well defined, held horizontally. Further north, a grave near Klein-Glein in the Sulm valley, Styria, tentatively dated from the fifth century B.C., contained a bronze citula with a lyre player holding an enormous four-stringed *kithara* in horizontal position. An easterly trade route, and a more familiar one, no doubt, led to Spain, where a fifth-century B.C. pottery goblet depicts a seated girl playing the lyre (the Greek colony of Massilia, the present-day Marseilles, had been founded about 600 B.C.).

Still further removed in space but within the realm of historical possibility is the occurrence of a north European lyre: Diodorus Siculus (first century B.C.) quotes a tantalizing passage from Hecataeus of Miletus, who lived in the late sixth and early fifth centuries B.C.; Hecataeus, whose works survive only in fragments, recounts that beyond the land of the Celts, that is, Gaul, there lies an island inhabited by Hyperboreans; this contains a spherical temple sacred to Apollo. Furthermore, the majority of the inhabitants played the *kithara* continuously in the temple and sang hymns of praise. Before dismissing this story as pure myth, it should be recalled that Hecataeus is said to have obtained some of his material from explorers such as the Carthaginians Hanno and Hamilco, and that Hamilco had explored some of the northern shores of Europe. It is tempting to see a description of Stonehenge in its glory, with lyre-playing Druids, but historians and prehistorians alike are just as willing to place the home of the Hyperboreans in southern Scandinavia, despite the fact that grave goods retrieved from Stonehenge cemeteries reveal that the inhabitants traded with the Mycenaean world—and the date is too late by far.

Diodorus also relates—on his own authority—that the bards of Gaul sang to an instrument resembling the lyre (*hi cum organis veluticum lyra cantant*) in his day. Here he is corroborated by Ammianus Marcellinus in the fourth century A.D., who also records their lyre playing. We know from the relief of a Roman musician's sarcophagus at Arles from this period that the classical form of *kithara* was still in use in southern France then. From the same century we have Thracian coins on which the figure of a *kithara*-playing Orpheus is struck, a relief from Enns (the ancient Lauriacum) in Austria with Orpheus playing a five-stringed *kithara*, and another Orpheus, also with a five-stringed instrument, from Dunapentele (the ancient Intercissa), Hungary: all Roman-style instruments. Yet another Orpheus holding a three-stringed *kithara* appears on a Roman mosaic from the Isle of Wight of this time, and the fifth-century poet-bishop Apollinaris Sidonius, a native of Lyons, also knew a three-stringed version. The mid-sixth-century lyre remnants found in 1935 at Abingdon, Berkshire, have provision for three strings.

Around the year 500 Clovis, king of the Franks, requested his brother-in-law, the Ostrogoth king Theodoric, to send him from Italy a *citharoede*; this is the last mention of the *kithara* in the classical sense of the word; shortly thereafter the name began to be transferred to several chordophones having a neck. But lyres were to remain symbols of classical culture, and in the sixth century the poet Venantius Fortunatus contrasted past with present when he wrote, a little wistfully perhaps:

> *Romanusque lyra plaudat tibi, barbarus harpa*
> *Graecus achilliaca, chrotta Britanna canat*

And if the Council of Cloveshoe in 747 mentions poets, a *citharista*, musicians, and jesters together, it is likely that a chordophone other than the lyre was meant, for the latter would not have been associated with jesters.

MEDIEVAL LYRES

Post-classical lyres were to assume a number of forms as they spread through Europe, thereby giving rise to many interesting if unconfirmed theories regarding their genesis and diffusion. Prior to 1000, the area of their distribution encompassed at least Britain, France, Germany, Scandinavia, Finland, and Estonia. Thanks to a number of instruments or parts of instruments recovered from excavations, we can follow their evolution during much of that period.

Two lyres from the sixth or seventh century have been found at Oberflacht in Württemberg: one measures 80.5 centimeters (ca. 32 inches) with a maximum width of 20.5 centimeters (ca. 8 inches), had six strings, and was made of a piece of hollowed-out oak with separate crossbar. The aperture between arms, resonator, and crossbar forms an elongated V, the instrument itself an elongated rectangle. Another lyre was retrieved from the arms of a male skeleton in a warrior's grave near Lupfenberg, again with provision for six strings, and of the same shape as the others, its crossbar also made separately, and of about the same age. A Frankish lyre of the early eighth century, formerly in Cologne but destroyed during World War II, had resonator, arms, and crossbar all carved from a single piece of wood, and six strings. Was it instruments such as these that the "kithara"-bearing Slav prisoners from the Baltic took to Thrace with them in the year 591, as recorded by the Byzantine Theophylaktos Simokattes? Two bridges, one of bone, another of amber, both flat, for a six- and a seven-stringed lyre, respectively, and both dating from the eighth century, are the only remains of chordophones from pre-Christian Sweden found so far.

These materials permit us to make comparisons with the lyres of antiquity: excavated early medieval specimens were made of a block of oak three to four centimeters thick—resonator and arms of one piece—with an inserted "crossbar," the latter no longer a rod but thickened and shaped to form the top. The oak block was hollowed and fitted with a thin wooden belly. In length these lyres varied from 40 to 80 centimeters (16 to 32 inches); their stringing method differed fundamentally from that of antiquity in that tuning pegs were inserted into the top in holes drilled from front to back, replacing the antique system of tuning rings and rods. A short projection at the bottom of the resonator served to secure the lower end of the strings (this device is also found on modern Ethiopian lyres). Broader but otherwise similar in structure is a five-stringed lyre, being held by King David enthroned, depicted in a northern Italian psalter of the late tenth century (Munich cod. lat. 343): David holds a plectrum in one hand, his tuning hammer in the other; his throne itself forms a giant lyre, but by contrast to the instrument he holds this takes the form of a classical *kithara*, as though the illuminator had had qualms about his concession to the modernity of the lyre in David's hands. Two Anglo-Saxon manuscripts of the early eighth and of the ninth centuries, respectively, show realistic rectangular lyres made of a single block of wood, with rounded tops and bottoms. The aperture between yoke and resonator is now greatly diminished; plectra are still in use, and all the strings are apparently being damped by the player's spread fingers. One of the instruments clearly has five strings; both are held in front of the body and resting on the player's knees, at a slight tilt, a position to be retained until the introduction of the bow.

The ninth-century French psalter now preserved at Utrecht and hence known as the Utrecht Psalter presents a curious medley of antique and contemporary features. Three types of lyre are portrayed, all based on forms of the ancient *kithara* and *lyra*: one resembles the *barbitos* except for the arms curving inward to join at the top, thus doing away with the crossbar; the player is grasping it at the top in a manner to be seen during the next three centuries in connection with other plucked and even bowed lyres. The second type is an elongated form of *kithara*, and might be contemporary if its arms turned inward instead of outward, for it has unmistakable tuning pins set in the crossbar; it terminates in a short stand, a charming fiction to be reinvented in the late fifteenth century by Filippino Lippi, and again—no longer fiction—by makers of the nineteenth-century lyre-guitars. The third type is no less than a straight-armed *kithara*, sounded to the accompaniment of two outsized pairs of crotals. In this, as in all other psalters, commentaries, and analogous religious texts, the artist's choice of material was limited by the wording of the text he was to illustrate, which accounts for the repeated occurrence of the same musical instruments connected with, for example, the Psalms. As the Latin terms for antique and obsolete or obsolescent instruments continued to be used, their significance was gradually lost and the old word was bestowed on a new instrument or on one whose name was unknown (the harp became *psalterium*, as did the lyre, which had been *cithara*), and, with the introduction of vernacular terms or of new instruments, confusion was compounded. In pictorial materials this procedure resulted either in an evocation of the past or in a combination of old and new such as, for example, the near-classical *kithara* seen in an eleventh-century Catalonian psalter, but with tuning pins and tuning hammer and resonator terminating in the same type of stand as that of the Utrecht Psalter.

Another ninth-century document, the archaizing Bible of Charles the Bald, must be mentioned for its illustration of a "fingerboard" lyre; all its strings are bunched together, passing over a narrow upward continuation of the resonator that divides the single space normally enclosed by the yoke into two spaces, thereby creating what looks like a fingerboard. Such a portrayal must derive ultimately from a misunderstanding of materials, based on Greco-Roman sarcophagi where *kithara* strings are rendered in stone *en bloc*, taking the form of a thin panel in the center of the arm-enclosed space (as, for example, on the Vienna Giustiniani Sarcophagus, formerly in Rome).

With the advent of the eleventh century, lyres undergo modifications leading to new forms: that of the fingerboard, the waisted, and the figure-of-eight lyres. The last of these appears to have been a short-lived development that took place in the Germanic countries, while the two former types were more generally distributed and longer lasting. All three were bowed, although lyres with and without fingerboard continued to be plucked. However, plucked varieties did not survive the Middle Ages.

Bowed lyres represent the final stage in the development of this ancient instrument. They first appeared in the early eleventh century and disappeared by the fifteenth, except in Wales, Scandinavia, Finland, and Estonia, pushed back by the ubiquitous fiddle. As folk instruments they are still bowed in "pockets" of Finland and Estonia. The three new forms arose simultaneously, undoubtedly in response to the introduction of the bow from the East and also to the specific requirements—structural or ornamental—of each area. Because bowed instruments require strings to be under greater tension than plucked ones, the lyre's frame had to be strengthened: the former yoke was enlarged and became more massive, the open area it enclosed was considerably diminished, ultimately becoming no more than a handhole (when this transformation was completed the lyre became a bowed psaltery). Furthermore, if all the strings are to be reached by the bow they must be bunched close together, at least at the bridge.

Considerable experimentation is evident from the various models depicted from the turn of the tenth to eleventh centuries: the bowed figure-of-eight form with its strange elongation—the length equals three times the maximum width—usually lacking a fingerboard, may not have been able to stand the extra strain imposed by the bow, for it soon disappears (but cf. the figure-of-eight fiddle, page 474); three such instruments of different sizes are figured in an eleventh-century German psalter at Klosterneuburg, with upper sections as large as the lower, and all three held in different positions: our earliest evidence of bowed chordophones built in a consort. A huge plucked figure-of-eight lyre with pronounced fingerboard appears in wood carvings of Hylestad Church, Norway, executed about 1175–1200, illustrating the story of Gunnar. The so-called round lyre was also in eight form, but squatter and with lower section larger than the upper, a plucked variety, bridgeless as far as we can tell, and quite frequently depicted. Such an instrument was copied from a now-destroyed thirteenth-century codex at Saint Blasius by Gerbert (1774), rare because it is inscribed *cythara teutonica*. It shows seven strings and no bridge, but it does show a tailpiece.

By now, differentiation along regional lines was taking place, particularly in those outlying regions where bowed lyres were to survive beyond the Middle Ages: Wales with its crwth (see page 374), the Scandinavian countries, Finland, and the coastal areas and islands of Estonia that were settled not later than the thirteenth century by Swedes. Our pictorial materials can be supplemented by the so far unique artifact we have from the later Middle Ages: a lyre and its bow excavated at Gdańsk (Dantzig) in 1949, dating from between 1255 and 1275. Made of a single block of wood some 40 centimeters (16 inches) long with straight sides, slightly trapezoidal, its diagonal top is bored from front to back with holes for five tuning pegs; the space between sides, top, and resonator—for we can no longer speak of a yoke—has been reduced in size to that of a circular handhole; it lacks a fingerboard. The lyre's state of preservation is such that even the remnants of a leather band were found attached to the front by a wooden nail. In form this is closer to the plucked *kantele* of Finland than any other bowed lyre, and probably represents the farthest development taken by the *kithara* of yore before its disappearance or transformation.

TUNINGS AND PLAYING TECHNIQUES

Early medieval plucked lyres had either five, six, or seven strings. As soon as the bow was applied to them they became fewer, with three or four the number most frequently seen in eleventh- and twelfth-century illustrations. Of these, only one was stopped, while the remainder acted as drones. Regardless of the presence or absence of the so-called fingerboard, that is, the central division of the upper section—actually a strut —the melody string was stopped by the player touching it tangentially either with the fingernail or with the fleshy part of the finger; it was never pressed against the central strut. This manner of playing is identical with that of the later northern European bowed lyres. In medieval illustrations the player's hand is seen reaching through the handhole or else around the instrument.

From the twelfth century on some bowed lyres appear with a greater number of strings—five or six—exceptionally even with nine; here it is believed that the strings may have been stopped. Bowed lyres are frequently seen rested against the chest, shoulder, or even chin, in contrast to plucked lyres, which were held in front of the body. We may thus safely conclude that, having taken over the bow from the medieval fiddle, the lyre also took over the latter's mode of playing, even to the point of discarding the strings it had in surplus to the fiddle. The oldest known fiddle tunings—those of Jerome of Moravia—agree with the oldest indications for tuning the *jouhikantele*. By adopting the bow, lyres were transformed into drone instruments. Thus the bowed lyres, fiddles, double pipes, organs, bagpipes, hurdy-gurdies, string drums, all testify to medieval man's predilection for a drone accompaniment to song or instrumental melody. With the development of organum into independent polyphony, drones were abolished or relegated to the realm of folk music, and the lyre had outlived its musical usefulness in art music.

ETYMOLOGY

Medieval literary sources are of little assistance to the historian concerned with the investigation of lyres because of the confusion in terminology. Clearest of the terms employed is the *lira* or *lire* of German literature. *Liren, harpfen, rotten* are often mentioned together in songs of the Minnesänger, and earlier, in the ninth century, Otfrid of Weissenburg wrote:

> *lira joh fidula*
> *joh managfaltu suegala*
> *harpha joh rotta* . . .

> lira and fiddle
> and several pipes
> harp and rote . . .

But later the *lira* becomes *Leir*, at a time when it can no longer pertain to the lyre, and we are left to surmise that it comes to designate the citole or even the lute or the harp.

Another name for the lyre was *chelys* ("tortoise"), a term employed not only in Greece but also in Rome, chiefly during the Christian era. At an early time this must have been translated into Old High German as *chrotta* or *hrotta*, tortoise (cf. the modern *Kröte*) and the cognate Old English *crud*, Old Irish *crot*, *cruit*, Kymric *crwth*, Old French *crouth*, leading to the medieval German *rotte*, modern English crowd or crowde, the troubadour's *rota* or *rote*, where, although the word forms used in the British Isles stand for the bowed lyre, on the Continent a different instrument was designated (see rote, page 215).

More difficult to decipher are the linguistic outgrowths of *kithara* (Latin, *cithara*). At a relatively early period this word came to designate any instrument with a neck. Our earliest source of this information known so far is al-Khwarizmi, who wrote in the tenth century that among the musical instruments of Byzantium there was a *qītāra* that resembled the *tunbūr*. This was a three-stringed, long-necked lute. In the thirteenth century one name of the harp was *cythara anglica* as opposed to the *cythara teutonica*, the lyre, and from then on *cythara* frequently denotes the harp. But in fourteenth-century France *cithara* is translated as *cithole*, and the French translator of Bartholomaeus Anglicus—presumably at a loss to understand a definition of Isidore's—renders *cythara barbarica* as *guisterne de barbarie,* or "gittern." In the end instruments with necks (i.e., the lute family in its wider, organological sense) prevail over the harps: guitar, *chitarrone, cetra, cistre,* and so on, are all philological derivatives.

POST-MEDIEVAL LYRES

THE CRWTH

Of the northern lyres that outlasted the Middle Ages the best known is probably the crwth. It did not disappear completely until the nineteenth century.

Its Kymric name is crwth, pronounced "crooth," plural crythau; its English name was crouth by 1310, crowd by the sixteenth century: one John Hogan was reprimanded in 1537 for "singing lewd ballads with a crowd or fyddyll" (although the reference here is probably to the rebec). Related word forms are the Old Irish *crot,* Gaelic *cruit,* Old High German *chrota* (all cognate with *rote,* see page 215). During the Middle Ages it was also known by the Latinized form *chorus.* In the twelfth century Gerard of Wales (Girardus Cambrensis) wrote that the *chorus* was in general use in Scotland and Wales, evidently a reference to the crwth, although *chorus* also designated other instruments at the time. Aimeri de Peyrac tells us in the fourteenth century that *chorus* had two pairs of strings tuned a fourth apart, presumably the same instrument seen on a seal dated 1316, once that of Roger Wade, a Welsh player, which shows a bow beside a fingerboard lyre with straight sides, rounded top and bottom, two soundholes near the lower end and—one judges— four strings. To the original four strings two more must have been added very early, for Welsh sources mention the crwth with its six strings as a bard's instrument from the eleventh century on, and a fifteenth-century poem specifically refers to the "two strings for the thumb."

After the sixteenth century the crwth is no longer mentioned in literature, and we lose trace of it until the eighteenth century, when it was rediscovered, then on the verge of extinction as but few people still knew how to play it. No crwth older than the eighteenth century has come down to us; the few examples that are preserved have an oblong body with flat belly and back, straight sides, closed at the top, handholes separated by a central fingerboard, and two circular holes cut in the belly; two off-board strings have been added to the four bowed ones, all of which are secured by rear pegs inserted in the top. The bridge is characteristically flat-topped, with one long foot reaching down through a soundhole to rest against the back, thus forming a combination bridge and soundpost; in order to shorten the scale of the treble strings it was set obliquely on the belly. Tunings and playing techniques that we know of derive from the eighteenth century when Daines Burnington, writing in *Archaeologia* III (1755), gave the tuning as $G°g'/c²c'd'd²$; another, dating from 1794, reads $g°g'/c²c'd'd²$—a more probable version of the earlier one—and a third is given in 1814 as $a°a'/e'e²b'b²$.

At this time the crwth was held almost in violin position, due presumably to the influence of the modern instrument. Both were of about the same size, but the crwth's open string length was close to that of a viola. One of the few genuine crwths left, now in the collection of the Gesellschaft der Musikfreunde in Vienna, is 60 centimeters (23½ inches) long, 29 centimeters (11½ inches) wide, and 6 centimeters (ca. 2⅜ inches) deep, with all six strings attached to a tailpiece, the two off-board drones set diagonally to the left of the fingerboard, hence independent of the stopping fingers, just as were those of the medieval fiddle. These off-board strings were bowed and could also be plucked by the player's thumb, thus explaining the passage from the fifteenth-century poem quoted above. Despite efforts to revive it the crwth became extinct by the nineteenth century, and today the word is used in Wales to denote any kind of stringed instrument.

NORTHEASTERN EUROPEAN LYRES

In relatively isolated areas of northeastern Europe the bowed lyre has fared a little better. In his distribution map for bowed lyres in northern countries, Otto Andersson, the late Finnish musicologist, showed a concentration immediately north and northeast of Lake Ladoga.

Probably the earliest record of a bowed lyre on Scandinavian territory is that of a twelfth-century stone carving at Trondhjem Cathedral, Norway, depicting a rectangular instrument, its handhole reduced to a mere slit in the upper left quadrant and what appear to be four strings; all are bowed and one is also being stopped. Substantially the same instrument, with its upper left slit and four strings, has been encountered in Finland under the name of *jouhikantele*; it rests on the player's right thigh while supported by his left in an upward slanting position. In the eighteenth century the *jouhikantele* had three horsehair strings tuned a fifth and a fourth apart (g° d' g'), later tuned in two fifths. During the latter part of the nineteenth century the number of strings was increased to five, and it seems that this increase caused the bow to be abandoned and the strings to be plucked. Further strings were added periodically—one specimen has as many as sixteen. Originally the few strings had been fastened to a horizontal string holder and led to tuning pegs inserted in the top.

Similar to the *jouhikantele* is the *tallharpa* of the Swedish settlements in Estonia with its very wide, often square, handhole. Formerly its three or four strings were of horsehair—a characteristic of northern chordophones—nowadays they are of gut or even metal; two are melody strings and the remainder are drones. The *eestikannel* found on Dagö Island, Estonia, up to the first quarter of this century differed from the *tallharpa* chiefly in having its body built up of slats and a horizontal crosspiece at the top; its four strings were tuned in fifths. Otto Andersson, the first investigator of northern bowed lyres, found that they had in common an almost rectangular body hollowed out of a block of wood or built up of thin slats, either a flat or rounded back, from two to four strings, a bridge, and a tailpiece. The upper section had one or two handholes; if two, these were separated by a longitudinal wooden division. The upper end was grasped by the player's left hand, the fingers passing through the handhole from the back; the strings were stopped tangentially either by the player's fingernails or by the upper part of the fingers. Those instruments having two handholes were played by moving the hand from one to the other during performance. Two-stringed varieties had a melody and a drone string, while those with three strings had two outer melody strings and a central drone; due to the looseness of the bow's hair and also to the flatness of the bridge, the drone always sounded when the melody strings were bowed.

LYRES IN NON-EUROPEAN CULTURES

Apart from East Africa, the only non-European area in which lyres are still played is northwestern Siberia, where the Ostyak, a people known to have migrated across the Urals in the Middle Ages and who are believed by some scholars to be of Sumerian descent (see harp, page 403) play a box lyre called *nares-jux*. *Nares-jux* means "musical wood," and *nares* may be derived from the Sumerian *nar* ("musician"). A people closely related to the Ostyak, the Vogul, play the same instrument but call it *sangkultap*.

Its rectangular resonator and arms are formed of a single block of wood to which a spruce soundboard is added; the cavity is then partly filled with a number of pebbles that rattle when the lyre is sounded. Museum specimens preserved in Helsinki measure up to 125 centimeters (49 inches), the size of the ancient Sumerian lyre. The player holds his instrument on his lap, plucking the strings with bare fingers, although sometimes the nails of the right hand are scratched across the strings. Both hands are used in playing; the melody lies in the right hand, while the left hand plays an accompaniment on the two highest strings. Both the Ostyak and the Vogul lyres are sounded in this fashion.

Lyra and *kithara* passed from Greece to Alexandrian Egypt, and ultimately underwent modifications of form, yet these ancient instruments have conserved their identities for the past two millennia and are still to be found in northeastern Africa. Ethiopia is their homeland in modern times, and they have scarcely spread beyond the sphere of influence of that country (the Egyptian *fellahin* form an exception; they play a five-stringed bowl lyre). Both bowl and box lyres are known in Ethiopia and among the Sebei, a Nilo-Hamitic people to the south; other areas know only the bowl lyre (Egypt, the Upper Nile, a region north and east of Lake Victoria, and the Nile-Congo watershed). Many a bowl-lyre resonator consists of a tortoise carapace, others are of wood with skin bellies laced to the back of the bowl, or even—as the "devil's harp" of the Masai in Kenya and Tanzania (called *kinandi-kinubi* in the vernacular)—of a tin basin covered with camel skin; the "devil's harp" is credited with paramount magical powers and is only produced at high festivities. In Uganda, the Soga and the Ganda sometimes substitute a calabash for the more usual tortoise carapace; their instruments have eight strings while those of their neighbors, the Madi and Lugbara, also of Uganda, have but four strings. The arms of these lyres are of wood, straight, and divergent.

Ethiopians play a variety of lyres said to represent the harp of David; this belief extends to both bowl and box lyres. The latter, according to tradition, were introduced from Egypt at a very early date. They are always played with a plectrum, but bowl lyres are generally, although not invariably, plucked with bare fingers. Ethiopian and Nubian playing technique is that inferred for ancient Egypt: all the strings are sounded simultaneously by the right hand, while the left hand stops those that are not required. The number of strings on African instruments varies considerably, from three to ten being reported from Ethiopia alone; they are attached to the yoke either by means of tuning rings of hide or by wooden tuning rods. The Ethiopian *kerar*, a bowl lyre, has five or six strings of gut today; if there are six, the treble string is duplicated at the octave; the lyre is held at a tilt, resting against the player's left hip in a near horizontal position, but a seated player may hold his on his left thigh. In either case, due to the tilt the right side of the bowl is lower than the left side, and consequently the highest-pitched strings are situated below the low-pitched ones, the latter now being on top and closest to the player. This stance may help us to understand the ancient Greek custom of indicating their pitches from the (low-pitched) top string down.

Box lyres of Ethiopia are considerably larger than the bowl lyres, attaining a total length of 100 to 120 centimeters (40 to 47 inches). Consequently they are rested in an upright position when played. In contrast to the bowl lyres, these are not popular instruments but are reserved nowadays for the accompaniment of songs having a religious character.

HARPS

To this category of instruments belong the primitive preharp chordophones best known as ground bows, but also as ground harps, and the harps proper. They have as a common distinguishing feature the plane of their strings, which does not parallel the instrument itself.

GROUND BOWS

Ground bows, or ground harps, are primitive chordophones still secured, as their name implies, to the soil. Nowadays their occurrence is limited to Central and East Africa, and to those areas of the New World to which they spread from Africa; but formerly the distribution was far wider, as is evidenced by encounters in Neolithic sites on several continents. Such implements consist simply of a flexible stick set upright in the ground, with a cord suspended from its upper end. The lower end of the cord is tied to the bark cover of a nearby pit, which serves as resonator, with the bark weighted down by stones or earth. Often a pot is placed in the pit to augment the volume of sound. The cord is then either plucked by the player's right thumb and forefinger while his left hand stops it, or the cord may be struck by a small stick. Among the Nepoko Pygmies of Zaire the performer plucks the string while beating the bark cover with a drumstick, to the accompaniment of a companion's singing. Sachs (1940) relates that sometimes the ground bow is played by several persons simultaneously. From Africa it reached the Caribbean; the *tambour maringouin* ("mosquito drum") of Haiti employs a sapling that can be flexed to change the pitch of the plucked cord.

Here we might well ask the question: when is a ground bow not a ground bow? and supply the answer: when it leaves the ground. A great step forward in its evolution is accomplished by making it mobile. This is done in Uganda by inserting a stick upright into one end of a log, while a gourd attached to the log's other end holds the cord taut. And the *tambour maringouin* is also made in a portable form consisting of a can, mounted on a plank, and a cord. Plank or log have replaced the pit: we are no longer dealing with ground bows but with protozithers, and in this stage of their development we find them no longer restricted to Africa and Afro-America but can observe them also in Asia. The Annamese *cai dan bao*, for instance, an instrument of great antiquity, consists of a flexible rod placed upright on a rectangular wooden resonator with a wire running from top of rod to resonator. The wire is plucked with a plectrum, as might be expected, and its pitch regulated by flexing the rod. A small hollow wooden ball—probably a gourd originally—is set below the juncture of rod and string to reinforce the sound. Only women and blind persons play it nowadays.

On the Indian subcontinent, primitive but ancient forms of the one-string chordophones, truly portable, can be followed in their evolution until they emerge transformed, not, as might be expected, into harps, but into primitive spike lutes. Here the resonator takes the form of a bucketlike container with open top and membrane bottom; the flexible rod is abandoned in favor of the player's arm, which is replaced in turn by a flexible shaft, later by a rigid one. In the final step the resonator is impaled on a rigid string bearer to form a primitive spike lute.

This progression can be followed in some detail: the *ānanda lahari* of Bengali mendicant singers has a typical bucket resonator with membrane bottom; the string is knotted to a small piece of cloth or hide, then passed through an aperture in the membrane (the knot prevents it from being pulled out while under tension). The other end of the string is fastened to a miniature replica of the bucket or to a knob furnished with a membrane and is held in the player's left hand; the bucket is then tucked under his left arm and the string held taut. Pitch it determined by that of the singer's voice, and the string is plucked with a plectrum. Because of the typical membrane cover of the resonator, this group of instruments was long referred to as plucked drums. Actually the membrane is an accessory only, a mirliton (see page 171) that does not create sound but merely serves to color it. In the next step the human arm is replaced by a more permanent yet still flexible device: a bamboo segment split for the greater part of its length; the ends of its two prongs, facing down, are attached to opposite sides of the bucket and a tuning peg is inserted in the upper end. By flexing the prongs the pitch can be lowered, but apparently no use is made of this facility.

A further advance is offered by the *tuntina* with its rigid pole attached to the outside of the bucket and extending far above it; some models have two strings. In the *kutam* of the Pulluvam, a tribe of serpent worshipers of Malabar, the resonator is a clay pot closed with vellum; formerly its string was fastened to a half gourd, now to a metal cup. Both cup and pot—the latter lying on its side—are fastened to a horizontal plank to maintain the string under tension: the rigidity of the original flexible pole or sapling has been progressively increased. The final development is exemplified by the *ektār* ("one string"), originally the central and southern Indian equivalent of the *tuntina*, but today it consists of a gourd resonator and a round stick, usually of bamboo, upon which the gourd is impaled. The long end of the stick carries a tuning peg for the single string, which passes over a bridge to the protruding stub of the stick, now transmuted into a spike. A peculiarity of the *ektār* is the piece of silk or woolen thread placed between string and bridge in order to enhance the "richness" of its timbre.

Old forms and new alike serve to provide a drone accompaniment to recitations of beggars and of mendicant monks on the subcontinent, either alone or in conjunction with a drum. A virtually continuous drone is obtained by plucking or striking the string repeatedly in quick succession. Not often are we given the opportunity of observing at one time so many phases of an instrument's development.

A modern New World version of the *ānanda laharī* surfaced in New York in 1965 in form of the "gut bucket," as it is called: a metal washtub is inverted, a broomstick attached vertically, and a length of catgut is affixed to stick top and washtub bottom. This is played by one member of a two-man team of street musicians whose partner manipulates brush drums on a large tin can.

HARPS

Harps are differentiated from other chordophones in that their strings run in a plane perpendicular to the resonator (the strings of zithers, lutes, and lyres follow a plane parallel to the resonator); a series of parallel strings are stretched diagonally between the resonator—also called body—and a neck. Those harps that have a pillar forming a connective link between body and neck are termed frame harps. The function of this pillar—also known as column—is to take the strain of the strings' tension and thereby permit higher pitches to be obtained. All modern Western harps are frame harps, as were some, but by no means all, harps of European antiquity. Outside Europe frame harps are rare; they were known to ancient and modern Syria, according to Sachs, and are encountered in Siberia today.

Columnless harps, or open harps, are generally classified either as arched or as angular harps; however, this classification is now held to be too rigid in that it does not allow for any intermediate types. Also, it has become increasingly clear that frame harps can no longer be considered as a separate species restricted to Western civilization, but rather that they must be considered as an order of angular harps. Arched harps are those with a curved neck rising away from the resonator, whereas neck and resonator of angular harps form a right angle or at least an acute angle. Arched harps are believed to be older than angular harps. Many investigators hold the harp to be a development of the polychord musical bow, and it seems certain that this applies to Negro Africa, at least. Elsewhere its genesis may have been different: its West Asian derivation in antiquity is both puzzling and problematic, for a harplike instrument drawn at Megiddo, Palestine, some 3,500–3,200 years B.C. consists of a small resonator with what is probably a closed frame above it, irregularly triangular; it could possibly represent a very large lyre. In the Aegean at least, harps preceded lyres (and later replaced them). Did both harp and lyre derive from some such common ancestor?

Harps are played in primitive and developed societies alike. Primitive harps are low in pitch in relation to their size, as they can withstand but little tension. Their resonator assumes many shapes—elongated, ovoid, or round—and the belly is often a membrane rather than of wood. Tuning of such instruments is effected either by means of movable tuning pegs, or by tuning rings. Ancient Egypt and Java made use of pegs best designated as tuning knobs, wedged into the neck from the rear and glued fast; they could not be turned, but did prevent the strings from slipping. Many modern exotic harps are tuned by bast or cloth rings, knotted to the strings of which they form prolongations, and turned several times around the neck; they can be moved slightly to tighten or relax the strings. The same system was in use in the ancient Near East and India. Most Asiatic harps still have tuning rings, whereas most African ones have fixed, that is, nonmovable, pegs. In some African harps the curved neck rests loosely against the bottom of the resonator until the tension of the strings holds it taut up against the underside of the belly. When playing instruments of portable size they can be held either vertically or horizontally; if horizontally, the resonator is sometimes supported against the performer's body. In antiquity, vertically held harps were plucked with the fingers of both hands, while those held horizontally were sounded with a slender plectrum held in the right hand; here the left hand appears to have acted as a damper.

HARPS IN ANTIQUITY

Arched Harps

In the ancient Near East, the arched harp made its appearance about 3000 B.C. in Sumer. Two such harps, held in a horizontal position, appear on a vase fragment from Bismaya (the ancient Adab) near Nippur from the early third millennium (formerly dated from the fourth millennium); one harp has seven strings, the other five; their players form part of a procession. Held vertically, a harp forming an obtuse arc is played in a banquet scene depicted on a plaque from Khafaje (Akkad) of 2800–2500 B.C., while a similar instrument but with neck terminating in a large sculpture figures in a banquet scene on a cylinder seal from Ur of the same period. Both harps show but few strings—five and four, respectively—but probably had more in reality.

Actual instruments have been excavated at Ur, dating from the mid-third millennium: one, its resonator decorated with a bull's or calf's head, is some three feet long and three and one-half feet high, with eleven strings; another is presumed to have had fifteen strings. The arched harp died out about 2000 B.C. in Mesopotamia, to be replaced there by the angular harp, only to reappear in the Middle Ages, presumably imported from Persia: a thirteenth-century metal bowl from Mesopotamia in the British Museum depicts an arched harp identical with that of Taq i-Bustan (see page 400). But it lived on in Egypt.

The Egyptian arched harp, now considered to be descended from that of Sumer, first appears in the Fourth Dynasty (2723–2463 B.C.). It is depicted as about as tall as a man, with very small resonator and long neck, and looks rather like a spade. Here also the tuning pegs are immobile. Such harps were held in an upright position, usually placed with the resonator touching the ground (which probably augmented somewhat the volume of tone), and the performer knelt. A new form, called shoulder harp in modern times, was played in the Middle Kingdom, depicted sparsely under the Fifteenth to Seventeenth (Hyksos) dynasties. A small instrument, it usually had but three or four strings, a scaphoid resonator, and a membrane belly. The name derives from its being carried on the musician's left shoulder with the neck projecting behind. But whereas in the Old Kingdom harpists had always been men, the shoulder harp was played by women. Indeed, the taboo against female players of harp and wind instruments at that epoch disappeared with the advent of the Middle Kingdom, and from then on we see women playing various types of harp as well as double pipes. Yet another form, known as the singer's harp, appears under the Eighteenth Dynasty (1580–1350 B.C.), perhaps an enlargement of the earlier spatulate form, with large, heavy body, shorter neck, and up to nineteen strings; and in some cases it was taller than the standing musician. A smaller, portable version also came into use, its neck usually set almost at a right angle and the instrument lifted off the ground by a slanting brace hooked on to the extremity of the resonator, thus serving as a stand, the harp resting at the same time against the player's knee. Such instruments are known as footed harps.

Very small arched harps, played by women, make infrequent appearances in the Greco-Roman world; the scaphoid resonator is about as long as the distance from elbow to wrist, and it has but few strings—perhaps a curiosity, certainly an import. We cannot give it a name, although *trigōnon* and *sambykē* have been suggested.

Today arched harps survive primarily in Africa and on the Indochinese peninsula, also among the Abchas of the Caucasus, the Vogul and several other western Siberian peoples. Remnants of a harp (an arched harp?) were discovered in a grave dating from about 400 B.C. at Pazyryk in the Altai Mountains of Central Asia—a grave of Scyth-related nomads.

Angular Harps

Angular harps first appear in the Aegean, during the third millennium B.C., as frame harps. Three small marble statuettes of a seated player holding a triangular harp have been found in graves of the southern Cyclades dated between 2200 and 2000 B.C. On all three the resonator assumes the form of a rectangular box resting on the player's right thigh, while the neck rises to the height of his head, so that the actual length may have been some 55 to 60 centimeters (22 to 24 inches). As the triangle is virtually equilateral, the neck has about the same proportion as the resonator. In Mesopotamia the oldest representation of an angular harp—an open angular harp—is that of a Babylonian relief from the Larsa period (2023–1761 B.C.) found in the Diyala region. Unlike the Cycladic instruments it is the string-bearing neck here that rests horizontally, while the cumbersome resonator is vertical, in the position to be assumed later by harps on the Greek mainland. Further north, at Ashnunnak in Akkad, on a plaque of the same period, a horizontally held angular harp is shown tucked under the player's left arm, its seven strings plucked with a plectrum. An open rectangular harp is also depicted on a cylinder seal from Cyprus, dated between 1600 and 1350 B.C., and a harp-playing figure on a small bronze stand, again from Cyprus, of about 1100 B.C., is seen in profile, holding an open angular harp with near-vertical resonator about twice as long as the round stick neck, to which perhaps fifteen or more strings are attached. Thus an eastern Mediterranean origin may be stipulated for the angular harp, which then appears, as an imported item, first in Mesopotamia, then in Egypt, and, proceeding westward, in Greece at a later period.

Assyria knew both horizontally and vertically held angular harps. An elaborate relief from Nimrud (the ancient Kalakh) of the ninth century B.C. shows one with elongated resonator, from which a slender stick-neck, terminating in an outstretched hand, projects upward. The player is stopping or damping the strings with his left hand, while in his right he holds a long plectrum. Vertically held harps from about the same time show a horizontal stick-neck and long, straight, upright resonator, the latter about twice the length of the former.

When it appears in Egypt under Amenhotep II in the fifteenth century B.C., the angular harp is treated as an alien instrument and does not gain full acceptance for several centuries. Always played in upright position, its round stick-neck rested on the player's lap with the narrow resonator held against the body, the strings running vertically. A number of ancient Egyptian harps, both of the arched and of the angular variety, have come down to us. From them as well as from fairly numerous paintings we know that their resonator bellies were of skin or wood and were sometimes painted. Wall paintings and reliefs frequently depict harpists, often in groups with other musicians or with a singer. Such materials and a relief from the grave of Idu in Giza (Sixth Dynasty) permit us to deduce that Egyptians employed highly developed playing techniques that included the sounding of stopped or half-stopped as well as of open strings, and the damping of strings by the flat of the hand. Egyptian harps were known by the generic name of *bnt* (not connected etymologically with the Sumerian *ban* or *pan*). Angular harps continued to be played in Egypt after that country had lost its independence.

Geographically situated between Mesopotamia and Egypt, Palestine might be expected to have received the harp at a very early stage of its history, or even—if we consider the Megiddo instrument already referred to—to have originated it. However, it seems to have been unknown there prior to the eleventh century B.C., when Israel became a kingdom. First mentioned in Samuel I, it is called a *nevel*, and seems to have been a vertically held angular harp, played with bare hands. A millennium later, Flavius Josephus (b. A.D. 37) wrote that the *nevel* had twelve strings. But it must be borne in mind that five and seven, together with their sums and multiples, were sacred numbers in the ancient East, Israel included, so that the *nevel*'s twelve strings may represent a purely symbolic number. About A.D. 200 Rabbi Johoshua comments that *nevel* strings were made of larger gut than those of the *kinnōr* (lyre) and were rough, from which we may conclude that the harp was pitched lower than the lyre.

The word *nevel* is clearly related to *nabla*, the Phoenician term for harp, which term the Greeks subsequently took over; indeed, Greek writers refer to the "Phoenician *nabla*" and at a yet later date, the Hellenistic writer Athenaeus (ca. A.D. 250) states that this instrument had come from Phoenicia. Certainly the Greeks identified it as an alien instrument, and harps played a very minor role in their musical repertory.

On the Greek mainland the earliest form met with is the frame harp. It appears on a bowl of the late geometric period, 750–700 B.C., a narrow triangle with but five strings. An Italiote krater by the Sisyphus painter made about 420 B.C. depicts a small frame harp with twelve visible strings and probably a few more, its resonator lying flat on the player's lap. On another krater by the same painter the curved resonator is projected upward above the player's head, while the neck with its tuning rings lies on her lap, reminiscent in its triangular form of Persian instruments. A large harp of this shape, possibly with a very slender pillar, certainly with about twenty-five strings, is played with both hands by a seated woman shown on a rock-crystal gem of the second half of the fifth century B.C. In the same century this type undergoes modification: the pillar is vertical and the resonator is prolonged horizontally to meet it, resulting in the shape of a reversed capital **D**. Made in different sizes, it coexists with and later replaces the triangular model. From about 400 B.C. on, the harp is depicted fairly frequently, always played with bare hands, that is, without a plectrum, and showing from thirteen to twenty strings. All are angular harps, most have a pillar. Both Greek vase paintings and Hellenistic terra-cotta statuettes quite often portray women harpists. Apart from the Cycladic statuettes and the Italiote kraters, it is the thin neck—not the resonator—that rests on the player's lap, with resonator upright and curving away from the player, regardless of whether or not a pillar is present. On all vertically held harps discussed so far, the shortest string is closest to the player.

Psaltērion was one name of the harp in Greece, *nabla* was another, and the word *trigōnon* was applied to an instrument so far unidentified but thought also to refer to the Greek harp; however, it might have indicated a triangular psaltery. Another unidentified chordophone of the Greek world was the *sambykē*, possibly an angular harp held upright. Al-Khwarizmi, writing in the late tenth century, identifies the *salbāq* as a stringed instrument of the Byzantines and Greeks resembling the *jank* (harp); *salbāq* is believed to derive from the Greek *sambykē*.

Angular harps were introduced to Rome in the second century A.D. by foreign girl players, and the harp may have been more popular there than it had been in Greece. In both areas it was held against the performer's left shoulder. And in neither culture does the presence of a pillar imply any structural modification of the other components: pillars are either straight but unexpectedly slender, or take on highly imaginative shapes—that of a swan was a favorite—forcing the conclusion that its presence does not indicate any change in tension of the strings. In fact the pillars of these Greek and Roman harps are more decorative than functional, and should be differentiated from those of the Cycladic harps, where they form an intrinsic part of the frame.

In the first century B.C. an almost rectangular frame harp is occasionally seen, very tall and narrow, later to be depicted in medieval Europe. Christian writers from the third century on frequently mention the *psalterium,* the form of which was usually said to resemble a reversed letter delta, but here the psaltery rather than the harp may be meant; we are on firmer ground with Saint Jerome, who renders *nevel* as *psalterium* in his Vulgate translation. Several early authors also mention an instrument with rounded resonator covered with a skin—a fair description of the Greek harp.

In antiquity the tuning devices—pegs or tuning rings—had been placed near the top of the instrument (on the neck) of most arched harps, and at the bottom of the instrument on the angular ones (with the exception of the Cycladic triangular harps). A structural shift was made in western Europe: the resonator was held as before, upright against the body, but the greater tension made possible by a solid pillar necessitated a change from tuning ring or fixed peg to movable tuning pin, and a series of these could be most conveniently reached at the top of the instrument, where the neck was now horizontal. This change took place some time in the first millennium, probably in Byzantium. We see the newly designed harp there in the tenth century (MS graec. 752, Vatican Library). All European harps from then on were built to this basic pattern. A few Greek and Roman harps, as well as the Byzantine one just mentioned, are shown with an elongated structure, forming more of a rectangle than a triangle.

HARPS IN POSTCLASSICAL EUROPE

We can follow the development of the Western harp, albeit falteringly for a while, from its earliest evidence in postclassical times on: that of the small, fragmentary instrument recovered in the Sutton Hoo ship burial of the seventh century, now preserved in the British Museum. This had but six strings, and is best considered as part of the grave goods rather than as a true musical instrument built for playing. Our first literary records hitherto believed to have reference to the harp actually relate to the rote, now known to have been a different instrument, and some early occurrences of the word "harp" or its cognates may not refer to the harp or to harp playing as such, but rather to the act of plucking strings, as for instance in the poem,

> *als Her David sein Rotten spien*
> *wan er darauf harpfen wolt*

> When Lord David espied his rote,
> then he wished to harp on it

or Chaucer's friar who "sung to the rote and harpying." Consequently we are not certain of the meaning of the oft-quoted line of Venantius Fortunatus, written about 600: *Romanusque lyra, plaudat tibi barbarus harpa.* And although the Old Norse word *harpa* is believed to have been a generic name for stringed instruments, and the word *harppu* or *harpu* denoted instruments other than the harp, we are reasonably sure that by the time Alfred the Great wrote (about 888) of *hearpunga*, he meant "a harping," and the Old English *hearpe* is conceded to have meant "harp." Also, the Old English *cytere, citere, citre*—all derived from the Greek *kithara* and not to be confused with the later cittern—also meant harp.

Around the year 1000 "lyre" was glossed as *hearpe* by Aelfric. But we need no longer rely on literary sources exclusively, for reliefs of stone crosses in Ireland dating from the ninth century to the eleventh are now generally acknowledged to represent harps rather than lyres: they portray instruments having pillars and held as harps would be. An eighth-century Anglo-Saxon manuscript and a ninth-century reliquary from Ireland also depict frame harps. The ninth-century Utrecht Psalter illustrates both open and pillared harps, and documents from the eleventh and twelfth centuries show either straight necks or undulating ones, with slightly outcurved pillar. In the twelfth century the *Hortus deliciarum* of Abbess Herrad of Landsberg (1167–1195) shows a harp with almost straight pillar and undulating neck inscribed *cythara*; here the tuning pins no longer appear at the top of the neck but are let into its side, as they are also on a harp with straight column that is depicted as being played by King David in the twelfth-century Codex 1879 of the Vienna National Library and in other works of the same century, as well as in the thirteenth-century manuscript formerly at the monastery of Saint Blasius, published in the eighteenth century by the prince-abbott

Martin Gerbert, with a harp inscribed *cythara anglica*. Wace's *Roman du Brut* (ca. 1155) has:

> *De sa forel ad sa harpe saké*
> *Et son plectrum ad enpoyné*
> *Se cordes a ben temprez*
> *Si ke ben se sunt acordez*

> From its bag he removed his harp
> And his tuning hammer he grasped
> To temper well the strings
> So that they were all well tuned

In this, as in other Old French literary examples, *plectrum* or *plectron* denotes a tuning hammer, not a plectrum in our sense of the word. Miniatures of the twelfth century on show players—often King David—holding a tuning hammer in the left hand.

By the thirteenth century English harpists were gaining a reputation on the Continent. Thus, in the chanson de geste *La prise de Cordres et de Seville* we read *Et d'Ingleterre i out des harpors* ("from England there were harpers").

All these instruments were angular harps, with the tuning pins inserted in the neck at the top and a pillar connecting neck and body, thus forming a triangle. Medieval harps had metal strings, strange as this may sound to us today. They were variable in size, with outcurved pillar, rather squat, had brays, and were played with both hands, one on either side of the strings, just as we play them today. Smaller models in the hands of standing or even walking musicians were kept in position against the player's body by means of a strap, sometimes visible on miniatures. Usually of wood, they may have been made of more costly materials on occasion: Beauneveû, in a miniature painted between 1380 and 1385 in the duke of Berry's Psalter, shows a white harp that we may take to be ivory, a brittle material little suited to withstanding tension (small ivory harps are occasionally met with in instrument collections).

Guillaume de Machaut in the fourteenth century mentions a harp with twenty-five strings, but neither size nor stringing were standardized in his day, and those depicted are usually smaller. Until about 1400 the harp remains squat and its pillar bulging in outline, after which a new form emerges, to be known as the Gothic harp, with very slender neck and pillar, pointed head, resonator of increasingly slender construction, and tuning pins mounted along the neck, prototype of the later European harp. By the mid-fifteenth century the squat type (called Romanesque harp by Sachs) was giving way to the new model, its almost straight pillar indicative of an increase in tension. The change of form was accompanied by a change in the manner of playing—the new instrument was at first held by one hand and played with the other, whereas theretofore both hands had been free to pluck the strings. Two regional varieties of importance during the Middle Ages were the Irish and the Welsh harps, discussed separately on pages 397 and 398.

From the late Middle Ages on the harp remained practically unchanged until the eighteenth century, except for an increase in size and in the number of strings. On pre-baroque harps the stringing is to the player's left, as it is on the modern pedal harp. Perhaps our best informants for the sixteenth century are Glareanus (1547) and Bermudo (1555). Glareanus depicts a slim and elegant instrument, which he describes as being five feet tall, having twenty-four strings, and a compass of F° to a°. His instructions for tuning it are to pull up the lowest string as high as it will go and to call it F (i.e., f°), then to proceed with the tuning by fifths (cf. the contemporary practice of calling the organ's low F or C keys indiscriminately F); he regrets the fact that harps were so little played in his day as the public preferred *clamoso* ("noisy") instruments; finally, he also describes the brays, a series of right-angled wooden or metal nails mortised into the resonator, and the snarl of the plucked strings when they struck against them. Brays are referred to as harp nails (*Nägel* in German) in medieval literature, and harps provided with such nails are known as bray harps. Among the instruments at the Stuttgart court in 1589 were "one small harp with brass nails throughout, in good condition, with its bag; is an octave [harp] made by Sixt Mayr; one *Quartharfe* [i.e., a fourth higher than usual] also made by Sixt; a new quadruple harp, also made by Sixt." Mersenne later wrote of the *harpions* [brays] *qui les font n'azarder, dont on a quitté l'usage pour écarter cette imperfection,* discontinued in order to avoid the nasal snarling. Although the instrument was obsolete on the Continent by Mersenne's time, Talbot (ca. 1700) could still write of the Welsh harp and its brays, "which give it a jarring sound." Typically, the Renaissance harp was a bray harp.

Bermudo also mentions a harp of twenty-four strings, pitched from "C below gamma ut" up (C°) and states that although others had twenty-seven strings there was no standard number. The low register of harps at this time is confirmed circumstantially by Giovanni Maria Trabaci, whose *Toccata seconda & ligature per l'Arpa* in Book II of his *Ricercate* (Naples, 1615) contains twice the mention "8° *bas*." Eustache Deschamps in the fourteenth century had noted that *la harpe tout bassement va*, not necessarily a reference to its classification as one of the *instruments bas* ("soft instruments") of the period, but more likely to its range. Bermudo gives many details of a practical nature, telling us that the strings corresponded to the natural keys only (without B♭), producing the pattern TTSTTTS, our major scale. But, he adds, there exist tricks to enable one nonetheless to perform pieces with chromatic tones: if when playing in the first mode on D you come to a cadence, place your finger on the D string to shorten it by a semitone to obtain the needed accidental; alternately, one can tune the fifteenth string (C) a semitone higher. On the other hand, when playing in the first mode with a flat, the seventh string (B) and its octave string can be lowered to obtain the necessary B♭. By such means all pieces are playable in all modes. He realizes that this may cause complications, as a given string might be needed both at its natural and its raised or lowered pitch; hence he considers the harp as an imperfect instrument for the music then performed: it lacks five chromatic strings per octave, and, if added, these could be colored for easy recognition. In another passage he implies the existence of "completed" harps having the compass of a clavichord, including the five additional strings per octave for the chromatic tones. Of great interest is his comment concerning the size of the strings: for the harp's present form they are disproportionate and produce a bad sound, being "three, four, or seven tones higher" than they should be, that is, too heavily strung. This is a particularly valuable comment in view of the well-known thick stringing of Latin American folk harps until now.

Latin American instruments, unchanged since their introduction by the Spaniards, preserve to this day a heavy resonator and thick strings, a straight, slight column and low neck, and have entered the domain of traditional music in many countries of the New World. Spanish harps are not frequently portrayed, but the Spanish painter Juan de las Roelas includes one in his *The Death of St. Hermenegild* (ca. 1600), with slender pillar, double-curved neck, and resonator surmounted by a scroll.

Chromatic Harps

The problem of providing accidentals as underscored by Bermudo was a vexed one indeed, and its solution was tackled in several ways. The double harp was one answer. Considerable confusion exists with regard to the Italian term *arpa doppia*. It seems to have denoted two distinct instruments, an ordinary and possibly very large harp, as well as the earliest form of chromatic harp, with two rows of gut strings, one for the diatonic, the other reserved for chromatic tones. Double harps are mentioned in Italy from about the mid-sixteenth century on, and the chromatic form appears to have remained in use until the end of the seventeenth century. Vincenzo Galilei (1581) ascribed invention of the *arpa doppia* to the Irish; Bottrigari mentions it in 1594; Monteverdi called for one in his *Orfeo* (1607); Praetorius (1619) depicts a cumbersome "great double harp"; Scipione Cerreto (1601) lists players of the *arpa a due ordini* then living in Naples.

Praetorius describes three kinds of harps: (1) ordinary harps with twenty-four or more strings and a compass of F° to c^2 or a^2, tuned diatonically; (2) double harps, chromatic from C° to $g\sharp'$ for the left hand, and chromatic from g° to c^3 for the right hand; (3) Irish harps with forty-three thick brass strings and a compass of C° to e^3. His double harp is provided with a separating soundboard, and he depicts it opened out to show both sides. His is a true harp, not an *arpanetta* (see page 219), of the kind occasionally met with in European collections and apparently of German manufacture. Of the double harp, Praetorius writes (*Syntagma III*) that it is as good in the bass as in the treble, must be played pizzicato, each hand answering the other "with trills, etc.," and requires a performer who can play a good counterpoint on it. His Irish harp is of great interest in that it becomes chromatic from the end of the second octave up, with B♭ as a natural, B♮ as an accidental, that is, an "F tuning." The ordinary harp he depicts has an outcurved pillar. That of the contemporary painting, *Hearing*, by the "Velvet" Brueghel in the Prado, Madrid, is a larger, nonportable instrument with perfectly straight pillar and high headed. Apparently the common harp was not standardized as to form or size.

Harps appear to have been among the most versatile of seventeenth-century instruments, participating with equal ease in drawing-room or tavern music. One may wonder which of the three types belonged to "the man who up to his death played the harp in the hostelries of Étampes [the reference is to 1625] and currently his son does so," known to Tallemant des Réaux. As to their size, Mersenne wrote: "One makes them the size one wishes, four or five feet, for example." The double harp lingered on well into the eighteenth century in certain areas. An example dated 1740 has fifty-eight strings, with tuning pins for the chromatic strings—twenty-six in number—inserted below the others, an arrangement found on other preserved chromatic harps.

A second answer to the problem of chromatic tuning was the triple harp. Originating in Italy in the late sixteenth century, it died out on the Continent a century later; at the same time it appeared in Wales, where it is still played. According to Mersenne it was invented thirty or forty years before he wrote by the Neapolitan Antonio Eustachio, chamberlain to Pope Paul V (1605–1621), and improved by Orazio Michi, composer and harpist. But the invention must have preceded Eustachio, since the Stuttgart court *Kapelle* records repairs to a triple harp in 1603 and the furnishing of eighty-nine "nails" and a tuning hammer for it. Of the three rows of strings, the center row was reserved for chromatic tones, plus two strings per octave duplicating two of those of the outer rows. Large instruments, they had a compass of four octaves at least, with long resonators and heavy necks. Very few early specimens survive: an undated instrument in the Museo Civico of Bologna is 193 centimeters (76 inches) tall, with ninety-four strings; Mersenne illustrates one with eighty-six strings. Early triple harps were low headed, triple strung throughout the compass; by the late seventeenth century high-headed models had come into use and were no longer triple strung throughout. The *Dictionnaire des Arts* of 1694 describes a triple harp with seventy-eight strings of brass and a four-octave compass. During the second half of the seventeenth century this instrument, which had traveled from Italy to France and thence north, was introduced to Wales, and by the late eighteenth century it had come to be regarded as the Welsh harp proper—which instrument it had presumably superseded; by the end of the nineteenth century it was played in Wales only by itinerant musicians and Gypsies.

Triple harps seem to have been *the* harps of Mersenne's time, but we have no record of their having been known in Wales before the end of the seventeenth century. Characteristically they have resonators built up of ribs, flat bellies, and straight columns. Stringing was on the right side of the neck. In Italy they lingered on until the end of the eighteenth century at least, if we may judge from an extant harp built in Vicenza in 1793. This instrument, 208 centimeters (82 inches) high, has a compass of just under five octaves and is gut strung. Welsh triple harps were likewise strung on the right side of the neck, played with the left hand on the treble, with the right hand on the bass strings, and were held at the left shoulder, that is, with the same playing technique as the Irish harp (see page 396); the strings were either toggled or pegged. On the European continent, however, triple harps were strung on the left side of the neck and held at the right shoulder, with the treble strings played by the right hand. The chromatic strings were plucked with the thumbs. Talbot (ca. 1700) comments that the triple harp was seldom used in consort but usually as a solo instrument. Although Mersenne illustrates a low-headed triple harp, no example of this type is known to exist today. At the end of the nineteenth century Welsh bards were abandoning the triple harp in favor of the pedal harp.

But the inconvenience of multiple rows of strings, and of strings too closely spaced for ease in plucking, was obviated in the late seventeenth century by the hook harp, with its new approach to the problem of chromaticism. This had a series of U-shaped hooks set in the neck for raising the pitch of a given string by a semitone, simply by shortening it. Although reputedly invented in the Tirol, there exists no evidence of its having actually originated there. Early models had hooks placed close to the C, F, and G strings, and later every string had its own hook. Harps tuned in F or in E♭ had B♭ as a "natural" string, B♮ as an accidental (the hook raised B♭ to B♮). Despite the fact that hooks could be set for any diatonic scale in which a piece was written, modulation would require the resetting of certain hooks, as would of course a change in tonality. But these improvements posed a new problem: while turning the hooks the player temporarily lost the use of one hand. This inconvenience was remedied in turn around 1720 by the invention of a pedal mechanism to act on the hooks and cause them to press against the strings, an invention that effectively ended the hook harp's usefulness as an art music instrument; however, it continued to be used by street musicians in Bohemia until the early twentieth century.

The invention of this important advance is generally attributed to two makers: the harpist Hochbrucker of Donauwörth and J. P. Vetter of Nuremberg. Five pedals, for C, D, F, G, and A, were connected to the hooks by wires passing through the hollow pillar, which pillar had, of course, to be straight (frequently the statement is made that harp pillars had to be straightened in the eighteenth century in order to accommodate a pedal mechanism, yet Virdung [1511] already depicts a harp with absolutely straight column). When, for example, the F pedal was depressed, all the Fs were raised by a semitone. Later the number of pedals was increased to seven. A signal disadvantage here was the displacement of hooked strings from the plane of the others, and the system ultimately gave way to that of the *béquilles* invented by Cousineau.

In 1739 Quirjn van Blankenburg described a pedal harp he had heard, together with its hidden mechanism; the player, whose name he gives as "Hohebrasken" (i.e., Simon Hochbrucker, the first virtuoso on the new instrument) informed him that his father had invented it. These early pedal harps were tuned to the key of E♭ and could be played in eight major and five minor keys. Jean-Henri Nadermann, the well-known Parisian builder, made use of this type of action—later known as single action—for his harps. By 1752 another Parisian harp maker, Pierre-Joseph Cousineau, together with his son Georges, had improved the pedals, done away with the hooks that pulled the strings out of tune, and substituted for them his own system of diminutive metal crutches, called the *système à béquilles*. In 1770 the Cousineaus doubled the number of pedals to fourteen in order to raise the pitch by a second semitone, and tuned their harps in C♭, in which scale they have remained until now.

The next major improvement was made by Sébastien Érard of Paris; while in London during the French Revolution he patented (in 1792) his improved single-action harp, doing away completely with the *béquilles* and replacing them with metal forks (*fourchettes*); these were rotating brass disks with two projecting studs that gripped the strings as they were rotated. More revolutionary yet was his 1810 patent for a Greek model harp with elaborate scrollwork, in which he reduced the number of pedals to seven and provided each with a half hitch and a whole hitch for raising the pitch by a semitone and a whole tone, respectively —the system known as double action—and adding a second fork for each string. (This half- and whole-hitch system was later incorporated in harpsichords.) His nephew Pierre Érard again modified the harp in 1836 by spacing the strings further apart and changing the pillar from Greek to Gothic.

A short-lived attempt was made later in the nineteenth century to provide a damper pedal (*pédale sourdine*) by adding an eighth pedal, the motion of which opened five shutters in the back of the resonator to diminish the volume of sound; some older instruments with an eighth pedal placed next to the D pedal are still encountered. Nowadays the pedals for the D, C, and B strings are placed to the performer's left, those for E, F, G, and A to his right. The modern concert harp has a compass of six and one-half octaves, from C′ to g⁴, and forty-six strings, but most present-day models are smaller. During performance the harp is tilted back against the player's right shoulder.

Nineteenth-century efforts to abolish the pedals resulted in a temporary revival of the chromatic harp, now once more forgotten. Jean-Henri Pape took out a patent in 1845 for a chromatic harp with two rows of strings crossing at one-half their length, one row for the natural, the other for the accidental, tones. Lyon of Paris, and Lyon and Healy of Chicago, subsequently made similar, if improved, models, and in 1894 Pleyel, Wolff & Cie of Paris patented a chromatic harp with metal frame.

In the first years of the twentieth century automatic harps were built, chiefly to serve as coin-operated machines placed in cafés. They remained popular as such in America until 1916. Powered by an electric motor, they played music from perforated paper rolls furnished with an automatic rewinder. The action consisted of horizontal plucking "fingers" attached to vertical levers, which in turn were controlled by the perforations of the rolls. Such "fingers" had already appeared on the claviharp (see page 398) of the preceding century, but it is doubtful that the inventor was aware of this.

The Irish Harp

Weathered stone crosses of Ireland erected between the ninth and eleventh centuries, their carvings now for the greater part indistinct, furnish our earliest documentation of the harp's presence on the island. From the eleventh century on we know that these instruments had typically a pronounced outward curve of the pillar, a low neck projecting beyond the pillar, and a very sturdy resonator; they were strung with metal strings as were their continental counterparts, and retained a brass stringing until the late eighteenth century, when they died out. Unlike most other harps, that of Ireland was rested against the player's left shoulder throughout its history, with the left hand plucking the upper register (nowadays the strings of that portion of the range are played with the right hand). The strings were attached on the left side of the neck and tuned on the right. In medieval times it accompanied the singing of epics, its metal strings plucked by long fingernails, but at the time of its abandonment it was played with the fleshy part of the fingers.

Early instruments were low headed, the neck projecting beyond the pillar, and relatively small—about 60 centimeters (2 feet) high—with perhaps thirty strings. In the sixteenth century a larger, still low-headed model is encountered, with a greater number of strings, such as that illustrated by Praetorius and described as having forty-three, with a compass of C° to e³ (see page 392). On the Continent it seems to have died out shortly after Praetorius wrote, but in Ireland a still larger model emerged about 1700, its pillar far less curved, the high-headed neck permitting considerably longer bass strings. String holes in the belly of older and later models were fitted with brass bushings to protect the wood from the strings; these were fastened to wooden toggles against the underside of the belly.

Several ancient Irish instruments are preserved, among them the so-called Brian Boru harp, now believed to date from the fourteenth century. Its resonator, and those of the other Irish harps, consists of a single block of willow with a separate back. Surviving older instruments have from thirty to thirty-two strings, later ones from thirty to fifty strings, traditionally plucked with long fingernails. Edward Bunting, writing about a meeting of harpers held at Belfast in 1792 relates that only one (Denis Hempson) played with long, curved fingernails; the other players pulled the strings up by the fingertips alone. Both the traditional mode of playing and the harp itself died out at this time. Subsequently a revival was attempted, led by a Dublin harp maker named John Egan, who by 1820 had produced a portable, gut-strung harp that stood about 90 centimeters (3 feet) high and had a three-octave compass. He placed seven finger levers on the inner curve of the pillar in the hope of making it competitive with the pedal harp. By depressing one of these, the corresponding string was raised by a semitone. This instrument is now known in Irish Gaelic as *cláirseach*.

The Welsh Harp

The national harp of Wales is the *telyn*, mentioned in Welsh poetry by the tenth century. According to Welsh laws known to us from the twelfth century although codified in the tenth, the *telyn* was one of the three indispensable possessions of a freeman. Originally supplied with horsehair strings, it had acquired strings of gut by the fourteenth century, at which time its wooden resonator seems to have been covered with leather. Early instruments had curved pillars, becoming straight in post-medieval times. Later they show a large resonator with a comparatively short, curved neck, and straight pillar. Talbot (ca. 1700) describes the Welsh harp as having the body made of one piece of wood, with thick, separate belly, slightly curved pillar, thirty-one or thirty-four strings, and also brays. Although the triple harp has since been identified with the Welsh harp, there is, according to Rimmer (1965–1966), no justification for associating it with Wales prior to the late seventeenth century, but its survival in Wales after it had died out elsewhere may account for the name. The Welsh harp itself was smaller than the triple harp and appears to have been superseded by the latter.

Keyed Harps

Attempts to construct harplike instruments controlled from a keyboard date back to the early seventeenth century. Philip Hainhofer saw in Dresden and recorded in his travel diary of 1629 *ain Instrument, dessen besaitetes Corpus, wie aine Harpfen, in die Höhe aufgerichtet ist, und das Clavier unten hat* ("an instrument, the strung *corpus* of which reaches upward, harp-wise, and has the keyboard at the bottom"). Mersenne refers to a new form of "spinet" of similar nature in use in Italy, notable for its lack of any soundboard; from his comment it is clear, however, that he had never seen one. In the same century a *clavi-arpa* is said to have been invented in Spain by Juan Hidalgo. According to Gerber, who calls it a new invention, the Württemberg organist Johann Kurtz built one in 1681 in the form of a spinet. Later, Joseph-Antoine Berger of Grenoble, then established in Paris, planned in 1765 to add a keyboard to an ordinary harp, but his working plans were stolen by an employee.

Continued improvement in pedal-harp construction during the course of the eighteenth century led to more complicated playing techniques, a factor that may have prompted early-nineteenth-century makers to create a keyboard instrument with harp sound. Of these builders, Johann Christian Dietz of Paris was the best known; he invented the claviharp (*clavi-harpe*) in 1813 (patented 1814), in the same year that John Bateman of London patented his clavi-lyra. On Bateman's instrument the strings were plucked by leather-covered tangents, on that of Dietz the silk-covered metal strings were plucked with a sideswiping motion by mechanical, hook-shaped plectra. These men and their successors gave their instruments the shape of a large harp with its pillar to the left, projecting above a shallow and low upright-piano case, devoid of soundboard, and with ordinary piano keyboard. Similar instruments were built up to the last decade of the nineteenth century, when Caldera of Turin and Racca of Bologna produced their *Calderarpa*. Here the strings were not plucked, as they had been on preceding models, but were struck by cloth-covered wooden bars, and the lowest strings even by hammers;

the harp shape was preserved. As an added attraction, claviharps could be furnished with pedals adopted from the piano, providing a choice of stops: bassoon, a roll of paper laid upon the bass strings; *forte*, the dampers removed; flageolet, a series of small pieces of felt pressed against the strings at half their sounding length; *piano*, a strip of soft leather moved against the strings. The force with which Dietz's claviharp gripped the strings was controlled by the player's touch; his stringing was unichord, each string being provided with its own damper.

The claviharp attracted attention outside the circle of mere musical amateurs: Liszt became interested in it and in 1883 wrote to the Milan publisher G. Ricordi suggesting that it could be profitably employed in the orchestra as well as in the drawing room. That it was not adopted by the orchestra is probably due to its tone, softer than that of a concert harp, and to the degree of precision required in the regulation of its action.

HARPS IN ASIA

Both types of harp known to ancient Mesopotamia—the arched and the angular—spread over the Asian continent, with the former type preceding the latter. Arched harps follow a sweeping arc, including Persia and Afghanistan, and through India to Burma; angular harps also take an eastward route, reaching Japan in Sassanid times (226–651). Horizontally held harps disappear after about A.D. 600, and, unless otherwise noted, all the following are or were held upright.

Arched Harps

These appear on Indian sculptures in the pre-Christian era and are connected with and were probably propagated by Buddhism and the patronage of Buddhist monarchs. During the reign of music-loving King Samudragupta in northern India (ca. 330–ca. 375), a number of coins were struck figuring the arched harp. Numismatists know them as the "lyrist" coins—a misnomer, for there were never any lyres in that area. The harps shown have elongated resonators and usually four visible strings, and are held with the player's left hand steadying the resonator while the right hand plucks. The neck is generally set at a very obtuse angle and the whole instrument forms a crescent; tuning rings seem to have been employed. The same playing position is still seen in Burma today, with the instrument's neck held diagonally away from the player's body. When Buddhism was forced to make way for Hinduism, the harp disappeared from Indian territory.

A closely related form is shown in Afghanistan in the sixth to seventh centuries; it is held in the lap, its neck pointing away from the performer, who plucks the strings with both hands. Now known to the West as the Kafir harp, locally as *waji*, the same instrument is still in use among the Kafir inhabitants of former Kafiristan (today's eastern Afghanistan and adjacent West Pakistan). It has a membrane belly and four or five strings secured to nonmovable tuning knobs, and is played with a plectrum that glides to and fro across the strings, while the left hand's function is to damp them. This is reminiscent of the manner in which some lyres are—and probably were formerly—played. We also find this harp in Burma, developed to a high degree of refinement, but there it is, alas, becoming increasingly rare. Harps are believed to have been introduced, together with Buddhist scriptures, from Bengal into Lower Burma around the fifth century. Formerly two types were known there, one with outcurving neck terminating in a sculptured phoenix, the other with an incurved neck. The former is first documented in a Chinese record of A.D. 802; in past centuries it had fourteen strings, neck and resonator of about the same length, and was characterized by the outcurved neck and sculptured head. This type is now extinct (in India it appeared at Amaravati about 220–400). The latter type developed into the current Burmese harp called *saung*, its name possibly derived from the Persian *chang*; it is slender, with scaphoid resonator and leather belly, and usually fitted with thirteen strings of silk. During performance, the *saung* is held across the player's lap, its strings plucked with both hands; primarily an instrument of vocal accompaniment, its secondary use is as a solo instrument. The arched harp is also figured on the Indo-Javanese stupa of Borobudur dating from about 800.

A late Sassanid relief at Taq i-Bustan, dated 590–628, shows many musical instruments, among which are no fewer than three types of harp: a horizontally held angular harp, a vertically held one, and an arched harp held vertically—the first appearance in this area of the arched harp. Evidence exists to support the thesis that it spread westward to medieval Mesopotamia before dying out.

Angular Harps

Among the musicians portrayed on a beautiful Greco-Indian frieze found at Airtam in Bactria, some three hundred kilometers southeast of

Samarkand, from the Kushan period (for dating, see page 410) is a harpist holding an angular instrument in upright position. Unfortunately it has been damaged, and the top of the resonator is missing, so that we cannot completely follow its increasing fullness and potential curve; it prefigures the Sassanid vertical harp that was to become so widespread. The horizontally held type made its last appearance on the above-mentioned Taq i-Bustan relief, and from then on the Asian harp is invariably held upright.

In Persia this form of harp was called *chang*, meaning "bent." During pre-Islamic times we hear of a widely varying number of strings, from thirteen to forty being mentioned. From miniatures of the fifteenth and sixteenth centuries we know that the harp was supported by the forearm at juncture of neck and resonator, leaving both hands free to pluck the strings. It was double strung throughout, which fact may account for the large number of strings in some descriptions of Eastern harps, and its upright resonator was about the same length as its round stick-neck. A tail-like curved appendix to the resonator reached halfway to the ground, its function apparently being that of adding weight to the bottom and thereby rendering the harp less top-heavy. Frequently it is depicted together with a frame drum or in instrumental ensembles, and sometimes it accompanied the reciting or singing voice. Still in pre-Islamic times the *chang* was introduced to Arabia, where it was called *jank* (this name was given to a different instrument in the eighteenth century), and from Arabia it traveled to Egypt, where it was still played in the fifteenth century; another route led from Arabia to Turkey. Fifteenth-century Turkish poets sing of it, and we hear of its use there up to the late seventeenth century, after which it is no longer mentioned. Turkish harps of the seventeenth century were virtually identical in construction to those of Persia, and this type pops up rather unexpectedly in Moorish Spain, where it is illustrated in the thirteenth-century *Libro de los juegos* (MS Escurial T.j.6).

Farther east, the angular harp did not appear in India before the Indo-Muslim period, and died out there some thousand years ago. Another route led through Eastern Turkistan over to China, whence it reached Korea and then Japan. China's angular harp, the *k'ung hu*, a development of the *chang*, was received from Turkistan about A.D. 400. On frescoes it is seen as having from sixteen to twenty-five strings. Unlike other alien instruments it never managed to establish itself, and it became obsolete during the Middle Ages. An illustration from the thirteenth or fourteenth century shows a harp with eighteen strings and a

Chinese angular harp, probably
ninth century. Shōsoin, Nara.

resonator about twice as long as the neck. Its Japanese counterpart, the
kugo, reached the islands from Korea, only to disappear during the
Heian period (794–1185) as a result of musical reforms, in the course
of which a number of instruments were eliminated. A Chinese instrument of the early Heian period—probably of the ninth century—survives
among the Shōsoin treasures at Nara in an extraordinary state of preservation (the instrument collection of the Shōsoin is undoubtedly the oldest
extant in the world). Structurally identical with the *chang*, it varies
only in that its "tail" is straight and that it is single strung; its twenty-
three strings are attached to (silken) tuning rings along the horizontal

neck. Other names of the *kugo*—such as *koto* and *tatekoto* ("standing *koto*")—bear witness to the fact that in Japan also the harp never succeeded in creating an independent identity for itself.

A curiously archaic form of harp is still played among the Ostyak. This Finno-Ugrian people migrated during the thirteenth century across the Urals to the Ob drainage of northwestern Siberia and then split into Ostyaks and Voguls; their ancestry is held by some anthropologists to be Sumerian. Of their two harps, the Ostyak *shotang* is angular, resembling that of ancient Egypt and is occasionally made with a pillar. Its meter-long resonator continues as a swan's neck, often terminating in a carved bird's head; from six to ten metal strings are held by turnable wooden pegs. Their *torop-jux* is a frame harp, also with a swan's neck, and has lateral pegs for from eight to ten strings. In form it is strangely reminiscent of an illustration in an eighth-century Anglo-Saxon manuscript and of a ninth-century Irish reliquary—the earliest representations of the frame harp in the British Isles. Ostyaks play the *torop-jux* by sounding the melody with one hand while accompanying themselves on the two highest strings with the other hand, a technique they also apply to their lyres.

HARPS IN AFRICA

Arched harps of modern Africa are held both vertically and horizontally. Their resonators are made of wood, calabash, or tortoiseshell, and assume a number of forms: scaphoid, ovoid, circular, trough shaped; the *kimasa* of the Soga of Uganda, now extremely rare, is even made as a footed harp. Bellies are of hide—tanned or not—or of snakeskin. Strings are made from a variety of materials, including leather, twisted raffia, camel gut, sinews of giraffe leg, and fiber.

The *ombi* of Gabon and Guinea has a trough-shaped wooden body, skin belly, and strings varying from four to eight in number made of fiber wound around long, immovable pegs; it is held horizontally, the resonator pressed against the player's stomach with both wrists, thus leaving the hands free for plucking. The *nanga* of Nubia is similar; here also, long wooden pegs prevent the strings from slipping. By contrast, the *enanga* of Uganda, with its circular or oval body, is held in the player's lap with the neck projecting away from him, in a position recalling the Burmese *saung*. A larger harp of Cameroun with scaphoid body is held obliquely across the body by a band passing over the right hand, leaving the fingers free to grasp the plectrum with which its strings are plucked. The *ardin* of the Mauretanian Moors exemplifies a variant type: here the neck rests loosely in the calabash resonator, to be held in position against the belly by the tension of the strings; these number between ten and twelve and are plucked while the tanned-skin belly is drummed upon simultaneously, both often accompanied by the rattling of metal rings attached to the top of the neck.

Angular harps are encountered in Central Africa and are notable for the acute angle that they form; devoid of pillar, they can withstand but little tension.

THE HARP ZITHER

A primitive hybrid form combining harp and zither, the harp zither is found only among the Sea Dayak of Borneo and in West Africa; it combines the principles of both instruments. On Borneo they are heterochord, whereas in Africa they are idiochord.

The Sea Dayak set a wooden box over a pit (the function of the pit is that of a resonator), furnish it with two vertical bridges, each notched to hold four strings, one above the other, while a nut at each extremity of the box is similarly notched.

In Africa the string bearer is a stalk of raffia palm, which may measure from 1.0 meter to 1.8 meters (40 to 71 inches) in length; from three to five "strings" are detached from its surface and raised, again one higher than the other, on a notched bridge. To augment the volume of sound, one, two, or even three calabashes may be attached to the palm stalk. Among the various peoples of West Africa who know the harp zither, only men may play it. It has been called Fan harp by some writers, but the Fan are far from being the only people to play it.

THE HARP LUTE

Indigenous to Africa, and found only there, is a chordophone combining features of both harp and lute—harp and spike lute, to be specific—and called harp lute by ethnomusicologists. Usually this consists of a large hemispheric gourd resonator covered with a skin belly stretched across the open top while wet, affixed by lacing or pegging, and traversed lengthwise by a round stick; the latter forms a neck at one end, a stubby spike at the other. A smaller stick pierces the resonator from side to side just beneath the belly and supports the bridge, a notched stick set upright upon it. The strings, variable in number, are attached to the neck by tuning rings, then pass at different heights via notches in the vertical bridge, to be fastened around the spike. The plane of the strings thus lies at a steep angle to the belly, as is true of all harps. Two small sticks project from the upper (handle) end of the resonator and serve as handholds.

The area from which the harp lute has been reported reaches from Senegal down to Nigeria, as well as inland from Mali. During performance the resonator is held pressed against the player's body, handle outward, middle fingers of both hands hooked over the handholds while the strings are plucked with thumbs and forefingers, a method similar to that of the pluriac (see page 182). While many instruments have straight, unadorned necks, others—from Guinea and Sierra Leone, for instance—have arched necks surmounted by copper plaques from which metal rings and pellet bells are suspended, to add their rattling sound to that of plucked strings. The *bolon* of the Ful of Sierra Leone has such a neck; its resonator is a large gourd, its belly a skin with the hair left on; instead of notches, its bridge is pierced with three holes for as many strings. Some larger instruments have many more strings; a Gambian one has twenty-two, for instance. The Malinke of Guinea play an outsized harp lute that attains a length of about 1.5 meters (ca. 60 inches) and has from fifteen to nineteen strings; on those having fifteen strings, the right hand plucks c♯°e°g°b°d′f♯′a′b′ and the left hand B°d°f°b♭°c′e♭′g′.

When Philip Hainhofer visited Dresden during his travels in 1629, he wrote in his travel diary of having heard there a "long new instrument," which he called *harpfen lauten* ("harp lute"). Unfortunately he gives us no description of it. But if we match this name with the illustration of a nameless "new" instrument of less than a decade earlier, that of Praetorius's *Theatrum instrumentorum* of 1620, we find that Hainhofer may in fact have heard a combination of harp and lute. Praetorius's anonymous instrument has an outsized, extra-robust lute body, short neck, and long pegbox bent forward (instead of backward as usual); a narrow string holder, probably of metal, is set obliquely on the belly. Twenty-four metal strings appear to have been attached to pins driven into the string holder in exactly the same manner as they were in the bandora and similar instruments, and are tuned by pegs inserted into the bent section of the neck. Thus we have a columnless harp with lute body for a resonator. The neck is unfretted, for all the strings are open ones.

It was probably this instrument that John Evelyn saw in Italy on August 9, 1661, at "Sir Fr. Prujean" (Francis Prujeane), called *polythore*, "an instrument having something of the harp, lute, and theorbo, by none known in England, nor described by any author, nor used, but by this skilful [*sic*] and learned Doctor." The caption of an undated seventeenth-century illustration by Randle Holmes indicates that similar instruments had from twenty-five to forty strings.

More than a century passed before this curious combination was revived. In 1798 Edward Light of London produced the first of a series of combination instruments, starting with a harp guitar that was intended to replace or improve the guitar in vocal accompaniments. A number of successive versions ensued, variously called harp lute, harp lute guitar, and so on, with a guitar head and neck plus a harp neck and column.

LUTES

In its wider sense the word "lute" designates any chordophone having a neck that serves as string bearer and handle, with the plane of the strings running parallel to that of the belly. Such instruments can be plucked, struck, rubbed with a friction stick, or bowed (in this sense, a violin is a member of the lute family). In the more restricted sense, lutes are plucked chordophones having a neck and bulging body, represented in the West first and foremost by the descendant of the Arabic *ʿūd*.

Plucked lutes fall into one of two categories known as long-necked and short-necked lutes. In the former the neck is patently longer than the body, its prototype being a wooden stick attached to an animal carapace or a bulging fruit shell, whereas in the latter the neck is shorter than the body, originating as a wooden body tapering off to form a neck and fingerboard. Of these, the older by far is the long-necked variety.

THE LONG-NECKED LUTE TO THE YEAR 1000

Investigators have concluded that the lute is almost certainly a northern instrument, and that it may have originated in the Caucasus or in present-day Russian Asia close to the Caspian. It first appears in Mesopotamia in the Kassite period (1600–1150 B.C.) or a couple of centuries earlier, with a small ovoid body and long fretted neck. The fact that it does not seem to have been used in Babylonian temple rituals tends to indicate a foreign origin, as does the late date of its introduction. In Mesopotamia it is always seen being played by a man. A lute depicted on a terra-cotta plaque probably of the seventeenth century B.C. in the Baghdad Museum has either two or three strings and a conspicuously small body. This type comes rapidly into common use and reaches Egypt during the Hyksos invasion (1680–1580 B.C.), at first portrayed sparsely and together with the shoulder harp, later more frequently, played by women only, and with a plectrum. A preserved, two-string lute dating from the Eighteenth Dynasty (1580–1350 B.C.) has a body of tortoise-shell, an animal-hide belly with six soundholes, and a neck 62 centimeters (24½ inches) long, which pierces the skin. Another instrument from the sixteenth or fifteenth century B.C., exceptionally with three strings, still had its original gut strings of about 1 millimeter diameter when found; this has a wooden body and hide belly, and plectra were found with both. Contemporary paintings show ovate or almond-shaped bodies and fretted necks. The neck penetrated the whole length of the body but did not emerge at the lower end. Strings were fastened to the bottom of the handle (underneath the belly), issued through a hole in the belly, and were secured by tuning rings at the upper end. In general two strings, rarely three, are shown. This type of lute survives in north-western Africa today.

A female lutenist is depicted on a Cretan bowl from 1500–1200 B.C., playing a two-stringed instrument undoubtedly modeled on an Egyptian original. On the relief of a lute player (known as "The Jugglers") at Alaca Hüyük in Anatolia, dating from the Hittite New Kingdom (1460–1190 B.C.), a new form is presented, having a waisted, almost guitar-shaped body and fretted neck; the lute is held horizontally, cradled at the elbow; it has two strings. On Carchemish reliefs from the tenth century the method of fastening the strings is visible: two lutes with small, ovate bodies have tuning rings wound around the top of the stick-necks; both instruments are held almost vertically.

Not until the fourth century B.C. does the long-necked lute appear in Greece, where it never came into common use, however. On a statue base of 350–320 B.C., probably by Praxiteles, now in the Athens National Museum, the seated figure of a Muse holds a lute with diamond-shaped body and rounded neck, a variation of the earlier models, but otherwise the *trichordon* ("three-stringer") as it was called, was the same instrument as that of the Eastern countries it came from, down to its fretted neck. Pollux, in the second century A.D., identifies *trichordon* with *pandoura*. This was the lute's Eastern name, thought to derive from the Sumerian *pan-tur* ("bow-little"). Such an etymology—which is far from assured—would point to the lute's derivation from a musical bow. In this connection the evolution of the ground bow into a full-blown necked chordophone becomes particularly meaningful (see page 380). Even now the long-necked lute of Armenia is called *pandir*.

From Greece the lute passed on to Rome. In late classical times it is sometimes seen with body still in the form of a spade but having a wider neck; three strings and frets are retained, but in Rome also it does not appear to have gained popularity. A new form, one with markedly incurved waist in a small, spade-shaped body, occurs in Coptic Egypt from the fourth to the eighth century A.D. Several examples of actual instruments are preserved in museum collections; these postdate by several centuries the short-necked lutes of similar shape but with larger bodies (for details of which, see page 411).

Long-necked *pandouras* were also played in Byzantium. A fifth-century mosaic in the former Imperial Palace of Istanbul represents a male lutenist holding an instrument with spade-shaped body, a neck that is by now no more than a rounded stick and that traverses the body, to emerge as a stub at the lower end—a spike lute—and three knobbed tuning pegs, two of which are inserted into the front, the third into the side of the neck. Equally important is the fact that the player holds a type of fan-shaped plectrum otherwise associated only with the Far East (see short-necked lutes, page 413). Another mosaic, this one of the sixth century and discovered in the nave of a church in Qasr el Lebia, west of Cyrene, Libya, contains an awkward rendering of a four-stringed, long-necked lute with disproportionately small body and outsized tuning pegs, inserted at an angle that seems to be a poor delineator's attempt to indicate frontal attachment. Frets are not visible on either mosaic. The shape of the tuning pegs foreshadows the T-shaped ones encountered on some Islamic *tanbūrs* (long-necked lutes) in our day, and the combination of frontal and lateral tuning pegs is still typical of many chordophones of the Moslem East, including northern India. Long-necked lutes did not arrive in India until the tenth century, probably in the wake of the Moslem invaders.

A Greek treatise of about 800 equates the *pandourion* with the *kobuz*, a lute—later also a fiddle—of Eastern origin, and mentions its three, four, or five strings and its seven frets. However, that the *kobuz* was a long-necked lute at that time is unlikely, for its namesakes known to us today are all of the short-necked variety. But that Byzantium continued to play the long-necked lute is clear from al-Khwarizmi's statement in the tenth century that the *qītāra* was an instrument of the Greeks and resembled the *tunbūr*, which we know to have had a long neck. In fact the *tunbūr* was, as we surmise from the etymology, a descendant of the Mesopotamian long-necked *pan-tur*. In al-Farabi's time (d. 950) the *tunbūr* had two strings, occasionally three, and five frets set at the upper portion of the long neck, frets that he attributed to the pre-Islamic period. The intervals they demarcated were microtones totaling a little over a minor third (representing the five top divisions of a forty-"fret" neck) and were, he informs us, in the process of being replaced by others having a larger compass, namely up to the interval of a fourth. At this time the strings appear to have been tuned a semitone apart; those of the Khorasan *tunbūr* were usually in unison, or else a semitone, even a tone, apart; all passed over a bridge, notched to prevent the strings from touching one another, and were rib fastened. Theorists frequently mention the *dastan*, a term employed for "fret"; it is derived from the Persian word *dest* ("hand"), and as such must originally have denoted stopping points. Although the short-necked *'ūd* was unfretted, the *tunbūr* really was a fretted instrument and has remained so ever since.

Use of a *tunbūr* as part of the grave goods at a tenth-century inhumation is recorded by ibn-Fadlan who set out in the year 921 on an embassy from the Caliph of Baghdad to the King of the Bulgars of the Middle Volga, who at that time dominated a large portion of the Balkans. On his way he witnessed the funeral of a chief man of the Swedish Rūs vikings. Prior to cremation on a ship the dead man was buried for ten days in a grave into which had been placed *nabīd* (an intoxicating drink), fruit, and a *tunbūr*, all of which were subsequently removed with the body. Whatever its name might have been among the Rūs, there seems little doubt that at this remote outpost—a riverside trading settlement—a long-necked lute was available.

A fourteenth-century Arabic commentary on the thirteenth-century *Kitab al-Adwan* of Safi ed-Din describes the *tunbūr* as having two strings tuned a fourth apart and a fretted neck. Smaller of body than the "lute" ('ūd), its neck was longer and thinner and its strings passed over a bridge. This last comment implies rib fastening. All told, this picture probably represents the *tunbūr* as it had been in al-Farabi's day.

THE SHORT-NECKED LUTE TO THE YEAR 1000

A Central Asian genesis has been postulated for the short-necked lute; this type may have originated among its Turkic populations and diffused west to Persia, east to China. It is first seen in Egypt in the Nineteenth Dynasty (1350–1200 B.C.), having probably come from Asia in Eighteenth Dynasty times, and was from the onset played with a plectrum. A unique terra-cotta statuette of the late second millennium, possibly of Cyprian origin but discovered in a Greek grave, is that of a woman holding a short-necked lute with pear-shaped body, one of the forms it was to retain for three millennia. Thereafter it is not seen again until the eighth century B.C., this time on clay figurines excavated at Susa, but unfortunately, beyond the fact that the bodies are ovoid, no details can be ascertained. It then disappears once more, to turn up in early Hellenistic times shaped like a future pandurina, and on a Hellenistic terra-cotta from Kom-es-Shukafa, Egypt, with slender body and clearly fretted neck.

Next it is depicted on art works of the Greco-Buddhist school of Gandhara from the first century A.D. The Gandhara instruments have large piriform bodies tapering to a neck, lateral tuning pegs, string holder on the belly, and a variable number of strings, from two (or two pairs?) to four or five, all of which features were to be perpetuated on both European and Near and Far Eastern lutes. Yet Gandhara instruments have one characteristic not found elsewhere: an indenting on each side of the body, giving the upper portion the appearance of an arrowhead, pointing downward on both sides. Sachs, who illustrates such an instrument (1940) calls them barbs (another is reproduced in Malraux [1954]). This form may have survived as today's bowed *sārindā*.

Contemporary with these is a sculptured frieze from Airtam on which several musicians are seen holding instruments, among them a short-necked lute. The stone frieze in question was found partly at Airtam, about three hundred kilometers southeast of Samarkand, and partly retrieved from the Amu Darya River, and had originally decorated the interior of a building, possibly a Buddhist temple, certainly dating from the Kushana period (first century B.C. to A.D. 176), and—according to

Picken—probably prior to A.D. 90, when the Kushana, known to the Chinese as *Yüeh-chih*, were forced to send tribute to China. The lute here depicted has an incurved, guitar-shaped body, a string holder for three strings, and four small C soundholes; the neck is missing, but from the disposition of the frieze it cannot have been very long. The strings are plucked with a plectrum while the lute is held horizontally. This form is not encountered in Europe or the Near East until the tenth century, but morphologically it agrees with the Byzantine bowed chordophones of the tenth and eleventh centuries. Quite possibly it represents the ancestor of our guitar. In India it appears, or reappears— for the Kushana kingdom comprised part of today's Afghanistan and of the Indian Punjab—after the Moslem conquest. Ovoid lutes with short necks are seen in southern India from the second to the fourth centuries, with five strings, lateral pegs, reversed pegbox, and string holder.

To Chinese sources we owe our earliest written records concerning the lute. In the *Shih Ming*, dating from between A.D. 126 and 270, it is stated that the *p'i p'a* originated among the (northern or western) barbarians, that is, foreigners, and according to the *Fen Su T'ung I* of about A.D. 200 it was of recent invention, had four strings and a length of three (local) feet and five inches, or about 90 centimeters (3 feet). Both texts mention to and fro motions of the hand, authorizing us to assume the *p'i p'a* to have been a lute from its inception rather than a form of zither subsequently transmuted into a lute. Furthermore, it was referred to as "that which is played on horseback," although this is not conclusive testimony. The indicated length is about that of the Japanese *gaku biwa*, introduced during the T'ang dynasty (618–907) and still played in the imperial court orchestra of Japan. A fragment of an essay on the *p'i p'a* from the third century mentions twelve *chu*, believed to indicate frets, as they are matched with the [twelve] pitchpipes. (For this paragraph, I have followed Picken [1965].)

Short-necked lutes are represented in China from the fifth or sixth century on. A Chinese seven-stringed-long zither miraculously preserved— together with several other musical instruments—at the Shōsoin of Nara, Japan, has been dated by van Gulik (1940) to the fifth century; a decoration upon its upper surface includes a lute player holding a *p'i p'a* with large, circular body, straight tapering neck, four strings attached to lateral pegs set in an apparently straight pegbox, belly stringholder, and fixed frets on both neck and body; a broad band is set from left to right across part of the lower belly. Chinese bas-reliefs from the first half of the sixth century also portray short-necked lutes.

A bent-necked *p'i p'a* is first referred to in the seventh century *Sui History*, where it is said to have come from Hsi-liang (modern Kansu Province) in the early fifth century; other sources permit us to equate

Chinese *p'i p'a*. Probably
ninth century. Shōsoin, Nara.

this form with the ovoid lute of foreign origin. The circular *p'i p'a* depicted on the Shōsoin zither is comparable to an actual instrument from the late eighth or early ninth century also preserved in the Shōsoin. This measures 1 meter by 39 centimeters (roughly 40 by 15 inches), has a circular body ornamented front and back, a very slender and slightly tapering neck, four lateral pegs, an elaborate string holder, and fourteen wooden frets spaced in groups of four, five, and five (counting from the top down), the last four of which are placed on the belly. Of two ovoid lutes from the same period and in the same collection, one has a bent-back neck, four strings, and a tear-drop shaped body very large in proportion to its short and slim neck; the other is straight necked, has five strings, almond-shaped body, and a broad band across the belly above the string holder. This band served the same purpose as the later tortoiseshell or wooden plaque of Near Eastern lutes, namely that of protecting the body from damage by the plectrum. The large, fan-shaped plectrum shown on a relief from a tomb in Chengtu, Szechwan, erected between 907 and 913, is of a type that has remained in common use in the Far East until now. With its emphatic, brushing strokes it could damage the delicate bellies, hence the need for protecting them.

The essential difference between these circular and ovoid body types is not only morphological but structural; in the former, body and neck always consist of separate parts clearly joined together, while ovoid bodies taper off indistinctly, the joint of body to neck not being marked; indeed, the body may be prolonged to form part or all of the neck.

Further west we find the *barbat* (pl. *barabit*) played in Sassanid Persia, represented from the fourth century A.D. on. The word itself is a corruption of the Greek *barbiton,* but as *barbat* also means "duck" in Persian, the instrument has been said to be so called because it is shaped like this animal, another instance of persuasive folk etymology. Around 600 we hear of *barabit* in the hands of Byzantine singing girls, and from Sassanian art objects we find it to be a short-necked lute with ovoid body, four strings fastened to lateral pegs, and belly string-holder. In the late ninth century ibn-Salama mentions frets in connection with the *barbat,* and in a tenth-century Arabic encyclopedia it is identified as a Persian lute. However, when ibn-Sina (Avicenna) described the same instrument in the eleventh century it was unfretted. This seeming contradiction is in keeping with our knowledge of the fretting of Arabic lutes: all theoretical writers from al-Farabi's day on go into considerable detail with regard to the correct emplacement of frets in order to obtain the specific

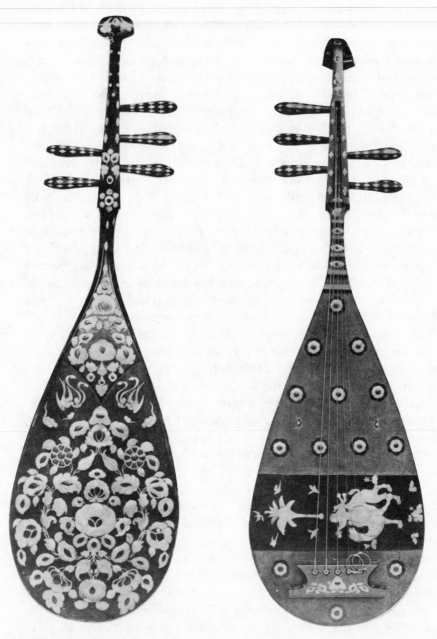

Chinese lute with almond-shaped body. Probably ninth century.
Shōsoin, Nara.

microtones desired, but as far as we know these frets remained theoretical stopping points serving mathematical demonstrations only—on short-necked lutes, that is—and actual ligatures were not applied then or now. By contrast, Near Eastern long-necked lutes were and still are fretted.

The Arabic *'ūd*, ancestor of our Western lute, appeared in Mecca in the sixth century, according to Farmer, and was said by al-Farabi to be the instrument most in favor in his lifetime, when it had four strings. The word *'ūd*, which became "lute" in the West, means "wood," specifically aloe wood. But it also means "tortoise," as Erlanger (1930) pointed out, and may consequently be considered a translation of the Greek word *chelys* (see lyres, page 365). Yet Sachs (1940) drew attention to an interpretation as "flexible stick," corroborating his assumption that early lutes were derived from the musical bow.

Al-Farabi not only mentions the *'ūd*'s frets, but states that they fulfilled the function of bridges (i.e., nuts)—but see the comment above. These frets, four in number, were named for the fingers that touched them, and al-Khwarizmi in the late tenth century also gives much detail regarding their correct emplacement. The strings could be plucked either with a plectrum or with thumb and forefinger, but as they were tuned in fourths, the perfect system (i.e., double octave) was not obtainable; in order to complete it two extra frets could be added for the little finger (but this, al-Farabi says, causes the inconvenience of obliging the player to slide his fingers a great distance from their normal position), or, if the existing tuning were modified to complete the scale, some tones would be lacking. Another possibility suggested was the addition of a fifth string tuned a fourth above the highest string, and this last option was the one adopted; indeed, Safi ed-Din in the thirteenth century knew the five-stringed *'ūd*. Al-Farabi's reference to the sliding of the fingers implies an absence of frets, for glissandi are possible only on a smooth fingerboard and, in modern times at least, are greatly relished by Near Eastern audiences. Although the *'ūd* was tuned in fourths, so-called abnormal lute tunings existed, the most common of which was that in fifths. A four-stringed lute so tuned enabled the performer to attain and even exceed the double octave. Tuning by ditones is also given as a possibility. But the ultimate solution led to the adoption of extra strings, and by the sixteenth century the *'ūd* had a total of six.

Postclassical lutes of Europe derive from these Arabic forebears, and although initially both long-necked and short-necked versions were in use, the dichotomy of the lute ends for practical purposes in the final adoption of the short-necked model in Europe—which was promptly given a longer neck than it had had; long-necked varieties continued a marginal existence as folk instruments. The reason for this preference is to be seen in the fact that short-necked lutes have a larger number of strings with a potentially far greater compass, which the West set about exploiting to the limit.

THE CLASSICAL EUROPEAN LUTE

At the time of their introduction to Europe the Arab lutes were unfretted, and Sachs (1920) has shown that European lutes remained unfretted until the fifteenth century. Lutes reached Spain with the Moslem conquest, but the short-necked type, destined to become the West's "classical" lute, is not encountered outside the peninsula until the thirteenth century, when it is both illustrated and mentioned in literature: as *leu* about 1270 in France, not until *King Richard* (ca. 1325) in England, although recorded there in 1306 when Janin le Lutour played at the Feast of Westminster. In Spain itself it is portrayed on tenth-century Hispano-Arabic ivories.

Instruments of different sizes are seen in the thirteenth-century *Cantigas de Santa María,* one of which has bass proportions, nine strings and as many pegs, probably representing four pairs and a chanterelle. The iconography of the fourteenth century shows lutes with pyriform bodies and Oriental roses, with neck so short there would be no room for frets, others with perfectly circular bodies and somewhat longer necks. Both types have pegboxes reversed at an acute angle, lateral pegs, belly stringholder, and four strings. Like the short-necked Arab lutes, they were unfretted and played with a quill-type plectrum. The lute spread rapidly throughout Europe and was played by amateurs and professionals, men and women, alike. Tuning of the four-stringed lute is said by later authors to have been CFAD, with the fifth string subsequently added to the treble, the sixth string to the bass. In 1396 the Duke of Orléans had a *joueur de viele et de lus* in his employ, foreshadowing the parallelism between lute and viol—due to the similarity of their left-hand technique—that would later induce Ganassi to write a tutor adapted to both instruments, and the Spaniards to call the two by a single name.

During the fifteenth century lutes continued to be plucked with a quill, but finger plucking was coming in, for Tinctoris (ca. 1484) mentions both manners of playing. By his day the number of strings had already been augmented to five or six (the sixth course is seen by 1500) with the two middle strings tuned to the interval of a major third and the remainder in fourths. A circular body form predominated until the mid-fifteenth century, judging from the iconography, after which it was replaced by the pear shape, and the plectrum was retained until the end of the century. The fifteenth century also witnessed the application of frets to the neck, at first four, later increasing to seven, eight, or ten. Originally of gut, during the decade of 1470–1480 they were replaced by fixed frets of metal, a signal in Italy at least for an increase in plucking with bare fingers. Tinctoris wrote of the lute that it had five and sometimes six strings, and that in order to obtain a greater volume of sound a second string might be added to any of the courses and tuned to its octave, except for the first string—here the reference would be to the chanterelle. Lute strings are usually made of gut, he continues, but the Germans invented others of low pitch made of brass and tuned to the (lower) octave. He is our earliest source of information on the geminating of lute strings and of the use of metal ones (*Leyrendrotzieher*, "lyre" wire drawers, were established at Nuremberg from 1414 on; "lyre" at that time could have referred to several instruments, such as lute, citole, or even harp).

The substitution of finger plucking for plectrum plucking denotes the passing from a monophonic to a polyphonic style of playing and the emergence of the lute as a true solo instrument. Tinctoris was greatly impressed by the lutenist who performed two-, three-, and even four-part music. The first music written specifically for the lute also dates from this century, and was notated then as later in tablature, with letters of the alphabet or numerals designating either the open string or the finger position on a given string and fret; hence pitches indicated by early writers must be conceived of as being at relative rather than absolute pitch. According to a late fifteenth-century manuscript (N 1117) at Trinity College, Cambridge, "to settle a lute loke that there be a Trebill, Secunde trebill, Meene, Tenor, and Basse. The secunde trebill to be sett a 4te from the trebill. The meene a 4te from the secunde trebill. The tenor a 3de from the meene. And the bass a 4te from the tenor," resulting in a relative tuning of CFADG. Gerle in 1532 gives the tuning of a six-stringed lute as A°d°g°b°e′a′.

Many sixteenth-century writers give instructions for the tuning of lutes, almost invariably with the counsel to pull up the chanterelle (called *Quint* [i.e., "fifth string"] by German writers, *canto* by Italian) as high as it will go without breaking. As neither stop nor thickness of string was standardized at that time, such advice is understandable; the Middle Ages had long before discovered that a chordophone sounds best when its strings are under maximum tension. Details of fretting are set forth in a manuscript (FX 11) of about 1575 of Basel University Library. Translated into the nomenclature employed above, the three lower frets were to be made of mean strings, the next two of second trebles, the following two of trebles, and the last of a "very small string indeed" for a total of eight frets. Earlier in the century only seven had been utilized.

By 1500 the lute had assumed its final and classical form, with large pyriform body, flat wooden top with rose-covered soundhole, pegbox reversed at an angle of about ninety degrees to the neck, and a vaulted resonator composed of a varying number of very thin ribs; some authors considered from nine to eleven the best, but as many as forty are encountered in practice. A wide variety of materials was employed: instruments in the Fugger family's *Kunstkammer* at Augsburg included in 1566 lutes of ebony, ivory, whalebone; of gray, black, and red *canna d'India*; of cypress, brazilwood, yellow and red maple, sycamore, yew, and even oak (and Galilei mentions pine and beech). But the best woods, according to Trichet (ca. 1640) were maple or sycamore (*érable*), yew, plum, cherry, or ebony. Mace (1676) and other writers of his day asserted that "air wood" was the best for lutes, with English maple next. Occasionally the word appears as "hairwood"; some modern writers take it to represent the German word *Ahorn*, ("maple") (the *a* is pronounced as in "father"). Yet it seems more logical to derive it from the French *érable* ("sycamore"), a word phonetically far closer. Ivory and ebony were generally considered tonally inferior, despite Trichet's recommendation.

In 1507 the first lute music was printed (by Spinaccino), and in 1511 the first book devoted entirely to musical instruments—Virdung's *Musica getutscht*—was published. This contains detailed instructions on lute playing and lute tablature, and depicts a six-stringed, seven-fret instrument: the golden age of the lute had started. Different-sized instruments were grouped by Judenkönig (1523) into regular and great lutes, the latter pitched a fourth below the former. He is already familiar with *scordatura*, that is, the lowering in pitch of the bottom string by a tone where necessary, in order to accommodate the compass of a given composition. A decade later, Lanfranco called the lute the most perfect of instruments; his was a six-course model, bichord except for the chanterelle, with the strings of the three lowest courses doubling at the octave. His tuning is A°d°g°b°e'a' (the same as that of his tenor viola da gamba) with a compass extending to e² on the seventh fret.

The lute was less popular in Spain, where the *vihuela* (see page 451) was preferred; that it had reentered the peninsula from the north is shown by its name, or rather, one of its names—*vihuela de Flandres*. As elsewhere, the lowest three or four courses of Spanish lutes were geminated in the mid-sixteenth century to form octaves; the tuning was that of the *vihuela*: G°c°f°a°d'g'. This appears to have been the most common tuning of the sixteenth-century lute, and by no means restricted to the Iberian peninsula. Later the guitar took over in Spain. A letter by Constantijn Huygens written in 1673 relates that J(acques) Gautier, perhaps the most celebrated lutenist of his day, played for two hours in the king's chamber in Madrid, whereupon the Spanish grandees present exclaimed: "*Grave lastima es que no tañe la guitarra*" ("what a shame he doesn't play the guitar"), tempting Gautier to "throw his lute at their ears."

One of the most popular tutors of the century was that of Adrien Le Roy, first published in France in 1557 (no longer extant) and then in English translations in 1568 and 1574. He mentions "the lutes of the newer invention with thirtene strynges," the last pitched a fourth below the bass, and advises "the little finger serveth but to keepe the hand from [i.e., firm] upon the beallie of the lute . . .," a playing position evident in so many paintings of the sixteenth and seventeenth centuries. It prevented the bulging and varnished resonator from slipping, but at the cost of immobilizing the right hand. This instruction was reiterated up to the end of the seventeenth century. The new seven-course lute of Le Roy developed into a nine-course model by the end of the sixteenth century, and the basic lute tuning, from G° to g', became known as the "old" tuning, as it no longer corresponded to the musical requirements of the times. The added strings were open bass strings called *cordes avalées* in French.

In 1600 Antoine Francisque published pieces for a lute *à cordes avalées* tuned B♭'E♭°F°G°B♭°f°b♭°d'g' in his collection entitled *Le trésor d'Orphée*. Another new tuning of the seventeenth century was the *accord nouveau* ("new tuning") A°d°f°a°d'f', significant for having continued in use in Germany into the eighteenth century, after the lute had been abandoned in other countries. In Italy, Caravaggio (d. 1610) had painted *The Lute Player*, now in Leningrad, with a six-course lute; but when Saraceni (d. 1620) copied the painting, he gave the lute seven courses. Banchieri (1609) tuned a seven-course lute F°G°c°f°a°d'g' with optional *scordatura* of the low string to C° or Bb'; his *leuto grosso*, or bass lute, was tuned a fourth lower, C°D°G°c°e°a°d'. His tuning indications are valuable, for they no longer represent relative pitches but absolute ones; they correspond to the keys of his organ.

From a *Short Treatise of Lute Playing* by John Dowland, appended to Robert Dowland's *Varietie of Lute Lessons* of 1610, we learn that "these Bases must be both of one bignesse, yet it hath been a general custom (although not so much used any where as here in England) to set a small and a great string together . . ." (i.e., at the octave), and "all the lutes I can remember used eight frets." Mathias Mason then invented three more frets, "the which were made of wood, and glued upon the belly, and from thence about some few years after, by the French Nation, the necks of the lutes were lengthened, and thereby increased 2 frets more, so that all those lutes . . . are of tenne frets" (i.e., had ten frets on the neck); "the first 2 frets are the size of a counter-tenor, the 3 and 4th great means, 5 and 6 small means, the rest trebles," with reference to string sizes. Seven years later, Jean-Baptiste Bésard was advising his readers that their lutes should have at least ten courses as used in Italy and France (he had been a pupil of Lorenzini in Rome); with little finger still glued to the lute's belly, technique for the right hand included stretching the thumb with all force as far as possible while holding the other fingers curved as though the fist were closed; he proposes all sorts of methods for increasing the span—including application of oil of tartar.

The alto lute (*Choristlaute* in German) remained the type instrument of a family embracing both smaller and larger sizes. Seven, eight, or nine courses were not uncommon in the first quarter of the seventeenth century (Praetorius gives the tuning of a nine-course lute as C°D°F°G°-c°f°a°d'g'), and archlutes (see page 426), with their second pegbox and off-board strings for the deeper pitches—needed especially for continuo playing—were in everyday use by then. Further additions of bass strings to the regular lute in order to meet the demands of continuo players required widening the fingerboard, consequently also the neck itself and the string holder, as well as lengthening the pegbox; furthermore, the body had to be made of thicker and broader ribs in order to withstand the extra tension. The number of strings passing over the fingerboard increased until it reached the limit imposed by the size of the human hand, so that finally strings had to be placed off board and given a separate nut and pegbox. Thus the archlute came into existence and the decadence of the true lute set in. Such was the impact of the archlute that Giustiniani could write (ca. 1628) of the lute's having been almost entirely abandoned in Italy since the introduction of the theorbo.

In the seventeenth and early eighteenth centuries old lutes were preferred to new ones for their sonority (as Trichet remarks, because the wood was seasoned), and this preference apparently included *mrs les Gautiers*, a French family of musicians and expert lutenists. (When the Queen Mother, Marie de Médicis, took up the lute under the aegis of "old [Ennemord] Gaultier [*sic*]" all her court started playing and, as Tallemant des Réaux relates, even Richelieu took lessons from him.) Old Bologna instruments were particularly favored. Jacques Gautier wrote to Constantijn Huygens that the old, nine-ribbed Bologna lutes had been made by Laux Maler; that mostly they were of medium size and not good for singing to; that Sigismondo Maler and others made a slightly larger one with eleven ribs; that a lute of Laux Maler's had been barred and necked (i.e., rebarred and renecked) by Master Nicolas, while another of the same maker had been sold that had only body and soundboard by Maler. Thus, although older instruments might be preferred, in practice they had to be modernized to accommodate the new strings. Huygens, long interested in the purchase of a Bologna lute—he had written Gautier from London requesting him to procure him a nine-ribbed lute—received a letter from G. P. Foscarini of Paris in 1648 informing him that he, Foscarini, possessed in Italy no fewer than five lutes by Laux Maler, found in a *guardarobba* of the late Duke of Urbino. Huygens replied, saying that there existed a few excellent lutes in Florence, to be had cheaper than in Paris: "The old-fashioned short necks can be lengthened according to the newer fashion." Not only were lutes enlarged or transformed into theorbos (Huygens also attempted to buy a large lute with the intention of having it rebuilt as a theorbo) but they were also cut down to make smaller ones. Such instruments were known as "cut" lutes; "cutting" included narrowing and shortening the neck.

But as the century wore on lutes gave way increasingly to archlutes; when Thomas Mace wrote his *Musick's Monument* (1676) as a memorial to the lute and its passing, he was, ironically enough, concerned with the theorbo-lute rather than with the true lute. By the end of the seventeenth century lute playing had declined everywhere except in

Lutes and citterns: (1) Paduan theorbo; (2) lute with off-board strings or theorbo'd lute; (3) choir [pitch] lute; (4) quinterna; (5) little mandora; (6) six-course choir [pitch] cittern; (7) small English cittern; (8) small fiddle, called *poche*. From Michael Praetorius, *Theatrum instrumentorum*, 1620.

Germany, in which country it acquired renewed importance and attention. But while Titon du Tillet in France was complaining (1727) of the lute's decadence, writing that the difficulty of playing coupled with its sparse use in concerts had caused it to be abandoned, "and I do not think one can find in Paris more than three or four old men who play it," such composer-virtuosi as Ernest Baron and the brothers Sivius Leopold and Siegmund Weiss were bringing lute playing to new heights of perfection in Germany.

The *accord nouveau* remained the basic tuning. A more robust build and the use of covered strings made possible the addition of more strings, yet confining them all to one pegbox. Baron, writing in the same year as Titon du Tillet, gives the tuning of an eleven-course lute as C°D°E°-F°G°A°d°f°a°d'f', with all the strings of equal length but only nine of which could be reached for stopping, that is, the lute had nine pairs and two single strings, and with the number of frets increased from nine for the E° and F° strings up to twelve for the two chanterelles, thereby increasing the compass to three-and-one-half octaves, C° to f². After the lute proper had been discarded, archlutes managed to hold their own a little longer, until the whole family was replaced by the easier and cheaper citterns and guitars, or exchanged for the louder and more sustained tone of the cello for thorough-bass parts.

A critical organological appraisal of the lute leaves no doubt that it was one of the most inefficient musical instruments ever conceived: the bulbous form of its large body made it most difficult to keep in position, while the varnish—necessary for resistance to dirt and dust—increased the chances of its slipping, so that for centuries lutes had to be rendered stationary by "glueing" the little finger of the right hand to the belly, thereby immobilizing the entire hand, to the detriment of dynamic variation (most modern performers have abandoned this technique); moreover, it was difficult to tune and the strings were always breaking. Mattheson's apt summing up (1713) is well known: a lutenist who has attained the age of eighty, he wrote, has spent certainly sixty years of his life tuning; and what is worse is that, among a hundred performers, particularly if they be amateurs, it is hard to find two capable of tuning properly; either the strings or the frets or the tuning pegs leave much to be desired; and he was informed that in Paris it cost as much to keep a lute in good condition as to keep a horse. His irony, it must be admitted, had a basis in fact.

A final attempt at updating the lute was undertaken in the mid-nine-

teenth century, when a lute body—frequently that of an old instrument
—was fitted with a guitar neck, fingerboard, and pegdisk, the resultant
hybrid being then called lute guitar. Some were given six single strings,
others five pairs of strings; sometimes neck and fingerboard were drilled
for the attaching of a *capotasto* to facilitate transposition without change
of fingering. Of the lute, only the shell was left.

ARCHLUTES

A new family of bass lutes arose in the sixteenth century in response to
the lutenists' requirements for additional bass strings. As the reach of a
player's hand is limited, fingerboards could not be widened indefinitely,
and so a number of open strings came to be placed off board, that is,
next to the fingerboard but not above it, and secured to a separate pegbox, more often placed above the first. This increase in length of the
neck was tantamount to transforming the short-necked lute into a
long-necked yet multistringed version, organologically equivalent to
having your cake and eating it. But whereas the bass strings of the true
lute were always stopped, the newer archlutes were characterized by
their open basses. Archlutes assumed several forms: the theorbo, the
theorbo'd lute, the *chitarrone*, and the angelica.

Lutes with a second pegbox were known as early as the mid-sixteenth
century: the Fugger collection in Augsburg contained by 1566 *ain
fischbaine Laute mit zwen Krägen* ("a whalebone lute with two necks"),
and experimental models continued to be made throughout the second
half of the century. Alessandro Piccinini, sometimes credited with invention of the theorbo, wrote (1623) that in 1598 he had caused to be
made by the Padovan luthier Cristoforo Eberle an experimental lute
with body long enough to carry bass strings, and with two string holders
spaced far apart (*et li fece fare per prova un liuto di corpo cosi lungo, che
serviva per tratta de i contrabassi, et haveva due scanelli molti lon-
tani . . .*). The appearance of his instrument may be judged by an
extant experimental model of 1595 signed by Vendelino Venere (Tieffenbrucker), formerly in Ambras Castle, now in Vienna: it has an elongated
oval body and short neck. Seven pairs of regular strings are attached
to a string holder placed about halfway up the belly, passing over a
fretted fingerboard, and three open strings are attached near the lower
end; of a total length of 147 centimeters (58 inches), 95½ centimeters
(37½ inches) are taken up by the body.

A different approach to the problem of bass strings is illustrated by another instrument in the same collection, dating from the same period. Here the unknown maker has maintained an elongated body form, ornamentally indented on its right side; each pair of the stopped strings is affixed to its individual small string holder, one positioned lower than the other, and the open strings likewise have separate string holders for each pair, also one below the other, but placed at the lower end of the belly and pegged to a second, extremely short neck. The highest three strings are attached to pegs set immediately into the rim of the body close to the main neck, a feature subsequently abandoned in western Europe art instruments, but which recurs in eastern Europe.

Piccinini's instrument proved to be a dud tonally, as he himself admitted, and later the long-bodied, short-necked forms were discontinued in favor of the now classical short-bodied, long-necked principle. If Piccinini did not conceive the archlute, he may at least be credited with inventing its name: *arciliuto*.

THE THEORBO

The theorbo—its etymology is unknown—is said by Giovanni Battista Doni to have been invented in Venice by Antonio Naldi, called Il Bardella, but the claim is questionable and has also been accorded to others. The first theorbos are believed to have been made in Padua and are mentioned by Giovanni Florio in 1598, at which time the word also occurred in France. From then on it became an increasingly popular continuo instrument, and remained in use as such up to the second half of the eighteenth century, and in Germany even longer.

The theorbo of Praetorius, which he calls Padovan, to distinguish it from the Roman *chitarrone*, was five feet long, with eight on-board strings and the same number of open ones, tuned D'E'F'G'A'B'C°D°/E°F°G°c°d°f°g°a°. On such large instruments, the greater distances between frets rendered any nimble-fingered lute technique impossible. In contrast to the lute—and this is one of the theorbo's distinguishing features—all the strings were originally single and did not become geminated before the eighteenth century, the period of the instrument's decline. It was differentiated from the lute by a second pegbox to accommodate the off-board strings, at first set in a vertical continuation of the neck, later above and to one side of the main pegbox, the two being separated by a short, S-curved neck. It retained the lute's fretting.

Praetorius gives the length of the on-board strings as over three feet, those of the open strings at about four and one-half feet. In the first half of the seventeenth century smaller theorbos were made in Italy, but neither their stringing nor their tuning became standardized. Around 1700 James Talbot lists the tuning of the English theorbo as G'A'B'C° D°E°F°G°/A°d°g°b°e'a', with each string paired to its octave up to A°, after which they were paired in unisons, the chanterelle remaining single, as usual. Another tuning, this one for a single-strung instrument, was A'B'C°D°E°F°G°/A°d°g°b°e'a'. Talbot also describes two sizes of French theorbo, a fourth apart in pitch, the smaller of which, tuned C°D°E°F°G°A°B♭°c°/d°g°c'e'a'd², preserved the relative tuning of the lute on its stopped strings. This remained a solo instrument and was to be called *théorbe en pièce* by Laborde (1780); the larger version was reserved for accompaniments.

THE THEORBO LUTE

Of the various archlutes, the theorbo'd lute, or theorbo lute, most closely resembles the lute proper. It retained the lute's pairwise stringing with single chanterelle, and had either a second nut for carrying one or two open strings, or else a second pegbox set in a vertical continuation of the neck. The body was smaller and the strings far shorter than those of the theorbo. Praetorius depicts a *testudo theorbata* with rib fastener, and described it as having seven or eight on-board courses of bichord strings, and six single off-board strings. However, neither extant instruments nor the iconography of the period bear out the rib fastening of his strings. He gives its tuning as F'G'A'B'C°D°/E°F°G°c°f°-a°d'g'. This instrument was taken up by the French seventeenth-century school of lutenists and by their followers abroad, and in Britain it became known as the French lute. It is the instrument to which Thomas Mace's famous *Musick's Monument* of 1676 is chiefly devoted—a theorbo lute with eight courses on the upper and four on the lower pegbox. Mersenne shows a small eleven-course *luth théorbé*, strung pairwise throughout except for the chanterelle and tuned C°D°/E°F°G°A°d°g°b°e'a', the four lowest strings duplicated at the octave, the remainder at the unison.

THE CHITARRONE

The *chitarrone* was but an enlarged version of the theorbo, with very long neck but slightly smaller body, and the two instruments were often confused. Praetorius mentions two varieties of theorbo, one gut strung, the other strung with steel and brass wires. The latter was the *chitarrone,* also known as Roman theorbo, of which Piccinini relates (1623) that it was in use in Bologna and that it had metal strings.

The word *citarone* occurs already in a Mantua document of 1524, but we cannot be sure of what it stood for then—possibly a bass *chitarra,* or guitar, as it does today. The *chitarrone* as we know it appears in great detail in the beautiful portrait of Lady Mary Wroth (d. 1586), daughter of the Duke of Northumberland, now in the National Portrait Gallery: a tall instrument with vertical pegbox set on a long, straight neck surmounted by a second pegbox for the off-board strings. The body is that of a smallish lute, the broad neck is fretted. Stringing of the *chitarrone* varied; Banchieri (1609) gives its tuning as G′A′B♭′C°D°E°F°-G°c°f°a°d′g′ (or d°), his chanterelle being marked *come piace.* A decade later Praetorius describes it as six feet long, with a body smaller than that of a (Paduan) theorbo, made not only in Rome but also in Prague—a measure of its popularity in his day—with six stopped and eight open strings tuned F′G′A′B′C°D°E°F°/G°c°d°f°g°a°. In the same year, Monteverdi published his seventh book of madrigals containing a *canzonetta a due voci concertata con duoi violini, chitarone o spineta:* it was to be a preferred continuo instrument for the remainder of the century. Moreover, the stopped strings were just short enough to permit their being fretted for solo playing.

But side by side with the specialized nomenclature that had developed, the word "archlute" continued in use as a general designation of bass lutes having open strings, an expression surely as accommodating as the term *Clavier* was to be. The trio sonata for two violins and *violone o arcileuto* of John Ravenscroft, published in Rome in 1695, could presumably be played by the owner of either theorbo, *chitarrone,* or even angelica.

THE ANGELICA

The angelica of the seventeenth and eighteenth centuries differs from other archlutes by having diatonically tuned strings throughout, thus obviating the necessity for frets, which were consequently dispensed with. Its very long neck carried sixteen or seventeen strings attached to the usual two pegboxes. All the strings were single, and except for this feature and for its lack of frets it was virtually identical with the theorbo, of which it may have been an offshoot, created with the object of obtaining greater sonority. Pepys mentions it in 1660, and Talbot at the end of the century calls it angel lute; he gives it sixteen strings, a diatonic tuning from D° to e′, a compass of just over two octaves. Although popular in Britain it seems to have been little played on the Continent; in fact, Fuhrmann (1706) states that it was an English instrument. Mattheson (1713) knew it and comments on its being easier to play than a lute, as it had more courses.

ARCHLUTES IN EASTERN EUROPE

The archlute was taken to eastern Europe and became widely known in eighteenth-century Poland and the Ukraine under the name of *torban*, a word derived from *tiorba* or *théorbe*. Early in the nineteenth century it enjoyed a short-lived popularity in central Russia, becoming extinct there by 1825, but in Poland it continued to be played until the last quarter of the nineteenth century and is still known in the Ukraine in a form having thirty or thirty-one open gut strings. The *torban*'s main pegbox carried five pairs of strings tuned in octaves, and two single chanterelles, plus four single strings called *pristrunki* to the right of the chanterelles, held by pegs set in the rim of the soundboard and sharing the common string holder, prolonged for this purpose across the right side of the belly. All *pristrunki* were open strings. *Torbans* were tuned to D°G°c°F°/C°D°G°c°f°g°a°, with the *pristrunki* sounding from b′ to a³ diatonically.

Pristrunki remind us of the extra treble strings on the early experimental archlutes described above (pages 424–425). They appear again in a modified form on a modern Russian chordophone called *bandura*, a short-necked lute with large, circular body, violin-type scroll, metal tuning pins set frontally at the base of the scroll, and numerous strings stretched over tiny individual bridges fanning out to the edge of the belly. An older archlute of the Ukraine also bears the name of *bandura*; this has an oval body and two pegboxes for six open and as many stopped strings.

REGIONAL LUTES

By the sixteenth century the long-necked Eastern lute had penetrated to southern Italy and Sicily, although it did not reach France or Germany until the early eighteenth century. Generally known thereafter by its Italian name, the *colascione*—the word may be an augmentative of *collo* ("neck")—has a small body and disproportionately long neck, attaining a length of about 2 meters (6½ feet). The entire neck bears movable frets, varying between sixteen and twenty-four in number. Originally furnished with but two or three strings, these were augmented to five or six during the seventeenth century. Initially a plectrum was utilized.

Although derived from the long-necked *tanbūr*, the *colascione* adopted the belly string-holder and occasionally even the reversed pegbox of a classical European lute. Seventeenth-century writers specify that its belly was sometimes half of wood and half of parchment, a typical Eastern arrangement. Tunings are given as $E°A°d°$, with the E omitted if the instrument had only two strings, or c' c^2 g^2—which should certainly read two octaves lower. In the 1767 edition of the *Encyclopédie méthodique* it was said to have three strings and sixteen frets; the 1785 edition reported it as being no longer in use. In Germany it took on extra strings. Mattheson (1713) writes of it as a continuo instrument with five or six strings in lute tuning; contemporaneously, Buonanni (1722) describes it as having two or three strings but illustrates it with five, calls it *calascione turchesco*, and says it was still played in the kingdom of Naples as well as by Turkish women. It continued as a folk instrument in Naples, played with a plectrum, together with a smaller form known as *colasciontino* or *mezzo colascione*.

When the Colla brothers concertized on the *colascione* in various European cities in the 1760s and 1770s, they called it a new instrument, from which one may perhaps infer that it was no longer known outside southern Italy. Today it is played only in Sicily.

Of the numerous regional lutes played in eastern Europe, several still bear the names of their Oriental forebears. The *kobuz* known to Byzantium as *pandourion*, for instance (see page 409), also known to Hungary in the Middle Ages, is mentioned in a German poem of the early fourteenth century (*Gottes Zeit* by Heinrich von der Neuen Stadt, cited in Sachs [1940]), described by ibn-Ghaibi (as *qūpūz*) in the fifteenth century as having a skin belly and five pairs of strings, penetrated to Turkey, where it had a wooden belly; spread to Romania (where it is called *qūbūz* in the older literature); Poland; and Russia as *cobza* (*kobza*). In Romania it has a mandolin-shaped body, very short neck, retains the Oriental multiple small soundholes on the belly and from five to twelve strings in mixed unison and octave pairs (e.g., $d°d'$ $a°a'$

d°d° g°g′g′), and is played either with a plectrum or with the bare fingers. The musical amateur, Felix Platter of Basel (d. 1614), had a *cobza* in his collection of musical instruments.

Again in the wake of Islam, the *qūpūz* spread east as far as Indonesia, where its descendant, the *gambus*, is usually bowed nowadays but also plucked, and west to Madagascar and Zanzibar—the Malagasy *kabosa* is identical to the *gambus*, pointing to its route of arrival. Other areas where the *qūpūz* exists are Latvia, the Ukraine, Arabia, and among the Kirghiz and Tatars (as *kobys*); the related modern Greek *koubouzi* is a bass lute introduced from Turkey. Turkic hunters of the Altai Mountains accompany themselves on *kobys* to entertain the master spirits of the *taïga*, as spirits are known to be attracted by the music and to show their gratitude by assisting players to take plentiful game. Kirghiz and some Siberian shamans induce their trances by dancing to the magical melody of a *kobuz* in preference to the more usual drumming.

Another east European lute, this one long necked, is the Russian *dombra*, whose name betrays its descent from the *tunbūr* (tnbr =dmbr). It is known to have had three strings in the sixteenth century. Today it has a rounded lute body, long fretted neck, three metal strings tuned in fourths, and a pegdisk, and is rib fastened. *Dombras* are played with a plectrum and made in several sizes. Among the Kazak and the Volga Kalmuck, as well as in Mongolia, they have triangular bodies and narrow, elongated necks with movable frets and two strings.

The balalaika, whose name first occurs at the end of the seventeenth century, is a descendant of this instrument. Older instruments had but two strings, augmented—probably in the nineteenth century—to three strings; modern instruments are characterized by a triangular body, long and thin fretted neck, rib-fastened strings, and simple pegdisk. The strings, usually single and of gut, can be tuned in a number of different ways, for example, e′e′a′, b°e′a′, or a°d′a′. Since its "improvement" by V. V. Andreyev, the balalaika, formerly an instrument of northern and central Russian peasantry, has been made in six sizes, and from a folk instrument has become a popular instrument. However, the Kamchadal of northeastern Siberia still play a two-stringed version, and Buryat hunters—also of Siberia—sing and play the balalaika to forest spirits who are fond of music and who show their gratitude by assisting huntsmen to catch many squirrels and sables.

Reference has already been made to the archlutes of eastern Europe.

LUTES OUTSIDE EUROPE

Outside Europe, the *tunbūr* still lives on as *tanbūr*, little changed since al-Farabi's day. That of the Near East is similar in appearance to the long-necked lutes of ancient Mesopotamia and Egypt. Popular ever since, it is found over an area extending from the Balkans to India, typically with small, piriform body, fretted neck, and pegs inserted directly into the neck from both front and sides (compare the ancient mosaics mentioned on page 408). When Villoteau, a member of Napoleon's scientific expedition to Egypt, examined five kinds of *tambura* played there, he found them all to have oval bodies, wire strings played with plectra, and still lacking pegdisk or pegbox, the pegs being inserted directly into the neck from front and sides. Favorite instrument of the Turks—Tinctoris, who heard it played when the Turks took Otranto in 1480, likened its shape to that of a large spoon with three strings—the Anatolian *tanbūr* now has four pairs of strings tuned a°c′d′d′ with frets providing the twenty-four microtones for the lowest octave of the Turkish system, which are played on the d′ d′ strings; for the upper octave there are fewer frets as a full complement would lie too closely together, and consequently some are suppressed. The player adjusts the intermediate upper octave frets according to the requirements of each piece. Turkish *tanbūrs* attain considerable dimensions, with a speaking length of as much as 106 centimeters (ca. 42 inches).

Further east, the *tambur* of Afghanistan has a hemispheric body and both melody and sympathetic strings, the former inserted into the neck by frontal, the latter by lateral, pegs. And even further east, introduced from Persia during the Middle Ages, the Indian *tambura* as seen on Mogul miniatures was a three-stringed, fretted instrument with thickened neck, almost semicircular body terminating in upswept "wings," later to become a classical drone lute with four strings (tuned to the interval of a fourth or fifth with octave unisons, such as c°c′c′g°) that are never stopped but merely plucked with the right forefinger. On modern instruments a mobile bridge permits easy adjustments of pitch to the range of the singer's voice; the large body is usually of gourd, lacquered, and the neck is of course unfretted. At present the *tambura* is giving way to the harmonium. Westward, the Turkish *tanbūr* was taken over by the Greeks, southern Slavs, Bulgarians, and Romanians, among whom it has from two to four metal strings, played with a plectrum.

As the *tunbūr* derives ultimately from the Sumerian *pan-tur,* so the *gunībrī* is descended, etymologically at least, from the *tunbūr* (pntr—tnbr—gnbr), and physically from the ancient Egyptian lute, which it still resembles. A favorite of the North African Arab populations, it retains such ancient Near Eastern characteristics as two strings attached by one frontal and one lateral tuning peg, an almost almond-shaped body, and a skin belly with multiple soundholes. A larger and decadent form is the *gunbrī,* principally an instrument of the non-Arabic northwest, popular among the Negroes of Morocco, Senegal, and Gambia, described in the eighteenth century as *kitāra kināwa* ("Negro guitar"). Of various models now in use, one with a large, rectangular body is played by members of the (Negro) brotherhood of the Gnawa of the Moroccan Shluh; tuning rings are still employed for tensing its three strings.

The *'ūd,* the short-necked lute to which Western music is so greatly indebted, is still played from Turkey to the Maghrib. In modern times a sixth pair of strings has been added in Turkey, resulting in the tuning d°d° e°e° a°a° d′d′ g′g′ A°, notated an octave higher. Elsewhere, five pairs of strings, or four pairs plus a single chanterelle, are standard, as is their relative tuning: tone, fourth, fourth, fourth (g°a°d′g′c²), adjusted to the compass of the vocalist, who sings an octave lower. Al-Kindi and Safi ed-Din (thirteenth century) already has five-stringed *'ūds* at their disposal. All medieval Arabic theorists describe their system in terms of lute strings, and hence all describe the lute as having frets, yet pictorial evidence is contradictory in that frets are just not illustrated. Specialists assert that it was fretless throughout Islam—not just in one country—so it is assumed that fretting was purely theoretical, intended for demonstration purposes only. Polyphonic playing is unknown and the first position is not exceeded, and, in any case, the shortness of the neck would not permit the stopping of intervals greater than a fourth. Nowadays it is around the lute that the North African orchestra groups itself. In Morocco, where older musical traditions prevail, the classical four-stringed lute may still be heard, tuned G°e° A°d° (i.e., in fifths between the two external and between the two internal strings). The main visual differences between the *'ūd* and the Western lute are the former's narrower neck, often its three large and circular soundholes, and the tortoiseshell plaque below the soundholes, placed there to protect the belly from damage by the plectrum.

The '*ūd* lived on not only under the name of lute but also as *lauta* (*la'uta, lavuta*). In Arab lands from Morocco to Iraq this is fundamentally the same instrument as the '*ūd*, but with a larger neck and less deeply vaulted back, and four pairs of strings tuned in fifths (c°g°d'a'). Modern Greece knows it as the *laouto*, and employs the same tuning.

A large family of different sized long-necked lutes is that of the *saz*, with small body, two or three strings, and movable frets; the treble string is a melody string, while the second, and third, if present, are drones. The relative pitches of its tunings are a° d'd'. It is played over a wide area including Turkey, Armenia, Azerbaidzhan, Georgia (where it is called *samusi*), and Yugoslavia.

The *tīrān* (plural of *tār*) constitute a group of Iranian lutes that are also played in adjacent areas—Armenia, Azerbaidzhan, Georgia, and Tadzhikistan—with body, usually rounded, hollowed out of a block of wood, movable frets, and from two to five rib-fastened metal strings played with a plectrum. The Georgian version, called *tari*, has an octagonal body and membrane belly. *Tīrān* are named for the number of their strings; thus the *dutār*, meaning two strings, is the bichord member of the family and the type instrument. With its small, pyriform body and silk or metal strings secured by either frontal or lateral T-shaped tuning pegs, it is reminiscent of its ancient Egyptian forebears. The poet Hafiz sang of it in the fourteenth century, and today it remains a favorite in Iran and in Turkistan. As its name indicates, the *setār* has three strings, the now obsolete *chartār* had four; the *panchtār* with its five strings is still played in Iran, Turkistan, and among the Uzbeks, and the six-stringed *shashtār* has been known since the Middle Ages. On illuminated manuscripts of the Safavid period (1500–1736), *tīrān* appear as instruments of exquisitely delicate workmanship. In the nineteenth century mulberry was the preferred wood for making the body, walnut that for the neck, deadborn kidskin for the belly. Most *tīrān* are played with a plectrum, but the *dutār*, nowadays little used, is plucked with the nail of the index finger, as is the *setār*.

Under the name of sitar, Iran's three-stringed *setār* became northern India's popular long-necked lute, appearing there in the Middle Ages. Its name is a misnomer nowadays, for modern instruments have from four to seven strings, held by both frontal and lateral pegs (in fact the sitar with three strings is called *tritantri vīnā*). Its body is made of gourd or hollowed wood covered with a wooden belly, and its broad neck carries movable frets that are repositioned for the different scales. Only one string serves for the melody; the rest are drones, sometimes enhanced by the addition of sympathetic strings tuned to the drones and echoing them. The tuning is g°c′f°c².

Numerous variants of this instrument, all characterized by broad, fretted necks, merge with the highly developed stick zithers of the subcontinent, to become known as *vīnā* in the south, *bīn* in the north. Several broad-necked lutes include in their names the word *kachapi*, *kacha*, *kancha*, and so on, words meaning "tortoise" in Sanskrit, Bengali, and Malayalam, thus giving rise to the belief that these instruments had originally been made of a tortoise carapace, but Sachs discovered that the *cedrela toona* tree is called *kachapa cedrela* in Sanskrit, and this etymology has since been accepted. Lutes named *kachapi* are found as far from the mainland as Sumatra and Celebes.

With a series of bowed, broad-necked lutes (described under fiddles), seemingly unchanged in form since their pre-bow days, the formerly accepted dichotomy of plucked versus bowed chordophones loses much of its force. In particular, a mid-seventeenth-century miniature by Bichitr in the Victoria and Albert Museum, London, depicts a long-necked lute with body semicircular in outline, terminating with upcurved "wings," and fretted neck of uneven width; this then metamorphoses into the broad-necked bowed *esrar*, its body modified by lateral cutouts instead of wings.

Yet another link exists between Iran and the long-necked lutes of the Far East, for *san hsien*, meaning "three strings" in Chinese, is a translation of the Persian *setār* and denotes the long-necked Chinese lute, which is known to have a West Asian origin. Its small body consists of a square or rectangular frame (originally circular), open back and front, these openings covered with snakeskin. A long, very slender neck pierces the body and carries three lateral tuning pegs. Nowadays it is furnished with a *capotasto* permitting changes of pitch; it is a singer's lute, and as such adjusts its compass to that of the voice it accompanies. It is played with a broad plectrum. A three-stringed instrument by this name was already mentioned in the *Chiao Fang Chi* of Ts'ui Ling-ch'in in the eighth century, but unfortunately no description is given. Hence we cannot be sure that the *san hsien* existed in its present identity before the Yüan dynasty (1260–1368). From China it is said to have reached the Ryukyus in 1392, introduced by traders. From there it entered Japan—as *san gen*, also meaning "three strings"—in the sixteenth century, when it was played with a finger plectrum (*tsume*), but the Japanese *biwa* players tried playing it with their horn plectra and ripped the delicate snakeskin belly. Consequently it was redesigned for local use, with enlarged body made square instead of round, and back and belly replaced by catskin.

Nowadays it is called *samisen*. Its silk strings are rib fastened, and their standard tunings are b°e′b′ or b°f♯′b′ or b′e′a′ (relative pitches); here again, the absolute pitch is determined by the range of the singer's voice. In practice the theoretical B of these tunings varies from a° to d′. The *samisen* is played with a wide, fan-shaped *bachi* (plectrum) that slaps against the belly—reinforced at this point by a piece of parchment—at the same time that it strikes the strings, producing a highly percussive sound; the broad striking end measures some 9 centimeters (3½ inches). Its Korean equivalent is now obsolete, but a Vietnamese version lives on, still with snakeskin top and back, three silk strings, and sliding ivory *capotasto*. Fretted long-necked lutes, their necks terminating in gracefully reversed arches, are played in Vietnam and other countries of the Indochinese peninsula.

Far Eastern long-necked lutes were not restricted to models with vaulted backs. Flat lutes, as noted earlier, appear at a very early date. They have either ovoid, circular, or octagonal bodies. The first category is exemplified by the Chinese *p'i p'a* and its derivatives, including the Japanese *biwa*; the second by the *ch'in p'i p'a*, nowadays called *yüeh ch'in* ("moon guitar"), and the Japanese *gekkin*, nowadays called *genkin*; the third by the *shuang ch'in* and the Japanese *genkwan*. China shares these lutes with Korea and the Indochinese peninsula. "Moon guitars," or circular lutes, have a vibrating metal tongue affixed to their interior; this rattles against the body when the instrument is played. A metal determinant in its ancient name may indicate that this is an extremely ancient practice; it is less likely to have referred to metal strings. Nowadays two pairs of strings tuned a fourth apart are usual, as are fixed frets on neck and belly; the strings are pressed down against the frets on some Japanese *biwas*, between them on others.

The Banjo

A West African long-necked lute, the banjo, was introduced into the New World by the slave trade, albeit not in its present form. Thomas Jefferson in his *Notes on Virginia* wrote that the Negroes called the instrument they had brought over with them, *banger*; he himself referred to it as *banjar* (the Senegalese still have a lute named *bania*). At first restricted to the southern plantations, it slowly moved north, to be adopted in the nineteenth century by colonial Americans and by them exported to Europe. But although banjos enjoyed a vogue in England, they were not accepted on continental Europe. In Britain as in North America they were popular in music halls and jazz bands, and particularly in blackface minstrel shows (from the very end of the eighteenth century on).

The modern instrument is of more sophisticated construction than were the early models, yet still of relative simplicity: the body, shaped like a tambourine, consists essentially of a parchment membrane stretched over a circular frame, tightened by screws, its back left open; a long neck pierces this frame, its fingerboard studded with raised metal frets; rib-fastened strings pass over a bridge to a pegdisk (the fretting of necks is relatively recent). Four gut or nylon strings are common, plus a "thumb" string, or drone chanterelle, so called because plucked by the thumb. This is only half the length of the other strings and is secured to a peg inserted halfway up the neck. The thumb string is often erroneously said to have been added by Joe Sweeney in 1847, but is depicted earlier.

At the turn of the eighteenth to nineteenth centuries instruments played on the plantations had a circular body apparently made of a gourd section, with parchment belly, a long and very simple flat neck broadening into a pegdisk, four rib-fastened strings, one of which was the thumb string; fingerboard and frets were absent. Later the number of strings was augmented to five, six, seven, or even nine; those with more than five, now obsolete, were played in Britain and known as British guitar banjos.

Nowadays the banjo is played either with a plectrum—in which case it is termed "plectrum banjo"—metal strung and with thumb string omitted, or it is played with bare fingers in which case it is called "finger-style banjo." The five-string finger-style banjo is the type instrument today, tuned g' (thumb string) c°g°b°d'. In the nineteenth century a number of hybrid forms were marketed both in the United States and in Britain, all short lived and ranging from attempts to combine the banjo with a ukulele or even a violin to the inevitable keyboard banjo.

THE MANDORA

The fourteenth-century terms *guitarra morisca* and *guitarra latina* referred to two entirely distinct instruments, both also called indiscriminately *guiterne*, gittern, *chiterna, Quiterne,* et cetera, for several centuries (see also guitar, page 448). "Moorish guitar" is believed to have designated a type of short-necked lute illustrated in the thirteenth-century *Cantigas de Santa María,* a rich source of information on instruments of the period, with almond-shaped body gradually tapering to a neck, a reversed pegbox with lateral strings, frontal string holder, and two small soundholes. Less clear representations occur earlier, starting with the tenth-century carving in San Leonardo in Arcetri near Florence. From the twelfth century on it receives the name of *mandura,* the *mandoire* of French literature. The word "mandora," derived from the Greek *pandourion,* places its identity on a firm basis, for the *kobuz* had been equated with *pandourion* in a Byzantine treatise on alchemy of about 800; consequently we may be sure of the Eastern parentage of our mandora.

The *mandoire, Quintern, guitarra morisca* or *moresca* or *morache,* as it was variously known, was a very small species of lute, distinguished by having body and neck of one organic entity, and a sickle-shaped pegbox often terminating in a carved head, later in a scroll or square butt. Body and neck of one continuous piece gave way with time to a body with vaulted back made of built-up ribs, and a fretted neck. In its early days the mandora appears to have had four or perhaps five strings and to have been plucked either with or without a plectrum; the iconography shows both string holders and rib fastenings. By the sixteenth century it was played exclusively with bare fingers.

Mandoras must have caught on very rapidly, for around 1300 Johannes de Grocheo wrote that the most important stringed instruments were the *psalterium, cithara, lyra* (ergo, psaltery, harp, lute), *quitarra saracenica* (our mandora) and the *viella,* and in 1349 the Duke of Normandy had among his minstrels a player of the Latin guitar and one of the Moorish guitar. Paulirinus (ca. 1460) writes that the *quinterna* was smaller than a *cithara* (lute), and later in the same century we hear unequivocally that *lutina quinterna vocant* ("the small lute is called *quintern*"). On a panel painted in 1458 by Paolo and Giovanni Veneziano, now in the Frick Collection, New York, an angel musician is plucking a mandora—notable for its elongated, sickle-shaped pegbox and frontal string holder—with a long quill (cf. the mandolin of Fra Angelico, as discussed on page 439).

In 1585 Adrien Le Roy wrote a tutor for the mandora, which has unfortunately not come down to us but is known only by Trichet's reference to it. Trichet (ca. 1640) stated that originally the mandora had

had no frets (mandoras portrayed in the *Cantigas de Santa María* do not appear to have had any) but had since acquired nine; that formerly four strings had been common but that in his day some players added a fifth or a sixth string, even geminating them, in which case the strings of a pair were tuned an octave apart; five- and six-course mandoras were known, he adds, as *mandores luthées*, clearly an attempt at emulating the lute. (Among the effects inventorized at the death of a musician's wife in Paris in 1639 were five mandoras with four strings, one with nine strings, and three *mandores luthées*, two of which are specified as being half-sized.) Strings were tuned to the intervals of a fourth, fourth, and fifth. Mersenne's mandora has its pegbox reversed like that of a lute, an almond-shaped body, and four strings tuned $c'g'e^2\ g^2$. Praetorius called it *Pandurina* or *Mandürchen* ("small mandora"), and gives its tuning as $g°d'g'd^2$; he also knew of the five-stringed version "said to be" much played in France, sometimes with a quill plectrum. Music for the five-course mandora was written from the early seventeenth century on, and this stringing does indeed appear to have been preferred in France. In fact,

Mandora. Detail from *The Coronation of the Virgin* by Paolo and Giovanni Veneziano, 1458. Copyright The Frick Collection, New York.

mandoras seem to have been little known outside the Romance countries. Toward the end of the century Furetière (1685) could still write of the four-stringed instrument, its chanterelle plucked by the index finger armed with a finger plectrum, with the other strings plucked by the thumb.

The elongated almond form was not the only one assumed by the mandora, for another and larger model had a pronounced pear-shaped body; in the fourteenth and fifteenth centuries we often see this plucked with a quill. Over the centuries it grows in size and develops a distinct neck. The smaller, almond-shaped version also developed a neck of its own—short and broad—and its body became ovate. When the larger type had evolved and coarsened considerably it became necessary to name each model differently: "mandora" was henceforth a term set aside for the large form, and the small one became known as *pandurina* or by other diminutives such as *mandoretta, Mandürchen*, or the double diminutive *Mandürinchen*. As it lacks a name of its own in English, we refer to it as *pandurina*.

The later and larger mandora, or mandola, as it was also called, came to look like a lute except for its shorter neck surmounted by a gracefully arched pegbox; until the eighteenth century its six courses of strings were bichord, at which time eight courses became common. Outside the Romance countries this variety seems to have been almost unknown. A rare and belated mention of the mandora in Germany is that of Johann Georg Albrechtsberger, who in his *Anweisung zur Composition* of 1790 qualifies it as a small species of lute with eight courses of gut strings, bichord except for the chanterelle, tuned $c°d°e°a°d'g'b'e^2$. After the mid-eighteenth century both types lost favor, and by the early nineteenth century were all but forgotten outside Italy, having been discarded in favor of the wire-strung mandolin.

THE MANDOLIN

Mandolins are distinguished from other closely related lute forms, such as the mandoras, by the pronounced increase in depth of vaulting at the body's lower end, the reversed pegbox, and metal strings. Were it not for its longer neck, a large mandolin could be mistaken for the Romanian *cobza*.

A painting by Fra Angelico (d. 1455) shows an early form of mandolin with a lute-type reversed pegbox and rib-fastened strings, held horizontally against the player's chest and supported by the left forearm. It is sounded by a short plectrum held between thumb and forefinger, judging from the position of the angel's hand; a strip of resistant material is affixed across the belly at the plucking point to protect it from potential inroads of the plectrum, an arrangement already encountered on Oriental plucked chordophones. Somehow or other—we cannot follow it—this instrument seems to have survived Renaissance and baroque in Italy; or perhaps it died out there and was reintroduced from the Balkans.

The mandolin in its modern form does not antedate the eighteenth or late seventeenth centuries. Its deeply vaulted back, puffed out at the lower end, is built up of ribs; the neck is fretted, the circular soundhole left open; the pegbox is now a pegdisk, no more than a flat rectangle; a low bridge is affixed to the belly, and the four pairs of metal strings are rib fastened and plectrum plucked.

In eighteenth-century Italy different models were produced in different towns, each with its own stringing and structural modifications. The instrument now called mandolin without further qualification is actually the Neapolitan version, with its four pairs of strings tuned g°d'a'e²; in other towns five pairs of strings were tuned like those of the *chitarra battente* (see page 454), and six pairs were also common. A bass size called *mandolone* or *arcimandola*, now obsolete, evolved in the eighteenth century, with seven or eight courses tuned F° (G°) A°d°g°-b°e'a', similar in all respects other than size and stringing to the Neapolitan mandolin. A tutor for the four- and six-stringed versions by Fouchetti was published in France in 1770, but music for them had been written earlier, and the mandolin had even made its way into opera by 1764 (in Arne's *Almena*). Auber still scored for it in his *Fra Diavolo* of 1830, after Mozart (the serenade in *Don Giovanni*) and Beethoven (a sonata for piano and mandolin) had composed for it. This popularity suddenly died out, and mandolins were not taken up again until the end of the nineteenth century. Today they are played in Italy as melody instruments, often to the accompaniment of a guitar; elsewhere they have been developed into a consort of different sizes, played in bands as soprano, with the mandora as alto and tenor, a *mandocello* as bass, and *mandobass* as contrabass.

THE CITTERN

The earliest form of cittern of which we have any knowledge, namely the citole, was widely distributed in medieval Europe, and a popular if not a favorite chordophone of thirteenth-century troubadours. The word itself is an Old French one and probably derives from *kithara* (French variants were *cithole, cithre,* the Italians called it *cetula, cetra,* and so on, showing the interchangeable *l* and *r*). Citoles are mentioned in French literature from about 1200 on (*Roman du Renard*), in English literature a century later (*King Alisaundre,* ca. 1310). By 1292, four *citoleurs,* makers of citoles, resided in Paris, according to the *Livre de la taille de Paris* of that year, and a "citoler" was mentioned in England in 1306. But its home, Tinctoris informs us (ca. 1484), was Italy, which is plausible. He describes it as having a flat body, four brass or steel strings with a reentrant tuning: tone, fourth, and tone back (*rursus*); the neck carried wooden frets and its strings were plucked with a quill. To his description we may add that the pyriform body and short neck appear to have been of one piece, that the strings passed from a flat pegdisk to a frontal string holder.

Tinctoris's information that it was played in Italy only by "rustics" to support light songs or dances is a far cry from its earlier presence in the hands of troubadours and in the poetry of Brunetto Latini, Dante, and Prodenzani, among others (Dante calls it *cetra*). During the fourteenth century it seems to have exemplified plucked chordophones, for Jean de Rompaygne is said to have played *tabour, harpe, viele, sitole—et joglerie.* German poetry of the period also speaks of *Zitole, Cistol,* or *Sistole.* In fact the late-thirteenth-century Minnesänger Heinrich von Meissen, better known as Frauenlob, echoes the *sons en citoles et en orgues* of Brunetto Latini (ca. 1265) with his *Zistol und orgelclang.*

An instrument of the Middle Ages, the citole's time was running out by the fifteenth century and it is no longer mentioned in literature after the early sixteenth century, by which time it had become transformed into the cittern.

This transformation took place in the course of the fifteenth century: when its string holder was exchanged for rib-fastened strings a bridge had to be added in order to raise the strings off the soundboard; the pegdisk with pegs inserted from the rear became a pegbox, often sickle shaped, with lateral pegs. The new instrument retained its pyriform shape, flat back, and central soundhole covered by a rose; the neck was short and carried twelve or more frets, by now made of brass. The quill plectrum of its predecessor was gradually abandoned, and metal strings were generally plucked with bare fingers, although a plectrum was used at least occasionally until the mid-seventeenth century. Both

Praetorius (1619) and Playford (1652) mention mixed brass and steel stringing. All these innovations were accomplished slowly; throughout the sixteenth century a combination of rear and lateral tuning pegs prevailed, the rear pegs inserted into a continuation of the neck, which by its form announced the later sickle shape. Praetorius depicts both the type with mixed tuning pegs and that with lateral pegs only. The number of courses was gradually augmented, but the original four were still standard in Praetorius's time; these could be tuned either in the French manner (a°g°d′e′) or in the Italian (b°g°d′e′). It can be no coincidence that the large interval is now that of a fifth, whereas Tinctoris knew it as a fourth; rather, this change is in keeping with the predilection for the interval of a fifth for developing chordophones of the sixteenth century, and those of the violin family par excellence. At this time, the courses consisted of pairs of strings while those of the citole had been single.

Literature for the cittern was written from the mid-sixteenth century on, in tablature; the *Mulliner Virginal Book* (probably 1553–1560) contains pieces for the cittern, including one for a five-course instrument tuned d°a°g°d′e′. Lanfranco (1533) describes a six-course *cethara* tuned DFECGA, with single strings except for the G and for the C string, which appears to have been duplicated at the octave. This tuning, with intervals of +3 −1 −3 +5 +1 (where + stands for up, − for down), is corroborated later by Praetorius, whose a° c°c′ b°g°d′e′ is the "old Italian" tuning of a six-course cittern, he writes. And in 1565 Adrien Le Roy wrote a tutor for the *cistre*. Galilei's comment (1581) that the cittern *fu . . . usata prima tra gli inglesi che da altri nazioni* ("was . . . used earlier by the English than by other nations") may refer to the appearance of cittern tablatures, rather than to citterns, in England at an early date. By the last quarter of the sixteenth century the instrument was sufficiently popular for an Innsbruck inventory to enumerate *4 alte Cithern*.

Late in the sixteenth century the need for an increasingly deeper compass resulted in the building of larger models. An Ambras inventory of 1596 lists tenor and bass sizes, and in the same decade we hear of an Italian bass cittern bearing the appropriate name of *cetarissima*—very much of a cittern; the Venetian composer Simone Balsamino (fl. 1594) is credited with its invention. Its seven courses of single strings tuned ADGCEGC in ascending order were played by means of a plectrum and the player's thumb.

The cittern's courses varied between four and twelve during the sixteenth and seventeenth centuries, and the number of tunings proliferated. Praetorius gives no fewer than two tunings for the five-course cittern, two for the six-course model—apart from that already referred to—one for the "great six-course cittern" with body twice the normal size and tuned a fourth lower than the regular six-stringers, and one for the twelve-course bass. In addition, a very small version called *citarino* in Italian and *englisches Citrinchen* or *englisches Zitterlein* in German, with half-open back, was known by the early seventeenth century, when it was introduced on the Continent from England. This instrument, Praetorius writes, was tuned $f^2a'd^2g^2$ or $f^2b\flat'd^2g^2$. In his *Polyhymnia* of 1619 he comments that it was rare and hard to come by. Apparently J. S. Bach's ancestor, Veit Bach, was fond of it, for Bach writes of him: *Er hat sein meistes Vergnügen an einem Cythringen gehabt, welches er auch mit in die Muehle genommen, und unter währenden Mahlen darauf gespielet.* ("He derived his greatest pleasure from a *Cythringen* [the German suffix *-gen* is nowadays spelled *-chen*], which he took with him to the mill and played during the milling"), for Veit was a miller by trade.

Though it retained its popularity during most of the seventeenth century, the cittern had already become a barbershop instrument, and this apparently on an international scale, for Praetorius bitingly characterizes the four-stringer as an *illiberale, sutoribus et sartoribus usitatem instrumentem*; in England it was placed at the disposal of barbers' patrons wishing to while away the time, and Trichet informs us that in France barbers played it themselves. Barbers seem to have long had a predilection for plucked instruments: already in 1355 . . . *accidit quod quidam varletus barbïtonsor in villa praedicta commorans petiit ab eodem quasi deridendo, si dictam guiternam sibi venderet* (". . . it happened that a certain servant-barber sojourning in the aforementioned house asked him almost scornfully if he would sell him said gittern"). John Ford's line in Act 2 of his *Love's Melancholy* (ca. 1630): ". . . a head-piece/ . . . barbers shall wear thee on their citterns" refers to the termination in form of a human head of some cittern pegboxes.

Literature for the cittern ceases—in England at least—around the mid-seventeenth century, and the instrument appears to have gone out of fashion shortly thereafter except in Italy, where the bass remained in use. Furetière (1685) states that the *cistre* was still much played there and describes it as being longer than the lute, with four courses of three unison strings, except for the second course, which had but two strings.

During the first quarter of the seventeenth century another small cittern, this one campaniform in outline, originated in Hamburg and became known as the *hamburger Citrinchen* in Germany and as bell cittern in England. It had five pairs of strings. Mattheson's concise formulation *Cithrinchen alias Huhr-Laute* implies a certain measure of popularity.

By the mid-eighteenth century citterns had lost much of their former elegance; the body was now of the same depth throughout and the duple stringing was gradually replaced by single strings of gut, rather than the traditional wire, as a result of the guitar's ascending influence. Many eighteenth- and nineteenth-century citterns have a series of holes drilled in the fingerboard between the frets for the attaching of a *capotasto*. This arrangement permitted transposition upwards by semitones while retaining the same fingering regardless of key, an innovation that caused it to become easier to play than the guitar and to remain competitive with the latter for a while. However, three new forms of cittern introduced from the mid-eighteenth century on went under the name of "guitar."

First in the series was an offshoot of the Italian cittern; it came into existence by 1740 and was so widespread in England that it was called the English guitar. Somewhat coarser than the true cittern and with fewer frets, its neck terminated either in a sickle head or in a fan-shaped tuning device with machine screws. The six courses, all of metal, were tuned c°e°g°e′e′g′—a far cry from the reentrant tunings so typical of the earlier cittern. A little later—about 1780—a second variety made its appearance in Germany, the *deutsche Guitarre* also called *Sister* in German (from the French *cistre*), originally with four, and by 1800 with seven, single gut strings, for the French had added three strings to the bass meanwhile—concessions to the guitar—written for in violin clef and tuned G°e°f°g°c′e′g′. Here also provision was made for a *capotasto* on the fingerboard. Museum examples are usually of very dark wood and heavy build.

Meanwhile the keyboard mania had broken out. The impact of the piano from the late eighteenth century on was such that practically every instrument, in order to meet with public acceptance, had to be furnished with a keyboard of sorts, however reduced in compass it might be. Consequently, the cittern known as English guitar was now updated, or "improved" in the language of the time, by the addition of a keyboard and was thereupon called the keyed guitar. Patents were granted in 1785 (to John Goldsworth) for actions taking the form of plucking or striking devices. In the former, a number of buttons on the right side of the body controlled levers that plucked the strings; in the latter, a detachable box with six keys and piano hammers was affixed to the body. These compromise instruments remained fashionable for a time, but they were not truly viable, and all were displaced by the guitar in the nineteenth century.

ARCHCITTERNS

The need for an increasingly deeper compass resulted in the creation of archcitterns by Italian and French makers, large instruments with two pegboxes and gut stringing, with from five to seven melody strings and six or seven off-board strings patterned on the order of the theorbo. The overall length was about 1 meter (40 inches). Known already in the seventeenth century, their chief use was, however, in eighteenth-century France and Germany. Praetorius depicts a twelve-course arch-cittern with incurved, guitarlike waist—he says it was as loud as a harpsichord—and gives it the following tuning: e° B♭° f°c°g°d°a°e°-b°d'e', with apparently four off-board strings. A typical later tuning was A°B°c♯°d°d♯°/ e°a°c♯'e'a'c♯² e². Most extant specimens are French of the late eighteenth century.

Two archcitterns originated in England, the seventeenth-century syron, with seven pairs of melody strings and as many single off-board strings, causing it to be known as the fourteen-stringed cittern, and the stump, created by Daniel Farrant at the turn of the sixteenth to the seventeenth century. Little is known concerning the latter, but a piece of music for solo stump calls for seven on-board and eight off-board courses.

The cittern family was versatile and long lived. Music was written for the solo instrument for over a century; it played an important part in broken consorts; its larger members were appreciated as thorough-bass instruments and accompanied the dilettante's voice. The tone of its metal strings was incisive; but after abandoning this feature and being otherwise debased to the level of an imitation guitar or piano, its further existence was no longer justified.

THE BANDORA FAMILY

Closely allied to the cittern is a group comprising the bandora (or pandora), penorcon, orpharion, and polyphant, the last two of which were played almost exclusively in England. Creations of the sixteenth century, none outlived the seventeenth.

THE BANDORA

The bandora was reputedly invented by John Rose, a London viol maker, in 1562. A thorough-bass instrument of bass size, it had a flat back and belly, lateral tuning pegs, the central soundhole and metal stringing of the cittern, but the one feature by which it was immediately recognizable was its scalloped silhouette, usually composed of three lobes. Its six pairs of metal strings, spun (that is, made of several fine strands twisted together as though to form a rope), according to Praetorius, were played with a plectrum. They were not rib fastened, as were those of the cittern, but instead were hitched to pins driven into a metal string holder on the belly. During the last decade of the sixteenth century the number of courses was augmented to seven, and string holder and nut were placed obliquely in order to give maximum length to the bass strings and simultaneously to reduce tension on the treble strings by shortening them. This necessitated a similar treatment of the frets. Tuning of the six-course bandora was C°D°G°c°e°a°, of that with seven courses C°D°G°c°f°a°d' (on the Continent only) or G'C°D°G°c°e°a°. The bandora is mentioned as early as Gascoigne's *Jocasta* of 1566 and is written for from the 1580s on. Agazzari knew it by 1609 (*Sacrae cantiones*) and is said to have played it well. A bandora was among the instruments belonging to the Berlin orchestra in 1667, but by 1697 William Turner could write that orpharion and bandora were among the "old English instruments" already laid aside.

Bandoras made admirable thorough-bass instruments; their metal strings were more incisive and louder than the gut-strung lutes, their compass nearly as great as that of the archlute, and their tuning was close enough to offer little difficulty to musicians wishing to play both instruments. They were also played in small, mixed ensembles, and some English literature exists for the solo bandora. It continued in use longer on the Continent than in Britain and was remembered at least up to the second half of the eighteenth century, for Adlung (1758) described a clavichord called *Pandoret*, so named for the alleged resemblance of its sound to that of the bandora, and Laborde (1780) is still able to point out the characteristic oblique bandora string holder.

THE ORPHARION

Except for its size, the orpharion was identical to the bandora, the former being about 1 meter (40 inches) long, and the latter about 1.2 meters (4 feet). The stringing varied slightly, as it had between six and nine courses. Tuned like a lute and written for in lute tablature, it was in fact a substitute and a louder lute. John Rose, inventor of the bandora, probably also created the orpharion: an instrument of his make dated 1580 survives. The orpharion is first mentioned in English literature by Drayton in 1590 and was probably played up to the mid-seventeenth century, its life span being about that of the English bandora. According to a tutor for lute, orpharion, and bandora of 1596, it was played with bare fingers. Rose's instrument of 1580 has a horizontal string holder, six courses of strings, and rear pegs; another, by Francis Palmer, dated 1617, has an oblique string holder and nut, and nine pairs of strings. Praetorius gives the tuning for an eight-course model.

THE PENORCON

The less important penorcon was intermediary in size between bandora and orpharion, but in other respects similar to both. Praetorius informs us of the tuning of the nine-course instrument: G'A'C°D°G°c°e°a°d', again, a lute tuning. The body was broader than that of the bandora, he writes, as was the neck, since it had to accommodate a greater number of strings. Quite possibly the nine-stringed "orpharions" still in existence should properly be called penorcons. Matters are not helped by Praetorius, as the numbers of his illustrations of these two instruments are reversed.

THE POLYPHANT

The polyphant, of which Playford wrote (1654) that it was "not much unlike a lute, but strung with wire" was often played by Queen Elizabeth, he states. This unusual instrument was a leftover from the period of experimentation with archlutes. It is often assumed to have been an orpharion, yet as eminent a musician as Playford might be expected to have known the orpharion and to have called it by its common name. More likely it was akin to the polyphone described by James Talbot at the end of the century. From him we gather that this was a form of archbandora: the body had scalloped sides, flat back and belly, body of the same depth throughout, metal strings, frets, and numerous small metal string holders, with the on-board strings divided into a set of five strings, one of six, a third of seven pairs, attached to as many individual string holders and played by the right-hand thumb, and a fourth set of nine single basses attached to six string holders and played with the left thumb. With so complicated a manner of playing, its early demise is understandable.

THE GUITAR

Guitars, characterized by their incurved ribs forming a distinct if gentle waist, may possibly be descended from the waisted lutes of western Central Asia such as that seen on the Airtam frieze of the Kushana period described on page 410, and may have been known to Roman Egypt. Four specimens of a wooden instrument that probably represent prototypes of the guitar have been excavated in Egypt and assigned to the period between the fourth and eighth centuries A.D., all with built-up bodies, sharply incurved ribs, and a long, narrow neck still bearing signs of having once carried frets and three or four strings. Similar instruments may have been introduced into Europe at a later date, but this is entirely conjectural: we cannot really trace them before the Middle Ages.

The earliest appearance on European soil of a waisted chordophone is possibly that of a Byzantine psalter of 1066 in the British Museum (Add. 19352), where a guitar-shaped instrument, albeit with pegbox and lateral pegs, is being bowed. Another forerunner of the guitar, this time plucked, is illustrated in the thirteenth-century Spanish *Cantigas de Santa María* in form of a chordophone with ribs, waisted body, fretted neck, and (probably) four strings. We hear a little later of the *guitarra saracenica*, and in the mid-fourteenth century Juan Ruiz, archpriest of Hita, juxtaposes *guitarra latina* and *guitarra morisca*. The Saracen and Moorish guitars were of course one and the same instrument; they are discussed under mandora (see page 437). The *guitarra latina*, on the other hand, is identified with the waisted guitar. Despite morphological differences, both types of *guitarra* became known during the Middle Ages as *ghiterra*, *ghiterna*, or *guiterna* in Latin, *guiterne* or *guiterre* on the Continent, gittern in England—words ultimately derived from the Greek *kithara* via the Arabic *qītāra*. They do not indicate the cittern, a different instrument despite the common etymology. Frequently confused, the disparity between cittern and the pre-guitar gittern had repeatedly to be pointed out, as, for example, by J. Carter in his *Specimens of the Ancient Sculpture and Painting* (1780): "Many writers have confounded the cittern with the gittern, from which it differs in shape very materially."

THE GITTERN

A 1349 source cited by Kastner (1852) lists a *joueur de la guiterre latine* and a *joueur de guiterne moresche* then in the employ of the Duke of Normandy; the *guitare latine* is mentioned in French literature in the same century. As long as guitar and mandora were still in the process of evolution the terminology remained confused, but from early descriptions, and above all from the relatively profuse sculptural and pictorial material, accurate knowledge of the gittern can be gained. At first the four-cornered body with its flat back was carved out of the same block of wood as its short, fretted neck (betraying its descent from the short-necked lute). More often the neck terminated in a pegdisk, less frequently it is depicted as a pegbox, in which case it sometimes took the form of an animal head (Charles V owned in 1373 *une guitare a une teste de lyon*, "a guitar with lion's head"). Strings varied in number from three to five—four were usual—and were often attached to a long tailpiece; in all cases they were rib fastened, and played with a plectrum. The shape of the body was not standardized.

Such instruments remained small, with a very short speaking string-length, and must have been of relatively high pitch. Gitterns are included in inventories of the fourteenth century, some mentioned as having sculptured heads, one even as being made of ivory. Machaut's *leus, moraches, et guiternes* (*Prise d'Alexandrie*) leaves no doubt that by then the *guitarra latina* was sufficiently popular to be called merely "gittern." Earlier in the century, around 1325, "harpis, luttes and getarys" were enumerated in *King Richard*. And already in 1429 we hear of a *magister de sone guitarra* in Spain.

In the fifteenth century the gittern's development made rapid strides; it increased in length, adopted a frontal string holder, the corners of the bodies became rounded, and in Spain it became transformed into the *vihuela*: Tinctoris (ca. 1484) described the latter as a flat instrument, unlike the lute, and in most instances (*ut plurinam*) incurved on the sides; he credited the Spaniards with its invention. In this connection it is interesting to note the four "gitterons" "called Spanish vialles" among the instruments of Henry VIII inventorized in 1547, a rare occurrence of the *vihuela* outside Spain. Orvieto Cathedral's frescoes, painted between 1499 and 1504, include an angel musician playing what is tantamount to a modern guitar, except for the curved pegbox terminating in a scroll and for the gentler incurve of its waist.

In England and France the four single strings gave way to three pairs of strings plus single chanterelle, all of gut, tuned d°g°b°e′, with the second string of each pair doubling at the octave. Music was written for this model from the mid-sixteenth to the mid-seventeenth centuries. The absolute pitch of its strings might vary, but Adrien Le Roy confirms that they were tuned to the intervals of a fourth, major third, and a fourth. This is the *accordatura* that Bermudo (1555), his Spanish contemporary, called the "new" tuning; it corresponded to that of the four inner strings of lute and *vihuela*. The "old" tuning differed solely by having an interval of a fifth in the bass. Old and new tunings were known to Mudarra (1546). In Germany, where it was known either by its Italian name of *chiterna*, or as *Quintern(a)*, the gittern generally had five single strings, occasionally four pairs. Praetorius gives their tuning as c°f°a°d′ or f°b°d′g′.

Instances of the true guitar appear by the middle of the fifteenth century; one is seen in a gittern tablature published between 1551 and 1553, with four courses of strings; the title page of another collection of gittern pieces printed in Paris at the same period shows an instrument identical to a guitar except for its animal head and lateral pegs. Yet Praetorius, more than half a century later, still illustrates an intermediary type with pegbox terminating in a sculptured head. A Parisian luthier whose estate was inventorized in 1551 left three *guiternes*, one of which had eleven strings; another luthier left in 1587 four gitterns made in Lyons. Gitterns enjoyed a tremendous vogue in France at this time, and the new form may have radiated to England and Germany from there. The situation was summed up by Bonaventure Desperriers in his *Discours non plus melancholiques que divers* published in 1556:

Ainsi demeure encore la vielle pour les aveugles; le rebec et viole pour les menestriers; le luc et la guiterne pour les musiciens, et mesmement le luc, pour la plus grand [sic] perfection, duquel en mes premiers ans nous usions plus que de la guiterne. Mais depuis douze ou quinze ans en ça, tout nostre monde s'est mis a guiterner, le luc presque mis en oubly, pour estre en la guiterne ie

ne şcai quelle musique, et icelle beaucoup plus aisée que celle du luc . . . en
maniere que trouverez aujourd'hui plus de guiternes en France qu'en Espagne.
("Thus there remains the hurdy-gurdy for the blind, rebec and viola for
minstrels, lute and gittern for musicians, and even the lute for its greater
perfection, which in my early years we used more than the gittern. But for
the last twelve or fifteen years everybody has taken up the gittern . . . for the
music of the gittern is far easier than that of the lute . . . so that today one
finds more gitterns in France than in Spain.")

An interesting passage, and one that probably constitutes the first of a
series of nostalgic complaints regarding the setting aside of the lute in
favor of the easier guitar.

THE VIHUELA

Spain had created a form of gittern all of her own in the fifteenth
century: the *vihuela*. This word, cognate with "viola" (see page 473),
was a generic term for chordophones, whether bowed or plucked, and
needed qualification in order to identify a specific instrument. Thus, although a *Libro de caballería* of 1460 refers to small fiddles as *miges
vihules*, more detailed terminology usually obtained: *vihuela de mano*
came to denote the finger-plucked variety, *vihuela de peñola* or *de
péndola*, the plectrum-plucked, and *vihuela de arco*, the bowed versions.
Their forms were identical: the above-mentioned fresco of Orvieto Cathedral also depicts both a plucked and bowed *vihuela* (we would call
the latter a large fiddle), twin instruments. In its more restricted sense,
vihuela denoted the classical plucked instrument of Spanish Renaissance
society, structurally identical with the contemporary guitar, but generally supplied with six courses of strings, as against four of the guitar.
The body was by this time elongated and very slightly waisted, extremely
shallow—the ribs of an instrument of the period are but 7.2 centimeters
(ca. 3 inches) deep—pegbox tilted slightly backward, movable frets on
the fingerboard, strings tuned like those of the lute ($G°c°f°a°d'g'$), and
plucked with bare fingers.

Luis Milan, who composed the earliest surviving *vihuela* music (*El
maestro*, 1535–1536), wrote for an instrument having five pairs of strings
and single chanterelle, but otherwise so similar to the coexistent guitar
that Bermudo (1555) could say it sufficed to remove the top and bottom
courses from a *vihuela* to transform it into a guitar. But variants with
five and seven courses also existed, and according to Bermudo, Guzmán

had composed for a seven-course *vihuela*, with the additional course placed in the treble and tuned a fourth higher. Bermudo also depicts a seven-course model, which he says was in use in his day. Fuenllana in 1554 included some pieces for a five-course *vihuela* as well as for the *vihuela a cuatro ordenes que dizen guitarra* ("the four-course *vihuela* called guitar"). A smaller descant model was also available, for Valderrábano wrote arrangements for two *vihuelas* tuned a fifth apart, the smaller of which he termed *discante*. But the six-course variety was short lived; its literature ends in the third quarter of the sixteenth century, and the five-course *vihuela*, from then on known as the *guitarra española* ("Spanish guitar"), predominated from then on, to become famous all over Europe in the seventeenth century. Both *vihuela* and guitar were traditionally written for in tablature.

THE SPANISH GUITAR

For a long time the terms gittern and guitar continued to be used indiscriminately, as, for example, in 1547–1548: *la vieille guiterre qu'on souloit nommer guisterne* ("the old guitar one used to call gittern"), yet Adrien Le Roy published in 1563 a *Tablature de guiterne*. In 1585 Jacques Cellier drew a four-course gittern with sickle-shaped pegbox in France, while a year later in Spain Juan Carlos Amat brought out the first edition of his *Guitarra española*, music for the five-stringed guitar.

Bermudo had already seen a five-course guitar, but with the extra string added to the treble, a fourth above the highest string, and had noted that it was shorter than the *vihuela*. The Spanish guitar, on the contrary, had its fifth course added to the bass, a fourth below the lowest string. The addition of this fifth course is usually attributed to Vicente Espinel of Madrid (1550–1624) later in the century. Both in Spain and abroad this version became known as the Spanish guitar; it gained a rapid foothold in Italy and spread from there to the rest of Europe. In its home country it became an instrument of the people, driving out the aristocratic *vihuela*.

Guitars of the seventeenth century had far narrower and more elongated bodies, and less incurved waists than those of modern instruments; the necks were proportionately long and narrow, carrying eight frets—ten by 1700—the large, central soundhole was covered by a rose, and except for the chanterelle all the strings were paired, those of the bass course being tuned an octave apart, an arrangement that had prevailed

Bermudo's drawing of a seven-course
vihuela with fixed frets. From Juan
Bermudo, *Declaración de los instrumentos
musicales,* 1555.

earlier. Another popular system consisted in having the strings of the two lowest courses sound in octaves. Such is the picture given by Trichet (ca. 1640). Shortly thereafter the chanterelle was also duplicated, and this stringing was maintained for about a century. But at some time in the first half of the seventeenth century the pitch was raised by a tone to A°d°g°b°e′; Espinel made use of both high and low tunings, but since Ruiz de Ribayez (1677) the higher pitch has prevailed.

Guitars became fashionable both in England and on the Continent (Tallemant des Réaux recounts that at a dinner given for Christine of France at the mid-century by Le Bossu, the silver table service was in the form of a guitar, as the princess was particularly fond of that instrument); and, though Praetorius asserted it was in the hands of charlatans and mountebanks, by the late seventeenth century it was accepted at court and in society, and makers such as Stradivari and Tielke did not hesitate to build them; a number of exquisitely ornamented instruments were turned out then. The extent of the guitar's popularity may be evinced from an amusing passage in the preface to John Playford's *Musick's Delight on the Cithren* of 1666:

. . . Nor is any *Musick* rendered acceptable, or esteemed by many, but what is presented by Forreigners; Not a City dame, though a tapwife, but is ambitious to have her daughter taught by Mounsieur La Novo Kirkshawibus on the Gittar, which instrument is but a new old one, used in London in the time of Q. Mary as appears by a book printed in English of instructions and lessons for the same about the beginning of Q. Elizabeth's reign, being not much different from the Cithren only was strung with gut strings, this with wyre which was more in esteem (till of late years) than the guittar.

Trichet, in addition to giving a description of the common seventeenth-century guitar, commented that it could also be built with a vaulted back. It is tempting to see here an allusion to an offspring of the guitar called *chitarra battente*, otherwise unknown prior to the eighteenth century, and then only as an Italian instrument. Here the body is deeper than that of the ordinary guitar, and both back and sides are built up of narrow longitudinal ribs, while the back is highly arched. The strings are of metal, hence rib fastened, and played with a plectrum; the belly is on two different planes, sloped downwards at the level of the low bridge. Trichet was, however, referring to a transition instrument. His contemporary, the painter Il Domenichino (d. 1641) has portrayed a guitar to all intents and purposes a *chitarra battente* except for its gut stringing, frontal string holder, and single-plane belly. Older specimens of the *chitarra battente* have five bichord courses, later ones five trichord courses, tuned d°g°c'e'a'. Simon Molitor writes in the preface to his *Grosse Sonate für die Guitarre allein* (Vienna, 1806) that on past journeys through Istria, Dalmatia, Albania, the Adriatic and Levantine islands, he had encountered a five-course guitar with metal strings; possibly these were *chitarre battente*, for in Calabria they were still played earlier in our century.

At the end of the seventeenth century the ordinary guitar's neck had been fitted with ten frets, and the strings of each course were tuned in unison, except that the chanterelle remained single. Half a century later the penalty of popularity had to be paid: guitars became instruments of amateurs par excellence, and it became necessary to simplify the playing technique. This was brought about by removing one string from each pair. Subsequently a sixth string was added to the bass end, tuned E°. The French do not seem to have adopted the extra string generally, but continued to write for the old and the revised instrument side by side. The tuning, E°A°d°g°b°e', is that in use today.

In the nineteenth century guitars were remodeled along more modern lines: the wooden tuning pegs were replaced by metal screws; the lower bouts were widened considerably, the rose was omitted from its sound-hole, now left gaping. Further changes have taken place in our own times: the body is now comparatively squat, the lower bouts are even wider, the neck is broader; the pegdisk has disappeared altogether to make room for a machine head, brass has replaced ivory for the frets, and the fingerboard has been lengthened right over the belly and reaches down to the soundhole. The interior barring of the belly, originally transverse, has become both longitudinal and heavier, and the string holder has been modified to withstand the pull of thicker strings. From an instrument of the drawing room or outdoor serenade, it has become one of the concert stage. Nowadays it is often strung with metal and played with a plectrum in order to obtain maximum volume of sound, despite the fact that its traditional playing method was based on finger plucking; alternately, it may have three courses of gut or nylon, the remainder of metal-wound silk. Transposition is facilitated by a *capotasto*.

Today the guitar is heard chiefly as a purveyor of popular music, but efforts to revive it as a classical instrument have been initiated, mainly by Spanish players. The modern guitar of Spain is made in a number of sizes: the type instrument, lowest in pitch, is called *guitarra*. Others, from large to small, are the *guitarra tenor, requinto, quitarro* or *tiple*, and *guitarillo*. Their tunings vary according to region and to type of music to be performed, and even the tuning of the type instrument is sometimes changed to conform to the predominant tonality of a piece.

BASS GUITARS

The need for extending the bass compass of the guitar made itself felt by the seventeenth century, and the example set by the archlutes was followed: off-board strings with their separate nut and string attachment ensued. Bass guitars of this nature, called *guitares théorbées* in French, are known to have existed in 1659 when Giovanni Battista Granata appended several pieces for a guitar calling for off-board basses to his *Soavi concerti di sonate musicali per la chitarra spagnuola*. In the eighteenth and early nineteenth centuries, models with two pegboxes were brought out in France under such names as *bissex* ("twice six") or *décacorde* ("ten-stringer").

HYBRID GUITARS AND OTHER DERIVATIVE FORMS

Various fanciful and mixed forms started appearing from the late eighteenth century on, proof that the heyday of the guitar was over: the lyre guitar, called *lyre anacréontique* by its Parisian maker, the luthier Maréschal, and known as Apollo lyre in England, had the form of a conventional *kithara* combined with a central guitar-type, fretted neck, pegdisk, and string holder. The appeal of its elegant form was diminished by the fact that it proved unwieldy to play, and according to a contemporary account could be used only for arpeggioed accompaniments to the voice. Nonetheless, it enjoyed considerable vogue as a drawing-room instrument all over Europe during the first three decades of the nineteenth century. The rage for guitars in the latter part of the eighteenth and the early nineteenth centuries resulted in yet another hybrid, the lute guitar, a guitar except for its lute body—often that of an older instrument; many an old lute was destroyed for the sake of this "transformation." Even a bowed guitar was produced, invented—if one may call it that—by Georg Staufer of Vienna in 1823; the size of a cello, it had a smooth guitar waist and twenty-four frets on its fingerboard. As it was subsequently imitated we may assume that it enjoyed a measure of popularity.

From Europe the guitar was taken both west to the Americas from

Spain, south to Africa by the Portuguese (as far as is known), and east to Java, also by the Portuguese on their far-flung expeditions to discover and open up new territories and in quest of slaves. Some South American instruments have become completely adapted to their new habitat, with resonator made of an armadillo carapace dried in a mold to give it the desired shape, and the five or six strings of the Spanish guitar. In South Africa a primitive guitar called *ramkie* has a wooden or calabash body; known to have existed by the first half of the eighteenth century, it is presumed to be of Portuguese origin and is now succumbing to the competition of cheap, ready-made European guitars. Portuguese sailors are also said to be responsible for introducing their *machete,* a cross between a guitar and a mandolin, into Hawaii in the 1870s, where it was transformed into the ukulele (the word means "flea"), a very small and simple form of guitar with reentrant tuning (g'c'e'a'). The Hawaiian guitar is a different instrument, a modification of the Spanish guitar, brought to the islands by American sailors and played in a characteristic position, namely laid across the seated player's knees. Its six metal strings pass over a nut so high that they cannot be pressed against the fingerboard but are stopped by the pressure of a steel bar held in the player's hand and made to glide along the strings over the frets, producing a glissando effect; the plucking fingers wear plectra. Both the position in which it is held and the manner in which it is played seem to derive from a fretted folk zither.

THE BANDURRIA

A hybrid with deep cittern body, very short fretted neck, and disproportionately long guitar-type pegdisk is known in Spain as the *bandurria.* Its six pairs of strings are attached to a string holder, fixed frets lie closely spaced on the neck, a large and open soundhole yawns, the strings are plectrum plucked. A smaller version, the *bandurilla,* and a larger one, *bandolón,* complete the family. In the Balearic Islands the type instrument is known as *manduarria.* One is tempted to identify the present-day *manduarria* with that mentioned by Juan Ruiz in the fourteenth century, but despite the identity of names we know nothing of the instrument at that time. Bermudo (1555) was the first author to describe it: it then had but three strings tuned either to fundamental, fourth, and octave—the older tuning—or to fundamental, fifth, and octave, and could be fretted or not. When it lacked frets, the strings scraped against the wood during performance (indicative of low tension); alternately it carried six or seven frets, but these were difficult to position accurately because of the shortness of the neck. Four strings or more could be accommodated on a *bandurria*, provided the narrowness of the neck permitted it—a far cry from today's build. The neck must have been narrow and long indeed, for having made the amazing statement: *De indias han traydo bandurria con cinco cuerdas* ("five-course *bandurrias* were brought from the Indies"), Bermudo continues: *y en el andaluzia se ha visto con quinze trastes* ("and in Andalusia they have been seen with fifteen frets"). Fifteen frets cannot possibly be accommodated on a modern instrument. In addition to a longer neck, we must also assume a lute-type, that is, vaulted, back, for only so can the cognates *mandora—bandora—bandurria* be explained, all ultimately derived from the Greek *pandourion*.

By the mid-eighteenth century the *bandurria* had acquired a total of five pairs of strings, tuned in fourths (c♯' f♯' b' e² a²); a sixth pair, tuned to d♯°, has been added since. *Bandurrias* are outdoor chordophones of southern Spain, played chiefly in a trio with lute and guitar. Apparently unknown outside the Iberian peninsula and the Balearic Islands, they were taken by the Spaniards to Latin America, where they flourish under the name of *bandola*.

THE ORGANISTRUM (HURDY-GURDY)

The etymology of the word organistrum is as frustrating as it is challenging: *organnae instrumenta* and *organum instrumentum* ("organlike instrument") have been proposed. A Latinization of the Old French *orgrenistre* is also a possibility; this denoted an organ player in the first quarter of the thirteenth century and was changed to *organistre* around 1300.

Better known in English by its modern name, hurdy-gurdy, the organistrum is a mechanically bowed chordophone known since the twelfth century. Appended to the works of Odo of Cluny (d. 942) is a short treatise entitled *Quomodo organistrum construatur*, which until recently was taken to be the earliest known reference to the organistrum. But the manuscript itself does not antedate the thirteenth century, and the treatise in question is now considered to be an anonymous work.

Our earliest documentation now stems from the mid-twelfth century, when the instrument appears on a sculpture from Santo Domingo of Soria, Spain, also in sculpture at the abbey of Saint Georges de Boscherville near Rouen, and in the *Hortus deliciarum* of Abbess Herrad of Landsberg, where it is identified by name (as organistrum). At about the same time it is mentioned in literature, either as organistrum or as *symphonia,* and in French as *symphonie,* from about 1155 to 1377, after which the term is used in a historical sense only or corrupted to *chifonie.*

Most of these early instruments have fiddle-shaped bodies in eightform, and three strings set in vibration by a hand-cranked wooden wheel at the tail end of the body. Nearly always a boxlike device is set alongside the neck, containing the rear portions of the key rods; these projected from the box, and when worked by the player their distal ends acted as nuts, stopping the strings. All three strings passed over the vertex of the wheel to a short and deep pegbox. Exceptionally, an instrument of different shape is portrayed or the key mechanism is omitted, in which case the strings were depressed against the fingerboard by hand as on a fiddle. Up to the mid-thirteenth century the instruments were very long, perhaps 1.5 to 1.8 meters (5 to 6 feet), too big for a single person to work both key rods and wheel; hence it was placed across the lap of two seated performers, one of whom cranked the wheel while the other manipulated the key rods. At this time the latter were rotating levers with a flat, perpendicular piece set on the rear section; they were turned, not pushed, so that each key stopped the three strings simultaneously. The twelfth-century *Hortus deliciarum* illustrates a rarer type without keyboard; this manuscript was destroyed by fire in the nineteenth century but fortunately two copies had been made earlier in the same century, the later of which distinctly shows frets on the neck, while the earlier copy does not.

The organistrum is now recognized as having evolved from the bowed fiddle, yet its characteristic wheel may have been derived, or at least inspired, by the "hemipherium," a semicircular nut of the monochord. As a descendant of the early fiddle, its object would have been primarily that of providing an alternative to bowing, and also to mechanize the stopping of strings by means of a built-in exact and invariable scale. It may be argued that its very size argues against this theory, yet bass fiddles too large to be played at the shoulder were held in a-gamba position before the organistrum existed.

In the late twelfth century an occasional pyriform instrument is seen,

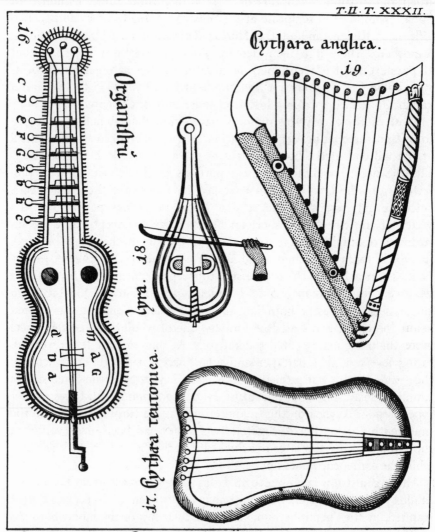

Organistrum. Copy of a now destroyed thirteenth-century drawing, made and published by Martin Gerbert in *De cantu et musica sacra*, 1774.

its form that of the contemporary fiddle, and in the thirteenth century a rectangular box type makes its appearance. A now lost thirteenth-century codex of Saint Blasius contained the diagram of an organistrum (reproduced in Gerbert [1774]) with a compass of one octave, C to C, including a B♭, and three strings. Only one key rod could produce sound at a time, even though the player might work one with each hand, simply because each rod determined the length of the open strings (the same principle as that of the clavichord's fretted keys), and as all strings were stopped simultaneously there could be no question of drones. However, it is most likely that the strings were not tuned in unison but to different pitches, resulting in the playing of (parallel) organum; indeed, the word *symphonia* was also applied to other instruments emitting two tones: bagpipes and two-headed drums come to mind.

Due to the nature of the key mechanism only slow playing was possible, and the pitch of these large, two-man models must have been of very low range. The wheel was rosined for the very heavy gut strings. A smaller instrument came into use in the mid-thirteenth century, played by a single person who could manipulate both wheel and keys. More important still, the system of key rods was changed at this time to one of non-rotating push levers that stopped one string only—from the side —and then fell back of their own volition, provided the organistrum were held in a slightly tilted position, as it has been ever since. Those strings not touched by the keys now sounded continuously as drones. This remodeling resulted in an instrument of higher pitch (shorter string length) and greater compass (one and one-half to two octaves) that could be played much faster than the old model. Its appearance coincides with the transformation of organ keywork and the emergence of the portative organ.

A study of the iconography shows that when two persons are depicted playing, the neck is about as often to their left as to their right, whereas when a single person plays the crank is worked by his right hand (only exceptionally with the left). Thus the left hand plays the melody, in contrast to the portative organ, where one player works both bellows and keys; and when the keyed fiddle appears, the crank hand becomes the bow hand.

An instrument of church and monastic school, the organistrum seems to have lost its position there in the course of the thirteenth century, possibly in favor of the up and coming portative, and in the fourteenth century it was relegated to blind players. Corbichon (*Proprietaire des choses, 1372)* is clear on this point: *On appelle en françoys une symphonie l'instrument dont les aveugles iouent en chantant les chansons de geste, et a cest instrument moult doux son et plaisant o oyr* ("In French one calls symphony the instrument played by the blind while singing *chansons de geste*, and this instrument has a very sweet sound and is pleasant to hear"), and Deschamps's oft-quoted phrase, *aveugle chifonie aura*, dates from about the same time. Instruments with five or six strings are also known by then (though Virdung depicts one with four strings in 1511), and in the fifteenth century a most modern version appears, further reduced in size, squatter, handier. A manuscript of the *Romance de Girart de Nevers*, of or before 1466, illustrates the words *la vyole pendu a son col* ("the viol suspended from his neck") by showing a man playing an organistrum suspended by a strap around his neck, a position that has remained in use until now. During the sixteenth century it attained its widest geographical distribution, at which time it was mentioned in Russia (as *rilya*), and may have been known as far north as Iceland, for an Icelandic bishop, John Arason (d. 1550) used the term *fon*, abbreviation of *simfon*, to denote an instrument having both strings and keys.

From an instrument of blind singers the organistrum became one of blind beggars, and with this change of status a new terminology came in. In French the terms *symphonie* and *chifonie* were replaced with *vielle, vièle à roue*, or *instrument de truand* ("itinerant beggar's instrument"); the new Latin equivalent was *lyra mendicorum* ("beggar's lyre"); the Old High German *Lira* had meanwhile been changed to *Leier* and was now transferred to the organistrum; in England it became known as cymbal before being called hurdy-gurdy (from 1749 on); and Italians knew it as *lira rustica, lira tedesca*. Both Mersenne and Trichet write of it as a beggar's instrument still, and at the end of the seventeenth century it served to amuse the common people (*les gens du peuple*). Of its four strings "the two outer are Drones tuned to 5ths, the two middle are Unisons," but the drones could also be tuned an octave apart.

Another transformation of the hurdy-gurdy took place in the eighteenth century, when from itinernant street musicians' hands it went into those of the French court *dilettanti: vielle* and *musette*, the latter a small bagpipe, suddenly became fashionable; but outside of France the hurdy-gurdy retained its previous status. The *vièle à roue* was refined and given a total of six strings, two of which—the melody strings— were called chanterelles, the remainder being drones. One of these, the *trompette,* was sometimes provided with a drumming bridge, similar to that of the trumpet marine, presumably its source. This could be set drumming or left silent at will. Both chanterelles were tuned to g′ and the drones played a continuous accompaniment of c°g°c′ if the tuning were to be in C, or, if in G, g°d′g′, one of the drones being suppressed alternately in each case. Some models had a special device for raising the *trompette*'s pitch from c′ to d′ without returning: an extra peg pressed the *trompette* against the edge of a fixed nut placed so as to shorten the string by exactly one-tenth of its length. Occasionally sympathetic wire strings were added to the right side; these were tuned c′e′g′a′ for the *vielle en guitare* tuning, or c°c′d°d′g′g′ for the *vielle en luth* tuning. Compass by the mid-eighteenth century had been enlarged to two octaves, g′ to g³, with twenty-three keys.

Old guitars, old lute and theorbo bodies, were sacrificed for transformation into *vièles à roues,* and from the last quarter of the eighteenth century on even miniature pipework was built into the body, a form known as *vielle organisée* (in English formerly as flute cymbal, now as organized hurdy-gurdy). Here pipework and bellows were housed inside the body, the crank operated both the wheel and the bellows, and the valves controlling wind admission to the pipes were worked by the keys. Organized hurdy-gurdies are a little larger than ordinary ones and also somewhat deeper, as they have to accommodate the small pipes and bellows; a register was provided to raise all the strings simultaneously off the wheel so that the organ part could be heard alone. Neither virtuosi nor composers were lacking; often they were united in one person. Charles Baton, a maker to whom extension of the compass is due, wrote several suites for the *vielle* and a history of the instrument, its *privilège* dated 1741.

Articulation in playing could be obtained by the wrist, hence known as the *coup de poignet,* as the wrist motion determines the manner and speed at which the wheel is rotated. Though the hurdy-gurdy never attained the same heights of fashion outside France as it did within that country, it did enjoy a measure of reflected glory elsewhere: Toepfer explained (1773) that the Germans were still setting marches, minuets, and polonaises for *Liren oder Leiern;* Haydn wrote five concerti and seven *notturni a due lire* for the king of Naples—delivered in 1786 and 1790, respectively, long believed to have been written for the bowed *lira,* outmoded a century earlier; and Donizetti's opera *Linda di Chamounix* (1842) contains two Savoyard songs with hurdy-gurdy accompaniment. Itinerant Savoyards still played it in the streets of London and Paris at the end of the nineteenth century. Its great popularity in France was cut short by the revolution, and when it was revived in the nineteenth century it was as an instrument of ambulant street musicians, who carried it suspended from a band around the neck; occasionally it may still be heard there. In certain provinces, notably Morvan and Berry, its utilization in popular music has maintained itself until now.

As a folk and mendicant's instrument it was also played in the mountains of Silesia until the middle of the nineteenth century, and up to the end of that century by like performers in the Austrian Alps; in Spanish Galicia it is still played although no longer made there. Further east it is played in the Ukraine, less in central and southwestern Russia, formerly by beggars, now as a folk instrument. The *rilya* there has two drones tuned a fifth apart, and single melody string. A characteristic form has been developed in central Russia with a body shaped like a flat violin, complete with F holes; this is often called *lira* or *kobza*. Such folk instruments can be differentiated from the art music varieties not only by coarser structure but also by their single melody string, a feature confirmed by museum specimens and already evident in Praetorius's drawing of a *Bauern-Lyre*. The keyless hurdy-gurdy with its four strings would also have had a single melody string, stopped by the fingers in the manner of a violin, with uninterrupted droning of the three others.

BOWED CHORDOPHONES

As a precursor of the bow, the friction stick is documented in medieval Chinese sources in connection with vaulted zithers and the spike fiddle *hu ch'in* that were subsequently to be bowed, except that in Wu-an County, Hopei, the vaulted zither *ya cheng* has retained its original name (elsewhere it is known as *la ch'in*) and is still "bowed" with a sorghum stem dusted with resin, as Picken (1965) has ascertained.

We first hear of the bow's existence from the *Kitab al-musiqi al-kabir* of al-Farabi (d. 950), who wrote that some instruments have strings that are rubbed by means of other strings or "something similar," and evidence points to Central Asia—possibly Khwarizm—as the probable place of its application to plucked or rubbed chordophones. Separate developments of the instruments may have taken place in Arabia and Byzantium, but, as documentary evidence is lacking, this is still surmise. Written sources confirm the existence of bowed chordophones in the Near East in the tenth century, pictorial sources their presence in Spain and Byzantium during the same century. No bowed instrument is depicted on the giant stupa of Borobudur in Java, erected about 800, nor do they appear in China unequivocally until the fourteenth century under the Yüan dynasty (1280–1368).

At the turn of the millennium ibn-Sina, better known to the West as Avicenna, mentioned the *rabāb* as an example of bowed instrument. Al-Farabi had described this as identical in structure to the Khurasan *tunbūr*, with long neck, piriform body, and rib fastener for its one or two single strings, or two pairs of strings. From a lengthy passage on the theory of intervals we gather that his *rabāb* could be fretted or not, but the lack of frets he considered a disadvantage, as making it difficult to stop the strings with precision. Of several possible tunings, that of two strings sounding a second apart seems to have been preferred. This instrument became known in Europe as the rubebe or rebec, and its evolution is traced below.

Medieval Islamic writers classed bowed chordophones as imperfect because of their weak tone and unappealing sound; in China they were folk instruments at first, the instruments of common people, as one source puts it. Pride of place in the high-culture areas of the East has always gone to plucked chordophones, never to bowed ones. All Central Asian bowed instruments are played in a-gamba position, and in this area only the top string is stopped, while the others sound as a continuous drone. Characteristic of the Turkoman, Uzbek, and Kirghiz folk music of our time is the organum at the fourth of both their vocal and their instrumental music; when playing bowed chordophones, two strings are frequently stopped together, resulting in parallel organum, reminiscent of that of our early Middle Ages. At least one surviving European folk fiddle is still played in double stops (see *Grobfiedel*, page 475), possibly and indeed probably a direct continuation of a method that originated with the first bowed instruments.

THE BOW

The bow as an instrumental accessory rather than as an instrument (i.e., musical bow) is of Asiatic origin, as stated above, documented by al-Farabi in the tenth century, and depicted in a Mozarabic Beatus commentary produced in Spain between 920 and 930 (Bibl. nac. MS 58, Madrid). Here several large, sharply curved bows of the type known as round bow are bent into a semicircle. Horsehair as a material is first mentioned in the East during the same century.

Three fundamental types of bow can be discerned in early illustrations: the first, a round bow, with its stick evenly curved and held in the center; then the bow formed by having the curve at one end only—the point—while the straight section forms a handle; finally, the stick may be straight in the center but curved at both ends. A primitive frog (also called nut) is formed by making use of a stick on which the stub of a branch has been left. On curved bows lacking this stub, the string may be fastened by knotting it or placing it in a cleft at the point, or by winding it around the stick at the lower (handle) end, and then either knotting it or again placing it in a notch (modern frogs, made of hard materials such as ebony or ivory, are attached to the lower end of the stick by a metal screw).

The round bow gave way by the turn of the tenth to eleventh centuries to an intermediary type, a long and slender bow, barely curved, leading to the twelfth-century model with curve at one end, shorter and apparently with a stub near the proximal end, to which the hair is fastened. This type has survived in Europe until today, in the hands of the southern Slav *guslares*. During the Middle Ages it co-existed for a while with the round bow until the latter disappeared (by the fourteenth century). Some early bows are seen as very short, others are twice as long as the instrument they sound. During the later Middle Ages the bow becomes increasingly flatter and assumes only a slight curve. The hair is loose and is tightened by the player's fingers, and in fact the *jouhikantele* bow continued to be so held until the nineteenth century; a certain amount of control was retained by such means until well after the invention of the *crémaillère*.

Until the turn of the millennium the bow is documented only in the Arabic and Byzantine empires (Spain formed part of the Moslem domains, it will be recalled), after which it is seen increasingly in the West. During the late Middle Ages some chordophones that had formerly been portrayed without bow, as those on the portals of French Romanesque churches, are henceforth played with one. Prior to the thirteenth century we cannot see details of hair attachment, but by then the prototype of the frog emerges in the form already described. The fiddle bow

King David playing a fiddle with a very long bow. French glass roundel, late thirteenth century. Ex-collection William Randolph Hearst.

is mentioned in the *Chronicum picturatum brunsuicense* in an entry for the year 1203, stating that *in dussem Jahre . . . sat de Parner des Mit-wirkens in den Pingxsten und veddelte synen Buren to dem Danse, da quam ein Donreschlach unde schloch dem Parner synen Arm aff mit dem Veddelbogen . . .* ("in that year . . . the parson fiddled on Wednesday of Whitsuntide for his peasants' dance, and a thunderclap came and cut off his arm with the fiddle bow . . ."). In the same century horsehair for bows is mentioned by Hugo von Trimberg, but had been known in the East since the tenth century.

Some of Urs Graf's drawings of the 1520s show a fiddle bow curved at one end, with a pronounced and high frog but no handle. A century later the frog is completely formed and no longer connected to the stick. In the second quarter of the seventeenth century the bow loses much of its convexity and by the mid-century is almost straight. Brazil-wood comes into use at about this time: Trichet (ca. 1640) mentions bows of brazil, ebony, and "other woods," and bows of *indianisch* wood are listed in Austria a little later; two bows of *cana d'India* were owned by the Verona Academia Filarmonica in 1562, probably brazilwood. Kremsmünster Monastery purchased *1 indianischer Violinbogen* in 1690, and two years later several of "Indian" wood.

The second half of the seventeenth century witnessed the appearance of the *crémaillère* as a serrated section holding the frog, to be replaced by a screw, probably around 1700, when the stick runs practically parallel to the hair. Jean Rousseau (1687) advised that the middle finger of the bow hand be on the inside of the hair, with thumb and forefinger holding the stick at least two or three finger breadths from the frog. About forty years later, Roger North wrote of the violinist Nicola Mateis, who came to England in the 1670s: "He . . . used a very long bow, resting his instrument against his short ribs . . . he taught ye English to hold ye bow by ye wood onely & not to touch ye hair wch was no small reformation," implying an advanced bowing technique for its time.

According to violin lore, Corelli (1653–1713) improved the bow so that the hair was at the same distance from the stick at both ends, and Tartini lengthened it, but these attributions are questionable. François Tourte (1747–1835, according to Fétis) has been credited with creating the modern bow by giving it a slightly concave curve, determining the best distance from hair to stick, lightening the head, arranging the hair in ribbon form by flattening it with a ferrule, and, finally, providing a metal screw for the frog. Actually, metal screws go back further than the Tourtes, and it is currently believed that François may have done no more than bring the art of bow making to a high degree of perfection, and possibly of standardizing its length to around 74 centimeters (ca. 29 inches). A second bow-making Tourte is referred to as Louis, although only his initial (L) is documented, as the late Rembert Wurlitzer informed the author. L. Tourte is frequently referred to as Tourte *père* but his relationship to François has not yet been established; despite efforts of recent researchers, the Tourtes remain elusive. L. Tourte has left us straight bows in mid-seventeenth-century style as well as later concave models, and the transformation of the bow is more likely—again, according to Rembert Wurlitzer—to have been his work than that of

François. Though introduction of the screw mechanism cannot be dated with any degree of accuracy, the ferrule may well be due to efforts of the Tourtes, and the amount of "spring" was standardized in their time; this is commonly adjusted on violin bows so that the hair almost touches the stick at the point of its greatest concavity. Cello bows, however, enjoy greater tolerances in their measurements. A list of musical instruments and appurtenances available at Bremner of London in 1765 included:

> violoncello bows pillard'd [i.e., fluted] or plane [*sic*]
> ditto with screws
> violin bows pillar'd or plane
> ditto with screws
> bows for small violins and kits

showing that bow screws were not taken for granted in England at the time. They had already been described in the first volume of the 1751 edition of Diderot and D'Alembert's *Encyclopédie*.

Much valuable information regarding violins is to be found in the *Carteggio* of the collector-dealer Count Cozio di Salabue, covering the late eighteenth and early nineteenth centuries, but he is frustratingly silent on the Tourtes, whose name he does not mention once, although he writes of the French school of bow making. Old bows, he states, did not produce a loud tone (*cavavano poco voce*); those of the Paris school and of the Mantegazza brothers are best; the highest quality of brazil-wood is the least red in appearance and is called pernambuco; other woods are either too "compact" or too elastic; the height of the head must virtually equal the curve of the stick; the length of the best bows is 25 Paris inches (67.6 centimeters or ca. 26½ inches) or 37 Roman architectural *onze* (68.7 centimeters or ca. 27 inches), we learn. These lengths are some six centimeters shorter than those of Tourte, his contemporary.

Jean-Baptiste Vuillaume, the Parisian luthier, experimented with further improvements in the nineteenth century, combining frog with stick, and also making hollow steel bows. The latter are no longer in use but remain highly prized as collector's items; he also invented a self-hairing bow.

Two different bow models exist for the double bass, to accommodate those players who bow palm down and those who prefer to bow palm up. The former make use of a "French" bow, which is merely an enlarged violin bow, while the latter prefer a Simandl model with far higher frog—a modification of the former Dragonetti bow. Actually the palm-up stance, formerly held in common with the viola da gamba, has become a "palm in" position, as the grip slants the player's palm toward his body. It is still the preferred position of double bass players in central Europe and the United States.

THE FIDDLE

An exhaustive study on the origins of the bow and of early bowed chordophones by Bachmann (1964) has brought together much new material and filled in many a gap in our sparse knowledge of the first centuries of their existence. The following pages draw heavily on this material for the early period.

When the bow reached Europe it was applied to chordophones already in existence there; some that had been plucked in the past were now played in the new way, permitting legato and sustained sounds. And sustained sound could be transformed into continuous sound if one string were given the role of a drone.

The first evidence of bowed chordophones in Europe so far known is the illustration (mentioned on page 466) in a Beatus commentary dating from 920–930, written and illustrated in Spain, that is, under Moorish influence and domination (MS 58, Bibl. nac., Madrid), where four large, bottle-shaped instruments are played by saints holding round bows: *habentes citharas dei.* Bachmann comments that in earlier Beatus commentaries the "citharas" were shown as plucked ones. These first fiddles are almost as tall as their standing players, are held vertically by necessity of this great size, and have three strings and round pegdisks. By the year 1000 smaller sizes with five strings appear in another Beatus commentary (BM add MS 11699), with elliptical body, still held vertically. A rebec type with reversed pegbox and lateral pegs is seen in Spain and Sicily from the turn of the millennium on, taken over from the Arabs; in Western Islamic culture this is played in the Oriental position, held upright, but Europe preferred a horizontal position for its smaller fiddles, including the rebec (the rebec is discussed separately on page 483). But despite the large body of pictorial and sculptural evidence at our disposal showing the fiddle in all phases of its development, a precise description of earlier instruments presents difficulties, as almost no two instruments are identical.

Bowed chordophones of the early period can be grouped as those having a flat pegdisk and pegs inserted from the rear, and those with pegbox and laterally inserted pegs. The pegbox variety is Oriental in origin; to it belong the rebec and Byzantine fiddles having a guitarlike waist. In general, early Byzantine bowed instruments have one more characteristic of the lute, namely the belly string-holder. It is the group of pegdisk chordophones that we find referred to as fiddles, a loose term originally applied to plucked as well as to bowed instruments over a wide geographic and linguistic area, from Icelandic and Old Nordic to Spanish and Italian. The word "fiddle" and its numerous cognates was in use in medieval times up to, but not east of, Germany; in Swedish and Norwegian sagas it denoted a plucked instrument; in Iceland at a later date, a bowed one with elongated, trapezoidal body, now extinct; the word is included in an Anglo-Saxon vocabulary of the first millennium and in Old High German in the ninth-century *Evangelienbuch* of Otfrid of Weissenburg, where it is specified as plucked. Byzantine sources show preponderantly two models: one with guitarlike waist, and bent-back pegbox; and another with pear-shaped body leading into a short neck, usually with belly string-holder. The first of these forms apparently continued in use and was still described in a Turkish treatise of the early fifteenth century. In Byzantium it is always depicted played at the shoulder, not in Oriental fashion.

From these two areas—Moorish Spain and Byzantium—the bow reached western Europe, and by 1100 many local plucked instruments were being bowed. In contrast to the Byzantine chordophones, most Western types have rib-fastened strings, a bridge, and a pegdisk. Regional patterns start appearing in the eleventh and twelfth centuries, with piriform fiddles predominating in the west, spade-shaped ones in the south (eleventh century in Spain, twelfth century in Italy), while in central Europe an instrument with almost circular body developed. All these were made from a single block of wood, hollowed out and covered with a thin wooden belly—some European folk instruments are still made in this manner; fiddles with built-up ribs do not appear until later. The hollow body construction has been found on all hitherto excavated medieval fiddles and lyres. Softwood was the preferred material for bellies from at least the fourteenth century on. During the eleventh and twelfth centuries, three strings preponderate, followed in the thirteenth century by five strings; an exception is made by the piriform instruments, which are frequently seen with but a single string in the twelfth and thirteenth centuries. Gut was the usual material, but occasionally we hear of the use of silk, a common material in the Orient. Metal strings are first mentioned in the thirteenth-century *Summa musicae* (Gerbert 1784 III).

Two distinct playing positions evolve, conditioned to a certain extent by the size of the instrument. Almost without exception, Oriental bowed chordophones were held upright, with the lower end resting against the player's knees or the floor. In Europe this position was inherited in areas of Islamic influence (see, for instance, the small piriform fiddle of the twelfth-century Palermo Capella Palatina fresco), and in all areas when playing the waisted form of fiddle, while piriform and elliptic instruments are held more or less horizontally or, if vertically, then with the lower end against the player's chest or shoulder, pegdisk pointing to the ground. From the onset, these two positions resulted in different bowing techniques: the vertically, a-gamba, held fiddles were bowed palm up, those assuming a more or less horizontal (or pegdisk down) position were bowed palm down. Exceptionally, a-gamba held fiddles are also seen bowed palm down.

A curious variety of larger instrument appears in the twelfth century with body in the form of a figure eight, the upper and lower sections—they cannot yet qualify for the designation of bouts—produced by a reduplication of the resonator. They are seen chiefly in England and northern France and may have originated there. This model undergoes constant modification, popping up periodically, until it finally disappears in the sixteenth century. Unwaisted forms continue to be seen up to the fifteenth century. It must be stressed that an incurving waist is no criterion for determining whether or not an instrument is bowed, for some plucked chordophones of antiquity already had this feature.

The circular central soundhole seen on so many early plucked instruments weakened the belly and/or interfered with emplacement of the bridge of bowed instruments, and therefore came to be replaced by a pair of smaller soundholes, elongated but variable in form, displaced to either side of the belly. The playing stance of plucked instruments was not changed when their strings were sounded by a bow; on the late twelfth-century portal of the Santiago de Compostela Cathedral a large fiddle with ornate body, plucked, is held upright against the player's body, pegdisk down; some of the bowed fiddles seen here are identical to others being plucked.

French literature of this period frequently mentions the *viele*, often together with the rote, and the twelfth-century *Roman de Thebes* unites these two with harps for vocal accompaniments:

> *qui chantoent o lor vieles*
> *et o rotes et o harpeles*

The word *viele* in the meaning of fiddle is replaced in French in the fifteenth century by *viole* or *vyolon*; its English equivalent, vyell (with variant spellings), still occurs in the late fifteenth century; the German *Fiedel* lingered on late, and one Zacharias der Fidelist is mentioned in a 1602 Weimar court document.

From the thirteenth century on, five strings were the classical number on European fiddles. (But cf. the rebec, page 483.) Around 1250 Jerome of Moravia gives us the first details of their tuning: D° Γ G° d° d°, but for secular music D° Γ G° d° g° was preferred, as he informs us. The D° was an off-board string plucked with the thumb; he states that this could be dispensed with, and many a-braccio fiddles do not show it. This penta-chordal stringing is confirmed later in the century by Elias Salomon. At the end of the thirteenth century, Johannes de Grocheo prefers the *viella* to all other stringed instruments, as it was capable of rendering all forms of music (. . . *Ita viella in se virtualiter alia continet instrumenta*); not only did it accompany a song but it was soon discovered to be apt for dancers, as we gather from the *Roman de Chauvenci*:

> *Et en milieu dance a viele*
> *chevalier contre demoiselle*

and professional instruction in playing could be obtained in the early fourteenth century, when, for instance, the minstrel master Simon of Ghent gave lessons in the art of fiddle playing during the fair of 1313. Supplementary information on tuning is forthcoming in 1372, when Jean Corbichon, who adds comments and explanations to his translation of Bartholomaeus Anglicus, describes the *vielle*'s center string as that from which the others are to be tuned (*la moyenne corde de la vielle ou de la guisterne qui accorde les autres*), a drone (cf. the modern *lira* and *gadulka* tunings, *sub* rebec).

In the following century we are fortunate in having a theorist-historian-composer, Johannes Tinctoris, write about the fiddle at the time it was also being painted by a preeminent artist of the period, Memling. The fiddle-playing angel of Memling's Antwerp triptych of around 1480 holds at the shoulder a guitar-shaped instrument with five strings, fretted neck, slightly reversed pegdisk, long tailpiece, bridge notched for each string so deeply that it has become more like a comb with teeth, very short fingerboard, and equally short stop. The same instrument is in the hands of an angel (wearing the same clothes) on Memling's reliquary of Saint Ursula, Bruges, with but minor variants—and the bridge is still a comb. Of the bowed *viole*, his contemporary, Tinctoris, knew three kinds: one, smaller than the lute, flat instead of tortoise shaped, with incurved sides in most cases; a second also differing from the lute in shape and with either three strings tuned in fifths—the more usual form—or with five strings tuned in fifths and unisons; these were disposed so that each could be touched separately by the bow, presumably over an arcuate bridge as seen on the paintings of Gaudenzio Ferrari and Grünewald described on page 496 (Tinctoris writes *tumide sunt extente*). His third viola is the rebec. His statement that each string of his second type could be bowed independently from the others shows that by the last quarter of the fifteenth century one major type of fiddle at least had discarded or transmuted its drones.

During the entire fifteenth century the five-stringed, guitar-shaped fiddle with seven frets on the neck and C holes, remained the classical model of northern countries; in Italy the oval or piriform version predominates for the first three-quarters of the century, after which the waisted model comes to the fore. However, a number of other types continue in use concurrently—or are newly created—variants of the main forms with either three or five strings, and do not disappear completely until their offspring, the *liras*, gambas, and violins, have rendered them obsolete.

EUROPEAN FOLK AND REGIONAL FIDDLES

Supplanted in most of Europe by the new Renaissance forms, the medieval fiddle did not die out entirely but is still to be found in some remoter areas. These constitute veritable "fiddle enclaves," retaining not only the elsewhere outdated instrument but also a playing technique descended from, if not even identical with, pre-Renaissance practice. Perhaps the best known of these enclaves is Jihlava (Iglau) in Moravia— it is also a linguistic enclave. Here a whole family of "medieval" fiddles have been made continuously since the sixteenth century to our knowledge, and earlier, as we surmise. Three sizes, the treble called *Klarfiedel*, the alto *Grobfiedel*, the bass *Plaschprment*, are modeled from a block of maple hollowed out and then covered with a fir belly into which rectangular soundholes are cut. The bridge is indented like a comb or, rather, like Memling's bridges were. Bass bars are lacking and the body remains unvarnished. The *Klarfiedel*'s four strings are tuned like those of a violin; the alto has only three strings, tuned g° d′ a′, that is, as the three lowest strings of the violin, on which only double stops are executed, since its function is to fill in the middle parts (one may speculate whether this is not rather a case of *a posteriori* justification and does not represent in reality a continuation of medieval droning practice). The cello-sized bass has four strings tuned C° G° d° d′, or occasionally C° G° d° d°, reminiscent of medieval tunings with paired unisons.

A three-stringed pegdisk fiddle with rounded corners is also played in nearby Bohemia today, held against the upper arm and steadied by a band passing over the player's left elbow and around the bottom of the fiddle to prevent it from slipping. This manner of holding an instrument may be compared with that in an illustration from a fourteenth-century Czech Bible (reproduced in Buchner [1956]) in which a four-stringed fiddle is held horizontally against the player's upper arm and supported by a band attached to the back of the pegdisk.

Among the West Slavic Wends of the Spreewald area of Lusatia (Lausitz), another linguistic island, the *husla* was played up to the mid-nineteenth century. Elsewhere in Lusatia it died out earlier. Slender and shallow, with incurved waist, its built-up body was similar in form to the keyed fiddle (see below); it had three strings (tuned d′ a′ e²), a pegdisk, both circular soundhole and rectangular soundslits, a short fingerboard, flat back, and evenly arched belly. Here again, the bass bar was dispensed with.

Keyed Fiddles

Apparently northern Europe preferred a mechanical means of stopping the strings to finger stopping, for we find bowed fiddles furnished with a key system analogous to that of the early hurdy-gurdy in Scandinavia, Denmark, and northern Germany. Our first evidence of such instruments is from a fifteenth-century fresco in an Uppland, Sweden, church, where a four-stringed, piriform, keyed fiddle is held horizontally across the player's chest, as were many other fiddles of the period, its back tilted against the performer's body to keep the slider keys clear of the strings; the slider keys emerge from a hurdy-gurdy type of box and point to the ground. This playing position was maintained throughout its history. The bow was moved almost vertically, and, in order to give the right arm greater freedom of motion, the fiddle is later suspended from a strap around the player's neck, a technique shared with several other folk instruments. By the end of the fifteenth century the figure-of-eight fiddle body replaced the pear shape, becoming more elongated in form in Sweden than in northern Germany.

Keyed fiddles are better known by the Swedish name of *nyckelharpa* ("keyed *harpa*") or their German equivalent, *Schlüsselfiedel* ("keyed fiddle"). Structurally they differ from the organistrum only by their lack of a wheel and by local variations in body shape. In all probability they are descendants of the organistrum or, more precisely, its adaptation to local requirements. The flat bridge ensured the simultaneous bowing of all strings, thus producing the same tonal effect as the hurdy-gurdy. An extant sixteenth-century instrument has provision for three strings, one of which appears to have served as melody string, the others as drones, and nine slider keys which, if the open string is considered to be c', produce a scale of d'e'f'g'a'bb'c² e² f².

Martin Agricola shows an unconvincing keyed fiddle in 1528, Praetorius a meticulously drawn one in 1620, with slider-key box open for our inspection; its melody string is separated on the flat bridge from the three drones, and the soundholes are cordiform, a characteristic of northern folk instruments. The resonator seems to be built up, in contrast to the Swedish instruments whose bodies, necks, and pegdisks were made of a single block of wood. After the seventeenth century we no longer hear of keyed fiddles in Germany, but in Sweden they continue in use and are still to be met with in Uppland today.

Nyckelharpas attained their greatest popularity in the seventeenth century, when they generally had three strings tuned a' (melody string) g° or a°, d', and a single row of slider keys. Early in the nineteenth century one or two melody strings and two or three drones were common, the former tuned a'c', the latter c°g°; the slider keys now increase in length as they approach the bridge. By then the instrument measured some 90 centimeters (3 feet) and had a "keyboard" of usually nineteen keys acting on the melody string as well as on three positions of the second string; some models have two sets of slider keys, a shorter set placed below the main set; up to eleven metal sympathetic strings were also added. Neither the number of strings and slider keys nor the tunings are standardized; a single melody string is common but a second may be present. The *nyckelharpa* is played with a short, loose-haired bow, the hair of which is tensed by the player's thumb, inserted between hair and stick.

The Gusle

A chordophone distributed among the South Slavs (including the Bulgarians) that bears no morphological relationship to the medieval forms of west and central European fiddles is the *gusle* (called *gusla* in Bulgarian). Its name derives from the Old Slavonic *gusti* ("to drone"); and, as most *gusles* have a single string nowadays, we assume the presence of a second one in the past.

Gusles are made from a single block of hollowed wood to resemble a ladle with slim neck. A peg inserted from the rear holds the horsehair string high off the neck; the belly is of dried sheepskin. Regional preferences determine the shape of the body—ovate or cordiform. Sizes are not standardized but vary from about 65 centimeters (25½ inches) to 80 centimeters (31½ inches) with proportionately small body: for *gusles* are descended from the old Eastern long-necked lute. When playing, the performer is seated; he holds his instrument vertically between the knees —in Montenegro players cross their legs—and stops the string with index, middle, and little finger, the weak fourth finger never being used. Lateral pressure is applied to the string by the fleshy part of the fingers, without pressing it down against the neck. If there is an additional string, this is tuned a second below the first. The player's left hand remains close to the tuning peg and does not change position except at the end of a piece, when it forms a glissando by sliding along the string. *Gusles* are played only to accompany the singing of epics, never for independent music, hence their restricted compass suffices, and no need for a more modern technique has been felt. *Gusle* bows are archaic: made of a forked branch bent to the required curve while wet, one tine is cut off short, leaving a stump through which a hole has been drilled to receive the hair; the long end is notched. High tension evenly distributed is demanded by the *guslar* to ensure that minimum pressure will make the string speak.

FIDDLES IN NON-WESTERN CULTURES

The Arabic lute *rabāb* is known to have been bowed since the turn of the millennium; according to al-Farabi it was shaped like a Khurasan *tunbūr*, slender, with long neck and pyriform body, one or two strings (tuned a second apart, if two), and devoid of frets. Other tunings, a third, fourth, or fifth apart, are referred to by him, and his suggestion of tuning to a fourth or fifth was later adopted. Yet because no Arabic pictorial material prior to the thirteenth century has reached us, we do not know how the *rabāb* of that time was held.

In North Africa today the name of *rabāb* is given to a different type of fiddle, now neckless (and spikeless), its narrow body forming a near-rectangle, with arched back, the body and pegbox made of a single piece of wood, belly of skin, and two thick gut strings; it is played with a short, curved, and heavy bow. Next to the lute it is considered the most popular orchestral instrument in Morocco; there, it rests obliquely on the seated player's knees, with left-hand fingers held between the two strings so that they can be stopped by lateral pressure. For orchestral participation the strings are tuned to d′ and a′ but, for accompanying men's voices, to D° and d°. (The long-necked type of *rabāb* is discussed with the spike fiddles, page 480.)

The long-necked lute *tunbūr* has continued in existence through the centuries, both as a plucked and as a bowed chordophone. With three strings it is the preferred plucked chordophone of Central Asia today, and frequently also appears as a bowed one. Among the Turkic peoples of Central Asia as well as in Anatolia, the word *iqliq* has designated a fiddle from the thirteenth century on; the term itself is a contraction of *oklu qobūz* ("bowed *qobūz*"), another lute. Allowing for regional variations, *iqliqs* have long necks, generally elliptic bodies, skin bellies, two rib-fastened horsehair strings, and rear tuning pegs. One string serves for the melody, the second is a drone.

Fiddles are played all over the Indian subcontinent, and particularly in the north, where they were introduced by Islam. Typical among them is a whole group of lutes that are both bowed and plucked. The *sarōd* of the Northwest, for instance, whose synonym, *rabōb*, betrays its origins, has body and short neck carved out of one block of wood, four melody strings, and a variable number of sympathetic strings. A glissando-legato style of playing is obtained by pressing the melody strings with the finger-nails and sliding them along the strings to the next required position, a technique made possible because the neck remains unfretted. When plucked, the *sarōd* is played with a plectrum. Another fiddle made from a single block of wood is the northern *sārangī*; it closely resembles the Moroccan *rabāb*, though it is far more cumbersome. Both have bodies with sloping, incurved sides continuing as a broad, thick neck, and a short, equally broad pegbox. The *sārangī*'s three gut strings are secured by lateral pegs; to these, one of metal is sometimes added, plus from eleven to fifteen sympathetic strings. Here also the strings are stopped by the player's fingernails.

A folk *sārangī* of most distinctive form, called the *sārindā*, is played all over the subcontinent by members of lower castes; the upper section of its body is far wider than the lower, from which it is separated by scooped-out "center bouts," the upper section forming downward-pointing barbs. This bowed version seems to derive ultimately from the ancient Gandhara lute, the only one to show a body division resulting in barbs. Another form of folk *sārangī* is the *ravanahasta*, its neck sometimes terminating in the form of an outstretched hand. Once taken by musicologists for an instrument of great antiquity and believed by them to represent the earliest instance of a bowed chordophone, the *ravanahasta* is now held to be a relatively recent creation.

Broad-necked lutes of the subcontinent may also be either plucked or bowed. Such is the *esrar*, a cross between sitar and *sārangī*, with waisted body, skin belly, movable frets on the broad neck, and both melody and sympathetic strings. In Afghanistan and northwestern India another form of *esrar*, the *dilruba* (from *rubāb*) is either plucked or bowed, while a southern Indian form assumes the imaginative and elegant shape of a peacock and hence is called *mayurī*, the Sanskrit name of that bird. Its body and neck are painted, the neck forming the peacock's tail. *Mayurīs* are bowed only; during the performance the bird's short legs remain on the ground or on a table, etc., and its tail rests against the player's shoulder. A *mayurī* is mentioned about A.D. 500, but we cannot tell whether it indicated a plucked predecessor of this instrument or not. Music in Indian village life often centers on primitive fiddles with half-coconut bodies attached to bamboo necks; in the west these may have parchment bellies, two strings, and lateral pegs; in the north and south wooden or skin bellies with the bottom left open, and the same stringing. The hair of the highly curved bow with which they are sounded passes between the strings as on the Chinese *hu* fiddles (see page 482) to which they appear to be intimately related.

Fiddles are not indigenous to Negro Africa and few are played there outside the areas of Islamic influence. Gourd or half-gourd fiddles with wooden stick handles and single strings are known in Guinea, played with very long bows. Fiddles are also known in Sierra Leone, and further south among the Masengo of Angola and among the Holo of the Congo basin a three-stringed wooden fiddle with stick neck and long lateral pegs betrays its European provenance by an open pegbox. (For Ethiopian instruments, see spike fiddles.)

As for the Americas, bowed chordophones are unknown to American Indians, with the exception of the nearly extinct "Apache fiddle," an instrument that is almost certainly of European inspiration. Apart from its use among the Apache, it is also played by the southern California Diegueño. The primitive chordophone is made from the hollowed stem of a mescal agave or flower stalk of a yucca, with string of horsehair or sinew. Usually there is but a single string on the short instrument, rarely there may be a second one; its short bow is semicircular, with horsehair attached by sinew.

Spike Fiddles

Lutes having a handle that pierces the body and emerges at the lower end were known in the second millennium B.C., when they appeared in western Asia and in Egypt (as long-necked lutes), and are referred to as spike lutes. Once the bow had come into existence it was applied to the spike lute, transforming it into a spike fiddle. Al-Farabi (d. 950) documents the spike, and indeed the first bowed instruments are likely to have been spike fiddles. An Arabian manuscript of the late eighth century mentions the *r-bab*, then a plucked scaphoid lute to be subsequently known as the *rabāb*. As a bowed instrument this form wandered as far as Spain, where it was taken over as the rebec (see page 483). At an unknown time the word *rabāb* was also given to the spike fiddle, which was then propagated under this name; both the instrument and the name are still in use.

Classic among the forms assumed by the spike fiddle is that of a half-coconut body, a divided or a membrane belly pierced by a long stick handle, lateral tuning pegs, usually three strings, and the spike on which it sometimes, but not invariably, rested when played. When al-Farabi wrote of it in the tenth century it had one or two strings, or even two pairs of strings, a bridge, and no frets (just as the modern instrument). With the Islamic expansion the *rabāb* spread through Anatolia and Syria across North Africa to the Maghrib, and east through Persia and Afghanistan to the Indian subcontinent—where it is now played by the Islamic population only—and to Southeast Asia. In all these regions it is played in a-gamba position, that is, held vertically. Only in areas where it was introduced in later times is it ever held a-braccio, as, for example, among the Muria of Bastar, India.

Numerous regional variants of construction and playing method attest to its adaptability: the *arababu* (from *rabāb*) of Halmahera in the Moluccas, for instance, has but a single string, which is either bowed or plucked; on Sumatra the *arbab* has a cordiform calabash body, two silk strings, and rear tuning pegs; on Java and southern Celebes the *rebab*, also made from a cordiform calabash, the back of which is pierced with small soundholes, has two metal strings. Here the pitch is modified both by the position of the player's fingers on the string and by the amount of pressure they exert (in the absence of a fingerboard), and *Bebungen* can be obtained by varying this pressure. The *rebāb* assumes a leading role in the Javanese *gamelan* (orchestra). On the Southeast Asian mainland, bodies of ivory and mother-of pearl inlay imitate the cordiform calabash.

Ethiopia's only bowed chordophone, the *masseneqo*, is a degeneration of the *rabāb*; its square or diamond-shaped body is a mere frame, covered front and back with parchment or hide, and the stick handle with rear peg for a single string pierces the body to emerge as a stub; the bow employed is the ancient round bow with a short handgrip. Its seated player holds the instrument with the knees, using all five fingers to stop the string; he is more often an *amzari* (wandering singer).

Another early name of the Near Eastern spike fiddle, tentatively documented from the tenth century on, is *kamānja*. In most of North Africa today, this term is either applied to the European viola or violin or it has become obsolete, as in Egypt. It can best be translated as "fiddle"— it is derived from a word meaning bow—for *kamānja agūz*, an obsolete Egyptian name, means "old fiddle," and *kamānja rūmī*, the equivalent of "Greek fiddle," denotes the Near Eastern *lira*. The *kamānja* is believed to have arrived in Byzantium via Anatolia in the eleventh or twelfth century; together with its bow it is represented in a thirteenth-century Byzantine psalter (Hamilton MS 119, Berlin, Kupferstichkabinett). Also known by its Persian and Turkish names (*ghizhak* and *iqliq*, respectively), it was described in a Turkish treatise of 1402–1404, from which we learn that its gut strings had been replaced by horsehair and were tuned a fifth apart, and the body was made of bronze. But such metal instruments were probably exceptional and we hear no more of them.

In some areas spike fiddles are large trapezoids rather than made of half coconuts or their imitations. Trapezoidal bodies are encountered in North

Africa among the Algerian Tuareg and the Moroccan Sus-Shluh. A version known as *khil-khuur* in Mongolia has two lateral pegs for horse-hair strings tuned a fifth apart, with pegbox carved in the form of a horse's head, the back and belly being of hide (among some tribes the body is circular). A similar arrangement is seen on Persian miniatures from the thirteenth century on. Exceptionally, the trapezoidal body is also met with in China.

In contrast to these instruments, all of which are played a-gamba, most Chinese spike fiddles are played a-braccio. Perhaps they should more properly be termed stub fiddles, for the spike is no more than a projecting stub. Their generic name, *hu ch'in* ("foreign *ch'in*"), is recorded by the ninth century, when they were plucked. A variety of *hu ch'ins*, all of small size, have either a cylindrical or a hexagonal body of bamboo or wood, the back of which is left open, the top covered traditionally with lizard or snakeskin; an exception is the *ti ch'in*, which has a hemispheric, half-coconut body and a long spike. Rib-fastened and passing over a bridge, the two strings or pairs of strings are usually tuned a fifth apart and are played with a short bow. That of the two-stringed versions has an unciform "frog" around which the hair is looped. For playing, the hair is detached, passed over one string and under the other, then looped to the frog. The bow of models with two pairs of strings, on the other hand, is attached permanently to the instrument by its hair, so that it cannot be removed from its position between the strings: the hair is parted into two lengths, one passing between the first and second strings, the other between the third and fourth strings, whose relative tuning is $f'c^2f'c^2$. On an "upbow," downbearing pressure is exerted on strings one and three, on a "down-bow," the bow is raised so as to touch the other two. Long rear pegs raise the strings well above the handle; they are looped to the neck, with the loop acting both as nut and as *capotasto*.

Fiddles such as these are played far beyond the confines of China proper; among the Sunit Mongols they are usually cylindrical, occasionally octagonal, with two pairs of silk strings tuned a fifth apart. Resting against the player's thigh, the strings are stopped either by the middle joints of the fingers or from underneath by the fingernails. Except for their larger size they correspond to the Chinese *su hu*; among the Kalmuck, the same instrument is called *biwa*. A very similar spike fiddle is played in Indo-china (where its generic name is *so*) and in Japan. Also played in Japan is a bowed form of *samisen* called *kokyu*, furnished with two, three, or four strings; if four, the two highest in pitch are unisons. When the performer plays in a seated position, the *kokyu* is given a spike, otherwise not. Of even greater interest than the instrument is its extremely long bow, measuring some 114 centimeters (45 inches), with loose hair held taut by the player's little finger, the stick itself held like a pair of chopsticks.

Apart from the elaborate ivory instruments of the Southeast Asian mainland, Cambodia, Laos, Thailand, and Vietnam still have a primitive form, identical with the *ti ch'in* of China, with a coconut body, wooden soundboard, and two pairs of strings. Further north in Bengal, the form is imitated in clay.

With such notable exceptions as participation in the Javanese *gamelan*, spike fiddles have remained folk instruments, capable of rendering solo melodies but more often furnishing the background for their players' voices.

THE REBEC

The rebec of medieval and Renaissance Europe that lives on today as a folk instrument in southeast Europe, is an adaption to Western use of the Near Eastern *rabāb*. This ancient plucked lute, documented from the eighth century on (see spike fiddle, page 480), is presumably identical with the plucked instrument mentioned by Theophylact Simocattes of Byzantium as *lira* in a reference to the year 583; certainly it was known by this name in western Europe when Otfrid of Weissenburg wrote of the *lira joh fidula* in his *Evangelienbuch* of the ninth century. Possibly the name *lira* derives, as Tinctoris reminds us, from the shape of its body—that of a tortoise carapace—but more likely from the fact that, as the instruments of antiquity died out, their names were bestowed in Byzantium on newly emerging ones. However, a bowed instrument is not yet implied.

With the spread of Islam the *lira-rabāb* traveled both east and west, probably after undergoing some modification of shape, for the tympani of Moissac and Chartres cathedrals, as well as that of Sainte Marie, Oloron, show lozenge-shaped, scaphoid, pyriform, and rounded types, all with pegdisks, some bowed, others plucked. The rounded rebec shape is first seen in the early eleventh century in Spain, held propped against the shoulder, and appears next in France. An elongated, scaphoid instrument introduced into Moorish Spain is depicted in the thirteenth-century

Cantigas de Santa María and may represent the *rabé morisco* (Moorish *rabāb*) of Spanish literature. Juan Ruiz distinguishes in the fourteenth century between the European rebec, which he calls simply *rabé*, and the *rabé morisco*.

From the thirteenth to the sixteenth centuries the rebec was known in western Europe as *rubeba*. Jerome of Moravia described this as having two strings tuned a fifth apart, and a compass of ten tones, from C to D. (Another thirteenth-century theorist, Pierre Picard, confirms the rebec's two strings a fifth apart.) A late-fourteenth-century writer, Heinrich of Kalkar (*Cantuarium*, ca. 1380), states that the highest pitched string on gitterns, rebecs, and *vielles* can be stopped to produce five or six tones, implying first that *vielle* and rebec were not considered identical, and then that the second string was a drone.

Meanwhile the *lura* or *lyra* had become so much a part of Byzantine music that in the late ninth century the Persian ibn-Khurdadhbib could call it "the *lura* of the Rumi," that is, of the Greeks. He gives it a wooden body, five strings, and says it was identical to the *rabāb* of the Arabs. At that time its strings would not have been bowed. An eleventh-century Latin-Arabic glossary renders *rabāb* as *lyra* (which term was in due course transferred to the *lira da gamba* and *da braccio*), and, in the West, twelfth-century illustrations of rebecs are inscribed *lira* (e.g., those of the *Hortus deliciarum* of Abbess Herrad of Landsberg, and a now-lost manuscript of Saint Blasius Monastery, published in Gerbert [1774]).

By the time the *rabāb* emerged as a full-fledged bowed rebec it had a small, usually piriform body and short neck, both made from a single piece of wood, a vaulted back, the Oriental rose in its soundhole that it was to keep for several centuries, and three strings tuned in fifths attached to lateral pegs, a type still depicted in the hands of Fra Angelico's angels in the second quarter of the fifteenth century. Later instruments were characterized by split-level soundboards, the raised upper section of which formed a continuation of the neck, with the bridge placed on the lower level. Exceptionally, rebecs were made of costly materials; thus we hear of payment being made in France in 1514 *pour ung chevalet d'argent que mondit seigneur a fait faire pour le rebec d'argent* ("for the silver bridge that my lord had made for the silver rebec").

Some idea of medieval playing methods may perhaps be gleaned from that of the *lira* as played in Yugoslavia today; there, the three strings usually have a (relative) tuning of g'd'a', the center string being a drone. Two strings, the drone and one of the outer strings, are always sounded together, and, although the highest string is stopped, the compass of a sixth is never exceeded. The lowest string is stopped less frequently, and then only by the thumb. *Liras* have no nut; instead, their three strings are raised high off the neck by elongated tuning pegs inserted from the rear. During performance they are held in the Oriental (i.e., upright) manner, on the player's lap, and in many areas the strings are stopped laterally by the pressure of fingernails rather than that of the finger.

As a folk instrument the rebec is still played in Europe, but as a "drawing room" instrument it survived perhaps longest in France, and French-made eighteenth-century rebecs are not uncommon. Yet Furetière (·1685) explains "rebec" as an "old word that formerly signified a three-stringed violin." This seeming discrepancy is explained if we realize that the kit is an offspring of the rebec; Trichet (ca. 1640) reports that there were still people who played the rebec in his day.

During the fourteenth and fifteenth centuries the rebec had little, if any, part in art music, being relegated to the playing of tunes for dancers. At some period of its existence, probably in the late fifteenth century, the pegdisk was abolished in favor of lateral tuning pegs, and this feature henceforth distinguished the western European rebec from the central and eastern European folk instrument. In the fifteenth century the nomenclature is still perfectly clear: both de Gerson and Tinctoris refer to the rebec unambiguously, but during the course of the sixteenth century terminology becomes confused with the rebec's admission into the sphere of art music, and the name was also applied to the new violin. Until the violin group was prominent enough to warrant names of its own we can often not tell which instrument is meant. Exceptionally, the 1551 inventory of a deceased Parisian luthier enumerates both rebecs and violins, and in a Florentine *intermedio* of 1565 a *ribecchino* and four *violoni* were among the participating instruments.

Agricola in 1528 depicts and describes a family of three-stringed rebecs called *kleine Geigen ohne Bünde* ("little fiddles without frets"); each has the characteristic split soundboard, and the neck and body are clearly of one piece. In his expanded version of 1545 he calls the same instruments *kleine 3 saitige Handgeigen* ("small three-stringed hand fiddles"), and adds *jeder will jetzt damit umgehen* ("everybody wants to play them now"). His tunings are in fifths: soprano g°d′a′, tenor c°g°d′, bass F°c°g°, all presumably indicated an octave below their true pitch, as they coincide (as given) with the three lowest strings of our violin, viola, and obsolete tenor violin. But in Agricola's day and for a good century thereafter the lowest string of the violin family of instruments was rarely utilized; furthermore, rebecs were smaller than members of the violin family, and the spritely playing for which they were noted could not have been achieved with slack, thick strings. That rebecs actually were made in three sizes is borne out by the fifteenth-century Orvieto poet, Simone Prodenzani, who writes of *suon d'archetto, rubebe, rubechette et rubicone,* and by such items as the listing of *4 grosse Rebebn* in a 1584 Kremsmünster inventory.

If the terms *Geige* and rebec are seen as synonymous, the French word *gigue,* derived from the Middle High German *gige,* is more ambiguous, as rebec and *gigue* are mentioned together in the late thirteenth century by Adenet Le Roi in his *Roumans de Cléomadès;* the same poem gives us *les gigeours d'Allemaigne,* pointing in this case to the northern origin of the word rather than of the instrument. However, *gigue* appears in numerous thirteenth-century French poems, never with rebec—except by Adenet Le Roi—often with *vielle.* Essentially a melody instrument, the *gigue* was in the hands of jongleurs in late medieval times and the preferred instrument of dancers, so much so that its name was transferred to the dance itself and we still speak of "dancing a gig."

The dukes of Lorraine employed "rebecs" continuously from 1509 to 1528; in 1568 the word is used in the court records in the pejorative sense of "street musician." According to documents of the English court, a "rebecke" was employed from 1518 on, and rebec players are mentioned in the records on and off thereafter until 1633. A possible explanation of their popularity may be found through comparison with the Lyons archives. There, during the first half of the sixteenth century, mention occurs of *rebequets*—rebec players. But from the moment the word *vyolon* appears, the professional designation of *rebequet* disappears, and some musicians listed as such up to about 1550 are given other appellations from then on. But not until Praetorius wrote do we find an unambiguous identification of *ribecchino* with violin. He states . . . *Bass-Tenor- und Discant-Geig (welche Violino oder Violetta picciola auch Ribecchino genennt wird) . . . seynd mit 4. Saiten . . .* (. . . Bass, tenor, and descant *Geig* [which is called *violino* or *violetta picciola* or *ribecchino*] . . . has four strings . . .). However, Italian seventeenth-century inventories of musical instruments make a distinction between violins and *ribecchini.* Praetorius inscribes his drawings of a three-stringed rebec and of an elongated kit *kleine Poschen/Geigen ein Octav höher,* and gives their tunings as $g'd^2a^2$ and a tone higher—an octave above the lowest three strings of the violin, and an octave above Agricola's descant *Geige*. The status of the rebec, at least in France, declined during the seventeenth century as it was apparently not able to withstand competition from the increasingly popular violins. We hear of a sentence passed in March 1682 in favor of the corporations of *ménétriers*, forbidding musicians to exercise their profession without having passed the professional examination required after a six-year apprenticeship; those who failed to pass were permitted to play only the rebec.

THE KIT

In the latter half of the sixteenth century a slender and diminutive offspring of the rebec established itself as a French dancing master's fiddle, housed in its master's coat-tail pocket when not in use, and hence appropriately called *poche de violon* ("pocket violin"). Its English name, kit, is older, but we do not know what instrument this may have designated during the earlier part of the sixteenth century—possibly the rebec.

During the two centuries of its existence the kit was made in a number of forms, as a miniature mandora, rebec, violin, or viola da gamba (the last two are later forms), or even scaphoid, hence Athanasius Kircher's Latinization of its name to *linterculus* ("little boat"). Its three strings were tuned $g'd^2a^2$ or a tone higher, according to Praetorius; if a fourth string were added it was to the bass, tuned a fifth below the g'. Scaphoid or club-shaped kits were occasionally built narrow enough to be enclosed in a hollow walking stick, in which case they were called *poches-canne* (nowadays *cannes-pochette*). Documents and iconography alike distinguish between ordinary kits (*poches communes*)—presumably such as that seen in the hands of a strolling player in Louis Le Nain's *Family of Peasants*—and more costly examples such as that inlaid with rubies, mother-of-pearl, and seed pearls inventorized after the death of a *violon ordinaire* to the king of France in 1625.

Praetorius illustrates a kit he calls *Posche* or, in another passage, *gar klein Geiglein*. Of its participation in string ensembles we are informed by Constantijn Huygens, who writes of a 1638 wedding celebration at The Hague, with excellent music of kits, lutes, and harp at supper, while later during a *partie de bague*—an outdoor game of skill—a chariot appeared with *luths, violons, violes, poches, et harpes*. Little played outside France, it continued in use in that country through most of the eighteenth century. Stradivari made two kits, one of which, now in the

Paris Conservatoire collection, formerly belonged to Antoine-Louis Clapisson, the composer and collector of musical instruments; he scored for it in his *opéra-comique, Les trois masques* (1866), where it accompanied a dance.

Monteverdi calls for a *violino piccolo alla francese* in his *Orfeo*, first performed in 1607; its notated compass, c′ to e♭², is believed to have sounded an octave higher; if this was so, the part could have been played on a *poche*, which would satisfactorily explain the *alla francese*, hitherto a stumbling block.

FOLK REBECS

Under the names of *rabel, arrabel,* or *rebab,* the rebec has survived into our century as a folk instrument in parts of southeastern Europe and in the Near East. When Carl Engel wrote (1874), the *rabel* or *arrabel* was in occasional use "among the country people" of Spain; it is still played in Estremadura. The name by which it was known to Byzantium, *lira,* has likewise come down to us, together with the instrument: today it thrives in Greece, Crete, and the Dodecanese, and as *lirica* (pronounced "liritsa") among Croatian speakers of Yugoslavia. Nowadays the pyriform body tapers to a short, ill-defined neck, it has a pegdisk for three strings, and the age-old Oriental a-gamba playing position has been retained, with the small instrument resting upon the performer's lap or crossed legs, its strings stopped laterally by the fingernails, thereby obviating the need for a fingerboard. Its tuning is in fifths, except that instruments with a drone are tuned to intervals of a fifth and reentrant fourth, for example, c′g°d′, as in the Dodecanese. The New Eastern *lira* kept its medieval name of *kāmanjā rūmi* ("Greek fiddle"). A Caucasian version named *skripka* ("the squeaky one") has three bowed silk strings and as many sympathetic ones.

One of the routes taken by the *lira* from Byzantium was through the Balkans and into Russia, where its descendants may still be found. Several of these derive their names from the Old Slavonic root *gudu* ("to sound a drone"), such as the Russian *gudok* and the Bulgarian *gadulka*: both of these are identical with the Greek *lira*. The word *gusla* is recorded in the tenth century as a Bulgarian folk instrument—whether bowed or not we cannot tell—but the term *gadulka* does not occur before the sixteenth century, at which time it was referred to indifferently as *gusla* or *gadulka,* and earlier references may be to either of these instruments (even today ambiguity reigns: the emblem of the Bulgarian *gusla* chorus is a *gadulka*). To avoid confusion, the term *gadulka* (or *gudok*, if reference is to the Russian instrument) will be restricted here to indicate the three-stringed rebec with pegdisk, while *gusle* and *gusla* will be reserved for the Balkan single-stringed *tanbūra*-type fiddle, *gusli* for the psaltery. Despite its notorious lack of mention in Bulgarian folk songs, the *gadulka* is currently widespread both as a solo and as an accompanying instrument, among Bulgarians and Gypsies alike. With rare exceptions it is played by men. Allowing for regional variations, today's *gadulka* measures from 40 to 55 centimeters (roughly 16 to 21½ inches) in length; body and neck are still of one piece. Of great interest is its soundpost, one end of which presses against the back of the body, then passes through the right semicircular soundhole to bear directly against the bridge; alternately the right foot of the bridge is prolonged to permit it to pass through the soundhole and rest against the back. *Gadulkas* may also have two and four strings; tunings vary and are usually reentrant, the center string being a drone. The first string is stopped by the player's fingernail, the others with the fleshy part of the fingers, but without pressing the strings against the neck. Lately *gadulkas* have been developed into treble-to-contrabass consorts for state ensembles.

In Russia the *gudok* was played from medieval times to the eighteenth century, but has now become obsolete. Of its three strings, only the highest pitched was stopped, the remaining two, drones, always being bowed together with it. In other respects it was identical to the *gadulka* and the *lira*.

Poland had the *skrzypce*, its name for the three-stringed *lira*, by the late Middle Ages, if indeed not earlier, and it has not entirely died out yet. According to the household accounts of Prince Sigismund of Poland while in Buda visiting his brother, Ladislas II of Hungary, in 1502, payment was made to *citharedi skrzypcom*—a term to delight any philologist —players of the Polish fiddle. (Two years earlier payment had been made, according to the same source, to *citharedis czyganom*. Gypsies playing the *skrzypce*?)

One reason for investigating in some detail such regional petrifacts of the rebec, quite apart from their intrinsic interest, is that they throw light—even if only a reflecting shadow—on Renaissance musical practices. In an age when the unfretted bowed instruments were still in process of gaining acceptance, there could be little question of dividing them into categories devoted to art and to folk music. Our judgment of today, implying that the rebec-*lira* of the sixteenth century had already become a folk instrument, while the violin was commencing its role as foremost of art music instruments, would not have been understood by a contemporary of, say, Jambe de Fer, who might well retort that the situation was exactly the other way around.

THE POLNISCHE GEIGE

German-language writers of the sixteenth century refer to a mysterious instrument, the *polnische Geige*, or "Polish fiddle," the identity of which has occasioned much speculation. Our chief informant on the subject is Agricola, but the expression also crops up in sixteenth-century inventories (e.g., Kremsmünster in 1584). Agricola uses the term to designate an unfretted, three-stringed, bowed chordophone tuned in fifths, its strings stopped in the Slavonic (and Old Nordic) fashion of lateral pressure by the fingernails; players reached in and stopped the strings with their fingernails instead of the more common method of using frets, and he comments that, due to the lack of frets, the fingering was more difficult. He could have added that the lateral stopping by means of the nails implies lack of a fingerboard against which to press them (these *polnische Geigen* are distinct from his rebecs). He opposes *polnische Geigen* to *welsche Geigen* (*welsch*, literally "foreign," at that time meant "Italian," and *welhische Gigen* are mentioned as early as 1315 in a German translation of the romance *Apollonius of Tyre*: they were probably large fiddles, played a-gamba). In other words, Polish performers employed their own fingering method, and this varied from the generally accepted techniques of Agricola's day.

Even before his time, Poles had played a descendant of the *lira* which they called *skrzypce* (see page 489), a word perhaps inhibiting enough to non-Slavs to warrant its easier rendering as "Polish fiddle." Wandering Polish fiddlers were certainly not unknown at the time; in 1511 three such entertainers were paid at Neustift (Novacella) Monastery (*item lb 1 pro libalibus tribus polonis qui fecerunt recreationem d. et f.* [*dominis et fratribus*] *in refectorio cum fidelis in die* S. Anne 1511), and Boyden (1965) reports that in 1555 the Burgomaster of Stralsund refers to the presence of four *polnische Geiger* in that city.

When Praetorius wrote, the term was obsolescent; his statement that *Kunstpfeifer* differentiated between the *viole da gamba*, which they called

Violen, and the *viola da braccio* called *Geige* or *polnische Geige* must be read in conjunction with his identification in another passage of violin with *ribecchino:* the unfretted *da braccio* instruments are lumped together and opposed to those that were fretted.

THE LIRA DA BRACCIO

The *lira da braccio,* preponderantly an instrument of the Italian Renaissance, is a development of the medieval fiddle, from which it evolved in the fifteenth century. It coexisted with the *viola da braccio,* with which it was frequently confused, ultimately to be replaced by it; Vasari (1568) speaks of the *lira ovver viola,* and Galilei (1581), in a much-quoted passage, of the *viola da braccio detta da non molti anni indietro lira* ("the *viola da braccio* called *lira* not many years ago"). Properly speaking, the *lira da braccio* is the treble member of a family including a somewhat larger model also known as *lirone da braccio,* and a bass called *lira da gamba.* In order to distinguish them from the antique *lyra,* some authors referred to the family as *lyra (lira) moderna.*

Characteristics of the *lire* are a squat violin shape, gentle waist, cordiform pegdisk, an almost flat bridge—to facilitate chordal playing—and wide fingerboard to accommodate five or more strings, in addition to which there were two off-board drones tuned an octave apart; the pegdisk was a boxlike affair with open back. Later instruments have a small, second nut for the off-board strings, resembling that of an archlute. Some of the earlier models lacked center bouts, and, instead, the lower bouts were marked off by pronounced corners. The smaller *da braccio* type was about the size of the tenor violin, 70 to 75 centimeters (27½ to 29½ inches) long; the larger, 80 to 92 centimeters (31½ to 36 inches). Smaller models are generally depicted held against the left shoulder, larger ones held lower. Lanfranco (1533) gives the tuning of the smaller version as $d°d'/g°g'd'a'e^2$. Both he and Bottrigari (1594) state that the *lira* was not fretted, and paintings up to around 1600 bear them out on this point. But Praetorius represents it with frets and gives two modified tunings: $d°d'/g°g'd'a'd^2$ and $d°g°/d'd'g'a'd^2$. The string, or even the two strings, nearest to the drones were stopped by the performer's thumb. Except for the drones and the doubled octave, Lanfranco's tuning is that of a violin, but, as we are dealing with an instrument the size of a tenor violin, it is tempting to conclude that the above tunings should read an octave lower or else be taken to indicate relative pitches. However, a

Transition type of fiddle-lira. Detail from *The Coronation of the Virgin* by Paolo and Giovanni Veneziano, 1458. Copyright The Frick Collection, New York.

glance at the short neck and the bridge placed comparatively high up on the belly as seen in sixteenth-century paintings indicate a short stop and suggest that the tunings are indeed meant as given.

A good example of a transition instrument, halfway between fiddle and *lira*, is depicted in the *Coronation of the Virgin* by Paolo and Giovanni Veneziano, dated 1458; one of the unusually well defined instruments, held by angels, is an ovate fiddle, a rather deep one, with pegdisk for four T-shaped tuning pegs, plus a fifth, lateral peg for an off-board string.

By the end of the century the transformation had been completed: the portrait of a musician tuning his *lira da braccio* with its five melody strings and single drone, by Cosimo Tura (d. 1495), shows the fully developed instrument, as does Bartolommeo Montagna's *Enthroned Madonna* of 1499. During the Ferrara carnival of 1506 the *intermedio* to a *pastorale* was performed by no fewer than eight *lira* players. An early transalpine reference comes from Judenkönig, when he describes a *geyge quod lyrae simillimum est*; and indeed it was played by masters of the ordinary *geigen* or *viole*, such as Andrea of Verona, who shortly after 1530 was known to *sona di viola con tasti et di viola senza tasti et di lira et di corneto* ("play fretted viols and unfretted 'viols' and *lire* and cornetti"), a curious combination. Later in the century Lomazzo (1584) includes Leonardo da Vinci, Alfonso da Ferrara, and Alessandro Striggio in a list of *lira* players, and then proceeds to name *viola da gamba* players separately; but he refers almost certainly to players of the bass *lira da gamba*.

With the passing of the sixteenth century the *lira da braccio* started its decline. First it took on frets. Praetorius, for instance, shows it with F holes and frets, in addition to its usual features. It was sufficiently well known outside the peninsula to be seen in several non-Italian paintings, and a *Geigenlyra* with seven strings occurs in a Kassel inventory of 1613; but in Italy the smaller sizes were being abandoned by this time. Mersenne is concerned chiefly with the *da gamba* model but gives a tuning for the *lyre à bras*, probably intended for the larger of the two arm-held sizes: e♭°e♭′/b♭°f°c′g°d′a°e′b°f♯′. But the information he furnishes us on all the *lire* reflects Italian rather than French practice, for he makes acknowledgment to Geronimo Landi, superintendent of music to Cardinal Barberini, as his source.

THE LIRA DA GAMBA

The bass member of the family, the *lira da gamba*, was almost unknown outside Italy and France. Having emerged in the mid-sixteenth century, far later than the *da braccio* versions, it fell into disuse in France by the mid-seventeenth century and in Italy some fifty years thereafter. Oddly enough, its earliest recorded mention appears to be that of a Graz inventory drawn up in 1577: *ain gar grosse geigen haist man lira da camba*. An enlargement of the squat violin form of the *lira da braccio*, but with proportionately wider neck and fingerboard, it had the same flat bridge and pegdisk of the smaller instruments, often a large circular soundhole covered by a rose in addition to its regular C or F holes—an archaism left over from its plucked predecessors. Moreover, the back was flat and the neck fretted. Its stringing varied between nine and fourteen melody strings and usually two drones, for which various tunings are given (Cerreto [1601]: G°g°/ c°c′g°d′a°e′b°f♯′c♯′; that of Praetorius is similar but for the drones and the lowest melody strings: G♭° d♭°/ A♭°e♭°B♭°-f°c°g°d°a°e°b°f♯° c♯′; Mersenne's is lower: C° c°/ D°d°G°g°d°A°-e°B°f♯°c♯°g♯°d♯°a♯°). Mersenne reports that this type of *lira* was little played in France; three years later, in 1639, Maugars heard it played in Rome, at just about the time when it exchanged its pegdisk for a pegbox and lateral pegs.

Few instruments have survived into our times. The Medici collection in Florence contained in Cristofori's day three *lire da gamba* with twelve, thirteen, and fourteen strings, respectively. Practically no literature is known for the instrument; Mersenne refers to it as accompanying the voice, but we may perhaps conclude that it was primarily an instrument for improvisation.

THE VIOLA DA GAMBA

The *viola da gamba*, commonly referred to nowadays as gamba or viol, emerged in the late Middle Ages, reached its zenith in the seventeenth century, became obsolete in the eighteenth, and was revived in the twentieth. Its component parts are substantially the same as those of the violin. Gambas differ, however, in the number and tuning of their strings—they have six strings tuned in fourths with a central third—deeper ribs, sloping shoulders, a proportionately longer neck, a flat back with canted upper section, plain corners, C holes, no overlap of belly and back beyond the ribs (some old Italian instruments form an exception to this rule), wider bridge and fingerboard, often a carved head in lieu of a scroll, movable frets on the neck—seven, plus one placed at the octave of the open string as a guide—and thinner strings. Furthermore, they are held vertically by seated performers, regardless of size, the larger models supported by the player's calves, the smaller ones resting on his lap or gripped by the knees. Traditionally, gambas have been bowed palm up. The proportionately thinner strings imply less tension, while the frets lend an open-string tone quality to all stopped strings, with each fret acting as a nut.

Fanciful *viola da gamba* with arched bridge and spike. *Child with a Viol* by Gaudenzio Ferrari, first half sixteenth century. Courtesy of the Detroit Institute of Arts.

The *viola da gamba* family represents the happy outcome of several centuries of gropings, during which a number of large fiddles played in an upright stance were created, modified, eliminated. A fiddle closely resembling a gamba is already depicted in the Bible of Saint Stephen Harding, now in the Dijon Municipal Library, completed between 1098 and 1109; the fiddle has rounded lower bouts, a marked waist, upper bouts with the gamba's characteristic sloping shoulders, apparently four strings attached to an ill-defined pegdisk, and what may be a tailpiece. A seated performer holds it vertically between the thighs, and is bowing palm up. Most twelfth- and thirteenth-century illustrations of fiddles played in gamba position are bowed palm up, but not all. However, no fiddle held in any other position (including the vertical position with pegdisk down) is so portrayed. In common with the violin it would seem that the final step in the gamba's evolution was the forsaking of pegdisk in favor of pegbox with lateral pegs. Judging by the iconography this was accomplished by the sixteenth century, although a single standardized pattern of construction was not adopted until somewhat later. Gambas in forms that seem highly fanciful to us today may be seen, for example, in the *Isenheim Altar* of Matthias Grünewald dating from 1510–1515, and in a Gaudenzio Ferrari painting—being bowed by a child—in Detroit; both have structural details in common and both have rounded bridge tops and are supplied with spikes; the more orthodox type of *grosse Geige* illustrated by Virdung and Agricola is also prominent in an ink drawing by Urs Graf of about 1525 (*Dancing Couple and Fiddle*). Such aberrant forms may have actually existed during the period of experimentation and transition.

From a very early stage in its development the gamba shared two distinctive features with the lute: its fretted neck and its tuning. Hence a player could avail himself of either instrument indiscriminately as far as the left hand was concerned; only the right-hand technique varied. Fretted neck and identical tuning of gamba and lute probably existed on the gamba-to-be by the second quarter of the fifteenth century, for Philip the Good, Duke of Burgundy, hired two blind lutenists in 1434 who were compensated as such through 1435; in the following year, however, the entries change to *joueurs de vielle* (viol players), with the musicians' names remaining as theretofore. In the same year a maker of "soft" instruments in Brussels was paid for two *vielles* made for the blind lute players in question; in the household accounts, the players are mentioned alternately as lute and as *vielle* players until 1456. There is no possibility of confusion of lute with *vielle* or vice versa, as in 1454 the blind musicians played the *vielle, et avec eulx ung leu bien accordé* ("and with them a well-tuned lute"). A Spanish nobleman describing the Burgundian court in 1438 refers to these particular players *que tañen vihuelas darco* ("who play bowed *vihuelas*"). Later, in 1523, Hans Judenkönig was to publish his *Ain schon künstliche underweisung . . . auff der Lautten und Geygen* in which he—as well as Hans Gerle (1532)—uses the term *grosse geygen* in the sense of *viola da gamba,* and shortly thereafter Silvestro Ganassi wrote his tutor for both lute and gamba.

By the end of the fifteenth century we learn of the large size that some fiddles could assume, when Bernardo Prospero relates that in 1493 Spanish musicians were brought from Rome to Mantua who played viols "about as big as I am" (*suonano viole grande quasi come me*). Unfortunately we know nothing of their shape. That large gambas were in use by 1500 we see from the iconography, and certainly the bass became the type instrument of the family in the first third of the sixteenth century. Martin Agricola's *Musica instrumentalis deutsch* (1528) has *grosse Geigen* with six strings for the bass size, five for the tenor/alto, as for the soprano; the tuning of his bass, given as GCFadg, is that of his lute; his tenor/alto duplicates the five upper strings of the bass, and his descant is tuned Fadgc. Lanfranco (1533), writing of the *violoni da tasti & da arco* ("fretted and bowed viols") states that *da Violone al Liuto altra differenza non vi e: se non chel Liuto ha le corde geminate: & il Violone semplici* ("The only difference between gamba and lute is that the lute has geminated strings and the gamba single ones"). He gives instructions for tuning a consort of soprano, tenor, and bass, with the soprano pitched a fourth higher and the bass a fifth lower than the tenor, which is at unison with his lute: A°d°g°b°e′a′. If a contralto is to be added, he states, it should be at unison with the tenor: most people prefer to tune their bass a fifth below the tenor (D°G°c°e°a°d′), which is an octave below the soprano, but some prefer it a fourth lower: E°A°d°f°b°e′. Incidentally, this was the preferred tuning of Alfonso della Viola, a renowned contemporary player, according to a manuscript notation made about 1536 by the owner of a 1515 cookbook.

By the time Lanfranco wrote, both gamba making and playing had attained a high degree of development. Shortly after July 1530, Andrea di Verona is recorded in the Trento State Archives as a player of the *viola con tasti* and of the *viola senza tasti,* as well as of the *lira* and cornett; English court records for 1532 mention three players of the "vyalls";

Alfonso della Viola was making a name for himself at the court of Ercole II of Ferrara in the 1530s, and Italian performers were engaged by the English court in 1540: Alberto da Venezia, Vincenzo da Venezia, Alexander, Ambroso, and Romano da Milano, Joan-Maria da Cremona. Playing of a "chest of vialls" was common enough to be depicted in the painting *The Castalian Fountain* (ca. 1540) of unknown authorship, privately owned in Zürich, with a bass, two tenors, and a descant gamba, in addition to a number of other instruments. (An earlier reference to *la musica delle quattro viole da arco* by Baldassare Castiglione in his *Il Cortegiano* may not refer to gambas, for it was written in the second decade of the sixteenth century, even though the term *viola d'arco* was later a synonym for *viola da gamba,* and is used as such by Galilei [1581] and Zarlino [1588]; both authors remark that the *viola d'arco,* lute, and *lira con tasti* have equal semitones, it may be noted.) In 1542–1543 the first tutor written predominantly for gambas appeared: Silvestro Ganassi's *Regola rubertina.*

From here on we are given some insight into the relationship between the fretted viols—the gambas—and the unfretted ones—the violin family. By Ganassi's time, gambists could play right up to the edge of the finger-board, whereas violinists did not exceed the first position. This advantage was of course due to the playing stance: the gamba was held firmly in position by the player's legs, thus leaving both hands free, while the violinist had to grip his instrument with the stopping hand. When Ganassi refers to virtuso players we may take this to indicate the degree of perfection that both instrument and playing technique had attained. Extant sixteenth-century gambas have wider upper and lower bouts in proportion to their length than do later models; their C holes are placed almost vertically in the middle of the center bouts, later to be slanted (but vertical C holes are also found on smaller eighteenth-century instruments); the bridge was lower and was placed below the soundholes. Several instruments of Antonio Siciliano and of his son Giovanni Battista are housed in collections on both sides of the Atlantic; Antonio seems to have been a maker exclusively, but his son is mentioned by Ganassi as *peritissimo del violon,* and his portrait was painted by Titian's son Orazio, probably in 1546. Vasari, to whom we owe this piece of information, refers to Battista as an *eccelente sonatore di Violone,* and Luigi Dentici (1553) records his participation in a concert at Naples. Moreover, either father or son—no first name is given—was in the service of Cardinal

Ippolito de' Medici, together with Francesco da Milano (Ippolito became cardinal in 1529 and died six years later).

From these data we are able to fix the Sicilianos' period of activity to the first half of the sixteenth century and to compare their "modern" and relatively squat model—flat back canted toward the shoulders, C holes with eyes facing out, sharply defined center bouts with corners, and, above all, the proportion of length to width—with near-contemporary dated instruments of a "medieval" type, one by Stephanus de Fantis in 1558, another by Cesare Bonoris in 1568. Both of these instruments are elongated, have guitar form, lack corners, the eyes of the C holes face in; the de Fantis has a vaulted, violin-type back, the Bonoris a flat, canted one. Strangely enough, between twenty and thirty guitar-shaped gambas have come down to us, dating from the sixteenth to the eighteenth centuries, all of which are undated except for the two just cited. This model then disappears from the world of art music, only to be reintroduced by Chanot in the nineteenth century, but then as a violin, not as a gamba. As folk instruments, this guitar form has been played from the Middle Ages until recently (cf. *husla*, page 475).

By the end of the sixteenth century a whole family of gambas had been developed, from double bass to soprano, with a second tenor serving for the performance of alto parts where needed. It is likely that a subcontrabass also existed by then, for a *double basse contre de viole* was among the effects of a Parisian maker in 1557 (another maker had left a *basse contre de viole* the year before), despite the fact that Praetorius was to state that the five-stringed subbass had been invented "recently." Banchieri (1609) gave the tuning of a *violone in contrabasso con tasti*, the fourth member of the gamba consort, as D′G′C°E°A°d°, a fourth below his bass and an octave below his tenor.

Valuable information is presented in Philippe Jambe de Fer's *Epitome musical* of 1556; gambas in France, he writes, had five strings tuned in fourths, although in Italy they had six strings; the *violes* (gambas) were played by *gentilhommes* and others, but the violin was employed for dancing, and properly so, in his opinion, for it was easier to tune, a fifth being *plus douce* to hear than a fourth, and violins were also easier to carry. Valid reasons indeed, and for a long time the relationship of gamba to violin was to remain analogous to that of organ to spinet. France was not the only country to have five-stringed gambas, though: Samuel Mareschall gives tuning instructions for a set of three gambas in

Viole da gamba. Left: by Giovanni Battista Ciciliano, Venice, ca. 1550; *right:* by an early-eighteenth-century English maker of the Norman Barak school. Note the soundhole location of the earlier instrument. Courtesy of Yale University.

1589, all of which had five strings only, and Praetorius also includes tunings for the five-stringed version.

Galilei (1581) believed the *viola da gamba* and *da braccio* families to be of Italian origin, possibly Neapolitan, the reason for his belief being that in Spain they were not made and but little played, which argument he also applied to England, France, and Germany. A better case for an Italian origin is to be found in the early German appellation of *welsche Geige* for the *viola da gamba*, *welsch*—literally "foreign"—being a German term for "Italian," as mentioned previously. Agricola had already written of *grosse welsche geigen*, and a purchasing agent for the Fuggers wrote from Antwerp in 1571 that he was expediting a chest of six *grosse welsche geigen* made in London by the Bassani brothers: two descant, two tenors, and a bass.

The latter part of the sixteenth century saw the addition of the *viola bastarda*, called lyra viol in England, documented from 1589 on. Intermediary in size between bass and tenor, it was often recognizable by an additional circular soundhole under the fingerboard. The name probably derives from its tunings, which follow the *lira* principle of mixed fourths and fifths, and thereby favor chordal playing; Banchieri (1609) speaks of the *lirone o viola bastarda* as though they were synonymous. Music for this instrument was always written in tablature; a large variety of tunings were in use, presumably to produce maximum sympathetic resonance of the open strings by having them tuned to the triad of the key each piece was to be played in. Around 1600 Daniel Farrant invented a lyra viol with sympathetic metal strings tuned in unison to the bowed strings, which fact tends to bear out the above supposition. This instrument became known in France as *basse de viole d'amour*. Praetorius specifies that the eight sympathetic strings were of steel and of spun (not wound) brass and attached to a brass string holder. But such instruments were in the main confined to England and were short lived, for Playford (1661) could write: "Of this sort of Viols I have seen many; but Time and Disuse has set them aside." The regular lyra viol was propagated on the Continent by English players: John Price was a cornett and *Bastardviolgeige* player at the ducal court of Württemberg by 1610; he imported a consort of viols from England two years later, and received a fairly large sum in 1616 for his invention of a gamba with twenty-four strings, which was made to his specifications by a local organ builder, probably on the lines of Daniel Farrant's earlier invention; and in 1626 one Johann Staden of Nuremberg requested the council's permission to send his son to study music and particularly the "viol bastarda" at the Brandenburg court for a year, under a "famous Englishman" named Walter Roy.

The preeminence of English players in the seventeenth century is also attested by Jean Rousseau in his valuable *Traité de la viole* of 1687. According to him, the *viola* passed from the Italians to the English, who were the first to compose for it and to play it in consort; early viols in France had five strings, he writes, were very large, and served for accompaniments; their bridge—very low—was placed below the soundholes, the bottom of the fingerboard reached down to the belly (*touchait à la table*); the strings were very thick and all were tuned in fourths: EADGC, and these viols looked like the *basse de violon* (cello). The neck was round and massive, and slanted too far forward (*trop panché sur le devant*); at the time of its remodeling a sixth string was added and the tuning was changed to that of "today," from D to D. Other sizes were also in use, a tenor, another and slightly smaller one served as alto, and a yet smaller model as soprano. These four sizes had been in use in Italy long before they became known in France; when such consorts were played in France, the tenor was tuned a fourth above the bass, the alto a fourth above the tenor, the soprano one tone above the alto. Viols were reduced to a size convenient for holding between the knees to distinguish them from the *grande basse de viole* (to which he has referred); the English reduced theirs in size before the French did, as can be judged by ancient English viols "that we in France esteem particularly," but it was the French who thinned the neck and "threw it backwards" for greater ease in playing, and there is no English viol but one is obliged to have a French type of neck put on it. Other historical comments of Rousseau's are to the effect that Sainte-Colombe added a seventh string in the bass (of the bass gamba) tuned to A', and introduced strings wound with silver. After some remarks on bowing and tuning (when playing in a consort, tune the C string first, but when playing with other instrument types first tune the A string), he reminds us that the soprano instrument is held gripped by the knees.

Rousseau's testimony is important and can be corroborated from other sources if necessary: his tuning of the old five-stringed French bass is that of Samuel Mareschall, the latter not a Frenchman, it is true, but born in Tournai—we would call him a Belgian today; and Rousseau's comments on the cello shape of some gambas is borne out by Christopher Simpson, who presents in his *Division Viol* of 1659 drawings of a violin-shaped gamba with C holes and fretted neck, and of a gamba of traditional form, accompanied by the somewhat disconcerting remark: "The Figure or Shape of a Division-Viol may be either of these; but the First is better for Sound." A passage in the Hills' classic, *Antonio Stradivari* (1902), also illustrates the hybridization of forms apparent in the mid-seventeenth century. Speaking of the earliest dated instrument of the violoncello type made by Stradivari (in 1667), the authors say:

It is a most interesting example, although it has been considerably altered, and we are able to recognize that the master tried to combine the principal features of both viol and violoncello, for whilst retaining the flat viol back canting off at the top, he adopted the violoncello outline, form of soundholes, and dimensions.

(It is in fact the similarity in body sizes of bass viol and cello that has made possible the rebuilding of bass gambas into celli, as the gamba has an average body length of 76 centimeters [ca. 30 inches], and the cello, one of 74 to 76 centimeters.)

Two different sizes of bass gamba had emerged in England in the seventeenth century, the larger consort viol, and a slightly smaller division viol, which was used for the playing of divisions, that is, extemporized figurations. The latter had a narrower waist to facilitate bowing, and the same tuning as a consort bass; both were played from notation—not from tablature. James Talbot, writing just before 1700, states that the consort viol was one inch longer in neck and body than the division viol, and broader, and that the lyra viol was smaller than the division viol by the same amounts.

As a latecomer to the gamba family, the *pardessus de viole* must be mentioned, a French soprano viol with five strings, tuned g°c′e′a′d², according to Rousseau, held upright on the player's knees; unfortunately it is also referred to as *quinton*, the name of a late-eighteenth-century hybrid of violin and viol, with the same tuning but the body of a violin.

Attempts were apparently made in the sixteenth and seventeenth centuries to play a-gamba instruments in a-braccio position, and not only the smaller models, but the cumbersome, low-pitched members as well. A seated gamba player holds his large instrument obliquely on his lap in Paolo Veronese's *Marriage at Cana* (1563), the Unton Mural shows one held guitar fashion across the knees, and a drawing by Abraham Bosse for Denis Gautier's *La rhétorique des dieux*, published in 1652, includes a whole quartet of gambas played a-braccio, the largest held almost horizontally across the player's chest; he is standing and his chin fits very nicely into the center bout. Six pegs and frets are visible, so there can be no mistaking the nature of these instruments. No satisfactory reason for adopting so awkward a stance has yet been proposed. Occasionally gambas were bowed palm down, but evidence of this is more rare; an example is that of an outdoor concert scene painted in 1641 on a ceiling of the former Pauline Monastery at Prague, now in the Municipal Museum there: a bass, alto, and soprano gamba are bowed palm down, and the bass is furnished with a spike, no less.

Today the four sizes of gamba in use have six strings each and are tuned as follows: soprano $d°g°c'e'a'd^2$, alto one tone below the soprano, tenor $G°c°f°a°d'g'$, and bass $D°G°c°e°a°d'$; the tenor is a fourth higher than the bass, the soprano a fifth above the tenor. But this was not always so.

Those sixteenth-century authors who knew only the five-stringed gamba do not indicate uniform tunings. Thus the bass gamba of Gerle (1532) sounded $D°G°B°e°a°$, that of Agricola (1545 edition) $F°A°d°g°b°$, and those of Mareschall, as of the later Jean Rousseau, $E°A°d°g°c'$; the tenors of Gerle and Mareschall were a fourth higher than their basses, while that of Agricola had four strings only, corresponding to the four highest strings of Gerle ($c°e°a°d'$); the soprano was in each case a fifth higher than the tenor. Mareschall, it will be noted, tunes his instruments in fourths throughout (cf. the Old French tuning given by Rousseau, above) while the others share the lute's intermediary interval of a third, but not necessarily in a central position. The indicated pitches of writers referring to six-stringed gambas fall into two categories and create a vexing problem by their discrepancies: the majority, including Lanfranco (1533), Ganassi (1542), Ortiz (1553), Salinas (1577), Marinati (1587), and Cerreto, Mersenne, Playford, Simpson, and Talbot in the seventeenth century, tune their basses from $D°$ to d', their tenors $G°$ to $g°$ (or $A°$ to a'), and their sopranos $d°$ to d^2; others, including Zacconi (1592), Banchieri (1609), Cerone (1613), and Praetorius (1619) tune their basses G' to $g°$, their tenors $D°$ to d', and their sopranos $G°$ to g' (Praetorius $A°$ to a'). In addition, Talbot gives that of his double-bass viol as an octave below his tenor, G' and up, yet Banchieri's *contrabasso* and Praetorius's *gar gross Bass* are D' to $d°$. These two sets of tunings present the following relationships:

Soprano	$d°$ to d^2	
Tenor	$G°$ to g'	Soprano
Bass	$D°$ to d'	Tenor
	G' to $g°$	Bass

Hayes (1930) already pointed out that no literature exists for a bass at the lower of the two tunings, and that an instrument large enough to yield such low tones would be unwieldy as a solo instrument. The suggestion that the set of low-pitched gambas actually sounded a fifth higher than indicated, with the G′ string of one bass having the same absolute pitch as the D′ string of the other, must be disallowed, for elsewhere in their texts both Banchieri and Praetorius ("low tuning" authors) give the pitches of violin strings as g°d′a′e².

This seemingly irreconcilable discrepancy can be resolved very simply once we accept that these pitches were exactly what their authors said they were and that only the nomenclature differed, a situation that obtains in our day with respect to several wind instruments, such as, for example, the alto flute of the United States, which is the bass flute of Britain. In the matter of gambas, one man's bass was simply another man's tenor. As far as their musical treatment of the gamba goes, Banchieri and Praetorius relegate the bass to a subordinate role, frequently that of doubling voices or other instruments, whereas Ganassi and Ortiz ("high tuning" authors) already confer independent parts in consort or even solo passages upon it. Praetorius has a curious and awkward passage in which he substantiates the foregoing conclusion, if one is patient enough to work his way through it. He writes (*Syntagma* II) of the English—already the foremost exponents of gamba playing—that when they *allein damit etwas musizieren*, that is, play a consort of gambas, they tune a fourth or fifth lower; this is a slip of the pen and should obviously read "higher," as appears from the next sentence:

also/ dass sie die untersten Saiten im kleinen Bass vors D; im Tenor und Alt vors A; Im Cant vors e rechnen und halten: Do sonsten/ . . . eine Quint tieffer/ Als nemlich der Bass ins GG; der tenor und Alt ins D; der Cant ins A gestimmet ist. Und das gibt in diesem Stimmwerck viel eine anmutigere prächtigere und herrlichere Harmonij, als wenn man im rechten Thon bleibet ("so that they count the lowest string of the small bass as D, that of the tenor and alto as A, that of the soprano as e; as otherwise . . . the tuning is a fifth lower, namely the bass in GG, the tenor and alto in D, the soprano in A. And that gives to this consort a far more splendid . . . resonance than when one remains in the ordinary pitch").

An English gamba consort thus was tuned, according to him, to the set of higher pitches as given above, and since gamba strings cannot be pulled up a fourth or a fifth (or let down, for that matter, if the instrument is still to sound like a viol—cf. Playford on this subject), the English must have played a consort of smaller instruments than those commonly utilized in northern Germany.

As a matter of fact, the two terminologies subsisted side by side until quite recently; in English, French, and American usage, the bass was considered to be the type instrument, whereas in Germany the tenor has been so considered; many inventories and museum catalogs employing the German classification enumerate a fair quantity of tenors but at best a stray bass; among the instruments owned by the Weimar court *Kapelle* in 1662, for example, were typically two tenor gambas, an alto, and a descant—and no basses; and the Collegium Musicum of Bern possessed in 1670 *1 Viola di Gamba oder Tenor-Geigen*. But this situation is now changing and a recent description of a historical gamba by an Austrian musicologist reads in part: "a tenor gamba (bass gamba, according to the old nomenclature) . . ."; actually this should read the other way round, but the intention is there. Ergo, an English bass and a German tenor are both tuned from D° to d' and both have the same dimensions, needless to say.

During the seventeenth century it became customary in England to accompany the gamba consort on a chamber organ, as we learn from writers such as Thomas Mace (1676) who knew viol fancies of three, four, five, and six parts with "the organ evenly, softly, and sweetly achording to all," and from Roger North, reminiscing (ca. 1728) that a chest of viols with an organ were seldom found wanting in a musical family: "But I must observe that the masters never trusted ye organist with his thro base [thorough bass] but composed his part." North also wrote of John Jenkins, who had died in 1678, that "he was once carryed to play on ye viol before K. Cha. I wch he did in his voluntary way, with wonderfull agility, and odd humours, as (for Instance) touching ye great strings with his thumb, while all the rest were Imployed in another way . . ." thereby anticipating Jean-Marie Leclair's famous thumb stopping of the violin G-string by the better part of a century.

In France the art of gamba playing flourished well into the eighteenth century, and as late as 1740 Hubert Le Blanc could write his fulminating *Défense de la basse de viole contre les entreprises du violon et les prétensions du violoncel*, but he was fighting a lost battle, for by the mid-century the gamba had been vanquished in France by the pretentious cello. A gamba made by Henry Jay, one of England's foremost builders, was offered for sale in Paris in 1766; it had cost 1,200 *livres*, and "1,500 were refused for it at the time the *viole* was in favor," as the advertisement stated. With the exception of Germany, the only member of the original family still in use in the late seventeenth century was the bass, and in the eighteenth century this became true in Germany also. Eighteenth-century references to the *basse de viole* or to the *viola da gamba* are always to the bass instrument. Carl Friedrich Abel played the gamba in public until 1787, the year of his death—he had lived in England from 1759 on, except for a two-year period—and the *musikalische Realzeitung* could report a year later that a pupil of his, a Miss Thicknesse, was England's leading gambist. It is unlikely that she had much competition.

With renewed interest in baroque music in the late nineteenth century a survival of gamba playing slowly got under way, and today instruments are being produced on traditional lines, and in consorts of bass, tenor, alto, and soprano. Some makers prefer to build their models with slightly projecting tables, as on the violin, to facilitate opening the instrument for repairs. Modern tunings are given on page 504.

THE VIOLONE

The *violone* of the sixteenth century was a *viola da gamba*; in fact Diego Ortiz (1533) uses the word as a generic term for gambas; subsequently it designated a double-bass gamba, later still it was a synonym of our double bass. The word occurs in an Este inventory of 1520. A somewhat later Verona inventory (1543) included *una cassa cum sette violoni*—they could not have been very large if they all fitted into one case—and a second chest containing 5 *violoni*. Another Verona entry, undated but of the same period, lists the above-mentioned instruments as *viole*. Not until Zarlino's *Sopplimenti* were published in 1588 are we sure that *violoni* belong to the class of fretted chordophones. By the end of the century the term is reserved for the large-sized gambas.

To Banchieri (1609) the *violone* was a six-stringed bass gamba, either the *violone da gamba* (tuned G′ up) or the *violone in contrabasso con tasti* (D′ up). As long as the violin family was still seeking an identity in the seventeenth century, the terminology remained confused. Praetorius called for *eine grosse Contra-Bass Geig/so die Itali violone nennen* ("a great contrabass fiddle/that the Italians call *violone*") in his *Polyhymnia* of 1619. Here he seems to consider it as an unfretted "fiddle," but in his *Syntagma* II he writes of the *violono* and its synonymous *grosse Viol da gamba*. In *Syntagma* III *die grosse Bassgeig* is also called *welsche Violone*

("Italian *violone*"). It seems that the name was bestowed on two different instruments: (1) an instrument the size of which was not standardized, occasionally made in violin form, that stood between double bass and cello, and is played today; (2) a contrabass viola da gamba. The first of these could be fretted or not. Eisel (1738) sums up the situation best by telling us that the *violone* had six strings tuned from G' up, but that there existed two other kinds, one with a larger body tuned a fourth lower (these two are Banchieri's *violoni*), and another large one having but four strings, the lowest of which was 16'C (C'). Some tune it an octave below the cello, he states, others prefer to tune it in fourths—still a hybrid, it would seem—and the Italians call it *violone grosso*. Two years later, Grassineau identifies it simply as a double bass with four strings tuned an octave below those of the cello. Leopold Mozart shows that standardization was, nonetheless, far from accomplished: the double bass, or *violon*, he writes, an octave lower than the cello, has usually four but sometimes three strings, while larger models have five; these last have fretted fingerboards to prevent the strings from flying off (*ausfliegen*) the fingerboard.

On the European continent today, small double basses are called *violoni*.

THE BARYTON

Similar in many ways to the bass *viola da gamba* was the *viola di bordone*, or baryton, which evolved in the first half of the seventeenth century and is commonly said to be a derivation of the lyra viol (*viola bastarda*), for one of its distinctive features is a circular soundhole beneath the fingerboard, in addition to regular C holes or flame holes, and another is the set of bass strings to which the instrument owes its name (baryton-bardon-bordone = drone). Yet despite its putative English origin its makers, composers, and players were chiefly from southern Germany and Austria, so that it is tempting to see in the baryton a direct descendant of John Price's gamba of twenty-four strings (see *viola da gamba*, page 501), which he invented in 1616 while employed at the Stuttgart court.

Structurally the baryton is characterized by a rather squat body, lower bouts lacking corners, a very broad neck partly covered by a fingerboard placed on its right, and very long and undulating pegbox terminating in a carved figure; of its two sets of strings, six or seven pass over the fingerboard, always of gut, the sympathetic wire strings below it and along the open back of the hollowed neck. The latter was always fretted. Not only did the metal strings resound sympathetically, but they were also plucked by the left-hand thumb.

Though the earliest preserved instrument (by Magnus Feldlen of Vienna) dates from 1656, no detailed description is forthcoming before that of Daniel Speer (1687): "Another viol . . . which surpasses them all; is titled Viola di Bardon . . ." Apart from its six bowed strings, he writes, it had extra lute (i.e. gut) strings affixed to the right side of the belly, plucked from time to time by the little finger of the right (bow) hand to create an echo effect, and in addition, brass and steel strings that passed close to the belly and along the back of the neck so that they could be plucked by the left-hand thumb. Actually no instrument with the added "echo" strings is known; these may have resembled the *pristrunki* of the east European *torban* (see archlutes, page 428). However, of 101 pieces for baryton contained in a manuscript collection of the Kassel Landesbibliothek, six call for just such a triple-strung instrument as that described by Speer: six bowed strings tuned to a D-minor chord, eleven "echo" strings tuned diatonically from e° to a′, and nineteen bass strings tuned chromatically from C′ up. The very broad neck needed for the accommodation of so many strings, and the plucking of the bass strings while bowing and stopping, made the baryton a most difficult instrument to play. Between ten and twenty sympathetic strings were usual, but exceptionally thirty are met with. In the foreword to his undated *Parthien* for baryton, known to have been published between 1695 and 1700, Johann Georg Krause requires a tuning of A°d°f°a°d′f′; the exactly contemporaneous manuscript of Talbot identifies the "viòl barytone" with the lyra viol, but pitched two tones lower, and with wire basses for the thumb. In fact the baryton was smaller; its body length varied from 60 to 66 centimeters (23½ to 26 inches), the overall length from 125 to 130 centimeters (49 to 51 inches). Majer (1732) gives its tuning as that of the regular gamba (D°G°c°e°a°d′).

Barytons were built as late as 1785, but are remembered today almost exclusively for their association with Haydn, who between 1766 and 1775 composed no fewer than 175 pieces for baryton for his patron, Prince Miklós Esterházy, most of which were destroyed by a fire in the eighteenth century. He required an instrument with bowed strings in gamba tuning—that given by Majer—and wire strings tuned to G° (A°) d°e°f♯°g°a°b°-c♯′d′. The year in which Leopold Mozart's *Versuch* appeared, 1756, is also that of our earliest preserved instrument; Mozart mentions nine or ten metal strings, touched and plucked by the thumb so as to form a bass to the bowed strings; Feldlen supplied his baryton with thirteen. Despite its Italian name, the baryton scarcely penetrated outside German-speaking countries, and it is perhaps fitting that our knowledge of it, starting in Vienna and Augsburg, should terminate in Vienna, where Vincenz Hauschka played it in public as late as 1823.

THE VIOLA AND VIOLINO D'AMORE

Two distinct chordophones have gone by the name of *viola d'amore*: the earlier was metal strung, with five strings, the later a hybrid form of *viola da gamba* with sympathetic strings.

The first type, an ordinary violin strung with four metal strings to which a fifth, of gut or wire, was sometimes added, was already played in the latter part of the seventeenth century. But metal-strung violins can hardly have been a novelty even then, for Praetorius had already praised their superior tone. From John Evelyn we learn that they had a name of their own; he notes in his diary on November 20, 1679, "the viol d'amore of five wire strings played on with a bow, being but an ordinary violin played on lyre-way by a German," and remarks on its sweetness of tone and its novelty. "Lyre-way" refers here to the tuning, and indicates that it was tuned like a *viola da gamba* rather than like a violin; this fact probably accounts for the *amore*'s name. A century later, Burney in his *General History of Music* recalled the composer Attilio Ariosti's playing the *viola d'amore* in London in 1716; he believed it to have been "the first time" that such an instrument had been heard in England. Fuhrmann (1706) comments dryly on the wire-strung *amore*: *wird verstimmt gespielt*, that is, played with scordatura. Mattheson in 1713 describes it as having four wire strings and one of gut, usually tuned to C major or C minor, thus confirming Fuhrmann, and Eisel in 1738 gives its tuning as g°c′d♯′ (or e′)g′c², with an alternate violin tuning from c° to e² in fifths, and adds that the Italians had recently brought out a model with seven strings, tuned F°B♭°d°g°c′f′b♭′, all of which were bowed (this lower tuning implies a greater string length, ergo a larger instrument). So far no author has mentioned sympathetic strings. But in 1732 Majer had written of two varieties of *viola d'amore*, a smaller one similar to a violin, and another, slightly larger than a viola, both with six strings;

a footnote informs us of the existence of sympathetic strings and probably constitutes the earliest reference to the second type of *amore*.

This second type, about the size of a viola, had a gamba body but was held and bowed like a violin. It lacked the gamba's frets, had flame holes, and often an additional circular soundhole; it is immediately recognizable by its elongated pegbox, which has to accommodate six or seven gut melody strings and as many sympathetic ones of wire. When Vivaldi wrote for this instrument around 1740 he required a tuning of $A°d°a°$-$d'f'a'd^2$. A similar tuning is common today ($A°d°a°d'f\sharp'a'd^2$ for a seven-stringed model, the low $A°$ being dispensed with on the six-stringed model, with the sympathetic strings tuned arbitrarily).

By the latter part of the eighteenth century the *viola d'amore* was almost forgotten, to be revived briefly by Meyerbeer in his *Les Huguenots* of 1836, after which it slumbered until the end of the nineteenth century. On the basis of chronology, it is probable that the two *amores* scored for by Bach in his *Passion According to Saint John* were of the earlier type.

Gambas with sympathetic strings had enjoyed a short-lived vogue in England at the beginning of the seventeenth century, when Daniel Farrant was credited with having invented a lyra viol with sympathetic wire strings tuned in unison to the bowed ones (see page 501). This fact had not escaped Praetorius, for he writes of an English *viola bastarda* with eight sympathetic metal strings. Possibly memories of these instruments lived on, for Leopold Mozart, after describing the *amore* with its six or seven bowed gut and as many wire sympathetic strings, writes of an *englisches Violett* resembling the former but for its having seven bowed and fourteen sympathetic strings, a different tuning, and a louder tone. Perhaps the elusive chordophone mentioned in some eighteenth-century Italian texts as *viola all'inglese* is the same English *violetta*.

The *violino d'amore*, or *violon d'amour*, as it was called in France, was a small instrument with five bowed strings tuned $G°d'a'd^2g^2$ and six sympathetic ones (Laborde in 1780 says four of brass), or four bowed strings tuned $e'a'd^2a^2$ and twelve sympathetic ones. They must have been at least moderately popular, for violins and *quintons* were rebuilt as *violons d'amour* (a *violon de Guerson* [sic] *disposé pour être monté en violon d'amour, à 16 cordes* was advertised for sale), and a *quinton* by Salomon dated 1773, strung with five bowed and as many sympathetic strings, is preserved in the museum of the Brussels Conservatoire.

THE VIOLIN FAMILY

THE VIOLIN

Perhaps the violin is the most difficult instrument to write about, for in its early days it had no name of its own, so that until the end of the sixteenth century we cannot tell with certainty to which of several possible instruments our sources refer. To this must be added the fact that over the centuries old instruments have been rebuilt and the evidence they might have presented thereby destroyed.

As we know it today, the violin has four strings tuned $g°d'a'e^2$; its arched back and belly are glued to the ribs in such a manner as to project slightly beyond the latter (this greatly facilitates opening the instrument for repairs), a neck covered by a fingerboard, continuing in a peg-box, and terminating in an Ionian scroll; its incurved waist forms the center bouts, often referred to in technical literature as CC; the outward-bulging upper and lower sections of the body form the upper and lower bouts, respectively. F-shaped soundholes, called FF or F holes, are cut into the belly near the edges of the center bouts; the bridge is placed between these, nowadays immediately in line with their cross strokes, formerly far lower down. The slight projection of back and belly (the latter known as tables) beyond the ribs can already be seen on a fiddle in a painting by Ambrogio or Evangelista Preda, commissioned in 1483, in the National Gallery, London.

Since the latter half of the nineteenth century it has been customary to attach chin rests—introduced by Louis Spohr in about 1820—to the left of the tailpiece. Prior to its adoption, the violin was held (in chronological order) at the chest, at the shoulder, slightly to the right of the player's neck, slightly to its left; in folk music it was even cradled against the left upper arm. Apparently violins and *viole da gamba* were varnished from their inception, an indispensable protection of their surface from rosin, as we may conclude from the fact that plucked chordophones had unvarnished soundboards.

That the violin evolved from the medieval fiddles is now a generally accepted fact, but its genesis seems to have been a slow and arduous one. Constant experimentation with numerous models of bowed chordophones in the late fifteenth and early sixteenth centuries led to the elimination of many forms, of parallel developments, and of multifarious stringings,

Fiddle with projecting tables, off-board string, and flat bridge. Detail of *An Angel in Green with a Vielle,* by Ambrogio or Evangelista Preda, commissioned 1483. Courtesy of the Trustees, the National Gallery, London.

prior to the final emergence of a family of chordophones originally small enough to be held on the arm in a horizontal position. At about the same time, another group appeared, larger, held vertically, and gripped by the legs. These two were known in Italian respectively as *viole da braccio* and *viole da gamba*, in German as *kleine Geigen* and *grosse Geigen;* the former were unfretted, the latter, fretted. Italian and German writers of the first half of the sixteenth century differentiate rightly between unfretted and fretted families, a distinction probably all the more necessary because the shapes of the various instruments differed sharply throughout this period. (However, medieval fiddles could also be fretted, as is clear from, for example, Memling's *Christ amid Musical Angels* [ca. 1480] in Antwerp, where an angel plays a classical five-stringed oval fiddle—classical, that is, except for the fretting on its neck.)

Judging by the pictorial evidence the decisive steps in the evolution of both the *da braccio* and the *da gamba* instruments were the standardization of number of strings, and the exchange of pegdisk for pegbox; organologically the most obvious reason for the latter would have been to permit greater tension. And greater tension implies higher pitch and/or greater brilliance of tone.

When Virdung (1511) writes of the *kleine Geige* he illustrates it with a rebec and classifies it among the "useless" instruments of his day (Virdung had anything but an affinity for folk music); Agricola in 1528 depicts a family of rebecs virtually identical with those of Virdung and calls them *kleine Geigen ohne Bünde* ("without frets"). A drawing by Dürer of a musical group (ca. 1515) includes a harp, a lute, and what would be a very small violin were it not for the pegdisk; it is held at the chest and had an estimated overall length of some 40 to 45 centimeters (16 to 17½ inches). If we momentarily disregard the question of standardization of stringing we may consider the fresco of Gaudenzio Ferrari at the Church of San Cristoforo in Vercelli near Milan of about 1530 (he lived there between 1529 and 1536) with its very small violin-shaped, three-stringed instrument having an unciform pegbox, and that of Saronno, painted by him 1535–1536, where a similar violin as well as a viola and a tenor violin are depicted; three pegs are visible on the two smaller instruments, otherwise they are true violins all, despite the fact that the F holes are reversed. In this connection it may be noted that George Hart (1884) mentions an Andrea Amati violin that originally had only three strings. With Gaudenzio Ferrari's models we can compare the very squat, violinlike instrument (the width is four-fifths of its length) in Gerolamo Giovanone's *Virgin and Child* of about 1520, with FF already facing each other, four strings, and unciform pegbox; however, the body outline is that of a pair of brackets: the corners occur where the center bouts should be.

The alto member of the family is generally considered to have evolved prior to the treble, that is, to the violin, and to constitute the type instrument, chiefly on the basis of its having retained the name of viola, a medieval appellation of the fiddle, whereas other members of the family are known by diminutives or augmentatives of this word. Certainly the oldest known *violino* part, written by Giovanni Gabrieli in 1597, is in alto clef and descends below g°, so that it must have been written for the instrument we now call viola. Actually the terminology does not become precise until the mid-seventeenth century. Praetorius, generally so clear, informs us that the descant viol or *violino* was tuned g°d′a′e², but he also refers to the same instrument as *Discant-Geige, kleine Geige, viola da braccio, violetta piccola, violino da braccio, rebecchino*, and goes on to say that *viole da braccio* were called *Geigen* or *polnische Geigen* by *Kunst-pfeifer*—in other words, by the practical, performing musicians of his time. Mersenne's information shows that in France it had become customary to call members of the *da braccio* family by the names of their written parts (*dessus, cinquiesme, haute contre*, all designating the same instrument).

Against this background we can attempt to trace the violin from the time of Giovanone and Ferrari. The word *vyollon* comes into use in the early 1520s. Boyden (1965) reports its occurrence in the accounts of the secretary-general of Savoy in 1523, when payment to *vyollons de Verceil* ("vyollon players from Vercelli") was made; in 1529 six *viollons* and other musicians received payment under François I, and in the same year a *rebecchino* (violin?) was played at a state banquet at Ferrara. By 1530 violin playing was established on sufficiently sound a footing for note to be taken of individual players. Thus the Trento State Archives house a list of musicians compiled shortly after July 1530 in which Andrea di Verona is mentioned, *el quale sona di viola con tasti et di viola senza tasti* ("who played the fretted and the unfretted *viola*"). From 1533 on François I had at his disposal "8 violins and players of the King's instruments"; in the same year Lanfranco wrote in his *Scintille* that the *violette da braccio & de arco*, which he also calls *violette da arco senza tasti* ("bowed fretless *violette"*), had only three strings, called *canto, mezzana,* and *basso;* the bass, however, had four strings, the lowest of which he called *contrabasso.* All were tuned in fifths, but no pitch names are given.

The Middle and New French spelling, *violon,* was used by the poet Clément Marot in 1537. In the same or in the following decade the Italian word *violino* occurs in the records of Pope Paul III (1534–1549), according to Boyden (1965), yet the older expression continued in use. Ganassi devotes a chapter of the second volume of his *Regola rubertina* (1543) to the playing of the three-stringed *violette senza tasti* and gives us the first specific tunings for them: soprano g°d′a′, tenor c°g°d′, bass F°c°g°; he voices disapproval of their lack of frets. His tunings are identical to those given by Agricola in his expanded version of 1545 for "hand fiddles," except that Agricola's bass, like that of Lanfranco, has four strings. The "hand fiddles" in question are a family of rebecs that had become popular in the interim, for *jetzt will jeder damit umgehen* ("now everybody wants to play them"). The pitches as given by Ganassi are those of the three lowest strings of our violin, viola, and tenor violin. An inventory taken at the death of a Parisian luthier in 1551 lists *grands viollons, petit viollon,* and rebecs—at last a clear differentiation is made between violin and rebec in written sources—and in 1553 a *taille* is mentioned. Nicola Vicentino could write in 1555 of the *viole da braccio senza tasti* or *viole con tre corde senza tasti,* but a year later the Frenchman Philibert Jambe de Fer in his *Epitome musical* describes the full-fledged, four-stringed violin tuned in fifths from g° up, which he calls *violon,* and also defines clearly the respective spheres of the violin and gamba families, that of the violins being restricted to dance and popular music. Here finally we have unambiguous evidence of the four-stringed violin. Unfortunately Jambe de Fer did not trouble to illustrate it; after all, it was not a gentleman's instrument.

Up to this point the relationship between rebec, fiddles (including the *polnische Geige*), and the developing violins is not really discernible; the Lyons archives frequently mention *rebequets, joueurs de rebec,* during the first half of the sixteenth century, but these professional designations disappear from the moment the word *violon* occurs, and several musicians designated as players of the rebec are called *violons* from then on. *Violons* are also recorded in 1548 in connection with the state entry of Henry II and Catherine de' Médicis: the new word is gradually coming into use, at least in the world of poets, musicians, and luthiers, as opposed to contemporary theorists.

Among early representations of the true violin is that in Pierre Woeiriot's portrait of the luthier Caspar Tieffenbrucker, completed in 1529 (strangely, it has C holes, while a *viola da gamba* next to it has FF). Rabelais's reference (1564) to *violons démanchés* seems to imply the inception of shifting, but such an interpretation is supported neither by the music nor by other documents of the next century or so. The obviously important role that France played in the early diffusion and perhaps even development of the violin remains to be investigated, but one conclusion to be drawn tentatively is that a North Italian—not a Neapolitan—origin for the violin is indicated (Vincenzo Galilei suggested in 1581 an Italian and "perhaps" a Neapolitan origin for both gamba and violin families), if only on linguistic grounds. And this problem brings to mind the *violini piccoli alla francese* scored for by Monteverdi in his *Orfeo*, first performed in 1607; these were probably kits (*poches*) with the stringing and tuning given by his contemporary, Praetorius.

Players who had been designated by the rather uncertain term of "violetts" in English court records in 1559 were listed six years later as *vyolons*, and when the *Tragedy of Gorboduc* was first performed in 1562, with Italian *intermedii* adapted to a series of "domme shows" preceding each act, "first the musicke of violenze began to play, during which came in upon the stage sixe wilde men clothed in leaues. . . ." Four violins and a *ribecchino* were played at a Florence *intermedio* of 1565. From such examples it becomes clear that the violin, at first favored for its incisive tone, but above all because it could be played standing or walking and was eminently portable (and also easier to tune than were viols) was rapidly gaining acceptance as an indoor instrument. Massimo Trojano goes as far as reporting, in his *Discorsi delli triomfi* of 1568, on virtuosi of the *viola da braccio* performing solo music *in camera*. Nonetheless their utilization in outdoor music was continued, for we hear of musicians agreeing to play at the Feast of Saint Michael in 1569 *six aubades de cornets de bouquin et de violons* ("six *aubades* of cornetts and violins") provided it did not rain, but, if it did, German flutes and sackbuts were to be substituted.

The country of classical violin making has always been Italy. By the time Gasparo da Salò (1540–after 1600) formed his school there, Brescia had already become a center of *lutherie*. However, the Brescian school was relatively short lived and became overshadowed by Cremona. Reputedly founded by Andrea Amati (ca. 1505–before 1580), who is generally credited with having given the violin its final form by changing the emplacement of the soundholes to their present position, the Cremona school flourished as chief center of violin making from roughly 1550 to 1760, first under the aegis of the Amati dynasty, which culminated with Nicolò Amati (1596–1684), then continued until 1740, when Gerolamo Amati died. Leadership then passed into the hands of Nicolò's pupil Antonio Stradivari (1644–1737), and to Giuseppe Guarneri del Gesù (1698–1744). Only one non-Italian master of the classical period gained an international reputation, Jacob Stainer of Absam near Innsbruck (ca. 1617–1683). Secondary centers of violin making were established at Venice and Rome. From about 1570 on Cremona violins had acquired a reputation beyond the peninsula; already in 1572 the flutist and violinist Nicolas Delinet was given fifty *livres tournois* for the purchase of a *violon de Cremone*, and an inventory taken after the death of a Paris musician in 1575 enumerates a *taille de violon* with its case, *façon de Crémone*; *2 tailles de violon, façon de Paris; 2 dessus de violon façon de Paris*, and a *poche de violon* (kit). Here, *façon de Crémone* signifies a Cremona pattern or model. Finally, in 1577, a contract was signed in Paris for the making of four *violons à la mode de Crémone*. From this time on, we see violin-viola-cello ensembles played at court and other formal indoor dances.

French inventories speak of *dessus, taille,* and *basse-contre,* and yet we cannot be sure whether these terms apply to our violin, viola, and cello, or rather to our violin, viola, and tenor violin. Zacconi (1592) is first to give us tunings for all four members of the family, albeit in a devious way, for his tunings are expressed as compasses. He specifies that the top string of the bass instrument is to be in unison with the bottom string of the soprano and to the second highest of the tenor. His soprano, which he calls *violino,* has a given compass of $g°$ to b^2, so that its strings must have been tuned as are those of our violin; his tenor has a compass given as F to A, which works out at strings tuned to FCGD and must have sounded $F°c°g°d'$, as our obsolete tenor violin (see page 532); his bass, B to D, works out as $B'F°c°g°$, and is our cello tuned one tone lower than customary nowadays. Now, although he has explicitly given the compass of his *viola da braccio* (which he also calls *violino*) as $g°$ to b^2, he says in another passage: *I violini ascendono sino a 17 voci, incominciando da C fa ut sino in Alamire* ("Violins rise to seventeen tones, starting on $c°$ up to a'''"); but from $c°$ to a' would be only thirteen *voci*. If we assume he meant a violin with strings *tuned* from $c°$ to a', these strings would sound c°g°d'a'—our viola—and thus complete a family of violin, viola, tenor violin, and cello.

A generation later Praetorius lists the various members of a thriving family:

gar klein Geig or *pochette* (the kit), g'd²a² or a tone higher
klein Discant Geig (the *violino piccolo*), c'g'd²a² or a tone lower
Discant Viol or *Violino* (the violin), g°d'a'e²
Tenor Viol (our viola), c°g°d'a'
Bass (our obsolete tenor violin), F°c°g°d'
Bass (our cello), C°G°d°a°
Gross Quint Bass viola da braccio (obsolete), F'C°G°d°a°

Surviving violins by early masters have less pronounced corners and more elongated soundholes than later instruments, but not the very highly arched backs they are so often credited with. Until the eighteenth century they were made in both small and large patterns, with a body length of 34½ to 37 centimeters (13½ to 14½ inches).

During the seventeenth century violins ran the gamut from barber-shop instruments—in Liége a barber accepted in 1644 an apprentice *pour travailler au barbage et jouer de violon* ("to work as a barber and play the violin")—to the celebrated V*ingt-quatre violons du Roi* created under Louis XIII (composed of six *dessus*, six *basses*, four *hautes-contre*, four *tailles*, four *quintes de violon*) and imitated by Charles II, whose King's Band of twenty-four violins was first heard in 1661. The art of violin playing in England was brought to such high standards by Thomas Balt-zar, who arrived in England in 1655, that according to Roger North "gentlemen . . . soon thrust out the treble viol." Anthony Wood, an eyewitness to Baltzar's playing in 1658, "saw him run up his Fingers to the end of the Fingerboard of the Violin, and run them back insensibly, and with all alacrity, and in very good tune, which he nor any in England saw the like before." There might have been but little impetus to develop such virtuosity at a time when "gentlemen played three, four, and five parts with viols, and that they esteemed a violin to be an instrument only belonging to a common fidler, and could not endure that it should come among them for feare of making their meetings to be vaine and fidling," as Wood wrote in his autobiography (quoted from Heron-Allen [1885]).

The necks of seventeenth-century violins were somewhat wider than

Members of the violin family and related instruments: (1, 2) small *poches*, fiddles an octave higher; (3) descant *Geige* a fourth higher [*violino piccolo*]; (4) regular descant *Geige* [violin]. (5) tenor *Geige* [tenor violin]; (6) trumpet marine; (7) *Scheitholt*. From Michael Praetorius, *Theatrum instrumentorum*, 1620.

they are today and about 1½ centimeters shorter, and the bass bar was shorter and far less massive. For the greater part of the century the G-string was put to little use; as Praetorius remarked (*Syntagma* III), the lowest string did not sound well (*keine rechte Harmoniam von sich geben*), for which reason he preferred employing the viola for parts calling for the low tones otherwise available from the violin G-string. Wound strings—silver over gut—are first heard of in connection with the *viola da gamba* in the last quarter of the century.

From the early eighteenth century on we can follow the interplay of musical taste, violin making, and playing. Raguenet in his *Parallèle des Italiens et des Français . . .* (1702) notes that in Italy violins were heavier strung than in France, and that the bows were longer; when he returned to France from Italy and went to the opera in Paris with the sound of Italian violins still in his ears, he found the French violins so feeble that he thought they were being played with mutes. A foretaste of the late-eighteenth-century remodeling is already evident in the records of Kremsmünster Monastery for the year 1720, when the big choir *violone* was taken apart, planed, both tables thinned, completely revarnished, and furnished with a new bridge; their "Cremonese violin" was repaired and revarnished; the fingerboard of another "old violin" was raised and repaired; yet another violin was revarnished. (More planing down of old instruments was to take place before the century was over.) The raising of the fingerboard in question was brought about by inserting a wedge between neck and fingerboard to tilt the latter away from the belly, an operation originally designed to compensate for the diminished arching of the belly due to pressure of the strings against the bridge over the years, but later it entailed an alteration in the height of the bridge with concomitant change of tone quality.

Rather surprisingly, Stradivari and Stainer are quoted by Eisel (1738) as makers of the best violins, and apparently the loudest, as he says they could be heard above a whole orchestra; one would have expected him rather to praise the Amatis, for during much of the eighteenth century the tone of Stainer and the Amatis (i.e., the high-arched models) was preferred and generally juxtaposed to that of Stradivari (low-arched models), and the zest for volume is not commonly met with until later in the century. By the third quarter of the eighteenth century a combination of advanced playing technique—from about 1750 on violinists started exceeding the seventh position, but not necessarily in *ripieno* playing—and larger audiences in larger halls created demand for instruments capable of producing greater volume and brilliance of tone.

These demands were met almost simultaneously in Italy and in France with a remodeling of the instrument (from ca. 1770 on). The neck, originally set at the same plane as the body, was now thrown back at an angle and slightly lengthened (up to 1 centimeter at most), the finger-board was lengthened (from 2 to 2.6 centimeters) and redesigned, the bridge made correspondingly higher, the tops of bridge and fingerboard made more convex, the bass bar made considerably stouter and some-what longer, and the soundpost thicker. Although thinner strings were then in use the tension was greater than it had been before the remodel-ing. Modern bass bars (averaging 27 to 28 centimeters) are encountered from about 1780 on. They were never standardized as to size but formerly they had perhaps half the mass over nearly the same length as they have nowadays. Gian Battista Guadagnini put a new bass bar in a 1730 Stra-divari for Count Cozio di Salabue (1755–1840), collector and later also a dealer in instruments by old masters, as early as 1776 (Stradivari bass bars have been reported at a length of 24 centimeters). Soundposts at the end of the seventeenth century were as thick as a goose quill, as Talbot wrote (ca. 1700), 3 or 4 millimeters at most, and have grown to a diameter of 6 to 7 millimeters today. Very few instruments indeed escaped this rebuilding.

Löhlein (in 1774) marks the end of an era when he describes the tone of a Stradivari as "thin." Two years later, in 1776, an "excellent Cremona violin by Amati *emmanché par Bocquet*" ("with neck by Bocquet") was offered for sale in Paris, and in 1777 Cozio sold a Guadagnini that had a slanted neck. In 1779 Gaetano Guadagnini presented Cozio with a bill on behalf of his father, Giovanni Battista, who was illiterate, for slanting the necks and otherwise modernizing violins. At about the same time it was also discovered that violin tone could be improved by thinning the wood, and the thinning of old instruments became the order of the day.

Much information on this whole subject of violin remodeling is con-tained in the writings of Cozio, who was in touch with the prominent makers of his day and whose papers have been published under the title of *Carteggio* (1950); however, as he writes in *patois* he is at times hard to follow. Specialists in modernizing violins were the Mantegazzas of Milan, father and son, it transpires; to them were sent classical instru-ments still in Italy and others from France. The Amatis and Stradivari had fastened their necks by means of four nails, Cozio relates, but new necks were held by three nails only (on modern instruments the neck is mortised into the upper block so that nails are not needed). Glue was held to adversely affect tone. Cozio inveighs against modern makers who thinned old instruments to lend them "oboe" tone quality, yet his friend Carlo Mantegazza thinned the bellies of Giuseppe Guarneris made between 1727 and 1730. Requests for instruments with necks lengthened *alla moderna* emanated from Paris and may even have originated there, for Cozio bid the Mantegazzas change the necks of some Amatis *all'uso di Parigi* between 1800 and 1810. The French school of *lutherie,* headed by Pique and Koliker, changed necks for the convenience of players, apparently at the request of teachers belonging to the velocity school— rounding them until they became semicircular. A new set of "rules" originated in Paris, traveled to Milan, and spread from there to the rest of violin-making Italy; these rules were the standardization of shape and width of neck and fingerboard; also, the Parisians replaced the maple tailpiece with ebony and were the first to change the form of the bridge, as Cozio writes.

Fingerboards of Stradivari varied from 19 to 21½ centimeters (7½ to 8½ inches), according to the Hills; modern ones are about 26½ centimeters (10½ inches) long. A rule of thumb for evaluating a fingerboard is given by Francesco Galeazzi (1791): its length is correct if, when placing the first finger in third position on the E string, the high A can be easily sounded without moving the hand; a fingerboard should provide a range of two octaves, that is, a finger placed on its extremity should cause the string to sound two octaves above the open string (this applies to the gamba fingerboard also); modern compositions, he states, cannot be played if it is shorter. More specifically, a leader in the *Allgemeine musikalische Zeitung* of August 1803, refers to the newly lengthened fingerboard as a convenience for violinists who are no longer satisfied with a compass of $g°$ to e^4.

As long as the body length varied slightly, not so much from maker to maker as from one instrument to another, no standard measurements could be applied. At the beginning of our century the luthier and collector Auguste Tolbeque indicated the length of that of a full-sized violin as 35.8 centimeters (see also *violino piccolo,* page 526). The speaking length, or stop, of a violin string nowadays is 33 centimeters (13 inches) or a fraction less, was probably less before the neck was lengthened and reset, yet probably greater in the seventeenth century before the bridge was set at its present emplacement between the strokes of the FF.

Small and medium-sized violins were abandoned because they could not supply the required volume of tone, as Cozio informs us, but by the end of the eighteenth century another crisis in the violin's history had arisen: pitch was creeping up. A German report of 1802 states that in a certain *Residenz* town smaller violins with a shorter stop were being taken up simply because the pitch had risen so high. Another report, this time to the German Academy of Sciences in 1822 (published in 1825) states that due to "today's" high pitch the stops of old Cremona violins had to be shortened by changing the bridge position, it being otherwise impossible to bring the strings up to pitch. Cozio is more precise: writing in 1823, he notes that strings were thicker than those employed in the mid-eighteenth century, and that tension was further increased by orchestral pitch having risen by *una voce* ("one tone"), or even more than the old *corista*. This fact seems to have been responsible for the change to thinner strings: after Ole Bull had concertized in Berlin in 1839, a critic commented that, like Paganini, Bull had strung his instrument with thin strings. The higher the pitch, the more brilliant the tone is a truth that was already known to medieval theorists, and brilliance of tone was perhaps never so well exploited as at this time: Ernst Chladni, the renowned physicist, reported hearing in 1825 a violin concerto in A performed by an excellent player who had transposed it to B.

As a result of acoustical experimentation, a French engineer and a French physicist, François Chanot and Félix Savart, respectively, brought out highly individual models independently of one another but at the same time. Chanot's first model, presented in 1817, was in guitar form, the result of abandoning corners (which are held to reduce vibrations), without overlap of the tables, having crescent sound slits (to prevent cutting across the grain more than absolutely necessary), with bass bar set along the exact center of the belly. Two years later he brought out a new model, this one with reversed scroll for easier access to the A-string in the pegbox; the tailpiece was discarded and replaced by a string holder on (and in) the belly, the bass bar was moved and restructured, and the emplacement of the soundpost was changed. Bowed guitar-shaped chordophones were not new: gambas have been occasionally so built from the sixteenth century on, and similar violins by several eighteenth-century makers are known, a natural result of abandoning corners for the above-stated reason. Savart's violin was trapezoidal, with straight sides, straight sound slits, flat tables, devoid of tailpiece but retaining the tailpin, and was known in England familiarly as "Savart's box fiddle."

These and other attempts at improving violin tone by constructing instruments according to acoustical principles were short lived, although they had an impressive *succès d'estime* in their day. Louis Spohr wrote in 1820 (in the *Allgemeine musikalische Zeitung*) that he had had his violin improved by Chanot, who shortened the tailpiece so that the string section below the bridge now sounded d♭² a♭² e♭² b♭³, an application of his, Spohr's, own invention; that this caused the violin to speak more readily, and the sympathetic vibration of their lower sections added greatly to the brilliance of tone. When preludizing in D♭, he continues, he was sometimes thought to be playing in D. Ingenious in construction, this is now forgotten (Spohr's chin rest, a boon to players ever since its invention, dates from this time but is not mentioned in the article in question).

Five-stringed violins, compromises attempting to combine violin and viola, have been made from the latter part of the eighteenth century on. The eighteenth-century *quinton* had a violin body except for its sloping shoulders, and was tuned d°d'a'd²g² to facilitate playing in the higher positions. Its use was chiefly restricted to France (the *quinton* is not identical with the *pardessus de viole*, a member of the *viola da gamba* family, nor with the *violino d'amore*). Usually, however, such instruments were combinations of violin and viola; if it was large, the fifth string was tuned to e², if small to c°. Some of the Chanot's guitar-shaped violins had five strings; their bodies were intermediary in size between violin and viola. The singer Farinelli mentions in his will of 1782 among other instruments: *altro violino (d'amore) a cinque corte* ("having five strings"), *ad uso di violino, o di viola*. This was probably a *quinton*, not a *violino d'amore* (see page 511).

Folk and Ethnic Violins

In different parts of Europe and the United States, violins are played as folk instruments, and either adapt features alien to their classical prototype or else the playing technique conforms to older traditions. Thus in certain areas of Romania a folk violin with five or seven additional sympathetic strings is played by the *lautar*, or professional minstrels, most of whom are Gypsies. A central and western Transylvanian ensemble comprises two violins and a double bass; the second violin has but three strings and its bridge is flat, so that all three are sounded simultaneously; consequently the playing is always in chords. In the Komitate Czik (Siebenbürgen), Hungary, a rustic violin of peasants and Gypsies, called *mozsika* (from the Latin *musica*), has normal stringing and tuning by fifths, but some specimens have an additional drone string. Most players utilize only three fingers for stopping the strings, and a peculiar local practice is that of never employing the first position. The *mozsika* is played together with the *gardon*, a folk violoncello. Poland formerly had a rustic violin with stumpy neck, F holes, short and broad pegdisk, and four strings tuned in fifths, a hybrid fiddle-violin.

Folk violins in Czechoslovakia in the late nineteenth century were held at the chin, tilted on edge so that the rib was uppermost. Bohemian Gypsy violins have unusually short necks and the F holes are cut higher than otherwise usual. Samuel Petri wrote (1767) that the Wends of Upper Lusatia still played a three-stringed violin lacking the G-string, a most interesting comment in view of our knowledge of the neglected fourth string in the early period of the classical violin. But the possibility cannot be overlooked that Petri may be referring to the *husla*, a fiddle (see page 475). Still further north, the Hardanger fiddle of Norway is, despite its name, a folk violin with four melody and four sympathetic strings, smaller in size than the regular violin, with short neck, flatter bridge, and more highly arched belly. According to tradition it was invented about 1670 in Hardanger, later to be improved by Isak Nielsen Botner (d. ca. 1780); the improvements are believed to have taken the form of added sympathetic strings inspired by the *violino d'amore*. Tunings vary, but ADAE seems to be preferred for the melody strings, DEF♯A for the sympathetic ones. This instrument is still in use. (For the *Klarfiedel* of Iglau, a petrifact of the medieval fiddle, see page 475.)

In the New World the violin continues to be played as a folk instrument in Oklahoma rural districts, held against the chest or even the waist; the first position is rarely exceeded. Characteristically it is played at dances.

An area where the European violin is played as an art music instrument (never in popular music) is North Africa. Algerian and Moroccan performers play seated on the ground, with the violin resting upright on the left knee (see also viola). Egyptian performers, however, hold it at the chin. In the whole area, the name *kamanja* is applied indiscriminately to viola and violin.

The Violino Piccolo

Small violins tuned a fourth higher than the ordinary violin ($c'g'd^2a^2$) were in use throughout the seventeenth and first half of the eighteenth centuries, that is, until the technique of playing the regular violin in high positions had become customary. They are often confused with the higher-pitched kits (see page 487). *Piccolos* must have existed by the late sixteenth century, for an Ambras inventory of 1596 lists two *claine Discant viole de braccio* as well as the ordinary violin. Monteverdi calls for *violini piccoli alla francese* in his *Orfeo* (performed 1607, published 1609), in addition to regular violins; the range of their parts is c′ to e♭² and it has been plausibly surmised—first by Andreas Moser—and is now generally accepted that the parts were intended for the *piccolo* as we know it, to be played an octave higher than notated. However, they could have been played on the French *poche* (kit), as notated, which would explain the unusual appellation.

Tuning of the *piccolo* in fifths from c′ did not vary from the time of Praetorius—who called them *claine Discant Geigen*—to Leopold Mozart (1756). Mozart points out that, although concerti had been composed for the *piccolo* in the past, such writing was no longer necessary, as "everything" could now be played on ordinary violins in high positions. Rendered superfluous from then on by the development of violin technique, the *piccolo* was retained solely as a teaching instrument for children.

Bach's tuning of the *piccolo* is sometimes a third higher than that of the violin, not the usual fourth (e.g., Brandenburg Concerto no. 1 in F, notated with the transposition of a third), possibly indicating that he disposed of a slightly larger model.

Auguste Tolbecque (1903) gives the following measurements for violins of smaller than standard size:

¼ violins: body 29.7 cm   stop 14.7 cm
½ violins: body 30.2 cm   stop 15.7 cm
¾ violins: body 33.2 cm   stop 17.4 cm

The stop is measured from the cross strokes of the FF to the nut.

THE VIOLA

In order to avoid confusion, the word "viola" without further qualification will be taken to denote the alto member of the violin family. Except for its size the viola is identical with the violin, as are its fittings, and as are the historical modifications of its neck, bass bar, soundpost, etc. Tuned a fifth below the violin, c°g°d′a′, it has a body length varying from approximately 38 to 44 centimeters (15 to 17¼ inches). Larger instruments, it should be noted, are classified as tenor violins (see page 532). If these measurements are compared with those of the violin it will become evident that the viola is proportionately too small for its pitch; theoretically it should be half again as large as the violin, but so big an instrument would be difficult to play in the a-braccio position. Musicians have been aware of this shortcoming for centuries, and attempts have been made sporadically to build an instrument capable of developing optimum tone. The most successful of such experiments was perhaps that of J. B. Vuillaume, who in 1835 introduced a broader and deeper model constructed along the acoustical principles worked out by the physicist Félix Savart, to give a fundamental pitch of F°, but difficulty in playing due to its size prevented its acceptance.

At the time that the violin, viola, and tenor originated, the intermediary-sized viola seems to have been the most important of the three and originally the type instrument of the family. This is borne out in part by its name, an abbreviation of *viola da braccio*, and in part by the treatment accorded it in the late sixteenth and early seventeenth centuries, a period when deeper ranges were being increasingly favored (the high-pitched, three-stringed fiddles were to become obsolete): Zacconi (1592) gives the c′g′d°a° tuning to the viola and calls it soprano; Giovanni Gabrieli wrote a *violino* part in alto clef for his *Sacrae symphoniae* of 1597 that descends below g° and therefore must have been intended for the alto instrument.

The earliest violas that have come down to us are of Italian make and can be roughly divided into two models: a smaller one with body length of about 41 centimeters and a larger with body length of about 44 centimeters (+16 inches to 17¾ inches); those of Gasparo da Salò (1540–after 1600) measure about 44 centimeters, and it seems that until the end of the seventeenth century the larger pattern predominated. From then on a smaller model was generally preferred, and this occasioned the cutting down of many an older instrument.

Violin and viola succeeded in replacing the higher-pitched members of the *viola da gamba* family earlier in Italy than elsewhere, and from Monteverdi on they had their place in the orchestra. The string section of Saint Mark's, Venice, in 1685 was top-heavy with altos: eight *violini*, eleven *violette*, two *viole da braccio*, three *violoni*, four *tiorbe* (theorbos), which by 1708 had changed to ten *violini*, three *violette*, one *viola da braccio*, one *violone*, three *tiorbe*; here, the term *viole da braccio* may have referred to bass instruments, that is, celli. The word *violetta* usually designated the viola, but occasionally also the alto *viola da gamba*.

At about this time, the custom prevailed in France of calling the viola by the name of the part it was to play; depending upon the compass scored for, it was either a *haute-contre* (C clef bottom line), a *taille* (C clef second line), or a *quinte* (C clef third line); in the eighteenth century the viola was additionally known as *alto, alto-viola, cinqième, quinte de violon*, or *violette*. During the age of Lully and the earlier eighteenth century, the middle voices frequently did not appear in print, it being left to copyists to write them out; thus, according to Lecerf de la Viéville (1704), Lully's secretaries *faisaient les parties intermédiares de ses oeuvres* ₊("made the intermediary parts of his works") the *haute-contres, tailles*, and *quintes*. Finally, Corrette could write in the mid-eighteenth century that these three, formerly differentiated by Lully, were now one. Lully's practice was evidently a common one, for the viola's role in the orchestra was of subordinate importance and consisted merely of doubling other string parts until such a time as it was given greater prominence by composers such as Bach and Handel. The Hills (1902) inform us that during the first half of the eighteenth century "there was almost a cessation of viola-making in all countries," coinciding with the dearth of contemporary chamber music containing a viola part. Indeed, as late an author as Quantz pointed out (1752) that the viola was of little consequence in music and that its players lacked ability. Frequently violas were in the hands of violinists who were more at ease with a smaller model, and consequently violas of this period—the mid-eighteenth century—were made with body lengths varying from 37½ to 39½ centimeters (14¾ to 15¼ inches). Then, when in the late eighteenth century the viola was given more important parts, a larger pattern prevailed once again. With the arrival in Paris of Carl Stamitz—composer, violinist, violist, and *viola d'amore* virtuoso—in 1770, the viola finally attained the status of a solo instrument. Today a large pattern with the fullest possible tone is preferred, especially in America, with body ranging between 40 and 43 centimeters (15¾ to 17 inches) in length.

Disregarding (or in ignorance of?) the fact that tenor violins existed, writers have frequently referred to the viola as a tenor, and this is particularly true after the disappearance of the tenor violin. A sales list of Longman & Broderip dated 1782 offered, among other instruments, violins, kits and small violins, tenor violins, and violoncellos; in fact, the majority of references to tenors prove on close examination to concern the alto instrument.

Hybrid Violas

Experiments to make the viola more competitive with the violin resulted in the creation of different types of hybrid, depending upon the maker's immediate aims. One type of instrument attempted to combine the features of violin and viola, while another strove to achieve improved tone and greater sonority.

To the first of these must be counted the *viola pomposa,* more accurately called the *violino pomposo,* a viola-sized instrument with an extra string tuned to e^2, in use from about 1725 to the end of the eighteenth century. Various late eighteenth- and nineteenth-century writers have ascribed its invention to J. S. Bach, and the myth persists, even though Bach never scored such an instument. Forkel and Gerber seem to be the sources of this misinformation, perhaps better called a misunderstanding, for both appear to have confused the *pomposo* with the *violoncello piccolo* (see page 526), an instrument for which Bach *did* write. In his *Musikalischer Almanach* for 1782, Forkel states that Bach invented the *viola pomposa,* a five-stringed instrument tuned like a cello with an extra treble string and a little longer than a viola, attached by a band so that it could be held *vor der Brust und auf dem Arme* ("at the chest and on the arm"). Two years later, Johann Adam Hiller quotes Forkel, but adds that the luthier Hoffmann built several *viole pompose* at Bach's request. Gerber, whose father had been a pupil of Bach's, goes a step further in the article devoted to the latter in his *Lexicon* (part I, 1790), in giving the tuning as that of a cello plus an e^2 string, and stating that its use afforded players the possibility of easier execution of high and rapid passages. Later authors compound the confusion.

The *viola pomposa* did nonetheless actually exist, and was best defined by Samuel Petri (1767) as "*violino pomposo,* which is of the size of a viola [*Bratsche*] and has five strings, so that it represents both viola and violin . . . is not much in use." Johann Gottlieb Graun, Telemann, and Lidarti are known to have composed for it. Graun's Double Concerto in D, *a 7 stromenti,* is for *flauto concertato, violino pomposo* or *violetta concertata,* and other strings. Another manuscript of the same piece calls for *violino o viola pomposa concertata.* Telemann wrote two short pieces for the *viola pomposa* by 1728, when he incorporated them into his *Der getreue Musikmeister;* both are duos for *flauto traverso e viola pomposa o violino.* Cristoforo Giuseppe Lidarti, cellist and composer, wrote a *Sonata a solo per la pomposa col basso* in Vienna around 1760. Koch sounds an echo by remarking in his *Musikalisches Lexikon* of 1802 that players occasionally made use of a viola with added violin E-string sometimes called *violino pomposo.*

But the *pomposo* was not the only viola with added violin E-string;

around 1788 another such instrument was devised by the violinist Michel Woldemar of Orléans and built probably by François Lupot. In 1800 we hear of the *Violalin* of Friedrich Hillmer of Leipzig, a viola with a fifth string tuned to e². Later in the century the idea was revived when the violist Hermann Ritter introduced (in 1876) a large viola, to which he subsequently (in 1898) had a violin E-string added, and named it *viola alta*. The term was not new; in the seventeenth and eighteenth centuries it had already denoted the viola. In our century, a somewhat retrogressive attitude to the viola was taken by Dessauer of Linz, who in 1901 invented his *Dessauerbratsche*, a viola with violin scale by means of which violinists were enabled to play the viola with normal violin fingering.

Lack of balance between viola size, normally restricted by the length of the human arm, and the resultant tone, was a source of preoccupation to players and luthiers alike, and from the mid-nineteenth century on structural solutions based on acoustical principles were actively sought. One of the earlier experimenters was J. B. Vuillaume, who produced in 1845 a very squat viola, almost square, in fact, to which he gave the name of *alto-ténor*. In 1854 the same name was bestowed upon a viola of Charles Henri of Paris, built with the entire left side larger than the right side. A year later Vuillaume designed his *contralto*, a deep-ribbed viola with lower bouts considerably wider than usual (he also built double basses with compensating wider-than-normal bouts). Twentieth-century experimentation has favored larger instruments with viola tunings but held like a cello; the 1926 *viola nova* of Hiller had a body length of no less than 54 centimeters (21½ inches), and a French *alto-moderne*, also called *viole-ténor*, of the 1930s, was another such instrument.

Ethnic Violas

Together with the violin, the viola is of course played in many non-European countries, but in none perhaps is its use more interesting than in Morocco, where both violin and viola were introduced in the eighteenth century, and where they are played in (Moroccan) art music as an integral part of the orchestra. The seated player holds his instrument upright, pegbox facing up, resting the body on his left knee; his left hand stops the strings and at the same time pivots the instrument so that the strings present themselves to the bow at the proper angle, for the bow moves in a horizontal line only, and is held palm up. The violin is tuned as it is in the West, but the viola has no fewer than three different tunings, the most common being d°a°d′b′, a tone higher than in the West;

the least common is the Western tuning, and a more popular one is, surprisingly, G°d°a°e′—that of the old tenor violin.

THE TENOR VIOLIN

Unknown in our day, the tenor member of the violin family, in the form of a larger version of the alto, became obsolete in the eighteenth century. Its overall length was some 70–75 centimeters (27½–29½ inches) with a body length in excess of 44 centimeters (17¼ inches) and a stop of about 50 centimeters (19½ inches). Its usual tuning was G°d°a°e′, an octave below the violin. In France the tenor's identity was disguised by the name *taille de violon,* which also meant "viola," while in Germany the term *Tenorgeige* frequently stood for the alto instrument, and in England tenor violin almost invariably did so, right up to the nineteenth century. Often only the indicated tuning of an instrument or the compass of an instrumental part taken in conjunction with the name authorizes us to postulate that a tenor is indeed required.

Gaudenzio Ferrari's fresco at Saronno, already mentioned in connection with the violin and viola, depicts a three-stringed violin of tenor size, and is the first source of our knowledge of the instrument. By 1553 a *taille de violon* is mentioned in France; this could, it is true, be a viola, but at that time is more likely to have referred to a tenor. No doubt can attach to Zacconi's (1592) tenor *viola da braccio* with its tuning F°c°g°d′, that given subsequently by most baroque writers, including Praetorius (who calls it a *Bass Viol da braccio* in *Syntagma* II, but in *Syntagma* III uses the term *Tenorgeige* as a synonym of *viol da bratio,* the alto instrument). However, Banchieri (1609) tuned his bass *viola da braccio* G°d°a°e′, and a near-contemporary inventory of instruments at the Kassel court, dated 1613, records "a large *tenor-Geige* with four strings," the lowest of which was tuned to G or to F. Many other German court inventories list tenors, but we cannot be sure whether or not the true tenor instrument is intended.

One of several tenor violins built by Antonio Stradivari has come down to us, originally part of a quintet of stringed instruments built for the Medici court. Known as the Tuscan viola, it dates from 1690 and is now preserved in Florence. The body length is 47.8 centimeters (nearly 19 inches); Stradivari's drawings, templates, and models for this very same instrument, as well as for its fittings, formerly in the Della Valle collection, are now housed in the Cremona Museum; they are marked "TV" for "tenor viola," in contrast to others inscribed "CV" for "contralta viola," the alto member of the quintet, now unfortunately lost (a violin and the cello of the set exist, in addition to the tenor).

The lack of music calling specifically for tenors makes it clear that theirs were intermediate voices in five-part ensembles, and the examination of compasses of parts written in tenor clef for "alto" instruments may suggest possible past employment of the tenor violin. With the reduction of five-part to four-part writing the tenor was doomed, and by the end of the eighteenth century it had fallen into oblivion. The early nineteenth century saw fit to re-invent it: proposals were made to build an instrument pitched between the viola and the cello, and even to call it "tenor violin," and in both the nineteenth and twentieth centuries a number of makers interested in experimentation came forth with models of their own, tuned exactly as the obsolete tenor had been. The *contraviolino* of Valentino de Zorzi, introduced in 1908, and the *Oktavgeige* of Johann Ritter of Mittenwald, with its exceptionally short body length of 42 centimeters (16½ inches), count among these. In general, though, the tenor is still a forgotten member of the violin family, and when encountered today it is usually mistaken for a child's small cello.

Sometimes the ordinary viola of Moroccan orchestras is tuned as was the tenor violin; its playing technique is described above, under viola (see page 526).

THE VIOLONCELLO

The violoncello, bass member of the violin family, sounds an octave lower than the viola, its four strings tuned to C°G°d°a°, and is played seated—again, one must say, nowadays. The word "violoncello," and its erstwhile synonym, *violoncino*, are both diminutives of *violone*, yet the etymology may be misleading. As far as we know, the cello emerged in the sixteenth century, probably by the mid-century, as a fullblown member of the *da braccio* family. Similar in construction to the violin though on a notably larger scale, the cello differs from it nonetheless in having relatively deeper ribs and shorter neck; also, its bridge is of proportionately greater height.

True celli made by Andrea Amati and his sons are among the earliest known (the so-called King Amati of Andrea Amati was made in Cremona in 1572) but few specimens and little information concerning them is available before the seventeenth century. A French document of 1570 cites a *bassecontre de violon façon de Venize* and another, *façon de Paris*, among the instruments having belonged to a deceased musician; and the *drei neue bassgeigen so man zwischen füeszen zu nemen pflegt* ("three new bass fiddles that one takes between the legs") of a 1577 Graz inventory may refer to the gamba rather than to the cello.

Seventeenth-century celli were either tuned as they are today or one tone lower (B′F°c°g°), the latter pitch being a fifth below that of the now obsolete tenor violin. Most English, French, and Italian writers of this century indicate the lower of the two tunings, but Praetorius gives the higher one. In English the instrument was usually referred to at that time as a bass violin; the Germans called it *Bassgeige*, but also by other names; the French term *basse de viole* denoted both the cello and other bowed instruments of bass range (the Italian bass *violino da braccio* was, however, the tenor violin). Nomenclature, particularly in French and German, is confused by the fact that the size of the cello was not standardized and that basses intermediate between double bass, *violone*, and cello existed. Some surviving seventeenth-century Italian celli are larger than later ones, others are known to have been cut down. Furthermore, no standardization on the matter of stringing existed until a late date, as five strings were formerly fairly common, and six are also occasionally mentioned, though here one suspects confusion with a gamba.

A number of older celli have reached us with a hole, or trace of a hole, in the center of their back. Such instruments are called "procession celli" because they were once played in religious processions, with a band passed through the aperture to enable the cello to be suspended from the player's neck, leaving both hands free to play. A Giovanni Grancino of 1677 with such a hole is described by Count Cozio di Salabue, and in their study of Antonio Stradivari the Hills (1902) relate that some northern celli were "Italianized" by the addition of such a hole.

Up to the latter part of the seventeenth century the cello's role was confined to supplying a bass line in concerted works, chiefly in the church, while any solo passages were reserved for the *viola da gamba*, which it was to rival and to finally displace in the following century. It was given a place of its own in the trio sonata, albeit a rather precarious one at times, as may be judged from such titles as the *Sonate a 2 & a 3 Con la parte del Violoncello a beneplacido* (1665) of Giulio Cesare Arresti, and until it had overcome the competition of theorbo, gamba, and *violone*. This was first accomplished in Italy: in a letter from Lucca dated 1657, Thomas Hill wrote: "The organ and violin they are masters of, but the bass-viol they have not at all in mind, and to supply its place they have the bass violin with four strings, and use it as we do the bass viol." Solo literature for the cello began to be written at the end of the century. Domenico Gabrielli of Bologna, composer and violoncellist, published in 1684 his *Balletti, gighe, correnti, sarabande, a due violini e violoncello con basso continuo*, followed by true solo pieces (*ricercari*) in 1689.

Though the louder tone of the cello compared favorably with that of the gamba in church and in larger halls, its size put it at a disadvantage when attempting to play rapid passages, so that from about 1700 on smaller instruments were built (cf. the division and consort basses of the gambas, page 503). The difference in string length between the two patterns amounted to up to 2½ centimeters (1 inch). The rather squat appearance of some disproportionately broad early celli, as seen, for instance, in Praetorius's illustration, had long given way to a more elongated form, but now all proportions were slightly reduced to meet the demands of a new school of Italian performers. However, it seems that for church music the larger pattern continued to be preferred, and the Hills state that not until the 1730s "and later do we find the makers finally abandoning the old tradition as regards dimensions." (The great majority of Stradivari's celli were of large size, it may be noted; some originally had five strings; most have since been cut down.) As late as 1752 Quantz makes it clear that the larger and thicker-strung pattern served for ripieno, and the smaller, with thinner strings, for solo work; he advises musicians who play both types of music to make use of different instruments and of different bows, that for ripieno to be haired more heavily.

In general the cello had no spike until the nineteenth century; large models were big enough not to require one, and smaller patterns could be set on footstools. But with the advent of solo parts a spike was found to be a great convenience to the standing performer.

The outsized five-stringed instrument depicted by Praetorius with a body length of some 85 to 90 centimeters (33½ to 35½ inches) is larger than a normal cello and would have been called *violone* or *Bassel* by a later generation. A number of such instruments of sizes intermediate between cello and double bass existed, some of which are discussed on page 540. In the early decades of the eighteenth century these intermediate instruments were being discarded in favor of the cello; they survived longest in German-speaking countries. Mattheson (1713) still knew the cello with five or even six strings, as did so late an author as Leopold Mozart (1756).

Italian players and instruments predominated on the Continent to such an extent that the youthful Johann Gottfried Walther, in his

Praecepta of 1708, could define the cello as an Italian bass instrument. Celli are first recorded at the Dresden court in 1714, when they were played by two Italians; in 1717 the string section of the court *Kapelle* consisted of eight violins, seven violas, and three celli, but by 1733 these had been augmented to twelve violins, four violas, four celli, and two double basses. Changing requirements and new ideals of tone quality were making themselves felt at the beginning of the eighteenth century, and Stradivari, for one, favored a heavier, that is a thicker, model from 1701 on—in the Hills' opinion in order to obtain a brighter and more penetrating tone.

Both the instrument and the manner of playing it had become refined: during the last decades of the seventeenth century the cello had been "a very hard and harsh sounding Base, and nothing so soft & sweet as now," according to Roger North, reminiscing in around 1728. More explicit on this subject is Michel Corrette in his cello tutor of 1741: "for about 25 or 30 years the *grosse basse de violon* has been discarded for the cello of the Italians, invented by Bononcini . . . its tuning is one tone higher than the former bass (B♭FCG)." Before the "invention" of the cello, he continues, the *grosses basses* played little more than *musique à grand choeur.* Now Bononcini had certainly not invented the cello, but passages such as these testify to the greater mobility of the instrument and to greater technical equipment of its performers, as well as to the influence of Italian musicians abroad. France had not admitted either the violin or the cello without protest, and was particularly tardy in accepting the latter. Hubert Le Blanc's famous pamphlet of 1740 was directed against both violin and cello, it will be recalled. And the new terminology was even less acceptable than were the instruments themselves, judging by the 1791 edition of the *Encyclopédie*, where among other definitions we find: "the *basse de Italiens* is called *basse de violon* by the French . . .," to which Framéry appends the terse comment: none of these instruments exists any longer but are replaced by the *quinte* (i.e., the viola) and the cello.

Celli of this period were undergoing a process of refinement: the necks were thinned to proportions more comfortable for the left hand, and, whereas the old, thick-necked models had been heavily strung, the remodeled version was provided with thinner strings. Orchestral musicians could finally play seated, grasping their instrument between the legs like a gamba, and consequently no longer required a spike, which was temporarily abolished. Playing while standing had fortunately gone out of fashion, and the seated posture possibly did more than any remodeling to improve orchestral technique, for, as one eminent musician of his day—Samuel Petri—put it: "When we play standing we cannot shift positions"; the left hand was now free to move.

With the interest accorded to acoustical experimentation at the turn of the eighteenth and nineteenth centuries, attention concentrated first on the violin and then was partly transferred to the cello. Chanot-type violoncelli were produced, nowadays condemned to museum cases as mere curiosities. One such instrument, built by Staufer of Vienna around 1824, was known as *arpeggione* or *Guitarre-Violoncell* or *guitare d'amour* because of its guitar fingerboard and stringing.

Violoncelli both smaller and larger than the common size have been made, with larger ones proliferating in the eighteenth century. Smaller models used for the teaching of children are generally referred to as three-quarter celli. Another small-sized instrument was the *violoncello piccolo*, in use in the first half of the eighteenth century and for which Bach wrote. Normally it was tuned like an ordinary cello and was probably intended for solo playing. Sometimes a fifth string was added in the treble, tuned to e'. Thus the five-stringed piccolo was exactly an octave below the *viola pomposa* (see page 530). Bach scored for the *violoncello piccolo* in nine of his cantatas (nos. 6, 42, 49, 68, 85, 115, 140, 175, 183); furthermore, the sixth of his suites for violoncello is for an instrument *à cinq acordes* (C°G°d°a°e'), the nature of which has been subject of much speculation. On a regular cello, a string tuned to e' would be apt to break easily, hence an identification with the *violoncello piccolo* has been suggested. Among the musical instruments inventorized in 1773 at the Cöthen court, where Bach had spent the years 1717 to 1723, was a *Violon Cello Piculo* with five strings, made by J. C. Hoffmann in 1731, another with four strings by J. H. Ruppert of 1724. Neither of these could have been used by Bach's musicians at Cöthen, of course, but we can attempt to match the name given to Hoffmann's cello with some of his extant instruments.

Hoffmann built a range of models from *violino piccolo* to double basses, but the only size in question here is that between viola and cello or, rather, between tenor violin and cello. To qualify for the designation of cello one would expect a deeper and more robust build than either tenor or alto could boast. The Heyer Collection of the Karl Marx University, Leipzig, contains two five-stringed instruments by Hoffmann, both with a body length of 45½ centimeters (nearly 18 inches) and rib depths of 9 and 8¾ centimeters (over 3½ inches), respectively; another by Hoffmann, in Brussels, also with five strings, is 7½ centimeters (3 inches) deep;

a Hoffmann in the estate of Wilhelm Rust, organist and later cantor of Saint Thomas's Church in Leipzig, who died in 1892, had a speaking string length of 41½ centimeters (16½ inches), body length of 45½ centimeters (18 inches), and rib depth of 3.8 centimeters (1½ inches), according to Kinsky, who adds that if strung with wound strings it could be tuned to C°G°d°a°e'. Similar instruments of other makers closely parallel these in their proportions (e.g., two in Leipzig with body lengths of 46 and 50 centimeters, depths between 8 and 9 centimeters, and one in the Bachhaus of Eisenach with body of 45½ centimeters and a depth of 8 centimeters). All are distinguished from alto and tenor violins by their squat appearance; perhaps they were called *violoncelli piccoli* in their day. Or was this merely another and a newer name for an already existing instrument?

Mattheson devotes a passage of his *Orchester* (1713) to the cello, part of which was copied verbatim or quasi-verbatim by Majer, Walther, Eisel, and Zedler (vol. 48, 1746): "The excellent violoncello, the *bassa viola* and *viola da spala* are small bass fiddles [*Bass-Geigen*] in comparison with the larger ones, with four, five, and even six strings, on which one can play all manner of rapid pieces, make variations and ornaments, with less work than on the larger machines." He continues: ". . . . particularly the *viola di spala*, or shoulder viola, makes a great effect when accompanying because it penetrates and can express the tone clearly. A bass [line] cannot be expressed more distinctly and clearly than on this instrument. It is attached by a band to the chest and thrown as it were on the right shoulder . . ." Having quoted this passage, Majer (1732) completes the last sentence by adding: "but by many it is held between the legs." He gives one tuning, that of the cello (C°G°d°a°), for all three instruments. *Viola da spalla* was therefore an early-eighteenth-century name for a small cello that could be held a-braccio or a-gamba; in the former position, so large and heavy an instrument would need support, and this could be supplied by resting it either on or below the right shoulder. In those days the smaller a-braccio instruments were held on the player's left, but the greater length of a *viola da spalla* would have required a diagonal position from left to right, in order to bring the top of the fingerboard within reach of the left hand. At the mid-century the reliable and helpful Adlung equated the *viola da spalla* with the cello. Italian authors seem to have used the term to distinguish a-braccio instruments from those of the gamba family; thus the luthier Tommaso Balestrieri wrote to Cozio di Salabue in 1776: *Vi sono due viole da spala d'Antonio e Girolamo Amati. . . . Tre altre viole da gamba degli stessi autori . . ."* Forkel's description of the *viola pomposa*'s playing stance is so close in wording to Mattheson's that one wonders if it is coincidence. However, it seems clear that the two instruments were not identical, but differed in size and in pitch.

Another small-sized cello held on the arm like a violin was the *Fagott-geige* of the seventeenth and eighteenth centuries (Italianized to *viola di fagotto*); it shared compass and tuning with those of the ordinary cello. Slightly larger than the viola, its low pitch was achieved by means of the wound strings that had come into use. Daniel Speer (1687) refers to its *schnurrende Saiten*, buzzing strings, whose bassoonlike quality may be responsible for the instrument's name. Perhaps it is not imprudent to conclude that the *violoncello piccolo*, the *viola da spalla*, the *Fagott-geige*, and the *Handbassel* all represent minor variants in size of one and the same instrument, and that the diversity of nomenclature is chiefly due to regional usage. Leopold Mozart in one passage equates the *Fagott-geige* with the *Handbassel*, in another he states that it was slightly smaller than the latter. And did Bach's "invention" consist in requiring J. C. Hoffmann, whom he knew in Leipzig, to add a fifth string to the *violon-cello piccolo*?

Folk Violoncelli: The Gardon

A folk instrument called *gardon*, similar to the cello, is played in Transylvania, but as a rhythm rather than as a melody instrument. Formerly it was hand made by its peasant performers from a block of wood; older specimens have a very short neck, elongated body, and long tailpiece. Some modern specimens have bodies of true cello form, but the more usual shape is that of a very large medieval fiddle—of which it is apparently a petrifact—either with sound slits or with FF. The three or four strings are secured to a conventional pegbox, and all are tuned to d°. Instead of being bowed, they are struck with a stick, and immediately after being struck, one of the strings is plucked. If the performer is seated, the *gardon* is held horizontally across the lap, but if standing, it is held obliquely by one hand, the soundholes on a level with the player's waist. Nowadays most of the performers are Gypsies, who play the *gardon* for rhythmic accompaniment to their violin-like *mozsika*.

THE DOUBLE BASS

Despite the fact that the double bass evolved as long ago as the sixteenth century, it has never become standardized in regard to size or even pattern, and only in comparatively recent times has a uniform stringing been adopted. As played today it has four strings tuned in fourths (E'A'D°G°), unlike the other members of the violin family; this smaller interval is necessitated by the larger dimensions of the fingerboard and resultant greater spread of the fingers when stopping. Orchestral instruments now in use may perhaps be said to vary in overall length from 180 to 220 centimeters (6 to 6½ feet), with an average body length of 112 centimeters (44 inches), and a stop of 107 to 108 centimeters (42 to 42½ inches). Disparities are still such, however, that German-speaking luthiers talk of full, three-quarter, and half-sized double basses, with body lengths of 112, 108, and 105 centimeters, respectively, calling them *violoni* (see page 507). They are still played on the Continent and counted as double basses. A study by Werner Bachmann distinguishes between five sizes of double bass: the *Bierbass*, quarter, half, and three-quarter sizes (*Violone*), and full bass; differing only in size, all with the same tuning. He gives their ratios to the proportions of the cello as follows:

> *Bierbass* 34:32
> Quarter bass 20:16
> Half bass 21:16
> Three-quarter bass 22:16
> Full bass 23:16

Stringed instruments of contrabass size make a brief appearance in tenth-century Spanish miniatures, then disappear until the Renaissance. Our earliest information concerning the double bass's emergence comes from written rather than from pictorial records, a reversal of the more usual sources of evidence: a *viola di contrabasso* was played in an ensemble in 1529 at Ferrara, a *basse contre de viole* formed part of a Parisian luthier's estate in 1557, and another *basse contre de viole, façon de Venise* appears in an inventory of 1570. A *sottobasso di viola* participated in 1565 at a Florence *intermedio*. To the same decade belong the first pictorial representations: both Veronese's *Marriage at Cana* of 1563, and Jost Amman's *Turnirbuch* of 1566 show an instrument of double-bass proportions with fretted neck, four strings, gamba-type flat back; and C holes are visible in the *Turnirbuch*. Another woodcut by Amman, for Schopper's *Eygentliche Beschreibung aller Stände, Künste, und Handwerke* of 1568, entitled *Drey Geyger* ("three fiddlers"), depicts a similar instrument from the back: the standing player is surpassed by the height of his instrument. Around 1600 Hans Haiden, inventor of the *Geigenwerk* (see page 308), built an extra-large contrabass, which for greater ease in fingering made use of a small keyboard. A passage in the Haiden family chronicle reads: *Eine überaus grosse Bass Geigen mit einem langen Kragen und einem Clavis, dass man nicht auf den Bünden mit hin und wieder greiffen dörffte . . .* ("An extremely large bass *Geige* with a long neck and a keyboard, so that one is not obliged to finger up and down the frets . . ."). This was the first of a number of outsized *contrabassi* to be made sporadically until the late nineteenth century.

Early Italian double basses have arched backs, later ones often but not invariably flat, gamba-type backs. The confused nomenclature of the seventeenth century, a time when the double bass was still in the process of elaboration, has given rise to the belief that it is (1) a member of the gamba family, (2) a member of the violin family. Praetorius himself is most ambiguous on the subject. Furthermore, any bowed chordophone with a lower than bass range was known as *violone* (see page 507), a term still applied to smaller double basses in Europe. Of the few old instruments that survive, those in gamba form have F holes. The *Gross Contra Bass Geig* of Praetorius has the sloping shoulders and frets of a gamba, otherwise a violin-type body with pronounced corners, F holes, a scroll, and four strings (the back is not visible). It corresponds in his table of pitches to the *gross Quint Bass* with, however, five strings, tuned in fifths: F′C°G°d°a°. This is clearly a violin type, and its sloping shoulders and fretted neck—the only gamba features—are concessions necessary to the handling and playing of so large an instrument, rather than proof of a hybrid genealogy.

For the rest of the century double basses were built for three, four, or five strings. Daniel Speer (1687) knew the three-stringed model tuned G′C°F°, that is, in fourths, a necessity in view of the large spaces to be bridged in fingering, and that with four strings, tuned as it is today (E′A′D°G°), and from then on we hear much of the three-stringed type, which came to be played in Italy and England, in addition to the German-speaking countries. Later German models tend structurally toward the gamba, with short, fretted neck, sloping shoulders, and flat back canted at the shoulder level to reduce body depth, high ribs, and more often with five strings (occasionally even six) tuned D′E′A′D°G°; these continued to be played in Germany until the mid-eighteenth century. Small double basses with an overall length of from 146 to 160 centimeters (57¼ to 63 inches) were carried in processions in the same manner as were the procession celli.

Talbot, writing about 1700, includes the double bass in his list of *viole da gamba,* and gives tunings for both the five- and the six-stringed models: F′ (or G′) A′D°F♯°A° and G′C°F°A°d°g°; the measurements he indicates are those of an average-sized orchestral instrument of today. Brossard (1703) expresses surprise that the double bass is not more often used in France, gives its body size as twice that of a cello and its pitch an octave below the latter. Yet in 1706 Marin Marais has already a double bass in his opera *Alcyone,* and in the following year Michel Pinolet de Montéclair became *contrebassiste* at the Paris Opéra. (In 1757 this institution had but one double bass player—not Montéclair, long retired by then—who played but once a week, on Fridays, *le beau jour* of that theater. This aristocratic tradition was still intact when Weckerlin wrote over a century later, in 1874.)

A violin-type double bass is showed by Majer in 1732, with the same tuning as Talbot's. Not until the mid-eighteenth century were the four-stringed models preferred. Quantz (1752) states that the effect is better if the *contraviolon* is of medium size and strung with four, not with five, strings: "the so-called German *violon* with five or six strings was rightly discarded"; this statement of his seems a little premature, though. If the music requires two double basses, he adds, the second may be somewhat larger than the first; what the latter loses in clarity it makes up for by its gravity (*Gravität*). Frets are indispensable, he goes on to say, to prevent the long, thick, and relatively slack strings from slapping against the fingerboard further down, thereby impeding vibration and causing a muffled tone. His remark concerning the abolition of five- and six-stringed German *violoni* must not be taken to mean that all double basses so strung were obsolete; it is merely a question of nomenclature. Leopold Mozart (1756) explicitly states that the large bass, *il controbasso* called *violon,* tuned an octave lower than the cello, usually has four, sometimes three strings, whereas the larger models have five. Regardless of size, all were tuned alike. The 1770s saw the reinvention by Carl Ludwig Bachman of Berlin of the machine-screw tuning system already known to Praetorius and later abandoned; apparently the early cogwheel device had not permitted sufficient accuracy in tuning due to variations of tension produced by the cogs.

Most double basses built prior to the mid-nineteenth century were originally intended to accommodate three strings, and their tone suffered when more were added. In the *Allgemeine musikalische Zeitung* of Leipzig for 1803–1804, a contributor wrote that, wishing to discover why old double basses sounded so poor, he opened one up and found the back and belly too thin; every player, he writes, knows that if a string breaks and he is obliged to play on three strings only, his instrument sounds "stronger and fuller"; the author therefore suggested limiting the strings to three and tuning them C′D°A°. Schubart comments (ca. 1788) on the common use of three-stringed contrabasses in the orchestra, but adds that for solo work a four- or five-stringer was indispensable. Francesco Galeazzi (1791) gives the tuning of the *contrabasso* as A′D°G°, but others, he says, tune it an octave below the cello, C′G′D°A°, or else G′D°A°e°. Three-stringed instruments lasted longest in Britain, France, and Italy, being in general use there when Carl Engel wrote in the 1870s. Their tuning was A′ (or G′) D°A° in England, A′ (or G′) D°G° in Italy. The three-stringed double bass lives on in parts of Europe as a folk instrument; in Sicily it is known as a *citarruni*.

In the early nineteenth century, the kind of music to be performed determined to a large extent the type of double bass to be played: large models with three strings served for simple orchestral parts, medium-sized ones with four strings were most commonly employed for solo work, while the smallest, sometimes called "half *violons*" or "German basses" were restricted to village dances. When the four-stringed Italian version was taken up again in the nineteenth century it was tuned D′G′D°G°; subsequently the two lowest strings were raised by a tone, and as need was then felt for a downward extension of the compass, the fifth string was restored, now tuned to C′. Later in the century the new "C-string attachment" carried the E′-string to the top of the head; the additional semitones could be stopped mechanically. In 1839 a French physicist of Corbigny was credited with having invented a keyboard to facilitate the execution of passages "otherwise impossible to play"—actually a rediscovery of Hans Haiden's idea designed to accommodate a three-stringed instrument, and a patent was granted in 1892 to a French organ builder named Duvivier for a *contrebasse à clavier* with detachable piano keyboard of thirty-five or thirty-eight keys.

By the mid-century the dilemma of sizes had still not been solved. A notice addressed to members of the Queen Square Select Society on November 6, 1846, is of interest in this connection. It reads:

At this meeting will be introduced to you a new instrument to which the name of Basso di Camera has been given, and which, uniting the compass of the

Double Bass, with a sufficient power for small parties, and possessing also a flexibility and smoothness nearly equal to the Violoncello, may be employed, it is conceived, with great advantage in the performance of chamber music.

Now the *basso da camera*, by no means a new instrument, was a small double bass known by a plethora of other names, chief among which were *Halbbass* ("half-bass"), and counted as a *violone*. Bottesini, one of the greatest double-bass players of all times, had a three-stringed *basso da camera* by Testore, and, although he had not played in England at the time this notice appeared, he had already made a name for himself on the Continent. Other soloists also favored the smaller model, and for the same reasons: clearer sonority and relative ease of playing. For the orchestra a larger model was needed to accommodate the low pitches required by composers of symphonic music. Yet the bottom string presented problems on the large instruments, and a late-nineteenth-century tutor pointed out that because the E-string was generally too slack and could not be tuned clearly, it was usually raised to sound F. When Beethoven's C-Minor Symphony—which calls for G′ in a solo passage—was performed in England, the passage had to be transposed up an octave, or else the A-string was lowered by a tone.

Ellis (1895) reported that the problem was overcome by winding a gut string with copper wire; by this means low C (C′) was obtained, and an instrument so strung was exhibited in London in 1872. But the extra strain caused thereby required strengthening the underside of the belly with four bars, the so-called elliptical tension bars that were originally designed for the violin and described, when exhibited in 1874, as "four strips of white deal, curved to an elliptical figure, passing parallel from end to end on the inside of the belly." From the foregoing we find that in the nineteenth century the pitch of the lowest string on a double bass varied from C′ up to A′ on the old three-stringer, via E′ and F′ for the four-stringers and G′ for the more recent three-stringed versions.

Nowadays bass players distinguish between a full bass with body length of about 122 centimeters (48 inches), these being chiefly of German make, and ordinary orchestral basses of so-called three-quarter length size. The bodies of Italian instruments do not exceed a length of 117 centimeters (46 inches), those of modern French workmanship average 114 centimeters (45 inches). Italian basses typically have F holes, a violin outline except for the sloping shoulders, either a vaulted or a flat back. J. B. Vuillaume designed his basses with elongated, tapering shoulders and compensating, wider-than-usual lower bouts, in an attempt to render his instruments easier to play (cf. his *contralto*, page 531).

Giant Double Basses

Giant double basses, actually subcontrabasses, have been built sporadically since 1600 or so, when Hans Haiden produced his outsized instrument, already described. Praetorius (1620) depicted an outsized *Bassgeige*. A giant in violin form but with flat back, a body of about 173 centimeters (68 inches) and of Italian seventeenth-century make is now in the Victoria and Albert Museum, London. Another, with seven mechanically bowed strings, was produced in Vienna in 1829. Vuillaume constructed two *octobasses*, one in 1849, now in Russia, and an improved version two years later, in the Paris Conservatoire collection. It is 4 meters (13 feet) high, its three strings (C′G′C°) stopped by pedal-operated levers, the bow set in a device similar to oarlocks. Finally, in 1889, John Geyer built a monster 4½ meters (15 feet) high in the United States.

Part Four

AEROPHONES

FREE AEROPHONES

BULLROARERS

Actually the bullroarer is a noisemaker rather than a musical instrument, for in no culture does it participate in music making nor, more important perhaps, does it emit a truly musical or rhythmic sound. Because of its intimate connection with ritual and with magic ceremony, the bull-roarer has been studied chiefly by ethnologists and anthropologists; its place in books on musical instruments has, however, become a tradition ever since Victor-Charles Mahillon described one in his monumental catalog of the Brussels Conservatoire collection, justifying its inclusion on the ground that its behavior was similar to that of a reed.

Bullroarers are slabs of wood, rhomboid, frequently but not necessarily carved, and pierced with a small hole at one end for attaching a length of cord. The cord is then held in the performer's hand (or attached in turn to a stick that he holds) and the wood is whirled through the air in circles, turning on its axis as it rotates. Velocity of rotation and size determine the pitch: the smaller the piece of wood, the faster it can be whirled, and the higher the pitch that can be obtained. The resultant sound is likened in various cultures to the roar of a bull, the howling of an animal or of a spirit, to thunder itself. Alterations of speed and angle to the ground bring about changes of sonority so that the same implement can be made to whimper or scream, moan or roar.

Ever since prehistoric times the bullroarer has been a fertility symbol; it has not ceased altogether to be played but may still be found in certain areas of each continent and the Pacific. Archaeologists have compared some shaped and carved antler plaques of the Aurignacian and Magdalenian cultures to the Australian *churinga* bullroarer, which they resemble strikingly; in addition, one or two of the Magdalenian plaques are pierced or notched, further suggesting identity with the bullroarer. Another area where the bullroarer is known to be of considerable antiquity is Egypt, where it appears in predynastic times, in the Negadeh II period (prior to 3300 B.C.).

The sound of a bullroarer is believed to be the voice of an ancestor, a spirit, or a deity, and thus plays an important role in various *rites de passage* in many parts of the world; at the same time it is taboo to women, who may never see it—in some areas, upon penalty of stillbirth or even death. It also represents, or becomes, thunder. Other societies put it to more practical use, namely that of driving or of stupefying game. Wood is the material commonly used for its fabrication, but whalebone baleen and ivory are utilized by the Eskimo; horn, hide, or bone by North American Indians; iron in Africa north of the Equator (but reserved here exclusively for magical rites connected with smithy).

The Australian *churinga* is made of stone or wood. Those of stone are never whirled; they are said to represent the voices of ancestors. Those of wood are made in many sizes. In Central Australia where thunder causes rain to fall, thereby bringing fertility, the bullroarer makes thunder. Boys of the Wiradthuri of New South Wales are not permitted to see one before the time of their initiation; during these rites it is swung while they cower, covered with blankets so that they hear it in utter darkness: it is the spirit of the sky god, the thunder. Later they learn to whirl it themselves. Similarly, in parts of tropical Africa newly circumcised or newly initiated boys may not see a bullroarer; their elders whirl it to frighten them as they remain in their huts after dark. At Cape York on the Torres Straits, two sizes of bullroarer are employed, a "male" that growls, and a "female" that shrieks, both of fearsome tone quality. The performer first swings them around his head to produce a buzzing noise, then he turns rapidly, facing the opposite direction, and swings them horizontally with abrupt backward and forward motions of the hand, causing them to emit a penetrating yelp.

Modern Egyptian bullroarers are elongated rectangles of wood, played predominantly by women when healing—a notable exception to the usual taboo; a number of holes may be pierced longitudinally to augment the dynamics with a sirenlike quality. Use of the bullroarer in Negro Africa in the fourteenth century is attested by ibn-Batuta, the great Moslem traveler. Nowadays it is associated with burial ceremonies among, for example, the Eyap of Cameroun. The same usage obtains among the Bororó of South America, and the Cuban descendants of the Yoruba make it in fish form and whirl it at funeral rites. The same form is found among the Ipuriná of Brazil. Among several North American peoples the bullroarer is both a bringer of rain or warm wind and a toy; it is currently undergoing a process of desacralization. In ancient Greece, however, it was still an implement of initiation rites. The scholiast of Clement of Alexandria, commenting on the Mysteries of Dionysus Zagreus, describes the *rhombos* as "a piece of wood to which a string is tied, and it is whirled round and round at initiation rites to make a whirring sound."

The transition from sacred to profane is completed in most of present-day Europe, where the bullroarer is now only played by children as a toy, except for a few districts among animal herders. The modern European bullroarer is also connected with thunder; having the same qualities as thunder, it *is* thunder, and the Scotch "thunner spell" treats like with like in homeopathic fashion and keeps thunder away by its whirling. Scotch herd boys formerly called their cattle home by swinging a bullroarer of their own making, whereupon the animals would throw up their tails and rush through the fields in a fury. The same device is used in Galicia, where it actually causes stampedes. The Bushman of South Africa swings his to drive game, and the now obsolete *berbaling* of Malaya chased a marauding elephant off the plantation.

BUZZERS

Related to the bullroarer is the buzzer, a disk, blade, or other form of wood, ivory, bone, etc., in the center of which two holes are pierced for fastening to a loop cord. Both ends of the cord are held by the player, who twists them and then pulls them apart; the string then twists and untwists itself again, and hums while being spun. Unlike the bullroarer, it spins only around its axis. In one form or another, buzzers are played nowadays in Africa, Asia, the Americas, and the Pacific, in Europe only as toys.

In certain areas buzzers assume the very form of the bullroarer, that of a blade, but it is always distinguishable by its two centrally located holes. This shape is found among the Lapps, the Greenland Eskimo, and the Yakuts of Siberia. But the disk form is more common, and indeed the device is usually referred to as "disk buzzer" in English and the German equivalent (*Schwirrscheibe*). Wooden disks are encountered in such far-flung areas as China, Togoland, Hungary, New Zealand (Maori), and among North American Indians, with other materials almost as widespread. Another feature shared with the bullroarer is its use by males only among many Amerinds, some of whom employ it as a fertility charm to bring rain or other weather favorable to the crops.

Two unconventional forms may be singled out for mention: that occurring in China, consisting of nutshells glued to a wooden disk, each nutshell having a split cut into it to make it whistle as it spins, and that of the Basque people: their *aballa* is nothing more than a shaped piece of paper inserted into a twisted cord, the cord being attached in turn to a stone; the whole contrivance is then thrown into the air, the paper whirring as it falls to earth.

A few decades ago, buzzers dating from the third century A.D. were discovered at a Coptic site at Kōm Aushīm in the Faiyûm, but nothing is known of the purpose they may have served in Egypt.

FLUTES

One of the oldest instruments of mankind, the flute is known to have existed by the Stone Age and is found among practically all peoples (aboriginal Australians form a notable exception). It is classified according to form, playing technique, or blowing device. Most flutes are tubular; they occur less frequently in vessel form.

TUBULAR FLUTES: ACOUSTICS

If the upper orifice of a tubular flute is used as its blowhole, it is said to be endblown, whereas if a blowhole is cut laterally into the wall it is termed sideblown. Of the two, endblown flutes are the older. From the position in which they are held when played, endblown flutes are referred to as vertical flutes—even when they are held obliquely—while the sideblown flutes are usually called transverse or cross flutes. The upper end of a flute is known as the mouth end (on cross flutes as well as vertical ones). The lower end may be open or closed, and if closed the instrument is known as a stopped flute. One fundamental law of musical acoustics is that an open pipe overblows its octave, a stopped one its twelfth (provided the width of the bore does not preclude overblowing), and this law applies to all tubular flutes. Usually but not always flutes are provided with fingerholes; on early and primitive flutes these are equidistant. Sometimes they also have dorsal thumbholes. Two or three flutes may be combined to form double or triple flutes, or sets of endblown flutes having different pitches may be combined to form panpipes.

A further distinction is made between ductless and duct flutes. The former may have a notch cut in the edge of the upper orifice, in which case we speak of a notched flute; the notch is usually beveled to facilitate speech; here the player partly closes the opening with his lower lip. Notched flutes can in turn be open, stopped, or half stopped by a hole pierced in the closing node (of the lower aperture). Sachs believed that stopped notched flutes—in some cultures these attain a length of 1½ meters (5 feet)—were older than open ones. Judging from excavated materials it would seem that ductless flutes with notches are older than those without. On many ductless flutes, including panpipes, the notch is absent. A variant is the so-called oblique flute, the upper orifice of which has been cut on the diagonal, the flute then being held obliquely (pointing down and to one side).

In duct flutes the air stream is directed by a narrow duct (also called flue or windway) against the sharp edge (lip) of a lateral aperture (vent). If a duct flute is very short we speak of it as a whistle (see page 582). Ducts can be internal or, exceptionally, external. Internal ducts, that is, those situated inside the tube, may be formed by a natural node, a block of wood or one of resin, while external ducts are often formed by a ringlike sleeve tied around the wall of the tube (ring flutes). Most internal ducts are terminal, and in such flutes the player blows directly into the duct. In other instances, however, the duct is central; here the player blows into the hollow tube that acts as wind chamber up to the duct, the block in this case formed by a blob of resin. Such flutes rarely have fingerholes; they are known in Asia, America, and the Pacific. Duct flutes containing a terminal block, or fipple, are also known as fipple flutes, and, if the upper ends are shaped into a beak to facilitate blowing, also as beaked flutes. The best-known European fipple flute, the recorder, is also a beaked flute. The combined duct and fipple head is also referred to as a whistle head, hence flageolets and recorders, for example, may also be called whistle flutes. The arrangement of fipple and duct at the lip of a flute's vent is in principle the same as the speaking mechanism of organ flue pipes. According to Sachs, flutes with a fipple preceded both the ductless endblown flute and the cross flute; and holeless flutes preceded those with fingerholes.

Sound production on cross flutes is similar to that of vertical flutes, except that here the sharp edge against which the player's breath is directed is that of a lateral hole. In primitive flutes this is placed near the center, in developed models close to the upper end. Cross flutes can be either open or stopped; open varieties are found on all continents and the Pacific, while stopped versions occur only in Asia, America, and the Pacific. The cross flute is first recorded in China in the ninth century B.C. but may be older, and is possibly of Central Asian origin.

Flutes have been made of a great number of materials, including bone, bamboo, dried fruit shells, wood, clay, ivory, metal, glass, and plastics. Of the very early bone flutes that have been found, those of bird bone are believed to be the oldest. These are generally devoid of fingerholes and yield but one tone—a signal rather than a musical instrument—whereas mammalian bones were often provided with fingerholes, four or more being the common number.

Tone production is effected by blowing either the fundamental or the harmonics (called overblowing). Pitch can be varied in a number of fashions, such as for instance stopping an open flute with the flat of the hand or against the knee, changing the sounding portion of a tube's length by providing fingerholes, and so on. Many early and primitive flutes (and some developed ones) have a bore too narrow to sound the fundamental; thus the lowest tone of its open tube is an octave above the fundamental. If the player blows harder, he will produce a tone a fifth higher (a twelfth from the fundamental); still harder, and he produces the double octave, and so on. On wider-bored tubes the fundamental will sound, and the first overblown tone is an octave higher. Hence, in order to play melodies it becomes necessary to create some artificial means for bridging the large gap between the lowest available tone and its overblown tone, and six fingerholes provide the solution.

The pitch standard of China during the Chou dynasty (1122–255 B.C.) was that of a flute cut exactly one (Chinese) foot long (229.9 millimeters); this produced the tone *huang chung*, which, according to Sachs, corresponded to the pitch of our f♯° and was probably identical to the Greek *mesē*. Japanese and Near Eastern pitch standards are d', a pitch also derived from the lowest tone of the vertical flute, that of Japan sounding 292 CPS. The European cross flute was also a d' flute historically (now a c' flute).

Flutes are closely connected with magical cults and still participate in many parts of the world at magicoreligious ceremonies; furthermore, as phallic symbols they are associated with fertility and rebirth, and are hence often encountered in ancient tombs, where they functioned as life charms.

SINGLE FLUTES

Flutes in Prehistory and Antiquity

A rock picture in the Paleolithic Magdalenian culture Trois Frères Cave, in Ariège, depicts masked and dancing sorcerers driving cattle; one of the sorcerers is holding to his mouth what is frequently described as a vertical flute, although some writers see it as a short musical bow. Certainly at a later date flutes were connected with hunting magic: a prehistoric palette of the fourth millennium B.C. from Hierakonpolis, Egypt, depicts a vertical-flute player disguised as a fox luring wild animals. Flutes have remained decoy instruments ever since—witness the rat catcher of Hamlin, better known as the Pied Piper, of Central European folklore; and their use by bird and game hunters to our day has been so successful that decoy whistles have been proscribed by law in many countries.

Our earliest tangible evidence of flutes is in the form of reindeer phalanges found in Europe and in North America, pierced on one surface, and of other animal bones pierced with blowhole as well as with several round fingerholes. A Stone Age flute of the Aurignacian culture with a rear thumbhole was found at Istoritz in the Basses-Pyrénées; an Iron Age jar of the pre-Roman period found in Jutland contained a deer-tibia fipple flute with square vent and three fingerholes; another Iron Age fipple flute, probably of the late pre-Christian era, was excavated at Malham Moor, Yorkshire; made of a sheep tibia, with two front and one dorsal hole, its mouthpiece shows well-defined tooth marks. (For other early flutes, see panpipes, page 589.) It seems as though Europe had manifested a preference for fipple flutes from the Neolithic on, in contrast to Asia and the Americas, where notched flutes have historically been the more popular.

In the Near East, flutes appear about 2600 B.C. in Sumer as shepherds' instruments. Vertical flutes dating from the Middle Kingdom have been excavated in Egypt, with wide bores and fingerholes spaced far apart. Ancient Egypt had but one word for both flutes and reedpipes (as did the

Greeks later); their flutes were of cane or of metal, 90 to 100 centimeters (ca. 36 to 40 inches) long, with from two to six holes bored at the lower end, blown without benefit of mouthpiece. On monuments they are often shown held obliquely, a position presumably made necessary by their great length, and are set against one side of the player's mouth. The upper end is not visible but can be conjectured as cut off diagonally. An elongated flute stopped at arm's length by the player's right hand is depicted in the New Kingdom tomb of Paatenemheb near Saqqara. Hickman (1961) measured preserved ancient Egyptian flutes showing diameters varying from 1.4 or 1.5 to 1.9 centimeters. Cross flutes remained unknown in Egypt until they were introduced in Roman times (from 30 B.C. on).

Our knowledge of flutes in classical antiquity is both sparse and problematic. When Aristotle speaks of soft-toned aerophones he may be referring to the flute and juxtaposing it to reed instruments, but this is by no means sure. A passage in Apuleius's *Metamorphosis* (second century) definitely indicates the presence of a cross flute: *Tibicines, qui per oblicum calamum ad aurem porrectum dexteram* ("Tibia players with their oblique instrument extended toward their right ear"). Furthermore, references occur to a mysterious *plagiaulos*; this has been identified with pipes such as those found at Meroë in the Sudan, having a short tube set obliquely near the upper end of the main tube (cf. aulos, page 658), the use of which has so far eluded specialists, although several theories have been put forward (one sees a blowhole or blowslit in the aperture of the short tube, another an arrangement for the insertion of a reed). A more plausible explanation of the term (*plagios* means "oblique") is that it denoted a cross flute, such as that appearing on a copy of a late fourth-century B.C. Greek original (not Etruscan, as formerly held). Other representations of the cross flute are found in Etruscan tombs, and terra-cottas of the Greco-Roman period leave us in no doubt as to their existence. The well-known relief head of a musician playing the cross flute dates from the second century B.C. and is taken from an Etruscan urn. Most of these representations are seen held at a slightly oblique angle, deviating somewhat from the horizontal. Apart from the single fourth-century B.C. occurrence, cross flutes do not appear in Greece proper, although they were adopted in Byzantium. The Romans do not appear to have made a great case of vertical flutes, yet they spread them far afield: a bone duct flute with six fingerholes and a one-hole whistle were found during excavations of Roman sites in the Rhineland.

Postclassical European Flutes

During the early part of the Middle Ages only endblown flutes were played, either singly or combined as double and even triple flutes, and in sets forming panpipes. These were joined, in western Europe in the twelfth century, in eastern Europe a little earlier, by the cross flute, an instrument that was to be and remain identified with foot soldiers for several centuries. The principal European flute up to the eighteenth century was the endblown recorder, an instrument subsequently neglected in favor of the now-classical cross flute, but in the later Middle Ages we hear much of the flageolet and the tabor pipe.

The flageolet. Like recorders, flageolets are fipple flutes with an inverted conical bore, contracting but slightly, and flaring for a short distance at the lower end of the tube. They are further characterized by having four front fingerholes and two dorsal thumbholes, and by overblowing the octave.

An endblown whistle flute of Asiatic origin reached the West in the eleventh century and from about 1180 on is called *flageol* in French, later *flageolet*, a name adopted in English. At first it appears to have been a simple pastoral instrument made of willow, for Colin Muset writes in the mid-thirteenth century:

> *Lors m'estuet faire un flajolet*
> *Si je ferai d'un saucelet* [willow]

and Machaut a century later mentions *flajos de saus* ("willow pipes"). But it rapidly gained entrance to more sophisticated surroundings, as may be gathered from the inclusion of a minstrel *Rex flaioletus* in a 1288 list of Philip IV's household officers. Though commonly made of wood or cane, metal was not unknown, for a copper flageolet, decorated and painted, was presented to the king of France in 1385 (*un flageolet de cuivre ouvré et peint que Mgr. donna au roy*). Galpin (1965) reproduces an English fourteenth-century miniature from Queen Mary's Psalter showing a goatherd playing a long vertical flute and stopping the lower end with his hand, just as we see similar flutes played in ancient Egypt. Simple vertical flutes continued to be played, but, apart from the emergence of the recorder, were increasingly relegated to pipe and tabor ensembles (see page 559), and identified with rustic music making in general.

Specific details as to bore and fingerholes are lacking until the sixteenth century. Burney ascribed the invention of the flageolet—that is, presumably, of its transformation—to the Sieur de Juvigny of Paris, who played it in the *Ballet comique de la Royne* of 1581: a short fipple flute with narrow, contracting bore and a beak, four front fingerholes, and two dorsal thumbholes. At any rate, the name "flageolet" has been associated with such an instrument ever since. A few years after de Juvigny's performance, Thoinot Arbeau (1589) writes of the *flageol & fluttot nommé arigot* ("the flageol and *flûtet* called *larigot*"), with its variable number of holes, depending upon size, the best being those with the aforementioned four front and two rear fingerholes. So that by then the old sheep bone, *larigot*, had become identified with the flageolet; and Cotgrave in 1611 could translate *larigot* as "recorder." Exactly a century earlier, Virdung had shown a very short fipple flute terminating in a slight flare, with four front fingerholes, and called it *Russpfeif* (Agricola called it *klein Flötlein mit vier Löcher*, "small four-holed flute"); it seems to correspond to the "little flute" prior to its putative improvement at the hands of the Sieur de Juvigny. An early-seventeenth-century flageolet, presented to the Guild of Saint Sebastian at Lokeren, Belgium, in 1608, is made of sheep bone and has two dorsal holes in addition to four front fingerholes. *Russpfeif* and *larigot* were, we may surmise, other names for the flageolet.

Still a pastoral instrument, it was also played by foot soldiers in the absence of fifes, as Trichet (ca. 1640) reports, and quotes Mersenne to the effect that good players could obtain semitones of the scale by half-stopping the fingerholes, a technique unknown to simple village folk. At that time it was still shorter than the standard flute (i.e., the recorder), and thinner, made of boxwood or of ivory. Pepys mentions it frequently in his diary for 1667 and 1668, shortly before it was superseded in England by the recorder.

By the eighteenth century two types of flageolet existed side by side, the regular and the bird flageolet. The latter was employed for teaching birds, particularly canaries, to sing, had an extremely high pitch, and was made in two sections with very narrow bore. Regular flageolets were longer, made in one piece, provided with a beak, and pitched in D (with low C available by closing all holes and half-stopping the lower aperture with the little finger). For the bird flageolet Grétry suggested writing some *petits airs en canon* ("little airs in canon form") to be taught to several finches, as he thought it would be amusing to hear part-singing by birds. In both types a sponge chamber was interposed between beak and fipple for the absorption of moisture from the player's breath; this is first mentioned in *The Bird Fancier's Delight* of 1717 and is thought to have originated with the bird flageolet. It remained a standard feature of all flageolets from then on.

The regular flageolet assumed an important role in the first half of the eighteenth century as orchestral precursor of the transverse piccolo flute, and was scored as *flautino* or *flauto piccolo* by, among others, Bach and Handel (also by Gluck and Mozart, but the piccolo had come into use in France by 1735).

Around 1750 the beak was replaced by a slender ivory mouthpiece, a short mouthpipe except for its flattened shape. This form subsequently became known in England as the French flageolet, to distinguish it from a new variety brought out by William Bainbridge from 1803 on, actually not a flageolet except in name. Bainbridge specializes in double and even triple "English flageolets"; these are discussed with other multiple flutes on page 586. The true flageolets acquired keys in the nineteenth century, sometimes as many as six, but keyless models continued to be made during the first half of the century. Thereafter, the keyed flageolet was transformed into its modern version, which makes use of the Boehm system of fingerholes and keywork.

Pipe and tabor. Ever since the thirteenth century, a one-man pipe and drum ensemble called pipe and tabor (pronounced "tabber" by purists) had been in use, first in northern Spain and southern France, and spreading in the next century until by the Renaissance it covered most of Europe: a sort of layman's precursor of the fife and drum combinations. Its chief function, that of playing for dances, was noted by Jean de Gerson (d. 1429), who described it as a two- or three-holed pipe joined to a drum. The pipe was known as *galoubet* in Provençal; *galoubet* and drum have historically provided the standard accompaniment for the Provençal *farandole*. In some other areas of southern France, however, the combination was one of pipe and string drum, the *tambourin à cordes*. Such ensembles are frequently depicted with the drum or string drum suspended from the player's left arm, drumstick held in the right hand and pipe in the left hand.

The pipe that formed part of the one-man duet had typically an almost cylindrical bore, two front fingerholes, and a rear thumbhole at the lower end of the tube, whence its familiar French name, *flûte à trois trous* ("three-holed flute"). Its early German name seems to have been *holre* or *holefloyte*, to judge by Ulrich von Lichtenstein's verse:

> *Darnach ein holrblaser sluoc*
> *Einem sumber meisterlich genuoc*

> Thereafter a *holr*-player beat
> A tabor masterly enough

Due to the narrowness of the bore the fundamental is barely obtainable and is not used, so that for practical purposes the scale starts on the second harmonic. An exception is formed by the *flaviol* of the Pyrenees, a very small flute with single fingerhole. As was true of other woodwinds in former centuries, the tabor pipe was, and generally still is, nominally pitched in D, although the *galoubet* has been built chiefly in B (natural) from the beginning of this century, and the Basque *chistu* is in G. All these pipes are devoid of keys.

From the early sixteenth century on the pipe was made in several sizes, and this is still true of the *Schwegel* of German-speaking areas, as well as of the *chistu*. Virdung (1511) illustrates only one size of *Schwegel* and remarks that pipe and tabor ensembles were played by the French and Netherlanders at dances and weddings, as though this were a foreign usage. Praetorius has the English play it; he already knew of two sizes, pitched in d' and g°.

The tabor of the ensemble was a small snare drum, its snare usually placed on the outside of the upper membrane; it was struck in the center of the head, right on the snare. This manner of playing can be followed on the iconography from the thirteenth century on. Occasionally the snare was stretched across the inner side of the membrane. The Provençal *tambourin*, companion to the *galoubet*, was formerly made from a hollowed tree trunk, preferably walnut, but is nowadays built up of slats; it has diminished in size over the years but is still a respectable 70 centimeters (27½ inches) long, with a diameter of 35 centimeters (13¾ inches), the only long drum of pipe and tabor ensembles. The lower and thinner of its laced heads is furnished with a snare. Played in the traditional manner described above, the ensemble is popularly known as the *tutupanpan*, from the sounds of its respective components. At the time Thoinot Arbeau wrote (1589) the *tambourin* was almost two feet long with a diameter of one foot, and snares on the lower head; it was played either with a stick or with the player's fingers. Elsewhere, as stated, the tabor is smaller. All these drums have small vents.

In England such ensembles survived at morris dances, chiefly in Ox-
fordshire, up to the 1860s, when they were replaced by fiddle and concertina. Rockstro, writing on flutes in 1890, recalled having heard "not
long ago" a performance in the streets of London. Today they are still
played in the south of France, and in the Basque country.

The recorder. The classical woodwind of Renaissance and Baroque
Europe was a vertical flute, a variety of flageolet characterized by its
wider, tapering bore, called recorder. Prototypes of the instrument can be
followed back to the twelfth century, and Sachs (1940) saw a flute with
tapering bore on a French miniature of the eleventh century. Known on
the European continent as "flute," later with qualifications derived from its
timbre (*flûte douce, flauto dolce*), or form (*flûte à bec, Schnabelflöte*),
it was called recorder in England by 1388 when the household accounts
of the Earl of Derby, later Henry IV, list *i fistula nomine Ricordo* ("one
flute called keepsake"); a "recorde" is mentioned in *The Squire of Lowe
Degree*, written ca. 1400. "Doucet" or "doucette" are other terms employed in fourteenth- and fifteenth-century English literature. When
Chrétien de Troyes (twelfth century) writes *sonent flaûtes et fresteles* in
his *Yvair, ou le chevalier au lion,* he is referring to recorders and panpipes.
And the *flaustes et traversaines* of Adenet le Roi's thirteenth-century
Roumans de Cléomadès indicate the straight and the sideblown flutes.

At the beginning of the fifteenth century recorders were being made
in several sizes, and at the end of that century the consort included a bass.
Virdung (1511) describes and depicts three sizes: bass f°, tenor c′,
soprano g′; and alto part could, if needed, be played on either tenor or
soprano. Furthermore, all three were built in two sizes, differing in pitch
by one tone, the choice of pitch depending upon the tonality of the
piece to be played (not unlike our C and B♭ clarinets). Silvestro Ganassi
in 1535 also mentions three sizes; his *La Fontegara* is the first tutor for
the recorder and already includes tonguing exercises; the three recorders
he illustrates are wide bored.

Instruments of this time were made of a single "joint," that is, one piece
of wood—commonly boxwood—or ivory, with a beaked mouthpiece, and
had a compass of about two octaves. The bore of Renaissance instruments
tapered slightly to the lower end—during the baroque more markedly so—
and ended in a small flare. Recorders had six front fingerholes and a
thumbhole until about 1470, when a seventh fingerhole was added, first
in Italy, somewhat later in the North, duplicating the little-finger hole in

order to accommodate right- or left-handed players, the unwanted hole being stopped with wax. Its total of nine apertures caused the recorder to become known in France as the *flûte à neuf trous*; Rabelais and Jambe de Fer (1556) allude to it only by this name. Fingerholes were equidistant on all models. Basses had one open key protected by a *fontanelle* (a short barrel or box-shaped cover slipped over the key, leaving only the touch visible) instead of duplicated little-finger holes, an arrangement necessitated by the wider spacing of these holes. Sixteenth-century authors give the fundamentals of the three sizes as $F° c° g°$, but in reality they sounded an octave higher. This custom of notating recorder music an octave lower than it actually sounded has persisted, although today alto and tenor are notated as they sound, and may derive from the fact that due to the paucity of overtones, recorders give the impression of being lower pitched than they are in reality; even Praetorius had difficulty in determining their true sound.

Apparently Italian instruments continued to be built with a wide bore long after it had been narrowed in the northern countries; when Saraceni (1579–1620) copied Caravaggio's *Lute Player* he changed the foreground to include a wide-bore Renaissance recorder, while Dürer's earlier woodcut, *The Men's Bath*, dating not later than the first decade of the sixteenth century, already depicts a recorder with extremely narrow bore. By the middle of the sixteenth century deeper basses were being made, and a contrabass in the Museo Civico of Verona is 2.85 meters (9 feet 3½ inches) long with one key protected by a *fontanelle*, another in the Steen Museum of Antwerp is 2.50 meters (8 feet 2½ inches) long, constructed in two joints, and originally had four keys for taking the compass down to $C°$—both instruments are believed to date from the sixteenth century.

German court records and inventories of the latter half of the sixteenth century mention instruments variously spelled as *Collone, Kolonen, Columnae*. These are recorders in the form of column flutes, endblown, turned on a lathe, and shaped to resemble a miniature column; the vent is disguised by a metalwork cover. The court of Baden-Baden possessed nine such "columns" in 1582; that of Stuttgart had a consort of ten in 1589, probably made in the court's own workshop, which had been founded eleven years earlier and could not keep up with the demands for musical instruments made upon it.

Seven sizes of recorder were being built in the early seventeenth century, as we know from Praetorius; each was constructed in two pitches a tone apart, as theretofore, and the two largest were played with crooks.

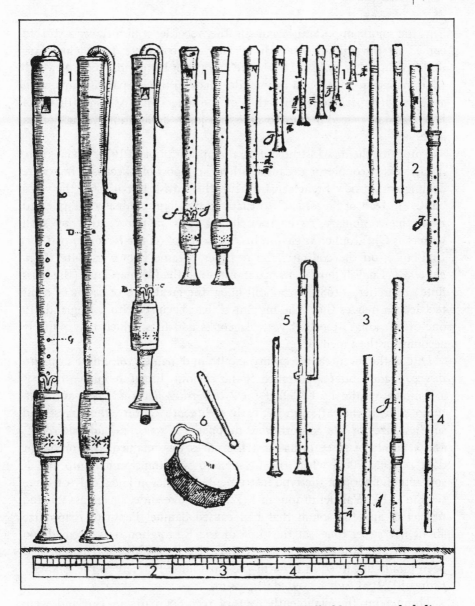

(1) Recorders, a whole consort; (2) *Dolzflöte* [vertically blown recorder] d′ g;
(3) cross flutes, a whole consort; (4) fife; (5) [tabor] pipe, bass and descant;
(6) small tabor, to be used with the [tabor] pipe. From Michael Praetorius,
Theatrum Instrumentorum, 1620. The bass cross flute is printed upside down,
and Praetorius's use of the term *Querflöten* here for cross flutes is in contradiction to his text.

But the most important event in the recorder's history was still to come: in the mid-seventeenth century its complete remodeling was undertaken either by Jean Hotteterre of Paris or by his entourage of wood-wind makers, resulting in a new model made in three separate joints, with a degree of taper about twice that of the older type. As the little-finger hole was now placed in the movable foot joint, duplication was no longer necessary.

Tutors for the new instrument do not appear prior to 1674. About then, or perhaps a couple of decades earlier, and possibly because they were dealing with a new French instrument, the British began using the word "flute" instead of "recorder," so that the old term gradually disappeared from the vocabulary, to be resuscitated early in our century by such writers as Christopher Welch in his *Six Lectures on the Recorder* of 1911. In France, on the contrary, the recorder became known as *flûte d'Angleterre* ("English flute"), in juxtaposition to the German flute (the cross flute). Furetière (1685), who still knew the great bass of seven to eight feet length, relates that "the big flutes" had been sent from England "to one of our kings" together with flageolets and fifes, which may possibly account for the appellation.

Late in the seventeenth century an alto in d′ named voice flute or *flauto di voce* made a brief appearance. So far the only literature known for it is a B-minor quintet by L'Oeillet for 2 *traversi*, 2 *flauti da voce*, and continuo. Shortly thereafter, in the early eighteenth century, the largest and smallest sizes of the consort were dropped (as was the *flauto di voce*), and a family of three or at most four sizes was retained. An important date is "ca. 1700," when the G soprano was transformed into the F soprano and became the type instrument. Mattheson knew only of three sizes in 1713, Walther of four in 1732. But the recorder's compass was too restricted, and the sound that had caused Samuel Pepys to rhapsodize about its "sweet tone" at the time of the Restoration, was deemed too feeble by the latter part of the century. By the 1790s the recorder had been totally discarded in favor of the cross flute. Framéry in the *Encyclopédie* of 1791 already regretted its passing.

Throughout the eighteenth century recorder parts in England were marked *flauto* or flute, just as they were on the Continent, and those for the cross flute were marked *traverso* or German flute. This terminology has caused considerable confusion in modern times, though it was clear enough in an age when the recorder was obsolete but not yet forgotten. An example in point is Busby's *Musical Dictionary* of 1802, where it is stated that the "Common Flute" "was formerly called the Flute a Bec. . . . It is now indifferently called the Common Flute and English flute, partly to distinguish it from the German flute. . . ."

Interest in the straight flute was renewed in the last decade of the nineteenth century (in 1896 a *multiflûte* that could be played either as a recorder or as a cross flute was patented in France) but its revival is due in great part to the efforts of Arnold Dolmetsch (from 1919 on). He took an English eighteenth-century instrument for model, and this type has been in use ever since, although wider bored Renaissance recorders are now produced on the Continent. Modern instruments are bored for two different fingerings, one known as the English fingering, which is that of old recorders, the other as the German fingering, in use in German-speaking countries.

Double recorders are discussed with other multiple flutes, on page 587.

The cross flute. The classical flute of European musical culture from the late Baroque on has been the cross flute. Like so many other European instruments, it came from the East, reaching western Europe under the aegis of Byzantium; there it is depicted in miniatures of the tenth century (Vatican MS graec. 752) and eleventh century (Codex Taphouse 14, Jerusalem Patriarchal Library; both reproduced in Bach-mann [1964]), in both instances held projecting to the right of the player, as they are today (but on an eleventh-century fresco in Kiev Cathedral, a minstrel holds his projecting to the left). Not until the second half of the twelfth century is a transverse flute depicted in the West, first in the *Hortus deliciarum* of Abbess Herrad of Landsberg, where it is called *tibia*. From the thirteenth century on it is mentioned in unambiguous terms; thus Adenet Le Roi's *Roumans de Cléomadès* enumerates *flahutes et traversaines,* and in another passage speaks of *flahutes d'argent traver-saines* ("transverse flutes of silver"). Guillaume de Machaut's *Prise d'Alexandrie* (fourteenth century) distinguishes between *flaustes traver-saines* and *flaustes dont droit joues quand tu flaustes* ("flutes you play straight when you flute"). A *flute traversaine* is recorded in a 1360 inventory of the Duke of Anjou's property. Miniatures of the period, such as in the Book of Hours of Jeanne d'Evreux of 1325, start illustrating cross flutes, yet the English word "floute" did not come into existence until Chaucer wrote it around 1384 in his *House of Fame.*

During the late Middle Ages cross flutes were chiefly identified with military instruments of Switzerland and Germany (see fife, page 571), from which countries they spread abroad under names such as *flûte allemande, flauta alemanna, Schweizerpfeife*. Their acceptance in art music was late, as their shriller and louder sound could not compete successfully with the soft and "sweet" tones of the recorder. Denis (1944) reports that, except for a single Flemish example of the mid-fifteenth century, the cross flute is not depicted in art works west or north of the Alps before 1500. Virdung (1511) knew only the military fife, but a few years later, in 1519, Arndt von Aich's songbook includes *etlich zů fleiten/ Schwegeln/und anderen Musicalisch Instrumenten artlicher zů gebrauchen* ("several for use with flutes, swegels, and other musical instruments"), where *fleiten* indicates recorders, and the swegels probably cross flutes (it is true that *Schwegel* designated the pipe of the pipe and tabor ensembles, but in southern Germany and the Alpine regions it was also the name of the cross flute). Cross flutes were already being built in different sizes, and if we can believe Rabelais, their mastery formed part of a gentleman's education: Gargantua was instructed in *flûte allemande* playing to this end.

Agricola in 1528 describes a family of flutes comparable to those seen in a 1523 drawing of Urs Graf (for details, see fife, page 571): a bass in C, tenor in G, soprano in D, the last of these a forerunner of our concert flute. His indications of woodwind pitches are unusually low and seem to be based on a pitch standard differing by about half an octave from that of later authors (but cf. problems of pitch arising in connection with organ and *viola da gamba*). Perhaps it is well to recall that with all six fingerholes closed the flute sounded d' and hence was said to be a D flute; by successively opening them, a diatonic major scale was produced. Once the C-foot had been added, the lowest tone became c'. Chromatic tones were obtained at first by cross-fingering combined with a flexible embouchure, later by extra holes covered with keys.

The bore of sixteenth-century flutes was cylindrical; they were made in one section and had no provision for tuning, a grave inconvenience. However, the pitch of individual tones could be "raised or lowered at pleasure by means of the fingers that stop the holes, little by little," to quote Salomon de Caus (1615), that is, by the partial opening and closing of fingerholes. Basses were being made in two sections, or joints, by the time Praetorius wrote. Boxwood was still the favorite material for all sizes, although smaller ones were occasionally made of glass: the inventory of Henry VIII's instruments includes "3 flutes of glasse and one painted like glasse in a case of black leather." Later, Mersenne was to include glass among the substances of which flutes were made, and in the nineteenth century two French makers were known for their flutes and piccolos of fine glass (of the quality known as *cristal* in French).

Praetorius's family of flutes (*Querpfeifen*) comprises a bass in g°, tenor in d′ (which he says was also used as soprano), and soprano in a′; thus the soprano of Agricola had become the tenor of Praetorius, and was to remain the type instrument from then on. All of these had a compass of two octaves, and Praetorius gives the type instrument an extra four "falset" tones in the treble, for a total of nineteen tones. By this time the military fife had been differentiated from the flute and each had its own fingering. In addition to these two varieties, Praetorius lists a third, the *Dulzflöte* or *Dolzflöte*, also called *Querflöte* (not to be confused with *Querpfeife*; in German, the word *Flöte* formerly identified vertical flutes, *Pfeife*, on the contrary, horizontal ones). These had the same six fingerholes and nineteen-tone compass as the regular flute (*Querpfeife*) but were sounded by means of a recorder embouchure cut into the back of the tube, on the side opposite the fingerholes (which explains the self-contradictory term *Querflöte*). Two sizes of *Dulzflöte* were made, in d′ and g°, the latter a two-piece instrument. To Trichet (ca. 1640) these were merely modified versions of the *flûte allemande*: *Aucuns font son embouchure par derrière et la tiennent joignant la poitrine pour l'entonner, et non de travers comme les autres flustes d'aleman, afin que par ce moyen les mains puissent plus aisément s'estendre jusques aux derniers trous tandis qu'on embouche* ("Some make its embouchure behind and hold it at the chest to sound it, not transversely like other German flutes, so that by this means the hands can more easily stretch to the last holes while playing"). This passage implies an unwieldy length of the bass flute, requiring an oblique or vertical playing stance, and indeed a late-sixteenth-century bass flute in Verona has a total length of 108.8 centimeters (nearly 43 inches) and is made in two sections; in order to be playable it has to be held in an oblique position.

Flutes of Trichet's day still had the nineteen-tone compass. His contemporary, Mersenne, illustrates a cylindrical instrument the bore of which he measured at 8 lines, or approximately 1.8 centimeters, for a length of some 59.5 centimeters (23 inches), a diameter that has varied very little since (counting the widest part of the bore on conoid flutes).

Growing musical demands made upon the single-jointed soprano in the seventeenth century caused its transformation in the mid-century; from then on it was built in three sections: head, middle, and foot joint. Around 1660 an additional hole was pierced and covered with a closed key for d♯′, placed on the barrel-shaped foot joint. Quantz ascribes this innovation to the French. Then, some twenty years later, presumably due to the efforts of the Hotteterres—an outstanding French family of woodwind makers and players—the bores of middle and foot joints were made conical, contracting toward the foot, while the head joint remained cylindrical. Ornamented with ivory bands, the "new" flute remained in use for over a century. Among the advantages of its conoid bore were greater mellowness of tone, less wind required for its production, and, above all, improvement in intonation of the flute's third octave. Furetière, who died in 1688, did not live to see the new instrument, but writes an obituary on the bass flute: this was double or quadruple the length of the ordinary flute, he states, and because of such a great length, a trombone or serpent was used in its stead.

A new era was inaugurated with the publication in 1707 of Louis Hotteterre le Romain's *Principes de la flûte traversière*, illustrating the conoidal, three-piece flute. Bach first wrote for the *flauto traverso*, the one-keyed flute, in 1717; up to then he had scored only for the recorder. For much of the eighteenth century composers referred to the recorder as *flauto*, and the cross flute was specified by terms such as *flauto traverso*, "German flute," *flûte traversière*. Quantz's great work on flute playing—far more than a mere flute tutor—appeared in 1752, and to him we owe much of our knowledge of the flute's history in the first half of the eighteenth century, and a great deal more about contemporary performance practices in general. He states that some thirty years previously, or about 1720, the foot joint had been lengthened to extend the compass down to c′ and c♯′; the long middle joint was divided into two sections, each provided with three fingerholes. The upper of these two sections, served by the left hand, was interchangeable with one of several *corps de rechange* of slightly differing lengths (Halle in 1764 wrote that some flutes were furnished with six such joints, and Tromlitz in 1791 recommended seven) to accommodate various deviations of pitch. After the flute's lowest tone had been changed to C, it gradually became known as a C flute, yet Samuel Petri (1767) called those flutes best whose D was at chamber pitch (*Kammerton*) D, and for a long time thereafter, flutes were still considered as being in D. The c′ and c♯′ open keys proved detrimental to the flute's tone quality and were abandoned, only to be reintroduced by the Italian flutist Florio in London some sixty years later.

Quantz already knew the cork screw-stopper, and claimed for himself the invention of the wooden head-joint tuning slide (a metal slide came into use a little later); he also caused an extra key to be placed on the foot joint for obtaining E♭ and improvement of intonation of certain other tones. Unlike flutes of other sizes, the "concert" flute was never treated as a transposing instrument, and the transposition of other sizes was calculated from C in every case. These other sizes, as listed by Quantz, were the *Quartflöte*, pitched a fourth lower than the type instrument, an orchestral flute in G called *basse de flûte* in the 1751 *Encyclopédie*; the *flûte d'amour*, a third lower; and the *kleine Quartflöte*, a fourth higher. Nearly extinct nowadays, the *flûte d'amour* has on occasion been made with the Boehm system.

Michel Corrette in his flute method (privilege dated 1735) wrote that in Paris "at present" were being made little octave cross flutes played in *tambourins* as well as in concertos written expressly for flute; among the composers of such concerti he mentions Quantz (who had spent several months in Paris in 1726). This information is in direct contradiction to that of Walther, who identified the *flauto piccolo* or *flautino* with the flageolet in his dictionary of 1732, but presumably the piccolo known to Corrette had not reached Germany by the time he or Quantz wrote. Early piccolos had a single key, later were made in two and even three joints with Boehm keywork; at present the orchestral models have separate head and body joints, with either a cylindrical or a conoid bore.

It seems likely that poor cross-fingerings were responsible for the flute's having become the first woodwind to be endowed with additional chromatic keys. Three closed keys (for f'g♯' b♭'), plus the original foot-joint key, resulted by 1760 in the four-keyed flute; with the reinvented c' and c♯', the six-keyed flute came into existence at about the same time. Once the c² and duplicate long key (f') had been added at the end of the century, the final development of the pre-Boehm flute had been reached.

A favorite woodwind of the eighteenth century, the flute had become so popular by the 1740s that it was fashioned in the form of walking sticks for lovers of the open air; a Dublin maker called them German cane flutes in 1748, and an advertisement appeared in Paris in 1767 for *flûtes en forme de canne*.

Once a flutist had familiarized himself with his flute's fingering system and mastered its vagaries of intonation, he was understandably not prone to experiment with new models, and, due to this conservatism, old keyless flutes continued to be played until the end of the eighteenth century in some areas. Thus an anonymous reviewer could note in the *Allgemeine musikalische Zeitung* of 1799–1800 that the number of flutists who played keyless [*sic*] flutes was steadily decreasing. The same paper had, the year before, pointed out that F, G♯, and B♭ keys existed on the flute—and should be used. But fundamentally the unresolved issue was one of tone quality or, rather, changes in this quality brought about by the manifold improvements combined with a general rise in pitch (in Germany), and in 1801–1802 the same publication accused the new and higher pitch of having transformed the gentle-voiced flute into a shrill military fife. Players had trouble adjusting to the many keys, and the bore, if narrow, was held accountable for weak tone or, if wide, for shrieking tone, and, if even, of rendering the second octave false and utterly unusable. Regarding foreign flutes, the 1825 issue commented that the bore of English and French flutes was so narrow that, although high tones could be produced easily enough, the low tones were very imperfect, as might be observed from the compositions for such instruments. Clearly it was time for Boehm to arrive on the scene.

Theobald Boehm, a Munich flute player, was in London in 1831 when he heard the virtuoso Charles Nicholson play a flute of very powerful tone with some larger than normal holes. Boehm realized that in order to match it he would have to completely redesign his own small-hole model. After much experimentation he produced one year later a revolutionary instrument in which he had systematically incorporated large holes throughout, placing them as closely as possible to the acoustically correct positions, changing the closed keys into open keys, and controlling them by means of rings. After further experiments, Boehm decided to exchange the conoid bore for a cylindrical one, as the greater volume of air would produce a fuller and clearer tone; furthermore, he redesigned the head, to which he gave a parabolic curve, while still larger fingerholes necessitated replacing the rings with padded finger plates (this cylindrical model, introduced in 1847, is still played). His earlier instruments were of metal, later ones of wood. Both are in use today; metal is preferred in America, wood in Europe.

The old bass flute was revived in the eighteenth century, pitched in c°, an octave below the modern concert flute; for bands it is also made in d♭° and e♭°. Both ends of the tube are folded in so that the overall

length is reduced to manageable proportions. However, no really successful model was produced prior to the *albisifono* of Abelardo Albisi of
Milan, brought out in 1910. Albisi's solution to the problem of widely
spaced fingerholes was to build a vertically held body, set the embouchure
in a horizontal tube that looks rather like the letter T, and work the keys
by extension rods. A winding in the upper portion of the tube reduces the
length.

The fife. The Swiss achieved military prestige by the end of the fifteenth
century (their fife and drum corps had already served in the battle of
Sempach in 1386). Swiss mercenaries had accompanied Charles VIII on
his Italian expedition; they formed an integral part of the French and
Italian armies, and, wherever the fighting led them, they were attended
by their fifes and drums, and the *Schweizerpfeife* ("Swiss pipe") was
known, esteemed, described, and depicted from the early sixteenth century on. For centuries the fife and drum corps was as much part of the
infantry as trumpets and kettledrums were of the cavalry, and long after
the mercenary troops had returned home the transverse flute was known
as the German flute or *flûte allemande*. A pen drawing by Urs Graf dated
1523 portrays a quartet of flute-playing *Landsknechte* (lansquenets) with
three of their instruments visible; the bass is twice the length of the
smallest, measuring perhaps 100 and 50 centimeters (40 and 20 inches)
respectively, with a third of intermediate size; one of the players carries
the bag, suspended from his wrist, into which they fit.

Technically, fifes are transverse flutes with a narrow, cylindrical bore,
six fingerholes, historically made of a single piece of wood, and devoid of
keys. Modern versions exist in metal and in plastic and sometimes have
an E♭ key, but differ from older models in that they are far shorter, perhaps half as long as they were in the sixteenth century.

The French word *fifre* does not occur before 1507, and then in connection with a drum, and in 1515 "oone Jacob phipher a drumslade that
was with Sir Thomas Bullayn" received payment at the English court
("drumslade" meant "drummer"). Three fifers and as many drummers
are referred to in the court records of Francis I (d. 1547). Some Renaissance inventories include large numbers of *Zwerchpfeifen* (a corruption
of *Querpfeifen*, "fifes" at this time), and several German courts seem to
have bought them wholesale, doubtless to ensure their being properly
tuned together: a case containing a dozen was purchased for the Württemberg court in 1578, another case of the same amount eight years later.

Thoinot Arbeau (1589) wrote that music for fifes was not notated but that it was improvised according to the rhythm (*cadence*) of the drum.

Details of pitch and compass are not forthcoming until Praetorius informs us that two sizes were in use when he wrote, one with a compass of g' to c³, and a lower-pitched model, d' to a²; the fingering of both differed from that of the flute, he notes. He is careful to distinguish between the *Schweizerpfeife* or fife and the *Querpfeife* or regular cross flute. Some twenty years later Trichet describes the Swiss fife as a short and narrow cross flute sounding louder than the regular flute, with the compass of a 15th (whereas the German flute had a compass of a 19th); it enjoyed a great vogue as a military instrument, but was not admitted as a *dessus* (treble) to the German flute because there already existed a small German flute designed for this purpose (this was the soprano flute, not the piccolo). By the 1660s the fife was admitted to the *ne plus ultra* of mixed ensembles in France: the *grande Ecurie du Roi* comprised twelve *trompettes*, twelve players of *violon, hautbois, saqueboutes & cornets*, three *hautbois de Poitou*, nine players of *phifres, tambourins & muzettes*. It could progress no further.

During most of the eighteenth century the fife's military status was unquestioned. With a two-octave compass, from d' to d³, it was in general use by the 1730s, but, whenever drums and fifes were incorporated into military bands, serious problems of intonation arose, so that bands started employing the *petite flûte* instead of the fife, as the former had a key and was thus less subject to sounding out of tune, if we are to believe the *Encyclopédie* of 1785. Despite this setback, a second size of fife came into use in the late eighteenth century and professional players carried both models. In the nineteenth century the fife was remodeled, given a conical bore and a little-finger hole for E♭, with or without a key, and an all-metal model was introduced. Today fifes are dying out, but can still be heard in all their shrill excitement, complete with E♭ key, in the various fife and drum corps of the Basel *Fasnacht*.

European Folk and Ethnic Flutes

Endblown flutes. The use of animal horn—that of cow, goat, chamois, or deer—for duct flutes reaches back to the Stone Age and long remained particularly important in northern Europe. As primitive fipple flutes that never entered the world of art music we hear of their existence in the fifteenth and sixteenth centuries. Called gait horn ("goat horn") in English, they are better known to organologists by their German name of

Gemshorn (chamois horn). The *Complaynt of Scotland* (1549) contains the earliest known reference to this instrument in English: "ane pipe maid of ane gait horne," and that is just what it was. With fipple inserted at the wide end it was bored for a variable number of fingerholes; Virdung depicts it in 1511 as also having a dorsal thumbhole. Agricola, who largely copied Virdung for the first edition of his book, depicted the *Gemshorn* in 1528, but suppressed it in the last, augmented, version of 1545. Was he no longer interested in folk instruments, or had it become obsolete? It seems to have been last depicted by Bianchini (1742), and then as a curiosity; he shows an instrument with three fingerholes and calls it a deer-bone pipe.

Sachs found an actual instrument in a Berlin arsenal, with six fingerholes and a vent at the tip, some 33 centimeters (13 inches) long, and the Bachhaus at Eisenach formerly possessed one from the Grisons measuring 17 centimeters (6¾ inches) with a single fingerhole.

During the fifteenth century it must have been fairly common, for the *cor de chamois* or *Gemshorn* organ stop existed by Schlick's time (1511). Such animal horns were presumably made and played by goat and cow herders in many areas and over a considerable period of time without attracting undue attention; in fact it has even been suggested (by Becker [1966]) that the *keras* of Pollux was just such an instrument.

Among the most versatile of western European endblown flutes must be counted the Italian *zuffolo*, a short fipple flute known from the fourteenth century on. Traditionally made of boxwood, it was but 8 centimeters (over 3 inches) long, conical in form, terminating in a flare, and with two fingerholes and a thumbhole. Of its total length, close to half (3.8 centimeters) was taken up by the whistle head. Yet on this tiny instrument no fewer than twenty-six semitones could be produced by an expert who knew how to exploit its possibilities to the limit. By blocking the lower aperture wholly or partly with the palm of the hand, and thereby transforming the *zuffolo* into a stopped or a half-stopped pipe, twelve semitones were produced; played as an open pipe, another eight consecutive semitones were obtained, and overblowing the stopped pipe produced six further semitones. Popularized abroad in the nineteenth century with this technique by the virtuoso Picco, it has been known since as the Picco pipe. The partial closing of a flute's lower aperture to change its pitch is a method encountered in many areas of the world. Romanian shepherds have a flute devoid of fingerholes on which they vary the pitch by such means.

A shepherd's flute as remarkable for its great length—about 1 meter (40 inches)—as the *zuffolo* for its shortness is the Slovakian *fuyara;* held vertically, a short, horizontal mouthpipe is inserted at some distance from the upper end so as to bring the fingerholes within the player's reach; it is recognizable at a glance, for the flute projects above the player's head.

Some flutes of the South Slavs are of Islamic origin, as might be expected. Such are the *caval* (*qawūl* further East) and *mali caval* ("little *caval*"). The former is a slender cylinder with a regionally variable number of fingerholes, usually played in pairs by two persons, and hence also made in pairs. Softwood is the material of choice—an exceptional choice for flutes, be it said—beveled at the upper end to form a sharp edge. Once a *caval* is finished, the wood is treated by oiling or buttering the whole instrument. Despite the fact that but little wind is required to play it, tone production is said to be extremely difficult. The fourth finger is never used in playing (cf. the Slavonic *gusle* players, page 477). In duets one performer plays the melody, the other furnishes a drone, or else both may play at the unison, with one flute embroidering the melody of the other. In Yugoslavia as in Turkey *cavals* are instruments of peasants and shepherds. The smaller instrument is in danger of dying out; formerly homemade and of wood, it is now factory made and consists of iron or brass tubing, with a conical bore. Its playing technique is reminiscent of Oriental reedpipe performance practice: constant, uninterrupted sound is produced by breathing while playing, with the oral cavity serving as a wind chamber; performers do not puff out their cheeks but utilize their tongue rather like a piston by its back and forth motions. Both regular and *mali cavals* are fingered with the second joint of the player's fingers, a widespread and ancient custom.

Another flute common to the Balkans and to Turkey is the *duduk.* In southwest Bosnia the tube is conical, but its bore is cylindrical; the mouthpiece is flared and the uppermost of its six fingerholes is never uncovered. Because of its width, the mouthpiece cannot be held by the performer's lips, but must be supported by forefinger and thumb. In this area it does not exceed 40 centimeters (16 inches) in length and is played chiefly by Muhammadans, who hum a deep drone while playing. On the other hand, *duduks* of eastern and southern Serbia attain a length of 1 meter (40 inches), with the top fingerhole bored at one-half of the tube's length. Long models have so narrow a bore that the fundamental octave will not speak at all unless the player utilizes his lower lip as a "beard," a word taken over from organ terminology to indicate a cylinder affixed under the ears of narrow-scaled flue pipes to assist their speech.

Sideblown flutes. As folk instruments of Europe, it is the vertical flute that preponderates by far; cross flutes are encountered less frequently, and then chiefly in the south.

Cane cross flutes are played in Iberian Estremadura, and at the other end of Europe the South Slavs make theirs of maple or chestnut wood and give them a wide, cylindrical bore.

Asian Flutes

Endblown flutes. Endblown flutes have been played in China ever since the twelfth or eleventh century B.C., and in early times were made of marble, copper, or other materials. Later they were associated with Confucian rites and were also welcomed by Buddhists; the flute is seen in the Yunkang, Shensi, Buddhist grotto reliefs of the Southern Wei period (ca. fourth to sixth centuries A.D.). Originally known as *hsiao* or *kuan* (a *kuan* is mentioned about 1100 in a Chinese poem, but see panpipes), we learn of its presence in the eighth century B.C. as a notched flute by the name of *yo*, so called because it measured exactly one *yo*, or Chinese foot (229.9 millimeters). Since it contained twelve hundred grains of millet (*chu*) it is thought to have originally been a grain measure. In addition to the one-foot *yo* there existed instruments of double and also of half this length, sounding an octave lower and an octave higher, respectively. Still at an early stage of its existence it is known to have had three fingerholes and to have become a dancer's instrument; as such it was gradually transformed into a dancer's wand and has served as a wand in ritual dances since the sixteenth century. Modern flutes of the same name are of bamboo, have five fingerholes and a thumbhole, and are notched. This instrument is known in Korea as *yak*; it retains the three fingerholes of the older Chinese type and is exactly one Chinese foot long. Both China and Korea share another form of *hsiao*, the *tung hsiao* (called *thung so* in Korea), which, in addition to four or five fingerholes and one or two thumbholes, has an extra aperture pierced close to the lower end and covered by a thin membrane: a mirliton device to alter the timbre. Finally, the *tai ping hsiao* must be mentioned; this is a whistle flute of bamboo with rear duct: its vent is cut in the back of the pipe opposite the fingerholes and is also furnished with a mirliton membrane (the *suling* of Thailand is another whistle flute with rear duct).

Japan's classical notched flute is the *shakuhachi*, received from China in A.D. 935 by Japanese Buddhist priests. Wide-bored, it terminates in a slight flare, with a lacquered interior permitting it better to withstand moisture from the player's breath. The pitch tone of Japan is taken from

A Japanese *komuso* playing the *shakuhachi*.

the *shakuhachi's* lowest tone, d', at 292 CPS and a standard length of 54.4 centimeters (ca. 21½ inches). Ever since the sixteenth century it has been played by *komuso*, at that time *samurai* who entered the priesthood and roamed through the country with the flute at their lips, and whose modern followers still wear a basket over their heads to escape recognition. This flute is always played by men, even in the *san kyoku* trio of flute, *koto*, and *samisen* that came into being in the nineteenth century. A shorter version, the *hitoyogiri*, first appeared in the Muromachi period (1534–1615), also played by mendicant priests; almost obsolete now, efforts are currently being made to revive it.

In India the classical flute is the cross flute, and the role of endblown flutes remains secondary; they are primarily instruments of herders. Typical of the more primitive varieties is the East Indian *venu*, which attains a length of 130 centimeters (4 feet) and is devoid of fingerholes.

Best known of the Near Eastern flutes is perhaps the *nay*, played over an area extending from Egypt to Iran (and known in the Maghrib as *qasaba*). Elongated and narrow-bored, it is seen on silver artifacts of the Sassanid period (A.D. 226–641) and can also be observed on Persian miniatures of later dates. Today in Iran it is made in different lengths, always of cane, and the traditional manner of playing by holding it between the lips has been changed recently to one in which it is gripped by the teeth, obliquely, on one side of the mouth. Five fingerholes and a thumbhole are usual, and on the larger *nays* a range of three octaves may be obtained.

Sideblown flutes. Cross flutes are depicted from the ninth century B.C. on in China and were probably known earlier. They may have originated in Central Asia. Both in China and in India the transverse flute was an instrument of art music; it appears on a Gandhara stone relief now in Lahore Central Museum, dating from the second or third century; with a very wide bore on Han dynasty (206 B.C.–A.D. 220) reliefs; on those of Borobudur (ca. A.D. 800); and in Andhra, central India, at the same time. Possibly the oldest Asian cross flute is the Chinese *ch'ih*, which originated as a stopped pipe with a central blowhole; in medieval times it had several fingerholes distributed on either side of the blowhole but not in line with it. Today it is an open cylinder of lacquered bamboo. Mahillon's reconstruction, based on sixteenth-century data, led him to conclude that the *ch'ih* had originally been a pitch standard and that it had also formed the basis for standards of length and hollow measures.

Another Chinese flute of great longevity, the *ti*, has a cylindrical wooden tube provided with six fingerholes, an aperture covered by a mirliton membrane next to the embouchure, and several vents. In former ages it was endblown but is now invariably sideblown. On the popular level, the Miao of southern China have six-holed cross flutes that are played by two men in unison when on their way to market in the towns.

Japan's major cross flute, the *riu teki*, was originally made of monkey bone; nowadays it is of bamboo turned inside out so as to have the insulating bark on the inside. The *sei teki* corresponds to the Chinese *ti* and has the same mirliton device.

India's *murali* is said to have been invented by Krishna himself; made of cane and furnished with from three to six fingerholes, it can also be played as a nose flute (see page 585), a characteristic it shares with other cross flutes of the subcontinent.

African Flutes

Endblown flutes. The North African *qawal* or *qawūl* (the *caval* of the Balkans), distributed over an area that extends from Turkey to Morocco, may well be descended from the ancient Egyptian flute. This may also be true of the *qasaba* of the Maghrib, with its five or six fingerholes placed in two groups, the only aerophone admitted to Arabic art music, about 70 centimeters (27½ inches) long, with a compass starting on the second harmonic. Berbers play their *qasaba* from one side of the mouth, with the flute reaching obliquely to the player's right. Those of Morocco are built in a number of sizes to conform to the pitch of the voice they may accompany.

Further south, endblown flutes are often blown in sets. Thus in Ethiopia a metal flute devoid of fingerholes is played in sets of three at dances, sometimes together with other instruments; in the southern part of the country they are also made of wood. In Uganda a stopped, endblown flute, also devoid of fingerholes, is made and played in sets of eight or even more. Bashi cattle herders of Ruanda make a notched flute of cane with two fingerholes near the lower end, fingerholes and notch obtained by burning; the flute's potentials are exploited to the full, for a compass of three octaves is obtainable, with seven tones to the octave; performers sing while they play (cf. simultaneous humming and playing in Yugoslavia, page 574). Similar flutes in Uganda are connected with the royal court. In the Congo basin, endblown flutes yielding but two tones are used at the hunt and as signal instruments; in South Africa stopped flutes may be made of bird bone, horn, hardwood, are often conoid and always small, with at most two fingerholes. The South African Karanga also have a two-holed flute whose performers sing while playing. Among the Sotho of South Africa it is an appurtenance of witch doctors. By contrast, shepherds and boys among the Bahaya of Tanzania play a horn whistle-flute having eight fingerholes.

Sideblown flutes. Cross flutes in Negro Africa serve for personal music making; Kenya cattle herders make ephemeral flutes from a stalk, furnish them with up to six fingerholes, and then throw them away shortly after use. More durable specimens are made of wood, often decorated with burned-in designs. Conoid cross flutes are found on the west coast (Sierra Leone), and in South Africa cross flutes may be either open or stopped and have up to four fingerholes. But in general the endblown flute seems to be preferred on this continent, perhaps because its musical possibilities are more flexible and less limited than those of the cross flute.

American Flutes

Endblown flutes. Flutes of South American Indians form an exception to the rule that all early or primitive flutes have equidistant fingerholes, for the notched flutes found in Peruvian tombs and dating from the beginning of the Christian era have unequally spaced fingerholes. Prehistoric Peru also had a flute, found elsewhere only in the Pacific (where it is still played), resembling a sea cucumber. This strange shape is halfway between a tubular and a vessel flute, and its occurrence on the South American continent is just one piece of the puzzle anthropologists are trying to solve, to wit, that of contact in pre-Columbian times between the peoples of Oceania and those of South America.

Notched flutes of ancient and modern Peru, of Bolivia, the Chaco, and along the Amazon, are known as *quena* or *quenaquena*. Poma de Ayala, the early-seventeenth-century chronicler, relates that the *quenaquena* or the *pinculo*—another flute—participated in all native festivals, always played by a man. Another ancient flute was the Aztec *tlapiztali*, a small, beaked whistle flute sometimes referred to as the "Aztec flute." Made of bone or clay, with or without fingerholes, those of clay usually had an elongated beaked mouthpiece and terminated in a disklike flare, not unlike that of the auloi seen on Etruscan frescoes. Ancient Central American clay flutes, usually provided with a single fingerhole, were sometimes modeled into shapes of animals or flowers or grotesque forms. Modern instruments of that region are not made of such traditional materials as cane, but bird bones are formed into small whistle flutes, or else animal skulls are fashioned into flutes by lengthening them by means of bird bones. Mention must be made of the whistle flute *pito*, about 30 centimeters (1 foot) long, with narrow bore, played in South America as a one-hand flute together with a small drum, exactly as the European pipe and tabor are played. Opinion is divided as to whether this strange combination is indigenous or not, but we know that panpipes and drums were played in a similar manner in pre-Incan times (see panpipes, page 594).

Among the organologically more interesting of North American Indian flutes is one of the Yuma of Arizona; made of cane, a natural node is left intact about halfway of the length to act as a baffle, and an aperture is cut between this and the upper end, partially wrapped with a piece of brown paper tied on with a string—an internal duct formed by the baffle and exterior cover. A cane flute of the Papago similarly has a central node left intact; here small holes, two in number, are pierced in the wall, one on each side of the node and connected on the surface by a groove. The player's forefinger is placed on the groove, thereby creating a duct, and is left there as long as the flute is played, while three finger-holes at the lower end furnish melodic possibilities.

Sideblown flutes. Cross flutes from the Chimú culture have been excavated from the coastal area of northern Peru, and are also figured on Chimú stirrup jars (of perhaps A.D. 1100–1450). In our times they continue to be played in South America, made of cane. Among the Umutina of the Mato Grosso, cross flutes are reserved for their death ceremonies: made of a cane segment, each flute has a small, rectangular blowhole below which a portion of the wall is cut away; this aperture is covered more or less by the player's right hand, according to the pitches desired, and these are obtained by a series of glissandi. As is true of all musical instruments of the Umutina, this is held by one hand only.

Flutes of the Pacific

Endblown flutes. Both endblown and sideblown flutes are played in this huge area, often intimately connected with rite or ceremony, and they may even constitute a bride-price. Thus Margaret Mead reports (1949) that among the Mundugumor of New Guinea, if a man lacks a sister to give in exchange for a wife, he will have to pay a valuable flute for her, resulting in a situation in which the symbols of male cult become equated with women and are nearly as valuable as are the latter. Elsewhere on

New Guinea, among the Arapesh, women flee when the flutes are installed.

Endblown flutes are ductless in this whole region; the *ki*, a whistle flute of the Marquesas Islands, is exceptional in this respect and is thought to be of European origin.

Some highly characteristic endblown flutes of the New Zealand Maori present the appearance of ornate sea cucumbers; they are made of stone, wood, or whale tooth (ivory). The tube of these instruments is conical with a tapering bore, the exterior rounded and finely carved, and a very short upturned neck bears the blowhole. Short and squat, they measure up to 12½ centimeters (5 inches), with a diameter of 3 centimeters (1¼ inches). Although the presence of this type of flute is now restricted to New Zealand, prehistoric specimens, albeit longer ones, have been found in Peru, as noted on page 579. A longer Maori flute, also ovoid with the widest part of the bore in the middle, is made of wood that has been split and hollowed; usually it has a single large central fingerhole carved to resemble a human mouth, and the stopping of this hole brings about a change in pitch; it is said to produce a booming sound. The Maori have also a carved flute that has been hollowed by fire, or split and hollowed, if made of wood—it is also made of bone—and played by men only with the object of attracting women. Ingenious, but at the other end of the scale of sophistication, is a trumpet of the Solomon Islanders made of two cylindrical tubes that doubles as a vertical flute.

Elongated, narrow-bored flutes, stopped at the lower end, are sacred in Papua, taboo to women, and played in pairs. With very great effort, three tones can be produced. The performer grasps the upper end of his flute with both hands, with thumbs lying along his cheeks, and blows into his hands; a U-shaped slot is cut from the top. In West New Guinea a one-holed vertical flute of the Ye-Anim can be coaxed by a local flutist to render a melody containing five different tones by the technique of half-stopping the fingerhole, stopping the lower end, and overblowing.

Sideblown flutes. Cross flutes of the Pacific vary widely. The Maori of New Zealand play a three-holed wooden transverse flute; in Polynesia cross flutes occur as double flutes (see page 589), either mouthblown or noseblown, and in Melanesia they are nearly always ceremonial. Typical are those played on New Guinea in pairs of unequal lengths, the longer considered male, the shorter female, and played antiphonally by men only. A ceremonial cross flute of the Kamaon and Sepik river areas of

New Guinea is connected with male initiation rites and always played in pairs, every family of the region possessing its own pair. Two varieties are made, one without fingerholes. On these the pitch is varied by lip tension and also by hand-stopping the lower end; the other model, a stopped flute, is often decorated with a sculptured head and has a single fingerhole. Some flutes of the Middle Sepik area have a large blowhole that can be made smaller by inserting the forefinger; this procedure facilitates the pairwise tuning. Other Melanesian cross flutes are up to 2 meters (6½ feet) long, with relatively narrow bore, emit but a single tone, and serve as drones; when played in sets of three, two players blow while the third takes a breath, hence uninterrupted sound is made possible while accompanying songs or death lamentations.

Whistles

Whistles are an extremely ancient form of flute: short, stopped pipes with ducts, they are devoid of fingerholes and yield only one tone. Sometimes a captive pellet or a pea is placed in the interior in order to create a trilling effect.

In the older European literature, whistle is synonymous with decoy whistle, as made for and by hunters and bird catchers to imitate specific sounds or calls of the game. As long ago as the thirteenth century we hear of precious metals being employed in France for the making of such *sifflets*. Bird decoys such as quail pipes also existed in other parts of the world—in China, for instance. Tibetans still have a signal whistle that is taken completely into the mouth in order to be sounded.

African whistles are sometimes made of horn, that of antelope, gazelle, and so on. Horn whistles are blown in South Africa to call dogs, and a sideblown whistle of the Wasongola of the Congo basin chases away evil spirits and is worn around the owner's neck as an amulet.

In America, effigy whistles of pottery were found in the Guatemala highlands dating from the late classical period (A.D. 700–1000); ancient Mexicans also possessed pottery whistles, a number of which have been found, some with enclosed clay pellet. The Sioux made bone whistles in modern times with a block of resin serving as fipple.

Aeolian pipes. Whistles sounded by the wind, known as Aeolian pipes, are found in China, Southeast Asia, and the New Hebrides. Some pipes are stationary—attached to a tree or building—others are mobile. A favorite form of the mobile variety is the pigeon whistle, a small pipe appended to the tail of a pigeon in order to discourage attack by birds of prey while it is in flight. In China such whistles may be tubular or globular, the former of bamboo, the latter of dried fruit husks or gourds with the top cut off and replaced by a whistle. Sometimes multiple whistles are made, with as many as fifteen tiny pipes disposed in three rows, or a number of smaller pipes are attached to the main pipe, causing the pigeon's flight to produce several pitches simultaneously.

Highly sophisticated forms of Aeolian pipe are found in Southeast Asia, one of which is the *bulu parinda* of Bali, Borneo, Java, and the Malay Peninsula, a large composite pipe hung in a treetop: a bamboo pipe up to 11 meters (33 feet) long with a longitudinal slit as well as several cross-slits. Analogous is the *bulu ribut* of the Orang Besiri and the Orang Mentera of the Malay Peninsula, actually a sort of Aeolian organ, since it consists of a series of stopped bamboo pipes, up to 8 meters (26½ feet) in length, furnished with slits of differing lengths and breadths, suspended from the highest treetop. Also on the Malay Peninsula, stopped pipes with beveled upper ends are attached to a device resembling a windmill, to be sounded by the breeze.

Flutes with External Ducts

Not all duct flutes have the duct situated internally; some have an external duct. The most common form of the latter is the ring flute, but it is by no means the only one. A stopped flute of Lithuania, for instance, has two saddlelike projections at its upper end, one for the player to rest his lips against, the other to create a sharp edge against which he directs his breath.

Ring flutes have an external duct chamfered in the wall and a ringlike sleeve tied around it. Such flutes are found in Asia and America. Celebes Islanders make theirs of bamboo, cut a hole below the upper terminal node, and then knot a piece of pandanus leaf around the aperture, leaving an air duct; they then add a bell of spirally wound leaf and four equidistant fingerholes. Concerning Java, Kunst wrote (1949) that the most popular solo instrument there was the ring flute *suling*. This is also of bamboo, with a notch cut at the upper end through both the terminal node and the tube, over which a bamboo ring is then tied, and from four to six fingerholes added. On Borneo the Land Dayak sometimes place the duct on the rear wall, that is, opposite the fingerholes. Further west, Nicobar Islanders play their ring flute as a nose flute, and in northern Burma a wax block may substitute for the usual bamboo ring.

A unique ring flute of the Indian Hopewell culture was excavated in 1959 and has been dated to about A.D. 200. Probably used in connection with funeral ceremonies, it is made of a human female radius; a vent is cut in the surface near the top, immediately below a copper ring; the decorated tube is devoid of fingerholes. In South America the ring itself is made of different materials, such as leather or bark, or the flute may have a wooden projection in which a gutter is cut to serve as a windway. Moliton Indians of the Colombia sierras play flutes that are 110 centimeters (43 inches) long, and set their external duct obliquely in order to be able to hold the flute at an angle convenient for reaching the fingerholes.

Piston Flutes

Piston flutes have adjustable plungers inserted in the lower end of the tube, and the pitch is varied by moving this in and out. As toys they are known in Europe, where they nowadays imitate the warbling of birds and hence are also called bird warbles. When automatic bird organs were built in the eighteenth century, their single pipe was a piston pipe; of the bird organ's two ratchet wheels, one controlled the wind supply, the other acted on the piston, both by means of connecting levers. Pierre Jacquet-Droz produced an automatic warble in about 1752 that gave an excellent imitation of trills and warbles.

Simple piston flutes are also played in parts of Asia, Africa, and the Pacific. Fingerholes, of course, are absent. Among the Papuans, piston flutes reach enormous proportions; they may be up to 2 meters (6½ feet) long, and are cult instruments, played at circumcision rites. The Tswana of South Africa make piston flutes of cane and use them as signal instruments, while on the Indian subcontinent and in parts of Indochina they are mere warbles.

Pointed Flutes

These curious instruments are found among buffalo hunters of Timor, Indonesia: wooden flutes with a doubly notched mouthpiece, barrel-shaped upper portion tapering to a near point at the lower end. Exactly the same instrument is encountered in parts of the "xylophone belt" of Africa, in Nigeria and East Africa, where they are made of many materials, including horn, and played either singly or in sets. Among the Lango of Uganda they are played in sets of five, made either of horn or its imitation in clay; each flute has three fingerholes. Other peoples in the same country have conical, wooden pointed flutes, and cut a cup mouth-piece in the upper end (for another aerophone with similar mouthpiece cut in the upper end, see cornett, page 773); the bottom tip is cut off and the extremity pierced with a small hole.

Nose Flutes

Any flute blown with nasal, rather than with oral, breath is termed a nose flute. And any form of flute can be sounded in this manner; thus the only common feature of nose flutes is their mode of playing. Indeed, many are sounded both as nose and as mouth flutes. Although they are, or were until quite recently, found on every continent, they are far more common in the Pacific than elsewhere (in Europe they occur only in Macedonia, except for the ubiquitous sheet-metal toy).

Nose flutes in Asia are found almost exclusively offshore, from the Nicobar Islands, where ring flutes are played nasally, west through Indonesia. The major exception to this distribution pattern is constituted by the Indian subcontinent, where a double flute is blown indiscriminately as a mouth or as a nose flute, and where cross flutes are also played nasally. In Africa a Congolese endblown nose flute is devoid of fingerholes, but modifications of pitch are obtained by partly stopping the lower end of the tube. On the South American continent, the Paressi-Kabishi of Brazil glue two gourds together to form a globular nose flute and provide it with two fingerholes. The Jivaro, better known for their head-hunting than for their flute-playing propensities, have a nose flute stopped at both ends of the tube, which reaches about 60 centimeters (2 feet) in length.

But the Pacific is the nose-flute investigator's realm of choice. In Melanesia and Polynesia the nose-blown flute has, in addition to its function as a musical instrument, great significance in ritual and in field-fertilizing ceremonies. In this area particularly it forms a link in the chain of many fertility traditions connected with the nose, for nasal breath is held to contain the soul. On some of the islands, and notably on Sarawak, the nose flute assists in that most mundane of rites—courtship. Details of its various playing techniques vary regionally: in Polynesia they are usually blown with the right nostril, in Melanesia with the left. But the overall manner of playing remains the same: as only one nostril is engaged, the other is either plugged up or closed by the player's hand while the fingers of that same hand are employed in stopping any fingerholes that may be present; some flutes have none.

As a rule, fingerholes of nose-blown flutes are smaller than those of mouth-blown ones, and the blowhole of transverse nose flutes is placed closer to the end; endblown flutes are held obliquely. A transverse flute is made on many Polynesian islands from a bamboo internode closed at both ends, with a blowhole pierced near the end; several fingerholes are then placed halfway down the tube, around its circumference. A similar instrument is known in Melanesia; in New Caledonia it can attain a length of 1 meter (40 inches). Globular flutes seem to be the preferred form of nose flute in Hawaii, where they are made of gourd or of calabash. The Maori of New Zealand formerly had an endblown nose flute of wood or of human bone, made in a variety of sizes and bores; those destined to become nose flutes were given a cylindrical bore.

MULTIPLE FLUTES

Double flutes fall into one of several categories: (1) those having parallel, connected pipes, usually with a duct, such as are found in Europe, Asia, America, and the Pacific; (2) double vertical flutes without duct, found in Africa; (3) double cross flutes. The last are played in Asia, Africa, and the Pacific. Typically they are of bamboo, either stopped at each end, with internal node and blowhole on either side of the node, or else they have open ends, one or both of which are closed by the performer's fingers, and a central blowhole. Acoustically the flutes of all these categories can be divided into those consisting of melody and drone pipe, and those permitting the simultaneous playing of two tones at different pitches; the latter are called chord flutes. A further form of multiple flute, the panpipe, is discussed separately.

Multiple Flutes in Europe

Double flutes have been played intermittently from the Middle Ages on in Europe. A passage from Machaut's *Prise d'Alexandrie* (fourteenth century):

> *Et de flajos plus de x paires*
> *C'est a dire de xx manieres*
> *Tant fortes comme des legieres*

> And more than ten pairs or twenty manners of flageols,
> Both loud and soft

seems to bear irrefutable testimony to their existence in his day. Tinctoris (ca. 1484) mentions in passing the use of double *tibiae* for performing two parts of a composition (an ambiguous term, however, for the Romans called their aulos, a reed instrument, *tibia*). But a little earlier, in 1457, payment was made to the player of a double flute, according to the household accounts of Charles the Bold, and in 1596 double flutes (*Doppelflöten*) participated with other instruments in a procession at Kassel on the occasion of the baptism of the landgrave's little daughter. From the sixteenth century we have two double recorders, one preserved at All Souls College, Oxford, made of a single block of wood, with shorter and longer connecting pipe and a common blowhole; another is in the Landesmuseum of Zurich, with equal fingerholes. And in the seventeenth century the musical diarist Samuel Pepys mentions "two pipes of the same note fastened together, so I can play on one and then echo it upon the other."

With respect to early pictorial materials we are on less sure ground, as the instruments are generally not clear enough to enable us to be sure of their means of tone production. Yet double recorders are recognizable in Simone Martini's scene from the life of Saint Martin (first half of the fourteenth century) in San Francesco Church, Assisi, with their beaked ends, held in divergent position, with one hand on each pipe; on a British fourteenth-century miniature (Brit. Mus. 10 E IV) reproduced in Galpin (1965), with pipes of equal length splayed apart, one hand on each pipe; on a Florentine engraving ascribed to Baccio Baldini (ca. 1470), titled *Music*; and equally unequivocal are those of Girolamo de Benvenuto's *Ascension of the Virgin* (ca. 1500), parallel pipes with shorter right-hand pipe. Double pipes shown in the sixteenth century appear to represent double reedpipes, and the double flute, one gathers, disappeared from western Europe at that time. However, it has remained very much alive in the Balkans to this day.

Chord flutes in the West have played a minor yet popular role in the diversion of their owners; the Brussels Conservatoire collection houses one dated 1717 with pipes of unequal length; a later specimen has pipes of even length and paired fingerholes, but one duct is longer than the other, causing the pipe to sound in thirds. Double and even triple English flageolets were made by William Bainbridge of London in the early nineteenth century, fabricated from a single block of wood and furnished with a single mouthpiece. His double flageolets were usually played in parallel thirds or, by overblowing the right pipe, in sixths; the added third pipe of his triple flageolets was a drone.

Parallel connected double-duct flutes are still popular among South

Slavs, whose playing techniques may represent or approximate medieval practices. The double *svardonica* of the Serbians consists of a single block of wood divided for half its length so as to form two pipes—a cross between divergent and parallel pipes—with paired fingerholes (a pair can be stopped with one finger) tuned very slightly apart so as to produce beats. In Herzegovina, the *dvogrle* has almost parallel bores, with tubes connected for the greater part of their length and sharing a common mouthpiece. This instrument is always held on the left side of the player's mouth so that the left pipe receives more wind than does the right, and thus sounds louder. *Dvogrles* are either played in parallel seconds with the same fingering for both hands, or else in unison with one pipe often serving to embroider the melody (double reedpipes of this area are played in the same manner). Different forms of the *dvoynice*, another flute, are played—chiefly by shepherds—all over Yugoslavia, always made from a single piece of wood; in Bosnia they are held on one side of the mouth, like the *dvogrle*, and for the same reason. Mostly such pipes are played with symmetrical fingerings, producing a series of parallel seconds, but some players have learned to use their hands independently. When accompanying dances, a drone may be hummed by the performer.

In all these areas the flutes assume a flat form, but in Dalmatia they are rounded and held at the center of the mouth so that both pipes can receive the same amount of wind. Another variety known in Serbia has six fingerholes on one pipe but none on the other, as it is a drone tuned to the second hole of the melody pipe. Croatian and Slavonian double flutes sound in parallel thirds, with the right-hand pipe always playing the upper voice. Traditionally these flutes are built in slightly divergent forms; only in Herzegovina are they parallel. Croatians furthermore have triple and quadruple flutes, played with the same technique as the *dvoynice*. The *troynice* has four fingerholes on the right bore, three on the center bore, none on the left bore, as this is a drone. Neither of these two instruments has reportedly become integrated as a folk instrument.

Among other areas of eastern Europe in which double flutes are still known to exist are Lithuania, the Smolensk *oblast* of the Soviet Union, and Bulgaria.

Multiple Flutes Outside Europe

Double flutes of Asia are distributed over areas north and east of India. In northern India, two single flutes are tied together to form double vertical flutes, and at least one form is also blown as a nose flute. Further north, in Tibet, two or even three whistle flutes are united in the same fashion, chiefly in pastoral areas. On the island of Flores, divergent equal flutes and long triple pipes with central drone are played together. China still knows divergent flutes, her only form of double pipe. The double flute of Japan, made of bamboo tubes glued together, is now played only by blind masseurs to announce their presence. Double cross flutes made by the Naga of Assam consist of a single long bamboo segment with central node, stopped at both ends by terminal nodes. The two stopped flutes thus created are a fifth apart in pitch; both are devoid of fingerholes.

This same type of double flute is played in the Transvaal, also stopped at both ends, with blowholes on either side of the central node, but here the flutes have three fingerholes spaced close to each end. Short double whistles of the Zulu and Xhosa peoples, made in imitation of the European police whistle, according to Kirby, sound an interval varying from a minor sixth to a major seventh.

Double whistles of clay, and even double whistling pots, have been found in Mexico, dating back to pre-Aztec cultures. They yield the interval of a second. Nowadays double flutes of cane are played in Bolivia, made of a long and a short tube. But the real country of multiple flutes is the Northwest Coast, where stopped whistles with up to six pipes are known. Standardization of form is nonexistent here: a piece of tree root 25 centimeters (10 inches) long is transformed into a trapezoidal triple whistle, or a slightly flared piece of wood may terminate in two short whistles, while the flare itself is pierced left and right by the heads of another two flutes. A different but no less interesting form of multiple flute is in use among the Suisi of northwestern Brazil, who take a cane segment of about 170 centimeters (5 feet 7 inches) in length, leaving its nodes intact so as to form five sections; in each of these a rectangular blowhole is cut, resulting in a quintuple flute. All five flutes are blown simultaneously by as many men during certain dances.

Double transverse flutes are played in several areas of the Pacific. Among the Fijians they assume the form of a stopped bamboo internode with blowhole pierced near each end. On a number of the Polynesian islands double flutes are sounded as nose flutes, and the Maori of New Zealand have a conoid flute called *pu torino* that they make both as single and as double flute.

Panpipes

A story is told of the god Pan, an inhabitant of rustic Arcadia: one day he pursued the nymph Syrinx, who fled to the river Ladon and became transformed into a reed in order to escape from him. Unable to distinguish her from other reeds, Pan cut several at random and formed them into a panpipe; some people call it syrinx. And to this day the panpipe remains nothing more than a set of vertical tubes of different lengths, tuned to a scale (except in South Africa among the Pedi) and joined together: a laborious and primitive equivalent of the single-fingerhole flute. Usually the tubes are stopped at the lower end. They are devoid of fingerholes and are blown across the upper ends; occasionally the rims are notched or beveled.

Organologists distinguish between those bound in raft form (raft pipes) —the more common variety—and those tied in a bundle (bundle pipes). Most raft pipes form a single row, but some may be arranged in two rows, one behind the other, in which case one row is generally stopped while the other is open. A large variety of materials has been employed in the making of panpipes, from a set of bird bones or simple canes cut so as to be stopped by a natural node, to a single block of wood or of stone from which all pipes are carved. Panpipes are found on every continent and in the Pacific area.

European panpipes. The earliest panpipes known so far are those removed from Neolithic cemeteries of the southern Ukraine, consisting of bird bones. One from Zhdanov, near Kiev, had seven or eight such pipes, decorated, and of different sizes, the longest measuring 10 centimeters (4 inches) with a 1.5 centimeter diameter: they have been dated to between 2300 and 2000 B.C. Another set of (undecorated) bird bones, composed of pipes varying from 12 centimeters to 5.5 centimeters in length, has been excavated at the village of Skatovka in the Saratov Region of the Volga and is said to have been assembled in the early second millennium B.C. From the cemetery of Przeczyce in Polish Lusatia comes a nine-tube panpipe of sheep or goat bones, dating from the eighth century B.C. (Four bone pipes found in Charente, France, hitherto believed to represent the oldest extant panpipes are no longer considered to be a musical instrument.) The earliest known Central European panpipes are of the late La Tène period.

Outside the zone of Hellenic culture panpipes were unknown in the ancient Near East (the Cycladic panpipes hitherto thought to date from the second half of the third millennium B.C. are now recognized as a fake). A fragment of a pottery figurine in the Louvre found on Cyprus and dating from the fifth century B.C. portrays a broken syrinx on which no more than parts of three pipes are left. In Greece proper the syrinx was connected with pastoral life, to judge by its occurrences in literature (e.g., Theocritus's shepherd songs); it formed a rectangle, usually with seven pipes, but as few as three and as many as thirteen have been depicted on art objects, and, although the pipes are all of the same length in appearance, we can assume the bores to have been graduated. Homer already knew it. A nine-tube panpipe is portrayed on the François Vase, a Greek krater painted about 570 B.C. and found in an Etruscan tomb at Vulci.

Although some makeup boxes in the form of a syrinx originated in the New Kingdom, panpipes were not played in Egypt until they were introduced under the Ptolemies at the end of the fourth century B.C. A thirteen-pipe specimen found in the Faiyûm, now in Alexandria, has a compass of $f\sharp^2$ to $d\sharp^4$.

During Hellenistic and Roman times the tubes are stepped, and they are also portrayed in this form by the Etruscans. Italic and Etruscan *situlae* from the late sixth century B.C. show five and six pipes, evenly stepped. The Romans called their syrinx *fistula*, and bequeathed both instrument and name to the alien peoples of their empire. A third century *patera* from Rennes shows a seven-pipe *fistula* irregularly stepped; an instrument with seven pipes carved out of a single block of wood was found in Roman Alisia (then Celtic Gaul, now Alise in the Côte d'Or), said to sound a diatonic scale. A comparison of other Gallo-Roman panpipes shows that all had a characteristic form, namely that of a rectangle with one lower corner cut off diagonally. Terra-cotta panpipes of this shape have also been found in the Roman Rhineland. During the entire period of antiquity only single-row pipes are depicted and have been excavated so far.

As pastoral instruments, it was perhaps natural that panpipes should pass into Christian iconography at an early date in the hands of the Good Shepherd himself. So depicted, and with a single sheep for audience, they appear on a Latin Christian epitaph of the fourth century (for the Orpheus-derived Good Shepherd playing the *kithara*, see page 366). Later, during the Dark Ages, when information flows so sparsely, the *fistula* continues in existence, and by the eleventh century emerges with its pipes stepped regularly in one continuous gradation. A nine-tube panpipe is played by the god Pan himself in an eleventh-century manuscript of Hrabanus Maurus's *De universo*, but, from the middle of the century on, panpipes appear in the more formal entourage of King David portrayed as a musician; thus in a Catalan psalter of that period one is being sounded in his presence, and in a psalter at Ivrea, also from the eleventh century, King David has become a shepherd and is playing them himself. In a twelfth-century French psalter at Cambridge, musicians are separated into two groups, one sacred, surrounding King David, the other profane, and it is among the sacred instruments that the panpipes are shown. The association with David continues in the iconography of the thirteenth century.

Meanwhile the instrument was flourishing in more worldly hands, and from the twelfth century on was known in French as *frestel*. Henceforth it was to be an instrument of village and countryside, of herdsmen and—in France and Spain—of itinerant tinkers, pig gelders, and the like, who signaled their presence by sounding their pipes. By the late nineteenth century panpipes in Europe were played only in rural areas and by a few ambulant musicians—typically, for example, by those of the English Punch and Judy shows. In Italy, in the villages of the Milanese countryside, bands of fifteen to twenty panpipers played during carnival to the accompaniment of bass drum and cymbals. Today the instrument survives in Europe as a child's toy or as a decoy for bird catchers (cf. Mozart's use of the panpipe in *The Magic Flute*).

European panpipes are always stopped, always in raft form, always consist of a single row of pipes. These are usually arranged in one continuous gradation, but in Slovenia they are also made in pyramidal form with the longest pipe in the center, and in Romania *nais* with a large number of pipes are assembled so as to form a concave curve at their upper end. Gypsy *nai* players of Romania can modify the pitch of a given pipe by about a quarter tone when partially covering the rim with their lips and tilting the instrument. To change the tonality of a set they insert shot or little balls of wax into the bores so as to shorten them by the required amount. In fact, all sorts of mechanical techniques are in use, both in Europe and in other parts of the world. In the Balkans, for instance, two players will form a duet, one playing the melody proper and the other adding a second voice on a lower-pitched instrument.

Asian panpipes. But the two areas where panpipes reach their highest state of development are East Asia and South America. Occurrences of similar or closely related musical instruments among East Asians and Amerinds are so marked that the possibility of coincidence is no longer considered. Panpipes are a case in point.

The ancient *pai hsiao* of China was a Confucian ritual instrument; its open notched pipes were arranged in raft form, with the shortest pipe in the center and the remainder placed in symmetrically stepped groups of *yang* (male) and *yin* (female) tones to either side. The precise number of pipes varied with the dynasties. Traditionally its form is said to have represented a phoenix with spread wings, and its tones those of the phoenix's voice. Still played in modern China, the *pai hsiao* now has sixteen pipes set in a decorative container, irregularly stepped on both sides, with the shortest pipe still in the center. The ascending pipes on the left emit *yang* tones, the descending ones on the right, *yin* tones, in a whole-tone sequence from a♭° to b¹:a°b°c♯′d♯′f′g′a′b′a♯′g♯′f♯′e′d′c′b♭°a♭°. This arrangement represents the junction of two originally separate sets of pipes; nearby, among the Karen of Burma, two separate sets are connected by a cord, illustrating an earlier stage in the development of the mainland instrument.

Both raft and bundle version are played in Indonesia. On Flores, bundle pipes are untied and their components distributed among four separate players, each of whom then sounds his own single tone. In nearby West Java some raft pipes are played in pairs, with one of the pair having from ten to fourteen small pipes, the other two or three large ones.

Panpipes in Africa. Panpipes are also played in pairs in East and Central Africa: the "little flutes," as they are called in parts of Uganda, are played in an ensemble of six performers divided into three pairs, and are accompanied by a drum. The Yombe of the Lower Congo area make raft pipes of six or eight pipes, and also a variety consisting of four stopped pipes having beveled embouchures, tied in two pairs; the longer pipe of each pair is considered to be the husband, the shorter pipe the wife. Inhabitants of Katanga play a version composed of from two to six pipes in sets of different sizes, three being a popular one. These also have raft form and are tied together with fiber, as are the pipes of most African syrinxes. A rare form is encountered among the Pedi of South Africa, who play an instrument made from the tail of a porcupine, with the quills acting as stopped pipes: these are not tuned.

Panpipes in the Americas. Pre-Columbian panpipes of the Americas were made of many materials; in addition to those of cane, ancient specimens also had bores hollowed out of a block of wood or stone, and even metal. A cane syrinx preserved in the British Museum has two parallel rows of seven pipes each, one row stopped, the other open; another is made from a block of soapstone with eight pipes, four of which have a lateral hole; when this hole is stopped the pitch is lowered by a semitone, so that a total of twelve semitones can be produced from the eight tubes. Among excavated objects of the Ohio Mound Builders (Hopewell culture) is a three-pipe syrinx made of cane sections in a copper housing. Radiocarbon dating has shown it to have been assembled about A.D. 100; two of its pipes are stopped with wooden plugs, and the third, center, pipe, is believed to have been stopped by the performer's hand.

Recent studies of the ancient Peruvian *antara* have widened our knowledge of these instruments considerably. Those of the early Naxca people, for instance, were wrought of individual clay pipes rolled around molds, then assembled in a graduated row to form a panpipe of from three to fifteen tubes, cemented together with clay. Small *antaras* having up to seven pipes were bored with a string hole, and a proportionately large number of paired instruments have also survived. A twin set of closed cane panpipes was excavated near Lima, its two sets of six pipes still tied into a complementary pair, with cotton string intact. *Antaras* are often found among grave goods, for the Naxca played them in their afterlife. In this life their use was restricted to men; women were not permitted to play them.

On a Mochica pottery vase two players are shown facing each other, their six-pipe *antaras* connected by a cord. In Bolivia today panpipes are played in exactly the same manner (the same arrangement among the Karen of Burma has already been noted). Another Mochica vessel depicts the player of a six-pipe *antara*—most representations are of the six-pipe variety—holding the ends of the two lowest pipes with his right hand, while his left fingers are held over the higher ones. Nowadays Indians of Lake Titicaca use precisely the same technique; they play slightly longer instruments with two rows of pipes, one row shorter than the other, the smallest pipe to the left [*sic*]. The instrument is held in the left hand, with the right hand forming a shield behind the pipes, the better to direct the wind. In general, excavated Peruvian instruments with two rows of pipes have an open and a stopped row; a single example has, however, come to light with both rows stopped, but here one of the rows is slightly longer than the other.

During the Ica period before the Inca conquest *antaras* with fewer than six pipes are seen on pottery in conjunction with a drum, played as an exact counterpart of the medieval European pipe and tabor ensemble, with panpipe held in the left hand. And in historic times the Quechua of Peru held their *huayra puhura* (meaning "air tube") in the left hand, with the right hand grasping a small stick for striking a small drum suspended from the left arm. *Huayra puhuras* consisted almost invariably of two rows of eight pipes each, one row behind the other: one row had stopped, the other open, pipes. Here also the treble pipes were to the player's left. The Quechua formed ensembles of these instruments with three pairs of pipes, one at intermediary pitch, a second an octave lower, a third an octave higher. As an individual panpipe produced only a portion of the diatonic scale, each of a pair furnished the tones lacking on his partner's instrument. Depending upon the melodic requirements, a given panpipe would be sounded successively or alternately.

Lasso de la Vega, in his early-seventeenth-century *Comentarios reales de los Yncas,* makes a similar report: he states that the Colla Indians of Peru played panpipes of four or five pipes bound together in two rows, and that they were made in different sizes, "like the four natural voices," soprano, alto, tenor, and bass. When one Indian had played, another would respond at the interval of a fifth or at some other interval, but never by playing together, *por que no las supieron concertar* ("because they did not know how to play them in concert"). Panpipes were also important during courtship, and Lasso reports that sometimes, when the player himself could be resisted, his instrument proved irresistible.

Nowadays the Cuna Indians of Panama play sets of two panpipes pitched a fifth apart; they are connected by a cord and referred to as man and wife (cf. usage among the African Yombe people, page 593). The Aymara of Bolivia and Peru also play sets, each instrument consisting of one or two rows of stopped pipes, and here again the shortest pipe is to the left; three or four different-sized panpipes form a set, tuned apart from one another at intervals of a fourth; the largest may attain 80 centimeters (31½ inches) in length; melodies are played in parallel octaves or in fifths. Today, the Aymara, as well as the Indians of Cuzco, hold their pipes in the left hand and strike a large and sometimes deep cylinder drum suspended from the left arm with a drumstick held in the right hand.

On modern two-row panpipes the second row is only half as long as the first and consequently sounds an octave higher; it performs the function of a color stop, to borrow a term from organ terminology, as the tone of a stopped pipe lacks harmonics. The player directs his breath against the main pipe, but the surplus reaches the shorter octave pipe, which enriches the tone of the big pipe by soft but audible sounds.

Panpipes in the Pacific. Exactly the same effect is obtained in Melanesia, where a parallel row of open pipes is added to the main row of stopped ones. Other Melanesian panpipes consist of open pipes only, each one of which the player stops with his finger as he wishes to make it speak, thereby causing it to sound an octave lower than the length of the pipe would suggest. Bundle pipes also are encountered frequently in this part of the world.

VESSEL FLUTES

Most flutes are tubular, but some are made as closed vessels, usually globular or ovoid, with a round blowhole. Prototype of the globular flute was a hollowed coconut or small gourd held at the mouth while singing, in order to distort the voice—a magical implement rather than a musical instrument. Globular flutes existed in Egypt in predynastic times as magical objects, later to become musical instruments, finally to degenerate to the level of a child's toy. As musical instruments they were made of such natural materials as gourd, coconut, or fruit shells, in areas where these grow: Asia, Africa, the Americas, and the Pacific; later they were imitated in clay, porcelain, and other substances.

Like tubular flutes, the larger the air chamber, the lower the fundamental pitch. Not all globular flutes are provided with fingerholes in addition to a blowhole, but when present they influence the pitch in a manner differing from that of the tubular flutes: here the pitch rises as the number of fingerholes increases, or, to express it in another way, the number of fingerholes closed—and not the order in which they are closed—determines the pitch. By calculated combinations of fingering, a large compass is obtainable with few fingerholes. Thus an investigator found that a two-holed globular flute of the Congo was capable of producing a (Western) scale of nineteen tones in chromatic sequence, although its Kongo players were unaware of its potentialities. On a modern Chinese *hsuan* the successive opening of its fingerholes, regardless of sequence, raises the pitch by about one tone per fingerhole opened. Apart from ancient Egypt, globular flutes were also known to prehistoric China, Bronze Age Hungary, pre-Columbian America, and are still played in many parts of the world, including sections of Europe.

EUROPEAN VESSEL FLUTES

Globular flutes, played in Europe since prehistoric times, are today chiefly confined to rural areas or else used as toys. From Russia to the Balearic Islands little clay whistles are made in form of a bird, usually with one or two fingerholes, sometimes with none at all. The latter, when partly filled with water, warble like birds, as the player's breath causes the water level to constantly vary; those with a single fingerhole emit pitches a third apart, in imitation of a cuckoo.

These simple little vessel flutes did not escape modernization: in the hands of Giuseppe Donati of Budrio, Italy, they were transformed around 1860 into the ocarina ("little goose"), an oblong instrument of clay or of porcelain with a whistle head, eight fingerholes, and two thumbholes. Since Donati's day the ocarina has been expanded into a whole family, ranging in size from soprano to bass, and supplied with a tuning piston to facilitate ensemble playing, so that it has now become a cross between a globular flute and a piston pipe. So popular did the "little goose" prove that nowadays any globular flute is called an ocarina. However, simple pottery flutes continue their existence as folk instruments in many areas— the Balkans, for one, at Belgian *kermesses* (fairs), for another. On Majorca pottery vessel flutes have traditionally represented a man on horseback, but today the man rides a motor scooter.

VESSEL FLUTES OUTSIDE EUROPE

One of the oldest globular flutes known is the *hsuan* of China. According to tradition it was invented in about 2700 B.C., and an actual instrument from the Shang dynasty (second millennium B.C.) was excavated at Anyang. Carved of bone, it is almost barrel shaped and stands about 5 centimeters (2 inches) high, with apical blowhole and five lateral fingerholes. Later instruments had from six to eight fingerholes and were of clay or porcelain; nowadays its lacquered ovoid clay body has from four to six fingerholes and apical blowhole. From China, where it became a Confucian ritual instrument, it was carried to Korea, where it is now made of clay; the corresponding instrument of ancient Japan was of stone.

African vessel flutes are commonly made of natural materials: the *ebumi* of the Congo region, so named because it is derived from the hollow berries of the ebumi tree, has a large blowhole and two fingerholes —the standard "equipment" of African globular flutes—although more are occasionally encountered; it is known by the same name in Uganda. Clay, gourds, and fruit shells are other materials converted into flutes on this continent. The Thonga of South Africa, the only South Africans to have globular flutes, blow theirs as though they were cross flutes.

Pre-Columbian vessel flutes comprise three categories: whistle flutes, fingerhole flutes, and whistling pots (which last are discussed separately below). Prehistoric globular whistles of gourd have been excavated at Hueca Prieta in northern Peru. Many others of pottery have been found in Mexico, mostly anthropomorphic, with a small clay ball in the interior that is set in motion by the player's breath, causing a typical whistle sound. Others, also of clay, are of the conventional type, with several fingerholes distributed over the surface. Similar instruments, some zoomorphic, were played in the Guatemala highlands around A.D. 700–1000. Pre-Columbian Peru had globular flutes formed of deer or guanaco skull, and today the Witoto employ a deer skull, complete with horns, making the vessel airtight by filling any cavities with pitch. Indians of the Peruvian Amazon now make globular flutes of beeswax, while the Paressi-Kabishi of Brazil make theirs of two gourds glued together, and play them as nose flutes. Vase-shaped clay flutes of the Brazilian Tucurima and the Ecuadorian Jivaro have a small blowhole on the lower portion; in some areas it imitates the roar of a jaguar.

North American vessel flutes are found only in a single area: Virginia–North Carolina, where they are made only of gourds. Some of the Indian players prefer them without fingerholes; others play both the whistle and the fingerhole varieties.

Small globular flutes made of natural materials are also played as nose flutes in the Pacific. Inhabitants of the Sepik area of New Guinea have a ritual globular flute made of a coconut, which instrument is taboo to women.

Whistling Pots

A form of globular flute peculiar to Central and South America is the whistling pot, better known by its Spanish name of *silbador*. Here two clay vessels, both globular and surmounted by necks, communicate by a tube reaching from neck to neck. Sometimes this conduit is tubular, sometimes a flat band. One neck, left open at the top, forms a blowhole; the other is closed but for a whistle head. Usually the pot with the whistle head is zoomorphic or anthropomorphic. If both vases are partly filled with water and the open neck is blown into, air is forced through the whistle head. However, modern whistling pots constructed on the same principles as ancient ones are played in quite a different fashion by Indians of Ecuador, Peru, and Chile, probably in a continuation of pre-Columbian usage: the pots are filled until the water level is above the juncture of conduit and neck, and then the *silbador* is rocked to and fro, so that the changes of air pressure cause it to warble like a bird. In fact, the pot's Nahuatl name is *tot-tlapiztali*, which means "whistling bird."

A nineteenth-century traveler to Chile related that Indians would suspend a whistling pot from the bough of a tree or from a beam by a cord, and then swing it backwards and forwards, producing "soothing sounds." Today a contemporary version of the traditional pot is being produced at Murcia, Spain, under the name of *botijito*; its function, as we might suspect, is that of imitating the warbling of birds.

THE ORGAN

The most complex as well as the most considerable of Western musical instruments, and that which has exploited its polyphonic potential to the utmost, the organ is basically a series of inverted flutes blown mechanically, engaged and disengaged from a keyboard. Modern organs with their pipework, wind supply, action, and keyboards are thought of as a single unit, but in reality the large majority are composites of several separate organs, each with its own pipework, action and keyboard, united partly or completely in a common case.

THE ORGAN IN ANTIQUITY

For a time, Sachs's theory of the organ's prototype, that of a set of mechanically blown panpipes, was accepted. Three Alexandrine figurines of about the first century B.C. (of which only one was known when he wrote) show a man holding panpipes with long bass pipes provided with rotating rings, fed by bellows held under his arm. Also considered as a potential prototype was the larger but still small bellows-blown *magrepha* of the Hebrews, a signal instrument known to have been in use during the last period of the Temple—possibly earlier—one of its functions being that of convoking the priests. Talmudic tractates describe it as having been an *amma* (about 50 centimeters) high, and as wide, with ten times ten pipes, probably a symbolic number. The word *magrepha* means "rake," and the instrument was probably named for its shape. However, it was contemporary with the early organ, and cannot be shown to have preceded it. But regardless of any putative precursors, the true organ's distinguishing feature is a keyboard, an arrangement that permits control of each individual pipe; mere mechanization of wind supply does not differentiate an organ from a bagpipe.

Invention of the organ thus awaited the creation of a keyboard, and this was achieved with the appearance of the *hydraulos*, or water organ. Tradition and Vitruvius (first century A.D.) ascribe its discovery to Ktesibius, an Alexandrian of the third century B.C. Hickmann has narrowed down its introduction to the reign of Ptolemy II Philadelphus (285–246 B.C.). It is of course far too complex an instrument to have sprung full blown from the head of Ktesibius, and his part in its evolution may have been simply that of applying some of Archimedes' mechanical findings to musical pipes. Writing on architecture, Vitruvius observes that Ktesibius investigated methods of making water clocks, discovered the principles of pneumatics, invented a pump for raising water, and made the first water organ. Other inventions or improvements of his included such mechanical toys as artificial birds made to sing by water power, to be beloved and imitated for centuries to come.

Pliny mentions Ktesibius' water organs briefly, while Hero, another Alexandrian (probably of the first century B.C. or A.D.) describes a water organ in his *Pneumatika*. Essentially a compiler, it is not clear which of the inventions described by Hero are his own and which those of Ktesibius. In addition to mechanical birds, he mentions automatic trumpets sounded by the force of compressed air, as well as a number of gadgets designed to impress, awe, and even frighten the spectators.

Our knowledge of the mechanics of the *hydraulos* is chiefly due to these two writers. They make it clear that the water organ differed from the "pneumatic" organ only by its wind supply and its size, and that water was not the motive force but merely acted to maintain even air pressure, with the air being supplied by one—or, more often, two—hand-worked pumps. In other words, the *hydraulos* was a pneumatic organ, the sole function of water being that of stabilizing the air pressure while the wind itself was supplied by pumps. Hero's *hydraulos*—if indeed it was his—had but one row of pipes, set over a conduit into which the air was forced, that is, a windchest. Each pipe had its own valve, closed by a wooden slider in which a hole had been cut; when the slider was pushed in, this hole gave the pipe access to the windchest. Each slider in turn was governed by a key (*ankōnistros trikolos*, "three-membered arm"), probably in the form of a carpenter's square with added arm, like a half swastika, to push it in, which key was returned by a horn spring.

The *hydraulos* of Vitruvius had provision for four, six, or eight rows of pipes with a longitudinal channel for each row. Sliders were inserted between an upper board, called *pinax*, and the windchest, pierced with holes to correspond to those of the *pinax*, and oiled for ease of motion. They were connected to the keys. The Anonymous Bellermann (first or second century A.D.) informs us that the *hydraulos* could be played in six *tropoi* (tonalities); thus four rows of pipes at this period must not be thought of as four ranks at different foot-pitch levels, nor of intentional varieties of tone color as on a modern instrument; rather, they may perhaps be compared in function at least to pipes connected with the split sharps of later organs (see keyboards, page 237).

The wind supply consisted essentially of pumps and a reservoir half filled with water; the latter formed the lower portion of the *hydraulos*. Inside was a metal *pnigeus*, a footed, bucketlike device placed open side down; a connection led from this to the small, boxlike windchest (*arcula*) above. Air from one, or more often two, hand-worked pumps was conveyed to the windchest, and as the pressure of the air in the chest was raised by the pumping, water was driven out of the *pnigeus* into the container. If the pressure in the windchest dropped, due either to the slowing of the pumping or to the flow of wind into the pipes, the displaced water flowed back from the container and the level in the *pnigeus* rose, thereby compressing the air above it and restoring pressure in the windchest. Thus the reservoir acted to keep the wind pressure continuous and steady, with the presence of the water assuring pressure between the pumping strokes, a *sine qua non* for playing. The water level of the *pnigeus* remained more or less constant while the organ was in use, in much the same way that the bag of a bagpipe remains inflated while the pipe is being played. Later, when the wind supply was furnished by bellows, the reservoir was discarded and the organ transformed from a cumbersome, nonportable instrument to a portable one small enough to be held in the lap.

The precise nature of the *hydraulos* was greatly clarified by the discovery in Carthage in 1885 of a clay model measuring some 18 centimeters (7 inches) in height, now in the Musée Lavigerie there, and of a smaller model now in the National Museum of Copenhagen. The former, made in A.D. 120, and inscribed with the potter's name, Possessor, shows three rows of pipes and a nineteen-key compass; the organist sits on a raised seat. Mosaics of the period show a high and narrow instrument with the organist's head projecting above the pipes, measuring perhaps from 2 to 3 meters (5½ to 9 feet) in height and from 1 to 1½ meters (40 to 60 inches) in width.

Bellows-blown organs were known from the second century on. Philo (second or third century) states in his *Pneumatika* that collapsible bellows forced air into organ reservoirs. More important is the statement of Julian Pollux in the second century to the effect that the *hydraulos,* in appearance similar to the syrinx, was filled with air in its lower portion, either by means of bellows if it were small or "by compressed water" (*hydati . . . anathlibomenō*) which drove out the air. Unfortunately this passage became known to medieval writers and, being no longer understood, was mistranslated. Thus the chronicler William of Malmesbury wrote about 1120 of hot water forcing air into the windchest: . . . *organa hydraulica, ubi mirum in modum aquae calefactae, violentiam ventus emergens implet concavitatem barbiti . . .,* thereby giving rise to the idea that the ancient water organ was powered by steam. The belief was current in the seventeenth and eighteenth centuries; Banchieri, for instance, could write (1609) that Pope Silvester II in 997 had fabricated an organ with pipes of gold sounded *all'impeto di un bollimento d'acqua* ("by the impetus of boiling water"), possibly the source of Praetorius's *ungestühme Gewalt des heissen Wassers* ("impetuous force of hot water"), echoed in turn by Caspar Printz in 1690. Forkel is probably the first author to realize that water in ancient *hydraulae* did not feed the pipes—he compares it to the wind pressure gauge.

A late writer, Claudian, states at the end of the fourth century that the action of the *hydraulos* was effortless. Numerous other writers refer to the water organ from about A.D. 200 up to the late fifth century, despite the fact that the waterless organ had already come into use, but as this new type was known for some centuries by the name of the older instrument, some of these literary references may in reality be to the bellows organ. One of the latest monuments to clearly show the *hydraulos* is a Roman sarcophagus in the museum at Arles, dated from the late third or early fourth century, with the typical altarlike container, two buckets for pumping, and some nine pipes. The Aquincum organ from the year 228 may well have been a pneumatic organ; it is described on page 604.

Too late to contribute to Hellenic music, by then on the decline, the *hydraulos* was distributed in the Roman world from Gaul to Africa; it was played at private banquets (Cicero), in the emperor's palace (Nero not only played but also improved the organ), at circuses, and is represented on mosaics, medallions, sarcophagi, and statuettes. After the sixth century it is not mentioned again in Europe until the ninth century, when Eginhard wrote of Georgius Venetus that he built an organ called *hydraulos* (in 826 or 828) for Louis the Pious (*organum quod Graece hydraulica vocatur*), proof that the old terminology was still in force at that late date. The Utrecht Psalter, created in France about 860, illustrates the word *organa* of the Psalms by portraying totally nonfunctional instruments, chiefly in the form of double organs. On the other hand, when the word *hydraulos* occurs in Talmudic commentaries it was as a synonym of *magrepha*.

An early writer known as Muristus, believed to have been a Greek, has been credited with inventing or improving some of the instruments he described, including the *hydraulos*. His treatise, translated from Greek into Arabic at some period before 988, is concerned with several instruments (see pellet bells, page 81) but not with the *hydraulos*. Musical automata with artificial birds singing in artificial trees were known both to Byzantium and to the Arab world, and Muristus's "organ" derives from these. His was a large copper vessel partly filled with water, with rudimentary action, supplied with wind by bellows on either side, and provided with from one to three pipes sounded simultaneously; Muristus called it the *argun al-buqi* ("the horn instrument"), and stated that the Greeks used it as a signal instrument in warfare, as it could be heard sixty miles away. The bellows "of Rum" (i.e., the Greeks) were round like those of a goldsmith, and trodden, he wrote. Muristus's "universal organ" (*argun al-gami*) consisted of three leather bags sewn together at both ends, with *zamri* (pipes) set atop the central bag—clearly not an organ but more likely some sort of siren.

The early pneumatic organ, then, was first known by the name of *hydraulos*—or Latinized to *hydraulus*—and for a while the two forms coexisted. Thus it is often impossible to differentiate between them in early texts. Windchest and pipework were identical, forming a unit that could be set upon an altar-shaped base containing a cistern or upon a table and worked directly by bellows; hence the great advantage of the bellows-blown organ was its portability. Judging from the iconography, these earliest blown organs were comparable in size to the future portative organs, whereas pumped organs were of positive organ dimensions. Pollux (second century) mentioned both kinds: a large instrument with air pumps and water pressure, and a smaller one furnished with bellows. Both appear to have been well known in his day.

In Rome the organ was known either as *hydraulus* or *organum* (pl. *organa*). The term was, however, used in the general sense of musical instrument before it came to specify the organ in postclassical Europe (the Greek *organon*, from which *organum* is derived, meant instrument in the sense of "tool"; Ptolemy, for instance, spoke of the astrolabe as an *astrolabon organon*). Saint Augustine (d. 430) still used the word in its wider sense: *Organa dicuntur omnia instrumenta musicorum. Non solum illud organum dicitur quod grande est et inflatur follibus, sed quidquid aptatur ad cantilenam . . . organum dicitur* ("All musical instruments are called *organa*. Not only is that called organ which is large and inflated by bellows, but any that is suitable for melody is called organ").

Our earliest unequivocal representation of the bellows-blown organ is that of a medallion fragment from Orange of the late second or early third century. This can be compared with the remains of an actual organ dating from the year 228—its date ascertained by the consulship referred to in its inscription—found in Aquincum near Budapest in 1932, the most important factor so far in our knowledge of ancient organs. Though badly damaged by fire, a number of metal parts survived. The windchest was originally of wood covered with thin bronze; including the keyboard, it was 18 centimeters (7 inches) high, 35 centimeters (14 inches) long, 10 centimeters (4 inches) wide, or, with projecting keyboard, 17 centimeters (7 inches) wide. Its longest pipe measured about 45 centimeters (18 inches). As the wind-supply system is totally lacking it is impossible to tell whether the *hydria,* as the instrument is termed in the dedicatory plaque, was a *hydraulus* or not. In its present condition—that is, without wind-supply system—it is small enough to be set on a table or even held in the lap. The bronze top of the windchest was pierced with fifty-two apertures in rows of thirteen each, corresponding to thirteen L-shaped keys and to four longitudinal metal grooves in the chest; the wooden keys, also covered with thin bronze, were attached by their upper ends to metal sliders bored with holes to permit communication with the grooves; thus they formed a manner of sliding key (forerunner of the medieval slider key), returned by means of a metal spring. Of the four rows of pipes, three were stopped, with the open pipes forming the back row. The front-row pipes were about half the length of those of the three other rows; all were made of 82 percent copper and 18 percent zinc, were 0.5 millimeters thick, cylindrical in form, with a soldered seam. Most interesting is the fact that the diameter was variable (early Western organ pipes had constant diameter), all of a very narrow scale. Experiments performed with some of the better preserved pipes show that the third and the eleventh pipe of the first row sounded an octave apart, and that the first row was apparently an octave higher than the second row. Moreover, the top of each pipe was furnished with a tuning ring. Each of the stopped pipes contained for almost its entire speaking length a wooden stopper that must originally have been movable. Some of the pipes were reconstructed by the organ builder, Oscar Walcker, who reported that it was almost impossible to obtain the fundamental on them but that they spoke promptly on very low pressure.

A center relief of the obelisk of Theodosius, erected in Constantinople during the last years of the fourth century, depicts the emperor in the Hippodrome with what appear to be two small organs, their bellows trodden by two youths; actually the relief depicts the front and rear aspects of one and the same organ. Here the wind trunk connecting bellows and organ is clearly visible.

THE ORGAN IN MEDIEVAL TIMES

With Cassiodorus (d. 575), a pupil of Boethius, who in his commentary on Psalm 150 mentions the organ's wooden *linguae* (keys), its soft and loud *cantilena,* and its towerlike shape (*quasi turris*)—the classical *hydraulus* in other words—the watershed between old and new is reached, the dying classical tradition, nascent western Europe, and the emergence of the Eastern empire. If Cassiodorus still knew or remembered the *hydraulus*, Isidore, bishop of Seville (d. 636) admittedly did not, for he could write in his *Etymologiae* of the *organum . . . cui folles adhibentur, hydraulum graeci nominant* (". . . worked by bellows, that it was called *hydraulus* by the Greeks). And when we learn from Saint Aldhelm (d. 709) of organs with "thousands" of gilded pipes, we are tempted to believe he is describing by hearsay an Eastern practice, that of gilding the pipes, rather than the instrument he had actually seen (the description of an organ in the *Interpretatio psalterii . . .* falsely attributed to Bede, who died in 735, is from Cassiodorus's Commentary on Psalm 150). Every chronicler of the period recorded the arrival in France in 757 (*organum in Francia venit*) of an organ sent to King Pepin by Emperor Constantine V Kopronymus; this was erected at Compiègne, and in 812 Emperor Michael I presented Charlemagne with one, accompanied by musicians who could play it, and set up at Aix-la-Chapelle (legend has made it a gift of Caliph Harun al-Rashid).

The difficulty of ascertaining just when the organ was admitted into the Christian church has been compounded by the fact that the word *organum* also denotes the earliest type of Western polyphonic music, so that references to *organum* in early documents are more likely to refer to singing than to the instrument. If the early church forbade instrumental music in connection with its services, it was with the memory of the role instruments had played in Greek and Roman rites, and their association—above all that of the organ—in circus (i.e., gladiatorial) displays. Fortunately the Psalms had listed those instruments suitable for use in the praising of God, among which were *organa*, interpreted in due course as organs. Although the importance attached by chroniclers to the imperial gifts from the Eastern empire give the impression that organs were unknown north of the Alps at that time, this cannot have been the case, although their presence was probably restricted to a few of the more important monasteries, and they may not have been made in the West. The earliest recorded occurrence of an organ in a church so far known, discovered by Jacques Handschin, is that of Cluain-Cremha, Ireland, in 814. Charlemagne's successor, Louis the Pious, caused an organ to be built for the palace at Aix-la-Chapelle in 826 (or 828) by the Venetian monk Georgius, as related by Eginhard, and in 872 Pope John VIII sent for the organ builder and player of Anno, bishop of Freising in Bavaria (later, in the sixteenth century, both Galilei and Zarlino recalled the tradition whereby organs were introduced to Europe from Greece via Hungary and Bavaria).

Yet throughout this and the following century organs must still have been relatively rare in the West. When the illustrator of the Utrecht Psalter (ca. 860) was faced with a passage containing the word *organa*, he portrayed double *hydraulae* intended for two players, with two sets of pumps, two cisterns, and two sets of pipes—instruments that could never have rendered any sound as depicted, and surrounded and surmounted by a nonfunctional framework, presumably the *turris* of Cassiodorus (in another psalter the verse from Psalm 137: *in salicibus suspendimus organa nostra*—rendered in the King James Version as "we hanged our harps upon the willows"—is charmingly illustrated with a series of miniature organs hung in the branches of a tree). Another fanciful interpretation of the organ is that contained in the Epistle to Dardanus by Pseudo-Jerome, also of the ninth century, a curious blend of half-forgotten realities and the symbolism so dear to the medieval mind; with its bellows of two elephant skins and its fifteen metal pipes, this organ could be heard *per mille passuum spatia*, from Jerusalem to the Mount of Olives.

Arabic civilization, so important to organology for its contribution of many musical instruments to the West, had no influence on the development of the organ; indeed it seems to have remained unknown in

Asaph playing the organ, a nonfunctional double instrument presumably inspired by the word *organa*. Detail of f. 272 v, Bibliothèque Nationale, MS latin 5371. Eleventh century.

the Moslem world, except for the latter's contacts with Byzantium. A valid explanation for this unexpected circumstance was offered by Gastoué, who suggested that organs were not apt for the rendering of Arabian microtone systems, and this may well account for their dearth. After Harun ben-Yahya, a prisoner of war taken at Ascalon was brought to Constantinople in 867, he described a Christmas banquet given for the prisoners of war, after which: "they bring in a thing called *al-urgana*," an object made of a square piece of wood resembling a wine press, covered with leather, into which sixty copper pipes are put, their pointed ends inserted for about half their length, their upper portions gilded; one pipe is always longer than its neighbor; at one side of the square is a hole into which bellows, shaped like smithy bellows, are inserted; two men are now brought in and blow the bellows and the master rises and plays the pipes. For someone who had never before seen an organ that is a very detailed description, and one to which his Arabic contemporaries and followers could add nothing.

Also in the ninth century, ibn-Khurdadhbih wrote of the skin bellows and iron pipes of the Byzantine organ, and interpreted the word *arganum* to mean "a thousand voices." Another early Arabic writer stated that "when a thousand men sing . . . with different sounds . . . that state of things they call an organum." Farmer has even suggested that "a thousand voices" may have been a nickname for the organ. When ibn-Rusteh wrote a description of Constantinople around 900, he included a report on an organ that had sixty bronze pipes on what looked like a square press, leather covered. Had he actually seen an organ or was he merely familiar with Harun ben-Yahya's writings? Al-Mas'udi, who died in 956, also mentions a Byzantine organ with bellows of skin and pipes of iron, and al-Khwarizmi, in his *Mafatih al-ulum* dating from between 976 and 991 defines *urganum* as an instrument of Greeks and Byzantines made of three large bags of buffalo skin tied together; mounted upon the head of the middle bag is a large skin, and mounted upon this in turn are brass pipes "having holes upon well known ratios from which are emitted pleasant sounds," to quote from Farmer's translation in the *Transactions of the Glasgow University Oriental Society* (vol. 7, 1957–1958).

From these brief references it should be clear that not only did the Arabs have no organ, but that they did not grasp the essentials of those instruments they had heard. Even later, the organ was never adopted by Islam and consequently remained incomprehensible to its followers, and when a Turkish traveler, Evlia Chelebi, visited Europe from 1662 to 1666 he noted that the Vienna cathedral organ had three hundred pipes (other organs he had already described had the same number of pipes) with twenty priests to pull each bellows.

That organs were common in the tenth-century Byzantium is known from Eastern sources: for the reception of a Moslem ambassador in Constantinople in 946, three organs were placed in the palace halls, one of which had gilded pipes, the two others silver pipes. And from the *Book of ceremonies*, authored or at least completed by Constantine VII Porphyrogenitus, in the first half of the tenth century, we learn of the custom of conducting a bride of noble birth to the bridegroom's house accompanied by the music of portable organs (the same document notes that Slavs were employed to "blow the organs," that is, as organ blowers), from all of which it may be gathered that the organ in Byzantium was a purely secular instrument.

From the tenth century on documentary and pictorial evidence begins to flow in western Europe; trodden bellows appear in northern France by the tenth century, as seen in the Stuttgart Psalter, and slider keys are also visible—wooden slats terminating in a handle by which they were pulled out to sound a pipe, pushed back to silence it, and, because one key looked exactly like another, the name of each one was written on its surface. Relatively small but not portable organs of the tenth to the seventeenth centuries were known as positive organs, and for several centuries they constituted the typical church organ. The monk Wolstan (d. 963) gives a description of an organ erected about 950 at Winchester in a laudatory Latin poem. Alas, very little of value can be gleaned from it, for Wolstan writes of a double organ built on a double ground, whatever that might be, requiring two players, each controlling his own keyboard; this consisted of twenty *linguae* (sliders) marked with the letters of the alphabet; "twice six" and fourteen bellows were needed, worked by seventy men (*septuaginta viri*); each slider had holes for ten pipes, for a total of four hundred pipes; an octave consisted of the *septem discrimina vocum* plus the "lyric semitone," presumably B♭. Furthermore, the organ made a deafening noise, he writes. As the poem was addressed to the bishop-donor, it can perhaps be classified as an early example of a bread-and-butter letter or, rather, poem, for two details only have the ring of contemporary realism, namely the marking of letters of the alphabet on the sliders and the presence of a synemmenon, a B♭. The duality of organ and player implies a literal translation of the word *organa* once again, the seven "voices" are taken from Virgil (and continue to occur throughout organ literature into modern times), the mystic number 70 apparently refers to the seventy (-two) Old Testament translators, unless it is a corrupt reading of *sex septemque*, which would then plausibly provide one blower for each pair of bellows. As for the vaunted four hundred pipes, the far smaller and surely far softer organ of Theophilus was not to be built for at least another century. Of one piece with Wolstan's poem is that of Walafried Strabo written earlier in praise of the Aix-la-Chapelle organ, for according to him a woman was so overcome with its *dulce melos* that this caused her death.

Outside the Eastern empire organ building was an art restricted to a few monasteries until after the turn of the millennium (Gerbert of Aurillac, the later pope Sylvester II, wrote in 986 to his friend and former teacher, Gerald of Aurillac, asking him to send an organ to Italy); indeed, it is probably safe to say that up to the eleventh century and possibly even later monastic churches were the only ones to contain an organ.

What these early instruments were like can be determined with a fair degree of accuracy, for the organ is one of the very few instruments whose development can be followed from documentary sources without having to rely for information on actual specimens or even on the visual arts.

Two codices of great importance for this purpose are the so-called Bern Anonymous (Codex B 56, Bern Municipal Library), probably written in northern France in the mid-eleventh century, and the somewhat later treatise of the monk Theophilus, possibly of Rhenish origin and written—again, probably—about 1100. Of these, that of Theophilus, titled *Schedula diversarum artium*, exists in several copies and is more detailed, being a book of instructions for the making of all objects connected with divine worship, and starting with the organization and equipping of a workshop for their fabrication.

That the barbarian invasions had brought about a great retrogression in technology has sometimes been disputed of late, yet its full extent becomes manifest when comparing details of the Aquincum organ with Theophilus's chapters on organ building, our first source of organ construction in the West; he goes to incredible trouble to make airtight joints and to achieve an airtight wind trunk, and to this end is obliged to take the curved branch of a tree and drill through it from both ends, then burn through the highly curved section in the center with a specially made tool—a metal "egg" on a long handle—to complete the channel. Theophilus's organ had an unspecified number of flue pipes made of copper soldered down the seam, all of the same diameter. His windchest, the *domus organaria*, is a slider-key chest of two and one-half "feet" in length; instructions are given for the making of two distinct types, one of wood with grooved upper section, the grooves being opened and closed by the slider keys; these were inserted between upper and lower portions of the chest, each slider pierced with a single hole, the thin board above pierced with as many holes as there were pipes to a key. Thus the slider keys controlled directly the admission of wind from chest below to grooves above.

His second type of windchest was of copper and its "action" of a different nature, for here the slider keys were pierced with as many holes as there were corresponding pipes and consequently the upper section was not grooved. Instead, the slider keys themselves controlled the admission of wind to the pipes after the wind had issued from the lower part of the chest through perforations in an intermediary copper floor, thence through the slider key—if it were pulled out—via a leaden lid to the foot of the pipes. This second action contained the elements from which the later slider chests were built. Slider keys of early Western organs do not seem to have been returned by springs—Theophilus mentions none—but, rather, by hand, so that playing could only have been slow. Theophilus makes his wind trunk long enough so that if desired the bellows could be placed *extra muros,* an indication that the wind-supply system was noisy.

Comparison with the treatise of the Bern Anonymous shows that the latter also had a slider-key chest, called *capsa,* and copper pipes. His organ had fifteen slider keys, lettered ABCDEFGABCDEFGAH [*sic*]. These were pierced as in Theophilus's copper windchest, with as many holes as there were pipes on a key; they could vary in number but might sound only as "single and double" (i.e., octave pipes), and, of these, as many as desired, "five, ten, or more." His slider keys were re-turned by horn springs; all his pipes had equal diameter, that of a pigeon's egg; they were made of very thin copper rolled on an iron pattern less than four "feet" long. A short wind trunk, the *fistula maxima,* was let in to the center of the windchest, and was supplied at the four sides of its further end with as many pairs of bellows furnished with nonreturn valves. Un-fortunately, the value of this treatise is impaired by its last passage: "For these pipes can be hydraulic if a waterfilled vessel is placed beneath and the wind draws water that flows back through the pipes with the sound." This bow to antiquity raises the question of whether his horn springs may not also have been reminiscences of yore (they had been mentioned by Hero). An appendix to this treatise, part of which also appears in Oxford Bodl. MS 300 (*incipit: Mensura isto modo finita*) and which may date from approximately the same time, has three pipes on each key, two fundamentals with an octave pipe between them; as the small pipes are "lacking" after the first ten tones (the second C), instruc-tions are given for filling the empty spaces with pipes of the lower octave; this can only mean that the treble pipes of an octave rank were too small in relation to their width to give speech, and the practice of what is now called repeating had to be resorted to.

Taken in conjunction, these two sources give a fair idea of the limita-tions and potentialities of the eleventh- or early twelfth-century organ, and contemporary illustrations help fill in the gaps: a small but not portable instrument, with a few rows of flue pipes consisting of funda-mentals and octaves only, sounded by pulling flat slider keys of slow manipulation, with wind supplied by numerous small bellows, probably quite noisy. Centuries later, Zarlino described the windchest of an ancient organ found at Grado in northern Italy, similar to that of the Bern Anonymous: it had equidistant holes in the upper surface for two rows of fifteen pipes each, lacked registers, and had circular perforations at the back for the introduction of bellows; it measured one *braccio* in length, one-quarter *braccio* in width (like most units of measure, this one varied in time and place, but if the later Roman *braccio* which was 70 centimeters, or 27½ inches, be considered, a length comparable to that of Theophilus's windchest is arrived at).

All early theorists and writers on organ-pipe scales mention their equal diameter; this factor would ensure variety of tone quality throughout the compass. Variable diameters are known to have been introduced in the twelfth century, presumably in connection with a compass extension, as the same width could not be maintained for more than two octaves or so due to difficulty of speech. Yet Handschin drew attention (in *Acta musicologica*, XIV, 1942) to a passage in Gerbert of Aurillac's mathematical works (of the late tenth century) concerning his *sphaera*, which had 7 *fistulae* . . . *quae hoc differunt a fistulis organicis quod per omnia aequalis sunt grossitudinis* ("seven pipes . . . that differ from organ pipes in that they *per omnia* have equal thickness"), and, as he had referred to the length of his pipe, this *grossitudo* must pertain to the width. But the emphasis must surely be placed on the words *per omnia*, used here in the sense of "throughout." Organ pipes in those days, as known from the treatises of both Theophilus and the Bern Anonymous, consisted of a cylindrical speaking section and a conical foot; ergo, the pipes of Gerbert's *sphaera* were of the same thickness, that is, diameter, throughout, unlike those of the organ, with their feet and body of differing diameters, and the *sphaera* may have represented a panpipe.

Medieval organ builders calculated their pipe lengths more often from the top pipe down (as did bell makers, probably the same individuals in those times), less often from the bottom pipe up; in either case the first pipe served as a standard for determining the length of all other pipes. Notker Labeo (d. 1022) seems to have been the first author to have suggested a scale proceeding from the bottom pipe up. Obviously he had practical experience, and his advice was worth taking, for serious problems of speech and intonation had to be overcome: one ell is too short a measure for the lowest pipe, he cautions, and two ells is too long for sonorous speech throughout the range, but one and one-half ells from the mouth up is a suitable measurement; the octave pipe will then be three-quarters of an ell long plus one half its diameter, and the fifteenth (top) pipe will be more than one-third of an ell (the ell of central Europe has historically been two local feet in length).

Of twenty-nine medieval treatises devoted to organ-pipe scales examined by Mahrenholz (1938), eight rely only on monochord measurements for their calculations, twelve make use of a combination of monochord lengths and end corrections. As most scales proceed downward the correction is calculated as a lengthening of the taller pipes; only six authors compute their scale from the bottom up. Once the pipes were made with variable diameters, those that were high pitched became relatively narrower and those that were low pitched relatively wider, thus reducing the need for end corrections.

By the twelfth century organs were sufficiently common to be mentioned in literary sources. Thus Wace's *Roman de Brut* of about 1155 has

> . . . *orgues sonner*
> *et clercs chanter et oraganueher.*

Throughout the twelfth century the organ compass did not exceed two octaves. Actions consisted of a slider chest with a groove for each key, every groove supplying all the pipes of its corresponding key. This type is still found, with modifications, in many organs today.

The thirteenth century saw a gradual extension of the compass, not yet fully chromatic. A compass of three octaves was to be attained in the fourteenth century, when it became fully chromatic. No longer restricted by virtue of their scarcity to the major churches, other forms of organ started appearing; smaller positives were furnished with short feet and placed on the floor or even on a table, one performer playing with both hands while a second person worked the bellows, either by hand or trodden. This type of positive was to become a domestic instrument, a secular house organ, and is seen resting on tables up to the seventeenth century, prototype of the later chamber organ. In Italy, larger models continued in existence until the eighteenth century. Pipework of the thirteenth century still consisted of flue pipes exclusively. Jerome of Moravia in the mid-century mentioned pipes of silver and lead; the use of pure tin, both expensive and very hard to work, was to become restricted to show pipes. Furthermore, at this time all were open pipes, for although stopped pipes had been known in antiquity they were not to be made again thereafter until the fifteenth century. Button-shaped keys, and occasionally T-shaped ones, appear on organs of the thirteenth century in place of the old and cumbersome sliders; when depressed they opened a pallet. This type was in turn replaced by domino-shaped keys that grew in length and width until they assumed the proportions described below in connection with the fourteenth-century Swedish organs.

Full chromaticism and compass increase of the fourteenth century necessitated placing the keys in two rows, one reserved exclusively for accidentals. Zarlino described as a curiosity an antique keyboard he had seen in which the bass keys were so wide that the interval of a fifth could barely be spanned, but on which the remaining keys diminished increasingly toward the treble. Such a disposition of manual keys is just what might be expected in organs built before the introduction of roller boards, yet having pipes of different diameters. The keyboard in question would seem to have been that of a positive of the thirteenth or fourteenth century.

Portative organs are first depicted during the thirteenth century (not during the twelfth, as has been claimed, due to a redating of manuscripts), to disappear again in the sixteenth century. During the three centuries of their life they served primarily in secular music, but also in religious processions. They were small enough to be carried and played simultaneously by one person, suspended from a strap passing around the player's neck and held at right angles to the body, the treble end projecting forward, with the bellows worked by the player's left hand. Higher in pitch than the positives, their original compass of two octaves increased to three by the end of the Middle Ages. All pipes were, of course, flue pipes. Early in their existence they added a couple of tall bass drone pipes (called bourdons) placed at the treble end.

Most portatives are depicted as having more than one row of pipes, and often two rows of key buttons are visible; this arrangement seems to have been a space-saving device only, and does not imply more than one pipe to a key. The keys were either button or T shaped, and wooden pipes are sometimes discernible on later instruments. Except for the drones, portatives were played monophonically and, owing to the position in which they were held, by two fingers only. Portative actions were simpler than those of larger organs; their windchests were not grooved, but, instead, pallets were placed immediately below the apertures of the pipe feet (in the fifteenth century, when their pipes could be arranged in an inverted V shape, a more complex action was called for). After their introduction, a clear distinction was made between the two types of organ: *orgues seans et orgues portatives*, the fixed "sitting," and the portable organ.

THE ORGAN IN THE FOURTEENTH AND FIFTEENTH CENTURIES

Large organs, formerly known as great organs, started appearing in churches in the fourteenth century. The term great organ is a later one, intended to avoid confusion with the smaller, auxiliary church organ; still later, as the organ expanded further and incorporated other sections, "great organ" became restricted in sense to indicate the main section of the compound organ and its pipework, controlled from the second lowest manual.

Some of the more important churches had a second, auxiliary, organ by the latter part of the fourteenth century; the Cistercian abbey of Meaux possessed in 1396 a great organ (*organa majora in occidentali fine ecclesiae*) and a small organ (*organa minora in choro*), in the west end of the church and in the choir, respectively; Saint Peter's, Leyden, had an organ and a "small organ" in 1400 that were termed "great" organ and "smaller" organ in 1426. It is in connection with two organs of this nature that a coupling system is first mentioned: archival records of Rouen Cathedral (published by Dufourcq, 1934–1935) document for the year 1387 payment *pro . . . innovationem seu reffectionem parvorum organorum quae debet facere cantare per se quando placebat, et quando placebit cantare seu ludere insimul cum magnis organis . . .* ("for . . . renovation of the small organ which must be made to sound alone at will, and at will sound together with the great organ . . .")—a prerequisite for creation of the chair organ.

Westminster Abbey had "two pairs" of organs in 1404; a "pair" of organs—an expression occurring in English and in French from the early thirteenth century on—denoted a single instrument (*une petite paire d'orgues* was inventorized as late as 1600 at the death of Pierre de La Barre). The term has never been satisfactorily explained. Analogies to pairs of scissors and other composites have been made but are unconvincing; more likely is the fact that the duality inherent in the concept of *organa* had not completely died out and was at the root of this conceit— a conceit subsequently passed on in England to the virginal. Such expressions as "a lytell payre of organs," "a great long payre," and "a lesser payr" occur at Holy Cross Abbey, Waltham, Essex, in the fifteenth century (cited by Harrison [1958]); in each case, reference is to a single instrument. "Pair" was then Latinized, and the Winchester College inventory of 1531 reads in part: *Item 1 par organorum . . . item aliud par organorum . . .*

Organ contracts were still in Latin for the most part, and *organa* was not then an obsolete term, as is evidenced by the following extract of the Gerona, Spain, chapter deliberations of 1473: *Et post multa verba concordavimus quod ipse* [the organ builder] *reparet dicta organa et deprimat modium per unum vel duos punctos dicta organa, que nimis alte fuerunt intonata,* that the organ builder should repair the *organa* and lower the pitch by one or two tones so that they should no longer be of such high intonation, where the *organa* under discussion are of course one instrument. English references to "single" and "double" organs are not uncommon a little later; they refer to the manual compass, that of a single organ not extending below Γ, that of the double organ extending further, for in letter notation the double letters (e.g., FF, DD, et cetera) were in use from Γ down. But this expression was to change its significance in the seventeenth century, when "double organ" denoted a great organ and its chair organ collectively (i.e., a two-manual organ), which we would nowadays qualify as two sections of a single organ.

Without doubt the fourteenth and fifteenth centuries were the most important in the history of the organ: the fourteenth century saw its expansion to two manuals and the invention of rollerboard, trackers, and pedalboard; the fifteenth century, that of registers. In fact, development had proceeded so far that by the mid-fourteenth century Machaut could already declare:

> *Et de tous instruments le roi*
> *Dirai-je, comme je le crois*
> *Orgue . . .*
>
> And of all instruments the king
> I would say, as I believe
> the organ . . .

Advances in technology and probably also the construction of large cathedral churches brought about an increase in manual compass, leading ultimately to the transformation of the relatively small church organ to the great organs, a feat accomplished by the late fourteenth century. With the invention of rollers and trackers the organ was free to expand, as builders were no longer obliged to place bass pipes to the left and treble pipes to the right in an unbroken line; henceforth they could be arranged in a V shape, an inverted V shape, and so on. The larger number of pipes necessitated placing them on a bigger windchest, augmenting the wind supply, so that extra and more powerful bellows were added. Pipework and chest were then raised above the level of the organist's head, and from then on they were enclosed in a case. Wooden shutters or a cloth curtain protected the pipes from dust and damage, and could also be closed if less volume were desired, as Praetorius was to point out in his *Syntagma* III; they existed locally as late as the beginning of the eighteenth century. Toward the end of the fourteenth century it became necessary to add a second manual, as continued expansion rendered a constant addition of grooves, pipes, rollers, etc. to the chest impossible. Hence a smaller, second, manual was supplied for the low-pitched pipes, as at first the compass extension was a downward one. This second manual was known as tenor manual; as a rule its pipes were placed in towers. A second manual existed in Rouen in 1386, and the tenor manual of the Cordeliers' organ (in Dijon?) contained ten keys in about 1440, according to Henry Arnaut.

Once again, light can be thrown on contemporary documents by the examination of actual instruments of the period, for we are fortunate in that the remains of no fewer than four organs of the late fourteenth century are still preserved in Sweden. All four have C as the lowest manual key, and on all four B♭ appears as a "white," that is, a natural, key. Of these organs, that of Sundre dates from about 1370, the others from the end of the century. The Sundre organ, built by a German named Werner, according to an inscription, has a single manual and a pedal. All its keys are now lacking, but spaces are provided for eighteen manual and eight pedal keys. Spacing of the manual keys indicates that these must have been approximately 5 centimeters (2 inches) wide, as the spaces themselves are 3 centimeters wide and 2 centimeters apart from one another. They provided for fourteen "white" and four "black" keys in the manual, for a compass of C° to g♯° in appearance, augmented by the eight pedal keys to close to three octaves. Remnants of a roller action are present, as are twenty-six pallets, or one for each key including the pedal keys.

The better preserved and thirty-odd-year-later Norrland organ stands 2.62 meters (8 feet 7 inches) high and 1.27 meters (4 feet 2 inches) wide and still possesses its manual and pedalboard, abstracts and rollers. The top of the windchest is 3 centimeters thick and forms the upper board; it is pierced for 141 pipes in all, and is grooved. All the pipes are missing, as is the wind-supply system; its manual keys, laid out in three tiers, one above the other, number fourteen natural and eight accidental keys (twenty-two keys), with a single key positioned above these two rows. The pedal had eight keys. Thus the manual compass, C° to a°, is already fully chromatic (with four accidentals per octave spaced pairwise). The natural keys project 6 centimeters beyond the case and are 3 centimeters wide; the accidentals have the same width but project only by 2 centimeters. Fourteen pallets are positioned immediately above the fourteen natural keys, but there are only four for the eight accidentals, two of which are supplied by each pallet. Two of the pallets servicing the accidental keys are located to the left of the larger group for the naturals, the other two are located to the right; as these are not exactly above their corresponding keys they must be activated by rollers. Letters of the alphabet were formerly written over each key and some are still legible, but regrettably all those for the upper row of accidentals are missing. In this connection it may be pointed out that the Robertsbridge Codex, dating from about 1325, and containing the earliest known organ music, calls for a compass of c° to e², and for the accidentals F♯,C♯,G♯,D♯,B♭,E♭, notated in tablature. (A third organ, that of Anga, also had letters inscribed over its keys, which numbered seventeen in the manual.)

Each pedal key of the Norrland organ had its own pallet, and these were in the same chest as those of the manual keys but were divided into two groups of four each, one at each end of the chest. As may be seen from the upper board, several pipes belonged to one pallet, those of the manual being situated in the center and standing six pipes to a pallet. Because registers had not then been invented, they all spoke together. A single key was placed on a third, upper tier by itself, as already noted; above this is an iron nail believed to have formerly held a latchet similar to that seen on Van Eyck's Ghent Altarpiece organ (painted 1432) to ensure that the key remained depressed. But here the key's function is said to have been that of opening a special valve at the bottom of the windchest.

Wide keys must have been standard even later than the time of the Swedish organs, for Praetorius saw keys two and one-half Brunswick inches wide, "that is, a good three fingers breadth," as he writes, on an old organ still standing in Minden, undated but older he thought, than that of Saint Egidius in Brunswick; the latter's dedicatory *carmina* were of 1456, and it had a keyboard on which he could reach only the interval of a fifth in what was otherwise a normal octave span.

Details of organs in Italy do not start flowing until late, to wit, not before the end of the fourteenth century. Prior to 1316 one is mentioned at Saint Mark's, Venice, for instance, but then it is in connection with repairs. And when pedals were adopted they were in the form of pull-downs hung from the manual keys. Santa Annunziata, Florence, had in 1379 an organ to the left of the high altar, some 6 ells (12 "feet") above the ground, and a pedalboard of twelve keys: *duodecim anulis de ferro . . . qui ligantur ad calculos pro tastando cum pedibus* ("with 12 iron rings [or springs?] . . . connected to pedal keys for playing with the feet"). Pedals of the Swedish organs were independent of the manuals, as has been shown, as were those of continental Europe north of the Alps in general, while those of Italy were hung from the manual by pulldowns, and this system continued in use there; indeed, the earliest expansion of manual compasses in Italy and Spain must be attributed to lack of an independent pedalboard in those countries. (Pedals were nonexistent in Britain until the eighteenth century and did not become common there until the nineteenth; the first, installed in the 1720s, were pulldowns.) Insofar as can be generalized, pedalboards in transalpine Europe had at first one stop, later a stop or two of their own, then drew others from the manual, finally became an independent division: the pedal organ.

Until such a time as individual rows of pipes could be drawn off, all pipes controlled by a given key spoke together. The pipework of these Gothic organs is known by the collective name of *Blockwerk* in German, *blokwerk* in Dutch. If we assume a fundamental pipe at 8′ pitch, the pipes of a *Blockwerk* that sounded simultaneously on its corresponding key would have been, from front to back, 1′ 1⅓′ 2′ 2⅔′ 4′ 8′ 4′ 2⅔′ 2′ 1⅓′ 1′, that is, fundamental, octaves, and quints. Aliquots were built up in this fashion on each key. Later, the *Blockwerk* was broken up to form a rank of fundamentals, with a *Vordersatz* (i.e., front pipes) in front and a *Hintersatz* (i.e., rear pipes) behind it, both of them mixtures. The *Hintersatz* developed into the *Grossmixtur* ("great mixture") of Schlick's age, wide-scaled principals, nonrepeating, composed at first of octaves and quints as the old *Blockwerk* had been, later also with tierces (Schlick compared its sound to the screaming of pigs).

A curious outcrop of the fifteenth-century organ was the *Hornwerk* of Gothic and Renaissance times, found only in Austrian territory, a signal instrument reminiscent of Arabic descriptions or even of the mythical horn of Alexander. It consisted of a number of flue pipes set on a chest of their own in a tower. All sounded simultaneously and for as long as the bellows continued to supply them with wind. They announced the hours and also summoned the faithful to worship. By the Renaissance such simple calls were no longer satisfactory, and the *Hornwerk* was consequently connected to a pinned barrel for the interpolation of tunes between calls. The pipework of the call was simply that of one tone of a cornett mixture, a triad, usually that of F or C major. Originally the pipes sounded from 4′ to ¼′ pitch, later they were extended downward. Several such instruments remain, one of them still in working condition— the well-known *Salzburger Stier* ("Salzburg bull")—erected at Salzburg in 1502, a mixture comprising 150 pipes renders a fifty-fold F major triad. In addition it also plays nine pieces of music. An imitation of the "Salzburg bull" was placed in Heilbrunn Castle park near Salzburg in 1750, and is also still in playing order.

Few details of pipe making in the fourteenth century are forthcoming, but Engelbert of Admont (d. 1331) states that the smallest pipe of an organ measured eight times its diameter (from the mouth up), yet not for another century does an author expatiate on this subject. He is Giorgio Anselmi of Padua (1434): long and wide pipes, he writes, emit a greater and deeper sound (*magis et gravem*), shorter and narrower ones a rougher and higher sound, so that organ pipes for churches should be relatively short, but those of organs in private houses can be longer and narrower, for the tone will be better and less penetrating. Pipes having seven and one-half times their diameter, he continues, have a rough and loud tone, those of seven times their diameter have a penetrating tone, those of nine times the diameter a sweet tone, while those over nine times the diameter produce a dull (*obtusus*) tone. Evenness of wind pressure was assured by then, for Anselmi alludes to it. Thus builders had at their disposal by the turn of the fourteenth to the fifteenth century the means of predetermining the tone quality of their pipes and of adjusting their scale to best fit the organ's surroundings, that is, the space to be filled by their sound. Yet this tool could be exploited only in part until registers had been invented and individual stops could be drawn off, which event had already taken place by the time Anselmi wrote.

Medieval bellows were trodden or of the smithy type. Rectangular, cuneiform bellows (known as diagonal bellows) came into use in the fifteenth century; the first hint given of their existence is in 1419 at York. A minimum of two bellows was necessary to ensure a continuous supply of wind, and on small organs, particularly procession organs, these were placed immediately behind the pipes. Their bottom plate was fixed; the upper, on which a leaden or other weight was placed, was free to fall back at a speed determined by the weight, after having been raised by the blower. Alternate rhythmical raising of each bellows provided steady wind pressure without the necessity of resorting to a reservoir. Trodden bellows either continued in use or were reintroduced for large organs; Praetorius depicts some of the twenty trodden bellows of Halberstadt Cathedral, requiring ten blowers; the bellows in question probably dated back to the fifteenth century, when the organ was renovated.

One of the most important and far-reaching events in the organ's history took place around 1400: the creation of registers. According to Dufourcq they may even have existed on large organs of the late fourteenth century. But the process of isolating every stop, or rather, of creating a stop by isolation from its peers, was a slow one, not to be accomplished consistently until a century or so later, somewhat earlier in France and in the Low Countries. Taken in conjunction with the preceding invention of roller and tracker, the creation of registers led to tremendous acceleration of the organ's development, and the musical potentialities that were increasingly exploited resulted in a flowering of organ literature and also ensured the instrument's preeminence in the West over all other musical instruments until the mid-eighteenth century (somewhat later in Germany).

First, the principal pipes—the fundamentals—were separated from their aliquots and could be played separately, then gradually the *Hintersatz* was broken up into component ranks, and in most countries imitative solo stops were added (i.e., imitative of orchestral instruments, the human voice, and so on). Italian and British organs formed an exception to this rule, being satisfied for the most part with principals at different pitch levels, called octave, twelfth, fifteenth, et cetera and devoid of mixtures. On the Continent, "principal" denoted the foundation pipes, and these could be either at 8′ or at 4′ pitch, depending on the size of the organ, but in Britain the term was restricted to pipes of 4′ pitch, with those of 8′ pitch being known as diapasons. Increasingly, these terms came to indicate the scale of the pipes. In Italy also, stops were named for their distance from their fundamental, for example, *ottava*, *dodecima*, and so on. This system continued to prevail in the fifteenth and sixteenth centuries; occasionally a flute or two would be added. A number of fifteenth- and early sixteenth-century dispositions consist of fundamental, octave, superoctave, quint, octave above, and flute. Elsewhere the stop indications were in pitch-feet right from their inception.

Italian builders were slower to adopt registers than were their northern colleagues. A contract between an organist and an organ builder of Padua, signed in 1439, called for the making of six positives having three registers each, yet the organ at San Antonio Daniata, Cremona, built in 1441, had none. Not until 1465 are registers mentioned unequivocally in an Italian church organ, that of Santa Maria della Pieve in Gemona. Rather ironically, the oldest extant organ with stops may be that of the south side of San Petronio in Bologna dating from 1470, with a stop for each rank of pipes on a spring chest.

The old form of windchest was an enlarged slider chest in which one groove was provided for each key (named for the slider, a thin wooden batten placed underneath a rank of pipes, with holes corresponding to the pipe feet). When the pipework was divided into registers an improved system was called for, resulting in the invention—probably in the Netherlands—of the spring chest. Here, each groove served all pipes of a corresponding stop, and each key had a separate spring valve (i.e., a pallet) in the groove. This type was preferred by builders of the Low Countries, but, allegedly due to the frequent breaking of springs, slider chests were preferred elsewhere as simpler to maintain and to repair. According to Praetorius, spring chests were invented around 1400; Werckmeister mentions one dated 1442. Werner Fabricius (1633–1679) described two types of slider chest, one of which must have been very old indeed: it was cut of very thick wood from which the grooves were hollowed (this would ensure their being airtight); he calls this a *gebohrte Lade* ("pierced chest"); the other kind had grooves built up of slats glued to a board.

Reference has been made to the second, smaller manual added to organs north of Italy in the late fourteenth century for playing the bigger pipes. This in turn led to the creation of a descant manual for treble pipes in order to counterbalance the by then overpowering bass. In France this appears to have developed into the *positif de dos*, the chair organ. Troyes already had a chair organ in 1433, Dijon one by 1440—the latter with 195 pipes, according to Arnaut—Zwolle one in 1447. But in France the chair organ was to remain restricted to a few ranks of pipes and never assumed the same importance as those of the Low Countries and Germany. There the development was of a somewhat different nature, as the *positief an de stoel*, later called *rugwerk* in the Low Countries, *Positiev zu Rücken*, later *Rückpositiv* in Germany—an indication of its position to the back of the organist—was not considered an integral part of the organ at first. "An organ and a positive behind" was a common expression in organ-building circles at the time, and it seems that the

Rückpositiv originated from the incorporation of a positive organ into the great organ (cf. the coupling of organs at Rouen in 1387, above). The pipes of the positive—now the chair organ—were enclosed in a separate case placed behind the organist's seat, but manuals of both instruments were soon to be superposed, that of the chair organ being the lowest manual of present-day organs, and called choir manual, a modern corruption of the word "chair" (and hence the equally erroneous term, "choir organ").

An important manuscript adds notably to our knowledge of the northern organ in the mid-fifteenth century, that of Henry Arnaut of Zwolle, physician, astronomer, and astrologer to Philip the Good, Duke of Burgundy, later also to Louis XI. It deals, among other things, with the construction of organs, keyboard chordophones, and the lute. Parts of the manuscript are in Arnaut's hand and date from around 1440; those portions devoted to organ scales and dispositions, and details of bellows construction are in other hands, in all probability those of organ builders, and have been dated on internal evidence to about 1447 by Dufourcq (1934–1935). From these writings it follows that the coupler was already in practical use, as was a manual compass of $B°$ to a^2, thirty-five keys (the organ of Sainte Marie de la Mer already had thirty-five keys in 1425, but many organs of that day had fewer). Furthermore, Arnaut indicates a scale of one-sixth for the lowest pipe, although some builders make it one-seventh, he says, and then reports one of one-fifth for the 4' pipe of the Dei Custodientes Church. Our next source of information on this subject, Schlick (1511), has double principals at one-fifth and one-seventh. These measurements represent the ratio of circumference to length. The wider scale afforded prompt speech, the narrower one a more delicate tone, but not always a prompt attack, and it may be for this reason that double principals were included in so many organs of the fifteenth and sixteenth centuries. Arnaut refers to those of Saint Cyr church (at Nevers?) with its twelve tenor pipes on a separate chest, and to those of the great organ of the Cordeliers. Another organ had single principals, but they were divided, and had a total of five registers.

In another hand, a chair organ of particularly sweet tone is described as having front principals of tin, auxiliary principals of lead placed to the rear, the latter very heavy and nearly three times as thick as those of tin. Its compass was $f°$ to f^3, three octaves, and in addition to the principals (triple from f^2 up), it contained an octave and a superoctave, for a total of 195 pipes. The Arnaut manuscript also contains an early and cryptic reference to reeds, cryptic because redacted in an abbreviated if not secret formula accompanied by two Latin phrases, and the novelty of reeds can be gauged by the fact that the writer found no Latin for them and was obliged to fall back on the French *anches*. It seems that they were governed from a manual of their own having eighteen keys and a compass of F° to b°, a downward extension from the usual B° or c°.

Another page, in yet another hand, describes the old Notre Dame organ at Dijon, remarkable for its compass of nearly four octaves, fully chromatic, from B′ to a²; a second organ of the same church had a compass of four octaves from F°, without the low F♯ and G♯. Both of these were unusually large for the time, except for the Italian and Spanish organs. As a final note to Arnaut's manuscript, the second organ of Notre Dame included a small mixture containing a tierce, believed to be the first of its kind. Some idea of the degree of development reached by the northern organs of this time may be gained from the fact that Amiens Cathedral organ had in 1429 no fewer than 2,500 pipes.

In Italy a second manual remained quite exceptional up to the end of the sixteenth century but, as already noted, manual compasses there were extended earlier; thus in 1435 San Antonio of Padua had fifty-six keys, Lucca Cathedral in 1442 had fifty-three or fifty-four. But even these are exceptions rather than the rule, for until the late sixteenth century forty-seven keys were more or less standard and these included the *contrabassi* for the pedals.

THE ORGAN IN THE SIXTEENTH CENTURY

Many organs of the fifteenth and sixteenth centuries were suspended against a church wall and are now known as "swallow's nests" in consequence. They can be observed in paintings of the period, for instance, that are attributed to Conrad Witz of about 1430, showing the Basel Minster organ, for a remodeled version of which Holbein the Younger designed the wooden shutters in 1523–1524 (they still exist), and Saenredam's interior of Saint Bavo, Haarlem, showing its organ of about 1500; the extant fifteenth-century organ, much renovated but not enlarged, at Sion, Switzerland, with its two principals, two octaves, two quints, and a mixture, is still perched aloft. A glance at the literature of the period to determine the use made of the organ's various components discloses that

The fifteenth-century "swallow's nest" organ of Saint Valère, Sion.

Adam Ileborgh composed in 1448 preludes requiring pedals (*Praeambulum bonum pedale sive manuale*) and that Conrad Paumann wrote in 1552–1555 for a compass of B° to f².

At about this time, reed and regal pipes were coming into use. Actually a regal pipe is not a pipe, properly speaking, for the reed alone sounds; originally it had no resonator at all and later an extremely short one, the timbre being affected by its shape rather than by its length. The regal was at first a portable instrument containing regal reeds exclusively. Its relationship to the organ was likened by Mahrenholz (1938) to that existing between the harmonium and the modern pipe organ: an independent form of instrument. The word "regal" is not encountered prior to the mid-fifteenth century and thereafter was often wrongly applied to portative or positive, particularly in England.

At first it consisted of a single row of reeds; later, in imitation of the organ it took on additional ranks. If a more substantial instrument were desired, small flute pipes could be added. By 1500 the multirank regal was being incorporated in toto into the organ, after which the name gradually ceased to denote an independent instrument. Regal reeds had meanwhile acquired short resonators of brass or of wood of different forms, and the material is sometimes indicated in the name of a regal stop, such as *Messingregal* ("brass regal"), as is its form, for instance, *Apfelregal* ("apple regal"). An *Apfelregal* is illustrated in the well-known early-sixteenth-century woodcut attributed to various authors showing Emperor Maximilian at Mass, with Paul Hofhaimer at the regal, a shallow box. The "apples" are globular resonators with a slit across the top to permit the wind to escape, taller in the bass although still low, and diminishing toward the treble. Praetorius states that a regal "pipe" sounding 8′ C (C°) was about five or five and one-half Brunswick inches high, square, and stopped, but with several holes pierced in the lower part, and that it was as sweet sounding as a curtal; that others were shorter and open, but of less sweet tone, and finally that reeds of the very small (book?) regals of Nuremberg and Augsburg make had too little space; their tubes were barely one inch high, and hence their sound was too snarling (*schnarrhaftig*). During the seventeenth century the short resonators were gradually abolished in favor of larger ones, whereupon the differentiation between regal and other reed pipes ceased. Cerone complained in 1613 that no instrument held its tuning less well than a regal, which, he claimed, was apt to go out of tune from one hour to another. A late form was the so-called Bible regal, a modern term given to small regals in book form (also called book regals) made from the sixteenth to the eighteenth century. Dom Bédos de Celles (1766–1778) shows a table organ with a rank of regal pipes and one of flue pipes; some makers, he writes, added a short cone to the reed to augment its volume. Regal and reed pipes are known collectively in German as *Schnarrwerk*, from their snarling tone.

All organ reed pipes were of the beating reed variety exclusively up to the end of the eighteenth century, when free reeds were first utilized. In such (beating) reeds, the metal tongue beats against the rim of a brass shallot enclosed in a tube usually of cylindrical or conical form. (Whereas the length of flue pipes from the mouth up is called body, regal or reed pipes are said to have tubes or resonators.) Shallot is called *rigole* in French, a word that may be at the root of *regal* in its organological sense. Since the tongue is the principal factor in determining pitch, the resonator's function is above all that of determining timbre by its shape, and influencing dynamics by its length. Pre-baroque tongues were characteristically thin and wide, a construction that favored the upper harmonics.

After the adoption of reeds the pipework of an organ consisted of flue, reed, and regal pipes. The former, in use ever since antiquity, have essentially a flue, or windway, between the edge of the languid and the lower lip, the languid consisting of a metal plate fixed horizontally inside the pipe at the upper extremity of the foot, with a beveled front edge (in wooden pipes, this is termed "block"); flue pipes are either open or stopped (i.e., closed at the top) or half-stopped. Made of metal at first, they were also made of wood from about 1500 on (wooden pipes occurred at Brussels in 1501). Basic pipework can be divided into foundation stops— the flue pipework alone—mutations, and mixtures. In mutation stops, the depressed key sounds a tone other than its own (e.g., if $c°$ were depressed, g' would sound). Mutations are always played in conjunction with foundations, never alone. (If the twelfth above a given key is sounded, the stop is called a twelfth, if the seventeenth a tierce.) Mixtures are composite stops, an outgrowth of the medieval flue pipework, with more than one pipe to a key, namely two or more of the fundamental's overtones, all controlled by one drawstop. The tonal position of mixtures is indicated by the foot-length of the biggest pipe on the $C°$ key, and in describing it, the number of ranks is usually indicated. This could be considerable; Praetorius gives the composition of a 42–44 rank *Grossmixtur*.

Although churches were by now provided with great organs, the older positives were often retained; thus Basel Minster had two organs and three positives for a while, and in 1473 employed an *organista cori* in addition to the regular organist. At the end of the fifteenth century the cathedral at Mainz had one large and two small organs, and Saint Stephen's Convent in Dijon had three "pairs" of organs in 1526. Initial expense and maintenance costs of a large organ were so considerable that many churches kept a second organ for rehearsal and practice purposes; Konstanz Cathedral had a second organ built in 1490 expressly to spare the great organ, and in organists' employment contracts a clause was occasionally inserted prohibiting organ playing except during services.

From about 1490 to the middle of the sixteenth century the manual compass usually terminated on F, often specified as "F below gamma-ut" in contracts, but organs more than any other instruments perhaps lacked standardization, both as to compass and as to disposition, due to their very expense. If a new organ had been erected shortly before a technological innovation took place or musical requirements became more demanding, it would have to continue in use for decades before any necessary improvements were made. For this reason it is difficult to pinpoint the degree of development of the organ at any precise date, quite apart from considerations of regional or national preferences, and therefore with indications of common manual compasses the sometimes considerable time lag must be borne in mind. But later in the sixteenth century a four-octave compass was in general use, Spain and Italy always excepted. Larger organs at the end of the fifteenth century, such as that of Hagenau in 1491, comprised tenor, descant, and positive sections—or pedal, manual, and chair organ, as we would term them today. A final development of the fifteenth century was that of the so-called split sharps, an attempt to overcome problems of intonation. (For details of these, see keyboards, page 237.)

In Italy the tonal ideal for an organ had been established by then and did not change; the new organ for Saint Mark of Venice built by Fra Urbino about 1490 (its shutters were painted in that year), was still in use in the eighteenth century. Its original disposition is known, as is the compass, a giant four octaves, F to F; it had nine registers all told: *contrabassi, tenori, ottava, decimaquinta* (fifteenth), *decimanona* (nineteenth), *ventesimaseconda* (twenty-second), *ventesimasexta* (twenty-sixth), *ventesimanona* (twenty-ninth), *flauti,* all serviced by *grandissimi* bellows placed behind the organ. Nearly two and a half centuries later Mattheson (1739) describes the same organ, still with its nine registers: *Sub-Principal* 24′ down to F, *Principal* 16′, *Octava, Decimanona, Quintadecima, Vicesima secunda, Vicesima sesta, Vicesima nona, Flauto* (he has inverted the order of fifteenth and nineteenth); all Italy is said to possess only organs with pulldowns, so there is in reality only one manual, he states, citing this organ as an example.

No Italian organ had two manuals before the mid-sixteenth century, and from then until the end of the seventeenth century such organs were built by foreigners and are found mainly in northern Italy. Santa Maria Maggiore, Trento, built in 1534–1539, is the first Italian organ known to have received two manuals; others followed, but the practice did not become general. Banchieri's description (1609) of the Pisa Cathedral organ, consisting of an *organo grosso* (great organ) as well as an *organetto di concerto dietro le spalle dell'organista* ("small concert organ behind the organist's shoulders") shows that chair organs were still uncommon, although by then they had been built at least as far south as Rome (Santa Maria in Aracoeli, 1586).

Divided registers became very common in Italy and on the Iberian peninsula during the second half of the sixteenth century, so that a second manual was not really missed; usually but not invariably the division occurred between b° and c′. It enabled organists to play in two different timbres on one manual. Dispositions remained basically unchanged from the previous century, and only from about 1530 on do Italian organs appear to have been built with more than ten stops. Reeds and stops not forming part of the *ripieno* were only adopted slowly; a *voce humana* appears from 1560 on in the treble of some organs, and Santa Maria, Gemona, became light-headed with drum and nightingale in 1568. Pedals remained undeveloped, representing as they did a downward increase in the principal compass; three- and five-tone extensions of this nature are mentioned in several sixteenth-century contracts. An independent pedalboard of twenty keys was called for in the 1537 contract for Brescia Cathedral, to be built by Gian Giacomo Antegnati.

Of the closely related Iberian instruments it is known that pedalboards remained small—that of Evora Cathedral in Portugal still has its six-key pedalboard built in 1562 and its single manual of forty-five keys; Toledo Cathedral organ, built in 1549, had two manuals of fifty-seven keys—all its stops were divided—and a double pedalboard (i.e., a divided one) with thirteen keys for the basses, thirteen for the trebles (its reeds placed *en chamade*, a glory of Spanish organs, was added during the seventeenth century). Santiago Kastner, who has a specialist's knowledge of Iberian keyboard instruments, writes (1936) that on many Iberian instruments the soprano could be played on the pedal and the bass on the manual, an arrangement that was, however, not confined to the peninsula at that time.

Arnold Schlick's book devoted to the organ, its playing, and its music, was published in 1511, a landmark in the instrument's history. That on which he played daily in southern Germany had two manuals, one for the *positiff zu rück* (chair organ), and a pedal; all its registers could be transposed up a whole tone (see keyboards, page 239), permitting him to play C with the D pipes, an uncommon arrangement at the time. He recommends a pedal compass of one and one-half octaves from F° to c°, with both low F♯ and G♯ (these keys were often omitted), and demands *Claves . . . in welcher auch einer zwo stym mit eim fuss greiffenn mag* ("pedal keys spaced so that the organist can play two 'voices' with one foot") showing his familiarity with the toe-and-heel technique.

Furthermore, he advocates accompanying the choir with two or even three "voices" (parts) in the pedal; thus the pedal was no longer a bass annex to the manual but had the same pitch and was capable of alternating with it. Eight or nine registers are all he recommends: the two principals (also called *coppel* or flutes) that could be drawn off from the *Hintersatz*, cymbal and remaining ranks; an octave, or in larger organs, suboctave; a gemshorn; *Rauschpfeifen* or a shawm; a cornett; a *hültze glechter* (xylophone) "that is unusual and curious to hear"; and a regal, "such as was first made five years ago for the emperor." In the pedals: principals at the same pitch as those of the manual, an octave, a trumpet or trombone. *Rauschpfeifen*, crumhorn, and trumpets were new stops, he states. Mixtures should have no more than sixteen to eighteen pipes on the highest key in a large church, and no quints and tierces such as the old builders made and were still to be found (i.e., no quints or tierces in close position).

The size of a mixture, he continues, should always be adjusted to that of the church; his bellows were trodden, nine or ten feet long, and supplied wind to the chest by an intermediary wind trunk (*Canal*); two builders anxious to innovate had furnished an organ with split keys some twelve years before he wrote, but they proved unsatisfactory and were consequently removed. His recommended length for the lowest pipe in the pedal, "F below gamma ut" (F°), drawn in the margin, measures 13 centimeters to be taken sixteen times, or 208 centimeters (ca. 6 feet 10 inches), but he gives no indication of the diameter. If this is calculated from our knowledge of other organs, a theoretical length of 224 centimeters (7 feet 4 inches) would result, which would be our present E♭ (for Schlick's measurements, I have followed Elis [1956]).

Having thereby indicated the most suitable pitch for accompanying the choir, Schlick proceeds to say that if one wishes an organ a fifth larger, then the C (*cfaut*, c°) in the pedal should have that same length, ergo, that of the F pipe. And if a still larger organ were desired, the lowest pipe should be made an octave greater than the indicated measure. In other words, an F key could sound F on one organ, C on another, a most confusing disposition (cf. Glareanus's usage of calling the lowest harp string F, regardless of its absolute pitch). Yet Schlick is not speculating idly; he is confirmed by Bermudo and Diruta later in the century, and by Praetorius in the next, and the fact has to be accepted that organs a fourth or a fifth apart in pitch coexisted; sometimes, as is clear from Praetorius, in the same time and even in the same church.

The reason and nature of this development is related to the organ's expansion. To the extent that one can generalize, organ manuals of northern continental Europe had a compass of two and one-half octaves during most of the fifteenth century, starting on C or B in the bass; from the last quarter of the fifteenth to the middle of the sixteenth century, this was increased to three octaves and a third, usually from F in the bass, then to three and one-half octaves, also from F; from then on until the end of the seventeenth century the most common manual compass was four octaves from C, with either short or long octave in the bass. When Schlick wrote, there would have been in existence older organs terminating on C or B, and new organs, or rebuilt older ones, terminating on F. Because of the great expense involved, the purchase or rebuilding of church organs was often put off, so that a great many nonmodernized organs continued in use. Douwes (1699), for instance, writes that some old organs with compasses of three octaves and a third (F° to a²), were still in existence, as were others with three octaves and a sixth (C° to a²), but that the majority of newer organs had four octaves (C° to c³), and that some were even larger.

Enlargement of an existing organ compass was usually brought about by adding new pipes and keys, but this was by no means an exclusive practice, as is evident from various organ contracts. Schlick suggests in effect leaving the pipes unchanged and merely renaming them in order to obtain a "larger" organ. Now the absolute pitch produced by depressing an organ key is a somewhat elusive factor, as the sound will depend upon the register(s) drawn; for example, changing from an 8′ stop to one of 16′ will lower the pitch by an octave, or changing it for a 4′ stop will raise it by the same amount; for this reason, Praetorius could talk of some old organ being a fourth higher *or* a fifth lower than those of his day.

When an organist performs as soloist, the absolute pitch of his instrument is for practical purposes immaterial, although musically a piece will suffer if it is "wrought out of its proper clef"; however, in playing an intonation, for example, it is essential that the choir be guided to a suitable pitch, and this cannot possibly vary by as much as half an octave —the interval of a fourth or a fifth. As Schlick's organ with the lowest pipe connected to an F key was of course at the same absolute pitch as that with the same pipe connected to a C key, transposition became mandatory on one or the other of the two instruments (in Schlick's case, with the C organ) whenever participation of a choir was involved, and this implied that the organist would have to master part of his repertoire in two distinct fingerings, with attendant complications caused by the necessity of using accidental keys tuned in unequal temperaments.

The same questions preoccupied Bermudo (1555). He wrote of organs commonly at seven and at fourteen *palmos,* and of another kind, pitched a fourth higher, at nine and one-half *palmos,* on which it was necessary to transpose down a fourth. Praetorius refers to the existence—particularly in Catholic churches—of organs a fourth higher or fifth lower than "our pitch"; these he considered the most convenient, and they were to be found in important collegiate churches of his day (smaller forms of organ were also affected: a regal pitched a fourth higher than the prevailing pitch is documented in the Württemberg court records for 1572–1573). And because of the expense involved, various expedients were resorted to in the sixteenth and seventeenth centuries when older organs were to be enlarged. One of these was the use of wooden pipes to extend the bass of a rank of metal pipes in order to save money on metal, but the added treble pipes would be of tin. The contract for renovating the organ of Saint Godard, Rouen, in 1632, stipulates that a principal at 8′ pitch of fine tin was to be extended to sound at 16′ pitch by means of an "augmentation of eleven big stopped pipes of wood," and the 6′ principal of the positive was to be extended to 8′ pitch by adding four "big wooden pipes to the bass." Similar conditions were laid down in the contract for the restoration of Notre-Dame-en-Vaux at Châlons-sur-Marne two years later.

But another, organologically far-reaching, expedient may throw light on Schlick's and Bermudo's organs: shortly before 1504, a contract for renovating the great organ at Saint Jan, s' Hertogenbosch, called for a new *principaelwerck* manual starting on F without the low F♯; although not explicitly stated, the old manual had started on B, for the contract goes on to specify that the top of the *hamy oft beduyr* (B♮) pipe be lengthened to sound a semitone lower. The old compass, B C C♯, and up, was thereby transformed to one starting F G G♯, and up (if the old B pipe had not been lengthened, the new compass would have started as F♯ G G♯). Saint Gall's Cathedral organ was renovated in the same year that Schlick published his *Spiegel* and contained a clause virtually identical to that of the s'Hertogenbosch contract: . . . *das bemal itz soll das fa werden* . . . (". . . the B♭ shall now become F . . .").

A renovation at Sainte Marie, Utrecht, of 1517, also requires change of the manuals, so that the key *dat nu cefaut is dat zal gammaut wesen end dat gammaut datter nu is, dat zall hy corten dat zal wesen effaut beneden dat cefaut, da gammaut are* . . . *befabemy* ("that is now C should become G, and the present G he should shorten, it is to become F below that G, then G A . . . B♭"); there the manual must have had a G short octave (see keyboards, page 236) with the lowest key apparently a B but sounding G (G/B C D D♯ . . .); after changing the C to G, the lowest pipe, now sounding a fourth lower than the second pipe, was shortened to sound only a tone lower and henceforth to serve as F, resulting in a manual with F G A B♭ . . . in the bass. The actual extension of compass took place in the treble where the new keys were added (small pipes cost less than large ones), as may also be seen from a contract dated 1500 concerning Saint Jean, Besançon, where it is explicitly stated *du b my ou commencent lesdites orgues en bas, en faire f fa ut, et adjouster six cleis en hault du clavier* ("of the B on which the organ starts in the bass, make F and add six new keys at the top of the keyboard"). Analogous instructions were contained in a contract for renovating the collegiate church of Stuttgart in 1580, their abbreviated form attesting to familiarity with the procedure: *In jedem Register soll er etlich pfeiffen oben im Diskant hinzumachen. Damit die grosse Pfeiff, so jetzt da F ist, hernach möge das C sein* ("In each register he is to add several pipes at the top to the descant. So that the great pipe which is now F may henceforth be C").

That such changes affected the organist practically may be judged from the existence of organ literature such as the *Intonazioni* of Giovanni Gabrieli, published in 1593, where an intonation in each of the twelve modes is followed by its transposition: seven modes are transposed up a fourth, three down a fifth, one down a fourth, one up a fifth; in each case it is the same piece of music that is so transposed. These intonations were taken over and embellished by Bernhard Schmid in his *Tabu-laturbuch* of 1607, also in the dual form of untransposed and transposed versions.

The concept of saving money on tin whenever possible did not die out with the Renaissance, for centuries later Abbé Vogler was to berate organ builders for persistently constructing their instruments at choir pitch rather than at the lower chamber pitch in order to benefit financially from the lesser length of the pipes.

To return to the sixteenth century: Renaissance organs north of Italy included both flue and reed pipes, with an increasing number of new timbres imitating the rich instrumentarium of the epoch. Chair organs retained their basic 4′ pitch, that of the main organ was at 8′ or at 16′. Up to the eighteenth century the preponderance of stops at higher pitches and also of mixtures lent a quality of great brightness and clarity to the organ.

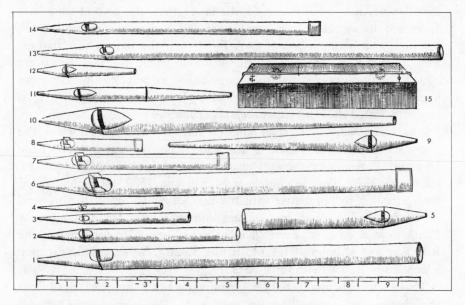

Early baroque organ pipes: (1) principal 8′; (2) octave 4′; (3) quinte 3′; (4) *Klein Octava* 2′; (5) open *Nachthorn* 4′; (6) quintadena 16′; (7) quintadena 8′; (8) *Nachthorn* 4′; (9) *Grossgedackt lieblich* 8′; (10) *Gemshorn* 8′; (11) *Spillflöte* 4′; (12) recorder 2′; (13) open *Querflöte* 4′; (14) *Gedackt Querflöte* 4′; (15) monochord. From Michael Praetorius, *Theatrum instrumentorum*, 1620.

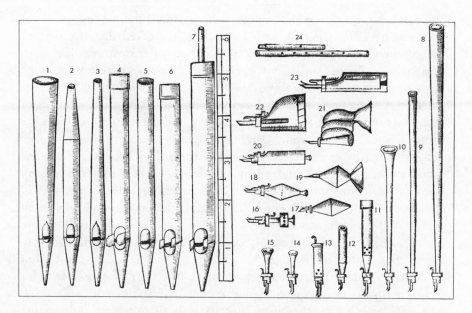

(1) *Dolcan* 4'; (2) *Coppelflöte* 4'; (3) *Flachflöte* 4'; (4) *Klein Bordun* 8'; (5) *Offenflöte* 4'; (6) *Gedackt* 8'; (7) *Rohrflöte* or *Holflöte* ("chimney flute") 8'; (8) trumpet; (9) crumhorn 8'; (10) shawm 8', 4'; (11) *sordone* 16'; (12) descant cornett; (13) racket 8', 16'; (14) *Messing Regal* 8'; (15) *Gedämpft* (muted) *Regal*; (16, 17, 18) crumhorns; (19–23) diverse *Barpfeifen*; (24) *Querflöte* ("cross flute"). (Note that no. 24 is not an organ pipe.) From Michael Praetorius, *Theatrum instrumentorum*, 1620.

Details of English organ building from the early sixteenth century are rare indeed, but in 1519 the contract for All Hallows, Barking, called for principals at 5' pitch with a bass at 10' pitch and a compass to "double ce fa ut" (C°). Saint Dunstan-in-the-West, London, had two organs in 1522, when "the organs in the quyer" and those "in the Rode lofft" (rood loft) underwent repairs—the latter an example of the English usage of placing an organ on the rood screen. Winchester College, Oxford, had three organs in 1531, one in the gallery on the north side of the choir, another in the pulpitum, a third in the chantry chapel; at the same time Eton had three "peare of organs." Later in the century Durham could also boast of having three organs, one of which contained wooden pipes only. English builders were partial to wooden pipes, of which they made considerably greater use, up to the end of the seventeenth century, than did their continental colleagues.

Chamber organs were not uncommon by this time; an unsigned instrument of 1592 is extant with its slides still worked directly, that is, not by drawstops. In the baroque period they often assumed the form of a large cupboard, and had a single manual and a variable number of stops; smaller models were also built to resemble flat-topped tables. In England, viol consorts were frequently accompanied by a chamber organ (see *viola da gamba*, page 506). During the Reformation, chamber organs played an important part as house organs for domestic music making; in many areas where the church organ had been banished—for example, the Protestant cantons of Switzerland—it was indeed the principal keyboard instrument until its displacement by the harpsichord in the second half of the eighteenth century. It may be added parenthetically that certain cantons were extremely slow to readmit the "devil's bagpipes" to Protestant service—not until the eighteenth century in the canton of Bern (first in Burgdorf, 1725), and in the canton of Zurich not until the nineteenth century. (Over 90 advertisements for chamber organs were placed in one Zurich weekly alone between 1730 and 1800, after which they were superseded by harpsichord and piano.)

THE ORGAN IN THE SEVENTEENTH CENTURY

The seventeenth century brought about changes in organ building in England, where reference occurs to a two-manual organ for the first time in 1606. When Thomas Dallam built a new organ for Worcester Cathedral in 1613–1614 he endowed it with two manuals, great and chair, with five stops on each, and an open diapason "CC fa ut a pipe of 10 foot long," as that of All Hallows, Barking, had been close to a century earlier. This gives a length of 5 feet for c° and 2½ feet for c′, a very low pitch, lying between our modern G♯ and A.

And this brings us to the question of the potential existence of organs "a fourth lower or a fifth higher" in England, for it is precisely in Worcester that a glimpse at the discrepancies of pitch is afforded. Around 1596 Thomas Tomkins became organist at Worcester Cathedral, a position he retained until 1646; a note to the *pars organica* of his *Musica deo sacra* (a note occurring only in the Saint Michael's College, Tenbury, copy) figures a semibreve on the F line of a bass clef and the text: *Sit tonus fistulae apertae longitudine duorum pedum et semiss: sive 30 digitorum geometricorum,* as Stevens (1957) relates, by Thomas's son and editor, Nathaniel (1599–1681), making it perfectly clear that f° equaled (or was to equal in performance of these compositions?) a 30-inch or 2½-foot long pipe; a very high F indeed, for as stated above, a 2½-foot pipe is closer to our G♯ or A.

Modern English musicians are well aware of the fact that Tudor church music is scored so low as to demand an upward transposition, whereas secular music of the same period was scored higher. But whatever the absolute pitch, it seems that in England as elsewhere a pipe of a given length could be called F just as well as C. In fact, Mersenne goes even further when he writes that the keyboard starts on C but that it can commence on whichever letter (i.e., key) one desires, and that the sound of each pipe corresponds indiscriminately to any key (. . . *que le son de chaque tuyau soit indifférent pour signifier le son de toutes sortes de lettres*).

English organs of the first half of the seventeenth century very often retained the earlier double principals; a second manual became common from the third decade on, but the pipework remained restricted to fundamental registers of principals and diapasons, plus flutes, twelfths, fifteenths, and twenty-seconds, reminiscent of the Italian tradition, and ignoring the wide variety of imitative instrumental stops that had been developed on the Continent. Both in England and in Italy, the organ was considered primarily as a complement to the human voice rather than as a solo instrument; André Maugars wrote from Rome in 1639: *Il semble que la plupart de leurs orgues ne soient que pour servir les voix, et pour faire paroitre les autres instruments* ("It seems that most of their organs are only for serving voices and for enhancing other instruments").

But the tradition of organ building in Britain came to a halt with the Ordinance of 1644 "for the speedy demolishing of all organs," culmination of Puritan pressures that had adversely affected building from the second half of the sixteenth century on. When construction was resumed after the Restoration (Samuel Pepys heard his first organ in 1660), it was influenced by and at first dependent upon an influx of foreign builders, or native ones who had sat out the troubles on the Continent, headed by Father Smith—Bernard Schmidt, a Dutchman according to Anthony Wood, writing in 1671.

It was not uncommon for British organs to contain wooden pipework exclusively (e.g., Durham, late sixteenth century; Exeter Song School, seventeenth century; a 1650 Loosemore positive at Blair Atholl Castle, Scotland) a procedure almost unknown on the Continent. Munich

Cathedral organ had once been famous for its wooden pipes said to have been round, turned of boxwood; Esaias Compenius built a small organ containing only wooden pipes in 1612, transferred four years later to Frederiksborg, Denmark, still in existence, and known to many music lovers from recordings. Praetorius characterized it *sehr herrlich* ("very splendid"), a modern writer on organs as "a freak." Which leads to the consideration that human ears may possibly have been irrevocably impaired by Cavaillé-Coll.

Post-Restoration construction in Britain did not differ fundamentally from earlier concepts; it continued with two manuals, total absence of pedalboard, paucity of solo stops, and a continued lack of both reeds and mixtures. Double principals and diapasons were being made as late as 1662 (Canterbury Cathedral). Father Smith introduced the echo organ in 1684, with its pipes placed in a closed box. He also built his Temple Church organ (1682–1684) with split B♭ and G♯ keys throughout the compass, a feature qualified by Westrup (1937) as "a luxury unique in England," and with a G short octave. On his Foundling Hospital organ two special slides above the drawstops changed E♭ to D♯ and B♭ to A♯, respectively.

Organ playing in Italy is said to have declined rapidly after the death of Frescobaldi in 1644, and building consequently to have stagnated; yet building continued to pursue undisturbed the traditions it had established by the early sixteenth century, sheltered from the impact of Puritanism, Protestantism, and the Thirty Years' War, and even profiting from the last to the extent that foreign builders enriched northern Italy with new ideas. Such an immigrant was Eugen Casparini of Sorau who settled in Venice in the late 1640s for a period of thirty years. To him seems due the invention of borrowing, by means of which an organ stop can be transferred from one manual to another, for his son Orazio wrote of his father's having built claviorgana with up to twenty variations of tone by transmission of the pneumatic (i.e., organ) sounds (*durch Transportirung der pneumatischen Stimmen biss etliche 20. Variationes gehabt*). It seems ironical that this particular invention should have taken place in Italy, land par excellence of the one-manual organ. Renatus Harris made use of this same borrowing of stops "by communication," as he called it in 1710; he employed double pallets, one controlled from the great, the other by the chair manual, with duplicate sliders for those stops to be borrowed.

Although by the latter part of the seventeenth century no more is heard concerning organs pitched a fourth or a fifth apart, absolute pitch continued to vary considerably from one town to another and from country to country, much to the detriment of woodwind manufacturing and playing, and exerting influence on musical practice and organ building alike. Two examples may serve to illustrate some of the practical implications: When Vicenzo Bolcione, organ and harpsichord maker of Florence, made two organs for Cardinal Ferdinand Gonzaga in 1612, he was careful to inquire at what pitch they should be built, for *in Roma si canta un tono [sic] più basso di qua* ("in Rome one sings a tone lower than here"), and in 1675 Giovanni Battista Mocchi, kapellmeister at the Neuburg Wittelsbach court, wrote to his employer from Rome that he would select the needed contralto singer for the court *Kapelle* with care: it would have to be a mezzo-soprano because German organs were pitched nearly two tones higher than those of Rome. Frotscher (1935) states that when Johann Walther arranged concerti, concerti grossi, and other works of Italian composers for the organ, he transposed them down between a tone and a minor third to allow for discrepancies in pitch. A 1638 contract for the cathedral organ of Mexico City throws an interesting light on conditions in the New World: the organ, to consist of great, chair, and pedal divisions, was to be built in Spain. But the great was to be somewhat lower pitched than was customary in Spain, because the voices of the viceroyalty were not of the same range as those of Spanish choirs; however, as the chair organ was intended for accompanying wind instruments, this section was to have the pitch of Spanish organs to obviate the necessity of transposing.

In Germany, efforts at unifying the several cornett, choir, and chamber pitches finally resulted in the building of (choir-pitch) organs with one or more chamber-pitch stops to permit an organist to play continuo without having to transpose. Breslau's Elisabethenkirche already had three chamber-pitch stops in 1717 in addition to its ten at choir pitch. A contract drawn up in 1750 for the same church, completed in 1761, called for chamber pitch exclusively—the finished organ had fifty-six stops—but this was still exceptional, although Glogow Cathedral's new organ of 1752 was at chamber pitch throughout. It took another century or so for chamber pitch to become the sole accepted standard. A manual for organists published in 1838 still refers to organs at choir and at chamber pitch and advises the organist to ascertain by means of an oboe how far from chamber pitch his instrument is tuned, so that he may transpose accordingly. Resistance to building at the lower chamber pitch (usually one tone lower than choir pitch, but sometimes a minor second lower) was hard to overcome, for several centners of tin could be saved on the low C pipes alone.

THE ORGAN IN THE EIGHTEENTH CENTURY

Among the innovations of the eighteenth century was the swell organ, first produced by Abraham Jordan of London in 1712, actually a rearrangement of the echo box (known from the mid-seventeenth century on) with the front side transformed into a large sliding shutter, devised in order to provide dynamic swelling of tone. It was worked by a cord passed over a pulley and operated by a pedal (the nag's head swell); later the front portion was composed of louvers. Another innovation was the overblown reed, created by extending the resonator to two or even three times its normal length. The top octave of Andreas Silbermann's clairon 4′ at Ebermünster, dating from 1730, is already overblown, and the earliest known reed stop overblown for its entire compass was by Lohelius of Prague in 1785 (overblown flue pipes were known to Praetorius; the then newly devised stopped *Querflöte* did not sound of its natural intonation, but rather by *übersetzen* or *übergallen*, he reports, due to the elongated proportion of the body. They were later forgotten, to be revived by Cavaillé-Coll in the nineteenth century).

By this time, taste in matters acoustical had become greatly modified, and the overall balance of organ tone underwent change accordingly, with the exclusion of some of the more penetrating solo stops and of mixtures, and with an alteration in the balance between high-pitched and low-pitched ranks, in favor of the latter. Samuel Petri epitomized the practice of his age when he wrote (1767) that playing had become very difficult during his century because, instead of church modes, all tonalities had come into use; since then, transposition had become more complicated, partly because of the uneven tuning of different tonalities and partly due to the short octave in manual and pedal, "and the whole bass has but a single F♯, G♯, and D♯, and the pedal only a single C♯," thus obliging the organist to transpose. Shifting keyboards remedied this situation to some extent. Three decades later and organ contracts could proudly announce: "at choir pitch in equal temperament," as did that of Saint Jacobi, Nordhausen, in 1796.

The swell organ had meanwhile been obliged to travel far in order to reach the Continent from England: Adlung knew it after the mid-century only as existing on English organs, and the Dutch author Joachim Hess (1774) described the organ of the Lutheran church in Curaçao, West Indies, started in 1770 by an English builder "in the taste of most English organs," which was to include specifically a "so-called swell echo"; Hess expressed the hope that it could also be met with "in our Netherlands church organs." But despite the swell, English organs remained poor cousins in relation to their European counterparts, due chiefly to their continued disregard for pedals. An entry in the records of Saint Paul's Cathedral, London, for the year 1720–1721 shows that payment was made to a "Musical Instrument maker" for adding six trumpet pipes in the bass, for use with or without a pedal, as well as payment "for the pedal and its movements"—the earliest evidence of an organ pedal in England so far known. Burney refers to Handel's visits to Saint Paul's to play the organ there "for the exercise it gave him in the use of the pedals" on his "first arrival" in England (Handel's first visit took place in 1710), but must be mistaken in his dating, for Renatus Harris in 1712 had sought in vain a commission to build a large organ with "pedals for the feet" for Saint Paul's. For the next century pedals remained quite exceptional and even then extended only for an octave or so, and in the first half of the nineteenth century they remained rare and suspect.

The Swiss-born Johannes Schnetzler, later John Snetzler, arrived in England shortly after 1738—the precise date is unknown—and made a number of both church and chamber organs. He is credited with the introduction of longer and narrower keys on organ manuals, and "skunktail" sharps, longitudinally inlaid accidentals otherwise associated with English spinets; in 1757 he built an organ for the German Lutheran chapel in London with a one-and-one-half-octave pedal, the first of such magnitude in the kingdom and, one must add, typically built for a foreign congregation. (Sir John Sutton, a great admirer of Snetzler's work, wrote [1847] that English pedals were inferior to those of Germany as they consisted only of one set of pipes, a large open or stopped diapason, and suggested removing them!)

A late-eighteenth-century innovator in organ construction was the versatile Abbé Vogler, who was first to introduce free reeds (in 1792), but they attracted no attention at the time, and it was not until after the spate of free-reed keyboard instruments had become accepted in the nineteenth century that the soft-toned free reeds were again incorporated in the organ. For a while they remained popular, but were then gradually abandoned by builders except for the clarinet stop. From the last decade of the century dates the simplification system of Abbé Vogler, considerably in advance of its time and hence a failure, just as his free reeds had been. The simplification aimed at reducing both space and cost of organs by omitting all show pipes and mixtures, these being deemed unnecessary: the front pipes were to be arranged according to size in order to simplify the wind supply system and the action; the entire pipework was to be enclosed in one large box provided with a swell, and the lowest-pitched stops were to have no pipes of their own but to consist solely of resultant ones. The phenomenon of resultant tones (also called combination tones) had been discovered by Tartini and by Sorge independently, but Abbé Vogler was first to exploit their possibilities for the organ. Saint Mary Magdalen, Biberach, contained an organ designed by him, with a "trias harmonica 16' pitch" composed only of a stopped 8', quint 5⅓', and tierce 3⅕'. The stop known as acoustic bass can sound at 64', 32', or 16' pitch, all the products of resultant tones created, for example, by placing a 16' top with a 2⅔' stop in order to obtain the resultant tone of 32' pitch; such procedure avoids the expense of very large pipes and saves considerable space.

THE ORGAN IN THE NINETEENTH CENTURY

Organ building and also organ playing were affected both adversely and favorably in the course of the nineteenth century. First of all, the breakthrough in knowledge, particularly that of the natural sciences, caused revision of school curricula, with drastic curtailment of choir training, which in turn led to deterioration of organ playing and cultivation, especially in small towns. German complaints anent the decadence of church music on this account are emphatic and frequent during the first half of the century. But the same increase in knowledge enabled Joseph Booth to invent the pneumatic lever, a vital component of modern actions that was developed by Charles Spackman Barker of Bath around 1832. Unable to interest builders in his own country, Barker took his pneumatic lever to Paris, where Aristide Cavaillé-Coll (1811–1899) recognized its potentialities and adopted it.

Cavaillé-Coll, the most important builder of his century, was creator of the romantic organ, a lush, symphonic instrument that responded to the new musical taste. He emphasized in his earlier instruments the new heavy-pressure reeds, the first of which was the grand ophicleide of

William Hill, 1834, on 12″ pressure, and he made extended use of total crescendo and diminuendo, thanks to Barker's new action. With the pneumatic lever no limits were imposed any longer on organ size, as a consequence of which organ history was made from the late nineteenth century on in concert, convention, and cinema halls rather than in churches, to culminate in monsters having up to a thousand stops working on up to 100″ pressure and played from up to seven manuals. Inevitably and happily, the reaction to these outsized one-man orchestras set in, spearheaded by Oscar Walcker's "Praetorius organ" of the 1920s—a return to the relative simplicity of the baroque—and a healthier atmosphere now prevails in organ building.

Modern organs are no more standardized than were those of yore, the number of stops and manuals, and even the type of action, still vary with maker and site. Today's larger organs have up to five manuals with a compass of five octaves, and a pedalboard.

Traditionally the pipework has been sounded by the intermediary of a mechanical or tracker action, in which a tracker pivoted to a sticker pulls the pallet open, thus involving backward motion. Roller actions combine backward with lateral motion—organs are divided into two sections known as the C division and the C♯ division (containing pipes for the CDEF♯G♯B♭ and for the C♯D♯FGAB keys, respectively)—by stickers that engage an intermediate roller communicating via a square with the tracker. But Barker's pneumatic action, created with the intention of procuring an easier touch, changed all this: with the new lever the keys no longer opened pallets indirectly; instead, they opened the valves of small, intermediary bellows. After a great deal of further experimentation, tubular-pneumatic and the yet more sophisticated electric actions were developed, presenting today's builders with a range of choices. In recent years a tendency has developed to go back to the old tracker action.

The ancient spring chests were transformed into springless *Kegelladen* (cone chests) by Eberhardt Walcker in 1842, taking their name from the conical valves; the mechanical model was in turn transformed into a pneumatic one in 1890. To the traditional pipework must be added the late-nineteenth-century polyphonic pipes, developed although not invented by Louis F. Debierre of Nantes, who by making a single pipe speak at three different pitches was able to suppress two-thirds of all bass pipes. More recently the Compton cube, invented by John Compton on the ocarina principle (see page 597) permits all tones of one octave to be sounded by two cubes, each furnished with several holes. From saving money and space by making one pipe or cube do the work of several pipes, it was just one more step to save considerably more money and space by eliminating the pipework altogether, and this took place with the twentieth-century creation of electrophonic organs that contain all necessary sound-generating parts in their console, and are moreover far cheaper and easier to maintain, as a slight turn of a screwdriver applied to twelve screws suffices to tune a whole organ. Sic transit . . .

ENHARMONIC ORGANS

When Italian theorists of the sixteenth century needed instruments on which to demonstrate the principles of what they believed to be resuscitated Greek genera, they had *arcicembali*—we now call them enharmonic harpsichords (see page 287)—built for this purpose. Organs, however small, were considerably more expensive to make, but for experimental purposes they offered the advantage of more permanent tuning (the equally great advantage of continuous tone was not exploited until the nineteenth century); in practical application, organs provided with microtones could in those centuries of unequal temperaments materially assist a choir's intonation. Salinas (1577), the blind Spanish composer, theorist, and organist, wrote of an organ at Santa Maria Novella, Florence, which he had not only heard but had often played, that had split sharps—a third "order" of keys, as he called them—for the enharmonic genus *ut commodius cantantium choro responderi possit* ("for the greater convenience of the choir in responding"). Bottrigari (1594) credited Nicola Vicentino of coining the term *arciorgano* for such instruments. Vicentino had designed two in 1572, he states, one of which was in Rome, built for the Cardinal of Ferrara, and another at Milan in Vicentino's care. A *herrlich* ("splendid") positive was brought from Italy to the archducal court near Graz "a few years ago," as Praetorius wrote (1619), with all sharps split, and a little later Doni in his *Compendio* of 1635 proposed an *organo panarmonico* with the octave divided into nineteen microtones, a favorite division of the theorists. This does not appear to have been built, and interest in enharmonic organs dies thereafter.

Both interest and organ were revived in the latter part of the nineteenth century and early twentieth century in connection with the experimental work of Helmholtz, Shohē Tanaka, and other investigators of European and extra-European tonal systems and tunings. Small experimental organs and harmoniums were constructed for them with specially designed keyboards; that of R. H. M. Bosanquet had two manuals, one with forty-eight microtones to the octave, the other thirty-six, all the pipes being stopped. But these also are now things of the past.

COLOR ORGANS

During the 1730s Pierre-Louis Castel, a Jesuit priest influenced by Newton's *Optics*, devised a *clavecin oculaire*, called color organ in English, and constructed a model later in the decade; by depressing a given key, a pallet was opened, and not only did sound issue from the corresponding pipe, but its complementary color appeared simultaneously in ribbon form, for the seven colors of the spectrum were made to correspond to the seven tones of the octave. Diderot, in an undated letter to Sophie Volland, alluded to its *petits rubans colorés* ("little colored ribbons"). It enjoyed a short-lived vogue, more as a curiosity than as a musical instrument. Scriabin later revived the idea of a color keyboard instrument, but this time a mute one, and scored his *Prometheus* (1913) for orchestra, piano, organ, choir, and mute color keyboard, where C was red, D yellow, and so forth, and the choir sang vowels with coloristic significance. Several other color "organs" have made appearances since, all of them mute.

MECHANICAL ORGANS

Musical Clocks

Musical clocks are a form of mechanical organ, usually very small indeed, powered by clockwork that sets a pegged barrel in motion at regular intervals (the principle of a carillon transferred to pipes); they may or may not contain a timepiece. Their history is one of increasingly smaller barrels being combined with increasingly smaller and higher-pitched pipes in increasingly smaller housings, starting with diminutive, automated carillons, to their full development in the late eighteenth century (and replacement by the miniaturized music box in the nineteenth century).

The larger instruments of the sixteenth and seventeenth centuries are better known as clockwork organs, due to their greater size. Usually they contained two ranks of pipes, a stopped 4' and an open 2'. Their organ components were made by an organ builder—often one of considerable repute—and the clockwork appurtenances by a clockmaker. Ornate showpieces with highly complicated movements were produced in this period, such as that sent by Queen Elizabeth as a gift to the Sultan of Turkey in 1599; the organ part of this instrument was made by Thomas Dallam, one of England's foremost builders, with an "open principal, unison recorder, octavo principal, flute, shaking stop, drum, nightingale," probably all at 4' and 2' pitch. Furthermore, it boasted a twenty-four-hour clock connected to eight moving figures; it could play for six hours without interruption and the lower portion of the instrument housed "a great barrel with a chime of very tunable bells."

The musical clock proper, always small, is a descendant of this marvel; it appears late in the eighteenth century. In general the automated flue pipes were housed behind the clockwork or in a special cupboard beneath it. Occasionally such clocks were combined with a stringed instrument, such as the musical-clock-cum-spinet made by 1687 by Mattäus Rungger, with a true spinet right down to the cardboard rose hidden in the interior of an ornamental clock; clockwork, cylinder, and bellows were placed under the soundboard. The little spinet has sixteen strings, the organ as many pipes inscribed with their pitch names (they sound a tone low by today's pitch standard). Stopped pipes were sometimes resorted to in order to avoid extremely high pitches; a late-eighteenth-century musical clock is known with sixty-four wooden pipes, all stopped.

German makers seem to have excelled at this type of workmanship, with Augsburg, Breslau, and Dresden as leading centers of production. Frederick the Great was fond of the *Flötenuhr*, and many musicians in court circles composed for it, including his flute master Quantz, Graun, C. P. E. Bach, and Kirnberger, while W. F. Bach, Mozart, Haydn, and Beethoven also wrote for it. Mozart complained in 1790 (à propos of *Ein stück für ein Orgelwerk in einer Uhr*, K. 594) that: "if it were a large clock and the thing sounded like an organ, it would please me," but it consisted solely of "small pipes that are high [pitched] and sound too childish to me." Of great artistic importance is the survival of no fewer than three musical clocks playing works by Joseph Haydn, and manuscripts of all the thirty-two pieces played have come to light. The clocks are dated 1772, 1792, and 1793, respectively; they have from seventeen to twenty-nine pipes, in each case a stopped 4' rank.

The musical clock, even though it might be made small enough to rest on a table, was not only an expensive acquisition but was at least as much of an art object as a musical instrument, so that when the music box, more quickly manufactured and hence more readily available, appeared with the latest tunes, musical clocks remained collectors' items, but obsolete ones. Henceforth the revolving cylinder continued to sound the organ pipes, but in a more plebeian manner: the rotation was accomplished by hand cranking.

Another development was that of the miniature organ popular in the 1760s, then known as music box, a transition instrument, both chronologically and structurally, between musical clock and idiophonic music box, its cylinder pinned with "minuets and country dances."

The Bird Organ

To the somewhat incongruous task of teaching songbirds to sing are due two types of automatic organs: the bird organ and its development, the barrel organ. The distinction made here is one of nomenclature only, as the majority of bird organs worked on the pinned barrel principle.

Since the late seventeenth century miniature mechanized organs have been hand cranked over and over again in the presence of caged birds in the expectancy that they would pick up the tune played to them. These little boxes with a handle had a few flue pipes, generally at 2′ pitch. The French called them *serinettes*, from *serin* ("finch") and by extension the word came to denote bird organs collectively. A typical instrument of the eighteenth century such as that described by Laborde (1780) might have had two miniature bellows, a windchest, thirteen pipes, and a barrel pegged with twelve tunes rotated by a hand crank. Usually the barrel required shifting in order to change the tune. Such organs were small enough to be set on the lap; *The Lady with a Bird Organ* by Chardin (d. 1779) shows a woman cranking a small box so held while she keeps an eye on her caged canary. Father Joseph Engramelle's *Tonotechnie* of 1775 contains detailed instructions for the "notating," i.e., the pinning, of *serinette* cylinders. The pitch of bird organ pipes was very high, starting at e^3 or even higher, the lower ones stopped in order to save space. With the advent of the French Revolution their use was abandoned.

The Barrel Organ

Structurally the barrel organ is but an enlargement of the bird organ: a mechanical and still portable organ. Possibly of Italian invention, it dates from the turn of the seventeenth to eighteenth century. One of the first makers was Giovanni Barbieri of Modena, from whose name the French term for the instrument, *orgue de Barbarie* ("Barbary organ"), was coined; this expression was first used in 1702 (later in the century its meaning was forgotten, as is apparent from the delightful advertisement, appearing in 1774, of instruments for sale: *un véritable orgue de barbarie fait par les sauvages* ("a true barbarian organ made by savages").

Essentially, a barrel organ consists of two or more ranks of organ pipes placed above the bellows in an enclosed cabinet; the pipes are controlled by a pinned barrel mounted on a metal spindle. The spindle is attached to a board and can thus be readily slid into position. Additional, interchangeable barrels were kept in a storage space provided in the cabinet. Each tune required one revolution of the barrel and several pieces of music were pinned side by side (on the smaller musical clocks, a given piece might occupy only half or a third of a revolution, so that the piece was played two or three times before the cylinder came to rest). As a space-saving device the bass pipes were stopped, and in at least one type of barrel organ, the *Wiener Werkl* of the 1860s, reed pipes were included to that end. Compasses were rarely chromatic because the tunes were transposed where necessary in order to require but few tonalities, the precise number depending upon the size of the instrument. Flat tonalities were not used. But the more elaborate barrel organs made for drawing rooms had barrels pinned with secular music requiring a wider range; for such models, more refined cabinet work and a larger compass were required, as the demand for longer and more complicated music—such as whole overtures—became expected of them. With the trend to longer and tonally more varied music they assumed undue proportions, until finally the orchestrion was born.

In England the barrel organ was, however, not always associated with mundane music making, for up to the middle of the nineteenth century many poorer churches and chapels possessed no organ, and a barrel organ served as a substitute, its barrels pegged with hymns, chants, psalm tunes, and even voluntaries. At least one well-known English builder, J. W. Walker, made barrel organs with an organ manual. Such combinations were known as "barrel and finger organs."

In the early nineteenth century an Italian builder named Gavioli, established in Paris, started making portable barrel organs; the first of these were sounded by means of perforated cardboard strips, folding bookwise, instead of barrels. They were small enough to be mounted on hand carts and wheeled about by street "musicians," the familiar "organ grinders." The street organs, as they became known, were a great success and lasted well into the twentieth century.

In 1731 Justinian Morse patented a "new organ" with "musick being prickt on both sides of leaves of half-inch wainscot, eight or ten psalm tunes being contained on a board about the size of a large sheet of paper," which could be worked by clockwork, jack, or winch, proper for use in church or chapel in small parishes unable or unwilling to bear the expense of an organist. Lacking as it did both pipework and blowing mechanism, the "new organ" can qualify only as a musical auxiliary, not as an instrument. It was, however, the forerunner of a nineteenth-century automatic player using a barrel rather than a flat board, the "dumb organist," an English device set upon an organ manual for depressing the keys automatically in the absence of a performer. This was a large, rectangular, boxlike container housing a barrel that was turned by a projecting hand crank. It was set on the keyboard, the appropriate keys of which were then depressed by trackers actuated by the barrel's pegs. Such auxiliaries were in use in some smaller English churches during the nineteenth century.

The orchestrion. When the monotony of the barrel organ no longer satisfied the public—the Germans had called it *Leierorgan* because of similarity to the hurdy-gurdy (*Leier*) sound—it grew into an imitation orchestra and was appropriately named orchestrion. Ranks of organ pipes of differing timbres were combined with various accessories to imitate the sound of orchestral instruments, and in due course the wooden barrel gave way to the newer perforated cards or rolls. The name, but not the idea, was new; in the mid-seventeenth century Athanasius Kircher described his machinamentum no. 7, a combination of organ pipes, hurdy-gurdy, and spinet that could imitate the lute, violin, and trombone, and which, like the above-mentioned "barrel and finger organs" could be played either from a keyboard or automatically by means of a pinned barrel. That his machinamentum was ever built is unlikely.

During their heyday in the nineteenth century, large orchestrions had up to forty registers of pipework and percussion, and as many as twelve barrels. Smaller but nonetheless elaborately finished instruments were supplied to private homes; these might have eight ranks of pipes with a chromatic compass of over five octaves, plus cymbals, drums, triangles, and so on. All operated on wooden barrels until 1887, the year in which Michael Welte patented "the use of paper rolls in connection with a pneumatic action." However, the barrels were pegged spirally, permitting them to revolve twelve times in the course of one piece, so that quite long compositions could be played.

One of the earliest orchestrions was in reality a portable organ built in Holland to the specifications of the versatile Abbé Vogler, and first played in 1789. Encased in a nine-foot cube, it had four manuals and a pedalboard, devices for obtaining crescendo and descrescendo on all registers, and was said to be capable of imitating a whole orchestra. But if the orchestrion is remembered at all today it is probably for the great *Panharmonicon* of Johann Nepomuk Mältzel, inventor of the metronome. At his request, Beethoven wrote a piece specially for it, *Die Schlacht bei Vittoria* (*Wellington's Victory*). The battle had taken place on June 21, 1813, and the music was performed in December of the same year (Beethoven also scored it for orchestra). In the *Panharmonicon* Beethoven disposed of no fewer than thirty-seven flutes, sixteen bassoons, thirty-eight clarinets, thirty-six oboes, eight trumpets, three French horns, two drums, two pairs of cymbals, triangle, and two kettledrums.

In the year 1815 Johann Gottfried Kaufmann and his son Friedrich, mechanical geniuses of Dresden, built a *Chordaulion* with open and stopped pipes that could imitate the sounds of both string and wind instruments. By increasing or decreasing the wind pressure, the sound could be modified dynamically without occasioning any change of pitch. One *Chordaulion* was shipped to Cuba in 1830; it could play thirty-four pieces of music and was operated by a weight raised by a hand crank without the assistance of clockwork—just like the English church-tower chimes of yore. Later, Friedrich Kaufmann built a larger model called *Symphonium*, with automatic piano, flutes, clarinets, clappers, and kettledrums. In a still later model, that of 1851, he incorporated several stops of free reeds.

Some idea of the size these instruments could attain is conveyed by the apollonicon of Flight and Robson of London, a monstrosity first exhibited in 1817, of 7.2 meters (24 feet) in height, 6 meters (20 feet) wide and deep. Its 1,900-odd pipes were disposed in forty-six registers and could be played either manually or mechanically on five manuals; these could be detached from the main body of the instrument to permit manual playing by five performers, no less, all facing the public. Three huge barrels were pegged spirally to permit playing long pieces. But despite the attention it attracted, the apollonicon was not a financial success, and in the end its makers demolished it.

After Welte had obtained his patent for perforated paper rolls in 1887, cylinders were gradually abolished; rolls cost less than barrels and took up far less storage space. But they required a modification of the action, making it both more complicated and more expensive. In the United States the orchestrion was in use sporadically—usually in the form of a coin-operated machine—until about 1930, and in Europe it lasted until even later.

A variant form existed in the calliope, a steam-driven organ (William of Malmesbury's dream come true at last) invented by the American, A. S. Denny. A row of pipes was connected to a steam boiler, pressure from which was controlled by valves, either from a keyboard or from a cylinder. When it first appeared in 1856 it caused a sensation; designed to attract people to fairs, showboats, and the like, from great distances, it could reach a public twelve miles away (from Jerusalem to the Mount of Olives).

REEDPIPES

DOUBLE AND TRIPLE PIPES

Throughout antiquity and into the Middle Ages, double pipes were the common form of reedpipes in the ancient Mediterranean world. They could be held and played in one of two ways: either as divergent pipes, one pipe held in each hand, with the mouthed reeds forming the bottom of a V, or as parallel pipes, often tied together, held with both hands, one above the other so that a given finger could stop a fingerhole on both pipes. Divergent pipes, identified by Curt Sachs and André Schaeffner independently of each other as having been sounded by double reeds, were an important feature of the eastern Mediterranean musical cultures. They appear to have preceded parallel pipes, believed by the two organologists to have been sounded by single beating reeds. But the question of matching form to type of reed has been reopened once more, and the above rule must now be considered as an oversimplification.

DOUBLE PIPES IN ANTIQUITY

Our earliest preserved specimens of double pipes are from the royal cemeteries of Ur, dating back to about 2700 B.C.: two very slender silver pipes, each with four fingerholes, and some 30 centimeters (12 inches) long, are believed to have formed a pair of divergent pipes; they are now preserved in the University Museum of Philadelphia, Pennsylvania. Some five centuries later we have evidence of the same pipes in the eastern Mediterranean: a marble statuette from the Cyclades dating from 2200–2000 B.C. is that of a player with one hand on each pipe. Israel of Biblical times had similar pipes made of cane, wood, or metal, called *hālil*. Translated by the Septuagint as "auloi," they were cylindrical in their early form, and despite the fact that they were primarily secular instruments they were played in the Second Temple (rebuilt 520–516 B.C.).

Parallel double pipes first appear in Egypt in the Third Dynasty (ca. 2700–2650 B.C.), but oddly enough, divergent pipes are not seen there until the Eighteenth Dynasty (1580–1350 B.C.). Parallel pipes of ancient Egypt were held either horizontally or diagonally; Hickmann, who has brought much new light to the history of Egyptian instruments, concludes that those held horizontally had downcut single reeds, those held diagonally, upcut ones, conforming to their modern counterparts, the *mashūra* and *zummārah* (surviving specimens from the New Kingdom period lack mouthpieces). Originally they had four, later five or six, fingerholes. Always a subordinate instrument in Egypt, by the New Kingdom the parallel pipes degenerated from art to folk instrument and have been played as such ever since. From their inception, Egyptian divergent pipes were played exclusively by women (quite exceptionally, in a few statuettes men are seen playing them). Their origin was thought by Sachs to lie within the Semitic world, somewhere between Asia Minor and Arabia; certainly their old Akkadian name, *halhallatu*, is cognate with the Hebrew *hālil*, and both were cult instruments, an indication that they had long been in use in those parts. In the Akkadian rite of immolating a bull prior to making a temple drum from its skin, the *kalu* priest sang to the sound of the bronze *halhallatu*, while the *hālil* was sounded on holy days in the era of the Second Temple.

All these pipes were originally made of cane; later the cane was replaced by metal in many areas, and for a long time the pipes continued to be made in cylindrical form. But on a Hittite relief of about 900 B.C. from Carchemish showing jugglers with lute and double pipes, the latter assume a slightly conoid shape; their conicity then increases, until by Roman times a pair of wide conical pipes on a bronze in the Landesmuseum of Trier are more reminiscent of natural horns than of reedpipes, and in the second century A.D. Jewish coins display pairs of conical oboes (pairs of conoid oboes united to form parallel pipes are always played with a common pirouette). Parallel pipes of the eastern Mediterranean underwent a similar metamorphosis: on a Syrian pottery vessel of between 100 B.C. and A.D. 100 in the Louvre, short conical pipes of equal length, probably tied together, are played by a priestess mounted on camelback.

Of their musical exploitation nothing is known, but Sachs inferred that, in ancient Egypt, of a pair of divergent pipes the right-hand one played the melody, whereas the left-hand pipe sounded a lower drone accompaniment; these deductions were made on the basis of finger positions on the pipes as seen on works of art, or present-day practice in other countries, such as India, and taking into consideration an excavated pipe having all fingerholes but one closed with wax.

From their Eastern homeland double pipes radiated to Europe in different migrational phases, for divergent pipes do not appear in Cyprus until the eighth century B.C., yet are unmistakably present on a sarcophagus from Hagia Triada, Crete, of the fourteenth century B.C. On a bronze figurine of the Hallstatt D period from Szazhalombatta, Hungary, a pair of double pipes is seen to terminate in vertical, disklike flares rather similar to, but larger than, those of some Etruscan pipes. Bone pipes with three, four, and six fingerholes, datable by contexts to the fourth or third century B.C., have been recovered from sites of former Greek colonies in Romania; we cannot tell, however, whether they were Dacian or Greek instruments.

About the first century B.C. a double-pipe player is sculptured, together with other musicians, on a Kushan-period frieze at Airtam, some three hundred kilometers south of Samarkand. Finally, with the Moslem expansion double pipes were carried as far as Southeast Asia. The Greek auloi in turn were dispersed in postclassical Europe; in western Europe they died out in the Middle Ages, but in the Balkans they have maintained an existence until now.

The Aulos

The divergent pipes of ancient Greece that we know as auloi are descended from these earlier Near Eastern instruments. In fact the Greeks themselves attributed their origin to Asia. Most important of the aerophones in classical antiquity, the aulos usually consisted of a very slender, cylindrical tube (from about 400 B.C. on, occasionally also conical for part of its length) made of cane, wood, or ivory and called *bombyx*, with a barrel-shaped socket (the *holmos*) at the upper end (that of the auloi found in Pompeii have a trapezoidal terminal), generally continued by a short, conical *hypholmion* into which the reed (*glōtta*) was inserted. Late in the nineteenth century the aulos was identified as a double-reed instrument by Victor-Charles Mahillon on the basis of personal examination in Italy and North Africa of monuments depicting auloi; he concluded not only that the reed was a double one and very similar to that of the Japanese *hichiriki* (a descendant of the Chinese indigenous shawm), but also that it had a similar keeper ring. His findings—prior to which the aulos had been taken for a single-reed instrument—were accepted by musicologists and organologists alike. Recently they have been questioned by Becker (1966), who, in a well-documented study, reexamines the evidence, reinterprets Theophrastus's famous passage on reed making, and concludes convincingly that the Greek aulos was usually played with a single reed but could also be played with a double reed. The term "aulos," it should be emphasized, included any kind of reedpipe, regardless of its means of tone production.

If Becker's interpretation of Theophrastus is correct, auloi in the latter's day were played specifically with upcut single reeds (as are most, but not all, double pipes of Mediterranean countries today). Cane for reeds, Theophrastus informs us, was cut during September (but, after about 350 B.C., in June, to obtain more elastic cane), laid out to season in the open, then scraped and cleaned in spring; in summer it was cut into segments at the nodes. Each internode furnished two reeds, so that when cut in half—that is, at half of the length—the *stoma* or mouth of each *glōtta* faced the cut (were upcut toward the node). Segments closer to the root were suitable for left-hand pipes, those closer to the foliage, for right-hand pipes; as a difference of bore is involved here, one may speculate that the left-hand pipe was the lower pitched of the two. Despite the numerous illustrations of the aulos, its reed usually remains invisible in the player's mouth or else is not sharply defined. Becker nonetheless shows a pair of auloi from an Etruscan fresco with two indisputable single reeds—downcut here. Parenthetically it may be noted that the clearly visible double reeds of the Pompeiian aulos player in the British Museum are the unfortunate result of a nineteenth-century restoration.

While playing, the performer held one pipe in each hand, for all classical auloi were double pipes—the single aulos did not come into use until postclassical times. Furthermore, instruments of the classical period were of equal length; those of unequal length or having conical bores are either distant ancestors or postclassical.

Frequently the performer is shown wearing a *phorbeia* (the Romans were to call it *capistrum*), a band passing over lips and cheeks to be fastened at the back of the head, with two apertures for introducing the pipes into the mouth. Known in Greece from the seventh century B.C. —it is seen on the Chigi Vase of about 640 B.C. in a military scene— and possibly of Aegean origin, its invention was attributed to Marsyas. So far it has not been seen worn by a female player (nor was it utilized in Egypt). Becker surmises that its function was that of supporting the lips when played with a double reed, and regards it as a forerunner of the pirouette. The player took the reeds completely into his mouth, inflating his cheeks to create an air chamber; played in such a manner, double reeds speak less easily and require greater power than do single reeds, and hence would have been played by men only.

Auloi appear in Cyprus in the eighth century B.C., as noted, but are not figured on Greek vases prior to 700, and then only sparingly for a while thereafter. During the classical period the number of fingerholes is believed to have been three and four, increasing later. From the fifth century on the number and disposition of fingerholes is said to have permitted playing in the three major Greek tonalities: Dorian, Phrygian, and Lydian. Several bone auloi from the second half of the seventh century have been found in the sanctuary of Artemis Orthia at Sparta. To the extent that the fourteen pieces can be fitted together they seem to have had three front fingerholes, one dorsal thumbhole, and possibly an additional fingerhole, now lacking (this would imply the use of two hands to a pipe, if the lower holes were in reality fingerholes), and a fragmentary bone tube with five front and one dorsal hole was taken from a late-sixth-century level at Brauron, Attica.

The only complete specimens from the classical age to survive are two wooden pipes from a tomb near Athens, now housed in the British

Museum (the Elgin Auloi), at present tentatively dated from between the fourth and the first century B.C. Their length is about 35 centimeters (14 inches); they have five frontal fingerholes and a dorsal thumbhole. Measurements of the bores of both instruments have proved contradictory: Kathleen Schlesinger (1939) found them to be strictly cylindrical, whereas A. Howard in 1893 had found a slight conicity of 2 millimeters and 3.5 millimeters, respectively. His experiments with reproductions built to these specifications showed that the harmonics were those of a stopped pipe, that is, they overblew the twelfth, a characteristic of cylindrical pipes (Howard also measured auloi found at Pompeii and ascertained that their bores were cylindrical). The Elgin Auloi are now generally admitted to be slightly conoid but are counted as cylindrical pipes because they overblow the twelfth.

Concerning the manner in which they were played we know virtually nothing; although the technique of overblowing was at their players' disposal, it is unlikely to have been exploited, as no present-day double or triple reedpipe, either European or extra-European, is overblown (and no overblow hole exists on any antique aulos). According to Plutarch, parallel-held auloi sounded a trifle lower than divergent ones. From the iconography we can deduce that they were played with the second finger joint, as are many modern folk instruments. Theophrastus refers to a change in the manner of playing, from aplastic to plastic, that took place in the mid-fourth century B.C. concurrently with an earlier cutting of reeds (in June), presumably, as has been mentioned earlier, to obtain more resilient material. Becker (1966) has interpreted this as a potential changeover from an uncontrolled reed vibrating freely in the mouth to a lip-controlled reed with less rigid tone.

Auloi in Greece had a role as cult, military, and social instruments. Aristoxenus enumerates five different lengths, in order to descending pitches: *auloi parthenoi, paidikoi, kitharisteroi, teleoi,* and *hyperteleoi,* together embracing a compass of over three octaves (cf. the different sizes of *launeddas,* page 662). Whenever playing was connected with the cult or with the military, the musicians were men, but at drinking parties they were girls. In the army, auloi performed the same task as did the fife in medieval infantry: Thucydides explains in his *Peloponnesian War* that, when the Argive and Spartan armies approached each other, the Spartans advanced slowly and to the music of auloi, which custom, he assures us, had no religious significance, but rather was intended to keep the men in step, marching at a steady pace without breaking rank. *Auletes* were not chosen for their musicianship, for Herodotus writes that in one respect the Lacedemonians resembled the Egyptians: heralds, *auletes*, and cooks took their trade by succession from their fathers.

From Greece the aulos passed to Egypt and, as far as is known, to Rome, although Rome may have been more influenced by the Etruscan *subalo* than by the aulos. Etruscan vases and tomb paintings of the sixth and fifth centuries show these played as double pipes. A cylindrical pair on a sixth-century black-figure amphora in the Museo dei Conservatori, Rome, terminates in thick, vertical disks, perhaps to indicate an acoustical adjunct, but generally Etruscan auloi are conical, sometimes ending in a flare. As cult instruments they had an important role at sacrifices and funerary rites. Auloi with three fingerholes appear to have existed in both Etruria and Rome; fingerholes were always bored near the mouth end, whereas any lower holes were vents, but from the total number of holes it is not always possible to determine which are fingerholes and which are vents. In Egypt both single and double auloi are first seen under Alexander and Ptolemy I (306 B.C.), according to Hickmann. Egyptian instruments preserved in Florence, Paris, and Turin measure 69.3 centimeters (ca. 27 inches), 65.9 centimeters (ca. 26 inches), and 59.5 centimeters (ca. 23½ inches), respectively. The left pipe of a pair is seen as slightly longer than the right pipe.

The Romans called their aulos *tibia*, the reed *ligula* or *lingula* ("little tongue"). Boxwood was a material appreciated by them for its manufacture, for the *buxus*, as the boxwood *tibia* was called, is mentioned frequently in literature. In late republican times the pipes are seen to grow longer, until they reach a length of some 60 centimeters (2 feet) or even more, and later ones have a larger number of fingerholes than did the auloi. Four ivory *tibiae* from Pompeii are provided with silver rings and no fewer than eleven, twelve, and fifteen fingerholes, only a few of which were in use at the same time, however, for a ring could be rotated over a given hole by its knob (*keras*) so as to open or close it as needed. This arrangement must not be thought of as analogous to our modern keywork, though, because the sleeves were preset and—as we see from their position—could not be reached by the player's hands during performance. Rather, they may be considered as an advance on the age-old method—still practiced—of stopping any unwanted holes with wax. Such was presumably the *tibia multifora* (many-holed pipe) mentioned by later writers. Instruments found at Meroë in the Sudan

in 1921 resemble those of Pompeii fairly closely, and are said to date
from pre-Christian times; they are furnished with rotary rings and have
up to twelve holes, some of which are square. Unfortunately not a single
one survived intact; instead, there exist sections of at least nine different
instruments, some of ivory with an outer casing of bronze, others of
wood, also with outer casing. Several have rotary sleeves provided with
kerata. Noteworthy is an oblique, tubular projection close to the top,
usually inclining toward the lower end, although a few point up. Pompeiian auloi share this peculiarity; it cannot by virtue of its emplacement
be either a blowhole or a fingerhole, and no reason has been found to
account satisfactorily for its presence. It has been suggested that such
pipes were known as *plagiauloi*, from *plagios* ("oblique"), (but cf.
flutes, page 556).

Roman *tibiae* depicted from the first to the third centuries usually
but not invariably show a series of upward protuberances arising from
the tube, prominent on the Phrygian aulos, that have been taken for
outsize knobs of rotary sleeves. But they are placed below the fingerholes
and thus could not have been utilized while playing, and furthermore
they are not connected to either rings or sleeves. Rather, they may be
seen as small, hollow plugs inserted in the toneholes; by raising the
latter artificially, the timbre would be changed but the pitch remain
unaffected. Becker presents photographic evidence identifying the protuberances as hollow plugs and likens them to registers.

A form of unequal pipes, the Phrygian auloi, also called *auloi Elymoi*,
are known to be of Cretan origin. Of the two pipes, one is straight, the
other has a short, upturned, conical bell as its prolongation. Such a
combination is seen on a fourteenth-century B.C. sarcophagus from
Hagia Triada, Crete, where the conoid bell is clearly visible as an added
component. After this unique appearance, Phrygian auloi are thought to
have proceeded to Asia Minor and thence west again; they were known
to the Etruscans and to the Romans, who took them over as *tibiae impares* or *buxum Phrygium*. They are not seen in Rome prior to the first
century A.D., but divergent pipes with horn bells are documented somewhat earlier in Spain, on a vase fragment believed to date from the first
century B.C. The larger pipe with the bell was generally held by the
player's left hand; it does not appear to have been a drone, for it is
often portrayed with fingerholes and with the above-mentioned plugged
holes; possibly it was played at parallel intervals to the shorter pipe.

Authors of the Roman era give contradictory descriptions of the *tibia*'s
tone; to some it is rough, threatening, strident; to others, soft and sweet;

such seeming discrepancies can be resolved if one considers the possibility that a given instrument could be played alternately with double and single reed. Also, it seems likely that the type of reed, as well as shape of the pipe, and resultant tone quality, may have to be considered in attempting to interpret the hitherto baffling references of Varro, Terence, and other writers to left and right pipes, *tibiae pares* and *impares*, *incentiva* and *succentiva*.

A particularly shrill form, the *gingrinas*, of Egyptian origin, was very short and hence high pitched; it served the Phoenicians and Greeks at funeral rites and on the anniversary of the death of Adonis, the solemn honors of which were known as *gingras*. The Romans called this variety *tibia gingrina*.

Tibia players of Rome had their own professional association, the *collegium tibicinum*, with administrators, a treasurer, and officers charged specifically with representing their interests at law. These *collegia* furnished performers for both public and private entertainment. By far the most important of the *tibicines'* functions was in connection with the state cult, and because their participation was deemed indispensable they benefited from certain jealously guarded privileges, much as the trumpeters were to do in baroque times. One such privilege was that of roaming the streets unhindered, even though masked and drunk, during the Ides of June or *quinquatrius* celebrations, finally assembling at the temple of Minerva, their patroness. Another was the right of participating in the sacred banquet of the Temple of Jupiter. When this privilege was abrogated in 312 B.C., the *tibicines* protested by withdrawing *en masse* to Tibur (present-day Tivoli), leaving Rome without players for the sacrifice (the *tibicines* officiating at sacrifices were originally Etruscans, according to the scholiast to Vergil). The Senate, duly concerned, sent a deputation to negotiate their return, but, as the *tibicines* could not be persuaded, the Tiburtians resorted to a strategy: in celebration of a feast day the players were invited to dine with different families, wine was not spared, and when sleep prevailed their hosts loaded them onto carts and transported them to Rome, where they awoke next morning to find themselves abandoned on the carts in the middle of the Forum. The population gathered in crowds and begged them to remain; they consented and, needless to say, their former rights were restored.

Carthage employed *tibia* players in like manner, for Plutarch relates à propos of their burned sacrifices that these were accomplished to the sound of *tibia* and *tympanum*, so as to drown out the cries of the sacrificial animals.

POSTCLASSICAL DOUBLE PIPES

A pair of crane-bone pipes was excavated in 1933 from an Avar grave near Jánoshida, Hungary, dating from the seventh or eighth century, still clutched in the skeleton's hand and originally bound together; it had five holes on the right pipe, two on the left pipe; this unequal number denotes diverging rather than parallel pipes, and we can safely identify them as reedpipes rather than as flutes—the earliest paired pipes found on European soil so far.

Divergent double pipes resembling classical auloi appear in European art works from the ninth century on. In many countries double pipes survived the Middle Ages in the form of folk instruments, either as plain parallel pipes or with an additional bell of horn or with a bag, sometimes with both. Divergent pipes have become extinct in western Europe and are currently dying out in Russia.

Divergent pipes are being held by a musician depicted in a tenth-century Beatus commentary in Madrid, and are also seen on an Andalusian-Moorish casket dating from 1004–1005 in Pamplona Cathedral. Cylindrical double pipes with two channels cut in a single tube and played with two reeds appear in the hands of a juggler in an eleventh-century Limousin manuscript (Bibl. nat. MS lat. 1118), with two rows of unequal fingerholes. A twelfth-century southern German manuscript (Bibl. vat. pal. lat. 39) shows conical divergent pipes in an illustration of King David and his musicians playing contemporary instruments, including a bowed fiddle. The thirteenth-century *Cantigas de Santa María* depict both parallel and divergent pipes, and also show a pirouette. And divergent pipes, slightly conical, one narrower and longer than the other, are shown in company with a pipe and tabor in the fourteenth-century *Smithfield decretals* (BM E. B.21, 949). In paintings and miniatures of the fifteenth century divergent pipes are more often cylindrical than conical. Of a pair of cylindrical divergent pipes in the Book of Hours of Catherine of Cleves (ca. 1440), that of the right hand is a narrow tube whereas the left-hand pipe has a narrow proximal section connecting to a wider section—a stepped bore analogous to that of some bagpipe chanters. The cupola at Saronno, painted about 1535 by Gaudenzio Ferrari, depicts among the numerous instruments both divergent and parallel pipes, all cylindrical.

During this entire period the reeds themselves are not normally visible, and we can but surmise as to whether single- or double-reed instruments were preferred. Although portrayed so frequently in the hands of angels, it is likely that at this time they were being increasingly relegated to the countryside, until they were able to survive only in mountainous areas least accessible to invasion by newer instruments. For a while Scotland may have been one such region, for we hear that around 1635 a witch, the wife of one Barton, stated that the devil, that is, the master of her coven, "went before us . . . playing on a pair of Pipes" at a meeting in the Pentland Hills (cited by Murray [1921]).

Up to the beginning of our century double hornpipes (see page 665) with parallel pipes were still played in the Basque country; both their name, *alboka* (from the Arabic *al-būq*), and the method of breathing while playing in order to produce continuous sound, point to a Near Eastern origin. Nearby, on the island of Iviza, two *xeremias* (folk clarinets) are sometimes combined to form a *reclam de xeremias*. Most double pipes played elsewhere in Europe, including double hornpipes, are parallel pipes, but an important exception is the Russian *brelka*, formed of two divergent pipes of unequal length, their idioglot reeds protected by a reedcap. Each pipe terminates in a large bell of horn or coiled bark. Early in our century the *brelka* was modernized by V. V. Andreyev of Saint Petersburg, who fitted single-pipe models with keys and incorporated them into his balalaika orchestra. Another Russian version, the *jaleika*, has parallel tubes with upcut reeds. The Cheremis of Kazan play parallel pipes of horn or tin embedded in a wooden gutter, with single upcut reeds and mouth horn. The right pipe has four fingerholes, the left—a drone—two rectangular fingerholes.

Albania and Yugoslavia have a group of double pipes called *diplye*, some of which are hornpipes, some bagpipes, yet others mere double chanters. Most are made of a single piece of wood with dual bores. Some have equal fingerholes, others unequal ones in a variety of dispositions. Shepherds around Lake Scutari make theirs of two canes tied together, with downcut reeds, with or without a horn bell. Both reeds are mouthed, their open ends being closed by the performer's tongue; breathing continues during the playing, in the Oriental manner, thus producing uninterrupted sound. With the exception of the second lowest tone of each pipe—they sound at unison—the pipes are tuned very slightly apart so as to produce beats. The southern Albanian *zummare*, a double hornpipe with five equal fingerholes, betrays by its name its derivation from the Moslem *zummāra*. Albanians and Yugoslavs alike play double duct-flutes and double reedpipes (with single reeds) side by side; that they are the only peoples to do so, and that their homelands border on the country of the aulos, cannot be coincidental.

TRIPLE PIPES IN EUROPE

Triple pipes were far less common at all times. A rare occurrence in medieval miniatures is that of a late-twelfth-century psalter (Glasgow, Hunterian Museum MS 229) where parallel triple pipes are rather crudely delineated. A Canterbury codex of the same period, reproduced in Becker (1966) depicts a harpy playing cylindrical triple divergent pipes of different lengths, and in the thirteenth-century *Cantigas de Santa María* cylindrical triple pipes of differing lengths are seen in parallel position, and what looks suspiciously like a pirouette is visible below the mouthed reeds.

The only European area where they are still played is Sardinia; the *launeddas*, for which a Phoenician origin was postulated by Sachs, has three cylindrical cane pipes of different lengths with single beating reeds, all of which are mouthed. Two pipes are for melody, while a drone is by far the longest of the three. Drone and left melody pipe are joined together but diverge sharply from the right pipe—the only divergent reedpipes still in existence. Medieval illustrations already show pipes of different lengths—a certain indication of the presence of a drone. Nowadays, when two *launeddas* lead the procession of Saint Efisio at Cagliari, their players employ the age-old technique of expanding the cheeks to transform the oral cavity into a wind chamber. Like the auloi, *launeddas* are made in various sizes, ergo pitches, and named accordingly: *mediàna-pipia* ("boy-girl"), *fiuda* ("widow"), *mòngia* ("monk"), *fioràssiu* ("musical ornament"), *zampogna* or *organù*, and *contrappunto*. The right melody pipe, called *mancosedda*, has five fingerholes, the left, or *mancosa*, only four. The fifth fingerhole of the *mancosedda*—in this case, either the highest or the lowest one—is closed with wax, depending upon whether one wishes to play the *pipia* or the *mediàna* scale. All three pipes are sounded simultaneously, the melody pipes in thirds and sixths, with symmetrical fingerings, and the reeds are taken entirely into the player's mouth in Eastern fashion. *Launeddas* are never overblown.

NORTH AFRICAN DOUBLE AND TRIPLE PIPES

Double pipes of North Africa are all furnished with single beating reeds; they are recognized as direct descendants of the ancient Egyptian parallel pipes. One of the most popular, the *zummāra*, is also found all over the Near East. Today its parallel pipes are invariably of the same length, cylindrical, and have the same number of paired fingerholes; these are roughly cut and impart a tremulous sound. Its reeds are upcut, in contrast to the otherwise similar Egyptian *mashūra*, a somewhat smaller instrument. The *mashūra*'s (heteroglot) downcut reeds favor the production of high tones; those of the *zummāra*, upcut, favor the low tones. Neither instrument is a hornpipe.

A Moroccan form played by Berbers has six fingerholes on each pipe that are covered pairwise with three fingers only—fore-, middle, and little finger—the weak fourth finger not being employed (this fingering has been noted already in connection with folk aerophones and chordophones, pages 574 and 477). Its compass is limited to six semitones, a diminished fifth, and is not exceeded by overblowing. Here again, breathing is in the Oriental manner, with cheeks expanded to form an air chamber. Another Near Eastern double pipe played over a wide area, the soft-toned *argūl*, has parallel cylindrical pipes with upcut reeds; the right pipe plays the melody while the left, usually larger, is a drone (if both pipes are of the same length the instrument is called a *qurmah*). This drone is made of several sections or extensions, permitting adjustments of pitch, and is always attached to the melody pipe. In North Africa all these reedpipes are known collectively as *zamr* (as is also a popular shawm).

Triple pipes of Egypt, called *trumway shubbuk*, are parallel with single reeds, and consist of a melody and two drone pipes, all of cane; the former is stopped by a node and has an upcut reed, the two latter have downcut reeds. Their bores deviate very slightly from a true cylinder. The drones are nearly twice the length of the melody pipe and terminate either in a common bell or in two separate ones.

ASIAN DOUBLE PIPES

On the Indian subcontinent double-reed aerophones were long preferred to those with single reeds; the double shawm is depicted in the first millennium A.D. on Java, at that time an Indian colony. Nowadays two cylindrical shawms (*sānāyī*) terminating in a flared bell are sometimes tied together in North India so as to form double pipes with separate reeds, but played with a common pirouette—the only known gemination of parallel double-reed aerophones. When two *sānāyī* are paired in this manner, fingerholes of one instrument are stopped with wax, leaving open only those to be sounded as drones. Yet in our day the subcontinent's preference goes to the only single-reed aerophone played there, known chiefly as *pūngī, tiktirī,* or *magudi,* depending upon the region, widespread in pastoral districts, and elsewhere found in the hands of such members of lower castes as snake charmers, professional jugglers, and acrobats. Engel (1870) wrote that during feats of jugglery and sleight-of-hand it was accompanied by a drum. *Pūngīs* have parallel pipes, the mouth ends of which are inserted into a globular gourd of calabash, then made airtight with wax; the gourd serves as air chamber and its elongated neck becomes a blowpipe. The left pipe is a drone. Recently it has also been made as a triple pipe, with an added long-necked, low-pitched calabash drone. Neighboring Assam has double pipes in the form of a hornpipe, with both mouth and bell horns.

In Southeast Asia double divergent pipes appear on the Khmer reliefs of Angkor Wat (eleventh to twelfth centuries) and in one form or another are still played. Those of Vietnam are cylindrical single-reed pipes with mouthed reeds; both are melody pipes and are tuned to near-unison so as to produce strong beats, a tone quality favored over an area extending from Vietnam to the Mediterranean. Offshore, several peoples of Borneo have double pipes of differing lengths, usually furnished with idioglot single reeds. On mainland China the *tui hsiao* is composed of two single-reed bamboo pipes.

DOUBLE PIPES IN THE AMERICAS

Double pipes are uncommon but not altogether unknown in the Americas. A singular form with internal single reed is played by the Camayura Indians along the Xingu River, Brazil: two cane tubes of unequal length—the longer considered male, the shorter female—are tied together; the longer measures some 2 meters (6½ feet). Both are devoid of fingerholes, needless to say. A natural node is left at about 30 to 40 centimeters (12 to 16 inches) from the top and is pierced; into the aperture so formed is placed an idioglot single reed. Pitch is controlled by the reed's emplacement in the septum.

Such internal reeds are more often associated with single pipes of the Amerinds.

HORNPIPES

By definition, "hornpipe" has come to mean any reed instrument furnished with a horn, either to protect the reed at the mouth end, or to prolong the chanter and fulfill the function of a bell, or both. Such instruments, with or without a bag for their pipe (see bagpipes, page 674), with single or double chanter, are played from India to Spain, and formerly were played all through western Europe. They are characterized by being sounded with single beating reeds.

Central Asia may well be the home of short aerophones played with a horn-protected reed: formerly China had a hornpipe with both a mouth and a terminal horn, and three fingerholes, said to have been of Central Asian origin.

In the West it is first depicted in the thirteenth-century *Cantigas de Santa María*. A medieval term for hornpipes having parallel pipes was swegelhorn; this had one or even two terminal bells, and its reeds were mouthed directly. Undoubtedly there is a close affinity between these and the many Asian aerophones with gourd-enclosed reeds, as well as with the European bladder pipe (see page 666). Mouth horn or gourd or mouth pipe not only protect the reed but also prevent its being mouthed, which in turn precludes the possibility of dynamic variation. When Chaucer translated into English the *Roman de la rose* around 1400, he coined the word "hornpypes" for the French *estives*, and in its narrower sense this word has since denoted a folk instrument formerly played in western Europe. On the Continent it seems to have died out in the Middle Ages, whereas in Wales and in Scotland it was played up to the nineteenth century.

The Middle English and Middle High German *stive*, as well as the French *estive*, is derived from the Latin *stipes* ("log" or "pole"), and occurs in the literature of the thirteenth century on both sides of the Channel. The French *Li biaus desconneus* by Renant de Beaujour, dating from around 1200, contains the lines:

> *L'un estive, l'autre viele*
> *Li autres gigle et calimele*

presenting aerophones and chordophones in consort. In the German *Parzifal*, it appears in company with a buisine, flute, and tabor. Many writers have rendered *stive* and *estive* as "bagpipe," but the *estive* is sometimes encountered in literature together with the Old French word *muse*, meaning "bagpipe," which clearly speaks against such identification. In 1235 and again in 1280, *estives de Cornouailles* occur, and this is the term that Chaucer translated as "hornpypes of Cornwall." A thirteenth-century glossary renders *estive* as *tibia*, generic term for bagless pipes. But whether these instruments had single or double pipes we do not know. Certainly the *estive* must have been a reasonably powerful instrument, for it was used by watchmen, according to the *Tournoiement de l'Antechrist:*

> En la tor du chastel omont
> As estives de Cornevaille
> Corna la guaite.

Celtic hornpipes have often consisted of bone rather than wooden pipes. The Welsh pibcorn was made of either material indiscriminately, judging from specimens preserved in collections ("pibcorn," by the way, literally means "hornpipe"). It has both a mouth horn and a terminal bell horn, a single reed, six front fingerholes, and a dorsal thumbhole. Although no longer played on the Welsh mainland, shepherds on Anglesey were reported by Engel in 1870 still to be playing it. Its counterpart, the pastoral stock and horn of southern Scotland, is now obsolete. Like the pibcorn, this could be made either of horn or of wood and had both mouth and bell horns. In Robert Burns's time it was already so rare that he had trouble obtaining a specimen, but in 1794 he could write triumphantly, "I have at last gotten one." Only two original specimens have been preserved, one with double bore and twice seven fingerholes and two thumbholes, the fingerholes so disposed that a pair could be closed by one finger. Other geminated hornpipes have been mentioned on page 661 in connection with double pipes.

THE BLADDER PIPE

The curious ninth-century Epistle to Dardanus by Pseudo-Jerome refers to an instrument called *chorus,* which is defined as follows: *chorus quoque simplex pellis cum duabus cicutis aereis, et per primam inspiratur, per secundum vocem emittit* ("a simple skin with two bronze pipes, into the first of which one breathes, the second emits sound"). This definition fits two different instruments equally well: the bladder pipe and the early bagpipe, and indeed the (now destroyed) thirteenth-century San Blasius Codex, copied by the prince-abbot Martin Gerbert in the eighteenth century, illustrates two distinct types of *chorus;* both have identical blowpipes and short chanters terminating in an animal's head, but whereas the air reservoir of the first is spherical and clearly a bladder, the second—far longer—is in the form of a pig—head, legs, and all, with

20.

vnū genᵒchœi

22.

dhū genᵒcoɾi.

Bladder pipe and early bagpipe. Copies of now destroyed thirteenth-century drawings, made and published by Martin Gerbert in *De cantu et musica sacra*, 1774.

the chanter issuing from its mouth, the blowpipe stuck in its back, and its body squeezed by the player. The hide bag justifies us in identifying this as a bagpipe. Perhaps foreshadowing the greater importance to be accorded the bagpipe, Nicholas of Lyra, the fourteenth-century exegete, glosses the above passage from the Dardanus epistle as *habet duas fistulas de ligno . . . et vocatur Gallice chevrette* ("it has two wooden pipes and is called *chevrette* in French").

The bladder pipe proper has a short blowpipe and a chanter furnished with a reed, the two pipes being separated by an intervening animal vesicule. One end of the blowpipe and of the reed are encased in the bladder, the latter extended by air pumped in by the player's breath while pressure is exerted on the bladder. The air stream sounds the reed, thereby making continuous, uninterrupted playing possible, a form of music making popular in the Middle Ages. Such instruments were played in Europe by the thirteenth century, at which time they were both depicted (San Blasius manuscript, *Cantigas de Santa María*) and mentioned (as *bladerpfif* in a poem of 1290), to become almost obsolete during the Renaissance. Today they survive only in Poland as a rare shepherd's instrument with one or two bladders, in Albania as a child's toy, among the Chuvash of the Soviet Union, and in European Turkey; in Brittany and Sicily they are sold at fairs as toys.

We do not know with what type of reed the medieval bladder pipes were furnished; modern Polish and Albanian varieties have single reeds. Albanian players squeeze the bag against their chest by means of their wrists, thus leaving the fingers of both hands free to play. Unfortunately medieval illustrations do not permit us to make any inferences as to early playing methods. From the thirteenth century until it is last depicted in 1612 in an etching by Wolfgang Kilian (who may merely be copying Virdung, incidentally) two distinct types are shown: one has a straight or nearly straight chanter and is almost cylindrical, the other boasts an upturned bell, sometimes with pronounced conicity. Of the two types shown in the *Cantigas*, one has an upturned bell, the other is a straight conical tube ending in a flare, with part of a second pipe showing (i.e., a double instrument). A rustic dance scene in the *Hausbuch* of Castle Wolfegg (ca. 1475) includes a bladder pipe with upturned conical tube and very large bladder; finally, in a design by Hans Holbein the Younger of about 1520, a group of peasants are seen dancing to the sound of bagpipe and bladder pipe; an upturned bell has been added to the chanter, the joint clearly marked by a boss. In the course of the sixteenth century the curved form lost its bladder but continued to protect its reed by inserting it in a small, rigid reedcap. This transformation became known as crumhorn (i.e., "crooked horn"), but until its emergence as a crumhorn the bladder pipe remained a folk instrument, participating in neither military nor art music.

That the bladder pipe was considered distinct from the bagpipe and the hornpipe is clear from the following lines of *The Complaynt of Scotland* of 1549, in which are enumerated the musical instruments played by shepherds:

the fyrst had ane drone bagpipe
the nyxt hed ane pipe maid of ane bleddir and of ane reid
the third playit on ane trump
the feyerd on ane cornepipe
the fyft playit on ane pipe maid of ane gait horne
the sext playt on ane recordar
the sevint plait on ane fiddil
and the last plait on ane quhissil

Called *vèze* in sixteenth-century France, this word was transferred to the bagpipe by Trichet in the seventeenth century—he assures us that it was the same as the *loure*; but *vèze* or *Platerspiel*, to give it its German name, is rarely mentioned in late medieval literature, possibly an indication that its identity was hidden under another name.

Although no instruments with soft air reservoirs are known in the East, several instruments with gourd reservoirs exist in India, and it is as yet a matter for speculation whether these represent forebears of the European vesicular form. The entire subcontinent, as well as Ceylon, has a pastoral and snake charmer's form of double pipe (see page 664) with single reeds inserted into a globular gourd or calabash rendered airtight with wax; in southern India it is even nose blown on occasion. However, the purpose of the gourd here is that of protecting the reed, while that of the flexible bladder was to create an air reservoir, two entirely distinct functions.

THE CRUMHORN

The crumhorn derives its name from the Old English *crump* ("crooked"), cognate with the German *krump* (*krumm* in modern German). This descendant of the upcurved form of the medieval bladder pipe, having exchanged its vesicular air reservoir for a protective wooden cap, became a reedcap woodwind of the fifteenth, sixteenth, and seventeenth centuries. Formed like the letter J, it was usually made of boxwood, had a narrow cylindrical tube and bore up to the last few centimeters, where both tube and bore widened. Six fingerholes and a dorsal thumbhole were standard. Its double reed was mounted on a staple enclosed in and completely hidden by the reedcap, a small perforated box that protected the reed (see reedcap shawms, page 695). The combination of double reed and cylindrical tube is most unusual in postclassical Western culture; one might perhaps say that the crumhorn had a double reed despite its cylindrical bore. As reedcaps allow only of indirect control of the reed, overblowing is precluded, and the compass is correspondingly restricted to a ninth. Crumhorns were built in different sizes, and the larger instruments, from the tenor down, were equipped with one key to extend the compass downward; fingering was that of the recorder.

Like the xylophone, the crumhorn is first mentioned as an organ stop (in Dresden, 1489), and since this must have been an imitation of the woodwind, crumhorns must have emerged in identifiable form by or shortly after the mid-fifteenth century. In Italy they appear in art works of the late fifteenth and of the sixteenth centuries: Carpaccio's well-known angel (1510) holds her instrument in a corner of her mouth, just like a cornett player. Zacconi (1592) was to call it a *cornamuto torto*, possibly because of its soft tone. The only surviving matched set of Renaissance *storti*, or *corni storti*, as they are usually called in modern Italian, is of his day: six boxwood instruments, once the property of Alfonso II d'Este (d. 1597), are preserved in the museum of the Brussels Conservatoire: a soprano of 47 centimeters (18½ inches), three tenors of 70 centimeters (27½ inches), a bass of 100 centimeters (ca. 40 inches), and a great bass of 117 centimeters (46 inches); the last two have keys for extending the compass downward by a fourth. The National Museum of Prague houses a great bass of 110 centimeters (43 inches), with a compass of G′ to d° and a tube length of 157 centimeters (62 inches). Such very large instruments were of necessity sounded by means of an added metal crook fitted to the reedcap. This is mentioned by the Nuremberg trumpet maker Jorg Neuschel in a letter to Duke Albert of Prussia in 1542, in which he offered for sale a set of ten crumhorns, *die Tenor haben auch Schloss und seindt wie die grossen Bass gemacht, das mans mit messen Roren plest* ("the tenors have a key and are made like the basses, which are sounded by a brass crook").

Virdung illustrates four sizes of crumhorn in 1511, and shortly thereafter Burgkmair (*Der Weisskunig*, ca. 1615) attests to their growing popularity; Hans Holbein the Younger included a crumhorn in nearly all the instrumental ensembles pictured in his woodcuts of the 1520s. From Germany it seems to have spread to Spain, for we hear in 1559 of *instrumentos que dizen orlos de Alemania, hechos a manera de cornetas* ("instruments called *orlos* of Germany, made in the manner of cornetts") among the property of Mary of Hungary. By 1571 five sizes had been made by the Bassani brothers, those inventive spirits employed at the English court. Praetorius could describe six sizes, from the sopranino, with its lowest tone c′, to the great bass, reaching down to F′. A late writer for the crumhorn was Schein, who appended a *padovano à 4* for crumhorns to his *Banchetto musicale* of 1617, and Praetorius gave instructions for setting a consort of crumhorns in his *Syntagma* III.

But it was in France that the *cromorne*, better known as *tournebout*, survived longest—into the eighteenth century—albeit in a transformed version. The classical sixteenth-century form had been included in ensembles of both "high" and "low" music; thus we hear of voices, trombones, cornetts, *storte*, flutes, lutes, harpsichord, and *organetto* participating at the wedding celebrations of Cosimo de' Medici in 1539, and the baptismal procession for the Landgrave of Hesse's little daughter in 1596 commanded no fewer than fourteen crumhorns, three fiddles, two lutes, two citterns, a harp, a regal, a trombone, shawms, a bagpipe, a psaltery, flutes, trumpets, drum, and kettledrums. Many inventories of the period bear witness to its widespread use, as, for example, those of London 1547 (Henry VIII's instruments), Verona 1569, Innsbruck 1571, Berlin 1582, Stuttgart 1589, and Kassel 1613. All of these would have been made of a single piece of wood, turned, then bored and bent. But by the mid-seventeenth century the *tournebout* was being constructed of two sections of wood hollowed out and fitted together again, then bound in leather for greater stability, just like the serpents. Our earliest information concerning this remodeling comes from Trichet (ca. 1640), who relates that the reed was mouthed directly, the reedcap— he calls it a little box—being placed over it after playing, in order to preserve it. And effectively the crumhorn in France was transformed into a more robust woodwind with wider bore (and greater volume), its reed carried on a crook, and in this form it gained admittance to the band of the Grande Écurie du Roi after the mid-century. Furetière (1685) states that six crumhorns were still serving in the King's Chamber, but only *aux grandes cérémonies*. And just as the serpent was to be developed specifically for church and for outdoor music in France, so the functions of the French *tournebout* may have been divided, for the orchestra of the New Church at Strasbourg (then an integral part of France) in 1685 consisted of six violins, two violas, two celli, a double bass, a flute, an oboe, two crumhorns, a bassoon, two horns, two trumpets, and kettledrums.

The extent to which the crumhorn may have been known and used

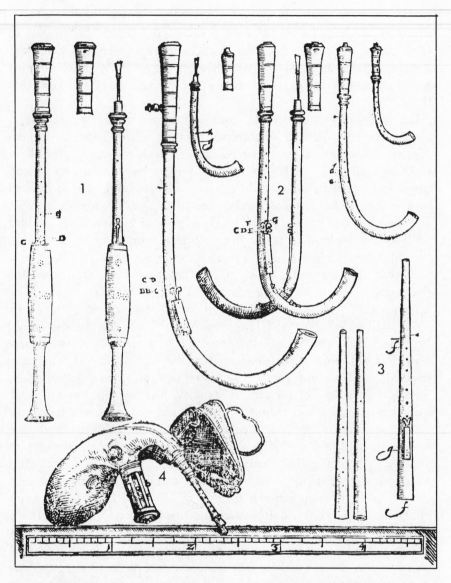

Crumhorns and other woodwinds: (1) *Basset nicolo*; (2) crumhorns; (3) mute cornetts; (4) bagpipe with bellows. From Michael Praetorius, *Theatrum instrumentorum*, 1620.

in England is at present hard to determine. Although virtually unmentioned in the literature, Henry VIII left several consorts of these instruments, and, according to Mersenne, crumhorns had reached France from England; Trichet goes as far as commenting that the *tournebout* was not as greatly in vogue in France as it was in Germany and England. Perhaps additional references will turn up in the future.

BAGPIPES

The first step in mechanizing the wind supply of a single or double pipe was attained with the creation of the mouthblown bagpipe or bladder pipe, followed by complete mechanization with suppression of the mouthpipe in favor of bellows. Characterized by their combination of reedpipe and air reservoir in form of a bag, bagpipes were at first invariably mouth blown, later also bellows blown. In either type, air reaches the reed in a steady stream causing the bagpipe to sound uninterruptedly. Bellows-blown varieties, in which bellows replace the mouthpipe (also called blowpipe) are not encountered outside Europe.

Two principal groups of bagpipes are distinguished, depending upon bore and reed of the chanter (melody pipe): (1) those with cylindrical bore and single reed, found in Europe east of Germany and Italy, Asia, and North Africa; (2) those with wide conical bore and double reed, found in western Europe, including Italy (both types are played in Italy). Exceptions to this rule of classification are the British small-pipe, which has a cylindrical chanter, and the *musette*, with cylindrical chanter and double reed. For purposes of classification, stepped bores, that is, those made in two or three joints of varying diameter, are considered to be cylindrical. Generally speaking, the melodic compass does not exceed nine tones, as most chanters do not overblow (the bellows-blown Irish bagpipe can be made to overblow the octave, and the chanters of some eastern European *kozas* can be overblown to extend the compass to two and one-half octaves). The bag forming the air reservoir is held under, and squeezed by, the player's left arm. In Europe it has traditionally been made of the skin of sheep, goat, or kid, whence such names as *Bock, cabrette, chevrette, koza,* and so on; and the heads of these animals are often carved on chanter stocks.

Age and homeland of the bagpipe are unknown. Certainly an Eastern instrument, and probably a Near Eastern one, it was designed for the production of continuous sound and, insofar as it was equipped with a double chanter or an independent drone, to provide the drone type of two-part music beloved of both the East and of medieval Europe. Reeds of the Eastern pipes are taken entirely into the player's mouth, not held between the lips as they have been in Europe since the seventeenth century. The Eastern player continues to breathe while playing, creating an uninterrupted sound; at a further stage of evolution the reed is protected by a gourd or animal horn that serves simultaneously as an air chamber (cf. hornpipes, page 664), and finally the gourd or horn is replaced by a flexible bag with a blowpipe. Primitive bagpipes with horn bells are still played in the Near East. The relationship between bladder pipe and bagpipe, if any, cannot be established, but both are of Eastern parentage and probably represent dual developments.

Coming from the East, the bagpipe was known to the Romans in the first century of our era, possibly earlier (Martial mentions the *ascaules* disparagingly). It may have continued in use in postclassical times, but if so we lose all knowledge of it until the ninth century, when the Epistle to Dardanus by Pseudo-Jerome describes the *chorus* as consisting of a simple skin and two brazen pipes, a blowpipe and a melody pipe. Although this description also fits the bladder pipe, it is more likely to relate to the bagpipe because the word *pellis*, used here, has the meaning of skin or hide, rather than bladder (for text, see bladder pipe, page 666). Arabic sources of information start in the eleventh century, with Avicenna and ibn-Zayla mentioning the *mizmār al-jirab*. To John Cotton, a theorist writing at the turn of the eleventh to twelfth century, the *musa* was the most excellent of instruments, combining as it did the use of human breath as in a flute, of the hands as with a fiddle (*phiala*), and of a bag as in an organ (this passage is iterated by Jerome of Moravia in the thirteenth century); John of Affligem in the early twelfth century also employs the Latin word *musa*, which becomes *muse* in French literature in the same century. A primitive form of bagpipe with short blowpipe, out-sized bag, short chanter—in all probability a double chanter, judging by its sausage shape—is depicted in a Lombard manuscript of the twelfth century. From the thirteenth century on bagpipes are increasingly illustrated and mentioned in literature. A thirteenth-century Byzantine psalter in Berlin includes a bagpipe in a group of instruments, and when Jean Lefebvre writes of the *chevrette d'Esclavonie* in the fourteenth century we realize how widespread its use must have become by then.

The drone is first mentioned in thirteenth-century French literature (*Le jeu de Robin* by Adam de la Halle: *pour le muse au grant bourdon*); early illustrations show it made of two or three joints with tenons to facilitate tuning. Nowadays a single drone is nearly always tuned two octaves below the chanter keynote; if there are two drones they are tuned in octaves or fifths; three drones are post-medieval and are now found only in the British Isles, also tuned in octaves and fifths. With the exception of *musette* and *zampogna*, western European drones have single reeds. Double pipes, ostensibly double chanters, but in reality one a melody, the other a drone pipe, were in use before the separate drone appears. Such double pipes exist in France and in the Balkans, and double drones are shown in the thirteenth-century *Cantigas de Santa María* (the *Cantigas* depict two bagpipes: one with slightly conoid chanter, prolonged by a conoid bell, and devoid of drone, the other with two chanters of unequal length, plus two double drones, for a total of six pipes); two independent drones appear in the early fifteenth century.

Bellows are first recorded in connection with a stillborn experimental instrument called *phagotum* by its inventor, Canon Afranio of Ferrara, details of which were published in 1539 by his nephew, Theseo Amboglio. In an attempt to extend the downward compass of the Pannonian *piva* (a bagpipe) that had a double chanter but no drone, Afranio built what was essentially two columns of turned wood, each with three parallel cylindrical bores united at the top, thus forming one airway, with fingerholes and keys, and each containing a metal reed, worked by bag and bellows strapped to the arm. This was accomplished prior to 1521. But possibly the first reference to bellows in connection with a true bagpipe is that of the sixteenth-century poem *Bergerie* by Remi Belleau (d. 1577):

> *Mais ta loure est entière, et le ventre en est bon*
> *L'anche, le chalumeau, le soufloir, le bourdon*
> *Ne perdent point de vent* . . .

> But the *loure* is whole, and the paunch is good,
> Reed, chanter, bellows, and drone
> Do not lose wind . . .

followed by an Ambras inventory of 1596: *ain sackhpfeifen, mit silber beschlagen, sambt seinem plaszbalg* ("a bagpipe garnished with silver, with its bellows"). Bellows were added to the Union pipes of Ireland a little earlier, about 1588, and to the French *musette* a little later, in the seventeenth century, and to other continental bagpipes at unknown times.

During the late Middle Ages the name of symphony was applied to bagpipes in Romance countries, but other instruments capable of emitting two sounds simultaneously had been given the same name. Dante (d. 1321) employs the derived word-form *sampogna* (*Paradiso* XX: *al pertugio/ della sampogna vento che penetra*), and Juan Ruiz, also in the early fourteenth century, *sampoña*. Word and instrument are still in use in parts of Spain and on the Balearic Islands, as in southern Italy, Sicily, and Malta (as *zampogna*), in Romania (as *cimpoi*—this has a double chanter terminating in a wooden bell), while the modern Greek *tsampouna* is etymologically derived from *zampogna*. Its very name, symphony, authorizes the belief that in its earliest stage the European bagpipe was provided with a double-bore pipe, one bore of which was a melody, the other a drone, pipe. Bagpipes played in Les Landes, southern France, still have chanter and drone bored in parallel channels from a single piece of wood, in appearance a double chanter.

The iconography shows us that at first the ostensible chanter was cylindrical, from which we may infer the use of a single reed, but in the late thirteenth century wide, conical chanters start appearing, at first in France, and soon all western European chanters were sounded with double reeds. It has been suggested that the introduction of the double-reed chanter took place in the wake of Arab expansion and was somehow connected with the Near Eastern shawm, yet the fact that up to the invention of the clarinet around 1700 no European art-music aerophone with single reed existed (single reeds were reserved for folk instruments) would tend to invalidate this theory. This partiality for double reeds in the West has not been explained.

Apart from its use as a pastoral instrument and as a provider of dance music, massed bagpipes participated in the Low Countries in secular ceremonies by the fifteenth century, with twenty-eight bagpipes forming part of the 1477 *ommegang* (a local procession) of Termonde. In the following century we hear of their military use: three Polish bagpipes were purchased in 1588 for the military band of the Württemberg court; Polish infantry regiments were equipped with bagpipes in the seventeenth century, a custom revived in the twentieth century. As military instruments, bagpipes survive in Britain and Ireland, and up to the

First World War, regionally in France also. Nevertheless, from the nineteenth century on bagpipes, whether played by the military or as folk instruments, have been dying out in continental Europe.

The Old French word *muse* probably referred to a large instrument, for its diminutive, *musette*, is encountered from the thirteenth century on and seems to have been a generic name for small bagpipes, and *cornemuse*, recorded from the fourteenth century on, came to denote bagpipes in general. It was the latter that accompanied both shepherds' and court dances, causing Eustache Deschamps (d. ca. 1406) to deplore the fact that the court should dance to the sounds of *cet instrument des hommes bestiaulx* ("this instrument of bestial men"). Later in the fifteenth century, during a forty-day celebration at the court of René II of Anjou, knights and their ladies were disguised as shepherds and shepherdesses, complete with bagpipes. This predilection of courtiers for the pseudo-pastoral life (including bagpipes) was to last until the French Revolution. Also in the fifteenth century, three *musette* players were among the personnel of Philippe le Beau's chapel musicians—one may wonder what their function was there—and accompanied him on his travels.

Among the now extinct *cornemuses* was the *cornemuse de Poitou* which differed from the ordinary model, according to Mersenne, by having a single drone, rather than two drones; its chanter was at unison with the *hautbois de Poitou* (see page 696) and the two were played in duet. Nowadays both the mouth-blown and the bellows-blown forms of *cornemuse* exist side by side: that of Les Landes with its double-bore chanter is mouth blown, while the *cabrette* of Auvergne has bellows, and in the Cantal region it is played together with the hurdy-gurdy to provide music for the *bourrée*.

THE MUSETTE

Despite its frequent mention in early French literature, we have no knowledge of the *musette*'s construction prior to the seventeenth century, when it appears as a very small, bellows-blown instrument. Remodeled in the eighteenth century, it became a fashionable and delicate toy of the nobility, with ivory pipes, its bag and bellows encased in matching silks and velvets. These two instruments, *cornemuse* and *musette*, despite the similarity of their names, represent two fundamentally different types: the *cornemuse* has conical chanter(s) with double reed, the *musette*, cylindrical chanters with double reed—an exception to the normal coupling of cylindrical bore to single reed; in this instance the exception is made possible acoustically by the *musette*'s very narrow bore (about 3 millimeters). Another difference between the two is that the *musette* sounded an octave lower, for its cylindrical tubes acted as stopped pipes.

In the beginning of the seventeenth century *musettes* had a single chanter devoid of keys, and a stubby drone formed like an elongated rackett (see page 704) with several channels, but, by the time Mersenne wrote, the chanter had acquired several keys, and shortly thereafter Jean Hotteterre added a second chanter, parallel to the first and sharing its stock, and known as the *petit chalumeau*; this extended the compass of the *grand chalumeau* (f' to a^2) up to d^3. The idea was not entirely new to western Europe, for Praetorius had shown a mouth-blown bagpipe with conoid chanter for each hand (g' to d^2 for the left, d' to a' for the right hand) on which two-part music could be played. But, in practice, was it? The sole example of this variety that he had seen was in the *Erzstift* of Magdeburg, and we are left to surmise whether this might have been an experimental model or a folk instrument.

Hotteterre's drone, or *faux-bourdon*, resembled a rackett, with parallel bores pierced longitudinally, interconnected pairwise to form longer channels. They opened on the wall of the tube, which was grooved to hold the tuning sliders called *layettes*. Furetière (1685) draws attention to the *musette*'s four drones on one cylinder; these were tuned C and G in octaves and were also fitted with double reeds. Because of the convenience offered by its bellows and the compact size of its drones, the *musette* became acceptable to the nobility, to courtiers and musicians alike—the only bagpipe to become a society instrument. But even then its repertoire remained folksy and bucolic; shepherd airs were played by *le tout Versailles* disguised as shepherdesses and shepherds in pastoral surroundings. Relatively few original compositions were written for it, though composers often imitated the effect of bagpipe drones, for example, Couperin in his various *musettes*, and later (1834) Berlioz in his *Harold in Italy*. A collection of pieces for *musettes* or hurdy-gurdy with thorough bass, entitled *Les défis* and published around 1740, depicts on its title page two gentlemen playing *musettes* from score and two ladies, seated nearby, playing a *musette* and a hurdy-gurdy; one can only hope their performance was antiphonal.

A *musette* chanter could also be detached from the bagpipe and played alone, in which case the reed was protected by a wooden reed-cap; when this was dispensed with in the nineteenth century, the chanter was transformed into a small, conical oboe in G, a fifth higher than the ordinary oboe, and marketed as a toy. The fashionable fad of *musette* playing had run its course by the 1770s, for Laborde (1780) assures us emphatically that *cet instrument n'est absolument plus d'usage* ("this instrument is absolutely no longer in use"). No other bagpipe received recognition as an instrument of the polite world, then or later; indeed, in 1721 bagpipes were expressly included in the "not musical" instruments that a professional German cornettist was forbidden to play.

REGIONAL FOLK BAGPIPES

After the revolution, bagpipes in France were played as strictly regional—chiefly northern—folk instruments. Among them must be mentioned the *biniou* of Brittany, mouth blown, traditionally played in octave unison with the *bombarde*, a folk shawm. During the 1930s the *biniou* disappeared, only to be gradually replaced by Scottish bagpipes.

Another bagpipe to combine narrow-bore cylindrical pipes and double reeds was the Italian *surdelina*. Trichet (ca. 1640) heard one in 1626 and called it a modern instrument; bellows-blown, it had two or three chanters of ebony with keys, and two drones; Trichet mentions that when all fingerholes were closed the pipes were silenced, thus they must have been stopped, as were the British small-pipes. Better known was the *cornamusa* of the Abruzzi with its mouth-blown chanter and two drones; traditionally, "vigorous peasants from the mountains play the cornemuse or other wind instruments in front of Madonnas [statues]" on Naples street corners during Christmastide, as Stendhal noted (*Journal* for 1811). Other mountainous regions of Europe where bagpipes are still actively played are Spain, Scotland, and the Balkans.

In Spain, the *gaita* undergoes regional modifications: thus, the *gaita gallega*, that is, of Galicia, is usually mouthblown, has single chanter and drone; the *gaita zamorana* has two drones, as does the *gaita tumbal*, the latter named for a now obsolete Andalusian dance. *Gaita* is related etymologically to *gajda* (or *gayda*) and *gajde*, names of the bagpipe in Slovakia, Slovenia, Serbia, Croatia, Macedonia, Bulgaria, Greece, Turkey, and—as *gajdy*—of Moravia, pointing to two routes of dispersal in Europe. The chanters of all these instruments are cylindrical, with single reed; both in Spain and in the Balkans they sometimes terminate in a cowhorn bell.

Before leaving the Balkans, a group known as *diplye,* the "twofolds," must be mentioned. All of these are double pipes in one form or another; some are hornpipes, some bagpipes, yet others are mere double chanters with neither bell nor bag. They are played over an area comprising Albania and Yugoslavia. In Herzegovina, and more rarely in Bosnia, *diplyes* are bagpipes, either mouth or bellows blown. Their chanters all have double bores, six pairs of fingerholes, and single reeds; in Dalmatia the same instrument is called *myesnica;* there the left bore has six fingerholes, the right but two or three. From this group we learn that one way of tuning a double-bored chanter is to bring the fingerholes of each pair into near unison, leaving them just distant enough to produce beats. Apart from modifying the tone quality, one effect of such a tuning is to make the pipes sound louder. If, as is likely, this represents late usage of an early technique, we may gain an idea of what the medieval double-chanter bagpipes sounded like. The *gaita-gajda* group remains an instrument of shepherds, and in the Balkans also of the peasantry who play at village dances, wedding processions, and the like, just as in the medieval West. In marked contrast to the British Isles, they are not martial instruments.

Northern Britain is without doubt one of the most active of the remaining bagpipe areas, and has exported its pipes for adoption by regional bands to France and to India. The mouthblown Scottish Highland pipe can be traced to the fifteenth century when it had a long blowpipe, conoid chanter, and two drones on the same stock. Today it boasts three drones—two tenors and a bass—spread out fanwise, with the bass tuned an octave below the tenors ($A°a°a°$). Somewhat smaller is the bellows-blown Lowland pipe, now obsolescent, made in regular as well as in miniature sizes (the latter with cylindrical chanter), both with three drones tuned like those of the Highland pipe.

Now extinct in Scotland, the small-pipe was formerly played both there and in Northumberland. It first appeared in the seventeenth century and is believed to be a descendant of the *musette.* A description of about 1700, when it was played on both sides of the border, draws attention to its salient characteristic, a chanter with twin bores. The usual eight fingerholes of the left bore sounded g' to g^2, with f' available from the open end; the right bore had four fingerholes for g' to c^2. The four lowest holes were paired, each pair being closed by a single finger; when the upper four tones of the main bore were played, that is, those lacking counterparts on the second bore, the latter sounded the low keynote as a drone. Only one finger was raised at a time, a system known as closed fingering: it is that of the *musette*.

The small-pipe's original drone was also similar to the *musette*'s; subsequent modifications brought about a three-drone model (tuned g°d°g′), and in the mid-eighteenth century another feature was developed, a stopped chanter. The great advantage of such an arrangement is that the bagpipe's inherent lack of all means of articulation was overcome to the extent that staccato playing became possible, as the chanter could be silenced by the simple expedient of covering all fingerholes. Apart from the extinct Italian *surdelina*, these are the only Western pipes to have such chanters. Today small-pipes are bellows-blown, indoor instruments of Northumberland only. Bagpipes were more widespread in England formerly than they are today. Typically, country morris dances could be accompanied by a fiddle or a bagpipe in the early eighteenth century.

A form of pipe so complicated that it has been called the "Irish organ" is the Union pipe of Ireland, intended for indoor playing by a seated performer—a less martial instrument is hard to imagine—with its three drones lying across the player's knees. In addition to a chromatic double chanter, in its present form dating back to the eighteenth century, it has also three or four regulators of varying lengths furnished with heavily sprung closed keys. Their purpose is to provide chords by striking the appropriate key; the lower end is closed by a stopper. The complex playing technique involves the striking of one key of each regulator with the lower edge of the right hand while simultaneously playing the chanter; this in turn can be transformed into a stopped pipe by closing it with the player's right knee. The twin bores are tuned in unison, with the second bore merely serving to augment the volume of tone.

Eastern Europe favors bellows as a means of wind supply; both the *duda* of Hungary, Poland, the Ukraine, and parts of Yugoslavia, with its double chanter set in a stock carved to resemble a goat's head, and its bass drone, and the *koza* of Poland and western Russia with single chanter capable of being overblown, and its bent drone terminating in a horn or metal bell, have goatskin bags and bellows. *Koza* means "goat" in Polish and translates into German as *Bock*, name of the now extinct German bagpipe depicted by Praetorius, when it was mouthblown; he shows its single chanter and bass drones terminating in bells of horn. These instruments have—or had—the Eastern type of cylindrically bored chanters sounded by means of single reeds.

Examination of some of the bagpipes played on the Indian subcontinent, the eastern limit of bagpipe distribution, shows that regardless of the number of pipes, they are sounded either as melody or as drone instruments, but never as a combination of both; in other words, a potentially polyphonic instrument is played monophonically. Thus the northern *nāgabaddha* has either one or two pipes, and, if two, the second acts as a drone with the melody pipe silenced. The *mashak*, also found in India, is likewise played either as a drone or as a melody instrument. Its southern counterpart, the *sruti upāngi*, is a drone only despite the fact that its cylindrically bored tube has six fingerholes; the five unwanted ones are plugged with resin. Thus the mere presence of a number of fingerholes on a pipe is no guarantee that it will be played as a melody pipe. Such may have been the prototypes of our Western instruments.

SHAWMS

The double-reed instruments known to antiquity were played pairwise (see double pipes, page 651). Several ancient Egyptian instruments that have come to light can be identified by their double reeds of straw, flattened at one end, rectangular in shape, and divided into two sections by a thread wound around the center, believed to represent a pitch-controlling device (cf. folk clarinets, page 728). With the advent of Islam the descendants of such aerophones were propagated east and west in two forms, cylindrical and conical. Both types were formerly played in Europe, but the cylindrical varieties have since died out (see crumhorn, *kortholt, courtaut, sordone*); both are still played in Asia.

During the twelfth century a double-reed woodwind of conical shape and bore was introduced into Europe from the Near East, probably by way of the Balkans and Italy. Known in modern times as the shawm, it remained in use until the seventeenth century, when it was replaced by its offspring, the oboe (an exception is made by Spain, where the shawm never became obsolete but survives as *chirimía* and *dolçaina*).[*] Spain received her shawms by a different route; the Arabic *al-būq* was known there by the thirteenth century. Spaniards called it *albogon,* but by Lope

---

[*] The word "shawm" and its equivalents in other languages is ambiguous in that it can denote both single-reed and double-reed aerophones. For the sake of precision, it will be applied only to double-reed aerophones in this book unless specified otherwise.

de Vega's day (d. 1635) its name has been changed to *albogue*. Now extinct, the name lives on in the Basque *alboka*, a double hornpipe.

The word "shawm" is derived from the Latin *calamus*, which gave rise to the Old French *chelemele* (twelfth to sixteenth centuries) as well as to the *chalemie* (fourteenth to seventeenth centuries); by the mid-seventeenth century *chalemie* had come to denote two separate instruments, the shawm and the *cornemuse* of shepherds. After 1500 the word *hautbois* was in general use in France for the higher-pitched shawms, and later also for the *hautbois de Poitou*, the *courtaud*, *basson*, and the oboe. Low-pitched shawms were in addition referred to as *grosbois*. Early English word forms are scalmuse, shalmye, shalmele, and so on, and from 1561 on the French word *hautbois* was also employed. The German *Schalmei* and its variants is cognate with the French and English terms. Both *chalumeau* and *Schalmei* are ambiguous, however, and especially so in the seventeenth century, in that we are often not sure whether they refer to a double-reed or to a single-reed instrument. Differences between these two types were less strictly defined in former times and the nomenclature more flexible than today.

Like its Eastern prototype, the European shawm was made of a single joint of wood terminating in a bell. The double reed was mounted on a conical metal staple and a wooden pirouette gave support to the player's lips. Seven front fingerholes—the lowest duplicated to accommodate left- or right-handed performers—were situated on the upper half of the tube, with the lower portion containing ventholes.

Shawms came into common use during the thirteenth century, and from the early fourteenth century on formed an integral part of town bands and also indispensable components of "loud" music. A larger size known as bombard appears in French miniatures of the thirteenth century, and is mentioned—as a musical instrument, that is—in the 1342 *Livre des mestiers* and in Italian and Spanish sources before references to it occur in England or Germany. After listing a number of "soft" instruments, Jean Lefebvre in his *Respit de la mort* of 1376 enumerates *muses, chalemelles, grosses bombardes nouvelles, trompes et nacaires*, all "loud" instruments, in an early juxtaposition of both members of the shawm family, and some eight years before the first mention in English literature of the shawm (by Chaucer in his *Hous of Fame* of about 1384: "cornemuse and shalmye"). The French word *bombarde*, from which the English and German equivalents are derived, originally denoted an artillery piece, an early, stone-hurling cannon that the new low-pitched shawm resembled in form. A Latin name for these big pipes was *burdones;* a fourteenth-century entry in the *Chronicle of Saint Albans* describes a Te Deum . . . *pulsato classico sonantibus chalamis* (*quos burdones appellamus*) *cum horologio,* a joyous service with trumpets sounding "and shawms (that we call *burdones*)" and the bells of the bell wheel ringing. Virdung (1511) illustrates a shawm and a bombard, both with pirouettes, the shawm with its seven fingerholes, the bombard with six and a swallow-tail key protected by a pierced fontanelle (a protective barrel or cylinder slipped over the tube).

Shawms had been developed into a whole consort by the sixteenth century, and thereafter the designation "shawm" was reserved for the soprano instrument, with all the larger sizes referred to as bombards. These larger models were actually elongated versions of the shawm, very slender, with narrow and slightly conical bore ending in a flare. In England the word "bombard" was little used as the term "tenor shawm" was preferred; in Germany, *Bombard* became corrupted to *Pommer* by the time Praetorius wrote, and in France the terminology alternated between *bombarde* and *hautbois,* giving us in 1590 the *double bas de hautbois autrement appelée bombarde* ("double-bass *hautbois* otherwise called bombard"). In addition to their six fingerholes, bombards had a key protected by a fontanelle, such as that depicted by Virdung, and some had in addition three or four extension keys, the so-called basset keys to carry the compass down.

Praetorius lists a total of seven sizes of shawm: a sopranino in b′ (*klein Schalmey*), soprano in d′ (*discant Schalmey*)—Mersenne was to call this a *dessus*—alto bombard in g° (*klein Altpommer,* called tenor shawm in England, the *taille* of Mersenne and the most frequently portrayed member of the consort), *Nicolo* in c°, *Bassett* or *Tenor Pommer* in G°—the bass of Mersenne—a *Basspommer* in C°, and finally the great bass in F′ (*Gross-Basspommer*) called *contrebasse* in French, also made as a quart bass in G′. These instruments ranged in size from about 50 centimeters (20 inches) for the sopranino to the monsters of some 290 centimeters (9 feet 8 inches) for the great bass in F′. An extant great bass in the National Museum of Prague has a tube length of 272 centimeters (ca. 9 feet), five keys, and a compass of E′ to b°. The same collection also houses a four-keyed bass with a tube length of 132 centimeters (52 inches) and a compass of A′ to e°; two tenors with single key and a length of 108 centimeters (42½ inches), compass c♯° to g′; and a one-keyed alto with tube length of 75 centimeters

(30 inches), compass e° to b′ (all compasses given in modern pitch).
The smaller sizes were played with a pirouette, but the reeds of bass
and great bass were mounted on a simple metal crook. The unwieldy
length of the basses presented problems of transportation and of performance; the frontispiece to Praetorius's *Theatrum instrumentorum*
(1620) shows a large bombard being played while its lower end is
supported by a second person; it was also played with the lower end
resting on the floor (cf. Tibetan and Chinese trumpets). But most of the
larger sizes were short lived, as the cumbersome basses were gradually discarded in favor of the more manageable curtals.

Shawms were perhaps the most versatile of all fifteenth- and sixteenth-
century instruments: in fifteenth-century England "shawmys of turnyt
buschboun" (turned boxwood) were pastoral instruments; a "shalmewer"
was engaged at the English court in 1511; and it was a wait's pipe from
the fifteenth century on. The wait was a tower watchman (*gait* in
French, both words descended from the Frankish *wahten*, "to watch"),
and by extension wait came to denote the wait's instrument, which
could be a shawm, cornett, sackbut, recorder, curtal; even chordophones
are occasionally mentioned in this connection. But the word "wait" became associated with the shawm from the fifteenth century on: a
nominale of that period glosses the Latin *colomaula* as "wayte pipe,"
and Palsgrave in 1530 defines the "wayte" as "an instrument, hauboys."
The term was still employed at the end of the seventeenth century, when
Talbot describes the treble wait as somewhat over two feet long, and
the tenor about two and one-half feet, which would correspond to the
shawm and alto bombard of Praetorius, and probably also to the two
instruments depicted by Virdung, though the latter are not drawn to
scale.

Shawms of different sizes continued to play an important part in
the loud music of the sixteenth and seventeenth centuries: at a service
performed in 1527 at Saint Paul's, London, on the occasion of a visit
by Cardinal Wolsey, "the Lord Cardinall began Te Deum the which
was solemnlie songen with the King's trumpetts and shalmes as well as
Inglish men and Venetians." Links between shawm and trumpet were
so close that in 1541 Duke Albert of Prussia included *1 tenor bomhart
sampt einen bass bomhart mit etzlichen roren* ("1 tenor bombard with
a bass bombard with several crooks") in an order given to Jorg Neuschel,
one of the foremost Nuremberg instrument makers of his day, and sup-

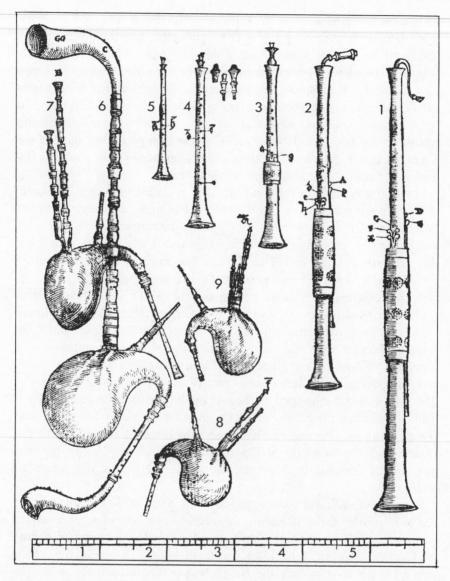

Shawms and other instruments: (1) bass shawm; (2) basset or tenor shawm; (3) alto shawm; (4) descant shawm; (5) small shawm; (6) great *Bock*; (7) shepherd's bagpipe; (8) *Hümmelchen*; (9) *Dudey*. From Michael Praetorius, *Theatrum instrumentorum*, 1620.

plier of trumpets to the Duke, who could thus be assured of matched pitches. Three shawms and a trumpet participated in the *ommegang* (local procession) of Louvain in 1594; three shawms and a cornett, curtal, and trombone made up the ensemble of musicians playing in an outdoor religious procession at Antwerp, as painted by Van Alsloot in 1616—and the same musicians playing the very same instruments appear in two contemporary paintings by Antoine Sallaert, depicting similar processions in Brussels.

Most shawms were pitched a tone higher than the cornetts and trombones, writes Praetorius. Furthermore, the keyless soprano (in D) presented difficulties in ensemble playing, for it lacked the F (it had an F♯); hence he recommends omitting the *käkend* ("strident") soprano and using only the lower-pitched bombards in consort playing. His advice does not seem to have been heeded, for as late as 1681 the Dresden court had among its instruments a case of five shawms—two descant, two alto, and a tenor—with gilt keys, three S-crooks, two *Balletten* (*palettes*, i.e., pirouettes) with two staples and five reeds. During the next forty years, from about 1680 to 1720, the shawm was gradually displaced by an improved, jointed version, the oboe, and the larger bombards that had managed to survive the competition of the curtal finally gave way to the bassoon.

A less common variety of baroque shawm with extremely slender build dates from this period, made in the Low Countries, Germany, and Switzerland, in soprano and tenor sizes. Both had unusually narrow bores terminating in a long, flaring bell, and both carried a fontanelle, though that of the soprano covered only a vent hole and was consequently non-functional; the tenor, however, was supplied with a key. Such instruments were still being made in the second decade of the eighteenth century, and according to Talbot (ca. 1700) the sound of the slender model was "sweeter" than that of the more robust wait.

A slightly later writer, Fuhrmann (1706), regrets that the *Bombardone* (bass bombard) of 16′ pitch should have been replaced by the French *basson* of 8′ pitch, an instrument not penetrating enough, in his opinion, for service in a large church, where a bass of 16′ pitch was a necessity. Only in Nuremberg, for centuries a center of wind-instrument making, did shawms remain in use, for the municipality showed an almost pathetic tenacity in keeping the old instruments alive and supported their players financially, so that in 1752 three *Pfeifer* (town musicians) could still be heard there, "one of whom blows a so-called old shawm, the second a bass, and the third a *Pommer* or Oboe, instruments that are either not at all in use now or barely so."

One form of shawm seems to have lingered on to the end of the eighteenth century, probably as a church instrument, and only in the canton of Bern. At the time of the Reformation, Bern had become Protestant and reacted strongly to the presence of musical instruments in its churches. They were banned, and musically the whole canton—its territory was then far greater than it is now—remained notoriously backward until the late eighteenth century. Nameless until Gustave Chouquet catalogued the example of the Paris Conservatoire collection, he chose to call them *basse de musette*, and they have been known as such ever since. A total of sixteen specimens have now come to light, all apparently of Swiss manufacture; in form they are similar to a large instrument illustrated in Borjon's *Traité de la musette* of 1672 except for the crooks, which on the Swiss shawms are coiled in a circle. *Basses de musette* have a wide, rapidly tapering conical bore, extremely thin walls, and vary in length from 127 to 132 centimeters (50 to 52 inches); they sound an octave lower than the oboe. Because of their positioning, two holes only are covered by the player's fingers, the remaining five by keys. Of the six specimens in the Bern Museum, one is dated 1777; all others are believed to be of approximately the same age.

THE OBOE

When the old, one-piece shawm was transformed into a jointed instrument in the seventeenth century, probably both invented and first played by Jean Hotteterre *père* and Michel Philidor II at the Court of France (in 1657), we begin to speak of it as an oboe. In England it was known by the older name of *hautbois* or hoboy, later as French hoboy; the German and Italian name, *oboe* (pronounced "oh-boh-ay"), is merely a phonetic reduction of *hautbois*, clearly an indication of its French provenance.

In a study of the oboe's early history, Marx (1951) concluded that in all probability Michel Philidor II refined the old shawm reed and, together with Jean Hotteterre the Elder, made an oboe around 1655 (Philidor died in 1659). Lully, who may be assumed to have been the leading spirit behind, and godfather to, the invention, scored for the new woodwind in his ballets and later in his operas. Emergence of the oboe was no accident, but the result of a studied attempt to provide a double-reed woodwind with a tone quality fit for refined indoor music making (shawms were thought of primarily as open-air instruments). Eminently successful, *le doux son des hautbois* was duly attested and the oboe's future assured.

Earlier in the seventeenth century the tenon and socket system of making joints had become known, so that the new oboe could be divided into three sections, and from then on it was invariably a jointed instrument, and thereby distinguished from the shawms. At the same time the bore was narrowed and the bell made smaller; the pirouette was abolished entirely, and the reed cut narrower and mounted on a staple. The old swallow-tail key, the open C key of the shawm, was retained, and a closed E♭ key was added, duplicated for left- and right-handed players. As to pitch, the oboe was made to sound a tone below the shawm, with a compass c′ to c³.

This new version met with immediate acceptance and was firmly entrenched by the beginning of the eighteenth century, when virtually every European band and orchestra had its pair of oboes; in fact the wind section of municipal and military bands were known in Germany as *Hoboisten* ("oboe players") well into the eighteenth century. The older shawm remained in use, and although both instruments were often called *hautbois* indiscriminately, a new nomenclature was in the process of formation. Thus Talbot, writing in the last years of the seventeenth century, distinguishes between the "English hautbois," or waits, the "schalmeye" or narrow-bore baroque shawm, and the "French hautbois," or oboe. Of the latter he writes:

The 7th hole is stopt by a great brass key by reason of Distance; on the same Joynt an 8th Hole on each side for right or left hand opened with a less Key . . . Its compass more proper for Consort than most Wind Instruments. Its sound lively & not much inferior to Trumpet: with a good reed & skilful hand it sounds as easy & soft as the Flute [the word flute denoted the recorder at this time].

The source of part of his information was the preface, signed J. B. and believed to stand for John Banister, to *The Sprightly Companion* of 1695, devoted to the French "hautboy": "For besides its Inimitable Charming Sweetness of Sound (when well play'd upon) it is also Majestic and Stately and not much inferiour to the Trumpet . . . ," and again: "For all that play upon this Instrument to a reasonable perfection know, that with a good reed it goes as easie and as soft as the Flute," an early tribute to the softer tone of the indoor instrument. A year later, in 1696, French oboes were purchased still further afield from their country of origin by the Austrian monastery of Kremsmünster, where in addition to *ein ganz Spill Hubua* ("a whole consort of oboes"), 3 *französische Schalmeyen* were acquired.

Printed tutors for the two- or three-keyed oboe started appearing in 1695 with the aforementioned *Sprightly Companion*, and do not cease until the late eighteenth century, as the long-lived, two-keyed model did not become obsolete until the early nineteenth century. Though c′ was always the lowest tone of the oboe, its absolute pitch varied according to whether a given instrument were built in "French tone," cornett tone, or chamber tone; it was quite common for two different pitch standards to be in use in one locality, in which case instruments at both pitches had to be at hand. An early tutor for flute, recorder, and oboe by Louis Hotteterre, so popular that it ran through numerous editions between 1707 and 1741, gives instructions for the embouchure: the reed should be placed between the teeth, right in the center, and should not penetrate the mouth by more than 2 or 3 *lignes* (5 to 7 millimeters) but, rather, placed so that it could be squeezed more or less, as desired, by the lips, and never touched by the teeth.

Still limited by the choice of keys available and demanding a complicated fingering, the oboe became part of the orchestra around 1720 and was scored for by, among others, Bach, Handel, and Haydn. Toward the middle of the eighteenth century the duplicate E♭ key was discontinued, since hand positions had become standardized by then. Two further keys were added for G♯ and A♯ by German makers, but the old two-keyed variety was still being made around 1820, and the four-keyed model did not become common prior to 1830. Up to the end of the eighteenth century oboes had no overblow (speaker) hole; this is a hole of small diameter placed above the fingerholes, usually but not necessarily dorsal, and covered by a key—the speaker, or octave, key; this greatly facilitates overblowing but is not indispensable.

Models at other tonal ranges were built, and the *oboe d'amore* (see page 694) came into being. By 1800 oboes were no longer scored in pairs but were given solo parts. Their influence in town and military bands had declined in the latter part of the eighteenth century; they were being displaced by the clarinet to the point that a writer in the *Allgemeine musikalische Zeitung* of 1812 suggested renaming the wind sections of these bands: they merited the name *Hoboisten* all the less, as "there is now not a single oboe among them."

Development in the nineteenth century progressed along uneven lines. Speaker keys became common around 1830; with the two- and four-keyed models still in use, six more keys were gradually added for a vent, low C♯, closed F♯ on lower joint, closed B♭ on upper joint, closed upper C, with a long-shank open key placed on the bell for b°, extending the compass downward. These ten keys, together with three extra levers for B♭, F, and D♯, suggested by Joseph Sellner, the German oboist, produced "Sellner's thirteen-keyed oboe." The original Sellner models were built by Stefan Koch, a Viennese flute maker, and despite subsequent improvements by other makers, German and Austrian oboes of today are substantially unchanged from the Koch-Sellner model. In 1825 Sellner also brought out a tutor for his oboe. Hitherto oboe making on the Continent had been predominantly German, with such notable woodwind masters as Grenser, Grundmann and his pupil Floth, all of Dresden, both experimenting and producing outstanding work.

But by the late eighteenth century it had become clear that the French and the Germans were developing very distinct tonal preferences, leading to the production of two different types of instruments in Paris and Dresden, which in turn resulted in the creation of an independent French school of oboe making in the second decade of the nineteenth century. A complete reform of the instrument was undertaken by such Parisian makers as Henri Brod and the Triéberts: bore, silhouette, and keywork were revised. The upper part of the bore was narrowed appreciably, the relative sizes and positioning of the tone holes were changed, the reed narrowed and thinned. Buffet of Paris produced a Boehm-system oboe in 1844, but this met with only limited success. Structural differences between the French and German models prevail to this day, the most noteworthy consisting in the proportions of the bore, that of French instruments still the narrower of the two. In general the French model is the more widely accepted and currently is also gaining a following in Germany.

The Taille des Hautbois

Oboes have been built in a variety of sizes, some smaller than the orchestral instrument and that intended for military use, others larger. Of the latter, the *taille des hautbois* is perhaps the oldest: dating back to the seventeenth century, it is probably not much younger than the type instrument, which it resembles closely except for size and for its pitch in F, a fifth below the common oboe. On most surviving examples the reed was carried on a detachable metal crook. Its written part was often abbreviated to *taille*. Another of its names was *quinte de hautbois*. In early eighteenth-century France the *taille* served mainly in military music; the famous collection of court music compiled by Philidor *l'aîné* (André Danican, d. 1740), includes marches and flourishes typically for two oboes, a *taille*, and a *basse de hautbois* (bassoon). In Britain, where it became known as the tenor hoboy, we first hear of it in Purcell's *Dioclesian* of 1690.

As was the case with other relatively low-pitched woodwinds, the tube's dimensions raised the problem of bringing tone holes within easy reach of the player's hands. On the tenor hoboy this was solved in different manners, one of which was described by Talbot (ca. 1700): "[the] holes which being at greater distance are bored more slantingly downwards that the tops may be covered with the Fingers." In general, English eighteenth-century tenors retained their straight construction but were made of only two sections, without a separate bell, with the reed attached to a long and sharply bent metal crook. This form was known as the "vox humana" from about 1750 to close to the end of the century.

On the Continent both shape and nomenclature varied, the more widely prevailing eighteenth-century terms included *cor anglais, corno inglese, englisches Horn,* or *oboe da caccia.* Contrary to British usage, the Continent showed a marked preference for curved or angled models; these forms brought the lower group of fingerholes within easy reach and closer to the player's body, and though some instruments were made with the flared bell of the regular oboe, others terminated in a globular, *amore*-type bell. Actually neither the origin of these terms, nor even the pairing of name with type of instrument, is clear. The earlier of these names is *oboe da caccia,* which instrument is believed to have been in use from about 1720 to 1760 or later; Bach scored for *oboi da caccia* in several cantatas between 1723 and 1740; they were at low chamber pitch, with d° (i.e., low chamber pitch d°) as their lowest tone. A German form of the word occurs as *Jagd-Hautbois* in Zedler (1735), where it is stated that the instrument in question was used during the hunt, and also mornings and evenings to play for the chief master of the hunt. Strangely enough, no such instrument is mentioned in the literature of the chase. Similar terms, such as *Wald-Hautbois, hautbois de chasse,* and *hautbois de forêt,* presumably apply to the same instrument. Two *hautbois de forêt,* each supplied with three *corps de rechange,* are enumerated in a 1780 inventory of instruments kept in Louis XVI's library at Versailles, but alas, without further detail. If indeed such large oboes were played on horseback, bending them or setting them at an angle would seem a logical solution to the problem of canting them close to the body. Whatever the name, these instruments were either curved to a crescent and covered with black leather, or made in angular form, also leather covered, and with flared or with *amore* bell.

The Cor Anglais

Shortly after the mid-century the adjective "English" appears in one language or another: *corno inglese, cor anglais, cor de chasse anglais, englisches Waldhorn*. The expression *corno inglese* starts appearing in Viennese scores around 1760, and this term has been matched with museum instruments of Viennese or Italian make, crescent shaped and with narrow bore. The only description of the *englisches Waldhorn* known to the author is that of Halle (1764), who states that "the English horns of wood are bent crooked and covered with leather, and are wide at the lower end, increasingly narrow toward the reed." He counts it as the highest pitched of the "horns," and relates that the reeds (*Rohrmund-stücke*) are made wider or narrower as required, to enable an instrument to be played at choir pitch. Now the *englisches Waldhorn* as described corresponds both in form and materials to a true hunting horn, the French *huchet*, a semicircular affair originally made of animal horn but later imitated in wood; two sections of wood were hollowed out and then bound together in leather. Taken together with Zedler's comment, this suggests the possibility that the *cor anglais* was at one time used as an imitation or substitute for the horn—not for the glorious duple- or triple-wound gentleman's horn that so elegantly encircled mounted huntsmen, but the short, curved signal horn of the attendant foot servants. As it had tone holes, the "English" version could additionally be used for serenading the master of the hunt.

Some slight confirmation of this hypothesis may be seen in the passage from the *Mercure de France* of 1749 (quoted in Pierre [1893]) in which the woodwind maker Charles Bizey advertised: *Il a inventé depuis peu des hautbois qui descendant au G ré sol, comme le violon, d'autres qui sont à l'octave du hautbois ordinaire, imitant parfaitement le cor de chasse* ("He invented recently oboes going down to G as does the violin, others at the octave of the ordinary oboe, imitating perfectly the hunting horn"). Apart from such speculation, one item of positive and valuable information emerges: it has often been stated that the *cor anglais* was made like a cornett, that is, of a piece of wood split lengthwise, hollowed out, rejoined, and covered with leather. This technique has been questioned recently on the grounds that the fingerholes would have to be drilled along that joint. Halle confirms these suspicions that instruments were bored straight, then bent (by heat) and covered to hide the resulting blemishes. The *cor de chasse anglais* is not mentioned until the late eighteenth century.

The present-day *cor anglais* is a straight model with the globular *amore* foot, based on the 1839 *cor anglais moderne* of Henri Brod, and played with a curved reed. Keywork and fingering are those of the oboe. Brod's instrument did not immediately displace the older, bent forms, but coexisted with them—at least in Italy—for about half a century. Its modern compass is from e° to a², and, like the *oboe d'amore*, it is treated as a transposing instrument and notated a fifth higher than it sounds.

The Oboe D'amore

Smaller and more recent than the *cor anglais* is the *oboe d'amore*, also called *hautbois d'amour*, an oboe in A, a minor third below the common oboe, made (outside France) with bulbous *amore* foot-joint that modifies the timbre by first allowing the air column to expand, and then compressing it by forcing it to issue through an aperture no greater than "a finger's breadth," as Walther observed. Both he and Majer stated (1732) that the *oboe d'amore* had been known since about 1720; its compass is given as a° to e² or higher. Older instruments had keys for b° and c′, but differed in structure: German instruments had a bulb bell, but the French retained the oboe bell. German composers were first to write for the *amore* as far as we know: Georg Telemann in his *Sieg der Schönheit* of 1722, and Bach from 1723 on. After the mid-century it was neglected, and nineteenth-century authors suggested it might have fallen into disuse because of the difficulties inherent in playing it in tune. Parisian makers revived it sporadically in the nineteenth century; Victor Mahillon of Brussels reconstructed one in 1874 for participation in Bach performances. His model had an oboe bell. A decade or so later both French and English makers started building models with bulb bell and full keywork. But except for Bach performances the *amore* is seldom heard today.

The Hautbois-Baryton

A large oboe, which for want of a better name is termed *hautbois-baryton* or baritone oboe, was pitched an octave below the type instrument. Probably originating at the turn of the seventeenth to eighteenth century, it seems barely to have survived the mid-eighteenth century. And its function is unknown. Few examples have survived and they offer little uniformity of design, except for their two keys.

The Heckelphone

A rival to the baritone oboe appeared early in our century when the firm of Wilhelm Heckel of Biebrich brought out its *Heckelphon* in 1904, pitched one octave below the oboe. Although it has a conoid tube, is played with a double reed, and has similar keywork, the heckelphone is in fact not an oboe at all, as its bore is far wider. Recognizable by its straight form, it terminates in a partly stopped bulb bell. In addition to the large model, two less successful sopraninos have been built, the *Terz-Heckelphon* in E♭ and the *Piccolo-Heckelphon* in F.

REEDCAP SHAWMS

Apart from shawms with mouthed double reeds, there arose by the sixteenth century several forms of double-reed woodwinds played with the reed enclosed in a protective cap. These are known as reedcap shawms. On all reedcap instruments the player exercised little control over the reed with regard to timbre and dynamics, and, because it could not be overblown, the compass of these aerophones was restricted to that of a ninth unless enlarged by keys.

The Nicolo

Of the seven sizes of regular shawms described and depicted by Praetorius, one—the *Nicolo*—is shown twice: once with a pirouette, and again with a reedcap and a rear thumbhole, lacking on his other shawms. Otherwise the *Nicolo* was the same in build as the tenor or basset shawn (except for the latter's basset keys). When capped, the *Nicolo* may have acted as bass to an ensemble of crumhorns, for Praetorius depicts it with a consort of these instruments.

The Rauschpfeife

One of the earliest of reedcap shawms to develop into a whole family were the German *Rauschpfeifen*, with their wide, conical bore terminating in a slight flare, seven fingerholes, and a thumbhole. The *Rauschpfeife* was known to Schlick as an organ stop in 1511, when he termed it a new stop; but, in order to be imitated as an organ register, the woodwind must have been known by the beginning of the century at the very latest. This short-lived instrument was depicted and named by Hans Burgkmair in his *Triumphs of the Emperor Maximilian* of 1512, and was already obsolete in Germany by the middle of the same century. It does not seem to have had a wide diffusion. A consort of six instruments is preserved in the Berlin collection, and a set of five, lacking their reedcaps, is housed in the National Museum of Prague. Praetorius knew only of the organ stop of that name.

The Hautbois de Poitou

A corresponding instrument of France was called *hautbois de Poitou;* it outlived the *Rauschpfeife* by well over a century. Here also the bore was conical, the seventh fingerhole was still duplicated for left- or right-handed players, and it had a thumbhole. In fact the only difference between the ordinary shawm and the *hautbois de Poitou* was its length, the disposition of its tone holes, and its reedcap, according to Furetière (1685). Mersenne lists three sizes, the largest of which was doubled back on itself like a bassoon, and had an open key protected by a fontanelle. Like most reedcap instruments (but not the *Nicolo*), the *hautbois de Poitou* probably originated as a folk instrument and was subsequently made in various sizes for ensemble playing. Though Mersenne's text is not clear, we may infer that the sizes in use in his day were a *dessus* (soprano), with a compass of c′ to d²; a *taille* (tenor), f° to g′; and a bass, C° to f°. Together with the *cornemuse de Poitou,* a bagpipe, these instruments formed a consort represented in the band of the Grande Écurie du Roi of Louis XIV. According to the French court calendar for the early 1660s, the Grand Écurie then comprised *12 trompettes, 12 joueurs de violons, hautbois, sacqueboutes & cornets* (trombones and cornetts); *4 haut-bois de Poitou, 9 joueurs de phifres* (fifes), *tambourins & muzettes.*

The Cornemuse

One reedcap shawm that certainly originated as a folk instrument was the French *cornemuse* of shepherds, also called *chalemie* after the mid-seventeenth century. This was merely a *musette* chanter detached from its bag, and with the double reed placed in a wooden reedcap for protection. We do not know when it originated, but it managed to maintain an existence as a reedcap shawm until the nineteenth century. By the eighteenth century it had dropped its earlier name and was called *musette;* it was this shawm chanter, and not the bagpipe, that gave its name to the *bal musette,* in which participation of a *musette* was formerly mandatory but now, alas, is replaced by an accordion. The reedcap itself was sometimes shaped into a beak that was then mouthed. In the course of the nineteenth century the reedcap was dispensed with and the chanter thereby transformed into a small oboe in G, sounding a fifth above the ordinary oboe, and marketed as a child's toy.

The Cornamusa

Probably unrelated to the foregoing despite its name is an elusive family of Italian Renaissance woodwinds, that of the *cornamusa.* Several Italian accounts of musical performances in the second half of the sixteenth century mention them. Massimo Trojano (1568) lists them together with the *dolzainas* that they must have resembled closely. Praetorius describes—as *Cornemusen*—a set of five instruments having apparently a cylindrical tube—his wording is not clear on this point—but certainly a single tube like that of the *bassanelli,* closed at the bottom, with several lateral vents through which the sound escaped, and devoid of keys. Each had a compass of a ninth, the soprano from b°, the alto from d°, the tenor from c°, another tenor from B♭°, and a bass from F°. Like the crumhorns, *schryari,* and bagpipes, the *Cornmusen* have a capsule over their reed, he writes. A bagpipe of the Abruzzi is also called *cornamusa,* and one may speculate as to whether the relationship between detached chanter (the *cornamusa* had two) and reedcap shawm might not have resembled that of the *musette.* In this context it may be noted that Greek Gypsies and shepherds play a shawm called *karamouza* (etymology: *cornamusa*), and also have a bagpipe of that name. But so far, the riddle of the *cornamusa-Cornemusen* has not been solved.

The Kortholt

Apparently little used and confined to Germanic countries of the late Renaissance was the *Kortholt,* also called *Kort Instrument,* or *Kurzpfeife,* all words denoting shortness—a reedcap rackett closely resembling the *sordone. Zwei Cort instrumenten genannt racketten oder Cornaldo* ("two short instruments named racketts or *Cornaldo*") figure in a Cleves inventory of 1610. Racketts were called *cortali* in Italian, and comparison of the *Kort instrument* and *cortali* is justified not only on etymological grounds, for the two had notable features in common: both were very short and their fingerholes were not disposed in a straight

line but were placed around the circumference according to the requirements of the bores. Praetorius briefly refers to this instrument by all
three of its names, commenting that it had the same length and proportions as the bass *sordone*, but the pitch of a tenor *sordone*, which
puzzled him. However, in his chart of pitches those of the *Kortholt* and
bass *sordone* are both given as B♭′ to g°. His drawing is that of a short,
cylindrical, *gedackt* (stopped) instrument with a two-channel bore—
also cylindrical—and provided with keys and reedcap. Unnecessary confusion with regard to the *Kortholt* has arisen from a nonfacsimile reprint
of Praetorius, in which the caption to his drawing reads: *Kortholt,
Basset oder Tenor zum Chorist-Fagott*, instead of the original: *Zingel
Kortholt. Basset oder Tenor zum Chorist-Fagott, G*, leading several investigators to postulate two kinds of *Kortholt*, whereas Praetorius is
merely referring to the "single curtal," elsewhere in his text spelled as
Zingelcorthol.

The Courtaut

The Old French word *courtaut* originally meant "bombard" or
"cannon," before it was transferred to a now obsolete French woodwind known chiefly from the descriptions of seventeenth-century authors,
although it was already mentioned by Jean Molinet (d. 1507) as a
musical instrument. It was a reedcap shawm with cylindrically bored
double channel in a single block of wood, from which the air escaped by
means of ventholes close to the top. In addition to its six fingerholes, two
groups of three short tubes, called *tétines*, projected obliquely from the
ascending bore through the wall of the tube, one group for left-handed,
the other for right-handed, players, the unneeded group being closed with
wax. The *courtaut*'s double reed was usually covered by a "little box," but
if played without its reedcap, the reed was mounted on a short crook.
The function of the *tétines* was to permit the player to cover two holes
with one finger, making use of tip and joint, placed flat, as Trichet puts it,
and thereby dispensing with keys, since the fingerholes could all be brought
within easy reach of the player's fingers. Both Mersenne and Trichet state
that the *courtaut* served as bass to the *musette*, and Mersenne likened
its appearance to that of a thick walking stick. No specimen has survived.
Writers still refer to it in the present tense late in the century, and
Furetière, having reminded us that it served as bass to the *musette* adds
that it is a big piece of cylindrical wood *dont quelquesuns font de grands
bourdons de Pélérins* ("of which some people make large pilgrim's
staves").

Though the *courtaut* was not identical with the English curtal (which had a conical bore), some contemporary English writers used the French word to designate the English instrument, with resultant confusion.

The Dolzaina

Among the less clearly identified Renaissance instruments is the *dolzaina*, putative reedcap shawm, called *douçaine* in French, and known to French literature from the thirteenth to the sixteenth centuries, when it apparently died out. It must have existed in at least two sizes or with two compasses, for the term *demi-douchaine* also occurs. In Spanish it was also known as *dulzaina*. As *dolzaina* it is mentioned in several southern German Renaissance inventories and by such Italian writers of the time as Massimo Trojano and Zacconi. Praetorius did not know of it. A rare English reference is that of "5 short instruments called Dulceuses" enumerated in the 1547 inventory of Henry VIII's instruments. Probably the *dulcina* of Tinctoris was another of its names; he describes it in the late fifteenth century as a kind of *tibia* with seven fingerholes, a thumbhole, and a limited compass. Hence the inference that the *dolzaina* was a cylindrically bored reedcap shawm. Zacconi (1592) informs us that the keyless *dolzaina* had a compass of a ninth, from c° to d′, and that given two keys it ascended to f′. This information agrees with Praetorius's description of the *Cornamusa*, except that the latter existed in five sizes. Following Kinsky's study of reedcap woodwinds (1925), several writers have identified the *dolzaina* with the *cornamusa*, but that the two cannot be identical is clear from Trojano's list of instruments played in 1568 performances, when both participated in several ensembles.

The Schryari

Yet another mysterious family were the *Shreierpfeifen* ("screaming pipes"), whose name was Latinized to *schryari*. Just as the *dolzaina* had been played in Romance countries, so the *schryari* were apparently restricted to Germanic territories. We find them enumerated in several inventories between 1540 and 1686, and also depicted by Praetorius. They were mentioned for the last time by Fuhrmann in 1706. A striking characteristic was their loud tone, but physically they resembled the elusive *Cornemusen*, says Praetorius. He shows a conoid tube, but we do not know whether the bore followed the outline of the instrument or might not have been cylindrical. *Schryari* were made in consorts of soprano in g°, tenor/alto in c°, and bass in F°; the compass, here again, was that of a ninth, and both tenor and bass models were furnished with keys to extend the range upward. Praetorius notes that the soprano was stopped, but had several lateral vents for the sound to escape by, and these are shown in his illustration. Among the woodwinds owned by the city of Augsburg for their town musicians in 1540 were a consort of five *Schreierpfeifen*. A year later, the Nuremberg trumpet maker, Jorg Neuschel, offered to Duke Albert of Prussia some *schreyende Pfeiffen* that he had received from Lyons and Venice, and which he claimed were far louder than bombards. Possibly the "screaming pipes" were played in Mediterranean countries as folk instruments under another name.

The Doppione

The *doppione* of the Italian Renaissance is referred to by Zacconi (1592) as occurring in three sizes, with compasses of c′ to d°, c° to d′, C° to d°, and, as these are all intervals of a ninth, we assume the *doppione* to have been another double-reed aerophone played with a reedcap, and probably having a cylindrical bore. Praetorius stated that he had never seen one. The very name (*doblado* in Spanish) suggests a duplication of some sort, probably that of the bore. Furthermore, Praetorius lists *doppioni* among those instruments having holes in front, in back, and on the sides, the others in question being racketts, *sordoni*, and *schryari*, thus suggesting that the *doppioni* may have been *sordoni* played with a reedcap.

EUROPEAN FOLK SHAWMS

Folk shawms never died out in certain parts of Europe, notably in northeastern Spain, Portugal, northern France, Italy, and the Balkans. The *dolçaina* or *dulzaina* of Old Spanish literature, the Iberian equivalent of the Italian *dolzaina*, still flourishes as a modified folk instrument, its sound transformed from the softness to which it owes its name into a loud and lively outdoor instrument, played with a broad reed mounted on a staple but without a pirouette. Its conical tube terminates in a bell. Some models are of wood, others of metal, with seven front finger-holes and either no keys at all or with simple keywork. Nowadays the *dulzaina* is invariably accompanied by a drum called *caja peñarandina*. The Basque people also play it, but call it *bolin-gozo*.

Better known due to its association with the *cobla* ensemble is the *chirimía*—the *charamela* of Old Spanish—now built in two sizes, a *tiple* ("treble") and *tenora*. Both are wide-bored conoid instruments still played with a pirouette and short, triangular reeds having a wide opening. The *tiple* is prominent in the North Catalonian *cobla* bands; pitched in F, it has a range of d' to g³ and is treated like a transposing instrument. The wooden body of the larger *tenora* terminates in a long metal bell; pitched in B♭, a fifth below the *tiple,* its compass is e° to c³; the downward extension of both models is due to keys. *Coblas* at the beginning of the nineteenth century consisted of pipe and tabor, one or two *tiples,* and a bagpipe; *tiples* of that period were keyless, made of boxwood, and had a turned pirouette. Apart from the fact that they were slightly shorter, they appear identical to the shawms of sixteenth- and seventeenth-century European art music; then, in the course of the nineteenth century, both *chirimías* were modernized and fitted with keywork. They are outdoor instruments par excellence, certainly the loudest of any modern woodwind, with a penetrating and slightly nasal tone quality. The Old Spanish term *charamela* lives on in Portugal, where it now denotes a folk shawm made in three sizes, called *bastarda, media,* and *charamelinha.*

An Italian folk shawm now restricted to the Abruzzi but that probably had a far wider dissemination in former centuries is the *ciaramella;* its conical bore ends in a short, flared bell; the double reed is tied to a staple but played without a pirouette. Nowadays the *ciaramella* is always accompanied by the bagpipe *zampogna.*

An abbreviated version of the French *bombarde* lives on in Brittany as a small folk shawm, a wide-bored instrument with detachable bell. Like the *ciaramella,* it is always played together with a bagpipe, in this case with the *biniou,* which it accompanies at the lower octave.

Depending upon the material from which they are cut, double reeds can be divided into a hard (European) and a soft (Asian) type, and in one area of Europe—the Balkans—both types exist side by side. The classic shawm of the Near East, the *zurna,* is found, under modified names, from the Balkans all the way East to China. In modern times, Gypsies from Persia introduced it to Yugoslavia, western Bulgaria, Romania, and Albania, where it is called *zurla* and played in the Oriental manner with puffed-out cheeks, a pirouette, and a soft reed of *durra* straw moving freely in the player's mouth. By contrast, the *sopila* of Yugoslavia, found chiefly on Krk Island and along the Croatian coast, is played with a pirouette and a harder, short, and wider reed of cane

(*Arundo donax*), gripped by the player's lips. *Sopilas* are made in two sizes and always played in pairs of a short and a long one. Quite untypically they are made of three separate joints—an indication of their relatively late origin—and prior to playing water is poured into the tube to swell the wood and thereby tighten the joints.

In the course of its dispersal, the Near Eastern *zurna* was introduced to the Magyars via the Balkan trade route in late medieval times, and became known there as *tárogató*, a word probably akin to *tarot*, a forerunner of the bassoon in France, and *tarota*, a shawm of Catalonia, both conically bored, double-reed aerophones. Originally devoid of fingerholes, the old folk instrument was not standardized; sometimes it had an ornamental tube, sometimes a plain one, and at other times a carved tube would be provided with fingerholes and terminate in a trumpetlike flare, or again it might be made with a bronze bell. Pitched in D, it was played with a pirouette and overblew the octave.

In the course of the eighteenth century, the *tárogató* became associated with the Hungarian national leader, Ferenc Rákóczy II (1676–1735), as a consequence of which it was revived a century later and raised to the status of a national instrument. Modifications were made in the mid-nineteenth century, and the instrument underwent complete transformation at the hands of Joseph Schunda of Budapest at the end of the century. When Schunda showed it at the Paris Exhibition of 1900 it had developed into a sort of wooden saxophone: double reed and pirouette had been replaced by a single reed placed on a clarinet-type mouthpiece, and additional keywork had been fitted. His type instrument was the soprano in B♭; others are now built in E♭ and A♭; Schunda also advertised tenors and basses.

From Hungary the *tárogató* reached Romania; in the Banat it has now replaced the clarinet in folk music.

A double-reed folk aerophone found in rural Slovenia and in Brittany is made of spirally wound strips of bark—often that of birches—and is notable for its reed of flattened soft straw, the same type of reed as that found on some ancient Egyptian reedpipes.

NON-WESTERN SHAWMS

Shawms in North Africa and Asia

Eastern shawms are of two varieties: either short, cylindrical, typically with seven front and two dorsal fingerholes; or longer, conoid, and typically with seven front and one dorsal fingerhole. The former is known in

the Near East as *'iraqīya*, a foreshortened reedpipe played nowadays chiefly
in Egypt, whose name points to its country of origin; its broad reed is exceptionally long—from 8 to 9 centimeters (3 to 3½ inches)—in relation to
its body length of from 18 to 23 centimeters (7 to 9 inches), and is held
in shape by a keeper ring. The same aerophone is known by different
names in North Africa (e.g., *surnā*, *ghaita*) but these are also bestowed
on the conical models.

Representative of the longer, conoid pipes, and perhaps best known
to Westerners because it also occurs in the Balkans, is the *zurnā* (called
zamr in the Maghrib), with its flared bell, seven front fingerholes, and
dorsal thumbhole. Near Eastern versions have vents near the lower end
that are utilized in connection with changes of the instrument's pitch:
a movable neck is constituted of a wooden cylinder partly cut away so
as to form a prong, rather like a clothespin, inserted at the upper end
of the tube; by turning the cylinder, the prong can be located under the
upper fingerholes, thereby blocking them, in which case the vents are
brought into play. The staple is set directly in the top of this cylinder
and invariably carries a pirouette. In the Caucasus, ensembles are formed
of a *zurnā*, a *duduki*, and a *duhul*, the *duduki* being a Georgian version
of the *zamr*, and the *duhul* a barrel-shaped drum.

With the spread of Islam *zurnās* were introduced from the Near East
and Persia to India, Indonesia, and China. The Persian *surnāy*, for instance, becomes the *sānāyī* of northern India, where two instruments are
sometimes combined to form a double shawm (see double pipes, page
651); generally, however, a single shawm is accompanied by a drone
bagpipe called *sruti upāngi*. The *sānāyī* corresponds to the *nāgasuram* of
southern India, a large shawm terminating in a metal bell, and played
together with the drone shawm, *ottu*. The latter is slightly longer than
the *nāgasuram* and has four or five holes pierced in the lower end; by
closing these, either partly or completely, the *sruti*, or keynote, of the *ottu*
is brought to the desired pitch.

A remarkable shawm, the *selompret* of Java and Madura, is played
with a pirouette in some areas, but in others a large wing-shaped *phorbeia* (page 655) of coconut is curved to fit the player's puffed-out
cheeks.

The *surnā*, another name of the Persian *sānāyī*, became the *sona* of
China, a shawm with flaring metal bell played with a flat pirouette; in
Shantung Province it is made entirely of metal. Chinese shawms differ
radically from one another, those of Islamic origin being conical in
form and in bore, while the indigenous *kuan tse* has a short, cylindrical

tube that does not overblow the octave, with seven equidistant finger-holes and one or two thumbholes, played with a reed some 7½ centimeters (3 inches) long, without a pirouette. Modern examples are sometimes made of bamboo; they are invariably short and do not exceed 28 centimeters (11 inches) in length, but during the Middle Ages the *kuan tse* appears to have been considerably longer. Nowadays both types of shawm have important roles at weddings, funerals, and other secular ceremonies, and in processions.

Another name of the *kuan tse* is *pi li*, known in Korea as the *p'iri*, to which corresponds the *hichiriki* of Japan (historically the majority of Japanese instruments were introduced from China via Korea). The *hichiriki* averages no more than 20 centimeters (8 inches) in length and has been in existence since the eighth century. Formerly made of hardwood and apparently with a cylindrical bore, it now consists of a bamboo segment lacquered on the inside and bound with cherry bark or wisteria bark; tube and bore are of very slightly inverted-conical form, but the conicity is so minor that, coupled with the fact that it does not overblow the octave, the *hichiriki* is classified as a cylindrical woodwind. It has seven fingerholes and two thumbholes. As is the case with other cylindrical shawms mentioned here, its thick double reed is maintained in shape by a keeper ring of cane; played without a pirouette, it forms part of the *gagaku* (court music) ensemble. A younger instrument is the *charumera*; this is a local adaptation of the Spanish *charamela*, which was taken to Japan in the sixteenth century.

Shawms in the Americas

Spanish *chirimías* were taken to the New World, probably in the early seventeenth century (the word *chirimía* is not known to have existed prior to 1600); once there, they spread over an area apparently extending from Mexico to Peru along the routes of Indian high cultures. The Lacandon of Mexico play a *chirimigo*, and in Peru the same instrument is called *chirisuya*—a rather poor linguistic joke. The Peruvian instruments are played with a pirouette and are characterized by a cylindrical bore. Their association in our day, not surprisingly in view of their origin, is with Catholicism.

THE RACKETT

A family of bass woodwinds noted for their typical stumpiness was played in the sixteenth and seventeenth centuries: stubby cylinders of ivory in which nine cylindrical channels were bored up and down, and connected alternately at top and bottom so as to form one continuous bore, with the channel finally emerging at the center of the top. The double reed, resembling that of the bassoon, was set on a staple and partly enclosed by a "pirouette" that was halfway between a true pirouette and a windcap—a flared cylinder. From ten to thirteen very small fingerholes were bored obliquely into the channels from all around the cylinder, to be covered by tip and middle joint of the player's fingers. Due to its cylindrical bore the rackett sounds as a stopped pipe (an octave lower than its tube length would imply); this fact, taken in conjunction with the weaving back and forth of the bore in order to obtain maximum length, made it possible to construct bass instruments of incredibly small stature. A cylinder measuring 12 centimeters (under 5 inches) in length, with a diameter of 4½ centimeters (under 2 inches) has, for example, a tube length of 90 centimeters (3 feet) or, counting staple and reed, 1 meter (40 inches).

The rackett is first mentioned in a Württemberg inventory of 1576 as *Ragett*; a year later, several *Rogetten oder Cortali* were listed in a Graz inventory. The designation *Cortali* appears in several Austrian documents and was apparently its Italian name. In a miniature of the Mielen Codex, Munich, Orlando di Lasso (d. 1594) is portrayed with musicians of the Duke of Bavaria's private *Kapelle*, one of whom is playing a rackett.

Praetorius lists four sizes, each with the compass of a twelfth (racketts do not overblow): a soprano $g°$ to d', alto/tenor $C°$ to $g°$, bass F' to $c°$, great bass D' to $A°$ or a tone lower. Of their tone quality he remarks that they sounded soft, almost like blowing through a comb (the *Encyclopédie* was to give a similar description some century and a half later, but adding "covered with paper," which is probably what Praetorius had in mind). It seems likely that they sounded "graceless" when played in consort, but agreeable when serving as bass to string or to other wind instruments. Praetorius's consort of racketts consisted of two sopranos, three tenors, a bass, and a great bass. In a contemporary inventory, that of Kassel in 1613, a consort of eight is enumerated: three sopranos, three tenors, and two basses. Mersenne records their use as bass to different ensembles.

Toward the end of the seventeenth century the rackett was completely remodeled by J. C. Denner of Nuremberg, according to Doppelmayr (1730), and emerged with conical bore, its reed now carried on a coiled or bassoon-type crook, the cylinder-pirouette abandoned and in its place a bassoon-type bell to lengthen the bore, sometimes with a mute in the form of a perforated cap; occasionally keys were even added. This later model became known as sausage bassoon or as rackett bassoon, and actually is a sort of miniaturized bassoon. No longer made of ivory, the new version was of wood, covered with leather or not. Museum specimens of the eighteenth century are not particularly rare.

Rackett-type woodwinds may have been made as carnival or masquerade instruments even before the more polished and diminutive form evolved, for an Innsbruck inventory of 1496 includes a consort of *Tartold wie Drachen geformiret* ("*Tartolds* formed like dragons"), and such a group, dating from the sixteenth century, is still extant; shaped like dragons, their painted bodies contain spirally coiled cylindrical tubing and are pierced with fingerholes, the coiled tails acting as a crook for the reed.

THE SORDONE

Closely allied to the racketts is the family of *sordoni*, as they were known in Italian—they lack a name in English—with narrow cylindrical bore running up and down one piece of wood two or three times, to terminate in a lateral aperture, and furnished with double reeds. As the name implies, their tone was soft and muffled.

Presumably of Italian origin, as the name would indicate, the *sordone* is first recorded in an inventory of instruments at the Innsbruck court about 1580, when "8 *Sordani*" [sic] are listed. They were known to Zacconi in 1592. Ambras had a consort of two basses, three tenors, two descants, and "1 smaller" descant in 1596, and it is probable that the only extant specimens, those of the Kunsthistorisches Museum of Vienna, once constituted the low-pitched members of this set. Today we call the Vienna instruments basses and great basses—there are two of each—for they measure roughly 87 centimeters (34 inches) and 90 centimeters (35½ inches), respectively.

Praetorius still knew the *Sordune*, grown by his time to a family of five: descant, alto/tenor, quart bass, quint bass, and great bass, each having the compass of a thirteenth; they had twelve tone holes, he wrote, and were not overblown (but, unlike the *courtaut*, they were not furnished with *tétines*). Larger sizes were played with metal crooks and "some" had two keys. Whatever their musical role at the time, it can no longer have been of importance when Praetorius wrote, for neither they nor the racketts are mentioned in Part III of his *Syntagma*.

BASSANELLI

Another family of double-reed woodwinds that failed to survive the Renaissance was that of the *bassanelli*, soft voiced and deep pitched, with narrow conical bore, the reed carried on a metal crook, six front fingerholes and an open key for the little finger. Our details come from Praetorius, who both describes and illustrates a soprano with the compass of d° to g′, tenor G° to c′, and bass c° to e° or f°. He ascribes their invention to the Venetian composer Giovanni Bassano, yet it is far more likely that they were named for the Bassano brothers, a gifted family of Italian musicians and instrument makers active in London (Anthony Bassano was one of seven sackbut players at the English court in 1581; Jerome played the recorder there). An inventory and a covering letter dated March 1571 show that these versatile men made lutes, bowed chordophones, cornetts, crumhorns, "flutes" and "great pipes," as well as other unspecified woodwinds: two great basses with four keys, two other basses serving as tenors to the above-mentioned basses, and two descants. Were these left unnamed because they were too new to have a name of their own? It is tempting to think that the reference might be to *bassanelli*.

The word itself does not seem to be documented prior to its appearance in a Graz inventory of instruments purchased between 1577 and 1590 (a descant, an alto, three tenors, and a bass). The court at Kassel possessed a chest of nine: four sopranos, an alto, three tenors, and a bass, "not all of the same shape," according to a 1613 inventory. No extant example is known (an instrument in Vienna described as a *bassanello* has proved to be a section of a bass flute).

Bassanelli is also the name of a seventeenth-century reed organ stop; Werckmeister (1705) reports it as almost unknown in his day, but the woodwind must have been reasonably well known to warrant its having been imitated in the organ.

BASSOONS

With instrumental compasses extending downward in the sixteenth century, the need arose for instruments of bass register less incisive and clamorous than the low-pitched brasses, for use with vocal choirs, and

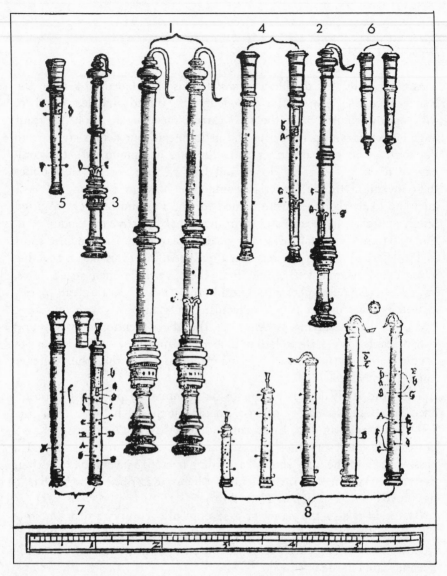

Bassanelli and other extinct woodwinds: (1) bass of the *bassanelli*; (2) tenor and alto *bassanelli*; (3) descant *bassanelli*; (4) bass of the *schryari*; (5) tenor, alto *schryari*; (6) *Cantus schryari*; (7) *Kortholt* or *Kurtzpfeiffe*; (8) a whole consort of *sordoni*. From Michael Praetorius, *Theatrum instrumentorum*, 1620.

experimentation with large sizes of double-reed instruments led to the creation, probably in Italy, of the bassoon's immediate precursor, the curtal.

THE CURTAL

Curtals, and later also the bassoons, differed from the contemporary shawms in that they were made either of a single block of wood with two parallel, conical channels bored up and down and connected at the lower end, or occasionally of two sections, each with half of the two channels hollowed out, then glued together and covered with protecting leather, a practice similar to that encountered in the making of cornetts. In both methods, a shortening of the overall length was brought about by creating duplicate channels, whereas the shawms had a single straight bore that rendered the larger sizes impractical for outdoor performance, but a curtal could conveniently be played by a walking musician. A short and slightly flared bell was set atop the bass terminal of the bore, and the reed was either mounted on a short crook or, as Mersenne writes, sometimes attached to a staple; finally, the curtal was furnished with two keys. On the European continent it was called *fagotto* in Italian, *fagot*, *basson*, or *tarot* in French, *Fagott* or *Dulzian* in German, and *bajón* or *fagote* in Spanish. Curtals were less strident in tone than the shawms, and this may explain some of their additional names, such as *dolce suono* and *Dulzian*.

We hear of these instruments first in the mid-sixteenth century: a *fagotto ed una dolzana* were purchased in Verona in 1546; a Spanish inventory of Queen Mary of Hungary's instruments included in 1559 *dos ynstrumentos de musica contrabaxos que llaman fagotes* ("two contrabass musical instruments called *fagotes*"), and a *fagote contralto* is mentioned in the same inventory. The English word "curtal" is met with in 1574 in the Hengrave Hall accounts. Not until 1577 do we learn of the existence of chests of curtals from a Graz inventory that lists a bass, two tenors, and a soprano *dolzoni*, also a chest of two basses, two tenors, a soprano, all described as *alte schlechte* [i.e., *schlichte*] *fagati* ("old plain *fagoti*"). The word *bajón* occurs in 1588 when a player in the royal band at Madrid, Melchior de Camargo, is identified as *bajón*. In Italy, *tromboni, cornetti, dolzaine et fagotti* accompanied singers at the wedding of Ferdinand I de' Medici at Florence a year later. Curtals figure in many English household accounts of the last quarter of the century, and sometimes an entry reads: "for an instrument called curtall." Tenors were known as single curtals, basses as double curtals. The bass was to become the type instrument, and, as it was at 8' range and pitched in C, it was known in Italy as *fagotto corista* and in Germany as *Chorist-fagott*. Some members of the family were made in both open and stopped (*gedackt*) versions in Germany, as we know from surviving sixteenth-century examples of tenor and bass sizes preserved in the Berlin collection, and from Praetorius who confirms the existence of both types. The fashion of making *gedackt* curtals persisted to the late seventeenth century; one made by Denner is now in the Leipzig University collection (former Heyer Collection), another of about the same period in the municipal museum of Brunswick. *Gedackt* models were covered with a perforated lid that muffled the sound; they also lacked a bell. Zacconi (1592) gives the compass of the *fagotto chorista* as C° to b' and mentions the existence of others pitched a little higher or lower, but without giving details.

When Calvisius wrote (1600), he was not familiar with the instrument, for he cites as choir pitch woodwinds only *cornua, Germanis Zincken, item, quae Italis Dulce soun dicuntur* ("cornetts, *Zincken* in German, likewise those the Italians call *dulce soun*"), yet by this time a whole consort of curtals had come into use, and curtal parts for music by Giovanni Gabrieli (d. 1613) survive. Praetorius enumerates the soprano with a compass of g° to c²; alto, c° to f'; tenor, G° to f' or g' (this was the single curtal); bass, C° to d' or g' (the double curtal or *Choristfagott*); two versions of a *Doppelfagott*, namely a *Quartfagott*, G' to f° or a°, and a *Quintfagott*, F' to e♭° or g°. It was the double curtal that was to be transformed into our bassoon. Small, high-pitched curtals are recorded primarily in Austria, Germany, and Spain. Judging by the iconography they were particularly popular in Spain, where they were called *bajoncillo* and were played in church, together with the *chirimía* and *bajón*, as well as in outdoor ensembles. By the early seventeenth century curtals were entering chamber music, and separate parts were written for them; thus Biagio Marini's *Affetti musicali* of 1617 included two sonatas with curtal parts, and two years later Philippe van Ranst described himself as *musicien et premier fagotist* [sic] *de la chappelle et chambre* of the Brussels court.

The French word *basson* came into use from 1613 on to denote the curtal; to Mersenne it designated specifically a bass curtal with bell lengthened so as to obtain a downward extension of the compass to B♭'.

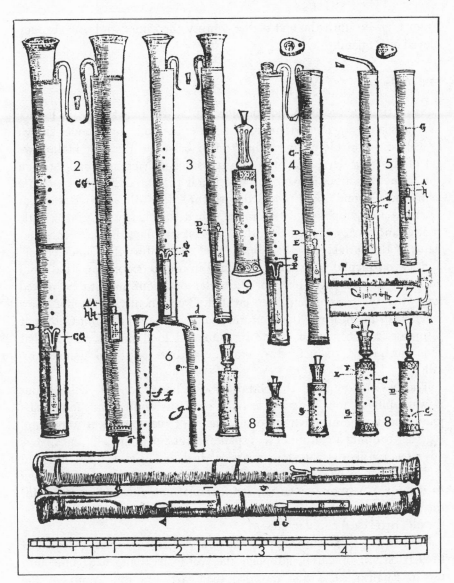

Curtals and rackets: (1) Bass *sordone* [seen] on both sides, GG; (2) double curtal down to GG; (3) open choir [pitch] curtal C; (4) *Gedackt* choir [pitch] curtal, C; (5) single *Kortholt*. Basset or tenor to the choir [pitch] curtal, G; (6) alto curtal, d; (7) descant or *exilent* to the choir [pitch] curtal, a: (8) consort of racketts. *Note:* At (1, 2, 3, 4, 5) the pitch names are placed against the holes that are closed, at (6, 7, 8) against the holes remaining open. From Michael Praetorius, *Theatrum instrumentorum*, 1620.

From then on until the end of the century the same word was also employed in England.

THE BASSOON

Some time before 1636 the one-piece curtal was transformed in France into a separately jointed instrument, the bassoon. It became known in England and Germany as the French bassoon. The first inkling we get of this new development is from passages in Mersenne and Trichet; the former describes a two-piece woodwind that he designates as *fagoté* or *lié* (i.e., bound), and provided with three keys, the latter states that "*bassons* are composed of two tubes joined together, one being a little shorter and narrower than the other," and resembling the *tarot* (another name of the curtal). For the remainder of the century the name "curtal" and its continental equivalents remained in use to denote impartially old and new instruments alike, for the older one continued to be played long after the bassoon had been created. Consequently we do not know which instrument it was that performed at the Festival of Saint George at Windsor in 1661, when "some instrumental loud musick was at that time introduced, namely, two double sackbuts and two double curtalls. . . ."

The bassoon retained the curtal's double-bored conical channel, but it was built of four separate sections or joints: butt, wing joint, bass joint, and bell joint, all traditionally made of maple or pear wood, and together forming a continuously expanding tube of some 240 centimeters (8½ feet). Like its ancestor, it was pitched in C; its compass was and is B♭′ to f² or a². Cesti's *Il pomo d'oro* (1667) seems to be the first opera to include a bassoon—or curtal, for that matter—with Lully writing for the new instrument in the next decade. Daniel Speer could still describe the old, two-keyed curtal in 1687.

Early in the eighteenth century the new version continued to be called French *basson* or curtal, although the word "bassoon" had come into use in English (it is first recorded in 1706). On the Continent the terminology was just as confusing, for *Dulzian* and *Fagott* were interchangeable in Germany, and *Basson* was yet another choice. Coexistence of the bombard, a bass shawm, and the curtal in the seventeenth century caused added confusion in the eighteenth century, when bombards were but a memory, with the result that writers used the word

Fagott to designate the earlier shawm, and Majer had to point out in 1732 that *Dulzian* and *Fagott* were one and the same instrument. The Italian word *fagotto*, first recorded in 1546 in Verona, denoted both curtal and bassoon. Fuhrmann tries to be helpful when, in 1706, he regrets that the *Bombardone* (a shawm) had been replaced by the French *basson*, which, in his opinion, was not penetrating enough for use in large churches, and explains that *Fagotto* or *Dolciano*, an 8′ *Dulcian*, is at choir pitch, and the *Bassone*, a French *Fagott*, was at chamber pitch. Here we run into niceties of pitch, and Fuhrmann's involved explanations boil down to saying that French bassoons were about a tone lower in pitch than German ones (cf. Mersenne's *basson*, page 712).

At the time of the curtal's transformation into the bassoon, a third key (for B♭) was added to the existing two (for D and F); Mattheson (1713), who knew both types, gives the bassoon's compass as C° to f′ or g′, with occasional downward extension to B♭′ or even A′. For just such an instrument Reinhard Keiser composed two suites for eight bassoons; he had visited Copenhagen and wrote in a letter dated 1720 that the King of Denmark had 8 *Bassons und Bassonetten* in his Grenadier Guards.

A singular type of keyed bassoon to which the name of *basson d'amour* has been given in modern times, had an *amore*-shaped bulb-bell made of brass; all surviving specimens seem to have originated in the same workshop—probably Swiss, as some came from churches of the canton of Bern. Unlike the true bassoon, these were played with pirouettes; some still have theirs attached to the crook.

Little-finger keys of all woodwinds, from the sixteenth to the eighteenth century, were equipped with swallow-tail touches permitting their use by either left- or right-hand finger. The bassoon was no exception to this rule, and, as long as it had no more than three keys (two for the thumbs, one for the little finger), it could rest against the left or right side of the player's body indiscriminately, or against his thigh when sitting. But after the addition of a fourth key by 1730, a position to the player's right became customary. Four keys remained standard for much of the century; Eisel depicts a four-keyed bassoon in 1738. Halle, however, mentions seven keys in 1764, a very early date indeed, as by the end of the century no more than six were common. As long as the bassoon's chief function remained that of a continuo instrument, independent parts were written for it only exceptionally (Quantz in 1752 required a bassoon for a chamber orchestra having but nine stringed instruments). Later in the century it received a staff of its own and was given solo parts; Mozart's bassoon concerto dates from 1774.

By the beginning of the nineteenth century complaints were being made about the bassoon's insufficient carrying power when played outdoors, and about its unequal tone quality in solo performance. These were answered by improvements made on an increasingly accelerated scale. One of the first was that of Carl Almenraeder, who brought the number of the keys up to 15 by 1827; at the end of that decade, the bassoon's compass had been extended to a total of nearly four octaves, from Bb^2 to ab^2. Covered tone holes were first designed by Charles Joseph Sax of Brussels, the father of Adolphe Sax, around 1820; the first bassoon with all covered holes was shown by him in 1825, and metal bassoons with covered holes were patented by him and by his son Adolphe from 1842 on. Adolphe Sax moved to Paris and brought out a twenty-three-keyed metal bassoon there in 1851. In the same year he demonstrated at the London Exhibition a brass bassoon with fingerholes placed at theoretically correct spacings, covered with finger plates. This caused a sensation, and Boehm examined it in Paris after the Exhibition was over, as a result of which he had some models of a Boehm-system bassoon made by Triébert of Paris, but, although shown in Paris in 1855 and in London in 1862, this system never caught on, as the keywork was too complicated.

Already in the nineteenth century two schools of bassoon making developed, French and German, with Heckel playing a preponderant role in German manufacture, Buffet one in France. The Heckel model is now played in America and most of Europe, France and Spain being notable exceptions.

Apart from the contrabassoon, the old bassoons of higher or lower than standard pitches have all become obsolete. Some of these are discussed below.

THE CONTRABASSOON

Our modern contrabassoon, pitched an octave below the bassoon and usually made of metal, is the product of a tradition going back to the turn of the sixteenth to seventeenth century, but did not take its present form until the nineteenth century. Today's instruments have an air column some 480 centimeters (16 feet) long, and, in order to reduce their overall length, the tube is bent back on itself several times, and all fingerholes are covered with keys, as they would otherwise be out of reach of the player's hand. The presence of two octave keys necessitates a playing technique slightly different from that of the bassoon. The usual compass is from C′ to f° or even c′ (notated an octave higher), but can be extended down to A² by slipping an inverted metal rim over the contra's bell rim.

Although curtals with lower ranges than that of the type instrument are known to have existed in the sixteenth century, the earliest mention of a true contrabassoon, that is, one pitched an octave below the bassoon, is by Praetorius, who relates that one Hans Schreiber was constructing a bassoon with C′ as its lowest tone. Such an instrument is enumerated in the 1626 inventory of instruments in the Barfüsser Church of Frankfurt on the Main, possibly that of Schreiber. For the remainder of the seventeenth century makers had better results with the smaller *Quart* and *Quint* basses mentioned by Praetorius. Talbot wrote (ca. 1700) of a "pedal or double bassoon FFF, touch as bassoon," but this again is an intermediary *Quint* bassoon.

Despite the many difficulties inherent in making such large instruments without recourse to modern tools and keywork, makers continued their efforts with apparent success, for large bassoons are called for in the scores of eighteenth-century composers. Bach's *Passion According to Saint John* requires a *bassono grosso*, a term occasionally used by German composers of the period. Burney (1785) relates that Stainsby, the flute maker, made a double bassoon for the coronation of George II in 1727, with the approbation of Handel, "but, for want of a proper reed or for some other cause," it could not be used then, nor indeed had it been in any band in England since, with the exception of a performance on it by Mr. Ashley of the Guards in the Handel Commemoration, as we are informed. Handel, Mozart, and Beethoven wrote for the double bassoon. Nevertheless, by the end of the eighteenth century the situation with regard to contras was not satisfactory, and the *Allgemeine musikalische Zeitung* complains in 1803 that bassoons do not carry in the open air, and *selbst der von den Engländern so berühmte Doppelfagott ist nur ein Schnarrwerk* ("even the double bassoon so praised by the English is only a *Schnarrwerk*") and at a recent performance of Haydn's *Creation* at Nordhausen the contrabassoon part was played on a serpent and "left the bassoon far behind." However, the Vienna court orchestra had a contrabassoonist on its payroll by 1807.

The development of military bands in the early nineteenth century and the need for contrabass instruments adapted to the needs of marching players gave considerable impetus to makers, forcing them to take up old experiments and to make new ones, with the result that a number of new models were produced. Their life span as military instruments was short, as the advent of the saxhorn spelled their doom, but they were able to maintain their position in the orchestra. Possibly because of the imputed weakness of carrying power and of their greater weight, wood was abandoned in favor of metal when a new generation of contras appeared in the 1830s. Stehle of Vienna brought out a brass contra in that decade, with fifteen keys; Schöllnast of Pressburg (Bratislava) patented his brass *Tritonikon* or *Universal Kontrabass* in 1839, with a tube length of 456 centimeters (ca. 15 feet) doubled back on itself five times; fifteen keys, of which fourteen were closed keys; and a compass of D′ to f°.

Another attempted solution to structural problems presented by keywork was the *Klaviatur-Kontrafagott* designed by Carl Wilhelm Moritz of Berlin in 1845, featuring a small, piano-type keyboard with fifteen keys; this short-lived instrument was not patented until 1856, a year after its inventor's death. The *Kontrabassophon* of Heinrich Haseneier followed in 1847, wooden and of entirely new design, with wide conical bore and a tube bent back on itself four times; its compass, C′ to c′, was effective only up to g°, as the high tones were not practicable, according to Alexander Ellis (1885). 1856 saw the appearance of Vaclav Cerveny's improved version of the *Tritonikon*, in tuba form, pitched in E♭, followed by a larger model in B♭, first shown at the Paris Exhibition of 1867, and by a subcontra in 1873, his *Subkontrafagott*, an octave below the contra and made of metal, no specimen of which has come down to us. Charles Mahillon of Brussels brought out his *contrebasse à anche* in 1868, actually a *Tritonikon* similar to that of Cerveny except for its compass starting on D′.

Subsequent makers intent on providing a satisfactory contra for military bands have by and large followed in Cerveny's footsteps. The modern contra is in tuba form with seventeen keys, of which two are octave keys. The tone holes are large enough to require no additional venting, so that a pianolike fingering is made possible. By 1880 Heckel had brought out a contra in modern form, and extended its compass down to A² in 1898. The manufacture of contras was not taken up in France until the second half of the nineteenth century, and makers there still prefer to work with wood rather than with metal.

HIGH-PITCHED BASSOONS

Curtals and bassoons pitched higher than the type instrument have existed intermittently ever since their inception and are mentioned from 1559 on (see also curtal, page 709). Of the various sizes known to Prae-torius, only the tenor maintained itself into the nineteenth century, at first as an instrument pitched in G, after 1830 also as an instrument in F, a fifth and a fourth above the type instrument, respectively, which positions gave rise to the unfortunate names of quint and quart bassoons, causing confusion with those bassoons pitched a fifth and a fourth *below* the type instrument. During the eighteenth century these high-pitched models were known in England as tenoroons; a Longman & Broderip catalog of 1782 lists "Bassoons/Tenoroons, or Vox humanas."

Octave bassoons, descendants of the tenor curtal (the single curtal) were called *fagottini;* these were still offered for sale in Belgium about 1830, together with small quints, regular bassoons, and contras. One function of these smaller versions was to occasionally replace the *cor anglais.* Other small models were the bassoon in D, one tone higher than the type instrument; the E♭ bassoon, called *Terzfagott* in German, a minor third higher, and in 1889 a French firm even showed a bassoon pitched a semitone higher than the regular bassoon. All these are now obsolete.

SINGLE-REED BASSOONS

Adolphe Sax is often cited as having been the first to couple a conical bore with a single beating reed in modern times, yet single-reed bassoons were already in experimental use in the eighteenth century. Gerber relates (1790) that a clarinettist named Johann Hesse (d. 1786) replaced the double reed of a bassoon by a beak and a single reed similar to those of the clarinet. Its pitch is not given. At an unspecified date in the eighteenth century the *dolcino,* an octave bassoon in B♭ (at 4′ pitch), furnished with a single reed, was played in military bands, only to be discarded in the early nineteenth century. These small bassoons equipped with single reeds seem to have had special appeal for the British, for Mahillon relates that in England around 1820 a single-reed *fagottino* was in use, capable of overblowing the octave; it had a clarinet-type mouthpiece. His collection of musical instruments, now incorporated into the museum of the Brussels Conservatoire, contained a similar instrument that had belonged to a clarinet teacher of the Royal Military Asylum of Chelsea prior to 1821; this also had a clarinet reed and beak. Around 1830 the Scotch bandmaster William Meikle invented his caledonica, a bassoon with single reed carried on a bassoon crook; an improved version was later brought out in London by George Wood, called *alto fagotto*, with shape, bore, and keywork similar to those of the bassoon. Several sizes were made, but only one example has survived, an octave bassoon in C, preserved in the Museum of Fine Arts, Boston.

THE SARRUSOPHONE

The modern sarrusophones, a family of brass instruments sounded by means of a double reed, are named for their inventor, the French military bandmaster Sarrus, and were first built by P. L. Gautrot of Paris, who took out a patent in 1856.

In creating this group, Sarrus was concerned with replacing the double-reed woodwinds—oboes and bassoons—of military bands with brass instruments of greater sonority, uniform timbre, fingering, and notation. And he may well have been influenced by the success of Adolphe Sax's brass reed instruments, the saxophones, for his fingering system is almost that of the saxophone. But, although his new instruments met with a very favorable reception and are still played, Sarrus failed in his aim of replacing the woodwinds.

All sarrusophones have wide conical bores ending in a flare. Apart from the two smallest sizes, built in straight form, the tube was doubled back on itself. His original group consisted of five sizes, from soprano in Bb to contrabass in Eb, augmented later by the addition of sopranino, baritone, and subcontrabass. The smaller sizes are now obsolete.

The contrabass was also built as an orchestral instrument, pitched in C, and has been scored for in a few orchestral works, chiefly those of French composers, for example, Saint-Saëns (*Étienne Marcel*, 1879) and Massenet (*Esclarmonde*, 1889).

REEDPIPES WITH SINGLE REEDS

As a rule single-reed aerophones, coupled predominantly to cylindrical tubes, assumed the form of double pipes in antiquity, as they do outside Europe today. For details of their history as such, see double pipes, page 651. Regarding the use of single instruments in Europe before the creation of the clarinet we know very little, and must rely on extrapolation from present-day folk instruments.

The Chalumeau

The *chalumeau*, wrote Trichet (ca. 1640) is (1) a rustic pipe made from a wheat stalk with a cut in its upper surface (i.e., an idioglot reed), half a foot long, such as are still played by children and young shepherds; it is also (2) the chanter of a *cornemuse* (bagpipe) played as a separate instrument. Furthermore, two other instruments were known by the same name and described by Walther and Majer, both in 1732, as (3) a small woodwind with seven holes and a compass of f' to a², and (4) a boxwood instrument with seven holes, two keys close to the mouthpiece, a thumbhole, and a compass of f' to a² or even c³. There exist soprano, alto, tenor, and bass *chalumeaux*, but due to the difficulty of the embouchure (*Ansatz*) they are very hard to play, and their range is not much more than an octave; hence one might just as well, Majer indicates, take up the flute (i.e., recorder) instead. Not an encouraging picture. Number three is presumed to have been a folk instrument and at the same time a primitive form of number four. Majer proceeds to devote a separate paragraph to the clarinet, with drawing and fingering chart. Nowhere does he mention the type of reed employed—nor is this visible from his drawing—but his clarinet and *chalumeau* number 4 are closely allied. (A *chalumeau* formerly owned by César Snoeck was 21 centimeters [8¼ inches] long, with an internal diameter of about 1½ centimeters, made of cane, supplied with six fingerholes and a thumbhole, and idioglot reed.)

Transformation of the *chalumeau* into a clarinet, as well as improvement of the *chalumeau* itself, was effected by Johann Christoph Denner of Nuremberg in the first years of the eighteenth century, according to Doppelmayr (1730). Information between the age of Trichet (or Mersenne—the only *chalumeau* he knew was the bagpipe chanter) and Denner is almost totally lacking. A tutor for the "new instrument called the Mock Trumpet" published in England in several editions from 1698 on has been shown to pertain to the *chalumeau*; it contains a chart for six fingers and thumb, and thereby demolishes the theory that a mock trumpet was a synonym of the trumpet marine.

Chalumeau and clarinet existed side by side for a while. A *chalumeau* is first known to have participated in art music in 1704 (in Marc Antonio Ziani's *Cajo Pompilio*), after which it was written for in numerous operas composed for the Vienna court in the first quarter of the century. Mattheson (1713) disliked their sound and preferred to hear them from afar (*Den sogenannten Chalumeaux may vergoennt sein, dass sie sich mit ihren etwas heulenden Symphonie des Abends . . . und zwar von weiten hören lassen*). The autograph of Handel's *Riccardo Primo*, composed 1727, contains *chalumeau* parts calling for a range of d' to c³. Often the word appears in scores as *shalamo, scialmo*, even *salmò*, long after the term "clarinet" had come into use. The two words continued to be employed for the same instrument for some half century.

With the publication of *Airs à deux Chalumeaux, deux Trompettes, deux Violons, deux Flûtes, deux Clarinettes ou cors de Chasse* by Estienne Roger and Le Cène of Amsterdam sometime between 1706 and 1716, we find the new name in print for the first time; the title of this work as it appears in their catolog presents variants, and is followed by *Airs à deux Clarinettes ou deux Chalumeaux, composées par M. Dreux*, no copy of which has survived. Yet the old name died hard, for Gluck's *Orfeo et Euridice* (1764) and his *Alceste* (1769) still contain *chalumeau* parts; in subsequent editions these become clarinet parts. But before 1739 Kremsmünster Monastery possessed two boxwood *Clarinett*, by which time the term was coming into common use.

CLARINETS

Orchestral clarinets are relatively modern descendants of the *chalumeau*, characterized by a cylindrical bore and the single reed with which they are played. Acoustically they perform as stopped pipes, sounding an octave lower than open pipes, with stress on the uneven harmonics and consequently overblowing the twelfth, not the octave. Hence the necessity for keywork more complicated than that of a flute or of an oboe, as the gap to be bridged is wider, and also for a different fingering system.

The Orchestral Clarinet

Denner's invention of the clarinet and improvement of the *chalumeau* —Doppelmayr credits him with both—must have fallen between 1700 and 1707, the year of his death. To him is perhaps due the discovery that the scale of fundamentals could be made to sound a twelfth higher if a venthole were pierced at the upper end of the tube, and also the all-important changeover from an idioglott to a heteroglot lamella. Denner made a *chalumeau* with an a' key and a rear b' key and gave this instrument a separate mouthpiece. Either he or his son and successor developed the bell, transformed the b' key into a bb' key, and placed it higher up so that it could serve additionally as a speaker key for overblowing the twelfth, and thereby added the high clarinet register to the existing *chalumeau* register.

Early clarinets were played with reeds 15 millimeters wide placed against the upper lip, and tied to the mouthpiece with twine. Mouthpiece and socket were of one piece, and our characteristic "barrel" is a development of the socket that appeared soon after the mid-century. The body joint had six fingerholes, and the foot-joint was pierced with twin little-finger holes. Pitched in C, these instruments were made of boxwood (the pitch of old clarinets cannot be determined by length alone, as the bore varied considerably). This model was played up to the mid-eighteenth century, long after a third key had been added. Majer gives its compass in 1732 as f° to a² or higher (Majer, Eisel in 1738, and the *Encyclopédie* of 1767, all illustrate a two-keyed *chalumeau*). To facilitate playing in different tonalities, the body was next divided into three sections, permitting the use of interchangeable joints of various lengths (called *corps de rechange* or *pièces de rechange*), and around the mid-century a fourth and fifth key were added; the old foot-joint was expanded into a bell. These developments are responsible for the clarinet's sudden emergence around 1750 as an accepted orchestral wind instrument, competing with the well-established oboe, and for a time even threatening to displace it; little by little it actually succeeded in doing so as far as military bands were concerned. Rameau scored for clarinets in *Zoroastre* and *Acanthe et Céphise* (1749 and 1751, respectively), and clarinets were played at the Paris *Concerts spirituels* from 1754 on and in symphonies of several composers including those of Stamitz, who introduced them to Mannheim in 1758. Specialized performers for the new instrument appeared in some orchestras by the 1760s, and in 1764 the first clarinet tutor was published: Valentin Roeser's *Essai d'instruction à l'usage pour ceux qui composent pour la clarinette et le cor.*

In the second half of the eighteenth century clarinet mouthpieces were narrower and their reeds shorter but wider than those of today; the pyriform barrel was developed, followed by the upper (i.e., left-hand) joint with its two keys, then came the right-hand, or lower, joint, sometimes made of one piece with the bell joint, which carried three keys. A sixth key was added around 1780. In 1795 Altenburg gave the clarinet's compass as from f° to d³ or f³. Because of problems of fingering and of intonation, clarinets were built at different pitches during the latter part of the century; apart from the type instrument in C, they were pitched in B♭ for performance in flat keys, and in A, B, and D for sharp keys. In Laborde's day (1780) the lowest was in G, with others available in AB♭BCDE♭ and F. Obviously the clarinettist's lot was not a happy one, but the various sizes at least spared him the difficulties inherent in fingering remote tonalities. Interestingly, a contributor to the 1783 edition of the *Encyclopédie* who signed himself "F. D. C." (Frédéric de Castillon?) states that, at the time he wrote his article on the clarinet, a musician passed through Berlin (where the writer then lived) who was able to play in all modes on a single six-keyed instrument.

At some unspecified time in the eighteenth century, probably around 1750, the principle of placing the reed against the upper lip was gradually abandoned in Germany, and it was henceforth to be held against the lower lip. Elsewhere this changeover did not take place until the nineteenth century, earlier in some countries than in others (an 1824 writer commented that half of all clarinettists still placed their reed in the old manner), and in Italy, according to Baines (1957), some clarinettists played with reed up "until quite recently." Nowadays it is held on the upper lip in rhythm bands and by all folk clarinettists, otherwise on the lower lip.

By 1800 barrels had become standard, and the five-keyed clarinet was still in favor despite the poverty of its *chalumeau* register. Alterations to the bore were undertaken at this time, and around 1806 John Marsh in his *Hints to Young Composers* could state that the clarinet "is generally substituted for [the oboe] in the country as not only easier to play, but more powerful." Carl Maria von Weber wrote solos for the improved version as early as 1811; the clarinettist Iwan Müller, then in Paris, brought out his omnitonic clarinet by 1812, pitched in B♭, which, according to its author, rendered the *corps de rechange* unnecessary. Other makers put forth the same claim. Of far greater importance was Müller's thirteen-keyed model of the same period. Modernization continued, with the flat brass keys giving way to cupped silver ones mounted on pillars (ca. 1840), and adaptation of the Boehm system to the clarinet by Hyacinthe Klosé of the Paris Conservatoire in association with Auguste Buffet, patented in 1844. But because of the revolutionary change in fingering involved, the old thirteen- and fourteen-keyed models continued in use, together with the new version.

Up to the late nineteenth century clarinets were made of boxwood or fruit woods, usually pear, either varnished or oiled, and subsequently

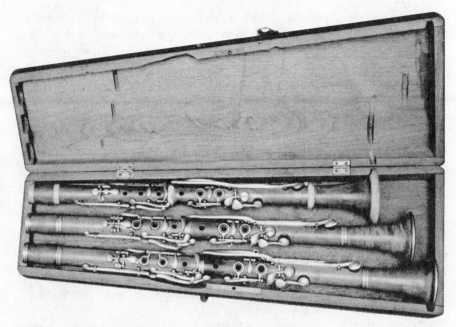

Set of A, B♭, and C clarinets, the *vademecum* of a clarinettist in the mid-nineteenth century. Courtesy of Yale University.

cocus and grenadilla became standard materials, while many others have been used experimentally. Today's type instrument is that in B♭, and the A clarinet, also played, has the same bore, mouthpiece, and barrel as the B♭ model. Flat parts are scored for the B♭, sharp ones for the A, instrument. Some countries have discontinued use of the A, and elsewhere the C is being revived. The Boehm system is not utilized in Austria, Germany, Holland, or the Soviet Union. The clarinet's lowest octave is known as its *chalumeau* register; this is followed by half an octave of intermediary register, and the clarinet register then starts with the overblown twelfth and continues for an octave, beyond which a further octave of extreme register is obtainable. The premature invention of a clarinet having simplified keywork, namely a small keyboard, is reported by Adlung (1758), a rustic dance instrument devised by a young peasant named Orval.

Higher- and Lower-Pitched Clarinets

During the eighteenth and nineteenth centuries clarinets were built in a variety of pitches, both higher and lower than the soprano (i.e., the type instrument), many of which have since been discarded.

The *ottavino*, a piccolo or octave clarinet, was built by Torosini in 1850, pitched in high C, but is now extinct; a *settimino* in high B♭, and the military *sestino* in high A, are the only remaining piccolos. Sopraninos in D, E, F, and G, known as *quartino* in Italy—they take their name from the F model—are now also defunct, but one in E♭ is still played in military bands of Britain. Altos in G, a fourth below the type instrument, were built in the eighteenth century; later they were pitched in F or in E♭ and became military band instruments after they had failed to gain a foothold in the orchestra. In appearance they resemble the basset horn, with which they are often confused. The bell of the modern version usually points up, while on older ones it pointed down.

Also pitched in G, but occasionally in A♭ or in F, a fourth, fifth, or sixth respectively below the type instrument, was the large *clarinette d'amour* of the late eighteenth century. Made up to around 1820, it had either a straight or an angular body terminating in an *amore*, or bulb-shaped, bell, and sometimes carried the mouthpiece on a curved metal crook. No literature for this instrument exists.

The so-called bass clarinets pitched in B♭ are actually tenors, as they are an octave below the type instrument. They have been made since 1772 at least, when Giles Lot of Paris produced his *basse-tube* furnished with several keys and said to have had a compass of three and one-half octaves. This was followed by the *Klarinettenbass*, designed in 1793 by Carl August Grenser the Elder of Dresden, the first in a series of similar instruments to be built in form of a bassoon. It had a four-octave compass starting on B♭′ and nine keys. The *basse-guerrière* of Dumas with its thirteen keys appeared in 1807, the *basse-orgue* of Frédéric Sautermeyer in 1812; the *glicibarifono* designed by Catterino Catterini about 1835, with its two parallel bores, was the last model to precede that of Adolphe Sax, then of Brussels. Sax brought out a perfected bass in or about 1838, rendering all earlier models obsolete, as serpentine or bassoon forms were no longer necessary once an acceptable straight form had been produced. Outwardly his bass (and ours today) resembles a narrow-bore saxophone, as both bell and mouthpiece are bent back to accommodate the player's reach. The only major change since then has been the application of the Boehm system in our own century. Other early basses were pitched in C and in A but these are now obsolete; older basses of all pitches were generally made of wood, sometimes covered with black leather, and had upturned metal bells. Sax reversed this curve, turning it downward.

Attempts were made in the early nineteenth century to produce a contrabass clarinet at 16′ pitch, in C or B♭, two octaves below the type instrument, but no successful model was introduced before that of Fontaine-Besson of Paris, patented in 1891. Efforts to provide new military band instruments of contrabass register resulted in the creation of, among others, the *contre-basse guerrière* of Dumas in 1808, the *Bathyphon* originally built by Eduard Skorra to the specifications of Wilhelm Wieprecht in 1839, and its close successor, the *clarinette-bourdon* of Adolphe Sax (ca. 1840, patented 1841), as well as the *mullerophone*, patented 1855 by Louis Muller of Lyons, in bassoon shape, intended to replace the contrabassoon. Finally, Fontaine-Besson patented their successful *clarinette-pédale* in 1891, and built it in both military and orchestral models. Several other wooden or metal contrabasses have been produced since, usually with conical bore, three U bends, and terminating in an upturned bell; those made in France were generally fitted with the Boehm mechanism. A subcontra in B♭ has been produced experimentally in recent years by Leblanc of Paris.

Combination Clarinets

During the nineteenth and the early twentieth centuries a series of combination clarinets were marketed, uniting several pitches in an effort to furnish orchestral players with a single instrument that would not require any *corps de rechange*. The first of these was by Jacques-François Simiot of Lyons around 1827, in B♭ with a separate upper joint in A, and an extendable bell. This was followed by the *clarinette multiphonique* of Frédéric Triébert of Paris in 1847; this could be crooked to C, B♭, or A. A metal version was introduced by Buffet-Auger *jeune* in 1862; Maino and Orsi brought out a *clarinetto a doppia tonalità* in 1887 in C, B♭, and A, with three slides; and a short-lived *clarino transpositore* by Agostino Rampone in B♭ and A appeared in 1901, with separate tone holes for each tonality.

The Basset Horn

Bassett, a German form of the Italian word *bassetto* (small bass), indicated in the seventeenth century a tonal position rather than a specific musical instrument, and was also applied to instruments of tenor range with downward extending compasses. By the eighteenth century the term had become associated particularly with a small string bass, and later in the century it was conferred upon a newly created woodwind.

Similar to an alto clarinet, the basset horn is a clarinet in F, having greater tube length and with an extended downward compass made possible by the basset keys; usually the bore is narrower than that of the clarinet. Whether these distinctions were always made in the past is a moot point, and many nineteenth-century references to the "clarinet in F" may disguise basset horns (in 1831 Henri Brod of Paris, oboist and oboe maker, sold a fourteen-keyed *clarinette en fa ou cor de basset*).

The basset horn was probably invented around 1770 by Anton and and Michel Mayrhofer of Passau, Bavaria, and was originally built in F or G, later in other tonalities also. Several different forms have existed historically: the first was sickle-shaped, like the *cor anglais* (from which instrument it may have received the "horn" of "basset horn"), with two basset keys. These early instruments were made of two curved sections of hollowed wood, glued together and covered with black leather to conceal the joints and to lend solidity, much in the manner of the serpents. Due to its curved shape it was occasionally referred to as *Krumhorn* in German-speaking areas.

The "box," an oblong piece of wood fitted at the lower end, contained —and protected—three parallel, interconnected bores that reduced the overall length, and carried a large, flaring bell. A new form, angular, appeared in Vienna by 1872. Here the tube was given a sharp bend instead of a curve, so that it could be made of straight joints of bored wood, linked by a very short elbow socket; the "box" was then made as a cube, either of wood or of metal, the instrument itself being of boxwood. This transformation was almost certainly due to Theodor Lotz of Vienna, credited by Cramer's *Magazin* of 1783 with improving the basset horn. By the end of the century the barrel was often curved and the bell set at an angle, and sometimes the bell was of the globular *amore* type.

Early in the nineteenth century it underwent further changes and was sometimes made in bassoon form, that is, with its "box" transformed into a butt and with bell projecting upward. Heinrich Grenser of Dresden is responsible for many of the changes that ultimately led to its present form: straight, with the reed carried on a curved barrel (called crook if made of metal, as it usually is nowadays), and terminating in an upturned bell, with the same bore and mouthpiece as the A and Bb clarinets. In fact, save for its crooked bell, the modern instrument has the appearance of an orchestral clarinet. Its compass is $F°$ to f^3, notated a fifth higher. In the first quarter of the nineteenth century Anton and Johann Stadler of Vienna added two more basset keys, and by 1824 up to fourteen keys were being supplied. Very popular in the late eighteenth and early nineteenth centuries, the basset horn then all but fell into oblivion. Mendelssohn still wrote for it in 1833, but from then on it led a precarious existence in German wind bands. A late reference, before Richard Strauss revived it in his *Elektra* of 1909, is that of Heinrich Welcker von Gontershausen in 1855, who states that they were usually built in F but also in D, E♭, E, or G. Predominantly a woodwind of German-speaking countries, the basset horn was known in eighteenth-century France as *contre-clarinette*, and in England at the turn of the eighteenth to nineteenth century as *clara voce* ("clear voice"). It had became known in Paris by 1774 and in London by 1789.

At the height of its popularity the basset horn was played with the reed either up or down; with reed up, a seated player could hold the instrument gripped between his knees, and to this purpose some models had flattened bells; with reed down, it could be held against the right thigh.

A contrabasset horn pitched one octave below the basset horn was brought out in 1829 by Johann Heinrich Streitwolf of Göttingen; shaped like a bassoon, it was fitted with nineteen keys of which four were basset keys, and with F' for its lowest tone. Thereafter, different models in F and in E♭ were produced by other makers.

THE SAXOPHONE

The most successful of Adolphe Sax's numerous creations was the saxophone, invented in 1841 while he was still in Brussels, and patented by him in France in 1846. Made of metal (originally of brass) with wide conical bore and slightly flared bell, the saxophone has a beaked mouthpiece similar to that of the clarinet and is played with a single reed. All but the two smallest sizes are bent back to terminate in a curved bell; the smallest are built in straight form. All overblow the octave, are fitted with oboelike keywork, and have a two-and-one-half-octave compass.

Sax devised the saxophone for both orchestral and military band use, and therefore the patent covered two groups of instruments, with a total of fourteen different sizes, from sopranino to contrabass; one group of seven was pitched alternately in F and C, for the orchestra; the other, also of seven, alternately in E♭ and B♭ for bands. All except the orchestral soprano in C are treated as transposing instruments. From its inception, the "sax" was scored for orchestra and opera, chiefly in France, and in

1845 it was also introduced into French military bands. By 1848 Sax had completed the family down to the contrabass (which was actually a subbass); a subcontrabass was added in 1904 by Conn of Elkhart, Indiana. Over the years the soprano in C, the alto in E♭, and the tenor in C, the latter known as melody saxophone in the United States, have proved the most popular. Currently a Boehm-system saxophone is in production by Leblanc of Paris.

FOLK AND ETHNIC SINGLE-REED PIPES

Europe

All single-reed folk aerophones of Europe are played with the reed up, that is, against the upper lip, as the reed is either cut from or placed on the same side as the fingerholes; the orchestral clarinet is the sole single-reed instrument to have reversed this position. Furthermore, the majority of the idioglot reeds are upcut (cut toward the mouth end) in Europe. Perhaps the reason for this is that with a very flexible lamella, pitch adjustments are possible by shortening the lamella through pressure of the tongue on the reed; this would not be possible if it were downcut. Some folk musicians regulate the pitch of their reeds by tying a thread around them; this can be moved up or down as required (the shorter the lamella, the higher the pitch), a practice inferred for some ancient Egyptian oboe reeds that have reached us with such threads intact.

Nowadays European single-reed folk aerophones are played mainly in rural or remoter areas, an indication that their distribution was once far wider. Some of the organologically more interesting survivals are the following: The *xeremia* of Iviza, one of the Balearic Islands, is made either with an idioglot or with a heteroglot reed and has a cylindrical tube provided with four fingerholes and a thumbhole; sometimes it is played in the form of double pipes, in which case it is called a *reclam de xeremias*. Shepherds of Portugal have a *chamada do carnaval* ("carnival call") made of oxhorn, a conical tube into the narrow end of which they insert a single beating reed. Such a combination of single reed with a conical tube is rare if not exceptional. The *chamada* serves only during the period between Christmas and carnival. Shepherds of eastern Europe make their folk clarinets of wood, and the Wends even go so far as to add four keys to theirs. Montenegro players are known to place hairs under the lamellae of their instruments if the lamella lies too near the tube, for fear that it might close up if accidentally touched by lip or tongue, and thereby render the pipe mute. Further north, in rural Lithuania, a folk clarinet has a cylindrical tube closed at the top, with idioglot reed taken in the player's mouth for its entire length.

Asia

Individual pipes of the single-reed type are not common in Asia. China has one, made of bamboo, but this also—and more frequently—occurs in the form of a double pipe. Among the several interesting varieties found in Indonesia are the bamboo pipes of Celebes, with heteroglot lamella affixed to a separate, tubular mouthpiece, and terminating in a disproportionately large bell of spirally wound leaves, reminiscent of the Russian *brelka* (see page 661); and also the Javanese *puwi puwi*, with its idioglot, downcut reed but tube with conical bore, another instance of the coupling of a single reed to an expanding bore. This instrument is provided with six fingerholes and a thumbhole, and is played with a reedcap.

Africa

In modern times, single-reed aerophones are played exclusively as double pipes in Northern Africa, and are relatively rare further south. However, the Ful of Sierra Leone make a characteristic reedpipe of slightly conical cane with an idioglot, upcut reed; to the bottom of the pipe they attach a gourd bell that has rectangular apertures cut in its walls, from which a number of fine metal chains dangle; they add their sound of clashing to that of the pipe. A unique form has been reported from Southeast Africa, namely a transversely blown reedpipe. Here the incision of the idioglot reed is so low down that the player is obliged to hold his instrument horizontally like a cross flute.

The Americas

Single-reed pipes are played both as single and as double pipes in South America; Indians of the Mato Grosso, of Guiana, and along the Amazon River play a single-reed instrument made of a 35-centimeter- (14-inch-) long cane section cut just above a node; a downcut idioglot reed of cane is then inserted in the pierced septum and glued fast. Fingerholes are absent, but melodies are produced by having each performer in an ensemble play his instrument when his turn comes. Pipes with gourd bells and heteroglot reeds are found among the Warrau of Venezuela; all are devoid of fingerholes. From Bolivia south to Paraguay, northern Argentina, and southern Brazil, a single-reed aerophone, also lacking fingerholes, terminates in a bell of horn, and is held with one hand while the other hand strikes a drum in the manner of pipe and tabor players of yore; this particular combination and playing method was probably introduced centuries ago by the Spaniards, but at least some of the aerophones in question are thought to be indigenous.

The Pacific

Reedpipes provided with fingerholes and played with a single reed have been reported from the Caroline Islands in Micronesia, and from the Marquesas in Polynesia, but in general the Pacific is not reedpipe territory; rather, flutes are the preferred form of aerophones here.

FREE-REED AEROPHONES

Free reeds are composed of a tongue (lamella) of metal or of cane and of its closely fitted frame. The tongue is attached to the frame at one end but left detached along three of its sides, so that it vibrates freely back and forth through the frame. Such reeds have been known to exist for at least three thousand years in Asia, and free-reed pipes are still made use of there, either singly or in such combinations as the mouth organ. Free reeds can also be utilized without pipes, as they are in the accordion, harmonica, and so on. In all of these tubeless free reeds the pitch is determined by length and thickness of the lamella. Tuning is effected by filing close to the free end to raise the pitch, or close to the fixed end to lower it. Unlike all other reeds, when a free reed is coupled to a tube, the tube serves only to reinforce the sound and does not determine the pitch.

FREE-REED AEROPHONES IN ASIA

China and Southeast Asia are areas employing both single and multiple free-reed pipes. One of the most ancient forms is an idioglot free-reed pipe reported from Nias Island. On the mainland a very short bamboo pipe, closed at both ends, has a free reed set in its wall, and is played in Peking puppet shows in imitation of animal or human sounds. In Shantung Province the same instrument is built as a double pipe of two bamboo segments, with a reed in the wall of each; the reeds sound about a semitone apart and are blown simultaneously.

Of a different nature is a group of instruments played in countries south of China. Some cylindrical cross flutes of Thailand have a free reed of metal inserted in the blowhole, resulting in a clarinetlike sound; the Padaung and the Karen of Shan State, Burma, have an endblown horn of curved buffalo horn, open at both ends, to which a free reed of cane is added, affixed transversely by wax. In these instances, modification of tone quality appears to be the objective sought by the addition of a reed, which is here plainly accessory.

While individual free-reed pipes can be used for monophonic playing, a number of them can also be combined so as to permit either monophonic or polyphonic playing, simply by arranging them in raft or bundle form in a common holder, and providing a common wind trunk. Such an arrangement, presenting certain elements of the organ as we know it in the West, is the Southeast Asian mouth organ.

The Mouth Organ

Known since about 1000 B.C., the mouth organ probably originated in southern China or in Chinese-influenced Laos (a Thai name of the instrument is "Laos organ"). Prototype of the mouth organ is a small, bowl-shaped gourd with a long natural neck, and a variable number of pipes inserted upright into the bowl, thus transforming it into an air chamber, the long neck serving as blowpipe. A free reed of metal or of very thin cane is let into the wall of each pipe near its lower end, and a tone hole is cut into the wall above the rim of the gourd. To enable a pipe to sound, this hole must be closed, for it acts as coupler between reed and pipe. As a free reed responds to both pressure and suction wind, the performer exhales and also inhales while playing.

Today, mouth-organ reeds in China and Japan are made of thin metal, but in Southeast Asia they are cut of thin bamboo. Set in the wall of mouth-organ pipes, these reeds have been likened in construction to miniature Jew's harps, consisting as they do of an elongated framework and a tongue; some bamboo mouth-organ reeds are idioglot and are thicker toward the free end, thereby heightening the resemblance.

The Asian mouth organ best known to the West is the classical Chinese *sheng*; this can be traced to about 1000 B.C. in literature and appears on bas-reliefs of the Han period Wu tombs in Shantung. As the immediate ancestor not only of the Western mouth organ but of all European free-reed instruments, it is of particular interest to organologists. According to tradition, its shape represents the phoenix (as does the stepped arrangement of the Chinese panpipe, already noted). After originating as a gourd or calabash it was reduced in size and refined to the point of discarding the gourd altogether; this was replaced by an imitation made of lacquered wood, and the original long neck was shortened to a stub. The slender pipes of cane are now always made in five stepped sizes, symmetrically arranged in an upright circle in the bowl, their sides flattened to ensure a close fit, and with a keeper ring of split cane passed over all the pipes to aid in maintaining them in position. The sounding length of each pipe is determined by a longitudinal slot in its back, and not by the total length of the tube.

Today the *sheng* is generally provided with seventeen pipes, but the total number may range from thirteen to nineteen; in the past, the precise number has varied with the era. Not all the pipes are speaking pipes, however; of a set of seventeen, for instance, four are dummies lacking reeds, their purpose being solely that of completing the symmetry. *Shengs* are always played polyphonically, in slow chords of three tones; the bowl is cupped in both hands, and the fingerhole of each pipe to be sounded is covered by one of the player's fingers. The reed itself was described in the last century by Hermann Smith as follows:

The lower end of each pipe is fitted with a little free reed of very delicate workmanship, about half an inch long, and stamped in a thin metal plate, having its tip slightly loaded with beeswax, which is also used for keeping the reed in position. One peculiarity to be noticed is that the reed is quite level with the face of the plate, a condition in which modern reeds would not speak. But this singular provision is made to ensure speaking by either blowing or suction. The corners are rounded off, and thus a little space is left between the tip of the reed and the frame for the passage of air, an arrangement quite adverse to the speaking of harmonium reeds.

Historically the *sheng* has been restricted in its use to cult and court music, and was occasionally also played at funerals. The modern *sheng* is a soprano instrument, but it may have sounded lower in former times when it was still made of a gourd and when its pipes were far longer than they are now. Such gourd mouth organs are still played in parts of southern China. The Japanese *sho* is indistinguishable from the *sheng* except for its lacquer ornamentation.

From its focal center, the mouth organ radiated to Korea and Japan, through all of Indochina and Bengal over to Persia. It was known to the Dong-Son culture of North Vietnam (fifth to second centuries B.C.), as is attested by a mouth-organ playing figure delineated on an elaborate kettlegong of that epoch, now in the Hanoi Museum. By the sixth century A.D. it had reached Persia, and around A.D. 800 it is seen on the sculptures of Borobudur, Java; it is also figured on art objects of Eastern Turkistan from the ninth to eleventh centuries. Among a group of musicians of the Sassanid Taq i-Bustan bas-reliefs dating from 590–628 are two players of mouth organs, and silver vessels of the Sassanid period and of the post-Sassanid eighth and ninth centuries depict mouth organs with pipes arranged in four stepped sizes, and a curved mouthpipe leading to a bowl that is no longer a gourd.

Mouth organs of gourd are still played over a wide area, and many are of the so-called raft type, that is, their pipes are set side by side (by contrast, those of the *sheng* are arranged in a form known as bundle pipes). Less elaborate instruments of Laos and North Borneo make use of long-necked gourds; several tall pipes, all of the same diameter, traverse the gourd by piercing it vertically, and project below; the joints are then made airtight with wax or other substances. Sometimes the neck is so long and the bowl so small that they form a near-cylindrical pipe ending in a bulge and acting as blowpipe, air reservoir, and pipe rack; the few untidily ordered pipes form two rows. This may be compared to the Laotian *khen*, a more elaborate instrument made in three sizes and comprising six, fourteen, or sixteen bamboo pipes of different lengths but identical diameter, also disposed in two rows, but with a small wind chamber of ivory or wood, and reeds usually made of silver.

Raft-pipe types of mouth organ are also found in Vietnam; one has two rows of seven pipes each, with the pipes of one row placed behind those of the other, graduated from long to short, those of the two rows sounding at different pitches. A small, almost globular gourd is impaled by extremely long pipes for some two-thirds of their lengths, with the longest placed close to the blowpipe; sometimes the biggest pipe measures 2½ meters (8 feet). Three sizes are played in Annam, corresponding in pitch to mezzo-soprano, alto, and bass. The Miao tribes have very large instruments of relatively few pipes, and although the longest pipe may vary from about 1½ meters (5 feet) to 4½ meters (13 feet), they remain light enough to be portable. Some of these instruments have six pipes, but the largest have no more than three. They are played by men, chiefly in groups of three, but also in pairs, while leading dances. The Karen of Burma possess equally large forms, but on their instruments the blowpipe has been shortened to a mouthpiece. Tribes of the Chittagong district of Burma also play a variety consisting of huge pipes that pierce a small calabash. On Sarawak, the lowest pipe of a six-pipe mouth organ commonly serves as a drone; there also it is an instrument for dancing, but it is additionally one of courtship.

WESTERN FREE-REED AEROPHONES

Mouth Organs

Oriental mouth organs may have been seen occasionally in Europe prior to the date usually assigned to their arrival, for a *charivari* performed in 1648 at the request of Louis XIV, with an assortment of both commonly used and of bizarre instruments that included several *orgues de Perse* ("Persian organs"), according to an unpublished *mémoire* quoted in Pierre (1893), and this can scarcely have been anything other than a mouth organ. Nothing further was heard concerning the mouth organ in Europe until it was pictured and described by Buonanni in 1722, and it was not until the nineteenth century that a Western counterpart was imagined. During the course of the eighteenth century several Chinese *shengs* were received in Europe, at first in eastern Europe. Johann Wilde, inventor of the nail violin, sojourned in Saint Petersburg from 1741 to 1764, when he learned to play the "delightful Chinese organ."

But the importance of its reeds was not brought out until a *sheng* was sent by Father Amiot, a Jesuit missionary in China, to Paris in 1777 by the overland route. It aroused great interest in Saint Petersburg, where it was examined by the Danish physicist Kratzenstein. Apparently considered too alien an instrument to warrant imitating, Kratzenstein suggested to the Saint Petersburg organ builder Kirsnik that he incorporate a rank of free reeds into an organ. But Kirsnik preferred to first experiment by including some reeds in his piano-organs in 1780 (the year in which Laborde's *Essai sur la musique* containing a study of the *sheng* was published). Later he contrived an organ register of free reeds, which his assistant, G. C. Rackwitz of Stockholm, incorporated in 1792 into an organ devised by Abbé Vogler. At the time Vogler introduced them to the public they did not attract attention, and only after they had become known through a spate of nineteenth-century free-reed keyboard instruments were they incorporated into the organ on any scale. Temporarily popular, most free-reed stops were later abandoned by pipe-organ builders, one exception being the clarinet stop.

Some four decades lapsed between the arrival of the *sheng* in Saint Petersburg and production of the first Western mouth organs, but in the intervening period its reeds were applied to other types of instrument.

Western free-reed aerophones can be conveniently grouped into four categories: (1) mouth organs, with wind supplied by the player's mouth; (2) reed organs, with wind supplied at first by the player's foot, later mechanically; (3) accordions with hand-operated wind supply, later mechanized; (4) free-reed automatophones with mechanical wind supply.

Considerable time elapsed between Kratzenstein's study of the *sheng* and the appearance of a Western type of mouth organ, the invention of which has been attributed to many makers. The reason for this delay is comprehensible: the outstanding feature of Eastern mouth organs is that each individual reed works on both pressure and suction wind, and consequently the adaptation of the *sheng* presented a very real puzzle. The latter is a most delicate and highly refined instrument, and the grosser varieties of Southeast Asia were unknown in Europe at the time Father Amiot sent his gift. And as mouth organs were totally unknown to the West, it is perhaps natural that the first attempts to exploit the new reed should have been in connection with a thoroughly familiar and widely distributed instrument of a related, if mechanized, nature, namely the organ. (A *Mundorgel*, literally "mouth organ," with its leather bag, made in Stuttgart in 1589, was probably a panpipe; the English term "mouth organ" when it occurs in the seventeenth and eighteenth centuries denoted either panpipe or Jew's harp.)

A single experimental mouth-organ model was produced by Friedrich Buschmann of Berlin in 1821, with fifteen steel tongues blown through small channels, and during that year and the next he took out patents for early forms of mouth organs. It was probably around this time that the *Neu Tschang* ("new *sheng*") was brought out by Reichstein in Germany, early models of which consisted of a wooden cylinder partially lined with a metal plate provided with six free reeds; these were spread equidistantly 1½ centimeters apart, with corresponding apertures in the wooden tube. The new *sheng* was held like a recorder. On blowing into the tube, all six reeds were sounded, forming a D major chord; by closing the tone hole nearest the embouchure the first reed, emitting the lowest tone, was silenced, *et ceteris paribus* until all holes were closed, causing the instrument to remain mute.

Similar instruments, both cylindrical and conical in form, were made in several other countries. An improved form of the new *sheng*, called *Psall-melodikon* by its maker, was invented in 1828 by Weinrich of Heiligenstadt near Erfurt; in shape a flattened cylinder, it had fingerholes and twenty-six keys of the brass-instrument type. In 1829 Charles Wheatstone of London patented his metal symphonium in the form of a shallow, upended box with single blowhole in front and key buttons on each side; this operated on pressure wind only and had at first silver, later, steel reeds.

Enough demand existed by then to warrant commercial manufacture of mouth organs, and this commenced in Vienna in 1829. The *Apollolyra*, identified in contemporary sources as an improvement of the *Psallmelodikon*, but which possibly owed more to Wheatstone, was the invention of Ernst Leopold Schmidt of Heiligenstadt near Erfurt in 1832, and had the form of a *kithara*. The flat wooden body had a blowpipe fitted to its top and forty-four reeds controlled by keys, with a four-octave compass. By the mid-nineteenth century the present horizontally held form had been created.

A new and extremely practical use was found for the mouthblown free reed in the second half of the nineteenth century, namely that of a substitute for the older pitchpipe. Circular devices were conceived, with free reeds in parallel grooves housed in a rotating disk, and furnished with a single blowhole. By rotating the disk, the major and minor triads of all tonalities could be obtained. Similar sets for indicating the pitch of individual tones are still in occasional use.

The modern mouth organ is standardized in all but size and compass; its reeds are mounted on a grooved metal box and sounded by the box being moved horizontally back and forth in front of the player's mouth. The grooves lead from the reeds to apertures on one of the long sides, into which the player breathes, supplying either pressure or suction wind, depending upon whether he exhales or inhales. Each groove constitutes a conduit from the exterior to two reeds of identical pitch, one of which works on pressure, the other on suction wind. The scale is a diatonic one so that several instruments have to be combined to permit changes of tonality. A departure from the now traditional form was made by Hoehner of Trossingen, a firm that has specialized in mouth organs since 1857; they introduced a "new" form—in reality, a reversion to the nineteenth-century type—a vertical model held like a recorder and operated by a series of push keys arranged so that one hand plays the diatonic, the other hand the chromatic tones. But despite such innovations, mouth organs in the West have remained more of a musical curiosity than anything else, lacking the tradition of a folk instrument, having no part in art music, and hence falling into the category referred to as popular instruments.

Reed Organs

Probably the earliest Western instruments to contain free reeds as the sole means of tone production were the automatophones, discussed on page 743. But even before these were fully developed, Johann Nepomuk Mältzl of Vienna is said to have incorporated some free reeds in 1804 or 1805 in a forerunner of his later *Panharmonicon*. He took his instrument to Paris, exhibited it, and sold it there. The Parisian organ builder Gabriel-Joseph Grenié saw it in 1807, and by 1810 he had produced the first keyboard instrument furnished exclusively with free reeds, a forerunner of the harmonium. He named his creation *orgue expressif*, which term is still used in France to denote the reed organ. Its single register was supplied by bellows worked by two pedals; the "expression" was a stop establishing direct contact between bellows and reservoir by means of the pedals, and permitted dynamic gradations for the first time in the history of the organ. Each of his reeds was surmounted by a pyriform tube, a resonator. No less a personality than Aristide Cavaillé-Coll of organ-building fame contributed an improved version of the *orgue expressif*; his *poïkilorgue*, first exhibited at the Paris Exposition of 1834, was built in the form of a small square piano, and had one rank of free reeds with a compass of C° to f°, and two pedals; that on the left worked the large bellows and that on the right varied the wind pressure and thus constituted an expression stop. Grenié had a pupil named Théodore-Achille Muller who continued improving his master's instruments, and in 1843 was able to patent a portable model that could be folded up into a rectangular box when traveling, an idea he may have borrowed from the *clavecin brisé* of Marius. His work contributed greatly to the perfecting of free reeds.

Concurrently with these developments in France, experiments were made in German-speaking countries, but their history is not easy to trace due to confusion of instruments and of makers in nineteenth-century source materials. As far as can be ascertained, it seems that Bernhard Eschenbach of Königshofen, Bavaria, devised a free-reed keyboard instrument about 1815—probably after earlier experimentation—which was capable of "expression" (crescendo and decrescendo). He claimed that his observations of the Jew's harp had suggested to him the design of his

Äoline (aeoline), as he called it. Eschenbach was not an instrument maker himself, and had his aeoline built by a piano manufacturer. It was successful from its inception and was promptly imitated.

At some time Eschenbach had apparently confided details of its construction to an organ builder named Voit (probably Johann Michel Voit of Schweinfurt, Bavaria) who produced the first in a series of imitations of the aeoline—improvements, as they were then called. Voit called his model *Äolodicon* and brought out several by 1818; he also did much to popularize free-reed instruments. Voit in turn did not remain without imitators, foremost among whom was Anton Häckl of Vienna, who for years was considered the inventor of the harmonium. Häckl built a *Physharmonica* in 1818, for which he obtained a five-year patent in 1821. His own instrument—other builders made them also—was a very small affair, measuring but 63 centimeters (25 inches) by 20 centimeters (8 inches) and standing 75 centimeters (29½ inches) high, with a four-octave compass. Originally it had been built for simultaneous playing with a pianoforte, underneath the keyboard of which it was placed, and was worked by two pedals, later transformed into treadles. Now long forgotten, it was successful in its day, and mid-nineteenth-century literature for the *Physharmonica* exists. Until well into the 1840s, all similar precursors of the harmonium were known indiscriminately as *Physharmonica*.

After Häckl, a sort of Greek revival in keyboard making set in, with *Äolo-melodicon, Claväoline, and Äolopantalon,* the latter an early combination of piano and reed organ built in 1824 by Jozé Dlugosz of Warsaw, in which each component instrument could be played separately if desired. Yet another aeolodicon appeared in the 1830s, that of Friedrich Sturm of Suhl, with two rows of reeds, one at 8′, the other at 4′ pitch, and a six-octave compass. Sturm claimed originality for his invention and, like Eschenbach, professed to have drawn his inspiration from the Jew's harp—he had heard a virtuoso perform on one in 1823—yet his model was merely an extension of the work of others, although in advance of similar instruments of his day. Meanwhile the *Physharmonica* had spread abroad, and John Green's seraphine, invented in England in 1834, strongly resembled it. This had a five-octave compass and the by-now-usual expression (later, any free-reed instrument working on the principle of the American organ was known in England as seraphine).

The harmonium. From the time Grenié had introduced free-reed keyboard instruments into France, the French had been leaders in the making and perfecting of free reeds, and in keeping with this tradition Alexandre-François Debain (1809–1877) brought out reeds of different thicknesses and widths and thereby obtained ranks of varying tone qualities, up to then an impossibility. He incorporated his new reeds in an instrument patented in 1840 under the name of harmonium.

The harmonium was the result not only of experimentation by his precursors, but also of Debain's own labors, for he had already produced a free-reed organ, the *organino,* some time between 1834 and 1840; this had two tones to a key, pitched an octave apart. Added flexibility provided by different timbres distinguished the harmonium from earlier instruments. One of its features was the use of pressure wind supplied by compression bellows, with each key controlling a valve that regulated the amount of wind to be admitted. Standard models had four divided registers, and a compass varying from four to five octaves from C°. Debain added an expression stop in 1843, the invention of Victor Mustel of Paris dating from the same year. In Grenié's early instruments, expression had been obtained by using pedals to compress air in the reservoir, whereas, in the harmonium, expression was produced directly by the pedals without recourse to any intermediary action, and was accomplished by installing a valve that bypassed the reservoir and communicated wind of variable pressure directly to the reeds by means of the bellows. Hence the dynamics were placed under the immediate control of the player, who determined the amount of wind to be furnished by his working of the treadles. Undoubtedly the most popular of harmonium stops, the expression was later also applied to the American organ. Some models were fitted with shifting keyboards, thereby permitting transposition of any interval, yet playing the music as notated, a boon to vocal accompanists. Debain himself led the way to further "improvements" by creating the piano-harmonium, which he patented under the name of symphonium in 1845. In the next decade another of Mustel's inventions, the double expression, was added (1854); this was nothing more than a divided expression stop worked by knee levers. Both as a cheap substitute for organs in small churches and as a household instrument, the harmonium was immensely popular for over a century, and lingers on today. Ultimately it was even mechanized, with its keys worked by pinned cylinders and perforated cardboard strips or metal disks; one such model was known as *musique perforée,* a small harmonium taking its name from the perforated cards patented in 1852 by Martin de Corteuil.

Once he had patented the name harmonium, Debain obliged his

competitors to resort to other designations for their products, few of which gave evidence of really new ideas. Of those worth mentioning are perhaps the *clavi-accord*, a compact, portable harmonium in which the keys, on being depressed, worked the bellows (1855); the *harmoniphrase* of Dumont and Lelièvre of Paris, exhibited in 1889, which was a chord harmonium (a forerunner of the chord organ); and Richard A. Brooman's trylodeon of 1860, in which the depth of touch controlled a variable number of reeds so that registration was effected by the player's fingers.

The harmonium's sustained tone made it admirably suited for acoustical experiments and demonstrations of different tuning systems, subjects that greatly preoccupied both musicians and scientists of the nineteenth century—a sort of renaissance of the Renaissance, as it were. Perhaps the best known of the experimental harmoniums built for such purposes in the last quarter of the nineteenth century was that of Shohē Tanaka of 1889, which could be tuned to pure intervals and had twenty keys to an octave; R. H. M. Bosanquet's harmonium had fifty-three microtones to the octave; Helmholtz had a two-manual experimental version built for his own work. Such instruments were dubbed "enharmonium" by Hans von Bülow. The maker of Tanaka's harmonium, Johann Kewitsch of Berlin, also patented (in 1892) a harmonium with each key constructed on two levels, the front portion slightly lower than the back portion, and the fronts tuned one syntonic comma higher than the backs, for the playing of pure thirds.

Portable, diminutive harmoniums in the form of a shallow, rectangular box (without stand) have been made in India since the 1920s, flooding towns and villages alike, to the great detriment of indigenous instruments. The playing is always monophonic, usually to accompany a voice. Ease of transportation and the fact that tuning is unnecessary are major factors contributing to their wide distribution both on the subcontinent and in Ceylon.

The American organ. One of the first French builders of harmoniums and allied instruments was Jacob Alexandre of Paris (1804–1876) who opened a factory in 1829. In the middle of the next decade a workman of his whose name has not come down to us, invented a new method of sounding free reeds, namely by suction wind, and Alexandre built a few instruments with suction bellows. Shortly thereafter, the employee emigrated to the United States, taking his invention with him. We know nothing concerning the fate of the free reed in America until harmoniums operating on suction wind were built by the firm of Estey at Brattleboro, Vermont, from 1856 on, and from 1861 also by Mason and Hamlin of

Boston. Since then practically all American-built reed organs have been constructed on the vacuum principle, while Europe remained true to the pressure reed. Suction-wind organs were originally known as melodium, melodeon, or cottage organ (if built in the shape of a cottage piano), in England also by the older name of seraphine; later, the term "American organ" was applied to all similar reed organs, and in that sense the name is still in use.

In American organs the wind is drawn inward through the reeds by means of suction bellows, and the reeds themselves differ from those of the harmonium as they are smaller and more highly curved, thus yielding a softer tone. But like the harmonium, models were not standardized as to compass or registers; a coupler, swell, and pedalboard, later even a celesta stop with its own manual, were optional additions. Alexandre continued experimenting and building, and in 1874 brought out the *orgue Alexandre*, familiarly known as *l'orgue à cent francs* ("the hundred-franc organ"), a tribute to its popularity, since some models cost a great deal more. This was a developed version of the American organ with broader and thicker reeds.

By 1861 the American organ could be played by perforated cardboard strips in France, when Joseph Testé, a piano maker of Nantes, received his first patent for a cartonium; this small instrument with a compass of but three and one-half chromatic octaves was hand cranked. Thereafter the mechanization of reed organs became general: one such instrument, exhibited in 1890 by the Limonaire brothers of Paris and called *limonaire* or orchestrophone, was hand cranked, its reeds sounded by means of perforated cards; drums, cymbals, and other idiophones were attached to the exterior. As an instrument of merry-go-rounds it remained in use in France up to the Second World War. The mechanized reed organ was also miniaturized into an imitation music box, with two rows of free reeds worked on suction wind provided by hand-cranked bellows, all housed in a compact box, and supplied by the British Organette and Music Manufacturing Company; this was a most popular instrument in nineteenth-century Britain.

Accordions

Eschenbach's aeoline of the early nineteenth century not only influenced the development of keyboard reed instruments, but also gave rise to a series of portable free-reed aerophones characterized by expandable bellows worked by the player's arm, culminating in the modern accordion with its felicitous combination of both pressure and vacuum reeds. Accordions consist largely of flexible, expandable bellows that supply wind to the reeds either by pressure or by suction, depending upon whether they are being compressed or expanded. One head is provided with a variable number of melody keys or buttons, the other with bass keys or chord buttons. Each key or button opens a valve that controls two reeds, one of which works on pressure wind and the second on suction wind—the principle of the mouth organ—so that the accordion continues to sound regardless of whether the bellows are being inflated or deflated. Different reeds may be connected by stops so that several can be played simultaneously on a single key; the chord buttons act on three reeds connected in such a fashion. With his left hand the player works the bellows and plays a bass accompaniment (consisting usually of tonic and dominant chords); with his right hand he plays the melody.

The accordion was invented by Friedrich Buschmann of Berlin in 1822; he called it *Handäoline* ("hand aeoline"). Seven years later the Viennese Cyril Demian was granted a privilege for an *Akkordion,* an improved version of the hand aeoline, and as this was henceforth the name by which such instruments were known, the accordion's invention is usually attributed to Demian. But, despite the terms of his privilege, Demian's instrument was promptly copied. As its name could not be used by his competitors they called their products *Handharmonika,* which term is still in use in many areas. These early models were diatonic, generally pitched in C, D, or G, and became chromatic around 1835.

A variant of the accordion was the concertina devised by Charles Wheatstone of London in 1829, a feature of which was the hexagonal shape of its heads. Concertinas were made in several sizes, from soprano to double bass, the original type instrument being the soprano. For a long time concertinas lay dormant until they were popularized by Giulio Regondi, a virtuoso performer and teacher who lived in London and who also composed for them. "Ordinary musical instruments," wrote Alexander Ellis (1885), "are intended to be tuned in accordance with equal temperament. . . . The English concertina, which has fourteen keys for the octave, is still usually tuned in the older Meantone temperament"; it has now joined the ranks of other forgotten free-reed aerophones.

The most important contribution since Buschmann's day was, however, the application of piano-type keyboards to the accordion, patented by Bouton of Paris in 1852 as *accordéon-piano* (piano-accordion). Makers everywhere have adopted it since. Today's models have a keyboard compass varying from two to four octaves, and an additional set of bass and chord buttons. One of the accordion's great advantages was that it could be played informally by an ambulant performer, yet in the next phase of its development this feature was abandoned, for Bouton built a *harmoniflûte*, also in 1852, that was simply a piano-accordion that could either be set in a stand with its bellows worked by a treadle, or else held in the lap. His idea was taken up by another French firm, which patented an accordion with bellows controlled by pedals.

The rage for mechanizing all types of instruments in the late nineteenth century did not spare the accordion: one version was made in the form of an upright frame, with bellows dangling from it, and the free reeds placed in its upper head were controlled by perforated cardboard strips; another version was sounded by means of a perforated metal disk. During the first quarter of the present century accordions were restricted in use to popular and rural entertainment, and their monotonous sound has caused them to be heard less and less frequently.

Two related free-reed instruments, with bellows worked by the player's hand, are the lap organ and the melophone. The former is also known as melodeon, elbow melodian, rocking melodian (from the rocking motion of its bellows), or teeter, and was made in New England from 1825 on for about a quarter of a century. Its deep, rectangular box was not too bulky to be held across the lap. Lap organs took over the accordion's key buttons; these were placed directly over the valves, so that the latter opened when appropriate key buttons were depressed. The player's left hand worked the diagonal double bellows, the lower chamber of which was a feeder. Also designed to be held in the lap was the melophone of Lecler, a Parisian clock maker, devised about 1837. His instruments were in the form of a guitar or hurdy-gurdy, with bellows operated by alternately pulling and pushing a U-shaped handle with the right hand, the left hand being engaged in playing the seven or eight rows of key buttons placed on its broad neck.

Free-reed Automatophones

The first automatophone to have contained free reeds is believed to have been that of Mältzl, referred to above, and free-reed automatophones imitative of lip-vibrated instruments were also built from the early nineteenth century on. Perhaps the most famous were those built by members of the Kaufmann family of Dresden, three generations of highly gifted musical instrument makers and "acousticians," as they were then called. Their earliest such automatophone was the *Bellonion* of Johann Gottfried Kaufmann and his son Johann Friedrich, first built in 1805, with twenty-four free-reed trumpets (free reeds set at the mouthpiece end of natural S-shaped trumpets) and two conventional kettledrums, all housed in a mahogany case and sounded by pinned cylinders. Friedrich Wilhelm III bought one for the Charlottenburg palace. It is related that in 1806 Napoleon, who was making his headquarters there, was rudely awakened in the middle of the night by a blast of the Prussian cavalry's attack signal; fortunately this was found to be emanating from the nearby automatophone, which had inadvertently been set off by one of his staff. The Kaufmanns' next instrument was an automatic trumpeter with clockwork built into its head for activating the mechanism, followed in turn by a *Salpingion* with nine trumpets and a pair of kettledrums; this instrument was imitated as *Salpinorganon* by van Oeckelen in 1824.

In the second half of the nineteenth century free reeds were being used in every possible manner: they were incorporated into music boxes; they were built into a horn by Jaulin of Paris in 1861 and sounded by twenty-seven piston valves arranged in keyboard fashion. Then came the period of unabashed imitation: the *orchestrino da camera*, for instance, was one of a series of small keyboard instruments patented by W. E. Evans of London in 1862, designed to substitute for the different orchestral instruments, such as clarinet, flute, French horn, oboe, bassoon, and so on. *Orchestrinos* had the same compass as did the orchestral instruments and imitated their sound; the free-reed clarinet and horn imitations even had transposing keyboards that could be shifted.

On the whole, free reeds did not prove to be of lasting interest in Europe; the automatophones are now forgotten, most of the ranks of free reeds incorporated into pipe organs were removed, mouth organs are now scarcely more than curiosities, and the harmonium has been replaced by the electronic organ. Only the accordion continues to be heard in the world of popular entertainment.

LIP-VIBRATED AEROPHONES

HORNS

Lip-vibrated aerophones originally made of animal horn or tusk, later imitated in wood or metal, are classed here as horns, in contradistinction to trumpets, which were originally made of a length of bone, wood, or bamboo. As Sachs pointed out, in Europe horns are more conical than cylindrical, and trumpets more cylindrical than conical, but this classification does not hold true elsewhere. Conicity cannot therefore be a criterion for classification, nor for that matter can length: the elcngated *lur* belongs to the horns, but some ancient Egyptian trumpets are only 60 centimeters (2 feet) or so long. Some writers solve this problem of definition by classing all horns as trumpets, using the term in a larger sense of lip-vibrated aerophones.

Primitive horns served magical ends rather than musical purposes and still do in some areas of the world. In Africa, for instance, they may be shouted or spoken into at the wide end, the object of such a procedure being to distort the voice. When they are played as musical instruments, horns are either endblown or sideblown, with endblown varieties predominating in Europe and Asia and sideblown ones preferred in Africa and South America. Ivory horns are sideblown in Africa, but were endblown in Europe ever since their introduction from Byzantium in the tenth century; on both continents they were considered as insignia of royalty.

Although the vast majority of horns are devoid of fingerholes, some folk instruments and obsolete European art-music instruments form exceptions. They are discussed separately, as fingerhole horns (see page 770).

HORNS IN PREHISTORY

Bronze Age horns of northern Europe named *lurer* (the plural of *lur*) have been found, chiefly in Danish peat bogs, but also in Sweden, on the west coast of Norway, in northern Germany, and in Ireland. The name, as applied to these horns, is a modern one, dating from the time the first *lurer* were excavated in Denmark in 1797. *Lur* is also the name of the alphorn in Scandinavia and derives from the Nordic *luðr*, horn. So far, close to fifty specimens have become known, all made of bronze, all with an entirely conical bore, and terminating not in a bell but in a flat, ornamental disk. Their age would seem to fall within the period roughly between 1100 and 500 B.C. Apparently they were always made in pairs; their form is that of an elongated S curve, the second part of which is twisted in a plane at right angles to that of the first section, and the two *lurer* forming a pair are always twisted in opposite directions.

From their length and form, scientists have concluded that the material of which they were originally made, that is, before their imitation in metal, was the horn of *Bos primigenius*. This would explain their peculiar curvature and also their pairwise appearance. Because the two of a pair are at the same pitch, it has been speculated that they may have been played antiphonally. The absolute pitch of those examined varies considerably, as does their length, which ranges from 1.51 meters to 2.38 meters (ca. 5 to 8 feet). A notable feature of the *lur* is its nondetachable mouthpiece of a form similar to that of a modern tenor trombone. From these details it will be apparent that the *lur* is often found in an excellent state of preservation, which is due above all to its discovery in moors.

From contemporaneous rock drawings, chiefly those along the east coast of Sweden, we know that they were played vertically with "bell up," that is, with the "bell" end projecting high above the player's head, and when depicted in pairs they curve away from each other. *Lur* players are frequently portrayed on northern cult ships, and hence the *lur*'s role will have been a ritual rather than a martial one. But the raucousness of its tone may well have led to its utilization in battle. The wide bore favored production of low tones, while the narrow upper (mouthpiece) end made that of high harmonics possible; the bore of a *lur* in the National Museum of Copenhagen expands from 6 millimeters to 60 millimeters over a length of 2 meters (6½ feet). A number of small metal plaques are suspended freely by rings from the tube of many specimens, close to the mouthpiece, doubtless intended to act as jingles. Similar jingles are encountered today on many wind and stringed instruments of non-Western cultures. Further south, a *lur* discovered in Ireland (the only one found there so far) is probably not older than 300 B.C., to judge from the ornamentation of its disk. Others, dated to the ninth century B.C., have been retrieved at Lübzin near Sternberg, not far from Wismar, in northern Germany, a site noted for other Bronze Age objects, including three horns.

Slightly different from the *lurer* are the curved Bronze Age horns recovered from Irish sites. They lack the twist of the former, and are assumed to be metal imitations of *Bos longifrons* horns. All told, over one hundred have been found, the oldest of which appear to date from the eighth century B.C. Archaeologists believe they have been played as late as the second century B.C. Some were endblown and had cast-on mouthpieces, others were sideblown through an oval lateral blowhole.

HORNS IN ANTIQUITY

In historical times, the horn is mentioned in Sumer as a ritual instrument about 2400 B.C., and is depicted there about 1250 B.C. Known as *si-im*, it was endblown, made of copper, and slightly curved in imitation of an animal horn. Babylonians of the second millennium B.C. also had curved horns, and on a Hittite relief from Carchemish of about 900 B.C., an endblown, slightly curved animal horn is visible. Horns were not in use in Egypt until a very late date (they are first seen under Alexander in the fourth century B.C.), although they had been known far earlier, for Amenhotep IV received a gift of forty horns in about 1400 B.C., seventeen of which were stated to have been oxhorns; all were covered with gold and some were even encrusted with precious stones. But "brass" instruments played a neglible part in Egypt's musical life, just as they were to later in Greece.

The Shofar

The ancient Hebrews called their horns by the generic name of *keren*; they were made of ox or of ram horn, emitted only a few tones, and were signal instruments exclusively. One of these was the ritual signal-horn shofar, the sole instrument to have survived into the twentieth century in the same form it had in antiquity. Its name is cognate with the Sumerian *sheg-bar* or *zag-bar*, the male wild goat or ibex, but although the ritual shofar may be made from the horn of any animal of the sheep or goat families, that of a ram is the more common. The shofar produces only two tones—the second and third harmonics—and very rough ones at that. A martial as well as a priestly signal instrument, its blowers let forth a powerful war cry to instill fear into the hearts of the enemy during battle, while priests sounded the "trumpets of killing," according to the Dead Sea Scrolls. The Mishnah relates that two different forms were employed in the Temple: that sounded at New Year and during the Yovel days was a straight ibex horn, its bell ornamented with gold; that sounded on fast days was a curved ram's horn with silver ornamentation. Furthermore, the Mishnah states that at Passover "a sustained, a quavering, and again a sustained blast were blown" on it. Identical blasts were sounded at other rites, "thrice repeated."

After the destruction of the second Temple (A.D. 70), the use of all cult instruments except the shofar was barred, and the shofar entered the synagogue hemmed in by rigid restrictions designed to preserve it unchanged from happier times: no improvement or modification that might affect the tone was permitted henceforth. Decoration by painting or covering the (natural) mouthpiece with metal were also forbidden; carving, however, was permitted. But no gold plating of the interior, no plugging of holes, no alteration of the length was allowed (the minimum permissible length of an approved ritual horn was three hands breadth). All processes of steaming or boiling were equally forbidden, according to both Talmud and Mishnah. Also forbidden were the use of horns of a cow, the repairing of a split horn or of one broken to pieces. In the apocalyptic literature the shofar assumes a new function, that of announcing Doomsday, which function became symbolically associated with the resurrection of Israel.

In the present century, the shofar is sounded ritually only at the New Year and on the Day of Atonement, when one blast is blown; in modern Israel it also announces the onset of the Sabbath.

A straight form of shofar with bent-back bell, rather like a shortened Roman *lituus*, is employed in central and eastern Europe, its bell often serrated. Such horns are now immersed in boiling water to soften them sufficiently for bending to the required angle. Elsewhere, however, the shofar had retained its unaltered animal-horn shape. Apart from their functions as cult and military signal instruments, shofars have been closely associated with magical beliefs and symbolisms from antiquity on, and even in present-day ritual use they remain covered and thus hidden from the congregation's eyes. (Sacred objects are similarly taboo in many other cultures; with regard to cult instruments we have merely to think of flutes, drums, and bullroarers in societies varying chronologically and geographically from ancient Greece to contemporary Australia.)

The shofar's magic manifested itself at the capture of Jericho when "seven priests bearing seven trumpets of ram's horn" sounded them seven times on the seventh day of the battle, and thereby caused the walls to fall down; their power was compounded by that of the magical number seven. Formerly, a shofar might also be blown if prayers for rain remained unanswered for a given length of time, or in the event of local disease, pestilence, and so on.

The Keras

The Hebrew word *keren* is cognate with the Greek *keras*, a horn whose invention was attributed by Athenaeus to the Tyrrhenians (Etruscans). Etruscans were certainly familiar with the curved horn and portrayed it on their monuments, but whether the Greeks received their horn from the Tyrrhenian West is doubtful. As a musical instrument the Greeks certainly made little enough use of it, and in the fourth century B.C. its name fades in favor of that of *rhyton*, a horn primarily used as a drinking vessel, but occasionally made of clay as a musical instrument, with or without fingerholes. Xenophon states (in *Anabasis* VII) that the Thracians used horns as signal instruments, and mentions a Thracian who sounded his *keras* during battle as long as the attack lasted, in order to frighten the enemy, a military tradition we can follow from the ancient Hebrews to the Crusades.

The Cornu *and the* Bucina

Etruscans also had a longer instrument, which they bequeathed to the Romans, who called it *cornu;* a specimen housed in the British Museum is about 1.20 centimeters (4 feet) long, made in several sections, and clearly shows its animal horn derivation; and, if its later form no longer betrayed its origin, its name served a reminder, for Varro wrote *Cornua quod ea nunc sunt ex aere, tunc fiebant bubalo e cornu* ("The *cornua* now of metal were formerly made from horns of the wild ox"). Another curved *cornu* from a grave in Alba Longa has a diameter of 70 centimeters (27½ inches). A short, animal-horn type appears on Italic vases.

Horns and trumpets of ancient Rome were chiefly instruments of the military, whose musicians were divided into four classes: *tubicines, bucinatores, cornicines, liticines.* Some of their instruments can be identified with certainty, others not. The *cornu* is unmistakable, for a funeral monument of a *cornicen* both shows and names his instrument. This was a large and powerful circular metal horn with narrow conical bore and slender bell. The tubing, some 3 meters (10 feet) long, formed a letter G; a wooden bar set transversely served both to steady the horn and to furnish a handhold; one end of the support rested on the player's left shoulder, and the other was held in his left hand, bell forward and above the head.

Two *cornua* excavated at Pompeii are about 3.3 meters (11 feet) long, have detachable mouthpieces of some 17 centimeters (nearly 7 inches), and are pitched in G. When playing, the performer held the mouthpiece to his mouth with his right hand. The *cornu* was not restricted to the soldiery, however, but was also played in the circus, possibly together with the *hydraulus;* mosaics show both instruments together, and the *hydraulus* is known to have been a circus instrument. *Cornua* were also employed during other important public and religious ceremonies. An amusing passage in Petronius's *Satyricon* relates that Trimalchion told some *cornicines* one evening to pretend that he was dead and to play "something beautiful" for the occasion; they obliged forthwith, but played so loudly that neighbors were awakened and, believing the house was on fire, broke the door down.

A Roman horn of uncertain form was the *bucina;* no monument identifies it. *Bucina* and *cornu* have often been confused, but the two had different functions. Both appear to have been made of horn originally, later of metal. In civilian life the *bucina* was a shepherd's instrument; it also called together assemblies of the people, and served as time keeper to announce the hours of the day; in military life it is known to have given "coarse" signals in battle, but was more frequently used to waken soldiers and in changing the watch.

HORNS IN POSTCLASSICAL EUROPE

The more primitive animal horns of antiquity continued to be played in the early Middle Ages. Often sounded without a mouthpiece at first, the later varieties were played with a cup-shaped mouthpiece, later still with one of funnel shape. At first these were an integral part of the instrument, then they became detachable. Up to approximately the seventeenth century—that is, up to the time when the trumpet entered the field of art music—mouthpieces of horns and trumpets were identical. Early medieval horns of Europe were signal instruments of hunters, watchmen, or the military, made of horn—often that of a cow—sometimes attaining a length of about 1 meter (40 inches), or that of a bugle, or their imitation in wood or metal. All were played with the bell pointing up, as they had been in antiquity, and as they still are in areas where natural, endblown horns are sounded. And, it may be noted, as they were in Europe until the hand-in-bell method of playing was introduced.

Byzantium furnished the West with horns of ivory as early as the tenth century (see oliphant, page 783); miniatures and literary references provide information starting with the eleventh century. From then on, the French designate as *graile* (from the Latin *gracilis,* "slender") a small horn of metal, and at the same time horns provided with fingerholes are first seen (fingerhole horns pursue a line of development leading to the Renaissance cornetts, whose progress is traced separately on page 772). In the twelfth century the *arain(e),* meaning bronze, was another French term for a metal horn, probably of short form as it is often mentioned together with the *trompe,* an elongated form described succinctly in a thirteenth-century *Art de chevalerie: Trompe est longue et etroite* ("The *trompe* is long and narrow"). *Cor, graile, olifant,* and *buisine* are mentioned in the *Chanson de Roland* (1100–1120). The *buisine*, recorded there for the first time, was a long, slightly curved martial signal instrument soon to be supplanted by a straight Saracen trumpet to which the name was then transferred; the *cor*, or *corne*, was of animal horn. The bugle, another rudimentary horn of the Middle Ages, had an independent if late development, summarized below.

Straight horns and trumpets were not always differentiated at this time, and words such as *graile* (or *grele*), *buisine*, and *tube*, could denote either a straight horn or a trumpet. By the thirteenth century less dependency need be placed on literary evidence, as documentary and pictorial elements become increasingly available. Thus in 1292 three *trompéeurs* (called *feséours de trompes* in 1297) were known to be working in Paris. Miniatures dating from 1379 of the *Livre du Roi Modus*, a book devoted to the chase, depict two types of hunting horn: one, slightly curved and perhaps a foot long, furnished with a large mouthpiece, is carried by foot-servants, whereas an oliphant-shaped horn is in use by mounted hunters. Signaling on either instrument was logically called *corner* ("to horn"). Perhaps the larger of the two was a *huchet*, the name given in the fifteenth century to a French hunting horn made of a semicircular animal horn (in the seventeenth century it was imitated in copper or in wood; if in wood, two sections were hollowed out and then bound together with leather). Black curved horns in the hands of huntsmen are visible in the Book of Hours of Catherine of Cleves (ca. 1440), probably leather-covered. A *gran cor qui se met en 2 pieces* ("a large horn that could be dismantled into two pieces") is mentioned in 1420, unfortunately without further details.

During the fifteenth century horns are seen to increase in size, an indication that the natural animal materials were being abandoned in favor of more tractable substances, and that plain signals were being elaborated into fanfares. Instruments of this period were still curved or semicircular, varying in length from the short hunter's horn of perhaps 30 centimeters (1 foot) to the curved metal *Herhorn*, a German military signal instrument of some 1½ meters (5 feet). Different models had now evolved to meet the requirements of increasingly specialized functions, foremost among which were the sounding of alarms and signals by waits (tower watchmen) and the military, the transmission of messages during the hunt, and signaling the arrival of posts.

Medieval watchmen's horns were on their way out by the sixteenth century (Virdung in 1511 depicts an S-shaped trumpet, by then virtually obsolete, as a *Thurnerhorn*, "wait's horn"), but hunting horns gain in importance and in complexity. Basically still comprising two sizes, *Zwaintzig gross und clain Jäger Horn in Riemen eingefasst* ("twenty large and small hunting horns set in straps") were included in the hunting equipment of castle Trausnitz near Landshut in 1562—the larger had become too cumbersome and was remodeled; the crescent shape was retained but it was given a small coil in the center. This transformation was unknown to Virdung, who depicts only a crescent hunting horn on a strap, and a very wide-bored, closely coiled instrument of snail-like appearance, the same that Praetorius was to call *Jägertrommet* a century later. Such a horn, made about 1575, is preserved in the Dresden Historical Museum; it measures 16½ centimeters (6½ inches) across the coils but has a tube length of about 165 centimeters (5½ feet). Mersenne still reproduces this type in 1636.

The horn with single central coil, in use in the sixteenth and seventeenth centuries, and now known as *trompe Dufouilloux*, was named for the author of a *Traité de vénerie* dedicated to Charles IX, the 1628 edition of which contains a woodcut depicting such an instrument; one preserved in Mechlin, Belgium, dated 1604, has a single coil formed close to the mouthpiece. Two years later, in 1606, Nicot differentiates between the hunting horn of natural horn or of ivory and the *trompe* made of brass: *Le cor du veneur n'est pas la trompe d'airain* ("The hunter's horn is not the brass *trompe*"), and more explicitly: *Ce cor d'airain entortillé à l'usage des veneurs* ("This brass horn coiled for the use of huntsmen"). Curiously, the Velvet Brueghel's *Hearing* in Madrid, a painting of about 1620, depicts no single-coil horn among the group of instruments obviously intended for the chase, which includes semicircular horns of metal and metal-tipped animal horn, very short signal horns with carrying straps, Virdung's "snail," and a far larger helically coiled horn, a whistle, and some decoy pipes. By then both the closely coiled helical form and the *trompe de chasse* had attained a tube length of sufficient proportions for the production of the first five or six harmonics.

When horns were first employed in Italian opera they were only to sound simple hunters' fanfares, just as trumpets had done somewhat earlier. Cavalli's *Le nozze di Tito e Pelei*, performed in Venice in 1635, calls for a *chiamata alla caccia* of four horns in C. Three decades later, Lully specifies *cors de chasse* for his divertissement, *La princesse d'Elide*, also for fanfares. The type of horn used for such early contacts with the world of art music is unknown, nor does Mersenne, writing at this time, offer any enlightenment; to him, *trompe* was synonymous with *cor de chasse*, crescent shaped and with a single central coil, more frequently played than the helically coiled model; his hunter's *huchet* is a smaller crescent, and his posthorn is nearly semicircular. There is a curious passage in which he remarks that hornists were capable of imitating trumpets so that the two instruments could not be told apart, a sure indication of the horn's expanding compass and of its bright timbre. From then on the distinction between venery and art music was to be clearly marked; decoys and hunting horns were "turned of stained and unstained [animal] horn" in accordance with a mid-seventeenth-century Nuremberg ordinance, while—probably in the 1650s—the French started remodeling the metal horn.

As long as it remained too short to render a consecutive scale (from the seventh to the thirteenth harmonics), the horn, and for that matter the trumpet also, was useless for art music. The trumpet may have developed sooner because of the greater difficulty inherent in producing the horn's long conical tubing. On early "snail" models, the close coils are seen as cylindrical, soldered to one another for stability, and the bell is insufficiently flared; hence a better and longer conical bore and a wider bell were the imperatives to which makers started applying themselves. Their efforts resulted in a new shape with short, cylindrical mouthtube and wider bell, and between the two, narrow-bore coils arranged in a large hoop; around 1660 the coils numbered two and one-half, reduced by 1680 or thereabouts to one and one-half, with a diameter of 45 centimeters (18 inches) or so, and a tube length of some 210 centimeters (7 feet). This circular, coiled horn was named French horn, a term first recorded in 1681. Experimentation along similar lines had probably been made far earlier and then abandoned, as may be inferred from a late-fourteenth-century choir stall of Worcester Cathedral carved with a figure whose circular horn encompasses his body, the bell projecting to his left, and from a 1502 edition of Vergil published at Strasbourg, containing a woodcut showing a large, hooplike instrument with three and one-half coils hung around its player's neck, the bell projecting outward from his left shoulder. But otherwise the hooped horn is not seen nor heard of until the third quarter of the seventeenth century (unless the stage direction in Thomas Nash's masque, *Summer's Last Will and Testament*, published 1600: "Enter Orion like a hunter, with a horn about his neck" called for the large hooped variety).

Mouthpieces of the sixteenth and first half of the seventeenth centuries were the same for trumpets and horns, as already noted, but the horn's transformation called for abandoning the old cup mouthpiece as new playing techniques were mastered and as a less harsh tone became desirable. The new French horn continued to be used for *chamades* and fanfares at the hunt, but it seems also to have gained acceptance in the orchestra very early in its existence, for two horns formed part of that of the New Church in Strasbourg in 1685. By then, or shortly thereafter, the "snail" model had become obsolete. Furetière (1685) knew plain crescent hunters' horns of brass, the *trompe* with one coil in the center, "and wound horns with eight or nine coils that are scarcely in use any more." The oldest preserved French *trompe* is dated 1689; it has a single coil and is now housed in the instrument collection of the Karl Marx University, Leipzig.

Count Franz Anton von Spork, Statthalter of Bohemia, musical connoisseur and great lover of the hunt, to whom Bach later sent the Sanctus of his *Mass in B Minor* and in whose honor he set a horn part in his *Peasant* Cantata—Count von Spork made his *grand tour* of Europe from 1680 to 1682. While in France he heard the new horn and had two of his servants trained to play it before returning home with several instruments, thereby laying the foundation for the Bohemian school of horn playing. From Bohemia the *Waldhorn*, as it was called in German from then on, spread to other German-speaking areas.

The French *trompe* took on additional tubing until its single loop had acquired a diameter of about 90 centimeters (3 feet); but, although it was elegant when draped across the shoulder of a mounted huntsman, it was cumbersome in the hands of all others, and especially those of indoor musicians. German and English hunting horns of the period, judging by extant instruments, had less tubing and smaller diameters. Toward the end of the century the wide-hooped *trompe de chasse* was reserved exclusively for the chase (and became known in Germany as *Parforcehorn*, horn of the *par force* hunt to hounds, formerly known as "hunting at force" in Britain), and for indoor players the hoop was reduced in diameter by winding it several times, and the bell was enlarged considerably until ultimately its diameter came to equal that of the hoop. This resulted in the new orchestral model, built at first in a variety of keys: C, D, F, G, and B♭, or else rebuilt into one of these, preferably F, the most popular key ever since the horn's earliest orchestral participation. Kremsmünster Monastery in 1710 paid a goldsmith for changing 2 *Jagdhorn, welche aus dem A gangen, solche umb einen ganzen Raiff weiter machen, damit solche aus dem F gehen* . . . ("two hunting horns which are in A, to enlarge these by a whole hoop so that they shall be in F"), and two "large horns" of theirs were to have a small amount of tubing removed so as to bring them into unison pitch with the organ. Orchestral players came provided with a whole set of horns, one for the key of each piece to be performed.

The Hamburg performance of Reinhard Keiser's opera *Octavia* in 1705, with horns scored for as *cornes de chasse* (Keiser's predecessor as director of the Hamburg Opera had beeen T. S. Cousser, a Lully pupil—and the model for Mattheson's *Der vollkommene Kapellmeister*—who had brought French instrumental style with him to Hamburg) was a milestone in the horn's history. More important by far, however, was the invention of the crook, which followed a few years later.

The earliest evidence for this innovation is a bill of Michel Leichnamschneider of Vienna, dated 1709, for a horn *Krummbogen* ("crook") to be fitted to an orchestral horn in order to change its fundamental pitch. By terminating the mouthpipe section in a socket, coiled crooks of varying lengths could be inserted between mouthpipe and tubing. The latter could then be lengthened as desired by the simple expedient of inserting one terminal crook into another, and from then on hornists could carry a single instrument and a set of crooks. Mattheson mentions the *Krummbogen* (1713) and writes that *corni da caccia* were much in vogue; the best were in F, and sounded fuller and filled in better than did the "screaming *Clarins*" (i.e., trumpets), because they were pitched a fifth lower. He relates that horns were employed in church, chamber, and theater, were pitched in F and (lower) C, and also in choir pitch G, but that for chamber music those in chamber pitch F were preferred. Majer in 1732 repeated the information concerning pitches, and commented that the horn was easier to play than the trumpet. In France, horns made their first appearance at the Paris Opéra in Campra's *Achille et Déidamie* in 1735; by 1748 La Pouplinière had imported both horns and horn players from Germany for his private orchestra in Pairs where, ironically, the instrument became known as the *nouveau cor de chasse allemand* ("the new German hunting horn").

During the 1740s the hand-in-bell technique, also called hand stopping, was developed. This new and revolutionary method was formalized by Anton Joseph Hampel, a Dresden hornist. Hampel had experimented with mutes, inserting them into his horn bell, and thereby raising the pitch by a semitone. He thereupon substituted his hand, and by partly

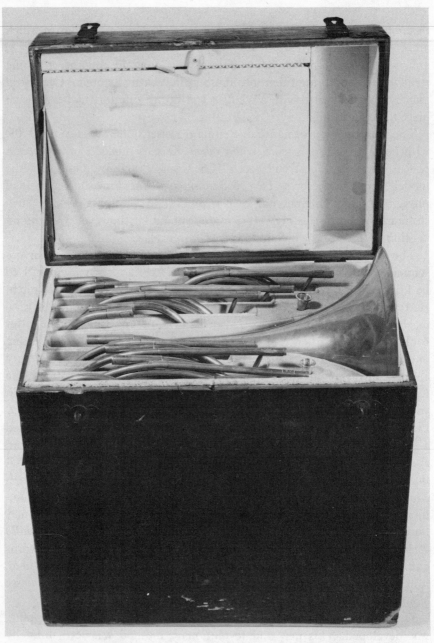

An early-nineteenth-century horn player's equipment: horn, nine crooks of different sizes and two mouthpieces. Courtesy of the Smithsonian Institution (on loan from Mr. Robert Sheldon).

stopping the bell in this manner found that he could change the pitch from a semitone to a whole tone or even more, and thereby bridge gaps between the harmonics. But this caused the sounds to become muffled—they became known as *sons etouffés*, or "hand notes"—a quality they retain today. The horn played in this fashion was a "hand horn"; it created a new timbre for the orchestra and enabled the performer to obtain a chromatic scale. It also led to a complete redesigning of both instrument and mouthpiece, in an attempt to eliminate the disparity between stopped and open tones, both as to quality and dynamics. Hitherto, horns had been played with a cup-shaped mouthpiece, and it is probably not until the hand-in-bell technique was developed that a remodeling was undertaken; first, the critical angle of impact, the grain (the narrowest point of the cup as it meets the shank), had to be rounded to assist production of a smoother, less raucous, tone; then, as the lower compass (the second and third octaves) was being exploited, support of the player's lips by the broad rim of a cup-shaped mouthpiece was no longer necessary and consequently the grain was all but eliminated, resulting in a funnel-shaped mouthpiece.

Once the new hand-in-bell method had been perfected and the new mouthpiece devised, the horn was regularly employed in the orchestra. But the new method made playing with terminal crooks most inconvenient as they were often compounded, so that the length of the instrument changed constantly. To remedy this situation Hampel subsequently (by 1753) succeeded in designing a model with central crooks, called *Inventionshorn* (from *in + ventus*, not from *inventio*); this was an ordinary French horn with crooks inserted in the center of the hoop instead of next to the mouthpiece as theretofore. The coils were cut into and bent, so as to form slides over which one of a series of U-shaped crooks was fitted. These were of varying lengths and served as tuning slides, so that a horn thus equipped could be brought to any pitch desired without adding to its length. The *Inventionshorn* was first built about 1754 by Johann Werner of Dresden to Hampel's specifications, and it is due to this device that the horn began to be used as a solo instrument (by 1760).

Keyed and Valved Horns

Another development followed shortly thereafter, when the Bohemian hornist Kölbel conceived the idea of obtaining a chromatic scale by means of tone holes covered with keys. Gerber (1790) states that Kölbel, a horn player at the Russian court, returned to Saint Petersburg by 1754 after extensive travels, and that he spent the next ten years perfecting his invention. The keys, probably two in number, were situated close to the bell; this was altered to an *amore* form and covered by a lid, a hemisphere pierced with numerous small apertures that lowered the pitch when closed—probably by a semitone. Because of its *amore* bell it was known in France as *taille d'amour* and in German as *Amorschall*. Kölbel's keyed horn was apparently not in use in the West before about 1770 and then enjoyed only a *succès d'estime*.

His attempt at creating a more flexible instrument was short lived, as it could not compete with the *Inventionshorn*, which was to come into general use, but a tribute was paid to it in the June 24, 1771, issue of the *Avant-Coureur*:

C'est une espece de cor-de-chasse mais avec des touches pratiquées dans le tuyau, qui se replie en quarté. Au moyen de ces touches on en tire des sons différemment modulés, comme dans les clarinettes; cet instrument est tres flatteur, il participe . . . du cor-de-chasse ordinaire, du cor Anglais, et du Hautbois. ("It is a kind of hunting horn but with keys in the tubing, which is folded. By means of these keys, tones of different registers can be obtained, as on clarinets; this instrument is very flattering, it partakes . . . of the ordinary hunting horn, the *cor anglais*, and the oboe.")

Johann Christian Bach wrote parts for the *taille d'amour* (e.g., in *Temistocle*, first performed in 1772). Although the *taille d'amour* itself proved to be a dead end as far as development of the orchestral horn was concerned, its underlying idea was an extremely important one and was later to be applied successfully to a whole new family of keyed brass instruments, starting with the keyed bugle.

Around 1776 an improved version of the *Inventionshorn,* called *cor-solo,* was designed by the Bohemian virtuoso Carl Thürschmidt, then living in Paris, according to Wilhelm Schneider (1834); as its name indicates, it was intended for solo concert work, and was furnished with inventions for G, F, E, E♭, and D. Another innovation was that of the tuning slide, due to J. G. Haltenhof of Hanau at the same time; the horn furnished with a tuning slide in addition to crooks became known in France as *cor à l'anglaise* (to be confused later with the *cor anglais*). The conservative Laborde (1780) defines this as a hunting horn with *coulisses* (slides); these enabled the total amount of tubing to be lengthened or shortened as desired, and were adopted in or by the 1780s on orchestral horns in France, elsewhere perhaps later. Also, short tuning bits were made in sets at about this time; it must be borne in mind that standardization of pitch is for all practical purposes a twentieth-century novelty, and that in the eighteenth and most of the nineteenth centuries pitches were far enough apart to render minor mechanical adjustments necessary: crooks could not be adjusted finely enough.

Further attempts at finding a solution to the problem of crook changing resulted in a series of duplex instruments, inaugurated by Charles Claggett of London in 1788 with his Eb and D horn to be played with a common mouthpiece, and permitting a rapid switch from one tube to that of the other. Continued attempts at achieving chromaticism led about 1815 to the building of his first omnitonic horn by J. B. Dupont of Paris, intended to obviate the need for changing crooks; there the crooks were incorporated in the horn and their length controlled by a graduated slide and dial, or by similar means; thus fixed, the *tons* were no longer *tons de rechange* (i.e., interchangeable) and were deemed able to transpose into all needed tonalities. Yet in 1818 Dupont patented an improved design with a slide, permitting up to nine changes of tonality.

From then on the problems of chromaticism were to be solved radically: in 1815 the horn player Heinrich Stölzel of Berlin had demonstrated the earliest valve. He and Friedrich Blühmel patented it jointly in 1818, but already in 1817 Stölzel had furnished the horn with two valves for the right hand, according to the *Allgemeine musikalische Zeitung* of Leipzig. A single valve was fitted in 1824 to the *cor saxomnitonique* of Charles Joseph Sax of Brussels (father of Adolphe Sax), to permit connection of the horn tubing with the fixed-crook tubing. Omnitonic systems of one kind or another continued in use until the end of the century; that of John Callcott in England (1851) involved the use of ten feet of cylindrical "crook coil"; that of Chaussier (1889) employed only four crooks, each with its own valve. Excessive weight and awkward manipulation caused the demise of these instruments.

From the 1830s on, three valves became the standard number, but as the right hand continued to be used for stopping, they were disposed for the left hand and have remained so ever since (other valved instruments are right handed). During the second half of the nineteenth century further refinements took place, including the enlargement of the bell until its diameter exceeded that of the coils. Later, the double horn in F and Bb appeared, a duplex instrument with two sets of valved crooks, now widely used in symphony orchestras. The single horn in (high) Bb is also in common use and has largely superseded the classical F horn. Most modern forms are fitted with three valves for lowering the pitch by a tone, semitone, and three semitones, respectively. Rotary valves are generally preferred, although piston valves prevail in some areas. In the United States a five-valved horn is also played; the fourth is a muting valve, the fifth a *Quartventil*, a valve that adds five semitones (the interval of a fourth) to the bottom of the compass in order to bridge the gap between pedal tone and the lowest tone available by the other valves.

Hunting horns were not discarded with the transformation of the natural horn to the crook horn; the *trompe de chasse* with its one and one-half narrow-bore windings that reached from shoulder to thigh in the mid-eighteenth century, survives in bands of the French military *chasseurs* with 2½ coils and considerably reduced diameter. And the ancient, spirally wound, wild-bore "snail"of Virdung was reintroduced in 1866 by Grégoire of Nancy, modernized, pitched in D, with no fewer than twenty coils, under the name of *trompe de Lorraine*. Nor were the smaller natural horns with their three or four coils abandoned: it is this version (never the *trompe de chasse*) that was played bell up, both in military bands and indoor music.

Folk Horns

Apart from the horns of art music and the hunt, rustic folk horns have remained in use among European animal herders. According to Furetière (1685), cow herders and shepherds of France transformed cow or ram horns into musical instruments by cutting off the tip and inserting a mouthpiece of elder wood. More recently, French shepherds have made *cornadouelles* in springtime of spirally rolled bark. Swiss goatherds assemble their flocks by sounding a horn in the morning to take them to pasture; the goats recognize the call and scamper out to meet them as they are released from their sheds. Both birch bark and goat horn are made into instruments in rural Finland, while Estonian shepherds sound horns made of wood or of goat horn.

The Post Horn

The post horn, historically a valveless brass or copper instrument, is of interest chiefly for its place in the chain of developments leading to the modern cornet. As signal instruments of postillons and mail-coach guards they occurred in a number of shapes. An early reference is that of 1562, when an inventory was taken of the hunting equipment at Castle Trausnitz near Landshut, which included *ain grosz Posthorn . . . mer ain clains Posthorn* ("a large post horn . . . another small post horn"). In the Germany of Praetorius's day they were coiled; in the France of Mersenne's, crescent shaped. By the late eighteenth century the French model had a diameter of some 30 to 45 centimeters (12 to 18 inches) and merged its identity with that of the military bugle horn. France also had a coiled form that looked like a very small French horn but with a single coil. The German *Reichspost* had three and one-half coils and a two-octave compass, but according to Halle (1764) those of Prussia were smaller and had a compass of a single octave. When Koch wrote (1802), the German post horn was identical to the French horn except for its smaller size. Nineteenth-century England produced, in addition to a coiled version small enough to fit into a pocket, a straight form with expanding bore, from 71 to 81 centimeters (28 to 32 inches) in length, traditionally of one piece, but later in the century a two-section, telescoping version was brought out. Three or even four tones could be coaxed from it.

French coiled post horns assumed the form of diminutive hunting horns, and had a theoretical length (that is, unwound) of some 135 centimeters (53 inches). Early in the nineteenth century these were fitted with crooks and tuning slides, and when about 1825 some were instead fitted with two valves, those having crooks and slides were called *cornet ordinaire* or *cornet simple*, to differentiate them from the valved model. The latter was the future cornet.

The Cornet

The old French post horn, wound into a single coil and resembling a small French horn, was fitted with two valves by Halary of Paris around 1825, and thereby transformed into the valved cornet. The new form was called *cornet d'harmonie*, later *cornet à pistons*; its early German name was *Posthorn mit Ventil*. In England the valved version was first known as cornopean, cornet, stop horn, or small stop horn, according to Clappé (1911). Halary himself called his new instrument *cornet d'harmonie*; he marketed it complete with crooks for C, B, A♭, and G.

The new valved instrument was prompt of speech and quickly became popular, both in wind bands—Wieprecht introduced it into Prussian army bands in 1833 as a replacement for the keyed bugle—and in the orchestra (Rossini: *Guillaume Tell*, 1829). By the mid-century it was in use in most of Europe and was being manufactured in several countries. Although early specimens exist in the original circular form, it assumed increasingly the appearance of a wide, stumpy trumpet, as builders continued to modify their patterns, making the bore partly cylindrical and widening it in their efforts to improve the tone quality, a subject of criticism for years to come. Early cornets were regarded, logically enough, as horns, and were played with French horn mouthpieces. To the initial two valves of Halary, a third was added in 1829 by Périnet. At first these were of the *Schubventil* and Stölzel types, later the Périnet valve was substituted. Valves were placed to the left of the bellpipe until the latter part of the nineteenth century; nowadays they are to its right.

Cornets were made primarily as sopranos in B♭ or A (in England in C), and as altos in E♭ (from 1830 on), all supplied with a number of crooks for other tonalities. For military bands there existed also a sopranino in E♭ and an octave cornet in A, high C, and B♭, the last-mentioned first produced by Cerveny in 1862. Cornets have been built down to tenor range, if the althorn and tenorhorn are included in this classification; actually the alto cornet, which was made both in trumpet and tuba form, fused ultimately with the althorn. Lower tonal positions were not possible to obtain because they would have required too narrow a bore for the low pitch required. Cornets have been built in a variety of forms and with different types of valves, but the trumpet shape equipped with piston valves is now standard; its bore remains conical and narrow.

A model known as echo cornet was made in the late nineteenth and early twentieth centuries, with a nondetachable mute controlled by a valve. The *Cornet-Instrumente* of Cerveny, patented in 1876, are not true cornets but are narrow-bore bugles played with a cup mouthpiece. Cerveny built them in circular form as band instruments, in a whole family ranging from sopranino to contrabass; they were adopted by German and Austrian military bands.

Of the lower pitched instruments, the tenorhorn is considered a true cornet, but many authors do not consider the althorn as such. Tenorhorns are usually built in B♭ and also in C and in A, but builders have now largely abandoned the original narrow cornet bore; those pitched in B♭ are called B♭ tenors in the United States. Althorns were considered by Eichborn (1885) to be descended from the valved trumpet; they appear a little later than the tenorhorns, around 1830. They are now made in trumpet, tuba, and helicon form, pitched in F and E♭, are standard components of brass bands, and are sometimes encountered in military bands also. The cornet's status was well summarized by the French musicologist, Michel Brenet: "the irremediable vulgarity of its timbre has kept it away from the symphonic or dramatic orchestra. But its ease of execution ensured its fortune in regimental bands, civilian fanfares, and dance orchestras."

The Bugle

Bugles were originally short animal horns, as their name implies. The Old French word *bugle*, derived from the Latin *buculus* ("bullock") was borrowed by the English in the thirteenth century, kept alive, and borrowed back by the French in 1814, albeit for a slightly different instrument. In medieval times the horn of a bugle served as a hunter's signal instrument; by late medieval times it had also been adopted as a signal instrument by tower watchmen, shepherds, and soldiers. Horns of this primitive material were still in existence in the fourteenth century, when reference was made to 3 *cornua de bugle*, and in 1378 an Englishman bequeathed *cornu meum magnum de bugle . . . ornatum cum auro* ("my large bugle horn, ornamented with gold"). Even in postmedieval centuries bugles retained their characteristic shape, that of a short, curved, wide-bore horn. They were then imitated in brass, copper, or silver, and when sounded they were held with the bell end pointing up.

In the last quarter of the eighteenth century the bugle was bent into a short semicircle for use as a military signal instrument, and as such it became known as bugle horn, a pleonasm. Its place was of course restricted to the infantry, as the cavalry was associated with the aristocratic trumpet, and the bugle, now of brass, continued to serve the infantry as it had in the past. The early nineteenth century witnessed another change of shape: the tubing was lengthened and arranged in a trumpetlike elliptical coil. Pitched in C or B♭, the new bugle's compass was from c' to g² (harmonics only), and from a military signal instrument it was transformed into a military band instrument. Known in France as *clairon*, it was able to serve in both capacities there. Alexis de Tocqueville describes in his *Souvenirs* (1893) the "diabolic" clamor produced by the call to arms sounded by *clairons* and drums during the troubles of 1848, when tension in Paris was at its height.

Keyless and valveless, the natural bugle has remained in use until now; its continuous wide conical bore has been retained, and it is played with a cup mouthpiece.

The keyed bugle. Shortly after the new elliptic form of bugle came into use, it was transformed into a keyed bugle by an Irish bandmaster named

Joseph Halliday, who applied five closed keys in order to bridge the gap between the second and third harmonic (c′ and g′). Halliday was granted a patent for this in 1810. The source of his inspiration may well have been the keyed trumpet of Anton Weidinger, an Austrian musician who had played it in England in the first years of the century. Halliday's instrument had a chromatic compass of c′ to c³. A sixth key, an open one, was added soon thereafter, and in this form the keyed bugle was introduced into British military bands under the patronage of the Duke of Kent, in whose honor it was henceforth known as the Kent horn. Not until 1815 did it spread to the Continent, where it was built in B♭. English instruments were made of copper with brass or silver keys and fittings, and pitched in C with a crook to B♭. On the Continent, where brass was the favored material, four more keys were added in due course, and a number of different sizes were built; in fact, Halary of Paris created a whole family of keyed bugles in 1817.

Despite the disadvantages inherent in their side holes, these instruments were played in military bands and orchestras alike until they were ousted by the flugelhorn, in Austria and Germany before the mid-century, and by the valved cornet elsewhere after the mid-century.

The flugelhorn. The flugelhorn (German: *Flügelhorn*), a valved bugle, is a direct descendant of the keyed bugle. Its etymology has never been satisfactorily clarified, but it may have been named in analogy to the *Bügelhorn* (German for "bugle"), from its use in the *Flügel* for the chase, or simply for the *Flügelmann*, who marched at the right-hand corner of the front ranks in German regimental bands.

Flugelhorns were first made in Austria, probably in Vienna, between 1820 and 1830. They retained the wide, conical bore and medium-sized bell of their ancestor, but with the passing of time makers increasingly narrowed the bore until it came to resemble that of a cornet; indeed the two can be differentiated externally only by the flugelhorn's larger bell. Furthermore, it came to be built in either trumpet, helicon, or even tuba form. Of its three sizes—sopranino in E♭ and F, soprano in B♭ and C, and alto in E♭—the B♭ soprano is the most popular; all share the compass and notation of the cornets. The flugelhorn was originally provided with three or four valves, but today three are the standard number; these are either rotary or piston types, depending upon the area. The mouthpiece is funnel shaped and differs from that of the cornet by its greater width and depth. Although it is almost exclusively an instrument of the wind band, the flugelhorn has on occasion been played in the orchestra for special situations; for example, in the early decades of the present century as a substitute in the high horn solo Quoniam of Bach's Mass in B Minor.

After the introduction by Adolphe Sax of his family of saxhorns, a number of which are known as *Flügelhorn* in German, nomenclature became almost inextricably confused.

The saxhorn. Adolphe Sax, best known for his saxophones, proceeded to narrow the natural bugle's bore, add valves, and to produce in 1843 a whole family of brass instruments he called saxhorns. They were patented by him two years later. But as valved bugles had already been known for some time, Sax's claim to the invention of a new instrument was heatedly attacked by rival Parisian makers, who demanded the revocation of his patent and who involved him in litigation. Viewed from the twentieth century, it becomes clear that his contribution—a very real one—consisted in blending a number of related but heterogenous brass instruments of his time, including the cornets, flugelhorns, tenorhorns, and tubas, into one homogenous pattern. All his saxhorns had a medium conical bore, medium-sized bell, and an upright form with valves fitted vertically on horizontal tubing, and were played with a funnel-shaped mouthpiece.

Initially all sizes were fitted with three valves, and, shortly thereafter, with four. The entire group was pitched alternately in E♭ and B♭, and to his original five sizes—soprano to bass—he added others, ultimately extending the family to a series of ten. In 1844 he built a set of saxhorns for the Distin family of musicians, coiled in circular form, but, by the time Georges Kastner depicted them four years later, Sax had already redesigned them with bell pointing up. Constantly experimenting, he changed the valve system around 1855, applying to the group his own system of six ascending valves that functioned by cutting out a given length of tubing instead of adding to it. Still not satisfied, he then patented (in 1859) a combination of three keys and three valves, and proceeded to apply these to his sopranino bugle. The three keys were located on the main tube not far below the bell, and raised the pitch by a semitone, tone, and three semitones, respectively. In creating this combination, Sax hoped to facilitate the playing of trills, to permit transpositions up to a minor third, and, finally, to obtain a fully chromatic scale by using only one valve and one key; but unfortunately this ingenious idea proved a failure.

After Chaussier's transposition device was brought out in 1889 it was fitted to the saxhorn, and the resultant instrument was then called *bugle omnitonique*: it could really be played in all tonalities.

Another development was the changing by Sax of some of his models from an upright form to a horizontal one. The final family included ten sizes, from octave to subcontrabass, with a *saxhorn baryton* and a *saxhorn basse*, both in Bb and differing only in timbre, as the bass had a wider bore than the baryton. As band instruments the saxhorns were extremely successful and are still played, though some of the smaller sizes have given way to the cornet. The confusion of nomenclature referred to above was further compounded by differences of opinion between French and Belgian makers as to the tonal positions of various models.

The ophicleide. Jean Hilaire Asté, commonly known as Halary, a Parisian instrument maker, was first to apply the principle of keys to low-register wind instruments. To him must be accorded the credit of abolishing fingerholes on the serpent–basshorn–Russian bassoon clan, and in doing so he created a bass keyed bugle. His task was notably different, however, from that of Halliday, inasmuch as he had to bridge a gap between fundamental and second harmonic, that of an octave. In 1817 he applied for a patent to cover three instruments that he called (1) *clavi-tube*, a modified keyed bugle; (2) *quinti-tube* or *quinti-clave*, a low-pitched keyed bugle later called alto ophicleide; and (3) *ophicléide* or *serpent à clefs*. The patents were withheld until 1821 on the grounds that his instruments were but improvements upon the *basse guerrière* of Dumas, which in point of fact they were not, as Dumas's instruments were low-pitched clarinets.

Halary's ophicleide was made of metal in U form. Some of his early models terminated in the open-mouthed serpent head of the Russian bassoon; their very large tone holes were covered with nine or ten keys, later with twelve, and, except for the first (nearest the bell), all were closed. The large mouthpiece was similar to that of a bass trombone. Type instrument of the family was the bass in C and Bb (actually a baritone), to which a contrabass in F and Eb (actually a bass) was added and sometimes called *ophicléide monstre*; the *quinti-tube* or alto ophicleide was made in F and Eb.

Ophicleides gained rapid admission to brass bands and even to opera (Spontini gave it a part in his *Olympie* of 1819), and was both imitated and improved by other makers, including Adolphe Sax. Joseph Riedl of Vienna, in about 1820, brought out a twelve-keyed bass, which he named *Bombardon;* a six-keyed soprano made of wood was shown in 1825 by Pierre Dupré whom Mahillon has described as an able builder with a mania for making in wood those wind instruments that his colleagues were engaged in supplying in metal.

With the invention of valves the construction of brass instruments was of course revolutionized, and those that did not lend themselves to transformation were discarded. A. G. Guichard of Paris tackled the problem of modernizing the ophicleide and in 1832 brought out his *ophicléide à pistons* in Eb, with three valves, and slides for C and Bb. More important was a five-year patent granted to him in 1836 for a single-valve version, which was in reality an early form of tuba in all but name. Around the mid-century the regular ophicleide started to be replaced by the new valved tuba, but was able to maintain itself in France for a few more decades. One of its functions there was to take the serpent parts in performances of "the older music." By 1880 it was almost obsolete, apart from Italy, where it continued to be played into the twentieth century.

The tuba. With his *ophicléide à pistons*, Guichard had effectively created the earliest *de facto* tuba, a valved, wide-bored, low-pitched bugle, terminating in a flared bell and played with a cup mouthpiece. Quite possibly Wilhelm Wieprecht, the designer of several successful wind instruments and reorganizer of the Prussian military bands, was acquainted with it, for tubas were built to his specifications beginning in 1835, the year in which he introduced a bass tuba in F to replace the bass trombone, and in which he was granted a joint patent with the Berlin wind instrument maker, Johann Gottfried Moritz. From then on tubas were built in various sizes, from tenor to subcontrabass, and in numerous shapes, resulting in an understandably vague terminology with reference to these instruments; F. L. Schubert (1862) did not differentiate between cornet, flugelhorn, or tuba, for example. The vertical form, with bell pointing up, has come to be identified as the typical tuba shape, and consequently any valved brass instrument so constructed is likely to be referred to as a tuba. Furthermore, the Eb bass tuba is still known as a bombardon in some areas, but if built in circular form it is called a helicon.

The Wieprecht-Moritz patent of 1835 was for an instrument in F with five valves of the type known as *Berliner Pumpen*—short piston valves of large diameter—two for the left, and three for the right hand, all lowering the pitch of the open tones. As the patent only covered a five-valved instrument it was soon circumvented by makers who copied it but were careful to restrict the number of their valves to three, four, or six, and who called the "new" instrument a bombardon. Perhaps they were unaware of Riedl's *Bombardon* and wished to compliment the ancient bass bombard. These early tubas had a relatively narrow conical bore; their advent was to spell doom to serpent, basshorn, and ophicleide alike, both in the orchestra and in the wind band.

Originally the bombardon had a wider bore than that of the tuba, but it was probably given the latter's proportions by the mid-century, as writers of the period no longer distinguish between the two. Rotary valves became standard on Austrian and German instruments; Vaclav Cerveny, a Bohemian maker, seems to have been one of the first to apply them, with his production of a bombardon in F displaying six such valves. Elsewhere the piston valve remains in use.

Tenor tubas were also built by Moritz but are now obsolete; only the larger sizes were viable.

The contrabass tuba in B♭ or C was an invention of Cerveny (1845) and has been made in upright (so-called tuba) form and also in circular form. The latter can be shaped either like a helicon or like a sousaphone, and the current models have a detachable bell and a double bend in the bell joint. The contra is known as a BB♭ bass (pronounced "double-B-flat") in bands.

Even larger versions were produced: a subbass in E♭′ was first built by Adolphe Sax in Paris in 1855, and later by Cerveny. Sax was also the first to build a subcontrabass; he pitched one in B♭² —an octave below the contrabass—in the same year. Since then other giants have been built in C′ and B♭², the largest of which are 2.40 meters (almost 8 feet) in height, with a tube length of no less than 13.68 meters (45 feet). Due to their unwieldiness, builders designed the larger tubas in circular (helicon) form for convenience in carrying, as their bell could then rest on the player's left shoulder while the tube passed under his left arm. Russia was the first country to adopt this form for her bands, with other European countries and the United States following.

For the performance of Halévy's opera *Le juif errant* in 1852, Sax built a series of saxtubas in circular form and of exceptionally powerful tone, shaped like Roman *bucinas*. Perhaps these were the instruments burlesqued in Offenbach's *La belle Hélène* of 1856:

> *Les deux Ajax*
> *Etalant avec jactance*
> *Leur double thorax*
> *Parmi le fracas immense*
> *Des cuivres de Sax.*

> The two Ajax
> Showing off with a swagger
> Their double thorax
> Amid immense blasts
> From Sax's brasses.

The euphonium. Concert master Sommer of Weimar designed in 1843 a wide-bored, valved bugle of baritone range, at first called *Euphonion* in Germany, later *Barytonhorn*. Originally it had a relatively narrow bore, was built in C, B♭, and A, and provided with three valves. Since then, furnished with four or even five valves, pitched in B♭ and C, it has been built in helicon, tuba, and trumpet form. In view of the lack of standardization in brass terminology, the euphonium, as it is now called, is also classed as a tuba or as a saxhorn, depending upon the form of a particular model. From the mid-nineteenth century on it successfully replaced the bassoon in German and Russian military bands. Today it remains popular in both military and wind bands, and disposes of a three-octave compass (B♭'/C° to b♭'/c²). A duplex version known as double euphonium also exists; by means of two independent tubes and two bells it can produce two tones at the same pitch but of differing timbres.

HORNS IN ASIA

Horns of Asia are endblown, played with a cup mouthpiece that is often cut out of the animal horn itself in more primitive instruments, or with a mouthpiece permanently affixed to those of metal.

In the north, a decoy horn of the Kan chin of Siberia is made of sections of hollowed wood bound with birch bark; it imitates the sound of a doe and hunters make use of it to entice the stag. Buffalo horn is a favorite material of herders in Southeast Asia, who sometimes add a free reed to the wall (cf. free reeds, page 730). China, a country so rich in trumpets, lacks horns. Yet they were known in antiquity, for the figure of a mounted knight from the Northern Wei dynasty (fourth to sixth centuries) is seen playing a short, curved horn, held bell up. The Tibetan *rwa dung* is believed to have originated in India rather than in China; the horn, usually that of a ram or antelope, is carved with symbols and is sounded during rites of exorcism.

India, equally rich in trumpets, is horn country par excellence. Several of its horns go by the name of *sringa* (*sing* in Hindi) on the subcontinent: a primitive cowhorn, its tip serving as embouchure; or a twisted goat's horn; also a crescent-shaped metal horn made of several sections—from two to five—of curved brass, with a thin brass rod connecting the extremities for greater stability, rather like the ancient Roman *cornu*; and finally the *rana sringa* (war horn), formerly a military signal instrument, now chiefly a ritual one. Undulating in imitation of a long-horned cow's horn, this *sringa* is composed of four brass sections joined together, with high ornamental rings covering the joints. These rings form bosses; they are hollow and are filled with rattling pellets, a characteristic of the metal *sringas*. Other features of the *rana sringa* are its fixed mouthpiece, and the custom of usually playing it in pairs, and always of holding it bell up. In Nepal the same serpentine, four-sectioned *sringa* is made of copper, and is—or was—occasionally made as a double instrument.

The Horniman Museum, London, houses an impressive double horn, S-shaped, with hollow, pellet-filled bosses, and two bells in form of human heads with gaping mouths, played by a common mouthpipe and sounding at unison. Like other horns of the subcontinent, its mouthpiece forms an integral part of the tubing. Designed to be played bells up, it was undoubtedly a cult instrument.

HORNS IN THE AMERICAS

Lip-vibrated aerophones of the Americas are almost exclusively trumpets; animal horns are, however, known to the Carajá of Brazil and are also played in Bolivia.

FINGERHOLE HORNS

When short animal horns are provided with fingerholes they offer the possibility of playing melodies, rather than simple calls or fanfares, for changes of pitch then can be controlled both by lip vibration and by varying the tube length, and, depending on the bore, overblowing may also be feasible. But just because of these combinations, intonation on such instruments is very hard to master. Notwithstanding, fingerhole horns have been made ever since antiquity, both in simple form as folk instruments, and in more elaborate form as participants in art music. Imitated in wood or even in ivory, the horn was gradually refined and narrowed until in Europe it emerged as the cornett.

THE FINGERHOLE HORN IN HISTORY

Our earliest knowledge of fingerhole horns, admittedly rather cloudy, is derived from ancient Greece, where the *rhyton*, a drinking horn (known as *keras*, "horn," prior to the fourth century B.C.) was occasionally made as a musical instrument, the horn shape imitated in clay, both with and without fingerholes. A post-Sassanid Persian silver vessel of about A.D. 700 clearly depicts a short, curved horn pierced with finger-holes. Similar instruments were in use in postclassical Europe, demonstrably from the eleventh century on, and probably earlier. The form most commonly seen in medieval miniatures is that of a conical, wide-bored, slightly curved horn of medium length; sometimes it is placed in the hands of Ethan in King David's entourage. But already in the eleventh century he is seen sounding a straight instrument terminating in an animal's head; whether this variety was still of horn or was already imitated in wood is impossible to tell. In the role of *tubae* announcing the Last Judgment such horns appear on the portal of Bamberg Cathedral, dating from about 1235: long, slightly curved fingerhole horns. During the same century they are first mentioned in French literature.

When the process of refinement and of further narrowing the bore transformed them into the cornett of Renaissance art music, they nonetheless continued to be played as folk instruments; shepherds and other animal herders of Estonia, Finland, Scandinavia, Russia, Yugoslavia, and some remote areas of the Iberian peninsula play them now. Outside Europe they are encountered only among the Bongo of the Sudan.

On all rustic fingerhole horns the tip of the horn is removed and the resulting orifice serves either as embouchure or, as with the extinct Latvian *aza rag*, a mouthpiece is added to it. This is also true of the Russian *rozhok* ("little horn"), a folk instrument showing marked similarities with the straight cornett. The *rozhok* is a straight tube with slightly tapering bore, traditionally made of two sections of hollowed wood and bound with birch bark, although lathe-turned specimens have been made recently. In the past, mouthpieces were turned in the tube of the *rozhok* proper, just as were those of the classical mute cornett, but nowadays a small mouthpiece is always added. The number of finger-holes varies from district to district, with five fingerholes and a thumb-hole being found among the herdsmen of the Vladimir and Ivanov districts northeast of Moscow, and four in the Olonets region. Herders play it to call their cattle, for solo music making, or for ensemble per-formances, and bands of *rozhkis* existed until the 1920s. *Rozhoks* in-tended for ensemble playing were made in two sizes pitched an octave apart; those for solo playing were of a size intermediary between the two. The resemblance between *rozhok* and the straight cornett of Western art music does not end with their form, for both were commonly held at one corner of the mouth; performers who placed their right hand uppermost are seen to hold their instrument at the left side of their mouth, and vice versa.

THE CORNETT

The cornett was nothing but a refined version of the medieval rustic fingerhole horn that worked its way into art music of the late Middle Ages and of the Renaissance. The thirteenth-century French *Sone de Nausay* speaks of *ces cors c'on sonne as dois* ("these horns played by the fingers"), and in English literature they are mentioned from the *Morte d'Arthur* (ca. 1400) on, as cornette, later spelled "cornet." In modern times this orthography has been changed to cornett in English in order to avoid confusion with the nineteenth-century valved brass instrument, written "cornet." The *coradoiz* (*cor à doigts*, "finger horn") changed its name in the sixteenth century to *cornet à bouquin* ("he-goat horn"); the Italian equivalent was *cornetto*, the Germans called it *Zink* (or *Chorzink*, because it was at choir pitch).

Two distinct types of cornett developed following the lines already laid down by their medieval precursors: the curved and the straight cornett. The smaller of the curved cornetts were slightly bent, larger ones were formed into an obtuse **S** by giving them a double bend. Both were made of a section of wood split lengthwise, hollowed out, then glued to-gether and bound with black leather for extra stability. Due to their color they became known on continental Europe as black cornetts. Typically they were octagonal in outline; occasionally they were made of ivory. Straight cornetts, on the other hand, were turned and bored;

they were generally not covered with leather, and hence the quality and even the color of the material employed in fashioning them was more important. Boxwood was preferred, but walnut, maple, and plum were also frequently worked. Because of their light color, boxwood instruments were referred to as white cornetts. Exceptionally, two leather-covered straight cornetts are enumerated in the Stuttgart court inventory of musical instruments dated 1589, one of the richest accumulations of any Renaissance or baroque court.

Straight cornetts were in turn divided into two categories: those played just like the curved ones, namely with a detachable cup mouthpiece of ivory, horn, metal, or wood, while a far less common sort known as mute cornett had its mouthpiece turned inside the top of the tube, like the *rozhok*. These turned mouthpieces were conical and merged with the bore without any angularity, the resultant tone being "gentle, soft, and sweet," as Praetorius wrote. Possibly the designation of "mute" is derived from the fact that this type of cornett accompanied or replaced the treble voice in a choir of singers; it was mute in the sense that it did not pronounce words. Under Louis XIII, three *dessus muets ou cornets* ("treble mutes or cornetts") replaced as many vocal parts in the royal chapel.

All cornetts had a conical tube with narrow bore and, at the time of their full development, six fingerholes and usually one thumbhole. To quote Zacconi (1592), they all had a natural compass of fifteen tones from a^0 to a^2, and the black cornetts could go another four, five, or six tones higher. Praetorius iterates this, but adds that some players reached e^3 and even g^3, while at the bottom of the compass g^0 and f^0 could be obtained by falset tones, that is, by slackening the lips (and a woodcut in Schlick [1511] shows a straight cornett with its lower end half-stopped by the player's hand). Built in several sizes, the type instrument was noted in its heyday for having the same compass as the violin, hence the numerous compositions for *violino ovvero* (or) *cornetto*. A trio sonata entitled *La Foscarina* by Biagio Marini of 1617 is for *doi violini o cornetti*, and a year earlier Thomas Stadler had appended to his *Harmoniae sacrae* a piece à 5 for two *cornetti over violini* and three voices, to mention but two less-known examples.

The smaller *cornettino* was pitched a fifth higher during the sixteenth and seventeenth centuries, but only a fourth higher in the eighteenth century in order to make its scale coincide with that of the contemporary flute (d' to d^3); German writers called this smaller version a *Quartzink* or *Kleinzink*. A larger form pitched in d^0, a fifth below the type instru-

ment, was usually fitted with a key for taking the compass down to C°
when closed; this was known as *cornone* in Italy, *basse de cornet à
bouquin* in France, tenor cornett in England, *Grosszink* in Germany—
Praetorius called it the *Gross Tenor-Cornet*; when its pitch was only a
fourth below the regular *Zink* it was known as *Quartzink*, a most confusing term. In addition, cornetts were pitched a tone or so below the type
instrument. As the latter were at choir pitch, the lower models were
presumably destined for participation in chamber-pitch groups.

Though Praetorius knew of only three sizes, Jacques Cellier had
enumerated no fewer than five in 1585: *dessus, hautecontre, taille*—the
three standard sizes—to which he added *sacqueboute* and *pédale*. These
large sizes were apparently no novelty in France even then, for in 1570
une basse contre de cornet was inventorized among the effects of a deceased musician. A bass pitched one octave below the type instrument,
and having the form of an obtuse S with a bell carved to resemble an
animal head, is preserved in the Paris Conservatoire Museum, which
also houses one of the only two surviving contrabasses: this carries four
extension keys and terminates in a down-pointing bell. A similar instrument, but with only two keys, is in Hamburg's Museum für hambur-
gische Geschichte. Some larger Italian cornetts ended in the form of an
open-mouthed animal head, just as some of their medieval precursors
had done.

Although the provision of fingerholes in a lip-vibrated instrument
greatly taxed the player's ability by demanding quite extraordinary control—"cornetts give a musician who wishes to play in tune as much
trouble as mercury gives an alchemist," wrote Fuhrmann (1706)—
cornetts were greatly favored from the fifteenth century on, by which
time they had assumed their final forms; they could be played very
softly when required, or loud enough to be included in tower music.
Furthermore, they were excellent substitutes for the forbidden trumpet
—forbidden by guild rules, that is—as well as for the unsatisfactory
soprano trombone. In other words, they represented a really flexible
addition to the woodwinds, as well as to the brasses, and as such they
came to replace both trumpet and soprano trombone in tower music and
town bands. In these capacities they lingered on in German-speaking
areas until the late eighteenth century, in some localities even well into
the nineteenth, long after they had become obsolete elsewhere (by the
end of the seventeenth century).

The transition from straight, wood-imitated fingerhole horn to the

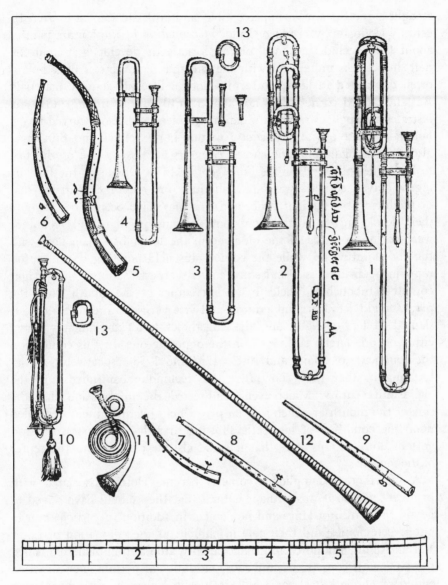

Cornetts and brass instruments of the baroque: (1, 2) quart trombones; (3) regular ordinary trombone; (4) alto trombone; (5) corno/great tenor cornett; (6) regular choir [pitch] cornett; (7) small descant cornett, a fifth higher; (8) straight cornett with a mouthpiece; (9) mute cornett; (10) trumpet; (11) hunter's trumpet; (12) wooden trumpet; (13) whole-tone crook. From Michael Praetorius, *Theatrum instrumentorum*, 1620.

straight cornett is almost imperceptible, and both are seen in fourteenth-century iconography. Taddeo Gaddi's *Coronation of the Virgin*, painted about 1335, includes an angel playing a perfectly developed straight cornett, her cheeks puffed out with the effort, and the lowest fingerhole is often duplicated in later fourteenth- and in fifteenth-century materials. But the curved cornett does not appear until later: Virdung (1511) illustrates a straight cornett with cup mouthpiece and also a curved fingerhole horn quite obviously made of natural horn; Schlick and Burgkmair also show straight but not curved cornetts. Ganassi is one of the first to illustrate both types in his *Fontegara* of 1535. Obviously the fashioning of curved cornetts was more laborious and complex than was that of producing the straight form, and this may have been a deterrent to their development. Furthermore, both playing position and technique were no longer those of the older horn; the latter had been held with the end pointing up while the cornett was held pointing down, or forward in open-air music; and since curved cornetts adopted the straight cornett's embouchure (held in the left corner of the mouth when the player's right hand was uppermost, and vice versa, as already noted), it slanted to left or right, and the fingerholes were consequently bored either on one lateral surface or on the opposing one. In this connection the comments of Majer and Eisel (1732 and 1738 respectively) are interesting in that they show that this technique continued into the eighteenth century. Majer even volunteered the information that the side of the mouth at which a given player held his instrument depended upon the condition of his teeth, showing that the true reason was forgotten. Both authors state that it could also be played from the center of the mouth.

As lip-vibrated aerophones cornetts became closely associated with trumpets, and so it was perhaps natural that they should have served to herald the arrival of kings and noblemen, in addition to participation in public ceremonies and their role in church: at the coronation of Louis XIII at Reims, a hundred musicians perched atop a triumphal arch hailed the king with cornetts exclusively. The duties of a trumpeter-cornettist employed at the Kassel court in 1536 included playing not only at court but also at dances and "whatever else" might be required of him, and at the baptism of the Landgrave's daughter in 1596 a band of ten trumpets, kettledrums, four trombones, two cornetts, two bagpipes, two shawms, eight fifes, and drums, provided the "loud" music. Nuremberg, renowned chiefly as center of brass instrument making, also furnished cornetts and other woodwinds in the sixteenth century. Duke Albert of Prussia corresponded with the Nuremberg maker Jorg Neuschel in 1541 regarding the purchase of various instruments, including *welsche* (Italian) curved cornetts and a set of six cornetts to be tuned together. Romans bought their trombones, flutes, and crumhorns in Nuremberg, but procured their *Zincken und Cornetti* from England, according to Duke Ernst of Bavaria, writing from Rome in 1574, whereas the Fuggers of Augsburg obtained their cornetts (and their clavichords) from Antwerp. Trade in musical instruments during the sixteenth century was both international and lively. In England cornetts were played in "private" theaters of the Elizabethan age, sounding flourishes and sennets as though they were substitutes for trumpets, and in *The Two Noble Kinsmen* "cornets, trumpets, sound as to a charge" for a tournament.

By the end of the sixteenth century the cornett had not only retained its position as a "loud" instrument for outdoor music but had also assumed considerable importance in both music *da camera* and *da chiesa*, chamber and church. In fact Calvisius (1600) names cornett and curtal as the principal church instruments, next to the organ, of course. Its role there was one of supporting the voices, while its range enabled it to soar above them, *paroissant comme une lumière brillante* ("appearing as a brilliant light"), to quote Trichet, and whoever has heard a cornett in concerted music must surely agree with him. Roger North, writing nearly a century later, expressed the same sentiment in rather different words: "What can yield a tone so like an eunuch's voice as a true cornet pipe?" he asked. In opera, Monteverdi had introduced it in his *Orfeo* of 1607, and as late a composer as Handel scored for it in *Tamerlane*, written in 1724.

During the latter half of the sixteenth and the first half of the seventeenth century—the *grand siècle* of the cornett—combinations of cornett and trombone were popular in church (*Encomium musices* of 1590, for example), in the hands of English waits, and in those of tower watchmen on the Continent. Locke composed an *Ayre for His Majesty's Sagbutts and Cornetts* for the coronation of Charles II. But Praetorius objected (1619) to the sound of the large *cornetto torto* or *cornone*, which he characterized as *unlieblich und hornhafftig* ("disagreeable and hornlike," that is, harsh), and advocated replacing it by a trombone.

Later the balance actually did shift in favor of the trombone, and the combination became a consort of trombones, except for the unsatisfactory soprano, replaced by a cornett. Additional impetus was given to such ensembles on the Continent at the end of the Thirty Years' War. Stuttgart, for example, inaugurated chorale playing from the tower "mornings, noons, and evenings with cornetts and trombone," which innovation was clearly religious propaganda destined to familiarize the population with chorales as rapidly as possible, and represented a break from the tradition of secular wind bands of the past. The golden age of the cornett was then coming to a close, and straight cornetts probably did not outlive the seventeenth century. The word *Zink*, which in the past had always required qualification, became synonymous with the curved cornett in eighteenth- and nineteenth-century usage.

In the course of the seventeenth century cornetts had been forced to submit to competition of the violin, and their musical importance was over by the early eighteenth century, after which they continued only as substitutes for the soprano trombone, chiefly but not exclusively for the performing of chorales. Their players were town musicians, and in Germany members of the cornettists' guild. The guild rules of 1721 stipulated a five-year apprenticeship with a master—or, if a boy had no money, six years without fee—after which he was freed but had to spend a further three years "abroad," working for other cornettists as assistant (journeyman); this period was known as the *Wanderjahre*. Thereafter, once he had passed an examination to qualify as town cornettist, he was declared a master. No cornettist, whether master, assistant, or apprentice, was permitted to play the bagpipe, hurdy-gurdy, triangle, "and other similar nonmusical instruments," no apprentice or assistant was permitted to teach cornett or trombone playing; if, however, in a small town some "honest person" should wish to learn how to play with the intention of honoring God in church, then he might teach him the trombone—but not the cornett.

Of the late composers for the cornett, Bach, Gluck, and Handel are the most prominent. Gluck assigned a part for the *trombone soprano o cornetto* in his *Orfeo et Euridice*, thereby leading Berlioz to believe that the soprano trombone had at one time been called *cornetto*. Bach scored for it in eleven of his church cantatas for the playing of chorales, either as upper voice to three trombones, or to support a *cantus firmus* in the soprano. Tower and town musicians continued playing their chorales for the balance of the eighteenth century (cornetts were still heard in Saint Stephen's Church, Vienna, in 1788), but in the nineteenth century town musicians were employed by only a few municipalities, and the last refuge of the cornett was among these and among tower musicians—nineteenth-century waits. In Schweinfurth it could still be found in the hands of both in the 1840s.

THE SERPENT

Structurally and acoustically, the serpent formed a bass to the cornetts from which it differed, however, in form. Tradition ascribes its invention to canon Edme Guillaume of Auxerre in 1590, and investigations of claims for greater antiquity as well as for an Italian origin have so far failed to upset this attribution.

The serpent is named for its winding S-shaped tube; its acute curves are necessary in order to bring the fingerholes of so large an instrument— the tube measured some 2 meters (6½ feet)—within reach of the player's hands. Like the curved cornett, the tube was of wood, covered with black leather, but the serpent had an extremely wide conical bore, and carried a brass crook on which the cup mouthpiece was mounted. For most of its existence this was of ivory or bone, on later military instruments often of metal. The fingerholes were spaced in two groups of three each; originally they were not provided with keys, but the reach was so inconvenient that by 1640 the lowest fingerhole came to be covered by a key protected by a fontanelle. Serpents were made in the same manner as the "black" cornetts; however, in nineteenth-century England they were built in short, overlapping sections, resulting in even more acute curves. English specimens of this period are thus readily recognizable by their relatively squat form, with the tube assuming U bends instead of the older S curves.

During the first century of its existence, if not longer, the serpent was almost exclusively an ecclesiastic instrument, doubling men's voices at the unison, and as far as is known its use was confined to France. From there it was disseminated, radiating to England, Flanders, and Germany. To Athanasius Kircher, writing in Rome in the mid-seventeenth century, it was still a French instrument. Praetorius makes no mention of it. Both Mersenne and Trichet give descriptions, though, from which it follows that serpents were then shorter than the eighteenth-century models were to be, and that their fundamental was considered to be E. From the eighteenth century on it was considered to be D, except in England, where it was indicated as C. Interplay of the huge bore, fingerholes, cup mouthpiece, and the performer's embouchure combined to create considerable leeway with respect to both compass and pitch, and indeed the former is said to have ranged between two and one-half and three and one-half octaves, due in part to the technique of slackening lip tension, whereby tones up to a fourth below the natural fundamental could be produced. Trichet writes that the tube was generally six feet long and that the best woods for its construction were walnut, plum, or sorb. Virtually every church had its serpentist; the *chapelle du Roi* in 1692 had three, but only two are recorded there in 1712.

The serpent was playing bass parts in instrumental ensembles outside the church by the mid-seventeenth century, and a century later it was employed in the orchestra of the Comédie Italienne, when a violinist named Simonet played one in fifteen performances of the *Chinois* (in 1756). Such frivolity was apparently short lived, for Laborde (1780) states that serpents were relegated to cathedrals (Burney, commenting on the service at Notre Dame in Paris of ten years earlier, had noted that little use was made of the organ, and that the voices were accompanied by a serpent).

Clumsy as it may have been, the serpent had the undisputed advantage of great power and a wide dynamic range, and eighteenth-century bandmasters were becoming aware of this. At the mid-century it succeeded in gaining a foothold in military bands while retaining its role in the church, thereby leading ultimately to its adaptation for such dual functions by branching into the *serpent d'église* ("church serpent") and the *serpent militaire* ("military serpent"), nineteenth-century terms to denote the older serpentine and the newly devised upright form. This infusion of new tone quality into military bands proved so successful that wind bands of other countries also incorporated serpents, with the consequence that they reached Germany about 1770, in which country they were manufactured from the turn of the eighteenth to the nineteenth century on.

By the end of the eighteenth century they had been accepted in orchestras—no longer played by violinists. The French émigré musician Louis-Alexandre Frichot, inventor of the basshorn, played the serpent in London orchestras in 1793 and 1794, and in Nordhausen a performance of *The Creation* was given with the contrabassoon part allotted to a serpent. German instruments of the period were described in an article by Gerber of 1803 as having a length of over eight feet, and a compass of no less than four octaves, from C′ to c², but adds that the lowest octave was created exclusively by the player's embouchure, with low C′ not always obtainable, and with all tones up to g′ almost inaudible out of doors. Substituting the serpent for a contrabassoon part became common practice in France, as contrabassoons were not made there until later in the (nineteenth) century.

With new life infused into it as a military band instrument, the serpent was gradually supplied with keys. By 1800 three closed keys were standard on the Continent, though four had been adopted in England a little earlier. Keys were continually being added, until a total of fourteen was reached. As the tendency was to increase the higher rather than the lower range, open extension keys were never used. Symphony and opera orchestras also benefitted by these improvements; Mendelssohn scored for the serpent, as did Beethoven and Wagner. It was still played in a Parisian church in 1870, and remained in use in many French village churches in the first quarter of the twentieth century; in Flanders, keyless serpents were still to be found in churches a little over a century ago.

Sheer bulk made the serpent both awkward and difficult to play when marching, while its fragility posed problems in military bands. Several solutions to these drawbacks were forthcoming: metal instruments of lighter weight were occasionally built around 1800; others, of wood, were made in horizontal form during the second quarter of the century. These terminated in a rather sharply flared bell; the fingerholes were spaced regularly along the tube, out of reach of the player's hands, so that all had to be provided with keys.

But the real breakthrough came in 1788 when a musician of the Collegiate Church of Saint Peter, Lille, named Regibo, built the first upright serpent with straight, doubled tubes. Little is known about his model other than that it could be dismantled into three sections, was both louder and easier to play than conventional models, and that it cost three carolins. Regibo opened the way for a whole series of bassoon-shaped "serpents," far easier to play than their precursors, as they could be held like a bassoon. First in this series was the *serpent Piffault*, brought out by Piffault of Paris in 1806 and also known as *serpent militaire*. Henceforth the latter term was applied to the numerous models, both of wood and of metal, that succeeded it during the ensuing half century, among which was the *ophibaryton*, a version with a straight bell in the form of a painted animal head. Ultimately the *serpent militaire* was replaced by the basshorn, which in turn gave way to the valved ophicleide and finally to the tuba. In 1835, the year in which the tuba was introduced, Gustav Schilling could still write that the serpent should not be lacking among instruments of bass register. Some bands, those of the Danish army, among others, retained their serpents until the mid-nineteenth century, and Spain actually had serpents in three bands as late as 1884. Instruments of very late date were occasionally built in the form of a tuba, but in leather-covered wood.

Contrabass serpents, double the size and pitched an octave lower than the standard instrument, were made in England in the mid-nineteenth century. One has survived; built around 1840, it remained in church service for some twenty years. It measures 4.75 meters (15 feet 7 inches) and stands 135 centimeters (4½ feet) high.

The Basshorn

Possibly inspired by Regibo's serpent, which could be dismantled, Frichot while in London invented one of metal in shape of a bassoon, with sections that could be taken apart. This was manufactured by G. (George?) Astor in London by 1800, the year in which Frichot brought out a tutor for it. Because it was made in England it became known as the English basshorn or *serpent anglais* (English serpent). Its appearance was that of a brass bassoon. In 1803 it had six fingerholes, a thumbhole, 2 keys (for F♯ and G♯) worked by the little fingers, and a cornett-type mouthpiece of horn. Compass, timbre, and fingering were those of the serpent. The serpent's six fingerholes were retained, situated as of old in two groups of three. Two more keys were added by 1813, when Choron credited it with the extraordinary compass of four and one-half octaves, fully chromatic, from A′ to d³, so that a basshorn could serve as soprano, alto, tenor or bass. Theoretically that is, for no single player could cover so enormous a range; a serpent mouthpiece was required for the bass register, an enlarged horn mouthpiece for the middle register, and a trumpet mouthpiece for the upper portion of the compass. Frichot had meanwhile returned to France, and in 1806 submitted to a committee of the Paris Conservatoire an improved version of his basshorn, which he called *basse-cor*. This was in turn improved by him and patented in 1810 under the name of *basse-trompette*, and presumably represents the version described by Choron. It was made completely of brass. Four slides were added in order to pitch the instrument in D for concert use, in C♯ for church performances, and in C for military bands; the remaining slide was a flat-pitch slide in C.

So popular were these improved serpents that a number of other, slightly variant forms, were built, starting with the second decade of the nineteenth century. The nomenclature also multiplied, with "Russian bassoon" and "bassoon serpent" emerging as favorite appellations. All were made in three or four detachable sections, two of which somewhat resembled the butt and wing joints of a bassoon. They either terminated in a wide brass bell or else in a fantasy bell painted to look like a serpent's head, with mouthpiece carried on a long **S** crook. This latter variety was known as Russian bassoon (also as *ophibaryton* in French). In a very amusing passage of his *Military Music*, Kappey (1894) relates having seen as a child an Austrian band with five or six such Russian bassoons in the front rank, "the bell of each being shaped like the open mouth of a huge serpent painted blood-red inside, with huge white teeth, and wagging tongue which moved up and down at every step," causing him to forget all about the music and to remember only "those terrible open jaws."

Different makers created their own models during the first half of the nineteenth century, some all metal, some of wood, others of wood with a brass bell. The various designs can be grouped into two distinct types: the basshorn with its two tubes inserted in a butt so as to form a **V**, and the Russian bassoon, with parallel tubes bored partly or even wholly in one piece of wood. From about 1815 to about 1830 basshorns were adopted in military bands in England and on the Continent, usually pitched in C but also in B♭, and for the Prussian infantry in E and F. Their great vogue lasted until the arrival of the ophicleide. Attempts were made in England and in Germany to create contrabass serpents, but these were little more than experimental.

The Oliphant

When the short, thick, and heavy horn of ivory reached the West from Byzantium in the tenth and eleventh centuries it was very properly called *cor d'olifant* ("elephant horn"). As such it appears in Old French literature from the early twelfth century on (as in the *Chanson de Roland* of about 1100, for instance). Later in the Middle Ages they became highly prized hunters' horns; in 1227 silver garnishes are mentioned: *4 cornua de ebore quedem* [*sic*] *sunt cum argento* ("four ivory horns, some with silver"). Whether the tusks originated in India or in Africa is not known, but as ivory horns have been played in Africa for centuries —they were first reported by Girolamo Merolla in 1692 from the Congo, where they could be owned only by royalty—it is likely that Africa was the source. Throughout their short history European oliphants were endblown.

HORNS IN AFRICA

The Oliphant. African counterparts of the oliphant were sideblown when Merolla wrote, and have remained so ever since. A lateral hole is pierced near the tip and the horn held horizontally with the lower (wide) end projecting to the player's right. Just as they had been in Europe, those of Africa are above all martial signal instruments. Oliphants called *katakyi* in Ghana are still insignia of royalty, but the Bakongo people have a word, *mpungi*, to designate horns in general, regardless of whether they are made of ivory, horn, or wood. In the Congo region ivory horns are imitated in wood by the Basoga, who protect the wide end by winding it with fiber; a most interesting if not uncommon method of sounding these horns exists among the Mangbetu of the same region, who change the pitch by alternately opening and closing a hole pierced in the tip of the tusk to the left of the player's mouth, so that the right hand is left free to support the heavy horn. To the west, in the "Bend," the Yoruba treat a sideblown tusk as though it were a "talking" drum: all tones and glides of the Yoruba language can be reproduced by the simple expedient of holding the palm of the hand at different angles to the bottom opening of the tusk while playing. In this manner whole messages, even poetry, can be transmitted over wide distances. A "talking" horn is also utilized by the Akan of Ghana for the transmission of messages, but theirs is not an oliphant.

Of the African oliphant it has been said that it can imitate the roar of a lion, the trumpeting of an elephant in fury; that it can render the sighs of a breeze or the whisperings of a lover's voice. Trills and tremolos can also be executed with great precision, a tribute to the musicianship and competence of its player.

Other African horns. The majority of African horns are not, however, made of such costly material as ivory; animal horn is standard, and when that is not available its form is imitated in wood. Like the ivory instruments, they are sideblown. A single word, *opi*, designates in Kwa languages (except Onitsa) indiscriminately a horn made of cattle horn and its wooden replica, as does *buru* among the West African Mandingo; this is a descendant of the now obsolete *buru*, trumpet of the Turks and Turkomans, who introduced it to North Africa, from where it spread not only to the Mandingo but also to Ghana, and to such West African peoples as the Mande and Susu, who call their signal horn *burifē*. Herders and hunters sound simple horns, often of cow (Ethiopia) or of antelope horn (Central Africa). More elaborate is a kudu horn of the Nuba people, prolonged by a mass of wax and possibly clay, in shape of an *amore* bell, with a slightly conical extension, attaining altogether the impressive length of some 110 centimeters (43 inches) and reserved for the exclusive use of important wrestlers.

Exceptionally, African horns are also played in sets. The Bahaya of Tanzania play antelope horns in sets of five or more, and if a single horn from the set is used when hunting it is given a different name.

TRUMPETS

Trumpets and horns are very closely related lip-vibrated aerophones; the former originated in a tube of bamboo, cane, wood, or bone, and were at first, therefore, straight instruments; later they were imitated in metal. Often a small gourd, horn, or other object was affixed to the lower end to serve as a bell. Horns, as already noted, were originally made of animal horn or tusk. Although trumpets are more cylindrical than conical in Western culture, and horns more conical than cylindrical there, this does not hold true elsewhere; ancient Egyptian trumpets, for example, have a conical bore throughout.

Man's earliest trumpets served magical rather than musical ends, and were first used as voice distorters. They were sung into, or shouted into, very much in the manner of a megaphone, for the purpose of warding off evil spirits. Wooden, megaphone-shaped trumpets are still in use in some areas of France, Switzerland, and Brazil, devoid both of mouthpiece and of bell. In many countries marine shells, usually conches, are blown as trumpets, and these also were voice distorters at first.

According to Sachs, the earliest types of trumpet, be they of wood or of shell, were endblown. These were followed by sideblown versions, such as are to be found now in Africa, South America, the Pacific, and as existed in Ireland during the Bronze Age (which extended far later there than elsewhere in Europe), all of them less developed than their endblown counterparts (the British Museum houses a bronze statuette from the Campania dating from about 470 B.C. representing a figure patently if inexplicably blowing a transverse trumpet).

TRUMPETS IN ANTIQUITY

From Bronze Age Babylon until now trumpets have served as martial instruments. Those of the Babylonian army were straight, made of several sections of wood bound together, and sometimes overlaid with gold. Excavations at Tepe Hissar and at Asterabad have yielded miniature votive trumpets in gold dating from the seventeenth century B.C. But we can trace trumpets back somewhat further on monuments, as the Akkadian Stele of Naram-Sin of about 2200 B.C. depicts a slender, narrow-bored, cylindrical trumpet with a very small bell.

In the Mediterranean area trumpets were generally both martial and temple instruments; those of the Egyptians, Israelites, some Etruscans, Greeks, and Romans were straight. In Egypt and Israel they were played in pairs—but not necessarily together—as were those of Afghanistan, India, and Tibet, all of which were made of metal, as are those of modern India. (Wooden trumpets of Lithuania, Romania, Chile, the Amazon forest regions, and Central America are also played pairwise, the performance being antiphonal with each instrument yielding only one or two tones—just as did those of classical antiquity.)

Verdicts of ancient writers concerning the trumpets of their time are invariably uncomplimentary: typical is that of Plutarch, who comments (*On Isis and Osiris*) that the people of Busiris and Lycopolis made no use whatever of *salpinges* (trumpets), because these made a sound like the braying of an ass. The hoot of an elephant is compared to "trumpeting" in English, but Jean de Meung went a step further when he wrote in the *Roman de la rose* of about 1280 of *olifanz . . . qui de son nés trompe et buisine* ("elephant . . . who trumpets and *buisines* with his nose"); a Turkish seventeenth-century author wrote that the *karranay*, a curved trumpet, sounded like the braying of an ass, but then the Turkish word for ass is *khar*, which might have influenced his judgment. And indeed the English language has but one word to denote the cry of an ass and the call of a trumpet: "the harsh resounding trumpets dreadfull bray" (*Richard II*).

Egypt received the trumpet, a military signal instrument, from King Tushratta of Mitanni (Upper Mesopotamia) in the fourteenth century B.C. Two trumpets were found in King Tutankhamen's grave, measuring 58.2 centimeters (ca. 23 inches) and 49.4 centimeters (19.5 inches), respectively. Both have a relatively wide and slightly conical bore, and short, flared bells. Separate mouthpieces were not then in use, but the ends are reinforced by a metal ring to serve as embouchure. Each trumpet emits one tone and an overblown tone, approximating c' and eb^2 on one instrument, bb° and e' on the other. Both were made of sheet metal, the smaller of bronze, the larger of silver, brazed along a longitudinal seam, and both contained a close-fitting wooden stopper. Trumpeters in ancient Egypt are usually but not invariably depicted in pairs. A bronze Egyptian trumpet of the Roman period, now in the Louvre, was also made of sheet metal, its tube brazed in the manner described; the bore is still conical, with the lower end forming a distinct bell; it cannot be sounded, but a facsimile rendered two tones.

Trumpets of the ancient Hebrews, called *hatzozroth*, were of silver, straight, and short, ending in a bell and played in pairs. Their length and form indicate their derivation from the Egyptian trumpet. Moses was commanded to "make thee two trumpets of silver; of a whole piece shalt thou make them," probably sheet metal, like their Egyptian ancestors, and Kirby (1952) suggested that the code of signals given in the Book of Numbers may well have been military code signals of the Egyptian pharaoh. Not only were the *hatzozroth* martial and cult instruments, but they became the insignia of priests at an early date, and "the sons of Aaron, the priests," were commanded to "blow with the trumpets" when making sacrifices.

The Talmud states that two silver trumpets were used in the rites of the Daily Whole Offering in the Temple, when "they blew a long, a quavering, and a prolonged blast." For such duties, fundamental and overblow tone would suffice; neither trumpets nor horns of antiquity were musical instruments in our modern sense of instruments capable of producing a musical scale. On the relief of the Arch of Titus at Rome, in a scene depicting the sack of the Temple, two late Hebrew trumpets are portrayed in the hands of Roman soldiers, straight instruments more akin to the Roman *tuba* than to their Egyptian prototypes.

A curious and unique bronze figure from the western Anatolia-Sporades area of the Mediterranean, dating from the turn of the eighth to the seventh century B.C., shows a man blowing a short, very wide trumpet terminating in a straight flare, with the player wearing a *phorbeia* (see aulos, page 655). This did not resemble the trumpet of the Greeks, called *salpinx*, a straight, conical instrument with a narrow bore—a conspicuously narrow bore, in fact—terminating in a bulbous bell of *amore* form. According to Greek tradition this was of Tyrrhenian (i.e., Etruscan) origin—they said the same of their horn, the *keras*—and apparently was always considered an alien instrument. Mentioned twice in the *Iliad*, it is not referred to again until the fifth century B.C., by, for example, Bacchylides and Aeschylus; the latter puts a Tyrrhenian trumpet into the hands of a herald who is to summon the Athenians.

Its earliest representation is probably that on a painted plate of ca. 520 B.C., where the player is shown wearing a *phorbeia*, as on the earlier Anatolian bronze. Later, *phorbeiai* were no longer shown in connection with trumpets but were retained for use with the auloi. A surviving *salpinx* in the Museum of Fine Arts, Boston, is made of ivory with a brass bell, and measures 158 centimeters (62 inches). As it was in Egypt, the Greek trumpet's function was restricted to the giving of military signals.

Xenophon (*Anabasis* VII) mentions the *salpinges* of rawhide ("raw bull skin") played by some Thracians; probably they were merely bound with rawhide for stability and protection, just as some woodwinds were to be bound with leather from the Renaissance on. But lip-vibrated aerophones played a negligible part in Greece compared to Etruria and, above all, to Rome.

A more widely disseminated trumpet was the Etruscan *lituus*, later taken over by the Romans, a straight, slender, cylindrical tube terminating in an upturned bell to form a letter J. Its prototype was obviously a curved animal horn attached to a straight wooden tube. On earlier Etruscan *litui* the hooked bell-end is connected to the tube by a strut. Later ones are indistinguishable from those of Rome, shorter, the tube becoming conical, the bell foreshortened and flared, but regardless of age they are always represented in pairs.

Mouthpieces of the Etruscan instruments were removable: of a pair of *litui* depicted in the Tomba dei Rilievi near Cerveteri, one has a mouthpiece of a different color (red) to that of the tube (yellow). In Rome, by contrast, the mouthpiece was not detachable. A late Etruscan specimen from Caere (Cerveteri), preserved in the Vatican Museum, varies from Roman models only by its greater length of 160 centimeters (63 inches). Mahillon examined it and found it to be pitched in G (two Roman *cornua* found in Pompeii were also in G, but an octave lower than the Vatican *lituus*); a Roman specimen found intact in the Rhine near Düsseldorf was pitched in A.

It is known that Roman *litui* served as cavalry signal instruments, but though they are frequently mentioned in literature they are rarely depicted or even referred to in military accounts. Fortunately a number of archaeological finds cover almost the entire period of their existence. A fourth-century B.C. Etruscan funeral scene shows the *lituus* held horizontally while played; this position did not change, for an Italo-Roman sarcophagus of the first century B.C. shows it being held in precisely the same manner.

Litui are depicted in early medieval manuscripts such as the ninth-century Bible of Charles the Bald, but their use at so late a date is questionable. However, the word *lituus* was certainly retained in postclassical times long after the instrument had died out, and in the Renaissance it came to denote the cornett or the crumhorn, in the eighteenth century also certain brass instruments; *litui vulgo Waldhorner . . . in* G were enumerated in a 1706 inventory taken at Osseg Monastery in Bohemia, and Bach's Cantata No. 18, *O Jesu Christ*, calls for *litui*, probably tenor trumpets in Bb. The term did not disappear completely until the latter part of the eighteenth century.

The Etrusco-Grecian *salpinx* was inherited by the Romans, who called it the *tuba*. By abolishing any remnants of a bulb bell they created a straight, wide-bored, conical trumpet that they played with a detachable mouthpiece of bone. The instruments of *tubicines*, trumpeters, on a marble relief of the first century B.C. have long, conical mouthpieces. Generally the *tubae* were made of bronze, rarely even of iron. Their triple role was (1) civilian—they appeared in the arena together with other instruments; (2) military—they served with the Legions; and (3) religious—they performed at certain sacred rites, and temple trumpeters, the *tubicines sacrorum*, held the rank of priest. Trumpets used at sacrifice were purified at a festival known as the *tubilustrum*, held at Rome on March 23 and May 23.

A puzzling term employed in antiquity, *tuba ductilis*, is believed to have referred to a *tuba* of metal hammered thin, but when applied to instruments of ancient Israel it probably indicated a metal trumpet in contrast to the *shofar*.

Yet another form of trumpet was known to Rome, and is seen on some Roman gravestones in Germany: that of a *tuba* bent into a surprisingly modern form of bugle, with two folds—a shortened instrument suitable for cavalry. The long, straight *tuba* would have been difficult to manage on horseback, but by bending it until it was reduced to about a third of its original length, the drawbacks inherent in signaling from the saddle might have been overcome. Here the mouthpiece seems to have formed an integral part of the tubing. Unfortunately, it has not yet been possible to match a name to this form.

Iron Age Celts had a martial trumpet called the *carnyx*, a long, hooked form with straight tube and bent-back bell, characteristically made in form of an animal head with open mouth, and played with a lead mouthpiece. Antiquity has left both descriptions and representations, and from the latter it is clear that, except for the design of the bell and an ornamental spine running the length of the tube, the *carnyx* resembled the Roman *lituus.* Celts had invaded the Po Valley at the end of the sixth century B.C., and scholars now are inclined to accept the hypothesis that they obtained their *carnyx* from Italy. Evidence of its presence has been found from Britain to Pergamon; it is first shown on the Pergamon Frieze of the early second century B.C. On Trajan's Column (second century A.D.) it is represented in the hands of Dacians, and a silver caldron found at Gundestrup, northern Jutland, also dating from the second century, is now recognized as being of Dacian origin. Here *carnyx* players are seen holding their instruments, not in the position one might expect, namely horizontally as were the *litui,* but upright, with the bell towering high above their heads. This position implies either that the tube was curved at the mouth end, or that a curved mouthpiece was inserted. If, as has been suggested, the open animal throat contained a movable tongue that added its rasping to the trumpet's bray, we can well imagine it in the historical role of all

Carnyx players. Detail of the Gundestrup Caldron, second century. Courtesy of the Danish Information Office.

martial instruments, that of terrifying the enemy. The same instrument is depicted on Celtiberian coins and on Belgic coins of Britain, showing a conical bore.

A number of Late Bronze Age hooked trumpets in the form of *litui* have been found in Ireland; their straight, cylindrical tubes were made in sections and joined to a curved, conical bell, with the joints covered by bosses. The bell end is always plain, that is, lacking the typical Celtic animal head, and the angle of the hook varies, some being more obtuse than others. All are patently metal replicas of a wooden tube prolonged by an animal horn, but whether they antecede the Etruscan *litui* or not is still an open question, for the age of the Irish instruments cannot be determined with any precision.

TRUMPETS IN POSTCLASSICAL EUROPE

Both the word *tuba* and the instrument itself were inherited by postclassical Europe, and, indeed, *tuba* has remained the Polish word for "trumpet" until now. As *tube*, a straight form of horn or trumpet is recorded in French literature of the thirteenth and fourteenth centuries, and the medieval Latin diminutive *tubecta* denoted a small, straight trumpet, probably equivalent to the *trombetta* of Dante. But, above all, the *tuba* is familiar to the West as the elongated trumpet always present in the hands of angels in illustrations of the Exultet text *Tuba sonet salutaris*; they may vary in form and even in material, for had not Cassiodorus (d. 575) defined the *tuba* as being made of horn or of metal? Hence it is not unusual to find in later medieval art works that the *tubae* sounding the Last Judgment consisted of one Tutankhamen-type straight trumpet, and one conical horn, or, as on the fresco of about 1200 now in the Archaeological Museum of Solsona, Catalonia, angels may be holding black (leather-covered?), elongated, slightly conical tubes, perhaps three feet long.

Early postclassical *tubae* were presumably still made on the Roman model, that is, with detachable mouthpieces. A Gospel book of the mid-eighth century (MS 51, Saint Gall Cathedral Library) includes a full-page rendering of the Last Judgment, its trumpet-blowing angels gripping their instruments halfway down with the right hand, the left hand covering their mouth and the mouthpiece, a gesture perhaps implying a wobbly juncture.

A straight trumpet of Arabian culture, also with conical tube, known as *nafir* since the eleventh century, was adopted by Spain as the *añafil* and is documented as such from the mid-thirteenth century (an Old Provençal glossary defined it as a *parva tuba cum voce alta*); its name was then Spanished to *trompeta morisca*. The crusaders certainly were aware of its presence, for it was the ferocious *cor sarrazinois* used in battle that they subsequently adopted and transformed into their *buisine*, a name theretofore reserved for large horns. The term was later taken into German as *busîne*, ultimately becoming *Posaune*, the present German word for "trombone."

Buisines had tapering tubes made of several sections, with their joints covered by ornamental bosses, and terminated in a wide bell. According to literary sources they could be made of brass, copper, or silver. Generally they were played in pairs. Such an instrument is illustrated in the thirteenth-century *Cantigas de Santa María* (in recent times, this type of trumpet has been called herald's trumpet). When the Doge of Venice proceeded in a vermilion-colored and silk-bedecked galley to Zara in 1202, he was preceded by four silver *buisines* and drums, and as the fleet sailed from Venice, "a hundred pairs of *buisines*, both of silver and of brass" were accompanied by drums and other instruments, as the crusader Robert de Clari relates in his memoirs. A shorter version of the *buisine* was also adopted, with cylindrical tube and wide, flared bell. From then on, European trumpets have been characterized by their long, cylindrical tube followed by a short, conical section. Perhaps these longer and shorter forms corresponded to the *tubae* and *tubectae* of silver ordered by Emperor Frederick II when he was in Arezzo in 1240; and the word *tubecta* may be a Latinized form of *trombetta*, mentioned by Dante.

Such early terms as *buisine, trompe,* or *tube* could designate indiscriminately both horn and trumpet, for the terminology was flexible in a period when lip-vibrated instruments were still in full development. The French word *trompe* was taken into English as "trumpe," to indicate a trumpet of brass. The growing number of names doubtless reflects not only extended use of trumpets at that time, but also discriminations of pitch; the *cleron* is mentioned in the thirteenth century together with *trompe* and *buisine*, its name already an indication of its higher range—not of a new instrument (. . . *cum tuba seu clarone*). Joinville, in his *Life of Saint Louis*, describes the sensation produced by the enemy's great clamor *de trompes, de nacaires* (kettledrums), *et de cors sarrazinois* in Egypt in 1250, intended to frighten the crusaders.

Despite the prevalence of Romance terms, the short trumpet continued to be known as *cor sarrazinois* up to the late fourteenth century, but its formidable aspects had been tempered with time and its use as a pastoral instrument is attested by a passage written in 1360: *2 bergiers dont l'un joue d'une fleute de saus et l'autre d'un cornet sarrazinois* ("two shepherds, one of whom plays a willow flute, and the other a small *cor sarrazinois*"). But at the same time it appears in the hands of court minstrels, for those of the Count of Poitiers, later Philip V, in 1313–1314 were a *ménestrel du cor sarrazinois*, two *trompéeurs*, a *ménestrel de naquaires ou tymballes*, a *ménestrel de trompette*. During the reign of Louis le Hutin as King of Navarre (1305–1316) payments were made to two minstrels listed as *trompeurs* (trumpeters), one minstrel of the nakers, one of the psaltery, and two whose instruments were not specified. Trumpet players were thus attached to princely houses in France as minstrels at a very early date, and at the same time their association with the kettledrum, here referred to as *naquaire* or *tymballe*, is already confirmed. Meanwhile primitive folk trumpets continued to divert the country populations: the Book of Hours of Jeanne d'Evreux (1325) shows a long and slender wooden tube to which a cowhorn is attached, complete with broad mouthpiece.

At about this time—around 1317—Giotto depicted straight trumpets made of three distinct sections, with very narrow tube and small bell, in his *Crowning of the Virgin*. Later in this century long trumpets are shown with banners suspended from bell to boss, and by 1380 the massing of trumpets at solemnities as bestowers of prestige had been developed. When Charles VI entered Reims he was preceded by more than thirty trumpets *qui sonnoient si clair que merveille*. But the great length of the straight trumpet was becoming a handicap, and by the end of the fourteenth century it was folded into an **S** shape, known as the *cor crochu* in French. A century later it had assumed the closer form we associate with the natural trumpet, and this was to remain the classical European instrument, standard until the end of the eighteenth century.

The late fourteenth and early fifteenth centuries were an era of major importance for the development of the trumpet, marking not only the creation of the modern folded trumpet, but also the transformation of the low-pitched model into the trombone: the first trombones were in fact called *trompettes saicqueboutte* ("sackbut trumpets"). These transformations may have taken place on French soil, where the

S-trumpet first appeared at the turn of the century, but is not seen in Italy until about 1420. Finally, problems caused by the trumpet's unique social status were resolved at the same time, with the instrument confirmed in its symbolism:

> Thou schalt be ryche whereso thou goo
> Men schul servyn the at mele
> With mynstralsye, and bemes blo

as Mundus tells Humanum Genus in *The Castell of Perseverance*, written about 1405 ("beme" is an Old and Middle English term for "trumpet").

Originally an attribute of worldly power in the East, the trumpet had been an instrument of princes and dignitaries, and was to retain this role in Europe until the eighteenth century. From the Middle Ages on, every self-respecting city had its own trumpeters, who were responsible to the municipal officers. Early in the seventeenth century the status of trumpeters in the German Empire was codified: only ruling princes, high nobility, cavalry forces (these were originally composed of noblemen, as they could afford to provide their own horses), and the Free Cities of the German Empire were permitted to retain trumpeters. Augsburg was the first town to receive an imperial privilege for keeping trumpeters—in 1434—at a time when other towns were permitted only to retain *Thürmer* (tower watchmen). Later, they also were granted privileges. Bitter rivalry ensued between those trumpeters who benefited from the promulgations of imperial privileges and the common musicians, including watchmen, as to limitations imposed upon use of the instrument, resulting in the organization of the privileged trumpeters into guilds with jealously guarded rights. Court trumpeters whose duties were secular rather than martial also participated in the court *Kapellen*, whence it was to be but a step to the opera.

According to the range in which they specialized, guild members were classified as clarin or principal players, the former consisting of the upper register of a trumpet, where the partials lie closely enough together to permit the playing of a scale, and for which a special mouthpiece was required. With the decay of the corporation system in the eighteenth century the days of the guild were over and the trumpet became free of restrictive practices. One duty of town trumpeter—often a tower watchman—as the town of Lübeck made clear to its new *Thürmer* in 1474, was *alle Abende zu blasen und zu spielen auf der*

Claritte wie es üblich gewesen (". . . to sound and play on the *clareta* as was formerly usual").

Trumpets folded into an **S** shape are commonly represented by the mid-fifteenth century, sometimes together with other forms. On the *Story of Holy Job* altarpiece in the Wallraf-Richartz Museum, Cologne, executed in 1485, Job's three friends are sounding as many different types of trumpet, one elongated and straight, another with a long fold running from near the mouthpiece to the base of the bell, and the third with a short fold in the center of the tube, ingeniously supported by the thumb on the far pipe, with main tube resting on the player's index finger, perhaps more elegant than practical a position. Giovanni Bellini's *Procession in Saint Mark's Square* (second half of the fifteenth century) includes players of straight, long trumpets with slightly flared bells, and also the newer folded model.

Another modification of the long trumpet took place at the mid-century, in northeast Europe to judge from the iconography, when a looped instrument appears. Two trumpeters in a battle scene of the Clovis Tapestries, completed about 1450, hold instruments that are cylindrical up to the terminal flare, made in sections with bosses at the joints, and bent into a rather small loop at the middle of the length; a short-lived but aesthetically satisfying variant. Another important modification of the fifteenth century was that changing the hitherto funnel-shaped termination into a modern, flared bell. But despite such improvements, old, straight models continued to be made until well into the sixteenth century in Italy.

Virdung (1511) includes woodcuts of three trumpets, which he calls *Feldtrumet, Clareta, Thurner Horn* ("field trumpet, *clareta*, wait's horn"). The first two are folded as the classical trumpet was to be, the *Thurner Horn* is still **S** shaped. His field trumpet had a wider bore than the more delicately built *clareta*, as well as a larger mouthpiece; that of the *clareta* is portrayed as almost funnel shaped. The "horn" of *Thurner Horn* was possibly a euphemism permitting tower watchmen to play an otherwise prohibited instrument, but more likely it was just a designation to differentiate the outdated model, still considered good enough for waits, from the newer version. As the field trumpets were not required to produce high clarin tones, one would expect them to have been shorter than the *clareta*, assuming that Virdung's *clareta* was indeed intended to emphasize the high register—although this relationship is not borne out by his woodcuts. However, in certain sixteenth-century Polish art works, mounted trumpeters are seen to carry distinctly shorter instruments than those on foot.

Clarin trumpets of the baroque had a bore slightly narrower than that of principal trumpets and were played with a broad, flat mouthpiece to facilitate the production of high partials. Nicot in 1606 states categorically that the *clairon* was the trumpet having the narrower tube, still in use among the Moors and among the Portuguese, who obtained it from them, and which elsewhere formerly served as treble to the tenor and bass trumpets. In another passage he defines the *clairon* as *la trompette claironnante pour estre gresle de tuyau* ("the trumpet clarion-voiced due to its narrow tube"); these passages were iterated by Furetière in the latter part of the century.

The secret art of tonguing was developed by the sixteenth century, and as early a writer as Agricola recommended that players learn the "diridiridē." Concurrently, the manufacture of brass instruments reached a high degree of perfection. Correspondence between the Nuremberg wind instrument maker Jorg Neuschel and his patron, Duke Albert of Prussia, affords insight into contemporary conditions; Neuschel received a large order in 1540, to include twelve German trumpets and twelve *welsche oder franczosische* ("Italian or French") trumpets, and a year later the Duke requested an estimate for a still larger order, including *12 deutzsche trommethen sampt mundstucken und claret-stucken, 12 welsche trummethen* ("twelve German trumpets with mouthpieces and clarin pieces, twelve Italian trumpets").

Nine months thereafter, Neuschel asks for information concerning the Duke's colors (for Albert was the first duke), so that the twelve *welsche* trumpets might be suitably "dressed," that is, provided with banners. (Banners and banner rings are seen on continental trumpets from the fifteenth century on, but are rarely appended to English instruments even at later dates.) Finally, in November 1545 Neuschel lists several royal patrons who had been satisfied with purchases from him of twelve German and twelve *welsche* trumpets and a pair of kettledrums; the Duke was not a generous prince, and Neuschel complains that he had to sit half a year making and matching a set of twelve trumpets, and that tuning them in unison was a great deal of work. It is not known wherein German trumpets differed from *welsch* models; from this correspondence it becomes clear, however, that German trumpets cost about half the price of Italian ones.

So marked a difference could not have been due to minor differences of pitch (i.e., length); there must have been either far more tubing involved, or more expensive materials, or both. The same terminology appears elsewhere, for the Württemberg court purchased 12 "trumpets" in 1583, another dozen in 1589, then 24 *welsche* trumpets in 1598. It is tempting to assume that these represented trumpet and trombone, a combination found at other sixteenth-century courts. Henry VIII had a corps of fifteen trumpeters and ten sackbut players, Elizabeth in 1571 had eighteen trumpeters and six sackbuts; toward the end of her reign the eighteen trumpeters were still employed, but the sackbuts had been reduced to two.

Folded trumpets were generally made of brass, on special occasions also of silver (for the coronation of Christian IV of Denmark in 1588 no fewer than sixty-four Danish and foreign trumpeters participated in the court festivities, all playing silver trumpets, some specially ordered from Nuremberg for the occasion); the metal was hammered on forms and then soldered, its joints concealed under ornamental garnishes with a boss or bell on the last joint. The embossed rim of the bell is known as a "garland," and it is here that a maker signs his handiwork. Brilliance of tone is due to the narrow and mainly cylindrical bore, and is enhanced by the even narrower clarin bore.

In their capacity as military instruments they were attached to the cavalry, and not only sounded signals and alarms but also helped maintain morale by their blaring. Chroniclers record that during the night preceding the battle of Agincourt (1415) the opposing armies lay in darkness and kept their spirits up by the continuous sound of their trumpets; the French regretted not having a sufficient quantity *pour eux resjouyr* and remained apprehensive. At court trumpeters functioned as heralds and couriers, accompanying their sovereign on journeys. They also played at the conclusion of their master's meals, and in provincial towns officials caused them to herald public proclamations and to play at ceremonial functions. From the 1560s on, trumpets were among the instruments played during dumb shows between acts in the English theater—for example, in Gascoigne's *Jocasta* (1566)—and an inventory of chattels of the Lord Admiral's Company at The Rose Theatre, taken in 1598, included three trumpets, a drum, and a sackbut; the company had paid eleven shillings and six pence for a drum, and twenty-two shillings for two trumpets a year later.

Their introduction to the opera took place in the first decade of the seventeenth century, in roles restricted at first to the playing of fanfares.

Monteverdi's *Orfeo*, performed in 1607 but not published until 1609, includes a toccata—called tucket in English at that time—for either four trumpets and kettledrums, or for five trumpets. The parts are designated as *clarino, quinto, alto e basso, vulgano, basso:* the age of specialization had set in. Seventeenth-century authors give the names of trumpet tones by which the parts were designated as follows:

Monteverdi (1609)		Praetorius (1619)	Fantini (1638)	Speer (1689)
C⁰		Fladder Grob	sotto basso	Flattergrob
c⁰	basso	Grob	basso	Grobstimme
g⁰	vulgano	Volgan	vurgano	Faul
c′		alter Bass	striano	Mittelstimme
e′	} alto e basso	(rare)		
		Alter-Bass	toccata	Prinzipal
g′	quinta	Principal or	quinta	Prinzipal
		Quinta or		
		Sonata		
c²	clarino	Clarin		Clarin (to g²)
				erster Clarin
				(to c³ or f³)

Praetorius's terminology is a clear reflection of Italian influence. In his *Syntagma* III he reports the use of trumpeters and kettledrums for *Sonades* in church, but adds a noteworthy warning: *Will/kan/oder darff man aber die Trommeten oder Heer-Paucken nicht gebrauchen . . .* ("If one does not wish/cannot/or may not employ trumpets and kettledrums . . ."), apparently with an eye to the guild. Trumpeters habitually play too fast, he wrote, because their instruments require so much wind, hence it is advisable for conductors to speed up slightly before trumpet entrances; the *Principal* or *Quinta,* sometimes called *Sonata,* is the tenor proper, he states, and directs and leads the whole ensemble of trumpets and kettledrums; the *Clarin* is the descant, and plays the melody line or the chorale, ornamenting it with running diminutions or coloraturas, as best he can; the *Alter-Bass* is like an alto and usually plays in thirds or fourths—rarely in fifths—with the *Principal* (this practice of doubling at a given interval was common; Kircher in 1650 furnished the upper part only of fanfares for two trumpets, with an annotation to the effect that the second player was to double the first at the interval of a lower third); the *Volgan* holds the fifth above the *Grob* and remains on one tone, g°; the *Grob* is the real bass and the foundation, and always plays c°; *Fladder*

Grob, finally, holds down the octave below the *Grob*, C°. It was customary for clarin and principal to move in octaves, particularly when playing chorales or other melodies. Clarin players who were familiar with chorales could play without music, but the *Alter-Bass* was advised to study his (independent) part; *Volgan, Grob, Fladder Grob*, and the kettle-drummer followed the principal player and did not require any music in order to find their parts. Indeed, most trumpeters could not read music, or, as Praetorius prefers to put it, they were musically inexperienced, and their repertoire as guild members was memorized without recourse to a written source. As to pitch, Praetorius states that formerly trumpets had been in D, a pitch still retained by field trumpeters, but that a few years before he wrote court trumpets had been lengthened so that their fundamental pitch was then C (Glareanus also considered the fundamental to be C).

When trumpets came to be played in ensembles with other instruments, problems of tuning and of pitch arose. Fine tuning was accomplished by terminal tuning bits, and for more radical changes—which amounted to transpositions—trombone crooks were attached. Praetorius in his *Polyhymnia* of 1619 discusses a piece of music in C, and suggests that if it is too high for the voice it should be transposed down a tone to B♭, in which case the trumpeters should put a whole-tone crook on their instruments; and a trumpet could also serve in soft-toned chamber music by introducing a mute, but as this raised the pitch by a whole tone, the trumpet could be restored to its natural pitch by means of a trombone crook. Foreseeing the possibilities of crooking to their logical conclusion, he suggested (*Puericinium*, 1621) the addition of trumpets to a piece written in G, but, because this tonality was a fourth lower than that of the trumpets, "I caused two whole-tone and one half-tone crooks (as one generally sets on a trombone)" to be added to the trumpets, thereby pitching them in G.

Some people, he reports (in *Syntagma* II) have trumpets wound like a post horn or snake (i.e., closely coiled) but these do not equal the regular trumpet in brilliance. He depicts such an instrument and calls it *Jäger-Trommet* ("hunter's trumpet"). A trumpet of this form appears in E. G. Haussmann's portrait of the Leipzig musician, Gottfried Reiche, painted prior to 1727 (an engraving of which is reproduced in Kinsky [1929]); Reiche holds the trumpet in one hand, and a sheet of music in the other hand contains a clarin part. This portrait has been cited as evidence for the use in the eighteenth century of closely coiled trumpets for clarin playing, yet such a practice is not otherwise documented. And on its sole authority, twentieth-century versions of this coiled type, provided with valves, have been made specially for Bach performances; they are less loud and far less brilliant than the folded natural trumpets.

Clarin playing, an art now dead, flourished in the seventeenth and eighteenth centuries, with the range usually divided between two players, one of whom specialized in the higher parts, the other in the lower parts, and both making use of special small-cupped, wide-rimmed mouthpieces. The middle parts, as well as military signals, were left to the principal players—field trumpeters were principal players—and the bass part was given to a bass player or to a kettledrummer. Altenburg, the last writer to treat of classical trumpet playing (1795) recognized two clarin, three principal parts, and one bass part. Girolamo Fantini, author of a trumpet tutor published in 1638, was also a remarkable clarin player, mastering the high ranges to a degree apparently unequaled by his contemporaries. From the title of his book it is clear that the trumpet had already become established in art music: *Modo per imparare a sonare/di tromba/ tanto di guerra/ quanto musicalmente in organo, con tromba sordina/col cimbalo e ogni altro instromento* ("Method for learning the trumpet not only in military but also in part music, with mute, together with a harpsichord or any other instrument"). He gives detailed instructions in the art of tonguing, the "pronouncing" of syllables by means of which the air flow is regulated (later this became a closely guarded secret among German guild players), and already made use of the eleventh harmonic, the trumpet's characteristically and notoriously weak tone, too low for $f\sharp^2$ but too high for f^2, and rarely encountered before the eighteenth century. Mersenne had received a report of Fantini's ability, apparently an erroneous one, and was puzzled at the overtone series he was credited with producing.

Mersenne furnishes a drawing of the wooden trumpet mute and notes that military trumpets were muted when the enemy was not supposed to hear the signals. Among his various suggestions was that of piercing tone holes in the yards in analogy to those of the serpent (more than a century later Kölbel was to apply tone holes and keys to the horn, but this destroyed its brilliance and fullness of tone), and that of learning to play a trumpet by the simple expedient of practicing on a detached mouthpiece; he also knew of a trombone-shaped trumpet, presumably a slide trumpet.

After the mid-century trumpets were increasingly admitted to opera;

the prologue to Cavalli's *Oronte* of 1656 contained an aria with trumpet obbligato, and in his *Artemisia* of the same year an aria was even accompanied by two trumpets; Legrenzi's *Eteocle e Polinice* of 1675 also called for trumpets. "Liberal fanfares of trumpet," as J. A. Westrup writes (1937), embellished songs and chorus of Purcell's martial *Dioclesian* of 1690; Alessandro Scarlatti frequently included trumpets in his operas of the last decade of the seventeenth century, and they were represented in Italian oratorios and cantatas from the same period on.

By the dawn of the eighteenth century composers had become aware of the trumpet's high register and had taken advantage of it, and, as long as the art of clarin playing flourished, this register was exploited for its brilliance. Christian Schubarth still associated its use with festive and majestic occasions in the 1780s. With the trumpets' entry into concerted music, tuning bits had been introduced for fine tuning, and crooks to alter the pitch by larger intervals. Tuning bits were straight metal tubes that lowered the pitch by lengthening the total tube length; but by adding one on top of another, the trumpet became too difficult to hold, so that bits came to be wound into a circle or else bent into a crook; but these had the disadvantage of making speech somewhat more difficult. Double crooks, the use of which had already been advocated by Praetorius, could lower the pitch by an interval as great as a third. Trumpets in England were usually in E♭, according to James Talbot, writing at the end of the seventeenth century, but could be crooked down to D, C, B, B♭, A, or A♭, as desired. In seventeenth- and eighteenth-century Germany, trumpets and cornetts were considered to be at choir pitch (*Chorton*) but could be crooked down a tone to chamber pitch (*Cammerton*), for *Chorton* C sounded at the same pitch as *Cammerton* D. Praetorius, it may be noted, uses the term *Cammerton* to denote the higher of the two pitches, contrary to other writers of his and later centuries, and to contemporary organ terminology. Whenever an organ was employed, it was of course imperative that all other instruments adapt themselves to its pitch, and some of the ensuing niceties of contemporary orchestration may be gleaned from a manuscript note to Kuhnau's cantata *Daran erkennen wir, dass wir in ihm verbleiben*, commenting (1) that the piece is set in B♭ choir pitch for strings, voices, and continuo; (2) that the trumpets are notated in C so that a tuning bit (*Aufsatz*) must be added at the mouthpiece to lower it to chamber pitch, and the kettledrums must be lowered down a tone to chamber pitch; and (3) that the oboes and bassoons must tune to chamber pitch, consequently, when their parts were copied they were transposed up a tone so as to agree (in pitch with the other instruments). Because orchestral trumpets were at *Chorton,* music written in *Cammerton* calling for their participation was set in D (*Cammerton*). Exceptionally, German trumpets of the period were pitched at *Feldton* ("field pitch"), a semitone higher than *Chorton;* these were considered to be in E♭ and could be crooked down to D choir pitch. A military F trumpet also existed; both this and the E♭ field trumpet were shorter than orchestral models, with the F trumpet sounding an octave higher than the horn.

Although the baroque trumpet had a theoretical range of four octaves, from C° to c³ (the fundamental was all but impossible to obtain), virtuoso clarin players could exceed this and continue the scale up to g³. Indeed, Adlung mentions a trumpeter who could bring forth g⁴ on his instrument, and sent information to this effect to Johann Walther for inclusion in the latter's dictionary. But Walther did not print it, either because of disbelief or forgetfulness.

Baroque trumpets were made of several sections soldered together, with the joints of yard and bow hidden by a garnish; however, more ornate trumpets may have had these joints fitted telescopically rather than soldered. Most players held their instrument with the right hand—by the boss if there was one—and, in order to better steady the embouchure, the mouthpipe passed to the right side of the bell pipe. For left-handed players this procedure was reversed. Sometimes pairs of left-handed and right-handed ceremonial trumpets are portrayed, and a matched pair by a member of the Haas family of trumpet makers is in the Gemeende Museet of The Hague. Requirements for clarin playing were an instrument of sufficient length, with a tube of at least 210 centimeters (7 feet), and a mouthpiece with shallow cup to facilitate the production of the higher harmonics. Throughout the seventeenth century a trumpet of about this length seems to have been standard, and baroque mouthpieces had longer shanks than do our modern ones. But by Mozart's day clarin playing was dead.

The last and very late writer to represent the tradition of eighteenth-century clarin playing, and to lament its passing, was Altenburg (1795). He no longer thought of trumpets as choir-pitch instruments in C, but rather as chamber pitched in D. German trumpets, he stated, were in D; the F trumpets were called French trumpets because they were played by the French (but see below) and were correspondingly shorter, and were also known as field trumpets in Germany; those in general use in

England, he informs us, were in G and were known in Italian as *tromba piccola*. In order to play in as large a number of tonalities as possible, and thereby increase the flexibility of the trumpet and kettledrum corps, different compromises were resorted to other than the employment of crooks; he cites the playing in A major by making use of a short English G trumpet and leaving a mute inserted, while a field trumpet could serve for performances of pieces in F, and the regular German trumpet could of course be crooked down to C, B♭, and B when necessary. French writers of the second half of the eighteenth century refer to their trumpets as commonly made in E, the tonality of marches and military ceremonies; they could be crooked down to E♭ and D, whereas trumpets in F could be obtained only on special order. It may be inferred that the E of French trumpets sounded at chamber pitch F of German ones, which would reconcile Altenburg's remark anent French trumpet pitches.

But neither compounded crooks nor different-sized instruments could overcome the need for a chromatic trumpet. The slide trumpet, by no means a new invention at this time, was one answer, and is discussed on page 805. Attempts were also made to provide the trumpet with tone holes, as Mersenne had suggested long before. A London correspondent of the *Allgemeine musikalische Zeitung* wrote in 1815 that some thirty years previously a British court trumpeter had played on a trumpet with tone holes, and that Dr. Close, the physicist, had devised horns and trumpets with seven tone holes but no keys for military purposes, the lack of keys being in order to avoid damage to instruments when played mounted, as military instruments often got rough treatment. This report is not altogether fictitious. German mounted trumpeters are rumored to have had a secret vent on their instrument, hidden by the wrapped cordage, and this was apparently true in some instances.

But more to the point is an English silver trumpet of 1787, made by William Shaw, with vents permitting changes of tonality. Of the four vents on the lower yard, three are covered by rotating sleeves, and the fourth by a key. Each raises the pitch by the interval of a fifth when uncovered, provided it is used in conjunction with the proper tube length: uncrooked in E♭, opening the first vent puts the trumpet in B♭ above; with a half-tone crook for D, the second vent puts it in A; with a whole-tone crook for C, the third vent puts it in G; and crooked to B♭, the key gives F. Such a system by no means abolished the cumbersome crooking but it did permit one change of tonality without a crook, and offered a relatively wide choice of tonalities with only three crooks. Perhaps it was to one of Shaw's trumpets that the Leipzig paper's correspondent referred.

Finally, around 1780, the *Inventionstrompete* was brought out, invented jointly by Michael Wöggel of Karlsruhe and by the well-known keyboard instrument maker, Johann Andreas Stein of Augsburg, an application of the mechanism of the *Inventionshorn* (see page 757). This short-lived version was followed by the "Chromatic trumpet and French horn" of Charles Claggett, prototype of later duplex instruments. Claggett's model, patented in 1788, was a double trumpet—or double French horn—consisting of two trumpets (or horns), one pitched in E♭, the other in D, and played with a common mouthpiece that could be switched instantly from the tube of one to that of the other. This in turn was supplanted by the *Stopftrompete* (*trompette demi-lune* in French), a natural trumpet of elongated half-moon shape, built in the first quarter of the nineteenth century and designed for transferring the hand-in-bell horn technique to the trumpet. One reason for its failure was too great a discrepancy between the open and the stopped tones. A keyed trumpet was built in 1801, devised by the Vienna court trumpeter Anton Weidinger, and originally made by Joseph Felix Riedl of Vienna, intended for bridging the gap between the second and the third harmonics (G and C). Shaped like the natural trumpet, it had fifteen closed keys, probably inspired by the earlier keyed horn of Kölbel, of which it was an extension. During the first half of the nineteenth century keyed trumpets were adopted in Austrian and Italian military bands, and introduced into opera in 1829 by Rossini in *Guillaume Tell*. The brevity of their success was partly due to the muffled tone resulting from side holes and soft pads, but above all to the invention of the valve (Leonardo da Vinci, who died in 1519, drew a straight trumpet with what look suspiciously like valves).

The first valves were square boxes of copper and were fitted to the cylindrical section of the tube, at first two of them, later three. Valved trumpets were built in F, and by 1828 also in E♭ and high B♭, the latter for German orchestras. By 1840 the valved trumpet had a place in most German opera houses. The F trumpet became rapidly popular in that country but was not adopted until later in France, where it first had to meet the competition of the *cornet à pistons* (cornet). However, by the end of the century it was being discarded in favor of the C and D models. Nineteenth-century England was particularly addicted to the slide trumpet, both in orchestral and military band, and little attention was paid to the ordinary trumpet there until the 1880s.

From the late nineteenth century on, makers started bringing out special trumpets for performance of the clarin parts of classical scores. Many of these were, and still are, known as "Bach trumpets." Some makers acted in the mistaken belief that their products constituted a true reproduction of the early-eighteenth-century trumpet, whereas their fundamental was actually an octave, a tenth, or even a thirteenth higher. One of these was a straight model in A, a fifth above the classical D trumpet, furnished with two valves; Mahillon of Brussels made a sopranino in d° both in straight and in folded form; yet another version was the "little F" trumpet pitched still a third higher. In the present century Otto Steinkopf of Berlin has recently introduced a very small, spirally coiled model.

Today the three-valve B♭ trumpet, pitched a sixth higher than the classical trumpet, is the most commonly used. Western Europe and the United States also avail themselves of the B♭ and C trumpet, a C trumpet that can be lowered to B♭; there exists a similar combination E♭ and D trumpet. Piston valves are now in use everywhere except for German-speaking countries and eastern Europe, where the rotary valve is preferred.

The Slide Trumpet

Efforts to meet the need for a chromatic scale on trumpets occupied and preoccupied makers for many a century, and one outcome of their experiments was to furnish them with slides. The trombone bears witness to their early success, for it is in effect nothing but a large slide trumpet.

Several German inventories of the late sixteenth and early seventeenth centuries mention the *Zugtrompete* ("slide trumpet"), sometimes together with the trombone, so that confusion of the two is not possible (a Marburg inventory of about 1601, for instance, lists as "new instruments" a case of flutes, two slide trumpets, a trombone, three straight cornetts, three shawms, and a wait's horn of brass). The word *Zugtrompete* has been matched in modern times with instruments seen in certain Italian, Flemish, and German pictures of the early fifteenth to the mid-sixteenth centuries, trumpets with elongated mouthpieces, the player holding his instrument with one hand, his mouthpiece with the other. Finally, a trumpet in Berlin dated 1651 has a very long mouthpiece that can be pulled out for 56 centimeters (22 inches) and will lower the pitch by as much as a third. This has been designated as a *tromba da tirarsi* (Italian for "slide trumpet").

However, neither pictorial materials nor the surviving trumpet itself can be considered representative of the slide trumpet; as far as the instrument is concerned, a sliding mouthpiece would in practice not stay in place while shifting larger intervals, and would be particularly troublesome in fast tempi—not to mention the problem of keeping a mobile shank airtight. As to illustrations, they show that the straight trumpet was played in precisely the same manner: one hand holding the mouthpiece to the player's mouth, the other supporting the instrument further along the tube. Good examples of this position are seen not only in European paintings but also in those of India, for example on a seventeenth-century Mogul miniature depicting the birth of the emperor Jahangir, preserved in the Victoria and Albert Museum, London; and a temple trumpet of southern India that lacks a mouthpiece is held with the end of the tube pressed against the player's lips. In other words, the fact that a trumpet is supported close to the mouth does not indicate the presence of a slide. *The Birth of Christ* by Jacob Cornelisz van Oostzanen of 1512 depicts both a folded and a straight trumpet held as described; and a pair of trumpeters, one left-handed, the other right-handed, in Hans Holbein the Younger's *Old Testament* series of woodcuts of 1523 are also holding the mouthpiece with one hand, the tubing with the other.

The question is a vexing one. Bach calls for a *tromba o corno da tirarsi* in Cantatas nos. 46 (*Schauet doch und sehet*) and 67 (*Halt in Gedächtniss*), and the parts for this instrument are not playable on the regular trumpet of Bach's day. Several alternative possibilities present themselves: one was a tenor trombone furnished with a trumpet mouthpiece; another was the instrument referred to by Kuhnau in 1700 as a *Trompete . . . nach ietziger Invention eingerichtet . . . dass sie sich nach Art der Trombonen ziehen lässt . . .* ("trumpet . . . arranged according to the present *Invention* . . . that can be pulled in the manner of trombones"). This was probably the same instrument as the slide trumpet of which Altenburg (1795) was to write later that ordinarily the tower watchmen and *Kunstpfeifer* used it for playing chorales, and that it was made like an alto trombone because *weil während dem Blasen hin und her gezogen wird* ("it was pulled and pushed while blown"). Altenburg, it should be noted, was preoccupied with reminiscences of his youth, the end of the "noble and heroic" period of trumpet playing, and was more concerned with the lamented past than with the present, in which he was obviously ill at ease. One further choice was the "flat trumpet" of late-eighteenth-century England, for which, among others, Purcell scored—in "A full anthem, Sung at the Funerall solemnity of

Queen Mary, 1694, accompanied with flat Mournfull Trumpets," and of which a single specimen, dated 1691, survives. Talbot (ca. 1700) gives valuable information concerning this model, after which it disappears:

In a Flat Trumpet the mouthpiece stands oblique towards right. 2nd Crook placed near left Ear & by it you draw out Inward yards, whereof one reaches to the Boss of the Pavillion [bell], the other to the 1st crook: its size with the yards shutt the same with common Trumpet. The crook at one end is joynted to an additional yard which incloses the fixed 2nd yard from the joynt of the 1st Crook to the beginning of the 2nd . . .

thereby disposing of the idea that an elongated mouthpiece shank served as slide, or that a slide was inserted at the mouthpiece. Talbot gives the range of a flat trumpet as from c° to c³, fully chromatic, far more concentrated if less extensive than that of the contemporary regular trumpet, and one that would permit Bach's *tromba da tirarsi* parts to be played on it.

Slide trumpets were still, or again—we do not know which—in use in the latter part of the eighteenth century. Laborde (1780) wrote of trumpets made with slides in the manner of the new horns—the reference here is to the *cor à l'anglaise*, a horn fitted with both tuning slide and crooks—and the *Encyclopédie* of three years later noted that they were preferable for orchestral playing. At about this time a modified version of the flat trumpet appeared in England, introduced by John Hyde, a trumpet major, in 1798 (Hyde claimed invention of the chromatic trumpet, but cf. the flat trumpet, above). Pitched in F, it was provided with the same crooks as the regular trumpet—E, Eb, D, C—as well as tuning bits, but the U bend connecting middle pipe and bell pipe was made so as to slide telescopically, being drawn back by the player's hand and released by means of a spring; but whereas the bell pipe of ordinary trumpets was held uppermost, on these instruments it was lowest.

Slide trumpets became the standard orchestral trumpets of nineteenth-century England: Covent Garden still utilized them in 1882, and they continued to be taught at the Kneller Hall School of Military Music as late as 1892. Indeed, they were occasionally used in the orchestra during the first decade of the twentieth century. On earlier nineteenth-century instruments the mechanism was generally controlled by two watch springs. A variety known as the Regent's bugle was built by 1815, both by Percival and by other London makers to the specifications of Johann Georg Schmidt, solo trumpeter of the Prince Regent. Designed to look and to sound like a bugle, it was actually a short and wide-bored slide trumpet in F, played with a deep cup mouthpiece, and probably owed its existence to the rivalry between Schmidt and John Distin, who popularized the keyed Kent bugle. The slide, with its 6 to 9 centimeter (2½ to 3½ inches) extension could lower the pitch by the interval of a fourth. In 1825 John Shaw took out a patent for "transverse spring slides for trumpets, trombones, French horns, bugles, and every other instrument of like nature." In the course of the nineteenth century many ordinary trumpets were cut down and rebuilt as slide trumpets in F, and the early clock springs gave way to spiral springs, ultimately to be replaced by elastic cords.

These types of instrument were not played on the Continent, where the regular trumpet was never neglected. Nonetheless, French makers brought out slide-trumpet models of their own in the first quarter of the nineteenth century. Legram, a Parisian regimental bandmaster, designed around 1820 a trumpet with slide that could be extended by two, four, or six and one-half *pouces* (inches) to lower the pitch by a semitone, tone, or three semitones, respectively, and in 1821 Schmittschneider of Paris patented his *trompette-trombone*, a trumpet with slide pushed forward like that of a trombone. But such instruments were rarely used, and today all slides trumpets are obsolete except for the very earliest of the entire series: the trombone.

The Trombone

One of the chief characteristics of fifteenth-century music is, from an organological point of view, the increasingly low pitches called for by composers. Not only did this necessitate further expansion of the organ compass, but it must also be held accountable for the creation of the bass trumpet, or trombone. When due to the demands for increasing depth the large S-shaped trumpet of the late fourteenth century became unwieldy, it was transformed into a *trompette saicqueboute* ("pull-push trumpet"), abbreviated in English to sackbut, known in Italian as *trombone* (augmentative of *tromba*), in German as *Posaune*, a corruption of *busîne*, Middle High German name for the trumpet. This development probably took place at the Burgundian court at the turn of the fourteenth to fifteenth century.

Trumpets of the late fourteenth century were shaped like a very flat S and were sometimes provided with a long-shanked mouthpiece; by transforming this into a mouthpipe, and the S curve into a U curve, the trombone came into existence. Virtually unchanged in form since then, modern instruments have the mouthpipe fixed to a parallel yard by a cross stay, while two outer tubes, joined at the lower end by a crook (called *potence* in French), slide telescopically over them. Early trombones had funnel-shaped bells, and these were retained until the eighteenth century, since when the bell has flared out; also, they were formerly made of far thinner metal. But the principle of telescopic slides has remained unchanged: when the slide is pulled back all the way, that is, toward the player, it is said to be in first position; in a Bb′ trombone this will sound the fundamental (Bb′) and its harmonics; if the slide is then pushed out a few inches it is said to be in second position, and its fundamental will then sound a semitone lower, or A′, and the harmonics will be those of A′, and so on. The three lowest fundamentals, however, can only be produced with difficulty.

State documents of the Burgundian court record the presence from 1421 on of a minstrel trumpeter, and in 1423 and 1425 his instrument, the *trompette de menestrel* was played together with *chalemies* and *bombardes* (shawms and bombards); later, the combination of shawm, bombard, and trombone was to become a standard form of outdoor ensemble, and the Burgundian references may already pertain to the new instrument. Toward the end of the century Tinctoris was to write of its use for the low parts of "loud" music. Its first unequivocal representation dates from the first half of the fifteenth century, while the term *sacqueboute* occurs from 1466 on in the sense of a musical instrument (for *saqueboute* was originally the name of a lance with a curved hook for disarming the opponent), and in 1468 the Duke of Burgundy's minstrels included a *trompette saicqueboute*, according to Olivier de la Marche, the Burgundian chronicler. The English term "sackbut" appears from 1470 on.

These older names continued in use until the eighteenth century, side by side with the Italian term *trombone*. "Shakbushes" were played at the court of Henry VII in 1495, and twenty years later the English court employed two "shakbushes" in addition to nine trumpeters; in 1513 trumpets, drummers, and sackbuts accompanied Henry VIII to France. Trombones of this time could be dismantled for ease of transportation, but their music was not restricted to fanfares or to participation in outdoor ensembles, for they were welcome adjuncts to mixed groups of singers and supporting instruments, and were often coupled with cornetts.

By the late sixteenth century trombones were being made in three sizes:

an alto in f° (or, with its slide pulled out, in B°), a tenor in B♭° (E° with slide out), and a bass in E♭° (with slide out, in A′), so that the three thus formed a continuous scale. The tenor was then, and has been ever since, the type instrument, and the word trombone without further qualification always denotes the tenor member of the family, a usage underscored in Germany by referring to it as the *gemeine Posaune* or the *rechte Posaune*, the common, or proper, trombone. A second and a tierce trombone are mentioned at Stuttgart in 1589, the tierce possibly pitched a minor third below the tenor, in G° (subsequently a bass in G° became standard in England).

Attempts at constructing a contrabass were made from the early seventeenth century on. According to Praetorius (1619) these fell into two categories: the first exemplified by a trombone twice as long as the tenor and pitched an octave lower, in B♭′, built by Hans Schreiber "four years ago"; the second type was less long but had slightly thicker tubing, and crooks for the deep tones (*Krummbügel*), and had been in service in various *Kapellen* for years, he reports. A contrabass by Isaac Ehe of Nuremberg, dated 1612, closely resembles Praetorius's drawing, and Jan Brueghel's *Hearing* of about 1620 in the Prado, with its double crook, comes very near his description of the second type of contrabass.

Such instruments were known in seventeenth-century England as double sackbuts and are referred to in a Campion masque of 1607. Quart and quint basses, in F′ and E′, respectively, were also made on the Continent at this time. Later in the century a soprano was added, pitched an octave above the tenor, but its acceptance was limited and it was soon to be replaced by the cornett; often it was confused with the alto trombone (Purcell's March and Canzona for four trombones of 1695 make use of a soprano). Minor adjustments of pitch could be made on all these instruments by terminal tuning bits, or the pitch could be lowered by half tones by means of crooks. As trombones participated in ensembles with other instruments early in their existence, these transposing crooks were fitted to them before they were applied to the trumpet, and in fact were transferred to the trumpet in the early seventeenth century.

Long after the trombone had been accepted in its own right and recognized as an instrumental entity, memories of its origin as a trumpet lingered on. Thus the *Mémoires des antiquités de Normandie* for 1614 note *une saqueboute ou trompette de six pièces en fin étain* ("a sackbut or trumpet of six pieces in fine tin"), and Mersenne still referred to it as a *trompette harmonique*. Perhaps this is the reason for the trombone's occupying a relatively high position in the instrumental hierarchy, although it never quite attained the status of the trumpet. Stuttgart town musicians for example, were forbidden in 1618 to play cornetts or trombones at "common" weddings, but might avail themselves only of fiddles and other stringed instruments on such occasions.

The contrabass was discarded in the course of the seventeenth century, and the soprano did not prove itself viable; its very short slide made it difficult to position a desired interval accurately, and the narrow bore must have caused the tone to be thin and even nasal. Consequently a consort of alto, tenor, and bass ranges remained. But as not even the alto was of sufficiently sure intonation, and the bass proved cumbersome, the tenor had become the solo player's choice when Praetorius wrote. Lack of flare in the bell, use of thicker metal, and flatter and more narrowly bored mouthpieces were responsible for the mellower and far softer timbre of older trombones, making them perfectly acceptable to small ensembles or even as an accompaniment to voice or strings; Paul Hainlein records in his diary that while in Venice in 1647 he heard in the Church of Saints Giovanni and Paolo an ensemble of four trombones and a single alto singer, with another singer echoing him from afar.

Then, when cornetts came to replace the higher-pitched trombones, the combination of cornett and trombone became a favorite ensemble until the early nineteenth century. Commenting on the role of the trombone in England, Talbot wrote (ca. 1700) that "the chief use of Sackbutt in England is in consorts with our Waits or English Hautbois. It was left off towards the latter end of K.Ch. 2nd & gave place to the Fr. bassoon . . ." (Charles II had died in 1685). Talbot limits his comments to the tenor and bass instruments.

Little is heard of the trombone during most of the eighteenth century. Mattheson (1713) stated that it was rarely heard outside the church, and Majer (1732) confined it to "churches and solemnities." If we are to believe him, the tenor and bass of his day had only four positions, an implication that the full seven were no longer available, and the alto and quint sizes had only three. Halle (1764) still knew, or knew of, soprano, alto, tenor, and the quart and quint basses, and specifies that the quart bass was at organ (i.e., choir) pitch. Burney (1785) reports on the difficulty of finding players of the "sacbut or double trumpet" for the Handel festival, and in the same decade Schubart noted that the trombone was neglected and played only by cornettists.

With redesigned bell, trombones staged an effective comeback in the late eighteenth century when they entered the orchestra as alto in E♭, tenor in B♭, and bass in E♭ (a rarer F bass is still played in Germany). In classical scores these were notated in alto, tenor, and bass clefs.

Among the more important innovations of the nineteenth century were the double slide and the valve. The former was invented in France with the object of obtaining all seven positions on so long an instrument with greater ease, and consisted of four parallel yards that made it possible to diminish by half the length required between each position; unfortunately it proved almost impossible to make them airtight, and hence the system was a failure. The double slide was in fact a reinvention, for a double-slide trombone by Jobst Schnitzer of Nuremberg, dated 1612, is in the instrument collection of Leipzig University. Valves also were a failure, but for tonal rather than for mechanical reasons; perhaps it is better to qualify them as a partial failure, for they remain in restricted use in several countries, furnished with three or four valves, but the natural instrument is by far the favorite.

The first valved trumpets were made experimentally in 1818, and further efforts led to the combination B♭/F trombone, produced from the 1830s on (called *Tenor/Bass Posaune* in German); this was a B♭ tenor fitted with an F "attachment" consisting of about 1 meter (40 inches) of coiled tubing brought into play by a rotary valve. By means of this valve an instrument normally in B♭ was lowered to F, and a similar attachment permitted the English bass in G to be switched to D. The Brussels Conservatoire houses a bell-in-air (upright) trombone in B♭ with five valves, transposable to an instrument in F by the fifth valve. One of Adolphe Sax's experiments resulted in the creation, in 1850, of his *trombone saxomnitonique*, which, by means of six piston valves and of seven separate bells, united seven instruments in one. Later in the century Chaussier's omnitonic system, originally devised for the horn, was transferred to the trombone, only to be abandoned shortly thereafter.

Another form of valved trombone was the *tromba contralta* in F, built in trumpet form and played with a trumpet mouthpiece. This was an invention of Rimski-Korsakov, and was introduced by him in his opera-ballet *Mlada* in order to obtain fullness and clarity of the low tones. More conservative valved models were developed and gained acceptance, among which was the *trombone da tracolla*, or shoulder-belt trombone, an instrument in helicon form intended for use by mounted bands; it encircles the player's neck and was formerly in use among Dutch military bicycle bands. A contrabass in helicon form with a slide mechanism, presumably

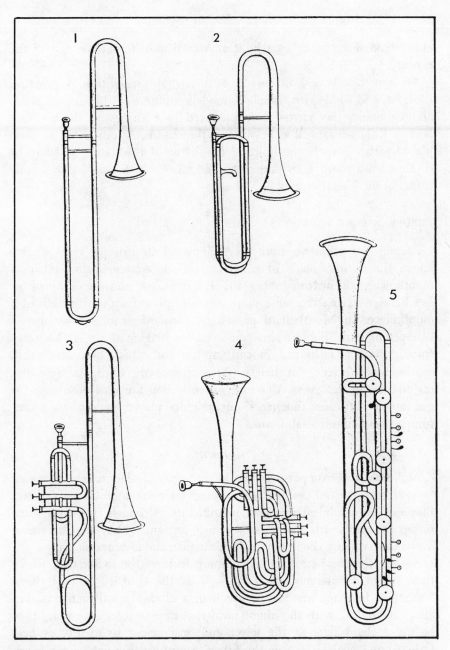

Trombones: (1) classical; (2) with double slide; (3) valved (by Riedl of Vienna); (4) vertical *trombone saxomnitonique* of Adolphe Sax; (5) *Bimbonifono* of Giovacchino Bimboni. From *Atti dell'Accademia del R. Istituto Musicale di Firenze*. Vol. 13, 1875.

also intended for bands, was built at Markneukirchen at the end of the century.

Modern trombones are made to three-bore specifications: narrow, medium, and wide, with wide-bore models common in the United States and Germany, the narrow bore preferred in France, and the medium bore in England as well as in most rhythm bands. A resurrected soprano played with a cornet mouthpiece joins the usual alto, tenor, and bass of rhythm bands, and goes under the abominable name of soprano slide cornet in the United States.

EUROPEAN FOLK TRUMPETS

Among the primitive trumpets still played in Europe, rural France knows the *burloir*, made of wood and in megaphone form, lacking a mouthpiece, an instrument of the Bourbonnais, and the *pihurne* of Les Landes, having the same shape and also played without benefit of a mouthpiece. In Montbéliard patois the *corniard* denotes a shepherd's trumpet of bark. Bark is also employed for making the rural Yugoslav *truba*, which is fashioned in early spring and which may attain 150 centimeters (5 feet) in length. Megaphone-type trumpets were not uncommon in the Swiss Alps until recently, but are now obsolescent if not obsolete. Other shepherds' instruments played over a wide area form a group known as alphorns.

Alphorns

Alphorns are trumpets of considerable age encountered in mountainous districts only, where because of their superior carrying power they can be employed as signal instruments. Although they have been linked by name with the Alps ever since antiquity, they are also found in the Carpathians, the Pyrenees, in Lithuania, and in Scandinavia.

Alphorns everywhere have as common features the material of which they are made, namely wood, as well as the conicity of their bore. Variations in shape are just as much of a chronological factor as they are geographical, with the oldest form that of a straight expanding tube having a slight flare at the lower end, insufficient to qualify as bell. Others are S shaped, as was the fifteenth-century trumpet, or are shortened by being folded like the natural trumpet, but most alphorns met within the Alpine regions today are straight, with an upturned bell. A typical modern Swiss instrument (with upturned bell) measures from

1½ meters to 4 meters (5 to 13 feet) and is made of two detachable sections so that it can be taken apart for transportation. Formerly all were played with a mouthpiece recessed into the instrument proper, rather like that of a mute cornett, but in many areas a separate cup mouthpiece is now common.

The alphorn was known to the Romans; Tacitus called it the *cornu alpinus*. In postclassical times this was changed to *lituus alpinus*, which term, abbreviated to *Liti*, is the name by which it was known in the canton of Unterwalden until about 1820. According to local tradition, Swiss alphorns were already used as signal instruments in certain villages in the fourteenth century. In the sixteenth century their length is given as eleven feet, at which time they were depicted as straight instruments held vertically. Praetorius illustrates one in the seventeenth century, also a straight model. As recorded in a 1689 description of their manufacture, alpine instruments were then fashioned from a log split lengthwise and hollowed out; the sections were then glued together with pitch and finally were bound with cherry bark.

Methods of both making and playing were simplified in the nineteenth century, when the bore was burned out of a single log—a young fir was preferred—and bound with bark or fir roots or even with cane; the bell was made separately and then fitted on. At the mid-century a separate, turned mouthpiece was inserted, and the length became standardized for a time to some 3 meters (10 feet). The old, straight form was played in the cantons of Appenzell and Schwyz, that with upturned bell did not develop until the eighteenth century and was native to the Bernese *Oberland*, and the folded, natural-trumpet shape was played in Uri, Unterwalden, and Schwyz. In Austria the old form maintained itself up to the nineteenth century but is extinct now.

Alphorns of all areas are made in the manner described; in most regions where they occur they are shepherds' instruments, but in Lithuania they were folk as well as signal instruments, and as such participated in processions, at weddings, and at other festivities; in the western Carpathians only women and children sound them.

The pedal tone (fundamental) cannot be obtained, but the Swiss alphorn yields from the second to the eighth harmonic or more, and a well-made instrument up to the sixteenth with ease. The fourth harmonic is typically too high and hence known as "Alphorn fa." In Switzerland cow herders formerly sounded their alphorn to assemble their herds and to communicate with one another, and in the nineteenth century it was still intoned as a signal for evening prayer in Catholic regions. But today it is chiefly a tourist and music hall attraction.

The idea of making such unwieldy instruments in different sizes, and tuning them for the performance of part music, seems to have originated with Ferdinand Huber of Switzerland, who in 1826 caused three alphorns to be tuned for ensemble performance; outside of Switzerland, two- and three-part playing was also practiced in Styria in the nineteenth century.

TRUMPETS IN ASIA

Unlike the trumpets of modern Europe, those of Asia never developed into musical instruments in the true sense of the word, as their potential range was not exploited. With only one, or at most two, tones at the player's disposal, trumpets were limited to temple and ceremonial use in the East, and in western Asia also to martial noisemaking and signaling. On the Asian continent distinctions can still be made between primitive bamboo instruments, those of bone, and, finally, those of metal. While European trumpets are characterized by a cylindrical bore for the greater part of their length, those of Asia are conoid, or else built up of cylindrical sections having different bores (stepped bores).

Bamboo is still in use among the Garo of Assam, who attach a curved buffalo horn to the lower end in order to form a bell. Another tribal people of Assam, the Naga, make their trumpets of several bamboo sections that telescope into one another, and to which they affix a bell of animal horn. Mouthpieces are lacking. Telescoping trumpets are typical of East Asia; in the high-culture areas these are of metal, but on Amboina and northern Celebes, bamboo forms the tubing of a relatively sophisticated trumpet made by partly inserting a tube into a larger one having the diameter of a man's arm and closed at the bottom; changes of pitch are obtained by moving the larger, distal, tube back and forth. Wood is the material of one of China's numerous trumpets, the *ta t'ung kyo*, when it is destined to serve in funeral processions, but for other occasions it is made of metal.

A human femur covered with human or yak skin constitutes a ritual trumpet of Tibet, to which a copper bell is sometimes added; often it is decorated with semiprecious stones and metal bands, and it is furnished with a mouthpiece of brass or copper. A similar instrument, also of Tibet, is made from a human tibia and is nowadays a mendicant's instrument. Further east, among the Kalmuck, a trumpet of human bone is also found. All of these were originally connected with the cult.

Metal trumpets are made in a variety of shapes: straight, long trumpets are blown pairwise, yet those of other forms may be played singly. Hooked trumpets, that is, those with a turned-back bell such as those known to the West in antiquity, appear briefly in Indian sculpture of the first century B.C., with zoomorphic bell, only to disappear thereafter. In China the popular form of the *la pa* has a curved-back bell, and the Cantonese *cha chiao* terminates in a hook, with flared bell.

The S-shaped *turya* of India is virtually identical to the earlier European natural trumpet, down to boss and bell. Like the *dhudka*, another S-shaped trumpet of the subcontinent with conical bore ending in a flare, and ornamental bosses concealing the joints, its serpentine aspect is enhanced by the position in which it is held, with bell high above the player's head. The possibility of a western Asiatic origin for these instruments cannot be dismissed, as curved trumpets were once played in Turkey. Older instruments, judging from miniatures of the Mogul epoch, had a long section of cylindrical tubing prior to the curve, a flaring bell, and greater overall length than later instruments. If unfolded they would have been longer than the contemporary straight trumpets with which they appear in outdoor wind and percussion ensembles, and that is doubtless the reason for which they were bent in the first place.

Long, straight trumpets with conical bore, known variously as *qarna* in Persia, as *kornai* in Turkistan, *karana* in northern India, are believed to have been introduced from western Asia; they are always played in pairs and are ceremonial instruments of princes and priests alike. They are depicted in Mogul miniatures with the player's right arm supporting the tube as far from the body as can conveniently be reached, while the left hand steadies it at the mouth—in exactly the same position some primitive trumpets are held by South American Indians, and as the long trumpet was depicted in Renaissance Europe. Southern India has a straight, cylindrical trumpet with conical bell of a type seen in Java about 1300, played in pairs, but with one peculiarity, namely, that one player sounds both instruments simultaneously. As mouthpieces are absent, the rim of the tube is pressed against the player's lips.

Mongolia and Tibet have a number of exceptionally long trumpets, often made in two or more telescoping sections, temple instruments always played in pairs. They were adopted by China, and although India was less influenced by them, it took at least one of its tubular trumpets from Mongolia. Red copper is the favored material for all these models. The conical tube of the Tibetan *dung chen* is so long it must rest on the ground or else be supported. Another Tibetan trumpet is made of several sections of conical tubing that telescope into one another and terminate in a large bell; because of its great length the bell end is either supported on a frame or held up by a novice. Its function is to sustain long tones in monastic services and mystery plays. Its Mongolian counterpart attains the extreme length of some 4.8 meters (16 feet) and its bell end is consequently given like treatment during performances. The long trumpets of northern China retained their position as temple instruments and were also played in pairs; with conical bore, sometimes exceeding 2.5 meters (10 feet) in length, they also were made of telescoping sections, and, as in Tibet, they were played with flat, disklike mouthpieces. Shorter versions of the *ta t'ung kyo* have become military and signal instruments in recent years, only one tone being sounded. Under its popular Chinese name of *la pa*, the Mongolian and Tibetan *ra pal* is probably the best known of all Oriental trumpets to the Western museum visitor. At its most compact, that is, when telescoped together, it measures about 1.5 meters (5 feet) and is distinguished by having a large bell. Japan inherited the *ta t'ung kyo* from China and modified it, making it at first of wood, long and heavy enough to require support during performance. In lieu of a bell, the modern version, which is of metal, has a long cylinder of wood or of metal into which the main section telescopes; it is played with a shallow, wide-rimmed mouthpiece like that of China. Still a ritual trumpet, it is a participant in funeral processions, but always in pairs.

TRUMPETS OF AFRICA

African trumpets are either endblown or sideblown. Those which are endblown emit either a single tone or they may additionally overblow the octave. They are considered symbols of virility but also heralds of death, and according to the observations of K. P. Wachsmann (1953) they are also associated with the cult of cattle. In some areas, notably in Uganda, regalia trumpets are linked to the institution of kingship (kettledrums are also linked to kingship there).

The original function of trumpets as voice distorters has already been mentioned; this age-old usage is still alive in Africa and may be observed in the northern Congo area among the Mbae, where the *kabile* trumpet, named for the *kabile* initiation rites at which it serves, is made from the hollow stem of the umbrella-wood tree, its upper end closed by a dried leaf and a lateral hole pierced nearby, into which the player sings or shouts; the disguised voice is then proclaimed to the uninitiated to be that of the *kabile* spirit. Secret society members among the Bambara of Mali employ for their rites narrow trumpets of iron into which they breathe, thus speaking mystically into the ear of their god Ko Man, while other initiates shake gourd rattles to provide rhythm for the dancers.

Nearly all trumpets of Negro Africa are sideblown. In South Africa endblown examples are so rare that Kirby (1934) considered a hooked, endblown trumpet of that region, named *icilongo*, to have undergone European influence; made of a bamboo tube, its lower end is fitted with an oxhorn. Among East African endblown instruments the *eggwara* of the Ganda may be mentioned: it consists of a conical and slightly curved tubular gourd provided with a gourd bell, the whole instrument then being encased in cowskin (*eggwara* is also the name of a sideblown trumpet of the Soga of Uganda, made of a conical gourd and likewise skin covered).

In the Moslem north and northwest, straight, endblown trumpets of metal predominate, diffused from the northeastern coastal area westward and thence south. From the eleventh century on the *nafir*, to give it its Arabic and Persian name, wandered westward, and still retains both name and identity in Morocco, that of an elongated, cylindrical metal trumpet with a bell, the trumpet of Ramadan, rarely played at other times (except at Fez, where it is sounded on important occasions). The *nafir* yields only the fundamental, sounded in blasts to coincide with the accented beats of an accompanying drum. Apart from its greater length—it varies from 130 to 150 centimeters (ca. 4 to 5 feet)—it is strikingly similar in form to the ancient Egyptian trumpets of Tutankhamen. The Hausa of the Sudan have a straight metal trumpet, about 180 centimeters (6 feet) long, made in three sections that can be taken apart during transportation; a signal instrument, its use is reserved for very important occasions. From the Hausa this trumpet passed to the Yoruba, and was also taken over by the Sudanic Nupe, who make it of bronze; it then penetrated to Cameroun, where it is a ceremonial instrument played in pairs. However, in Cameroun it consists of a bamboo tube with an elongated copper bell. Due to its great length the player must stretch out one arm to support the tube, while the other steadies it at his mouth, a position already noted on two continents.

Sideblown trumpets of Africa are often made of a branch or the root of a tree, or even of bamboo. Sometimes the lower end is closed; if open, the player may half-close it with one hand to change the pitch. Formerly the Babembe of the Middle Congo region made sideblown trumpets from straight, conical tree roots opening up to form a natural "bell"; these were ritual instruments connected with ancestor worship.

Association with royalty is by no means restricted to endblown trumpets in Africa, for a set of sideblown *kanga*, short trumpets of the Alur of Uganda covered with cowhide, forms part of the sultan's regalia. In the same area, conical sideblown trumpets are made of two hollowed sections of wood covered in leather. Wood and ivory bound in skin are combined in some Congolese war trumpets. Bamboo was already employed for the *malakat* of Ethiopia when Laborde wrote (1780); a copper or elongated gourd bell was affixed to a bamboo tube covered in skin, and the bell was attached by a section of curved horn so as to project perpendicularly to the tube.

The object of encasing such instruments was to prevent cracking or damage to the often fragile tubing, and to keep the instrument airtight. Sideblown bamboo trumpets of the Somali, not encased in any protective material, are dipped into water before they are played; here the object is of course to swell the wood and thereby render it airtight. Among the Kambatta of southern Ethiopia long, narrow-bored trumpets announce death; longer models (2.75 meters or 9 feet) announce that of a man, shorter ones (2 meters, or 6.50 feet) that of a woman; they are of plain bamboo, sometimes provided with a cowhorn bell.

The coupling of trumpet and drum goes back demonstrably to the sixteenth century in Africa, and probably far earlier, for a bronze plaque from Benin of that period now in the Lagos, Nigeria, Museum, depicts a sideblown trumpet and a cylinder drum in the hands of royal musicians.

TRUMPETS OF THE AMERICAS

Tubular trumpets of the Americas are, or have been, made of clay, gourd, wood, cane, or metal, both with and without mouthpieces.

Furthermore, evidence of metal trumpets in pre-Columbian Peru is furnished by writings of the Conquistadores, who mention both silver and copper, and a silver trumpet 77 centimeters (29½ inches) long ending in a funnel-shaped bell is cited by Sachs as being in the Ethnological Museum of Berlin. On the entire continent, as is also usual elsewhere, trumpets are played by men only. Alexander von Humboldt, the nineteenth-century naturalist and traveler, reported that the *botuto* of Indians near the Orinoco was considered an object of veneration and that no woman was permitted to see it.

Indians of Guiana had an ancient clay instrument with two or three bosses that they played chiefly during mourning or death dances, while the Inca possessed a wooden *acocotl,* named for the wood (*acocotl*) of which it was made. This survives in modern Mexico with a long, narrow-bore tube of some 3 meters (10 feet), bell, and mouthpiece, and is now referred to as *clarín.* Wooden trumpets are played in pairs by youths of the Amazon forest region; sacred instruments, neither women nor the uninitiated are permitted to see them, and when not in use they are kept hidden in the bed of a forest stream, which thereby also becomes taboo. Straight cylinder trumpets of the Araucanians of Argentina and Chile also have a narrow bore and terminate in a gourd bell. Their usage demonstrates a peculiar blending of cultures, for they are played both at puberty rites and on Good Fridays. On the latter occasions they are sounded from a tower. Additionally, young folk play them as desacralized solo instruments. The Araucanians also have a straight wooden trumpet terminating in an upturned oxhorn bell.

Trumpets of gourd were already known to the Aztecs; in Brazil today the Bororó join three or four gourds together with wax and perforate them so as to form one continuous tube. Endblown cane trumpets of the Brazilian Tucurima have a bell made of armadillo tail and a built-in mouthpiece: the cane is cut off immediately above a node, which is then pierced in the center and acts as a support for the player's lips. Along the Upper Amazon the Tucuna make conical trumpets 4 to 6 meters (13½ to 20 feet) long and of rolled bark, strengthened by tying the tube at intervals to a long stick. During the daytime it serves as an occasional signal instrument, but at night it is sounded during girls' puberty rites and is taboo to women. When not in use it is kept under water to preserve the bark and to prevent women from seeing it. Similar trumpets of rolled bark are played by the Ipuriná of the Rio Purus. Sideblown trumpets of the Carajá of Brazil are of wood and terminate in a gourd bell, while those of the Canella, another Brazilian people, are made of cane tubes extended by an oxhorn bell.

Three forms of clay trumpet existed in ancient Peru, a straight, a coiled, and a third one imitating the form of a shell trumpet. Mochica coiled trumpets terminated in a flared bell; some pointed horizontally from the player, others straight up, or down, or at an oblique angle. The total tube length (i.e., if straightened) of surviving museum specimens varies from 36 to 59 centimeters (14 to 23 inches), reduced by coiling to a maximum of 30 centimeters (12 inches). They were played by means of a cup mouthpiece. The remains of one specimen in the National Museum of Peru, dating from about A.D. 500, appear to have been folded in a close S shape.

TRUMPETS OF THE PACIFIC

Trumpets of this area also can be either endblown or sideblown. Those that are sideblown occur in New Guinea and New Zealand. Among the endblown varieties may be mentioned a half-stopped bamboo instrument, its lower end closed by a node in which a small hole is pierced, played in the Solomon Islands; another from the same island group is made of two cylindrical tubes of differing lengths and diameters; when joined together, the resulting instrument can function either as a trumpet or as a vertical flute. A straight wooden trumpet of the New Zealand Maori conforms even less to the traditional standards of natural trumpets; its length varies from 90 to 250 centimeters (3 to 8 feet) and consists of wood that is split, hollowed, and then bound together; it terminates in a bell made by splitting open a portion of the tube and inserting pieces like gores. Some models are conical throughout, others are cylindrical. Either close to the carved mouthpiece or to the lower end, a free tongue of wood is placed inside the tube; the two irregularly shaped pieces forming the tongue are both attached to the wall of the tube so as to face each other, leaving a narrow windway between them. The smaller upper piece acts as a mobile ulula and its vibration is said to enrich the tone. In wartime this served as a signal instrument (Maori instruments are lip-vibrated trumpets containing a sound modifier; their nature differs entirely from the reedpipes of some American Indians who insert an interior reed. Cf. Maori shell trumpets, below).

But the most remarkable of all Pacific aerophones, and perhaps the best known, at least among specialists, is the northwestern Australian *didjeridoo.* Here, a branch or slender tree trunk some 120 to 150 centimeters (4 to 5 feet) long, with a diameter of 5 to 10 centimeters (2 to 4 inches), is furnished with a resin-coated wax mouthpiece or rim, and the lower end of the tube is inserted into a tin-can resonator, or else it may be supported off the ground before the seated player's feet. The entire tube is painted. Its playing technique, as described by Collaer (1965), is most impressive: the performer inhales through the nose, fills his oral cavity with air—to maintain equal pressure, as in a wind chamber—then proceeds to blow uninterruptedly, uttering imprecise syllables all the while. As is the case with all primitive trumpets, only one tone is available, but here another tone, a fourth higher in pitch, can be obtained by a good player. *Didjeridoos* are ritual instruments connected with circumcision, sunset, and funerals, yet they also symbolize life forces.

A variety of both endblown and sideblown wooden trumpets are sounded on New Guinea, with those that are endblown being the more common. They are notable for their very wide bores, often stepped twice.

SHELL TRUMPETS

Marine shells are blown as trumpets the whole world over. Often they are derived from the shell of a conch, as a consequence of which they have been called conch trumpets; but in addition to conches, cowrie shells have also been converted into musical instruments, so that the term "shell trumpet" is to be preferred. Among the shells that have been so transformed are the *Cassis cornuta, Cassis tuberosum, Charonia tritonis, Cymatium nodiferum, Cymatium tritonis, Strombus galeatus, Strombus giga, Triton australis, Triton tritonis, Turbinella rapa,* and the *Xancus pyrum.* Like other trumpets they are either endblown or sideblown, and in general they produce but a single tone, although they can sometimes be made to overblow. To transform a shell into an endblown trumpet it is necessary to remove its tip; the spiral at the tip end forms a natural mouthpiece very like the cup mouthpiece of some brass instruments, and the larger spirals form a regular tube. Sometimes a lateral hole is pierced instead, permitting the shell to be sideblown.

A gem from the Idaean Cave on Crete, dating from between 1850 and 1550 B.C., depicts a woman, possibly a priestess, blowing a triton shell, apparently sideblown. Such shells have frequently been found in graves from Neolithic times on, and may also have been known to ancient Mesopotamia. Triton, the Greek sea god, whose special attribute was a seashell, was a son of Neptune, at whose bidding he caused the ocean to roar or to subside by blowing his shell. In later times the *kochleos* was referred to by Euripides, and today it continues in use among Greek islanders as an endblown signal instrument.

Formerly shell trumpets were more widely distributed in Europe than they are now; during the War of the League of Augsburg in 1689 they are said to have replaced the fifes and drums of a corps of *miquelets* in Roussillon, France, and their sound was judged to be a most martial one indeed. In nearby Billon, Puy-de-Dôme, the same instruments are, or were up to the late nineteenth century, used as replacement for bells during Easter Week; they were blown from church towers to summon the congregation. Elsewhere in modern Europe, on Majorca, fish vendors blow a shell trumpet to announce their presence.

Shell trumpets are believed to have magical powers in many parts of the world, and in others even to be inhabited by demons. Thus shells are blown by the Solomon Islanders of Bougainville Straits to expel demons credited with having brought epidemics; the Poso Toradja of Celebes blow a shell trumpet to summon the wind spirit in the event of a calm at sea, and also make use of it as a signal instrument. Sachs found that on Madagascar alone it was sounded at circumcision and ancestral rites, as warning and marine signals, as a wind charm, at musical performances, and as a means of communicating over long distances by means of long and short blasts.

Some shell trumpets are covered or ornamented with metal bands, even with semi-precious stones; in certain areas they are encased in a net and suspended from the player's neck, elsewhere a metal mouthpiece may be added. The Maori of New Zealand fit a short wooden mouthpiece to their endblown shells and on occasion modify their sound by placing a piece of hardwood in the spiral (cf. Maori wooden trumpets). On Tahiti a long bamboo mouthpiece is inserted into a lateral hole pierced close to the tip; this can be so long as to assume several times the length of the shell itself.

Imitations of shells in more permanent materials are found in parts of Asia: among the Khmer of Cambodia both the natural shell and a cast bronze imitation thereof were in use by priests as lustral water containers, as well as signal instruments for heralding the king's approach, with those serving as trumpets differentiated from the ritual objects by their blowhole. Such shells are shown on the medieval bas-reliefs of Angkor

Wat. Similar shells of bronze have, surprisingly, been unearthed about 140 miles up the Niger River, showing that shell trumpets were another instrument that West Africa shared with Southeast Asia. In ancient China shell trumpets were held by inserting the hand into their natural opening, and shells are still so played by Buddhist priests and also by boatsmen as signal instruments.

On the Indian subcontinent the *bakura* of the *Rig-Veda* was a martial instrument sounded to frighten the enemy; in the *Mahabharata* two blasts on Arjuna's sacred conch scattered the foe. Later it was taken over into religious and civil ceremonies; in modern times the endblown *shanka*, made of a smooth, white *Turbinella rapa*, sometimes with added mouthpiece or decorated body, is a cult instrument exclusively, given an important part in many ritual ceremonies. From India the shell trumpet was carried to inland Tibet, which, being far removed from any ocean, had to rely upon its neighbor to furnish it with *Xancus pyrum* shells. Fa Hsien, who started out on his travels to India in A.D. 399, relates that, at a Buddhist shrine in what is now eastern Afghanistan, those in charge beat on a large drum, blew a shell trumpet, and clashed copper cymbals. More recently, the nineteenth-century French missionary, Father Huc, heard shells blown to summon priests for prayer when in Tibet. Shell trumpets were considered the most warlike of instruments in the chronicles of medieval Ceylon, where in addition to their martial use they were also sounded at festivals and processions. In Japan also they were martial instruments originally.

As cult instruments of ancient Mexico, priests of the rain god sounded endblown shell trumpets whose intimate association with religion is apparent from their very name, *tecciztli*, derived from that of the god Tecciztcatl. They are also known to have been in use in Peru some two thousand years before the Conquest, in the early Chavín period, and were believed to be inhabited by powerful demons. The *Strombus galeatus* found there does not live in Peruvian waters and was brought in from as far away as the Isthmus of Panama. Because they were difficult to obtain they were both costly and were considered as "aristocratic" instruments: they alone were deemed fit for burial with chieftains to make their afterlife happier. The practical Mochicans, however, made clay imitations of the rare shell, with blowhole always pierced on top. In the days of the Inca their principal use was martial, and large prizes were given in exchange for the highly valued objects, and both the instrument and its player were held in great esteem. In North America shell trumpets occur but rarely; the Zuñi employ them in their horned water snake dance.

In the Pacific area, on Viti Levu, one of the Fiji Islands, a fingerhole pierced at the end of the shell is alternately opened and closed, thereby effecting a change of pitch, a rare instance of the application of finger-holes to a shell. Two different shells are transformed into trumpets in western New Guinea, the *Charonia tritonis*, which is always sideblown, and the *Cassis cornuta*, sometimes sideblown but more often endblown; in Papua other marine shells are also sideblown, and serve for signaling.

Glossary

ACTION. Mechanism forming the connection between key and pipe (e.g., of an organ) or key and string (e.g., of a piano).

AMORE BELL. A bulbous bell, as that of the *oboe d'amore*.

BACKCHECK. Piano-action component that checks (brakes) the hammer as it falls back.

BALANCE RAIL. Wooden rail of keyboard chordophones containing the pins on which the keys pivot.

BELL. The flared or bulbous lower end of many aerophones.

BELLY. Synonym of SOUNDBOARD.

BELLY RAIL. The wooden member to which the keyboard end of a soundboard is glued, running the width of the instrument.

BENTSIDE. The curved side of a harpsichord, piano, or spinet.

BOUTS. The upper, center, and lower sections of an instrument of the violin or *viola da gamba* family.

BRIDGE. A wooden member either set loosely upon or glued to the belly of some chordophones, over which the strings pass. Not to be confused with STRING HOLDER.

BRIDGE PIN. Metal pin inserted into the bridge of a keyboard chordophone.

CAPOTASTO. A movable nut tied or clipped to the fingerboard of some plucked chordophones.

CAPOTASTO BAR. The metal pressure bar of a piano, acting as a nut.

CHANTER. The melody pipe of a bagpipe.

CHANTERELLE. The highest-pitched string of some chordophones of the lute class.

CHEEKPIECE. The short side of a harpsichord or spinet case at the treble end of the keyboard.

CHOIR. On harpsichords, a set of strings, one for each key, controlled by one jack slide.

CLOSED KEY. Of woodwinds, a key that remains closed when not in use.

CORNERS. Of a violin, etc., the almost pointed terminals of upper and lower bouts, facing the center bouts.

827

COURSE. A string of a lute, guitar, and related instruments; or two or three strings lying close together, sounded together, and tuned to unison (rarely at octave) pitch.

CROOK. (1) a curved tube that carries a double reed (cf. STAPLE); (2) a detachable piece of tubing added to a brass instrument to alter its pitch; (3) the bent tubing that connects two yards of, for example, a trombone.

CROSS-STRUNG SCALE. The same as OVERSTRUNG SCALE.

DIVERGENT PIPES. A pair of pipes held, one in each hand, so as to form a V shape, and played together.

DOWNCUT REED. An idioglot single reed cut toward the lower end of a woodwind.

DRONE. A pipe or string that sounds a sustained tone.

DROPLEAF. A wooden board, hinged to the front of some early keyboard chordophones, that hung down when open.

FIPPLE. A terminal block at the mouth end of certain flutes.

FLAGEOLET TONES. Harmonics produced on certain chordophones by touching a string lightly so as to form a node, instead of stopping it completely, as by depressing it against a fingerboard.

FLAT SCALE. Said of a piano having all strings on one level, as opposed to an OVERSTRUNG SCALE.

FLUE. A narrow duct for the passage of wind. Also called windway.

FLUE PIPE. Organ pipe in which the tone is produced by wind passing through a flue immediately below the mouth.

FONTANELLE. Box- or barrel-shaped, perforated cover slipped over some longer Renaissance woodwinds to protect the key.

FRET. Fixed or movable division of a fingerboard, neck, or even belly of some chordophones, to indicate stopping points.

FROG. That part of a bow which serves to tighten the hair. Called NUT in Britain.

GUIDE. A fixed, perforated batten that holds the lower part of jacks in place.

HARMONICS. (1) The fundamental and overtones of a given tone; (2) synonym of FLAGEOLET TONES.

HITCHPIN. On keyboard chordophones, the pins to which strings are attached or over which they are hitched.

HOPPER. Short for grasshopper—the escapement lever or jack of a piano.

JACK. (1) Action component of plucked keyboard instruments, a thin rectangle of wood that bears the plectrum and usually also a damper; (2) an intermediary action member of pianos, also called sticker, HOPPER.

JACK SLIDE. A mobile batten perforated to hold one row of jacks.

KEY FRAME. The wooden frame that carries the keys of a keyboard.

LIP. (1) of a bell, the rim; (2) of a flute, the sharp edge of a lateral aperture.

LUTHIER. A maker of chordophones of the lute class.

NOTE HOLE. Synonym of TONE HOLE.

NUT. (1) A raised ridge glued to the top of the neck of lutes, violins, and related instruments, determining one end of the string's speaking length; (2) on keyboard chordophones, a straight member serving the same purpose, opposite the bridge; (3) British name of the FROG.

OCTAVE KEY. Synonym of SPEAKER KEY.

OFF-BOARD STRINGS. Strings of an instrument of the lute class that do not pass over a fingerboard, but beside it.

OPEN KEY. Of woodwinds, a key that remains open when not in use.

OPEN STRING. One that is not stopped, as that of a harp.

OVERBLOWING. The production of overtones on a wind instrument.

OVERSTRUNG SCALE. Said of a piano with bass-string section strung diagonally across the main body of strings (cf. FLAT SCALE).

PEDAL TONE. The fundamental of a wind instrument.

PEGBOX. Boxlike structure surmounting the neck of some chordophones, for lateral insertion of the pegs.

PEGDISK. A flat piece of wood into which the tuning pegs of medieval fiddles, ancient and modern guitars, etc., are inserted from the back.

PINBLOCK. Synonym of WRESTPLANK.

PIROUETTE. Wooden disk or cylinder, that serves as a lip rest on some reed instruments.

PLECTRUM. (1) A device for plucking strings, whether held in the hand, worn on a finger, or attached to the jack of a harpsichord, etc. (2) In medieval times, the tuning key of a harp or a fiddle bow.

RACK. A board containing sawcuts in which the backs of the keys of a clavichord, and so on, ride up and down.

REEDCAP. A small wooden cap fitted over the double reed of some Renaissance woodwinds, with a blowhole on top.

REGISTER. (1) A row of harpsichord jacks or its slide; (2) on organs, a slider.

RIB FASTENING. Of chordophones of the lute class, any method of attaching strings to the lower end of the ribs, as on a violin (as contrasted with a STRING HOLDER placed on the soundboard).

RIBS. (1) The individual staves of a lute body; (2) the side walls of a violin, and certain other chordophones.

SCALE. (1) The relationship of organ pipe length to diameter or circumference; (2) the relationship of a string's length to its pitch.

SHOW PIPES. The front pipes of an organ.

SLIDE. See JACK SLIDE.

SLIDER. Of an organ, a thin wooden batten placed beneath a rank of pipes, with holes for the pipe feet, that could be moved so as to admit wind or not.

SOUNDBOARD. The upper surface of many a chordophone, to which the strings transmit their vibrations.

SOUNDBOW. The most resonant portion of a bell, immediately above the lip (rim).

SPEAKER KEY. Or octave key, facilitates overblowing on certain woodwinds.

SPUN STRINGS. Several lengths of metal strings twisted together, as of a cable (cf. WOUND STRINGS).

STAPLE. Of woodwinds, the straight metal tube that carries a double reed (cf. CROOK [1]).

STOCK. Short wooden tube inserted in a bagpipe bag to hold the pipe(s).

STOP. (1) A rank or register of organ pipes, named from the control system that "stops" wind from entering the pipes; (2) transferred to the harpsichord, this term denotes a register; (3) of a violin, etc., the distance from the cross stroke of the F holes to the upper edge of the belly; (4) the speaking length of strings of instruments of the violin family, measured from the cross stroke of the F holes to the nut; on gambas, from the top of the bridge to the nut.

STOPPED. (1) Of aerophones, any tube closed at the end farthest from the wind supply; (2) of strings, the shortening of a string, as by the fingers on a violin.

STRING HOLDER. A wooden bar glued to the belly of some chordophones, such as lutes, to which the strings are attached. Not to be confused with BRIDGE.

STRING PLATE. Metal plate of a piano for attaching the strings.

TABLES. Of a violin, etc., the back and belly.

TAILPIECE. Of a violin, etc., a fitting to which the lower end of the strings are attached.

TAPE CHECK ACTION. An upright piano action with tape check (now called bridle strap) to speed the hammer's return.

TONE HOLE. Any aperture in the wall of an aerophone that affects its pitch. Called NOTE HOLE in Britain.

TOUCH. The portion of a woodwind key touched by the finger when depressing it.

TRACKER. In an organ, a strip of wood forming part of the connection between a key and a pallet.

TUNING PEG. A mobile wooden peg, moved by hand, to which one end of a string is attached.

TUNING PIN. A metal pin, moved by means of a tuning hammer, to which one end of a string is attached. Also called WREST PIN.

TUNING RING. (1) A mobile ring of leather or other material to which one end of a string is attached; (2) an adjustable metal ring for tuning the metal flue pipes of an organ.

UPCUT REED. An idioglot single reed cut toward the mouth end of a woodwind.

UPPER BOARD. Of an organ, the board over the windchest that holds the feet of the pipes.

VENT. (1) An aperture in the wall of an aerophone that assists speech but does not shorten the air column; (2) the window of a fipple flute, cut just below the fipple; (3) a small hole in the body of a drum to let air escape.

WINDWAY. Synonym of FLUE.

WOLF TONE. (1) Of keyboard instruments, the accumulated "errors" of non-equal temperament tunings, often heaped on the G♯ key and also on the E♭ key, causing a dissonant effect; (2) of chordophones, a pronounced difference in timbre and dynamics of usually a single tone.

WOUND STRINGS. Strings consisting of a core around which a wire is coiled (cf. SPUN STRINGS).

WREST PIN. Synonym of TUNING PIN.

WRESTPLANK. Block of wood—today laminated—into which the wrest pins, or tuning pins, are driven. Also called PINBLOCK.

YARD. One of the long tubes of a trumpet or trombone.

Works Referred to in This Book

Adlung, Jacob. *Anleitung zur musicalischen Gelahrtheit* (written 1754). Erfurt, 1758.

————. *Musica mechanica organoedi*. Berlin, 1768 (posthum.).

Agricola, Johann Friedrich. Addenda and comments to Adlung (1768).

Agricola, Martin. *Musica instrumentalis deutsch*. Wittenberg, 1528 (Exp. ed., 1545).

Al-Khwarizmi. *Mafatih al-ulum*. Translated by Henry George Farmer, in *Transactions of the Glasgow University Oriental Society*, vol. 7. 1957–1958.

Altenburg, Johann Ernst. *Versuch einer Anleitung zur heroisch-musikalischen Trompeter- und Pauken-Kunst*. Halle, 1795.

Amat, Juan Carlos. *Guitarra española*. Barcelona 1586 *et seq*.

Anselmi, Giorgio (of Parma). *Musica* (written 1434). Edited by Jacques Handschin, in *Musica disciplina*, vol. 2. Rome, 1948.

Arbeau, Thoinot. *Orchésographie*. Langres, 1589.

Arnaut, Henry. *Les traités d'Henry Arnaut de Zwolle et des divers anonymes*. Edited by G. Le Cerf and E. R. Labande. Paris, 1932.

Bach, Carl Philip Emanuel. *Versuch über die wahre Art das Clavier zu spielen*. Berlin, 1753.

Bachmann, Werner. *Die Anfänge des Streichinstrumentenspiels*. Leipzig, 1964.

Baines, Anthony. *Woodwind Instruments and Their History*. London, 1957.

Banchieri, Adriano. *Conclusioni nel suono dell'organo* (written in 1606). Bologna, 1609.

Banister, John. *The Sprightly Companion*. London, 1695.

Baron, Ernst. *Untersuchung des Instruments der Lauten*. Nuremberg, 1727.

Bartholomaeus Anglicus. *De proprietatibus rerum*. Translated, and with comments, by Jean Corbichon. 1372.

Becker, Heinz. *Zur Entwicklungsgeschichte der antiken und mittelalterlichen Rohrblattinstrumenten*. Hamburg, 1966.

Beckmann, Johann. *Beytrage zur Geschichte der Erfindungen*. 2nd ed. Leipzig, 1786.

Bédos de Celles, Dom François. *L'art du facteur d'orgues.* Paris, 1766–1778.

Bermudo, Juan. *Declaración de instrumentos musicales.* Osuna, 1555.

Bésard, Jean-Baptiste. *Isagoge in artem testudinaram.* Augsburg, 1644 and 1717.

Bessaraboff, Nicholas. *Ancient European Musical Instruments.* Boston, 1941.

Bianchini, Francesco. *De tribus generibus instrumentorum veterum . . .* Rome, 1742 (posthum.).

Blankenburg, Quirijn van. *Elementa musica.* S'Gravenhage, 1739.

Blüthner, J., and Gretschel, H. *Der Pianofortebau.* Weimar, 1886.

Bonanni, Filippo. See Buonanni, Filippo.

Bontempi, Giovanni Andrea. *Historia musica.* Perugia, 1695.

Boone, Olga. *Les xylophones du Congo Belge.* Annales du Musée du Congo Belge, Ethnographie, série III. Tervueren, 1936.

Borjon, Charles Emmanuel. *Traité de la musette.* Lyons, 1672.

Bottrigari, Ercole. *Il desiderio.* Venice, 1594.

Boyden, David. *The History of Violin Playing.* London and New York, 1965.

Brenet, Michel. *Dictionnaire pratique et historique de la musique.* Paris, 1926.

Breslauer Sammlungen. See *Sammlung von Natur . . . Geschichten.*

Brossard, Sébastien de. *Dictionnaire de musique.* Paris, 1703, 1705 *et seq.*

Buchner, Alexandr. *Musical Instruments Through the Ages.* London, n.d.

Buonanni, Filippo. *Gabinetto armonico pieno d'istromenti sonori.* Rome, 1722.

Burney, Charles. *A General History of Music.* London, 1776–1789.

———. *An Account of the Musical Performances in Westminster Abbey . . . in Commemoration of Handel.* London, 1785.

Busby, Thomas. *Musical Dictionary.* London, 1802.

Calvisius, Sethus. *Exercitationes musicae duae.* Leipzig, 1600.

Casparini, Adam Orazio. In *Breslauer Sammlungen,* 1718.

Caus, Salomon de. *Les raisons des forces mouvantes.* Frankfurt on the Main, 1615.

Cellier, Jacques. *Recueil de plusieurs singularités.* MS ca. 1585.

Cerone, Pietro. *El melopeo.* Naples, 1613.

Cerreto, Scipione. *Dell'arbore musicale.* Naples, 1608.

———. *Della prattica musica.* Naples, 1601.

Chales, Claude de. See Dechales, Claude-François Milliet.

Choron, Alexandre-Étienne. *Francoeur, L. J.: Traité général des voix et des instruments d'orchestre. Nouvelle édition revue et augmentée par A. Choron.* N.p., 1813.

Chouquet, Gustave. *Le musée du conservatoire national de musique. Catalogue descriptif et raisonné.* Paris, 1884.

Citolini, Alessandro. *La tipocosmia.* Venice, 1561.

Clappé, Arthur A. *The Wind-Band and Its Instruments.* New York, 1911.

Clutton, Cecil, and Niland, Austin. *The British Organ.* London, 1963.

Collaer, Paul. *Oceanien.* Leipzig, 1965.

Comenius. See Komenský, Johann Amos.

Corbichon, Jean. See Bartholomaeus Anglicus.

Corrette, Michel. *Méthode pour apprendre aisément à jouer de la flûte travesière.* Paris and Lyons, *privilège* 1735.

————. *Méthode pour apprendre le violoncelle.* Paris, 1741.

Cozio di Salabue, Count Ignazio Alessandro. *Carteggio* (written at different times, from the last quarter of the eighteenth century to his death in 1840). Transcribed by Renato Bacchetta. Milan, 1950.

Dechales, Claude-François Millet. *Cursus seu mundus mathemathicus.* Lyons, 1674.

Denis, Valentin. *De muziekinstrumenten in de Nederlanden en in Italië* . . . Leuven, 1944.

Dentice, Luigi. *Duo dialoghi della musica.* Naples, 1553.

Diruta, Girolamo. *Il transilvano.* Venice, 1597.

Doni, Giovanni Battista. *Annotazioni.* Rome, 1640.

————. *De' trattati di musica.* 2 vols. Florence, 1763 (posthum.).

Doppelmayr, Johann Gabriel. *Historische Nachrichten von den nürnbergischen Mathematicis und Künstlern* . . . Nuremberg, 1730.

Douwes, Claas. *Grondig ondersoek van de toonen der muzijk.* Franeken, 1699.

Dufourcq, Nobert. *Documents inédits relatifs à l'orgue français.* 2 vols. Paris, 1934–1935.

Dupont, Wilhelm. *Geschichte der musikalischen Temperatur.* Nördlingen, 1955.

Eichborn, Hermann. *Die Trompete in alter und neuer Zeit.* Leipzig, 1881.

Eisel, Johann Philipp. *Musicus autodidacticos.* Erfurt, 1738.

Eliade, Mircea. *Shamanism.* Translated by Willard Trask. Bollingen Foundation, 1964.

Elis, A. See Lunelli, Renato.

Ellis, Alexander J. See Helmholtz, Hermann L. F.

Encyclopédie ou dictionnaire raisonné des sciences, des arts et des métiers. Edited by Diderot and d'Alembert. 1751–1780 and subsequent eds. (*Encyclopédie méthodique* . . . 1782–1832).

Engel, Carl. *A Descriptive Catalogue of the Musical Instruments in the South Kensington Museum.* London, 1870 (2nd ed., 1874).

Engramelle, Marie-Dominique-Joseph. *La tonotechnie.* Paris, 1775.

Erlanger, Baron Rodolphe. *La musique arabe.* 2 vols. Paris, 1930.

Faber, Nicolaus. *Musicae rudimenta.* Augsburg, 1516.

Fantini, Girolamo. *Modo per imperare a sonare di tromba.* Frankfurt, 1638.

Farmer, Henry George. See Al-Khwarizmi.

Fischhof, Joseph. *Versuch einer Geschichte des Clavierbaues.* Vienna, 1853.

Forkel, Johann Nikolaus. *Musicalischer Almanach für Deutschland auf das Jahr 1782 [1783, 1784, 1789].* Leipzig.

Frotscher, Gotthold. *Geschichte des Orgelspiels.* 2 vols. Berlin, 1935–1936.

Fuhrmann, Martin Heinrich. *Musicalischer Trichter.* Frankfurt an der Oder, 1706.

Furetière, Antoine. *Essai d'un dictionnaire universel* . . . Amsterdam, 1685.

———. *Dictionnaire universel* . . . The Hague, 1690 (posthum.).

Gafori, Franchino. *Theorica musicae.* Milan, 1492.

Galeazzi, Francesco. *Elementi teoretico-pratici.* 2 vols. Rome, 1791–1796.

Galilei, Vincenzo. *Dialogo della musica antica e moderna.* Florence, 1581 (facsimile reprint Rome, 1934).

———. *Discorso intorno all'opera di messer Gioseffe Zarlino.* Florence, 1589.

Galpin, Francis W. In *An Illustrated Catalogue of the Music Loan Exhibition* . . . *at Fishmonger's Hall, June and July, 1904.* London, 1909.

———. *Old English Instruments of Music.* 4th ed. London, 1965.

Ganassi, Silvestro. *Regola rubertina.* 2 vols. Venice, 1542–1543.

———. *La Fontegara.* Venice, 1535.

Garcilaso de la Vega. See Lasso de la Vega, Garcia.

Gerber, Ernst Ludwig. *Historisch-biographisches Lexicon der Tonkünstler.* 2 vols. Leipzig, 1790–1792.

———. *Neues historisch-biographisches Lexicon der Tonkünstler.* 4 vols. Leipzig, 1812–1814.

Gerbert, Martin. *De cantu et musica sacra.* 2 vols. Saint Blasien, 1774.

———. *Scriptores ecclesiastici de musica sacra potissimum.* 3 vols. Saint Blasien, 1784.

Gerle, Hans. *Musica teutsch* . . . Nuremberg, 1532.

Gérold, Théodore. *La musique au moyen âge.* Paris, 1932.

Glareanus, Henricus. *Dodecachordon.* Basel, 1547.

Gombosi, Otto. *Studien zur Tonlehre des frühen Mittelalters.* In *Acta musicologica,* vol. 12, 1940.

Gradenwitz, Peter. *Music of Israel.* New York, 1949.

Grassineau, James. *A Musical Dictionary.* London, 1740.

Gulik, R. H. van. *The Lore of the Chinese Lute.* Tokyo, 1940.

Halle, Johann Samuel. *Werkstätte der heutigen Künste.* Berlin, 1764.

Harding, Rosamund. "Harpsichord," in Grove's Dictionary of Music and Musicians, sup. vol. London, 1944.

———. *The Pianoforte.* Cambridge, 1933.

Harrison, Frank Lloyd. *Music in Medieval Britain.* London, 1958.

Hart, George. *The Violin.* 2nd enl. ed. London, 1884 (first ed. 1875).

Hayes, Gerald R. *Musical Instruments and Their Music,* vol. 2: *The Viols and Other Bowed Instruments.* London, 1930.

Helmholtz, Hermann L. F. *On the Sensations of Tone.* Translated [and annotated] by Alexander J. Ellis. 2nd ed. London, 1885.

Heron-Allen, Edward. *Violin-Making as It Was and Is.* 2nd ed. London and New York, n.d.

Herrad von Landsberg. *Hortus deliciarum.* Edited by A. Straub. Paris 1879–1899 (text), Strasbourg, 1901.

Hess, Joachim. *Disposition der merkwaardigste Kerk-Orgelen* . . . N.p., 1774 (reprinted Utrecht, 1945).

Hickmann, Hans. *Ägypten.* Leipzig, 1961.

Hill, W. Henry; Hill, Arthur F.; and Hill, Alfred E. *Antonio Stradivari.* London, 1902.

Hiller, Johann Adam. Biography of Franz Benda, in *Lebensbeschreibungen berühmter Musikgelehrten und Tonkünstler.* Leipzig, 1784.

Hipkins, Alfred James. "Pape, Jean-Henri," in Grove's Dictionary of Music and Musicians. 3rd ed. London, 1946.

———. In Helmholtz, L. F. (q.v.).

Hotteterre, Louis. *Principes de la flûte traversière* . . . Paris, 1707.

Howard, A. A. *The Aulos or Tibia,* in *Harvard Studies in Classical Philology,* vol. 4, 1893.

Hubbard, Frank. *Three Centuries of Harpsichord Making.* Cambridge, Mass., 1965.

Hummel, Johann Nepomuk. *Ausführliche* . . . *Anweisung zum Pianofortespiel* . . . Vienna, 1828.

Izikowitz, Karl Gustav. *Musical and Other Sound Instruments of the South American Indians.* Göteborg, 1935.

———. *Le tambour à membrane au Perou,* in *Journal de la Société des americanistes,* vol. 23. Paris, 1931.

Jambe de Fer, Philibert. *Epitome musical.* Lyons, 1556.

Jones, A. M. *Africa and Indonesia.* Leiden, 1964.

Judenkönig, Hans. *Ain schon künstlich Unterweisung* . . . *auff der Lautten und Geygen.* Vienna, 1523.

Kappey, Jacob Adam. *Military Music.* London and New York, 1894.

Kastner, Georges. *Les danses des morts.* Paris, 1852.

———. *La harpe d'éole et la musique cosmique.* Paris, 1856.

Kastner, Santiago. *Musica hispanica.* Atica, 1936.

Kinsky, Georg. *Musikhistorisches Museum von Wilhelm Heyer in Cöln. Katalog,* vols. 1 and 2. Colonge, 1910 and 1912.

———. *Doppelrohrblattinstrumente mit Windkapsel.* In *Archiv für Musikwissenschaft,* vol. 7, 1925.

———. *Geschichte der Musik in Bilder.* Leipzig, 1929.

Kirby, Percival R. "Ancient Egyptian Instruments." In Hinrichsen's 7th Music Book. 1952.

———. *The Musical Instruments of the Native Races of South Africa*. London, 1934.

Kircher, Athanasius. *Phonurgia nova*. Kempten, 1673.

———. *Musurgia universalis*. Rome, 1650.

Koch, Heinrich Christoph. *Musicalisches Lexicon*. Frankfurt on the Main, 1802.

Komenský, Johann Amos (Comenius). *Orbis sensualium pictus quadrilinguis*. Nuremberg, 1666.

Kuhnau, Johann. *Musicalischer Quacksalber*. Dresden, 1700.

Kunst, Jaap. *The Music of Java*. The Hague, 1949.

Kützig, Carl. *Das Wissenschaftliche der Pianoforte-Baukunst*. Bern, 1844.

Laborde, Jean-Benjamin. *Essai sur la musique*. Paris, 1780.

Lanfranco, Giovanni Maria. *Scintille di musica*. Brescia, 1533.

Lasso de la Vega, Garcia. *Comentarios reales . . . de los Yncas*. Lisbon, 1609.

Le Blanc, Hubert. *Défense de la basse de viole contre les entreprises du violon et les prétensions du violoncel*. Amsterdam, 1740.

Lecerf de la Viéville, Jean-Laurent. *Comparaison de la musique italienne et de la musique française . . .* Brussels, 1704.

Lehmann, Johann Traugott. *Gründliches . . . Stimmsystem*. Leipzig, 1827.

Le Roy, Adrien. *Brève et facile instruction pour apprendre la tablature de cistre*. Paris, 1565.

Löhlein, Georg Simon. *Anweisung zum Violinspielen . . .* Leipzig, 1774.

Lomazzo, Giovanni Paolo. *Trattato dell'arte della pittura*. Milan, 1584.

Lorber, Johann Christoph. *Lob der edlen Musik*. Weimar, 1696.

Lunelli, Renato. *Der Orgelbau in Italien*. Translated, with comments, by A. Elis. Mainz, 1956.

Luscinius, Ottmar. *Musurgia*. Strasbourg, 1536.

Mace, Thomas. *Musick's Monument*. London, 1676.

Mahillon, Victor-Charles. *Catalogue descriptif et analytique du musée instrumental du Conservatoire Royal de Musique de Bruxelles*. 5 vols. Ghent-Brussels, 1880–1922.

Mahrenholz, Christian. *Die Berechnung der Orgelpfeifenmensuren*. Kassel, 1938.

Majer, Joseph Friedrich Bernhard Caspar. *Museum musicum*. Halle, 1732.

Malraux, André. *Lunes en papier*. Paris, 1921.

———. *Le musée imaginaire de la sculpture mondiale*, vol. 2. Paris, 1954.

———. *Oraisons funèbres*. Paris, 1971.

Marcuse, Sibyl. *Musical Instruments: A Comprehensive Dictionary*. New York, 1964.

Mareschall, Samuel. *Porta musices*. Basel, 1589.

Marinati, Aurelio. *Somma di tutte le scienze*. Rome, 1587.

Marpurg, Friedrich Wilhelm. *Historisch-critische Beytrage* . . . 5 vols. Berlin, 1754–1778.

———. *Kritische Briefe über die Tonkünst*. 3 vols. Berlin, 1759–1763.

Marx, Joseph. "The Tone of the Baroque Oboe," in *The Galpin Society Journal*, vol. 4, 1951.

Mattheson, Johann. *Das neu-eröffnete Orchestre*. Hamburg, 1713.

———. *Critica musica*. Hamburg, 1722–1725.

———. *Der vollkommene Kapellmeister*. Hamburg, 1739.

Mead, Margaret. *Male and Female*. New York, 1949.

Merolla, Girolamo. *Breve e succinta relatione del viaggio nel regno di Congo*. Naples, 1692.

Mersenne, Marin. *Harmonie universelle*. 2 vols. Paris, 1636–1637.

MGG. See *Musik in Geschichte und Gegenwart*.

Mizler, Lorenz Christoph. *Neu-eröffnete musicalische Bibliothek*. Leipzig, 1739–1754.

Montal, C. *Anweisung das Pianoforte selbst stimmen zu lernen*. Mainz, 1835.

Mozart, Leopold. *Versuch einer gründlichen Violinschule*. Augsburg, 1756.

Mudarra, Alonso de. *Tres libros de música en cifras para vihuela*. Seville, 1546.

Murray, Margaret A. *The Witch-Cult in Western Europe*. Oxford, 1921.

Musik in Geschichte und Gegenwart. Kassel, 1949–.

Norlind, Tobias. *Systematik der Musikinstrumente*. Hanover, 1939.

North, Roger. *The Musical Gramarian* (MS ca. 1728). Edited by Hilda Andrews. London, 1925.

Ortiz, Diego. *Tratado de glosas sobre clausulas* . . . Rome, 1553.

Paul, Oscar. *Geschichte des Claviers*. Leipzig, 1868.

Paulirinus, Paulus. *Tractatus de musica*. Edited by Joseph Reiss, in *Zeitschrift für Musikwissenschaft*, vol. 7, 1925.

Pepys, Samuel. *Diary* (covering the years 1760–1769). Various eds. since 1825.

Petri, Johann Samuel. *Anleitung zur praktischen Musik*. Leipzig, 1767.

Piccinini, Alessandro. *Intravolatura di liuto et di chitarrone*. Bologna, 1623.

Picken, Laurence. "The Music of Far Eastern Asia," in *New Oxford History of Music*, vol. 1. London, 1957.

———. "Early Chinese Friction-Chordophones," in *The Galpin Society Journal*, vol. 18, 1965.

Pierre, Constant. *Les facteurs d'instruments de musique*. Paris, 1893.

Playford, John. *Booke of New Lessons for the Cithren and Gittern*. London, 1652.

———. *A Breefe Introduction to the Skill of Musick* . . . London, 1654.

———. *Musick's Recreation on the Viol, Lyra-way* . . . London, 1661.

————. *Musick's Delight on the Cithren*. London, 1666.

Pontécoulant, Louis-Adolphe. *Organographie*. Paris, 1861.

Porta, Giovanni Battista. *Magiae naturalis*. Naples, 1558.

Powne, Michael. *Ethiopian Music*. London–New York, 1968.

Praetorius, Michael. *Syntagma musicum*, parts II and III. Wolfenbüttel, 1619.

————. *Theatrum instrumentorum* (addendum to *Syntagma* II). Wolfenbüttel, 1620.

Price, Frank Percival. *The Carillon*. London, 1933.

Printz, Caspar. *Historische Beschreibung der edlen Sing- und Kling-Kunst*. Dresden, 1690.

Puliti, Leto. *Cenni storici*. Florence, 1874.

Quantz, Johann Joachim. *Anweisung, die Flöte traversiere zu spielen*. Berlin, 1752.

Raguenet, François. *Parallèle des Italiens et des Français en ce qui regarde la musique*. Paris, 1702.

Ramis de Pareja, Bartholomé. *De musica practica*. 1482. Edited by Johannes Wolf. Leipzig, 1901.

Rattray, R. S. *Ashanti*. Oxford, 1923.

Ribayez, Lucas. See Ruiz de Ribayez, Lucas.

Rimbault, Edward Francis. *The Pianoforte*. London, 1860.

Rimmer, Joan. "The Morphology of the Triple Harp," in *The Galpin Society Journal*, vols. 18 and 19, 1965–1966.

Robert de Clari. *La conquête de Constantinople*, in *Historiens et chroniqueurs du moyen âge*. Paris (Pléiade), n.d.

Roberts, Helen. In *Yale Publications in Anthropology*. 1936.

Rockstro, Richard Shepherd. *A Treatise on . . . the Flute . . .* London, 1890.

Rose, Algernon. "A Private Collection of African Instruments," in *Zeitschrift der internationalen Musikgesellschaft*, vol. 6, 1904–1905.

Rousseau, Jean. *Traité de la viole*. Paris, 1687.

Rühlmann, Julius. *Die Geschichte der Bogeninstrumente*. Brunswick, 1882.

Ruiz de Ribayez, Lucas. *Luz . . . por las cifras de la guitarra española*. Madrid, 1677.

Russell, Raymond. *The Harpsichord and Clavichord*. London, 1959.

Sachs, Curt. *Reallexikon der Musikinstrumente*. Berlin, 1913.

————. *Handbuch der Instrumentenkunde*. Leipzig, 1920.

————. *A History of Musical Instruments*. New York, 1940.

Salabue. See Cozio di Salabue, Count Ignazio Alessandro.

Salinas, Francisco. *De musica*. Salamanca, 1577.

Sammlung von Natur- und Medezin-, Kunst- und Literatur-Geschichten. Breslau (periodical). (Known as *Breslauer Sammlungen*.)

Schilling, Gustav. *Universal Lexicon der Tonkunst*. Stuttgart, 1835.

Schlesinger, Kathleen. *The Greek Aulos*. London, 1939.

Schlick, Arnold. *Spiegel der Orgelmacher*. Heidelberg, 1511.

Schneider, Wilhelm. *Historisch-technische Beschreibung der musicalischen Instrumente*. Leipzig, 1834.

Schott, Caspar. *Mechanica hydraulico-pneumatica*. Würzburg, 1657.

Schubart, Christian Friedrich Daniel. *Ideen zu einer Ästhetik der Tonkunst* (written in 1784). Vienna, 1806 (posthum.).

Schubert, Franz Ludwig. *Katechismus der Musik-Instrumente*. Leipzig, 1862.

Seder, Theodore A. "Old World Overtones in the New World," in *University Museum Bulletin* (Philadelphia, Pa.), vol. 16, 1952.

Simpson, Christopher. *The Division Viol*. London, 1659.

Smith, Hermann. Quoted by Alexander J. Ellis in Helmholtz, L. F. (q.v.).

Speer, Daniel. *Grundrichtiger . . . Unterricht der musicalischen Kunst*. Ulm, 1687.

Steger, Hugo. *David rex et propheta*. Nuremberg, 1961.

Stellfeld, Jean-Auguste. *Bronnen tot de geschiedenis der antwerpsche clavicimbel-en orgelbouwers*. The Hague, 1842.

Stevens, Denis. *Thomas Tomkins*. London, 1957.

Sutton, Sir John. *A Short Account of Organs Built in England from the Reign of King Charles the Second to the Present Time*. London, 1847.

Talbot, James. Music MS 1187, Christ Church Library, Oxford, ca. 1700. In *The Galpin Society Journal*, vol. 1 et seq., 1948 ff.

Tallemant des Réaux, Gédéon. *Historiettes* (written 1657–1675). 1834.

Tans'ur, William. *The Elements of Music Displayed*. London, 1772.

Thon, Christian Friedrich Gottlob. *Abhandlungen über Klavier-Saiten-Instrumente*. Weimar, 1843.

Thureau-Dangin, F. *Rituels accadiens*. Paris, 1923.

Tinctoris, Joannes. *De inventione et usu musicae*. Ca. 1484. Edited by Karl Weinmann. Regensburg, 1917. Excerpts and English translation by Anthony Baines in *The Galpin Society Journal*, vol. 3, 1950.

Titon du Tillet, Evrard. *Description du parnasse françois*. Paris, 1727.

Tocqueville, Alexis de. *Souvenirs*. n.p., 1893.

Tolbecque, Auguste. *L'art du luthier*. Niort, 1903.

Töpfer, Johann Christian Carl. *Anfangsgründe zur Erlernung der Musik*. 1773.

Trichet, P. *Traité des instruments de musique* (*vers 1640*). Edited by François Lesure. Neuilly-sur-Seine, 1957.

Trojano, Massimo. *Discorsi delli trionfi*. Munich, 1568.

Tromlitz, Johann Georg. *Ausführlicher . . . Unterricht die Flöte zu spielen*. Leipzig, 1791.

Trowell, M., and Wachsmann, K. P. *Tribal Crafts of Uganda*. London, 1953.

Turner, William. *A Compleat History of the Most Remarkable Providences*

. . . 1697. Quoted in *The Galpin Society Journal*, vol. 10, 1958.

van Gulik, R. H. See: Gulik, R. H. van.

Vasari, Giorgio. *Le vite de' più eccelenti architetti, pittori, et scultori italiani* . . . 2nd ed. Florence, 1568.

Vega, Garcilaso de la. See Lasso de la Vega, Garcia.

Vincentino, Nicolo. *L'antica musica ridotto alla moderna prattica.* Rome, 1555.

Virdung, Sebastian. *Musica getutscht und ausgezogen.* Basel, 1511.

Wachsmann, K. P. See Trowell, M., and Wachsmann, K. P.

Walther, Johann Gottfried. *Praecepta der musicalischen Composition* (preface 1708). Leipzig, 1955.

―――. *Musicalischer Lexicon.* Leipzig, 1732.

Wanzlöben, Sigfried. *Das Monochord als Instrument und als System.* Halle, 1911.

Welcker von Contershausen, Heinrich. *Der Clavierbau.* Frankfurt, 1870.

―――. *Der Flügel* . . . Frankfurt on the Main, 1853 (new ed. 1870).

―――. *Neu eröffnetes Magazin musicalischer Werkzeuge.* Frankfurt on the Main, 1855.

Wellesz, Egon. In *New Oxford History of Music*, vol. 2. London, 1954.

Werckmeister, Andreas. *Die nothwendigsten Anmerkungen . . . wie der Bassus continuus . . . könne tractiret werden.* Aschersleben, 1698.

―――. *Organum gruningense redivivum.* Quedlinburg, 1705.

Westrup, J. A. *Purcell.* London, 1937.

Zacconi, Ludovico. *Prattica di musica.* 2 vols. Venice, 1592, 1619.

Zarlino, Gioseffo. *Istitutioni harmoniche.* Venice, 1558.

―――. *Sopplimenti musicali.* Venice, 1588.

[Zedler, Johann Heinrich]. *Grosses vollständiges Universal Lexicon.* 64 vols. Halle, 1732–1754.

INDEX NOMINUM

Abel, Adam, 293
Abel, Carl Friedrich, 507
Adam de la Halle, 675
Addison, Robert, 241
Adenet Le Roi, 561, 565
Adlington, William, 89
Adlung, Jacob, 71, 100, 230, 254, 257, 269, 276, 285, 286, 292, 296, 327, 328, 330, 351, 446, 538, 723, 802
Aelfric, 388
Aeolian Piano Company, 357
Aeschylus, 59, 788
Afranio, Canon, 675
Agazzari, Agostino, 446
Agricola, Johann Friedrich, 259, 285, 326
Agricola, Martin, 27, 476, 485, 487, 490, 496, 497, 501, 504, 514, 516, 566, 567, 573, 796
Aimeri de Peyrac, 200
Albisi, Abelardo, 570
Albrechtsberger, Johann Georg, 439
Aldhelm, Saint, 605
Alessandro degli Organi, 284
Alessandro of Modena, 301
Alexandre, Jacob, 307, 354, 740, 741
Al Farabi, 199, 409, 410, 413, 415, 431, 464, 465, 466, 480
Alfonso da Ferrara. See Alfonso della Viola
Alfonso della Viola, 493, 497, 498
Al Jahiz, 184
Al Khwarizmi, 373, 409, 415, 608
Al Kindi, 432
Almenraeder, Carl, 714
Al Musudi, 184, 608
Alsloot, Denis van, 687
Altenburg, Johann Ernst, 167, 721, 800, 802, 806
Amalarius of Metz, 5, 17

Amat, Juan Carlos, 452
Amati, Andrea, 514, 517, 533
Amati, Gerolamo, 518, 538
Amati, Nicolo, 518
Amiot, *Père*, 734
Amman, Jost, 540
Ammianus Marcellinus, 367
Ammerbach, Elias, 284
Andersson, Otto, 376
Andrea of Verona, 493, 497
Andreyev, Vassil Vassilyevitch, 214, 430, 661
Anselmi, Giorgio, 620
Antegnati, Francesco, 263, 284
Antegnati, Gian Giacomo, 629
Apollodorus, 52
Appunn, A., 37
Apuleius, 80, 89, 556
Arbeau, Thoinot, 126, 166, 558, 560, 572
Archiotti, 318
Arena, Antoine d', 244
Aretino, Pietro, 284
Ariosto, Attilio, 510
Aristotle, 556
Arnaut, Henry, 224, 235, 244, 245, 248, 249, 260, 261, 291, 292, 617, 622, 623, 624
Arne, Michael, 440
Artusi, Giovanni Maria, 288
Asté, Jean-Hilaire. See Halary
Astor, G., 782
Athenaeus, 385, 748
Auber, Daniel-François-Esprit, 440
Augustine, Saint, 12, 200, 604
Avicenna. See Ibn Sina

Babcock, Alpheus, 339, 343
Bach, Carl Philip Emanuel, 255, 315, 316, 646

843

INDEX RERUM

857